Quilters' Travel Companion

5th Edition 1998 - 2000

Published by: Chalet Publishing
32 Grand Avenue
Manitou Springs, CO 80829
(719) 685-5041

Edited by:
Audrey Swales
Anderson

With all my love, this book is dedicated to my husband, Marlow.
Thank you for your support and hours of assistance.

How to Use this Guide

Whenever you're away from home be sure to take your *Quilters' Travel Companion* (QTC). You never know when you might have an opportunity to check out a shop. This guide includes featured listings for over 1350 quilt shops in the United States and Canada. There is a description of each shop, including hours, featured merchandise, plus address and phone number. In addition, we provide a local map which will help you to drive right to their door. Look for the many shops who are offering discounts if you show them your QTC. Also we include the addresses of over 1000 other shops.

The shop listings are organized by state. We provide a state map which will enable you to tell at a glance where each of the featured shops is located. The number on the state map will also be found with the shop listing. In addition, for each state we include listings of area quilt guilds and other shops located in that state.

We've tried hard to include every shop in the country, but we're sure that we've missed some.
If you know of one we've missed drop us a note or call us at (719) 685-5041.

There are two basic ways we see you using our guide:
1) Whenever you're traveling on business or vacation check out your route and see what shops you may be close to. The state maps should give you an idea if you'll be in the vicinity of a store. Then if you have time or can make time give yourself a break and STOP !

Since beginning these guides in 1992, I have certainly realized that I used to drive right by shops on my travels, but not stop because I didn't realize they were close.

2) Or go WILD and take a few days with family or friends and plan a whole trip going from shop to shop. Many shops are in historic / tourist places so your trip just may lead you into an unexpected adventure. Either way, enjoy exploring all the great shops scattered across this country. We would be grateful if you'd tell them that QTC got you there.

We have made every effort for the information in this book to be up-to-date and accurate. Unfortunately shops do move, change hours, or go out of business; so if you want to be sure before you go a phone call might be prudent. All the featured shops' information was correct when published. Also note that many new telephone area codes have been added across the country and many more new ones are planned.

Map Conventions used in the QTC:
a) Our state maps only include major roads; please use our maps in conjunction with commercial maps.
b) All maps are oriented with North at the top.
c) The shops are marked either by a square with the street address inside (i.e. 100) or by a star ☆

* = traffic light	■ = Business or landmark
┼┼┼┼┼┼┼┼ = Railroad	A Gray line or area = water
Dashed line = state border	● = City

Chalet Publishing's mascot, Max.

About the Guild Listings: The only way we get this information is from the shops we work with or from our customers. We tried to include more information about the guilds this time (i.e. meeting times and places). Unfortunately, many times we were not provided with complete information. If you are interested in a particular guild, we suggest contacting a shop in that area for more information. We hope providing this information leads to some fun times.

About the new Web Site Index: Shopping on the net is becoming more and more an alternative to actually being there. Many shops have web sites, please visit them when you need a fix and can't get there in person. The last few pages of the book include some shops that are just in cyberspace. Most of the addresses do not include the necessary http://. As savvy surfers you probably knew to add that prefix, but we thought we'd better mention it.

A Comment About Our New Size: We're sure that some people will like the new full size and some won't. Just wanted to let you know that we had to change it due to success—at the old size it would have been too thick for the binding to hold up.

Contents

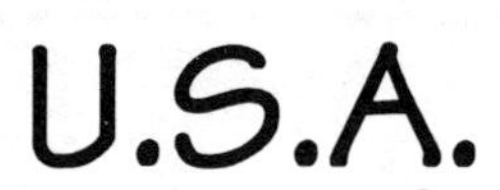

U.S.A. Featured Shops

Canadian Featured Shops

Have a Great Trip

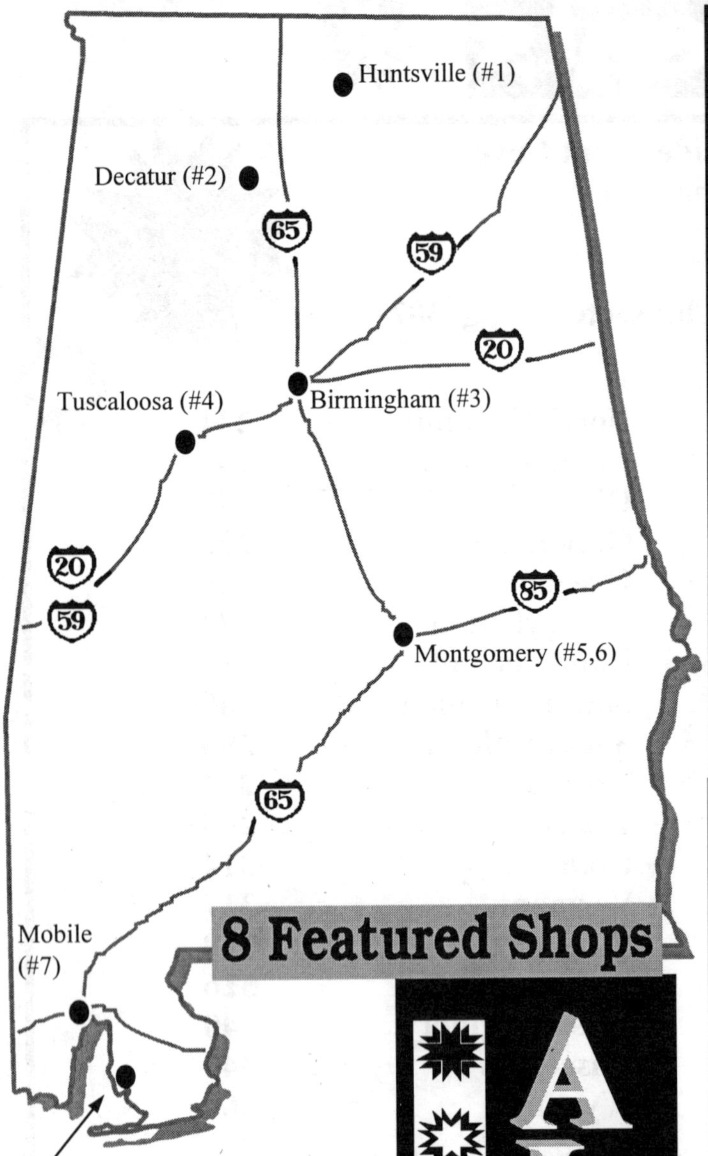

Huntsville (#1)
Decatur (#2)
Birmingham (#3)
Tuscaloosa (#4)
Montgomery (#5,6)
Mobile (#7)
Fairhope (#8)
65 59 20 85

8 Featured Shops

ALABAMA

Alabama Guilds:

Birmingham Quilters Guild, Birmingham

Enterprising Quilters, P.O. Box 31114, Enterprise, 36330

Hartselle Quilt Lovers' Guild, Hartselle Library, 35640

Heritage Quilters of Huntsville, P.O. Box 6885, Huntsville, 35824 Meets: 3rd Thursday 7 p.m. at Faith Presbyterian Church, corner Whitesburg Dr. & Airport Rd.

Azalea City Quilters Guild, Mobile Meets: 2nd Tuesday at 10:30 a.m. at United Methodist Church Contact: Clara Charlesworth (228-497-5490).

Kudzu Quilter's Guild, 3933 Croydon Rd., Montgomery36109

West Alabama Quilters Guild 305 Caplewood Dr., Tuscaloosa, 35401 Meets: 2nd Saturday at 9:30 a.m. at Department of Transportation, 1000 28th Avenue

Huntsville, AL #1

Mon - Thur 10 - 5
Thur til 6
Sat 10 - 4

Patches & Stitches

817-A Regal Drive 35801
(205) 533-3886
Owner: Linda Worley
Est: 1978 3500 sq.ft.

Complete line of quilt supplies, classes, books, and needlework; including cross-stitch and needlepoint. Also mail order.

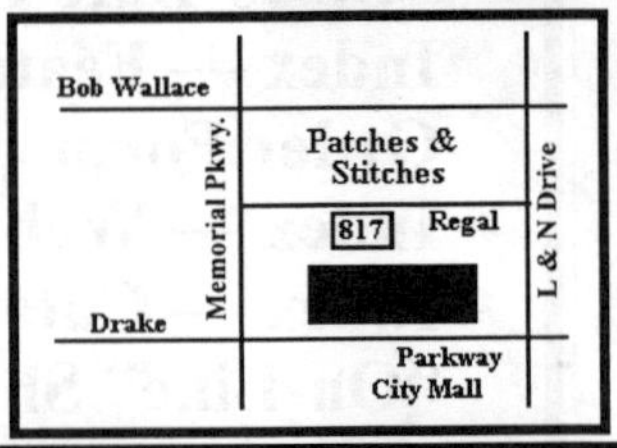

Bob Wallace
Memorial Pkwy.
Patches & Stitches
817 Regal
L & N Drive
Drake
Parkway City Mall

Decatur, AL #2

Mon - Fri 10 - 5
Sat 10 - 4

The Crafty Bear Shop

2208 Danville Rd. S.W. 35601
(205) 351-0420
Owner: Helen DeButy
Est: 1988 1800 sq.ft. 600 Bolts

Cotton Fabrics, books, patterns, supplies, and classes. The friendliest quilt shop for service, inspiration and sharing of ideas.

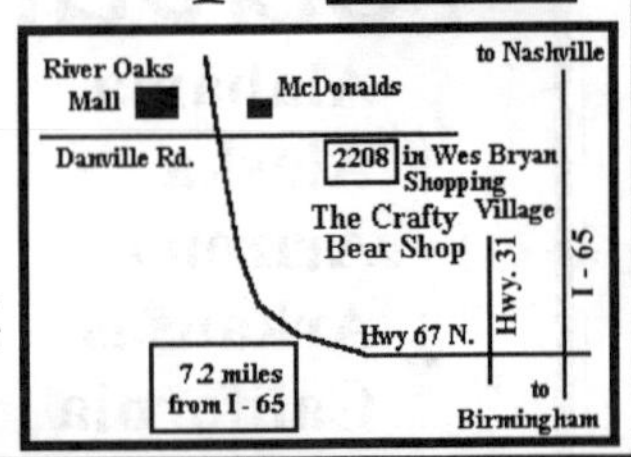

Birmingham, AL #3

Quiltmaker's Workshop

Est: 1994
1500 sq.ft. 2000+ Bolts

Mon - Fri 9 - 5
Sat 10 - 5

2403 1st St. NE
35215
(205) 854-4485
Owner:
Annie Woods

Everything you need for Quilting Start to Finish.

Large selection of 100% cotton fabrics. Great selection of Books, Patterns, Notions, and the latest Gadgets.

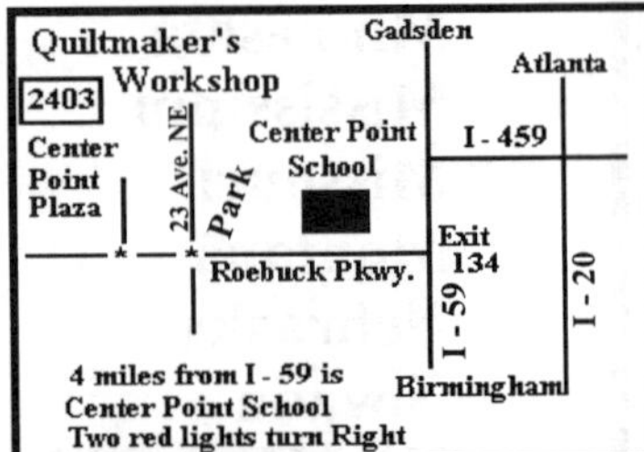

Classes for Beginning, Intermediate and Advanced Students.

Serious Quilters Club Quarterly Newsletter

Carolina Lily Quilt Shop

100% Cotton Fabrics from Leading Manufacturers
Books, Patterns, Frames and Quilting Notions
Classes and Custom Machine Quilting Offered.

2516 - C University Blvd. 35401
(205) 752-8700
Owner: Joy W. Robertson
Est: 1997 1000 sq.ft. 1500 Bolts

Mon - Sat
9:30 - 5:30

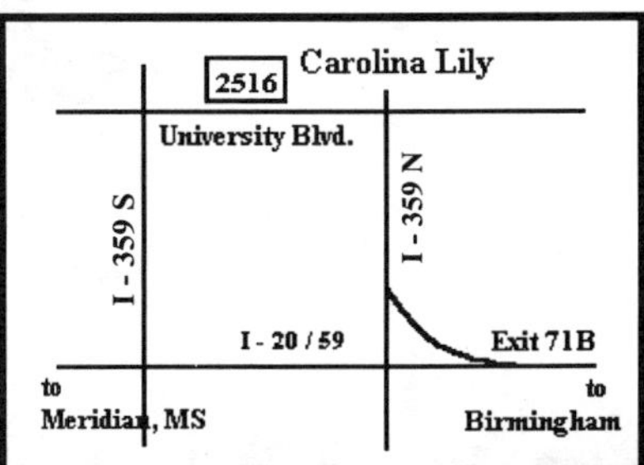

Tuscaloosa, AL #4

Montgomery, AL #5

Tues - Fri 9:30 - 5
Sat 9:30 - 3

Kudzu Blossom Quilt Shop

3666-E Debby Dr. 36111
(334) 288-8108
Owner: Janice Jarrett
Est: 1997 1500 sq.ft.

A wonderful shop to meet all your quilting needs. Lots of great fabrics, books, patterns, and quilting supplies.

Montgomery, AL #6

Mon - Fri 9 - 5:30
Sat 10 - 3

Rose of Sharon

4032 Troy Hwy. 36116
(334) 281-9775 Est: 1994
Owner: Sharon Wilson

100% cotton fabric, thread, stencils, notions & variety of classes. Quilted items for sale. Restoration work & machine quilting available.

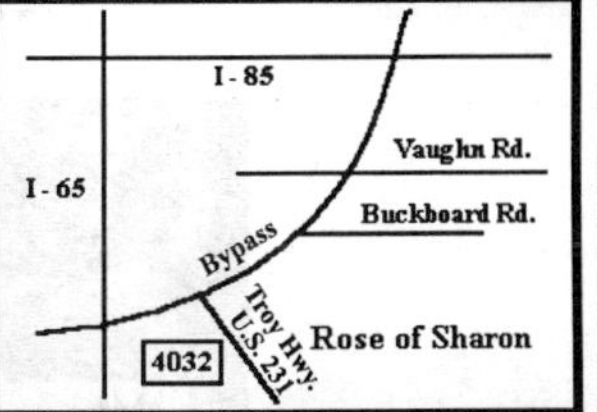

Mobile, AL #7

Tues - Fri 10 - 5
Sat 10 - 3

Quilters' Market

6345-K Airport Blvd.
Piccadilly Square 36608
(334) 343-6004 Est: 1997
Owner: Charlotte Vinson
1300 sq.ft. 1500 Bolts

Quilting supplies, books, classes, 1500 bolts of 100% cotton fabric and machine quilting.

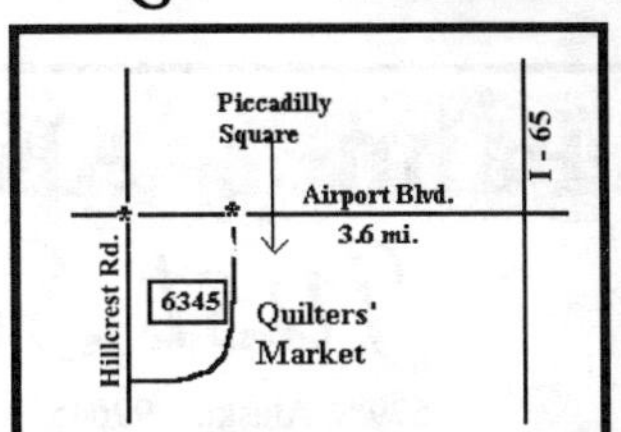

Fairhope, AL #8

Mon - Sat 10 - 5

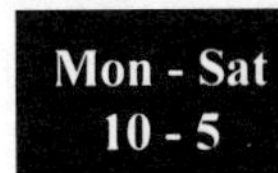

Bears by the Bay — Quilting, Too

26 S. Section St. 36532
(334) 928-8989 Fax: Same
Owner: Nancy Scott
Est: 1994
1850 sq.ft.

Unique atmosphere for the serious Teddy Bear collector and the Quiltaholic. Books, classes, notions, patterns, 1500 bolts and growing.

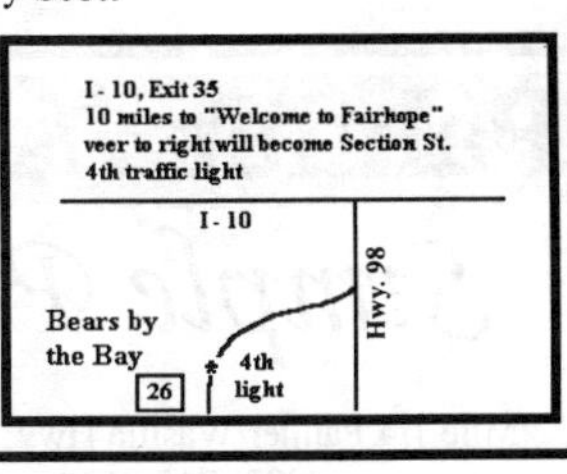

Other Shops in Alabama:

Alexander City	Midtown Fabrics, 26 Main St.	205-234-2394
Anniston	Cloth Patch, 2120 Noble St.	205-237-9972
Foley	Quilt Connection 21188 Miflin Rd.	334-943-4641
Jasper	Grandma's Treasures, Parkland Shp Ctr	205-221-5263
Madison	Cattywampus, 1871 Slaughter Rd.	205-864-0280
Mobile	Fabric Works, 5441 Highway 90 W.	334-666-0285
Northport	The Quilted Heart, 401 20th Ave.	205-345-5809
Pelham	Southern Textiles, 2775 Hwy. 31 S	205-664-1811
Pike Road	Jo's Sew & So, 834 Maryweather	334-281-1785
Russellville	Parker's Discount, Hwy. 24 E	205-332-4539
Wetumpka	Creations Galore, 105 E. Main	334-567-6096

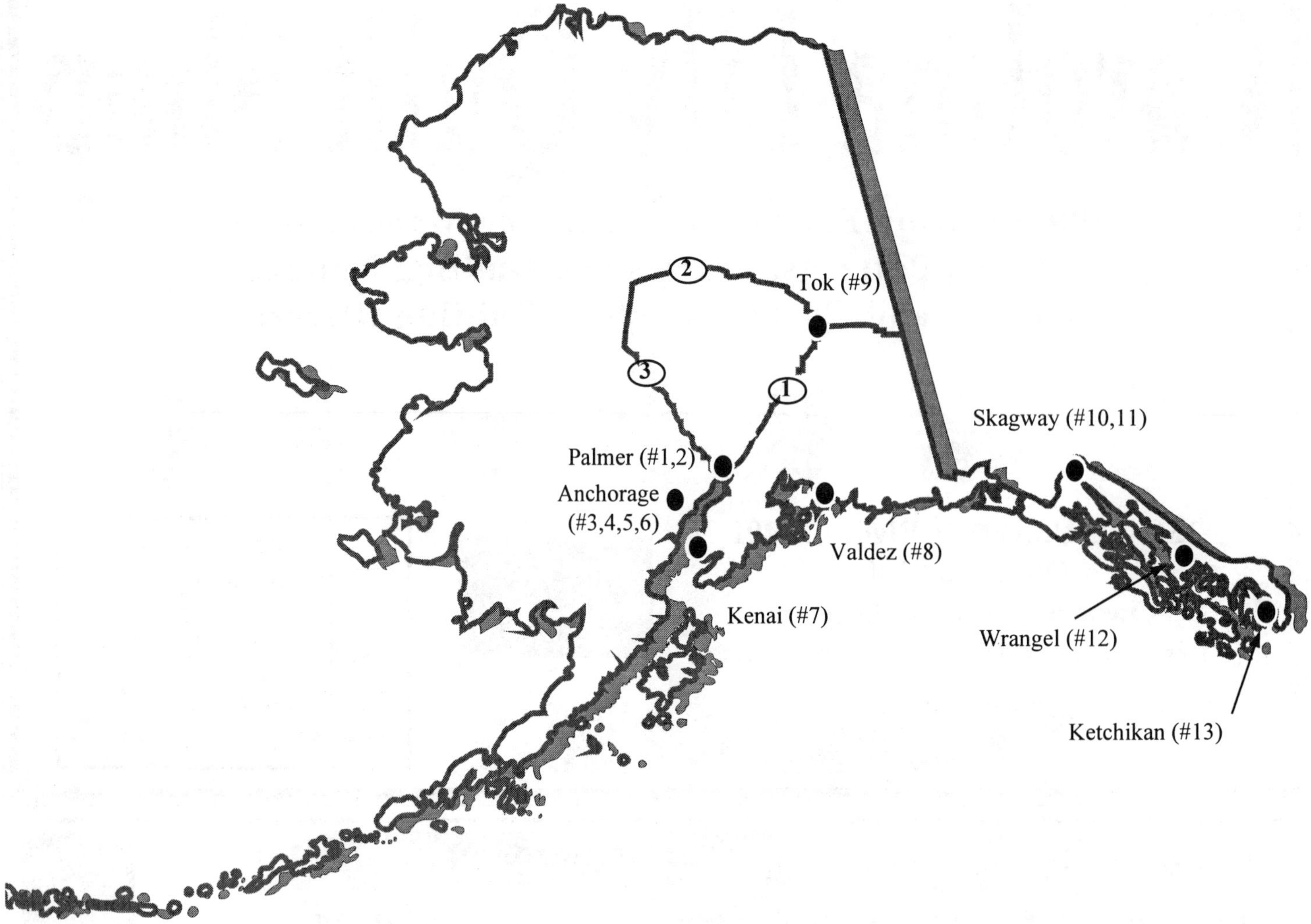

Tok (#9)
Skagway (#10,11)
Palmer (#1,2)
Anchorage (#3,4,5,6)
Valdez (#8)
Kenai (#7)
Wrangel (#12)
Ketchikan (#13)

Palmer, AK #1

Mon - Sat
10 - 6

Simple Pleasures

Mile 1/4 Palmer/Wasilla Hwy. 99645
(907) 745-8630
Est: 1985 900+ Bolts

Quilting Fabrics, Books and Notions.
Country Home Accessories. Gifts.
Friendly Country Atmosphere.

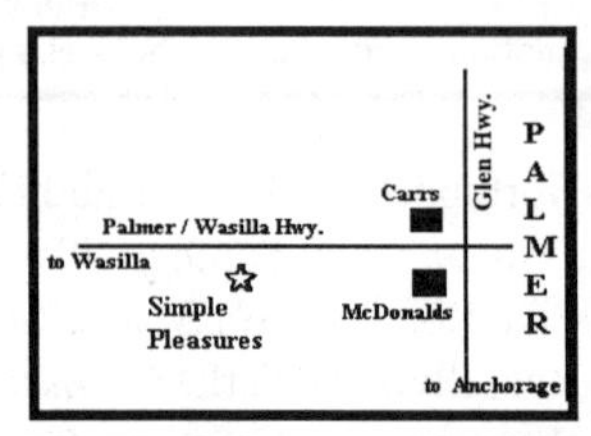

Palmer, AK #2

Just Sew

579 S. Alaska 99645
(907) 745-3649
Owners: Jim & Cheri Cooper
2400 sq.ft.

All your quilting and needlework supplies. 100% cottons, books, patterns, notions, cross-stitch supplies, yarn, and lots more!

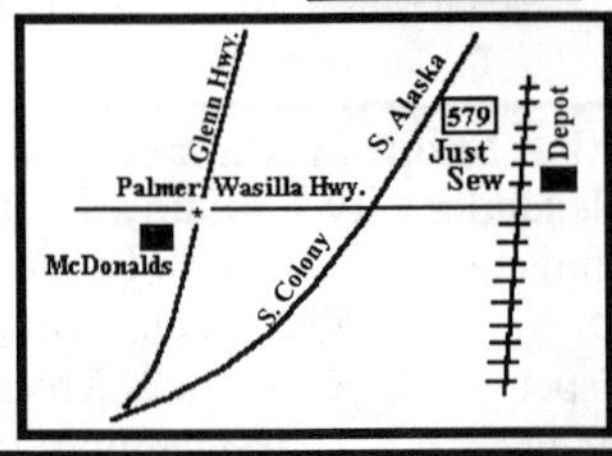

Anchorage, AK #3

Mon - Sat 11 - 6
Sun 12 - 4

The Whiffletree

9420 Old Seward Hwy. 99515
(907) 344-5922
Owners: Rich & Diane Melms
Est: 1983 1000 sq.ft.

Full line antique store with quality antique Quilts, tops, blocks, doilies, bedcovers, tablecloths, hankies, buttons, trims and laces.

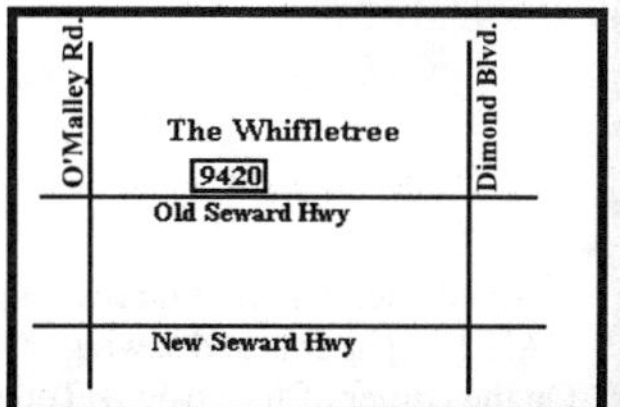

Anchorage, AK #4

Mon- Fri 10 - 7
Sat 10 - 6
Sun 12 - 5

The Quilt Tree

5520 Lake Otis Pkwy,
Suite 105 99507
(907) 561-4115
Fax: (907) 561-4406
3000 sq.ft. 2000 Bolts

Large selection of quality 100% cotton fabric, unique Alaskan patterns, books, notions & supplies. Experienced, helpful staff.

Anchorage, AK #5

Mon - Wed 10 - 8
Sat 10 - 6
Sun 12 - 5

Three Sisters' Fabric Boutique

1120 Huffman #10 99515
(907) 345-8041 Fax: (907) 345-7801
E-Mail: mbell@micronet.net
Owner: Marla Bell
Est: 1968 3000 sq.ft.
Samples Sent on Request

Finest Fabrics for Quilting, Bridal & Eveningwear, Costuming, and Outerwear. Designer Fabrics & Buttons. Alaskan Prints. Full Service Fabric shop.

Anchorage, AK #6

Mon - Fri 10 - 6
Thur til 8
Sat 10 - 5
Sun 12 - 5

Quilt Works

3120 Denali St. #4 99503
(907) 563-9773 Fax: (907) 563-9772
Owner: Sue Bergerson
Manager: Karen Tomczak

Over 2000 bolts of 100% cotton fabric. Excellent selection of books, patterns, and Alaskan patterns.
Put your pin on our visitor map!

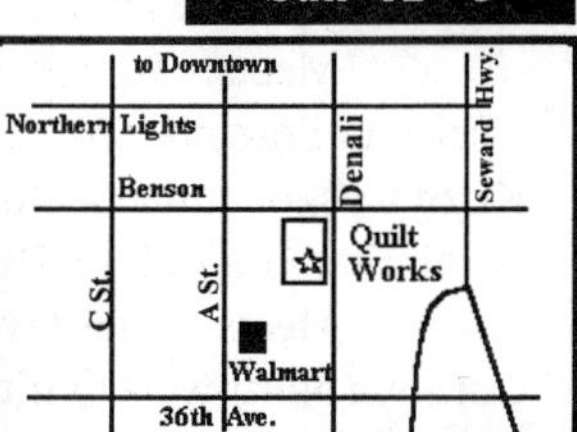

Kenai, AK #7

Tues - Fri 10 - 4:30
Sat 10 - 1
or by Appt.

Kenai Fabric Center

115 N. Willow 99611
(907) 283-4595 Fax: (907) 283-5609
Est: 1970 4000+ Bolts

Quilting Fabrics & Classes, Fashion & Outerwear fabrics, Husqvarna/Viking & White Sewing Machines & Sergers, Notions, Yarns, Books, Family-owned.

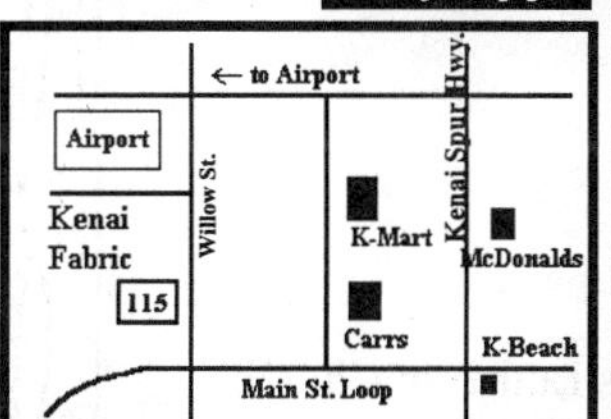

Valdez, AK #8

Mon - Sat 10 - 5

The Calico Whale

354 Fairbanks Dr. 99686
(907) 835-4263 Fax: (907) 835-5263
E-Mail: Koszarek@Ak.net
Owner: Trudy Koszarek
Est: 1995 1500 sq.ft.

Good selection fabrics, books, patterns, quilting supplies, needlework and local handmade gifts.

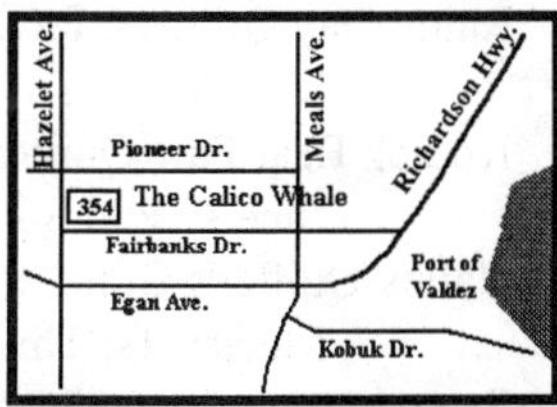

Tok, AK #9

Mon - Sat 10 - 5

The Quail's Nest

P.O. Box 480 99780
(907) 883-4353
Owner: Lynne Burton

Alaska Quilt Patterns
— Books & Notions —
— 100% cotton fabric —
Gifts and craft supplies.

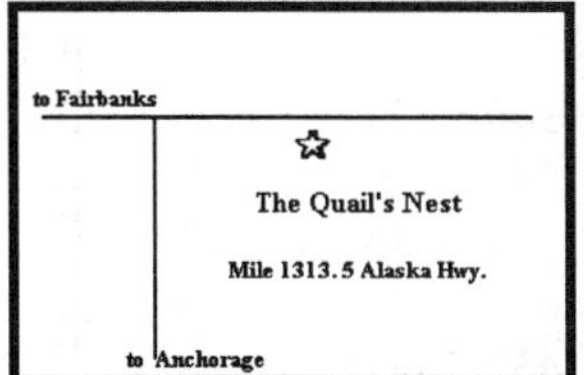

Skagway, AK #10

Mon - Sat 10 - 5

Dirce Ann's Fabrics

P.O. Box 284 412 8th Ave. 99840
(907) 983-2376 Fax: (907) 983-3114
Owners: Dirce & Dennis Spurrier
Est: 1993

Alaskan Wildlife Fabrics, 100% Cotton Quilting Fabrics, Northern Patterns, Quilting Supplies, Yarns, Homemade Gifts & More.

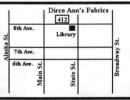

Dirce Ann's Fabrics
412
8th Ave.
Library
Alaska St.
7th Ave.
6th Ave.
Main St.
State St.
Broadway St.

Skagway, AK #11

We provide lodging year round.

The White House

8th & Main St., P.O. Box 41 99840 (907) 983-9000
Fax: (907) 983-9010 E-Mail: whitehse@ptialaska.net
Owners: The Tronrud Family

Come relax in our ten room Inn in historic and picturesque Skagway.
Built in 1902, our newly remodeled inn still features all the comforts of home such as private baths, telephone and a hardy homemade breakfast.
With a quilt on every bed we are the perfect get-away for anyone who loves the romance of quilts and Alaska.

Wrangell, AK #12

Mon - Sat 11 - 5

Angerman's Special-Tees

P.O. Box 849 99929
(907) 874-3611
Owners: Barbara & Dick Angerman

Full Service Fabric Store
Alaskan Outdoors style. Husqvarna Viking dealer. Custom Tees and womens Woolrich.

One Block from Cruise Ship Dock. Two Blocks from Ferry Terminal One mile from Airport

Ketchikan, AK #13

Mon - Sat 10 - 5:30

Silver Thimble Fabric Shoppe

2450 Tongass Ave. 99901
(907) 225-5422
Owner: Betty T. Gale Est: 1984

Available: Quilting fabrics, supplies, Alaskan patterns and sewing machines.
On the corner of Jefferson & Tongass Ave.

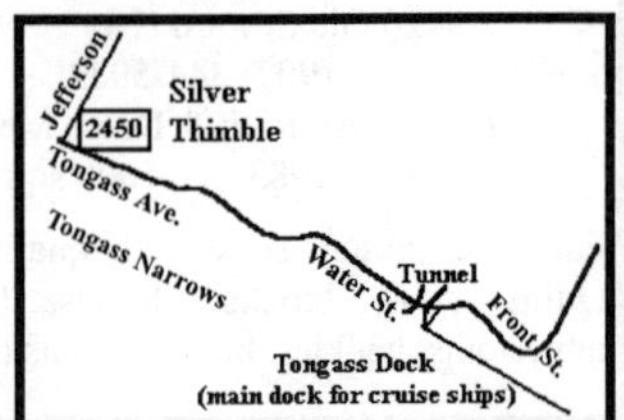

Alaska Guilds:

Chugach Mountain Quilters Guild
Anchorage Log Cabin Quilt Guild, P.O. Box 202582, Anchorage, 99520
Meets: Thursdays at 10 a.m. or 1st and 3rd Thursday at 7 p.m. at Central Lutheran Church, 15th & Cordova, Anchorage
Christian Stitchin, 8621 E. 17th Ave., Anchorage, 99504
Kozy Kusko Quilters, Box 126, Bethel, 99559
North Star Guild, P.O. Box 520973, Big Lake, 99652
Meets: Tuesdays 10 a.m. to 5 p.m. at the Mid Valley Senior Center
Cordova Northwest Quilt Guild, Box 1995, Cordova, 99574
Craig Quilters, Box 142, Craig, 99921
Tundra Patchwork Quilter's Guild, P.O. Box 347, Dillingham, 99576
Meets: 3rd Saturday (Oct. thru May) at the High School Home Ec Room
Cabin Fever Quilters Guild, P.O. Box 83608, Fairbanks, 99708
Meets: 3rd Tuesday at Fairbanks Lutheran Church
Capital City Quilters, 8533 E. Valley Ct., Juneau, 99801
Rainy Day Quilters, P.O. Box 1256, Ketchikan, 99928
Meets: 4th Tuesday at First Lutheran Church
Kodiak Bear Paw Quilters, Box 3856, Kodiak, 99615
Meets: 2nd Sunday various locations
Valley Quilter's Guild, P.O. Box 2582, Palmer, 99645
Meets: 1st Thursday (except Aug.) 6:30 p.m. at St. Johns Lutheran Church
Petersburg Quilters, Box 217, Petersburg, 99833
Ocean Waves Quilters, Box 1771, Sitka, 99835
Redoubt Quilters Guild, P.O. Box 2992, Soldotna, 99669
Meets: Thursday 10 a.m.
Tok Quilters, Box 229, Tok, 99928
Valdez Artist Guild, P.O. Box 1401, Valdez, 99686

Other Shops in Alaska:

Anchorage	Alaska Designs, 4801 Jumar Rd.	907-346-3779
Anchorage	Calicos & Quilts, 11900 Industry Way #7	907-345-4839
Cordova	Calico Corner, P.O. Box 320	907-424-3285
Cordova	Forget-Me-Not Fabrics, P.O. Box 1109	907-424-3656
Fairbanks	Hands All Around, 927 Old Steese Hwy.	907-452-2347
Fairbanks	Snow Goose Fibers, 3550 Airport Way #6	907-474-8118
Fairbanks	Quilts Unlimited, 1918 Jack St.	907-452-1918
Haines	Seams Like Yesterday, P.O. Box 1167	907-766-2265
Homer	Sew & Reap, 3657 Main St.	907-235-7648
Homer	In Stitches, 4270 Pleasant Way	
Juneau	Tina's Fabrique Boutique, 9397 La Perouse	907-789-3666
Kodiak	The Stitchery, 202 Center Ave., Suite 310	907-486-5580
Sitka	Calico Cross Stitch, 223 Lincoln St.	907-747-5122
Soldotna	Robin Place Fabrics, 105 Robin Pl.	907-262-5438
Soldotna	Finer Point, 105 Shady Ln., P.O. Box 2517	907-262-1405
Wasilla	Alaska Dyeworks, 300 W. Swanson Ave.	907-373-6562
Wasilla	Stitches, 4901 E. Parks	

ARIZONA

17 Featured Shops

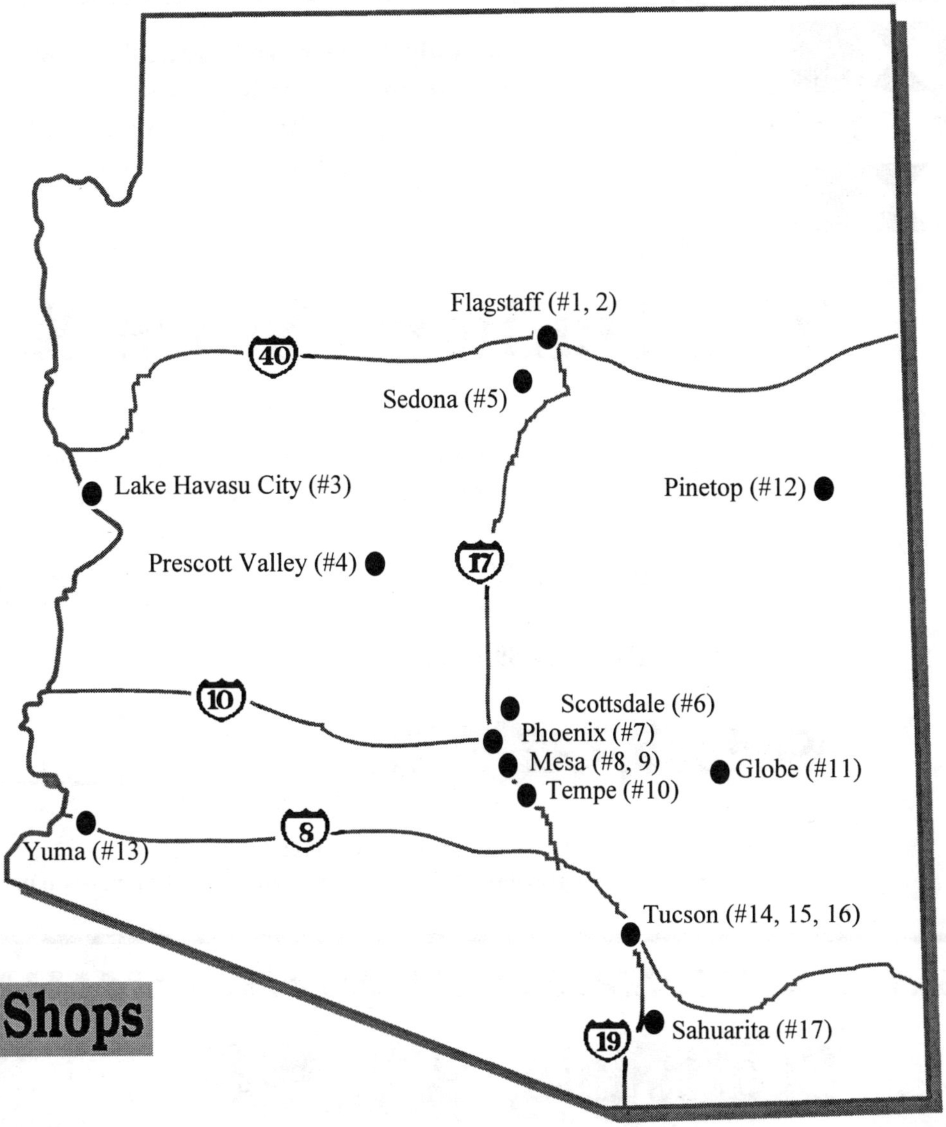

Flagstaff (#1, 2)
Sedona (#5)
Lake Havasu City (#3)
Pinetop (#12)
Prescott Valley (#4)
Scottsdale (#6)
Phoenix (#7)
Mesa (#8, 9)
Globe (#11)
Tempe (#10)
Yuma (#13)
Tucson (#14, 15, 16)
Sahuarita (#17)
40
17
10
8
19

Flagstaff, AZ #1

Mon - Sat 9 - 5:30

Odegaard's Sewing Center

19 W. Aspen 86001
(520) 774-2331 In AZ (800) 360-2331
Fax: (520) 774-4668
Bernina, Pfaff, Viking, Singer

Large selection of 100% Cotton Fabrics, Quilting Books & Patterns. Southwest Fabrics and Notions.

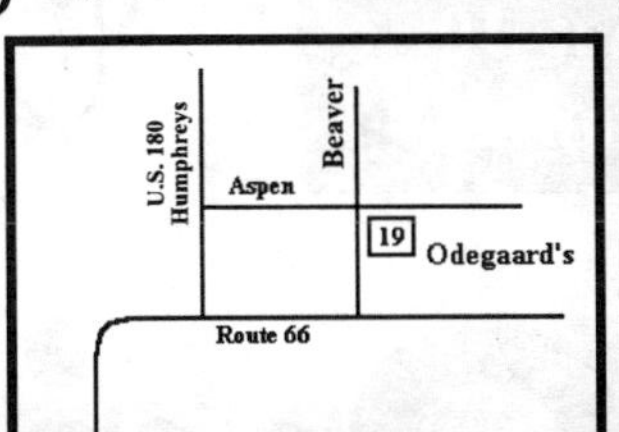

Flagstaff, AZ #2

Mon - Sat 10 - 5

Pine Country Quilts

1800 S. Milton Rd., #13 86001
(520) 779-2194 Green Tree Village
Owner: Kris Hetz

Fabrics for the traditional and contemporary quilter. Books, notions, and unusual gifts. Sheer pleasure on the way to the Grand Canyon.

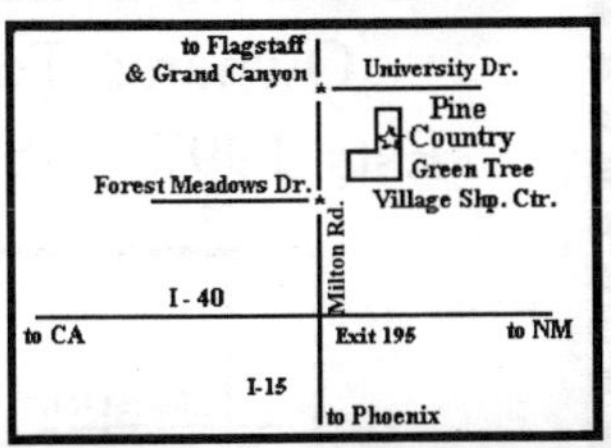

Lake Havasu City, AZ #3

Mon - Fri 8 - 5
Sat 8 - 3

Sew What?

21 S. Acoma Blvd. 86403
(520) 453-4040 Fax: (520) 453-3023
Owner: Jeanette Kennedy
Est: 1995 1500 sq.ft. 2500 Bolts

Largest selection of fabrics, books, patterns, & quilting supplies on the Colorado River and the American Home of the London Bridge.

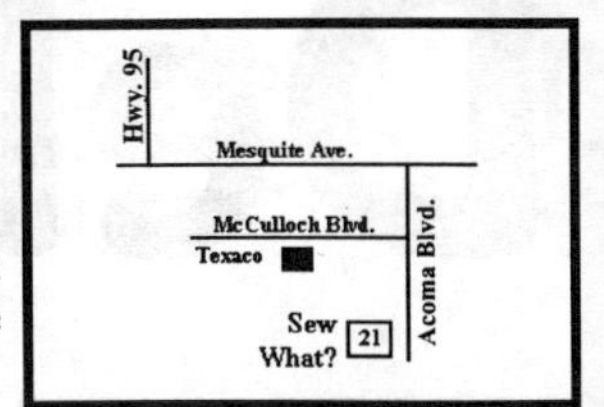

Prescott Valley, AZ #4

Tues - Fri 9 - 5
Thur til 9
Sat 9 - 4

A Quilter's Dream

8742 E. Hwy. 69 86314
(520) 772-0864
Owner: Muriel L. Gregg

Beautiful 100% Cotton Fabrics. Great Selections of Books, Patterns & Notions. Unique Gifts. Classes for all Levels of Quilting.

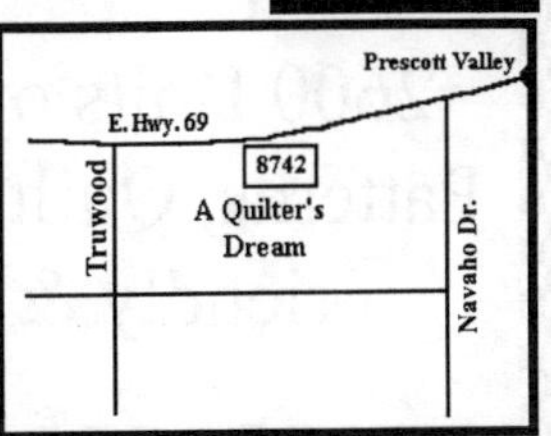

Not only do we have beautiful fabrics, we also have beautiful views! We've added a Quilters' Gallery with artwork and traditional & antique quilts. Come Visit!

The Quilter's Store & Gallery

Quilting Supplies — Classes — 100% Cotton Fabrics
Personalized Instruction Available

(520) 282-2057
Marge Elson, Proprietor
3075 West Highway 89A 86336

Sedona, AZ #5

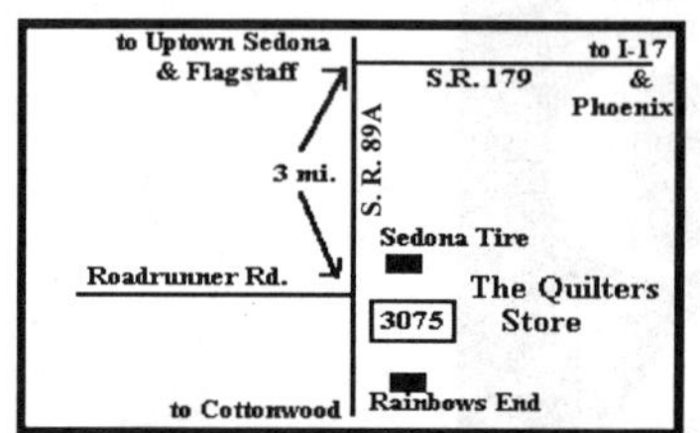

Monday - Friday: 9 a.m. - 5 p.m.
Saturday: 9 a.m. - 4 p.m. **Sunday**: 12 p.m. - 4 p.m.

Scottsdale, AZ #6

7318 E. Shea Blvd. #106 85260
(602) 368-9598 Fax: (602) 368-0595
E-Mail: TMARTIN007@aol.com
Owners: Tom & Anita Martin
Est: 1997 3500 sq.ft. 2600 Bolts

Mon - Fri 10 - 7
Sat 10 - 6
Sun 12 - 5

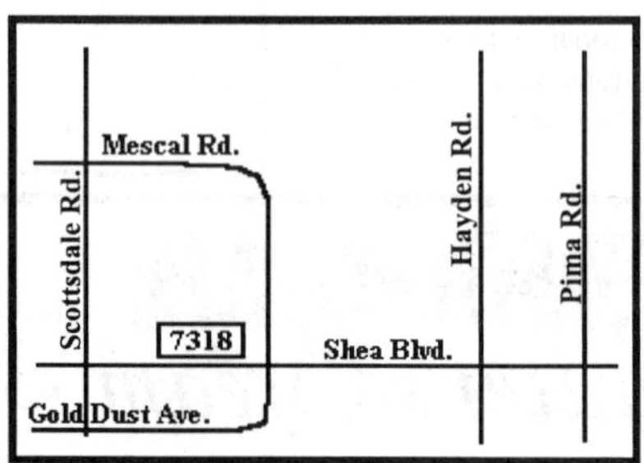

2600 Bolts of 100% Cottons, Books, Patterns, Quilting Notions, and Classes. Friendly & Knowledgeable Staff.

Quilters Delight

Phoenix, AZ #7

Mon - Sat
9:30 - 5:30
Tues till 9

The Quilted Apple

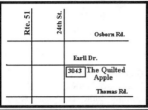

3043 North 24th St. 85016
(602) 956-0904
Free Catalog Owner: Laurene Sinema
Est: 1978 4600 sq.ft. 2200 Bolts

100 % cotton fabrics, books, patterns, notions, classes. Specialize in fine hand quilting. Bernina Sewing Machines.

Rte. 51
24th St.
Osborn Rd.
Earll Dr.
3043 The Quilted Apple
Thomas Rd.

Mesa, AZ #8

Mon - Fri
9:30 - 5:30
Thur til 8
Sat 9 - 4

Common Threads

142 W. Main 85201
(602) 668-0908
Web Site: members.aol.com/commonthd
Owners: Gail & Greg Biesen
Est: 1995 5000 sq.ft. 1800 Bolts
Quilting supplies, Fabric, Books, Patterns; Classes. We also have a Block of the Month. Viking Sewing Machines.

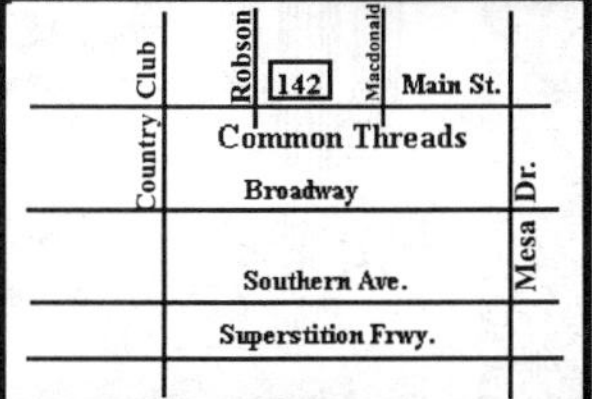

Mesa, AZ #9

Quilter's Emporium

7516 E. Main St. #3 85207
(602) 654-8143 Fax: (602) 654-8165
E-Mail: QuiltrsEmporium@juno.com

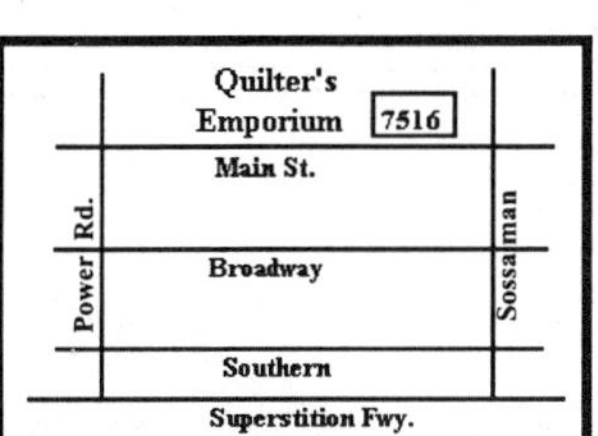

Large selection of fabric (2000 bolts), books, patterns & quilting supplies. The friendliest quilt shop for service, inspiration and sharing of ideas.

Mon - Fri
9:30 - 5:30
Sat 9:30 - 4

Tempe, AZ #10

Est: 1982

the Quilter's Ranch

227 East Baseline Road #J2 85283
(In Mill Towne Center)

Friendly, knowledgeable staff
Cozy and inviting environment
From batiks to southwest to homespuns;
something for everyone!

(602) 838-8350
E-Mail:
quiltersranch@juno.com

Mon - Sat 9:30 - 5:30
Thurs til 9
(Sept. - May) Sun 12 - 4

Owner: Susan Visotsky

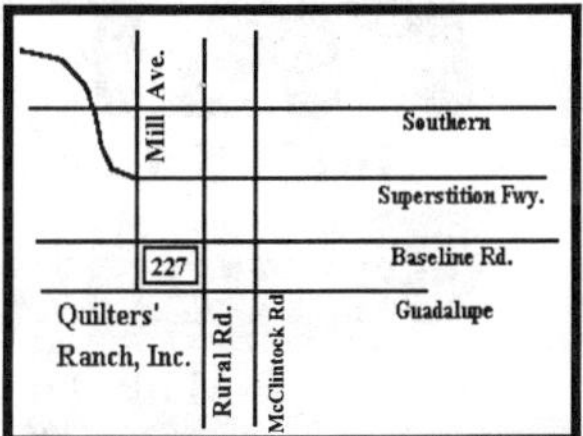

Globe, AZ #11

Tues- Sat
9 - 5:30

Country Corner

383 South Hill Street 85501
(520) 425-8208
Owners: Johnny & Janice McInturff
Est: 1986 6000 sq.ft.

Quilts, Fabric, Notions--Antiques Hardware, Tack, Boots, Vet Supplies, Chain saws--parts and service.

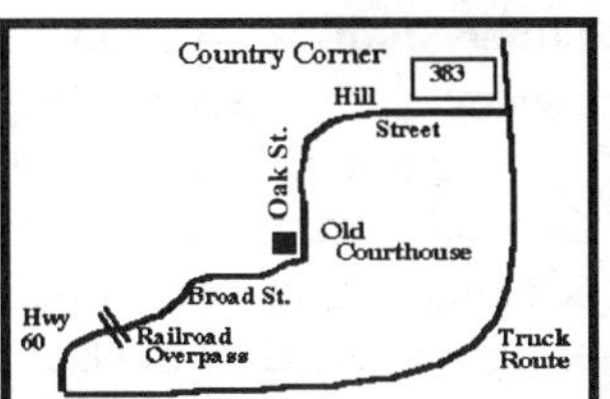

Pinetop, AZ #12

Mon - Sat
10 - 5

The Bent Needle

159 W. White Mountain Blvd. 85935
(520) 367-2770 Fax: (520) 532-7340
E-Mail: BNQUILTS@WhiteMtns.com
Web Site: Same
Owner: Becki Reissner
Est: 1998 1600 sq.ft. 800 bolts
Complete Quilt Store. Fabrics, Notions, Books & Patterns. In store long arm quilting. Fun and Friendly

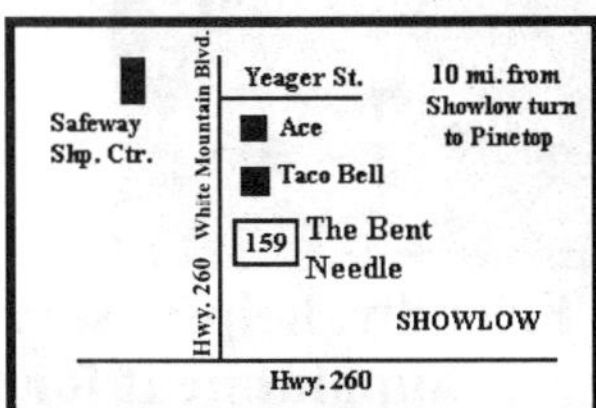

Arizona Guilds:
Arizona Quilters Guild, P.O. Box 82416, Phoenix, 85071
Mountain Top Quilters, P.O. Box 12961, Prescott, 86304
Tucson Quilter's Guild, P.O. Box 14454, Tucson, 85732
Meets: 2nd Wednesday 9:30 a.m.
at St. Francis Cabrini Church

Yuma, AZ #13

Mon-Sat 10 - 5

Traditions and Olde Town Quilters

251 S. Main St. 85364
(520) 343-0522 Fax: (520) 343-0534
Owner: Penny St. Mars
Traditions carries over 600 bolts of fabrics, all 100% cotton, unique quilting and crafting tools, primative doll patterns and organic potpourri. Full service machine quilting as well as "Unfinished Business", just bring us your unfinished project and we'll finish it for you.

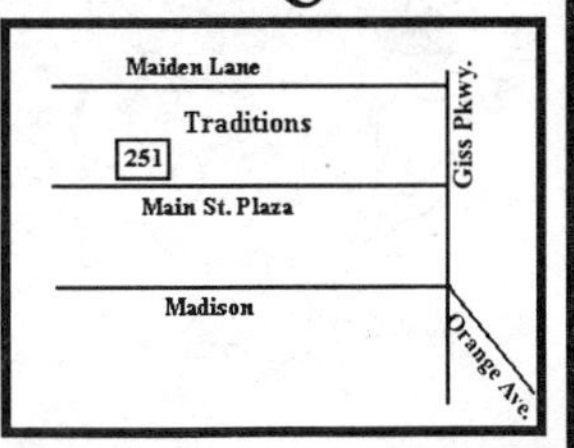

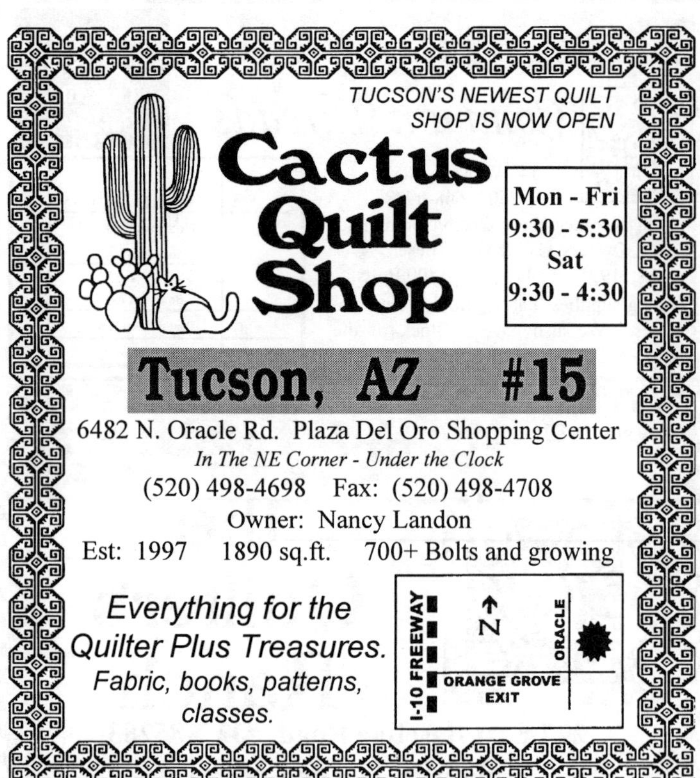

Tucson, AZ #14

Mon - Sat 9:30 - 6
Sun 12 - 4

Precious Hands Needleworks

2917 E. Grant Rd. 85716
(520) 325-8010
Owner: Cathy Dargel
Est: 1994 2000 sq.ft.

Bountiful Cotton Fabrics, Quilting Supplies, Classes, & Notions. We also offer machine quilting, come see a demonstration!

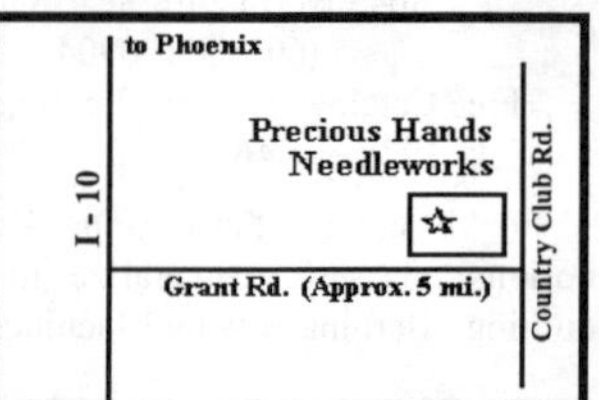

Tucson, AZ #16

Mon - Sat 9:30 - 5

Quilt Basket, Inc.

6538 C E. Tanque Verde Rd. 85715
(520) 722-8810 Fax: (520) 722-7720
Owner: Peggy Peck
Est: 1990 1500 sq.ft.

Lots & Lots of beautiful fabrics ....
Everything for today's busy quilter ....
Come see us !
"A friendly place for all your quilting needs"

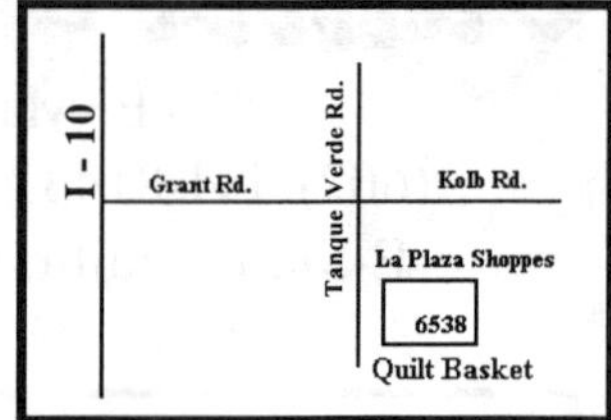

QUILTERS DESERT

(520) 648-1533
hm: (520) 393-1237
for Appointments

16121 S. Country Club Rd. 85629

Sahuarita, AZ #17

E-Mail: fabric@quiltersdp.com
Web Site: www.quiltersdp.com
Owner: Phyllis Sirrine Est: 1985

Mon - Fri 9 - 5
Sat 9 - 12

Summer Hours (June, July, August) Fri & Mon 9 - 5 or by Appt.

to Tucson
I - 19
1800 sq.ft. Stuffed with Bolts & Flat Folds.
Helmet Peak / Sahuarita Rd.
Exit 75
Country Club Rd.
Quilters Desert Patch
to Green Valley

Friendly, helpful service. We're happy to open by appointment for travelers in the summer. Great selection of cottons.

Other Shops in Arizona:

Dewey	Sun Country Quilts-Mary Wilson, 12 Smoki Trail, HC 61, Box 446	520-632-7422
Glendale	Heart Strings, 7157 N. 58th Dr.	602-937-3713
Kingman	Aunt Tee's Attic, 615 E. Beale St.	520-753-2825
Kingman	Stitch N Lock & Fabric Dock, 2017 Stockton Hill Rd.	520-753-2614
Lake Havasu City	Cactus Fabric Shop, 2011 Swanson Ave.	520-855-2229
Mesa	Sally's Fabrics, 2647 W. Baseline Rd.	602-839-0154
Mesa	Sally's Fabrics, 1235 E. Main St.	602-833-7201
Paradise Valley	Quilted Bear, 6316 N. Scottsdale Rd.	520-948-7760
Payson	The Quilters Cottage, 408 W. Main St.	520-474-2952
Phoenix	Mom's Quilting & Yarn Shop, 6842 N 14th St.	602-265-1953
St. Johns	Calico Corner, 55 E. Cleveland PO Box 1519	520-337-4046
Tucson	Quilters Bee, 3860 N. El Moraga Dr.	520-743-0391
Tucson	Sew-Vac Sales & Service, 5933 E. 22nd St.	
Tucson	Antiques American, P.O. Box 13709	520-745-5631
Yuma	Quilting Bee, 2370 W. 32nd St.	520-726-3000

9 Featured Shops

Eureka Springs (#1)
Rogers (#2)
Pea Ridge (#3)
Fayetteville (#4)
Conway (#5)
Little Rock (#6, 7)
Stuttgart (#8)
Greenwood (#9)
71
40
55
30

Eureka Springs, AR #1

7 Days A Week 10 - 5

The Cotton Patch Quilts

1 Center St. 72631
(501) 253-9894 or (888) 784-5899
Fax: (501) 253-5066
Owners: Rosemary Helms
3100 sq.ft. 1000 Bolts

Largest Selection of Hand Quilted Quilts. Amish, Mennonite & Local. 2nd Location in Branson, MO—Engler Block Mall.

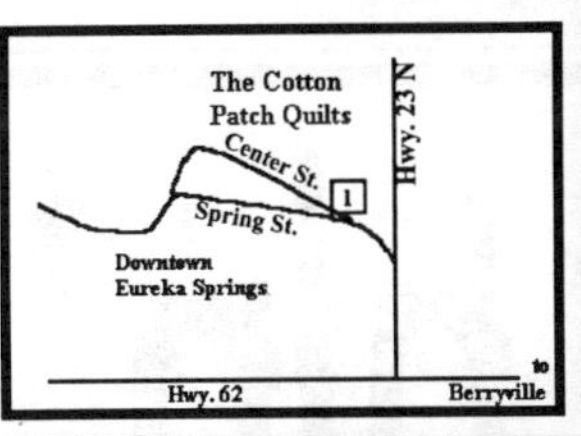

Pea Ridge, AR #3

Tues - Fri 9 - 5
Sat 10:30 - 2:30

Country House Quilting

16324 N. Hwy 94 72751
(501) 451-8978
Owners: Charlotte & Ronald Foster
Est: 1982 1600 sq.ft.

Fabrics, Notions, Quilts, Machine Quilting. Supplies, Books, Patterns, Q-snap frames, Classes.

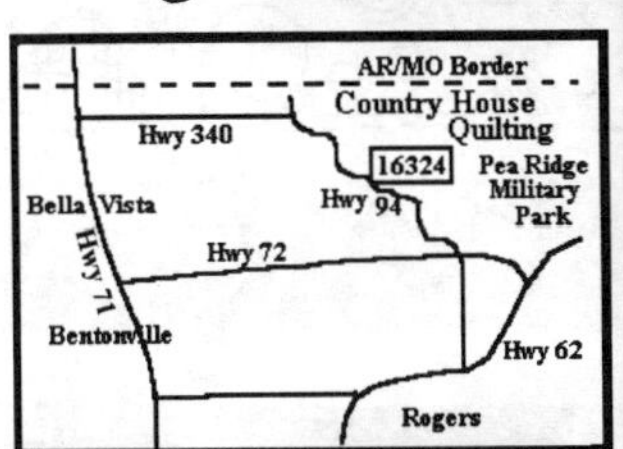

Fayetteville, AR #4

Mon - Sat 10 - 5

Quilt Your Heart Out

125 E. Township #11 72703
(501) 587-0307
Owner: Lila Rostenberg
Est: 1993 1000 sq.ft.

800 Bolts of 100% cotton fabric. Lots of patterns, books & notions. Homespuns, 1930's & 1800's reproduction pieces.

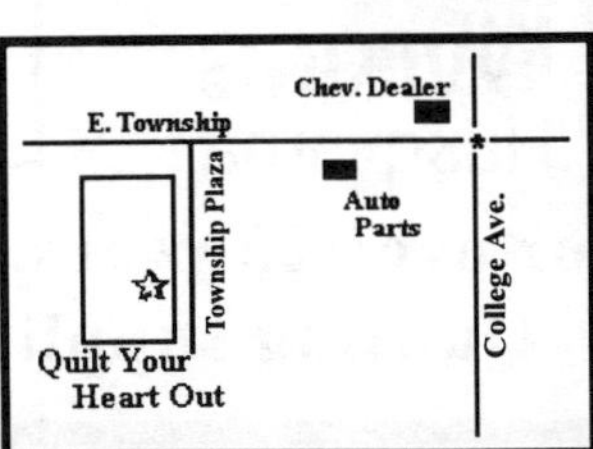

Patchwork Emporium

Shop For Sale

Rogers, AR #2

218 S. 1st St. 72756
Est: 1981
(501) 636-3385
Owner: Nora Cope

Mon - Sat 10 - 4

"A Complete Quilt Shop !"

2000 Bolts of Fabric—100% Cottons,
2500 Patterns & tons of Books, Notions.
Rug Hooking Kits, Felted Wool Kits.
Handmade Gifts.
Lots of Quilts! Models! Ideas! Classes!

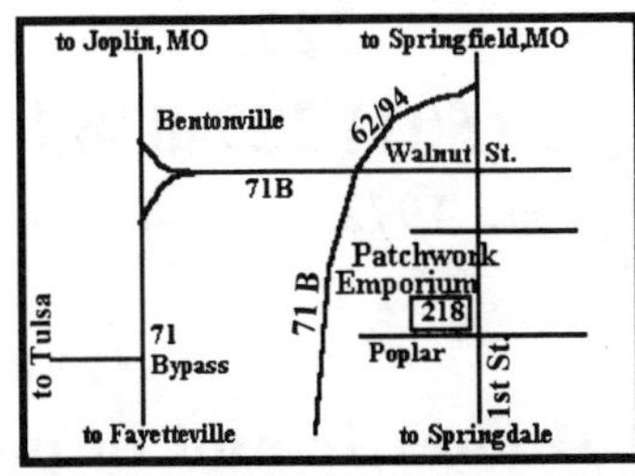

4 or 5 miles from Bypass

Idle-Hour Quilts & Design

Tues - Sat
10 - 5

2216 Washington Ave. 72032 (501) 329-3323

Owner: Jaynette Huff Est: 1992 1400 sq.ft.

Your Complete, Full-Service Quilt Store.

Offering superior quality supplies,
fabrics (Over 2000 Bolts)
notions, books, frames, and classes.
Free Newsletter

Conway, AR #5

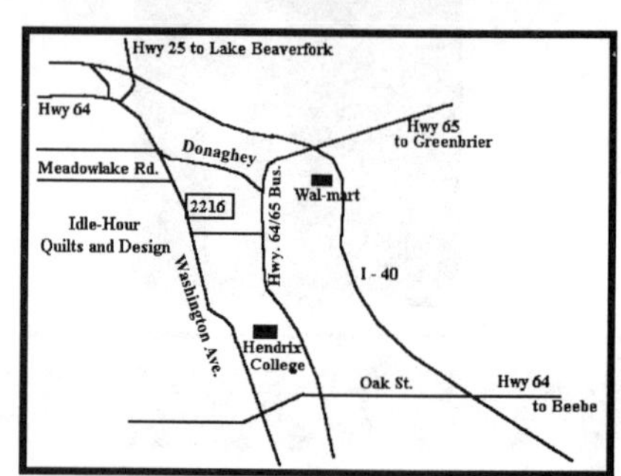

Whether you are a new quilter who needs help with the basics, an intermediate quilter taking steps to stretch and develop your skills, or an accomplished quilter-extraordinaire! IDLE-HOUR QUILTS AND DESIGN can deliver the quilting service and supplies you need, promptly and professionally.

The Stitchin' Post

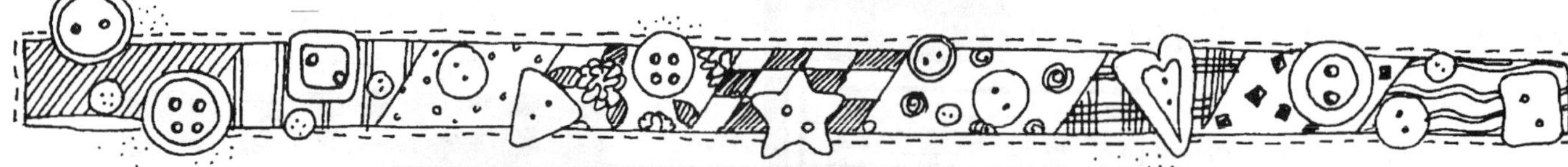

Little Rock, AR #6

10301 Rodney Parham Rd.
(In Breckenridge Village)
72227
(501) 227-0288
Est: 1972 3600 sq.ft.

Mon - Fri
10 - 5:30
Sat 10 - 5

VIKING
Husqvarna

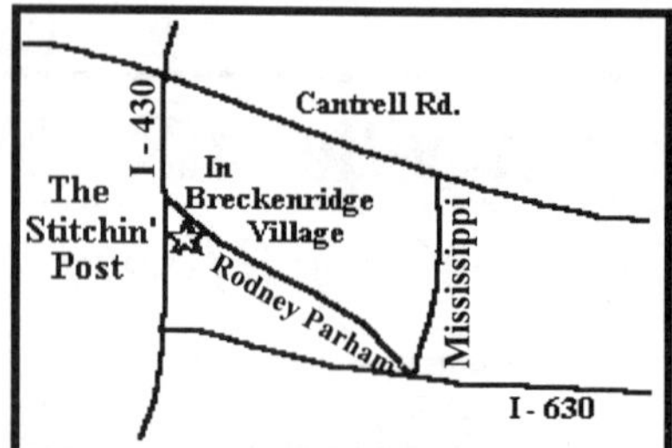

Serving quilters for over 25 years.
Domestic and imported cottons. Quilting supplies and classes.

Little Rock, AR #7

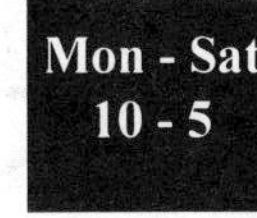

Stitches

10720 Rodney Parham 72212
(501) 225-4202 In Trellis Square
Owner: Marie Henry
Est: 1993 1100 sq.ft.

Little Rock's Premier Quilting Shop. Features over 800 bolts of wonderful fabrics. Friendly, knowledgeable employees.

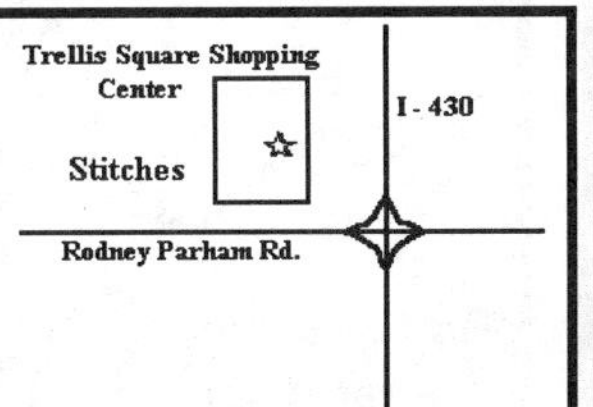

Stuttgart, AR #8

Mon - Fri
9:30 - 5:30
Sat 10 - 2

The French Seam

2014 S. Main St. 72160
(870) 673-8156 Fax: (870) 673-6280
E-Mail: french-seam@futura.net

Authorized Bernina dealer. Quilting, heirloom, silk ribbon, fashion fabric and notions. Machine embroidery supplies Ultrasuede and tapestry. Machine repair.

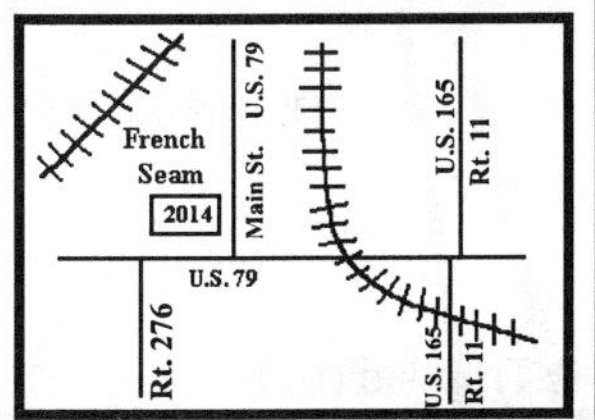

Greenwood, AR #9

Mon - Fri
9 - 5
Sat 10 - 3

Main Street Fabric

20 N. Main, P.O. Box 908 72936
(501) 996-7349
Owner: Oleta Kennedy
Est: 1990
1600 sq.ft. 1600 Bolts

Great selection of 100% Cotton Fabric, Books, Patterns, Notions, Supplies. Classes Avail. Approximately 10 miles south of Exit 12

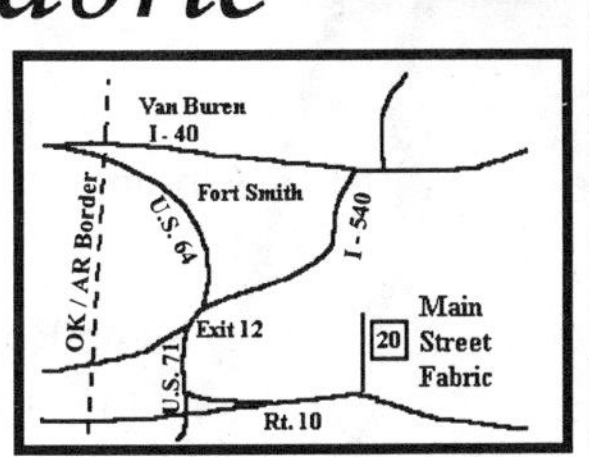

Arkansas Guilds:

Saline County Quilters Guild, 224 W. South St., Benton, 72015
Q.U.I.L.T., 823 Lakeside Dr., Fayetteville, 72701
Belle Point Quilters' Guild, P.O. Box 3853, Fort Smith, 72913
Meets: 4th Monday (except Dec.) at
Wesley United Methodist, 2200 S. Phoenix
Arkansas Quilters Guild, 4219 Sugar Maple Ln., Little Rock, 72212
Hill 'n Hollow Quilters Guild, Box 140, Mountain Home, 72653
Hope Quilter's Guild, 624 Cale Rd., Prescott, 71857
Quilt United, Rt. 2, Box 308-B, Rogers, 72756
Quilt Guild of NW Arkansas, P.O. Box 6739, Springdale, 72766

Other Shops in Arkansas:

Ash Flat Homestead Stitches, HC 67, Box 256 870-994-2033
Batesville The Fabric Conn., 151 W. Main St. 870-793-2405
Batesville Marshall Wholesale Fabrics, P.O. Box 2313 870-793-2405
Booneville General Store, 200 W. Main St. 501-675-4017
Camp Quilts & Things, R.R. #1, Box 573 501-895-2518
Conway The Quilt Patch, 273 Hwy. 36 501-796-2282
Eureka Springs Honeysuckle Rose Quilts & Gifts 89 S. Main St., Box 285E 501-253-5146
Eureka Springs Cameo & Country Craft Shoppe Hwy 62 East 501-253-8299
Eureka Springs Sharon's Quilts, R.R. #1 501-253-7889
Eureka Springs The Gingham Goose, 7 N. Main 501-253-9141
Fort Smith Heirlooms Quilt Shop, 1415 N. 38th 501-782-6839
Gurdon Judy's Fabric Outlet, 109 E. Joslyn 501-353-2300
Hot Springs Log Cabin Crafts, 450 S. Rogers 501-767-6624
Hot Springs National Park Quilt House Antiques 5841 Central Ave. 501-525-1567
Huntington Mama's Log House, 3715 E. Clarks Chapel Rd.
Little Rock Sew Smart, 9700 N. Rodney Parham Rd. 501-223-2317
Lowell Makin Memories Fabric Shop 5731 Primrose Rd. 501-756-9502
Mena Quilts, Inc., 607 N. Mena St. 501-394-2024
Mountain Home Remember Me Quilt Shop, 914 S. Main 501-425-7670
Mountain View Remember Me Quilt Shop, 220 W. Main, 501-269-3352
Omaha Quilting Bee, 24790 U.S. Hwy. 65 N 501-426-5466
Paragould Hillcrest Quilt Shop, 8802 Hwy 412 W 501-236-1988
Pelsor Country Palace Ozark Crafts, HC 30 Box 108 501-294-5366
Pelsor Nellie's Craft Shop, HC 30 Box 102 501-294-5317
Russellville Ozark Heritage Craft Village, I-40 & Hwy 7 501-967-3232
Springhill Massey's Hog Heaven, 589 Hwy. 65 N 501-679-6400
Tumbling Shoals Daisy Patch, 2366 Heber Springs Rd. N 501-362-8988
Yellville Sleeping Owl Crafts, Hwy. 14 S 501-449-5299

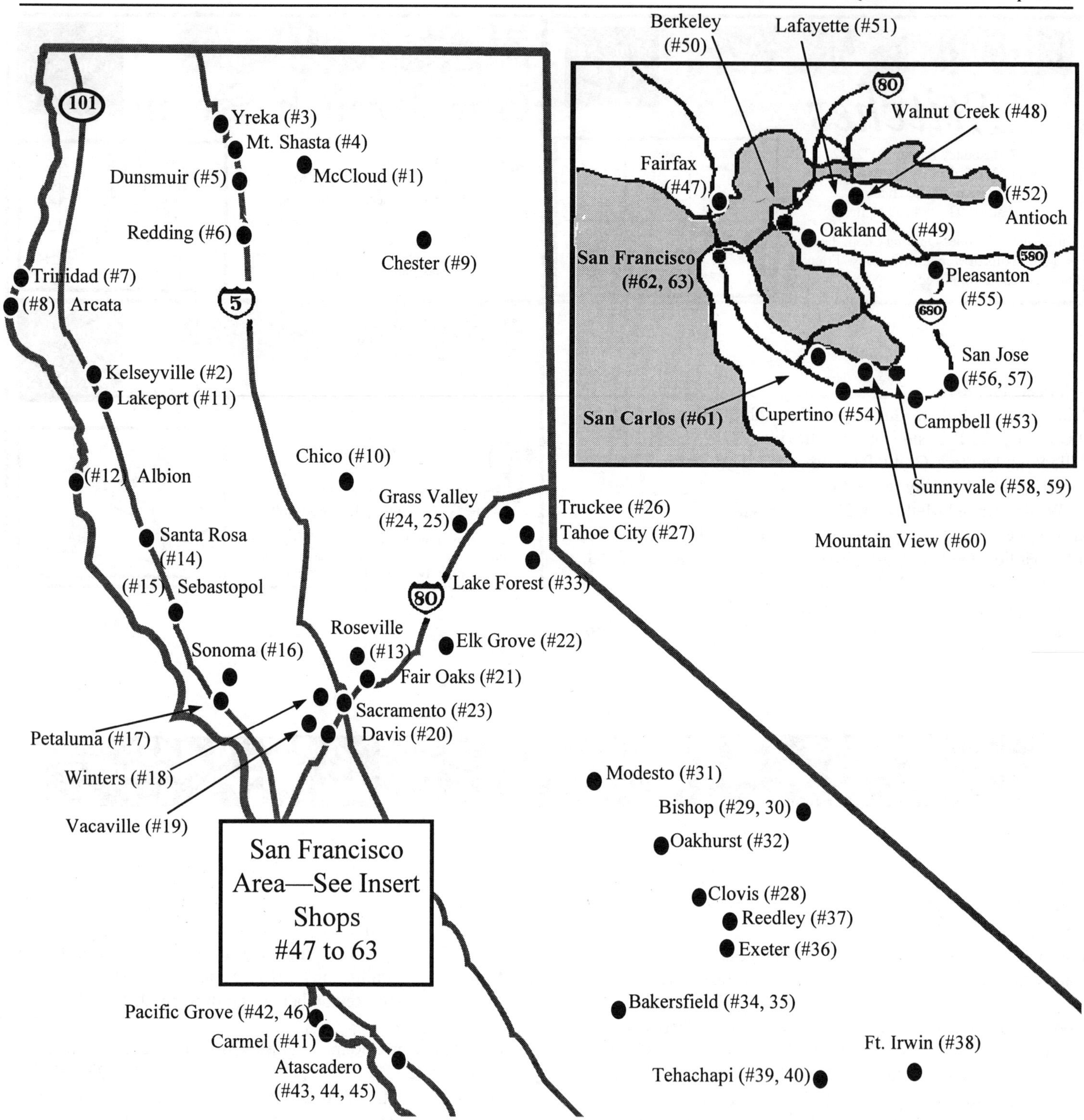

Berkeley (#50)
Lafayette (#51)
Walnut Creek (#48)
Fairfax (#47)
(#52) Antioch
Oakland (#49)
San Francisco (#62, 63)
Pleasanton (#55)
San Jose (#56, 57)
San Carlos (#61)
Cupertino (#54)
Campbell (#53)
Sunnyvale (#58, 59)
Mountain View (#60)
80
580
680

101
5
80
Yreka (#3)
Mt. Shasta (#4)
McCloud (#1)
Dunsmuir (#5)
Redding (#6)
Chester (#9)
Trinidad (#7)
(#8) Arcata
Kelseyville (#2)
Lakeport (#11)
Chico (#10)
(#12) Albion
Grass Valley (#24, 25)
Truckee (#26)
Tahoe City (#27)
Santa Rosa (#14)
(#15) Sebastopol
Lake Forest (#33)
Roseville (#13)
Elk Grove (#22)
Sonoma (#16)
Fair Oaks (#21)
Sacramento (#23)
Davis (#20)
Petaluma (#17)
Winters (#18)
Vacaville (#19)
Modesto (#31)
Bishop (#29, 30)
Oakhurst (#32)
Clovis (#28)
Reedley (#37)
Exeter (#36)
Bakersfield (#34, 35)
Ft. Irwin (#38)
Tehachapi (#39, 40)
Pacific Grove (#42, 46)
Carmel (#41)
Atascadero (#43, 44, 45)

San Francisco Area—See Insert Shops #47 to 63

For Southern California See Page 31 Shops #64 thru #105

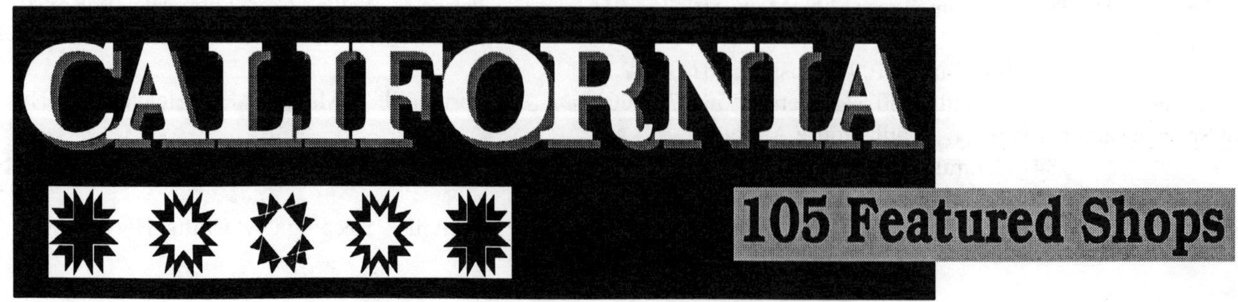

"The Oldest & Largest Quilt Shop in Northern California"

McCloud, CA #1

207 Quincy Ave. P.O. Box 347 96057

(530) 964-2500

E-Mail: quiltldy@snowcrest.net

Mon - Sat 10 - 5

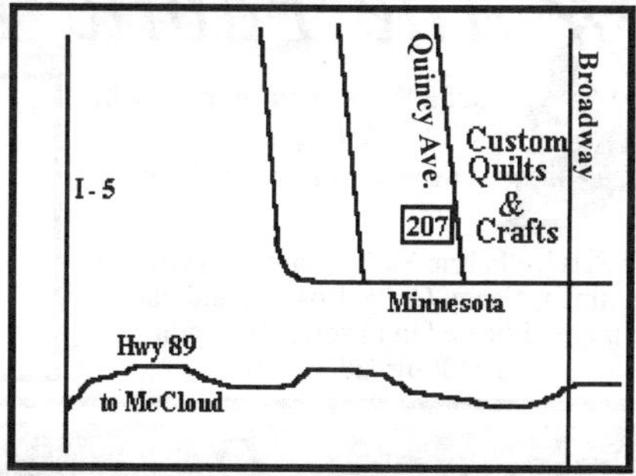

Home of McCloud Quilt Weekends.
Enjoy 2 full days of undisturbed quilting in historic McCloud.
Call, write or e-mail for information.

Books, Patterns, Supplies. Friendly, Knowledgeable Service.
Over 1000 Bolts of FABULOUS FABRICS

Quilted Treasures

BLUE LAKES
UKIAH
UPPER LAKE
NICE
LUCERNE
LAKEPORT
Clear Lake
GLENHAVEN
CLEARLAKE OAKS
FINLEY
HOPLAND
KELSEYVILLE
WILLIAMS
CLEARLAKE PARK
CLEARLAKE
GEYSERVILLE
LOCH LOMOND
ADAMS SPRINGS
SEIGLER
HOBERGS
COBB
LOWER LAKE
WOODLAND
MIDDLETOWN
SANTA ROSA
CALISTOGA
NAPA
IGNACIO
SACRAMENTO
GOLDEN GATE BRIDGE
CARQUINEZ BRIDGE
SAN FRANCISCO
OAKLAND

1 hour from Hwy. 5
45 min. from Hwy. 101

3925 Main St., P.O. Box 1189 95453
(707) 279-0324 Fax: (707) 279-4430
Pamela Francis, President
Anne Barquist, Vice President

Kelseyville, CA #2

- Thousands of premium cotton fabrics
- Flannels, batiks, ikats, silk, rayons, and fleece for fine sewing.
- Books, patterns, and notions
- Quilts on display
- State of the art *Gammill Hand Guided Quilting Machine*
- Knowledgeable, friendly staff

Mon - Fri 10 - 5:30
Sat 10 - 4

For all your Quilting needs!

Yreka, CA #3

Tues - Sat
10 - 5:30

Fabric Country & Needlecraft

333 W. Miner 96097
(530) 842-5550
Est: 1987 2200 sq.ft.

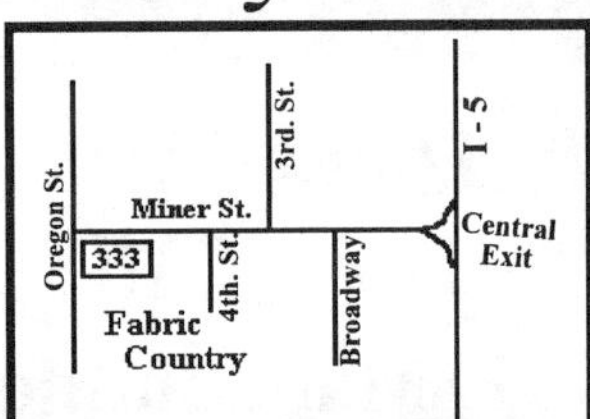

A most unusual store. Full service fabric store specializing in quilting and wedding fabrics. Pfaff sewing machines too. We also carry yarn, needlework & gifts.

Mt. Shasta, CA #4

Tues - Sat
10 - 5

Sew Unique

412 S. Mt. Shasta Blvd. 96067
(530) 926-0768 Fax: (530) 926-4908
Owner: Tina Seres Est: 1989
1400 sq.ft. Large Inventory

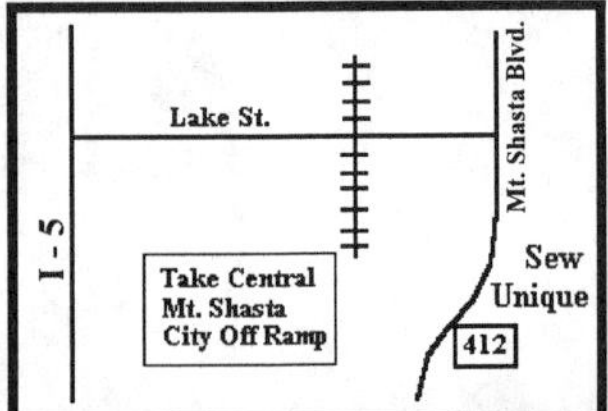

Designer fabric, quilting supplies, books and gifts. Classes and Quilting Retreats. Call for newsletter. Fun, Friendly Store. New Home Dealer.

Dunsmuir, CA #5

Mon - Sat
10 - 5

The Fabric Train

5853 Sacramento Ave. 96025
(530) 235-4519
Owners: Bill & Ann Sanford

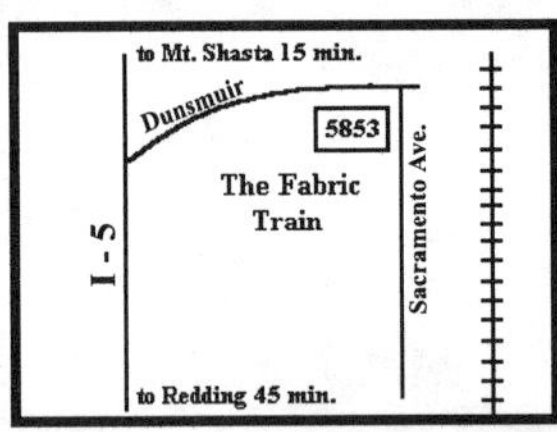

Full Service Fabric Store. Large selection of Hoffman, Nancy Crow, Rosebar and many more. Located in historic Dunsmuir. "The Railroad Town"

Redding, CA #6

Mon - Sat
9 - 6
Sun 11 - 5

Ben Franklin Crafts

961 Dana Dr. 96003
(530) 221-8313 Fax: (530) 221-8387
Owners: Fred & Judy Zerull
Est: 1965 9000 sq.ft. 3500 Bolts

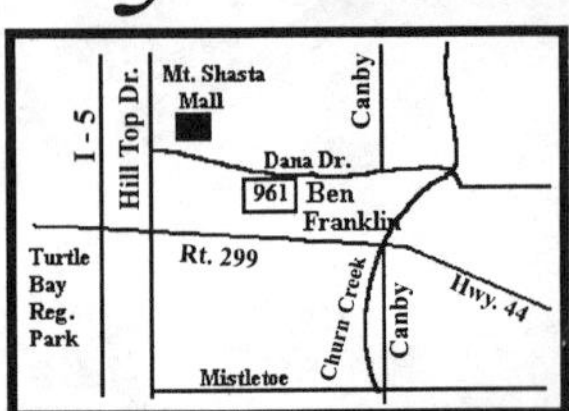

Visit our complete quilt department; stitchery, patterns, books, notions and fabrics: P&B, Benartex, Hoffman, Nancy Crow, Moda and many more.

Trinidad, CA #7

Open 6 days
9:30 - 5:30
Closed Tues

Ocean Wave Quilts

529 Trinity St. 95570
(707) 677-3770
Owner: Sandi Globus
Est: 1994 800 sq.ft. 1000 Bolts

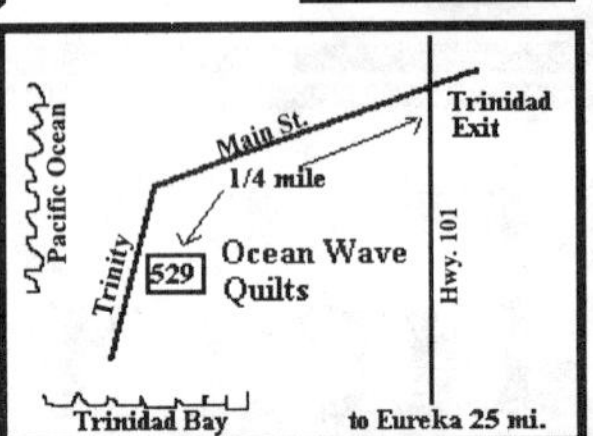

A unique shop containing fabulous fabrics, books and notions located in a historic fishing village nestled between redwoods and beaches.

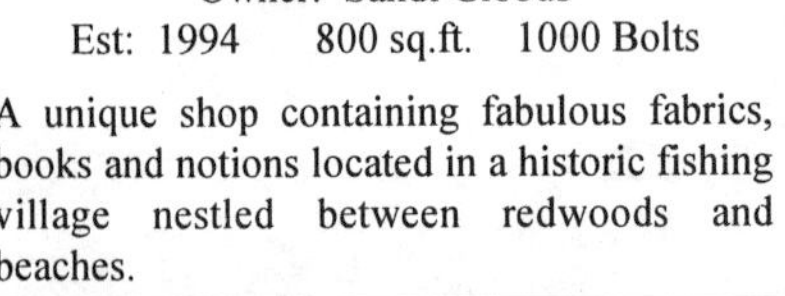

Arcata, CA #8

Mon - Sat
10 - 5:30
Sun 11 - 4

Fabric Temptations

942 'G' Street 95521
(707) 822-7782
Owner: Lennie Est: 1984
Swatch Set $4

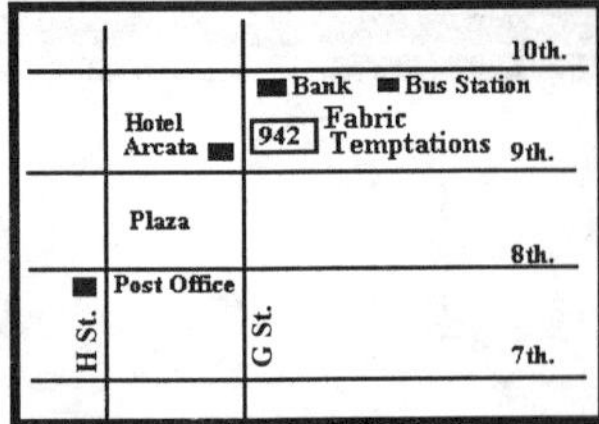

Natural Fiber Fabrics. Liberty of London. Battings: Cotton, Silk, Wool & Polyester. Quilting & Sewing Supplies. Mail order.

Chester, CA #9

Oct 1 - April 30
Mon - Sat 10 - 5
May 1 - Sept 30
Mon - Sat 10 - 5
Sun 12 - 4

135 Main St. #6E
P.O. Box 546
96020
Est: 1992
1500 sq.ft.
1200 Bolts

Owners: Jenifer Paine-St. Clair
& Sharon Paine (530) 258-3901

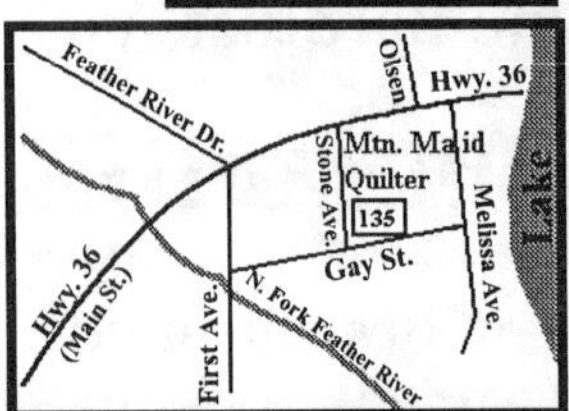

Fabric, Notions, Specialy Yarns, X-stitch, Dyes, and Silk Ribbon. We're next to beautiful Mt. Lassen and Lake Almanor. Classes Offered

Chico, CA #10

Mon - Sat
10 - 5:30

Honey Run Quilters

1230 Esplanade 95926
(530) 342-5464
E-Mail: hrquilt@shocking.com
Web Site: www.shocking.com/~hrquilt/
Owner: Sharon Berg

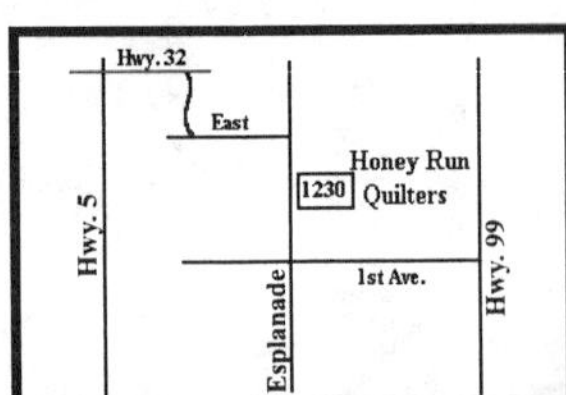

The latest in fabrics, books, patterns & notions.
Friendly, knowledgeable service.
Good Parking. Coffee's always on!

Lakeport, CA #11

By Chance
or Appt.

Kerrie's Quilting

2695 Hartley Rd. 95453
(707) 263-8555
Owners: Harry & Kerrie Hershey

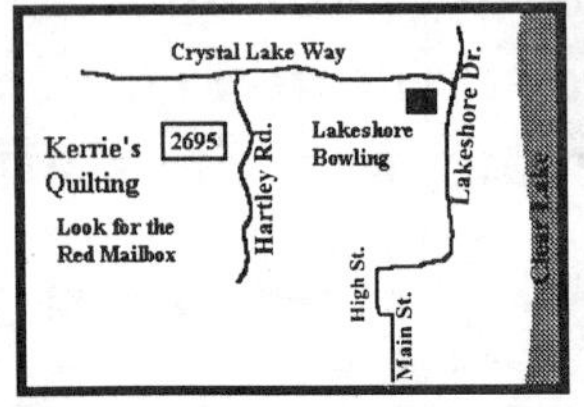

Authorized Elna dealer, cotton fabrics, books, classes, retreats. A friendly small town shop in the country.

Albion, CA #12

Phone for
Appointment

Rainbow Resource Co.

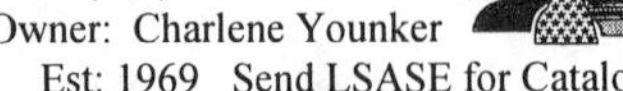

P.O. Box 222 95410
(707) 937-0431
Owner: Charlene Younker
Est: 1969 Send LSASE for Catalog

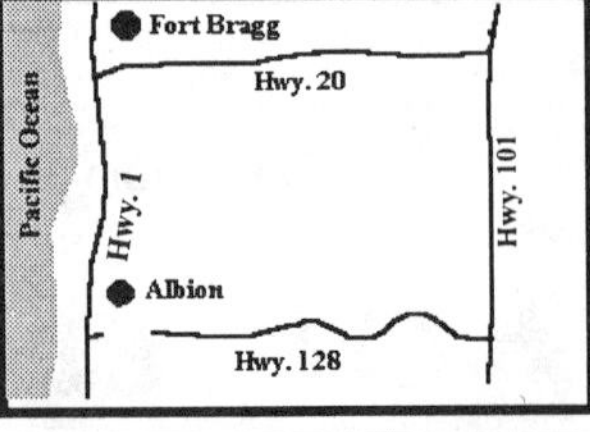

My own line of hand silk-screened fabric for quilters, along with related fabrics from various companies. Unusual Buttons, & Fun Stuff.

Roseville, CA #13

Largest Selection of Patterns in Northern California

The Stitching Station

1000 Sunrise Ave. 95661
(916) 773-0296
Fax: (916) 773-0294
Owner: Sandra Satnowski
Est: 1989 2400 sq.ft.

Mon - Fri 10 - 6
Sat 10 - 5:30
Sun 12 - 4

If you're a quilter, you've heard about The Stitching Station. We have the most unique array of Quilting supplies in the Sacramento area, with a large selection of show quality quilts and doll models on display.

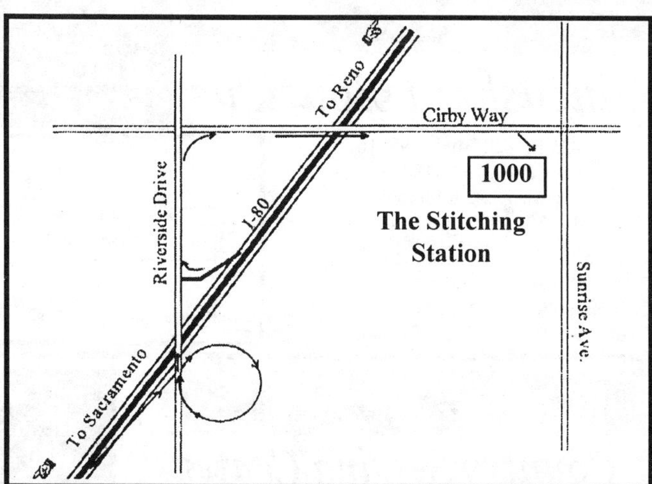

From Sacramento: Take I - 80 east (towards Reno) to the first Roseville exit, Riverside Dr./Auburn Blvd. Follow the signs to Riverside Dr. (pass through the underpass, circle around and cross over the freeway). Turn right again at the second stoplight, Cirby Way. Follow Cirby Way approximately 1 mile, and turn right just before Sunrise Ave. The Stitching Station is on the right.

From Reno: Take I - 80 west (towards Sacramento) to the Riverside Dr. off-ramp. Turn right onto Riverside. Turn right again at the first stoplight, Cirby Way. Follow Cirby Way approximately 1 mile, and turn right just before Sunrise Ave. The Stitching Station is on the right.

Fabric, Books, Supplies, Notions, Doll Patterns, Quilting Classes. Large selection of 30's reproduction fabrics and a great collection of Homespuns.

Santa Rosa, CA #14

Mon - Sat 10 - 6
Sun 12 - 5

TREADLEART

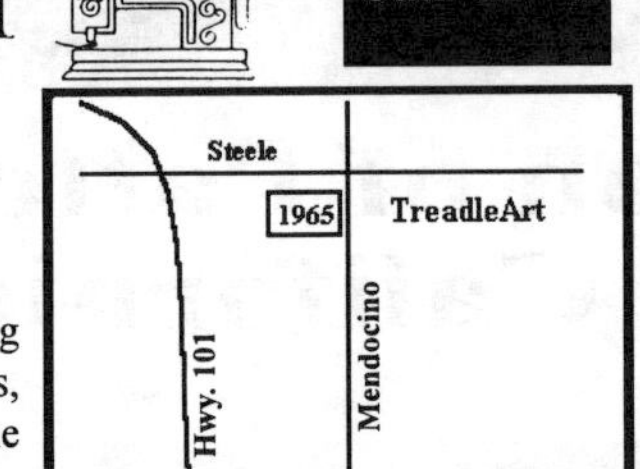
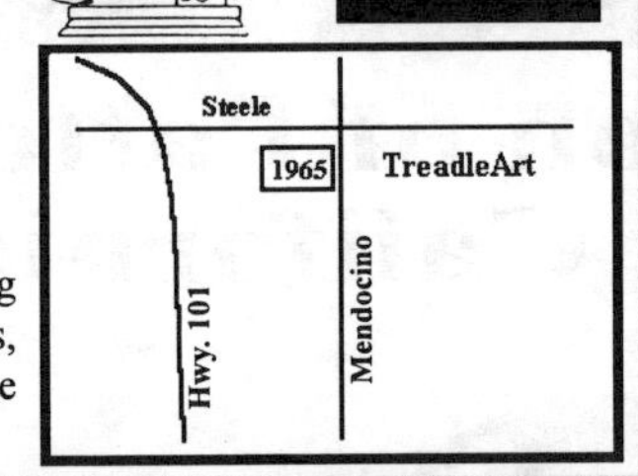

1965 Mendocino 95401
(707) 523-2122
Owner: Janet Stocker
Est: 1994 2300 sq.ft.

Supplies for all your quilting and sewing needs. 5000 bolts of fabric, patterns, books, stencils, decorative thread, machine accessories notions.

Sonoma, CA #16

Mon - Fri 9:30 - 6
Sat 10 - 5:30
Sun 11 - 4

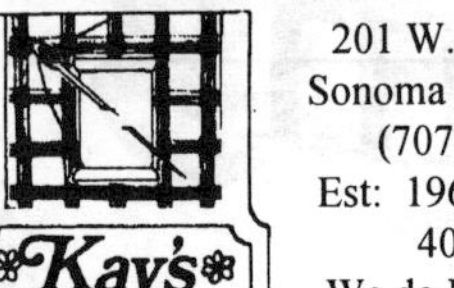

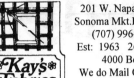

201 W. Napa St. #14
Sonoma Mkt.Pl. 95476
(707) 996-3515
Est: 1963 2600 sq.ft.
4000 Bolts
We do Mail Orders &
Invite Fabric Requests.

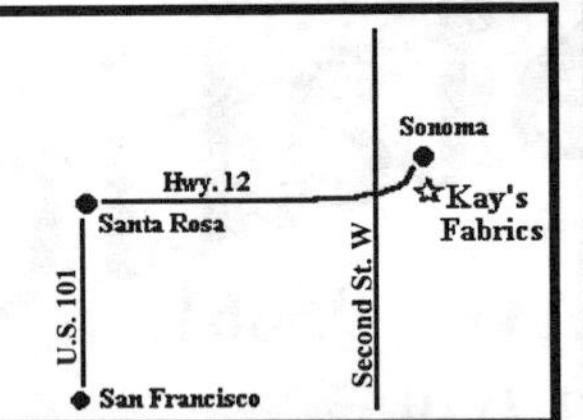

Complete line of quilting fabrics, books, patterns and notions. Hoffman, RJR, VIP, Kona & Many Unusual Fabrics.

Sebastopol, CA #15

SPECIALTY: JAPAN

EASTWIND ART

Owner: Joanne Newcomb
Established 1973

P.O. BOX 811 SEBASTOPOL, CA 95473
(707) 829-3536 kitagami@eastwindart.com

Web page:
www.eastwindart.com

Patterns: Japanese crafts, clothing, quilts, accessories

Fabrics: Japanese prints, indigo, shibori, kimono scraps

Sashiko: Needles, thread, stencils, indigo fabric, books

Books: Japanese designs, paper dolls, quilting, clothing

Gifts: Miniature cast iron tea pots, note cards, charms, etc.

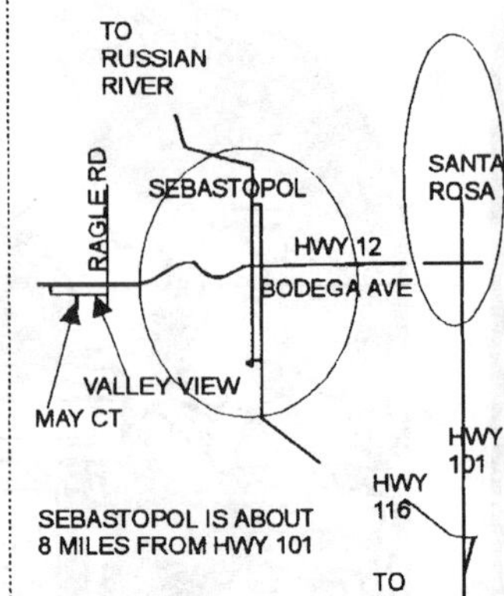

Petaluma, CA #17

Mon - Sat 10 - 5:30
Thur til 7:30
Sun 12 - 4

200 G St. 94952
(707) 763-0945
E-Mail: angels@QuiltedAngel.com
Web Site: www.QuiltedAngel.com
Owner: Susie Ernst
Est: 1991 2200 sq.ft. 2850 Bolts

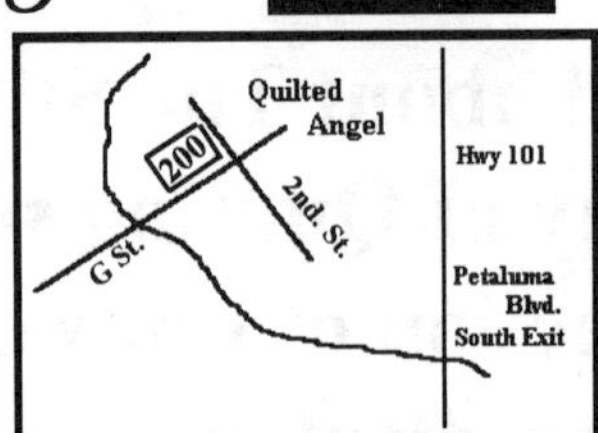

A "destination" Quilt Store. Fabrics from all major suppliers, books (600 titles) notions, patterns, doll supplies & classes.

Winters, CA #18

Tues - Sat 10 - 4:30
Fri til 9

Cloth Carousel & Quiltworks

9 Main St. 95694
(530) 795-2580
Owner: Laurie A. Sengo
Est: 1995

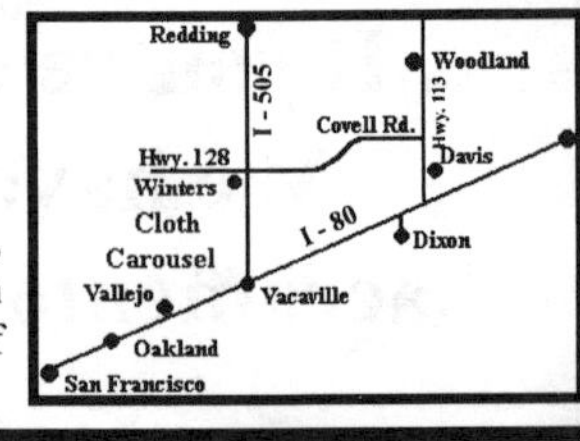

Specializing in service. 850 bolts, notions, books, classes. We offer quality custom machine quilting. Eleven miles North of Vacaville off I - 505.

Vacaville, CA #19

Hours by Appt.

The Unique Spool

407 Corte Majorca 95688
(707) 448-1538
Web Site: www.uniquespool.com
Owner: Roberta Dent

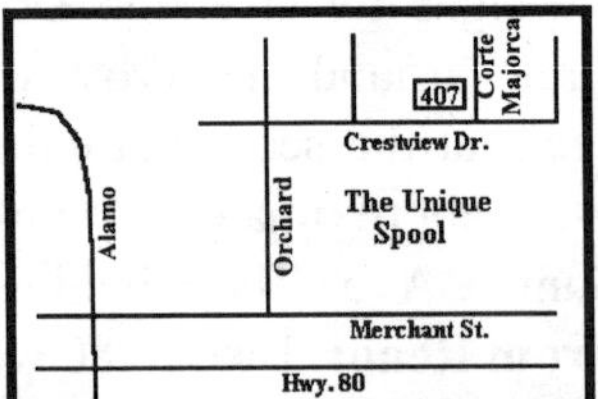

African and Australian Fabrics plus domestic prints, ethnic quilt patterns, notions & quilt frames.

Davis, CA #20

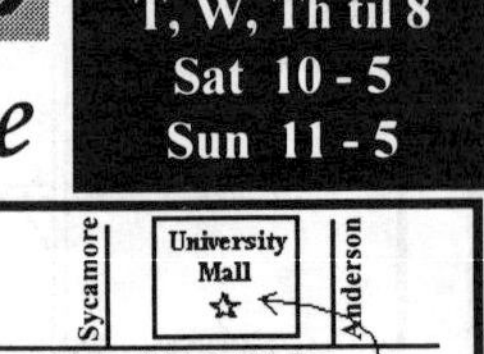

Pincushion Boutique

825 Russell Blvd. 95616
(916) 758-3488
Owner: Beth Murphy
Est: 1977 1000 sq.ft. 3000 Bolts

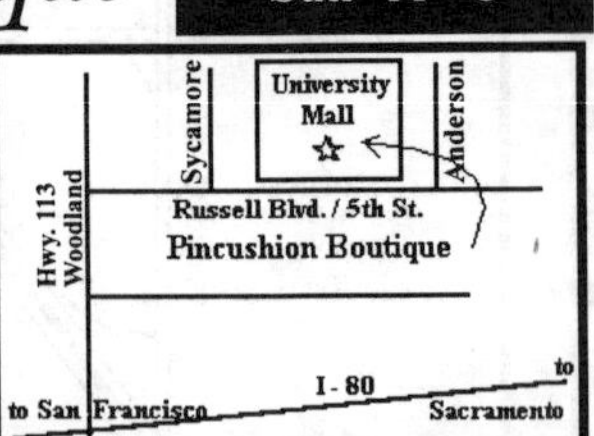

Home of Sweet Treat Medleys.
2000 Hoffmans 1000 other.
Helpful quilters on Staff.
Mail Order & Sweet Treat Subscription.

Fair Oaks, CA #21

Mon - Sat 9 - 5
Wed & Thur til 8

Tayo's Fabrics & Quilts

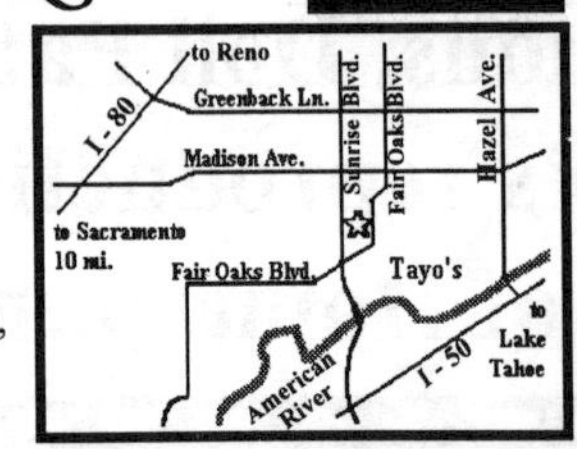

10127 Fair Oaks Blvd. 95628
(916) 967-5479 Fax: (916) 721-1933
Owner: Shenna Mealey Est: 1983

Fabrics, books, patterns & notions for traditional & contemporary quilting, cloth dolls, wearable art & fashion sewing. Classes. Personal & friendly service.

Elk Grove, CA #22

Mon - Fri 10 - 6
Sat 10 - 5

Country Sewing Center

9639 E. Stockton Blvd. 95624
(916) 685-8500
E-Mail: cntrysew@elkgrove.net
Visit our Web-Site: www.elkgrove.net/csc
Owners: Susan & Bill Zimlich
Est: 1993 2400 sq.ft. 800+ Bolts

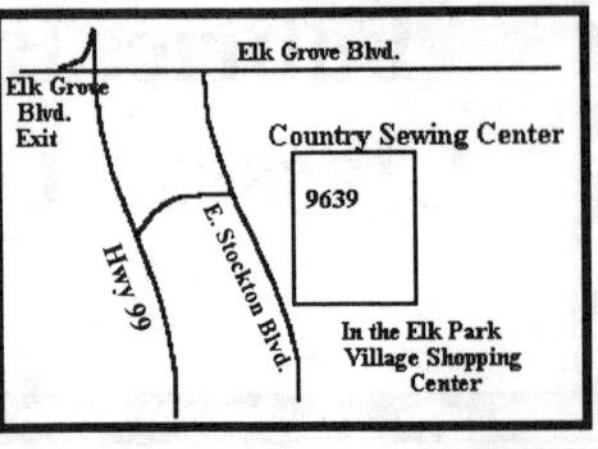

15 minutes south of Sacramento on Hiway 99. Great selection of 100% fabrics, books & notions. Friendly, small-town service.

Material Girls

Sacramento, CA #23

2617 Alta Arden Expressway
95825
(916) 485-4252
Fax: (916) 485-4272
Owners: Terri Lanning,
Dawn Licker, & Phyllis Day
Est: 1997 2500 sq.ft. 2500 Bolts

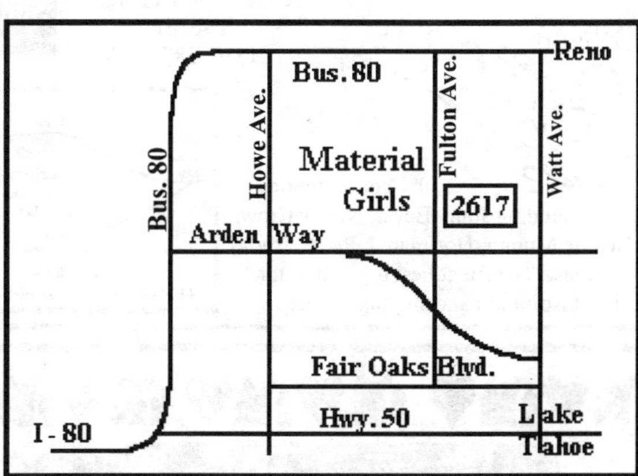

"Friendliest Shop in Town"

A great selection of :

- Quality 100% cotton fabric
- Books & Patterns
- Notions
- Classes Offered
- Quilting Machine on Premises.

Monday 10 - 8
Tuesday - Saturday 10 - 6
Sunday 12 - 4

Grass Valley, CA #24

Mon- Sat 10 - 6
Sun 11 - 4

Fabrications

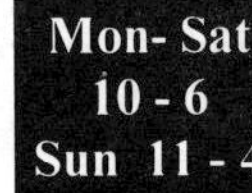

Free Catalog

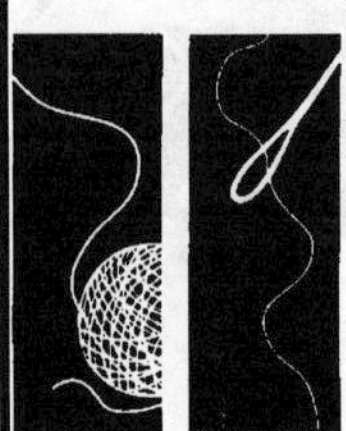

120 W. Main St. 95945
(530) 272-4412 Est: 1995
Fax: (530) 272-1450
E-Mail: fabric@gv.net
Web Site:
FABRICATIONS-GV.com
Owner: Judith Bernard
3000 sq.ft. 2000 Bolts

W. Main St.
Richardson St.
Fabrications
120
Mill St.
Neal St.
S. Auburn St.
to Hwy. 20 & Reno
Hwy. 49
to Hwy. 80 & Sacramento

Grass Valley, CA #25

Mon - Fri 9 - 8
Sat 9 - 6
Sun 10 - 6

Ben Franklin Crafts

11598 Sutton Way 95945
(530) 273-1348

Large Selection of 100% cotton fabrics from leading manufacturers; battings and quilting books. Friendly and personal service.

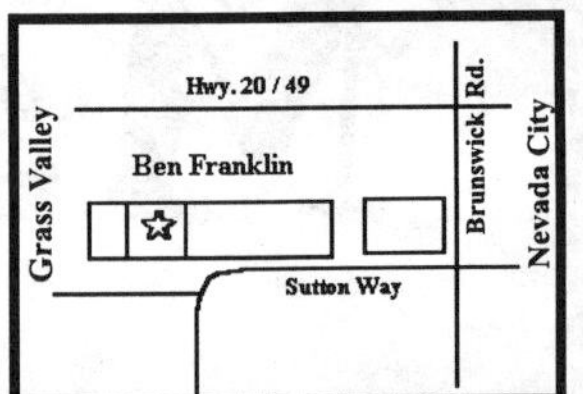

Truckee, CA #26

Mon - Sat 9:30 - 5:30
Sun 10 - 5

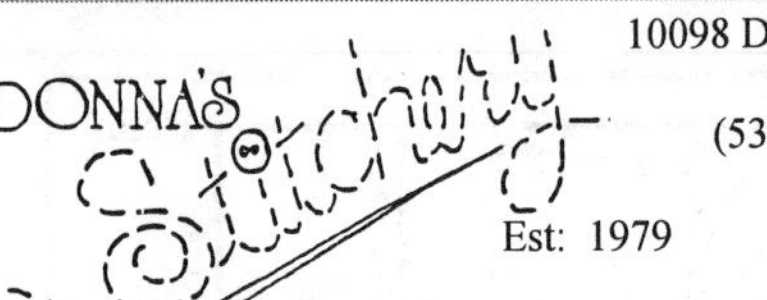

10098 Donner Pass Rd.
96161
(530) 587-6708

Est: 1979

100% cotton fabrics including Jinny Beyer, Nancy Crow, Moda, Debbie Mumm, Hoffman & P&B. Books and Notions. The friendliest quilt shop for service, inspiration and sharing of ideas.

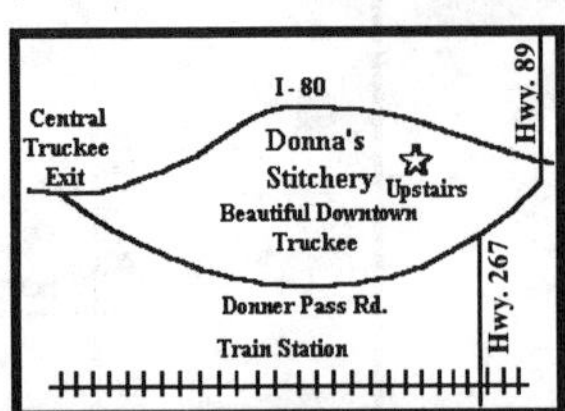

Tahoe City, CA #27

10 - 5
Closed Wed.

Mountain Stitchery

295 N. Lake Blvd., P.O. Box 1420 96145
(530) 583-9301
Est: 1978 700 sq.ft. 700 Bolts

Large variety of gorgeous quilts in stock or we'll make yours to order! Great selection of unique fabrics, wallhangings and dolls.

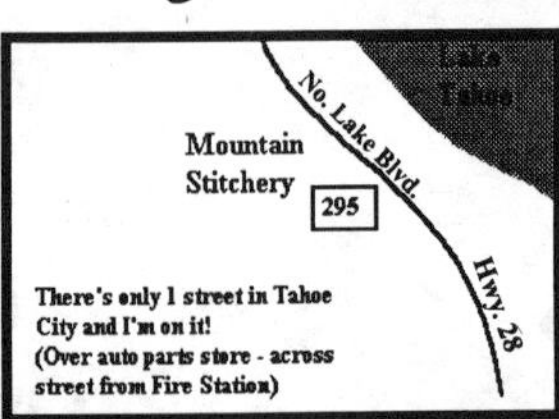

Clovis, CA #28

QUILTERS' PARADISE

339 Pollasky
93612

(209) 297-7817
Owner:
Jennifer Wheeler
Est: 1978
5000 sq.ft.

- **helpful, friendly service**
- **great selection of newest fabrics, books, patterns and notions**
- **silk ribbon, doll and bear making supplies**
- **new merchandise arriving daily**
- **mail orders & special orders welcome**
- **Visa, Mastercard, & Discover**

Just What the Shop Name Says!!

Mon - Fri 10 - 6
Sat 10 - 5
Sun 12 - 4

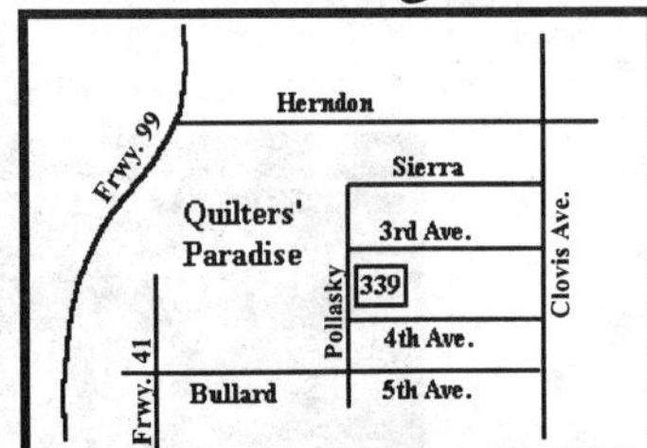

Bishop, CA #29

Mon - Sat 10 - 5:30

Sew It Seams

124 N. Main St. 93514
(760) 873-5635
Owner: Nancy Wood
Est: 1995 2200 sq.ft. 700 Bolts

Large Selection of Quality Fabric. Books, Patterns and Quilting Supplies. Classes Available. Machine Sales & Service. Friendly& Personal Service.

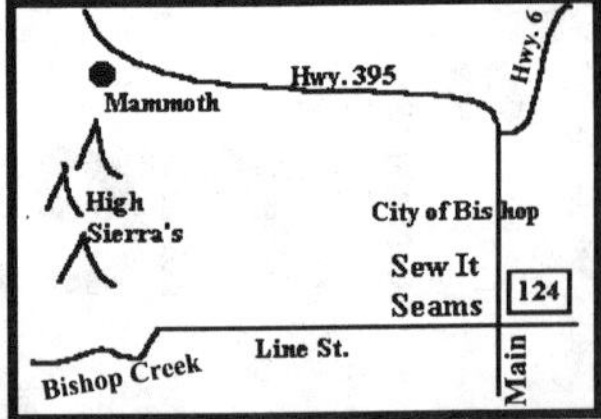

Bishop, CA #30

Mon - Sat 10 - 5
Sun 1 - 5

The Fabric Store

1343 Rocking W. Dr. 93514
(760) 873-6808
Owners: Charlie & John Waldriff
Est: 1982 1280 sq.ft. 700 Bolts

A Sewer's Haven
Classes in Quilting & Sewing

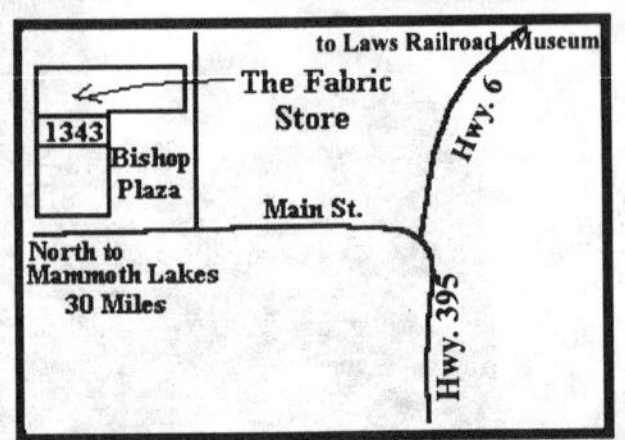

Modesto, CA #31

Mon - Fri 9:30 - 5:30
Sat 10 - 5
Sun 12 - 4

R. Lily Stem Quilts

909 W. Roseburg Ave. Suite B 95350
(209) 577-1919
Owner: Marilyn Nelson
Est: 1986 3200 sq.ft.

Fabulous fabrics, books, patterns, cross-stitch, custom comforters, classes and great service ! Authorized Bernina Dealer.

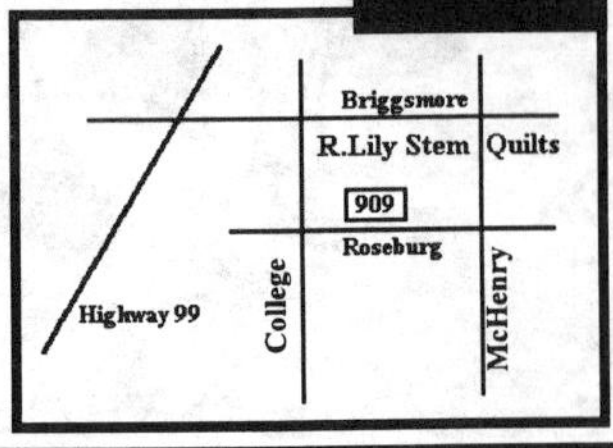

Oakhurst, CA #32

Arlene's Calico Country

Located in the Enterprise Center
(209) 683-SEWS
Owner: Arlene Hartman
40092 Hwy. 49 93644
Est: 1990 2600 sq.ft.
Over 4000 Bolts of FABRIC!!!

A QUILTER'S HAVEN

Quilting Supplies • Silk Ribbon Embroidery Supplies • Fabric • Books T-Shirts • Sweatshirts • Beads • Yarn • Afghans • Lace • Ribbon • Notions DMC • Gifts • Bess Lap Hoops & Border Bars • Gift Certificates • Classes

Happy Birthday
Come in on your birthday for a 25% discount on any fabric purchase.

50% OFF on selected fabrics in our Treasure Trunk all year!

40% OFF
at least 1 or 2 quilt books & patterns every month!

We carry Hoffman, Maywood, Norcott, Alexander Henry, Nancy Crow, P&B, Kona Bay, Bali, Moda, Spiegel, Marcus Brothers, Roberta Horton, RJR, South Seas, Concord, Debbie Mumm, Hi-Fashion, Mission Valley & many more.
All the latest Collections !

Bolt End Sale
40% Off !!
Last Day of the Month

Quilt - Pak of the Month Club!
Join Now!

Enjoy new fabric each month! You get the newest and most popular fabrics *fast*! 5 color coordinated fat quarters for $8.50 plus $1.95 for shipping. Q-PAK of the month offered only on an automatic credit card billing system. When you order, provide your credit card number and expiration date, authorizing us to charge your Q-PAK to it each month. Return your Q-PAK for any reason, your credit card will be credited, and you'll continue to receive future Q-PAKs. You may cancel your membership at any time. Sign up for your quarterly mail order list and newsletter. We ship fabric! (1 yard minimum cuts). Send us a swatch of what you're looking for. If we have it, we'll ship it!

Mon - Sat
9 - 5
Open Sundays Memorial Day thru Labor Day 11 - 4

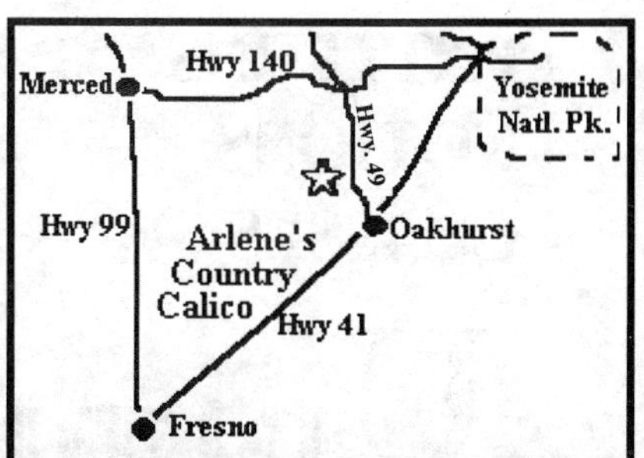

Material Possessions Quilt Shop

Mon - Sat
10 - 5:30
Wed til 9

22600-C Lambert St. Suite 905
Lake Forest, CA 92630
(714) 586-3418
Fax: (714) 586-7125
Proprietor: Wendy Hager
Est: 1995 5000 sq.ft.

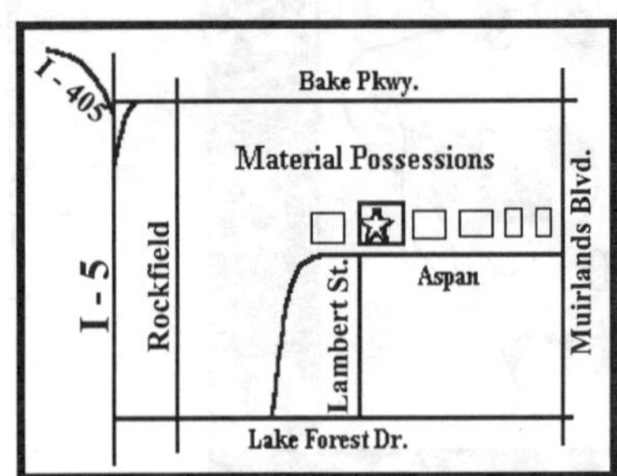

Lake Forest, CA #33

We cater to all of your quilting needs. The shop carries a wonderful selection of 100% cotton fabric from numerous manufacturers. We specialize in authentic Japanese fabrics, batiks and hand-dyed fabric. Come browse through our 200 book titles or many wearable, quilt, applique and soft craft patterns. We have an extensive silk ribbon department and carry a full compliment of YLI and hand-dyed silk ribbon, perle cotton, and silk threads. We offer a wide variety of classes in a spacious classroom. Our classes are for all levels and there are many wonderful teachers to choose from.

E-Mail: matpos@material possessions
Web Site: www.materialpossessions.com

The Bobbin Spinner

Mon - Thur 9 - 6
Fri & Sat 9 - 5
Sun 11 - 4

Bakersfield, CA #34

- FABRICS (100% Cotton)
- BOOKS
- PATTERNS
- NOTIONS
- CLASSES

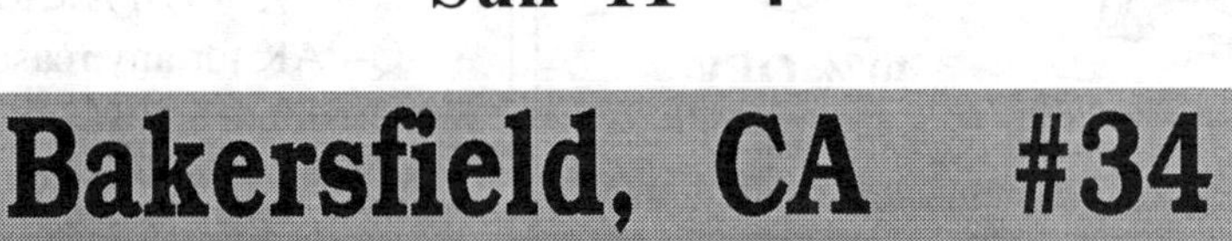

(805) 325-5244
3401 Chester Ave.
Suite J 93301
Owners: Sharon & Ray Payne
Est: 1994 1500 sq.ft.

Unique Country Fabrics

Bakersfield, CA #35

Mon - Fri 10 - 5:30
Sat 10 - 5

Strawberry Patches

6439 Ming Ave. #C 93309
(805) 835-1738 Fax: (805) 835-0406
Owner: Suzanne Zingg
Est: 1985 2500 sq.ft.

Voted one of America's Top Ten quilt shops by American Patchwork & Quilting Magazine. Selection, Service, Smiles.

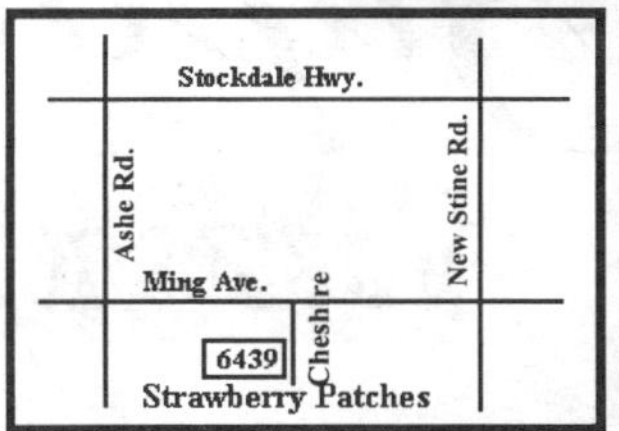

Exeter, CA #36

Tues - Fri 9:30 - 5:30
Thur til 7
Sat 9:30 - 4:30

Thimble Towne

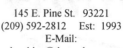

145 E. Pine St. 93221
(209) 592-2812 Est: 1993
E-Mail:
hawkins@theworks.com
Owner: Kathy Hawkins
100% cotton fabrics; books and patterns galore; mail order welcome; newsletter; classes

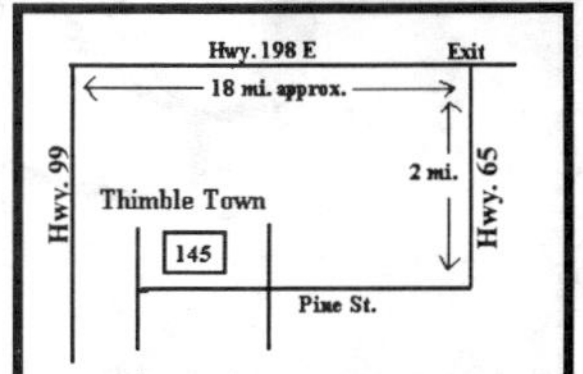

Reedley, CA #37

Mon - Fri 9:30 - 4:30
Sat 10 - 2

Mennonite Quilt Center

1012 "G" St. 93654
(209) 638-3560 2500 sq.ft.
Mgrs: Jeanne Heyerly
& Kathleen Heinrichs 450 Bolts

100% Cotton Fabrics, notions, Books, Patterns, & Battings. Quilters on site Monday mornings. Quilt show year around. Tours Avail.

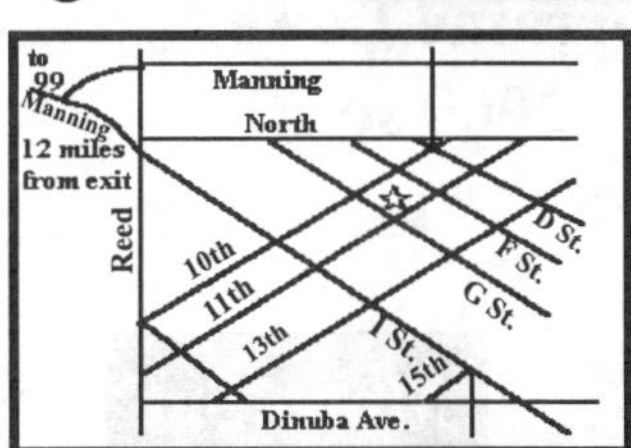

Fort Irwin, CA #38

By Chance or Appt.

Annie's Attic

3918 Tiefort Dr. 92310
(760) 386-1224
E-Mail: asfarq@aol.com
Owner: Annie Farquhar

100% Cotton Fabrics, Quilting Supplies, Books and Gifts. Personalized Service.

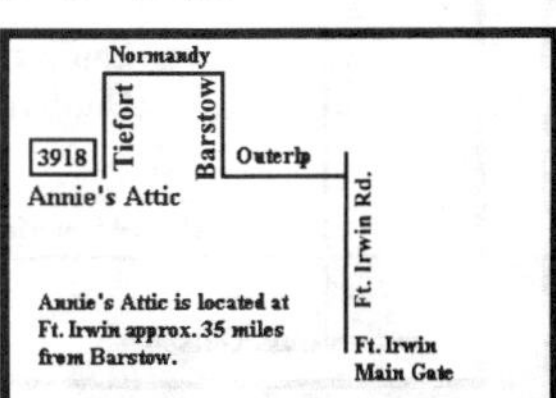

Tehachapi, CA #39

Tue - Fri 10 - 5
Sat 10 - 4

Clear Creek Homeworks

The Quilting & Fabric Shoppe
20608 South St. 93561
(805) 823-9108
Owner: Ann Webster

A shoppe of distinction for the most discriminating quilter.
A palette of extraordinary colors and patterns to stimulate your imagination.

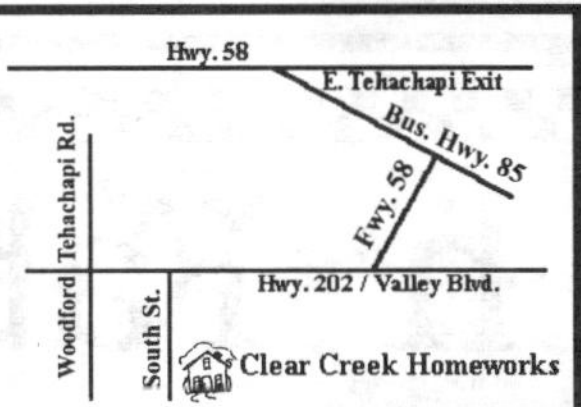

Tehachapi, CA #40

Tues - Fri 9:30 - 3:30
Sat 10 - 2

* 5 Heart Quilts & Fabric *

Est: 1993
900 sq.ft.
1000 Bolts

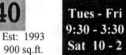

122 E. Tehachapi Blvd. #C
(805) 822-8709 93561
Owner: Claudia Blodget Priddy

A Quilters Heaven with all of the Colors - 100% Cotton, Hoffman, Alex. Henry, Northcott, Benartex, Books, Notions and Classes - For Your Needs.

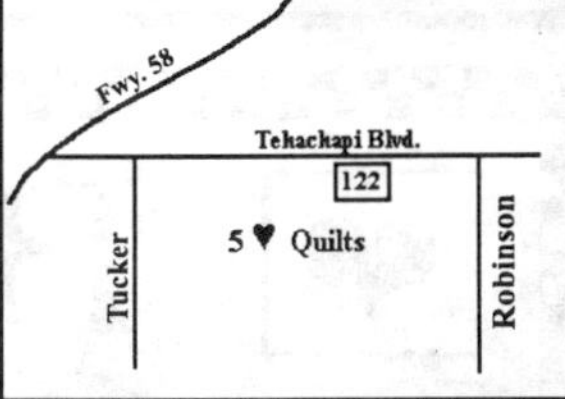

Carmel, CA #41

7 Days a Week
11 - 5

California QuiltMakers

Ocean Ave. at Monte Verde
P.O. Box 7237 93921
(408) 625-2815
Owners: Pat Fryer & Pam Howland
Est: 1995 500 sq.ft.

Quilts for Sale. Quilted Clothing.
Books, Patterns
Fabric Pieces.

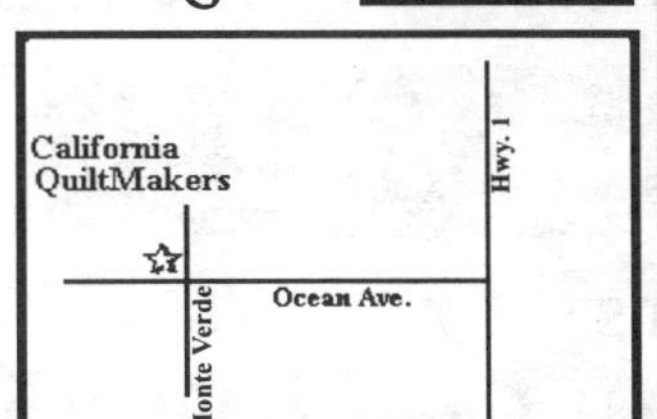

Pacific Grove, CA #42

Mon - Sat 10 - 5:30
Sun 12 - 4

The Hand Maden

620 Lighthouse Ave.
(408) 373-5353
Owners: Olivia & Don Shaffer
Est: 1983 3000 sq.ft.

3000 bolts of quilters cotton. All supplies & patterns needed. Extensive Needlework selections. Viking Machines.

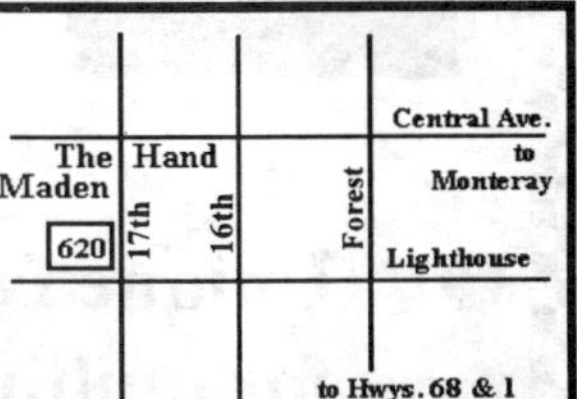

Atascadero, CA #43

Mon - Sat 10 - 5

The Country Sampler

6155 El Camino Real 93422
(805) 466-7282 Fax: (805) 466-7392
Owners: Teri Gentry & Maureen Bryan

Come discover the appeal & friendship of an old time general mercantile. Everything for your quilting needs, as well as unique gifts & clothing. Specializing in applique.
Newsletter and mail order clubs for Fabrics, Thread & Block of the Month Available.

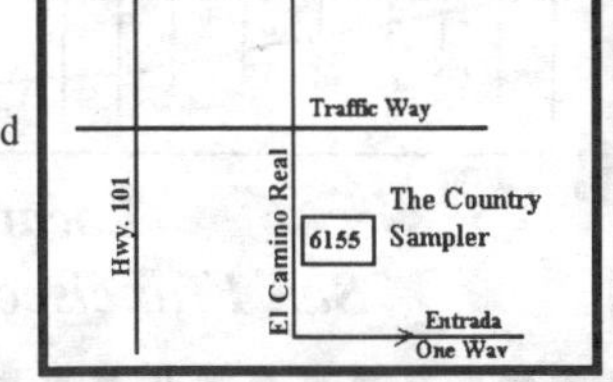

Atascadero, CA #44

Mon - Fri 10 - 7
Sat 10 - 5
Sun 12 - 5

Sew Fun

8775 El Camino Real
93422 (805) 462-9739
Owner: Marilyn (Lynn) J. Barksdale
Est: 1996 2400 sq.ft. 3500 Bolts
Great selection of fabrics, books, patterns.
The latest in quilting supplies.
Friendly and helpful staff.
New Home sewing machine sales & service.

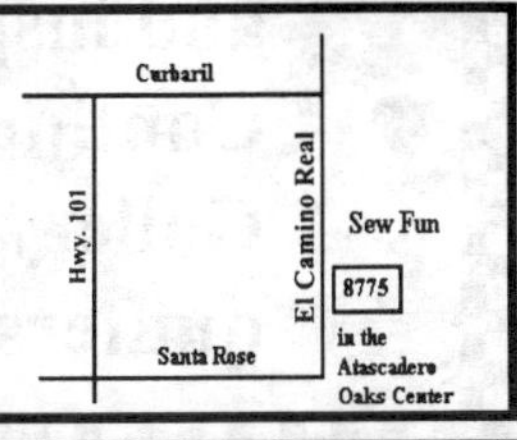

Atascadero, CA #45

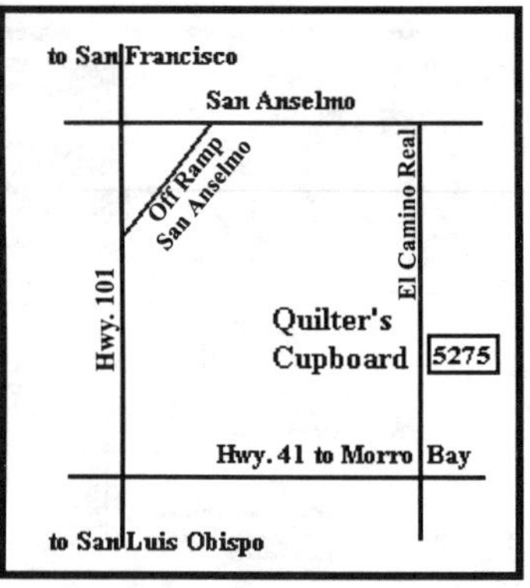

5275 El Camino Real 93422
(805) 466-6996
Fax: (805) 466-6555
Owner: Lorraine Lowe
Est: 1997 2000 sq.ft.

Mon - Sat
10 - 5

COMPLETE QUILT STORE
with over 2000 bolts of 100% cotton fabric, stencils, notions, books, patterns, classes & gifts.

Back Porch Fabrics

157 Grand Ave. at Central 93950
(408) 375-4453 Fax: (408) 375-3755
E-Mail: backporch@csi.com
Owner: Gail Abeloe Est: 1996

Mon - Sat
10 - 5
Sun 12 - 4

Pacific Grove, CA #46

- Unique fabrics, books and patterns for quilting and wearable art.
- Home of the "Back Porch Press" pattern company.
- Try on model garments for sizing and inspiration.
- Continuous shows in our Quilt Gallery featuring prominent, local quilters.

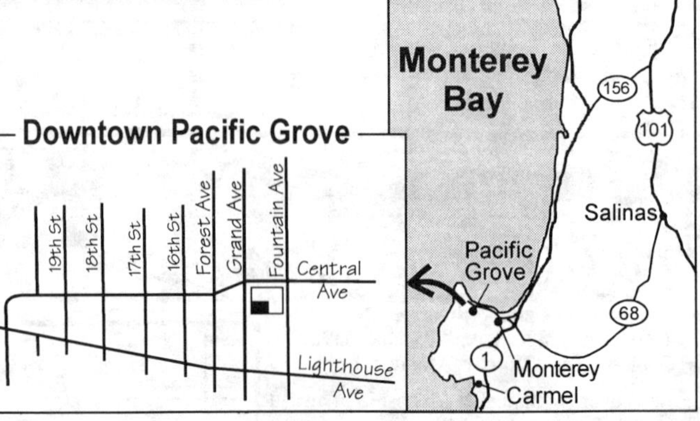

Located 90 miles south of San Francisco on the Monterey Peninsula.

Fairfax, CA #47

Mon - Sat 10 - 6
Sun 12 - 4

Rainbow Fabrics

50 Bolinas Rd. 94930
(415) 459-5100
Owner: Rose Taber

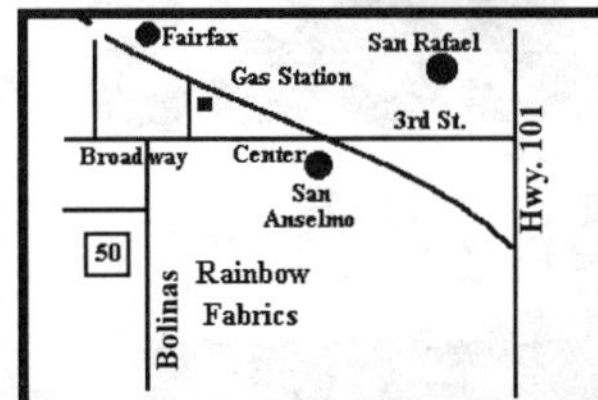
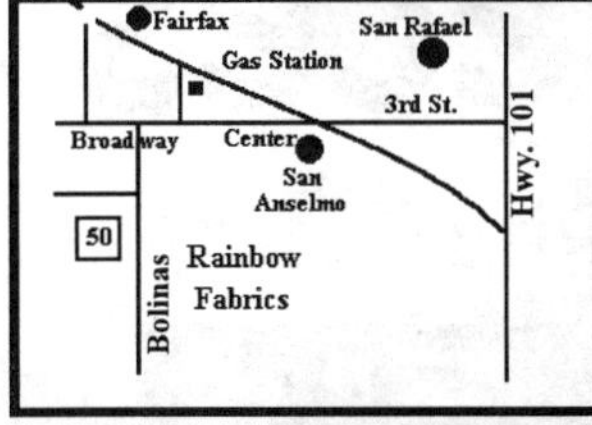

Unique country store. Cotton, Rayons, Books, Beads, Notions. Open daily.
Helpful staff
Classes for Adults and Children

Oakland, CA #49

Mon - Fri 9:30 - 8
Sat 9:30-5:30
Sun 11 - 5:30

POPPY FABRIC

5151 Broadway 94611
(510) 655-8850
(800) 55-POPPY
Owner:
Paul Eisenberg
Est: 1971
5000 sq.ft.

College Ave. to Berkeley
Poppy Fabric
5151
Broadway
51st. St.
Pleasant Valley Rd.

Dress and Decorator Fabrics with a large amount of imported and specialty fabrics.

Walnut Creek, CA #48

ThimbleCreek

1536 Newell Ave.
94596
(925) 946-9970
Owners:
Janey Edwards &
Roxie Wood
Est: 1994 6000 sq.ft.
4000 Bolts

Wonderful quilts on display in a spacious, friendly, atmosphere.
ThimbleCreek Gallery now open
featuring new exhibits every 6 weeks.
Great selection of books, patterns, notions, fabric & classes !

Mon - Fri
9:30 - 5:30
Tues & Thur til 8
Sat 9:30 - 5
Sun 12 - 4

Walnut Creek
N. 680
24
Mt. Diablo Blvd.
Lafayette
S. 680
California
Thimble-Creek
S. Main St.
1536
Newell Ave.

Berkeley, CA #50

Mon - Fri 9:30 - 6:30
Sat 10 - 6
Sun 11 - 5:30

Stonemountain & Daughter Fabrics

2518 Shattuck Ave. 94704
(510) 845-6106 Est: 1981
Owners: Suzan & Bob Steinberg
6000 sq.ft. Thousands of Bolts

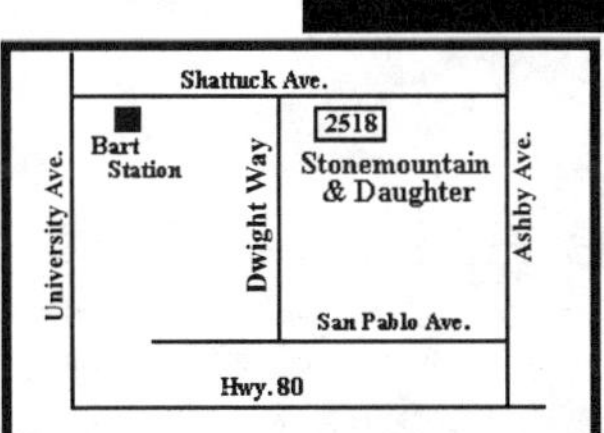

Huge Selection of Quality, Unique Cottons at affordable prices! Ethnic, Quilting & Basic Cottons. Wools, Silks, Rayons, & Linens also Available.

Lafayette, CA #51

Mon - Fri 9:30 - 5:30
Thur til 8
Sat 10 - 5
Sun 12 - 4

Cotton Patch

1025 Brown Avenue 94549
(925) 284-1177
Proprietor: Carolie Hensley
Est: 1978

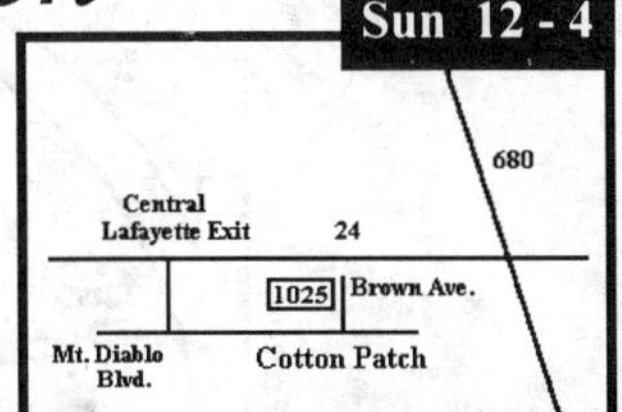

Cotton prints, solids, batiks, African, Japanese fabrics. 500 book titles, gifts, notions, etc.

Antioch, CA #52

Mon - Fri 9 - 8
Sat 9 - 6
Sun 10 - 5

Ben Franklin Crafts

Independently owned & operated
2710 Delta Fair Blvd. 94509
(925) 778-3850 Fax: (925) 778-5829
E-Mail: BFC5938@aol.com
Owners: Ted & Jo Decker
Est: 1988 2500 sq.ft. 1500 Bolts

Beautiful Fabric, Quilting Supplies, Books & Patterns. "You're not just a customer, You're also our Friend."

Campbell, CA #53

Mon - Fri 10 - 6
Thur til 8
Sat 10 - 5
Sun 12 - 4

Golden State Sewing Center

2435 South Winchester Blvd.
(408) 866-1181 95008
Owners: Margrit Schwanck
Est: 1951 1600 sq.ft.

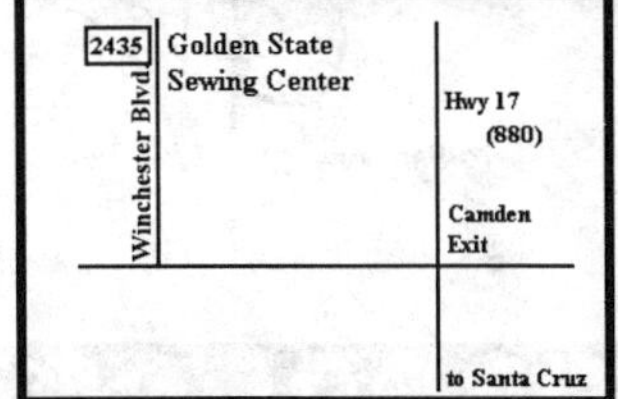

A great place for those addicted to Quilting and Cross Stitch !
Oldest Elna Dealership in the Valley.

Cupertino, CA #54

Mon - Fri 9:30 - 6
Thur til 8
Sat 9:30 - 5

Whiffle Tree Quilts

10261 S. DeAnza Blvd. 95014
(408) 255-5270
Web-Site: http://www.jandaweb.com
Owners: Louise Horkey
Est: 1982 1280 sq.ft.

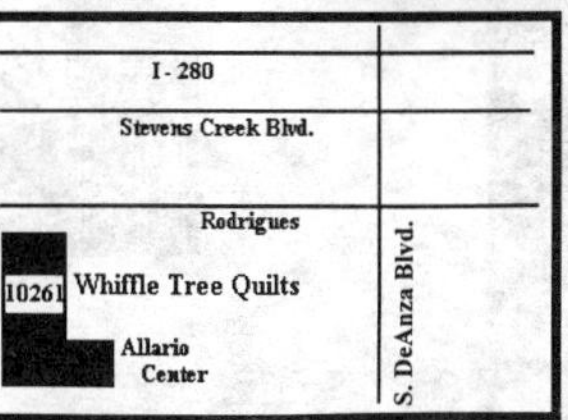

A terrific store full of fabric, patterns, & notions & books. The user-Friendly quilt shop in the heart of Silicon Valley!

Going To Pieces

1989 F Santa Rita Rd

Pleasanton, CA #55

(510) 462-9340
fax (510) 462-4135

Established 1981
Owner: Judie Eichenbaum
2400 sq.ft.

Store Hours:
Monday - Friday 10-7pm
Saturday 10-6pm
Sunday 11-5pm

Large selection of 100% Cotton Fabrics,
Books and Patterns
for Dolls, Quilts and Wearable Art
Surface Design Supplies
Silk and French Wired Ribbons
Beginning to Advanced Classes
Quarterly Sales
Free Newsletter

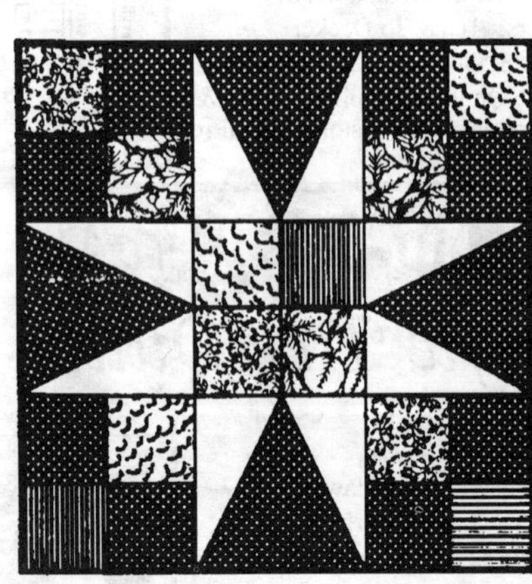

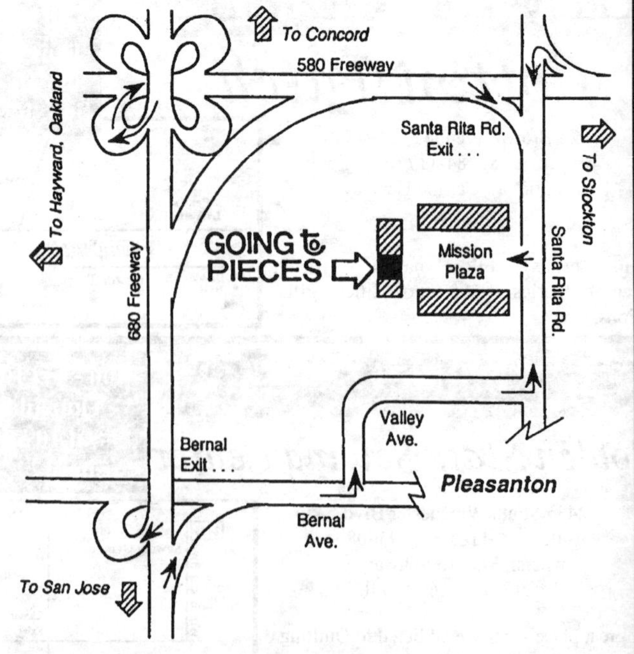

San Jose, CA #57

Tues - Sat 10 - 4

American Museum of Quilts and Textiles

60 S. Market St. 95113
(408) 971-0323 Est: 1977
Non-profit Public Benefit Museum

Regularly changing exhibits of Quilts and Textiles.
Museum Store has extensive assortment of books on quilting.
Call for Directions.

Sunnyvale, CA #58

Mon - Fri 10 - 6 Sat 10 - 5

Carolea's Knitche

586 South Murphy Ave. 94086
(408) 736-2800
Owner: Carolea Peterson
Est: 1973 1400 sq.ft.

The very latest in Hoffman, Alex Henry, Jinny Beyer, Kaufman, Tony Wentzel, Gutcheon . . . Mail orders welcome.

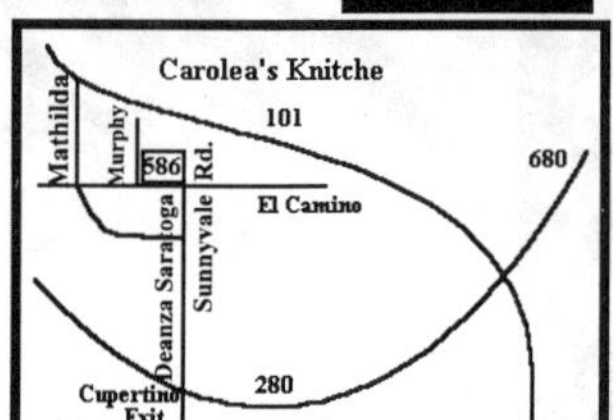

Est: 1973

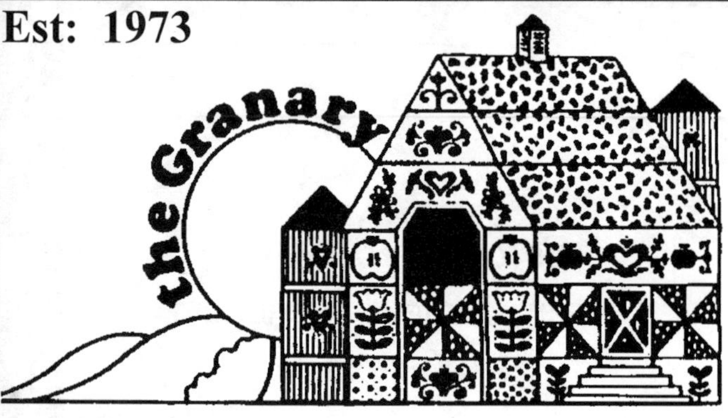

Mon - Thur 10 - 6 Fri & Sat 10 - 5 Last Sunday of the Month 10 - 4

1326 S. Mary Ave.
94087
(408) 735-9830
Owner: Karen Yancey

Sunnyvale, CA #59

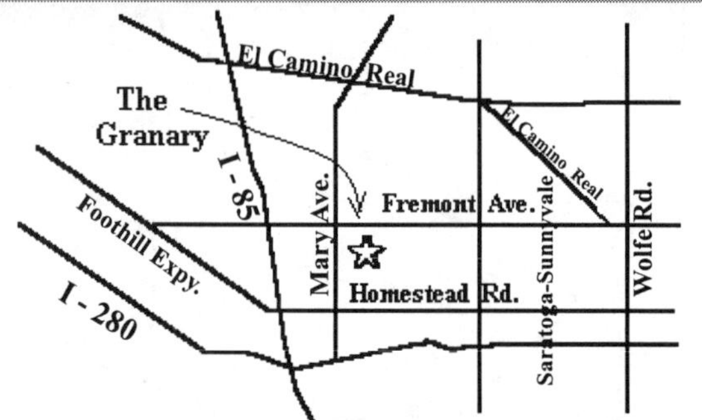

1200 bolts of 100% cotton fabric.
Quilting Supplies, Patterns, Classes.

Mountain View, CA #60

Mon - Fri 9 - 8:30 Sat 9 - 5 Sun 11 - 5

Eddie's Quilting Bee

264 Castro St.
94041 (650) 969-1714 Est: 1976
(888) QUILTER (784-5837)
E-Mail: quiltbee@quiltingbee.com
Web Site: www.quiltingbee.com
Owners: Eddie & Diana Leone 2500 sq.ft.

Husqvarna VIKING WHITE BERNINA

2500 Bolts of Cotton, 750 Books,
Classes, Notions & Appraisals.

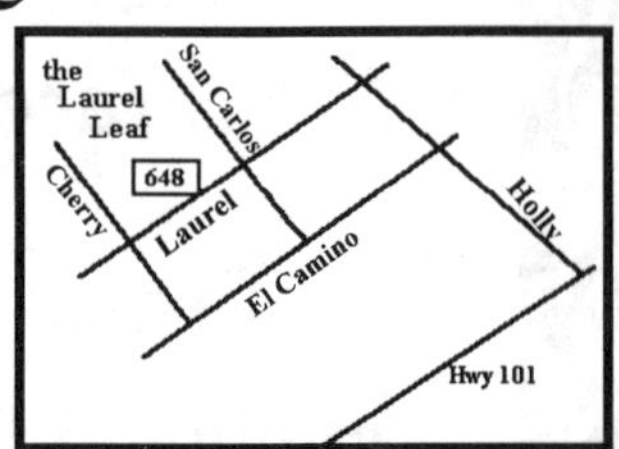

San Carlos, CA #61

Mon - Sat 10 - 5

The Laurel Leaf

648 Laurel Street 94070
(650) 591-6790
Owner: Julie Murphy
Est: 1983 2200 sq.ft.

100% Cotton Fabric, Books, Patterns,
Quilting Supplies, Classes.
10 Min. South of San Francisco Airport

San Francisco, CA #62

Mon - Fri 10 - 6 Sat 10 - 5:30 Sun 12 - 5

Mendels
Far-Out Fabrics

1556 Haight St. 94117
(415) 621-1287 E-Mail: sales@mendels.com
Web-Site: http://www.mendels.com
Owner: Bette Mosias 3900 sq.ft.

Lots of wonderful cotton fabrics, unusual ethnic - large selection textile dyes, paints, great buttons, trims and an art supply store.

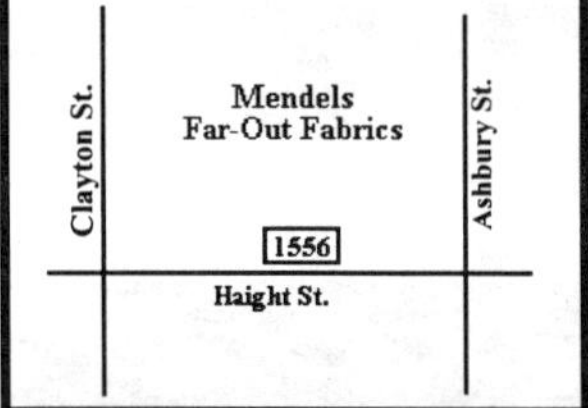

San Francisco, CA #63

Mon, Wed, & Fri 10 - 6 Thur 10 - 8 Sat 10 - 5:30 Sun 12 - 4

2608 Ocean Ave. 94132
(415) 337-1355 Fax: (415) 337-1383
Owner: Gretchen G. Nelson
Est: 1996 1500 sq.ft.

The only store in San Francisco devoted exclusively to meeting your quiltmaking needs. Featuring fabrics, books, patterns, notions & classes.

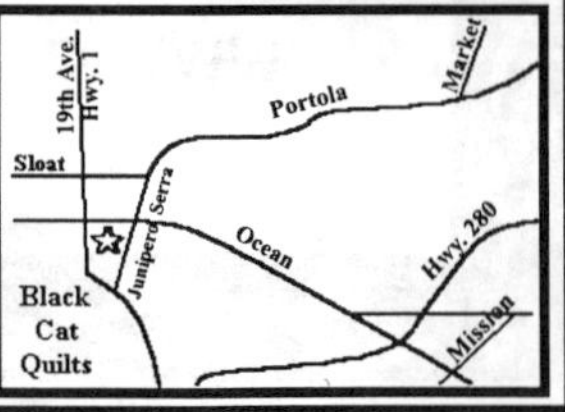

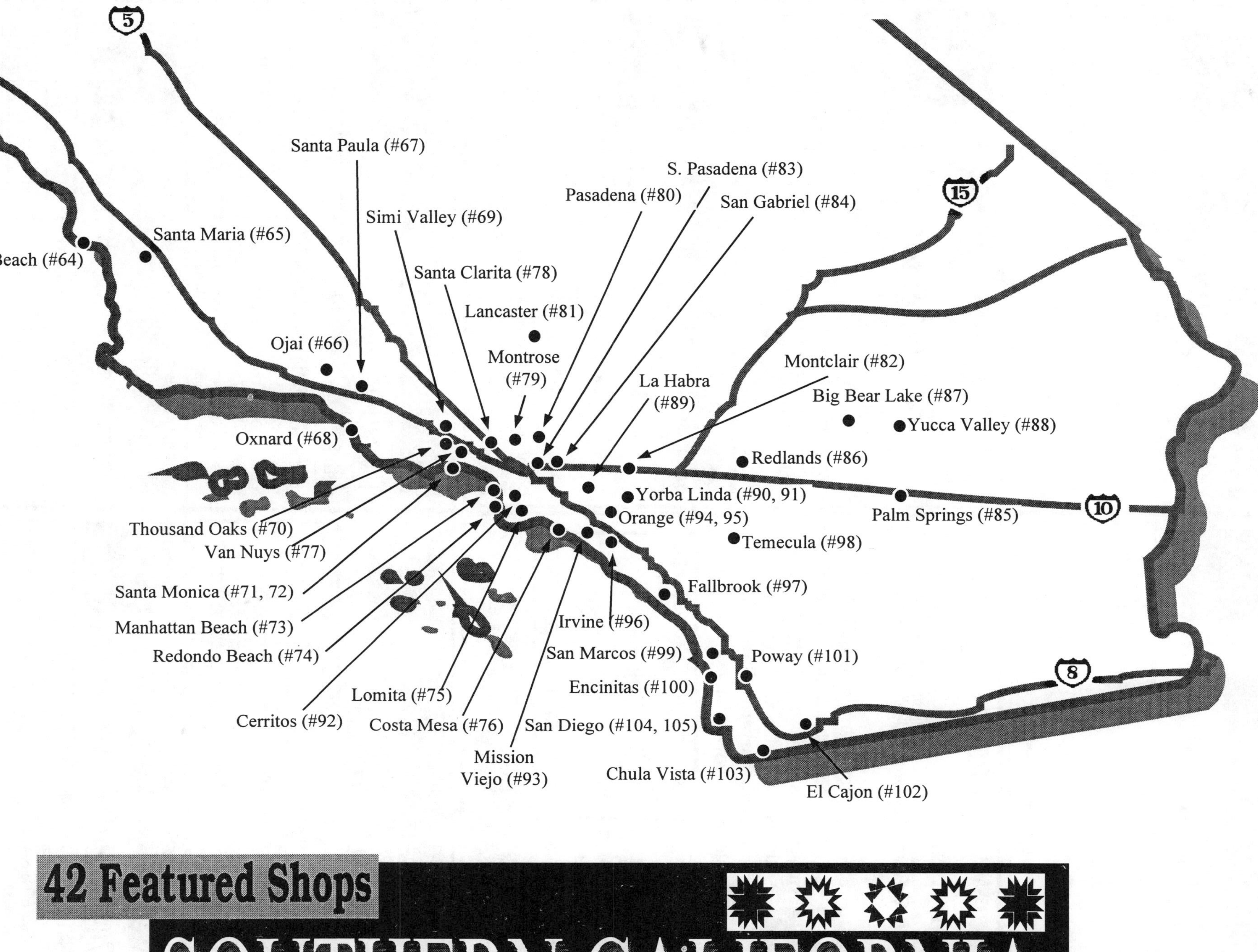

5
15
10
8
Pismo Beach (#64)
Santa Maria (#65)
Santa Paula (#67)
Ojai (#66)
Oxnard (#68)
Simi Valley (#69)
Santa Clarita (#78)
Lancaster (#81)
Montrose (#79)
Pasadena (#80)
S. Pasadena (#83)
San Gabriel (#84)
La Habra (#89)
Montclair (#82)
Big Bear Lake (#87)
Yucca Valley (#88)
Redlands (#86)
Yorba Linda (#90, 91)
Orange (#94, 95)
Palm Springs (#85)
Temecula (#98)
Fallbrook (#97)
Thousand Oaks (#70)
Van Nuys (#77)
Santa Monica (#71, 72)
Manhattan Beach (#73)
Redondo Beach (#74)
Cerritos (#92)
Lomita (#75)
Costa Mesa (#76)
Mission Viejo (#93)
Irvine (#96)
San Marcos (#99)
Encinitas (#100)
San Diego (#104, 105)
Poway (#101)
Chula Vista (#103)
El Cajon (#102)
42 Featured Shops
SOUTHERN CALIFORNIA

Pismo Beach, CA #64

Tues - Fri 10 - 5
Sat 10 - 4

Quiltin' Cousins

470 #C Price St. 93449
(805) 773-4988
Owners: Shawn Lombardo & Gerri Kautz

The "cousins" will greet you with their knowledge and friendly inspiration. Fabric, books, notions, patterns, gifts and classes.

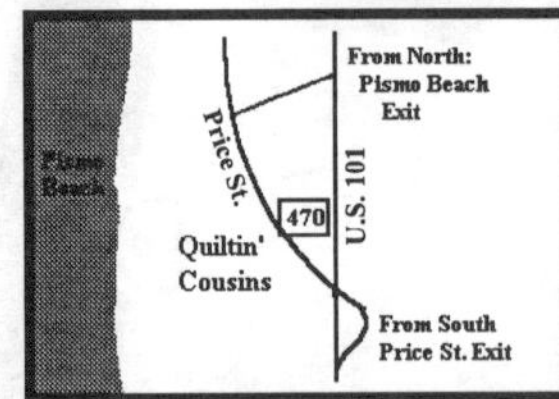

Santa Maria, CA #65

Mon - Fri 10 - 5
Sat 10 - 4

Sally's Quilt Quarters

1765 - B South Broadway 93458
(805) 925-1888
Owner: Sally Testa
Est: 1986 950 sq.ft.

Bolts of 100% Cotton Fabric, books, notions, classes and always friendly Service !

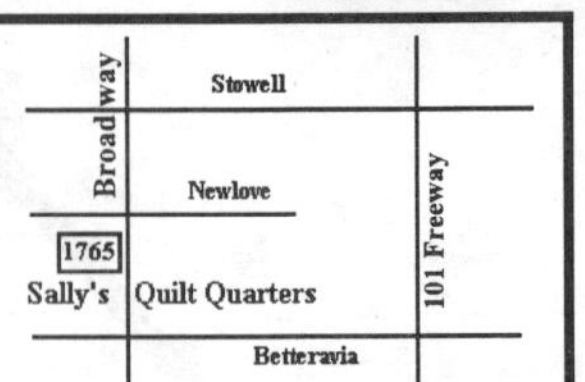

HEARTWARMERS Mercantile

"Where it feels good to shop"

Wed - Sat 10 - 5:30
Sun 11 - 4

Fine 100% cotton dry goods, quilt & doll supplies, books, handcrafted clothing & vintage quilts are tucked in every corner of this historic home. Quilts repaired.

E-Mail: hartwrmr@west.net

On-line newsletter at: www.west.net/~hartwrmr

310 E. Matilija St.
93023
(805) 640-1187
Proprietress:
Lou Ann Schlichter
Est: 1994

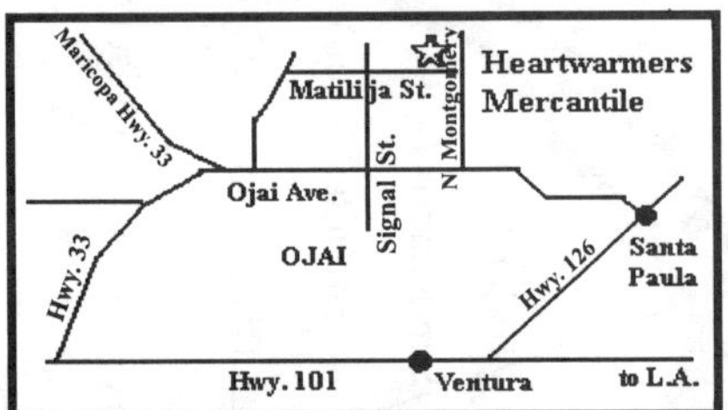

Ojai, CA #66

Santa Paula, CA #67

Mon - Sat 10 - 5
Sun 12 - 4

Fabric Depot

866 S. Main St. 93060
(805) 525-4556 E-Mail: fabdepo
Owners: Cynthia & Fred Davis
Est: 1992 3500 sq.ft. 2000 Bolts

Full range of fine quilting cottons; tapestries, flannels. Notions, patterns, books, fancy ribbons, soft crafts. Classes. Pfaff sewing machines.

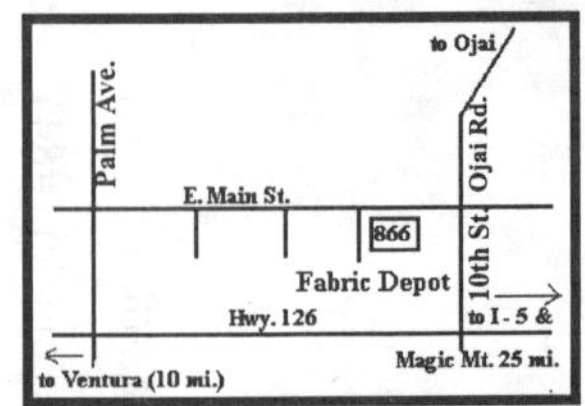

Oxnard, CA #68

Mon - Fri 9:30 - 8
Sat 9:30 - 6
Sun 11 - 5

Fabric Well

3075 Saviers Road 93033
(805) 486-7826
Owners: Ray & Bev Hicks
Est: 1975 13,200 sq.ft. 1000+ Bolts

One of the Largest Selections of Quilting Fabrics and Supplies you will find anywhere.

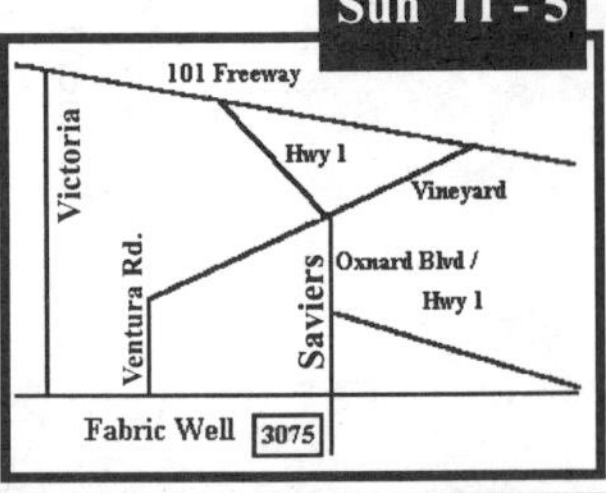

Simi Valley, CA #69

Tues - Sat 10 - 6

WHISTLE STOP
Quilt Station

4395 Valley Fair St. 93063
(805) 584-6915
Owner: Judy Ragan
Est: 1984 1500 sq.ft. 1600 Bolts

Full line Quilting.
Classes. Antique Quilts.

Thousand Oaks, CA #70

Mon - Thur 10 - 6
Fri & Sat 10 - 5

Mary's Quilt Inn

1772 Avenida de los Arboles #E 91362
(805) 241-0061 Owner: Mary Freeman
Est: 1978 1575 sq.ft. 900+ Bolts

We offer a large variety of fabrics, classes, quilting supplies, books & patterns.

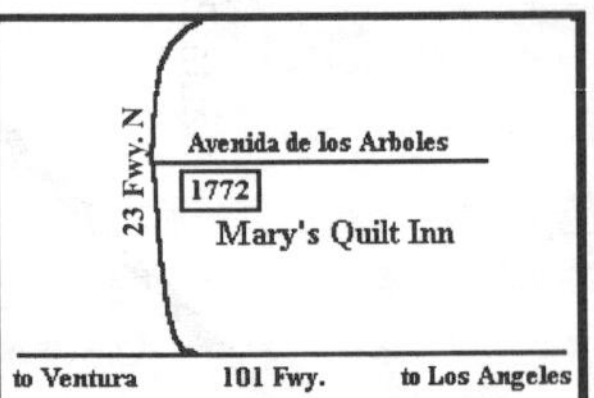
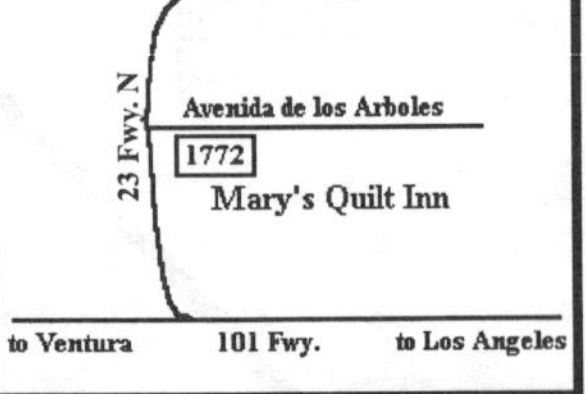

Santa Monica, CA #71

Mon - Sat 10 - 6
Sun 12 - 4

McGuire's Quilt & Needlework

521 Santa Monica Blvd. 90401
(310) 395-7753
Owner: Gerry McGuire
Est: 1982 900 sq.ft.

100% Cotton fabrics, books, patterns, and notions. We have Computer Software to design your quilts for sale.

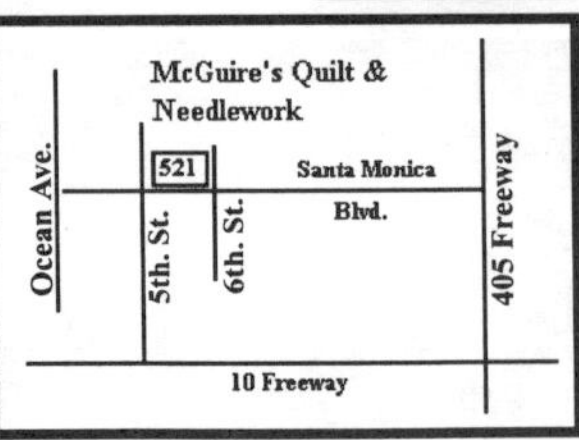

Santa Monica, CA #72

Mon - Sat 10:30 - 5:30
Sun 1 - 4

Crazy Ladies & Friends

2451 Santa Monica Blvd. 90404
(310) 828-3122
Owner: Karin Sheard
Est: 1977 1300 sq.ft. Classes

The Quilt Shop that offers words of encouragement. 3000 Bolts of Cotton Fabric chosen with the Quilter in mind.

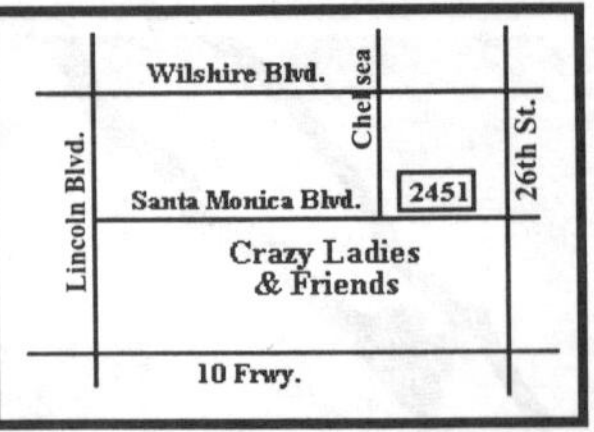

Manhattan Beach, CA #73

Mon - Sat 10 - 6
Sun 11 - 4

Luella's Quilt Basket

1840 N. Sepulveda Blvd.
(310) 545-3436 90266
Owner: Luella Fournell
Est: 1988 1400 sq.ft.

We are a Premier Viking Dealer and offer a wide variety of Fabrics, Classes and quilting supplies.

L.A.X.
Rosecrans
Manhattan Village Mall
Marine Ave.
1840 Luella's Quilt Basket
Sepulveda Blvd.
San Diego (405) Frwy.
Hawthorne Blvd.
Manhattan Beach Blvd.

Redondo Beach, CA #74

Mon - Thur 10 - 7
Fri & Sat 10 - 6
Sun 11 - 5

THE COTTON SHOP FINE FABRICS

(310) 376-3518
1922 Artesia Blvd. 90278
Est: 1959 8400 sq.ft. 2000+ Bolts
Full Line Fabric Store with Large Quilting Dept. Probably the Largest Selection of Hoffman Prints in Southern California

Lomita, CA #75

Mon - Sat 10 - 6
Tues til 9
Sun 12 - 5

TREADLEART

25834 Narbonne Ave. 90717
(310) 534-5122
Owner: Janet Stocker
Est: 1978 7000 sq.ft. Catalog $3

Supplies for all your quilting and sewing needs. 5000 bolts of fabric, patterns, books, stencils, decorative thread, machine accessories, notions.

TreadleArt
San Diego Fwy. (405)
Torrance
Carson
Sepulveda
Lomita
Pacific Coast Hwy.
Hawthorne
Crenshaw
Narbonne
Western
Normandie
Vermont
Harbor Fwy. (110)

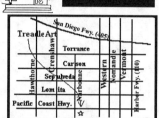

Costa Mesa, CA #76

Mon - Fri 10 - 9
Sat 10 - 5:30
Sun 10 - 5:30

Piecemakers Country Store

1720 Adams Avenue 92626
(714) 641-3112 Owners: 35 Piecemakers !
Est: 1978 12,000 sq.ft. 2000 Bolts
E-Mail: mail@piecemakers. com
Catalog $2.00 Web Site: www.piecemakers. com
Complete line of quilting supplies, fabrics, books, notions, dolls, handmade quilts, unique gifts & hundreds of classes every month. Four Craft Fairs per year call for information.

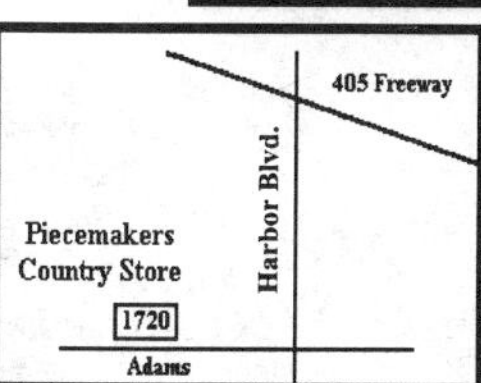

Van Nuys, CA #77

By Appointment Only

Sandy White Antique Quilts

14936 Gault St. 91405
(818) 988-0575 Est: 1985
E-Mail: s423@gte.net
Web Site: www.quiltlady.com

Lovely Selection of Appealing **ANTIQUE QUILTS** for both Home and Office,
For the Collector and Decorator.
Call for Show Schedule.

Please Call for Directions

Montrose, CA #79

Mon - Sat 10 - 5
Sun 12 - 4

Quilt 'n' Things, Inc.

2411 Honolulu Ave. 91020
(818) 957-2287 Fax: (818) 957-2207
E-Mail: qltnthings@aol.com
Owner: Donna Senecal 2000 sq.ft.

Classes, notions, books. More than 2500 bolts of fabric - all 100% cotton. Expert Assistance. The friendliest shop in Southern California.

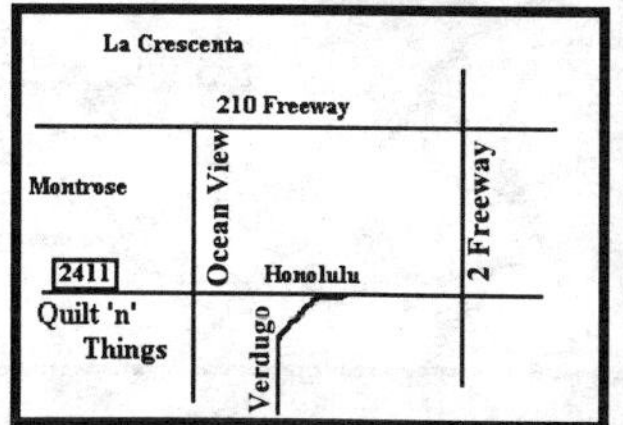

Loving Stitches QUILT SHOPPE

Owner: Marge Soper
Est: 1990
26111 Bouquet Canyon Rd. #B6 91350
(805) 254-1296

Over 1500 Bolts of Fabric - Classes - Largest Selection of Plaids in S. California - Buttons - Patterns - Books - Gift Items - Notions
Machine Quilting
Authorized Bernina Dealer

FULL SERVICE QUILT SHOP!

Please call for directions—We are expanding and may be moving.

Mon - Fri 10 - 5
Sat 10 - 4
Evenings during classes

Santa Clarita, CA #78

Pasadena, CA #80

Mon - Fri 9:30 - 7
Sat 9:30 - 6
Sun 12 - 5

Bearly Stitchin Sewing Center

2245 E. Colorado Blvd. 91107
(626) 796-2118 Fax: (626) 796-3966
E-Mail: bstitchin@earthlink.net
Est: 1986 3100 sq.ft. 2000 Bolts

Complete selection of 100% cotton fabrics. Bernina and Husqvarna Viking sewing machines, books, notions, machine accessories and cabinets.

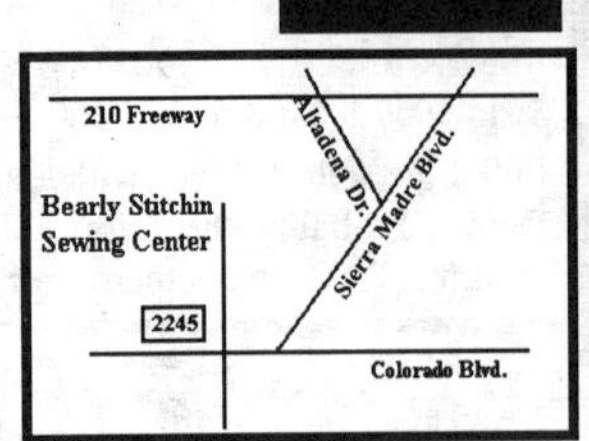

Lancaster, CA #81

Mon 12 - 6
Tues - Thur 9:30 - 6
Fri 9:30 - 5
Sat 9:30 - 4

Quilters' Cabin

43923 N. 15th St. West At J-8
(805) 948-2118 93534
E-Mail: qcabin@dtw.com
Cabin Keepers: Lewis & Gayle Farmer
Est: 1988 1100 Bolts

Lots of Wonderful 100% Cottons, Notions, Books, and Bernina Sewing Machine Dealer.

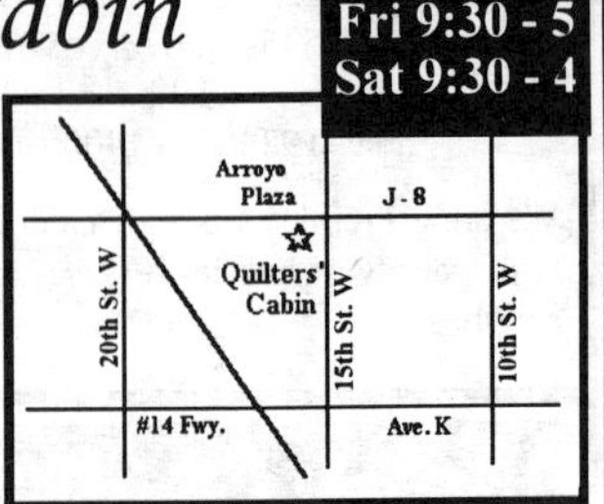

Montclair, CA #82

Marie White
Carolyn Reese
Since 1981

Mon - Sat 9:30 - 5
Sun 12 - 3

5436 D Arrow Highway 91763
909-985-9000
Fax: 909-985-9163

So. California's Largest, Most Complete Quilt Shop

3000 bolts of 100% cotton
300 book titles
More than 1000 craft and quilt patterns.
Large selection of notions
Gift items for Quilters and their friends.
We do mail order
Use the Central Ave. exit on I - 10

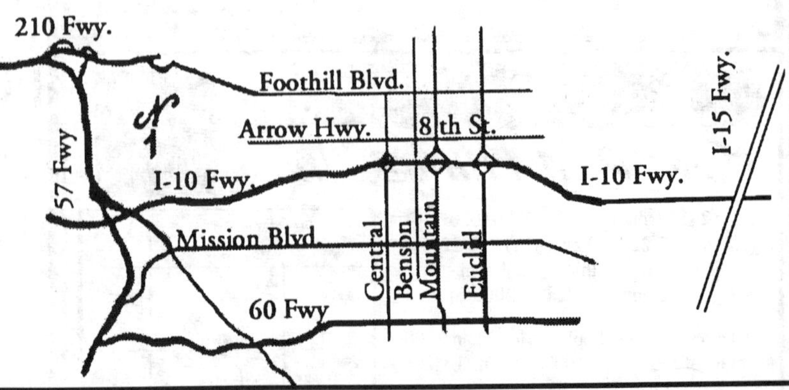

"SEW HAPPY" EST. 1995

#83

"THE PLACE TO GO IF YOU LOVE TO SEW"

STORE HOURS: MONDAY - SATURDAY 10:00AM - 6:00PM

STORE SIZE: 2000 SQUARE FEET

OWNERS: MARSHA AGUIRRE AND LINDA HALL

OUR FRIENDLY AND KNOWLEDGEABLE STAFF IS AVAILABLE TO ASSIST YOU WITH YOUR QUILTING AND SEWING NEEDS! PLEASE STOP BY AND VISIT US WHEN YOU ARE TRAVELING THROUGH THE LOS ANGELES AREA.

WE SPECIALIZE IN:

- ☆ LARGE SELECTION OF 100% COTTON FABRIC (APPROX. 2000 BOLTS OF FABRIC QUILTER'S WILL LOVE)
- ☆ QUILTING BOOKS AND CRAFT PATTERNS
- ☆ LARGE SELECTION OF RIBBON AND BUTTONS
- ☆ EXTENSIVE STOCK OF QUILTING & SEWING NOTIONS
- ☆ SILK RIBBON AND RELATED NOTIONS
- ☆ SOCCER BANNER FELT (LARGEST SELECTION IN THE AREA)
- ☆ ADULT QUILTING CLASSES
- ☆ CHILDRENS' SEWING & QUILTING CLASSES (AGES 5-18)

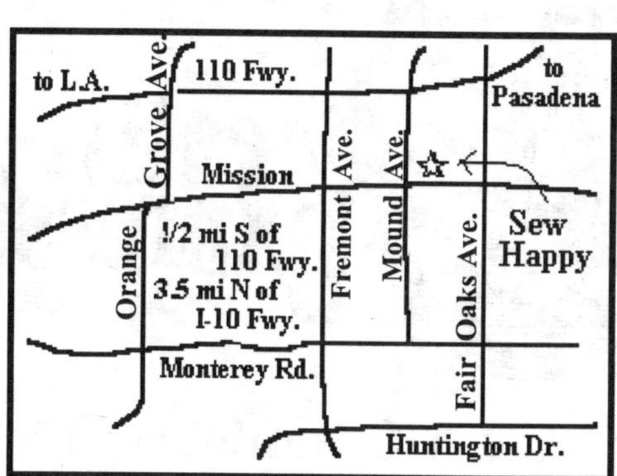

OUR NEWSLETTER/CLASS SCHEDULE IS AVAILABLE UPON REQUEST.

ON-LINE SALES ARE AVAILABLE AT: www.sewhappy.com

"SEW HAPPY," 1500 MISSION STREET, SOUTH PASADENA, CA 91030 (626) 799-7087 FAX (626) 799-3324

A Quilter's Dream

...if you love to quilt or love a quilter.

8958 E.
Huntington Dr.
91775
Owner: Susan Prescott

Mon - Sat 10 - 5:30
Sun 12 - 4

(626) 441-0740

E-Mail:
susan@greenheart.com
Web Site:
www.aquiltersdream.com

Come visit our ever-growing fabric selection, we specialize in batiks, 30's reproduction prints and unique buttons. 100% Cotton Fabrics, Quality Notions & Classes.

San Gabriel, CA #84

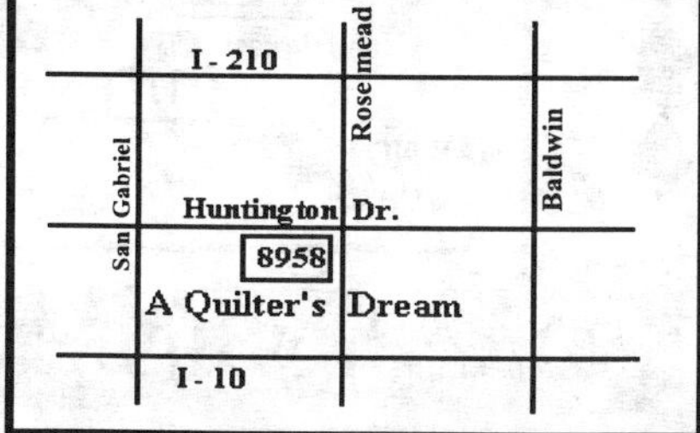

(760) 327-2587

1111 South Palm Canyon Drive
Palm Springs, CA 92264
STORE HOURS
Mon - Sat 9:00 am - 5:00 pm
Sun 12:00 pm - 5:00 pm

We are A Complete Quilt Shop

We stock only the finest quality 100% Cotton Fabrics in solids and prints. Our very full line of notions, books and stencils is complemented by our personal service and instruction in our monthly collection of classes.

From the Exquisite to the Exotic . . .

Creative Expressions is also a Complete Bead Shop Featuring beads from all over the world from size 14 seed beads to large African Trade Beads
- Crystals - Sterling Silver - Semi-precious Stone -

Classes available in quiltmaking, beaded jewelry, and wearable art and more.
- Call for a free class schedule -

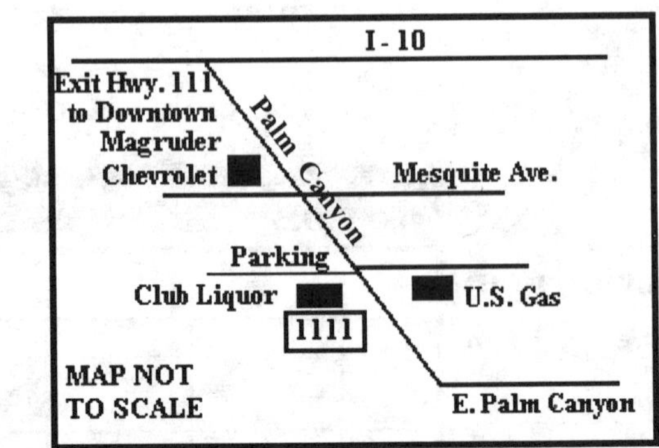

Palm Springs, CA #85

Redlands, CA #86

Est: 1986

The Calico Horse

461 Tennessee St. Suite J 92373
(909) 793-1868 or 824-6198
Fax: (909) 793-5868
E-Mail: calhrse@aol.com
Owners: Debra & Doug Grantz
Beverly & Bill Dean
1580 sq.ft.

Mon - Fri 10 - 6
Sat 10 - 5

I-10
Tennessee Exit
Colton Ave.
The Calico Horse
461
Tennessee St.
Redlands Blvd.

Large selection of 100% cotton fabrics and supplies including flannels & reproduction fabrics. Patterns & Books. Orange crate labels on muslin. Friendly, expert advice. Mail Order Available.

Big Bear Lake, CA #87

Mon - Sat 10 - 5

The Patchwork Peddler

4217½-A Big Bear Blvd.
92315
(909) 878-4629
Owner: Candace Wright - Wilkerson

A Shop for Quilters
Fine Fabrics — Notions — Patterns
Classes — Specializing in Beginning Quilting

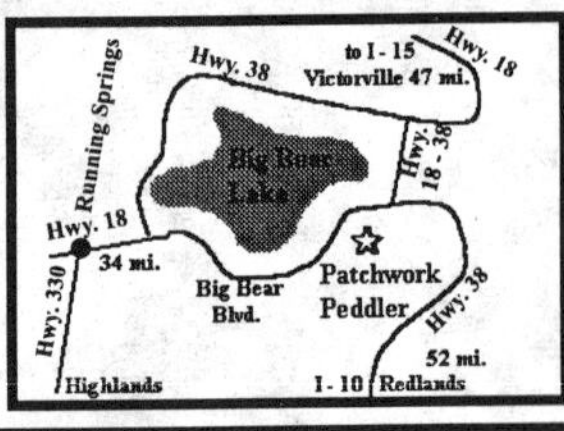

Yucca Valley, CA #88

Tues - Sat 10 - 4

Stitchin & Quiltin

57365-C 29 Palms Hwy. 92284
(760) 365-1744
Owner: Linda Neal

Free Classes with purchase of Materials.

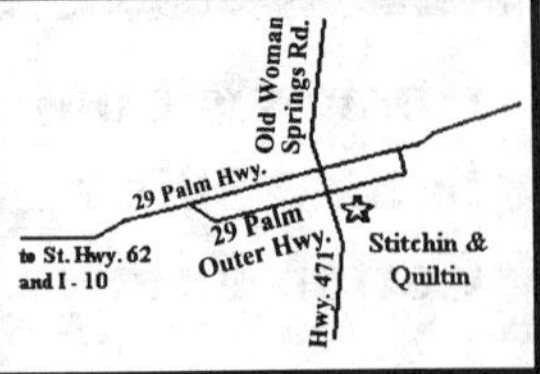

3500 Bolts of 100% Cotton Fabric Notions, Patterns, Books, Classes, Friendly Service.

Calico Corner Quilt Shop

2094 W. LaHabra Blvd.
90631 Est: 1984
(562) 694-3384
Owner: Sheila Ingersoll

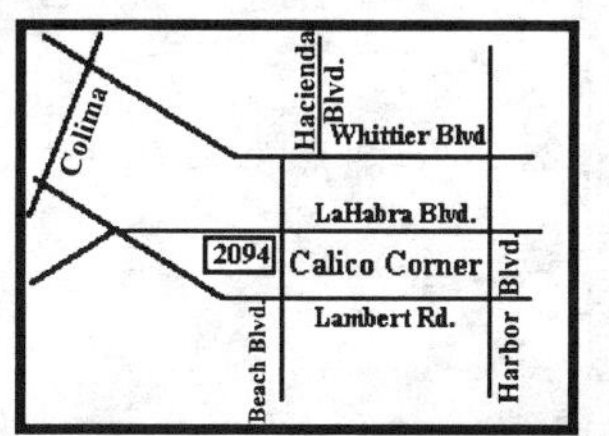

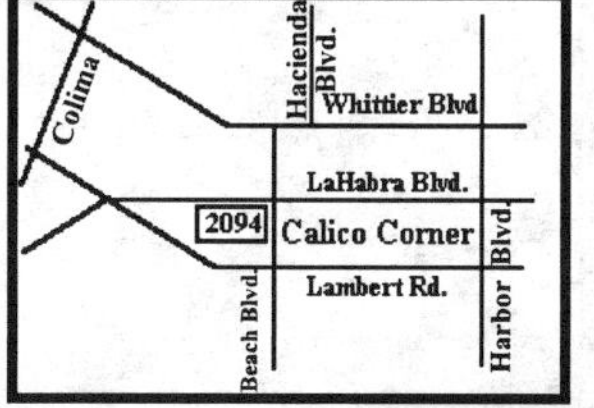

LaHabra, CA #89

Mon - Sat 10 - 5

Yorba Linda, CA #90

Mon - Fri 9:30 - 5
Sat 9:30 - 4
Sun 12 - 3

The Calico House

4825-D Valley View Ave. 92886
(714) 993-3091
Owners: Jane, Janice, Cari
Est: 1981 1500+ Bolts

Complete Quilt Shop.
Books, Fabrics, Notions, Classes.
Helpful, Friendly Staff

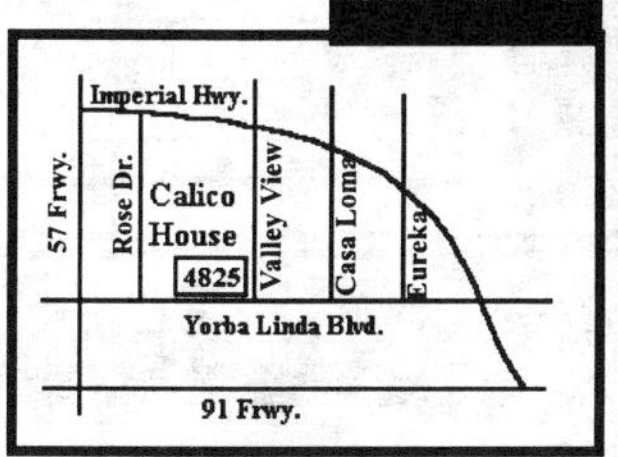

Yorba Linda, CA #91

Cerritos, CA #92

TALL Mouse ARTS & CRAFTS

Huge selection (2500+ bolts) of the finest 100% cotton fabrics.

Complete quilting supplies, notions, books and patterns. **PLUS** cross-stitch, ribbons, buttons, beads, stencils and complete scrapbooking and rubber stamp department with die-cut machine. Day & evening classes. Friendly service.

Quilt & Crafters Heaven

17506 Yorba Linda Blvd.
92886
(714) 996-0101

Family Owned & Operated for 31 years

13233 E. South St.
90703
(562) 865-0800

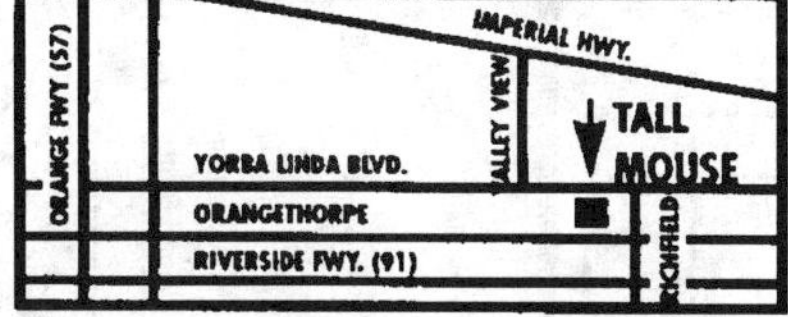

15 minutes from Disneyland

OPEN 7 DAYS
Mon - Fri 9:00 - 9:00 pm
Sat 9:00 - 6:00 pm
Sun 10:00 - 6:00pm

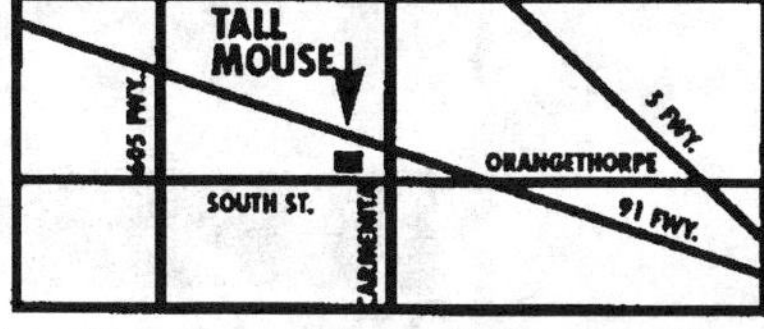

2 miles from Knott's Berry Farm

WE VALUE YOUR OPINION!
E-mail us your comments, suggestions or crafty questions at netmice@tallmouse.com or Fax at (714) 996-3939
www.tallmouse.com

Retail & Wholesale
Discounts to Seniors

2 Great Locations!

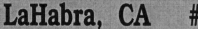

TWO SHOPS

Leah's Fabric Gallery

Mission Viejo, CA #93

Mon - Fri 10 - 9
Sat 10 - 7
Sun 12 - 6

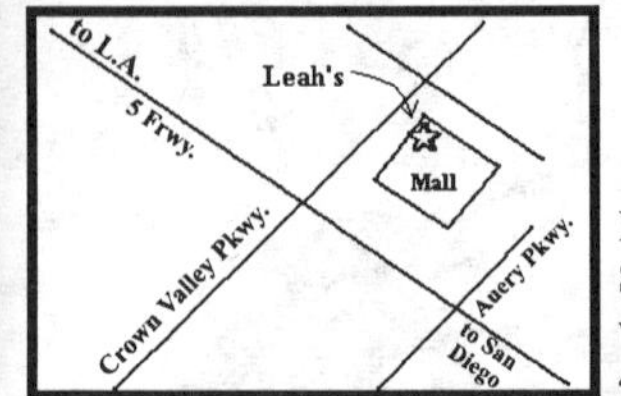

294 Mission Viejo Mall 92691
Crown Valley Parkway
(714) 364-6372
2800 sq.ft. 3000 Bolts

Large selection of cotton fabric. Specializing in 30's, 1800's, Batiks, wonderful flannels prints & solids. 400 book titles, 300 Patterns—novelty buttons—inspirational models.

Orange, CA #94

Mon - Fri 10 - 8
Sat 10 - 6
Sun 12 - 5

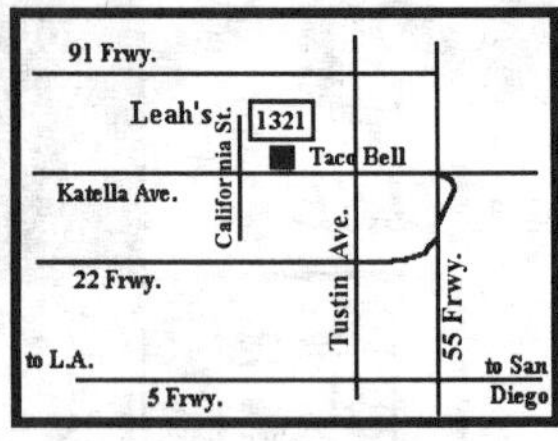

1321 E. Katella Ave. 92867
(714) 639-3245
Fax: (714) 639-2213
Est: 1969 4000 sq.ft. 4000 Bolts

Orange County's largest selection of Quality Quilting Fabric—400 Book Titles—300 Patterns—Novelty Buttions—Gifts for Quilters—Wonderful Models

Irvine, CA #96

Mon - Fri
9:30 - 6:30
Sat 10 - 6
Sun 12 - 5

FLYING GEESE FABRICS

14210 Culver Dr. Suite D 92604
(714) 552-3809
Owner: Bonnie Boyd Est: 1986

Newest Quilt Fabrics, Books, And Patterns. Great Selection of Buttons for Clothing and Quilt Embellishment. Classes

American Roots

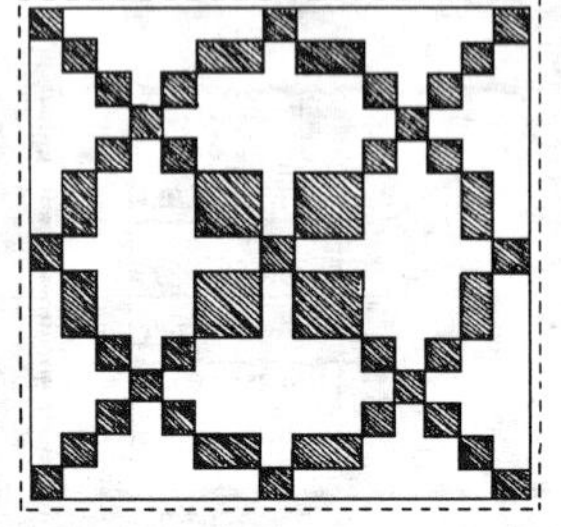

Mon - Sat 10 - 5 Sun 11 - 5

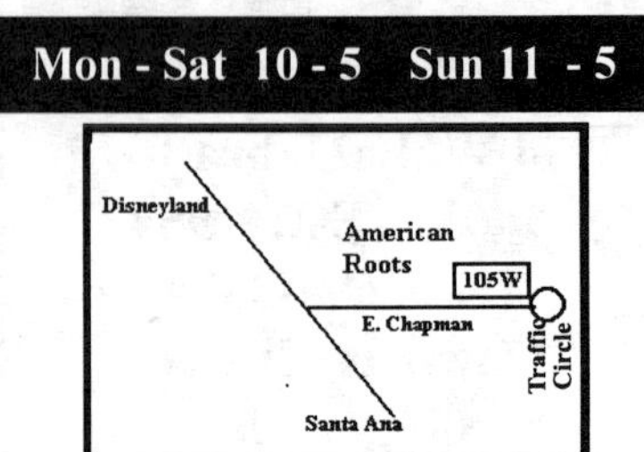

105 W. Chapman (714) 639-3424
Featured Dealer: Sandy White Antique Quilts

Orange, CA #95

Group Shop specializing in Country Antiques, as pictured in Country Home Magazine. Large inventory of **ANTIQUE QUILTS** c. 1860-1930 in a cozy atmosphere. Just off the Orange Circle.

We Cater to Quilters !

Sharon Walters — Owners — Dolores Coleman

Mon - Sat 9:30 - 4:30

129 S. Vine St 92028
(760) 723-3060
Est: 1990 800 sq.ft.
1500 Bolts

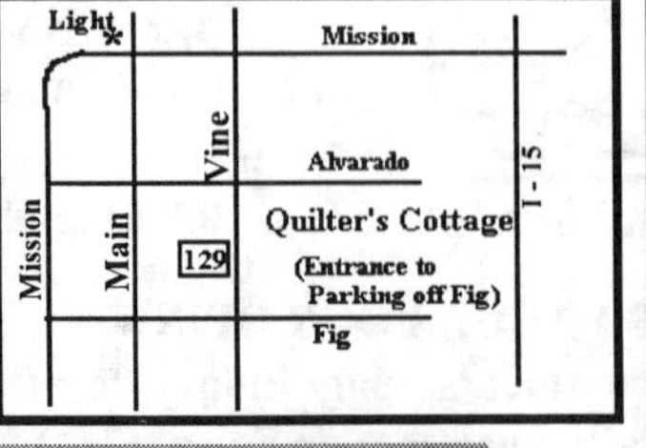

Fallbrook, CA #97

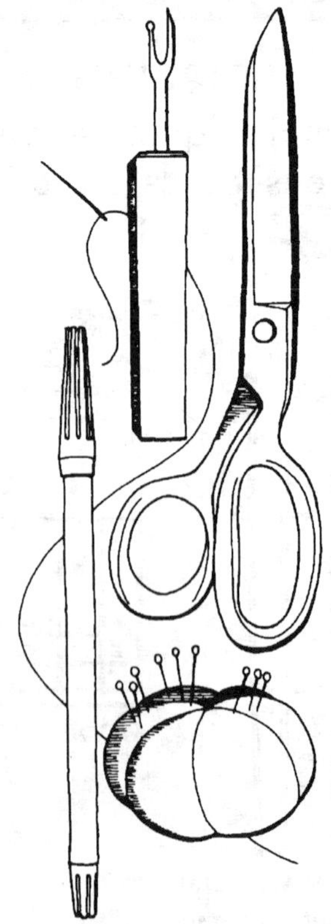

27574 Commerce Center Dr.
(909) 693-3213 92590

Fax: (909) 693-3216
E-Mail: woerthgot@aol.com
Owners: Jo Charity, Linda Musial, & Aileen Woerth

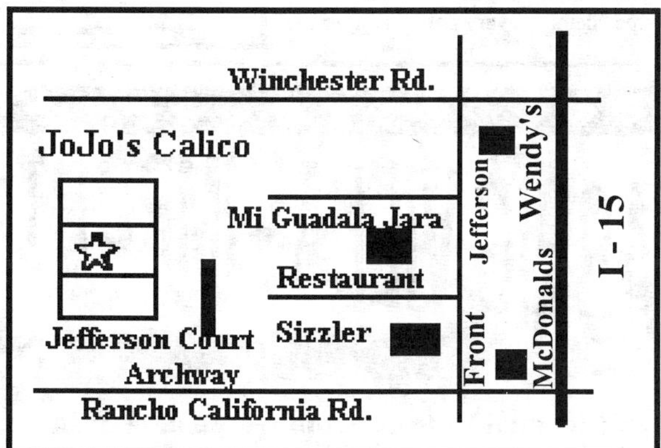

Heading South on I - 15: take the Winchester (79) exit and go west. Turn left at the first intersection (Jefferson). Proceed south on Jefferson approximately 3/4 mile. Turn right into our driveway, directly across the street from the Country Inn Motel, just south of the 3-story Urgent Care - Industrial Center building. If you pass the Sizzler Restaurant, you've gone too far.

Heading North on I -15: take the Rancho California Rd. exit and go west. Turn right at the first intersection (Front St.). Front becomes Jefferson approximately 1 mile north of Rancho California Rd. Turn left two driveways past the Sizzler and look for our sign. We are next to CC & Co, the costume shop.

3000 Bolts of Fabric
Books & Patterns
Notions & Classes
Gifts & Quilts

Mon - Sat
9:30 - 5:30
Sun 12 - 4

Temecula, CA #98

San Marcos, CA #99

Mon - Fri 9 - 5
Tues till 9
Sat 9 - 4

Quilt in a Day

1955 Diamond Street 92069
(760) 591-0081 or (800) 777-4852
Fax: (760) 591-4424 1500 sq.ft.
Owner: Eleanor Burns Est: 1978

Education Center, Showroom featuring large selection of 100% Cottons, books, quilting supplies, Video Production Studio.

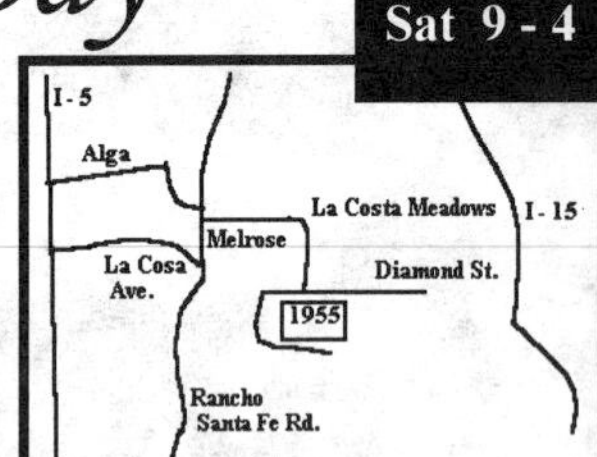

Encinitas, CA #100

Hours By Appt.

Claire's Collection

3461 Bumann Road 92024-5716
(619) 756-5718

Antique Quilts, Tops & Blocks. Old fabrics, buttons, trims. Sewing accessories —old & new— Linens, bedcovers, feedsacks, aprons, handkerchieves, and some antiques.
Quiltkeepers.

North of San Diego. From I - 5 take Encinitas Blvd. Exit. Distance is about 7 miles inland (20 min.) Call for exact directions. IT'S AN ADVENTURE !

Poway, CA #101

Mon, Fri Sat 9 - 5
Tues, Wed Thur 9 - 8

Zook's Warehouse for Quilters

12625 Danielson Ct. #111 92064
(619) 486-0696 Fax: (619) 486-1618
Owner: Kristin Zook
Est: 1994 3800 sq.ft. 1700 Bolts

A full service quilt shop carrying fabrics, books, patterns, notions and gifts.
Mail Order Avail. Free Catalog

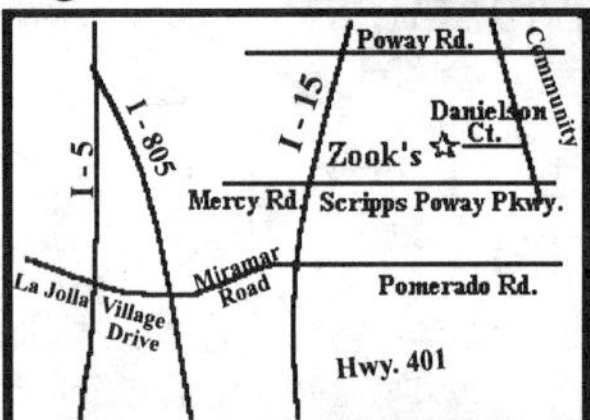

El Cajon, CA #102

Mon - Sat 10 - 5
Sun 12 - 3

Patchwork Plus

2650 Jamacha Rd. #129 92019
(619) 670-9445
Fax: (619) 670-3969

Patchwork Plus offers the latest cotton fabrics, quilting books and notions — plus classes. We have free "demos" every Saturday morning!

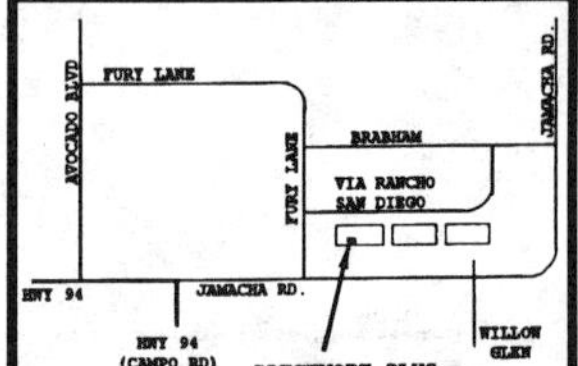

Chula Vista, CA #103

Mon - Sat 9:30 - 5:30
Sun 1 - 5

Quilters' Choice

423 Third Ave. 91910
(619) 425-2545
Owner: Nancy Letchworth
Est: 1992 1000+ sq.ft.

100% Cotton Fabric, Books, Patterns, Notions, Classes and Always Friendly Service.

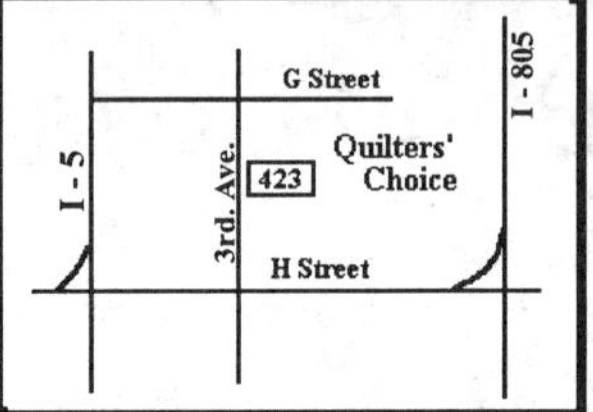

FABRIC VILLA - IMPORTS

San Diego, CA #104

Hand-loomed Cottons from Guatemala & India, African Prints, Batiks, Ethnic Braids, Cuna Indian Molas, Unique Assortment of Printed Cottons.

Mon - Fri 10 - 6
Closed Sat Sun 11 - 3

6364 El Cajon Blvd.
92115
(619) 286-4364
Est: 1974
1200 sq.ft. 5000 Bolts

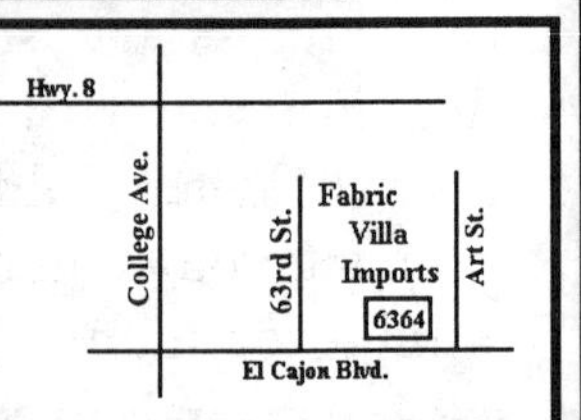

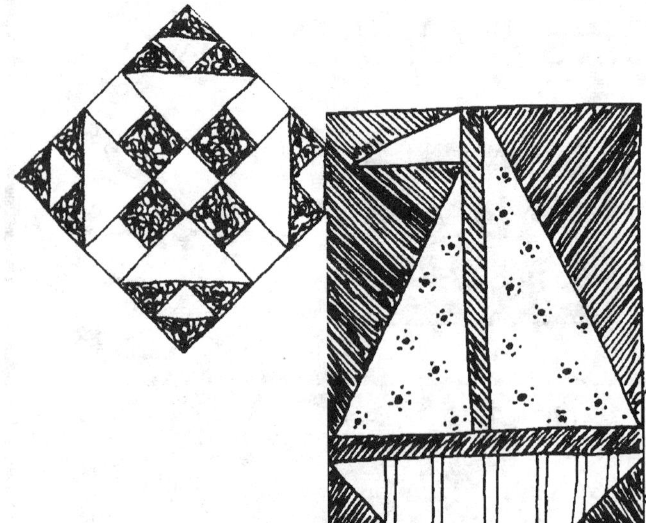

San Diego, CA #105

Rosie's Calico Cupboard

7151 El Cajon Blvd. Suite 'F' 92115

(619) 697-5758 Fax: (619) 465-8298 E-Mail: rozgonzalez@earthlink.net

A Full Service Quilt Shop
Catering to Quilters and Crafters Since 1983

Offering over 4900 sq.ft. (stocked to the brim) with over **8000** bolts of **First Quality** 100% Cotton Prints, plus Books, Batting, Notions, Patterns, Thread, Silk Ribbon, Quilting & Crafting related gift items, New & Old Antique Quilts, a 'Trunk Full of over 500 lbs of Buttons', plus much, much more and all at Everyday **DISCOUNT** prices.

- Well stocked sale rack with values from 25 to 75% off suggested Retail Prices.
- New stock arriving daily.
- 1100 sq.ft. Classroom with a full calendar or Quilting & Crafting Classes all year round.
- Mail Orders and Special Orders Welcome
- Visa, MC, Discover, American Express, ATM Cards Accepted
- Once a year '24 Hour Fall Quilters Madness' held in November. (Call for exact date)

Open Seven Days a Week

Monday - Friday 9 - 5
Wednesday til 8
Saturday 8 - 5
Sunday 11 - 5

Hwy. 8 (East or West) — take 70th St. exit, travel south on 70th St. for 1/2 mile to El Cajon Blvd., turn left (east) onto El Cajon Blvd., travel for a block-and-a-half. We will be on the south side of the street in the College Plaza Center.
Hwy. 94 (East or West) — take the Mass. exit, travel north to University Ave., turn left, follow to 70th St., turn right, follow to El Cajon Blvd., turn right, travel 1 1/2 blocks.

I-80
El Cajon Blvd.
7151
Rosie's
Tower
Stanford
70th St.
71st St.
Harbison
University Ave.

California Guilds:

East Bay Heritage Quilters, P.O. Box 6223, Albany, 94706
Delta Quilters, P.O. Box 154, Antioch, 94509
Pajaro Valley Quilt Assoc., P.O. Box 1412, Aptos, 95003
Independence Hall Quilters, P.O. Box 842, Arnold, 95223
South County Quilt Guild, P.O. Box 656, Arroyo Grande, 93421
Foothill Quilters Guild, P.O. Box 5653, Auburn, 95604
Cotton Patch Quilters, P.O. Box 9944, Bakersfield, 93389
Carquinez Strait Quilters, P.O. Box 1101, Benicia, 94510
Busy Bear Quilt Guild, P.O. Box 6513, Big Bear Lake, 92315
Desert Quilters Guild, 410 W. C St., Brawley, 92227
Citrus Belt Quilters, P.O. Box 626, Bryn Mawr, 92318
Camarillo Quilters Assoc., P.O. Box 347, Camarillo, 93011-0347
Meets: 2nd Tuesday (except Aug.) 9:30 a.m.
at Orchid Bldg., 816 Camarillo Springs Rd.
Santa Clara Valley Quilt Assoc., P.O. Box 792, Campbell, 95009
Valley Quiltmakers Guild, P.O. Box 589, Canoga Park, 91305
Chester Piece Makers, P.O. Box 1702, Chester, 96020
Meets: 2nd Monday 7 p.m. at Memorial Hall, Gay St.
Anne's Star Quilt Guild, P.O. Box 4318, Chico, 95927
LA Quiltmakers Guild, 16167 Augusta Dr., Chino Hills, 91709
Clear Lake Quilters Guild, P.O. Box 5323, Clear Lake, 95422
Pacific Flyway Quilters, 1974 Wescott Rd., Colusa, 95932
Inland Empire Quilt Guild, P.O. Box 2232, Corona, 91718
Diablo Valley Quilt Guild, P.O. Box 1884, Danville, 94526
Gold Bug Quilters, P.O. Box 516, Diamond Springs, 95619
Mountain Star Quilters, P.O. Box 647, Downieville, 95936
Sunshine Quilters, P.O. Box 20483, El Cajon, 92022
Redwood Empire Quilters Guild, P.O. Box 5071, Eureka, 95501
North Wind Quilters, P.O. Box 2891, Fairfield, 94533
Fallbrook Quilters Guild, P.O. Box 1704, Fallbrook, 92028
Folsom Quilt & Fiber Guild, P.O. Box 626, Folsom, 95763
Piecemakers Quilt Guild, P.O. Box 2051, Fremont, 94536
San Jaquin Valley Quilt Guild, P.O. Box 5532, Fresno, 93755
Orange Grove Quilters Guild, P.O. Box 453, Garden Grove, 92642
Meets: 2nd Wednesday 9:30 a.m.
at First Baptist Church, 12761 Euclid Avenue
Glendale Quilt Guild, P.O. Box 5366, Glendale, 91201
Pine Tree Quilt Guild, P.O. Box 3133, Grass Valley, 95945
Meets: 1st Tuesday at Hennessey School, S. Auburn St.
Log Cabin Quilters, P.O. Box 1359, Hayfork, 96041
Valley Quilters, P.O. Box 2534, Hemet, 92545
Mountain Quilters, P.O. Box 603, Idyllwild, 92349
Coachella Valley Quilt Guild, 43-761 Towne St., Indio, 92201
Flying Geese Quilters, P.O. Box 19608-154, Irvine, 92713
Meets: 2nd Monday at 6:45 p.m.
at Irvine Presbyterian Church, 5 Meadowbrook
Friendship Square Quilt Guild, P.O. Box 681, La Habra, 90633
Antelope Valley Quilt Association, P.O. Box 4107, Lancaster, 93534
Tokay Stitch-N-Quilt Guild, P.O. Box 1838, Lodi, 95241
ADA Quilt Guild, 3460 Wilshire Blvd, Los Angeles, 90010
Westside Quilters Guild, 1019 Walnut Wood Ct., Los Banos, 93635
Bear Valley Quilters, Los Osos
Sierra Valley Guild, Loyalton, 96118
Quilters Etc., P.O. Box 2507, Lumpock, 93438
Heart of California Quilt Guild, 415 Camden Way, Madera, 93637
Manteca Quilters, P.O. Box 1558, Manteca, 95336
Gateway Quilters, P.O. Box 3793, Merced, 95344
Country Crossroads Guild, P.O. Box 577063, Modesto, 95355
Piece by Piece Quilters, 114 Cochrane Rd., Morgan Hill, 95037
Piecemakers By-the-Sea, P.O. Box 963, Moss Beach, 94038
Meets: 3rd Thursday 7:30 & Last Sunday 11 a.m.
at Canada Cove Mobile Home Rec. Hall, Half Moon Bay
Napa Valley Quilters, P.O. Box 405, Napa, 94558
Los Angeles County Quilt Guild, P.O. Box 252, Norwalk, 90651
Sierra Mountain Quilters Guild, P.O. Box 1359, Oakhurst, 93644
Mountain Quilters Guild, Oakhurst Library, Oakhurst
El Camino Quilt Guild, P.O. Box 1952, Oceanside, 92051
North Cities Quilt Guild, P.O. Box 2432, Orange, 92859
Meets: 4th Monday 7 p.m. at Placentia Presbyterian Church
Orange County Quilters Guild, P.O. Box 3108, Orange, 92665
Meets: 2nd Tuesday at 6:45 p.m.
at Portola Junior High, 270 N. Palm Dr.
Oroville Piecemakers Quilt Guild, P.O. Box 1604, Oroville, 95965
Monterey Pen. Quilters Guild, P.O. Box 1025, Pacific Grove, 93950
Southern CA Council of Quilt Guilds, 2342 W. Avenue N.,
Palmdale Ridge Quilters Guild, P.O. Box 1668, Paradise, 95969
Northern CA Quilt Council, 3935 Sloat Road, Pebble Beach, 93953
Petaluma Quilt Guild, P.O. Box 5334, Petaluma, 94955
East Bay Heritage Quilters, P.O. Box 6223, Petaluma
Sierra Gold Quilt Guild, P.O. Box 1078, Pine Grove, 95665
Cactus Sew-Ables Quilt Guild, P.O. Box 317, Pioneertown, 92268
Quilters of Contra Costa Cty, Box 23871, Pleasant Hill, 94523
Amador Valley Quilters, P.O. Box 955, Pleasanton, 94566
Porterville Quilters, P.O. Box 1881, Porterville, 93257
Friendship Quilters, P.O. Box 1174, Poway, 92074
Meets: 2nd Monday 7 p.m. at Tierra Bonita School
Redding Quilters Sew-ciety, P.O. Box 492581, Redding, 96409
Peninsula Quilters, P.O. Box 2423, Redwood City, 94064
Meets: Alternates day and night
at San Mateo Garden Center
San Fernando Valley Quilt Assoc., P.O. Box 1042, Reseda, 91337
Rocklin Pioneer Quilt Guild, P.O. Box 126, Rocklin, 95677
Schoolhouse Quilt Guild, P.O. Box 356, Rosemead, 91770
River City Quilters Guild, P.O. Box 15816, Sacramento, 95852
Canyon Quilters, P.O. Box 22465, San Diego, 92192
Seaside Quilt Guild, P.O. Box 9964, San Diego, 92109
San Francisco Quilters Guild, P.O. Box 27002, San Francisco, 94127
Meets: 3rd Tuesday 7:30 p.m.
at Bridgemont High School, 501 Cambridge St.
Peninsula Stitchery Guild, 15780 E. Alta Vista Way, San Jose, 95127
Beach Cities Quilters Guild, Box 322, San Juan Capistrano, 92693
Meets: 2nd Thursday 6:45 p.m.
at St. Edwards Church, La Primavera, Dana Pt.
San Luis Obispo Quilters, San Luis Obispo
North County Quilting Assoc., P.O. Box 982, San Marcos
Marin Quilt Lovers, P.O.Box 6015, San Rafael, 94903
Mt. Tam Quilt Guild, P.O. Box 6192, San Rafael, 94903
Meets: 2nd Tuesday 7:30 p.m. at Aldersgate Methodist
Church. Contact: Susie Ernst (707) 763-0945
Coastal Quilters Guild, P.O. Box 6341, Santa Barbara, 93106
Santa Clarita Valley Q. G., P.O. Box 802863, Santa Clarita, 91380
Santa Maria Valley Quilt Guild, P.O. Box 5075, Santa Maria, 93456
Meets: 2nd Wednesday (Sept. - June)
at St. Andrews Methodist Church
Santa Rosa Quilt Guild, P.O. Box 9251, Santa Rosa, 95405
Moonlighters, P.O. Box 6882, Santa Rosa, 65406
Legacy Quilters, 9320 Lake Country Dr., Santee, 92071
Wandering Foot QG, P.O. Box 943, Sierra Madre, 91025
Southern CA Council of Quilt Guilds, 1857 Temple Ave., Signal Hill, 90804
Simi Valley Quilt Guild, P.O. Box 3689, Simi Valley, 93093
Meets: 2nd Wednesday 7 p.m. at Senior Center
Sonoma Valley Quilters, 1463 Mission Drive, Sonoma, 95476
Sierra Quilt Guild of T.C., P.O. Box 43, Standard, 95373
Tuleburg Quilt Guild, P.O. Box 692151, Stockton, 95269
Tehachapi Mountain Quilters, 30300 Lower Valley Rd., Tehachapi, 93561
Valley of the Mist QG, 27475 Ynez Rd., Temecula, 92391
Almond Country Quilters, P.O. Box 914, Templeton, 93465
Pacific Piecemakers' Guild, The Sea Ranch
Conejo Valley Quilters, Thousand Oaks, 91362
Meets: 4th Monday 6:30 p.m.
South Bay Quilters Guild, P.O. Box 6115, Torrance, 90504
Valley Oak Quilters, P.O. Box 1093, Tulare, 93275
Turlock Quilt Guild, P.O. Box 66, Turlock, 95381
Night Owl Quilters Guild, P.O. Box 5019, Upland, 91786
Vallejo Piecemakers, P.O. Box 5515, Vallejo, 95381
Desert Winds Quilt Guild, P.O. Box 1989, Victorville, 92392
T L C Quilters' Guild, West Covina, 91791
Afro-American Quilters, 22544 Califa, Woodland Hills, 91367
Valley Quilt Guild, P.O. Box 1463, Yuba City, 95992
Cactus Sew-Ables Quilt Guild, P.O. Box 298, Yucca Valley, 92284
Meets: 1st Monday 9:30 a.m.
(2nd Monday in September and January)

Other Shops in California:

Altaville	Country Cloth Shop, 457 S. Main St.	209-736-4998
Anaheim	M & L Fabrics, 3430 W. Ball Rd.	714-995-3178
Atascadero	The Yardstick, 8310 C El Camino Real	805-461-1228
Auburn	Thyme to Sew, Gold Ctry Mall, 994 Lincoln Way	530-888-6420
Berkeley	New Pieces Fabric, 1597 Solano Ave.	510-527-6779
Berkeley	Ninepatch, 2001 Hopkins St.	510-527-1700
Berkeley	Kasuri Dyeworks, 1959 Shattuck Ave.	510-841-4509
Burbank	Q is for Quilts, 620 S. Glenoaks Blvd	818-567-0267
Camarillo	David Sanders Co., 1221 Calle Suerte	805-389-4699
Camarillo	Baron's Fabric, 379 Carmen Dr.	805-482-9848
Citrus Heights	Your Hearts Desire, 6308 Mugho	916-729-0729
Etna	Wooden Spools, 538 Main St., P.O. Box 728	530-467-5633
Fremont	Quilting Bee Sewing Center, 39161 Farwell Dr.	510-494-9040
Gilroy	Nimble Thimble, 55 W. 6th St.	408-842-6501
Granada Hills	Patchwork N' Things, 12355 Jolette Ave.	818-360-2828
Grass Valley	Quilt Loft, 762-C Freeman Ln.	916-274-0250
Half Moon Bay	The Pin Cushion, 757 Main St.	620-726-4247
Healdsburg	Fabrications, 118 Matheson St.	707-433-6243
Kernville	Sewing for You, 142 Tobias St., P.O. Box 821	760-376-3220
La Mesa	The Country Loft, 8166 LaMesa Blvd.	619-466-5411
Lancaster	Cozy Quilts, 701 W. Ave K, Suite 121	805-945-1207
Los Angeles	Azabu-Ya, 1953 Westwood Blvd.	310-446-1831
Los Gatos	The Makings, 786A Blossom Hill Rd.	408-356-7770
Los Gatos	California Quiltz, 21892 Bear Creek Rd.	408-354-9580
Madera	The Quilted Grape, Opening in Sept. 98	209-674-3142
Mammoth Lakes	Fabrications, 126 Old Mammoth Rd.	760-934-5682
Manhattan Beach	Once Upon a Quilt, 312 Manhattan Beach	310-379-1264
Mendocino	Crossblends, 45156 Main St.	707-937-4201
Modesto	Helens Yardage, 1331 Crows Landing Rd.	209-526-0903
Mokulemne HIll	Pamela Hill, 8500 Lafayette St.	209-286-1217
Morro Bay	The Cotton Ball, 475 Morro Bay Blvd.	805-772-2646
Mountain View	Buttons & Bolts Factory Outlet, 264 Castro St.	650-965-9712
Newhall	Aunt Ida's Attic, 24251 San Fernando Rd.	805-253-9141
Northridge	Boothill Patches, 18711 Parthenia St., #5	818-882-8753
Oxnard	Me & Thee Quilts, 200 Iowa Pl.	805-988-0995
Paradise	Fabric Friends Studio, 148 Pearson Rd.	916-877-3564
Petaluma	Chanticleer Antiques, 145 Petaluma Blvd. N	
Pico Rivera	S & J Quilts, 7860 Paramount Blvd.	310-942-7784
Quincy	Quincy Emporium, P.O. Box 450	916-283-0716
R.S. Margarita	De'cor Aum Enterprises, 22431-B 160 Antonion Pkwy, #485	
Rancho Cucamonga	Quilters Haven, 7662 Ramona	909-987-1607
Redding	Sew Simple, 3001 Bechelli Ln.	916-246-9310
Redwood City	Adams Notion & Yardage, 2090 Broadway	415-366-1711
San Anselmo	Quilt Complex, 69 Olive Ave.	415-453-7140
San Diego	The Shepherdess, 2802 Juan St.	619-297-4110
San Leandro	Quilters Three, 743 Rodney Dr.	510-895-9249
San Luis Obispo	Betty's Fabrics, 1229 Carmel St.	805-543-1990
San Marcos	Calico Station, 727 Center Dr. #117	619-480-8568
San Pedro	Quilt Sails, 1312 W. 37th	310-548-7094
Santa Ana	Quilting Possibilities, 2207 S. Grand Ave.	714-546-9949
Santa Cruz	Hart's Fabric Center, 1142 Soquel Ave.	408-423-5434
Santa Maria	Betty's Fabrics, 1627 S. Broadway, P.O. Box 5257	805-922-2181
Sky Forest	Sew Fun, 28589 Hwy 18	909-337-1521
Solvang	From the Heart, 1576 Copenhagen Dr.	805-686-0758
South Pasadena	A Quilters Dream, 1024 Mission St.	626-441-0740
Summerland	Sally's Alley, PO Box 876	805-565-5504
Torrance	Sew Fun, 16908 Prairie Ave.	310-542-7838
Truckee	Truckee Fabrics & Quilts, 11429 Donner Pass Rd.	916-582-8618
Tulare	Allens Fabric & Notions, 110 S. K St.	
Valencia	Quilted Heart, 24201 Valencia Blvd. #1371	805-255-0771
Weaverville	Stitch Witchery, 1310 Nugget Ln.	916-623-6891
Woodland Hills	Baron's Sewing Center, 22914 Victory Blvd.	818-348-7012
Woodland Hills	The Quilt Emporium, 4918 Topanga Canyon Blvd.	818-704-8238
Yuba City	Quilts & Simple Pleasures, 1654 Nedean Dr.	916-755-2705
Yucaipa	Apple Tree Gifts, 38392 Oak Glen Rd.	909-797-3130

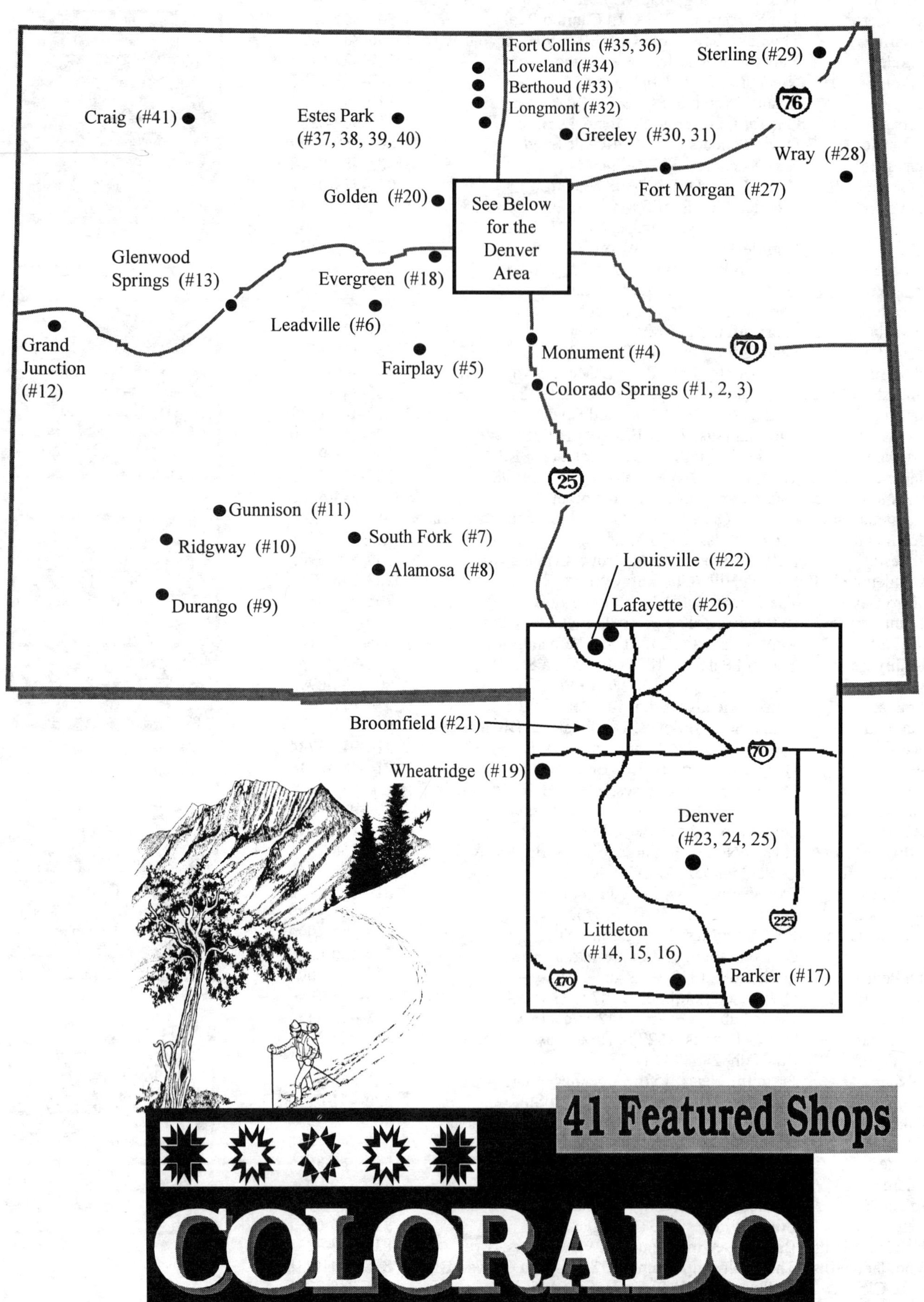

Fort Collins (#35, 36)
Loveland (#34)
Berthoud (#33)
Longmont (#32)
Sterling (#29)
76
Craig (#41)
Estes Park (#37, 38, 39, 40)
Greeley (#30, 31)
Wray (#28)
Fort Morgan (#27)
Golden (#20)
See Below for the Denver Area
Glenwood Springs (#13)
Evergreen (#18)
Leadville (#6)
Grand Junction (#12)
Fairplay (#5)
Monument (#4)
70
Colorado Springs (#1, 2, 3)
25
Gunnison (#11)
Ridgway (#10)
South Fork (#7)
Alamosa (#8)
Durango (#9)
Louisville (#22)
Lafayette (#26)
Broomfield (#21)
Wheatridge (#19)
70
Denver (#23, 24, 25)
225
Littleton (#14, 15, 16)
470
Parker (#17)
41 Featured Shops
COLORADO

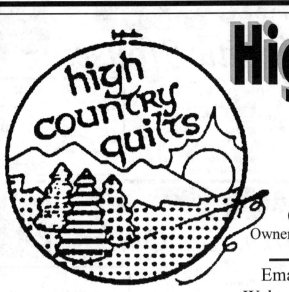

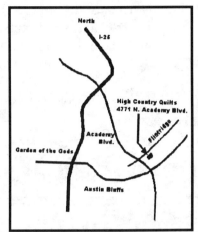

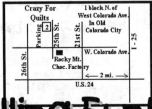

Monument, CO #4

The Quilted Cottage
& Diane's Collectibles

341 Front St. (719) 488-2558
Owners: Karen Hadfield & Diane Tremaine

Together we offer quality quilting fabrics & notions, clothing decor & gift items. Quilt-craft workshops. Primitive & Countrystyle antiques and furnishings. Enjoy the old world charm of shopping in Historic Monument Village!

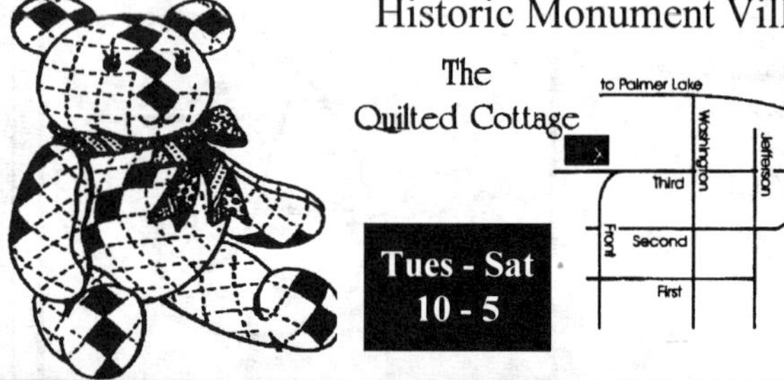

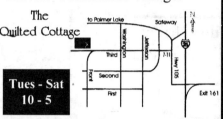

Tues - Sat 10 - 5

Fairplay, CO #5

7 Days A Week 10 - 4

Treadle House

443 Front St., P.O. Box 557 80440
(719) 836-0985
E-Mail: treadle@chaffee.net
Owner: Tricia Benes
Est: 1995 3000 sq.ft. 1000+ Bolts

Quality fabrics, notions, books for quilting but we also have cross stitch supplies, yarns and we're a gift shop too!

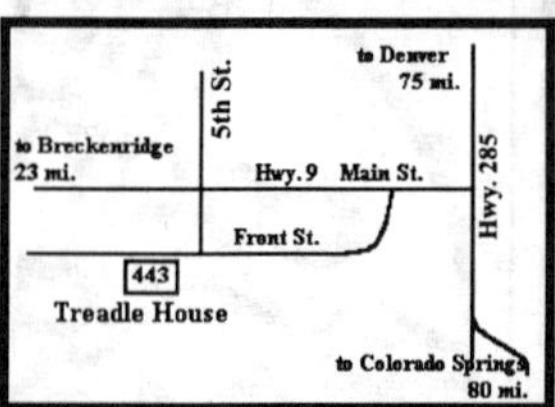

Leadville, CO #6

Hrs. Vary Please Call First

Mtn. Top Quilts

129 E. 7th St. 80461
(719) 486-3454
Owner: Gwendolyn Shepherd
Est: 1983 E-Mail: ccsmtq@sni.net

Quilts—old and new, vintage fabric, old quilt blocks and quilt tops. Hundreds of antique buttons. Vintage clothes & sewing collectables.

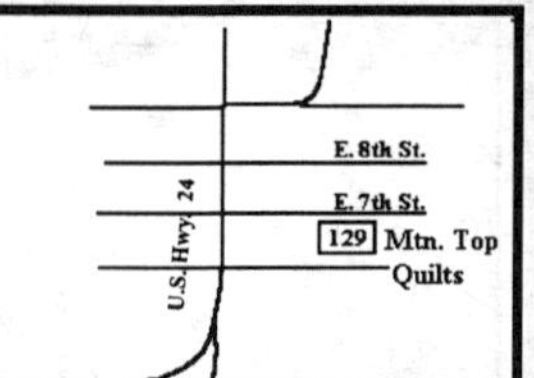

South Fork, CO #7

Tues - Sat 10 - 5

Fabric Trunk

31070 Hwy. 160
P.O. Box 451 81154
(719) 873-0211
Owner: LaWanna Pair
Est: 1993 700 sq.ft

Fabrics, Patterns, Notions, Classes. One Day Classes for those Visiting. Quilts, Books, and Gifts.

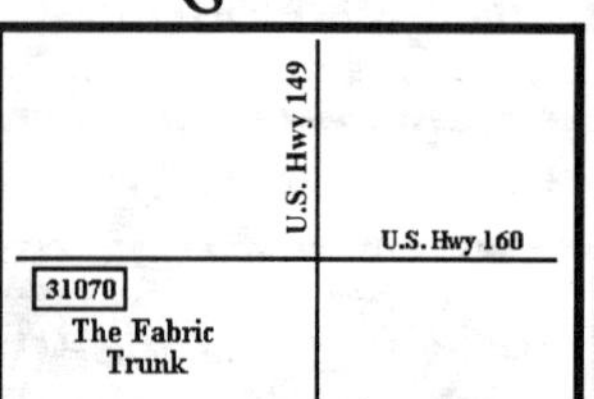

Alamosa, CO #8

Mon - Sat 9:30 - 5:30

Gray Goose Fashion Fabric

614 Main St. 81101
(719) 589-6982
Owner: Janet Davis
Est: 1985 2000+ Bolts

100% Cottons & Fashion Fabrics, notions, quilting supplies, books, and patterns. Daytime, evening and Saturday Classes.

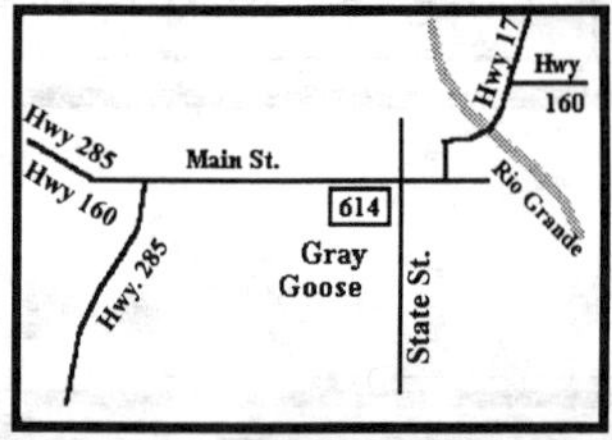

Durango, CO #9

Summer 10 - 5:30 Winter 10 - 5 Sun 12 - 4

Animas Quilts

600 Main Avenue 81301
(970) 247-2582
Owner: Jackie Robinson
Est: 1988 2600 sq.ft. Free Catalog

"A quilter's paradise" on the western slope of Colorado. 1000 Bolts of wonderful cottons! Home of international teacher & author, Jackie Robinson. Plus more

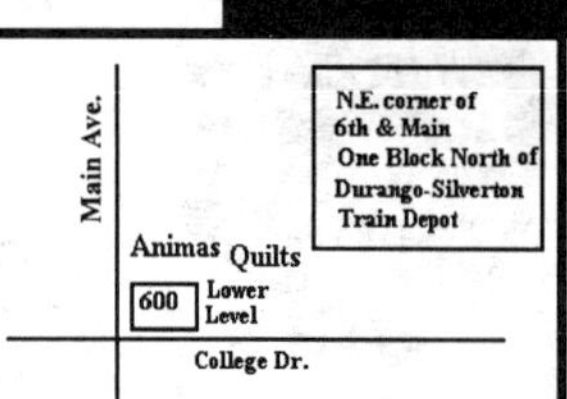

Ridgway, CO #10

Winter: Daily 10 - 5 Summer: Daily 10 - 6 Wed & Fri til 8

Piecemakers Country Store

550 Hunter Pkwy. 81432
(970) 626-4348 600 Bolts
NOW OPEN IN COLORADO !
www.piecemakers.com Catalog $2

Classes, fabrics, handmade quilts and dolls, original books and patterns. Times and Seasons Quilt Calendars and Cards. Gifts and clothing.

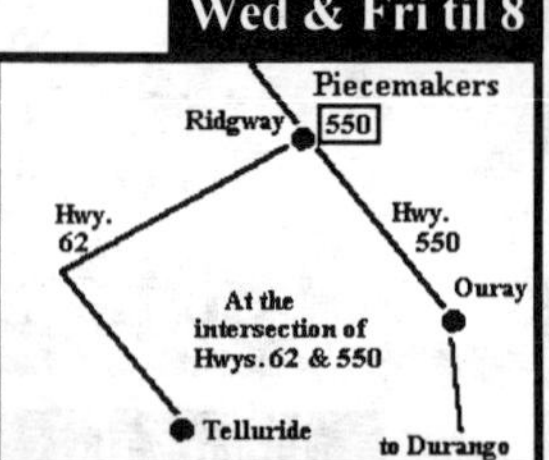

Gunnison, CO #11

Mon - Sat 9 - 5:30 Sun 12 - 4

E & P Sewing Emporium

135 N. Main St. 81230
(970) 641-0474 (800) 736-4281
Owners: Ellen Harriman & Pat Venturo
Est: 1985 2000 sq.ft.

We are a full-service sewing store offering New Home Sewing Machines, quilting and sewing classes. Home of the Rainbow Quilt Festival in mid-August.

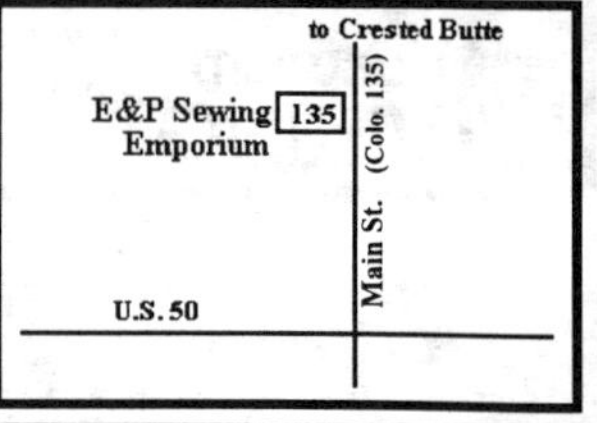

Grand Junction, CO #12

Mon - Sat 9:30 - 5:30

Hi Fashion **Fabrics, Inc.**

2586 Patterson Rd. 81505
(970) 242-1890 Est: 1965
Owners: Arlene & Jeff Vogel 11,500 sq.ft.
3000 Bolts Cottons, 8000 Bolts Overall

Huge Selection of Quilting Cottons, Books, and Supplies. Complete Line of Other Fabrics: Bridal, Fashion, Outer Wear, Drapery & Upholstery.

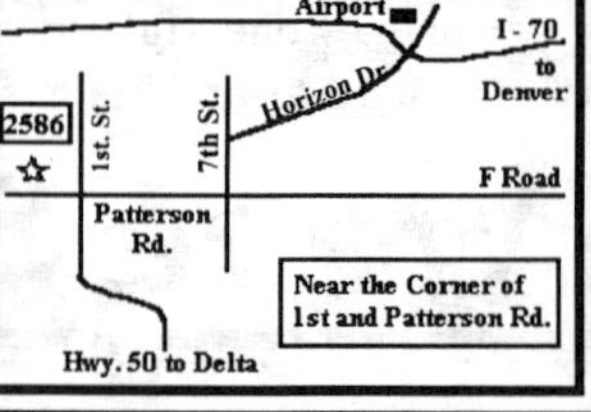

GLENWOOD SEWING CENTER

822 Grand Ave., Glenwood Springs, CO 81601
(970) 945-5900 or (800) 371-5967
E-Mail: glenwoodsew@compuserve.com
Owners: Bob & Sandy Boyd
Est: 1977 5000 sq.ft. 2500 Bolts

Mon - Sat 10 - 6
Sun 11 - 4

Glenwood Springs, CO #13

- Over 2,500 bolts
- Full line of books & notions
- Quilting classes & workshops

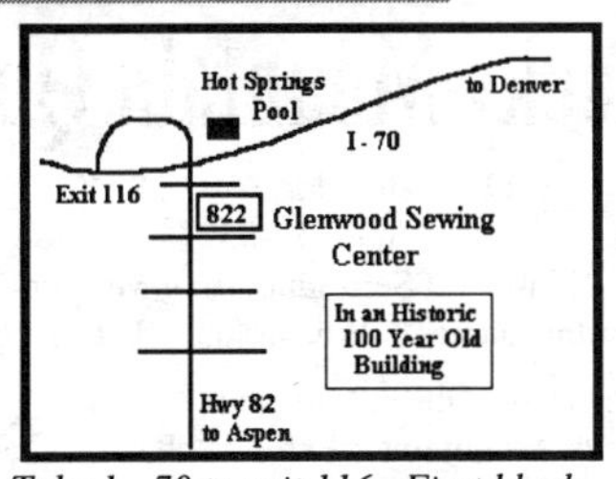

Take I - 70 to exit 116. First block after the bridge in downtown.

Littleton, CO #14

Mon - Wed 10 - 8
Thurs - Sat 10 - 5
Sun 12 - 4

The Creative Needle

6905 South Broadway #113 80122
(303) 794-7312
Web Site: www.thecreativeneedle.com
Owner: Marge Serck
Est: 1978 3500 sq.ft. 2000 Bolts

One stop for quilting, cross-stitch, heirloom and smocking. Elna machine sales and service.

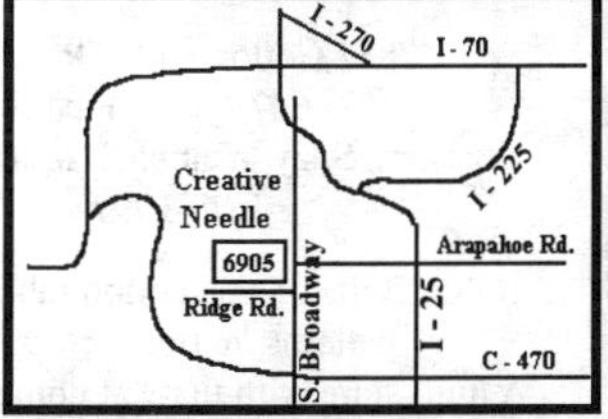

Littleton, CO #15

Mon - Fri 9:30 - 8
Sat 9:30 - 6
Sun 12 - 5

2777 W. Belleview 80123
(303) 730-2777 or (800) 996-6902
E-Mail: df@denverfabrics.com
Web Site: http://www.denverfabrics.com

Denver's Largest Selection of Fabrics, Buttons, Notions, and Patterns. Also Quilting Books, Patterns & Supplies

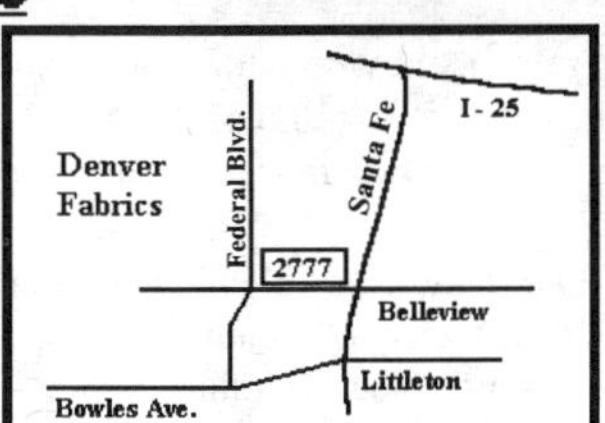

A Unique Quilt Shop

Littleton, CO #16

5950 S. Platte Canyon Rd. #D1 80123
(303) 798-2556
Owners: Toni Phillips
& Juanita Simonich
Est: 1994 1800 sq.ft.

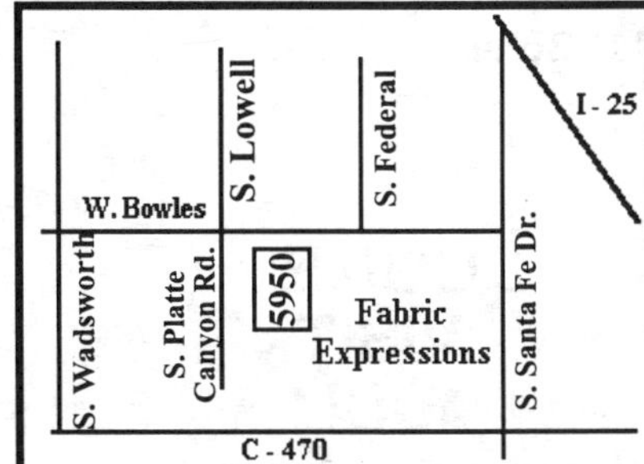

Mon - Fri 9:30 - 6
Tues til 8
Sat 10 - 5

100% Cottons! Homespuns, Flannels, Plaids, Prints, Solids. Books, Notions, Classes.

Catalog of Our Patterns SASE
Monthly Block of the Month Club

Home of "Fabric Expressions" patterns & books.

Parker, CO #17

Mon - Fri 10 - 5 Sat 10 - 4

High Prairie Quilts

17872 Cottonwood Dr. 80134
(303) 627-0878 Fax: Same
Owners: Suzy Weinbach & Jeannie Ivis
Est: 1997

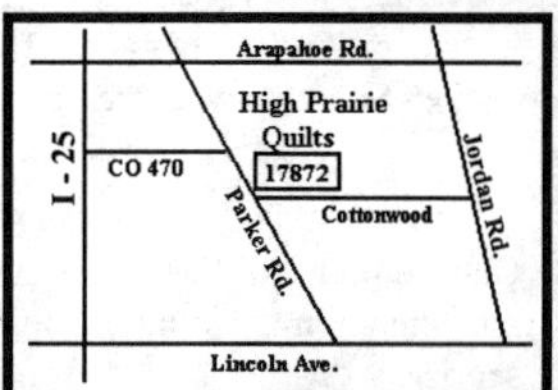

1000+ Bolts of fine cotton fabric, books, patterns, notions, classes.
A quilt store with that "at home" feeling.

Evergreen, CO #18

Mon - Sat 10 - 5 Sun 11 - 4

The Quilt Cabin

6947 Hwy. 73 80439
(303) 670-4798
Owners: Nancy O'Connor & Holly Engelken
Est: 1996 Free Catalog

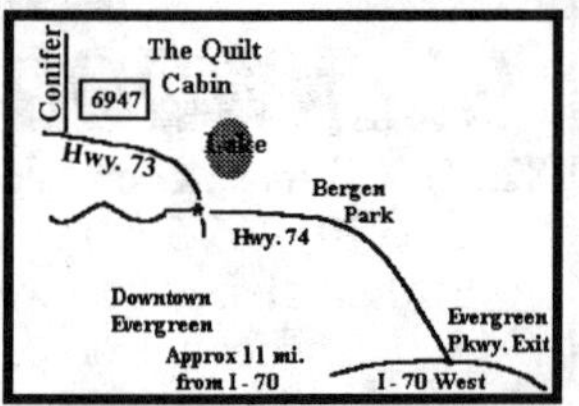

Great Selection Quilting Fabrics and Supplies. Reproductions & Flannels and Plaids our speciality.

Wheatridge, CO #19

Mon - Fri 9:30 - 5 Sat 9:30 - 4

Harriet's Treadle Arts

6390 West 44th Ave. 80033
(303) 424-2742
Owner: Harriet Hargrave

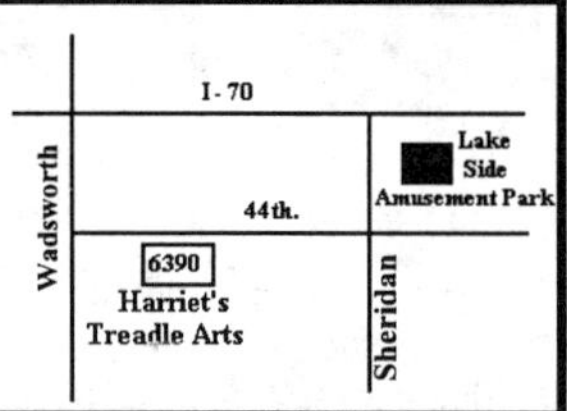

Our shelves are bulging with beautiful bolts!
Wide variety of notions.
Denver's oldest Bernina Dealer.
Come See Us ! !

Golden, CO #20

Tues - Sat 10 - 4

Rocky Mountain Quilt Museum

1111 Washington Ave. 80401
(303) 277-0377
Non-Profit Self Supporting Museum
Adm: James J. Prochaska Est: 1990

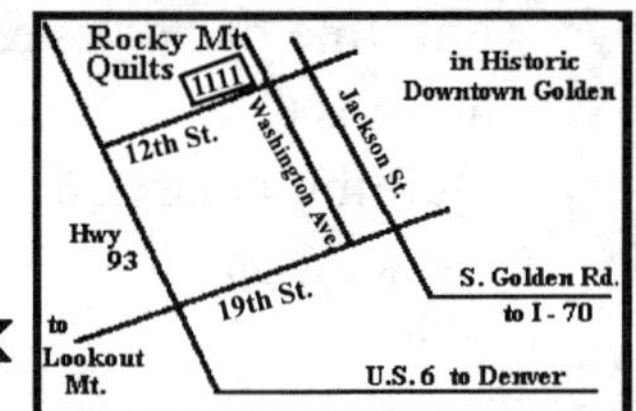

The only Quilt Museum in the Rocky Mountains. Exhibits change every two months. Send S.A.S.E. for schedule. Admission $1.

Broomfield, CO #21

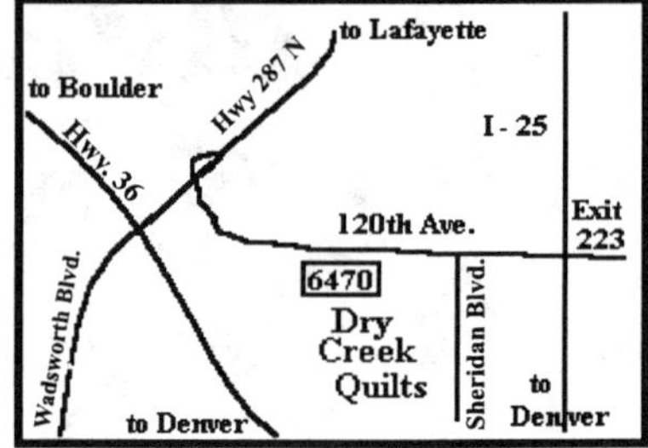

VILLAGER SQUARE SHOPPING CENTER
One mile West of Sheridan Blvd.
6470 W. 120th Ave., Unit D-3 80020
(303) 465-2526
Owner: Patty Albin
Est: 1995
1700 sq.ft.
1000 Bolts

COME VISIT US!

Everything for Quilters: Top Quality 100% Cottons, Quilting Books, Patterns, Notions, Viking Sewing Machines & Classes. FREE Inspiration and Advice.

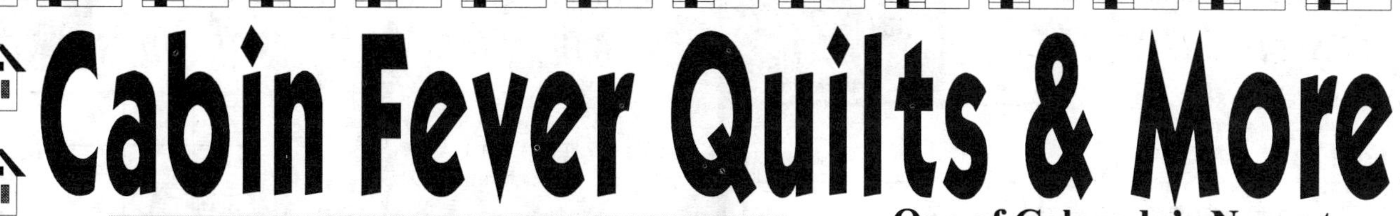

1075 S. Boulder Rd. #135 80027
(303) 664-1877 Fax: (303) 664-1887
Owners: Kathy Lewis & Monika Koenig
Est: 1996 1500+ Bolts

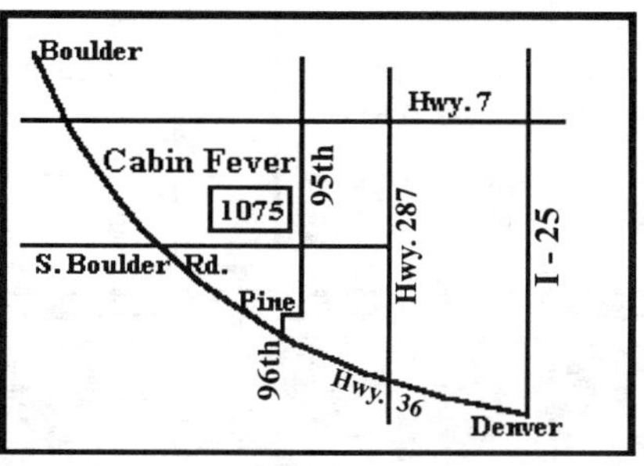

Mon, Tues,
Wed 10 - 6
Thur & Fri
10 - 9
Sat 10 - 5
Sun 12 - 4

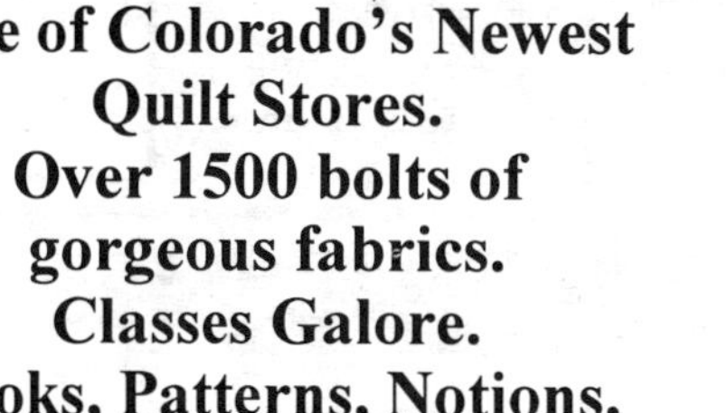

One of Colorado's Newest
Quilt Stores.
Over 1500 bolts of
gorgeous fabrics.
Classes Galore.
Books, Patterns, Notions,
Pfaff Machines.
Tons of Pre-cut Quarter Yards
and Fat Quarters.
Friendly, Expert Staff.
Open 7 Days a Week
(except holidays).
Convenient Hours.
30 minutes from
downtown Denver.

Denver, CO #23

8970 East Hampden Ave. 80231
(303) 740-6206 or (800) 474-2665 Fax: (303) 220-7424
Web Site: www.greatamericanquilt.com
Owners: Nancy Smith & Lynda Milligan Est: 1981 3000 sq.ft.

Great American Quilt Factory

Welcome !

3000+ Fabrics, Books, Notions, Patterns, Classes.
Photo transfer and machine quilting services.

Mon - Fri
9:30 - 6
Wed til 8:30
Sat 9:30 - 5
Sun 12 - 5

Home of:

Publishers of:
Dream Spinners, I'll Teach Myself,
and Possibilities books.
Free Catalog for ***Possibilities***

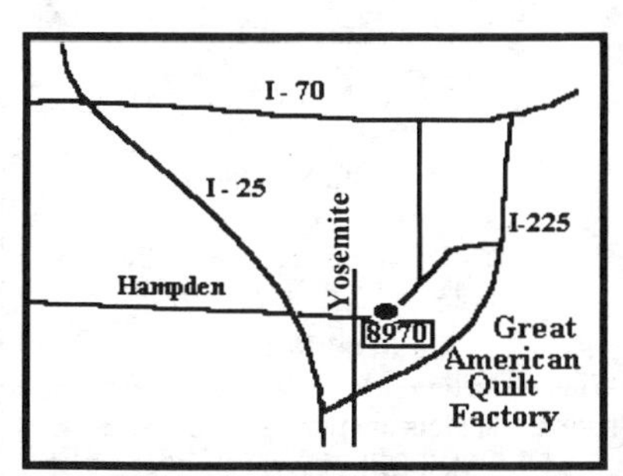

Denver, CO #24

Mon - Fri 9:30 - 5:30
Sat. 9:30 - 4:30
Sun 12 - 4

Quilts in the Attic

1025 South Gaylord St. 80209
(303) 744-8796
Est: 1972 1200 sq.ft.
Owners: Nancy O'Connor & Holly Engelken

Fabric - all 100% cotton - Books, Patterns, Batting, Notions. Ideas and Friendly Service. Classes.

Denver, CO #25

Mon - Sat 11 - 5
Sun 12 - 3

The Country Line Antiques & Quilts

1067 S. Gaylord St. 80209
(303) 733-1143
Owner: Genna Morrow Est: 1988

Antique Quilts from $20 to $2000 Also—quilt scraps, pieces, & "cutters" Gifts made from Antique quilts our specialty. Vintage Buttons, Linen & Laces.

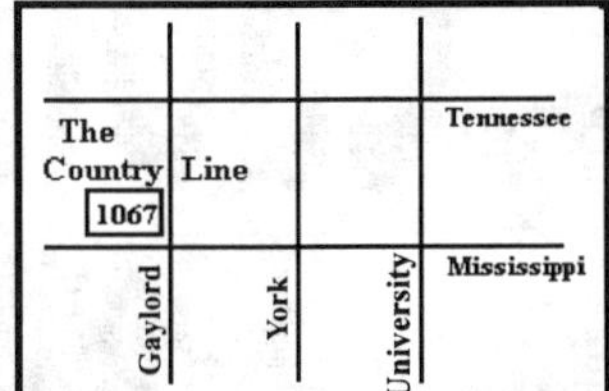

Lafayette, CO #26

Hours Vary Please Call First !

Artistic Creations

825 Sparta Dr. 80026
(303) 665-2388 Est: 1987
Owners: Bobby & Lewis Lombardi

We sell, trade, collect Antiques, Buttons, Quilts, Folk Art, Dolls, Bears, Books, Notions, Brass Charms.
Custom Picture Framing. Special Orders

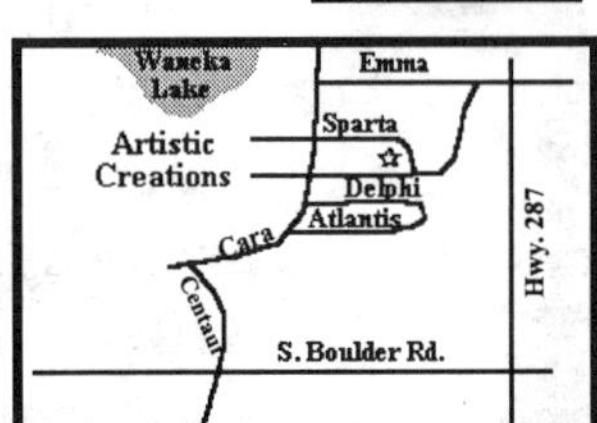

Ft. Morgan, CO #27

Mon - Sat 10 - 5

inspirations

324 E. Railroad #100 80701
(970) 542-0810
Web Site: www.inspirations-quilts.com
Owners: Ginger McCafferty & Nancy Hocheder

Top quality fabrics, quilt books, patterns, & kits, doll, bunny & bear patterns, notions, supplies & gifts.

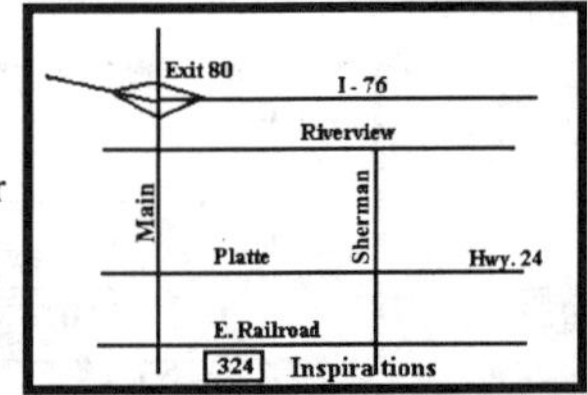

Wray, CO #28

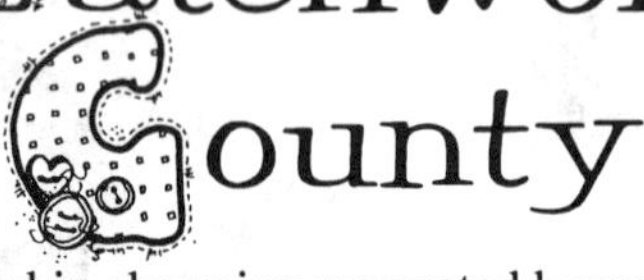

Mon - Fri 9:30 - 5:30
Sat 9:30 - 3

Located in charming renovated house built in 1902 one block east off Main.
Latest fabric, Patterns, books, notions.
Patchwork County—"*Where The Inspiration Is Free!*"

140 E. 4th St. 80758
(970) 332-5676
Owners: Dana Barnett & Claudia Fix
Est: 1994

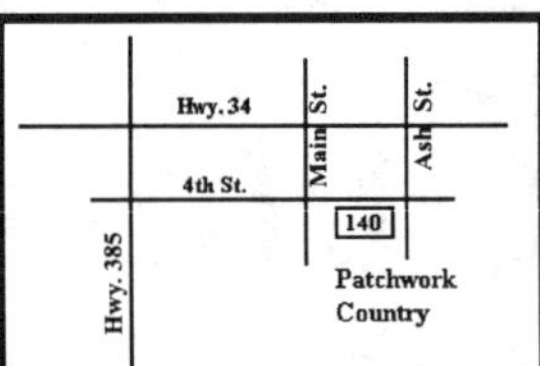

Sterling, CO #29

Est: 1987

Quilts-N-Creations

(970) 522-0146
201 Ash P.O. Box 991 80751
Owners: Everett & Dorothy Duncan
Mgr: Leta Propst
Asst. Mgr: Shauna Houser

Mon - Sat 9 - 5:30

1000 Bolts of Printed & Solid Cottons
Bridal Headquarters for N.E. Colorado including Bridal Fabric & Trims. Tuxedo Rentals with over 70 varieties to choose from. Authorized Bernina Dealer.
Custom sewing including crafts, quilts, garments or Bridal.
Custom, Traditional & Heirloom Quilting.

Greeley, CO #30

Mon - Fri 9 - 5:30
Sat 9 - 4:30

Country Crafts & Supplies

903 E. 18th St. 80631
(970) 353-1774
Owners: Jean Baker & Sherry Baker
Est: 1983 1200 sq.ft. 1000 Bolts

Quilters' Heaven
Wide selection of 100% cotton fabrics, notions, and lots of critter and doll patterns.
Mail Orders Welcome.

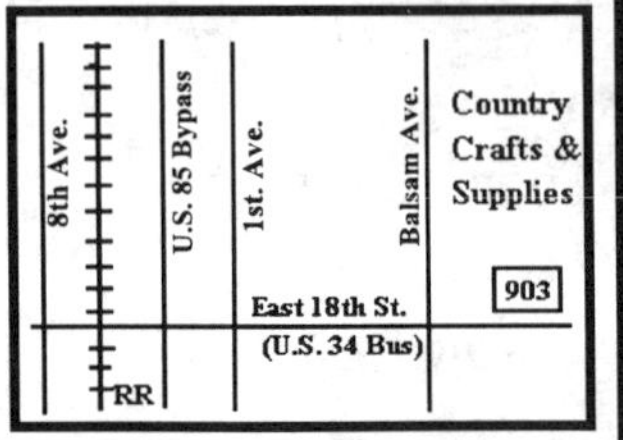

Greeley, CO #31

Mon - Fri 9:30 - 5:30
Sat 10 - 4

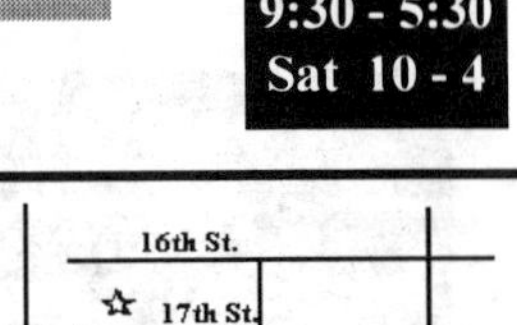

2308 17th St. 80631
(970) 356-0335
Owner: Ruth Dixon
Est: 1978 1800 Bolts

Needlework Shop. Quilting Supplies, Hand Knitting Yarns. Needlepoint, Hardanger and Cross Stitch

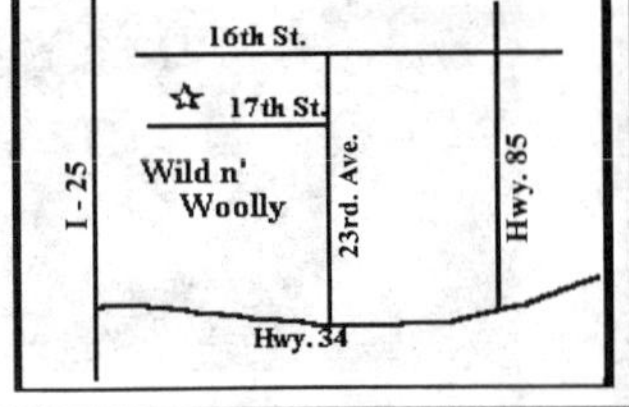

Longmont, CO #32

Mon- Sat 10 - 5:30
Mon & Thur til 7
Sun 12 - 4

The Patch Works

700 Ken Pratt Blvd. #101 80501
(303) 772-3002
Owner: Terri Miller Est: 1988
2000 sq.ft. 800+ Bolts

Friendly atmosphere, clean bathroom, lots of fabric, books, patterns, notions. Some one-day classes available.

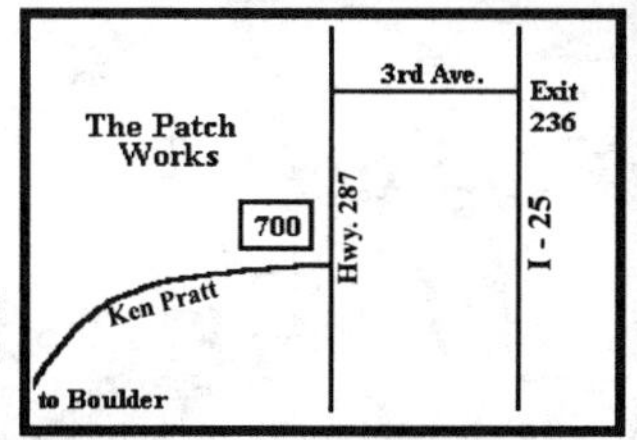

Berthoud, CO #33

Mon - Fri 9:30 - 6
Sat 9:30 - 5
Sun 1 - 5

Carriage House Quilts

516 Mountain Ave.
(970) 532-3386 or (888) 553-8381
E-Mail: Carriagehousequilts@juno.com
Owner: Mary M. Moody-Cox
Est: 1996 2000 sq.ft. 1000 Bolts

Quilt Supplies, Classes, Books
100% Cotton Jewel-Tone Fabrics
"The Quilter Friendly Store."

Loveland, CO #34

Mon - Fri 10 - 5
Sat 10 - 2

Treadle Quilts

444 N. Cleveland Ave. 80537
(970) 635-9064
Owner: Kim D. Garber
Est: 1993 2000 sq.ft.

Machine Quilting
Lessons, Fabrics
Books, Notions, Patterns

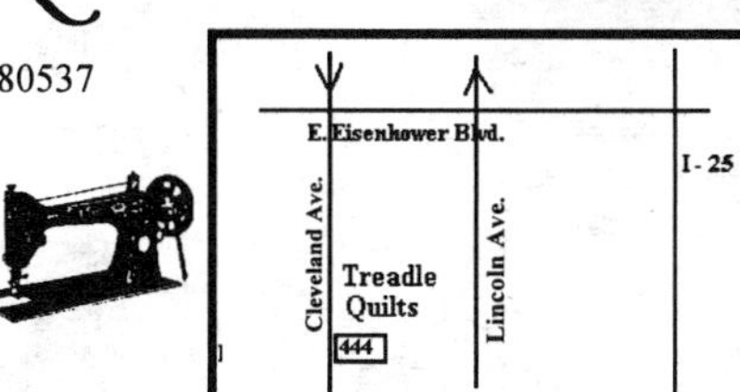

Ft. Collins, CO #35

Tues - Sat 10 - 5

Calico "Cat"

148 W. Oak 80521
(970) 493-0203
Owner: Lorraine Williams
Est: 1985 2000 sq.ft. 1000 Bolts

'All' the Books. Patterns Galore !
(100 Solids) Beautiful Yarns,
Wearable Arts, Quilts, Dolls, Animals

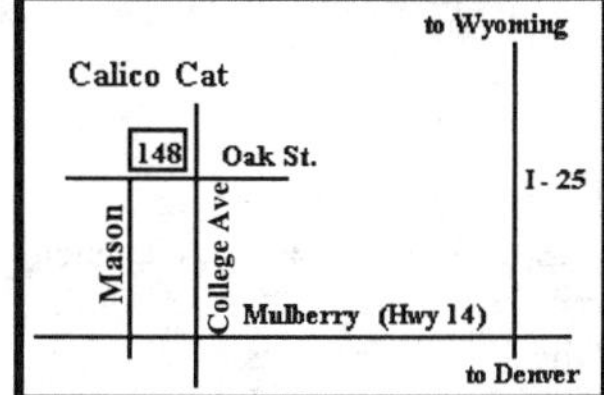

Ft. Collins, CO #36

The Fig Leaf

3500 S. College 80525
(970) 226-3267
Owners: Rob & Laura Shotwell
Est: 1982 8500 sq.ft.

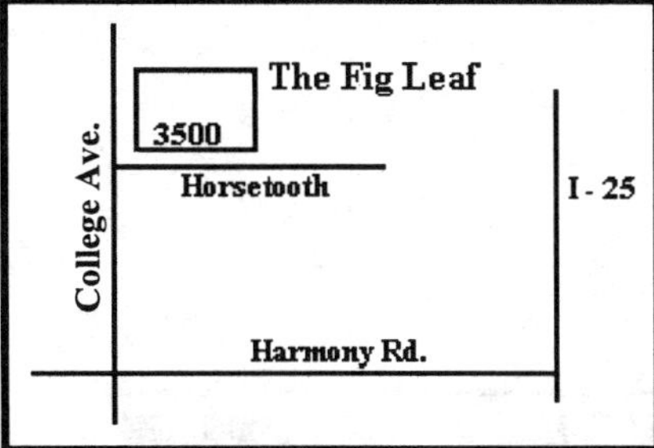

Mon - Fri 10 - 7
Sat 10 - 6 Sun 12 - 5

Located in two shops inside "The Square"

The Fig Leaf — Over 2500 bolts of fabrics, books, patterns, notions and gifts.
The Fig Leaf, Too — Country Furnishings & accessories.

Estes Park, CO #38

Open Daily Summer Closed Sun & Mon Winter

Mountain Lady Quilt Shop

205 Park Ln., P.O. Box 436 80517
(970) 586-5330
Owners: Connie Westley

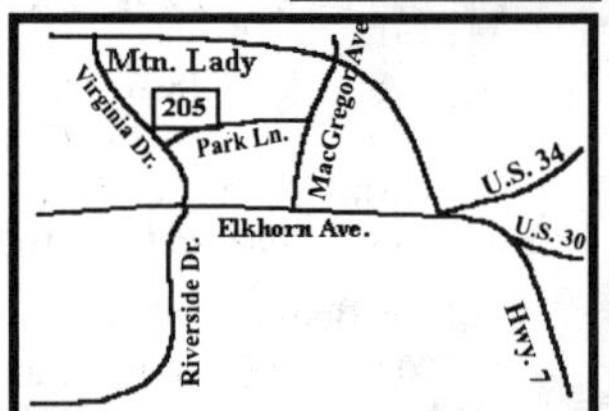

Everything for Quilters and Rug Hookers. Classes & Workshops Scheduled "just for you". American Made Quilts, Custom Quilts, Pfaff Machines, Mail Order.

Estes Park, CO #39

Year 'round 10 - 5 Closed Wed.

Maggie Mae's Quilts 'N

242 Moraine Ave. P.O. Box 4857
(970) 586-4257 80517
Owner: Margaret McCormick
Est: 1990 1200 sq.ft.

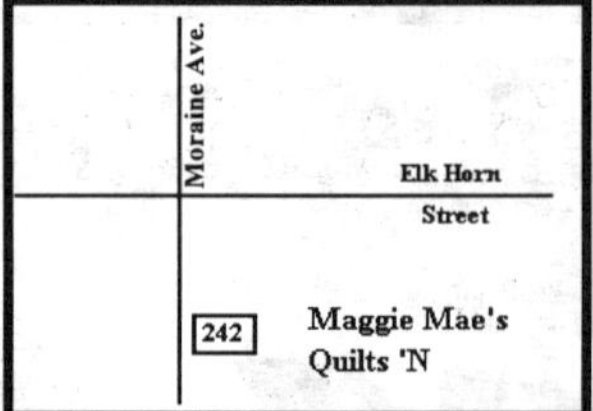

Featuring Patterns by Colorado Designers, both quilting and cross stitch. Kits - Handmade Wooden Quilt Racks - Fabrics - Christmas Projects & Unique Wearables.

Estes Park, CO #40

Mon - Sat 10 - 5 Sun 12 - 5 in the Winter Extended hours in the Summer

Traditions Remembered

800-B Moraine Ave., P.O. Box 3454
(970) 586-8598 80517
Owner: Beverly Peterson
2000 sq.ft. Free Catalog

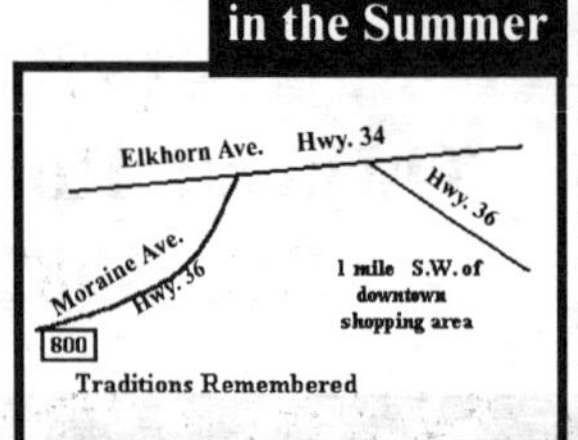

Quilting Fabrics & Notions * Wildlife Patterns, Antique Fabrics, Feedsacks, Laces, Patterns, Antique & New Buttons! * Old quilts, tops, blocks & UFO's! Gifts & finished items.

Estes Park, CO #37

7730 CO Hwy. 7 80517
(970) 586-2862 Fax: (970) 586-2095
Est: 1988 1000 sq.ft.
Owner: Elaine Winslow

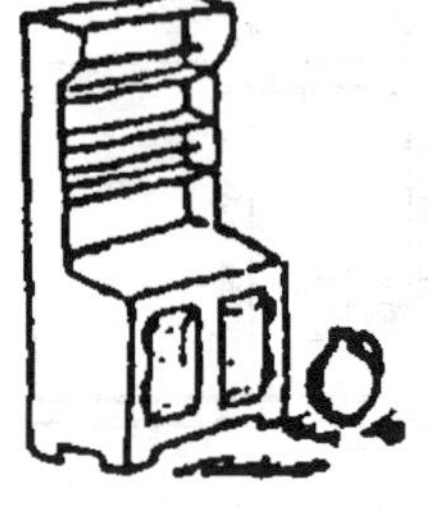

Daily 10 - 5 Best to Call First

Specializing in 19th century American country furnishings & decorative items. Antique quilts, fabrics, sewing treasures, gifts & collectibles.

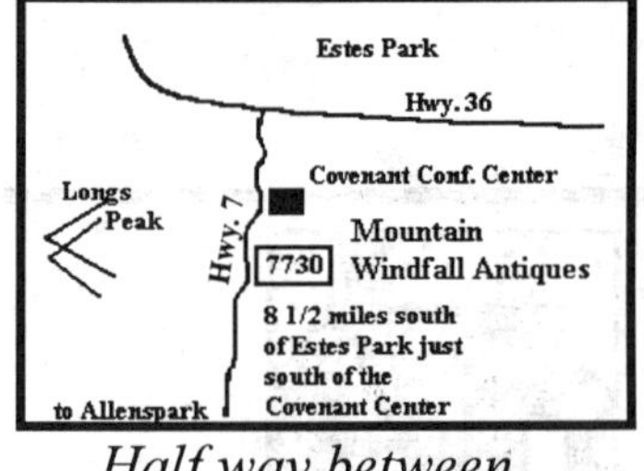

Half way between Allenspark and Estes Park

Craig, CO #41

Tues - Fri 10 - 5:30 Sat 10 - 4:30

Rose of Sharon Quilt Shop

356 Ranney St. 81625
(970) 824-7414 Fax: Same
E-Mail: rosqs@cmn.net
Web Site: www.cmn.net/~rosqs
Owner: Sharon Lausin

100% Cotton Fabric, Books, Quilt Patterns, Notions, Classes, Quilts & Gifts. New Home Sewing Machines—Sales & Service. Vacuum Repairs, Bags & Belts

Colorado Guilds:

San Luis Valley Quilt Guild, 6750 Juniper Ln., Alamosa, 81101
  Meets: 3rd Saturday 1:30 p.m.
  call the Gray Goose (719) 589-6982 for location
Colorado Quilting Council, P.O. Box 2056, Arvada, 80001
Piecemaker Quilt Group, Aurora
Royal Gorge Quilt Council, 1402 1/2 Sherman Ave., Canon City, 81212
Piecing Partners, Colorado Springs, 80925
  Meets: 3rd Wednesday 9:30 a.m. at Faith Presbyterian, 1529 N. Circle
Colorado Springs Quilt Guild, P.O. Box 8069, Colorado Springs, 80907
  Meets: 2nd Thursday 6 p.m.
  at Pulpit Rock Church, 301 Austin Bluffs Pkwy.
Great American Quilters, 8970 E. Hampden Ave., Denver, 80231
  Meets: 1st Tuesday 7 p.m. at Great American Quilts
African American Quilters and Collectors Guild, Denver
La Plata Quilter's Guild, P.O. Box 2355, Durango, 81302
Arapahoe County Quilters, P.O. Box 5357, Englewood, 80155
Estes Valley Quilt Guild, P.O. Box 3931, Estes Park, 80517
  Meets: 2nd Wednesday 7 p.m. at Various locations
Alpine Quilters, Genesee
Colorado West Quilt Guild, 1320 Houston Ave., Grand Junction, 81501
Rocky Mt. Wa Shonaji, Littleton
Front Range Cont. Quilters,
  7133 Gold Nugget Dr., Longmont, 80503
San Luis Valley Quilt Guild, Monte Vista Coop,
  Monte Vista, 81144
The Barn Quilters, Monument
  Meets: 2nd & 4th Friday 9 a.m.
  at Woodmoor Community Center,
  1691 Woodmoor Dr., downstairs
Pride City Quilt Guild, 60 Portero Dr., Pueblo, 81005
Monarch Quilt Guild, Salida
Delectable Mountain Quilter's Guild,
  P.O. Box 774383, Steamboat Springs, 80477
  Meets: 3rd Monday
Columbine Quilters, Wheat Ridge

Other Shops in Colorado:

Arvada	Pincushion Fabric, 8662 W. 84th Circle	303-426-9967
Aspen	Katie Ingham Antique Quilts, 257 Glen Eagles Dr.	970-925-2595
Boulder	Elfriede's Fine Fabrics, Arapahoe Village Shopping Ctr.	790-447-0132
Breckenridge	Honeysuckle Rose Quilts, 211 S. Main, P.O. Box 7338	970-547-9654
Broomfield	Barb's Fabric Outlet, 9103 W. 103th	303-424-2727
Buena Vista	Bev's Stitchery, 202 Tabor St.	719-395-8780
Cahone	Ann Neely's Quilting Shop, 14064 Hwy. 666	970-562-4655
Cedaredge	Katie's Kloth & Kreations, Box 1093	970-856-7878
Colorado Springs	Mill Outlet Fabric Shop, 2906 N. Prospect	719-632-6296
Conifer	Log Cabin Patchworks, 27051 Barkley Rd.	303-838-7343
Denver	D'Leas Fabric Affair, 2719 E. 3rd. Ave.	303-388-5665
Denver	Exeter River Trader, 1212 S. Broadway	303-744-7049
Fort Collins	Calico Country, 4604 Terry Lake	970-493-2751
Fort Morgan	Quilting Corner, 328 Main St.	970-867-9066
Golden	Leman Publications Quilt Gallery, 741 Corporate Circle	303-278-1010
Hotchkiss	D C Fabrics, 148 E. Bridge St.	970-872-2688
Lakewood	Sew Far Sew Good, 10555 W. Jewell Ave. Apt. #14-208	907-279-7656
Littleton	Designer Fabrics, 8966 W. Bowles	303-978-9914
Longmont	Bernina Sewing Center, 510 4th Ave.	303-776-6704
Loveland	Country Wishes & Wants, 120 E. 4th	970-635-0132
Merino	D & J Country Antiques, P.O. Box 29	970-842-5813
Steamboat Springs	Pieces of the Past, 626 Lincoln Ave.	970-870-8684
Sterling	Sew Together, 320 N. 4th	970-521-0258

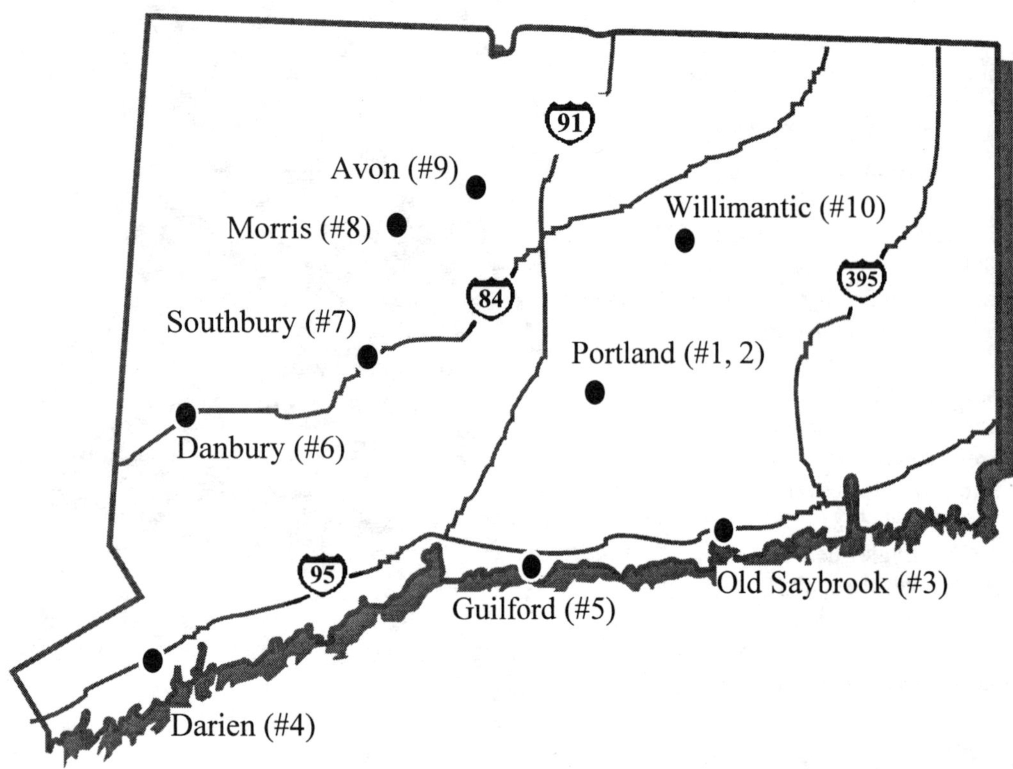

Connecticut Guilds:
Clamshell Quilt Guild,
Box 3, Hartford, 06385
Thames River Quilters,
New London, 06320
Greater Hartford Quilt Guild,
P.O. Box 310213,
Newington, 06131
Trumbull Piecemakers,
34 St. Mary's Ln.,
Norwalk, 06851
Heart of the Valley,
Portland, 06480

10 Featured Shops

CONNECTICUT

Portland, CT #1

Tues - Fri 10 - 5
Sat 10 - 3

Patches & Patchwork

216 Main 06480
(860) 342-4567
Owner: Jane Wilk Sterry
Est: 1980 1200 sq.ft.

We carry the unusual in fabrics. Latest books, patterns and notions. Classes. Antique quilt repair! Commission quilts

Portland, CT #2

By Appointment

Carolyn's Quilting Bee

73 Ames Hollow Rd. 06480
(860) 342-1949
Owner: Carolyn Johnson
Est: 1980

Located in the Blacksmith Shop of an 18th Century Farm.
Visitors are always welcome.

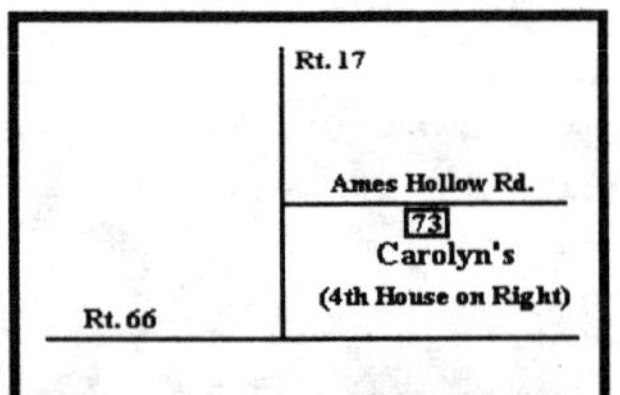

Old Saybrook, CT #3

Mon - Sat 10 - 5

Saybrook Quilts

210 Main St., Cinema Plaza 06475
(860) 388-2295 Fax: (860) 388-5885
E-Mail: Fenwoodmwm@aol.com
Owner: Marcia Moore 1000+ Bolts

Great selection of quality 100% cotton fabrics, books, patterns, notions, classes, quilts & crafts for sale.
Custom Machine Quilting done on premises.

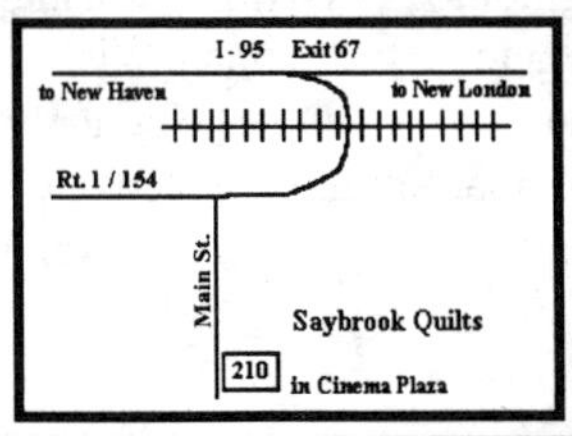

Darien, CT #4

Mon - Sat 10 - 5

Appalachian House

1010 Boston Post Rd. 06820
(203) 655-7885 Est: 1973
6 Rooms in a picturesque House

A non-profit Craft Shop. We provide a Market Place for Mountain Crafts People Dependent on their Skill and Talent for their Livelihood.

Directions from I-95 North--Take exit 11--Turn Left--Store is on the Right 1/4th mile on Rt.1
Directions from I-95 South--Take Exit 11--Turn Right--Store is on the right after 1st Traffic Light.

Calico Alley

1310 Boston Post Rd. 06437
Strawberry Hill Plaza
(203) 458-6122
Owner: Melinda Cacamis
Est: 1992

IT'S WORTH THE DRIVE

2500+ Bolts of Designer Fabric & 100% Cottons, Notions, & Supplies. Authorized Viking and White Dealer.

MON - FRI 10 - 5 SAT 10 - 4 SUN 12 - 4

Your Fat Quarter Headquarters
8000+ Fat Quarters

COME SEE US SOON !

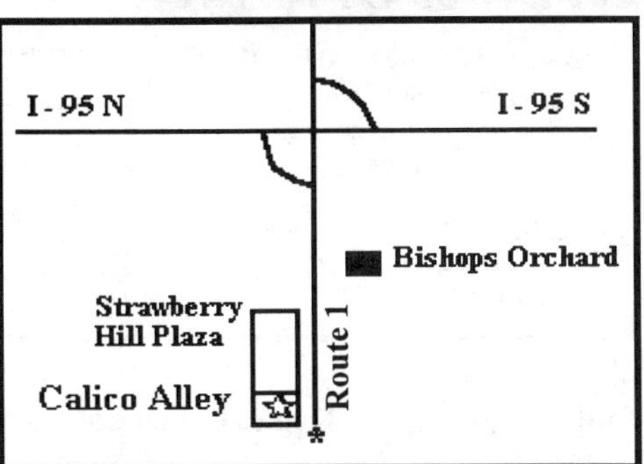

Within minutes of Shoreline Trolley Museum & Thimble Islands
45 minutes from Mystic Seaport
60 minutes from Foxwoods Casino.
From I - 95N take Exit 57.
Take a Right.
We are 3/4 mile on the Right.

Danbury, CT #6

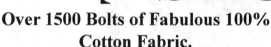

THE QUILT SHOP

Over 1500 Bolts of Fabulous 100% Cotton Fabric.

Area's Authorized Bernina Dealer

BERNINA® AUTHORIZED DEALER

Featuring Complete Line of Machines & Accessories.

Plus a Tremendous Selection of Books & Classes.

FOR ALL YOUR QUILTING SUPPLIES

16 Padanaram Rd.
Rt. 37 06811
(203) 743-0543
Fax #: (203) 797-0936
Owner: Ginny Murphy
Est: 1994 1600 sq.ft.

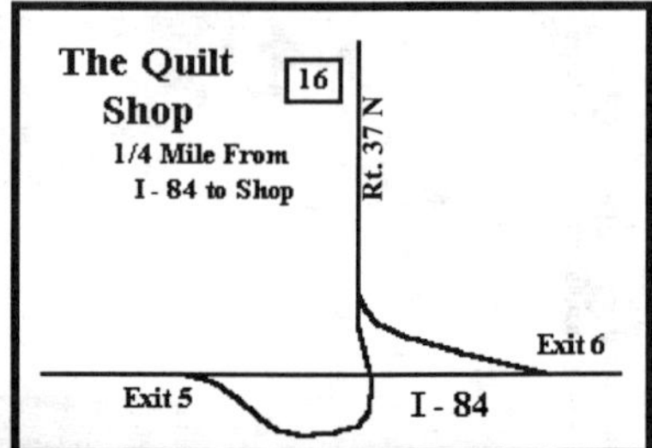

Mon - Sat 9 - 5
Thur til 8 Sun 12 - 4

Southbury, CT #7

Dagmar's Fabrics

1481-6 Southford Rd. (Route 67) 06488
(203) 262-1206
Owner: Dagmar Ferguson
Est: 1989 2500+ sq.ft.

Mon - Fri 9:30 - 6 Sat 9 - 5

Area's largest selection of quilting books, patterns, & supplies. Knowledgeable, Friendly Staff, Quality Fabrics - over 3000 bolts. Classes. Gift Certificates Authorized Viking Dealer

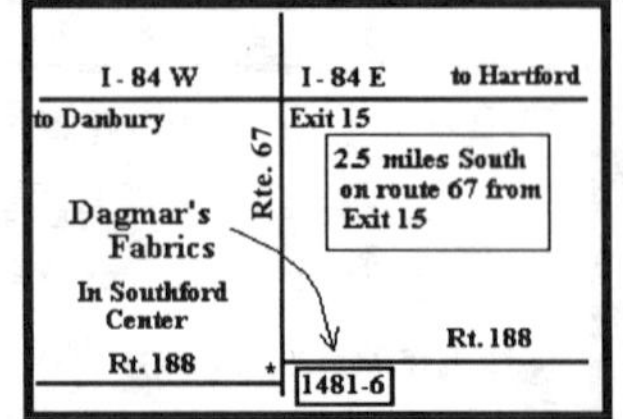

Morris, CT #8

Wed - Sun 10 - 5

The Fabric Barn

11 Watertown Rd. (Rt. 63)
(860) 567-5823 06763
Owner: Marjorie Munson
Est: 1978 800 sq.ft.

Full stock of calicos and quilting supplies. Specializing in remnants and closeouts. Call for info. on classes. Open all year.

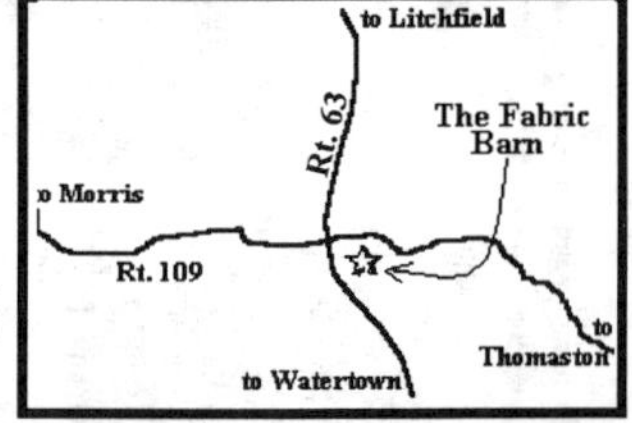

Avon, CT #9

Tues - Sat 10 - 5

Patchwork Cottage

17A E. Main St. (Rt. 44) 06001
(860) 678-0580
Owner: Patricia-Anne Barker
Est: 1997

Beautiful 100% Cotton Fabrics
Books, Patterns, Notions, Classes.
Handmade Gifts.

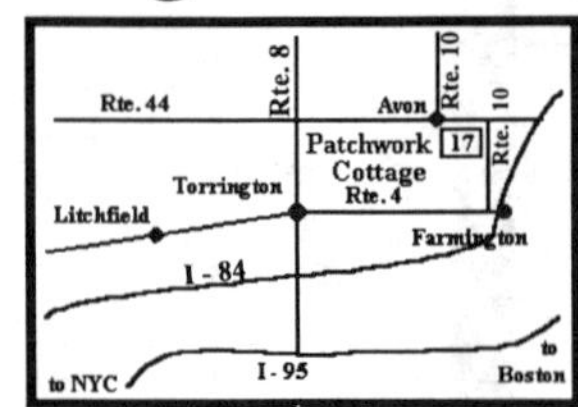

Other Shops in Connecticut:

Cheshire	Calico Etc., 116 Elm St.	203-272-2443
Clinton	J & N Fabrics, 55 W. Main St.	860-669-5310
Colchester	Colchester Mill, 51 Broadway	860-537-2004
Glastonbury	Close to Home, 2717 Main St.	860-633-0721
Salem	BG Calico, 6 Centre St.	860-859-3417
Stamford	Gingham Dog & Calico Cat, 219 Bedford St.	203-327-5740
Torrington	Gingham Rocker, 84 Main	860-482-9364
Torrington	Eleanor's Fabrics, 29 Water St.	860-489-9237

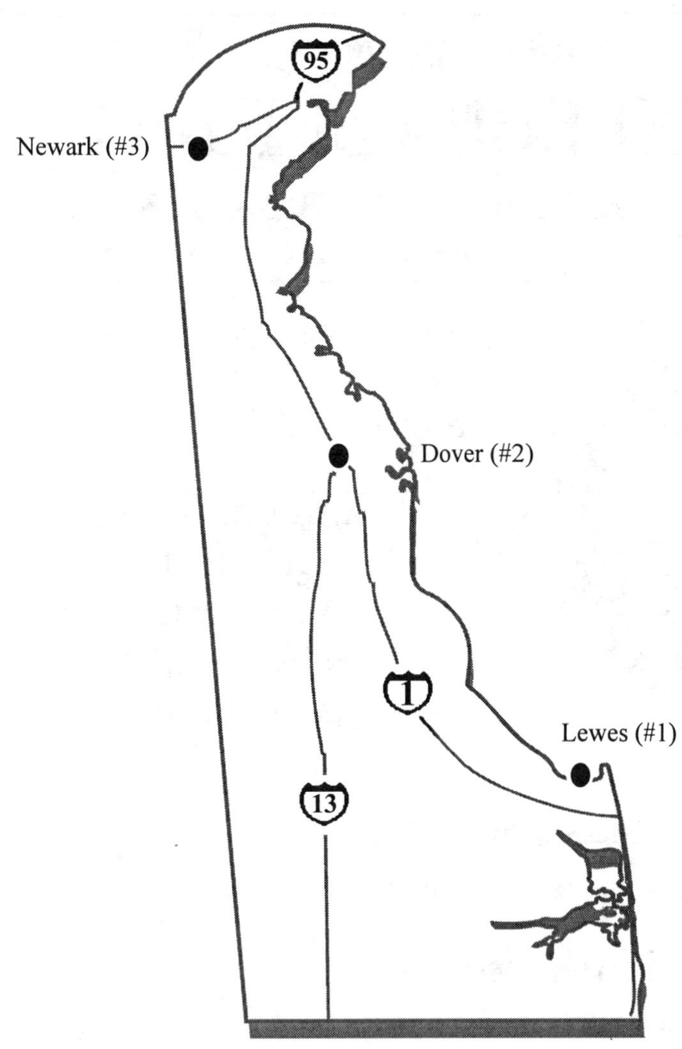

- Fabric
- Notions
- Cross Stitch
- Classes
- DMC

At the "Beacon Motel"
528 E. Savannah Rd.
19958
(302) 644-0556
E-Mail: mcfee@ce.net
Owner: Maryann McFee
Est: 1995 2000 sq.ft.

"We are located just over the drawbridge on Savannah Road @ The Beacon Motel"

Lewes, DE #1

Dover, DE #2

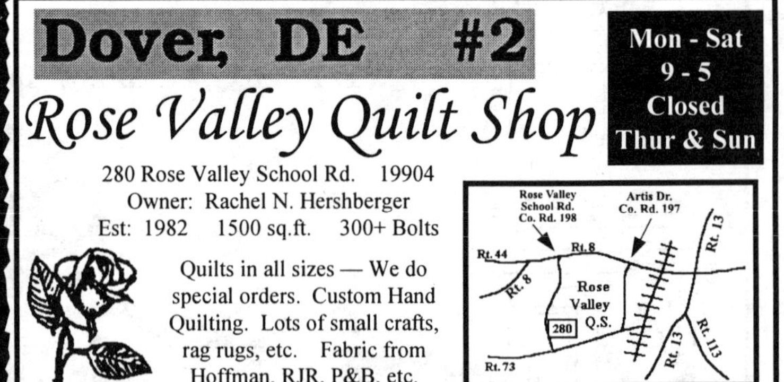

280 Rose Valley School Rd. 19904
Owner: Rachel N. Hershberger
Est: 1982 1500 sq.ft. 300+ Bolts

Quilts in all sizes — We do special orders. Custom Hand Quilting. Lots of small crafts, rag rugs, etc. Fabric from Hoffman, RJR, P&B, etc.

Another Shop in Delaware:
Laurel Homestead Shoppe, Rt. 64, Box 179
302-875-2017

1800 Capital Trail,
Suite 2
Newark, DE 19711
(302) 737-5699
quilthive@aol.com

HOURS

10 - 5 Monday thru Saturday

Open til 8 PM Wed & Thur

1 - 5 Sunday

2800 sq. ft. of all the fabric, gadgets and goodies that quilters love

- the latest 100% cotton fabrics, books and patterns
- classes from beginning hand and machine quilting to advanced Baltimore Album-style applique

Newark, DE #3

LOCATED AT THE CORNER OF KIRKWOOD HIGHWAY AND HARMONY ROAD

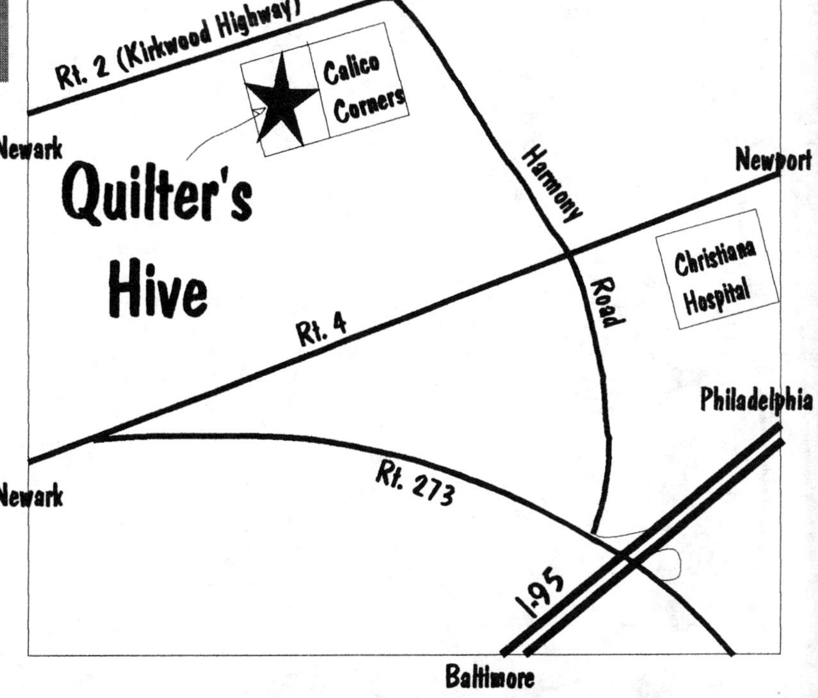

TAX FREE SHOPPING CLOSE TO I-95

From I-95 take Exit 3 on to Rt 273 West (towards Newark) - Turn right on Harmony Road at the first traffic light - Follow Harmony Road for 2.1 miles and turn left into the Calico Corners/Quilter's Hive parking lot (just before the 5th traffic light)

Niceville (#1)
10
(#13) Orange Park
St. Augustine (#3)
Gainesville (#2)
Palatka (#4)
Ocala (#14)
Ormond Beach (#6)
Belleview (#5)
South Daytona (#27)
Dade City (#8)
Leesburg (#7)
Maitland (#15)
Lakeland (#17)
Orlando (#10, 11, 12)
Titusville (#28)
Dunedin (#18)
Rockledge (#29)
Clearwater (#24)
Winter Haven (#16)
Kissimmee (#9)
Largo (#19)
Melbourne (#25)
75
Palm Bay (#30)
Ellenton (#20)
95
Sebring (#21)
Wabasso (#31)
Ft. Pierce (#32)
Palm City (#34)
Fort Myers (#23)
Jupiter (#33)
Sanibel (#22)
Coral Springs (#36)
Delray Beach (#35)
Royal Palm Beach (#26)
FLORIDA
36 Featured Shops

Niceville, FL #1

Mon - Sat 9:30 - 5

Terri Cloth, Inc.

93 John Sims Pkwy. 32578
(850) 678-7283
E-Mail: tccloth@aol.com
Owner: Terry Casey
Est: 1989 2200 sq.ft.

On the Florida Panhandle, we have the largest selection of 100% cotton from leading manufacturers. Notions, Books & Patterns.

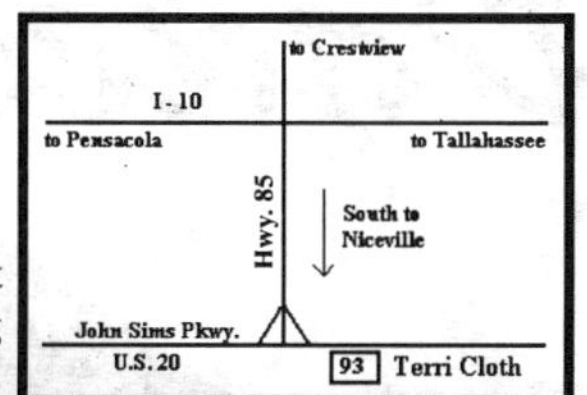

Gainesville, FL #2

**M, T, W, F 10 - 5:30
Th 12 - 8:30
Sat 10 - 4**

My Favorite Quilt Shop

3911 NW 13th St. 32609
(352) 372-4720 Fax: (352) 372-1222
Owner: Mary E. Derry Est: 1995 2500 sq.ft.
E-Mail: MaryEDerry@msn.com

North Central Florida's finest Quilt Shop.
E-Z on-off I - 75 Take Exit #77.
WE LOVE QUILTERS

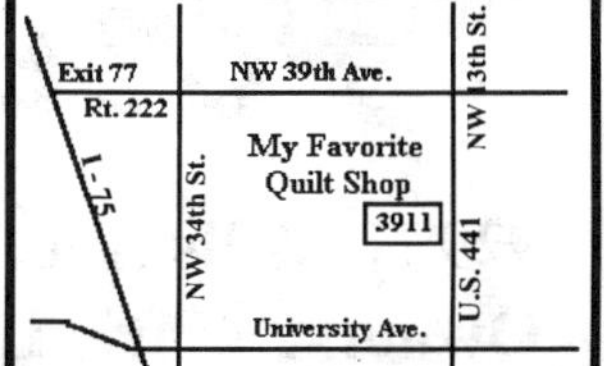

Saint Augustine, FL #3

**Mon 10 -6
Tues - Fri 10 - 5
Sat 10 - 4**

Material Things

77 Saragossa St. 32084
(904) 829-3778
Owner: Joyce Snyder
Est: 1991 1575 sq.ft. 1000+ Bolts

Most beautiful selection of 100% cottons in the area. Wide variety of books, patterns, notions and classes.

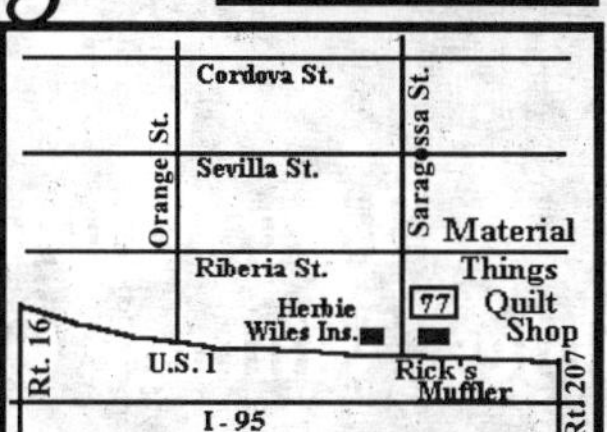

Palatka, FL #4

**Mon - Fri 9 - 5
Sat 9 - 2**

Quilted Pleasures

2403 Crill Ave. 32177
(904) 329-5226
Owner: Brenda Gaston

100% Cotton Fabric, Quilting Supplies, Books, Patterns. Day / Night Classes. Wool, Cotton, Poly Batting
M/C & Visa accepted

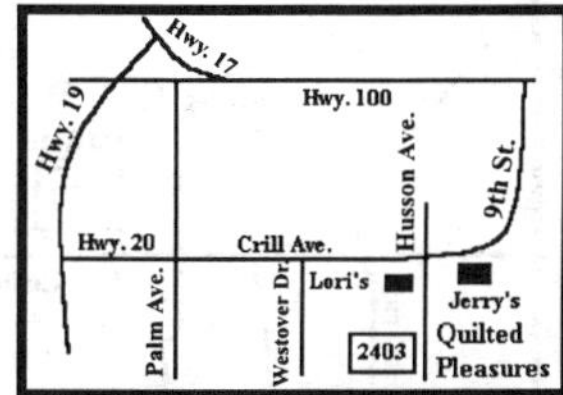

Belleview, FL #5

**Mon - Fri 9 - 5
Sat 9 - 3**

Fabric Stash

11012 SE 62nd Ave. 34420
(352) 245-3989
E-Mail: fabricstash@bigfoot.com
Owners: Janet Bunn & Gayle Blades

A Quilt Shop and More!
Quality notions, books, patterns & upscale 100% cotton fabrics, warm & personal assistance. Premier Viking Dealer.

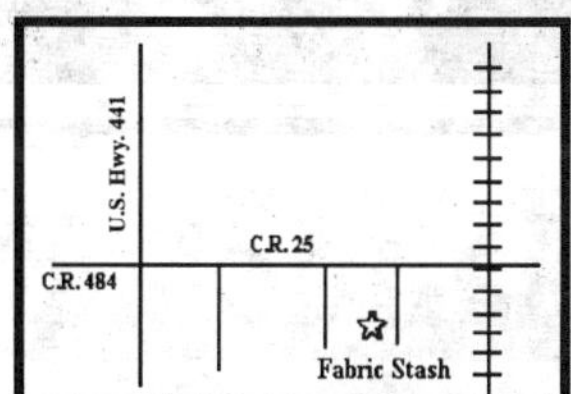

Ormond Beach, FL #6

Mon - Sat 9:30 - 4

Grammy's Quilt Shoppe

489 S. Yonge Street U.S. # 1
(904) 673-5484 32174
Owner: Mary K. Tate
Est: 1981 1800 sq.ft.

Fabrics -- Notions Books -- Patterns
Gifts -- Classes Everything for the Quilter !

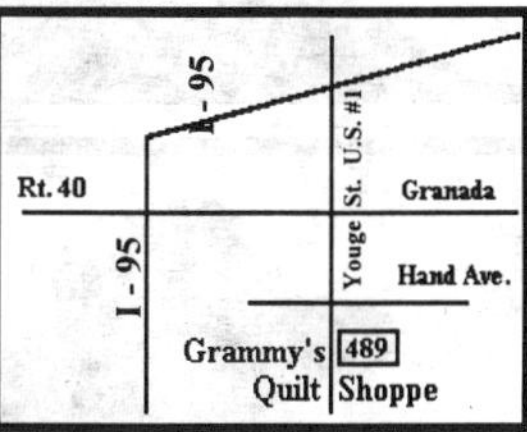

Leesburg, FL #7

**Mon - Fri 10 - 3
Sat 10 - 1**

The Magic Thimble Quilt Shop

2501 W. Main St. #110 34748
(352) 728-4445
E-Mail: zoequilt@Lcia.com
Owner: Zoe Krcelic
Est: 1993 1000 sq.ft. 600+ Bolts

A friendly, full service shop offering individual attention. Quilting & Silk Ribbon Embroidery. Classes Available.

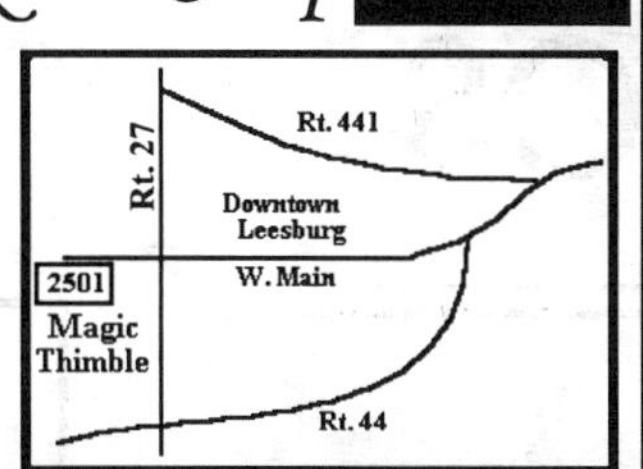

Dade City, FL #8

Mon - Sat 10 - 5

Quilts Etc.

13230 South Hwy. 301 33525
(352) 567-0444
Owners: Suzanne & Bill Stewart
Est: 1988 4000 sq.ft. 2000 Bolts

Fabric, Quilting Supplies, Books, Patterns. Custom Machine Quilting & Wide Selection of Pre-cut Fabrics.

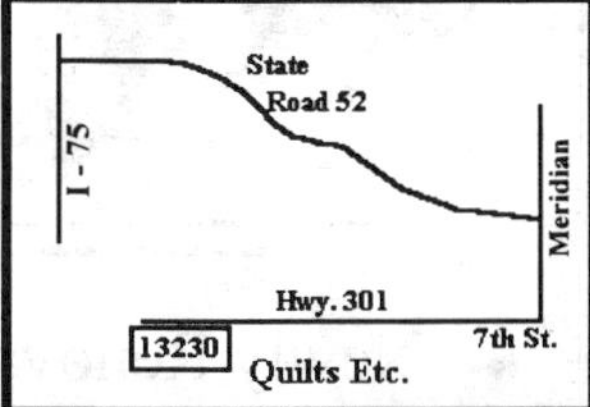

Kissimmee, FL #9

**Mon - Fri 10 - 6
Tues til 9
Sat 10 - 5**

Queen Ann's Lace

715 East Vine Street 34744
(407) 846-7998
Owners: Ginny & Tom King
Est: 1991 1400 sq.ft.

3500 Bolts of 100% Cotton
plus supplies, notions, & patterns
Everything you'll need.
Decorative Art Painting & Doll Supplies.

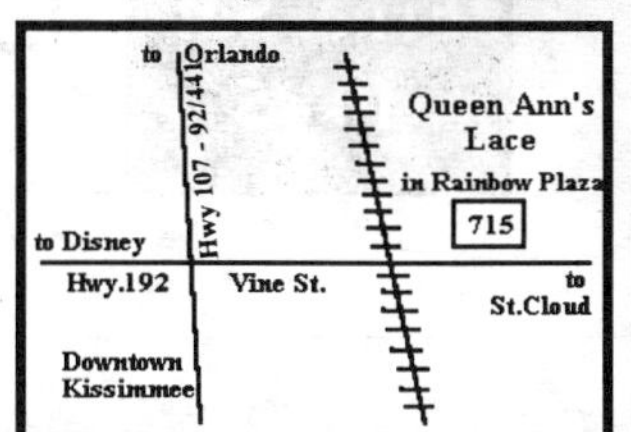

Orlando, FL #10

Mon - Sat 10 - 5

Patchwork Cottage Quilt Shop

2413 Edgewater Dr. 32804
(407) 872-3170
Owner: Tracy Stein

100% Cottons, Quilting Supplies, Books, & Patterns. Classes.
Good Times to be had here!

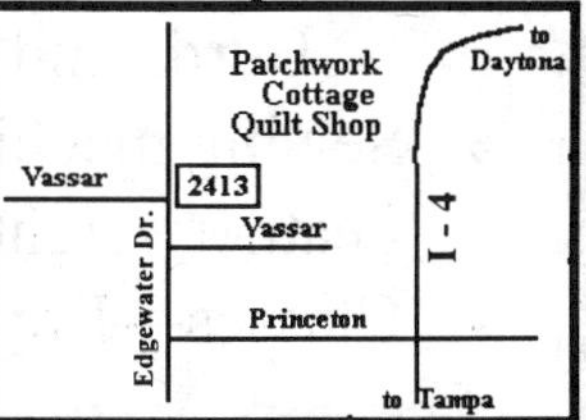

Orlando, FL #11

Firefly Antiques

929 N. Mills Ave. 32803
Owners: Chris Lee & John Roberts
Est: 1985
(407) 898-7888

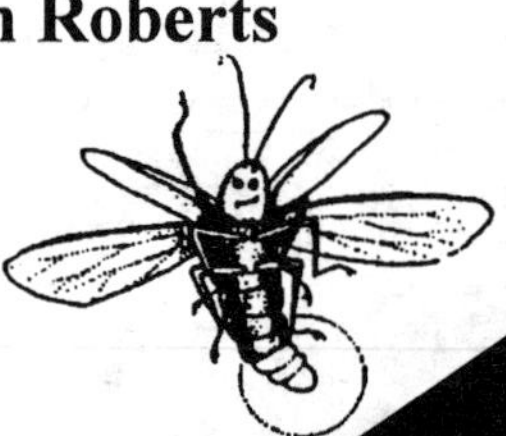

A Full-Line Antique Shop Generally with 15 - 20 Older Quilts

The Most Eclectic Selection In The Micky Mouse Region

Collectibles, Vintage Clothing & Jewelry

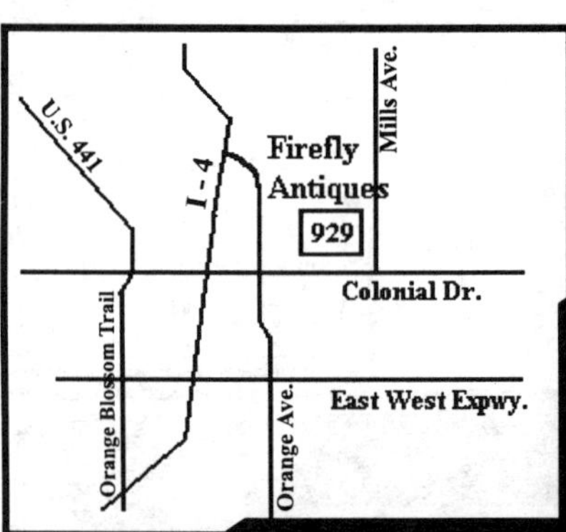

Monday - Saturday 11 - 5
or by Appointment

Orlando, FL #12

In "Ocoee"
Just 10 miles west of Orlando
114 W. McKey St. 34761
(407) 656-1624
Over 3000 Bolts

- Newly Renovated & Expanded!
- Quilting Fabrics, Books, Patterns, Supplies & Notions
- Silks, Linens, Wools and other fine fabrics
- Also available:
  Burda and McCall's patterns
- Sewing machine repair
- Featherweight Specialists
- Classes—Day, Evening & Weekend.

Mon - Thur 10 - 6
Fri & Sat 10 - 5

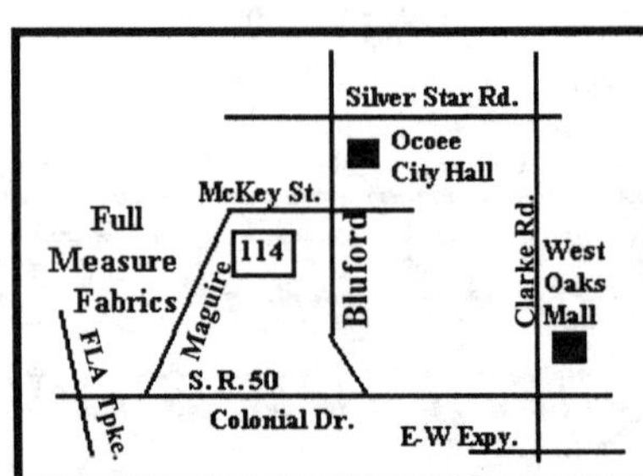

From Florida Turnpike: take Colonial Dr. (E)/Ocoee exit
From East-West Expressway: take Clarke Rd./Colonial Dr. (W) exit
From I - 4: take Exit 41, Colonial Dr. (W)

Orange Park, FL #13

Calico Station

Monday - Thursday 9 - 9
Friday 9 - 5
Saturday 10 - 5
Sunday 12 - 5

1855-6 Wells Road 32073
(904) 269-6911
Owner: Faye Heyn Est: 1980 2500 sq.ft.

The Largest Quilt Shop in N.E. Florida

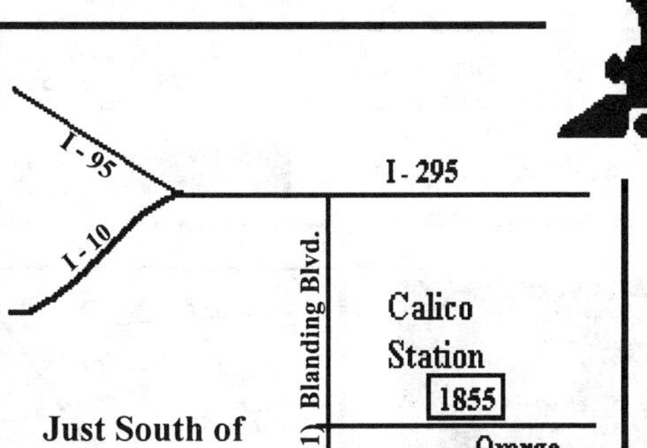

Over 2000 bolts of 100% Cotton Fabrics.

Classes, Special Orders, Notions, Books and Patterns. Large Selection of Stencils.

Quilts for Sale

Whippoorwill Station

Hours: Mon - Fri 10 - 6 PM
Sat 10 - 3 PM

Ocala, FL #14

"Distinctively Different"

3115 E. Silver Springs Blvd. 34470
(352) 690-1914 E-Mail ~ Whip3437@aol.com
Owners: Billie J. Clark and Shirley E. Klingele

Ocala's newest and foremost Quilt shop

Distinctively different comes to mind when you explore our quilt and gift shop, you will find 100% cotton fabric for the Quilter's dream. We also have a wonderful selection of fabric for your next craft or sewing project. Over 1,500 bolts of fabric and growing. We invite you to browse our gift area also for that just right gift....

Northcott.... Hoffman.... RJR.... P&B....
Moda.... Kings Road.... Liberty of London....
In The Beginning.... Nancy Crow.... Clothworks....
Vintage & Reproductions.... Etc.etc.etc....

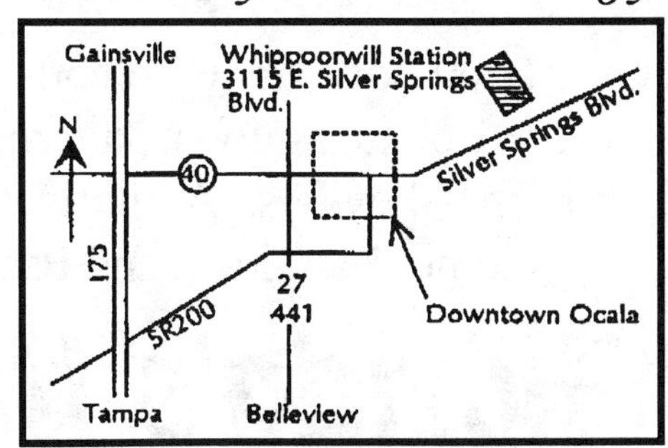

Classes forming.... Call for a schedule....
and sometimes we carry a selection of the TY beanie Babies!

SEWING STUDIO

9605 S. HWY. 17-92 32751
(407) 831-6488

WE ARE THE LARGEST STORE IN CENTRAL FLORIDA FOR ALL YOUR SEWING NEEDS! COME VISIT US!

- ★ Full Quilting Dept.—Fabrics, Patterns, and Books
- ★ Full Line of Quilting Notions
- ★ Smocking & Heirloom Fabrics, Patterns and Plates
- ★ Huge Selection of Bridal & Evening Wear Fabrics
- ★ Full Line of Lycra Swimwear
- ★ Costuming Fabrics, Linens, Silks & Much, Much More
- ★ Elna, Brother and Singer Sewing Machines and Sergers Many, Many Models to choose from.
- ★ Check out our new Euro-Pro Quilters Companion Sewing Machine!
- ★ Don't Forget to Visit our Bargain Annex—Next Door!
- ★ We have many 'Hard to Find' Items!

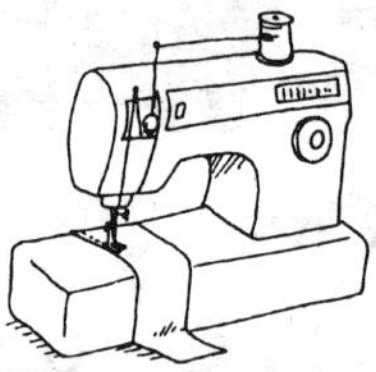

Maitland, FL #15

We service and repair any make or model sewing machine or serger, including industrial. We make house calls! (60-Day Warranty)

BERNINA brother elna Singer

Mon - Fri 9:30 - 8:30
Sat 9:30 - 5:30
Sun 12 - 5

Winter Haven, FL #16

Call for directions
Just 25 minutes off 1-4
near Cypress Gardens

AK Sew & Serge

1602 6th Street SE 33880
(941) 299-3080 or (800) 299-8096
Family Owned and Operated

Mon - Fri 9 - 8
Sat 9 - 5:30

Over 5000 bolts of 100% cottons, heirloom fabrics, fashion and designer fabrics under one roof. Books, notions, patterns, and supplies. Call or stop in for our schedule of classes and special events. Authorized dealer for Viking, White, Elna, New Home, Singer, Pfaff, Janome, Babylock, and Esante. Your one stop source for all of your sewing needs.

Florida's Premier Sewing Center

Granny's Trunk

4644 Cleveland
Heights Blvd. 33813
(941) 646-0074
Fax: (941) 646-4329
Owner: Pamela Bell
Est: 1981 1500 sq.ft.

Mon & Tues 10 - 6
Wed - Sat 10 - 5

to Tampa | Exit 18 | I - 4 | to Orlando
Memorial Blvd. (Hwy. 98)
Airport Rd.
Highland Dr.
Florida Ave.
Cleveland Heights
4644
Granny's Trunk

Over 2,000 Bolts of 100% Cotton Fabrics from the Best Companies.
We carry the latest in Books, Patterns, and Quilting Notions.
As well as Heirloom, Smocking and Silk Ribbon Embroidery supplies.
We have a small selection of quality fabrics for clothing.
We sell and service Bernina Sewing Machines.
We have beautiful models and sometimes they are for sale.

Lakeland, FL #17

Dunedin, FL #18

Rainbow's End

941 Broadway (Alt 19) 34698
(800) 353-1928 or (813) 733-8572
Web Site: www.rainbows-end.com
Owner: M. Facsina Est: 1982 6900 sq.ft.

Over 5000 Bolts of Cotton Fabric. Complete line of Notions. Over 1000 Books and Patterns. Crazy Quilting, Beadwork & Silk Ribbon Embroidery.

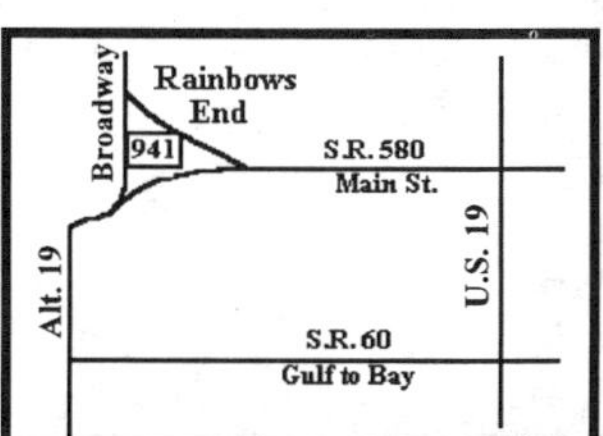

Mon - Sat 10 - 5
Mon til 8

Largo, FL #19

The Quilt Stop, Inc.

Mon - Fri 10 - 5
Sat 10 - 3

7250 Ulmerton Rd. #D 33771
(813) 532-4566
Owners: Michael & Cheryl Solt
Est: 1997 1200 sq.ft. 1000+ Bolts

Over 1000 Bolts of Fine Fabrics.
Notions, Books. Classes - Year Round
Friendly, knowledgeable personnel.

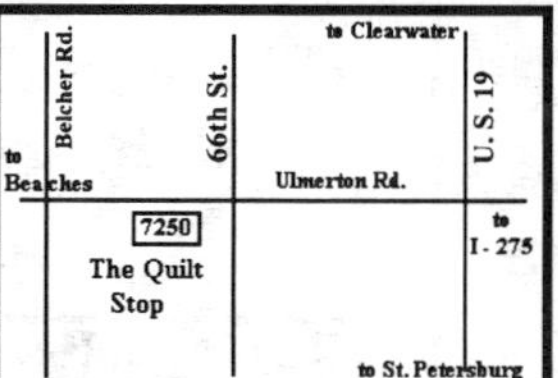

Ellenton, FL #20

Patches Galore, Inc.

Mon - Fri 9 - 6
Sat 9 - 4

6210 Hwy. 301 N 34222
(941) 722-5523
Owners: Lynn Briscoe & Lois Ankrom

Over 1000 bolts 100% cotton, Classes in Quilting and Sewing. Notions & Books. Authorized Bernina Dealer.

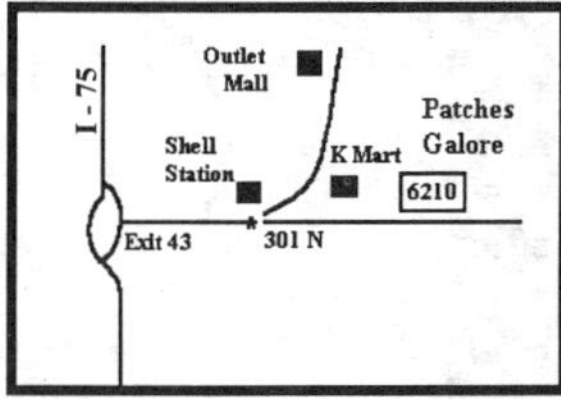

Sebring, FL #21

Crafty Quilters

4920 U.S. 27 South 33870
(941) 382-4422 Est: 1990
E-Mail: shdee@strato.net
Owners: Dee Dee Bedard & Lois Ucciferri

Mon - Fri 9 - 5
Sat 9 - 3

For all your Quilting Needs.
Quilting Frames.
Classes Available.
Factory Authorized Dealer of New Home & Babylock.
Repairs on all Machines.

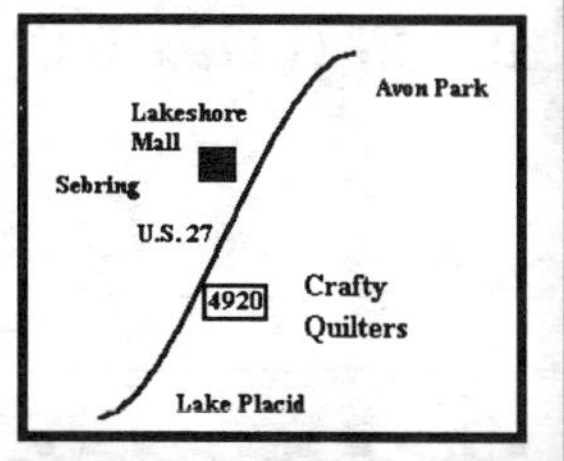

Sanibel, FL #22

Three Crafty Ladies, Inc.

Mon - Sat 9:30 - 5

1620 Periwinkle Way 33957
(941) 472-2893

Over 1500 Quilting Fabrics featuring batiks and fish, shell, and tropical prints—including Hoffman. Quilting patterns, books and supplies.

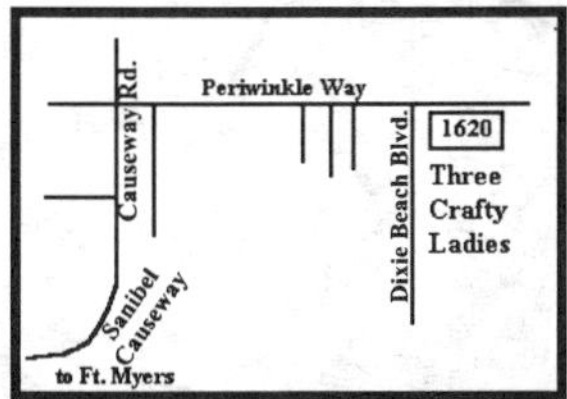

Ft. Myers, FL #23

Mon - Fri 10 - 5
Sat 10 - 4

The latest in Quilting Fabrics & Supplies.
Cross Stitch Samplers.
Rug Hooking & Doll Supplies.

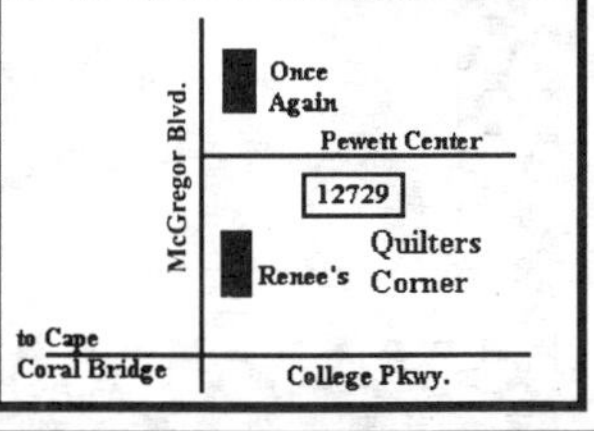

Country Quilts "N" Bears, Inc

1983 Drew Street 33765
(813) 461-4171 Est: 1986 2200 sq.ft.
Owners: Marilyn & John Humphries

Clearwater, FL #24

Country Store with a Christian Heart

Mon - Fri 9 - 5
Tues til 9
Sat 9 - 4

Drew St.
1983
Country Quilts "N" Bears
Hercules
Belcher
U.S. 19
Rt. 60 (Gulf to Bay)

A fully stocked quilt shop —
1600 bolts of cotton fabrics.
Large selection of flannels.
Friendly Service.
Classes in quilting, country clothing, & miniature bears.
Beginner bears, advanced and limited edition Teddy Bear classes taught by Francy Gordon.
Mohair, luxury plush acrylic fur, glass eyes, joints and Bear accessories available.

South Daytona, FL #27

Mon - Fri 9:30 - 4:30
Sat 9:30 - 3

Pelican Quiltworks

905 Big Tree Rd. 32119
(904) 761-8879
Owner: Michelle Ross

Quilting, silk ribbon and cloth dolls. We stock 1000 bolts of 100% cotton fabric. A complete line of Grannie Suzannie paper foundation patterns and kits is available. A wide variety of books and patterns available. Classes offered.

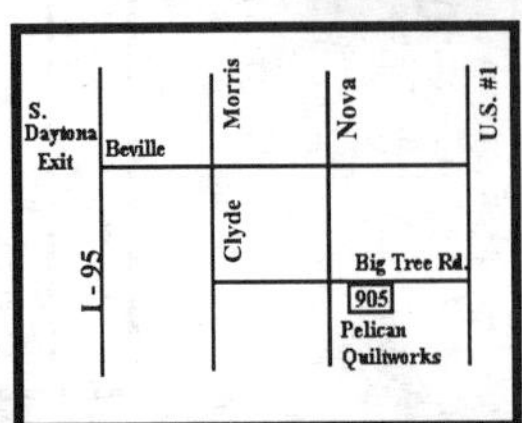

Titusville, FL #28

Mon - Fri 10 - 5
Sat 10 - 2

Fabric Emporium

3190 S. Hopkins Avenue 32780
(407) 267-6080
Owner: May Jane Mazurek
Est: 1883 2400 sq.ft.

Quilt Shop — Fabrics, supplies, books, patterns, & Notions. Classes. 90" Sheeting

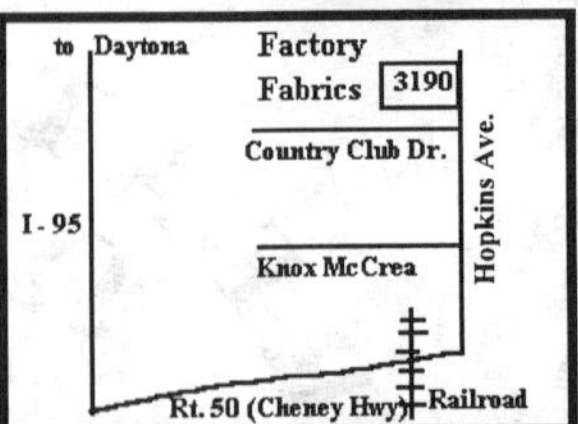

Rockledge, FL #29

Mon - Fri 10 - 5
Sat 10 - 3

Dawn's Fabric Cottage

1012 Flordia Ave. 32955
(407) 636-3822 Est: 1995
E-Mail: dawnhaun@juno.com
Owner: Dawn Haun 1000 sq.ft.

Machine Quilting Service. Group or private classes. Friendly, Creative, Knowledgeable staff. Across from Don's Sewing Machine authorized PFAFF Dealer..

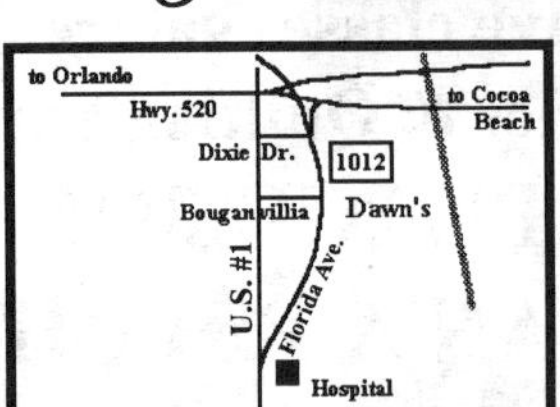

Palm Bay, FL #30

Mon - Fri 9 - 4:30
Sat 10 - 4

The Quilt Stash

2000 Palm Bay Rd. 32907
(407) 722-3306
Owner: Patti Goodwin Est: 1995

Hand guided quilting machine.
100% cotton fabrics, books, notions, and classes.

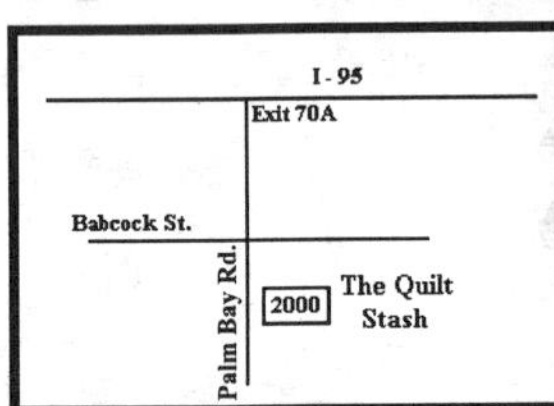

Wabasso, FL #31

Mon - Sat 10 - 7
Sun 1 - 5

Marilou's Quilting & Sewing Center

8802 N U.S. 1, P.O. Box 337 32970
(561) 589-0011 Fax: (561) 388-5722
Owners: Stan Kahn & Marilou Keen
Est: 1996 2400 sq.ft. 800 bolts

Custom Machine Quilting, Quilting Supplies, Fabric, Books, Classes, Husqvarna Viking Sewing Machines, Sales and Service. Quilts and Crafts for sale.

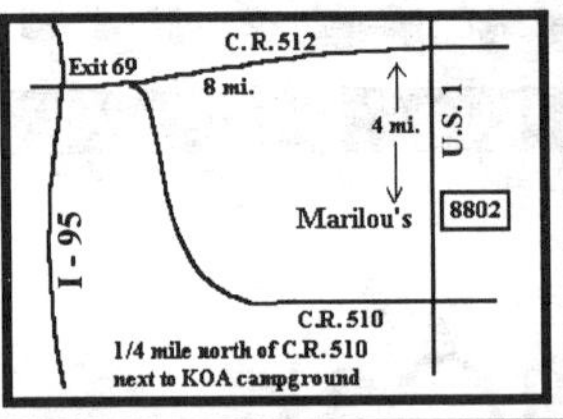

Ft. Pierce, FL #32

Mon & Wed - Sat 9 - 5

Tomorrow's Heirlooms

1840 S. King's Hwy. 34945
(561) 461-9510
Owners: Theresa & Earle Field
800 Bolts

100% Cottons, Quilting Patterns, Quilting Supplies, Instruction Books.

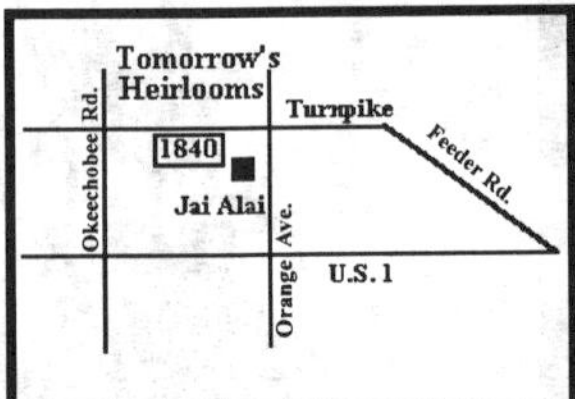

Quilters' Choice

1500 bolts of 100% cotton. Complete selection of Notions, Books & Patterns. Authorized Bernina Dealer. Great classes and friendly service. Machine Quilting Service Provided on our Gammill Quilt Machine.

1695 West Indiantown Rd. 33458
(561) 747-0525 Fax: (561) 747-0267
E-Mail: quilterschoice@msn.com Est: 1992
Owner: Vivian Irwin 3000 sq.ft.

Mon - Fri 10 - 5
Sat 10 - 4

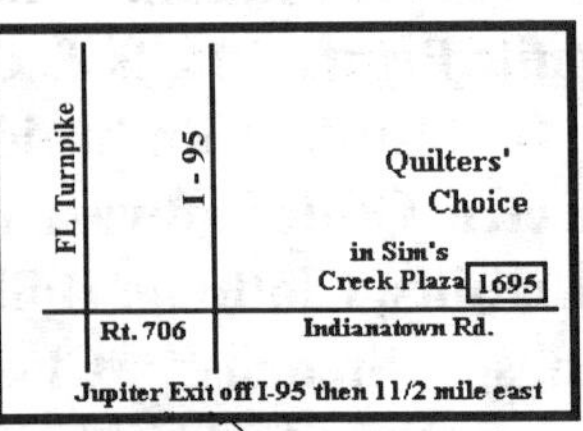

Jupiter, FL #33

Palm City, FL #34

Mon - Fri 10 - 5
Sat 10 - 3

Needles and Pins

3019 SW Martin Downs Blvd. 34990
(561) 220-9198 Fax: (561) 223-8396
E-Mail: mstarita@gate.net
Web Site: www.needlesandpins.com
Est: 1986 2100 sq.ft. 2000+ Bolts

Quilting Cotton and supplies. Also Imported Swiss Batiste; Swiss, French and English laces for Heirloom Sewing.

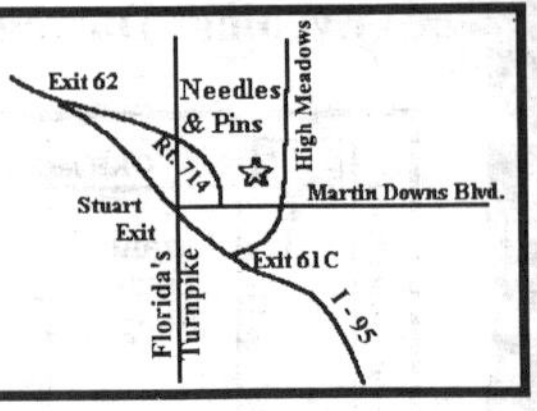

Quilters Marketplace

524 E. Atlantic Avenue 33483
(561) 243-3820

Delray Beach, FL #35

Home of the book *"Tropical Punch"*
by That Patchwork Place.
Owner: Marilyn Dorwart
Est: 1987 950 sq.ft

Mon - Sat 10 - 5

1200 bolts of 100% cotton including a beautiful array of tropical and Bali fabrics. Complete Notion Dept. Many patterns and a large selection of books. Gifts and a Friendly Staff.

I - 95
Woolbright
Atlantic Ave.
Linton
U.S. 1 South
U.S. 1 North
524
Quilters Marketplace

Coral Springs, FL #36

Mon - Sat 10 - 5
Sun 12 - 4

Country Stitches

11471 W. Sample Road 33065
(305) 755-2411
Owner: Gayle Boshek Est: 1982 3200 sq.ft.

Your one stop Quilting Shoppe.
Over 4000 bolts of fabric and patterns !
You'll be glad you came !

11471
Country Stitches
Sample Rd.
Sawgrass Expressway
University Dr.
I - 95
I- 595

Florida Guilds:

Gold Coast Quilter's Guild, P.O. Box 710, Boca Raton, 33429
Manatee Patchworkers, P.O. Box 356, Bradenton, 34206
Brooksville Women's Club, 131 S. Main St., Brooksville, 34601
Central Florida Quilters Guild, P.O. Box 180116, Casselberry, 32718
Creative Quilters of Citrus Cty.,7165 W. Riverbend, Dunellen, 34433
Southwest Florida Quilters Guild, Box 2264, Ft. Myers, 33901
Palm Patches Quilt Guild, P.O. Box 07345, Ft. Myers, 33919
Tree City Quilters Guild, Inc., PO Box 140-698, Gainesville, 32614
Citrus Friendship Quilters, 3384 S. Diamond Ave., Inverness, 34452
Honeybee Quilters Guild, Jacksonville
Florida Keys Quilters, PO Box 1251, Key Largo, 33037
Ocean Waves Quilters, 6421 S. Mitchell Manor Circle, Miami, 33156
Naples Quilter's Guild, P.O. Box 3055, Naples, 34106
Pelican Piecemakers, 2636 Sunset Dr., New Smyrna Beach, 32168
Flying Needles, Niceville
Meets: 2nd & 4th Thursdays 10 a.m. at First Presbyterian Church, 1800 Hwy. 20 E
Stitch Witches, 9020 2-C S.W. 93rd. Lane, Ocala, 34481
Country Road Quilters, P.O. Box 4082, Ocala, 34478
Meets 1st & 3rd Thursday 7 p.m.
Honeybee Quilters Guild, P.O. Box 0003, Orange Park, 32067
First Coast Quilters Guild, Orange Park
Country Stitchers, 2043 Sue Harbor Cove, Orlando, 32750
Cabin Fever Quilter's Guild, P.O. Box 891, Orlando, 32802
Meets: 1st Tuesday 7 p.m. at Marks St. Senior Center, 99 E. Marks St., Holds Bi-annual quilt show--next one is Jan. 23 & 24th 1999 at Central Floriad Fairgrounds
Racing Fingers Quilt Guild, P.O. Box 730544, Ormond Beach, 32173
Largo Cracker Quilters, Palm Harbor
Saint Andrews Bay Q. G., P.O. Box 16225, Panama City, 32406
Pensacola Quilter's Guild, P.O. Box 16098, Pensacola, 32507
Seaside Piecemakers, Satellite Beach, 32937
Pine Needles Quilters, P.O. Box 535, Silver Springs, 32688
Meets: Thursdays 10 a.m.
Ocean Waves Quilt Guild, P.O. Box 43-1673, South Miami, 33243
Possum Creek Quilters, P.O. Box 430, Sparr, 32091
St. Augustine Piecemakers, St. Augustine
Belleview Busy Bee Quilters, P.O. Box 936, Summerfield, 34492
Sunshine State Quilters Assoc., 1113 Albritton Dr., Tallahassee, 32301
Quilters Unlimited of Tallahassee, P.O. Box 4324, Tallahassee, 32315
Quilters' Workshop, 12717 Trowbridge Ln, Tampa Bay, 33624
Lake County Quilters Guild, P.O. Box 1065, Tavares, 32778
Palm Beach County Q. G., P.O. Box 18276, West Palm Beach, 33416

Other Shops in Florida:

Avon Park	Quilting by Design, 118 U.S. Hwy 27 S	941-453-2622
Big Pine Key	Samantha's, 30883 Dolgado Ln.	305-872-2235
Crestview	Granny's Attic, 396 S. Main St.	904-682-3041
Daytona Beach	Pieces & Patches, 1425 Tomoka Farms	904-252-5588
Delray Beach	Nanny's Attic, 124 N. Swinton Ave.	561-278-8877
Ft. Myers	Fabric Mart II, 6900 Daniels Pkwy. #15	941-482-5250
Gulf Breeze	Fabric Yarn & Sew Much More, 2823 Gulf Breeze Pkwy	904-932-1751
Jacksonville	Calico Corners, 4725 San Jose Blvd.	904-737-6930
Jacksonville	Quilting Connection, 8011-11 Merrill	904-743-2332
Lake Worth	Sew 'N Tell, 2913 29th Ln.	561-642-4710
Lakeland	Fabric Warehouse, 3032 N. Florida Ave.	941-680-1325
Maitland	Sew From the Heart, 110 N. Orlando	407-628-8739
Marathon	Joanne's Discount Depot, 12188 Overseas Highway	305-289-1166
Miami	Quilt Scene, 9505 S. Dixie Highway	305-666-0166
Mossy Head	Calico Country Fabrics, P.O. Box 1280	904-461-2309
Orange Park	Country Crossroads, 799-3 Blanding	904-276-1011
Palm Harbor	Classic Cloth, 34930 U.S. Hwy. 19 N.	813-785-6593
Pembroke Pines	The Quilt Shop, 7161 Pembroke Rd.	954-963-5656
Pensacola	The Thread & Needle Crossing, 1805 Creighton	904-478-4058
Plant City	Quilter's Corner, 113 W. Reynolds	813-754-9344
Port Charlotte	Charlotte County Sewing Center, 3280 Tamiami Trail	941-629-2202
Port St. Lucie	Quilters Haven, 8406 S. Federal Hwy.	561-343-9011
Sarasota	Classic Cloth II, 3985 Cattleman Rd.	941-379-5316
South Daytona	Brian's, 333 Beville Rd.	904-760-6444
St. Petersburg	Sewing Circle Fabrics, 408 33rd Ave. N.	813-823-7391
Tampa	Quilted Sampler, 4109 S. MacDill Ave.	813-831-8997
Tampa	Necchi Singer Sewing Centers, 104 Fletcher Ave. E.	813-960-0377
Tampa	Grand Ole Ctry. Store, 8709 40th St. N.	813-980-6330
Venice	Deborah's Quilt Basket, 337 W. Venice	941-488-6866

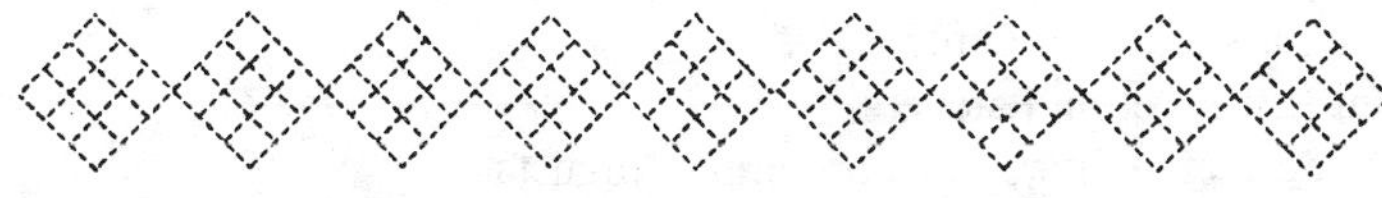

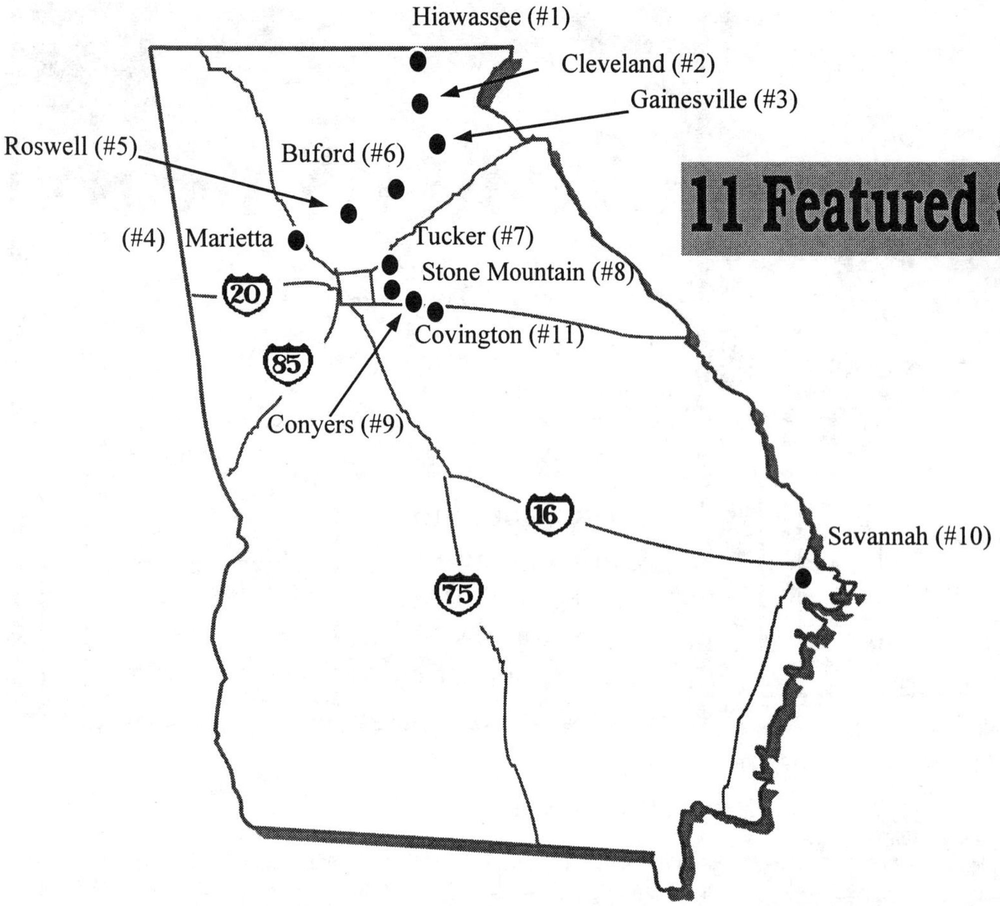

Hiawassee (#1)
Cleveland (#2)
Gainesville (#3)
Roswell (#5)
Buford (#6)
(#4) Marietta
Tucker (#7)
Stone Mountain (#8)
Covington (#11)
Conyers (#9)
Savannah (#10)
20
85
16
75

GEORGIA

11 Featured Shops

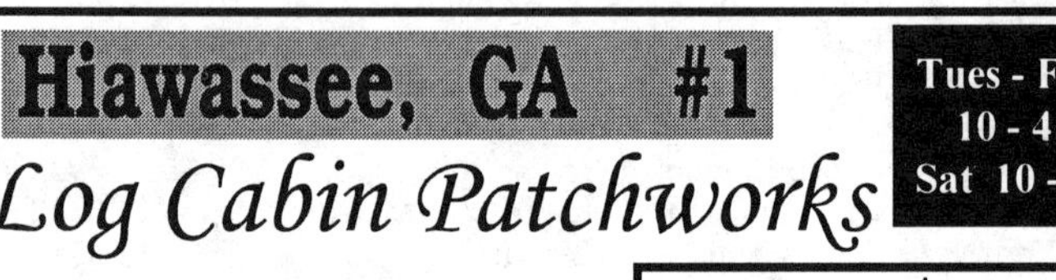

Tues - Fri 10 - 4
Sat 10 - 1

35 S. Main St. 30546
(706) 896-7275
Est: 1981 600 sq.ft. 1200 Bolts

Set in a Log Cabin from the mid-1800's. We specialize in Thimbleberries, Homespuns, Flannels and Reproduction fabrics.

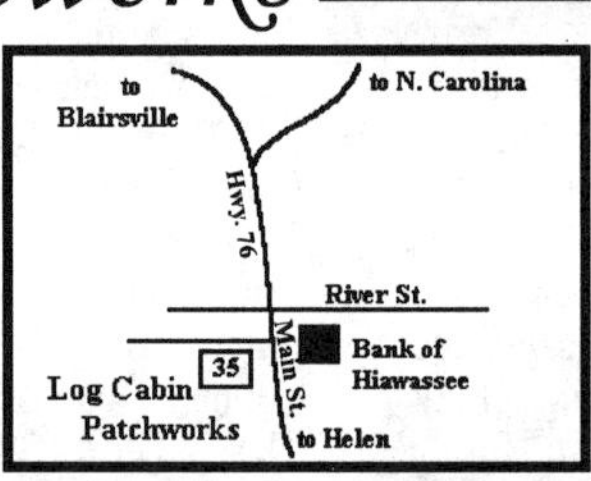

Cleveland, GA #2

Everyday 10 - 6

The Calico Barn

Rte. 384, 3599 Duncan Bridge Rd. 30528
(706) 865-9029
Owners: Grace Giebert & Jacqueline Stoner
Est. 1992

Over 1500 Bolts of Designer Fabrics, Patterns, Books, Stencils, and Quilting Supplies.

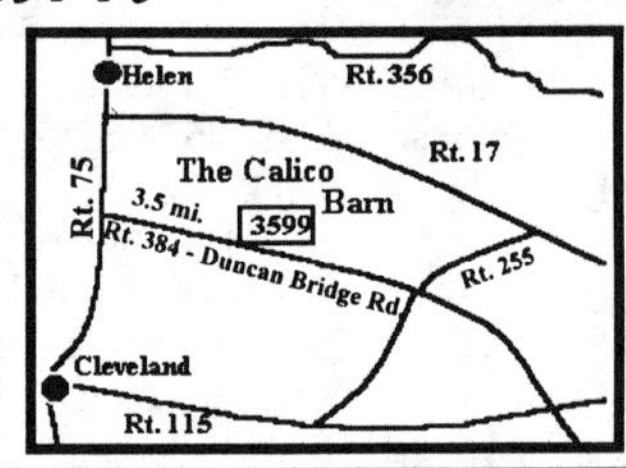

Gainesville, GA #3

Mon - Sat 10 - 5

2415 G Old Cornelia Hwy. 30507

(770) 536-3959 Fax: Same
Est: 1991 2500 sq.ft.
Owners: Leslie Peck & Sally Babcock
Located North of Atlanta, we offer over 2400 Bolts of 100% cotton fabrics, books, patterns, notions, classes & INSPIRATION. Rug hooking wool and supplies.

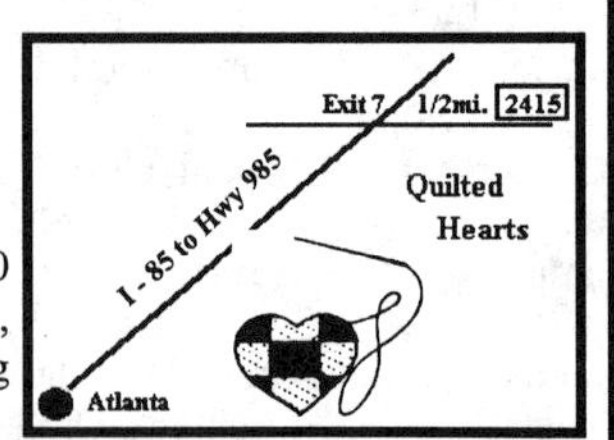

Georgia Guilds:

Wiregrass Quilter's Guild
Flint River Cotton Patchers
Sew Perfect Quilters of Georgialina, Augusta
 Meets: 1st Thursday 10 a.m. at Lumpkin Rd. Baptist Church
Mountain Laurel Quilters Guild, Clarkesville, 30523
 Contact: Florine Johnson, PO Box 1712.
 Meets: 3rd Thursday at 1 p.m.
 at Grace Calvary Episcopal
Gala Quilters Guild, 1816 St. Elmo Dr., Columbus, 31901
Cotton Boll Quilt Guild, Covington
 Contact: Marilyn Titman, (770) 786-1221
Hall County Guild, 5845 Hidden Cove Rd., Gainesville, 30504
N. Georgia Quilt Council, 7292 Cardif Pl., Jonesboro, 30236
Allatoona Quilters' Guild, Marietta
East Cobb Quilter's Guild, P.O. Box 71561, Marietta, 30007
Georgia Quilt Council, Inc., 2752 Long Lake Dr.,
 Roswell 30075
Calico Stitchers, P.O. Box 13414, Savannah, 31416
 Meets: 3rd Monday 7 p.m. at The Woods,
 7564 Hodgson Memorial Dr.
Ogeechee Quilters, Savannah
Yellow Daisy Quilters, P.O. Box 1772, Stone Mountain, 30086

Marietta, GA #4

Tiny STITCHES

2520 E. Piedmont Rd.
Suite H 30062
(770) 565-1113

New Chastain
Exit 2
I - 75
I - 575
Bells Ferry
Canion Rd.
Blackwell Rd.
Ebenezer
Sandy Plains
Barret Pkwy.
2520
Exit 116
Piedmont Rd.
Tiny Stitches

Visit Georgia's Largest Quilt Shop

We are a fully stocked quilt shop
— Over 4000 bolts of cotton fabrics — over 500 book titles —
Large selection of the newest notions
Besides friendly service we have classes in quilting, clothing, and soft sculptured dolls.

Just off I-75, Tiny Stitches is a convenient stop for the traveling Quilter. Exit 116, east onto Barrett Pkwy. This becomes E. Piedmont, we are located at 2520 E. Piedmont.

Est: 1992

We will gladly do mail order.

Visit our website: www.tinystitches.com

Mon - Sat 9:30 - 5:30

Roswell, GA #5

Calico Quilter

14 Elizabeth Way
30075
(770) 998-2446

Est: 1983 2000 sq.ft.

Owners:
Ellen Jennings &
Elizabeth van den Heuvel

Mon - Fri 10 - 6
Sat 10 - 5

Calico Quilter
14
Canton
Elizabeth Way
Magnolia
Alpharetta Hwy.

In addition to the fabrics & notions you would expect to find in a traditional quilt store, we also carry a wide selection of high quality & specialty threads. We have ribbons including silk ribbon & French wire edged ribbon. The store carries a wide assortment of unusual and beautiful books. We also have patterns and notions for quilted clothing.

Mon 1 - 5
Tues - Fri
10 - 5
Sat 10 - 3:30

1700 bolts of 100% cotton Fabrics, Books, Patterns, Notions and Batting. Thimbleberries (both Flat & Flannel), Hoffman, P&B, etc. Classes Offered.
Toll Free: (888) 784-1773

1879 Buford Hwy. #3 30519
(707) 271-0408
Owners:
Daryl & Richard Hood
Est: 1996

we are here
GA 20
BUFORD HWY
I-985
I-85
I-285
to Atlanta

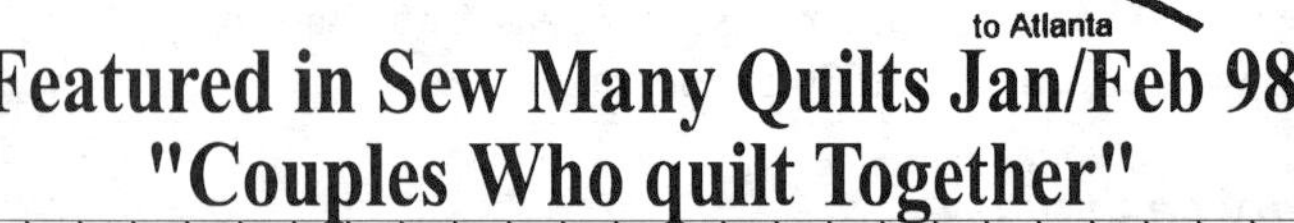

Tucker, GA #7

Dream Quilters

Mon - Fri
10 - 5:30
Thur til 7
Sat 10 - 4
Sun 1 - 5

2343-A Main Street 30084
(770) 939-8034
Owners: Jan Holdorf
Est: 1991 1988 sq.ft. 1500 Bolts

The latest in cotton fabrics, books, patterns & notions.
A nice place to visit.

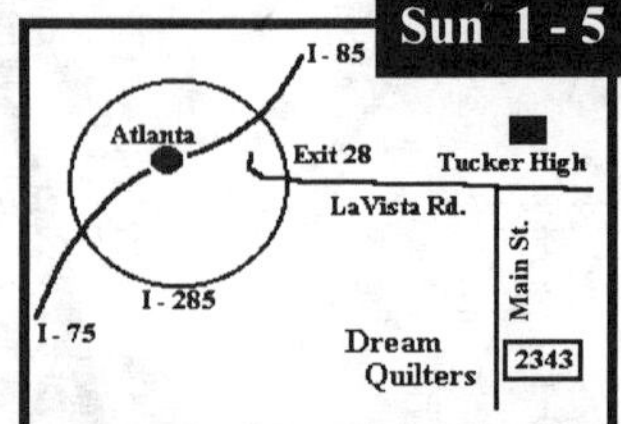

Stone Mountain, GA #8

Village Quilt Shop

Mon - Sat
9 - 5
Thur til 8

975 Main St. 30083
(770) 469-9883
Owner: Joyce P. Selin
Est: 1981 1200 sq.ft.

A "One-stop Quilt Shop"
Quilts -- Quilting Supplies -- Books
Fabrics -- Notions Class schedule Available.

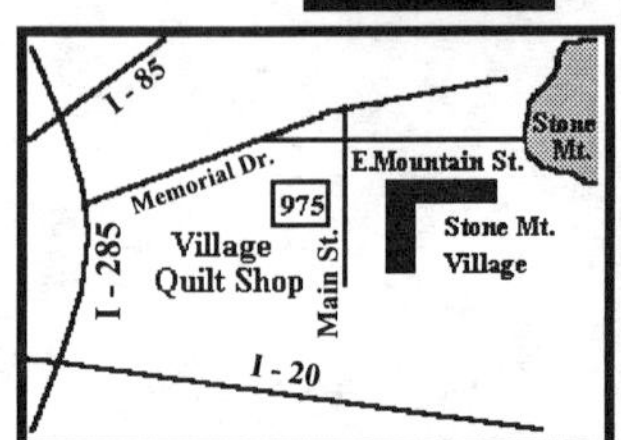

Conyers, GA #9

Mon - Fri
10 - 6
Sat 10 - 5

925 Commercial St. 30012
(770) 388-0789
Fax: (770) 388-0790
Owner: Patricia Lines Est: 1996

"Everything you need to make a quilt & more!"
Quilting Classes, Sewing Classes, Doll Making & Silk Ribbon. elna sewing machines.

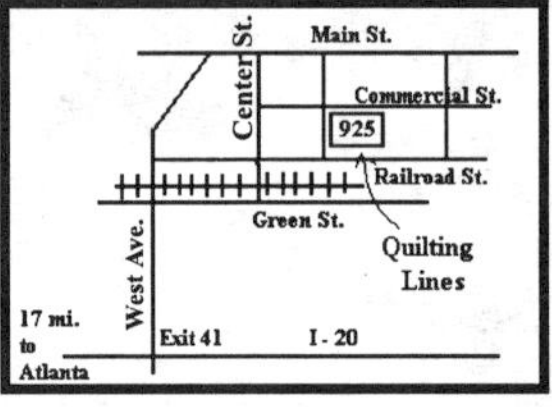

Savannah, GA #10

Colonial Quilts

Mon - Sat
10 - 6

11710 A Largo Dr.
(912) 925-0055
E-Mail: CQuilts11@aol.com
Savannah's Quilt Shop

Located in historic Savannah, we offer a wide array of fabric, notions, classes, books and patterns for quilting, cross-stitch, French sewing, smocking, etc. Complete Jinny Beyer palette.

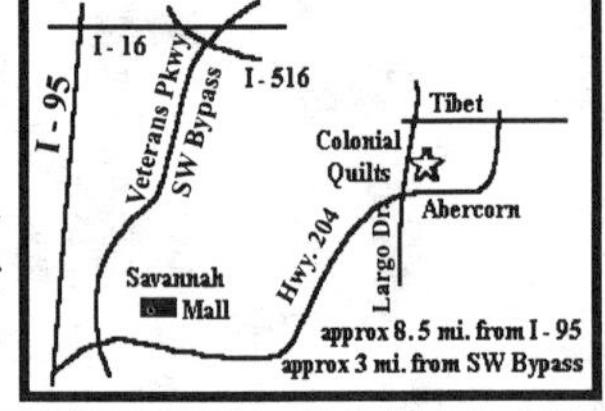

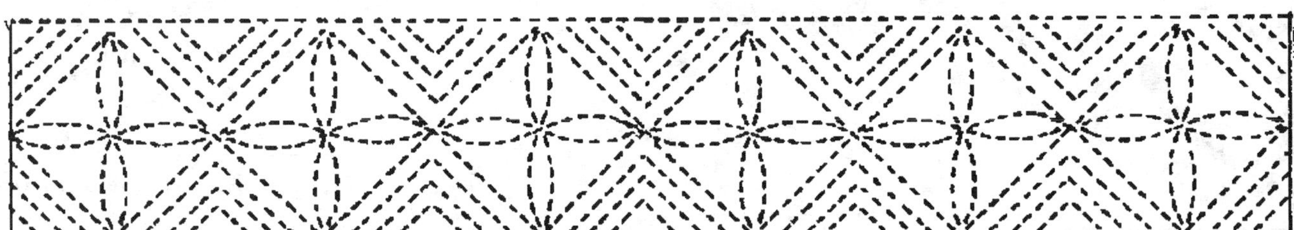

Other Shops in Georgia:

Bainbridge	Janet's Fashion Fabrics, 124 E. Broughton St.	912-246-5674
Blairsville	Corn Crib, 101 Pat Haralson Memorial Dr. #C	706-745-3426
Blue Ridge	The Cotton Patch, Inc., 965 Main St.	706-632-2300
Columbus	Southern Sewing Center, 2507 Manchester Expressway	706-327-1231
Fayetteville	Quilters Corner, 690 N. Glynn St. #C	
Kennesaw	Beautiful Rugs & Quilts, 3333 George Busbee Pkwy.	770-421-9100
Lumpkin	Westville Historical Handicrafts, Inc., P.O. Box 1850	912-838-6310
Macon	Patchwork Station, 4357 Forsyth Rd. #130	912-471-8288
St. Simons Island	Stepping Stones Quilts, 301 Skylane Rd.	912-638-7128

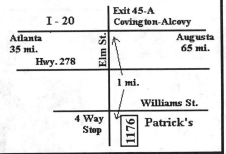

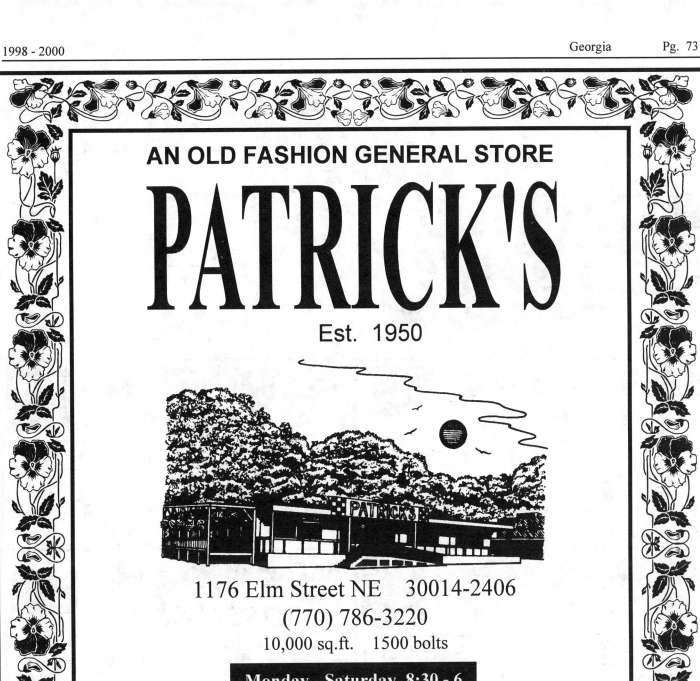

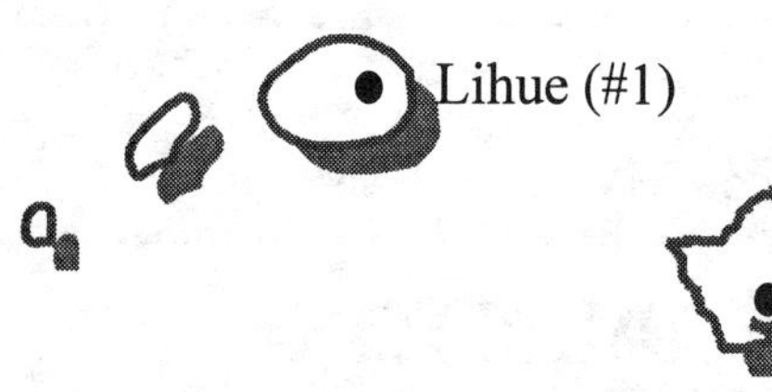

Lihue (#1)

Honolulu (#2)

Kahului (#3)

Kamuela (#4)

Kailua-Kona (#5)

Volcano (#6)

Hawaiian Guilds:
Mauna Kea Quilters' Guild, P.O. Box 2249, Kamuela, 96743
Meets: 2nd Saturday 9 a.m. at Thelma Parker Library, Waimea
Ka Hui Kapa Apano O'Waimea c/o Topstich, P.O. Box 2631, Kamuela, 96743
Meets: Last Saturday 9 a.m. at St. James Church
Maui Quilt Guild, Maui,
Meets: 1st Tuesday for info call Charlene Hughes (808) 572-8864
Hawaii Quilt Guild, 172 Kaopua Loop, Mililani, 96789

HAWAII

6 Featured Shops

Lihue, HI #1

Mon - Sat 9 - 5

Kapaia Stitchery

P.O. Box 1327 96766
3-3561 Kuhio Hwy.
(808) 245-2281
Est: 1973 Visa, MC, Discover

We Love Quilting !
Send $24 (postage included) for our original "pineapple" Hawaiian Quilting Pillow Kit—Dk. Green/Natural. Hand Applique 18" x 18"

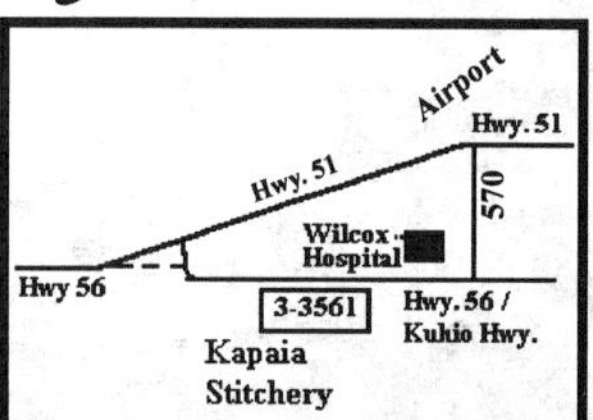

Honolulu, HI #2

Mon - Fri 10 - 6 Sat 10 - 4

Kwilts 'n Koa

1126 12th Avenue 96816
(808) 735-2300 Fax: (808) 737-2300
Orders (800) 787-1855
E-Mail: KwiltsnKoa@aol.com
Owners: Kathy Tsark & Tsarkie
Catalog $10 yr.—4 issues
Est: 1991 650 sq.ft. 100+ bolts
Hawaiian quilting classes, patterns, kits / supplies; Hawaiian gifts & Koa wood.

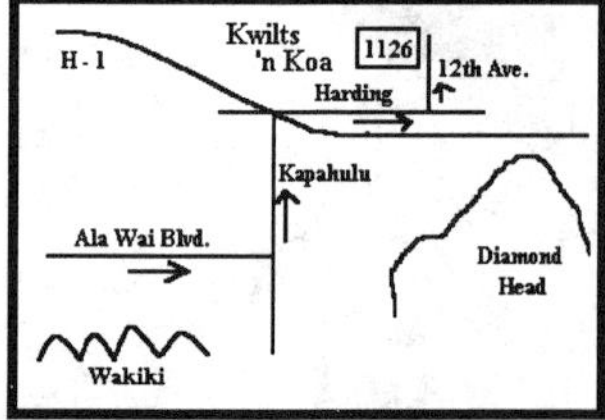

Kahului, HI #3

Tues - Fri 9 - 6 Sat 9 - 5 Sun 9 - 3

The Maui Quilter

244 Papa Place, Unit 12 96732
(808) 877-4850 Fax: Same
E-Mail: MauiQuiltr@aol.com
Owners: Dianna Grundhauser & Kathy Bento
Maui's best source—100% cotton fabrics, latest quilting & silk ribbon supplies & books. Weekly Hawaiian quilting and other classes. Friendly staff.

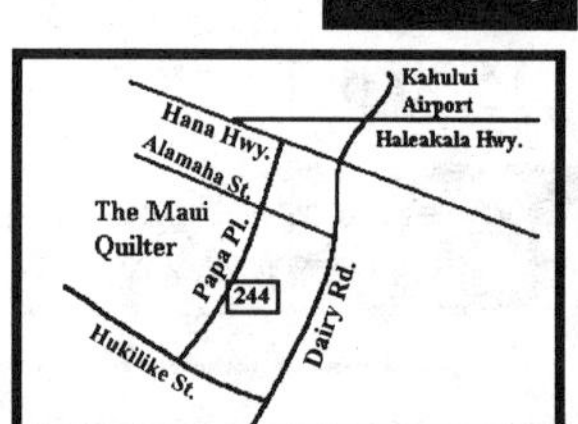

Kamuela, HI #4

Mon - Sat 9:30 - 4

Topstitch

Holomua Center, P.O. Box 2631 96743
(808) 885-4482
Owner: Ellie Erickson Est: 1978

A fine collection of cotton fabrics including tropical prints, quilting solids, and batiks. Needlecraft supplies and Hawaiian Quilts.

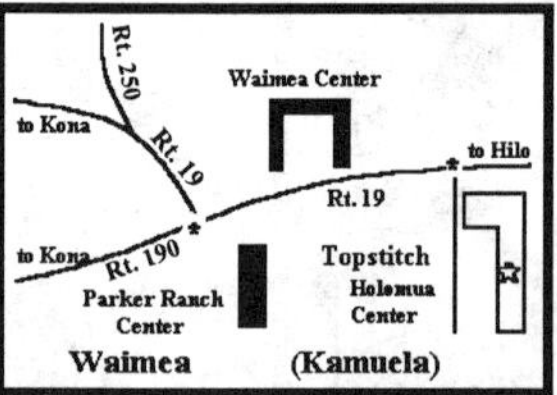

Kailua-Kona, HI #5

By Appt. Only

Kona Kapa, Inc.

P.O. Box 390136 96739
(808) 326-7119 Fax: Same
E-Mail: konakapa@aloha.net

Beautiful Hand-stitched **Hawaiian Quilts,** Wall Hangings, Cushion Covers, Hot Pads, Kits & more.
Home office—call for an appointment.

Volcano, HI #6

7 Days a Week 9:30 - 5:30

Kilauea Kreations

P.O. Box 959 96785
Old Volcano Hwy.
(808) 967-8090

Hawaiian Quilt Shop and local art.
Ready made to make you own.
Everything you need.
Fabric, Notions, Books, Kits

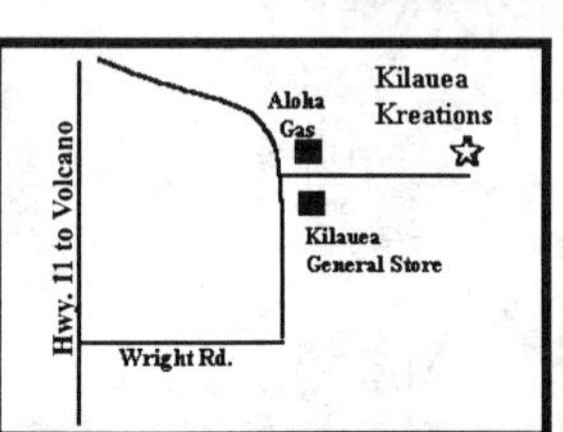

Other Shops in Hawaii

Aiea	Homspun Harbor, 98-029 Hekaha St. #24	808-488-5844
Honolulu	Hawaiian Quilt Connection, 2525 Kalahaua # 220B	808-599-776
Honolulu	Kaimuki Dry Goods, 1144 10th Ave.	808-734-2141
Honolulu	Quilts Hawaii, 2338 S. King St.	808-942-3195
Honolulu	The Calico Cat, 1223 Koko Head Ave.	808-732-3998
Kahului	Sew Special, 275 W. Kaahumanu Ave.	808-877-6128
Kamuela	Upcountry Quilters, P.O. Box 2631	808-885-7666
Lahaina	Quilter's Corner, P.O. Box 1562	808-661-0944
Wahiawa	The Pineapple Patch, 64-1550 Kamehameha Hwy.	808-622-3494

11 Featured Shops

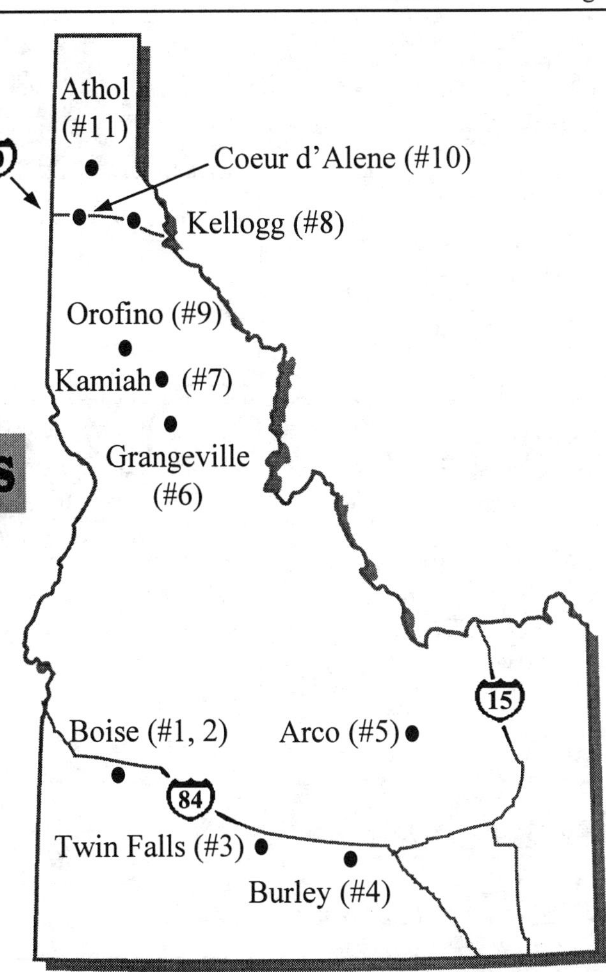

The Quilt Shop

Mon - Sat
10 - 6
Sun 12 - 4

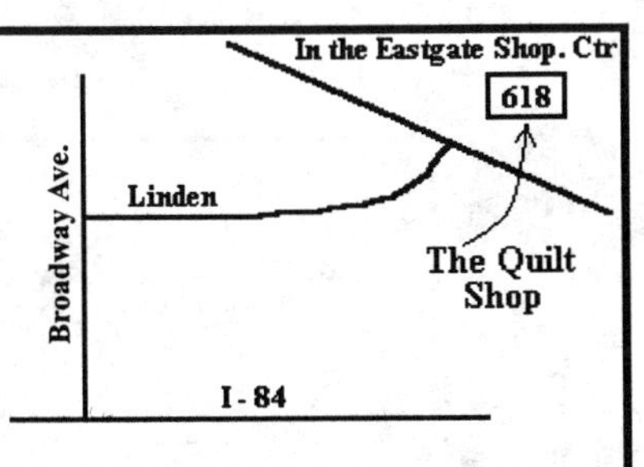

618 E. Boise Ave. 83706
(208) 387-2616
E-Mail: QuiltBoise@aol.com
Owner: Kathy Sterndahl
Est: 1994
2300 sq.ft. 1400 Bolts
Custom Machine Quilting

Boise, ID #1

We specialize in 100% cotton fabrics, books, notions, classes, friendly service and all the help you need.

Boise, ID #2

Mon - Sat 10 - 6 Sun 12 - 5

The Quilt Crossing

6431 Fairview Avenue 83704
(208) 376-0087
E-Mail: qltxing@worldnet.att.net
Owner: Patty Hinkel
Est: 1987 3000 sq.ft. 1200 Bolts

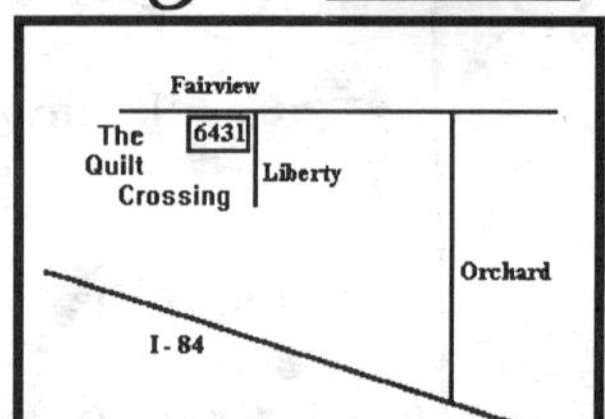

Specializing in distinctive 100% cotton fabrics, classes, books, gifts & quilt / soft sculpture patterns.

Twin Falls, ID #3

Mon - Sat 10 - 5

Carole's Quilts

677-A Filer Ave. 83301
(208) 733-7879 or (888) 249-9050
E-Mail: cquilts@safelink.net 2000 sq.ft.
Web Site: www.safelink.net/cquilts
Owner: Carole Dugan 600+ Bolts

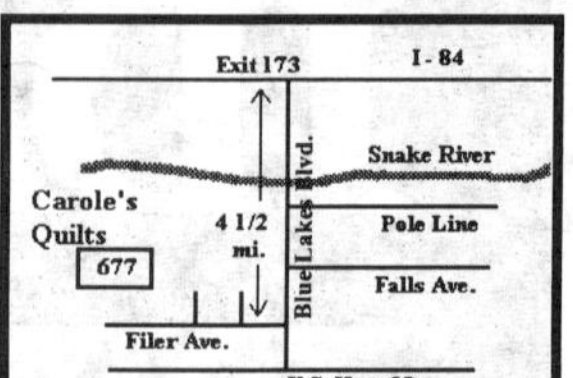

Small Shop Dedicated to Quilters.
Books, Patterns, Magazines, Notions, Kits, Classes — 100% cotton Fabrics.

Burley, ID #4

Mon - Fri 10 - 8 Sat 9:30 - 6 Sun 1 - 5

Snake River Plaza 83318
(208) 677-3573
Est: 1995
Mgr: Carleen Clayville
12-1500 Bolts

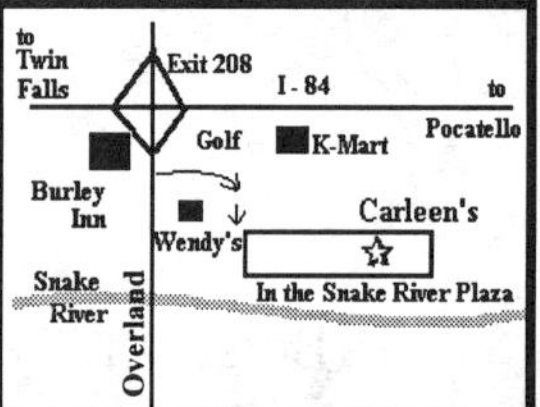

4000 sq.ft. of fabrics. Mainly Quilting Cottons. 65 - 70 shades of solids. Imported yarns, selected crafts. Bridal & better dress. Local consignment gifts & florals.
E-Mail: carleen@cyberhighway.net

Arco, ID 

Mon - Sat 10 - 6

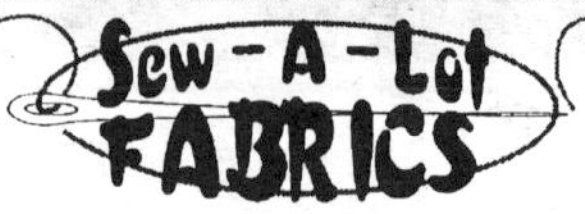

101 W. Grand Ave. Rt. 1, Box 26
(208) 527-3586 83213
Owner: Roxana Lewis Est: 1994

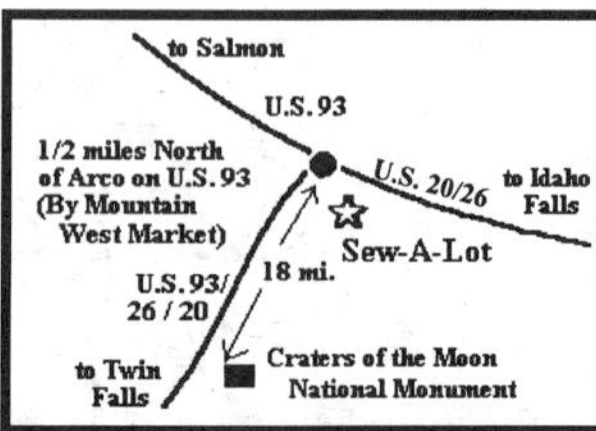

High Mountain Hospitality is our specialty. Lots of fabrics, books, notions & quilting supplies. Quilts & Crafts from the Lost River Valley.

Grangeville, ID #6

Mon - Sat 9 - 5:30

Melinda's Fabric

207 W. Main St. 83530
(208) 983-0254
Owners: Arleta Workman & Melinda Funke Est: 1987

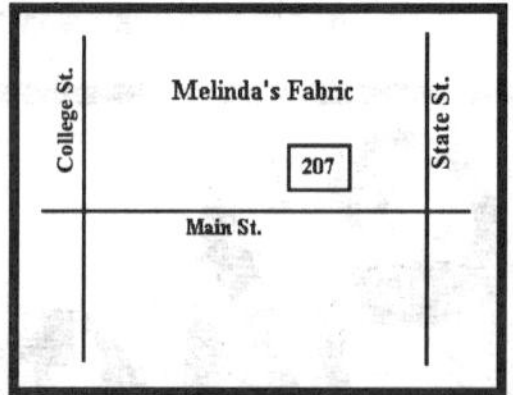

Grangeville's only Quilt Shop.
Over 2500 bolts — all 100% Cotton — including Hoffman, RJR, Benartex, Kauffman, Moda.
Books, Patterns, Notions.

Kamiah Kustom Kwilting

A Machine Quilting Service!

Gammill quilting machine used to do quilt finishing. Classes offered on a pre-arranged basis. I carry some fabrics and quilting supplies needed for classes.

Kamiah, ID #7

P.O. Box 278 83536
(208) 935-2431
Owner: Joyce Anderson
Est: 1992

By Appt. Only

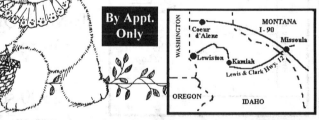

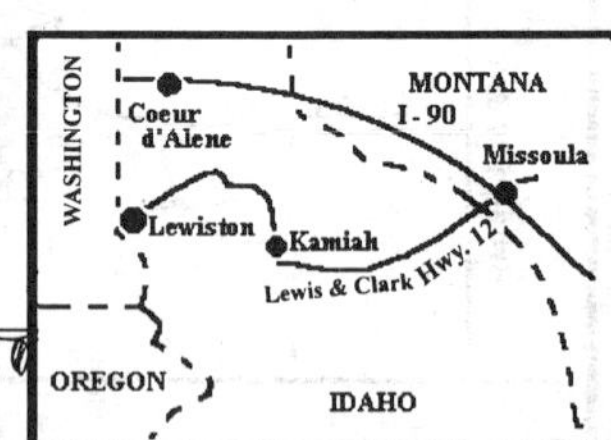

Silver Needle Textile

Mon - Sat 9:30 - 5:30

Unique North West Cottons
100% Cottons — Patterns
Quilting Supplies — P&B Cottons
Sweat Shirts — Souvenirs

Kellogg, ID #8

205 Main St. 83837
(208) 783-1194

Mgr: Scherry Colhoff
1800 sq.ft.

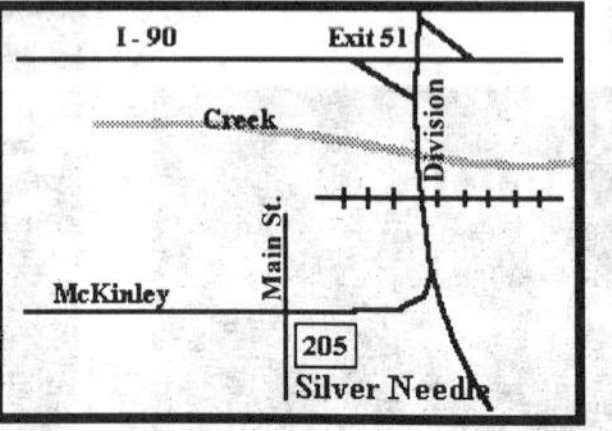

Orofino, ID #9

Tue 10 - 8 Wed - Fri 10 - 6 Sat 10 - 4

LURA'S FABRIC SHOP

10494 Hwy. 12 83544
(208) 476-7781
Est: 1981
Owner: Lura Mullikin
Web Site: Coming Soon

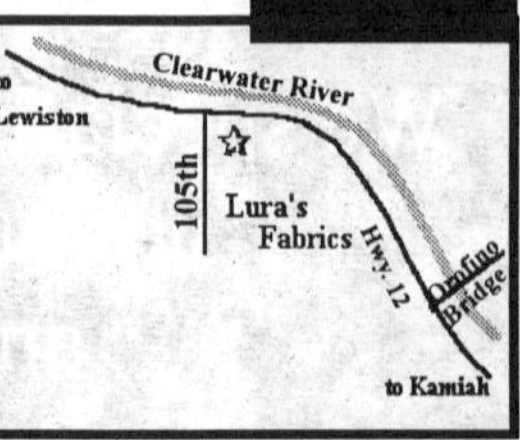

Great Selection of 100% Cottons. The latest Quilting Books & Patterns. Pfaff Sewing Machines & Sergers. Quilting Notions & Gadgets. Complete line of Kwik Sew Patterns. Classes. **"We cater to quilters!"**

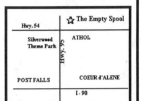

Idaho Guilds:

Lost River Hospital Auxillary, P.O. Box 145, Arco, 83213
Piecemakers, 9 W. River Rd., Blackfoot, 83221
Twin Falls Quilt Guild, 11602 Reutzel, Boise, 83709
Boise Basin Quilters, P.O. Box 2206, Boise , 83701
  Meets: 3rd Tuesday (except July & Dec) 7 p.m.
  at Church of Christ, 2000 Eldorado St.
Mt. Harrison Quilt Guild, Burley
Syringa Quilters Group, 15844 Wrightway Ln., Caldwell, 83605
  Meets: Tuesday 10 a.m. at First Christian Church
Bits and Pieces, P.O. Box 1082, Challis, 83226
Ladies of the Lake, W. 9300 Fighting Creek, Coeur d'Alene, 83814
Council Mountain Quilters, P.O. Box 829, Council, 83612
Sew Help Me Quilters, Elk City, Meets: Last Tuesday 7 p.m.
Valley of Plenty Quilters, 615 E. Locust, Emmett, 83617
  Meets: 1st & 3rd Thursday 10 a.m.
  at Nazareen Church, 1144 N. Washington Ave.
Sew-Ciety, 207 W. Main, Grangeville, 83530
  Meets: Every Tuesday 7 p.m.
North Idaho Quilters, P.O. Box 777, Hayden, 83835
  Meets: 4th Monday every other month starting in Jan.
Mt. Harrison Quilters, Rt. 2, Box 2150, Heyburn, 83336
Clark Fork Valley Quilters, 1370 Peninsula Rd., Hope, 83836
Snake River Valley Quilt Guild, 1450 Paul St., Idaho Falls, 83401
Idaho Falls Quilters, 1884 Melody Dr., Idaho Falls, 83402
Central Idaho Quilters, P.O. Box 278, Kamiah, 83536
  Meets: 1st Tuesday 6:30 p.m.
  at Chamber of Commerce, 518 Main St., Kamiah
Panhandle Piecemakers, P.O. Box 39, Kootenai, 83840
Seaport Quilter's Guild, P.O. Box 491, Lewiston, 83501
  Meets: 4th Monday 7 p.m.
  at Pautler Senior Center in Clarkston
Oneida Quilting Guild, 620 W 600 N, Malad, 83252
Pine Needle Quilters, P.O. Box 587, McCall, 83638
  Meets: Monday 7 p.m. (Sept - May) at McCall Library
Palouse Patchers, P.O. Box 9795, Moscow, 83843
EL-Y-HEE Quilters, Mountain Home
Nampa Friday Quilters, 210 Fay Ln., Nampa, 83686
  Meets: Friday 1 p.m. in member's home
Clearwater Quilters, P.O. Box 2748, Orofino, 83544
  Meets: 2nd Thursday at Community Center
Happy Hands Quilt Club, 40 Davis Dr., Pocatello, 83201
Lemhi Piecemakers, Box 59, Rt. #1, Salmon, 83467
Valley Piecemakers, 905 Main, St. Maries, 83861
Sawtooth Mountain Mamas, P.O. Box 33Q, Stanley, 83278
  Meets: 2nd Thursday 7 p.m. in member's home
Desert Sage Quilters, P.O. Box 812, Twin Falls, 83301
Thread Bears, 690 Adobe Dr., Weiser, 83672

Other Shops in Idaho:

Bonners Ferry	Gini Knits, 7225 Main St.	208-267-5921
Challis	Patchwork Pig Pen, 600 Main St.	208-879-5606
Chubbuck	Mill End Fabric, 4415 E. Burnside Ave	208-238-1388
Coeur d'Alene	Lyle's, 600 E. Best Ave.	208-765-9627
Eagle	Seams Etc., 124 E. State St.	208-939-8227
Grace	Fabulous Fabrics, P.O. Box E	208-425-3821
Idaho Falls	Quilts 'N' Things, 1375 E. 49th N	208-524-2439
McCall	Granny's Attic, 104 N. Third St.	208-634-5313
McCall	Mountain Fabrics, 123 E. Lake	208-634-8450
Moscow	Quilt Something, 1420 S. Blaine	208-883-4216
Nampa	Alice's Fabrics, 511 12th Ave.	208-467-2771
Pocatello	Quilt Shop, 4155 Yellowstone Ave.	208-237-6619
Pocatello	Happy Hands Quilting, 208 Cottonwood Ave.	
Pocatello	Mill End Fabrics, 4415 E. Brunside Ave.	208-238-1388
Post Falls	Joanne & Bucks, E. 511 Seltice Way	208-773-1488
Rigby	Middleton's Cozy Quilts, 3904 E. 600 N	208-745-7120
Salmon	McPherson's, 301 Main St.	208-756-3232
Sandpoint	The Cotton Mill, 402 Cedar St.	208-263-0824
Soda Springs	Nifty Needle, 120 S. Main	208-547-2441
Weiser	Kalico Korner, 455 State St.	208-549-0410

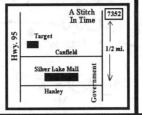

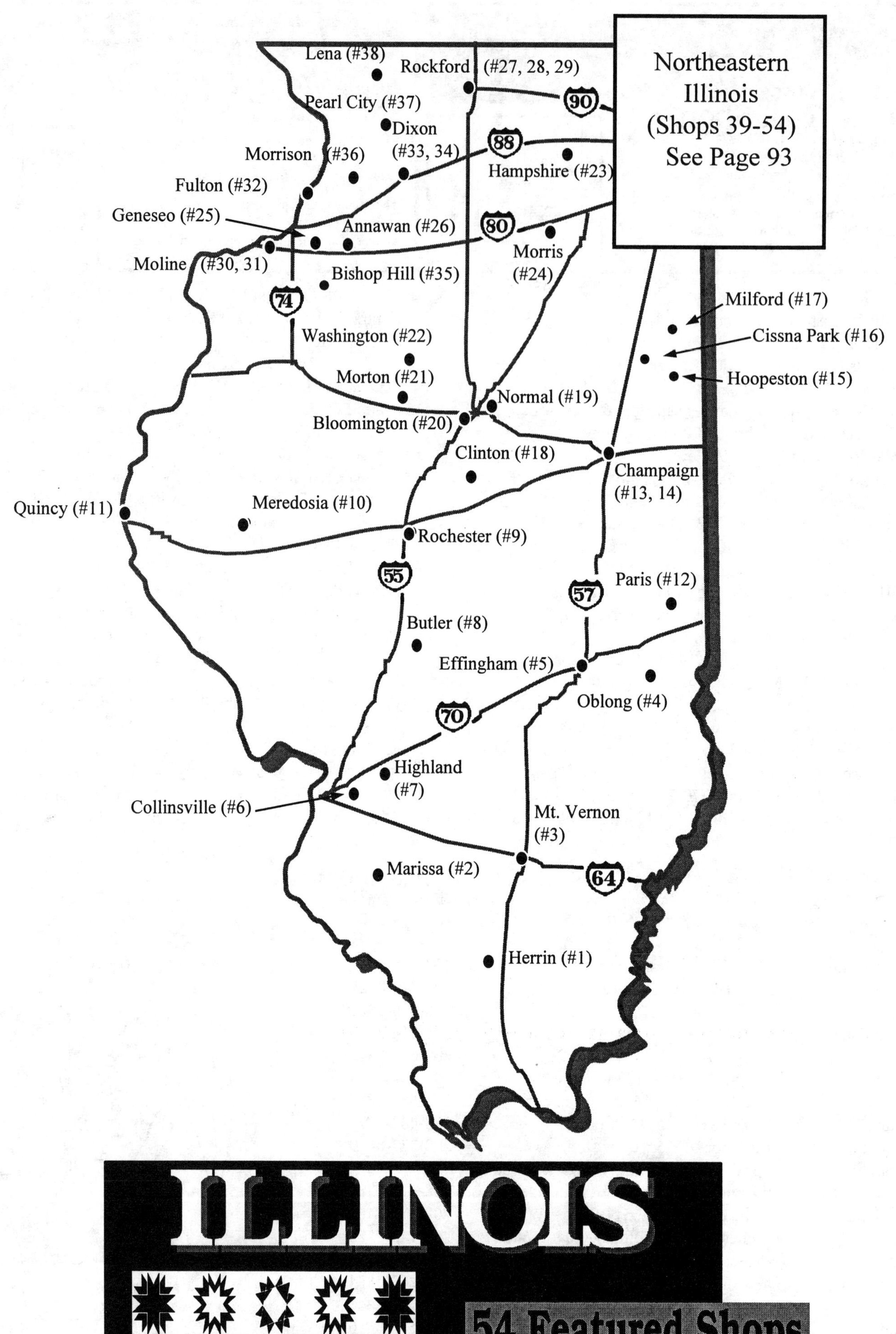
Northeastern Illinois (Shops 39-54) See Page 93
Lena (#38)
Rockford (#27, 28, 29)
90
Pearl City (#37)
Dixon (#33, 34)
88
Morrison (#36)
Hampshire (#23)
Fulton (#32)
Geneseo (#25)
Annawan (#26)
80
Morris (#24)
Moline (#30, 31)
Bishop Hill (#35)
74
Milford (#17)
Cissna Park (#16)
Washington (#22)
Hoopeston (#15)
Morton (#21)
Normal (#19)
Bloomington (#20)
Clinton (#18)
Champaign (#13, 14)
Quincy (#11)
Meredosia (#10)
Rochester (#9)
55
57
Paris (#12)
Butler (#8)
Effingham (#5)
Oblong (#4)
70
Highland (#7)
Collinsville (#6)
Mt. Vernon (#3)
Marissa (#2)
64
Herrin (#1)

ILLINOIS

54 Featured Shops

The Greatest Quilt Shop in Scenic Southern Illinois

The Cottage Quilt Shop

1221 S. 16th St.
62948
(618) 988-8742

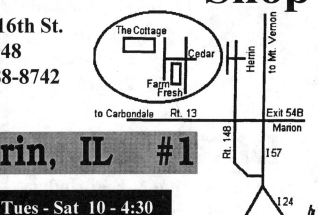

The Cottage
Cedar
Farm Fresh
Herrin
to Mt. Vernon
to Carbondale Rt. 13
Exit 54B
Marion
Rt. 148
I 57
124
Paducah KY

Herrin, IL #1

Tues - Sat 10 - 4:30

100% Cotton Designer Fabric.
Fabric Lines Include:
Hoffman, Benartex, South Seas,
P&B, Timeless Treasures, Hi Fashions and more.
Books, Notions, Classes. Knowledgeable, Friendly Staff.

Marissa, IL #2

Mon, Tue, Thur, Fri 9 - 5
Sat 9 - 2

Fancyworks

106 N. Main 62257
(618) 295-2909
Owner: Cindy Galle
Est: 1991

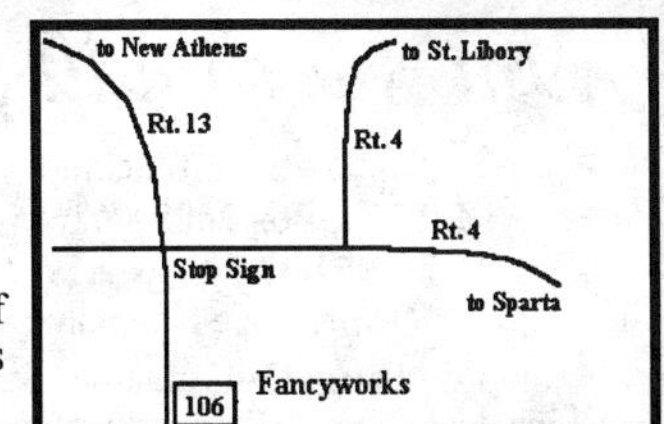

RJR Fabrics, Moda & more. Full line of quilt supplies, notions and books. Classes Available. Authorized Bernina Dealer

Mt. Vernon, IL #3

Mon - Fri 9:30 - 6
Sat 10 - 5

Mt. Vernon Sewing Mart

4112 Broadway 62864
(618) 244-5856
Owner: Dana Tabor 2000 sq.ft.

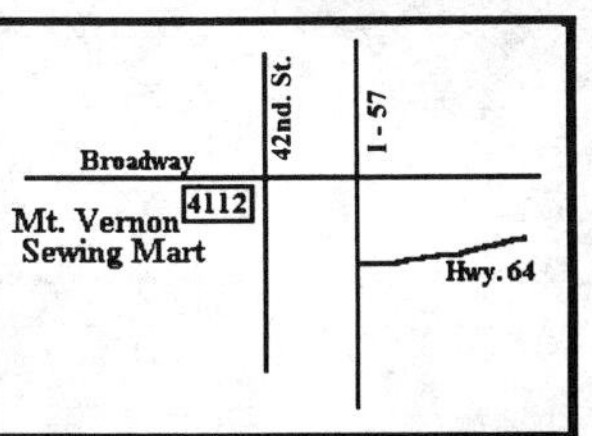

Fabrics, Quilting Supplies. Viking Sewing Machines & Sergers. Patterns, Books, Smocking Heirloom. Come & Browse.

Oblong, IL #4

Mon - Sat 9 - 5
Evenings by Appt.

The Village Stitchery

108 E. Main
62449
(618) 592-4134 2400 sq.ft.
Owner: Lisa Pinkston Est: 1982

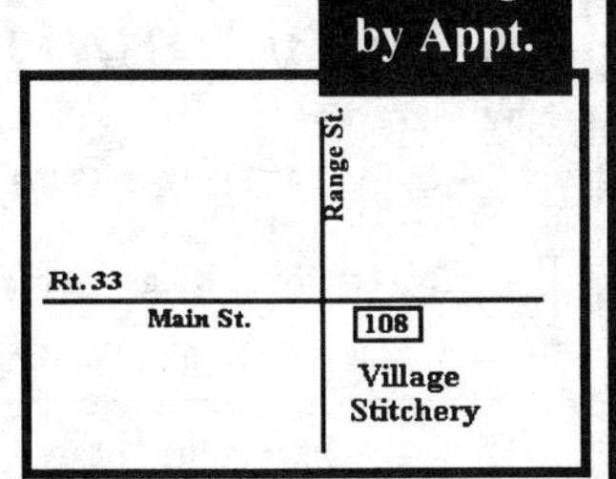

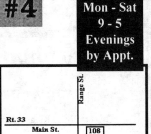

Visit our unique shop which carries a complete line of fabrics and supplies for the beginning to expert quilter.

Effingham, IL #5

Mon - Sat 9 - 5

Dusts' Quilt & Craft Shop

We are getting 911, so our street names and numbers are changing, call if you need directions. R.R. #1 Box 310 62401
3 1/2 miles from Rt. 33 turn off
(217) 536-6756 2000 Bolts

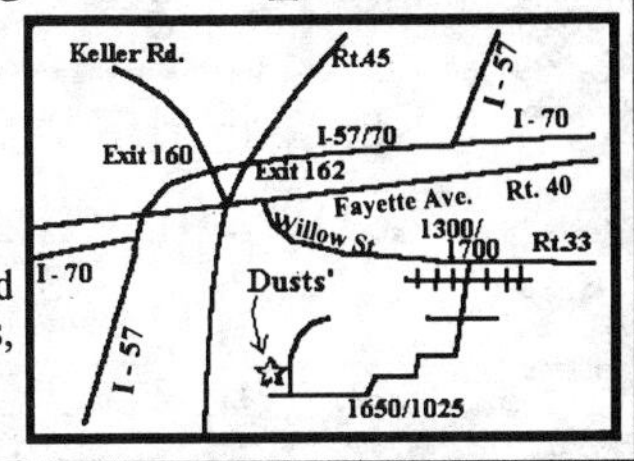

Large selection of fabrics, books, patterns and stamped textiles for embroidery. Notions, laces, embroidery flosses, crochet thread
Low Prices.

Collinsville, IL #6

110 W. Main St. 62234
(618) 345-3661
Owner: Mary Solomon
Est: 1990 2000 sq.ft.

Mon - Sat 9 - 4

Over 2500 Bolts of 100% Cottons
Designer Fabrics too
Books, 1000+ Patterns
Threads.

BERNINA®

Bernina Sewing & Embroidery Machines and Sergers

Cross Patches

Only 12 min. from downtown St. Louis

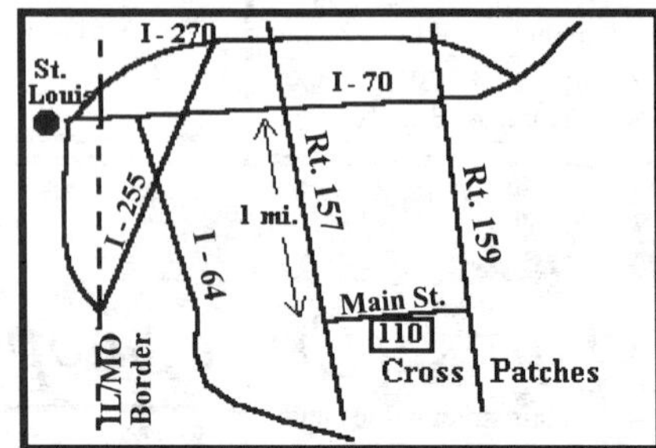

Show us this AD and we will give you a 10% (one time) discount on Fabric purchases.

Highland, IL #7

Mon - Fri 9 - 5
Sat 9 - 4

Rosemary's Fabric & Quilts

812 Ninth St. 62249
(618) 654-5045
Owner: Rosemary Seifried
Est: 1988

Largest Quilt Shop in St. Louis Area
Over 3000 Bolts of Fabric.
Everything a Quilter Needs!

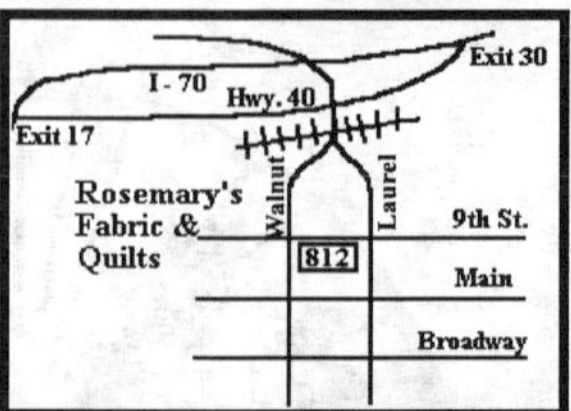

Butler, IL #8

Open Thursdays Call for Directions

Calico Quilt Frames

Mail Order: 14323 Il. Rt. 127 62015
(217) 532-2676 Owner: Judy Tucker

Quilting Frames: Single block to Full size, for quilting & needlework - Hinterberg, Norwood, Q-Snap, roll & mini-gear frames & more.
Speed Cutting tools. Stamped embroidery.
Discounted DMC Pearl Cotton.
Limited in-stock quantities of some frames.

Rochester, IL #9

Wed 10 - 8
Thur, Fri, Sat 10 - 4

peace & Applique

At the time this publication was being put together we were moving to Rochester and did not know our new address. We expect to be on Main St. We'd love to see you!

Owners: Gretchen Quist & Lois Weissberg
Please call for the new address at: (217) 498-7430
Top of the line cottons, flannels and homespuns.
Come enjoy our new shop.

Meredosia, IL #10

Tues - Fri 8 - 5
Sat 8 - 12
Or by Appt.

Forest Sewing Machines & Aunt Sue's Quilt Shop

Naples-Bluffs Blacktop
R.R. #1, Box 268B 62665
(217) 754-3729 Est: 1971
Owner: Sue Hileman
Authorized New Home-Janome Sewing Machine dealer. Quilt Shop with over 700 bolts of 100% cotton fabrics & quilting supplies.

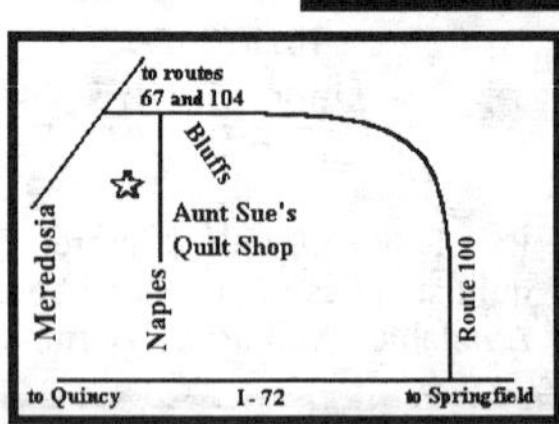

Quincy, IL #11

Mon - Fri 8 - 5:30
Sat 9 - 1

Quincy Quality Quilting

123 N. 6th St. 62301
(217) 223-3507
Owner: Joyce Riggs Est: 1995

Custom Machine Quilting.
Quilts custom made for you and for sale.
Other quilted items.
Christmas and Holiday gifts. Plus Classes.

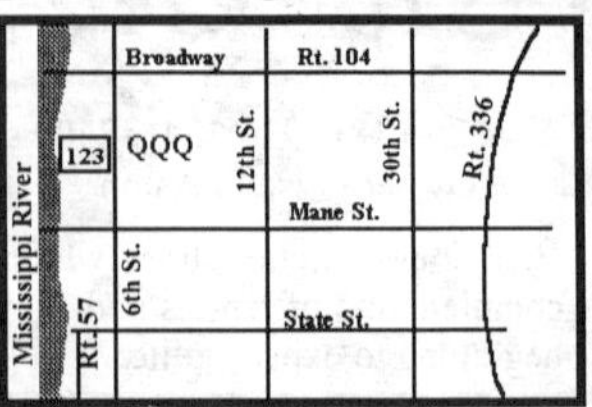

Paris, IL #12

Mon - Sat 9 - 5 Fri til 8

Lori's Pins 'N Needles

109 N. Central Ave., P.O. Box 815
(217) 465-5541 61944
E-Mail: loris@comwares.net
Owner: Lori Bridwell
Est: 1980 2000 sq.ft.

Over 1000 Bolts of 100% Cotton. Quilt Backings, Battings, and Large Selection of Books & Patterns. Authorized Viking Dealer.

Champaign, IL #13

Mon 9:30 - 8 Tues - Sat 9:30 - 5:30

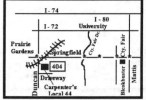

LONDA'S Sewing Etc.

404 S. Duncan 61821
(217) 352-2378
Fax: (217) 352-3389

Est: 1990
6000 sq.ft.

E-Mail: sewez45@aol.com
Owners: Londa & Charles Rohlfing
Top quality quilting, fashion and bridal fabrics, plus fine yarns. Pfaff and Elna Sales & Service. Wonderful classes and special events.
Come ... browse!

Champaign, IL #14

Mon - Sat 10 - 5 Sun 12 - 4

The Treadle

53 Marketview 61820
(217) 359-8636

Over 5000 Bolts of Calico Prints. Largest selection of quilt books, quilt patterns, craft patterns in the state of Illinois.

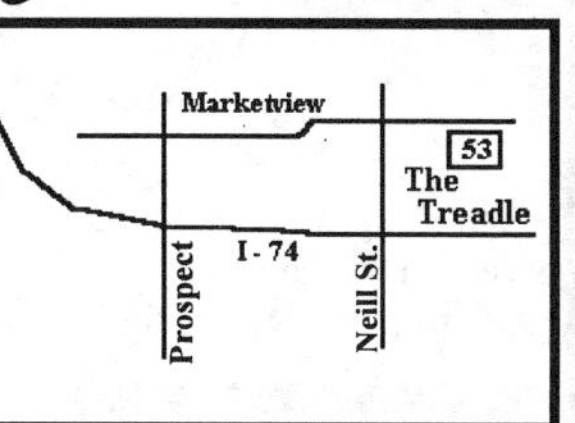

Hoopeston, IL #15

Mon - Thur 9 - 5:30 Fri 9 - 6 Sat 9 - 5

Hoopeston Fabrics

222 E. Main St. 60942
(217) 283-7125 Est: 1980
E-Mail: SewBout@VermRivrilnet.org
DBA: Sewing Boutique 1800 sq.ft.

Lots of Hoffman's P&B's, Concords.
Books & Patterns Classes Galore
Authorized Viking Sewing Machine Dealer.
In Downtown Hoopeston

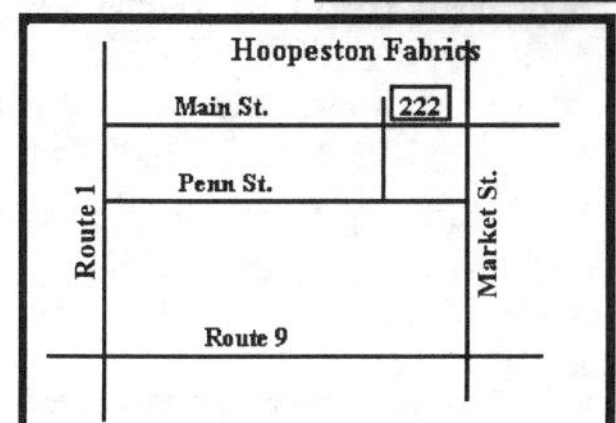

Prairieland Quilts

Unique selection of Books, Patterns, gift items, Quilt frames and supplies. Wide variety of classes. New Home sewing machines sales and service on all sewing machine makes & models. Machine quilting service available. Quarterly Newsletter with stories, tips, recipes, humor and new products for quilters. Mail order with free shipping on orders over $25.00.

Mon - Fri 9 - 5 Sat 9 - 3

JANOME NEW HOME

107 N. 2nd. St. (Rt.49) 60924
(815) 457-2867 (800) 391-2867
Owner: Suzanne Bruns Est: 1993

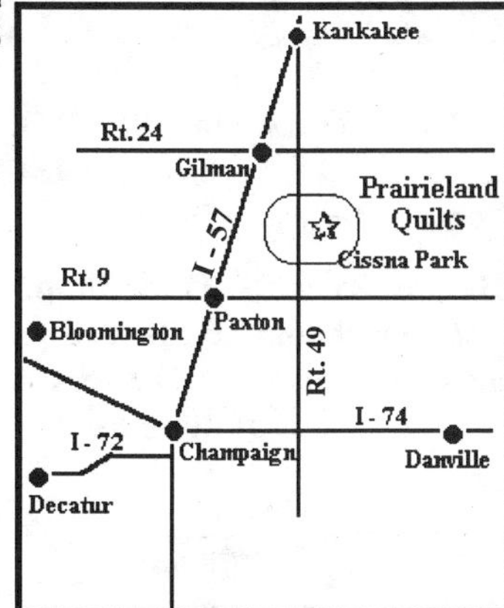

Bring your 'Travel Companion' with you and receive a one time 10% discount on your purchase.

Cissna Park, IL #16

Milford, IL #17

Tues - Fri 9 - 5 Sat by Appt.

Dixie Cloth Shop

130 East Jones 60953
(815) 889-5349
Owner: Arlene McKinley
Est: 1982 2400 sq.ft.

"Outline" Machine Quilting a Specialty 90" Preprinted Quilt Tops. Cheaters Cloth (Microwave Quilting) Backing 90" - 120" all Colors. Finished Quilts. Mail Order

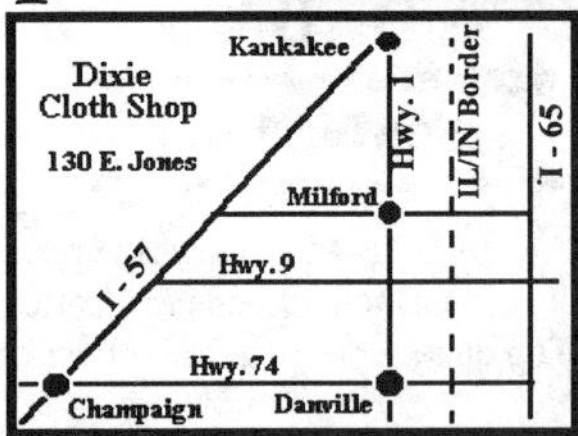

Clinton, IL #18

Mon - Wed & Fri 5:30 - 8:30 Sat 9 - 5 Sun 1 - 5

Quilters Delight

419 S. Walnut 61727
(217) 937-0159
Owner: Shirley Jo Monkman

Fabrics, Batting, Sewing Notions, Needles and Threads, Books and Patterns, Classes and Much More.
"Blessed are the "Quilters" for they are life's piece makers."

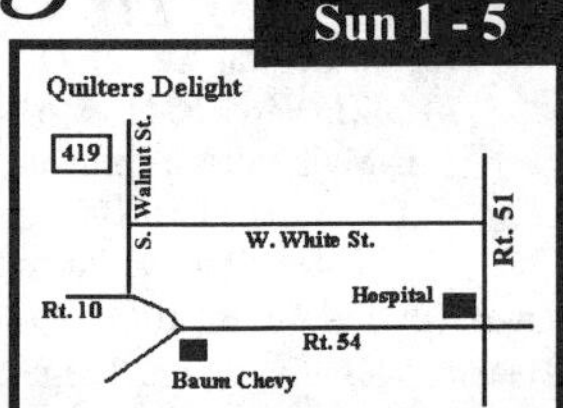

Normal, IL #19

Mon - Fri 9:30 - 6 Sat 9:30 - 5 Sun 12 - 4

Sewing Studio

1503 E. College, Suite C 61761
(309) 452-7313
Owners: Margaret Couch
Est: 1983 2600 sq.ft.

Quality quilting and fashion fabrics. Quilting & sewing classes, books. Quilting & heirloom supplies & notions. Bernina / Viking / White Dealer

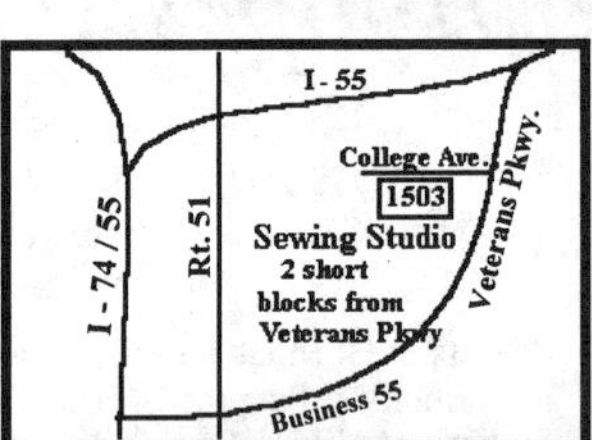

Bloomington, IL #20

Mon - Sat 10 - 5 Sun 12 - 4

The Treadle

2101 Eastland 61704
(309) 662-1733

Over 5000 Bolts of Calico Prints. Largest selection of quilt books, quilt patterns, craft patterns in the state of Illinois.

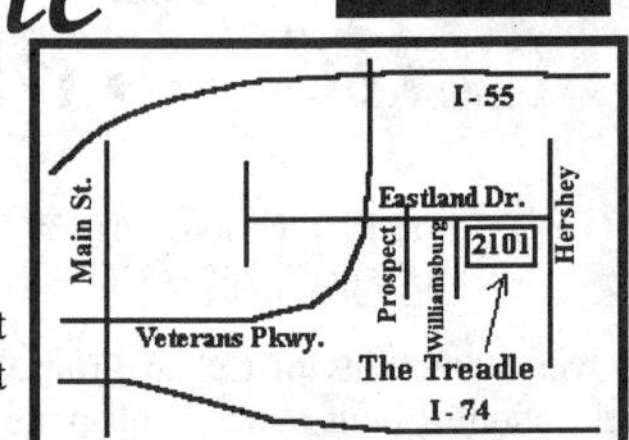

Morton, IL #21

Mon - Thur 9:30 - 8 Fri - Sat 9:30-4:30 Summer Mondays only til 8

The Quilt Corner

2037 S. Main Street 61550
(309) 263-7114
Owner: Karen Ehrhardt
Est: 1988 2500 sq.ft. 3000 Bolts

Complete line of Quilting Fabrics, Books, Patterns & Notions. Complete line of Silk Ribbon

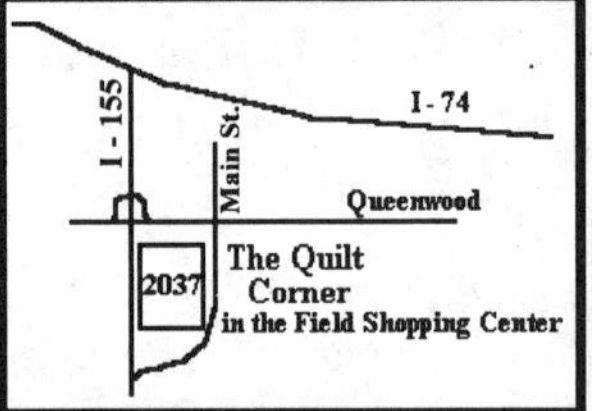

Washington, IL #22

Peg & Lil's Needle Patch

"The friendly place for happy Stitchers"

Mon 10 - 7 Tues - Fri 10 - 5 Sat 10 - 4

FABRICS - 1500 bolts 100% cottons
QUILTING - Large selection of Fabrics, Books, Patterns, Rotary tools, Stencils and Classes.
CRAFTERS - Patterns & Homespuns Lots of Samples on display.

Davenport, IA
Chicago
Peg & Lil's Needle Patch
Washington
U.S. 24
Peoria
Bloomington
Hwy 121
I - 74
Indianapolis
I - 55
10 miles East of Peoria on the square Downtown
Springfield

127 Peddlers Way 61571
(309) 444-7667
1400 sq.ft. Est: 1985
Owner: Lillian Cagle
Authorized Pfaff Sewing Machine Dealer

Hampshire, IL #23

Judy's Quilt 'n' Sew

252 S. State St., P.O. Box 908 60140
(847) 683-ISEW (4739)

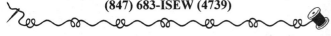

Hampshire's best Quilt Shop. A nice selection of fabric, notions, books and thread. An even nicer selection of friendly experienced Quilters to help you with your special quilting needs.

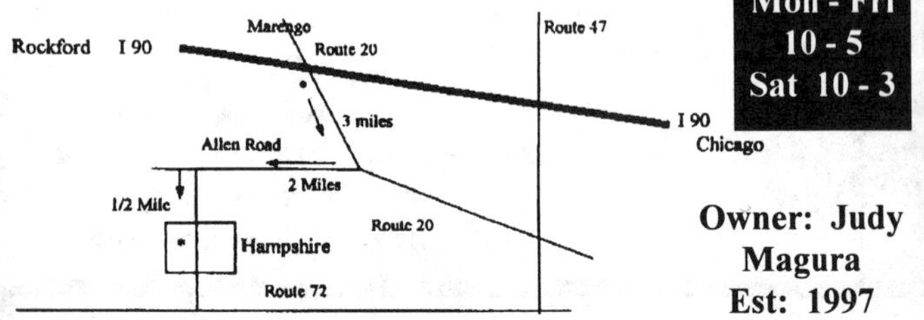

Mon - Fri 10 - 5 Sat 10 - 3

Owner: Judy Magura
Est: 1997

Morris, IL #24

Mon - Wed 9 - 5:30 Thur 9 - 8 Fri 9 - 5:30 Sat 9 - 5

The Fabric Center

301 Liberty St. 60450
(815) 942-5715
Owner: Lonnie Booker
Est: 1974 6000 sq.ft.

Largest New Home Dealer in Illinois. Thousands of bolts of Quilting Cottons—discounted everyday. Bridal & Fashion Fabrics.

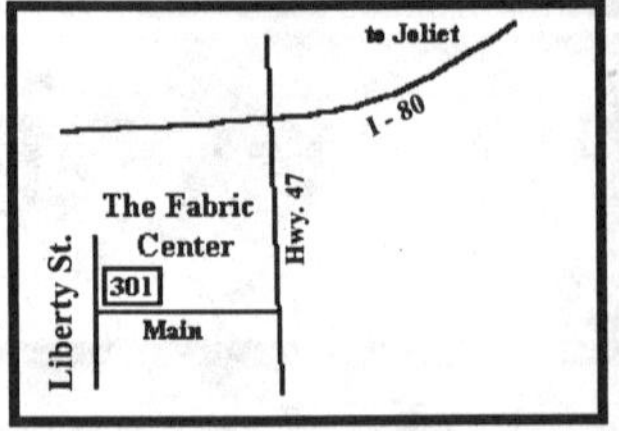

Geneseo, IL #25

Mon 10 - 4
Tue - Fri 10 - 5
Sat 10 - 3

Quilt Quarters

100 N. State St. 61254
(309) 944-2693
Owners: Roger & Dianne Peterson
Est: 1992

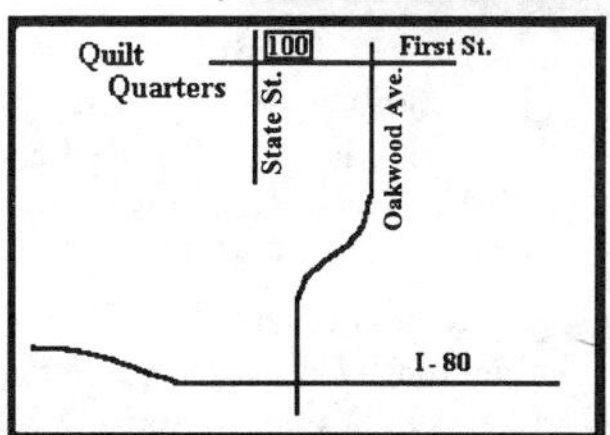

Satisfying Quilters and their needs.
Fabrics, books, patterns, notions, and "how to" classes. Hand made gifts by local artists.

Annawan, IL #26

Mon - Fri 10 - 5
Sun 1 - 5

Memory Lane

303 W. Front St. 61234
(309) 935-6366
E-Mail: memlane@geneseo.net
Owner: Mary Moon
Est: 1994 2800 sq.ft.

1000 bolts 100% cotton. Newest books, patterns, notions. Friendly service with a smile. Antiques & collectibles for the family to explore.

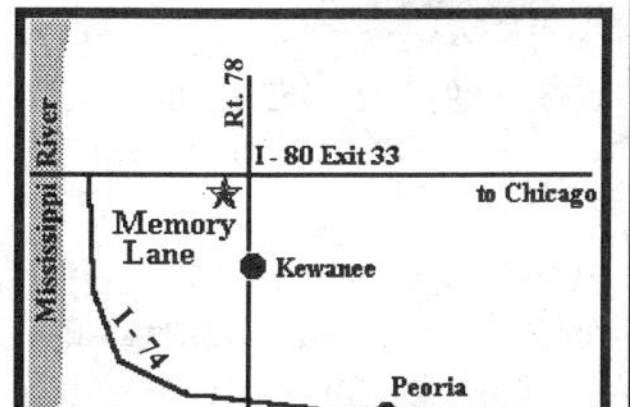

Rockford, IL #27

Mon - Fri 9:30 - 5:30
Thur til 7
Sat 9:30 - 4:30

929 S. Alpine - Storefront 106
61108
(815) 226-1272
E-Mail: quilts@cottonpeddler.com
Web Site: www.cottonpeddler.com
Proprietor: Kathy Goral

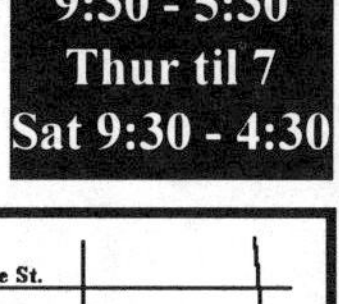

Old fashioned quality and dependability with knowledgeable staff.
Courtesy is always in style.

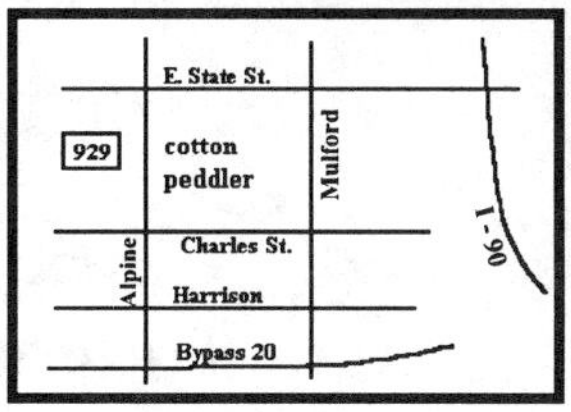

Rockford, IL #28

Mon - Sat 10 - 5
Sun 12 - 4

Quilter's General Store

6903 Harrison Ave. 61108
(815) 397-5160
Owner: Jan Ragaller

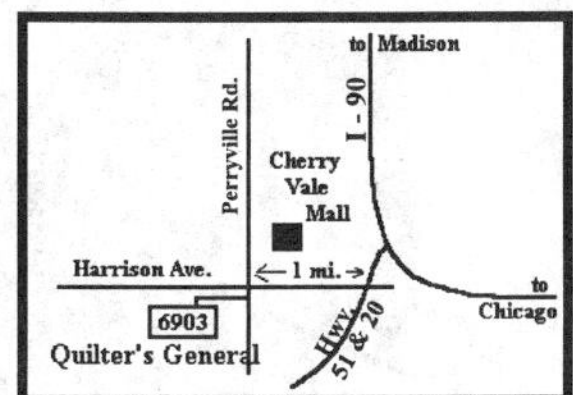

This "country in the city" shop boasts 1000+ bolts of cotton fabric, books, patterns, notions and a friendly, helpful staff of quilters.

Rockford, IL #29

Quilter's Haven

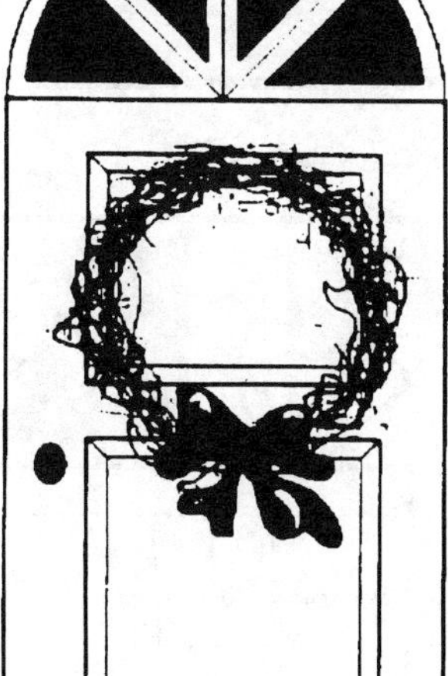

Quilter's Haven carries a wide variety of 100% cotton fabrics, books, and patterns.
In addition we carry supplies for rug hookers.
We offer a unique combination of classes and have several samples to inspire you!
Friendly, individual attention is what we are known for.

4616 E. State St. 61108
(815) 227-1659
Owners: Stephanie Gauerke & Cathy Johnson
Est: 1995 1200 sq.ft.

Mon - Sat 10 - 4 Wed til 7

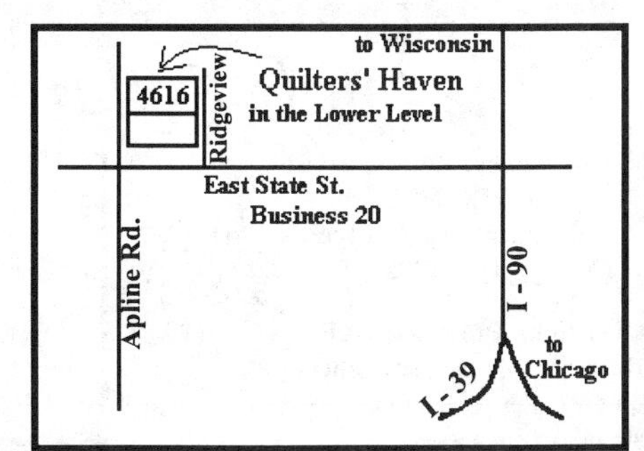

Moline, IL #30

Mon - Fri 10 - 5
Sat 10 - 2

Quilts By the Oz

3201 - 23rd. Ave. 61265
(309) 762-9673 or (800) 735-9673
Owner: Harlene Rivelli
Est: 1987 2400 sq.ft.

3000+ bolts 100% cotton. Large assortment of Books, Patterns, Notions, Bulk Buttons, Machine Quilting--White Sewing Machines Tri-Chem Paints Quilts & Quillos

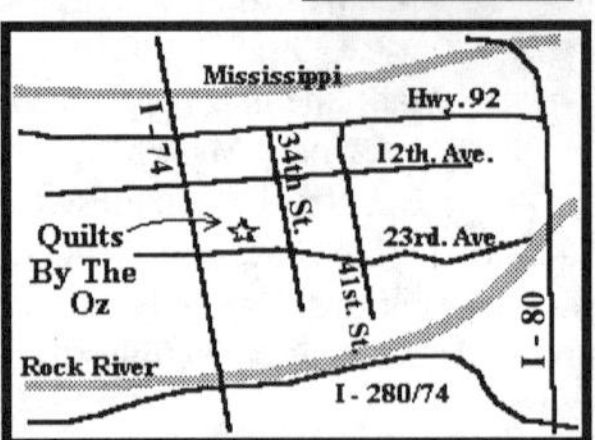

Moline, IL #31

Mon - Thur 10 - 5
Wed til 9
Fri & Sat 10 - 4

Not Just Quilts

2521 - 53rd St. 61285
(309) 764-9836 Est: 1995
E-Mail: NJQ01@aol.com
Web Site: www.rightonweb.com/NJQ.html
Owner: Cindy Hodson 1600 sq.ft.

Large selection of fabrics including flannels and homespuns. Country gifts, patterns, books, basket supplies and notions. Friendly Staff.

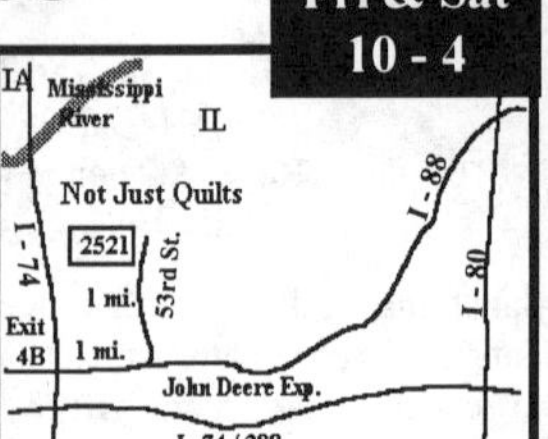

Featured in the American Patchwork & Quilting Shop Sampler 1998.

Fabric, Notions, Books, Patterns, Stencils, Machine Quilting, Classes and two floors of antiques and collectibles.

Fulton, IL #32

1108 4th St. Fulton, IL 61252
(800) 676-2284 or (815) 589-2221

Hours: Tues - Sat 10 - 5 Sunday 12 - 5
Closed Mondays and Holidays

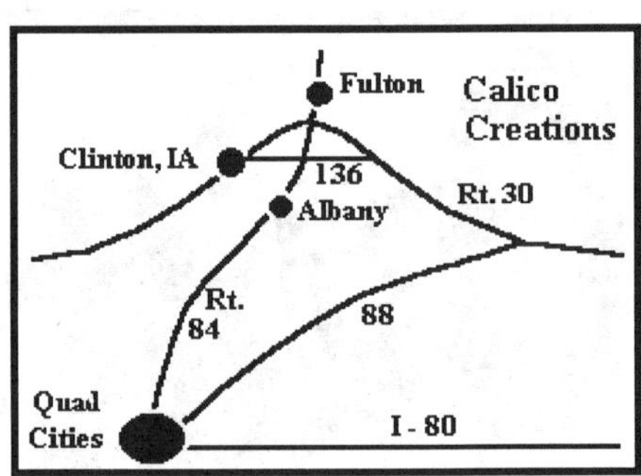

Owner: Jane Huisingh
Est: 1986 8,000 sq.ft.

Dixon, IL #33

Tues - Sat 10 - 5

The Quilt Cellar

541 Penrose Road 61021
(815) 288-5594
Owner: Sue Ramage
Est: 1992

Over 600 Bolts of P&B, Benartex, Marcus, and other quality fabrics. Quilting supplies and classes.

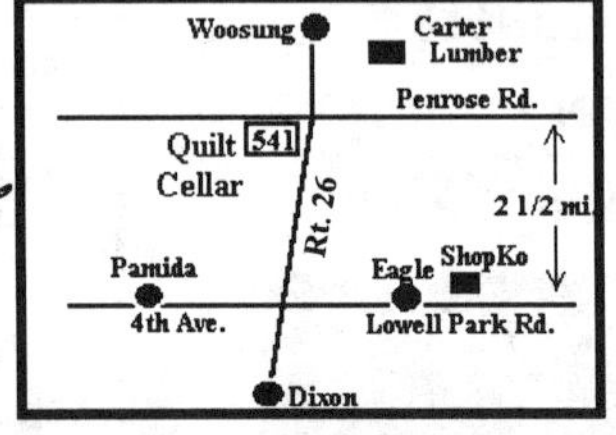

Dixon, IL #34

Mon - Fri 9 - 5:30
Sat 9 - 5

Viking Sewing Shop

302 W. 1st St. 61021
(815) 288-3219
Est: 1971 1200 sq.ft.

500+ Bolts of quilt fabric. Batting & quilt supplies. Machine quilting. Sewing Machines.

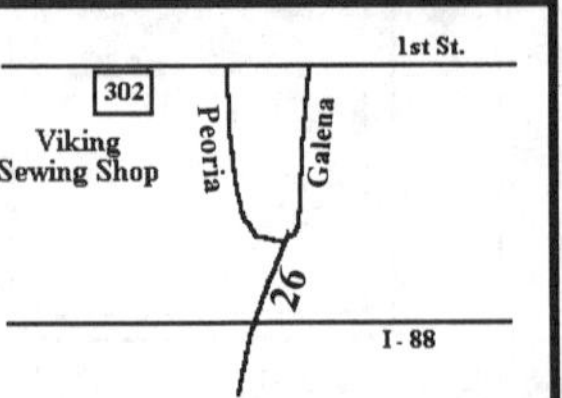

Bishop Hill, IL #35

April - Dec
Daily
10 - 5

The Prairie Workshop

Box 23 61419
(In the Historic 1846 Village)
(309) 927-3367 Shop Est: 1983
Owner: Betty Robertson

Fabric, Quilting Supplies, Books, Handmade Items
In the Historic Village of Bishop Hill, Illinois

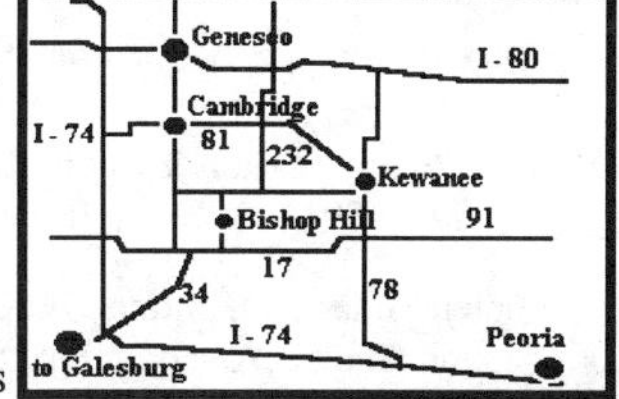

Morrison, IL #36

Tues - Sat
10 - 5

CONstantly Stitching N' More

13690 Lincoln Road 61270
(815) 772-2833
Owner: Connie Barr
Est: 1992 5000 sq.ft.

Machine Quilting, Fabric, Notions, Books, Patterns, Quilt Classes. Basket Weaving Classes. Gift Items. Ready Made Crafts. Antiques.

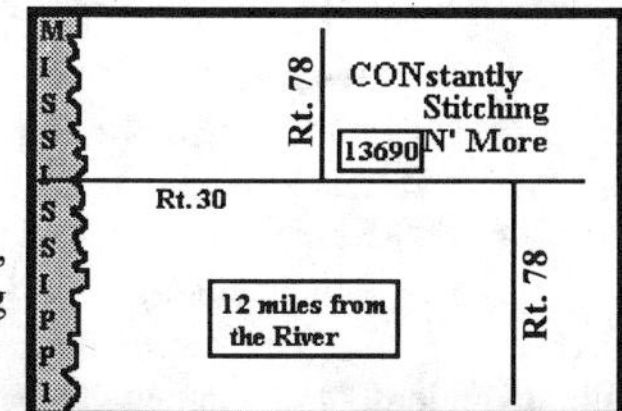

Pearl City, IL #37

Mon, Wed & Fri 11 - 7
Tues & Thur 3:30 - 7
Sat 10 - 5
Sun 11 - 5

Sew many Antiques

140 - 160 S. Main St., P.O. Box 55
(815) 443-2211 61062
Owners: Jill & Dave Kempel and Vicki & Dave Olsen
Est: 1992 4300 sq.ft. 1200+ Bolts

Filled with over 1200 bolts of fabric, patterns, books, gifts, and antiques. We offer classes, retreats & always a friendly welcome.

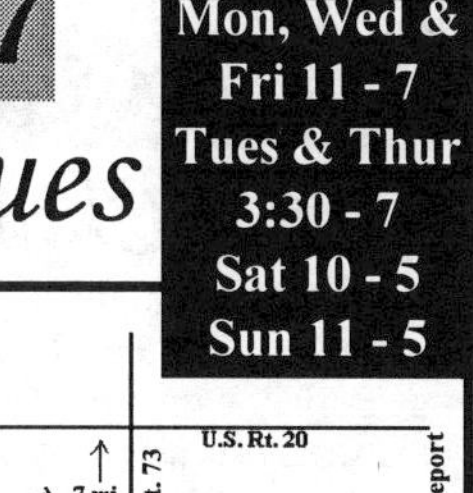

Lena, IL #38

Mon - Fri
10 - 6
Sat 9 - 4

Quilted Treasures

209 E. Main St., P.O. Box 93
(815) 369-9104 61048
Owners: Jean & Cy Breit

"A unique blend of fabrics & quilts in a charming old home." Fabrics, Books, Patterns, Antique & New Quilts. Handcrafted Gifts.

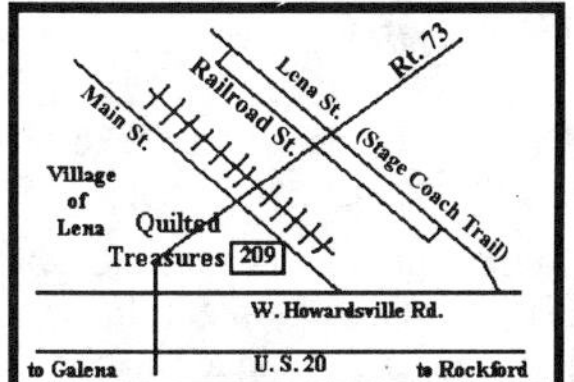

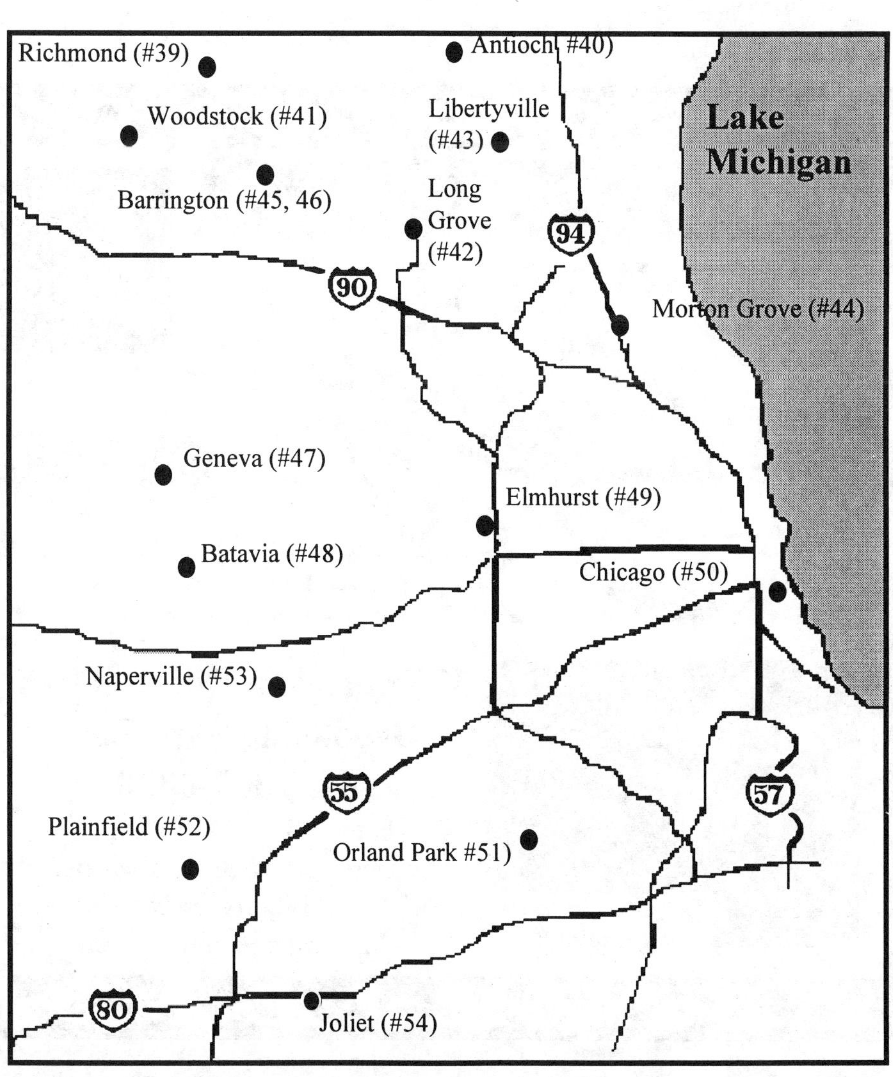

Richmond, IL #39

Mon - Sat 10 - 5 Sun 12 - 5

Sunshine and Shadow Quilt Shoppe

5608 Broadway 60071
(815) 678-2603 2000 + Bolts
Owner: Linda Rullman Est: 1991
In Historic Richmond among Antique & Unique Shops

Purveyor of fine fabrics, books, patterns, quilting notions, doll making items, sundry gifts & Collectibles. Classes Offered.

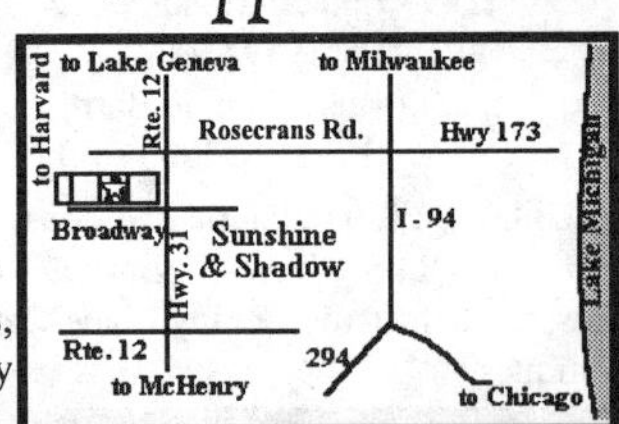

Antioch, IL #40

Tues - Sat 10 - 4 Sun 12 - 4

Quilter's Dream, Inc.

902 Main St. (Rt. 83) 60002
(847) 395-1459
Owners: Wendy Maston & Robin Kessell
Est: 1994 1200 sq.ft.

A complete line of Quilting Supplies & 100% cotton fabrics. A very unique town. We love visitors. Stop in & chat!

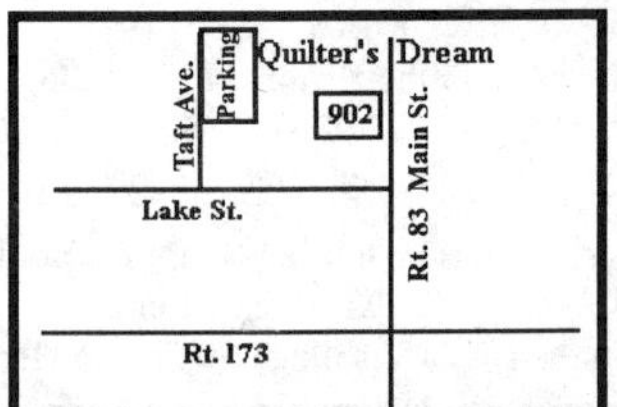

Woodstock, IL #41

Mon - Fri 9:30 - 5:30 Thur til 8 Sat 9:30 - 5 Sun 12 - 4

The Quilt Studio, Inc.

129 Van Buren St. 60098
(815) 338-1212
Owner: Diane Webster
Est: 1994 2000 sq.ft

Fabric, Quilting Supplies. Ready-Made and Custom-Made Quilted Items. Sewing Collectibles & Antique Quilts.
Quilt Racks & Handcrafts.

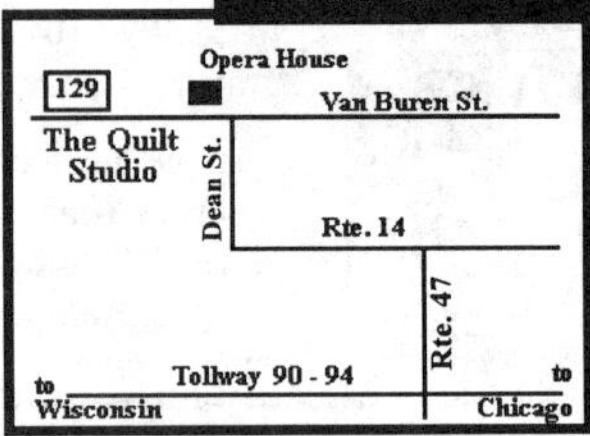

Long Grove, IL #42

Mon - Sat 10 - 5 Sun Noon - 5

Prints Charming, Ltd.

221 R.P. Coffin Road 60047
(847) 634-1330 Fax: (847) 634-1405
E-Mail: Printschrm@aol.com
Owners: Joan & Steve Attenberg
Est: 1978 3000 sq.ft.

Oldest quilt shop in northwest Suburban Chicago. 100% Cottons, Quilting Notions, Classes. Hundreds of unique craft patterns and supplies.

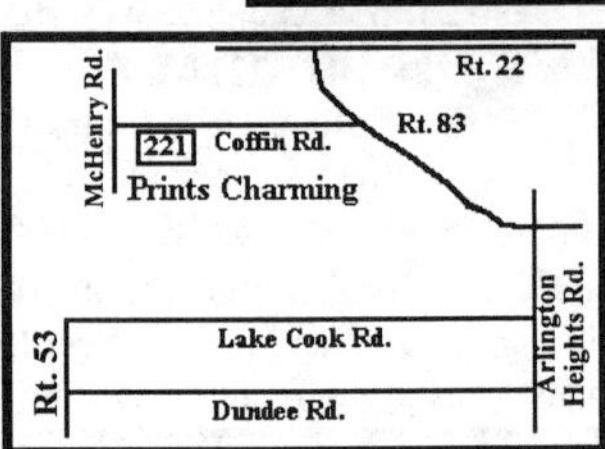

Libertyville, IL #43

Mon - Thur 9 - 9 Fri & Sat 9 - 5

LIBERTYVILLE Sewing CENTER

Large Selection of :
- Calicos featuring Hoffman.
- Quilting Supplies.
- Buttons
- Threads
- Sales & Service -All Makes & Models

When You're Ready for the Best® VIKING
Nothing Sews Like A Bernina. Nothing. BERNINA®
baby lock

The Quilter's Dream Sewing Center 2080

326 Peterson Rd. 60048
(Brookside Shp. Ctr.)
(847) 367-0820
Est: 1982 4500 sq.ft.
Owners: Linda & Rick Mosier
E-Mail: Libertysew@aol.com
Web Site: Coming Soon

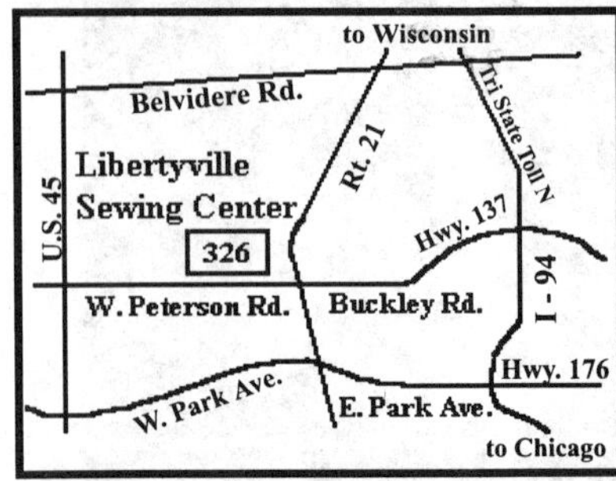

Exit Hwy. 137 from North or South
Exit Hwy. 21 from North only
Exit Hwy. 176 from South only

(847) 966-1882

Morton Grove, IL #44

Just North of Chicago

Cotton Pickers' Fabrics

5926 Dempster
60053

Mon - Sat
10 - 5
Sun 12 - 4

5000 sq.ft.

The Midwest's Largest Quilt Supply Shop

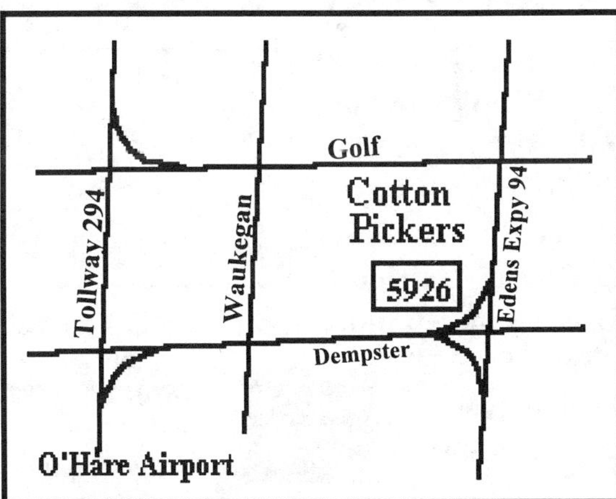

We carry 4000+ different calicos

400 Books — Stencils — Patterns

Over 100 Quilts Displayed

Barrington, IL #45

Mon - Sat 10 - 5
Tues & Thur til 8
Sun 12 - 4

Barrington Sewing Center, Inc.

762 W. Northwest Hwy. 60010
(847) 304-4500
Owner: Sharon Turskey
Est: 1994 2400 sq.ft.

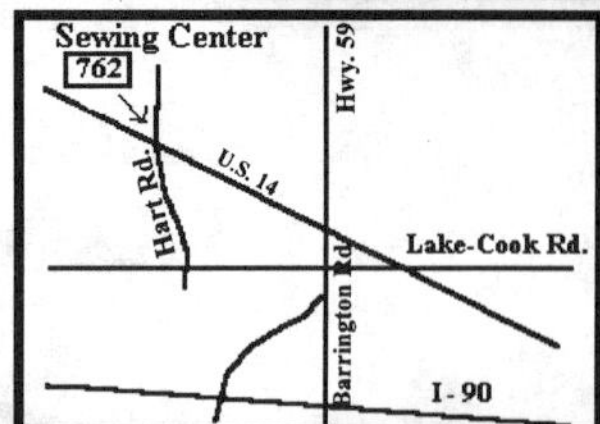

Unusual 100% cotton fabrics. Tons of Batiks! Books, Patterns, Notions, Classes. Viking Sewing Machines.

Barrington, IL #46

Tues - Sat 10 - 4

A Touch of Amish

130 Applebee 60010
(847) 381-0900
(888) 5-QUILTS (578-4587)
Owner: Lynn Rice
Est: 1986 2500 sq.ft.

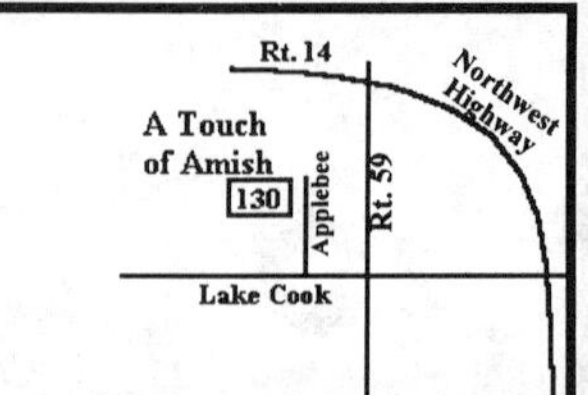

Wonderful fabrics, books, patterns, custom quilting, free weekly demonstrations, and always great service.

Geneva, IL #47

Mon - Sat 11 - 6

Quilted Fox

322 Hamilton St. 60134
(630) 232-4888
Owner: Sara Buchholz
Est: 1978 2800 sq.ft.

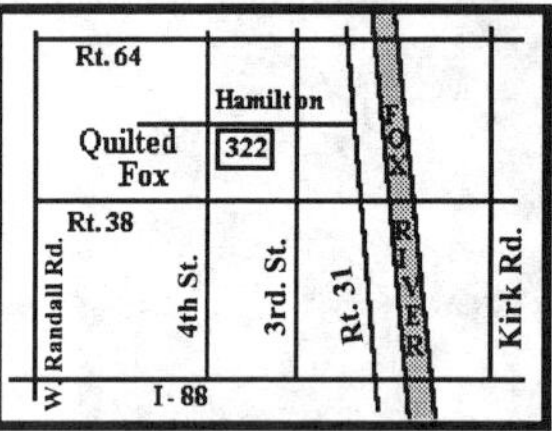

Large selection of unusual & better fabrics: including Liberty—Hoffman Japanese, etc.
Pfaff sewing machines.
Custom Quilts & Art Clothing.

Batavia, IL #48

Mon - Fri 10 - 5
Thurs til 8
Sat 10 - 4
Sun 12 - 4

Quilting Books Unlimited

1911 W. Wilson 60510
(630) 406-0237
Owner: Rob Roberts
Est: 1983 3000 sq.ft.

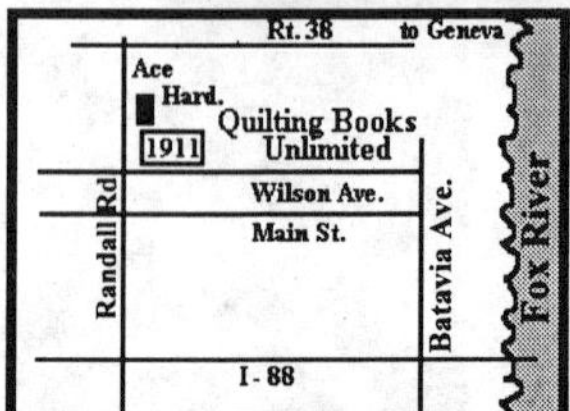

Boasting a collection of over 1000 quilting books, we are the only resource you'll ever need for hand-made quilts, quilting supplies, 100% cottons, and classes. Country Gifts too.

Elmhurst, IL #49

Fabrics Etc. II

We have 1200+ bolts for quilting and 500+ bolts of knits & other fabrics. We have books, Stretch & Sew Patterns, Heirloom Laces & much more. Baby Lock & New Home Machines

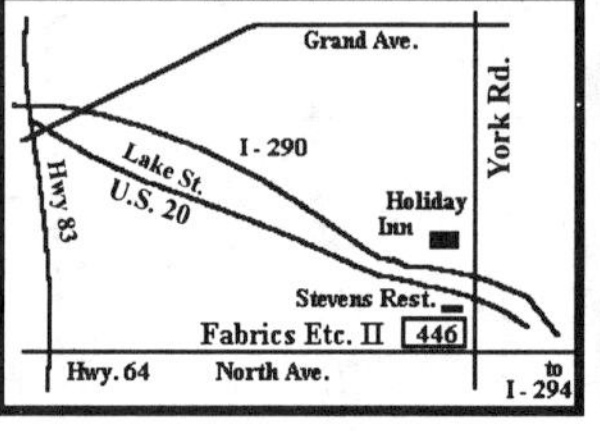

446 N. York Rd.
60126
(630) 279-1482
Est: 1995
2000 sq.ft.

Mon - Sat 9:30 - 5

Chicago, IL #50

By Appointment Only

The Quilt Cottage Gallery

Lake Shore Drive
in Lincoln Park
(312) 404-5500 Est: 1978

American Antique Quilts in Excellent condition displayed in beautiful home setting. Dealers welcomed. Lincoln Park in downtown Chicago

the quilters' Cotton co.

Orland Park, IL #51

Est: 1988
2000 sq.ft.
Owners: Grace McCuan & Donalda Pierik
7046 West 157th Street
60462
(708) 614-7744

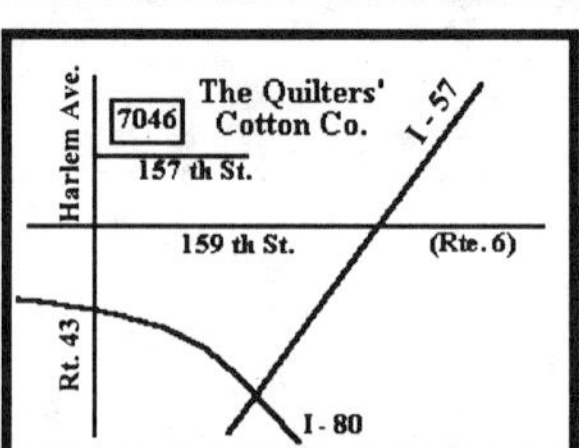

2500+ Bolts of 100% Cottons — Alexander Henry, Benartex, P&B, RJR, Hoffman, Kaufman, Marcus Brothers, Spiegel, Roberta Horton, Homespuns— Mission Valley, Red Wagon Wool & Wool for rug hooking, Flannels, 250+ Books, 150+ Pattern Companies
Great selection of notions, classes.

Mon 12 - 9
Tues-Sat 10 - 4
Thur til 9

HAND-SEWN TOUCH

601 W. Lockport St. (RT. 30), P.O. Box 176, Plainfield, IL 60544
Downtown, 2 Blocks West of Rt. 59, corner of Lockport & DesPlaines

Plainfield, IL #52

(815) 436-6236 "IT'S WORTH THE TRIP"

TUE-WED-FRI-SAT 10:00-4:00 THURSDAYS 10:00-7:00

— Uniquely Packaged FABRIC COLLECTIONS
— Books & Patterns with FABRIC STARTER PACS
— Over 1800 BOLTS including Reproductions, Traditional, Contemporary, Batiks, Flannels, Plaids, Florals for Watercolor and More!

We opened HAND-SEWN TOUCH in 1995. Each week we have new customers both locally and from out-of-state. Many comment on our unique presentation of fabrics, wide variety of selections, and spacious well-lit environment. Several customers (and husbands) have stated HAND-SEWN TOUCH is one of the nicest quilt shops they've been in. We will continue to work diligently to maintain a standard of high quality in a pleasant & helpful atmosphere, and we hope you have an opportunity to visit soon.

Raymond & Arlene Smolich, Owners

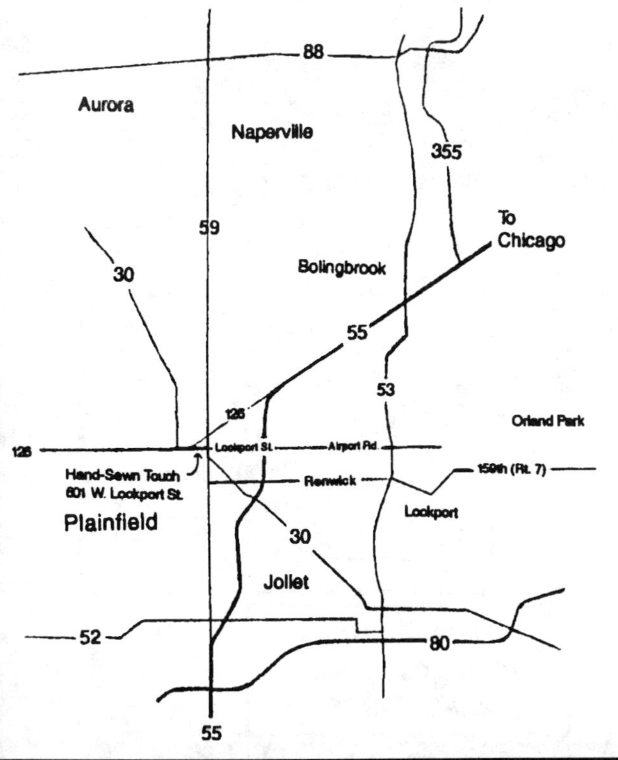

From 55 South - Exit at Rt. 59
From 55 North - Exit at Rt. 126
(Weber Rd. is the exit before Rt. 126)
From 80 - Exit at 55 North, then at Rt. 59

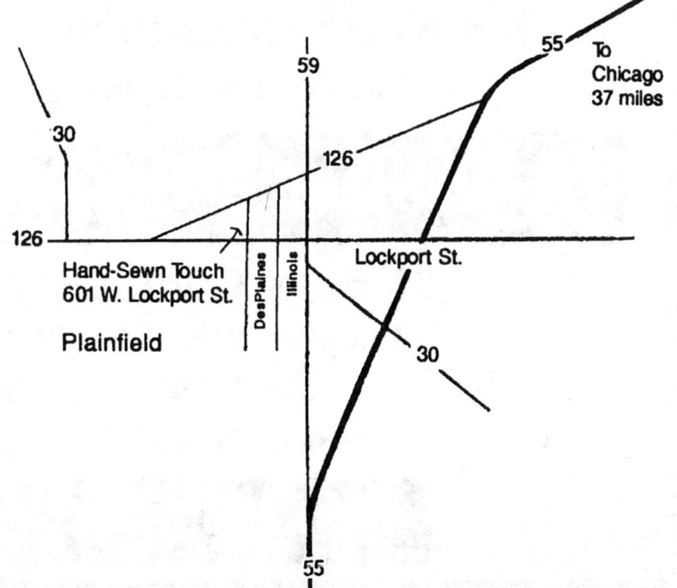

Naperville, IL #53

790 Royal St. George Dr. #119
(630) 420-7050 60563
Owners: Beryl & Sarah Coulson
Est: 1981 4260 sq.ft.

Stitches N' Stuffing

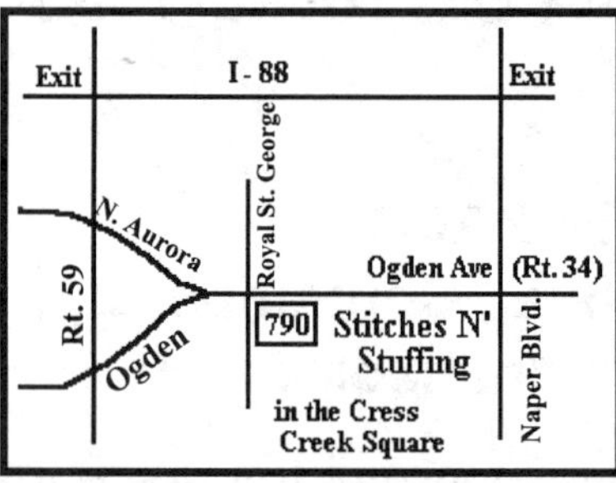

Facing Ogden Ave (Rt. 34)
In the Cross Creek Square

4000+ Cotton Fabrics, Homespuns,
Liberty of London. Patterns, Books, Notions.
Authorized Bernina sales/service
Smocking, Cross - Stitch, Heirloom Supplies.

Quilters & Crafters Heaven

Joliet, IL #54

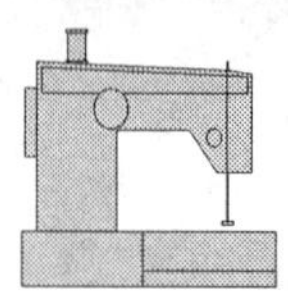

Roberts Sewing Center

255 North Chicago St. 60432 (815) 723-4210
Owner: Ken Roberts Est: 1930 2500 sq.ft.

"A Quilter's Paradise"

4000 Bolts Cotton Fabric
The Lowest Prices in Illinois
Pfaff - - Singer - - Brother
Home & Industrial Machines

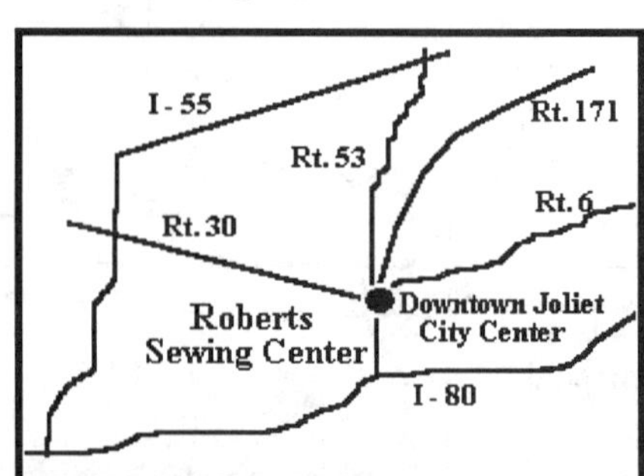

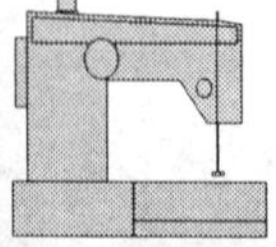

Mon - Sat 9 - 5

Bus Tours
Please Call Ahead
800-273-9111

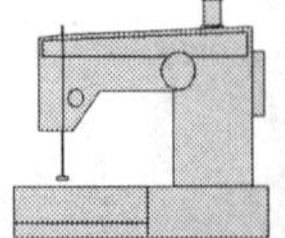

Illinois Guilds:

Mercer County Quilters Guild, P.O. Box 5, Aledo, 61231
Original Heartland Quilter's Guild, P.O. Box 1435, Alton, 62002
Northern Lake Cty Quilters' Guild, P.O. Box 418, Antioch, 60002
N.W. Sub. Quilter's Guild, P.O. Box 146, Arlington Heights, 60006
Prairie Green Quilt Club, P.O. Box 23, Bishop Hill, 61419
Meets: 4th Tuesday every other month 7 p.m.
at Bishop Hill Colony School
Hands all Around Q. G., 205 Fairway Dr., Bloomington, 61701
Meets: 1st Thursday at First Christian Church, 401 W. Jefferson
Country Crossroads Quilt Guild, P.O. Box 214, Butler, 62015
Friendship Star Quilt Guild, 333 Alicia Dr., Cary, 60013
Quiltworks, 2125 Stoner Dr. E, Charleston, 61920
Garfield Ridge Quilt Group, 6249 W. 59th St., Chicago, 60638
Chicago Quilter's Guild, 10406 S. Moody, Chicago Ridge, 60415
Salt Creek Patchmakers Quilt Guild, Clinton, 61727
Meets: 3rd Thursday at Warner Library
The Good Shepherd Quilters, Collinsville
Algonquin Quilt Guild, 550 Lochwood Dr., Crystal Lake, 60012
Vermillion Valley Quilters, 616 Bryan, Danville, 61832
Decatur Quilter's Guild, P.O. Box 415, Decatur, 62525
Petunia City Quilters, 541 Penrose Rd., Dixon, 61021
Faithful Circle Quilters, P.O. Box 9171, Downers Grove, 60515
Loose Threads, 1555 Sherman Ave. #124, Evanston, 60201
Country Crossroads, Forreston
Quilters Plus, 480 Butternut Trail, Frankfort, 60423
River Cities Quilters Guild, P.O. Box 306, Fulton, 61252
Meets: 3rd Tuesday 7 p.m.
at First Presbyterian Church, 701 - 11th Ave.
Geneseo Quilt Guild, Geneseo, 61254
Meets: 2nd Monday 7 p.m. at Geneseo Community Center
Prairie Start Quilters Guild, 33 W. 848 Cherry Ln., Geneva, 60134
Pope County Senior Citizen Quilters, Box 93B, Golconda, 62938
Tri-State Quilters Guild, 338 Park Dr., Hamilton, 62341
Prairie Quality Quilters, 307 Lake Shore Dr., Hanna City, 61536
Village Quilters, P.O. Box 538, Harvard, 60033
Shawnee Quilter's, 1221 S. 16th St., Herrin, 62948
Meets: 3rd Friday at The Cottage Quilt Shop
Hinsdale Embroiderer's Guild, P.O. Box 284, Hinsdale, 60521
Joliet Quilt Guild, 1121 Alann Dr., Joliet, 60435
Heritage Quilters Guild, 1228 Buell Court, Joliet, 60435
So & Sews, 1500 W. Kennedy Rd., Lake Forest, 60045
Piecemakers, Lane
Meets: 4th Thursday at Lane Christian Church
Stagecoach Quilter's Guild, Lena, 61048
Meets: 4th Monday 7 p.m. at Lena United Meth. Church
N. Lake Cty. Quilt Guild, 2121 Old Elm Rd., Lindenhurst, 60046
Prairie Piecemakers Quilts, 15850 W. Shady Ln., Lockport, 60441
Illini Country Stitchers, Box 112, Mansfield, 61854
Tuesday-Odd-Thursday Quilters, Box 112, Mansfield, 61854
Kimball Thimble Quilt Guild, 675 Clark St., Marseilles, 61314
Prairie Quilter's Guild, 802 W. Walnut St., Mason City, 62664
Country Quilters, 824 Banbury Rd., McHenry, 60050
Meets: 1st Thursday 7 p.m. at Shepard of the Hills Lutheran C.
Meredosia Quilt Guild, Meredosia
Meets: 3rd Tuesday at Aunt Sue's Quilt Shop
Massac Quilt Guild, 201 Oak Dr., Metropolis, 62960
Mississippi Valley Quilt Guild, Moline
Kaliedoscope Quilters, 59 Hickory Ridge Dr., Morton, 61550
Quilt Sitters Circle, 59 Hickory Ridge Rd., Morton, 61550
Cedarhust Quilters, P.O. Box 341, Mt. Vernon, 62864
Dupage Textile Art Guild, 1200 Yorkshire Dr., Naperville, 60540
Hearts 'n Hands Quilt Guild, P.O. Box 416, O'Fallon, 62269
Mendota Nine Patch Q. G., 303 W. Walnut St., Oglesby, 61348
Illinois Valley Quilter's Guild, P.O. Box 1001, Ottawa, 61350
Bee Quilters Guild, P.O. Box 815, Paris, 61944
Meets: 4th Monday 6 p.m. at Chester Sutton Center
Pieces & Patches, P.O. Box 184, Park Forest, 60466
Gems of the Prairie Quilters, P.O. Box 9543, Peoria, 61612-9543
Meets: 1st Wednesday at 6:30 p.m.
at First Christian Church, 6400 N. University
Heart of Illinois Quilters, 5105 W. Greenridge Ct., Peoria, 61615
Pride of the Prairie Quilt Guild, P.O. Box 501, Plainfield, 60544
Covered Bridge Quilters`, Princeton
Quinsippi Needleworkers, 202 N. 30th St., Quincy, 62301
Quincy Quilt Guild, 3123 Lewis Dr., Quincy, 62301
Illini Prairie Quilters, Robinson, 62449
Meets: 4th Monday 7 p.m. at Crawford Co. Christian Center
Sinissippi Quilters, P.O. Box 1556, Rockford, 61110
Itasca Quilt Guild, 516 Avebury, Roselle, 60172
Roselle Quilting Circle, 315 Chatham Lane, Roselle, 60172
Nimble Thimbles Q. G., 422 Highnoor Dr., Round Lake Park, 60073
Knot Just Quilters, 280 E. Concord, Sheldon, 60966
Heritage Quilters of S. Suburbia, P.O. Box 932, South Holland, 60473
Q.U.I.L.T.S., P.O. Box 7502, Springfield, 62791
Prairie Piecemakers, Box 163, St. Joseph, 61873
DeKalb City Quilters, P.O. Box 385, Sycamore, 60178
Salt Creek Quilt Guild, P.O. Box 214, Western Springs, 60558
Centennial Quilters, 5808 Wolf, Western Springs, 60558
Illinois Quilters, Inc., P.O. Box 39, Wilmette, 60091
Stagecoach Quilters, 9336 W. Lake Rd., Winslow, 61089
Woodstock Quilters, 1664 Eastwood Dr., Woodstock, 60098
Kalico Kwilters Bee, E. Van Emmon, Yorkville, 60560
Prairie Point Quilt Guild, 9103 Ament Road, Yorkville, 60560

I ♥ QUILTING!

Other Shops in Illinois:

Alton	Patchwork Plus, 108 W. 3rd. St.	618-462-8565
Arthur	Melrose Quilts, R.R. #1, Box 133A	217-543-2844
Arthur	The Calico Workshop, 228 South Vine	217-543-2312
Arthur	Quilts & Crafts, R.R. 1, Box 185A	217-543-2702
Avon	The Clothesline Quilt Shop, 102 N. Main	309-465-3850
Barrington	Finn's Fabrics, 113 North Cook,	708-381-5020
Bishop Hill	Village Smithy, 309 N. Bishop Hill St.	309-927-3851
Carpentersville	Grist Mill End, 39 E. Main St.	847-426-6455
Carpentersville	Quiltmaster Inc., 1 S. Wisconsin	708-426-6741
Carthage	Country Pastimes, 541 Main St.	217-357-3765
Charleston	Needle Nook, Rt. 4, Box 182	217-345-4048
Dunlap	Quilt Crossing, 1719 W. Woodside Dr.	309-243-9028
Edwardsville	Edwardsville Sewing, 110 N. Main	618-656-4272
Effingham	Calico Shoppe, 1108 N. Merchant St.	217-342-6628
Elmhurst	Granny's Goodies, 116 N. York St.	630-834-0666
Evanston	Quilting B, 1729 Central St.	847-328-9642
Hinsdale	Hearts & Hands, 10 W. Hinsdale Ave.	630-654-0844
Hutsonville	Apple Blossom Quilt Shop, St. Rt. 1	618-563-4388
Lebanon	Material Things, 618 N. Monroe St.	618-537-2157
Liberty	Pam's Quilt Shop, R.R. #1, Box 106	217-645-3871
Long Grove	The Patchworks, 223 R. P. Coffin Rd.	847-634-0330
Mascoutah	Patchwork Corner, 200 N. Jefferson St.	618-566-2652
Nashville	Lee's Fabric, 212 E. St. Louis St.	618-327-8866
Odin	Mary's Vogue Shop, 105 Green	618-775-8371
Pinckneyville	Quilters Heaven, 1007 S. Main St.	618-357-5531
Pittsfield	The Pin Cushion, 510 N. Jackson St.	217-285-6923
Princeton	Old Times--Quilter Heaven, 954 N. Main	815-872-9841
Quincy	Jean Lyle, P.O. Box 289	217-222-8910
Rockford	Gingerbread & Calico, 4125 Charles St.	815-399-5194
Springfield	A-1 Quilters, 1052 E. Stanford Ave.	217-789-4223
Sycamore	Tomorrow's Treasures, 310 E. State St.	815-899-7060
Sycamore	Made Just For You, 338 W. State St.	815-895-8122
Tinley	Park Sew Creative, 15953 S. Harlem	708-429-6056
Waterloo	Warm Expressions, 1047 Gilmore Lake	618-939-3606
West Frankfort	Calico Country Sewing Ctr., 310 S. Logan	618-932-2992
Wyanet	Country Seams, 114 N. Walnut	815-699-7295

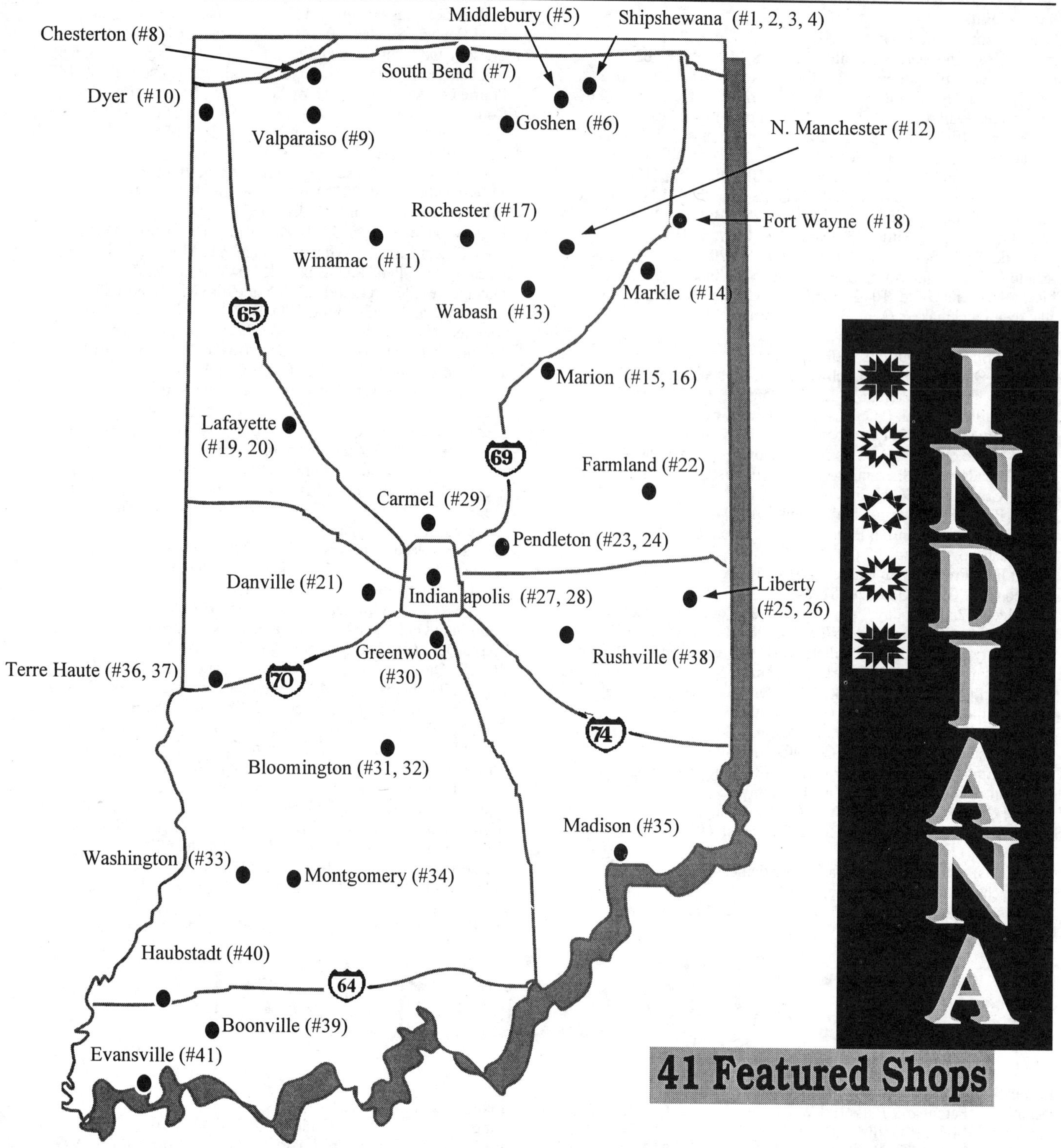

Middlebury (#5)
Shipshewana (#1, 2, 3, 4)
Chesterton (#8)
South Bend (#7)
Dyer (#10)
Goshen (#6)
Valparaiso (#9)
N. Manchester (#12)
Rochester (#17)
Fort Wayne (#18)
Winamac (#11)
Markle (#14)
Wabash (#13)
65
Marion (#15, 16)
Lafayette
(#19, 20)
69
Farmland (#22)
Carmel (#29)
Pendleton (#23, 24)
Danville (#21)
Indianapolis (#27, 28)
Liberty
(#25, 26)
Greenwood
(#30)
Rushville (#38)
Terre Haute (#36, 37)
70
74
Bloomington (#31, 32)
Madison (#35)
Washington (#33)
Montgomery (#34)
Haubstadt (#40)
64
Boonville (#39)
Evansville (#41)
INDIANA

41 Featured Shops

Shipshewana, IN #1

**Mon - Fri 8 - 5
Sat 8 - 4:30**

Spector's Store

305 S. Van Buren (Ind. 5)
P.O. Box 347 46565
(219) 768-4439

Full Line of Fabric and notions. Quilt and Craft supplies. Hand stitched, quilted items. Wallhangings & Quilts. Excellent Values on Solid & Printed fabrics.

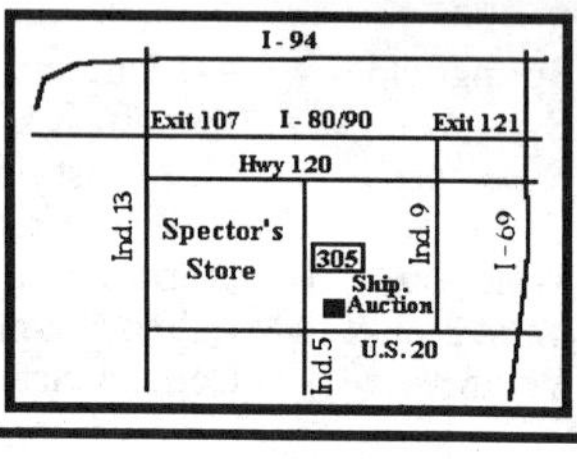

I - 94
Exit 107
I - 80/90
Exit 121
Hwy 120
Ind. 13
Spector's
Store
305
Ship.
Auction
Ind 9
I - 69
Ind.5
U.S. 20

Shipshewana, IN #2

Mon - Sat 9:30 - 5

Rebecca Haarer Folk Arts and Antiques

165 Morton St. 46565
(219) 768-4787
Owner: Rebecca Haarer
Est: 1971 Free Brochure

Antique Quilts — gathered from this area. Amish Quilts, dolls, rockers, old fabrics, feed sacks, and stencils. Amish Quilt Lectures.

I - 80/90
Hwy. 120
Hwy. 13
Hwy. 5
Shipshewana
Rebecca
Haarer Quilts

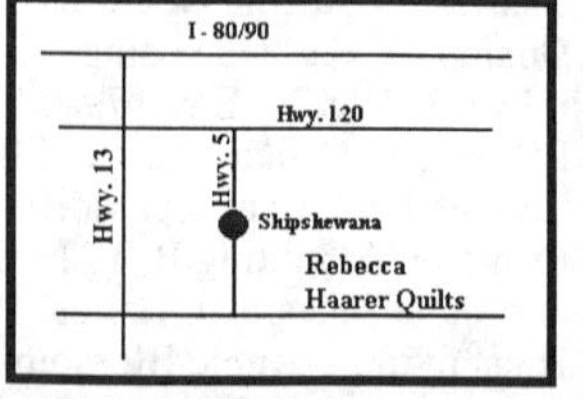

Shipshewana, IN #3

Lolly's Fabrics

Superior selection of quilting fabrics, stencils, & notions. Specializing in new & custom-made quilts and wallhangings.

Mon - Sat 9 - 5

228 W. Main,
P.O. Box 277 46565
(219) 768-4703
Fax: (219) 768-7304
Owners: Alvin & Elsie Miller
Est: 1980 2600 sq.ft. 2500 Bolts

Exit 107
Toll Road
Exit 121
U.S. 120
Lolly's
228
Main St.
Ind. 13
Ind. 5
Ind. 9
U.S. 20

SHIPSHEWANA, IN #4

"Find the basic and the unusual!"

- Over 10,000 bolts of fabric. (over 3,000 bolts of quilting type fabrics) Brands include: Hoffman, Benartex,
- Concord, P & B, Marcus Bros., Mission Valley, Mumms the Word, Moda, Rose & Hubble, RJR, V-I-P, Springs, Alaska hand dyed fabrics, homespuns, quilter's flannel, and many more. Also fashion, bridal and home decorating fabrics (Waverly, John Wolfe, & Robert Kauffman). Silk, velvet, wool, linen, denim, calicos, and many hard to find fabrics.
- Accessories, trims, patterns, sewing notions, quilting supplies, and books.
- Clothing and shoes for all ages.

Visit a family tradition that still places friendly service, quality merchandise and value as their highest priority.

Open: 8:00 - 5:30, Monday - Saturday
Closed Sunday
Will Mail-Order. Credit Cards Accepted

YODER'S SHOPPING CENTER
P.O. Box 245, St. Rd. 5
Shipshewana, IN 46565
(219) 768-4887
www.shipshewana.com/fabrics
e-mail: fabrics@shipshewana.com

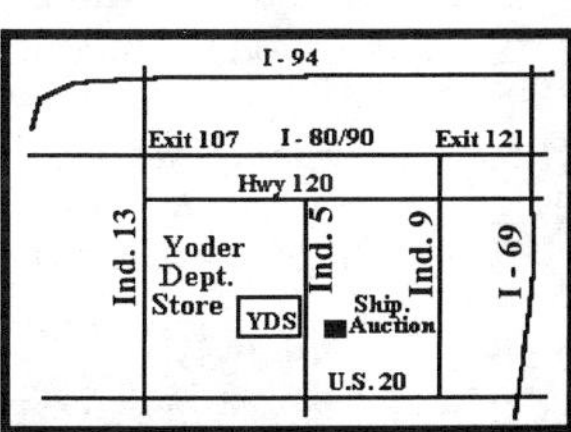

Middlebury, IN #5

Mon - Sat
10a.m. -
Evening Hrs.
April - Dec.

Quilts by Esther

Est: 1986
1200 sq.ft.
Owner:
Esther A. Hershberger
Web Site:www.info@ quiltsbyesther.com
AT ESSENHAUS Village Shops

P.O. Box 405
46540
(219) 825-9471

- **Quilts**
- **Wall Hangings**
- **Cotton Fabrics**
- **Over 600 Quilt Stencils**
- **Books**
- **Free Inspiration**

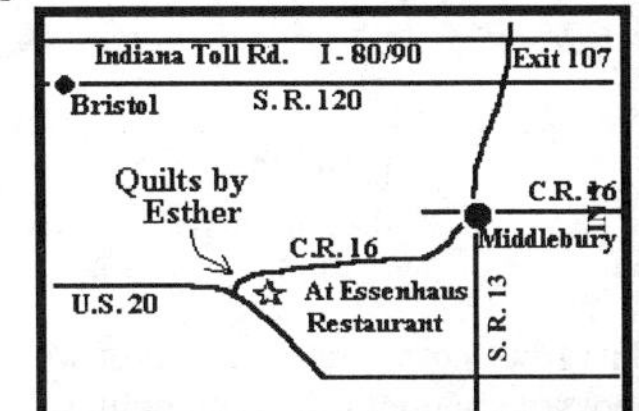

Goshen, IN #6

Mon - Fri
9 - 5:30
Sat 9 - 4

Meredith's Sewing Corner

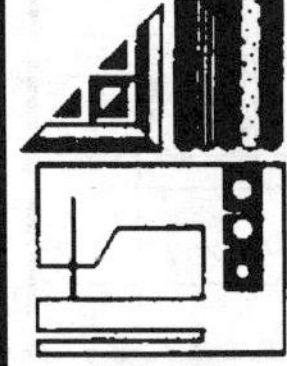

712 W. Lincoln Ave. 46526
(219) 533-3414

6000 square feet a full fabric store, needle crafts and Bernina Sewing Machines. Wonderful displays. Great prices.

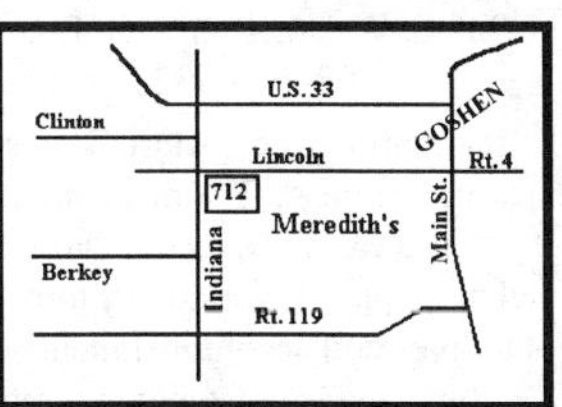

South Bend, IN #7

Heckaman's Quilts & Yarns

63028 U.S. 31 South 46614
(219) 291-3918

- Quilts for Sale
- Custom Orders Welcome
- Let Us Quilt for You
  Hand or Machine Your Top
  or Ours—Several Designs
- We Repair Old Quilts
- Supplies, Stencils, Books, Fabric
- Quilt Hangers, Hoops
- Hinterberg Quilt Frames on Display
- Beautiful Yarns, Books, Supplies.
- Brittany Needles And Much More!!
- Ashford Spinning Wheels
- Schacht Weaving Looms

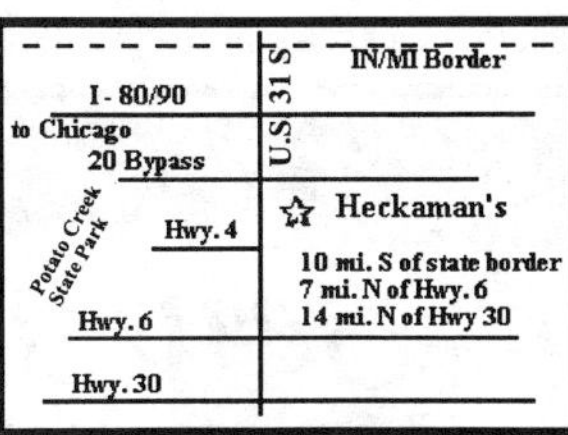

Mon - Sat
10 - 5
Or By Appt.

Chesterton, IN #8

Tue Thurs Fri 11 - 4:30
Wed 11 - 7
Sat 10 - 4

Pieceful Quilts

119 Broadway 46304
(219) 926-2182
Owner: Sandy Stahl
Est: 1994 1000 sq.ft.

1200 bolts of 100% cotton fabrics, flannels & wools. Hoffman, RJR, South Seas, Benartex, P&B, and more. Newest patterns & books. Classes Offered.

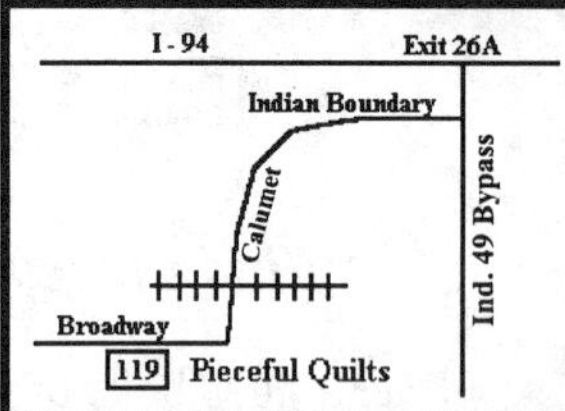

Valparaiso, IN #9

Mon - Fri 10 - 5
Thur til 7
Sat 10 - 3

Needle & Thread

60 Jefferson 46383
(219) 462-4300 Est: 1990
Owner: Marlene Rock 1500 sq.ft.
1200 Bolts Free Newsletter

Visit our old Victorian house filled with everything for quilting, cross stitch, tatting, hardanger, stencilling, silk ribbon emb. & knitting. Classes.

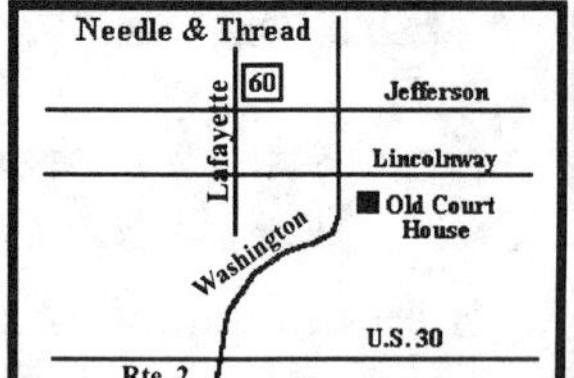

Dyer, IN #10

Mon & Thur 10 - 8:30
Tues, Wed & Fri 10 - 6:30
Sat 10 - 5:30

Quilter's Haven

Over 3,000 Bolts of 100% Cotton Fabrics. Large selection of Patterns, Books & Notions. All levels of Classes.

Sand Ridge Plaza (Rt. 30)
1060 Joliet St. 46311
(219) 322-4624
E-Mail: QuiltHaven@aol.com
Owner: Judith Ann Bremer
Est: 1994 1800 sq.ft.

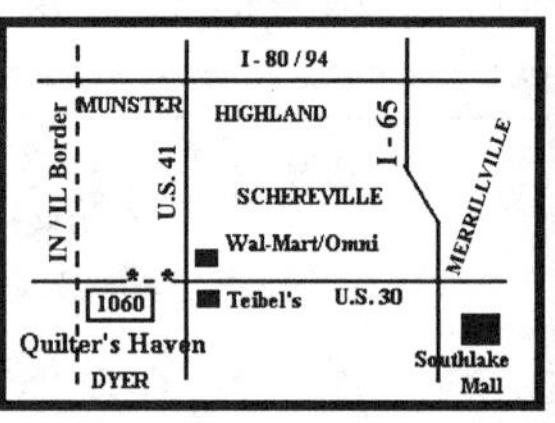

From the corner of U.S. 30 and U.S. 41: Go west on 30 to the second stop light. Turn left, immediately turn into Sand Ridge Plaza. Quilter's Haven is on the west end of the plaza.

Winamac, IN #11

Tues - Sat 9 - 5

The Country Patch

102 N. Monticello St. 46996
(219) 946-7799 Est: 1992
Owner: Eddie Ploss

New and Unique Quilt Shop featuring 100% cotton 650+ bolts. Springmaid, RJR, Etc.

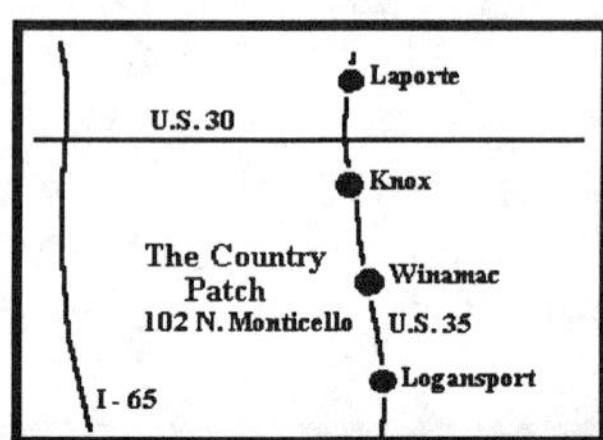

N. Manchester, IN #12

Mon - Fri 10 - 5
Sat 10 - 4

Creative Threads

229 E. Main St. 46962
(219) 982-2359
Owners: Jim & Shirley Mishler

We carry quality 100% cotton fabrics, quilt patterns, books & notions. Classes are available — Personal Service.

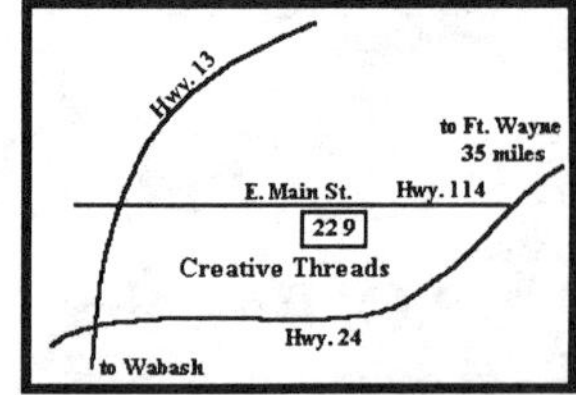

Wabash, IN #13

Mon - Fri 10 - 5:30
Sat 10 - 5

Nancy J's Fabrics

1604 South Wabash 46992
(219) 563-3505 Est: 1980
Owners: Nancy Jacoby & Miriam Peebles
website: www.qcos.com/nancy-js/

The latest & greatest Fabrics. Books and Patterns for quilts, & dollmaking.
Plan to spend a day in Historic Wabash!

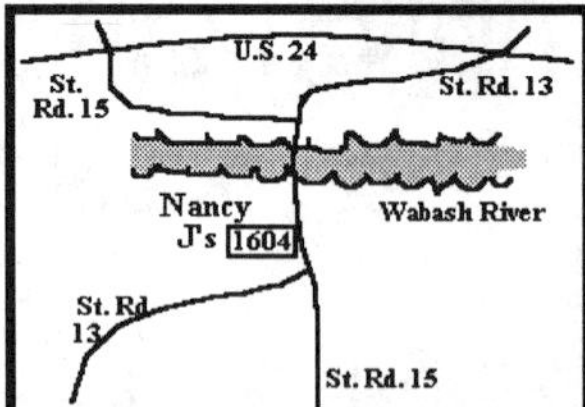

Markle, IN #14

Mon - Fri 6 - 8 pm
Sat 9 - 1
or by Appt.

Stitchin' Corner

225 Lee St., P.O. Box 175 46770
(219) 758-2217
E-Mail: gordon@qws.com
Est: 1995 320 sq.ft.

Small but cozy, we carry top quality fabrics, books and notions for both quilters and cross stitchers. Hand made gifts.

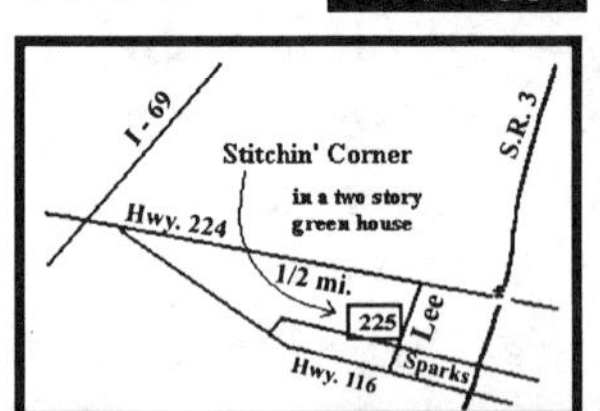

Marion, IN #15

Mon - Fri 10 - 6
Sat 10 - 3

Sew Biz

3722 South Western Ave. 46953
(800) 500-3830 or (765) 674-6001
Fax: (765) 674-5992 Est: 1983
E-Mail: sewbiz@comteck.com
Owner: Donelle McAdams 3,500 sq.ft.

Viking & White Dealer. 100% cottons, books, patterns, classes, dolls, bears, bunnies, etc. A place to share ideas and get inspired.

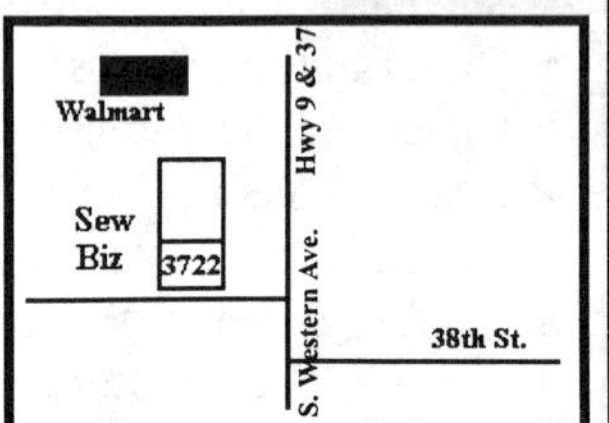

Marion, IN #16

Please Call First

The Quilters Hall of Fame

926 S. Washington, P.O. Box 681 46952
(765) 664-9333 Fax: Same

Renovation of the Marie Webster Home is now in progress. The museum is not yet open. Please call for update. Our mission is to celebrate quilting as an art form, by honoring the lives and accomplishments of those who have made outstanding contributions.

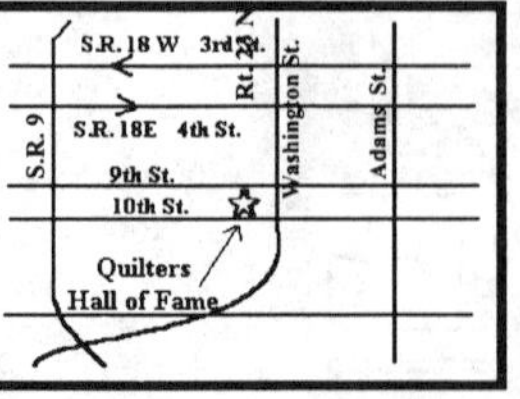

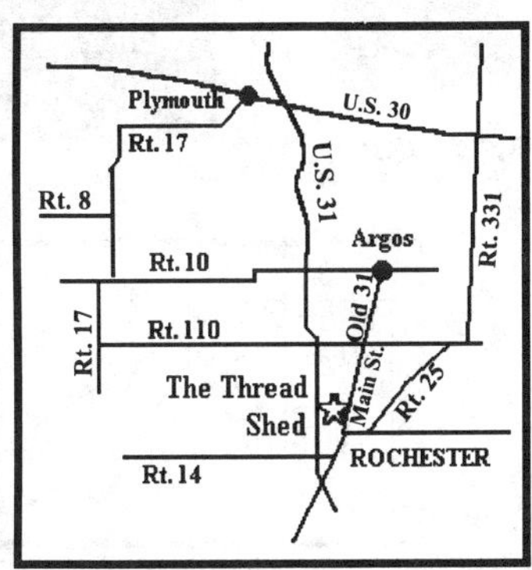

The Thread Shed

610 Main St. 46975
(219) 223-4959
E-Mail:
threadshed@rtcol.com
Owner: Carol M. Richmond
Est: 1978
2800 sq.ft.
1200+ Bolts

Located in historical downtown Rochester we offer a complete line of notions, patterns, threads etc. To complete your quilt we carry Quilters Dream Cotton. For Cross Stitchers we have patterns, DMC floss and fabric. Authorized Husqvarna Dealer and repair service. Complete with Internet Station. Classes offered and plenty of free advice.

Rochester, IN #17

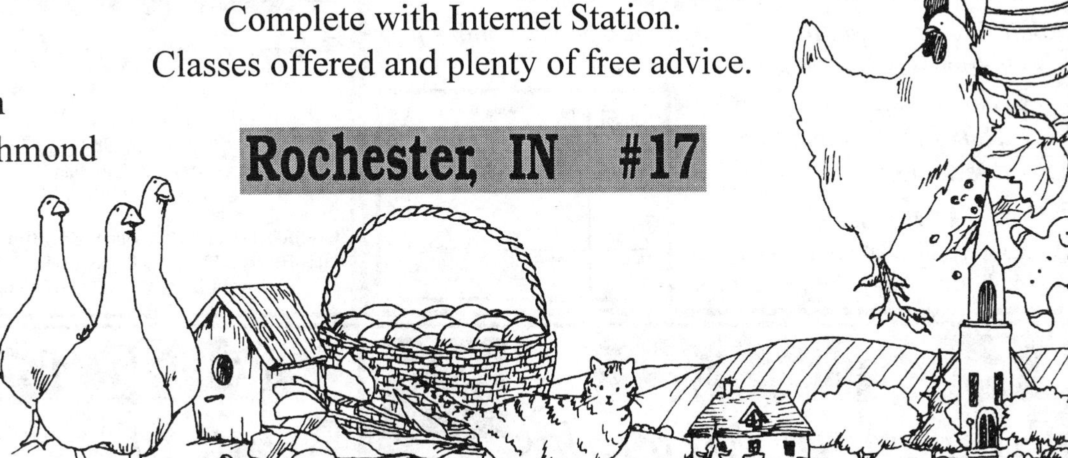

Mon , Tues, Wed, Fri 9 - 5
Thur & Sat 9 - 2

Fort Wayne, IN #18

Patchworks Shop

2910 Lake Avenue • Fort Wayne, Indiana

"In the Old Brick House"

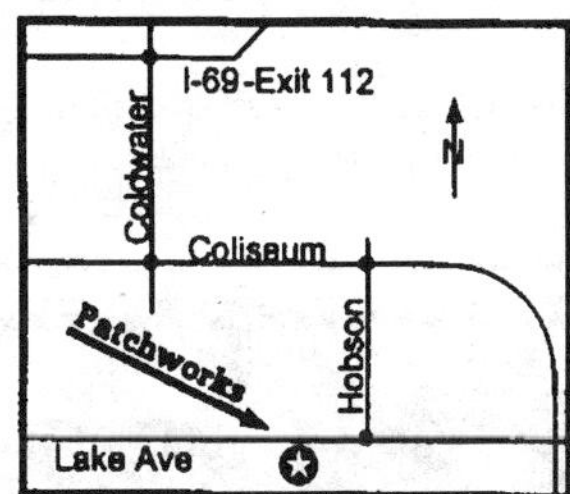

- **Homespun Cotton Fabric**
  One of the largest selections anywhere.
- **Reproduction Cottons**
  Choose from our huge *I want it to look old collection.*
- **Batik Cottons**
  For the contemporary & applique lovers.
- **Cotton Flannel**
  Great for clothing, quilts and crafting.
- **Over "3000" Bolts of Fabric**
- **Your Headquarters for Quilting & Craft Patterns, Books and Supplies** We're always on the look out for *What's New!*
- **Premier VIKING Dealer**
- **Mail Order Available**
  PO Box 15834, Fort Wayne IN 46885

— One of Indiana's most unique fabric & quilt shops —

Phone: 1-800-44PLAID
(219) 422-5277
FAX: (219) 424-5432
e-mail: PATCHFTWAY@aol.com

— Hours —
Monday-Wednesday-Friday-Saturday.....10 am to 5 pm
Tuesday-Thursday..... 10 am to 7 pm

Home of the
Stash-O-Matic Fabric Club
50-5" squares of the newest fabric mailed quarterly
$30 per year or $8 quarterly

Lafayette, IN #19

Tues - Fri 10 - 5
Sat 9 - 2

Sally's Sewing Basket INC.

"We sell Sewing Excitement!"

326 Brown St. 47901
(765) 423-4744
Fax: (765) 423-5448
Owner: Sally Carter
Est: 1994 800 sq.ft.

Authorized PFAFF Dealer

Sally's carries quality quilting fabrics, books, notions for:

- *Quilting and Wearables*
- *Cross-stitch, Hardanger & Silk Ribbon Embroidery*
- *Classes too.*

Web Site:
www.sallys.lafayette.in.us
E-Mail: info@sallys.lafayette.in.us

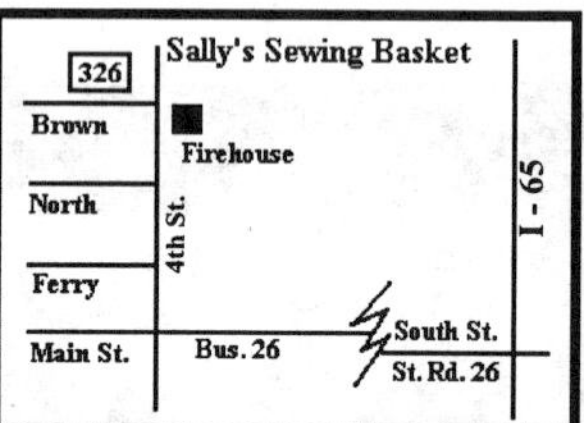

Lafayette, IN #20

Mon - Sat 9:30 - 5:30

The Paisley Pincushion

2007 Kossuth St. 47905
(765) 447-4996 Fax: (765) 447-7075
Est: 1995 2700 sq.ft. 3000 Bolts

Bernina Dealer & Quilt Store
With over 3000 bolts of fabric, books, patterns, notions, classes.

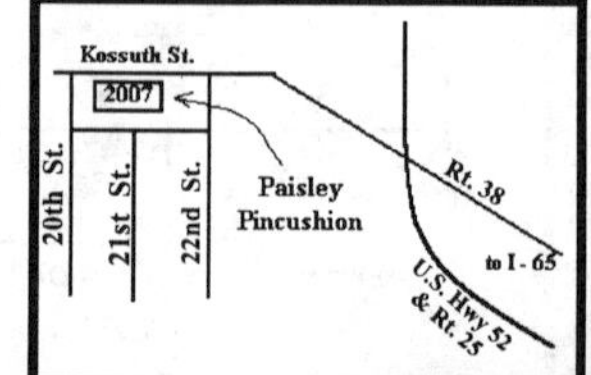

Danville, IN #21

Mon - Fri 9 - 4
Sat 10 - 2

Venture's Quilting Center

35 Lawton Ave. 46122
(317) 745-2989
Owner: Linda Moreland
Est: 1987 3300 sq.ft.

Over 700 bolts of 100% cotton Fabrics. (Hoffmans, Jinny Beyers, VIP's, Etc.) Books, Notions, Batting, Backings, Classes and Samples Galore.

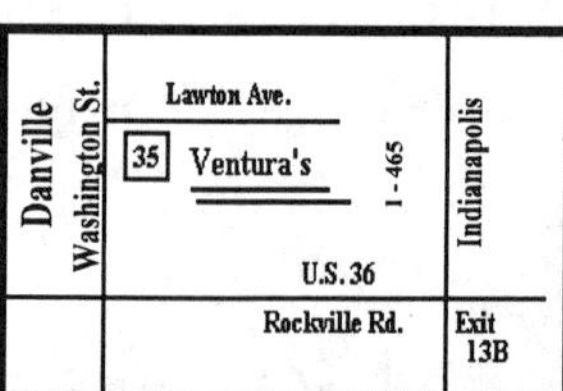

Historic Farmland, IN #22

Tues - Sat 10 - 5

Homespun Memories

108 W. Henry 47340
(765) 468-7472
Owner: Jennifer Kindred

Specializes in exclusive quilting fabric, notions and classes.

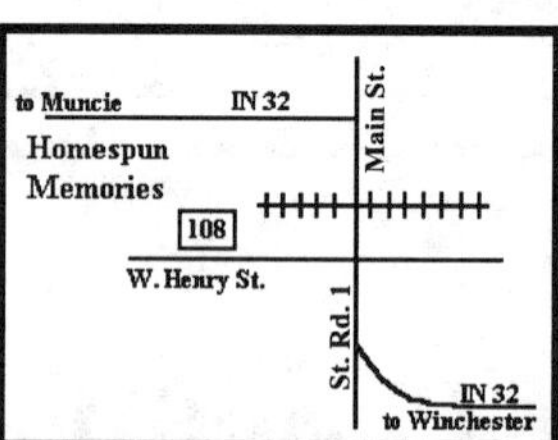

Pendleton, IN #23

Mon - Sat 10 - 5
Sun 1 - 5

Needle in the Haystack

132 West State St. (Hwy 38) 46064
(765) 778-7936 (800) 779-7936
Owner: Tammy Vonderschmitt
Est: 1981 4000 sq.ft.

Bernina Dealer & Repair. Fabric, Quilting supplies, Books, Patterns, hand and machine quilting services, Classes. Cross- stitch, craft patterns and supplies.

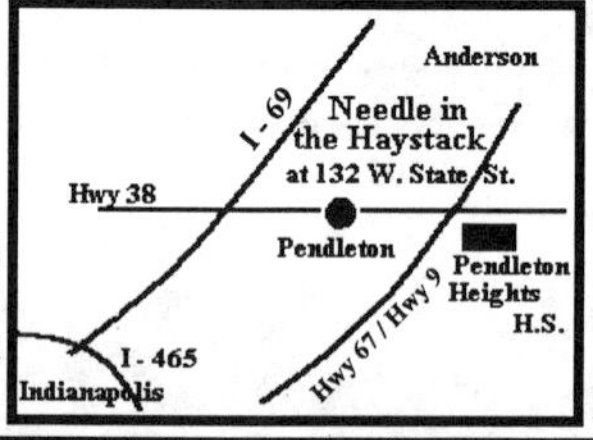

Pendleton, IN #24

Ruth's Legacy, Ltd.

104 W. High St. 46064
(765) 778-2488
Est: 1996 1800 sq.ft.

Mon - Sat 10 - 5
Sun 1 - 5

The very latest fabrics from Hoffman, RJR, Benartex, Maywood Studio & more. Classes, Patterns, Notions & friendly Service. Over 35 different cat prints. Large selection of batiks. Distinctive Gifts & Collectibles such as Deja Vu, Clothtique Santas, Mosa Porcelain and Rosie's House Guests.

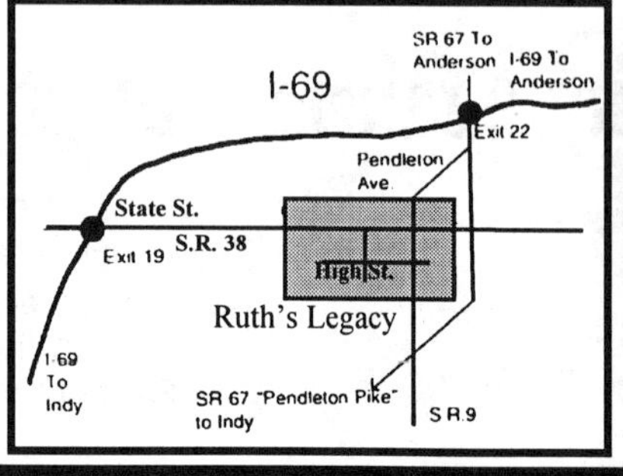

Liberty, IN #25

Mon - Fri 9 - 5
Sat 9 - 3

Stitching Nook

41 W. Union St. 47353
(765) 458-6443
Owner: Diana Bruns
Est: 1982 800 Bolts

100% Cotton Fabrics, Quilting Notions, X-Stitch, Framing, Classes, Machine Sales, and Friendly Personal Attention

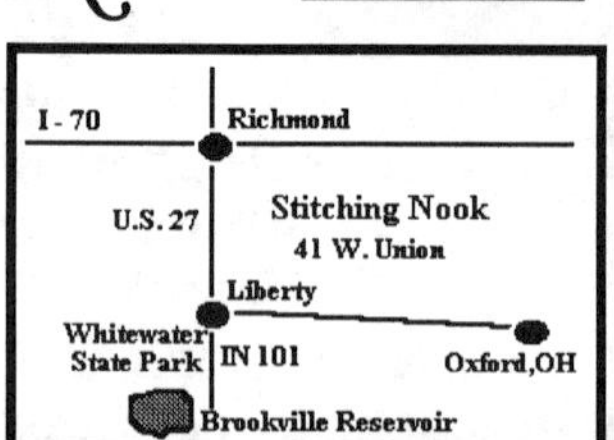

Liberty, IN #26

Mon - Fri 9 - 3
Sat 9 - 4
Or by Appt.

Pohlar Fabrics

6439 S. State Rd. 101 47353
(765) 458-5466 or (800) 357-3152
Owners: Kenny & Rose Pohlar
Est: 1984 1150 sq.ft.

Over 2000 bolts of brand name 100% cotton fabrics, sewing & quilting notions, books, patterns and ready made gifts. Machine Quilting.

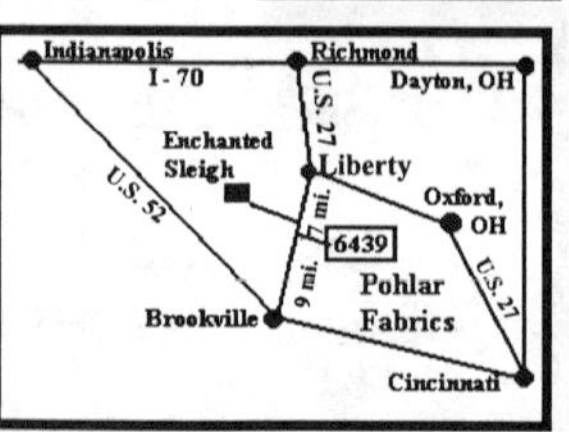

1748 E. 86th Street Northview Mall
46240 (317) 844-2446 or (800) 840-2241
Owners: Karen Loser & Jeanne Moosey
Est: 1978 2400 sq. ft. 3000 Bolts

Mon - Sat
10 - 5
Thurs til
8:30
Sun 12 - 4

Indianapolis, IN #27

Come in... visit us for a unique Quilt shop experience. Our staff of friendly, expert quilters is always ready to assist you with all your quilting needs.

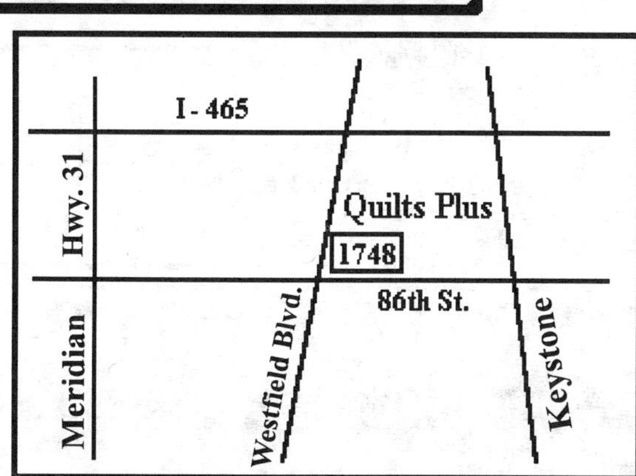

Quilt Quarters

2 Locations

3133 E. Thompson Rd.
46227
(317) 791-1336
Est: 1995
3000 sq.ft. 3000+ Bolts

Mon - Sat 10 - 5
Thur til 8:30

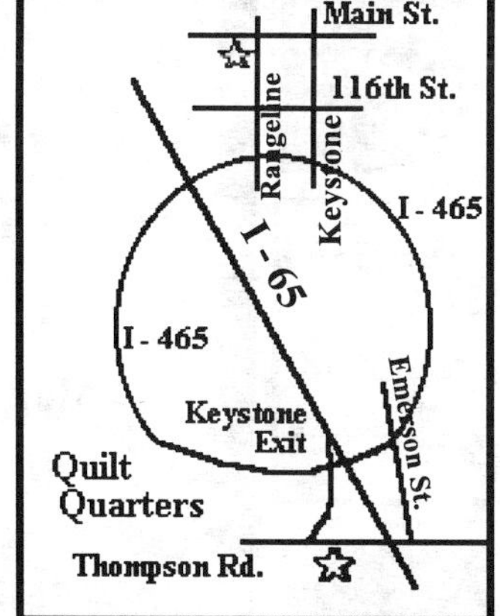

1017 W. Main
(317) 844-3636 46032
Owner: Kaye England
Est: 1989
4000 sq.ft. 4000+ Bolts

Mon - Sat 10 - 5
Thur til 8:30

Indianapolis, IN #28

Carmel, IN #29

Wonderful selection of traditional and non-traditional fabrics.
Bernina Sales and Service.
Patterns, Books, Notions, Stencils, Classes, Helpful Staff

Est: 1973 **Greenwood, IN #30** 4000 sq.ft.

The Back Door, Inc.

2503 Fairview Place #W 46142
(317) 882-2120
E-Mail: dttes@indy.net
Watch for our new Web Site
Owners: Linda Hale & Teri Dougherty

Mon - Thur 9:30 - 9
Fri 9:30-6 Sat 9:30 - 5
1st & 3rd Sundays Jan - Labor Day
All Sundays Labor Day to Christmas

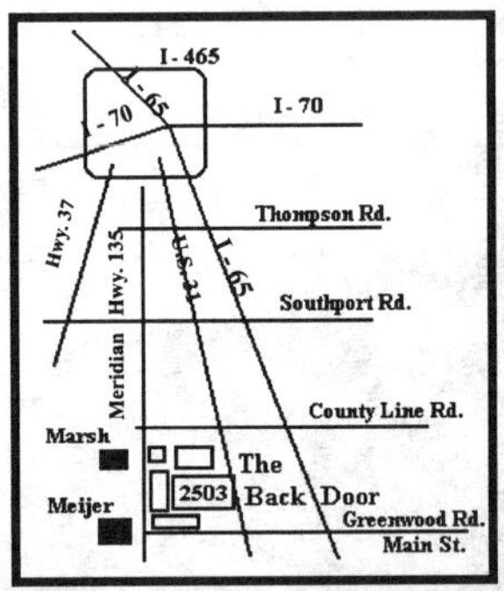

Full line of quilt supplies, bear and dollmaking, tolepainting, and many, many samples.
A Great place to shop!

Bloomington, IN #31

Mon 10 - 6
Tues - Sat
10 - 5

Fountain Fabrics

301 N. Morton St. 47403
(812) 333-1335

Full service quilt shop. Quilting fabrics and supplies plus books, patterns, notions, classes, and custom designed quilt projects.

1 Block NW of Courthouse Sq. Corner of 7th & Morton Sts. Located in the Historic Depot across from the Bloomington Antique Mall

Bloomington, IN #32

Mon - Sat
9 - 7
Sun 12 - 5

FABRIX

4027 W. 3rd St. 47404
(812) 339-2005
Owners: Tina & Charles Allgood
Est: 1997 3000+ sq.ft. 1900+ Bolts

Full service fabric shop with pre-cut quilt kits, notions and classes. Pfaff Dealer. Visit our Home Gallery of handcrafted products. Handicap Accessible

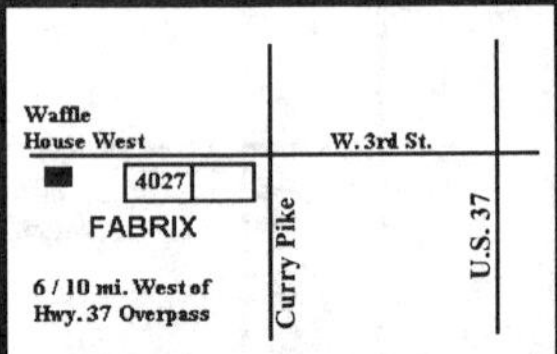

Washington, IN #33

Mon - Sat
10 - 5

The Stitching Post

400 East Main Street 47501
(812) 254-6063
Owner: Mary Dell Memering
Est: 1986 1500 sq.ft.

Southwest Indiana's largest selection of quality quilting fabrics--3000 bolts 100% cottons including Plaids & Hoffmans. Quilting supplies, notions, books, & patterns.

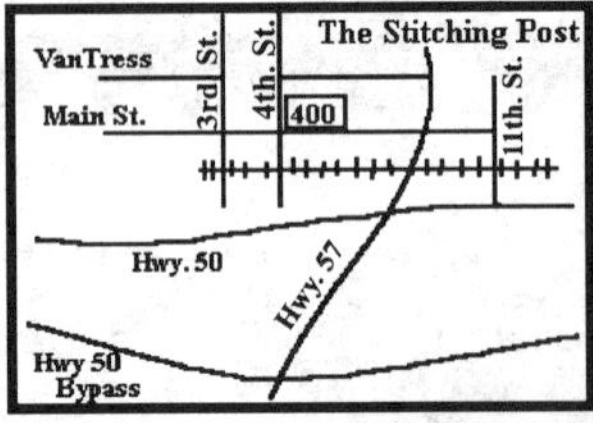

Montgomery, IN #34

Mon - Sat
Daylight
Hours

David V. Wagler's Quilts

R.R. 1 Box 73 450 E. 200 N.
(812) 486-3836 47558
Owners: David & Anna Wagler
Est: 1980 1900 sq.ft. 1500+ Bolts

Hand Made Quilts on display. Quilts made to order, applique, pieced, & wholecloth tops. 100% Cotton Fabrics, Stencils, Books, Patterns, Kits

Madison, IN #35

Mon - Fri
10 - 5
Sun 1 - 5

Margie's Country Store

721 W. Main St. 47250
(812) 265-4429
Owner: Marjorie Webb
Est. 1970 900 Bolts

Quality fabrics, books, patterns. Many samples to inspire you. Gracious service. Large line of gifts and home decorations.

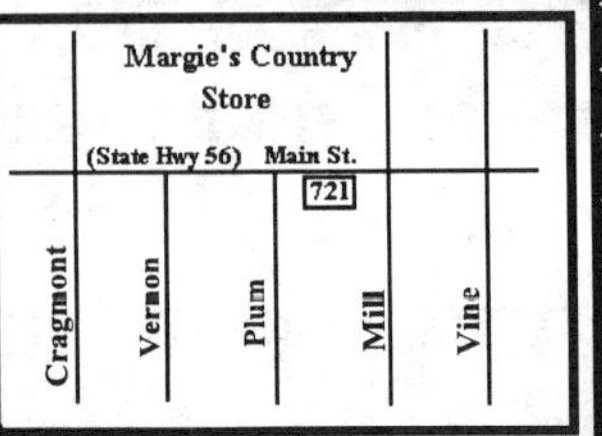

Terre Haute, IN #36

South 25th Street Fabrics

Mon - Fri 11 - 6
Sat 10 - 4

1031 S. 25th St. 47803
(812) 232-0299

* *

100% Cotton Fabrics

Mail Order Available
Sales!!
Babylock
Newsletter

* * * * * * * * * * * * * * * * *

IN STORE COUPONS

SEWING MACHINES NOT INCLUDED
$5.00 off / of $25.00 or more purchase
$10.00 off / of $50.00 or more purchase
$20.00 off / of $100.00 or more purchase

* * * * * * * * * * * * * * * * * * * *

1907 S. 3rd. St. (U.S. 41)
47802
(812) 232-0610
Owners: Basil & Chris Ave
Est: 1974

Mon - Fri
10 - 5
Sat 10 - 4

100% Cotton Fabrics, Quilting Patterns, Books,
Notions, Supplies, Quilting & Sewing Classes
Knowledgeable & Helpful Staff
Custom Monogramming
Sublimation and Screen Printing
Authorized Pfaff & Brother Dealer
Service on all makes sewing machines

Hullman
McKeen
1907
Quilts & More
Vorhees
U.S. 41
I - 70

1 mile North of I - 70 on U.S. 41

Terre Haute, IN #37

Rushville, IN #38

PRIDDY FABRICS

114 W. 2nd 46173 (765) 932-4717

♥ **5000 Calicos & Homespuns. Quilting & Applique Books, Stencils.**

♥ **Craft Patterns and Ceramic Buttons.**

♥ **Fashion & Bridal Fabrics, Notions, & Fashion Patterns.**

♥ **Nice Selection of Handmade Gift Items.**

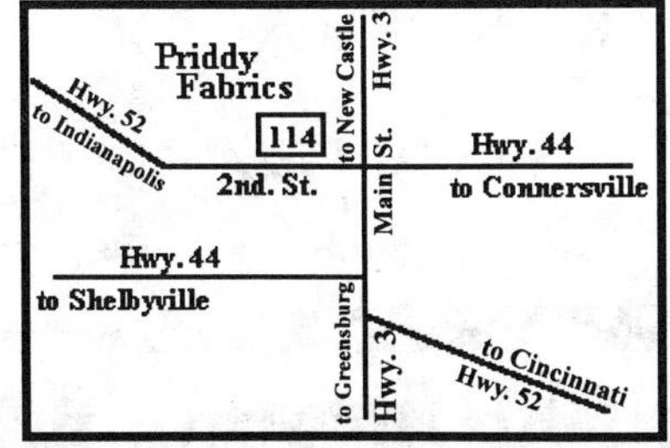

Owners:
Frances & Robert Priddy
Est: 1972
3130 sq.ft. 10,000 Bolts

Mon, Tues, Thur,
Fri, Sat
9 - 5
Wed 9 - 12

Boonville, IN #39

123 S. 2nd. St. 47601
(812) 897-5687
E-Mail: villagmerc@aol.com
Owners: Betty & Steve Cummings
Est: 1992 3000 sq.ft. 3000+ bolts

Mon - Sat 10 - 5 Thurs til 8

20 min. east of Evansville; 10 min. south of I - 64, exit 39
West side of the Historic Town Square

Turn of the century charm boasting a fantastic collection of 100% quilting cottons & homespuns. Hundreds of quilting books; patterns for quilts, critters & clothes; kits; silk ribbon supplies. Large selection of ceramic buttons; notions, stencils plus unique gifts for the quilt enthusiast. Quality crafts & antique consignment an added bonus. Be inspired by our many samples of wall hangings, clothing & critters. Kits available or to order on any project. Ongoing classes scheduled.

to Evansville
I - 64
Exit 39 at Lynnville
12 miles
BOONVILLE
2nd. St.
Main St.
The Village Mercantile
123
Courthouse Square
3rd. St.
Hwy 62
Locust St.

VICTORIA'S TEA ROOM

2nd Floor, Village Mercantile
Mon - Sat 11 - 3 & Thurs 5 - 8

Plan to join us for a delightful lunch, or come Thursday evening for a specially planned and prepared dinner. Scrumptious homemade everything, specializing in soups, desserts, hot grilled sandwiches, pasta salads, breads, flavored coffees & teas. Our chicken and tuna salads are the best. Have you ever tasted a Tomato Pie?

Plan to spend the day with us - You won't be disappointed!

Haubstadt, IN #40

Tues 2 - 8
Fri & Sat
10 - 4

Quilts n' Bloom

R.R. #1, Box 53 47639
(812) 768-6009
Owners: Kathy & Rick Will

Quilting supplies, Books, Patterns, quality cotton Fabrics, Classes, Featherweight Parts & Service, unique garden supplies, Shepherd Seeds, Country Setting & Flower Garden.

Water Tower
Maple St.
Quilts n' Bloom
Main St.
U.S. 41
Hwy. 68
I - 64
Exit 25

Evansville, IN #41

Quilter's Barn

Full service shop.
Fabrics, Classes, Books, Patterns. Specializing in beautiful handcrafted oak & walnut quilt frames, quilt racks, shelves and hangers. Quilt til the cows come home in a warm country atmosphere.

Tues, Thurs, & Sat
10 - 4

7915 Marx Rd. 47720
(812) 963-6336
Owner: Bettye J. Sheppard
Est: 1988

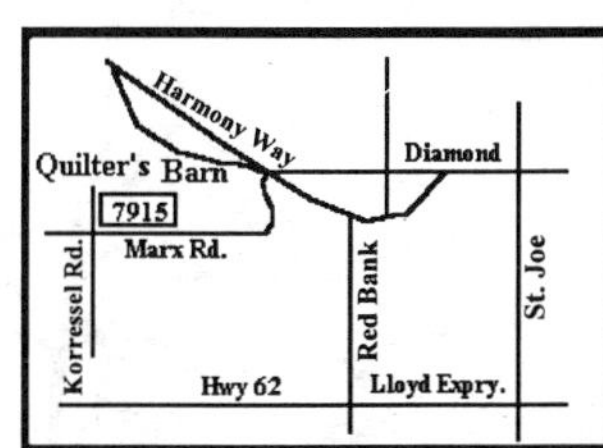

Indiana Guilds:

Anderson Evening Guild, 1112 North Dr., Anderson, 46011
Redbud Quilter's Guild, 111 E. 12th St., Anderson, 46016
Americus Quilting Club, P.O. Box 312, Battleground, 47920
Quarry Quilters, P.O. Box 975, Bedford, 47421
Bloomington Quilters, P.O. Box 812, Bloomington, 47402
Clay City Calico Quilters, Box 107, Clay City, 47841
Columbus Star Quilter's Guild, P.O. Box 121, Columbus, 47202
Conner Quilters Guild, 704 W. Third St., Connersville, 47331
Quilt Patch Quilt Club, 210 Elm St., Corydon, 47112
Heritage Quilters, P.O. Box 8, Crown Point,46307
Love 'N Stitches, 116 S. Muessing, Cumberland, 46229
Hendricks County Quilters Guild, Danville, 46122
Heartland Quilters, 55922 Channelview Dr., Elkhart, 46516
Calico Cut-ups, 10013 Teton Court, Fort Wayne, 46804
Crossroads Quilt Club, 3625 Amulet Dr., Fort Wayne, 46815
Qu-Bees Quilt Club, 1512 Irene Ave., Fort Wayne, 46808
Spring Valley Quilt Guild, 7164 W. Reformatory Rd., Fortville, 46040
Greenfield Guild, 3842 E. 200 S., Greenfield, 46140
Quilt Connection Guild, 2321 Willow Circle, Greenwood, 46143
Meets: 1st Thursday 7 p.m. at Community Church of Greenwood
Hill Valley Quilting, 607 W. Ralston, Indianapolis, 46217
IQ's, 3370 N. Highwoods Dr., Indianapolis, 46222
Quilt Connection Guild, 6630 Yellowstone Pkwy., Indianapolis, 46217
Meets: 1st Thursday 7 p.m. at Community Church of Greenwood
Quilter's Guild of Indianapolis, P.O. Box 50345, Indianapolis, 46250
Meets: 2nd Thursday 7 p.m. at Washington Township School Administration Center, 3801 E. 79th St.
Common Threads, Lafayette
Meets: 3rd Wednesday 7 p.m. at Hanna Comm. Ctr., 1201 N. 18th
Dune Country Quilters, P.O. Box 8526, Michigan City, 46360
New Paris Puzzle Quilters, 10729 CR 46, Millersburg, 46543
Hands All Around Quilt Club, 10729 CR 46, Millersburg, 46453
Carolina Quilters, 413 Conduit Rd., Mooresville, 46158
Evening Quilter's Guild, 4001 W. State Road 28, Muncie, 47303
Muncie Quilters Guild, 812 W. Cromer, Muncie, 47303
Pioneer Women of Brown County, P.O. Box 668, Nashville, 47448
Hoosier Favorite Quilters, 1715 Duart Ct., New Haven, 46774
Common Threads Quilt Guild, 5811 S. 500 W., New Palestine, 46163
Indiana Puzzle Quilt Club, 68535 CR 23, New Paris, 46553
Raintree Quilters Guild, P.O. Box 118, Newburgh, 47629
Meets: 1st Wednesday 6:30 at St. Theresa School, 700 Herdon Dr., Evansville
Spring Valley Quilt Guild, Pendleton
Meets: 1st Monday 6:30 p.m. at Pendleton Public Library
Stitch & Chatter Quilt Guild, 221 W. Seventh St., Portland, 47371
Piecemaker's Quilt Guild, 211 N. Main St., Salem, 47167
Sew-n-Sew Quilt Club, 19887 Alou Lane, South Bend, 46637
Vigo County Quilters Guild, 1907 S. 3rd St., Terre Haute, 47802
Randolph County Art Assoc., P.O. Box 284, Union City, 47390
String-along Quilt Guild, P.O. Box 2363, Valparaiso, 46384
Indiana State Quilt Guild, 3059 Sullivan, W. Lafayett, 47906
The Old Tippecanoe Quilt Guild, P.O. Box 707, W. Lafayette, 47902
Meets: 1st & 3rd Tuesday 7:15 p.m. & the Wednesday after at 9:30 a.m. at Morton Community Center, 222 N. Chauncey, North Lafayette
Spinning Spools Quilt Guild, 4111 CR 16, Waterloo, 46793

Other Shops in Indiana:

Berne	Hilty's Dry Goods Store, Hwy. 27 N	
Brazil	Dorothy's Quilts & Crafts, R.R. # 17	812-446-5502
Brownstone	Quilt N Baskets, 209 S. Sugar St.	812-358-2338
Farmland	Quilts & Quilting, Cty. Rd. 600 W	765-468-7052
Goshen	Calico Point, 24810 County Rd. 40	219-862-4065
Grabill	Country Shops, 13756 State	219-627-6315
Loogootee	The Fabric Shop, 219 1/2 N. JFK	812-295-3362
Lynnville	Betty's Quilts, 244 W. 3rd St.	812-922-3642
Madison	Joan's Quilts & Crafts, 115 E. Main St.	812-265-2349
Michigan City	Joann's Books, 718 Franklin St.	219-874-6402
Middlebury	Ctry Quilt Shoppe, 200 W. Warren	219-825-9309
Monroe	Wilmen's Country Store, 421 E 100 S	
Monticello	Needles in the Haystack, 116 N. Illinois	219-583-9332
Morrisville	Colonial Outlet, 490 E. St. Clair	317-831-0026
Nashville	Fabric Addict, 175 Old Schoolhouse	812-988-4993
Nashville	A Time to Remember, 145 E. Gould St.	812-988-8463
Odon	Hopes and Seams, 105 W. Main St.	812-636-4393
Richmond	The Fabric Shack, 1027 E. Main	765-962-4943
Salem	Craft Town, North Side of Public Sq.	812-883-6860
Shipshewana	Fabric Outlet, 440 S. Van Buren	219-768-4501
South Bend	Erica's Craft & Sewing Center, 1320 N. Ironwood	219-233-3112
South Bend	Whitney's Fabric Outlet, 1117 E. Ireland Rd.	219-291-0960
Vernon	Heritage Crafts, 23 E. Brown St.	812-346-7933
Wanatah	Prairie Point Quilt Shoppe, 213 N. Main	219-733-2821
West Lafayette	The Country Girl, 1185 Sagamore Pkwy. W.	317-497-1790
Zionsville	Liberty Farmhouse, 25 Cedar St.	317-873-1776
Zionsville	Country Corner, 70 E. Hawthorne	317-873-6728

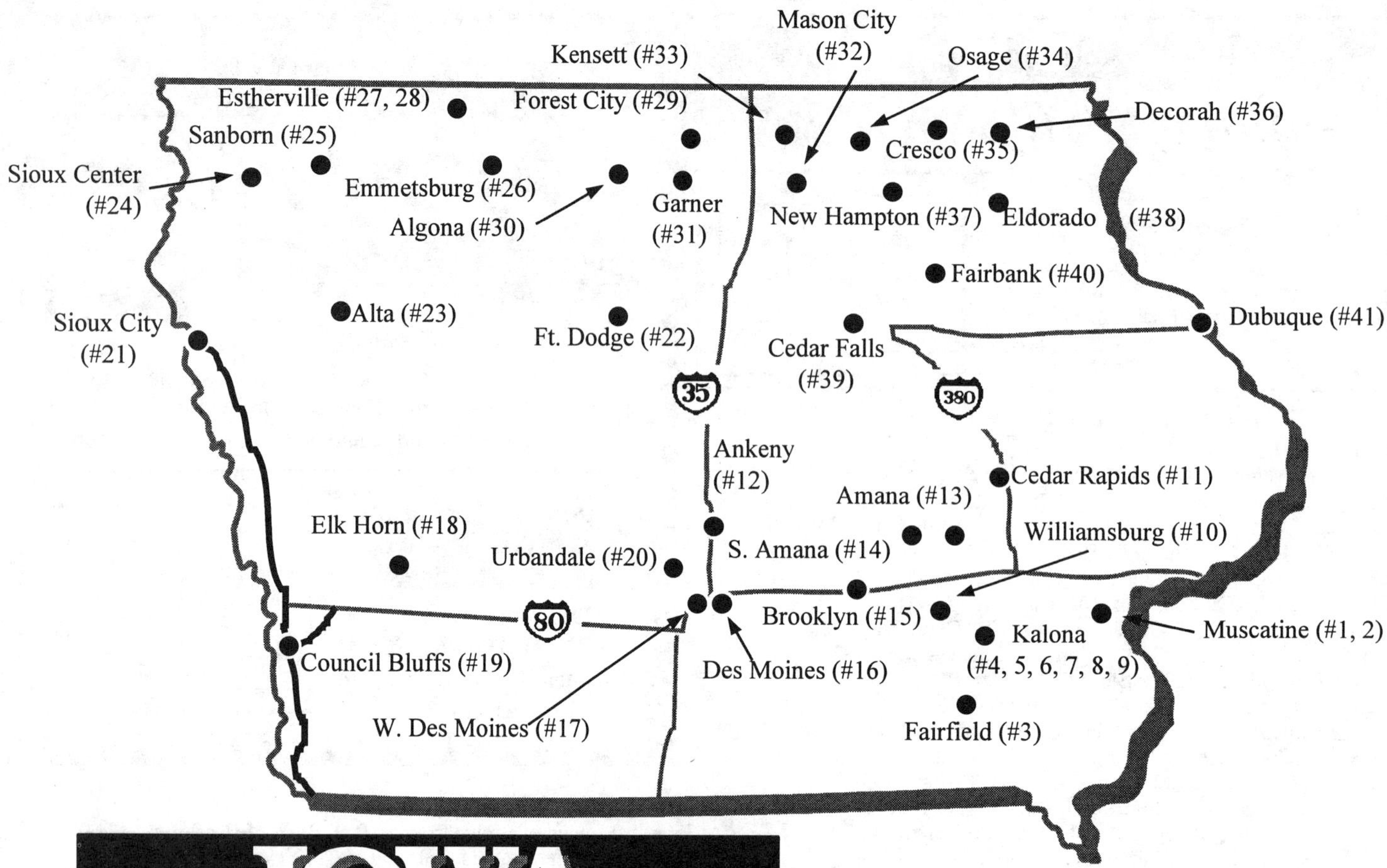

Mason City (#32)
Kensett (#33)
Osage (#34)
Estherville (#27, 28)
Forest City (#29)
Decorah (#36)
Sanborn (#25)
Cresco (#35)
Sioux Center (#24)
Emmetsburg (#26)
Garner (#31)
New Hampton (#37)
Eldorado (#38)
Algona (#30)
Fairbank (#40)
Sioux City (#21)
Alta (#23)
Ft. Dodge (#22)
Cedar Falls (#39)
Dubuque (#41)
35
380
Ankeny (#12)
Cedar Rapids (#11)
Amana (#13)
Elk Horn (#18)
Williamsburg (#10)
Urbandale (#20)
S. Amana (#14)
80
Brooklyn (#15)
Kalona (#4, 5, 6, 7, 8, 9)
Muscatine (#1, 2)
Council Bluffs (#19)
Des Moines (#16)
W. Des Moines (#17)
Fairfield (#3)

IOWA

41 Featured Shops

The Cotton Shop

Est: 1996

317 E 2nd St. 52761
(319) 262-5709
Owners: Sabrina Smith & Kathi Morgan

Mon - Fri 9 - 5:30
Sat 9 - 5

Muscatine, IA #1

A hands-on store offering classes & support for quilters & crafters. Fine 100% cotton fabrics, Kunin Felts, patterns, books, & handcrafted gifts.

Bypass 61
Hwy. 61
Hwy. 22
The Cotton Shop
9th - Washington
Walnut St.
Mulberry St.
Bus. 61
Park Ave.
Cedar St.
Sycamore St.
Iowa Ave.
2nd St.
Mississippi River

Muscatine, IA #2

Mon - Thur 9 - 5:30
Fri 9 - 8
Sat 9 - 5

Neal's Vacuum & Sewing Center

309 E. 2nd St. 52761
(319) 263-4543 or (800) 362-4543
Fax: (319) 263-8073 Est: 1951
E-Mail: nealssew@muscanet.com

Over 3000 bolts of fabric, books, patterns, and notions. Viking & White sewing machines and sergers. Lots of Personal Help!

Mulberry St.
Bus. 61
3rd St.
Walnut St.
2nd St.
Neal's
309
Rt. 22
Cedar St.
Mississippi Dr.
Mississippi River

Fairfield, IA #3

Mon - Sat 9 - 5

The Sewing Room

1903 Hwy. 34 W 52556
(515) 472-7540 (888) 793-2722
E-Mail: sewroom@kdsi.net
Est: 1989 Owner: Joann Fritz

2800 sq.foot, well lit, 3500 bolts quality fabrics, over 200 book titles. New Home sewing machines. Silk ribbon supplies. Handicap accessible.

The Sewing Room
1903
2.2 mi.
Town Square
Auto Mall
Hwy. 34
1/2 mile west of the Super 8 Motel

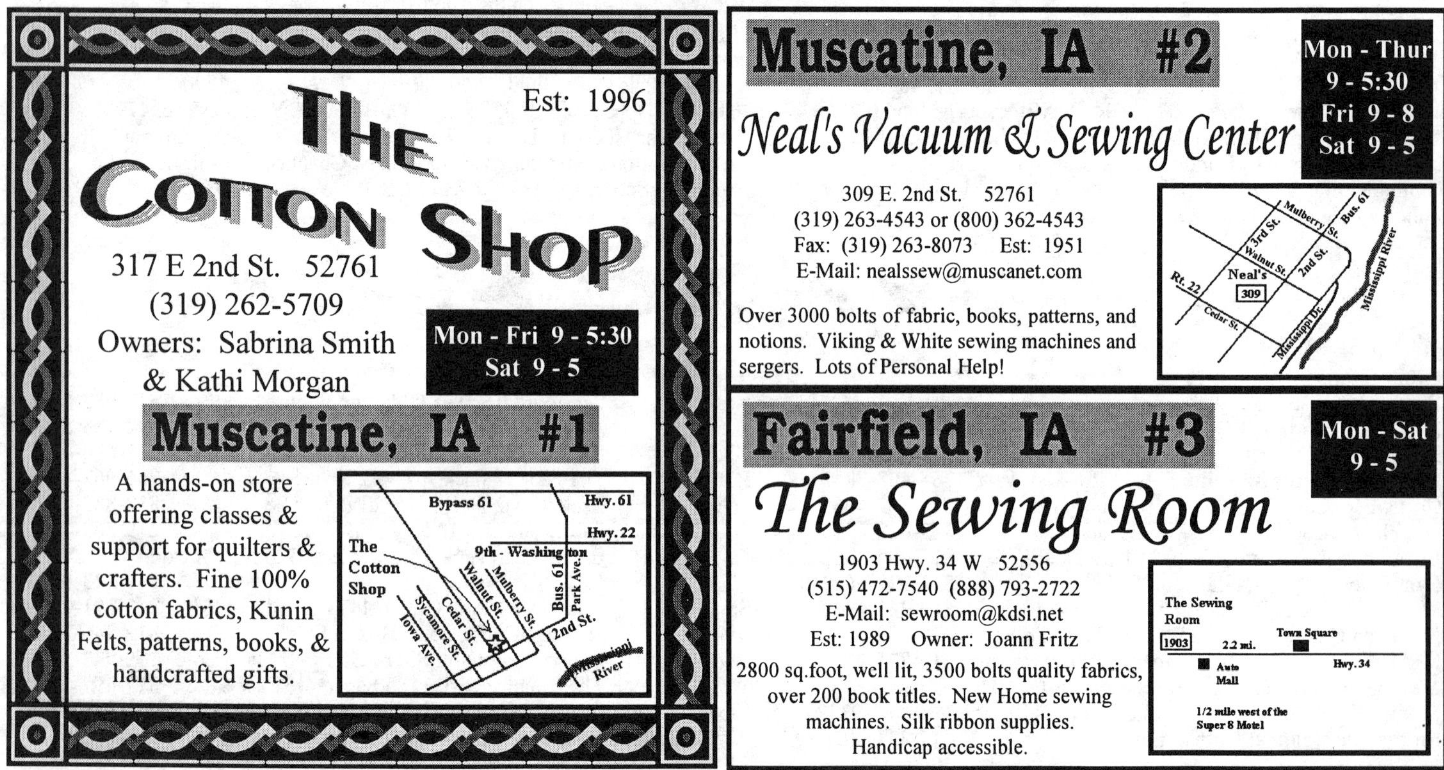

Kalona, IA #4

Mon - Sat 10 - 5

Woodin Wheel

515 "B" Ave. 52247
(319) 656-2240
Owner: Marilyn Woodin
Est: 1973

Downtown Kalona 5 Blocks off Highway 1

Over 250 New & Antique Quilts for Sale plus a Private Quilt Museum.

Kalona, IA #5

Mon - Fri 9 - 5 Sat 9 - 3 March - Oct Sat 9 - 5

Stitch 'n Sew Cottage

207 4th St. P.O. Box 351
(319) 656-2923 52247 Est: 1981
Owners: Dorothy, Paul & Cande Schumann & Niva Burkholder
"Where Ma Saves Pa's Dough"
Fabrics, Notions, Quilting Supplies Pillow Forms, Embroidery Supplies, batting. 1000+ Bolts

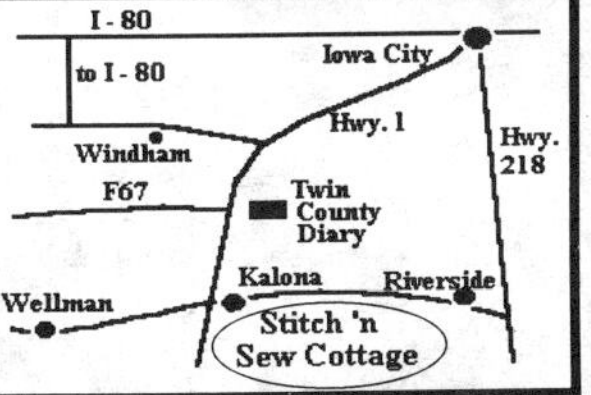

Kalona, IA #6

Mon - Sat 9 - 5

Kalona Kountry Kreations

2134— 560th St. S.W. 52247
(319) 656-5366
Owner: Sara M. Miller
Est: 1977 2500 sq.ft.

We have 5000 - 6000 bolts of fabric, both domestic & imported. Plus quilts, new & antique.

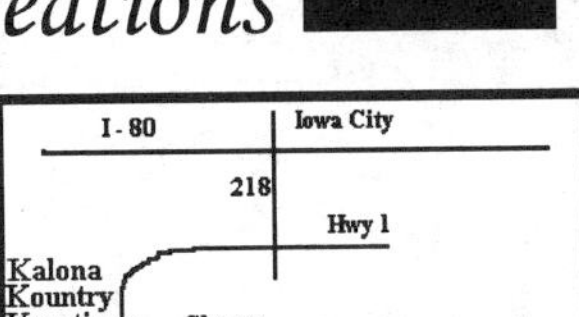

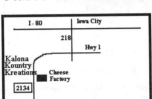

Kalona, IA #7

Mon - Sat 8:30 - 5 Thur til 7

Ellen's Sewing Center

405 "B" Ave., P.O. Box 252 52247
(319) 656-3303
E-Mail: colette@kctc.net
Est: 1975

Large selection of Quilt Books, Quilt Supplies, Fashion Fabrics. Bernina Machines & Supplies.

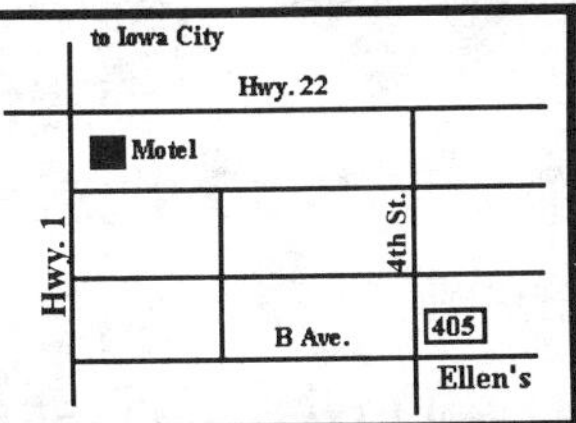

Kalona, IA #8

Mon - Sat 9 - 5

Willow Creek Collectibles

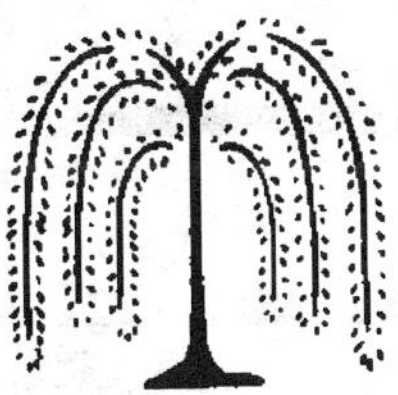

418 B Ave. 52247
(319) 656-3939
Owner: Juanita Troyer

Over 3000 Doll Craft Patterns, Hundreds of bolts of Homespun and novelty print fabrics.

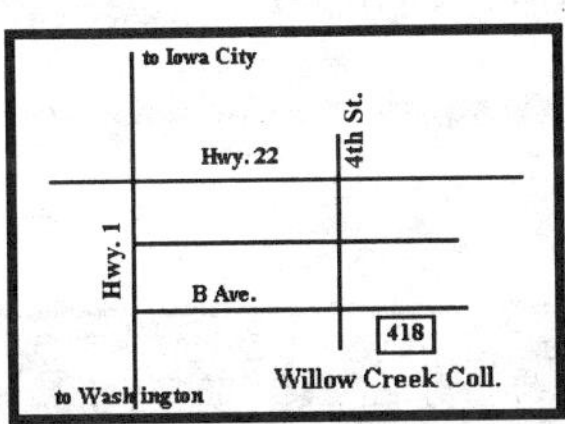

Kalona, IA #9

Mon - Sat 9 - 5 Evenings by Appt.

109 1st. St. Hwy 1 52247
(800) 233-4189 Est 1982

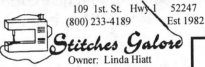

Owner: Linda Hiatt
Free Bi-Monthly Newsletter

Elna & Pfaff Dealer. Sewing instructors & supplies they use—includes quilting, smocking, tatting, Brazilian Emb & more.

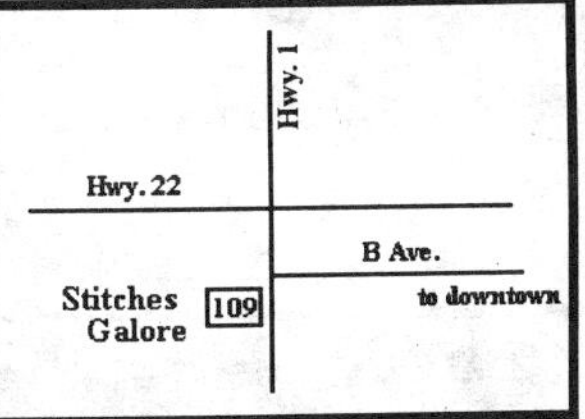

Rainbows & Calico Things

Wed - Sat 9 - 4 Other Times by Chance or Appt.

Homespun Fabrics, Books, Patterns, Notions, Rulers - Olfa Products, Battings, Electric Quilt Software & a great selection of 100% Fine Cottons (1000 bolts) by Hoffman, P&B, Benartex, Moda, RJR, Marcus and more.

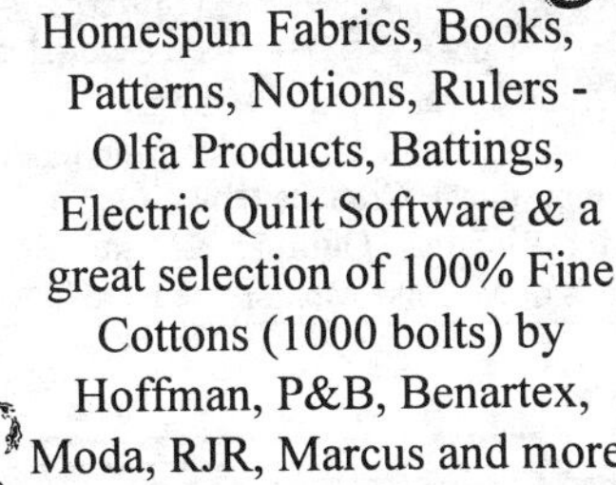

2811 240th St. 52361
(319) 668-1977
Owner: Barbara Wardenburg
E-Mail: barbaraw@avalon.net
Est: 1994 1100 sq.ft.
Web Site: www.avalon.net/~barbaraw/quiltshop.htm

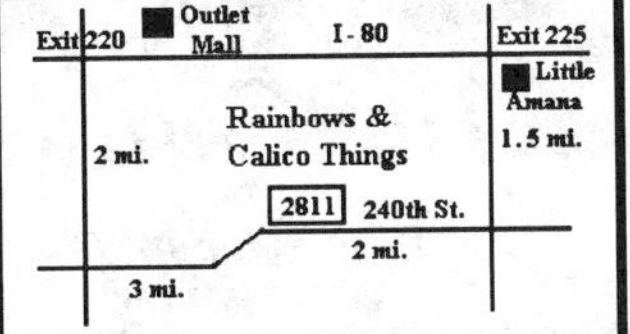

A unique shop located on a three generation farm just outside of historic Williamsburg, Iowa.

Williamsburg, IA #10

Cedar Rapids, IA #11

Mon - Fri 10 - 4:30 Sat 10 - 4

The Quilting B

224 Second St. SE 52401
(319) 363-1643
Owner: Beverly Thornton
Est: 1986 750 sq.ft.

Complete Line of Supplies & Notions. Doll and Santa Patterns Yarns for Santa Beards & Doll Hair. Finished items for sale.

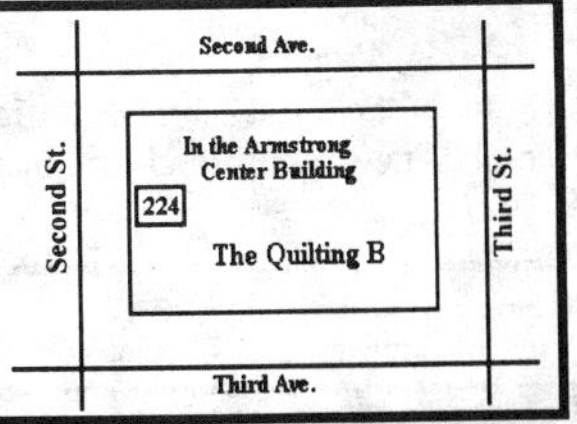

Ankeny, IA #12

Mon - Fri 10 - 5:30 Thur til 8 Sat 10 - 5 Sun 12 - 4

Country Clutter

305 S.W. Walnut St. 50021
(515) 964-2747 Est: 1985
Owner: Deb Heller Group Appts. Available

Cozy Quilt Shop featuring 800+ bolts of fabric, quilt books, counted cross-stitch, & 100's of doll patterns. We now offer many quilt notions & have a wonderful teaching staff including Jill Reber from Master Piece Products. **A Quilter's Dream!**

Hwy 69 Ankeny Blvd.
1st St.
I - 35
S.W. Walnut
S. W. Third
Under the Red Awnings
305 Country Clutter

Amana, IA #13

Open Daily
Mon - Sat
10 - 5
Sun 12 - 4

Heritage Designs
Needlework & Quilting

4517—220th Trail 52203
(319) 622-3887
Est: 1976
1200 sq.ft. 1200+ Bolts

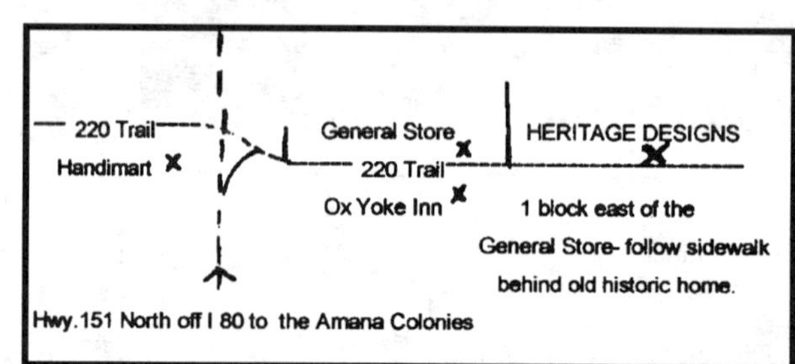

On the main street in the historic village of Amana, just off I - 80, an exclusive shop featuring unique quilting & needlework supplies & accessories.
Books, patterns, notions, ceramic buttons, cross-stitch and more.
Renowned for our fat quarter table & coordinated bundles!
Hoffman/Bali's - RJR - Moda - Benartex - Kaufman - Indo/wovens - Alexander Henry - Kona - M&M Fab/SSI - cherrywood/hand-dyed & others. Designer Favorites!

South Amana, IA #14

Mon - Sat
9:30 - 5
Sun 12 - 4

Fern Hill Gifts & Quilts

103 - 220th Trail 52334
(319) 622-3627 Fax: (319) 622-6382
Est: 1987 3400 sq.ft. 3000 Bolts

Relax & linger in our fabric loft with 3000 bolts of the latest fabrics. Antiques, antique quilts, new quilts and wallhangings await your arrival.

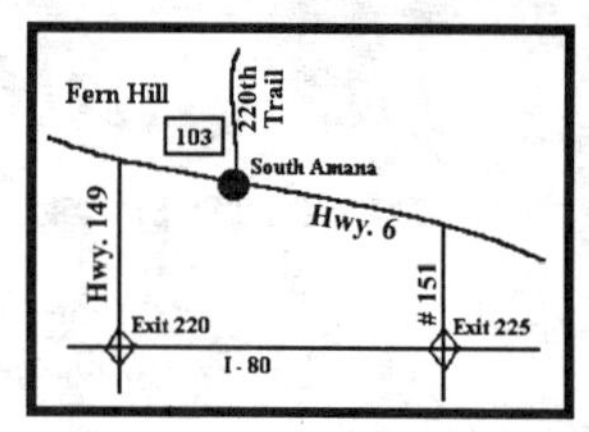

Brooklyn, IA #15

Mon - Sat
8 - 6

Coast to Coast

118 W. Front St.
52211
(888) 522-7712
Free Newsletter

12,000 yards of Quality Cotton Quilting Fabric (Debbie Mumm, Moda, Homespuns), Craft Patterns, Rubber Stamps, Silk Ribbon. Quilting & Craft Supplies. Lots of Models. Memory items & ideas.

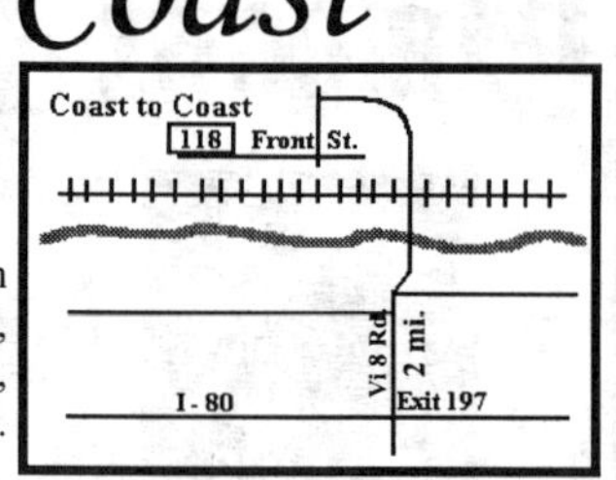

Des Moines, IA #16

Mon - Fri
10 - 5
Sat 10 - 4

Creative Sewing Center

3708 Ingersoll Ave. 50317
(515) 279-0019 Fax: Same
E-Mail: csew@earthlink.net
Owner: Lynda Charleston
Est: 1992 2500 sq.ft. 1200 Bolts

Large Selection of Fabrics, Books, Patterns, & Notions. Horn Cabinets, Euro-Pro Irons. Viking & White Sewing Machines & Sergers.

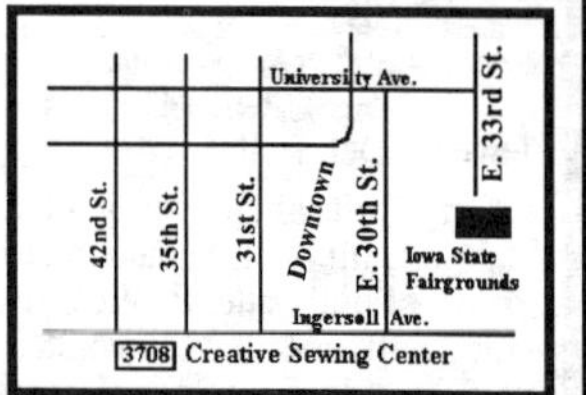

West Des Moines, IA #17

M -S 10 - 5
Thur 10 - 7
Sun 1 - 4

The Quilt Block

325 5th Street 50265
(515) 255-1010
Owner: Mary Miller
Est: 1987 3000 sq.ft. 2000 Bolts

Full line quilt supply store--fabrics, notions, books, patterns. Authorized Bernina dealer.

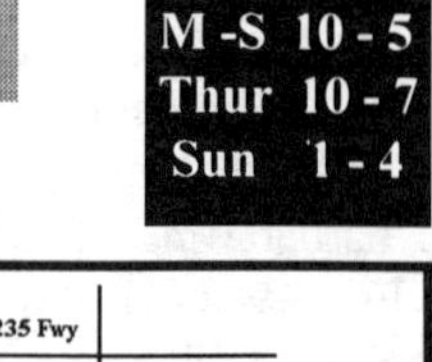
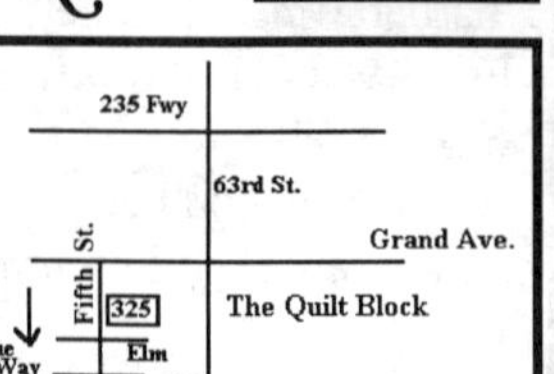

Elk Horn, IA #18

Prairie Star Quilts

4132 Main St. 51531
(712) 764-7012
Owner: Julie Larsen
Est: 1986 1500 sq.ft.

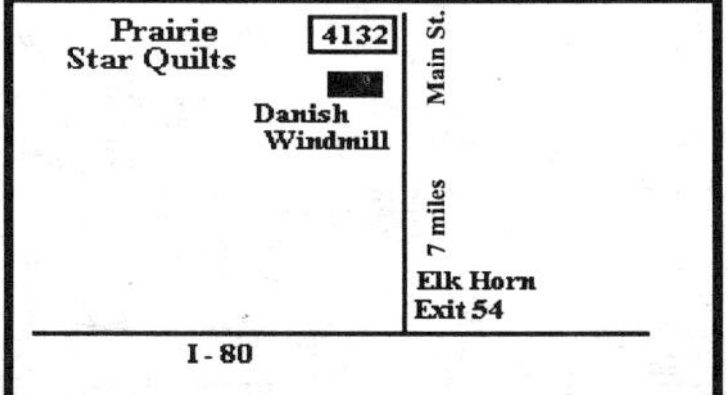

Mon - Sat
10 - 5

We Love Mail Order

Over 1500 bolts of 100% cotton fabric.
MODA, RED WAGON
HOFFMAN, MARCUS
THIMBLEBERRIES

Custom Machine Quilting

We specialize in flannels, home spuns & reproduction fabric. Also kits and original block of the month designs.

Council Bluffs, IA #19

Kanesville Quilting Gingham Goose

19851 Virginia Hills Rd. 51503
(712) 366-6003
Owners: Mavis Hauser & Karen Krause
Est: 1990 3000 sq.ft.

Spacious, well lit shop, filled with 100% cotton fabrics, books, patterns, notions, and the latest magazines. We do machine quilting on your tops. Our friendly staff are always ready to assist you with your quilting needs.

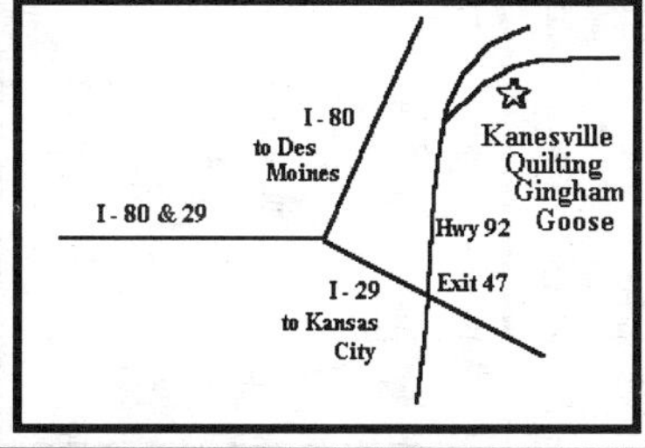

Mon - Fri
10 - 5:30
Sat 10 - 4

East on Hwy. 92

Urbandale, IA #20

Mon - Sun
9 - 5

Living History Farms

2600 N.W. 111th 50322
(515) 278-2400 24 Hr. Info. Line
Non-Profit Agricultural Museum

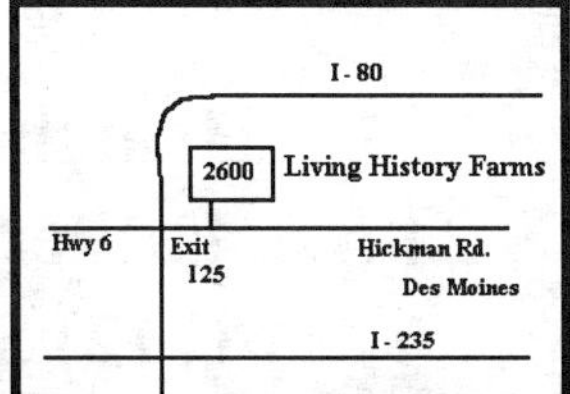

Our farm is a 600 acre, open-air farming museum. We display a portion of our collection of 300 quilts Oct. 1-4. Other gifts and crafts may be purchased in The Marketplace.

Fort Dodge, IA #22

Grandma's Quilts, Crafts & Needlework

1422—1st. Ave. North 50501
(515) 955-1521
Owner: Mary Consier
Est: 1987 2000 sq.ft. 4-500 Bolts

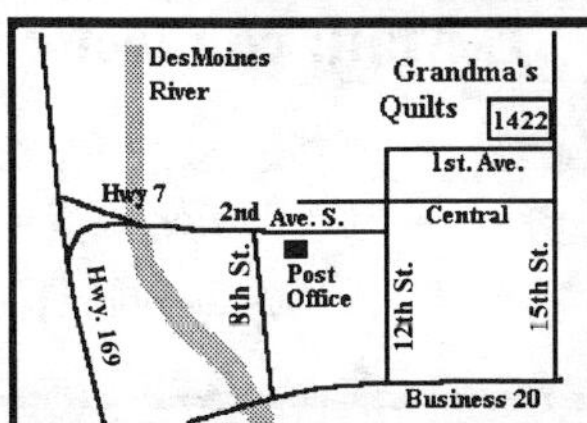

In a House built in 1896 with a black wrought iron fence. We carry crafts, fabric, and lots of books and patterns. We also carry yarn.

Heart & Hand Dry Goods Co.

Sioux City, IA #21

1551 Indian Hills Dr. 51104 (712) 258-3161
Owners: Ann Brouillette & Lerlene Nevaril
Est: 1996 2000 sq.ft. 1200 Bolts

Mon - Fri 10 - 5:30
Thurs til 8 Sat 10 - 5

We feature an antique-filled atmosphere that compliments the quilting fabrics, patterns & books, sewing notions, gift items and greeting cards. Mail orders, swatch service, newsletter & machine quilting available.

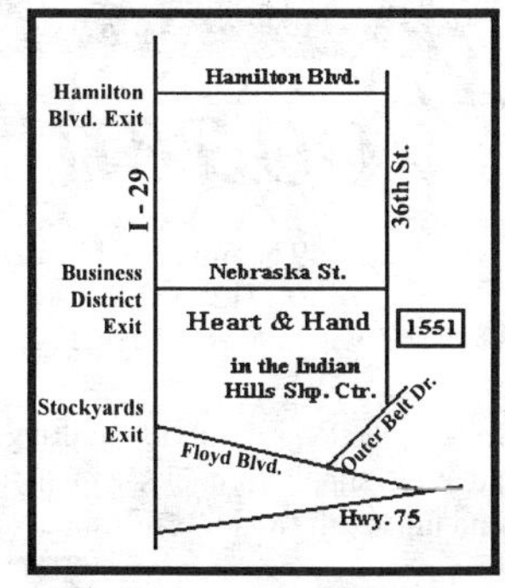

Alta, IA #23

Mon, Tue, Thur, Fri 9:30 - 5:30
Thur til 8
Sat 9:30 - 3

The Quilt Shoppe

206 S. Main 51002
(712) 284-2724
Owner: Pat Patten
Est: 1987 1200 sq.ft.

All cotton fabrics, books, patterns, notions, classes. Consignments welcome. Personalized helpful service for all your quilting needs.

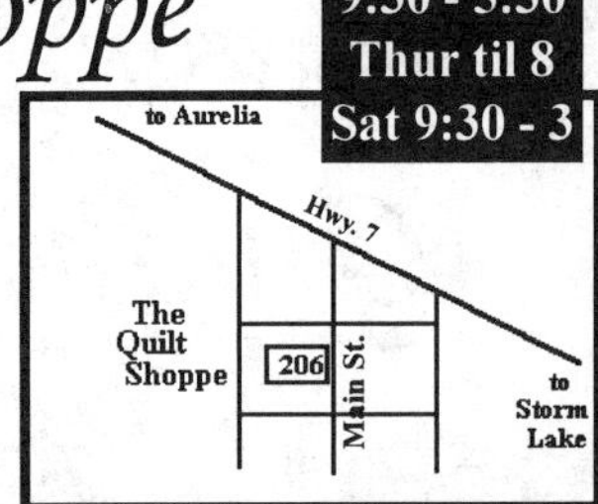

Sioux Center, IA #24

Mon - Sat 9 - 5:30
Thur til 9

Roelofs

24 3rd St. NW 51250
(712) 722-2611
Owner: Dixie Roelofs
Est: 1976 2000 sq.ft.

Quilting Fabrics & supplies; Fabric craft patterns and supplies; wall hanging kits; hemstitched flannel receiving blankets ready for crochet edge.

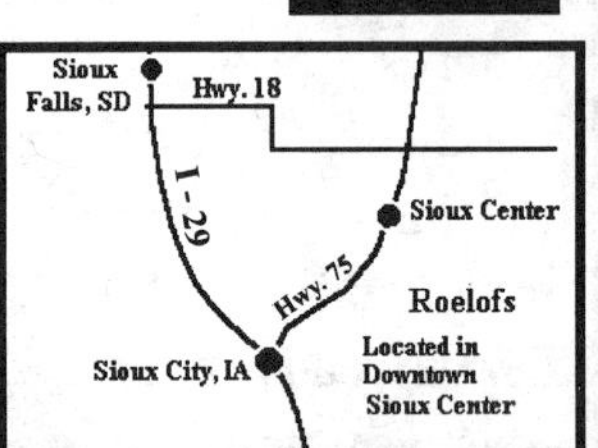

Sanborn, IA #25

Tues - Sat 10 - 5:30

Quilter's Coop

6063 - 280th St. 51248
(712) 736-2204
Owner: Judy Flanagan
Est: 1992 1280 sq.ft. 800 Bolts

Cotton Fabrics, Notions, Patterns & Books, Original Patterns, Country feel in an old Chicken Coop.

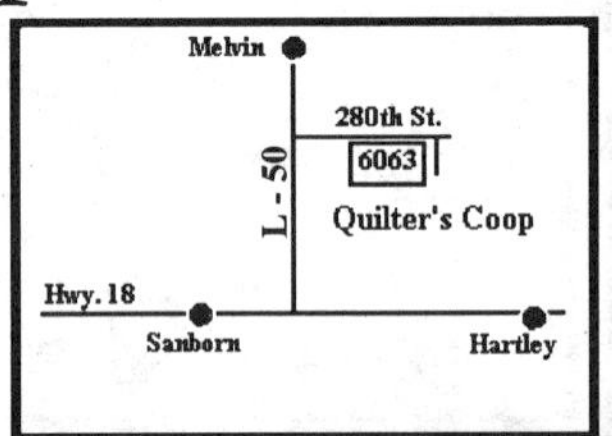

Emmetsburg, IA #26

Mon - Sat 9 - 5
Thur til 8

Calico Cupboard

2201 Main St. 50536
(712) 852-2098
Owner: Deborah Hite
Est: 1981 2500 sq.ft. 700 Bolts

Large selection of quilting fabrics, notions, books, quilt & craft patterns and stencils. Great classes and friendly service !

Calico Cupboard
2201
Broadway
Hwy 4 & 18
U.S. Hwy 18
Corner of Hwys 4 & 18 - downtown Emmetsburg
Hwy 4

Estherville, IA #27

Mon - Sat 9 - 5
Thur til 8

Wooden Thimble

9 N. 5th St. 51334
(712) 362-2561
Owner: Mary Hart Est: 1984

Large selection of fabric, quilting, cross-stitch and craft supplies, books and patterns. Many hand made gifts and lots of friendly service.

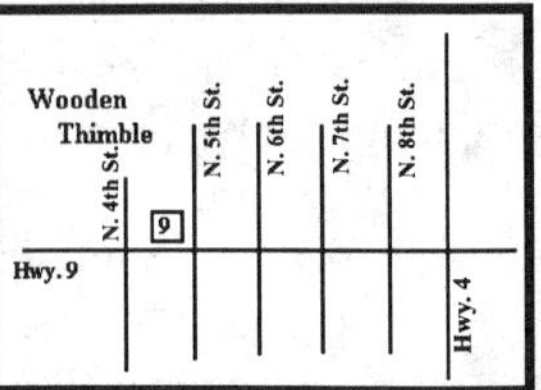

Heartland Americana

Shop Estherville's original 1910 City Hall & Fire Station building where you find three "open levels" housing a wonderful *Quilt Shop, Gift Shop,* and *Gallery* with custom framing.

Our full service Quilt Shop has over 2000 bolts of 100% cotton fabrics by Hoffman, Benartex, South Seas, Marcus Brothers, Mission Valley, P&B, Red Wagon, Dan River, RJR, Monarch and many others. A great place to buy your next quilt book (250+ titles) along with patterns, books and notions.

Bernina Sales & Service
Come in and sew on one of our Berninas, *(you can't beat our prices)*
Many classes offered throughout the year.

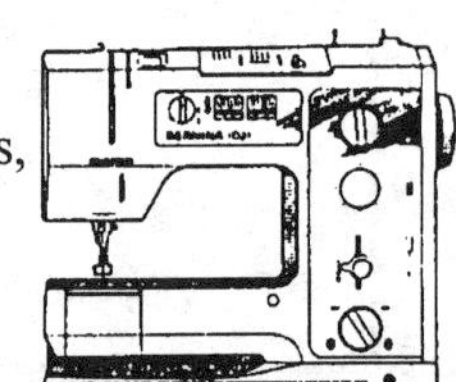

Join **"Fabric Express"** (our fabric club), and swatches of our newest fabrics will be delivered to you each month. Also receive:

* 20% birthday discount & other discounts!
* a free pattern of your choice in December
* complimentary yard card with subscription
* monthly freebies and other perks!!

Annual membership is $21.00 (Includes tax).

We accept Visa, Mastercard, & Discover!!

Open 9-5:30 M-F,
Thur. until 8 pm, Sat until 5 pm

Heartland Americana
24 S 6, Estherville, IA 51334
(712) 362-2787
Toll Free (888) heartld

 # 28

Visit our web site at www.heartlandamericana.com

E-Mail: connect@heartlandamericana.com

(located 1 block South of library square, across from the Dairy Queen!)

We welcome tour buses and mail orders!!

North Iowa's Newest Quilt Shop!

109 N. Clark St., Forest City, IA 50436
(515) 582-2438

Forest City, IA #29

Professional Machine Quilting
Wide Variety of Fabrics & Patterns
Pre-packaged Fabric Kits & Bundles
Favorite Quilting Accessories
Quilting Classes
Frequent Buyer Club

Enjoy our local Victorian Tea Room, Gourmet Coffee & Dessert Shops & Other Specialty Stores!

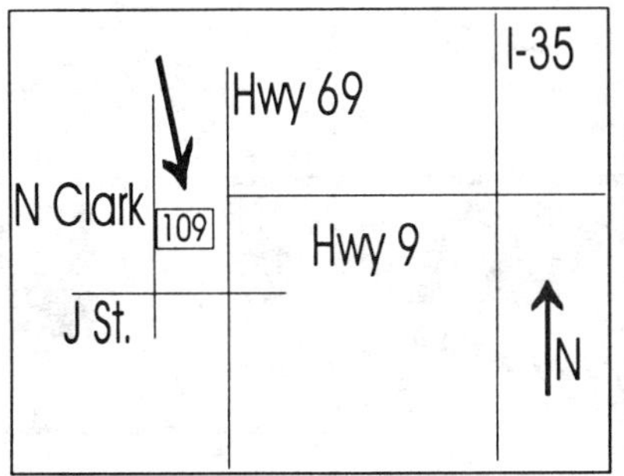

"We look forward to meeting you!"

Owners:
Roz Hemberger
Manette Lamping
Shelley Robson
Established: 1998

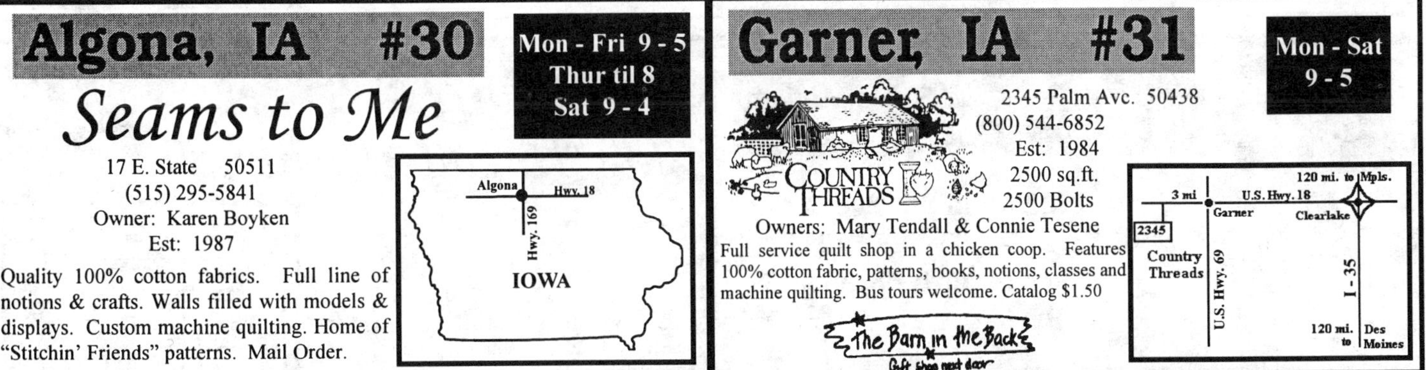

Algona, IA #30
Mon - Fri 9 - 5
Thur til 8
Sat 9 - 4
Seams to Me
17 E. State 50511
(515) 295-5841
Owner: Karen Boyken
Est: 1987
Quality 100% cotton fabrics. Full line of notions & crafts. Walls filled with models & displays. Custom machine quilting. Home of "Stitchin' Friends" patterns. Mail Order.
Algona
Hwy. 18
Hwy. 169
IOWA
Garner, IA #31
Mon - Sat
9 - 5
2345 Palm Ave. 50438
(800) 544-6852
Est: 1984
2500 sq.ft.
2500 Bolts
Country Threads
Owners: Mary Tendall & Connie Tesene
Full service quilt shop in a chicken coop. Features 100% cotton fabric, patterns, books, notions, classes and machine quilting. Bus tours welcome. Catalog $1.50
The Barn in the Back
Gift shop next door
3 mi
U.S. Hwy. 18
120 mi. to Mpls.
Garner
Clearlake
2345
Country Threads
U.S. Hwy. 69
I - 35
120 mi. to Des Moines

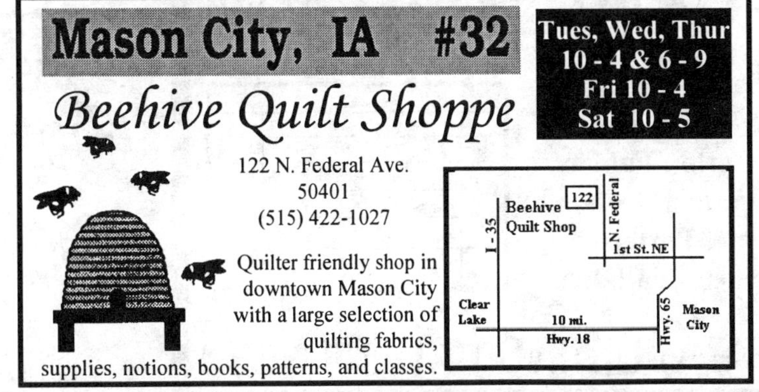

Mason City, IA #32
Tues, Wed, Thur
10 - 4 & 6 - 9
Fri 10 - 4
Sat 10 - 5
Beehive Quilt Shoppe
122 N. Federal Ave.
50401
(515) 422-1027
Quilter friendly shop in downtown Mason City with a large selection of quilting fabrics, supplies, notions, books, patterns, and classes.
Beehive Quilt Shop
122
N. Federal
I - 35
1st St. NE
Clear Lake
10 mi.
Hwy. 18
Hwy. 65
Mason City

Kensett, IA #33

Tues - Fri 9 - 5 Sat 9 - 3

Heart & Sew Quilts

908 Maple St. 50448
(515) 845-2234
Owner: Holly Adams

1895 Cottage in the Country.
Handmade quilted items, miniature to bed sizes.
Wallhangings, Santas, Valances, Vests,
Ornaments, Books & more.

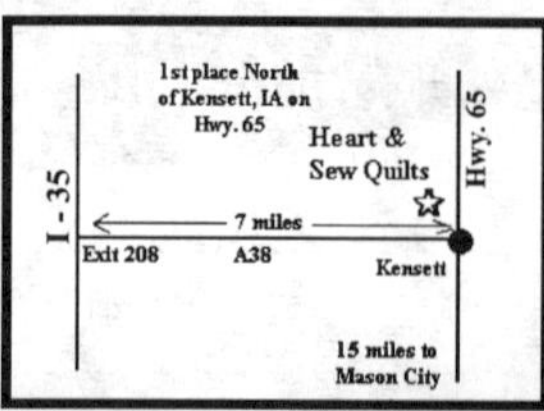

Osage, IA #34

Mon - Sat 9 - 5 except Fri til 6

The Fabric Shoppe

705 Main St. 50461
(515) 732-3669
Owner: Pam Schaefer - Smith
Est: 1988 1900 sq.ft.

Over 3000 bolts quality 100% cotton fabrics. Large selection of books, patterns, & notions. Classes. Well worth the trip!

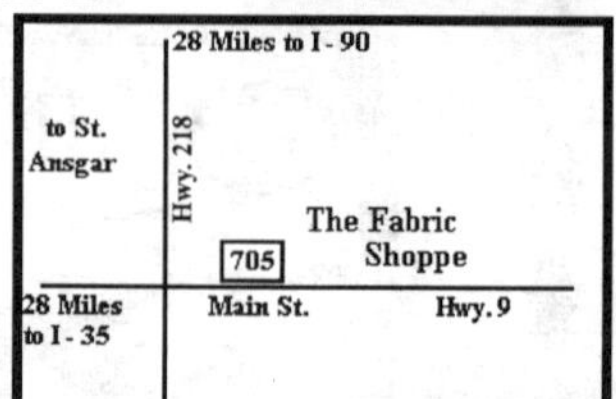

Cresco, IA #35

Tues - Fri 10 - 5 Sat 10 - 4

Just A Little Something

105 2nd Ave. SW, Hwy 9 52136
(319) 547-5064 Est: 1997
Owner: Crystal D. Monson
Web Site: New in March '98

Great Selection of Quality Fabrics. Books, Patterns, Notions. Old Fashioned Friendly Service. Bernina Sewing Machines Sales & Service. Quilting Classes.

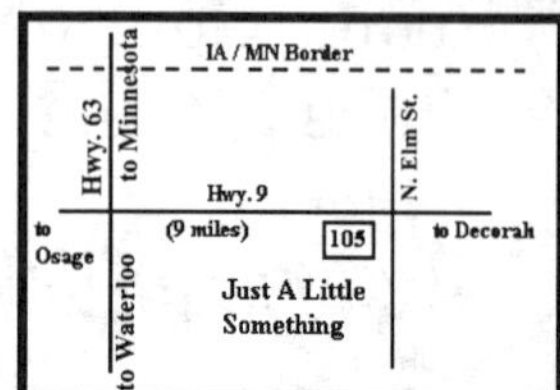

Decorah, IA #36

Mon - Fri 9 - 5 Thur til 9 Sat 9 - 4

The Sewing Basket, Inc.

519 W. Water St. 52101
(319) 382-4401
Owner: Darlene Frana

Quilting Fabrics, Notions and Books. Classes held throughout the year. Viking Sewing Machines Sales and Service.

New Hampton, IA #37

Mon - Fri 9 - 5:30 Thurs til 8 Sat 9 - 5

Material Magic

22 E. Main 50659
(515) 394-2461

Large selection of 100% cotton fabrics, books, patterns & quilting supplies. Custom machine quilting. Hand-made crafts. Classes offered.

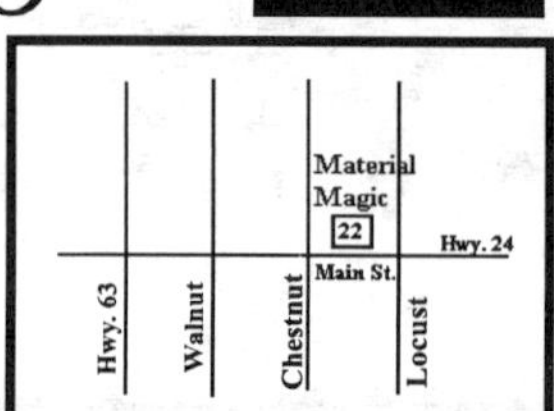

Eldorado, IA #38

Mon - Sat 7 - 6

Eldorado Store

29014 State St. P.O. Box 1 52175
(319) 422-3097
Est: 1996 2800 sq.ft. 1250 Bolts

An original store since 1880
where you will find a great selection of current Thimbleberries, flannel, Moda, Marcus and others.

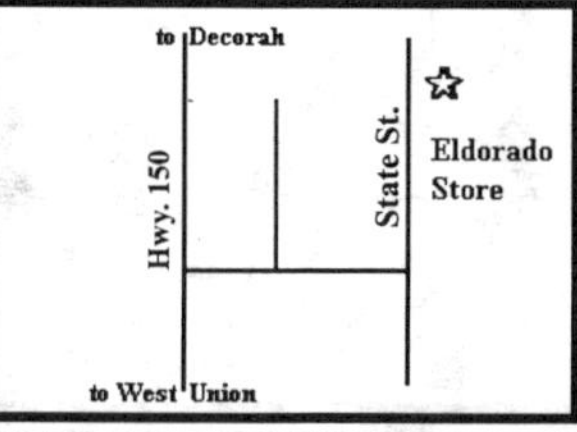

Cedar Falls, IA #39

Tues - Sat 10 - 5

212 Main St. 50613
(319) 277-8303 Est: 1993
Owners: Marlys Kauten & Barbara Newcomer

THE QUILT EMPORIUM

Full Service Shop.
Featuring—2000 Bolts of 100% Cotton Fabric
Large Supply of Notions, Books, & Patterns
Mail Order Available.

Downtown
1st. St.
IA 57
2nd. St.
212 Quilt Emporium
3rd. St.
4th St.
5th St.
Washington
Main St.
State

A GREAT QUILTING EXPERIENCE!

Fairbank, IA #40

Mon - Sat 9 - 5

Jo's Thread & Thimble

105 Grove St. 50629
(319) 635-2119
Owner: Jo Haberkamp
Est: 1974 2500 sq.ft.

N.E. Iowa's finest quilt shop. Very large selection of fabrics, notions, patterns, books, and quilting supplies.
Quilted Gift Items Also.

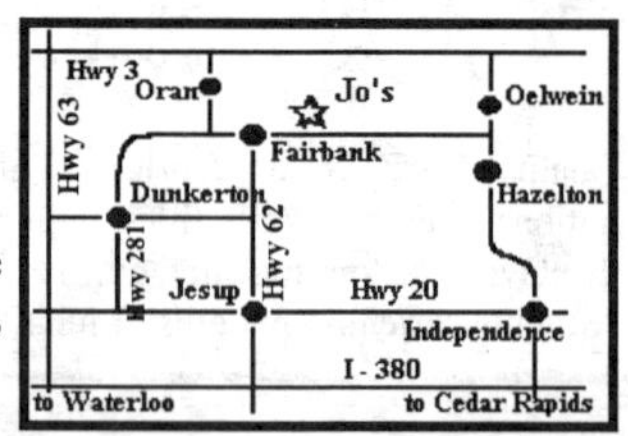

Dubuque, IA #41

Tues - Sat 10 - 5

Bluff Street Sampler

392 Bluff St. 52001
(319) 588-4106
Owners: Marlys Kauten & Barbara Newcomer

Located on Bluff Street in the heart of historic Dubuque.
Quilting Supplies Galore.

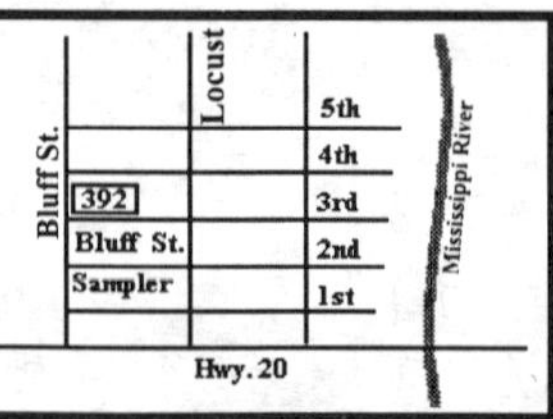

Iowa Guilds:

Quilt Sew-ciety, 206 S. Main, Alta, 51002
Meets: 1st Wednesday 7 p.m.
at Lakeside Presbyterian Church, Storm Lake

Ankeny Area Quilters Guild, P.O. Box 961, Ankeny, 50021
Meets: 2nd Tuesday 7 p.m.
at Neveln Community Center, 320 SW Schat St.

East Iowa Quilters, P.O. Box 1382, Cedar Rapids, 52406

Cherokee Quilt Batts, 217 S. 9th St., Cherokee, 51012

Lake Area Quilter's Guild, Clear Lake
Meets: 1st Thursday 7 p.m.
at City Hall Community Room

Mississippi Valley Q. G., P.O. Box 2636, Davenport, 52809

North Star Quilt Guild, Estherville
Meets: 2nd Monday at Public Library

Fort Dodge Area Quilters, P.O. Box 881, Fort Dodge, 50501
Meets: 2nd Tuesday 7 p.m.
at Senior Citizen Center, 118 N. 12th St.

Iowa Quilter's Guild, Box 65, Garden City, 50102

Fabricators, Gilbert
Meets: 3rd Monday
at Gilbert Luthern Church, 135 School St

Old Capitol Quilters Guild, Iowa City

Quilting for Fun, 1305 Yewell St., Iowa City, 52240

North Iowa Quilters Guild, P.O. Box 1163, Mason City, 50402
Meets: 2nd Wednesday

Northeast Iowa Quilter's Guild, P.O. Box 43, Monona, 52159

Melon Patchers, P.O. Box 1286, Muscatine, 52761
Meets: 4th Thursday 7 p.m.
at Grace Lutheran Church, 2107 Cedar St.

Clip & Stitch Quilters Guild, c/o Material Magic,
22 E. Main, New Hampton, 50659
Meets: 3rd Monday at New Hampton Community Center

Sioux Prairie Quilters, 1689 2nd Ave. SE, Sioux Center, 51250
Meets: 1st & 3rd Monday (Sept - May)
and once a-month (June - Aug.)

Siouxland Samplers, P.O. Box 162, Sioux City, 51102
Meets: 2nd Monday at 7 p.m.
at Council Oaks Community Center

Four Seasons Quilt Guild, P.O. Box 178, Sloan, 51055

Kountry Quilter's, Wellman, 52356
Meets: 3rd Monday 7 p.m.
at Wellman Catholic Church, small fun group

Des Moines Area Quilt Guild, 6222 University Ave.
West Des Moines 50265
Meets: 4th Tuesday 1 or 7 p.m.
at WDM Methodist Church

Iowa Country Heartland Quilters, Williamsburg
Meets: 3rd Monday 7 p.m.
at Presbyterian Church on Hwy 149

Other Shops in Iowa:

Altoona	Back Door Fabrics, 106 2nd St. S.E.	515-967-2321
Amana	The Gingerbread House, Main St.	319-622-6346
Anamosa	Cristy's Design Quilting & Crafts, 122 E. Main	319-462-4195
Boone	Memory Lane, 715 Carroll St.	515-432-3222
Burlington	The Sew 'N Sew Shop, 3206 Division	319-752-5733
Burlington	Sandi's Sewing Connection, 415 S. Roosevelt Ave.	319-752-2226
Cedar Rapids	West Side Sewing Machine Shop, 418 First St.	319-365-3075
Chariton	Ben Franklin Quilt Shop, 907 Braden Ave.	515-774-2496
Chariton	The Sampler, 102 S. Grand	515-774-2116
Conrad	Conrad General Store, 101 N. Main St.	515-366-2043
Corydon	J's Nook, 105 S. Franklin	515-872-2709
Creston	Knits & Other Notions, 209 W. Montgomery	515-782-8874
Davenport	Frankies Sew & Sew Center, 901 E. Kimberly Rd.	319-391-2010
Davenport	Jensen's Antiques, 2017 13th St.	319-322-4905
Denison	Memory Lane Fabrics, 28 N. Main St.	712-263-8383
Des Moines	Bartlett's Quilts, 820 35th St.	515-255-1362
Dubuque	Dubuque Sewing & Vacuum, 3430 Dodge	319-588-1308
Fayette	Country House Cottons, P.O. Box 375	319-425-4384
Fort Madison	Catricia's Needles 'N Brushes, 713 Avenue G	319-372-9270
Griswold	Quilting Party, 442 Main St.	712-778-2332
Humbolt	Janice's Keepsake, 19 6th St. S	515-332-5683
Indianola	Stitching Place, 110 W. Ashland Ave.	515-961-5162
Iowa City	Textiles Inc., 109 S. Dubuque St.	319-339-0410
Iowa Falls	Sewing Machine Co., 520 Washington Ave.	515-648-2379
Kalona	Country Livin', 1369 Hwy. 1	319-656-3773
Kalona	Yoders Antiques, 432 B Ave.	319-656-3880
Keokuk	Fabric Boutique, 606 Main St.	319-524-2932
Keokuk	Stitch N Crafts, 114 Bel Air St.	319-524-9593
Keosauqua	La Donna's Quilting Shop	319-592-3666
Marion	Connie's Quilt Shop, 785 8th Ave.	319-373-9455
Marion	Sanctuary Antiques, 801 Tenth St.	319-377-7753
Monona	Suhdrons's The Mall, 120 W. Center	319-539-2135
New Market	Helen's Quilting Boutique, R.R. #1, Box 228	712-585-3678
Newton	Nina's Quilt Patch, 213 W. 2nd St. N	515-791-2272
Oelwein	Louann's Fabrics, 21 E. Charles	319-283-5165
Ottumwa	Homespun Traditions, 1111 N. Quincy	515-682-6136
Ottumwa	Calico Connection, Rural Route 6	515-682-1197
Parkersburg	The Stitchery, 903 Muller	319-346-1691
Pella Vande	Lune Fabrics, 701 Franklin St.	515-628-3350
Postville	Sudron's Fabrics, 138 W. Greene	319-864-3919
Red Oak	The Country Heart, 210 Coolbaugh	712-623-3927
Red Oak	Quilting on the Square, R.R. #3	712-623-3884
Rudd	Laughing Lady Quilt Shop, 416 Chickasaw St.	515-395-2638
Sheldon	Sheldon Fabric, 301 9th St.	712-324-4598
Sigourney	In My Sewing Room, 104 E. Washington St.	515-622-2212
St. Olaf	Country Calico, R.R. #1, Gunder Rd.	319-783-2445
Storm Lake	Country Stitches, 1122 N. Lake Ave.	712-732-5419
Strawberry Point	Keppler Krafts, 35536 Hwy. 13 N	319-933-6069
Volga	Crazy Little Quilt Shop, 510 Washington St.	319-767-4125
Waukon	Joyce's Quilt Lodge, 920 2nd St. NW	319-568-4188
Webster City	Gingerbread House, 309 Bank St.	515-832-1492
West Des Moines	Donna's Dolls & Country Collections, 234 5th St.	515-274-2522

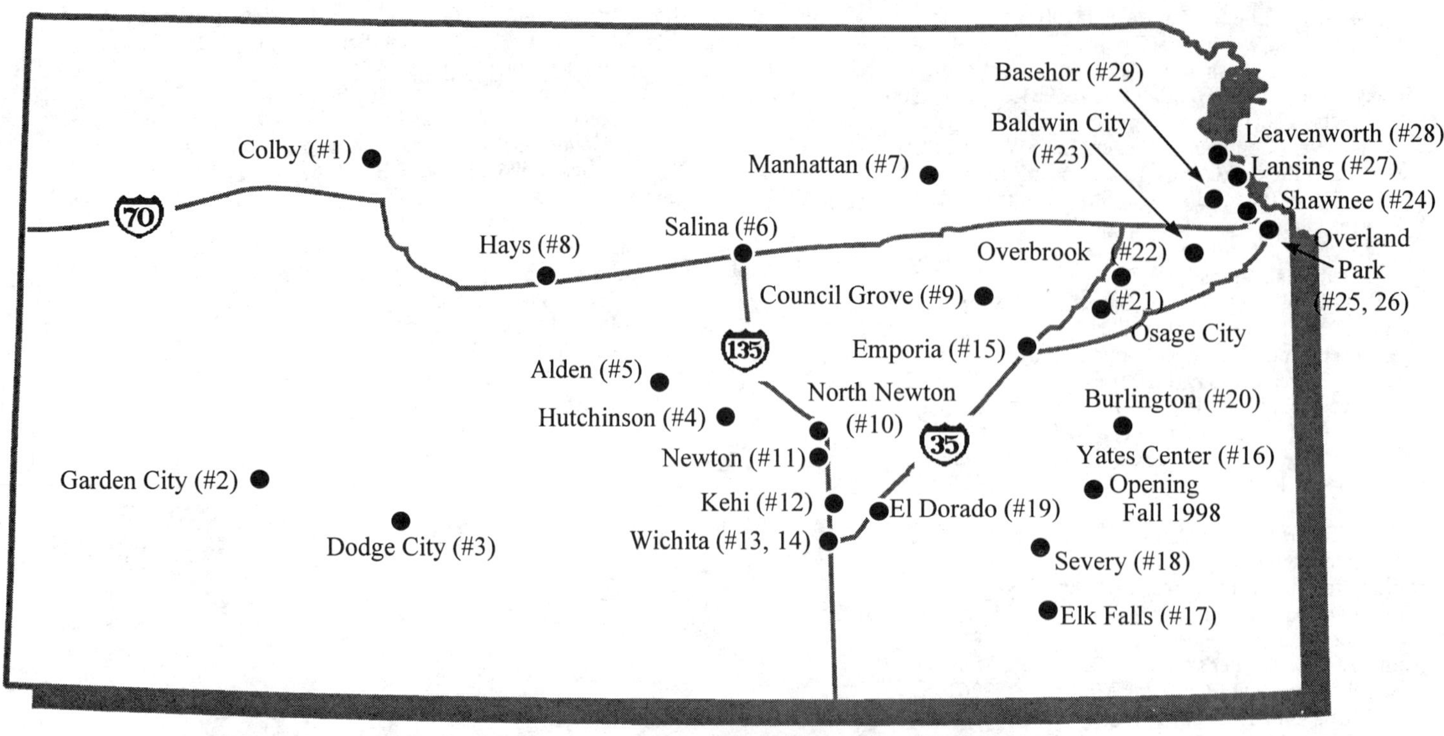
Colby (#1)
Garden City (#2)
Dodge City (#3)
Hutchinson (#4)
Alden (#5)
Salina (#6)
Manhattan (#7)
Hays (#8)
Council Grove (#9)
North Newton (#10)
Newton (#11)
Kehi (#12)
Wichita (#13, 14)
Emporia (#15)
Yates Center (#16)
Elk Falls (#17)
Severy (#18)
El Dorado (#19)
Burlington (#20)
(#21)
Overbrook (#22)
Baldwin City (#23)
Shawnee (#24)
Overland Park (#25, 26)
Lansing (#27)
Leavenworth (#28)
Basehor (#29)
Osage City
Opening Fall 1998
70
135
35

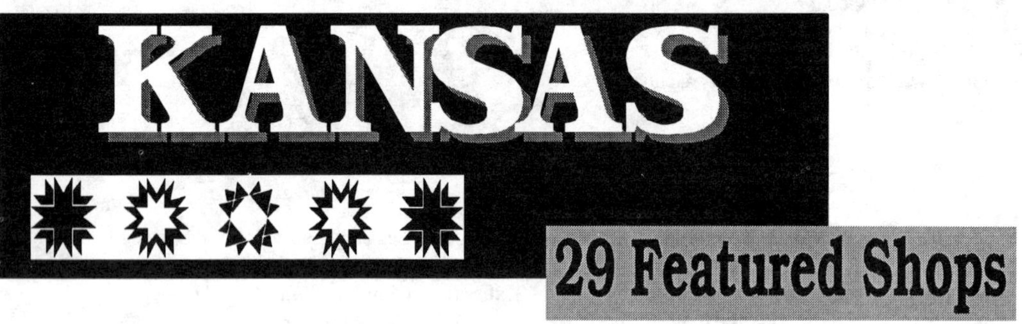
KANSAS
29 Featured Shops

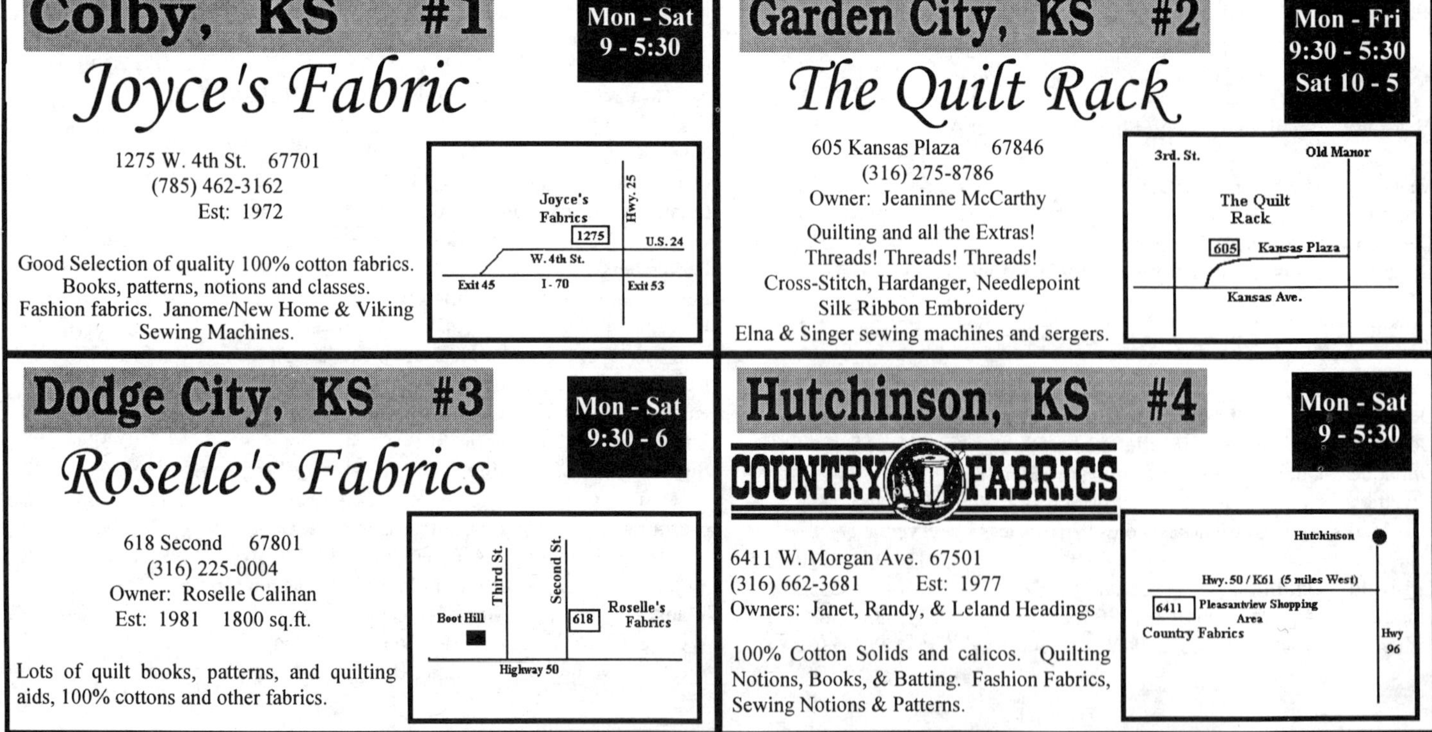
Colby, KS #1
Mon - Sat 9 - 5:30
Joyce's Fabric
1275 W. 4th St. 67701
(785) 462-3162
Est: 1972
Good Selection of quality 100% cotton fabrics. Books, patterns, notions and classes. Fashion fabrics. Janome/New Home & Viking Sewing Machines.
Joyce's Fabrics
1275
Hwy. 25
U.S. 24
W. 4th St.
Exit 45
I - 70
Exit 53
Garden City, KS #2
Mon - Fri 9:30 - 5:30 Sat 10 - 5
The Quilt Rack
605 Kansas Plaza 67846
(316) 275-8786
Owner: Jeaninne McCarthy
Quilting and all the Extras!
Threads! Threads! Threads!
Cross-Stitch, Hardanger, Needlepoint
Silk Ribbon Embroidery
Elna & Singer sewing machines and sergers.
3rd. St.
Old Manor
The Quilt Rack
605
Kansas Plaza
Kansas Ave.
Dodge City, KS #3
Mon - Sat 9:30 - 6
Roselle's Fabrics
618 Second 67801
(316) 225-0004
Owner: Roselle Calihan
Est: 1981 1800 sq.ft.
Lots of quilt books, patterns, and quilting aids, 100% cottons and other fabrics.
Third St.
Second St.
Boot Hill
618
Roselle's Fabrics
Highway 50
Hutchinson, KS #4
Mon - Sat 9 - 5:30
COUNTRY FABRICS
6411 W. Morgan Ave. 67501
(316) 662-3681 Est: 1977
Owners: Janet, Randy, & Leland Headings
100% Cotton Solids and calicos. Quilting Notions, Books, & Batting. Fashion Fabrics, Sewing Notions & Patterns.
Hutchinson
Hwy. 50 / K61 (5 miles West)
6411
Pleasantview Shopping Area
Country Fabrics
Hwy 96

Prairie Flower Crafts

27 years collecting cotton fabric for quilts.

Large selection of RJR, Thimbleberries; Hoffman; Bali; South Sea Imports; Clothworks by Fabric Sales Co.; Kona Bay; P&B Fabrics; Benartex; Liberty of London, Etc.

Alden, KS #5

205 Pioneer St.
67512-0158
(800) 527-3997
E-Mail:
PrFlrCraft@aol.com
Owner: Sara Fair Sleeper
Est: 1970 5370 sq.ft.

Mon - Sat 10 - 4:30

Salina, KS #6

Mon - Fri 9:30 - 5:30
Thur til 6:30
Sat 9:30 - 5

Quilting Bee

120 S. Santa Fe 67401
(785) 823-9376
Owner: Shirley Wolf
Est: 1979 4000 sq.ft.

4000 Square Feet devoted to cotton quilting fabrics, notions, books, and classes. All major fabrics, lots of plaids. 3500 bolts.

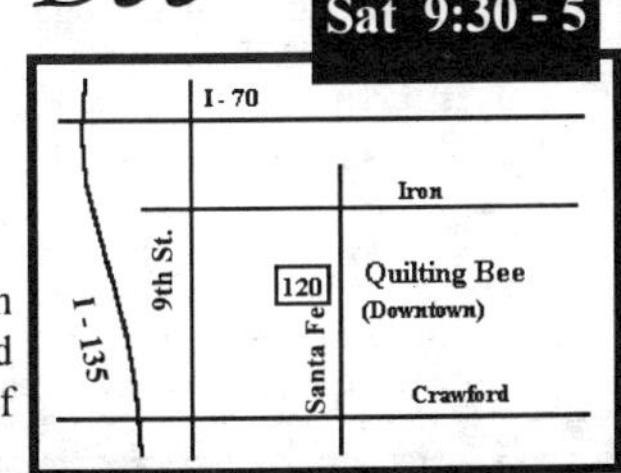

Manhattan, KS #7

Mon - Fri 11 - 5:30
Thur til 7
Sat 10 - 4

Ideas Unlimited Quilt Shop

523 South 17th 66502
(785) 539-6759
Owners: Dorine & Stan Elsea
Est: 1987 1500 sq.ft. 3000 Bolts

Unique fabrics for quilts & fashions. Large selection of books & patterns for quilts and pieced garments.

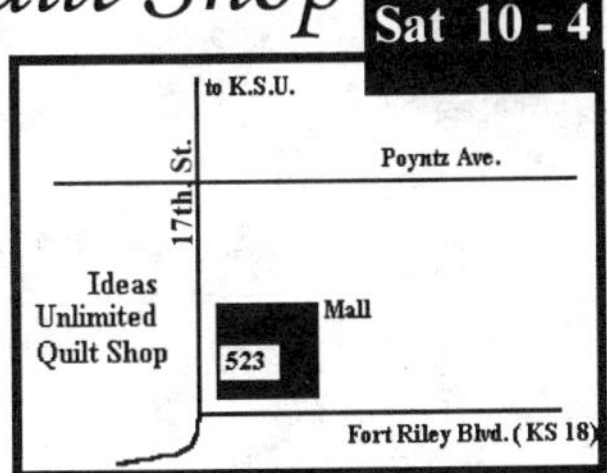

Hays, KS #8

Quilt Cottage Co. & Cross Stitch, Too!

Mon - Fri 9 - 5:30
Sat 10 - 3

202 Centennial Center (corner of Centennial and Vine) 67601

(785) 625-0080

Est: 1994 3000 sq.ft. 1400 - 1500 Bolts
Owners: Debbie Huebner & Kari Schultz

Top quality quilting fabrics.
The area's finest selection of books, patterns and notions.
Cross-stitch fabrics, patterns & DMC floss.

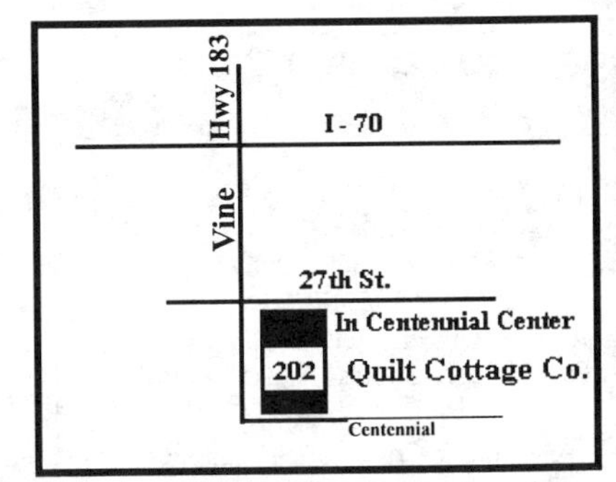

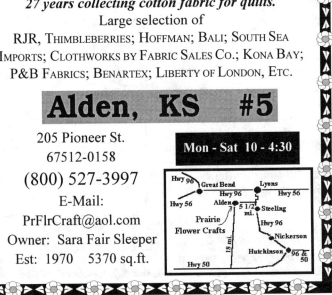

Council Grove, KS #9

Mon - Sat
10 - 5

Prairie Pieces

217 W. Main St. 66846
(316) 767-6628
E-Mail: twoquilt@midusa.net
Owner: Toni Steere
Est: 1990 1500+ Bolts

Full line quilt shop. Hoffman, Moda and other fabric lines. Gift items and antiques. Small town service with a smile.

The Quilt Shop, Ltd.

2511 N. Main • N. Newton, Ks 67117

Owners: Laura Flaming & Wilma Schmidt
Est: 1988 1120 sq.ft. 3000 Bolts
(316) 283-2332

Mon - Fri 9 - 5
Sat 9 - 1

Wide choice of fabrics, books, patterns & notions. Experienced, friendly shop. Personnel offer help and extend a warm welcome.

Exit 34
I - 135 to Wichita
27th
The Quilt Shop
2511
N. Main
24th

North Newton, KS #10

Newton, KS #11

Charlotte's Sew Natural

Fabrics • Patterns • Buttons
Trims • Notions • Classes

710 N. Main
67114

(316)
284-2547

Owner: Charlotte Wolfe

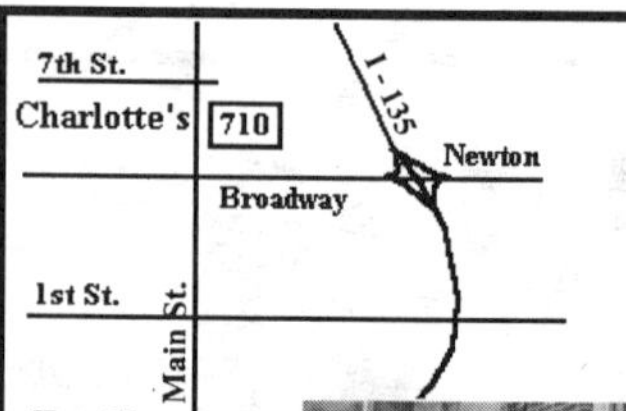

Mon - Fri
9:30 - 5:30
Thur til 8
Sat 9:30 - 5

Specializing in beautiful fashion fabrics: cotton rayon linen wool.

Kechi, KS #12

Mon - Sat
10 - 5

Kechi Quilt Shop

200 E. Kechi Rd., P.O. Box 357 67067
(316) 744-8500
Owners: Janet Robinson & Shirley Padding
Est: 1996 1000 Bolts

A cozy little shop situated in the "Antique Capital of Kansas"
Cottons, stencils, books, patterns, notions.

to Kansas Coliseum
Kechi Quilt Shop
200
Exit 14
61st. N
2 mi.
I - 135
to Wichita

Wichita, KS #13

Mon - Sat
9:30 - 5

Gramma's Calico Cupboard

1945 S. Hydraulic 67211
(316) 264-0274
Owner: Betty Webb
Est: 1982 3500 sq.ft. 5200 Bolts

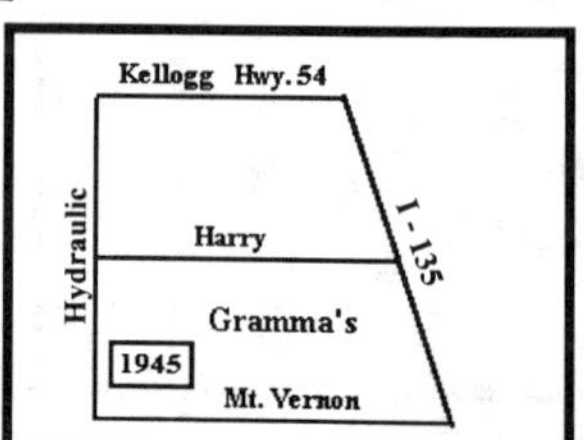

Quilting & Craft fabric & supplies.
Christmas room open all year.
Antiques, gifts including Muffy Vanderbear.

Wichita, KS #14

Prairie Quilts

Mon - Fri
9 - 6
Sat 9 - 5:30

1010 S. Oliver (Parklane Shopping Center)
(316) 684-5855 67218
Owner: Shirley Binder
Est: 1996 1300 sq.ft. 1500 Bolts

Complete Selection of Quilting Supplies. Fabrics, Books, Patterns, Notions & Classes.
Ask About our Block of the Month Program.

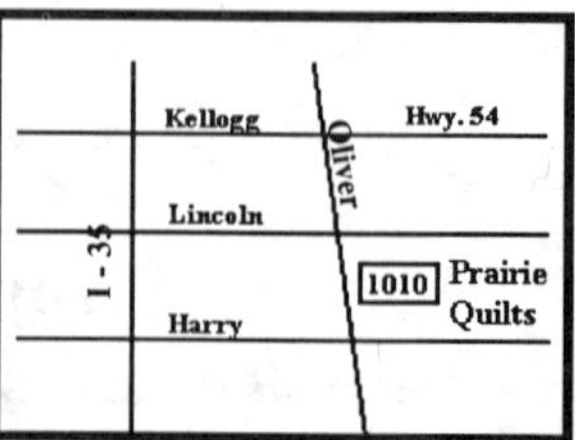

Est: 1992

1800 sq.ft. 1500+ bolts
Owner: Colleen Janssen

Fabric Corner

416 W. Sixth Ave. 66801
(316) 342-3040

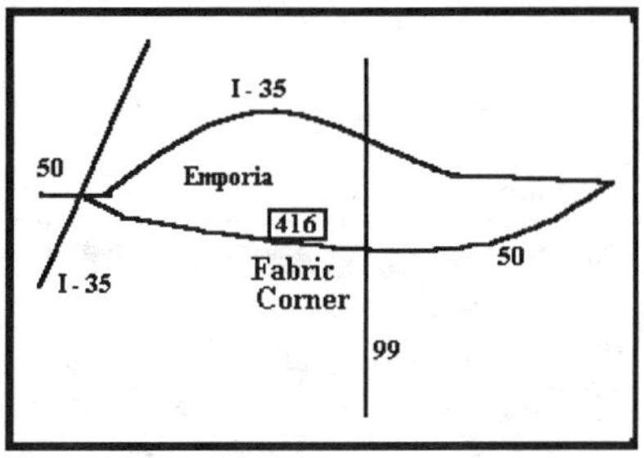

I - 35
50
Emporia
416
Fabric Corner
50
I - 35
99

Emporia, KS #15

Quilting classes, supplies and fabrics - Hoffman, RJR, Jinny Beyer, Springmaid, P&B & South Seas.
We also carry a wide selection of craft and applique patterns.
We carry over 250 book titles from publishers such as: That Patchwork Place, Quilt in a Day, C&T Publishing, and many others.

Mention This Ad and Receive 10% off your purchases.

Mon - Fri 9 - 6 Sat 9 - 5

Emporia is located in the heart of the Kansas Flint Hills on two major highways, which makes Fabric Corner easily accessible on your next trip through Kansas. With an abundance of service and lots of good conversation, we're sure this is one quilt shop you'll be glad you stopped in.

The Quilt Shop

Hwy. 54 201 E. Mary
(316) 625-2693

Yates Center, KS #16

Full Service Quilt Shop.

Super selection of 100% cottons, batting, Quilt Books, Notions, Quilts for Sale.
Original Oregon history Quilt Blocks, Light House and Covered Bridges. Kansas Court House Blocks (one in a series of 12.)
We do machine quilting and sell quilting machines.

Owner: Lynn Hobbs

Mon - Sat 9 - 5

Formerly The Quilt Shop of Reedsport, OR. This shop will be opening in the Fall of 1998

Elk Falls, KS #17

Tues - Fri 10 - 5:30 Sat 10 - 4

Quilts & More

Located in a "Living Ghost Town"
in the Heart of the Kansas Ozarks
9th & Montgomery, P.O. Box 38 67345
(316) 329-4440
Owner: Edie Baker

Custom machine quilting, cotton fabrics, patterns, notions, & more. We specialize in novelty quilting.

Needle In A Haystack

Severy, KS #18

R.R. #1, Box 174 67137
(316) 736-2942
Fax: (316) 736-2222
Owner: Lois Klepper
Est: 1991 3000 Bolts

Mon & Wed - Sat 9 - 5 Sun 1 - 5 Summer Hrs. 7 day a week

Fabric - Books -
Notions
Machine Quilting
Handcrafted items
for sale.

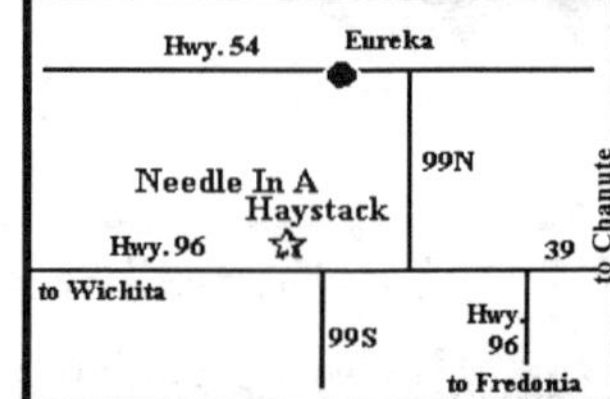

El Dorado, KS #19

Mon - Fri 10 - 5:30 Sat 9 - 5:30

Sew N Sew

(316) 321-7600 309 S. Vine 67042
Est: 1992 Owner: Karen Hayes

Featuring Hoffman, P&B, Moda, Rose & Hubble and other fine fabrics. Books, notions, gifts, classes and an abundance of fun!

Exit
to Emporia
N. Main
Central
Exit
Pine
Sew N Sew
Ash
S. Vine
little brown house w/ big parking lot
to Wichita
309

Come See Us !

Burlington, KS #20

Mon - Sat 10 - 5:30 Sun by Appt.

Silver Threads & Golden Needles

321 Neosho 66839
Owner: Jerry Anne Hoyt
(316) 364-8233
Est: 1985 2000 sq.ft.

Quilters Discount
Custom Machine Quilting. Fabrics, Patterns, Notions, Crafts, Gift Items, Quilting Supplies & Craft Patterns.

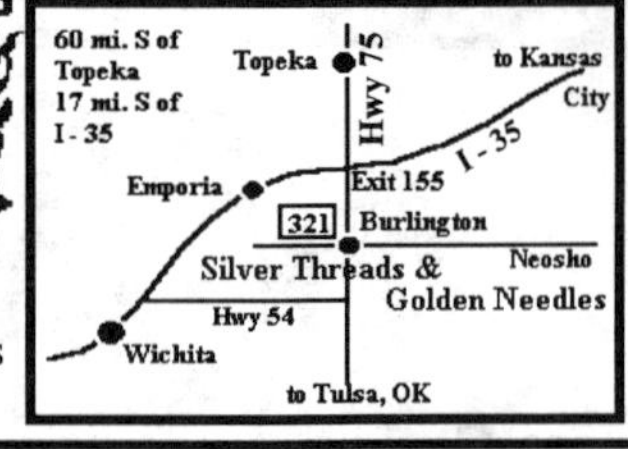

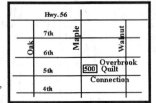

Osage City, KS #21

Tues - Fri 9 - 5 Sat 9 - 3

Calico Cupboard

513 Market 66523
(785) 528-4861
Owners: Lewis & Lora Lee Meek
Est: 1983

We specialize in machine made quilts ! Usually 100 or more in stock ! **OR** choose from our 1000 bolt inventory for a custom order. Fabric also sold by the yard.

5th.
6th.
Market / Hwy 31
Calico Cupboard
513
30 miles southwest of Topeka

Overbrook, KS #22

Tue - Sat 10 - 5

Overbrook Quilt Connection

500 Maple P.O. Box 50 66524
(785) 665-7841 or (888) 665-7841
E-Mail: oqcquilt@overbrookquilts.com
Web Site: www.overbrookquilts.com
Owners: Roxane Fawl & Carolyn Meerian
Est: 1994 4300 sq.ft.

1500 bolt inventory, books, patterns, notions, classes. Mailorder. Free flier.

Hwy. 56
7th
Oak
Maple
Walnut
6th
5th
500
Overbrook Quilt Connection
4th

Baldwin City, KS #23

Mon - Sat 9:30 - 5

713 8th St. 66006
(913) 594-3477 Est: 1986
Owner: Sharon A. Vesecky

Quilting supplies, books, patterns, fabric—Hoffman, Jinny Beyer, Debbie Mumm, Nancy Crow, Springs, Concord. Needlework supplies. Gifts. Machine Quilting. Kansas Products.

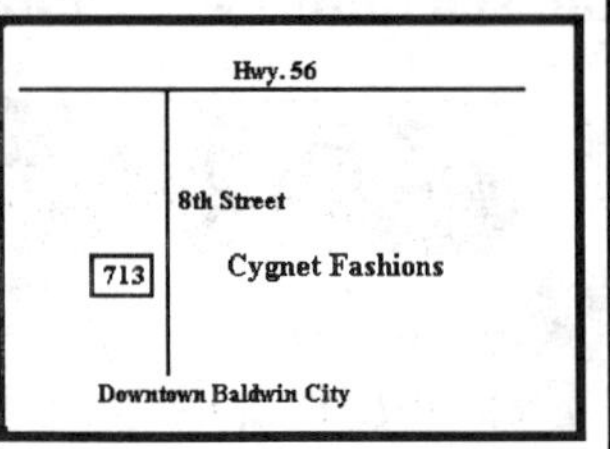

Prairie Point

Fabrics, Quilting and Cross-Stitch Supplies

Located in Suburban Kansas City
7341 Quivira Rd
#24 Shawnee, KS 66216
(913) 268-3333
Toll Free (888) 268-5606

Your mail orders are welcome!

- > 3,000 of the best new fabrics including flannels, novelty prints, ethnic designs, country homespuns and prints, contemporary jewel tones, 1930's and Civil War era reproduction prints, Bali Batiks, Japanese and more !
- Wide assortment of notions
- >1,000 books and patterns
- Cross-Stitch specialty fabrics, designer charts, Mill Hill buttons & beads, and Sampler threads.
- Fine silk thread from Tire and YLI for appliqué.
- Designer and On the Surface Threads
- Pinweaving supplies
- 10% discount to guild members on all in-store purchases.

If you can't find it, give us a call and we'll special order the notion, pattern or book you've been looking for.

Store Hours:
Monday - Thursday 10:00 - 8:30
Friday & Saturday 10:00 - 5:30
Sunday 1:00 - 5:00

Learn to pinweave beautiful vests and quilts. Order *Pinwoven Treasures* from us today!

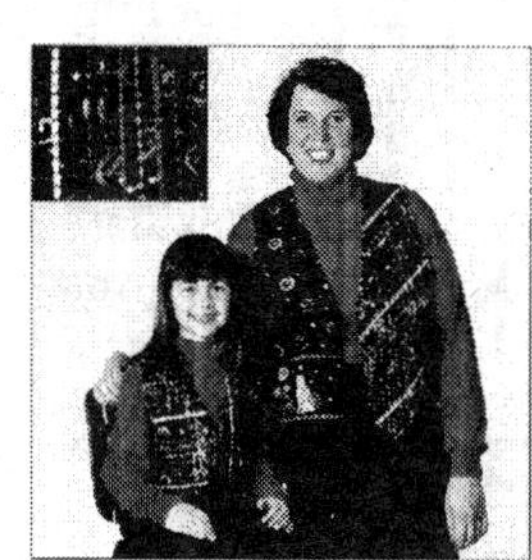

Dressy and elegant or playful and zany, these pinwoven vests are great fun to make and wear

Stop in for a visit. With so many inspirational samples, your're bound to find a project you just can't resist!

Overland Park, KS #25

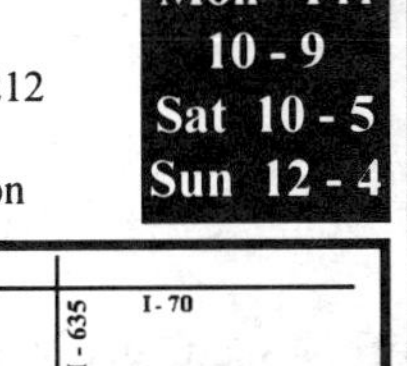

7917 Santa Fe Dr. 66212
(913) 648-2SEW
Owner: Elaine Johnson
Est: 1969

Mon - Fri 10 - 9
Sat 10 - 5
Sun 12 - 4

Large Selection of Brand Name 100% Cottons.

Specializing in quilting & kids prints. Notions & Sewing Supplies, Classes & Workshops. Premier Husqvarna Viking Sewing Machines.

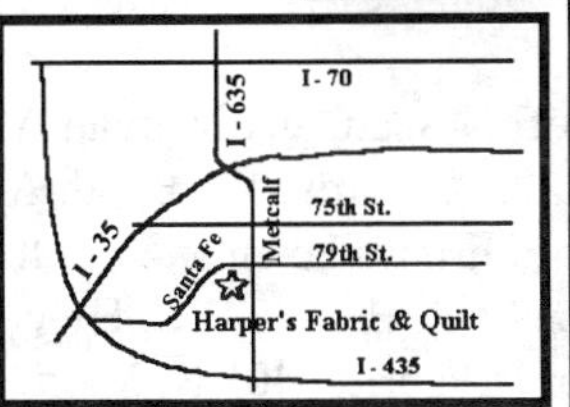

Overland Park, KS #26

The Saltbox Sampler

Mon - Fri 9:30 - 5:30
Tue & Thur til 8:30
Sat 10 - 4

4663 Indian Creek Plwy. (106th & Roe)
(913) 642-0180 66207
Owner: Charlene Buchanan
Est: 1983 1300 Bolts

Cottons for quilting & sewing, notions, books, loads of homespun fabrics.
Cross stitch fabrics & supplies.
Wonderful samples. Classes.

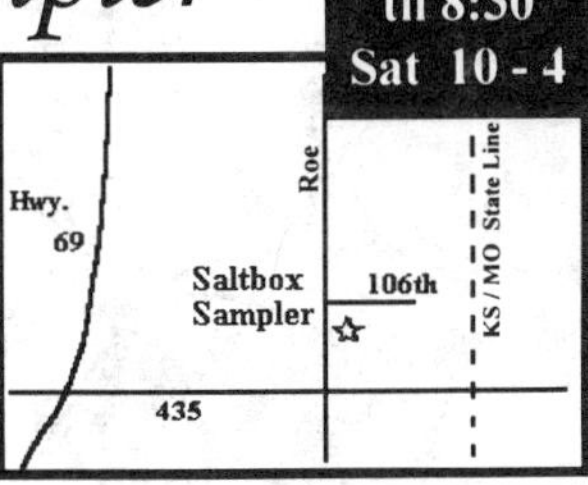

Kansas Guilds:

Silver Needles Quilt Guild, 5500 S. Ohio Rd., Assaria, 67416
Maple Leaf Quilters Guild, P.O. Box 563, Baldwin City, 66006
Meets: 4th Thursday 7 p.m. (except Nov & Dec, 1st Thur in Dec) at Baldwin Senior Center
Tonganoxie Sunflower Quilt Guild, P.O. Box 33, Basehor, 66007
Meets: 2nd Monday 1 p.m. at Jenell's Quilt Patch
Emporia Regional Quilt Guild, P.O. Box 1403, Emporia, 66801
Central Kansas Thread-Benders, 1400 Truman, Great Bend, 67530
Big Creek Quilt Guild, 1061 Catherine Rd., Hays, 67601
Heart of Kansas Quilt Guild, P.O. Box 271, Hutchinson, 67504
Sunflower Quilter's Guild, P.O. Box 69, Iola, 66749
Quilters Guild of Greater K.C., 1617 W. 42nd St., Kansas City
Kaw Valley Quilters Guild, 924 Vermont, Lawrence, 66044
Sunflower Piecemakers, c/o Quilter's Quarters, Leavenworth, 66048
Meets: 2nd & 4th Thursday 7 p.m. at Lansing City Hall, Lansing
Needles & Friends Quilt Guild, P.O. Box 72, Liberal, 67901
Olathe Quilters Guild, 151st Street & Blackbob Rd., Olathe, 66061
Santa Fe Trail Quilt Guild, 500 Maple, Overbrook, 66524
Meets: 1st Tuesday 7 p.m. at Overbrook Quilt Connection
Miama County Quilters Guild, P.O. Box 453, Paola, 66071
Little Balken Quilt Guild, Inc., P.O. Box 1608, Pittsburg, 66762
Meets: 3rd Monday 7 p.m. at Presbyterian Church, 6th & Pine
Silver Needles Quilt Guild, P.O. Box 1132, Salina, 67402
Meets: 3rd Monday 7 p.m. at Presbyterian Manor, 2601 E. Crawford (Annual quilt show in late October)
Kansas Capital Quilters Guild, Topeka, 66606
Meets: 2nd & 4th Tuesday 7 p.m. at Women's Club, 5221 SW West Dr.
Prairie Quilt Guild, P.O. Box 48813, Wichita, 67201
Meets: 2nd Tuesday 7 p.m. at Downtown Senior Center, 200 S. Walnut
Kansas Quilters Organization, 1721 Weile, Winfield, 67156
Walnut Valley Quilters Guild, 1615 East 20th Ave., Winfield, 67156

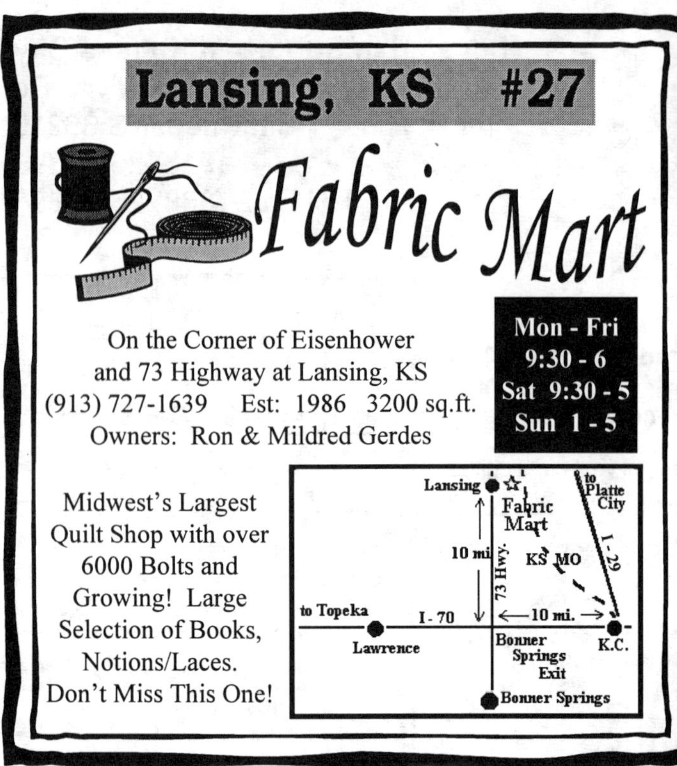

Leavenworth, KS #28

The Quilter's Quarters

Mon, Tues, Thurs, Fri, Sat 9:30 - 5:30
Wed 12 - 8

Minutes from Kansas City, The Quilter's Quarters is dedicated to providing the best possible customer service in the friendliest atmosphere. Quilters will truly find a home in our civil war vintage building where the surroundings may be antique, but the fabric and ideas are cutting edge. Unlike a fabric museum, our merchandise is constantly being updated. You will find our large selection of fabrics, notions, books, kits, plus new and antique quilts just outside the front gate of historic Fort Leavenworth. All guild memberships honored with a 10% discount. Ask about our Fifty-yard Club, buy 50 yards and receive 5 yards free!

402 S. 5th St. 66048
(913) 651-6510
E-Mail: QLTRSQLTRS@aol.com
Owner: Jerry Ann Stube
(founder of the area's largest quilt guild: The Sunflower Piecemakers.)

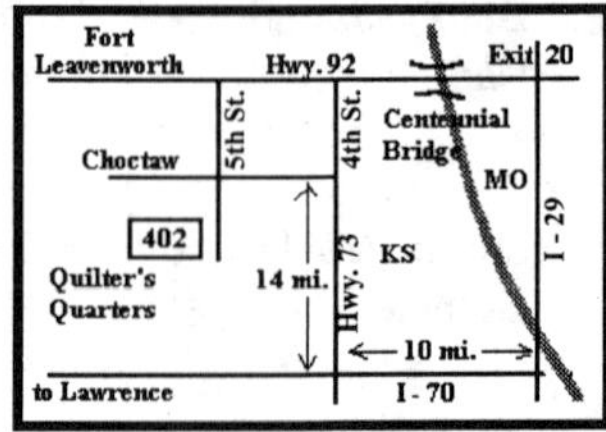

Basehor, KS #29

Jenell's Quilt Patch

Mon - Sat 9 - 6
Wed til 8

155th & State Ave., P.O. Box 172
(913) 724-4610
Owner: Jenell Noeth
Est: 1995 1300 sq.ft.
Carrying a large selection of your favorite fabrics.
Hundreds of books, notions, classes. Machine Quilting-many patterns to choose from.

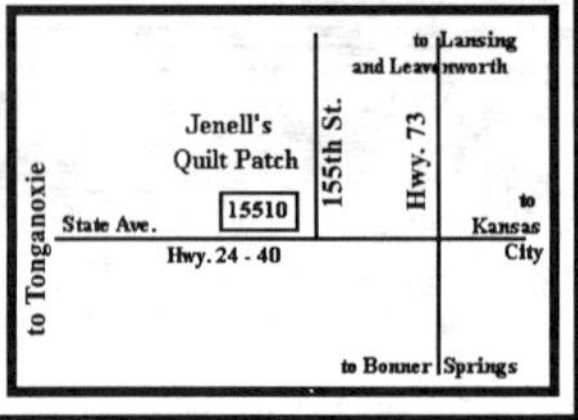

Other Shops in Kansas:

Abilene	Quilt Patch, 305 N. Cedar St.	913-263-1825
Anthony	Pride of the Prairie Quilt Shoppe, 131 W. Main St.	316-842-5945
Clay Center	Clione's Collections, 709 5th St.	913-632-3839
Dodge City	Charlie's Quilt Shoppe, 503 Central Ave.	316-225-7720
Downs	Stuff N Such, 801 Morgan Ave.	913-454-3416
Emporia	Quilts & Yardage, 7 E. 6th Ave.	316-343-3850
Fort Scott	Rose Erma's Sewing & Quilt Shop, 7 N. Main St.	800-959-4353
Galva	The Quilt Barn, 221 E. Hwy. 56	316-654-3400
Garden City	Bar K Fabrics, 401 N. Main St.	316-275-7689
La Crosse	Patchwork Parlor, 812 Main St.	913-222-3536
Lawrence	Sarah's Fabrics, 925 Massachusetts	913-842-6198
Lawrence	Stitch on Needlwork Shop, 926 Massachusetts St.	913-842-1101
Lawrence	Schoolhouse Studio, 803 1/2 Massachusetts	913-865-0738
Lincoln	Calico Country	913-525-6377
Marysville	Fabric Center, 818 Broadway	913-562-2601
Norton	The Sewing Box, 128 S. State	913-877-3821
Oakley	J & E Crafts, 129 Center Ave.	913-672-4842
Ottawa	Chris' Corner, 229 S. Main St.	913-242-1922
Oxford	Variety Shoppe, 106 S. Summer St.	316-455-3698
Seneca	Picture This, 420 Main St.	913-336-3296
Topeka	Wallace's Stitchin Post II, 4004 S.W. Huntoon St.	913-272-5930
Topeka	Bennett's Sewing Center, 2125 N. Kansas Ave.	913-232-9117
Wichita	The Sewing Center, 2101 W. 21st St.	316-832-0819
Winfield	The Sewing Basket, 211 E. 9th Ave. #A	316-221-4517

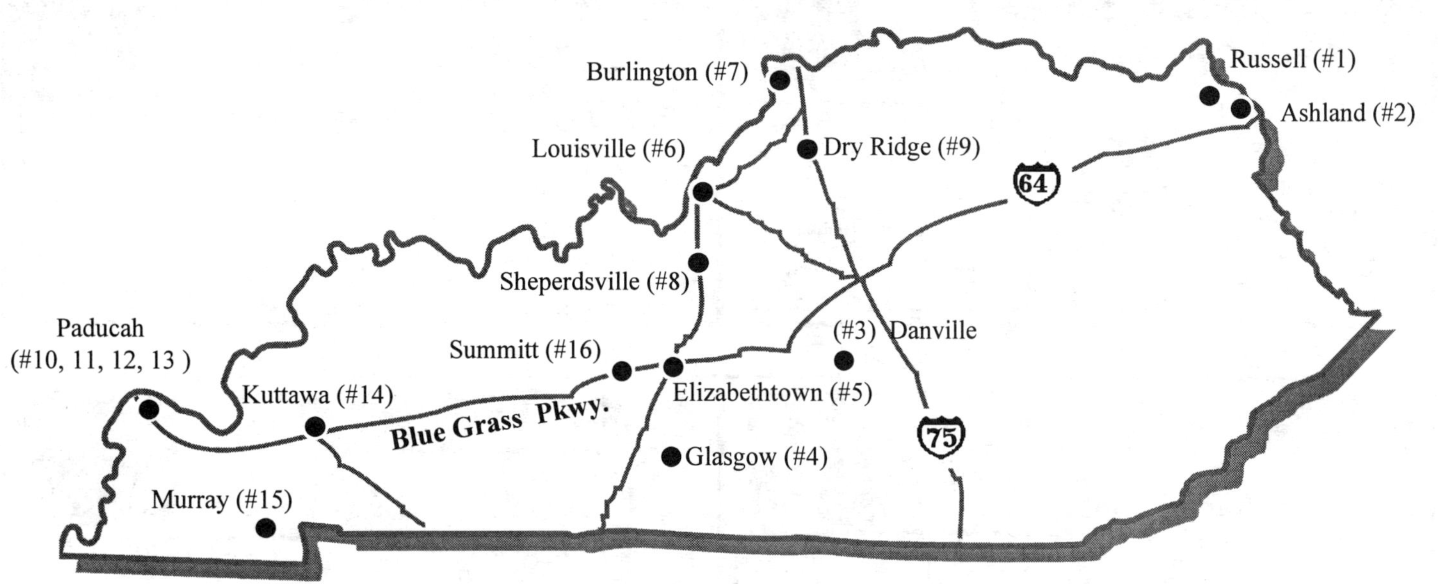

Historic Russell, KY #1

401 Belfonte St.
41169
(606) 836-9920
Owner:
Melvina Blair

Est: 1995

Mon - Sat
10 - 5

Finest Fabrics & supplies for the quilter and sewing enthusiast. Plus Bernina sewing machines & supplies.

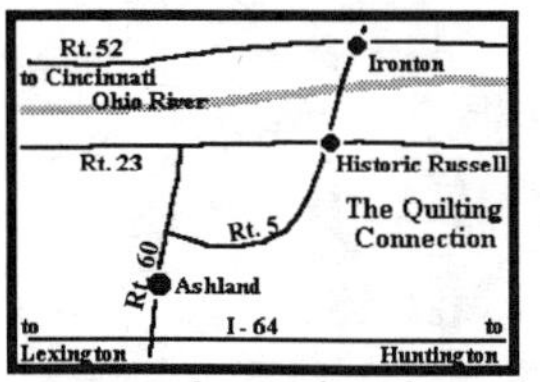

You'll find everything you need right here.

Ashland, KY #2

Mon - Sat
10 - 5
Wed 2 - 5

Craft Attic Quilt Shop

2027 Hoods Creek Pike 41102
(606) 325-1212
Owner: Donnie Maggard
Est: 1982 1500 sq.ft. 1000 Bolts

100% Cotton Fabrics.
Full Line of Quilting Supplies.
Books , Stencils , Classes

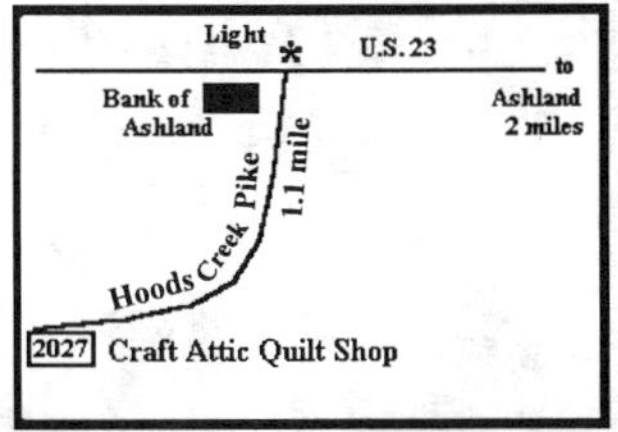

Danville, KY #3

Mon - Sat
10 - 6

World Wide Fabrics

104 Man O'War Blvd. 40422
(606) 236-1175
Owners: Earl & Jean Steinhauer
Est: 1976 4000 sq.ft.

Authorized Bernina Dealer
Calico Cottons Quilting Books and Supplies
Bridal Fabrics and accessories. Complete line of Notions, Drapery & Upholstery

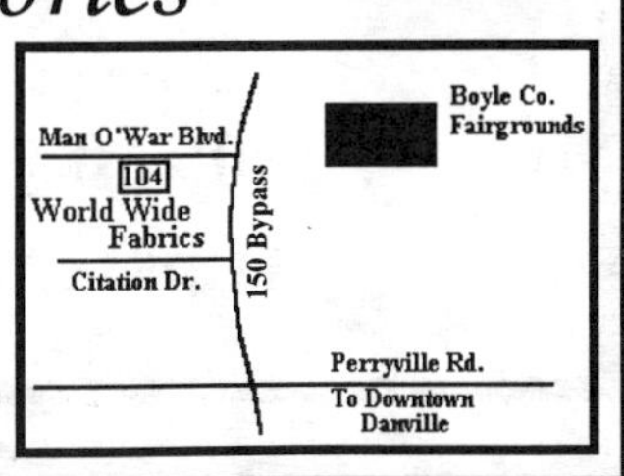

Glasgow, KY #4

Tues - Fri 10 - 4
Sat 10 - 3

The Barn Cat Quilting Shoppe

2897 Matthews Mill Rd.
42141
(502) 646-5468
Owners: Philip & Dorothy Bunch

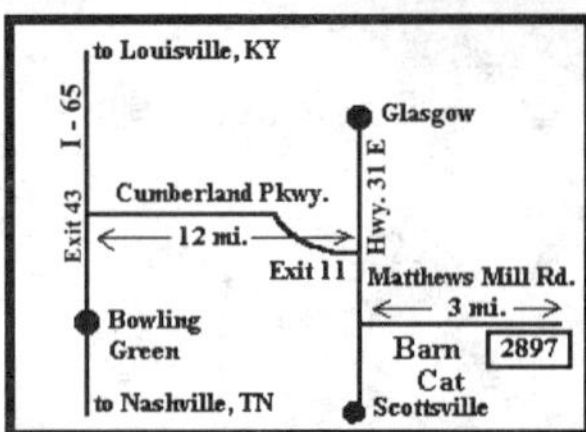

Top name Fabrics, Notions, Books, Patterns and Classes. If you're passing thru on a Monday & would like to stop feel free to call.

Elizabethtown, KY #5

Tues & Thur 10 - 9
Wed & Fri 10 - 6
Sat 10 - 3

Uniquely Yours Quilt Shop

2973 Rineyville Rd. 42701
(502) 766-1456
Owner: Mary Sennott

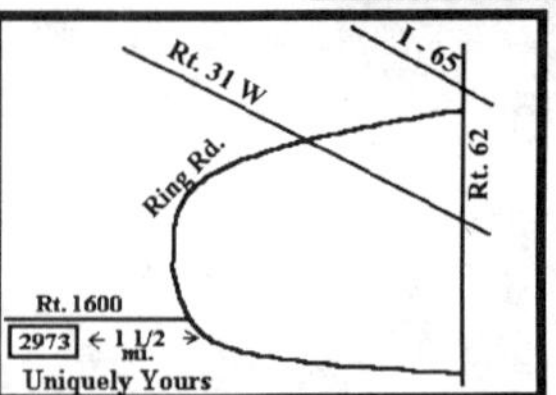

Over 600 bolts of beautiful 100% Cotton Fabrics. Books, patterns, notions and classes. Friendly, professional advice. Quilts for sale.

Louisville, KY #6

Mon - Fri 10 - 5
Sat 10 - 4

Happy Heart Quilt Shop

7913 3rd. St. Rd. 40214
(502) 363-1171
Owner: Yvonne Fritze
Est: 1985 3000 sq. ft.

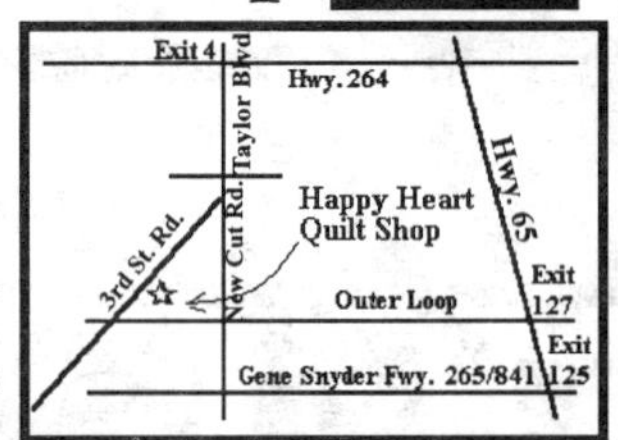

3000 bolts of fabrics including Hoffman, RJR, Jinny Beyer, P&B, Liberty/London. Quilt Kits. Extensive line of books, patterns and notions.

Burlington, KY #7

Mon - Sat 10 - 6
April - Oct 3rd Sun 12 - 5

Cabin Arts

5878 N. Jefferson St. 41005
(606) 586-8021
Owners: Linda Whittenburg & Sarah O'Neil
Est: 1992 1300 sq.ft. 1500 Bolts

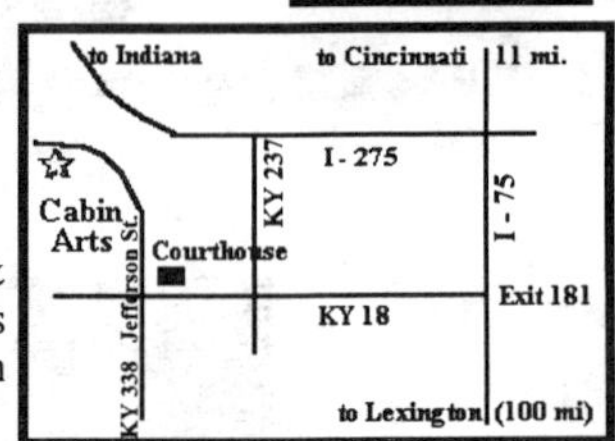

Quality Quilt Fabrics plus notions, books & more. Local Handcrafted Treasures. Classes Available. Located in historic district in 1850's Log Cabin.

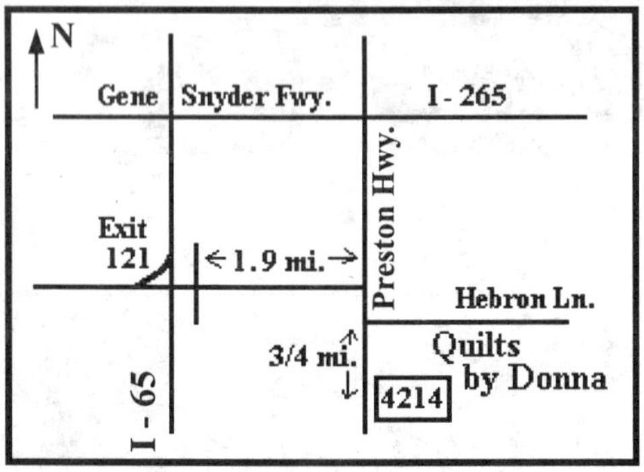

N
Gene Snyder Fwy. I - 265
Exit 121
<1.9 mi.>
Preston Hwy.
Hebron Ln.
3/4 mi.
Quilts by Donna
4214
I - 65

Shepherdsville, KY #8

(888) 810-1003

4214 N. Preston Highway 40165

Mon 9 - 8
Tues - Fri 9 - 6
Sat 9 - 5

Owner: Donna Sharp
Est: 1982 1800 sq.ft.

Quilts by Donna

Bring This Coupon to get 25% off all Fabric Purchases.

100's of bolts of fabric. Books & Patterns Tops, Etc. Up to 100+ Finished Quilts.

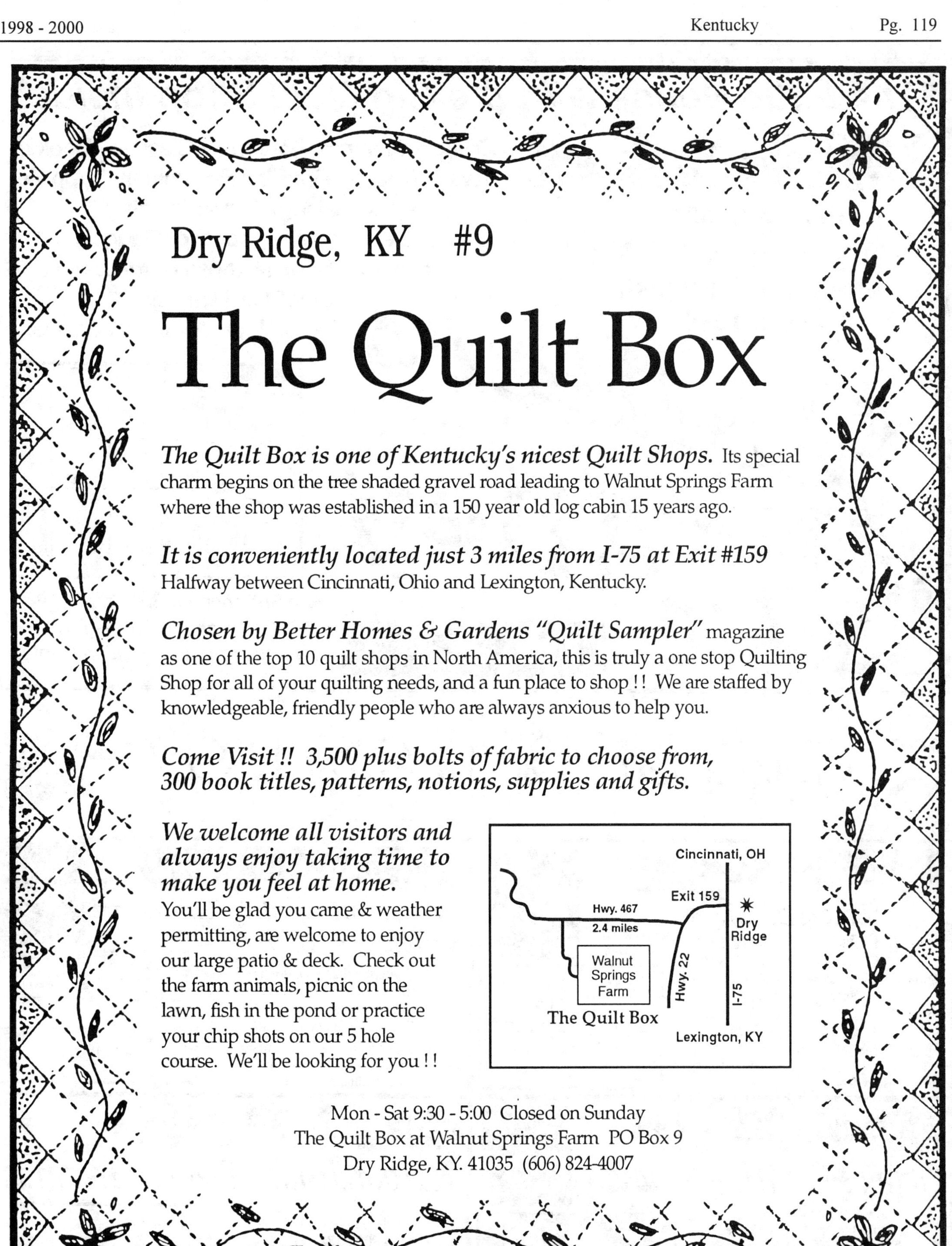
Dry Ridge, KY #9
The Quilt Box
The Quilt Box is one of Kentucky's nicest Quilt Shops. Its special charm begins on the tree shaded gravel road leading to Walnut Springs Farm where the shop was established in a 150 year old log cabin 15 years ago.
It is conveniently located just 3 miles from I-75 at Exit #159
Halfway between Cincinnati, Ohio and Lexington, Kentucky.
Chosen by Better Homes & Gardens "Quilt Sampler" magazine as one of the top 10 quilt shops in North America, this is truly a one stop Quilting Shop for all of your quilting needs, and a fun place to shop !! We are staffed by knowledgeable, friendly people who are always anxious to help you.
Come Visit !! 3,500 plus bolts of fabric to choose from, 300 book titles, patterns, notions, supplies and gifts.
We welcome all visitors and always enjoy taking time to make you feel at home.
You'll be glad you came & weather permitting, are welcome to enjoy our large patio & deck. Check out the farm animals, picnic on the lawn, fish in the pond or practice your chip shots on our 5 hole course. We'll be looking for you !!
Cincinnati, OH
Exit 159
Hwy. 467
2.4 miles
Dry Ridge
Walnut Springs Farm
Hwy. 22
I-75
The Quilt Box
Lexington, KY
Mon - Sat 9:30 - 5:00 Closed on Sunday
The Quilt Box at Walnut Springs Farm PO Box 9
Dry Ridge, KY. 41035 (606) 824-4007

"The Little House with the Big Quilt Shop Inside"

Paducah, KY #10

(502) 443-5673
420 North 4th St. 42001
Owner: Pat English
Est: 1989

Designer Fabrics - Patterns - Classes - Books
Newest Notions-Brazilian Embroidery Supplies
Lace Making - Fabric Painting
Quilter's Jewelry - Tools or Gadgets
We do mail order on all those Hard-To-Finds
Janome/New Home &
Babylock Sewing Machines.

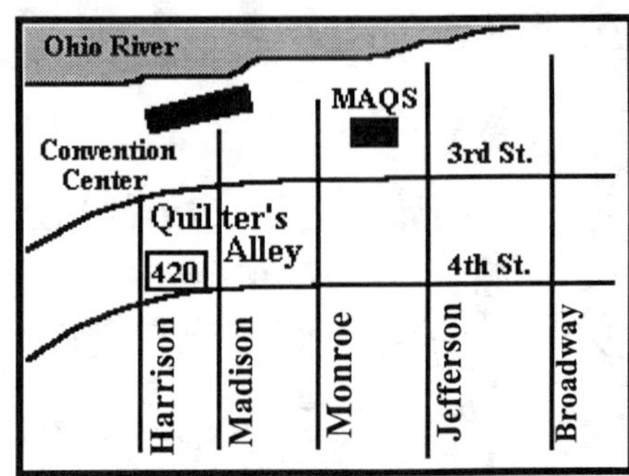

Mon - Sat 10 - 5

Entrance on 3rd St. at 419
New Parking Area—Right across from Convention Center

Paducah: Quilt City U.S.A.

Paducah, KY #11

Hancock's

Mon - Fri 9:30 - 7
Sat 10 - 6
Sun 1 - 5

3841 Hinkleville 42001 (800) 845-8723
fax: (502) 442-2164
Est: 1969 50,000 bolts 65,000 sq.ft.
Owner: W.R. Hancock Free 60 page Catalog
www.Hancocks-Paducah.com
America's largest selection of Hoffman, Alexander Henry, P&B, Benartex, Jinny Beyer, Nancy Crow & Debbie Mumm Fabrics. Also a huge stock of Waverly and P/Kaufman drapery and upholstery fabrics.

I - 24 | 3841 Hancock's | Exit 4 | Hinkleville Rd.

Paducah, KY #12

Museum of the American Quilter's Society

Open Year round
Tues - Sat 10 - 5
April - Oct Also Sun 1 - 5

215 Jefferson St., P.O. Box 1540
42002-1540 Est: 1991
(502) 422-8856 Fax #: (502) 442-5448
E-Mail: maqsmus@apex.net
Changing exhibits of over 150 new and antique quilts on display.
A Quilter Must See!

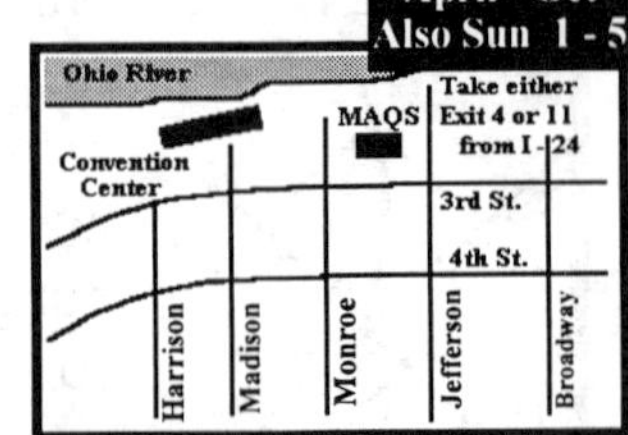

Paducah, KY #13

King's Quilting Studio

Open 10 - 5
Closed Tues & Sun

119 N. 4th St. 42001
(502) 444-7577 Fax: Same
E-Mail: sara@paducahquilts.com
Web site: www.paducahquilts.com
Owner: Sara Newberg King

Quilts, wallhangings, wearables, patterns. Silk ribbon embroidery, dyes, silks, books, classes, hand-dyed fabrics & ribbons, mail order.

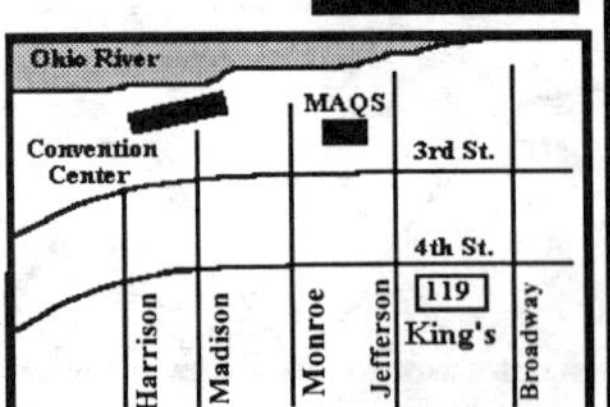

Kuttawa, KY #14

Harbor House Bed & Breakfast

1730 Lake Barkley Dr.
(502) 388-4012
Owners: Lee & Betty Bird

Specializing in Sewing or Quilting Retreats

From Paducah, KY:
—Go on I - 24 to Exit 40 (Kuttawa/Eddyville Exit)
—Go west 1/2 mile to exit #295
—Turn left and follow road around to 1730 Lake Barkley Dr.

Murray, KY #15

Tues - Sat 10 - 5

The Magic Thimble

813 Coldwater Road 42071
(502) 759-4769
Owner: Peggy Smith
Est: 1986 1000 sq.ft. 300 Bolts

100% Cotton Fabrics, Patterns. Friendly Atmosphere & knowledgeable staff

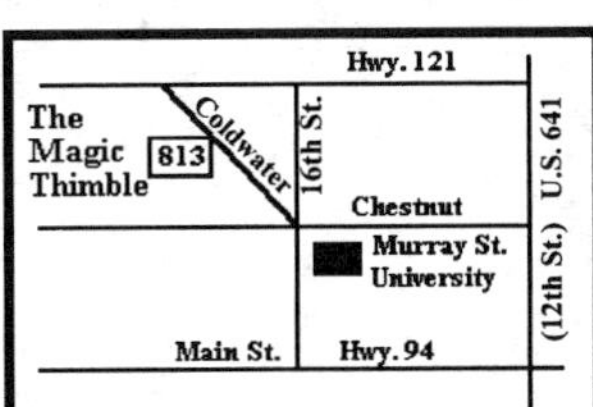

Summit, KY #16

Mon, Tues, Wed, Fri, & Sat 10 - 5

Quaint Quilts

16117 Leitchfield Rd. 42783
(502) 862-9708
Owner: Kathryn Richardson
Est: 1985 672 sq.ft.

Quilts, Curtains, Machine & Hand Quilting, Oil Paintings, Prints, Basketry, Rugs & Rug Weaving. Approx. 100 printed quilt top fabrics.

to Elizabethtown
Hwy. 84
Summit Rd.
16117
Quaint Quilts
to Sonora & I-65
U.S. 62
to Leitchfield
Western KY Parkway

Kentucky Guilds:

Covington Quilt Guild
Gone to Pieces Quilt Guild, 2027 Hoods Creek Pike, Ashland, 41102 Meets: 1st Monday 7 p.m. at Craft Attic Quilt Shop
Stringtown Quilters' Guild 4706 Limaburg Rd., Hebron, 41048 Meets: 3rd Thursday 7 p.m. at Florence Baptist Church
Contact: Linda Whittenburg at (606) 586-8021
Louisville Nimble Thimbles, P.O. Box 6234, Louisville, 40206
Graves County Piecemakers, Rt. 3, P.O. Box 236-2, Mayfield, 42066
Murray Quilt Lovers, P.O. Box 265, Murray, 42071 Meets: 3rd Tuesday at 6 p.m. at Calloway County Public Library
Owensboro Quilters Guild, Owensboro, 42301
Quilt And Sew On, Paducah Meets: 2nd Tuesday 6:30 p.m. at Kentucky Oaks Mall Community Room
Murray Quilt Lovers, P.O. Box 975, Paintsville
Licking Valley Quilters, 907 Mary St., Villa Hills, 41017

Other Shops in Kentucky:

Allensville	Grandma's Cupboard, 5760 Russellville Rd., Hwy 79	502-483-2461
Barbourville	Kno Discount Fabric, Hwy. 229 & 25 E	606-546-9362
Benton	Needle & Thread, 817 U.S. Hwy. 68W, P.O. Box 78	502-527-1300
Corbin	The Kentucky Quilt Co., 1878 Cumberland Falls Hwy.	606-523-4393
East Bernstadt	Quilting B, 1870 E. Hwy. 30	606-843-2803
Elkton	Julia's Fabric Shop, 103 S. Weathers Ln.	502-265-2038
Frankfort	Treadleworks, 235 W. Broadway St.	502-223-2571
Lewisburg	Quilt Shop, 308 8th St.	502-755-4843
Lexington	Quilter's Square, 140 Moore Dr.	606-278-5010
Louisa	Sewing Cottage, R.R. # 4, Box 1530	606-638-3102
Louisville	Baer Fabrics, 515 E. Market St.	502-569-7016
Louisville	The Smocking Shop, 3829 Staebler Ave.	502-893-3503
Louisville	The Quilting Shop, 7100 Preston Hwy.	502-962-8232
Magnolia	The Jewel Box, 10075 N. Jackson Hwy.	502-528-3087
Middlesboro	Heavenly Scent Flower Shop, 205 Exeter	606-248-8985
Murray	Murray Sewing Center, 700 N. 12th St.	502-753-5323
New Castle	Quilt Stitchin, P.O. Box 387	502-845-4987
Owensboro	Donna's Stitchery Nook, 3400 S. Hummingbird Loop	502-685-0404
Paducah	Sewing Center of Paducah, 842 Joe Clifton Dr.	502-442-1661
Paducah	Web of Thread, 1410 Broadway	502-575-9700
Paducah	English's Sewing Machines, 7001 Benton Rd.	502-898-7301
Paducah	Michael Stewart Antiques, 136 Lone Oak Rd.	502-441-7222
Perryville	I Love Quilts, 334 Buell St.	606-236-8800
Philpot	The Quilting Place, 5996 Old Kentucky 54	502-729-2290
Pineville	Kathy's Needle & Thread, P.O. Box 118 Route #2	606-337-6753
Renfro Valley	O Shep Originals, Hwy. 25	606-256-5018
Salyersville	Quilting Shop, 664 E. Mountain Pkwy, PO Box 998	606-349-1303
Somerset	Mill Outlet, 4502 S. Highway 27	606-236-5173
Whitesburg	Cozy Corner, 210 E. Main St.	606-633-9637

11 Featured Shops LOUISIANA

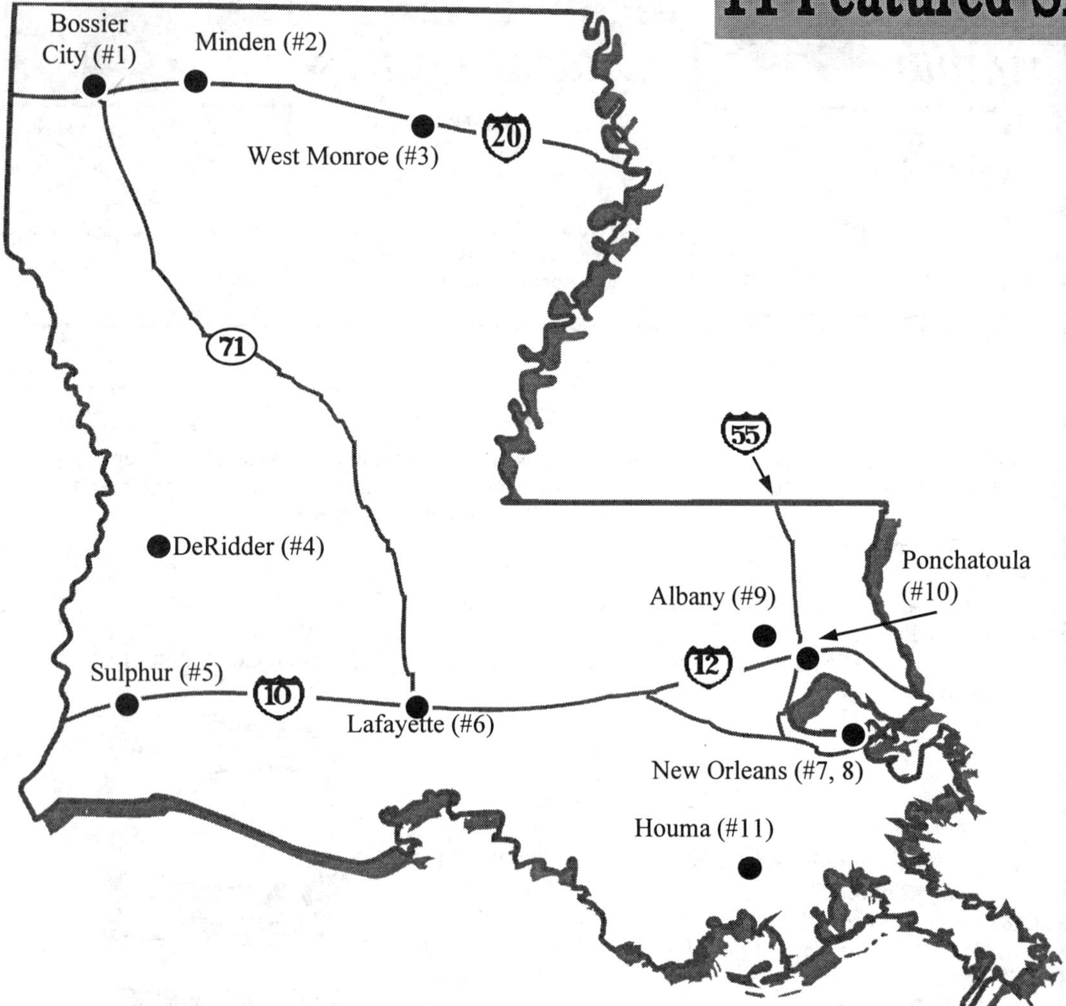

Bossier City (#1)
Minden (#2)
West Monroe (#3)
20
71
55
DeRidder (#4)
Ponchatoula (#10)
Albany (#9)
12
Sulphur (#5)
10
Lafayette (#6)
New Orleans (#7, 8)
Houma (#11)

Bossier City, LA #1

Mon - Sat
10 - 6

Fabric Boutique

Heart of Bossier Shopping Ctr.
1701 Old Minden Rd. 71111
(318) 742-0047 Fax: (318) 742-5934
Owner: Shirley C. Warren
Est: 1986

Unique combination of classes, quilting supplies & fabrics. Authorized Bernina, Sewing Machine dealer.

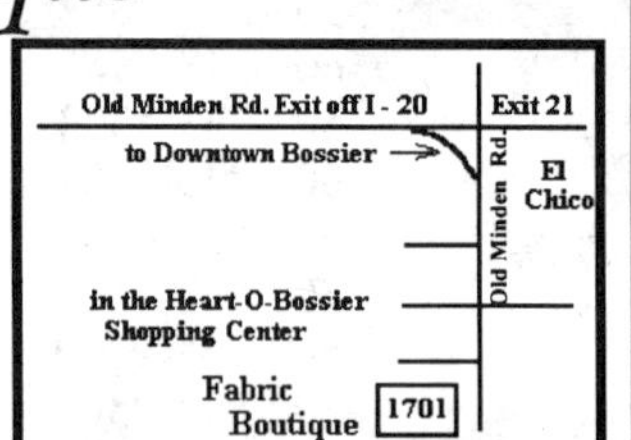

Minden, LA #2

Tues - Fri
9 - 5
Sat 10 - 2

The Little Country Quilt Shop

534 Old Arcadia Rd. 71055
(318) 377-2462
Owner: Nona Sale
Est: 1983

We have approx. 1000 bolts. All the latest books, patterns, & supplies. Also a variety of classes. Plus we have old and new quilts for sale.

From I - 20 take Exit 49. Go North 3&1/2 miles to the 2nd blinking light. At the light turn right for 1/4 mile to Parish 131. Shop is 1 mile on the left. Watch for Signs ! !

West Monroe, LA #3

Mon - Fri
9 - 5
Sat 10 - 2

Quilt 'N Stitch

6049 Cypress St. 71291
(318) 396-6020
E-Mail: qultstch@bayou.com
2000+ Bolts

The store is located in a house where antiques nestle amoung the many fabrics, books, and notions.

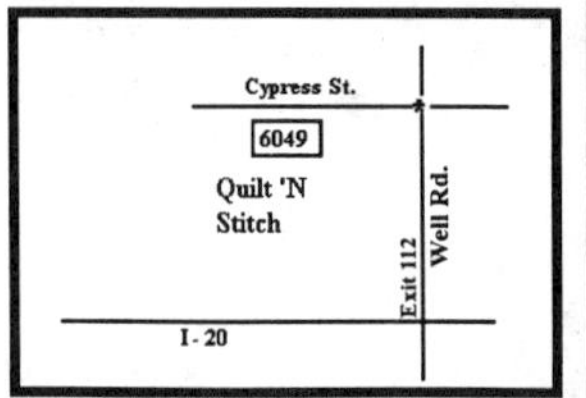

DeRidder, LA #4

Tues - Fri
9:30 - 5:30
Sat 10 - 5

The Sewing Room

109 N. Washington Ave. 70634
(318) 462-4944
E-Mail: srich@worldnetla.net
Owner: Sandra Rich

Large selection of top quality 100% cottons and other quilting supplies. Classes.
New Home Sewing Machines.

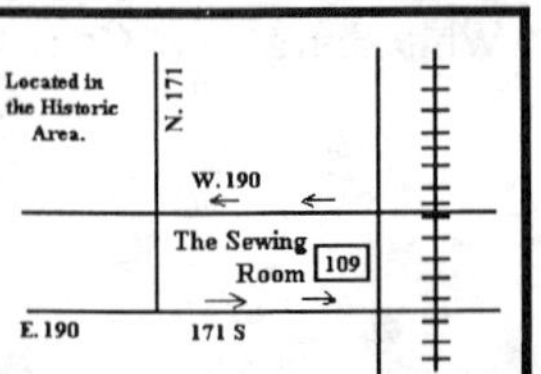

Sulphur, LA #5

Mon - Fri 9:30 - 5 Sat 10 - 3

Mary Ann's Fabric Cottage

2304 A Maplewood Dr. 70663
(318) 625-4223
Est: 1994 1200 sq.ft. Free Newsletter
400 Bolts of Cottons.
500 bolts of Fashion Fabrics.

Great selection of 100% cotton fabrics, lots of Fat Quarters, books, Quilt supplies, patterns, notions and silk ribbon. Classes also.

I-10
Exit 21
1/4 mi.
Maplewood Dr.
1/2 mi.
2304
Fabric Cottage
Cities Service Hwy.
Post Oak Rd.
Beglis Pkwy.

Lafayette, LA #6

Ginger's Needleworks

Usually Open
Tues - Thurs 10 - 5 Sat 11 - 3
Closed to work Quilt Shows:
See our Booths at Paducah, Houston, Dallas, and many other smaller Quilt Shows.

905 East Gloria Switch Road
(318) 232-7847 70507
Owner: Ginger Moore Est:1984
450 sq.ft. Quilting 200 sq.ft. Yarns

Quilting fabrics, notions, supplies and quilts for sale. Yarns.

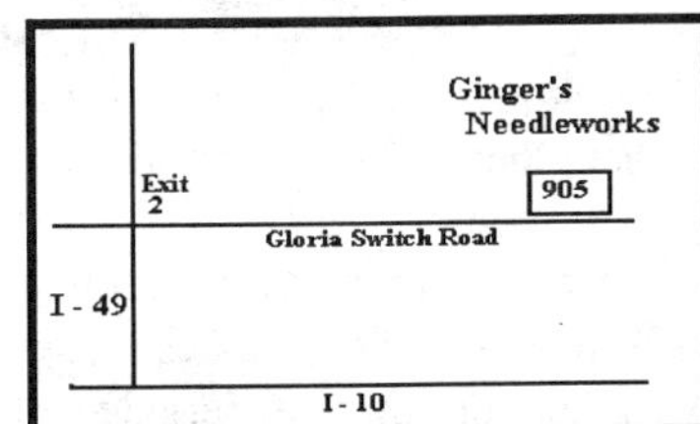

CATALOG $1 Send us your name & address, Attn: Dept QTC

New Orleans, LA #7

7 Days A Week 9 - 6

Quilt Shop in New Orleans

816 Decatur St. 70114
(504) 522-0835
Owners: Janelle & Richard Garrett
Free Catalog

We offer a variety of hand-quilted items; patchwork quilts, pillow covers and clothing. Our clothing is of exquisite traditional or contemporary design that is very unique.

Bourbon St.
Royal
Conti St.
St. Peter
St. Ann
Chartres St.
Canal St.
Jackson Square
Quilt Shop 816
French Market
Clay St.
Mississippi River

New Orleans, LA #8

(800) 453-6998

Mon - Sat 10 - 5

Quilt Cottage

801 Nashville Avenue 70115 (504) 895-3791
Owners:
Carol Schiaffino
& Jeanne Lincks
Est: 1981 2000 sq.ft.

Your Complete Quilt Shop !

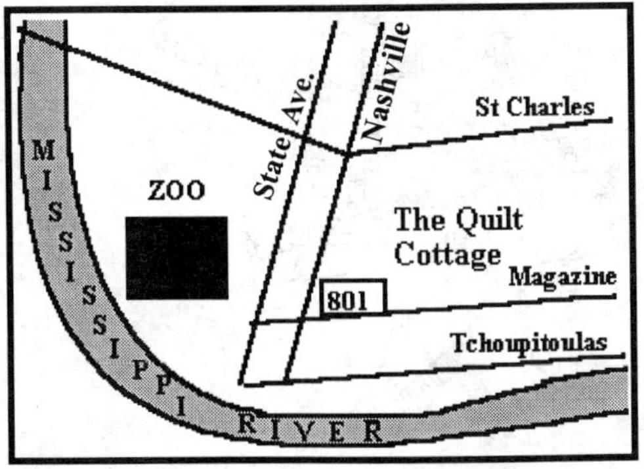

Room full of 100% cotton fabric. Over 1000 Bolts. The latest books, notions, & Patterns. New, Antique, Custom made quilts. Repair.

Send us your name and address and we'll send you our free newsletter three times per year.

Material Girls | LA Hwy 190 | Montpelier Ave. | 29937 | Albany LA | I-55 | Hammond LA | I-12 | to Baton Rouge | Exit 32 | to Slidell | 1 1/2 miles N of I-12 | to New Orleans

Mon - Fri 9 - 5 Sat 9 - 3

Material Girls' Quilt Shop

29937 S. Montpelier Ave. P.O. Box 1375, 70711
(504) 567-5269 E-Mail: mtrlgrls@i-55.com
Owners: Peggy Peacock, Rhonda Smith & Judy Jensen
Est: 1997 2000 Bolts

Albany, LA #9

Looking for a friendly atmosphere, a place to come and just hang out? Then Material Girls' Quilt Shop is here for you. Our goal is to make our down-home quilt shop - with our friendly and helpful personnel, great selection of fabrics, notions, supplies, classes, patterns, books and more - just the place for you to experience a little bit of quilter's heaven.

Ponchatoula, LA #10

Mon - Sat 10 - 5 Sun 12 - 5

Yesteryear Antiques & Quilts

165 East Pine 70454
(504) 386-2741 Est: 1982
Owners: Pat Zieske & Lee Barends

We do Custom Made Quilts !
We have samples and fabrics at the shop for you to look at - you choose your own pattern and colors. We'll quilt on your tops too!

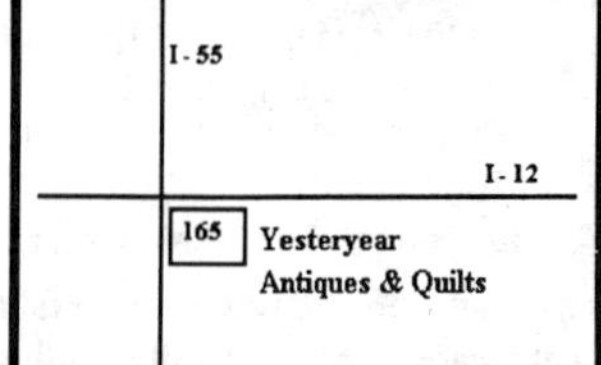

Houma, LA #11

Mon - Sat 10 - 5

Jo's Cloth Cottage

205-C Bayou Gardens Blvd. 70364
(504) 879-4602Est: 1982 2500 sq.ft.

Jo's is a creative sewing idea center which specializes in classes, fabrics & supplies for quilting, heirloom sewing, fashion & serger sewing. Lots of models and sewing ideas pack our 2500 sq.ft. store.

Take Hwy. 90 out of New Orleans 55 miles to Hwy 24. Jo's is in the Old South Square across from the Southland Mall on Bayou Gardens Blvd.

Louisiana Guilds:
Strawberry Patch Quilters, Albany
Common Thread Quilters' Guild, 1402 Meadowbrook Dr., DeRidder, 70634
Meets: 2nd Tuesday 6 p.m. & 3rd Tuesday 2 p.m. at The Sewing Room
Heritage Quilt Guild, Jonesboro, 71251 Meets: 1st Wednesday 9:30 a.m. at Jackson Parish Library
Gulf State Quilting Assoc., P.O. Box 8391, Metairie, 70011
Jefferson Parish Quilting Guild, 711 Ridgelake Dr., Metairie
North LA Quilters Guild, Monroe, 71201
Meets: 1st Thursday 1 p.m. & 6:30 p.m.
at Auacheta Extension Office.
North Louisiana Quilters, Monroe
Meets: Morning Stars Chapter--1st Tuesday 9:30 a.m.,
Sunshine Chapter--1st Thursday
1 p.m., Moonlight Chapter--1st Thursday 6 p.m.
Call (318) 396-6020 for locations
Southern Samplers, 165 E. Pine St., Ponchatoula, 70454
Red River Quilters, P.O. Box 4811, Shreveport, 71134
Meets: 1st Monday 1 p.m. & 6:30 p.m.
at Broadmore Prebyterian Church.
Holds annual quilt show.
Also classes and workshops offered.
Seven community projects.

Other Shops in Louisiana:

Baton Rouge	Peaceful Quilter, 12318 Jefferson Hwy	504-751-3551
Gibson	Alice & Lee's Quilts, 6233 Bayou Black Dr.	504-575-2389
Lafayette	Heymann's Fabrics, 456 Heymann Blvd.	318-234-1211
Many	Sybil's Fabric Shop, 805 W. Georgia Ave.	318-256-0402
Metairie	The Quilting Bee, 3537 18th St. #15	504-456-2304
New Orleans	Alder Sewing & Vacuum Center, 8217 Oak	504-866-8050
New Orleans	Krauss Dept. Store, 1201 Canal St.	504-523-3311

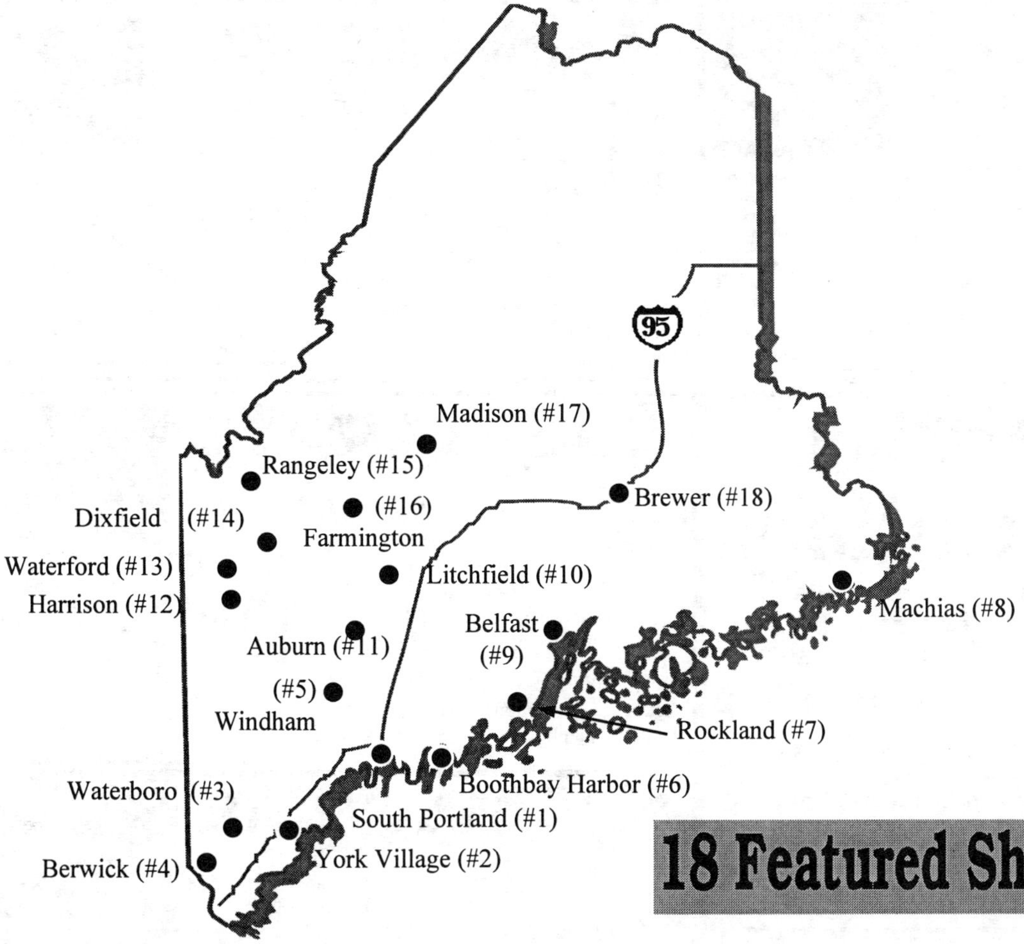

MAINE

18 Featured Shops

Madison (#17)
Rangeley (#15)
(#16) Farmington
Dixfield (#14)
Waterford (#13)
Harrison (#12)
Brewer (#18)
Litchfield (#10)
Belfast (#9)
Machias (#8)
Auburn (#11)
(#5) Windham
Rockland (#7)
Boothbay Harbor (#6)
Waterboro (#3)
South Portland (#1)
York Village (#2)
Berwick (#4)
95

EVERYTHING QUILTERS NEED

PineTree Quiltworks is a full service quilt shop that also offers quilting supplies via mail order catalog.

When you visit Maine, visit PineTree. Only a few minutes from I-295, Pine Tree's a great place to stock up on vacation quilting supplies.

Store Hours:
Mon - Fri
10 - 4:30
Tues til 8:30
Sat 10 - 2

fabric, of course • 100% cotton sewing & quilting thread • machine quilting supplies synthetic & natural-fiber batts • hoops & hoops on stands • measuring tools & rulers value viewers • design mirrors • basting systems • pencils & markers • note cards rippers • clippers • snippers • scissors • fabric care products, including Retayne, Synthrapol, Orvus Quilt Soap and Conservator's Choice™ acid-free tissue paper • paper foundations • patterns . . . and interested quilters who'll answer questions & help with fabric selection

PineTree Quiltworks

South Portland, ME #1

585 Broadway 04106
Shop: (207) 799-9535 Mail Order: (207) 799-7357
Phone or write to request a catalog,
or E-mail us: pinetree@quiltworks.com
Web Site: http://quilt.com/pinetree

DIRECTIONS
From I - 295: Take exit 6A to Forest Avenue South. Bear right off the exit; follow signs to Route 77. You'll be on State Street; bear right at the bottom of the hill and cross the bridge into South Portland. You'll be on Broadway. Watch on your left; PineTree is immediately after Dunkin Donut and Kentucky Fried Chicken before you reach the first set of lights.
LOOKING FORWARD TO SEEING YOU!

York Village, ME #2

May 15 - Oct 12
Mon - Sat 10 - 5
Sun 12 - 5
Winter by Appt.

Rocky Mountain Quilts

130 York St. (Rt. 1A) 03909
(800) 762-5940 or (207) 363-6800

Antique Quilts, Tops & Blocks plus Vintage Fabrics (1770 - 1950). Restoration and Custom Quilting.

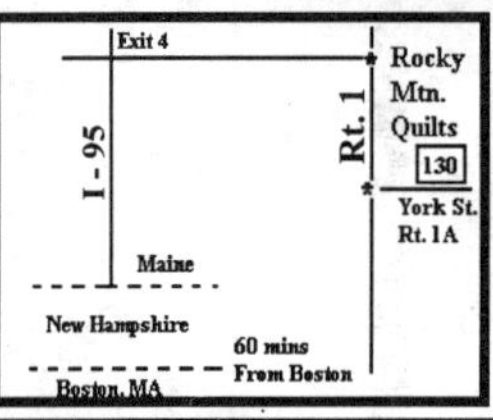

Waterboro, ME #3

Mon - Fri
9:30 - 5
Sat 9:30 - 3

Route 202 04087
(207) 247-4665
Est: 1988
Owner: Betty Ann Hammond

Fine Cotton Fabrics, Quilting supplies, Books, Quality Yarns, Pattern Books for Knitting & Crocheting, Floss and more! Classes Available.

Berwick, ME #4

Cottage Herbs

A Craft and Quilt Shop

151 Diamond Hill Rd. 03901 (207) 698-5507

Large Selection of Homespuns and Country Fabrics
Many Books, Patterns, Notions
Quiltmaking ★ Dollmaking ★ Dried Arrangements
Classes Avail. ★ Baskets, etc. ★Specializing in Dried Flowers

Wed - Sat 10 - 5
Sun 1 - 5

Owner: Nancy Riley
Est: 1980

DIRECTIONS:
(We're easy to find)
Just Follow the signs on Route 9 in Berwick

Windham, ME #5

Mon - Fri
9:30-4:30
Tues til 8:30
Sat 9:30-4

Calico Basket Quilt Shop

40 Page Road 04062
(207) 892-5606
Owner: JoAnne Hill
Est: 1982 1300 sq.ft.

Over 3000 Top Quality Fabrics. The Latest Books, Notions, Craft Patterns, and Quilting Supplies.

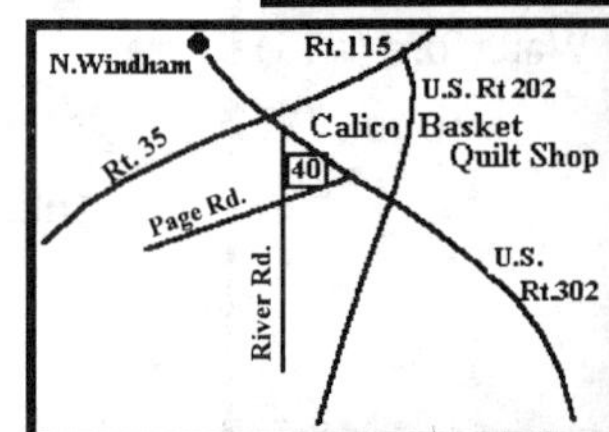

Boothbay Harbor, ME #6

Summer
7 Days 10 - 8
Winter
Tues - Sat 10 - 5

14 Boothbay House Hill 04538
(207) 633-2007
E-Mail: rroberts@ctel.net
Est: 1998
1000 sq.ft.
500+ Bolts
Quilt Shop & Fiber Arts Gallery.
Designer fabrics (Hoffman, Bali Batiks, African batiks, silks) supplies, notions, beads, embellishments & gifts for quilters.

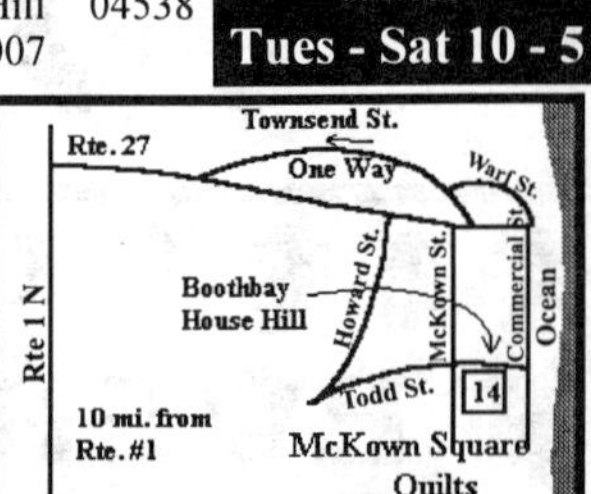

Rockland, ME #7

Mon - Sat
9 - 6
Sun 12 - 5

Fabric Bonanza

195 Park St., Rt. 1 04841
(207) 594-2555 Fax: (207) 594-2556
E-Mail: bjf@midcoast.com
Web Site: www.midcoast.com/~bjf
Owners: Joel & Barbara Fishman
Est: 1976 8000 sq.ft. 1500 Bolts
Over 1500 bolts of 100% cotton top quality quilting fabric, supplies, books and patterns. Located on Route 1 in Mid-Coast Maine.

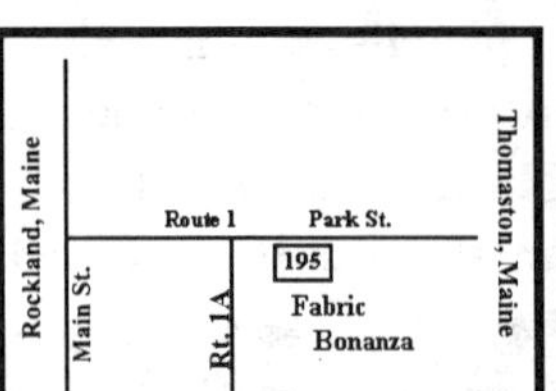

Machias, ME #8

Tues - Sat
10 - 4

Gingham Fabrics

Route 1 East
Mail: Box 286, Cutler, ME 04626
(207) 255-8238
Owner: Linda M. Throckmortow
Est: 1977 1700 sq.ft.
Eastern most quilt shop in the USA. Look for the geodesic dome midway between Ellsworth and Calais.

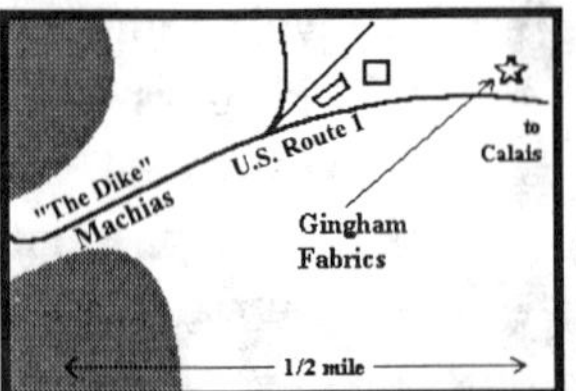

Belfast, ME #9

7 Days a Week
9 - 5

Nancy's Sewing Center

HCR #80 (Rte. 3) 04915
(207) 338-1205
Owner: Nancy E. Black
Est: 1984 1200 sq.ft.

1000 Bolts of Fabric. Notions, quilt Supplies, Classes.

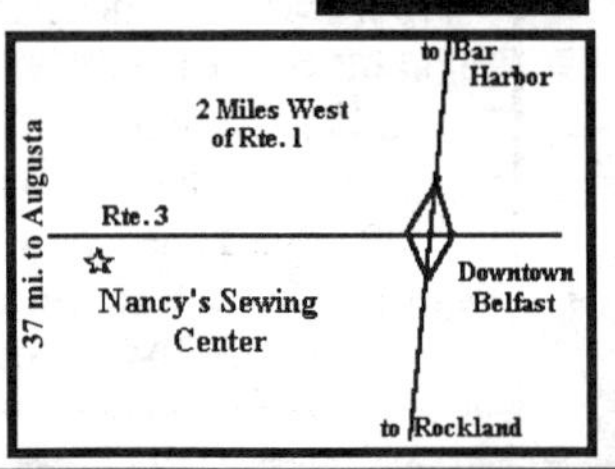

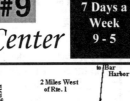

Litchfield, ME #10

Mon - Sat
10 - 5
Sun by chance

The Busy Thimble

Hallowell - Litchfield Rd.
Rt. #1 Box 1040 04350
(207) 268-4581 Est: 1990
e-mail: bsythmbl@ctel.net
Owner: Cynthia Black 1000 sq.ft.

A Quilter's Paradise
More than 1100 bolts of 100% cotton fabric.
Complete Library & Notions galore!

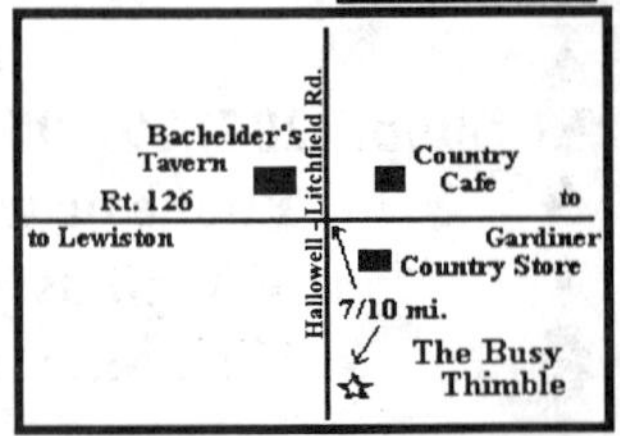

Auburn, ME #11

Mon - Fri 10 - 6
Sat 10 - 4

Quiltessentials

1146 Minot Ave. 04210
(207) 784-4486
Est: 1994

Full line of Quilt and Basket Making supplies & classes. Unique selection of 100% cotton fabrics, books & notions. Handmade Baskets

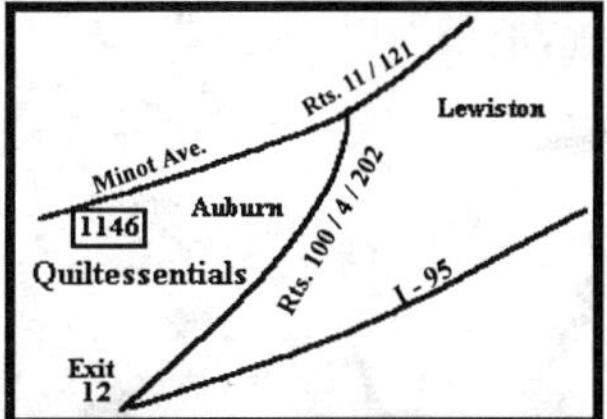

Harrison, ME #12

8 - 4
Most Days
Call Ahead to be sure

Jan's Golden Needle

RFD #1, Box 173-A, Zakelo Rd. 04040-9712
(207)583-2654 or (888) 615-4517
E-Mail: jgneedle@megalink.net
Web Site: www.megalink.net/~jgneedle
Owner: Jan Friend Est: 1996

Call us for fine workmanship, workshops, getaways, & antique restoration. Custom quilting, cross-stitch designs, hand work our specialty.

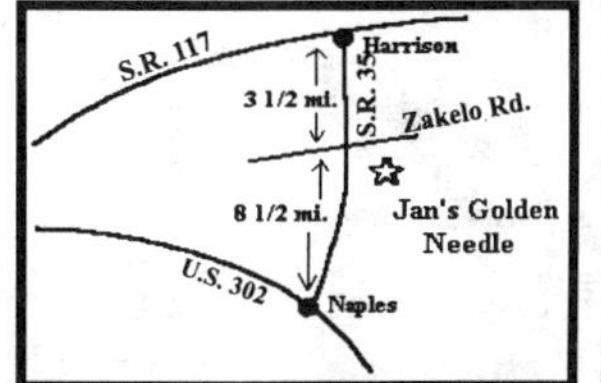

Waterford, ME #13

Mon - Thur 9 - 6
Fri - Sun 9 - 9

Kedar Craft

Rt. 35, Box 61 04088
(207) 583-6182 Fax: (207) 583-6424
E-Mail: kedar01@aol.com Est: 1989
Web Site: members.aol.com/kedar01
Owner: Margaret Gibson 1000 Bolts

Fine 100% Cotton Fabrics, Notions, Classes, Books. FOR SALE: New and Antique Quilts, Wallhangings and much more.
Located at Kedarburn Inn.

Dixfield, ME #14

Tues 9:30-8
Wed - Fri 9:30 - 5
Sat 9:30 - 1

Log Cabin Craftworks

31 Main 04224
(207) 562-8816
Owner: Norine Clarke
Est: 1981 350 bolts 2500 sq. ft.

Located in the foothills of Western Maine we offer a variety of Fabrics, Current Books, Tools and Notions.

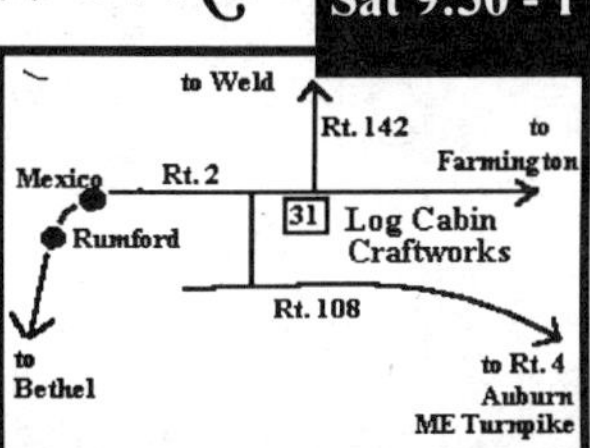

Rangeley, ME #15

Tues - Sat 10 - 5

Threads Galore Quilt Shop

11 Pleasant St., P.O. Box 219 04970
(207) 864-5752 Est: 1996
E-Mail: dperk@rangeley.org
Owners: Carol & Dan Perkins

Hand guided Machine quilting.
Fabric, Books, Notions, Classes.
Quilted items for sale.

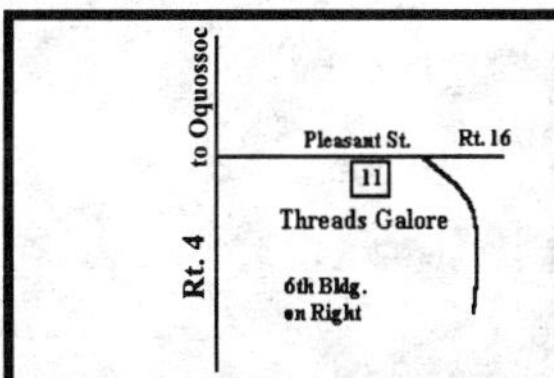

Farmington, ME #16

Mon - Sat 9 - 5
Sun 11 - 3

Fabric Inn

R.R. #4, Box 5057 04938
(207) 778-4288
Est: 1976 2000 sq.ft.

The store for all your sewing and quilting needs. Name brand fabrics, books, patterns & notions. New Home sewing machines sales and service.

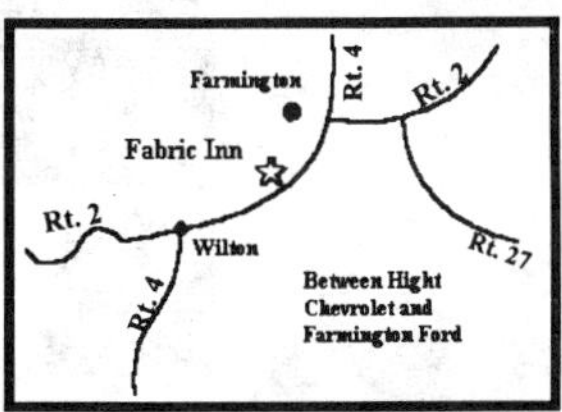

Madison, ME #17

Mon - Fri 9 - 6
Sat 9 - 5
Sun 12 - 5

The Fabric Garden

Web Site: www.somtel.com/fabricgarden
Rt. 201 North 04950
(207) 474-9628
Owner: Michaela Murphy
Est: 1978 2400 sq.ft.

Inspiring Collection of Fine Quilting Cottons.
Wonderful Silk Ribbon Emb. Supplies.
Quilts for Sale.
"A Fabric Lover's Home Away From Home."

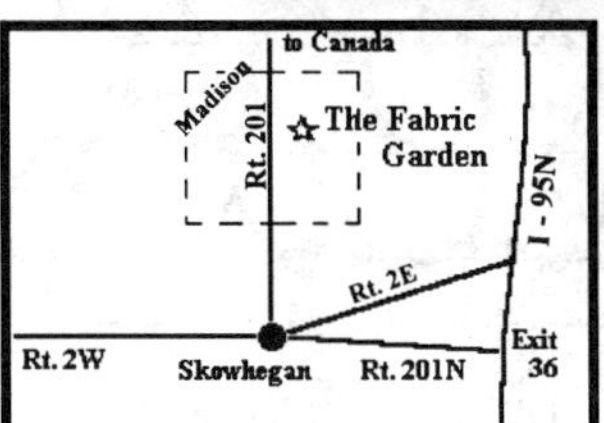

Brewer, ME #18

Mon - Fri 9 - 5
Sat 9 - 4
Sun 12 - 4

Cotton Patch Quilts

46 Betton St. 04412
(207) 989-9932 Fax: (207) 989-6288
E-Mail: CottnPatch@aol.com
Owners: Dawn Emmons & Sondra Spencer

Beautiful 100% cotton fabrics, books, notions, Quilts for sale, & classes.
A Quilter's Haven in scenic central Maine.

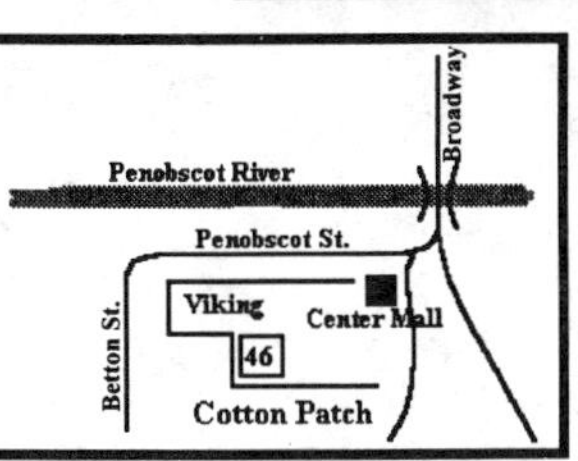

Maine Guilds:

Friendship Sampler Quilters, 112 Bog Rd., Belfast, 04915
Meets: 2nd & 4th Thursday 10 a.m.
at St. Margaret Church, 49 Court St.

Down East Chapter, Pine Tree Quilters Guild, Box 286, Cutler, 04626
Meets: 4rth Thursday at 1 p.m.
at Porter Memorial Library in Machias

Rangeley Quilters Guild, Rangeley
Meets: 1st & 3rd Thursday (Sept - June) 7 p.m.
at Rangeley Congregational Church

Pine Tree Quilter's Guild, RD Box 252, Turner, 04282

Nimble Thimbles, Community Center, Windham, 04062

Other Shops in Maine:

Bar Harbor	Sewing by the Sea, RFD #1, Rte 102	207-288-4266
Freeport	Quilt & Needlecrafts, 22 Main St.	207-865-3224
Jefferson	Country Creations, Route 32	207-549-7424
Lisbon Falls	Mill Fabric Center, 2 Ridge	207-353-8421
Milo	Roses & Old Lace, 27 W. Main St.	207-943-5017
Newcastle	Alewives Fabrics, R.R. #1, Box 480	207-563-5002
Newport	Robyn's Nest Fabrics, Rt. 7	207-368-2419
North Edgecomb	On Board, Route 27, Booth Bay Rd.	207-882-7536
Pittsfield	Quilter's Dream, 9 Easy St.	207-938-3524
Presque Isle	Fabrique Shoppe, 375 Main St.	207-764-6191
Rumford	The Pin Cushion, 94 River St.	207-364-2888
Saco	Patchwork Boutique, 304 Beach St.	207-284-7287
Wiscasset	The Marston House, P.O. Box 517	207-882-6010

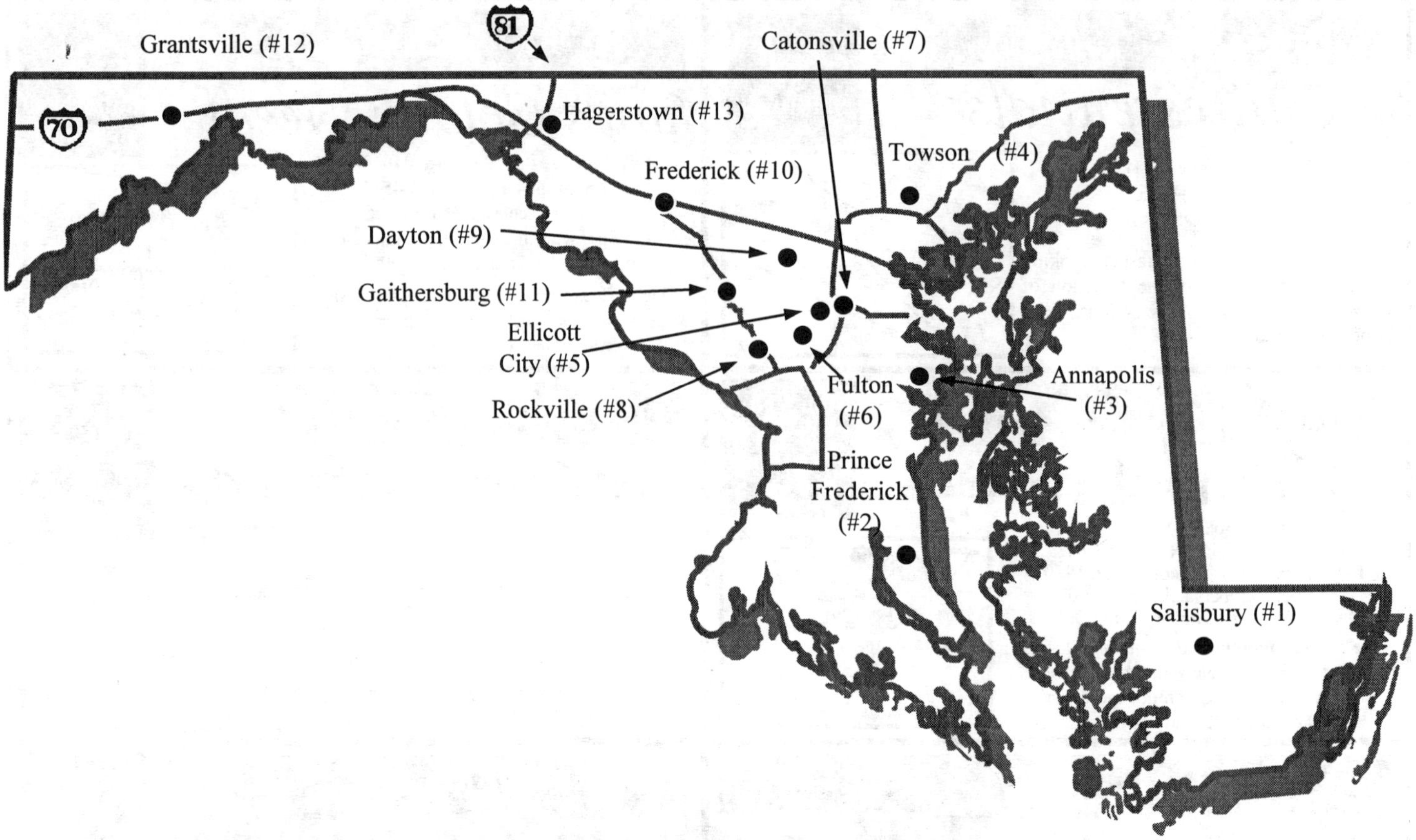

81
Grantsville (#12)
Catonsville (#7)
70
Hagerstown (#13)
Towson (#4)
Frederick (#10)
Dayton (#9)
Gaithersburg (#11)
Ellicott City (#5)
Rockville (#8)
Fulton (#6)
Annapolis (#3)
Prince Frederick (#2)
Salisbury (#1)

Maryland

13 Featured Shops

QUILT SHOP
OPEN
FABRIC
NOTIONS

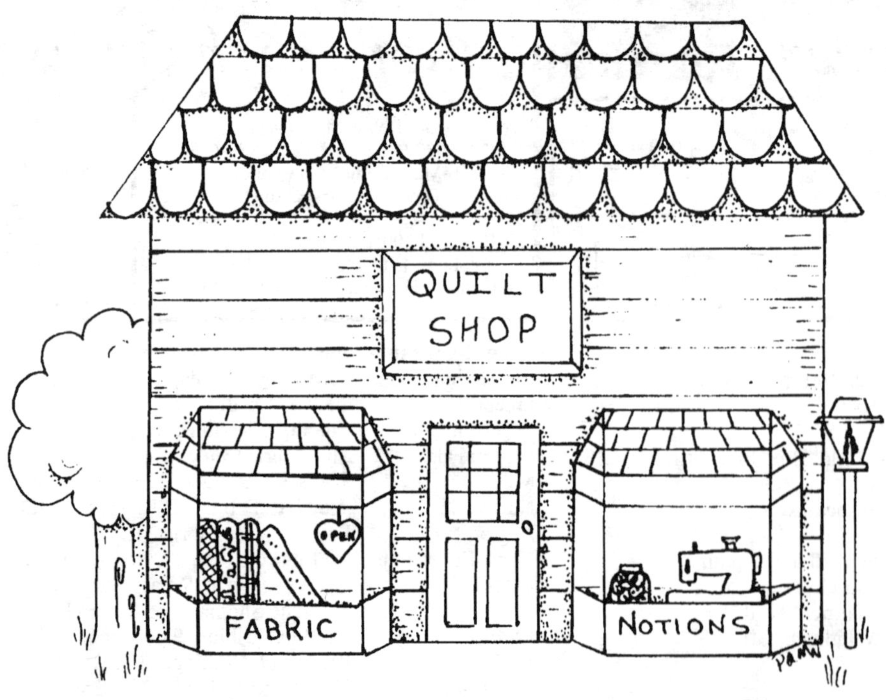

Salisbury, MD #1

Mon, Wed, & Fri 10-8
Tue, Thur, & Sat 10 - 6

Jenny's Sewing Studio

311 Civic Ave. 21804
(410) 543-1212
E-Mail: jenny@shore.intercom.net
Web-Site: www.jennys-sewing-studio.com
Owner: Jennifer Friedel
Est: 1982 3200 sq.ft.

Full service quilt shop & sewing machine dealer. (Bernina, New Home, Pfaff, Singer) Over 2000 bolts of fabric and approx. 30 classes offered.

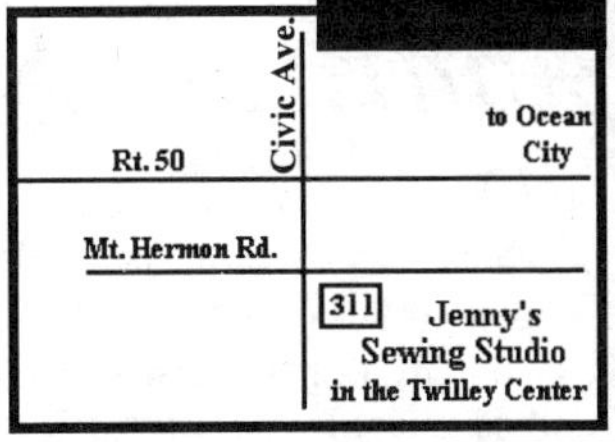

Civic Ave.
Rt. 50
to Ocean City
Mt. Hermon Rd.
311 Jenny's Sewing Studio in the Twilley Center

Prince Frederick, MD #2

Mon - Thur 9 - 6
Fri 9 - 7
Sat 9 - 4

Calvert Quilting Shop

MD Rt. 4 at Industry Lane 20678
(410) 535-0576 Fax: (410) 535-1197
Est: 1966 2000 sq.ft. 2000+ Bolts

We carry major manufacturers of Quilting Products. 100% Cotton, Name Brand Fabrics, Notions, Cutting Equip., Classes. New Home Sewing Machine Sales and Service.

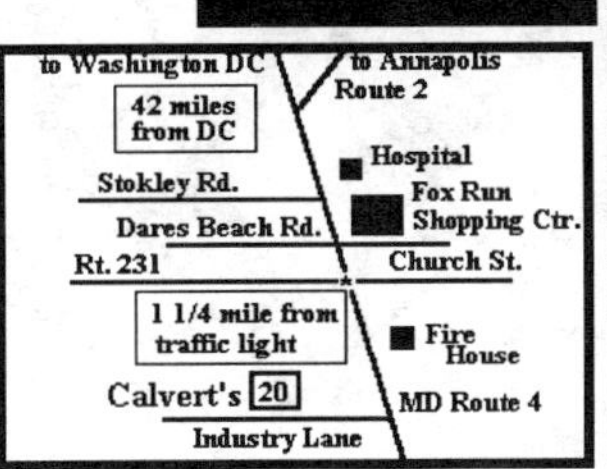

Cottonseed Glory

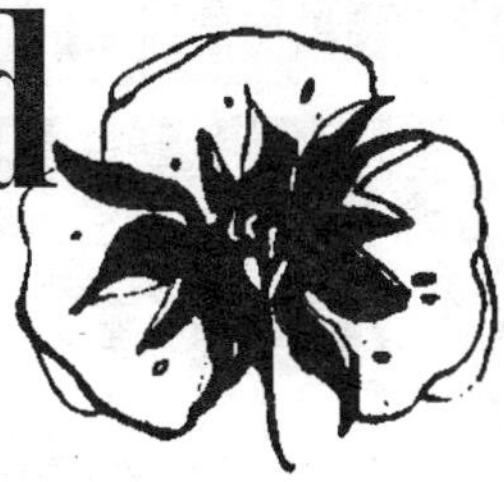

Est: 1978

3500 bolts from over 40 manufacturers.
Books, Gourmet Notions,
PATTERNS, PATTERNS, PATTERNS!

Mon - Sat 10 - 5
Sundays 1 - 4
(No Sun hours June - Aug)

4 Annapolis St. 21401
(410) 263-3897
Owner: Pat Steiner

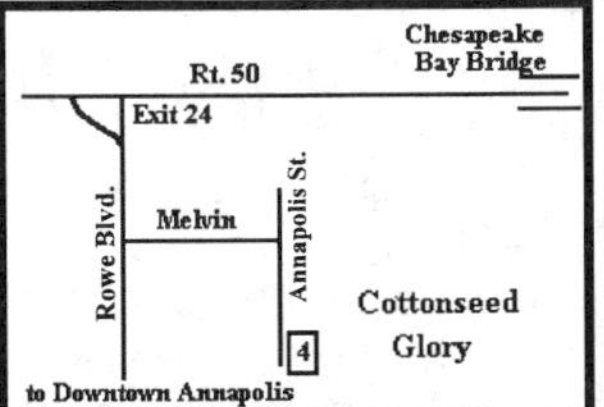

Visit Both Locations

BEAR'S PAW FABRICS

Towson, MD #4

8812 Orchard Tree Lane 21286
(410) 321-6730
(800) 761-2202
695 to Exit 29B (Loch Raven Blvd.)
-right on Joppa Rd.
-right on Orchard Tree Lane
-5th store on left

Ellicott City, MD #5

8659 Baltimore National Pike (Rt. 40)
(410) 480-2875 21043
(888) 877-4898
695 to Exit 15B (Route 40 W)
-Rt. 40 West to Ridge Rd (Howard Cty)
-U-turn at Ridge
-Store immediately on right

FINE SELECTION OF QUILTING FABRICS, NOTIONS, PATTERNS AND BOOKS.

Fulton, MD #6

P.O. Box 243 20759
(301) 465-7202
E-Mail: stocklin@erols.com
Web Site: www.erols.com/ stocklin

By Appt. Only

I-695
Baltimore, MD
Rt. 216
Fulton
I-95
I-495
Washington, DC

Owner: Inge Stocklin Est: 1989

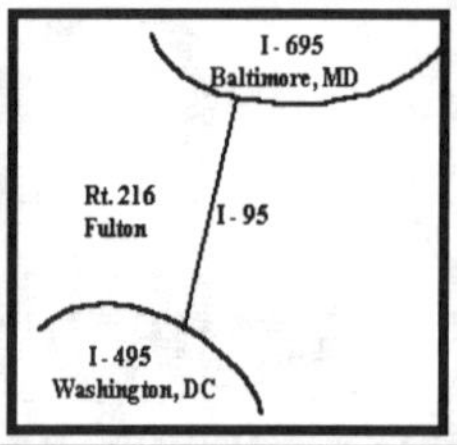

Quilt restoration, appraisals, lectures, shows. Patterns of lighthouses and motifs from the Chesapeake Bay.

Catonsville, MD #7

Mon, Wed, Thur 10 - 8
Tues, Fri, Sat 10 - 5

Seminole Sampler

71 Mellor Ave. 21228
(410) 788-1720
E-Mail: seminolesampler@erols.com
Est: 1980 3360 sq.ft.

3000 Bolts; Cottons; Complete Line of Quilting Supplies; Unsurpassable Service; New Home/ Janome Sewing Machines; Neighbors: Stitching Post, Weavers Place.

Rockville, MD #8

Mon - Fri 10 - 7
Thur til 9
Sat 10 - 6

Anna Marie's Fashion Fabrics

2011 Veirs Mill Rd. 20851
(301) 762-8491
Owner: Anna Marie & Jack Roberts
Est: 1970 3000 sq.ft.

Extensive selection of quality fabrics for quilts and fashions - Patterns - Notions Trims - Buttons - Hard-to-find items - Expert advice from friendly knowledgeable staff.

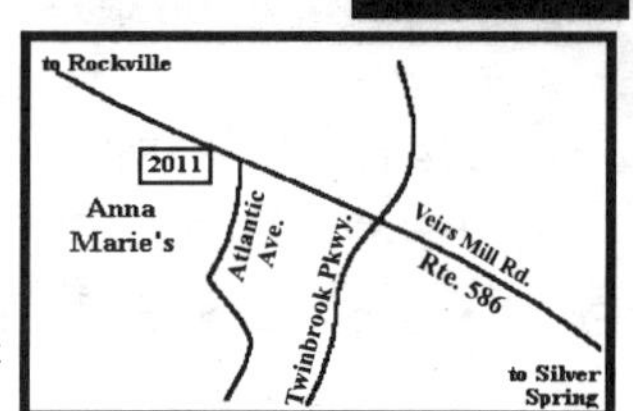

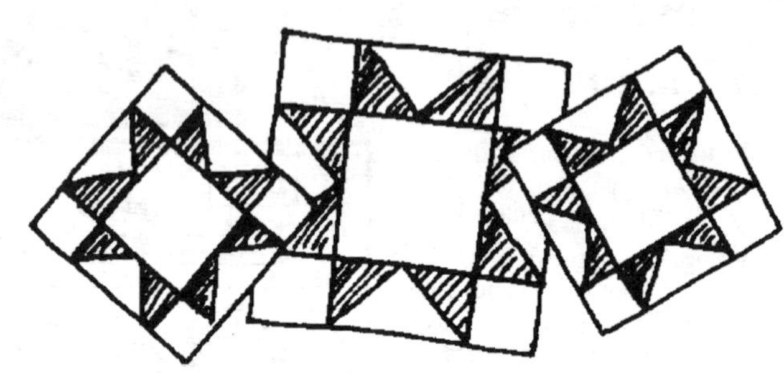

Dayton, MD #9

- Friendly, knowledgeable staff
- Classes (2 classrooms)
- Books
- Patterns
- Notions wall
- Machine quilting services
- Quilts for sale
- Free Newsletter

The Quilt Block

4714 Linthicum Rd.
21036
(410) 531-5723
Owner: Diane Janoske
Est: 1995
1600+ Bolts

Mon - Sat 10 - 5

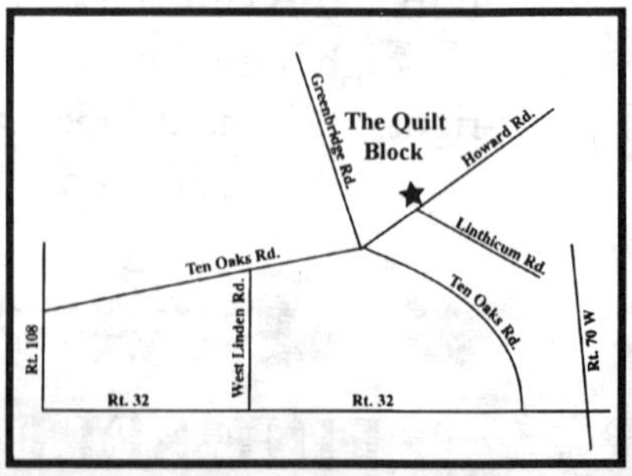

Greenbridge Rd.
The Quilt Block
Howard Rd.
Linthicum Rd.
Ten Oaks Rd.
Ten Oaks Rd.
Rt. 108
West Linden Rd.
Rt. 32
Rt. 32
Rt. 70 W

A Quilter's Heaven

Frederick, MD #10

310 E. Church St. 21701
(301) 695-7199
Web Site: pw2.netcom.com
/~cpowell2/needles.htm

Mon - Sat 9 - 7 Sun 12 - 5

Located in historic Everedy Square & Shab Row shopping area. Within easy walking distance of many specialty shops, restaurants, antique shops and historical sites, including the National Museum of Civil War Medicine.

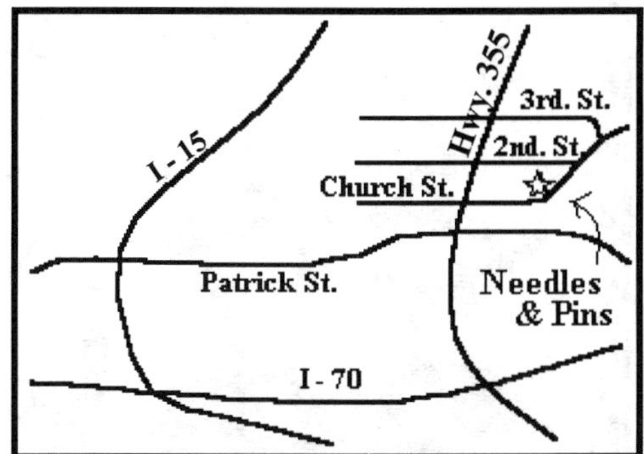

Needles 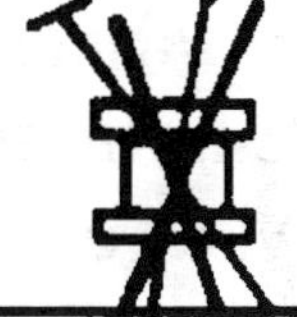 Pins

quilting ✂ dollmaking ✂ needlework

We have over 1000 bolts of the highest quality cotton fabrics for quilting, dollmaking and clothing including: P&B, RJR, Mission Valley Textiles, Kona Bay, Clothworks, Peter Pan, Benartex, Rose & Hubble and more.

Hundreds of patterns for dolls, Santas, snowmen, wallhangings, clothing, quilts, clothing for the popular 18 inch dolls, bears and more. Largest display of doll hair in region. We carry patterns by elinor peace bailey, Sally Lampi, Magic Threads and many, many others. Holiday patterns available year round.

Full line of Kunin Rainbow, Shaggy and Plush felts.
Hobbs cotton battings by the yard; Polydown Stuffing;
Books, notions, tools of the trade.

We also stock counted cross stitch patterns and fabrics not sold in the chain stores. Anchor embroidery floss and pearl cotton. Hand dyed threads.

Gaithersburg, MD #11

Mon - Sat 10 - 6
Sun 12 - 5
Class Eve.

15926 Luanne Dr. 20877
(301) 527-0598 Est: 1995 1800 sq.ft.
Owners: Susan & Gary McLaughlin

CAPITAL QUILTS

Great selection of high quality fabric and a full range of books, patterns, & notions. Featuring patterns by local artists. We're proud of our many classes. Service is friendly & helpful. Bring in your 'Problem Pieces'. Easy Access by Public Trans.

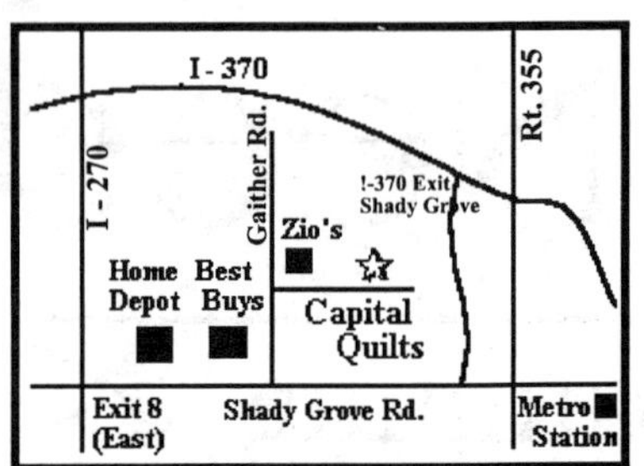

We Are Very Easy to Find!

Grantsville, MD #12

Mon - Sat 9 - 5

Four Seasons Stitchery

P.O. Box 218 116 Main St. 21536
(301) 895-5958
Owner: Jane Benson
Est: 1985

Most Complete Quilting Shop in the Tri-State area. Over 1000 bolts all cotton fabrics. Books, Notions & Cross Stitch Supplies.

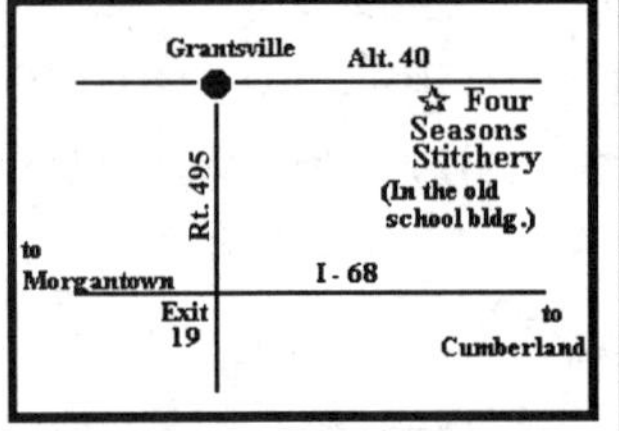

Maryland Guilds:

Annapolis Quilt Guild, 98 Spring Valley Dr., Annapolis, 21403
Meets: at St. Andrews Church, Forest Dr.
Baltimore Heritage Quilters' Guild, P.O. Box 66537, Baltimore, 21239
Flying Geese Quilt Guild, P.O. Box 1894, Bel Air, 21014
Faithful Circle Quilters, 5012 Lake Circle W, Columbia, 21044
Friendship Star Quilters, P.O. Box 8051, Gaithersburg, 20877
Lydia Guild, 2770 Crooked Oak Ln., Hebron, 21830 Meets: 2nd Monday 7 p.m. at Rockawalkin UMC, newly formed--mostly beginners
Creative Needle Quilters, 946 Natinal Hwy., LaVale, 21502
Schoolhouse Quilters' Guild, 888 Weires Ave., LaVale, 21502
Eternal Quilter, 346 Chalet Dr., Millersville, 21108
School House Quilts, Salisbury, c/o Joan Norman, 4705 Fleming Mill Rd., Pocomoke, MD 21851
Meets: 3rd Wednesday 7 p.m. at Holly Center, Snow Hill Rd., Salisbury

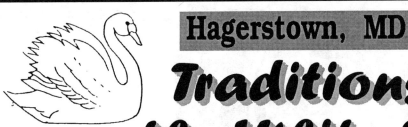

Hagerstown, MD #13

Traditions at the White Swan

Authorized Bernina Dealer

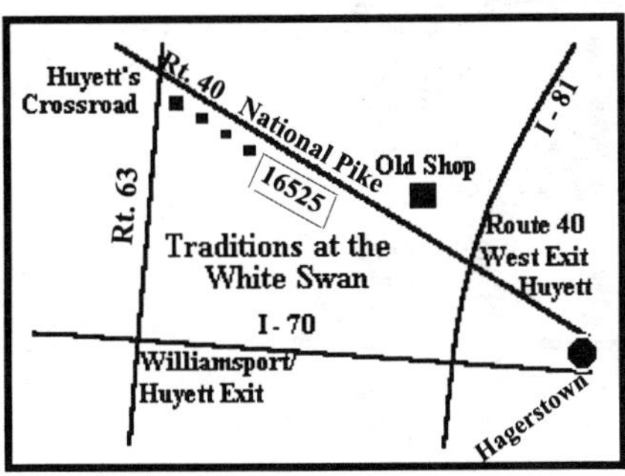

3½ miles West of town

Largest Quilt Shop in the area with everything for the quilter— beginner thru advanced.
2500 bolts of fabric including— Hoffman, RJR, P&B, Benartex, Marcus Brothers & Mums the Word.
Notions, Books, Patterns, Stencils, & Classes

June - Aug
Tues - Sat 10 - 5
Sept - May
Mon - Sat 10 - 5
Sun 1 - 5

16525 National Pike 21740
(301) 733-9130 Est: 1985
Owners: Dick & Wendy Shank 1700 sq.ft.

Other Shops in Maryland:

Baltimore	Blanks, 6709 A Whitestone Rd.	
Baltimore	Harbor Quilting, 3500 Parkdale Ave.	410-462-4022
Bethesda	Amish Quilts & Furniture, 7910 Kentbury Dr.	301-656-1644
Boonsboro	Old School Fabrics, 230 Potomac	301-432-6195
Chester	Peggy's Sewing Center, 100 Helfendein Ln.	410-643-7202
Chestertown	The Yardstick, P.O. Box 3	410-778-0049
Columbia	Milltown Quilters, 5238 Farm Pond Ln.	
Easton	Lilies of the Field, Easton Plaza Shp. Ctr.	410-822-9117
Flintstone	Cathy's Country Quilts, 12712 Murleys Branch Rd. NE	301-478-2589
Hagerstown	Wilson Sew & Vac, 21680 Leitersbury Pk.	301-790-3526
Rockville	G Street Fabrics, 11854 Rockville Pike	301-231-8998
Upper Marlboro	Stitches & Sew On, 9020 Trumps Hill Rd.	301-627-2990

Shops in Washington DC:

Washington	Appalachian Spring, 1415 Wisconsin Ave. NW	202-337-5780
Washington	Daughter of Dorcas, 1109 Abbey Place NE	
Washington	Appalachian Spring, 50 Massachusetts Ave. NE	202-682-0505

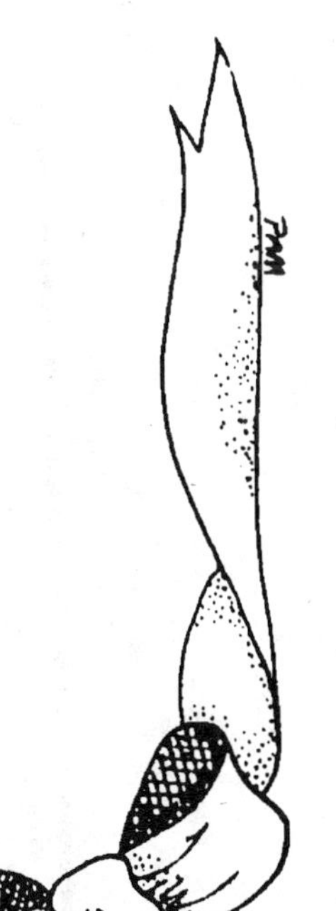

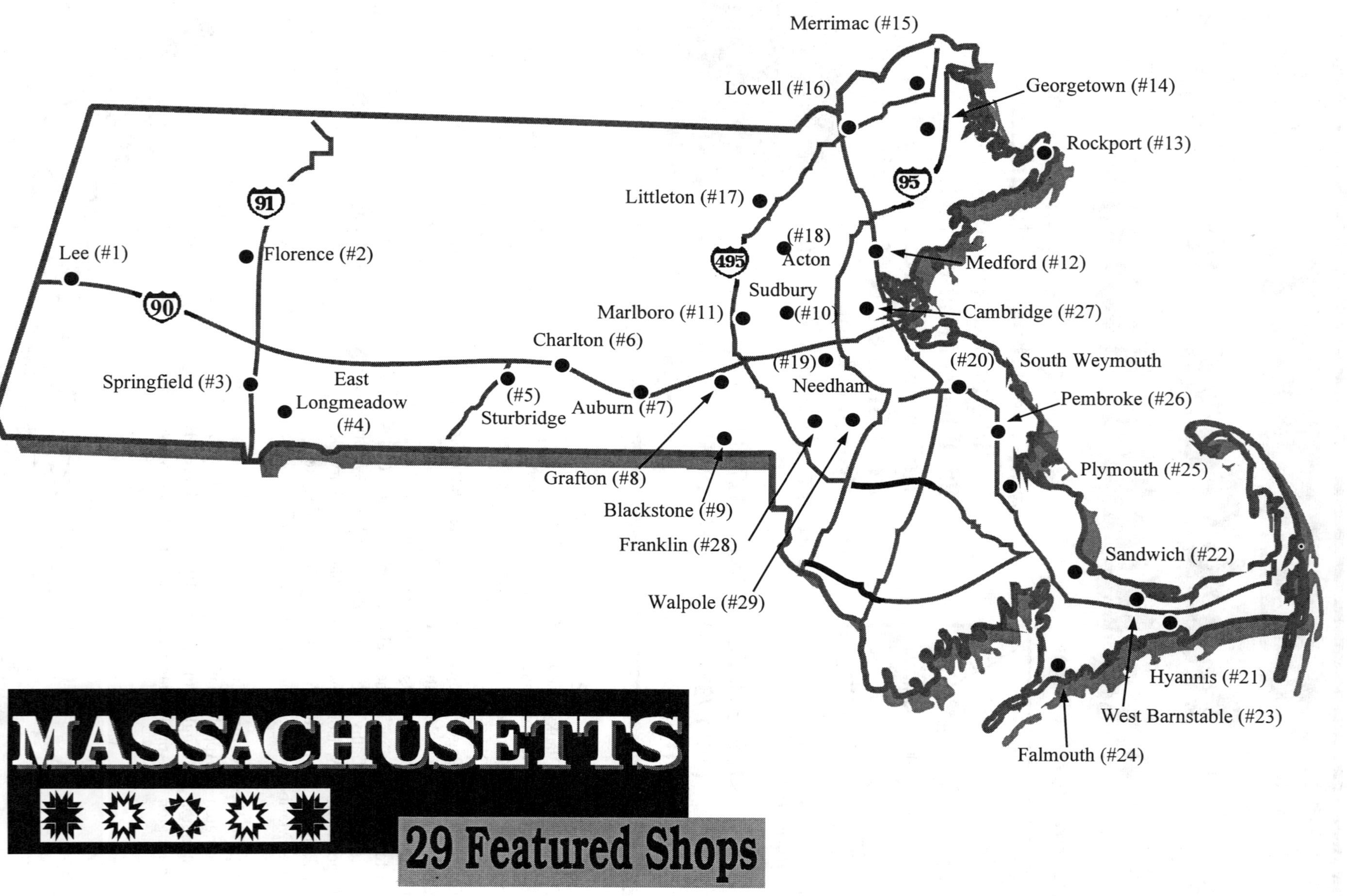
MASSACHUSETTS
29 Featured Shops
Merrimac (#15)
Lowell (#16)
Georgetown (#14)
Rockport (#13)
Littleton (#17)
(#18) Acton
Medford (#12)
Lee (#1)
Florence (#2)
Sudbury (#10)
Marlboro (#11)
Cambridge (#27)
Charlton (#6)
(#19) Needham
(#20) South Weymouth
Springfield (#3)
East Longmeadow (#4)
(#5) Sturbridge
Auburn (#7)
Pembroke (#26)
Grafton (#8)
Plymouth (#25)
Blackstone (#9)
Franklin (#28)
Sandwich (#22)
Walpole (#29)
Hyannis (#21)
West Barnstable (#23)
Falmouth (#24)
91
90
495
95

Lee, MA #1

Mon - Sat 10 - 6
Sun 12 - 6

Pumpkin Patch

58 W. Center St. (Rt. 20)
(413) 243-1635 01238
Owners: Susan & Dan Sullivan
Est: 1985 800 sq.ft.

Located in the beautiful Berkshires!
Cotton fabrics, books, patterns, etc. . . .
Classes, machine quilting . . . .
Bernina Sewing Machines

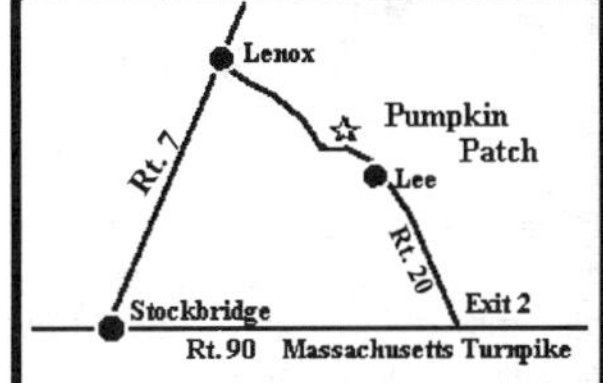

Florence, MA #2

Calico Fabrics

52 Main St. 01062-3165
(413) 585-8665
E-Mail: calico.fabrics@the-spa.com
Owner: Joan Trecartin
Est: 1980 1000 sq.ft.

Mon - Fri 10 - 5
Sat 10 - 3
Winter Suns 12 - 3

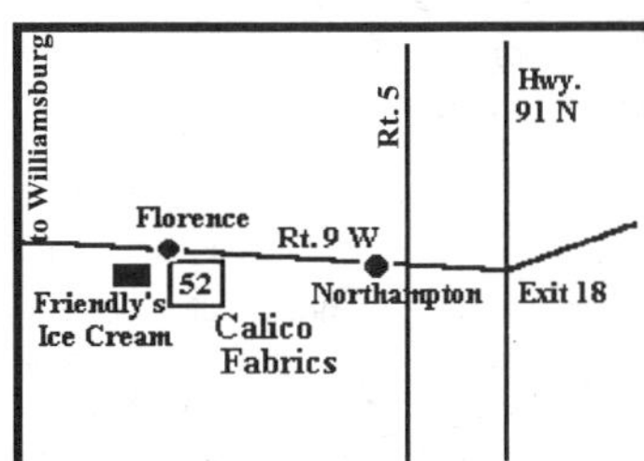

Choose from 1600+ bolts of top name Fabrics. Hoffman, RJR, P&B, Kaufman, Moda, Kona Bay. Books, Quilt Supplies and Classes.
Handicapped Accessible

Largest Quilt Shop in the Area!

Springfield, MA #3

Mon - Sat 10 - 4

Double T Quilt Shop

219 Berkshire Ave. 01109
(413) 737-9605
Owner: Jean Thibodeau
Est: 1983 1000+ Bolts Samples $4

We carry a wide stock of fabrics from Hoffman, A.Henry, Libas, MEH, P&B, Bali and Guatemalan types. Plus Books and Notions.

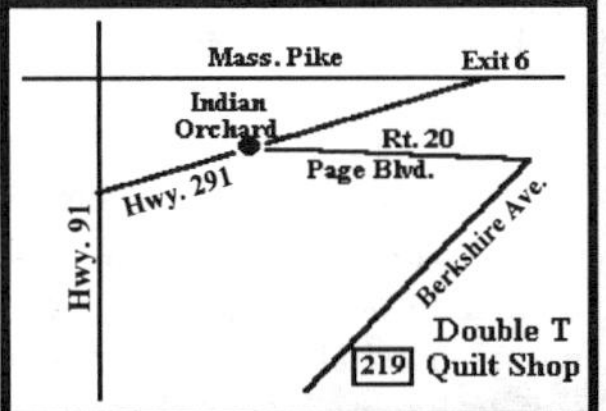

East Longmeadow, MA #4

Mon - Thur 10 - 9
Fri & Sat 10 - 5
Closed Mondays in July & Aug.

Thimbleworks

56 Shaker Rd. 01028
(413) 525-4789

Sewing Machine Center

Great selection of 100% cotton Fabrics, Books, Patterns & Quilting Supplies. Authorized dealer for Pfaff & New Home.

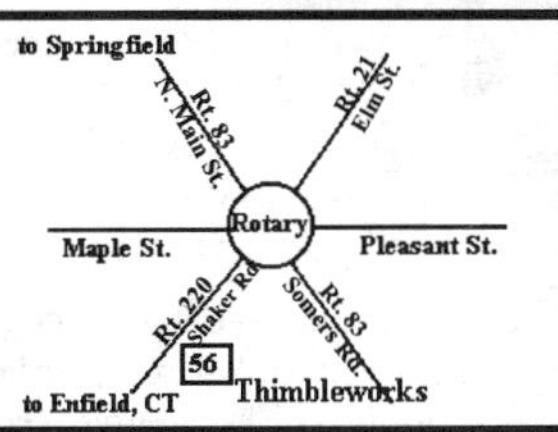

THE Quilt AND Cabbage

Enter a warm, friendly & relaxing atmosphere of 800+ bolts, best selection of quilting stencils, books, patterns, & notions. Custom quilted items, pillows, & sweatshirts. Leave with inspiration, treasures & a smile.

P.O. Box 534 01566
538 Main St. (Rt. 20)
(508) 347-3023

Sturbridge, MA #5

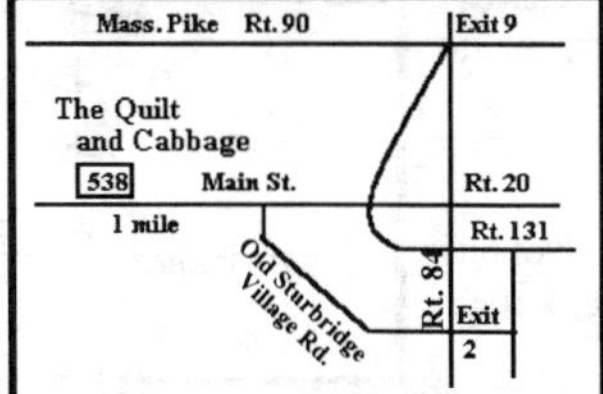

Mon & Wed - Sat 9:30 - 4:30
Sun 11 - 4
Closed Tues

Est: 1991

Charlton, MA #6

Mon - Sat 9:30 - 6:30
Fri til 9

THE FABRIC STASH

16 Sturbridge Rd. (Rt. 20)
01507
(508) 248-0600
Owner: Laurel Wilber

"The Stash" is a full Service Fabric Store with friendly, helpful service. We have an extensive line of Quilting Fabric as well as apparel and home decor.

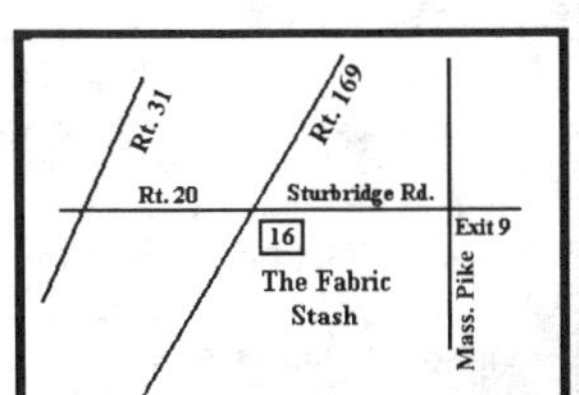

Auburn, MA #7

Mon - Wed 10 - 8
Thur - Sat 10 - 5

Appletree Fabrics

59 Auburn St. 01501
(508) 832-5562
Owner: Lois Therrien Est: 1991

Over a thousand bolts of beautiful cotton prints, solids & homespuns.
Large selection of books & patterns.
Handcrafts for sale. Classes.

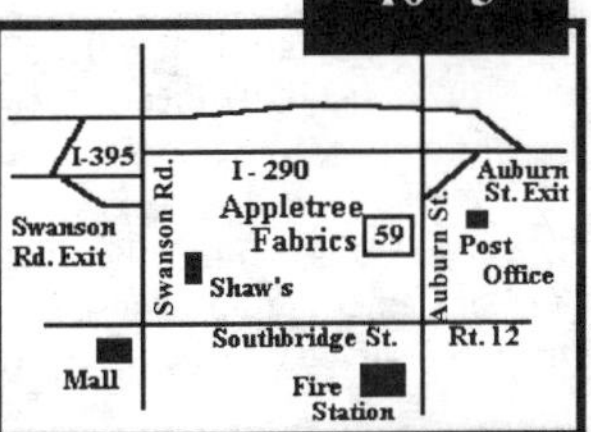

Grafton, MA #8

Tues - Sat 10 - 5 Sun 12 - 5

Calico & Co.

2 Grafton Common (Rear) 01519
(508) 839-5990
Owner: Joanne & Richard Erenius
Est: 1984 1000 sq.ft. 500 Bolts

Helpful & Friendly Service & Supplies for your every Quilting & Cross Stitch need. Classes to inspire your creativity.

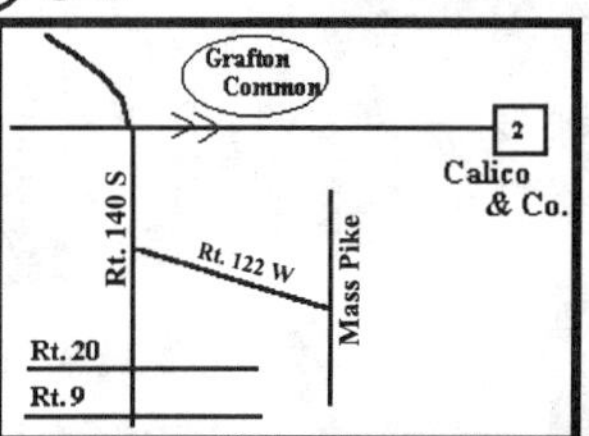

Blackstone, MA #9

Tues - Sat 10 - 5 Thur til 8

Quilter's Quarters

157 Main St., Rt. 122 01504
(508) 883-4140
Owner: Kathy Lemay
Est: 1995 1000 sq.ft.

Gorgeous selection of the best quality cottons along with supplies, books & patterns. Classes. Come browse in our relaxed atmosphere.

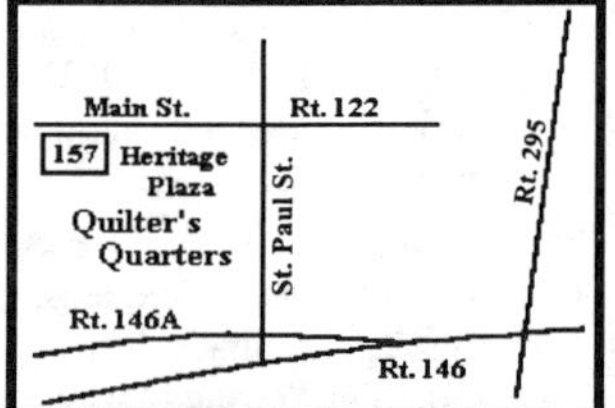

Sudbury, MA #10

Mon - Thur 9:30 - 9:30 Fri & Sat 9:30 - 6

Quilted Or Not

385 Boston Post Rd.
(978) 440-9505 01776
Est: 1992 1500 sq.ft. 1000 Bolts
Catalog $9 per year

Fine fabrics, quilting supplies & books, unique gifts. Classes, midnight parties & events. Chocolate is always served. Free Newsletter.

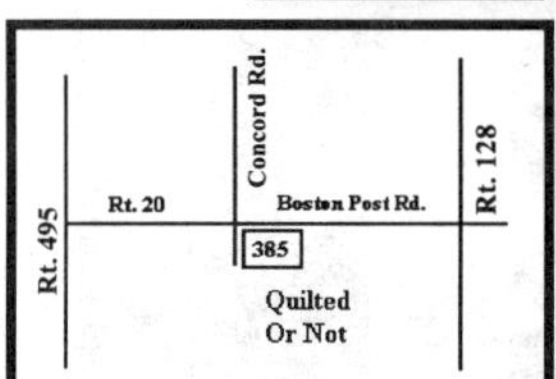

Marlboro, MA #11

Tues 12 - 5 Wed - Sat 10 - 5 Thur til 7 Sun12-5 (Nov-May)

A Quilters Garden

33 Main St. 01752
(508) 485-5481
Owner: Mary L. Walter Est: 1995
1000 sq.ft. Class Brochure Avail.
"A Place where ideas Grow"
A friendly and inspirational shop offering unusual fabrics, books, notions & techniques. Look for Batiks, African & hand-dyed fabrics.

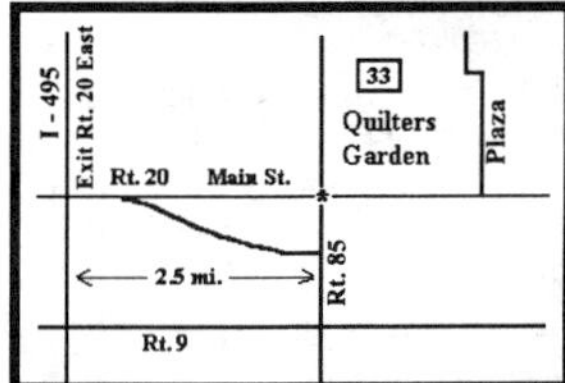

Medford, MA #12

Mon - Fri 9:30 - 5:30 Sat 11 - 5

Quilter's Hideaway

84 High St. 02155
(781) 395-3603
E-Mail: KPPARECE@aol.com
Owner: Katherine Parece Est: 1993

Over 1500 bolts of fabric, including batiks, 1930's repros, Japanese prints. Largest selection of quilting stencils in the area. Gift items, 100's of books, notions.

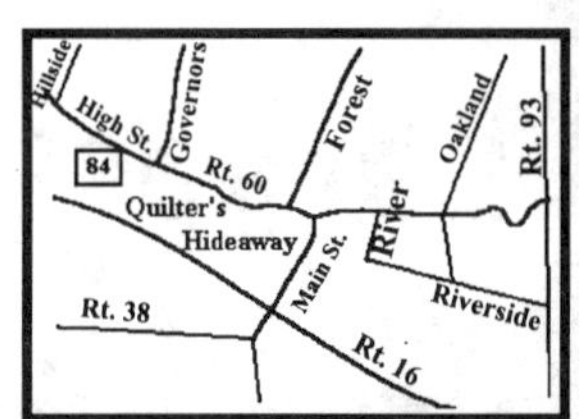

Rockport, MA #13

Tues - Fri 9 - 5 Sat 9 - 3

Rockport Quilt Shoppe

2 Ocean Ave. 01966
(978) 546-1001
Fax: (978) 546-2193
E-Mail: gdwhite@shore.net
Owner: Gloria White

Antique Quilts—Large Stock on Hand. Vintage Linens. Textile Restoration. Custom Work. Decorative Accessories.

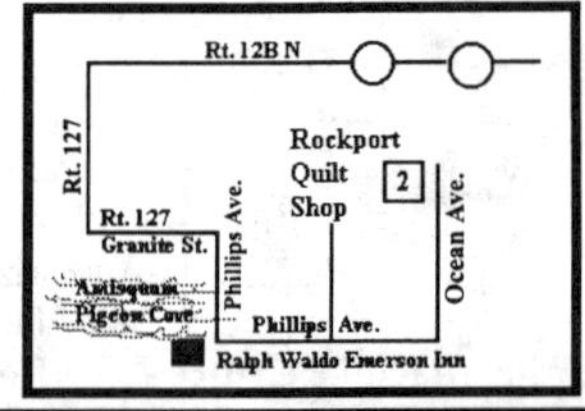

Georgetown, MA #14

Tues - Sat 9:30 - 4:30 & Thur 6 - 9 p.m.

The Crazy Ladies at The Quilted Acorn Shoppe

33 Library St. 01833 Est: 1983
(978) 352-7419 Schedule of Classes & Sales
Owners: Cynthia Erekson & Sandra Schauer

Unique combination of Folk Art Painting, Quilting Supplies, Fabrics and Classes specializing in an "Antique Look". Many Homespuns Doll Patterns, too!!

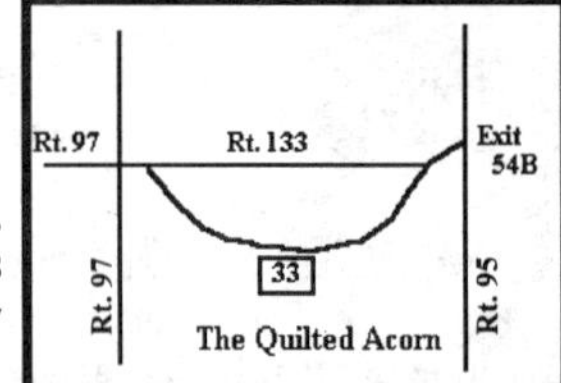

Merrimac, MA #15

Mon - Fri 9 - 5 Tues & Thur til 7 Sat 9 - 4

Red Barn Sewing & Yarn Center

90 West Main St. Rte. 110 01860
(978) 346-9292
Owners: Helen Gosselin & Linda Ouellette
Est: 1978 2000sq.ft. 1700 Bolts

100% cotton fabrics, fine yarns, patterns, books, supplies. Authorized New Home/Janome Sewing Machine Dealer. Quilting, Knitting & Sewing Classes. *Celebrating 20 years.*

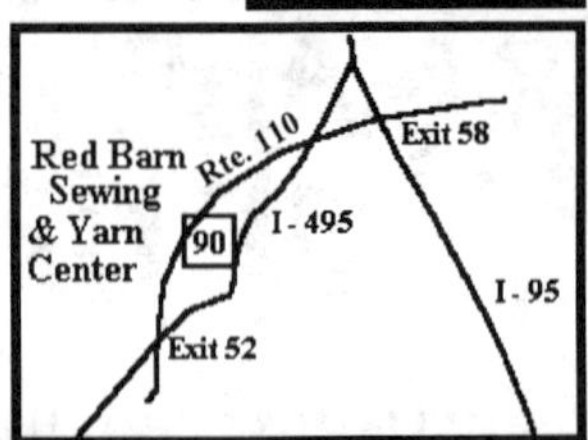

Lowell, MA #16

Tues - Sat 10 - 5 Sun May - Nov 12 - 5

The New England Quilt Museum

18 Shattack St. 01852
(978) 452-4207 Free to Members
Adm: $4, $3 Seniors & Students

Directly across from the National Park Visitor Center. From Boston's North Station trains are served by a bus every 15 minutes.

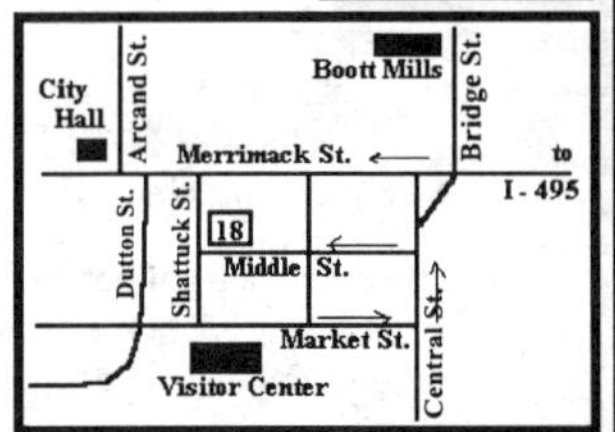

Littleton, MA #17

M, T, Th, F 10 - 5 Sat 10 - 3:30 Sun 12 - 4 (Sept-April)

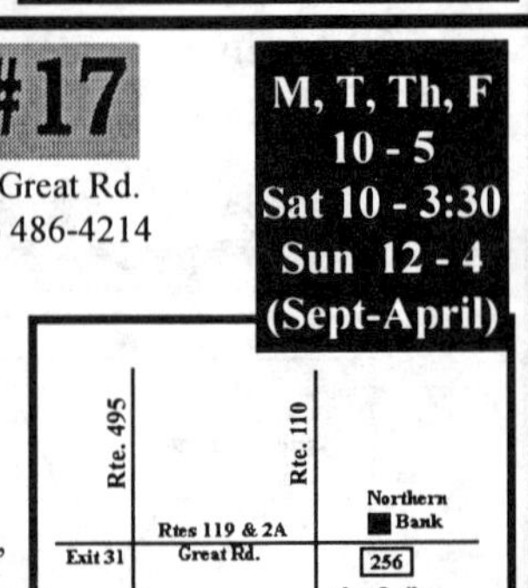

256 Great Rd.
(978) 486-4214
Owner: Gerre Clements

100% Cotton Fabrics, Books, Patterns, Notions, Quilt Racks, Hand Painted Quilt Labels, Custom Quilts.

Ralph Jordan's

... your Quilt Destination

Everything for your Special Quilting Projects from beginning to end . . . and More.

Over Two Thousand 100% Cotton Prints:
Plaids & Solids by Hoffman, RJR, South Seas, Concord, Moda, P&B, Peter Pan, Alexander Henry, Spiegel, Momen House, Benartex, Quilters Only and Hi-Fashion.

A complete selection of quilting books, patterns, templates, stencils, scissors, rotary cutters, mats, hoops and much, much more.

We also offer over 80 classes in quilting and crafts for beginner to advanced students.

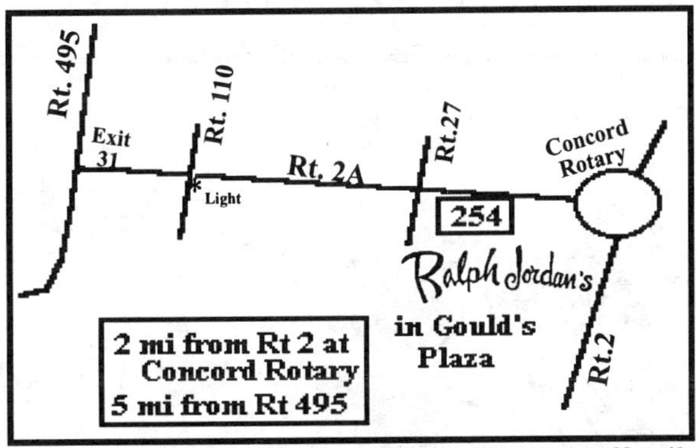

We honor All Quilt Guild Membership cards for 10% off quilt fabric, books and notions. (AQS, NEQG, and EQA included!)

254 Great Rd. Rt. 2A Goulds' Plaza 01720
(978) 263-0606

Tues, Wed, Thur 9:30 - 9:00
Mon, Fri, Sat 9:30 - 5:30
Sunday 12:00 - 5:00

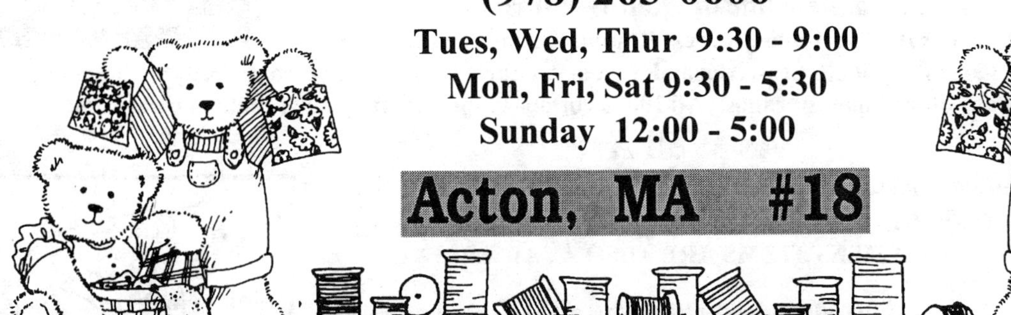

Acton, MA #18

The Button Box

Needham, MA #19

1081 Great Plain Ave., Route #135 02192
(781) 449-1810
Owner: Catherine Gentile
Est: 1995 1500 sq.ft. 2000 Bolts

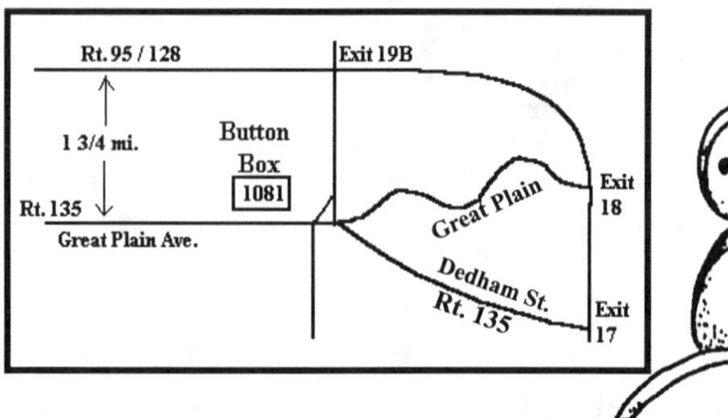

Mon - Sat 9:30 - 5:30
Wed & Thur til 8
Sundays 12 - 5
Sept. thru June

10% discount when you show a guild membership card, exclusive of other discounts.

Documentary/Vintage Reproduction and Contemporary Fabrics our Specialty.
Beautiful Japanese Sateens.
The Best Button Shop in Massachusetts, over 11,000 styles and sizes.

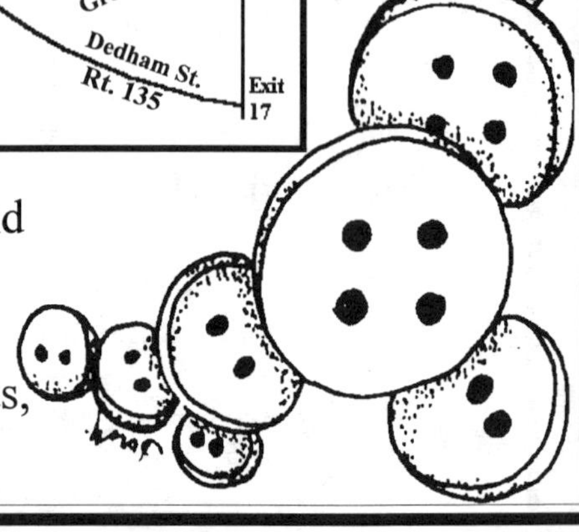

South Weymouth, MA #20

"A SHOP DEDICATED TO QUILTERS."

"WHERE CUSTOMERS ARE PATRONS AND PATRONS BECOME FRIENDS"

Mon - Thur 10 - 9
Fri & Sat 10 - 5
During July & Aug
Close Sat at 3

We carry a complete line of Quality Fabrics.
Including: Hoffman, RJR, Fabri-quilt, Robert Kaufman, American Classic, Hi-Fashion, Monarch, Kona Bay, South Seas, Alexander Henry, Fabric Country, Benartex, P&B, Springmaid, John Kaldor and many other famous brands. All 100% cotton--Approximately 2000 Bolts to pick from.

As Well As:

Batting, books, patterns, & stencils. A complete line of notions.
WE DO SPECIALTY WORK & COMMERCIAL QUILTING
CONSIGNMENT ITEMS ARE ALSO AVAILABLE

1500 Main Street (Route 18)
02190-1306 Est: 1989
(781) 340-1351

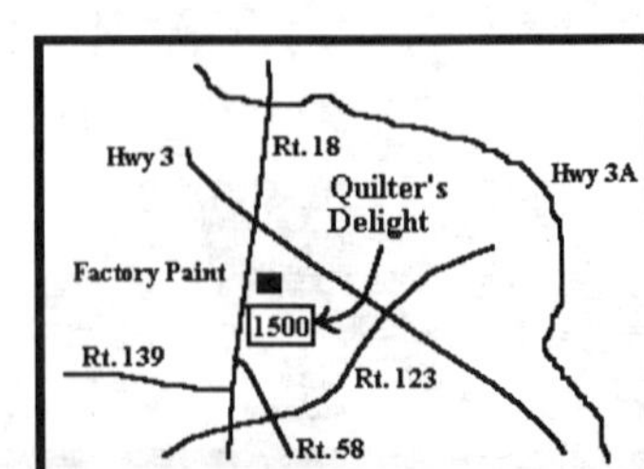

Largest Quilt Shop on Cape Cod

Hyannis, MA #21

Mon - Sat 10 - 6
Sun 12 - 4

765 Main St. 02601
(800) 393-8050
(508) 771-0011
Est: 1987 3500 sq.ft.
Owner: Helen Weinman

Mc/Visa Welcome
Bus Tours Welcome

5000+ Fabric Bolts:
(Hoffman, RJR, P&B, Moda, Hi-Fashion, Kona Bay, Robert Kaufman, Liberty of London, Debbie Mumm & Nancy Crow)
Fantastic Book & Pattern Selection

Embellishments, Fancy Threads,
Silk Ribbon, Buttons,
Fancy Velvets.
Workshops
Free Newsletter
Mailorder

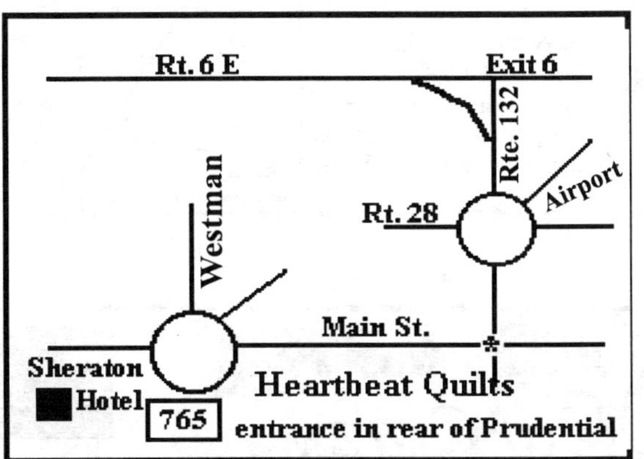

5000+ Bolts of Fabric

Scissor & Spool

FABRIC AND NOTIONS

Tradewinds Plaza
290 Rte. 130
02563
(508) 888-5669
Fax: (508) 888-8924
Owner: Marie Baron
Est: 1991 2200 sq.ft.

Over 4000 Bolts of 100% Cottons

Hoffman, RJR, Momen House, Alexander Henry, Bali, Benartex, Mission Valley, Debbie Mumm, Maywood Studio, Nancy Crow, Northcott Silk, and Many More!

MANY NEW FABRICS ARRIVING DAILY !!

Friendly, Helpful Service. Books & Patterns and More!

**Mon - Sat 9:30 - 5:30
Fri til 6:30
Sun 12 - 5**

Bus Tours Welcome!
We Also Ship Anywhere

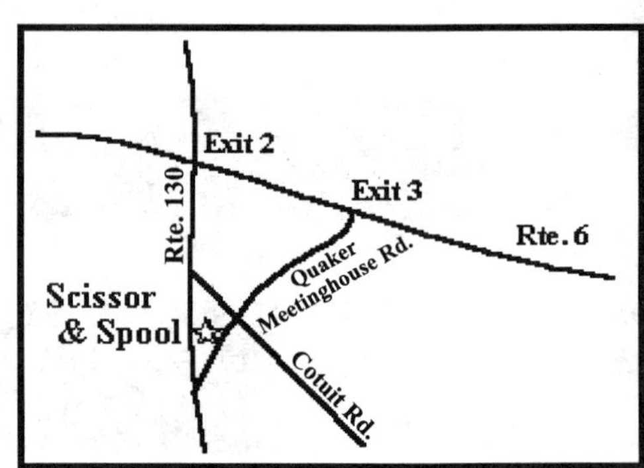

West Barnstable, MA #23

**Mon - Sat 10 - 5:30
Sun 12 - 5
Thur Eves.**

Tumbleweed™

Corner of Rt. 6A & Rt. 132
(508) 362-8700 02668
Est: 1985 3200 sq.ft.

Wonderful fabric gathered from the best mills for quilts, clothing and home decoration where the contemporary mixes with the traditional.

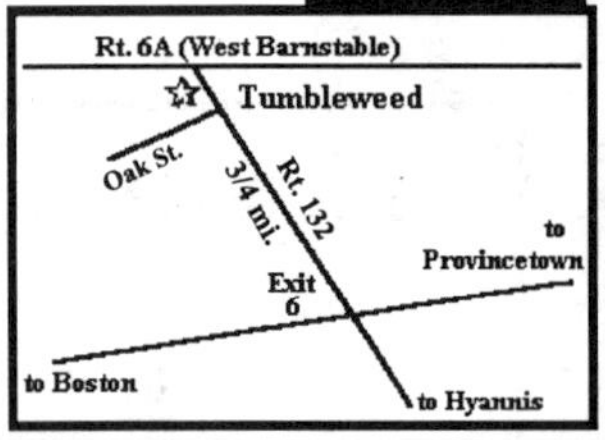

Map: Rt. 6A (West Barnstable); Tumbleweed; Oak St.; 3/4 mi.; Rt. 132; to Provincetown; Exit 6; to Boston; to Hyannis

Falmouth, MA #24

Offering Fabric • Quilt Supplies • Classes

97 Davis Straits Rd. 02540
(508) 495-4000 Fax: (508) 495-4401
Owner: Linda McCarthy Est: 1998

Open Year Round

Featuring a Barn full of inspiration! Offering both Quilts for Sale and Kits to make you own Cape Cod Memories.

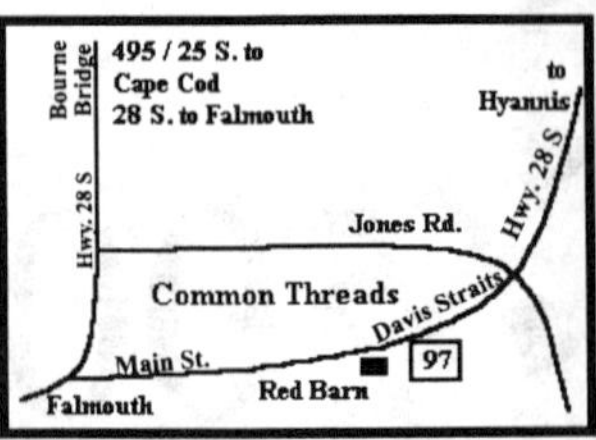

Plymouth, MA #25

Mon - Sat 9 - 4:30

Sew Crazy

5 Main St. Extension Rt. 3A
(508) 747-3019 02360
Owner: Dottie Krueger
Est: 1977

Elna, Pfaff, & New Home Sewing Machines.
Over 900 bolts of fabric and more coming.
Notions & Lots of Patterns.

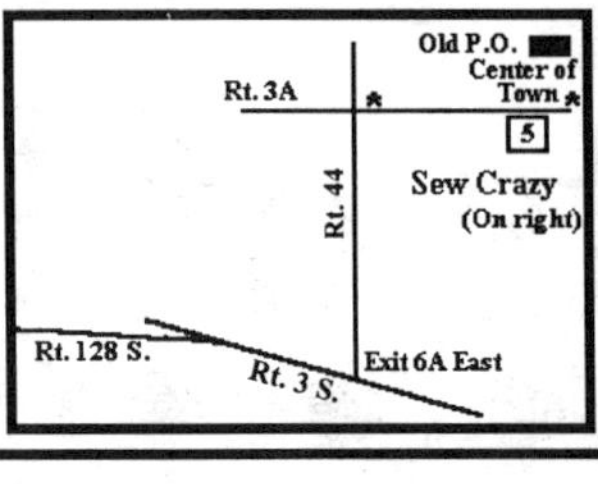

Map: Old P.O.; Center of Town; Rt. 3A; 5; Rt. 44; Sew Crazy (On right); Rt. 128 S.; Rt. 3 S.; Exit 6A East

Pembroke, MA #26

Mon - Sat 10 - 5:15
Sun 12 - 5
Thur Eves.

Tumbleweed

158 Center St. 02359
(781) 293-6400
Est: 1973 1000 sq.ft.

Large selection of fabrics, hundreds of books, notions, batting & more. In a pre-civil war house. Classroom in barn.

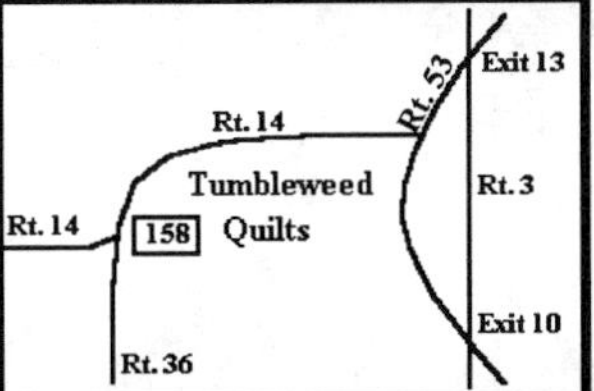

Cambridge, MA #27

Mon - Sat 10 - 6
Thurs 10-7
Sun closed

Cambridge Quilt Shop

95 Blanchard Rd. 02138
(617) 492-3279
Owners: Lynn Gorst & Margaret Lawler
Est: 1996 1100 sq.ft.
E-mail: quilt@acunet.net

Our shop maintains 1200 bolts of fabric and over 400 current quilt books, plus the latest in quilting supplies and classes!

Franklin, MA #28

Mon - Fri 9 - 9
Sat 9 - 5
Sun 12 - 5

The Franklin MILL STORE

305 Union St. 02038
(508) 528-3301

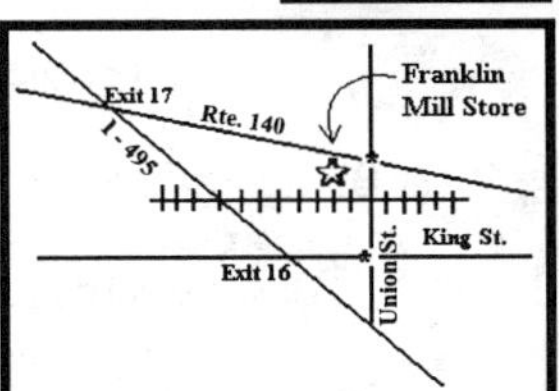

A varied and voluminous supply of Fine Fabrics, Yarns, Custom Draperies & Window Treatments.

Walpole, MA #29

Mon - Sat 10 - 6
Wed & Thur til 8:30
Sun by Chance

Quilts Ltd.

958 Main St. 02081
(508) 668-0145
Owners: Margaret Ransom & Lynn DiRusso
Est: 1983

We carry all your quilting needs. Over 1000 bolts of quality cotton fabric.

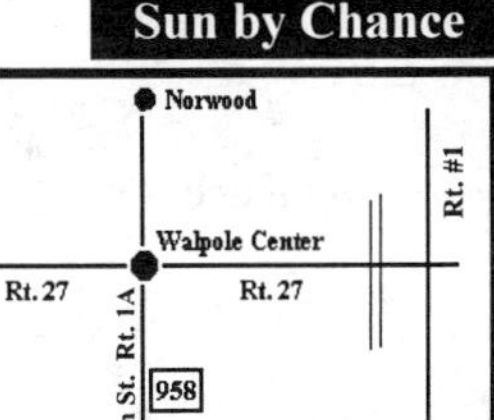

Massachusetts Guilds:

Hands Across the Valley, P.O. Box 831, Amherst, 01002
Pioneer Valley Quilters, P.O. Box 202, Aqawam, 01001
Quilter's Connection, 12 Monadnock, Arlington, 02174
Plymouth Country Cranberry Quilters, P.O. Box 149, Carver, 02330
Chelmsford Quilters Guild, P.O. Box 422, Chelmsford, 01824
Concord Piecemakers, Concord
Berkshire Quilt Guild, 47 W. Sheffield Rd., Great Barrington, 01230
    Meets: 2nd Tuesday eve. at Searles Middle School
Merrimack Valley Quilters, P.O. Box 1435, Haverhill, 01831
    Meets: at Holy Angels Church, Plaistow, NH
New England Quilters Guild, P.O. Box 7136, Lowell, 01852
Barberry Quilters of Cape Cod, P.O. Box 1253, Orleans, 02653
Yankee Pride Quilt Guild, P.O. Box 833, Pittsfield, 01202
Wayside Quilters, Sudbury
Tewksbury Piecemakers, Tewksbury
Squanicook Quilt Guild, Townsend
East Coast Quilters Alliance, P.O. Box 711, Westford, 01886

Other Shops in Massachusetts:

Arlington	Fabric Corner, 783 Massachusetts Ave.	781-643-4040
Boston	North End Fabrics, 31 Harrison Ave.	617-542-2763
Brewster	The Yankee Craftsman, 230 Route 6A W	508-385-4758
Cambridge	Sew Low Discount Fabrics, 473 Cambridge St.	
Dorchester	Ross Common Quilts, 15 Fairfax St.,	617-436-5848
East Brookfield	Calico Crib Quilt, 108 Howe St.	508-867-7389
Falmouth	Fabric Corner, 12 Spring Bars Rd.	508-548-6482
Framingham	Fabric Place, 136 Howard St.	508-872-4888
Framingham	Rachel's Fabrics, 337 Worchester	508-872-1141
Gloucester	Quilted Gallery, 77 Rocky Neck Ave.	978-283-7978
Greenfield	The Textile Co., Inc., Power Square	413-773-7516
Greenfield	Bear's Paw Quilts, 1182 Bernardston Rd.	413-773-9876
Holden	Betsey's Sewing Conn., 1085A Main	508-829-6411
Ipswich	Loom N' Shuttle, 190 High St.	508-356-5551
Lawrence	Malden Mills, 46 Stafford St.	978-685-6341
Medway	Sisters, 97 Summer	508-533-7407
Newton	Quilted Giraffee Inc., 50 Winchester St.	617-332-7633
North Chelmsford	Quilters Corner, 65 Tyngsboro Rd.	508-459-8354
Pocasset	Quilts & Things, 674-B MacArthur Blvd.	508-563-5551
Rehoboth	The Store on 44, 224 Winthrop St.	508-252-5640
South Hadley	The Calico Shop, 40 Searle Rd.	413-536-3245
South Hamilton	Cranberry Quilters, 161 Bay Rd.	508-468-3871
Southampton	S. Hampton Quilts, 162 College Hwy.	413-529-9641
Springfield	Osgood Textile Co., 30 Magaziner Pl.	413-737-6488
Vineyard Haven	The Heath Hen Yarn & Quilt Shop Tisbury Market Place	508-693-6730
Vineyard Haven	Beas Fabrics, State Rd., P.O. Box 1296	
Wakefield	Susie Kate's Quilt Shop, 1117 Main St.	617-245-3302
Wales	Ilona's Whim, 10 Stafford Rd.	413-245-3827
Woburn	Fabric Place, 300 Mishawun Rd.	781-938-8787
Worcester	Shirley's Sewing Center, 452 W. Boylston St.	508-853-8757

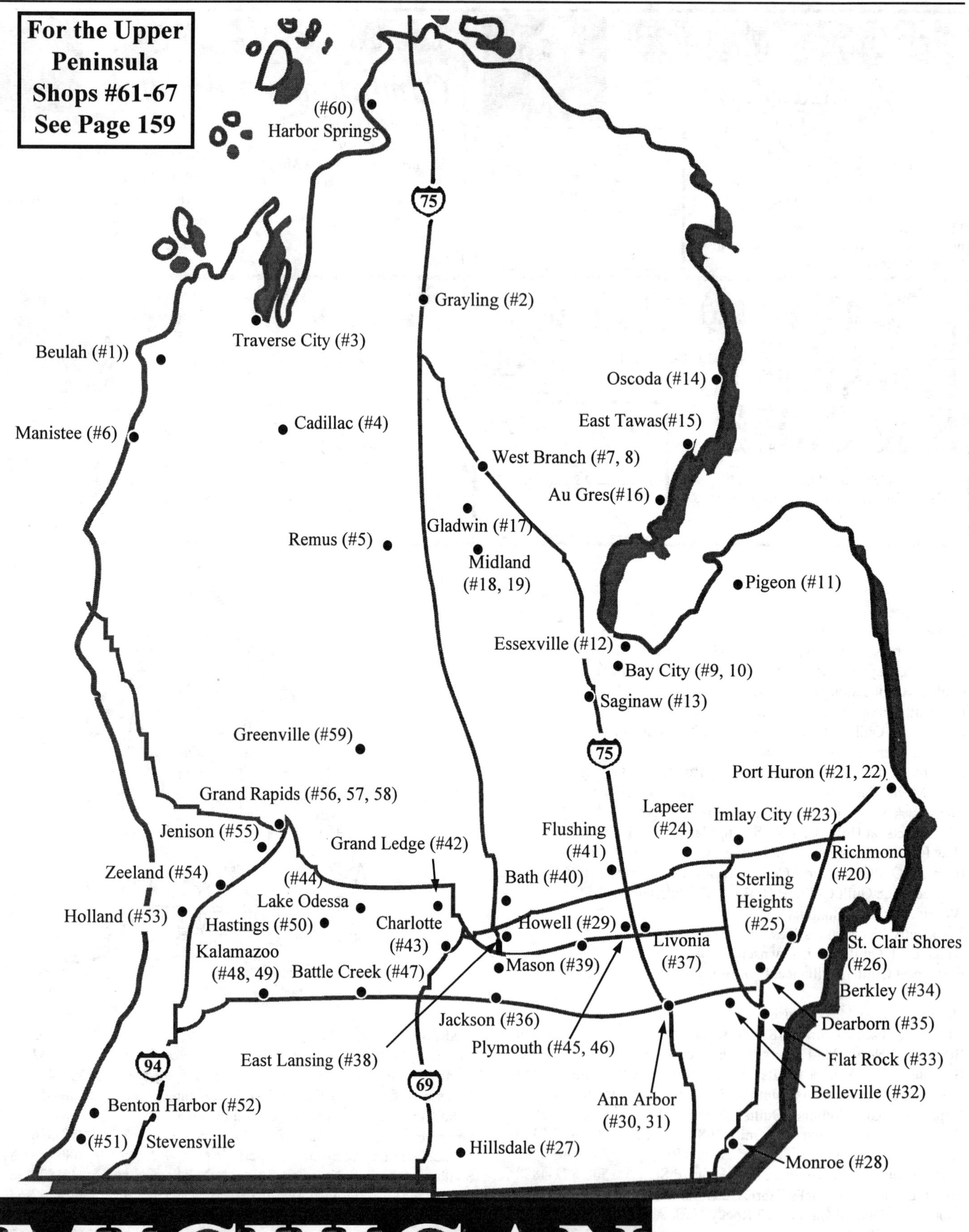
For the Upper Peninsula Shops #61-67 See Page 159
(#60) Harbor Springs
75
Grayling (#2)
Traverse City (#3)
Beulah (#1))
Oscoda (#14)
Manistee (#6)
Cadillac (#4)
East Tawas(#15)
West Branch (#7, 8)
Au Gres(#16)
Gladwin (#17)
Remus (#5)
Midland (#18, 19)
Pigeon (#11)
Essexville (#12)
Bay City (#9, 10)
Saginaw (#13)
Greenville (#59)
75
Port Huron (#21, 22)
Grand Rapids (#56, 57, 58)
Lapeer (#24)
Imlay City (#23)
Flushing (#41)
Jenison (#55)
Grand Ledge (#42)
Richmond (#20)
Zeeland (#54)
(#44)
Bath (#40)
Sterling Heights (#25)
Lake Odessa
Holland (#53)
Hastings (#50)
Charlotte (#43)
Howell (#29)
Livonia (#37)
St. Clair Shores (#26)
Kalamazoo (#48, 49)
Battle Creek (#47)
Mason (#39)
Berkley (#34)
Jackson (#36)
Dearborn (#35)
Plymouth (#45, 46)
East Lansing (#38)
Flat Rock (#33)
94
69
Belleville (#32)
Ann Arbor (#30, 31)
Benton Harbor (#52)
(#51) Stevensville
Hillsdale (#27)
Monroe (#28)
MICHIGAN
67 Featured Shops

Bring Your Quilt Group Up North for a "Quilters' Day Out"

Complete line of Fine Quilting Supplies.
Fabrics, Books, Patterns, Notions and Quilt Kits.
Can't find an out of print book? Give us a try.

We offer a variety of Basic to Advanced Quilting Classes.
Let us set up a special class for your Quilting Group.

Let our friendly and experienced staff help you select the supplies for your next project.

We have a unique collection of handmade Wallhangings, Quilts, Woven Throws, and Rugs.
Norwegian Sweaters
Folk Art, Heritage Lace Curtain, & Scandinavian Gifts.

Margie Ann's Quilt Shop

(616) 882-4024
194 South Benzie Blvd., P.O. Box 655 49617
Owner: Rebecca Zerfas
Est: 1980 2500 sq.ft. 2000+ Bolts

Mon - Sat
10 - 5
Call for
Summer Hrs.

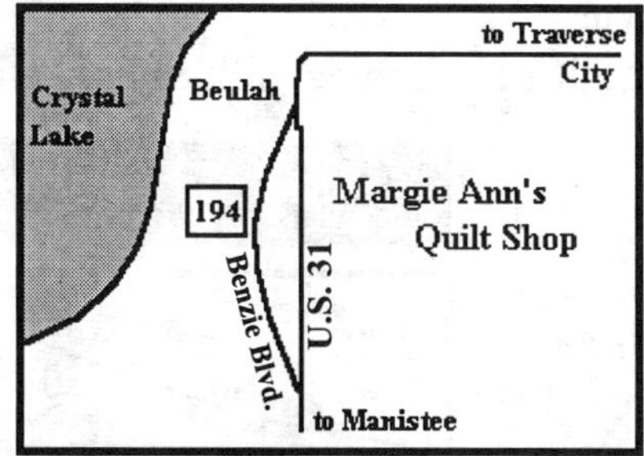

Beulah, MI #1

Grayling, MI #2

Mon - Sat 10 - 5

The Ice House Quilt Shop

509 Norway Street 49738
(517) 348-4821
Owner: Jill Wyman Est: 1980

A unique shop for the person seeking quality in all quilting supplies.
Gifts--Gourmet Foods.
We've added a Bed & Breakfast!
B&B Phone (517) 348-6630

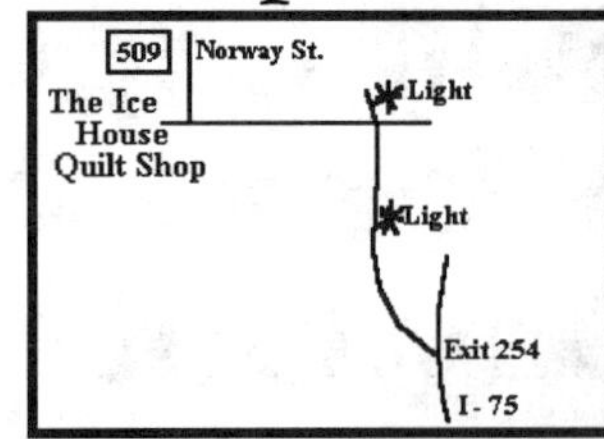

Traverse City, MI #3

**Mon, Wed, Thur 9:30 - 8
Tues & Fri 9:30 - 5:30
Sat 9:30 - 4**

A Selective Stitch

1425-F S. Airport Rd. W 49686
(616) 946-2554 Fax: (616) 929-7275
E-Mail: selectiv@freeway.net

Beautiful quilting fabrics. Fine quality bastiste. A great collection of flannels, fleece and ribbings. Sewing machines, cabinets, and sewing classes.

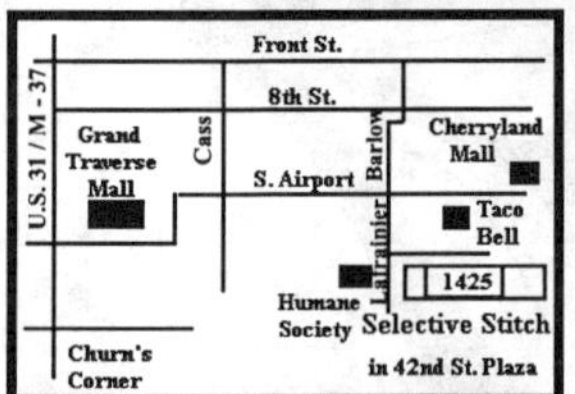

Cadillac, MI #4

Mon - Sat 9:30 - 5:30

Julie Ann Fabrics

109 S. Mitchell 49601
(616) 775-8301
Owners: Gerald & Ruth Britton
Est: 1973 2000+ Bolts

Great selection of quilting fabrics, books, patterns, notions. Classes. Pfaff, Janome, White, Husqvarna sewing machines & sergers sales & service.

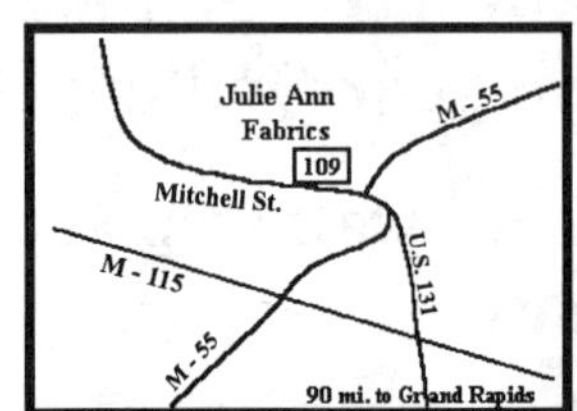

Remus, MI #5

**Mon - Fri 9 - 5:30
Sat 9 - 4**

Towne Fabrics, Gifts, & Crafts

135 W. Wheatland Ave. 49340
(517) 967-8250
Owners: Ann Jensen and Jann Parks
Est: 1989 2300 sq.ft.

Quilts supplies from fabrics to frames. Also reed and cane supplies. Our staff is knowledgeable & caring.

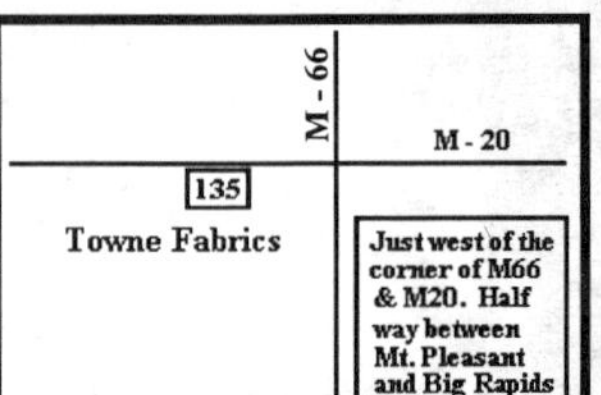

Manistee, MI #6

The Quilted Heart

607 Parkdale (North U.S. 31) 49660
(616) 723-7069
Owner: Judy Dunlap Est: 1989

- Fabrics - Cottons, Flannels, Felts, Homespuns
- Patterns, Books, Quilting Supplies
- Kits for quilts - Large & Small (Samples throughout the shop)
- Folk Art Clothing
- Country Wares
- Classes - quilting, clothing, silk ribbon, etc.
- Mail Order

MasterCard VISA DISCOVER AMERICAN EXPRESS

Mon - Sat 10 - 5

Call for info on fax, e mail & web-site addresses to be in place by summer 1998.

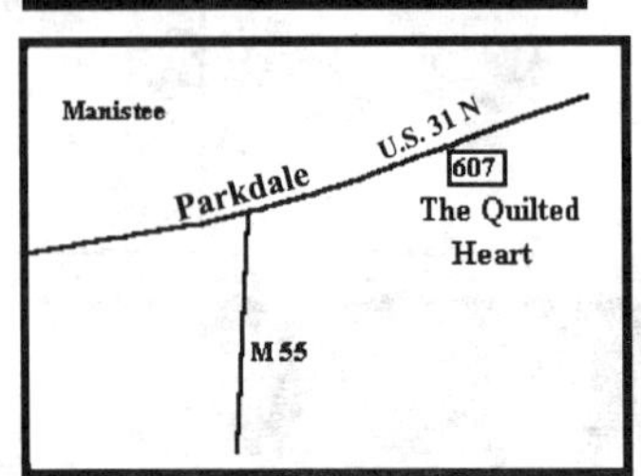

Unique Setting in an old Farmhouse

West Branch, MI #7

**Winter Hrs. Vary
May thru Dec.
Mon - Thur 11 - 4
Fri & Sat 10 - 5**

Crocker's Attic

3156 W. M-55 48661
(517) 345-1780 Est: 1993
E-Mail: crocker@voyager.net
Owner: Jolee Crocker 300+ Bolts

Primitive homefurnishing and gift shop featuring Moda, Indo, and Mission Valley Homespuns, Deb Strain Patek-Brannock, Thimbleberry, Mumm prints and more.

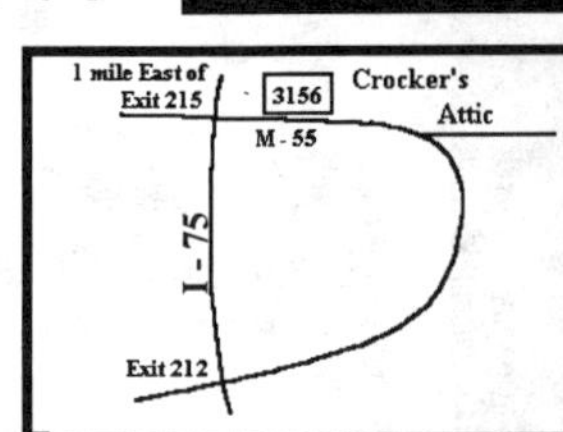

West Branch, MI #8

**Mon - Fri 9 - 6
Sat 9 - 5**

Button Hole

218 West Houghton 48661
(517) 345-0431
Owner: Darlene Jones
Est: 1981 3300 sq.ft.

We have Everything for the Quilter ! ! Located in a Victorian, downtown West Branch on Business Loop I - 75

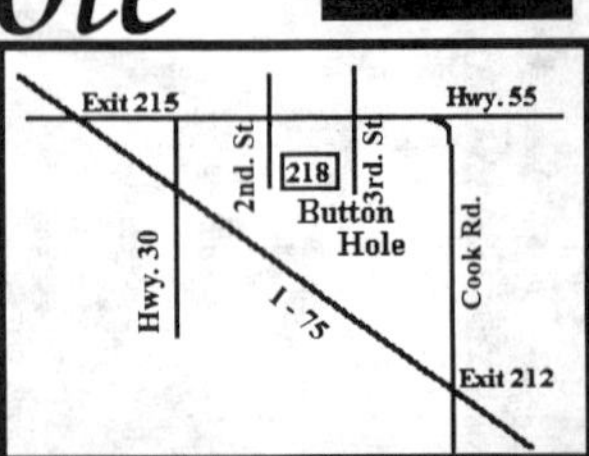
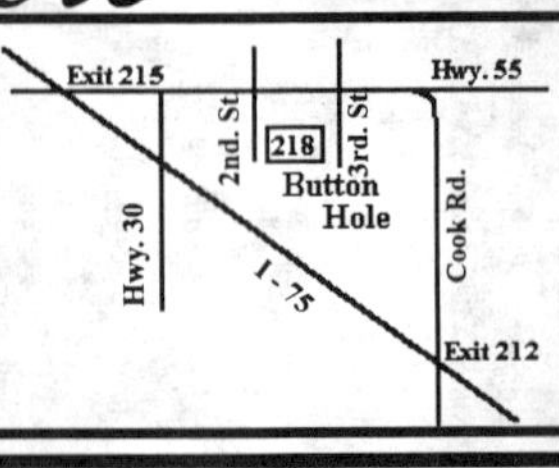

Bay City, MI #9

**Mon - Fri 9 - 5
Sat 9 - 3**

Snail's Trail Quilt Shop

214 S. Henry 48706
(517) 895-9003
Fax: (517) 894-2549
Owners: Pat LaRoche & Kathy Baker

Fabrics including Hoffman & South Seas. Crafters, you'll love our Button Crock! Large Selection of Patterns. Classes. Featuring wearable art.

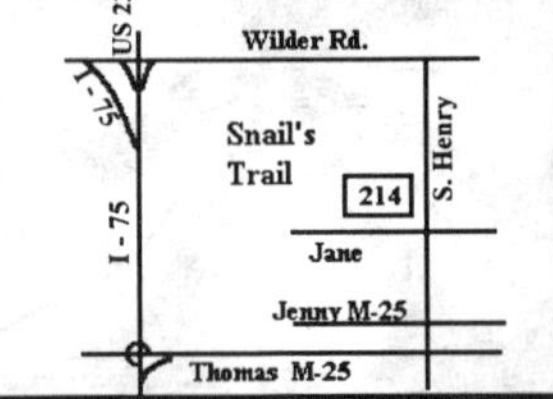

The Fabric Fair

"6 Rooms of Fabric"

Bay City, MI #10

206 Fifth St. 48708
(517) 893-8971
Owner: Bunny Rosenbrock
Est: 1955 7000 sq.ft.
10,000+ Bolts

THE STORE EVERYONE IS TALKING ABOUT!

Quilters Cottons • Homespuns • Quilting Supplies • Silk Ribbon by the Yard
French Wired Ribbon • Exquisite Bridal Room • Headpieces
Finished Veils • Silk• Ultra Suede • Pendleton Wool
Hours: Mon thru Fri 9:30 - 7 • Sat 9:30 - 5 • Closed Sunday

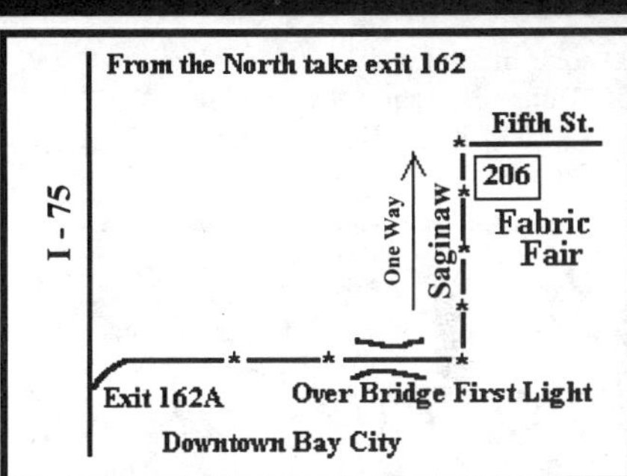

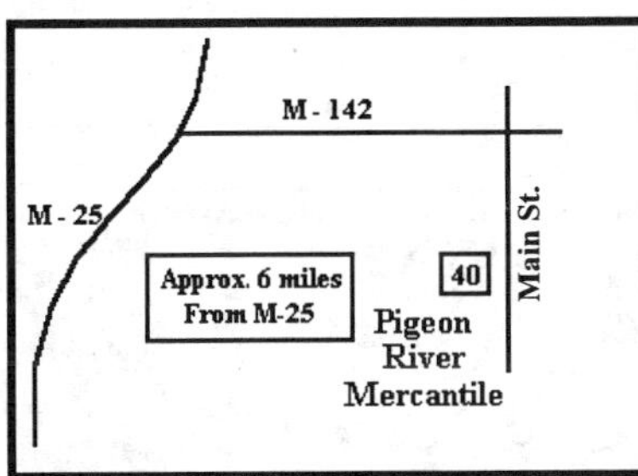

We're located in Michigan's Thumb! Come see us in Huron County and enjoy our beaches, trails, and back roads. Explore Huron County's delightful small towns for a week or weekend of fun!

Call Toll Free 1-888-453-4554 for FREE Block of the Month by mail info!

Home of Graywood Designs patterns & Block of the Month quilts with THANGLES

Wholesale info available

At The Mercantile you will find:

100% Cotton Quilting Fabrics
Patterns -- Notions -- Threads
Elna sewing machines
Great selection of Fat Quarters
We have THANGLES!
Cross Stitch Designs
Linen, evenweave, aida
DMC floss and perle cottons
Lots of specialty threads
Classes in quilting & stitching
We're housed in two storefronts of a former dimestore. . .tin ceilings, wooden stairway, vintage linoleum floors!

Visit our Website at www.quiltinpigeon.com

Pigeon River Mercantile & Wool Co

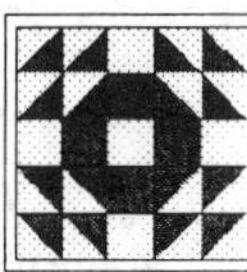

One of Ten shops featured in the 1998 Quilt Sampler Magazine!

"Home of Fine Fabrics & Creative Quilts"
40 South Main Pigeon, MI 48755
517-453-2311 TOLL FREE 1-888-453-4554 FAX 517-453-4313
Hours: 10 am-5:30pm M-Sat
Summer months: Open on Sundays Noon - 4 pm

#11

Essexville, MI #12

Mon - Sat 9:30 - 5:30 Closed First two Weeks of July & Sat in July & Aug

Marjorie's

1602 Woodside 48732
(517) 893-8611
400+ Bolts of Calico

My three specialties are Calicos, Bathing Suit Fabrics, & Lingerie Fabrics. Notions. We also teach many classes.

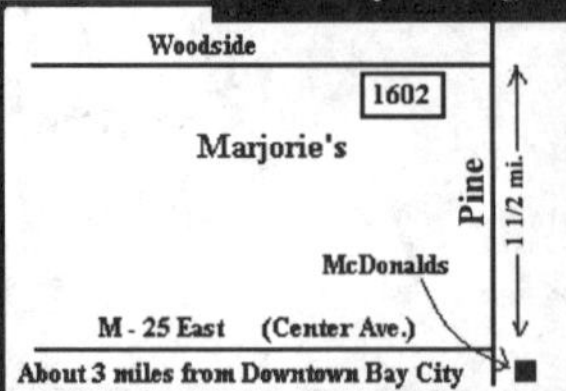

Saginaw, MI #13

Mon - Sat 9 - 4 Thur til 7

The Fabric Stash

3541 State St. 48602
(517) 790-9317
Owners: Karen Butler & Joanna Wardin

We carry fine cotton fabrics, books, notions and quilting supplies. We also feature baskets, pottery and custom gift baskets.

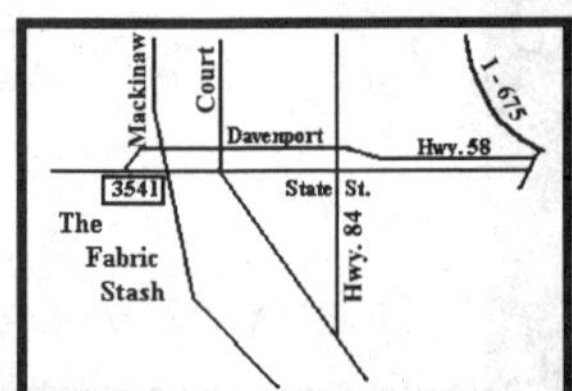

Oscoda, MI #14

Mon - Sat 10 - 5

Loose Threads Quilt Shop

208 S. State St. 48750
(517) 739-7115 3500 sq.ft.
We Accept Visa, MC & Discover

Over 3500 sq.ft. of Quilters Heaven ! More than 2500 Bolts of Fabric by Benartex, Hoffman, Spiegel, Jinny Beyer, P&B, & More. 300 Quilt Books.

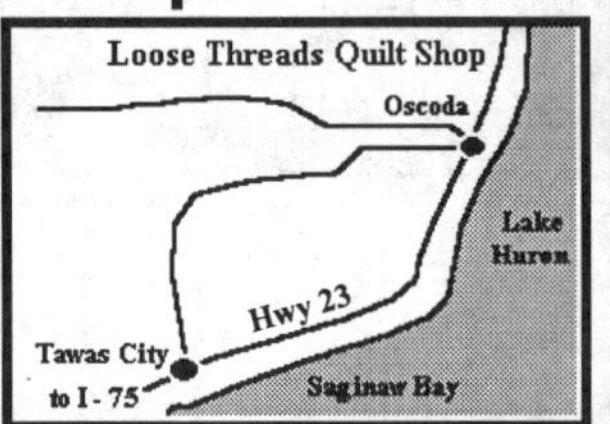

East Tawas, MI #15

Mon - Sat 9 - 5

Cotton Patch Quilt Shop

306 Newman St. 48730
(517) 362-6779
E-Mail: ctnpatch@alpena.cc.mi.us
Web Site: www.oscoda.com/ctnpatch/index.htm
Owner: Doni Butzin
Est: 1996 3000 sq.ft. 2600 Bolts

Full Service Quilt Shop.

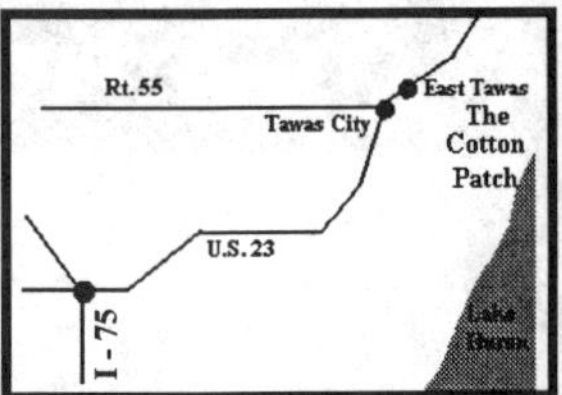

Au Gres, MI #16

Tues - Fri 10 - 4:30 Sat 10 - 12

Bayview Calicos

3631 E. Huron (U.S. 23) 48703
(517) 876-6933
Owner: Evelyn Griffore
Est: 1988

Quilt fabric and supplies. Classes.
Christmas year round.
"Where Friendly Quilters Meet"

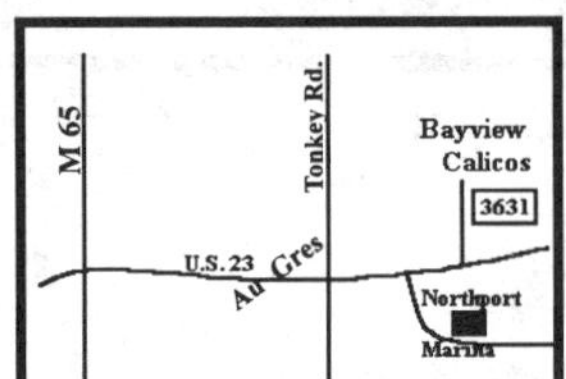

Gladwin, MI #17

Tues - Sat By Appt.

The Log Cabin Fabric Shoppe

1901 Lakeshore Dr. 48624
(517) 426-1422
Owner: Cherie Thornton

We are now located in a beautiful shop in the country. Come visit our brand new barn full of quilting delights.

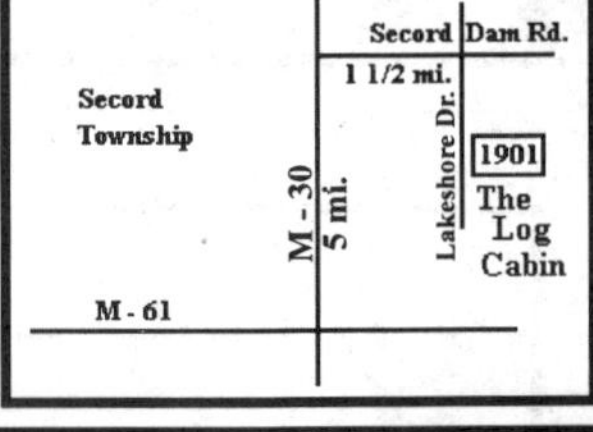

MATERIAL MART

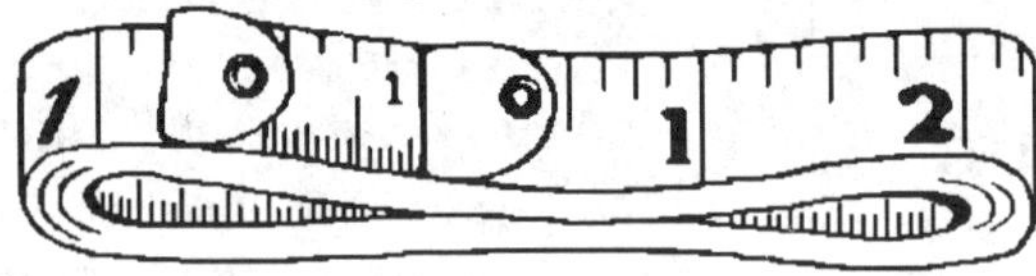

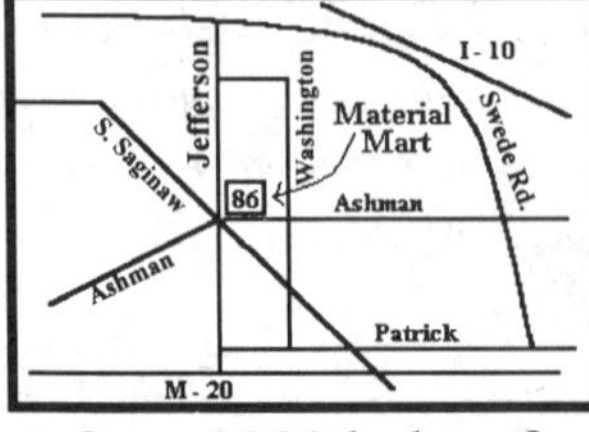

86 Ashman Circle 48640
(517) 835-8761
Fax: (517) 835-9820
E-Mail: matrlmart@aol.com
Web Site: www.materialmart@husqvarna.com
Est: 1971 4100 sq.ft.

Over 3000 bolts of top designer fabrics, latest notions & quilt books. Friendly, knowledgeable staff.

Mon - Fri 9:30 - 9 Sat 9:30 - 5 Sun 12 - 5

Midland, MI #18

Midland, MI #19

Mon - Thur 10 - 7 Fri & Sat 10 - 5

Quilted Giraffe

1124 Eastman Ave. 48640
(517) 837-2666 Fax: (517) 837-1487
E-Mail: qgiraffe@aol.com
Est: 1996 2500 sq.ft.

Large selection of 100% quality cottons, supplies, and classes. A year-round mini quilt show. Fun, Friendly and Knowledgeable Staff.

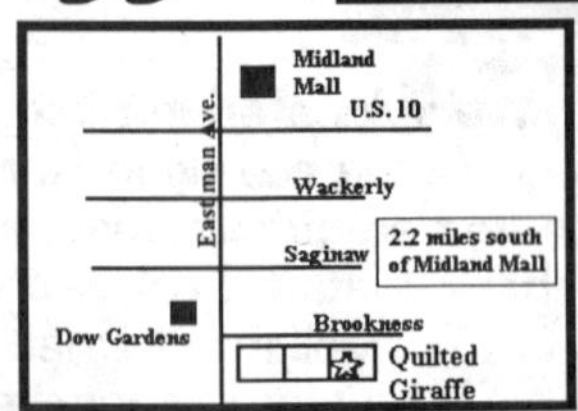

Richmond, MI #20

Tues - Thur 10 - 5 Fri 10 - 7 Sat 10 - 4

Sew Together

69295 Main St. 48062
(810) 727-1555
Owners: Gina Kaszynski & Susan Weinert

A large variety of cotton fabrics, many different threads and embellishments. Huge assortment of books and patterns

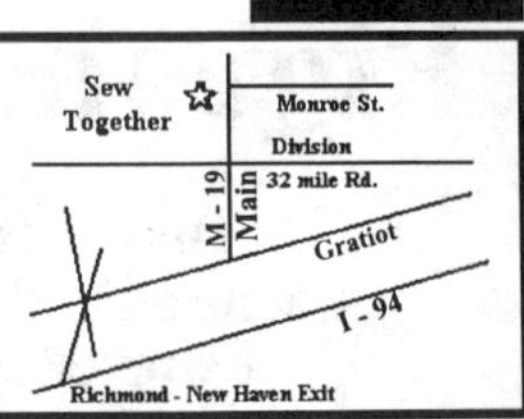

Port Huron, MI #21

Sew Elegant

Quilt Shoppe

3909 Pine Grove Rd.
48059
(810) 982-6556
Fax: (810) 982-6996
E-Mail: elsew@aol.com
Web-Site:
www.sewelegant.com
Est:1986 4880 sq.ft.
Owner: Linda Anderson

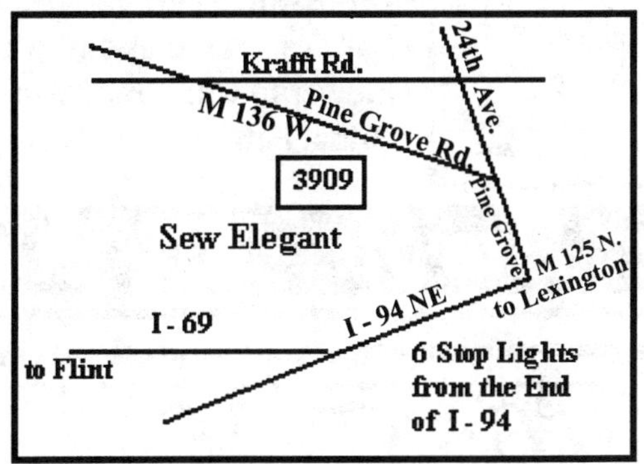

Eastern Michigan's Largest Quilt Shop!
Our Shop is full of 100% cotton Fabrics--
over 8,000 bolts

Mon - Sat
10 - 5:30
Sun 12 - 4:30

VAST SELECTION OF
BOOKS, PATTERNS AND
SEWING NOTIONS
FOR QUILTERS.

PFAFF MACHINES
SALES & SERVICE

Fabric • Yarn • Crafts • Stitchery

mary maxim Inc.

EXCLUSIVE NEEDLEWORK and CRAFTS

. . . the idea place

2001 Holland Ave. 48060
(810) 987-2000
Fax: (810) 987-5056
Web Site: www.marymaxim.com
Est: 1956 20,000 sq.ft.

Mon - Sat 9:30 - 6
Fri til 9 July - Jan
Sun 11 - 5

FREE CATALOG

- Quilting Supplies • Books
- Yarns • Baskets • Craft Kits
- Cross-Stitch • Wood Items
- Fabrics • Needlepoint Kits
- Flowers • Christmas Kits
- Bridal Fabrics and Accessories

Mary Maxim
2001
Pine Grove
Holland Ave.
Blue Water Bridge to Canada
I - 94
Take I - 94 or I - 69 to end, then M-25 to Holland Ave.
I - 69 to Flint
to Detroit

Port Huron, MI #22

The Pincushion

Imlay City, MI #23

113 East Third Street 48444
(313) 724-7065
Owner: Joyce Schihl
Est: 1971 1800 sq.ft.

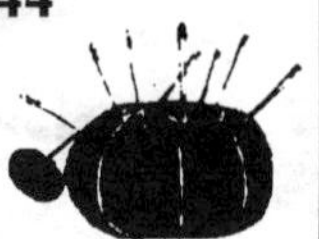

Quality Quilting Supplies & Fabrics. Extensive Books & Pattern Selection. Buttons by the cup or each. Cotton, Wool & Polyester Batting. Small Town Friendly Service. Our Customers are our Friends.

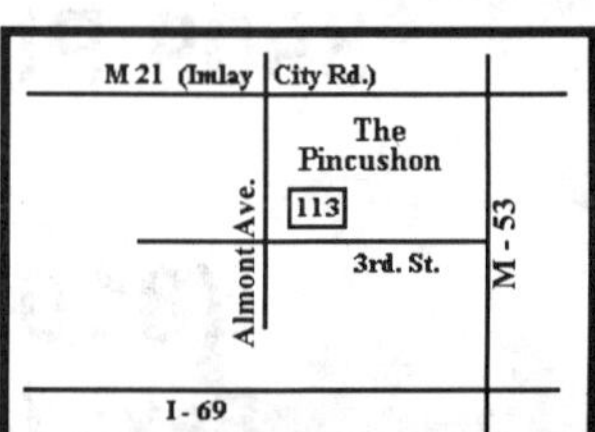

Mon - Fri 9:30 - 5:15
Sat 9:30 - 5

Jill's Fabrics

& Costume Rental

2268 N Lapeer Rd. 48446
(810) 667-4025 Fax: (810) 667-4622
E-Mail: jills@cardina.net
Visit our Web Site at: http//www.Lapeermall.com/jills/
Owner: Jill Hurd Est: 1988

Mon - Fri 9 - 6 Sat 10 - 5

Lapeer, MI #24

Large Selection of 100% Cotton Fabrics Quilting Supplies, Books, Templates, Stencils, Classes. Pfaff & New Home Sewing Machine Sales & Service. Helpful & Friendly.

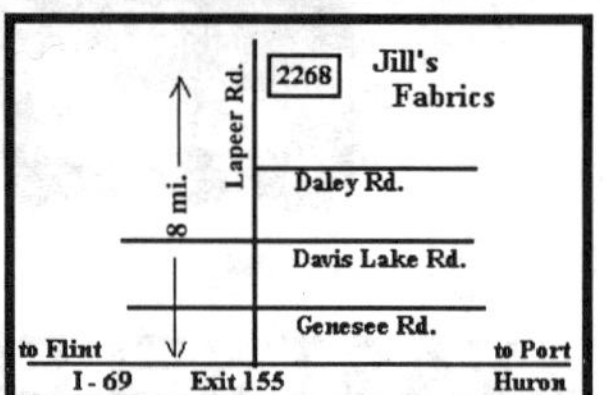

Sterling Heights, MI #25

4090 17 Mile Road 48310
(810) 979-7422
Gretchen L. Tatge
Est: 1983

Quilt-n Friends

1500 bolts of 100% Cotton Fabrics
Notions ... Books ... Patterns
Gifts ... Machine Quilting
Newsletter every 2 months ... Friendly Staff
Classes Year Round ... Michigan's Finest Teachers

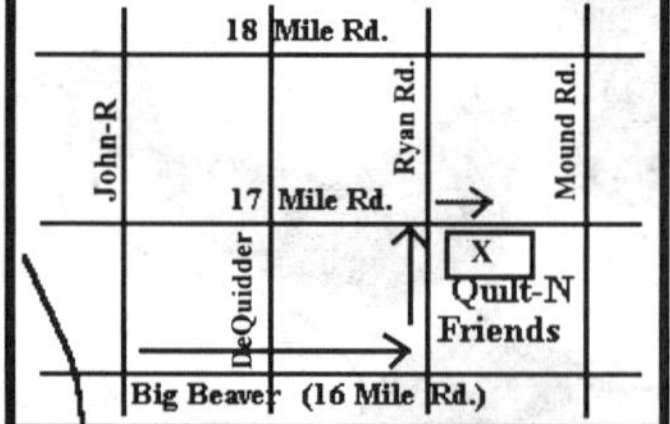

"The Complete Quilt Shop"

Mon - Fri 9 - 5 Sat 9 - 3
Mon & Thurs Eve til 8:30

St. Clair Shore, MI #26

Mon,Tues, Fri 10 - 6
Thur 10 - 9
Sat 10 - 5

The Quilters Patch

31384 Harper 48082
(810) 293-1999
Owner: Beverly Maxvill
Est: 1981 1200 sq.ft.

Author of Victorian Patchwork & Embroidery Meredith Books—many original designs available for Quilts & Blocks. Fabrics-Notions-Books.

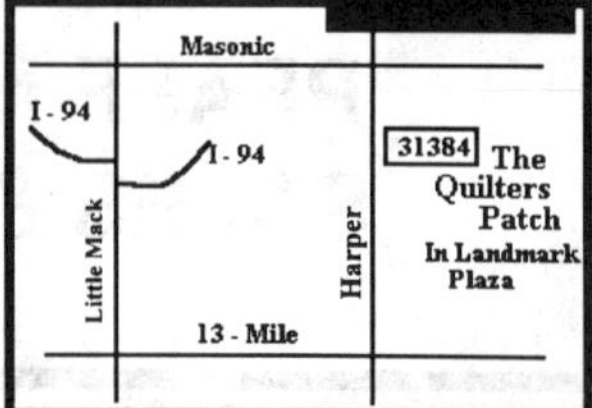

Hillsdale, MI #27

Mon & Fri 9:30 - 8
Tues, Wed, Thur 9:30 - 5:30
Sat 9:30 - 5

My Favorite Things

33 N. Broad St. 49242
(517) 437-4577
Owner: Betty White Est: 1989

Nice things come in small packages—that's us!
Highest quality cotton fabrics, quilt notions and classes. New Home / Janome Dealer.

Monroe, MI #28

GERWECK'S HOMESPUN FABRICS

15221 S. DIXIE HWY. 48161
SOUTH MONROE PLAZA
(313) 242-9528

Hours: Mon-Sat 10:00-5:00
(fall & winter) Tues 10:00-9:00
Closed Sundays
Bus Tours Welcome

South Monroe Plaza (Krogers)
15221
R.R.
Telegraph
S. Dixie
Dunbar
Jones
Scott
Front
Elm
Frenchtown Square Mall
Monroe St.
Dixie
Manufacturers Market Place
La Plaisance
I-75

Minutes from I-75 use exit 11

MasterCard
VISA

Over 3,000 bolts of fabrics 1,500 plus of books and patterns
Complete supply of notions
100's of samples to inspire you
Gift items for quilters & Sewers
Complete line of PFAFF sewing machines Classes
Personal, helpful, and friendly service
Quality machine quilting service
7 years experience
Backings & battings available up to 120" wide

One of Michigan's largest quilt shops. with 4,000 sq. feet of quilting!

Howell, MI #29

The Stitchery

1129 E. Grand River Ave. 48843
(517) 548-1731
Owners: Susan Reid
Est: 1980 4000 sq.ft.
New Home / Janome Dealer

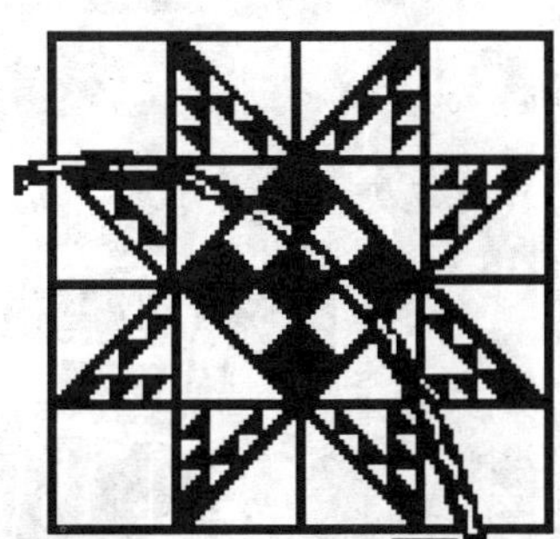

100% Cotton Prints including Hoffman, RJR, Moda, Marcus, Peter Pan, Northcutt's "Quilt for a Cure", Kona Bay, Kona Cottons, South Seas, Debbie Mumm, Alma Lynne, Clothworks & RJR. 108" Quilt Back Prints.

Silk Ribbon Embroidery Supplies, Wools for rug Hooking & Primitives, plus many Books, Supplies, Notions & Classes

M-59
Michigan
Latson
U.S. 23
Grand River
1129
The Stitchery
I-96
D-19

Mon - Fri 9 - 6
Sat 9 - 4
Call for Quilt Guild Outings Special Discounts

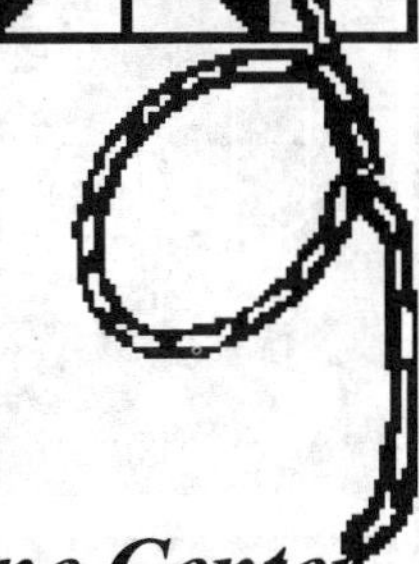

Livingston County's Largest Quilt Shop & Sewing Machine Center

Ann Arbor, MI #31

Mon - Wed 10:30 - 5:30
Thur 11 - 7
Fri & Sat
Winter 10 - 5
Summer 10 - 4

THE LOOKING GLASS QUILT SHOP

1715 Plymouth 48105
(734) 662-2228
Owner: Carla Aderente

A full line quilt shop with wonderful fabrics, books, patterns, and notions. Come Say Hi !

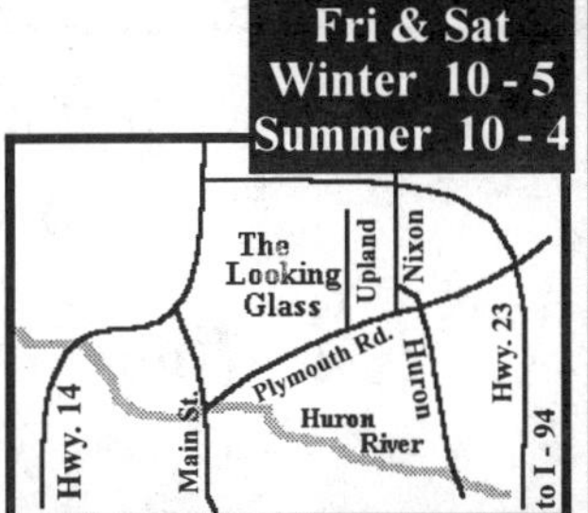

Belleville, MI #32

Mon - Sat 10 - 6
Sun 12 - 5
Other Hours by Chance Or Appt.

Threads 'n Treasures Quilt Shop

129 South St. 48111
(313) 697-9376 Fax: Same
Owner: Kay Atkins Est: 1996

Batting, Big Discount on Books, Notions. Lessons. Quilts for Sale. Hand Quilting. Fabric, Silk Ribbon and other treasures. Will Special Order.

Flat Rock, MI #33

Tues - Fri 10 - 5
Sat 9 - 3

Cotton Pickin' Quilts, Inc.

26261 E. Huron River Dr. 48134
(734) 783-5406 Fax: (734) 783-5412
E-Mail: cttnpckn@ili.net
Owners: C J Martin & Sally Regan

100% Cotton Fabrics —
Hoffman * South Seas * RJR * P&B *
Marcus and many others.
Quilting Notions, Books, Patterns & Classes.

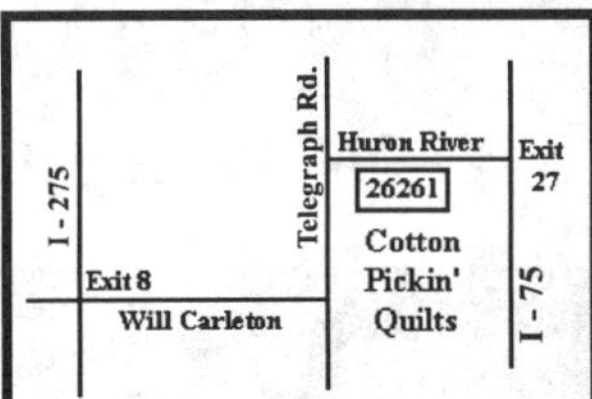

Berkley, MI #34

Mon - Fri 10 - 6:30
Sat 10 - 5
Sun 12 - 3

Guildcrafters Quilt Shop

2790 West 12 Mile Rd. 48072
(810) 541-8545
Owner: Jo Merecki
Est: 1982 2500 sq.ft.

3500 Bolts Largest Quilting Fabric, Notion, Stencil & Book supply in the area. Classes, Gifts. Friendly Service.

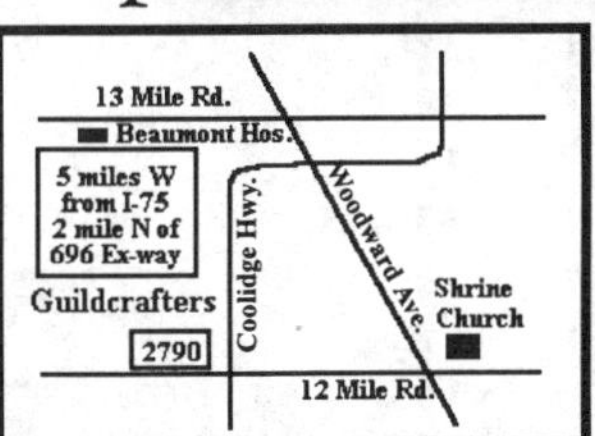

Bits 'n Pieces #35

100% Cotton Fabrics
Lessons, Supplies & Kits
Books & Patterns
Mail Order Available

BERNINA
Authorized Dealer
Sales * Service * Repair

1033 Mason
Dearborn, MI 48124
(313) 278-8681

Owner - Julie Hale Est. 1981

Mon -- Sat 10 - 5 Tues & Thurs 'til 7

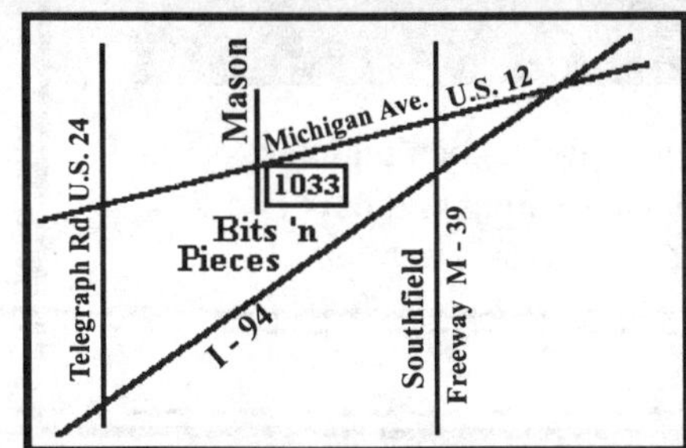

Jackson, MI #36

HEARTS ALL AROUND

2614 Kibby Road 49203
(517) 789-8228
Owner:
Barbara Markowski
Est: 1983 3000 sq.ft.
1400 Bolts

Mon - Fri
10 - 5:30
Sat 10 - 4

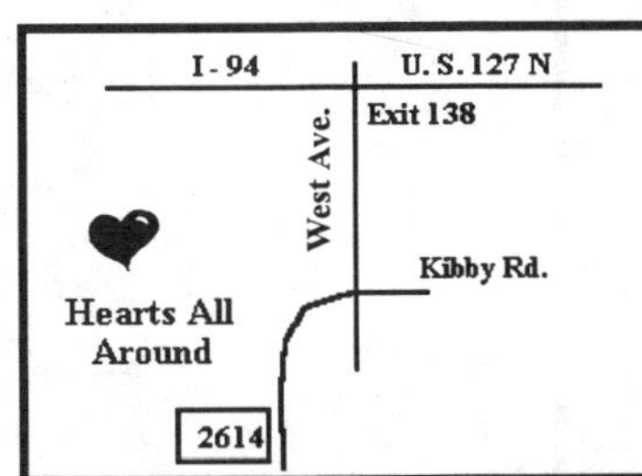

Fabrics, books, patterns, quilt "gadgets", classes! Sewing machine cabinets, craft tables, specialty threads, specialty fabrics. Machine quilting services. Authorized Pfaff sewing machine dealer.

PFAFF SALES & SERVICE

The Finishing Touch

A MACHINE QUILTING SERVICE

Jean Coleman
Designer

Hours by Appointment

(734) 425-6385

36749 Angeline Circle 48150

Livonia, MI #37

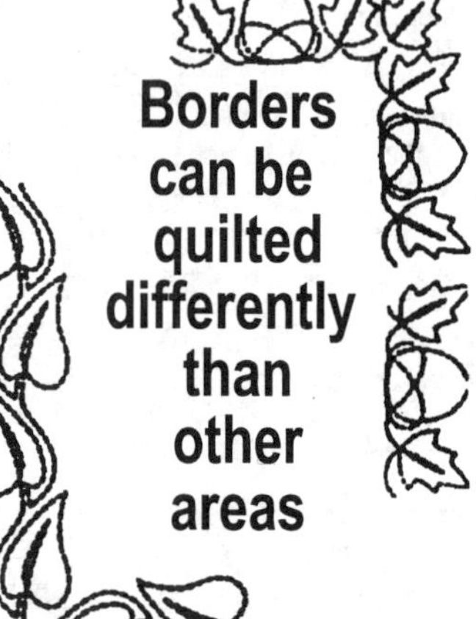

We have great block Designs
and we can now do perfect circles.

CREATIVE QUILTING is a unique service of machine quilting pieced tops in a manner which will enhance the overall design of the quilt by individualizing block, sashing and border designs. There are many designs to choose from including perfect circles and cross hatching.

America's largest quilt shoppe, COUNTRY STITCHES, is a Quilter's Heaven

- Over 6000 bolts of 100% cotton fabric line the shelves.
- A continuous quilt show and year-round Christmas displays offer ideas and inspiration.
- Over 1,500 classes a year cover topics from quilting to basic sewing to machine arts.
- Friendly, knowledgeable staff are trained and ready to help with your creative project.

Treat yourself to Country Stitches, truly a unique quilt shoppe.

Bring this ad and receive 50% off any item (maximum value $25). (not good with other discounts)

Country Stitches

Hours:
Monday - Friday
9:30 am - 9 pm
Saturday
9:30 am - 6 pm

One block east of US 127 on Lake Lansing Rd., across from Meijer, East Lansing.

Call **517-351-2416** or **1-800-572-2031** for more information and a free brochure.

East Lansing, MI #38

Mason, MI #39

Mon - Fri 9 - 8
Sat 9 - 5:30
Sun 12 - 5

Kean's Store Co.

406 S. Jefferson St. 48854
(517) 676-5144

Large selection of quality fabrics, bear supplies, mohair, quilt books, patterns, books, & notions. Bring a friend, spend the day, lots to see!

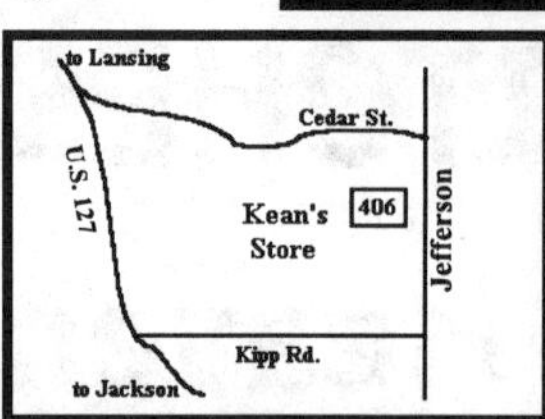

Bath, MI #40

Tues 10 - 7
Wed & Thur 10 - 6
Fri 10 - 5
Sat 10 - 4

Quilting Memories

13630 B. Main St. 48808
(517) 641-6522
Owner: Dorothy Mills
Est: 1994 1500 sq.ft.

Complete supplies for quilters. Silk Ribbon, Brazilian Embroidery. Offer weekend and evening classes. Great assortment of quilters cottons.

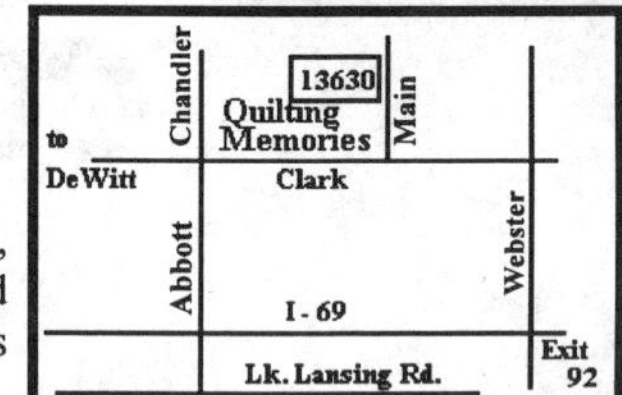

Flushing, MI #41

Tues - Sat 10 - 5
Sun 1 - 4 Closed Mon
Closed July

100% Cotton fabrics.
Quilting books & patterns.
Notions.
Lots of classes.
Warm and personal service.
Quaint setting.

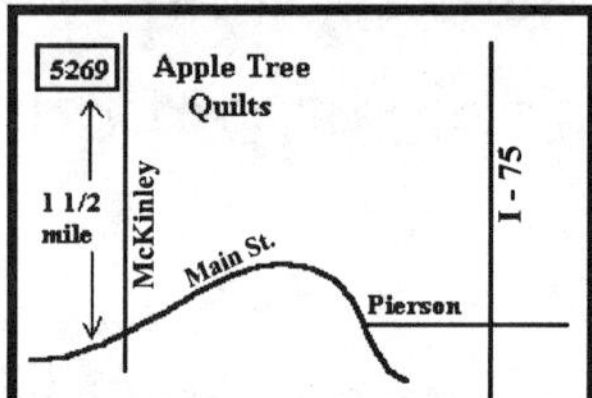

APPLE TREE QUILTS

5269 McKinley Rd. 48433
(810) 659- 4190
Owner: Judie Martin
Est: 1996
2000 sq.ft. 1000+ Bolts

Grand Ledge, MI #42

Mon - Fri 10 - 6
Sat 10 - 3

Fabrics 'n' Moore

202 S. Bridge St. 48837
(517) 627-0744
Owner: Sharon Moore

Quilting supplies, 100% cotton, classes, fashion fabrics, Heritage Lace, notions, books & patterns. Machine quilting available.
"Friendly Service is a Tradition"

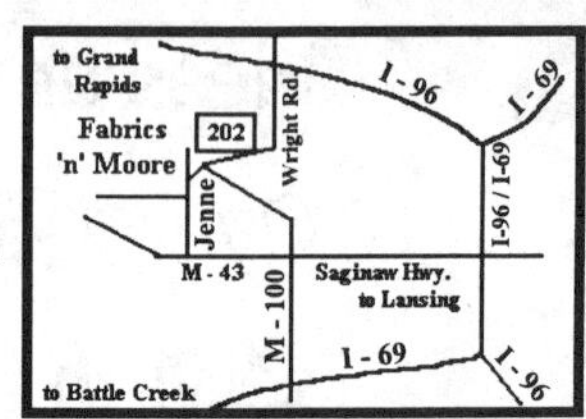

Plymouth, MI #45

Village Patchwork

AT THE DEPOT

IN PLYMOUTH'S OLD VILLAGE

Over 1000 Bolts of 100% cotton fabrics
Books, Patterns, Notions & Classes
Special Orders, Gift Certificates

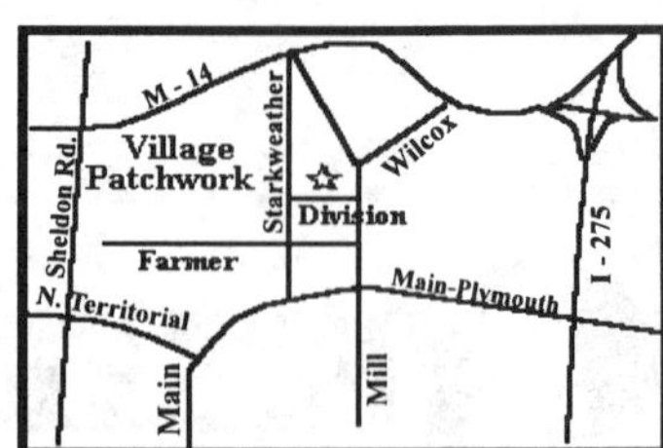

Machine Quilting Service Available.
Mail Order Available.

Mon - Fri 10 - 5
Thur til 7 Sat 10 - 4
Labor - Memorial Day
Sundays 11 - 4

Show Us Your QTC and received 10% off Your Purchases
(One Visit Only)

900 Starkweather 48170
(313) 453-1750
Owner: Jan Williams
Est: 1989 1400sq.ft.

Charlotte, MI #43

Mon - Sat 10 - 5:30

Hen House of Charlotte

211 S. Cochran 48813
(517) 543-6454
Owner: Nancy Conn
Est: 1974

A craft shop specializing in quality materials including 100% cotton and homespun fabrics, Stenciling, X-Stitch, Tole Painting and Basket Supplies

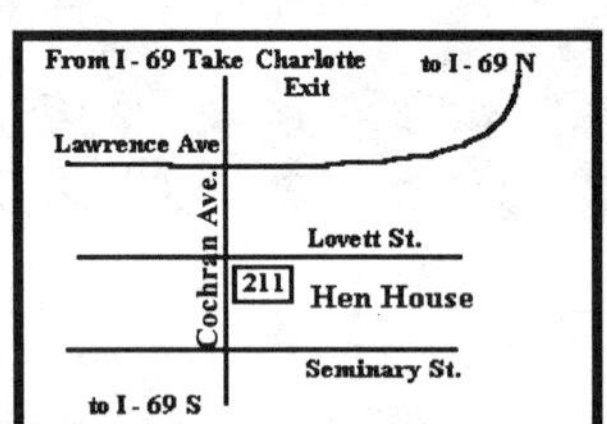

Lake Odessa, MI #44

Mon - Sat 9 - 5:30

Katie's Stitch 'N' Stuf

1017 4th Avenue 48849
(616) 374-8535
Owner: Kathleen Stuart
Est: 1986 1200 sq.ft. 600 Bolts

Quilting Fabrics, Large Selection of Templates, Books, Craft Supplies, Yarn, Counted Cross Stitch, Crochet Threads, Classes Available.

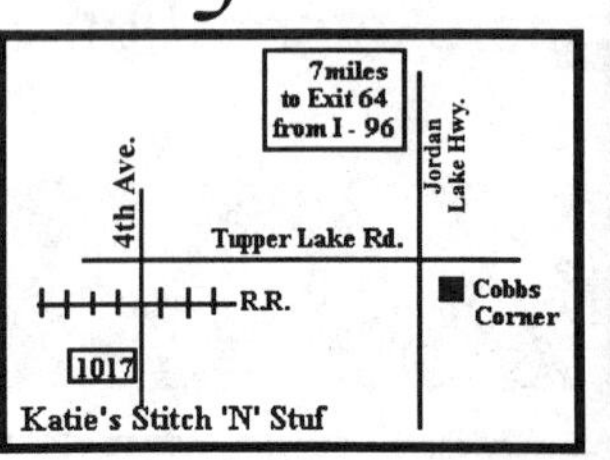

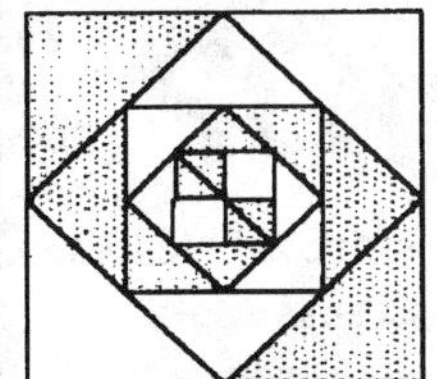

In the Heart of Beautiful Downtown Plymouth

QuiltWorks

Plymouth, MI #46

580 Forest Avenue #4
Plymouth, Michigan 48170
(734) 207-8708

Your place for contemporary cotton fabrics for quilting and clothing. Let our friendly, knowledgeable staff help you make your project come to life. Books, patterns, books, notions, classes... complete quilting supplies for the novice to the expert. Large selection of Hoffman batiks

Monday - Saturday
10 - 5
Tuesday open to 7

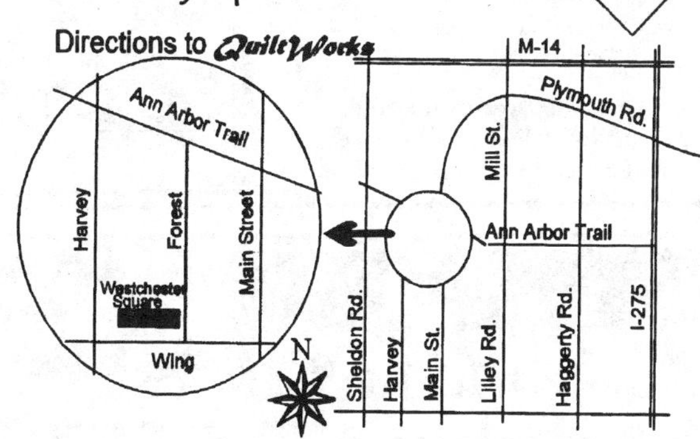

The Quiltery

1540 East Columbia Ave. 49017
(616) 965-2116
Est: 1981 2500 sq.ft.
Owner: Lynne Evans

Tues - Fri 10 - 5 Sat 10 - 1

HUGE selection of quality 100% cottons by Hoffman, RJR, Jinny Beyer, P&B, Benartex, Red Wagon, Gutcheon, Roberta Horton, and others; Complete line of notions, books, patterns; Bernina Sewing Machines. Call for a free newsletter listing classes & sales.

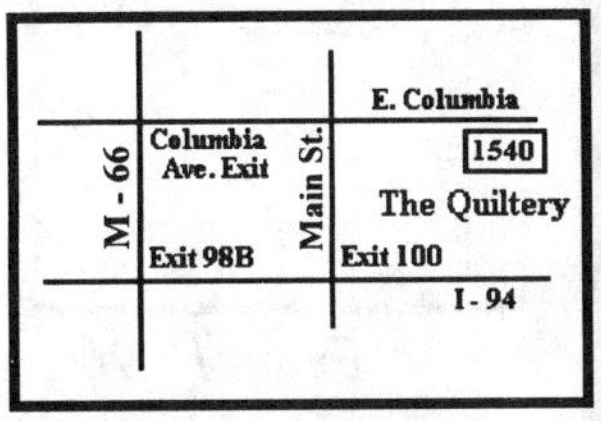

E. Columbia
Columbia Ave. Exit
M - 66
Main St.
1540
The Quiltery
Exit 98B
Exit 100
I - 94

Battle Creek, MI #47

Kalamazoo, MI #48

Viking Sewing Center

**Mon - Fri 9 - 5:30
Wed til 7
Sat 9 - 4**

5401 Portage Rd. 49002
(616) 342-5808
Owners: Phil & Julie Rotzien
2500 sq.ft.

1000+ bolts of 100% cotton fabric. Quilting, heirloom, garment and specialty sewing classes. Viking & White sewing machine sales & service.

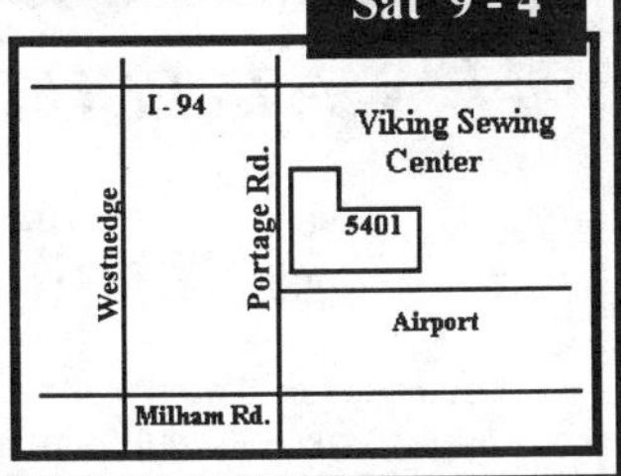

Kalamazoo, MI #49

Quilts Plus

**Mon - Fri 10 - 6
Sat 10 - 4**

4426 W. Main 49006
(616) 383-1790
Owner: Kathleen Edwards
Est: 1997

Fabrics, Classes, Quilting Supplies, Books, Patterns, Wool Rug Hooking Kits, Quilting Hoops and Frames. Samples Galore.

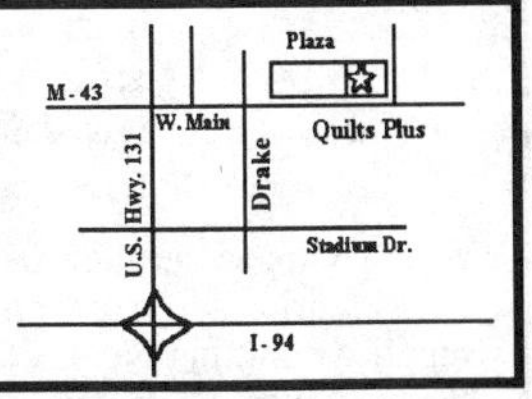

Hastings, MI #50

Sisters Fabrics

Mon - Thur 8 - 5:30
Fri 8 - 7
Sat 9 - 5:30

218 E. State St. 49058
(616) 945-9673

Large selection of calico, books, patterns, quilting supplies, Pendleton wool, fleece, dress fabrics, JHB and Streamline buttons, etc.

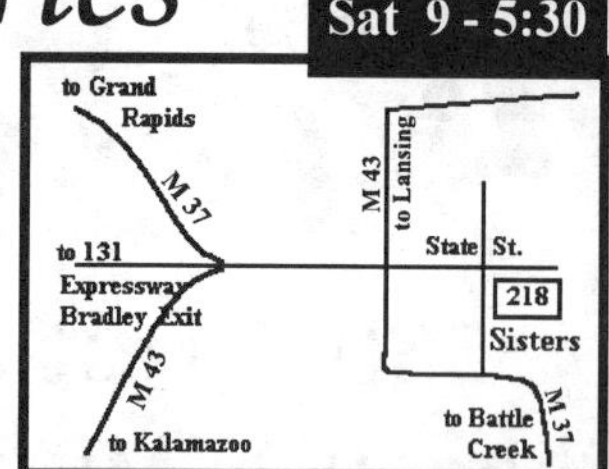

Benton Harbor, MI #52

Carol's Quilt Cottage

Tues - Fri 10 - 5
Sat 10 - 4

1985 Zoschke Rd. 49022
(616) 849-4065
Owner: Carol Frosolone
Est: 1997

Available will be a wide variety of notions, patterns, books, quality 100% cotton fabric, and many gift ideas. Full service quilt shop.

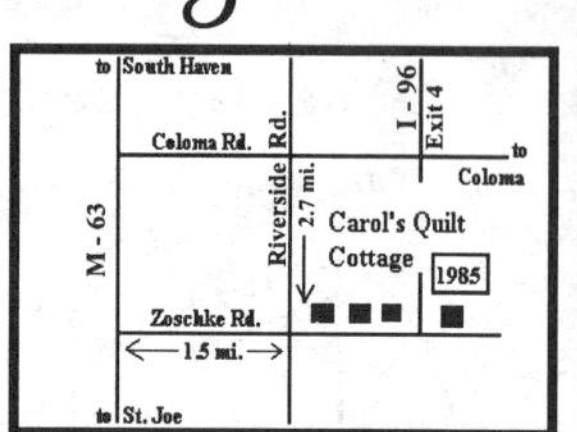

Loving Stitches QUILT SHOP

Est: 1996

Owner: Holly Martin

We have expanded & now have even more fabric in stock!
Patterns, books, supplies. Classes Available.
See Our perennial garden in season.

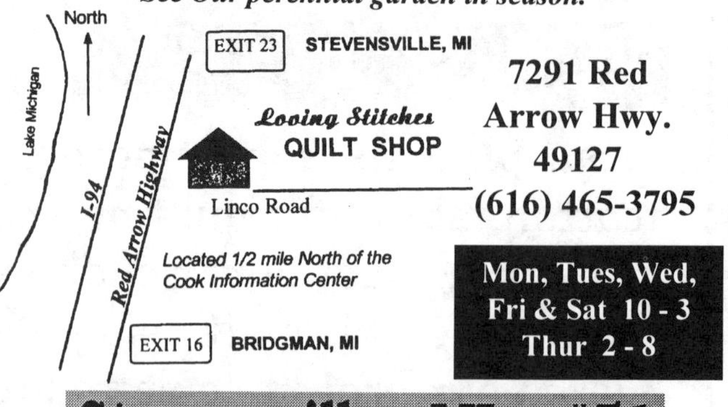

7291 Red Arrow Hwy.
49127
(616) 465-3795

Mon, Tues, Wed, Fri & Sat 10 - 3
Thur 2 - 8

Stevensville, MI #51

Holland, MI #53

Field's World of Fabrics

Mon - Sat 9 - 9

281 East 8th 49423
(616) 392-4806
Owner: Jack Veldman
Est: 1953 9000 sq.ft.

Packed with Fabrics !
5000+ Bolts
Many Unique Prints.

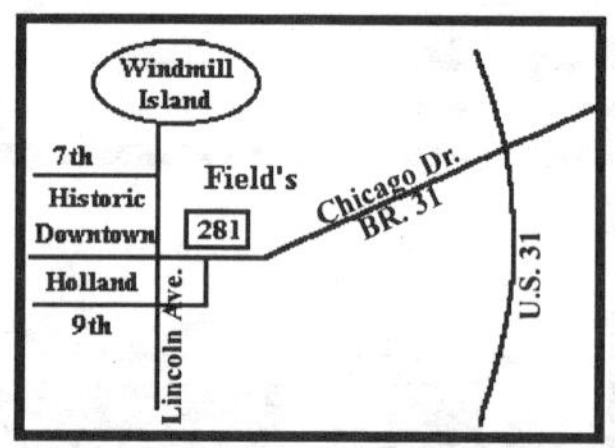

Zeeland, MI #54

It's Stitching Time

Mon - Fri 9 - 5:30
Fri til 8
Sat 9 - 2

150 E. Main 49464
(616) 772-5525

Complete Needlework and Quilt Shop.
Over 350 Quilt Books.
Lots of patterns, fabric, rulers.
A Quilter's Dream Shop.

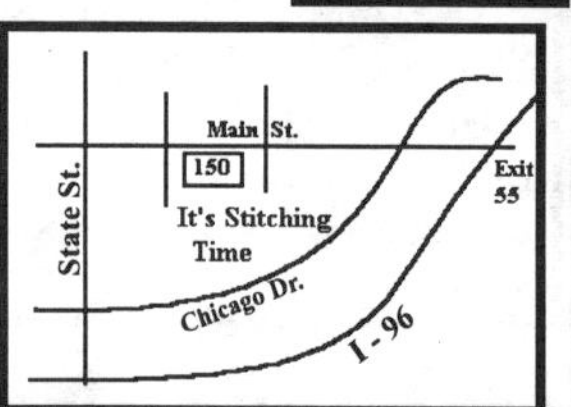

Jenison, MI #55

Country Needleworks

Mon - Sat 9:30 - 9

584 Chicago Dr. 49428
(616) 457-9410 Est: 1981
Owners: Cheryl Van Haitsma & Barb Langerak

Your complete needlework shop carrying: quilt fabric & accessories, cross-stitch supplies, knitting yarns, largest stamping center in West Michigan. Giftware.

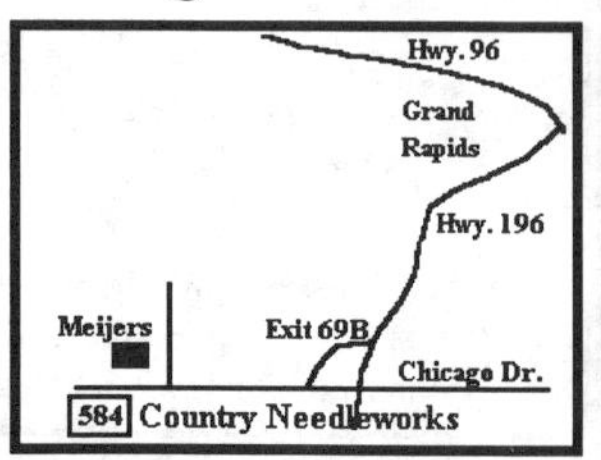

Grand Quilt Co.

Grand Rapids, MI #56

Eastbrook Mall
3605 28th St. SE 49512
(616) 942-6707
Fax: (616) 942-6904
E-Mail: Katquil@aol.com
Est: 1997 2400 sq.ft.

2,000 Bolts of 100% Cotton Fabrics— Hoffman, Benartex, etc. Patterns, Books, Notions, Threads. Silk Ribbon Embroidery, Gift Certificates, Gifts, Handmade Quilts.

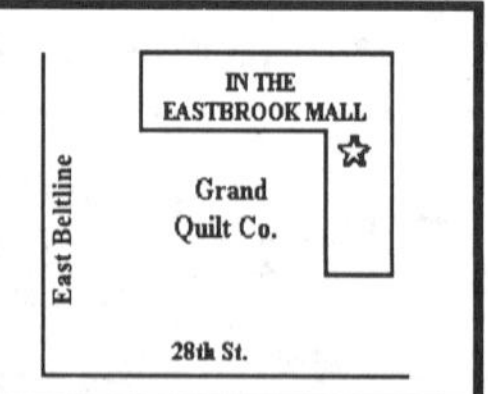

Mon - Fri 10 - 9
Sat 9:30 - 7
Call for Summer hours June through August

From I - 96 Take Exit 43A
2 miles to Mall

Lowest Prices in the Great Lakes Area on Hobbs Batting!

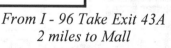

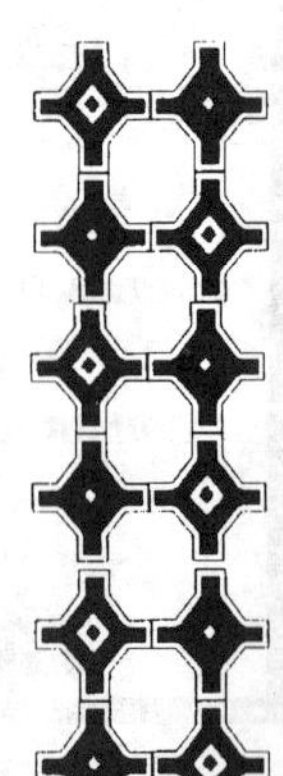

Attic Window Quilt Shop

Grand Rapids, MI #57

Large selection of fabric, books, patterns, and notions.
Antique reproduction fabrics. Special order and hard-to-find items.
Classes, mail order and more.

1035 Four Mile Rd. NW 49544
(616) 785-3357
Fax: (616) 785-3358
E-Mail: ssquilt@aol.com
Owners: Sally Johnson
& Gay Bomers

Mon 10 - 8
Tues - Fri 10 - 5:30
Sat 10 - 3

Est: 1997 2800 sq.ft.

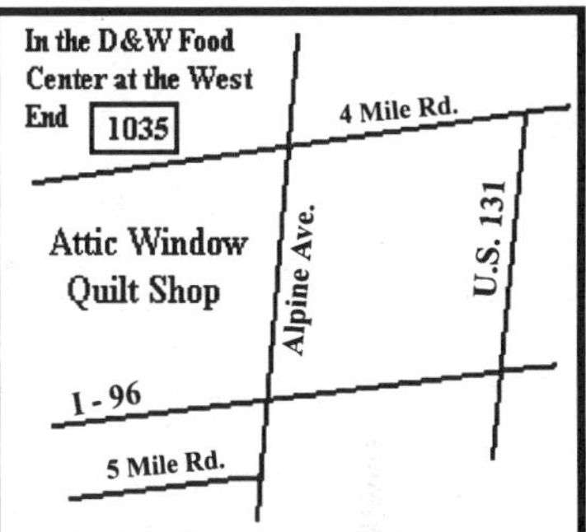

SMITH OWEN

Sewing & Quilt Center

Western Michigan's largest Quilt Shop

Check on the latest in books, notions, and patterns. Many Quilts and Wallhangings on Display.

Mon & Thur
9 - 8
Tues, Wed,
Fri 9 - 5
Sat 9 - 3

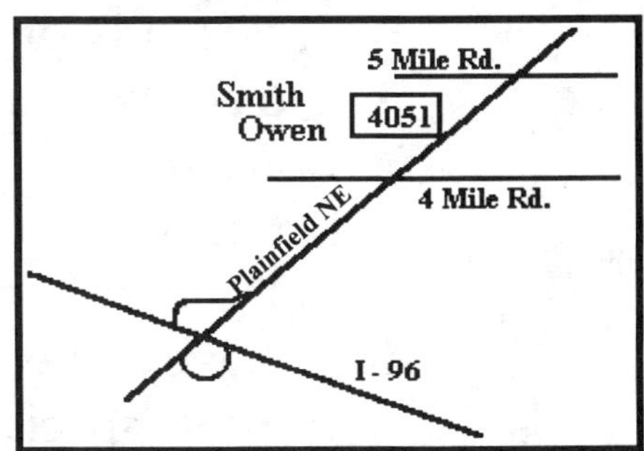

Grand Rapids, MI #58

4051 Plainfield NE 49525
(616) 361-5484 Fax #: (616) 361-8727

Over 3000 bolts of quilting fabric.

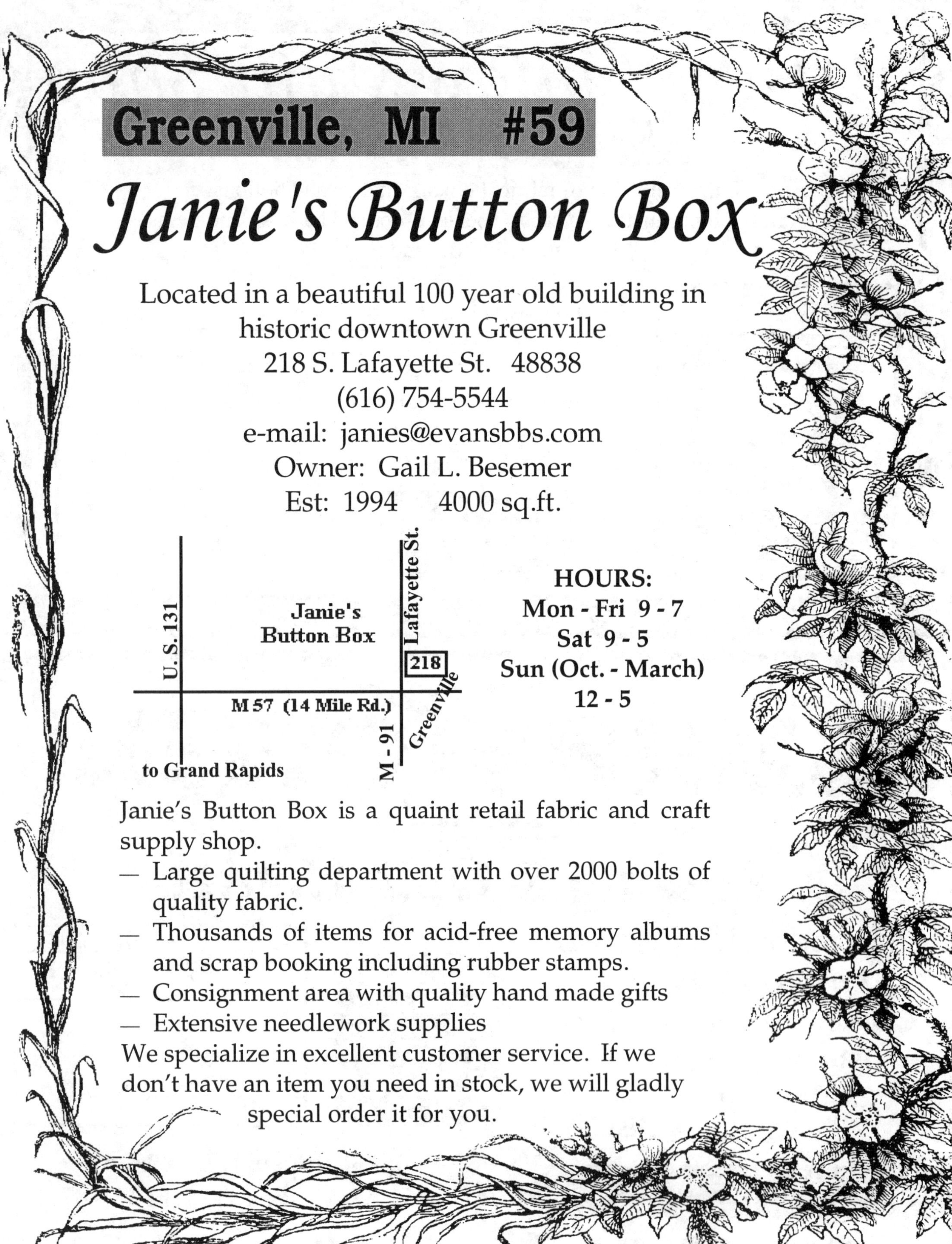

Greenville, MI #59

Janie's Button Box

Located in a beautiful 100 year old building in historic downtown Greenville
218 S. Lafayette St. 48838
(616) 754-5544
e-mail: janies@evansbbs.com
Owner: Gail L. Besemer
Est: 1994 4000 sq.ft.

HOURS:
Mon - Fri 9 - 7
Sat 9 - 5
Sun (Oct. - March) 12 - 5

Janie's Button Box is a quaint retail fabric and craft supply shop.

- Large quilting department with over 2000 bolts of quality fabric.
- Thousands of items for acid-free memory albums and scrap booking including rubber stamps.
- Consignment area with quality hand made gifts
- Extensive needlework supplies

We specialize in excellent customer service. If we don't have an item you need in stock, we will gladly special order it for you.

Note: Harbor Springs is <u>not</u> on the Upper Peninsula just very Northern Michigan

Harbor Springs, MI #60

Mon - Sat 10 - 5 Year - round

Quilting Barn

1221-A West Conway Road 49740
(616) 347-1116 Est: 1978 850 sq.ft.
Owners: Dolores P. Boese
& Karen Boese Schaller

Emmet County's Complete Prof. Quilting Store. We have over 2000 bolts of 100% cotton fabric and 19 years of experience.

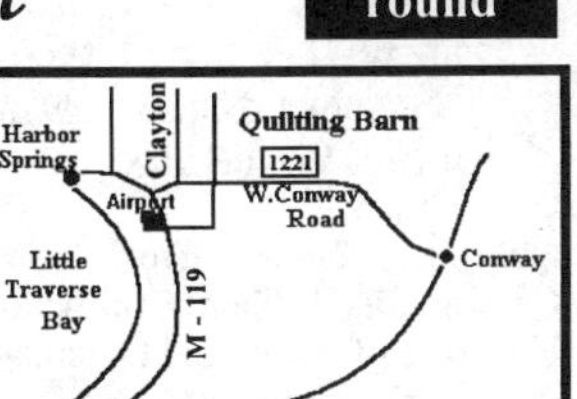

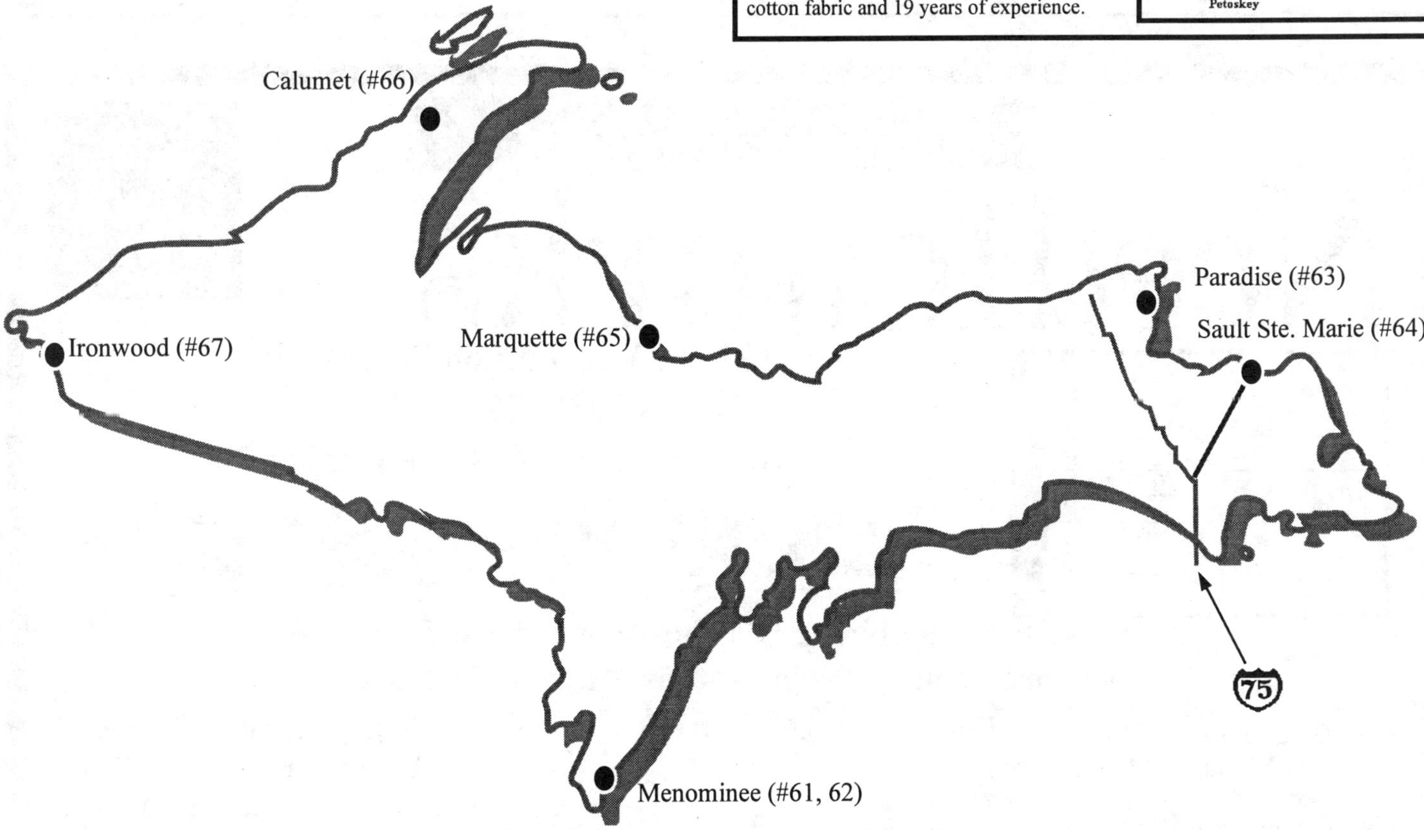

Calumet (#66)
Ironwood (#67)
Marquette (#65)
Paradise (#63)
Sault Ste. Marie (#64)
75
Menominee (#61, 62)

7 Featured Shops MICHIGAN'S UPPER PENINSULA

Menominee, MI #61

**Mon - Fri 10 - 5
Sat 10 - 4
Oct & Nov
Sun 12 - 4**

Country Treasures

W 6607 2.5 Lane 49858
(906) 863-6368 Est: 1993
Owner: Nancy Zeratsky
5500 sq.ft. 1000+ Bolts

100% Cotton Fabric for Quilting and Crafts. Notions, Books, Patterns, Craft Supplies, Wood, Cross Stitch, Beads, Flowers & much more. Classes

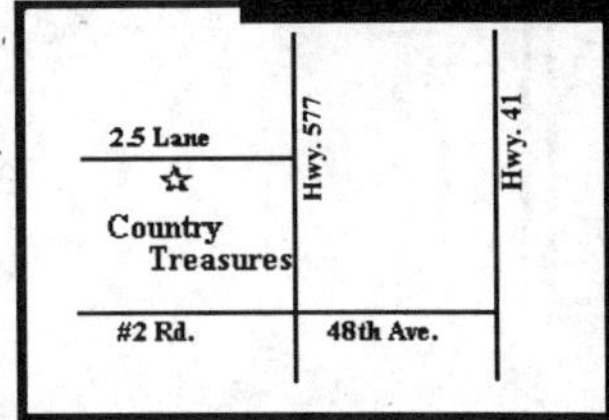

Menominee, MI #62

**Mon - Fri
9:30 - 5:30
Thur til 8
Sat 10 - 4
Sun 1 - 4**

Quilter's Haven, Ltd.

707 1st St. 49858
(906) 864-3078
Owner: Chris Caselton
Est: 1996 2000 sq.ft. 1500 Bolts

A friendly quaint quilt shop along the beautiful shore of Lake Michigan.
Notions, books, patterns galore!!

Paradise, MI #63

Summer
Daily 10-7
Winter
10 - 5
Closed Tue
Sun 12 - 5

Village Fabrics & Crafts

32702 W. Hwy. M-123 P.O. Box 254
(906) 492-3803 49768
Owner: Vicki Hallaxs Est: 1986

Quilting, Counted Cross Stitch, Plastic Canvas, Silk Ribbon Emb. Unique Crafts. Hundreds of Books and Patterns— Many of Area Attractions. Gifts.

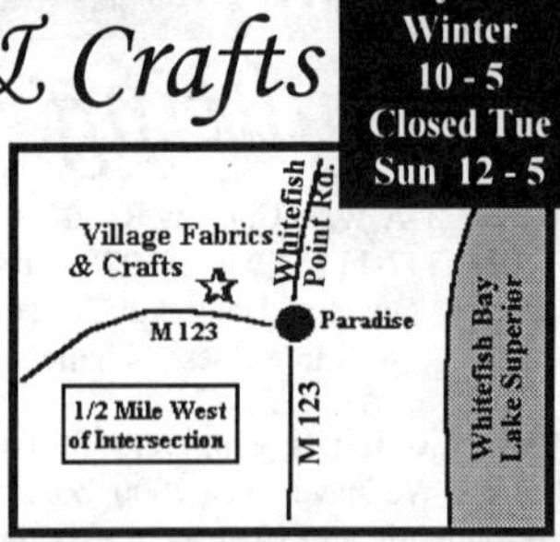

Sault Ste. Marie, MI #64

Mon - Fri
9 - 5

Gloria's Happy Hooker

Quilting & Needlecraft Supplies

M - 129 (2733 Ashmun St.) 49783
(906) 635-9937
Owner: Gloria Larke

Fabric, Yarns, Cross Stitch Supplies, Books & Accessories. Home of the Famous Soo Locks.

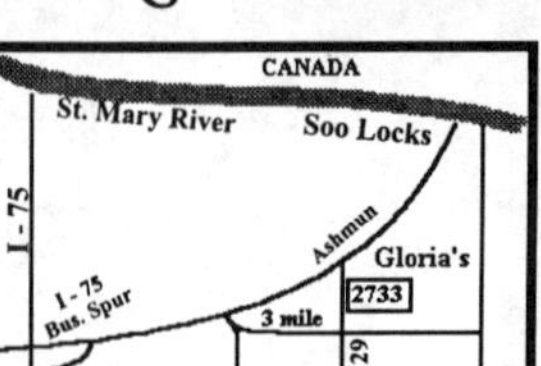

Marquette, MI #65

Mon - Sat
10 - 5
Fri til 6
Sun 12 - 4

Needleworks

Bluff St.
Third St.
Front St.
Hwy. 41 W
Washington St.
121
Needleworks
Bank
Main St.
U.S. 41 S
Spring St.
Lake Superior

121 W. Washington St. 49855
(906) 228-6051
Owners: Robin & Alice Robinson

A unique shop combining Quilting & outerwear fabrics for the northcountry sewing enthusiast. FEATURING:

<u>Cottons</u> by Kaufman, Momen House, Hoffman, Roberta Horton, Moda, P&B and more...

YKK zippers • unique buttons • Kwik Sew & Burda patterns • books • Australian quilting magazines • Classes

<u>Outerwear</u> fabrics including; berbers, Brand Name fleeces, supplex nylons, corduras, flannels, quilted linings, lycras, ultrex and more ...

A fun shop to visit! The coffee pot is always on.

Calumet, MI #66

Mon - Sat
9:30 - 5:30
May 1 - Sept 30
10 - 5
Oct 1 - Jan 1

Traditions

U.S. 41, Rt. #1, Box 86 49913
(906) 482-8674 Est: 1993
Owners: Barb Heinonen, Carol Eskola
Carole Ryynanen & Sue Pietila

Books, Fabrics & Supplies for Quilting, Smocking, French Hand Sewing & Silk Ribbon Emb. Also unique Hand Made Gifts.

CALUMET
HANCOCK
HOUGHTON
Lake Superior
US 41
to MARQUETTE
Half-way Between Hancock & Calumet

The one who dies with the most fabric ...
WINS!

Ironwood, MI #67

The Fabric Patch

Owners: Arlene Wanink, Ruth Potter, & Joanne Kuula
121 N. Lowell St. 49938
(906) 932-5260 Fax: (906) 932-5004
E-Mail: fabric@portup.com Est: 1981

Mon - Thur 9:30 - 5
Fri 9:30 - 6
Sat 9:30 - 4

Quilting, Rubber Stamping and Craft Headquarters of the North. Largest Selection in Michigan's Upper Peninsula and Northern Wisconsin.

Choose from over 3500 Bolts of Quilting Fabrics Huge Selection of Quilting Books and Craft Patterns.

Authorized Dealer for Husqvarna Viking and White Sewing Machines & Sergers.

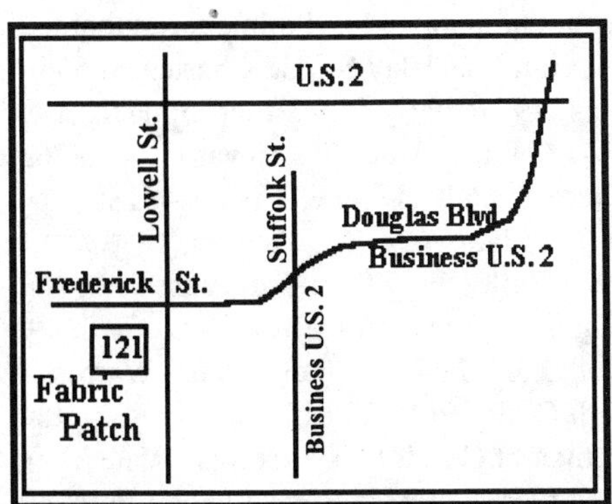

Ongoing Block of the Month Kits
Call or Stop In for Details

Mail Order Available.

Michigan Guilds:

Trinity Piecemakers, 9077 Allen Road, Allen Park, 48101
U of M Women's Quilters, 2481 Trenton Ct., Ann Arbor, 48105
Greater Ann Arbor Quilt Guild, P.O. Box 2737, Ann Arbor, 48106
Meets: 3rd Saturday (odd # months, except May)
at Washtenaw Community College, Morris Laurence Bldg.,
Nationally known Speakers and classes offered
Michigan Quilt Network, P.O. Box 339, Atlanta, 49709
Thunder Bay Quilters, P.O. Box 960, Atlanta, 49709
McKay Library Quilters, 105 S. Webster Street, Augusta, 49012
Berrien Towne & Country Quilters, 4218 E. Tudor Rd.
Barrien Springs, 49103
Cal-Co Quilters' Guild, P.O. Box 867, Battle Creek, 49016
Bay Heritage Q. G., 321 Washington Ave., Bay City, 48708
Silk City Quilters' Guild, 108 Hanover, Belding, 48809
Meets: 1st Wednesday 6:30 at the Community Center
Western Wayne Cty Quilting Guild, 129 South, Belleville, 48111
Pieceable Friends, 1991 E. Lincoln, Birmingham, 48009
Needlework & Textile Guild, 3219 Woodside Court,
Bloomfield Hills, 48013
Casual Quilter's, 5418 Ethel, Brighton, 48116
Brighton Heritage Quilters, 10281 Carriage Dr., Brighton, 48116
North Star Quilters, 8436 E. 48th Rd., Cadillac, 49601
Keweenaw Heritage Quilters, Calumet, 49913
Rivertown Patchworkers, 1849 Richmond, Cheboygan, 49721
Thumb Thimbles Quilt Guild, 5140 English Rd., Clifford, 48727
West Michigan Q. G., 13646 48th Ave., Coopersville, 49404
Evening Star Quilters, 1034 Carla Blvd., Davison, 48423
Meets: Last Wednesday 6:30 p.m.
at Davison Senior Center, 334 N. Main
General Dearborn Quilt Soc, 915 Brady Road S., Dearborn, 48124
The Monday Night Quilters, 79939 40th St., Decatur, 49045
St. Raymond's Quilters, 20212 Fairport, Detroit, 48205
The Crazy Quilters, 51106 Glenwood Rd., Dowagiac, 49047
Island City Piecemakers, P.O. Box 14, Eaton Rapids, 48827
Victorian Quilters Guild, P.O. 149, Empire, 49630
Bay deNoc Q. G., 606 Ogden Ave., Escanaba, 49829
Care & Share, 4052 Fairgrove Rd., Fairgrove, 48733
Greater Ann Arbor Q. G., 36437 Saxony,
Farmington, 48335
Crazy Quilters, 7870 Peninsula, Farwell, 48622
Genesee Star, G-4324 W. Pasadena, Flint, 48504
Meets: 3rd Friday 9:30 a.m.
at Nazarene Church, 2254 Dye Rd.
Evening Star, 5327 Hopkins, Flint, 48506
Genesee Star Quilters, 614 S. McKinley,
Flushing, 48433
Rumpled Quilts Kin, P.O. Box 587,
Frankfort, 49635

Tall Pine Quilt, 2073 Baldwin, Fremont, 49412
North Country Piecemakers, P.O. Box 10, Glennie, 48737
Au Sable Quilt Guild, P.O. Box 198, Grayling, 49738
Claire County Crazy Quilters, 5189 Hamilton, Harrison, 48625
Tuesday Night Crazy Quilters, 18 N. Center St., Hartford
Tulip Patch Quilting Org., 600 Woodland Dr., Holland, 49424
Composing Threaders, 144 N. Trybom Dr., Iron River, 49935
Carrie Jacobs-Bond Composing Threaders, Iron River
Pieces & Patches Quilt Guild, Box 6294, Jackson, 49202
Log Cabin Quilters, 6632 Woodlea, Kalamazoo, 49004
West Michigan Quilter's Guild, P.O. Box 8001, Kentwood, 49518
Meets: 4th Tuesday 7 p.m. of Jan, Mar, May, July, Sept, Nov
at Calvary Christian Reformed Church
Lansing Area Patchers, 3305 Sunnylane, Lansing, 48906
Capitol City Q. G., 7131 Willow Woods Cr., Lansing, 48917
Thimble Buddies Q. G., 3167 Roods Lake Rd., Lapeer, 48446
Lewiston Lakes Quilt Guild, P.O. Box 512, Lewiston, 49756
Anchor Bay Quilters, 5757 N. River Rd., Marine City, 48039
Marquette County Quilters Assoc., PO Box 411, Marquette, 49855
Meets: 1st Wednesday 7 p.m. at Marquette Township Hall
Northwood Quilt Guild, Menominee Meets: 2st Monday
contact: Chris Caselton (906) 864-3078
Quilters Squared Quilt Guild, 2715 Whitewood Dr., Midland, 48640
Meets: 2nd Tuesday at Quilted Giraffe
Midland Mennonites, 364 E. Gordonville, Midland, 48640
Patchers at the Lake Shore, 926 Wellington Ct., Muskegon, 49441
Niles Piecemakers, 1347 Louis St., Niles, 49120
Greater Ann Arbor Quilt Guild, 22452 Meadow Brook, Novi, 48375
Calico Patch Quilters, 1550 W. Drahner Rd., Oxford, 48371
Little Traverse Bay Quilters Guild, P.O. Box 2022, Petoskey, 49770
Meets: 2nd Wednesday 7:30 p.m. at NCMC College
Pinckney Quilting Sisters, 11383 Cedar Bend Dr., Pinckney, 48169
Island City Quilters, 180 S. Sherwood, Plainwell, 49080
Plymouth Piecemakers, 11768 Turkey Run, Plymouth, 48170
Portage Quilt Guild, 6278 Redfern Circle, Portage, 49002
Loose Threads, 37550 Hebel Rd., Richmond, 48062
Oakland County Q. G., 282 Rose Briar Dr., Rochester Hills, 48309
Piece to Peace Quilting Club, 3914 Mission, Rosebush, 48878
Piecemaker's Quilt Guild, Saginaw
Meets: 3rd Wednesday 7 p.m.
at Presbyterian Church, 2665 Midland Rd.
Keeping the Piece Quilt Guild, Sault Ste. Marie, 49783
Friendship Ring Quilt Guild, 305 E. Harrison St., Shelby, 49455
Wyandotte Museum Quilters, 13407 Pullman, Southgate, 48195
Piecemakers Quilt Guild, 202 Jay St., St. Charles, 48655
Tri County Q. G., 4619 Hatherly Place, Sterling Heights, 48310
Sunrise Quilters, 318 N. McArdle Rd., Tawas City, 48763
Eton Center Quilters, 7946 McKinley, Taylor, 48180
Trenton Quilters, 3398 Norwood Dr., Trenton, 48183
Cass River Quilters' Guild, 6977 Sohn Rd., Vassar, 48768
Northern Lights Quilt Guild, 1315 Dewey, Wakefield, 49968
Greater Ann Arbor Q. G., 29807 Autumn Lane, Warren, 48093
Metro Detroit Quilt Guild, 6148 28 Mile Rd., Washington, 48094
Barrien County Coverlet Guild, P.O. Box 529, Watervliet, 49098
Quilt-N-Friends, 6332 Aspen Ridge, West Bloomfield, 48332
Rifle River Quilt Guild, 2831 Highland Dr., West Branch, 48661
Meets: 4th Tuesday 7 p.m. at Ogemaw Hills Free
Methodist Church, 1 mile west of downtown on M - 55

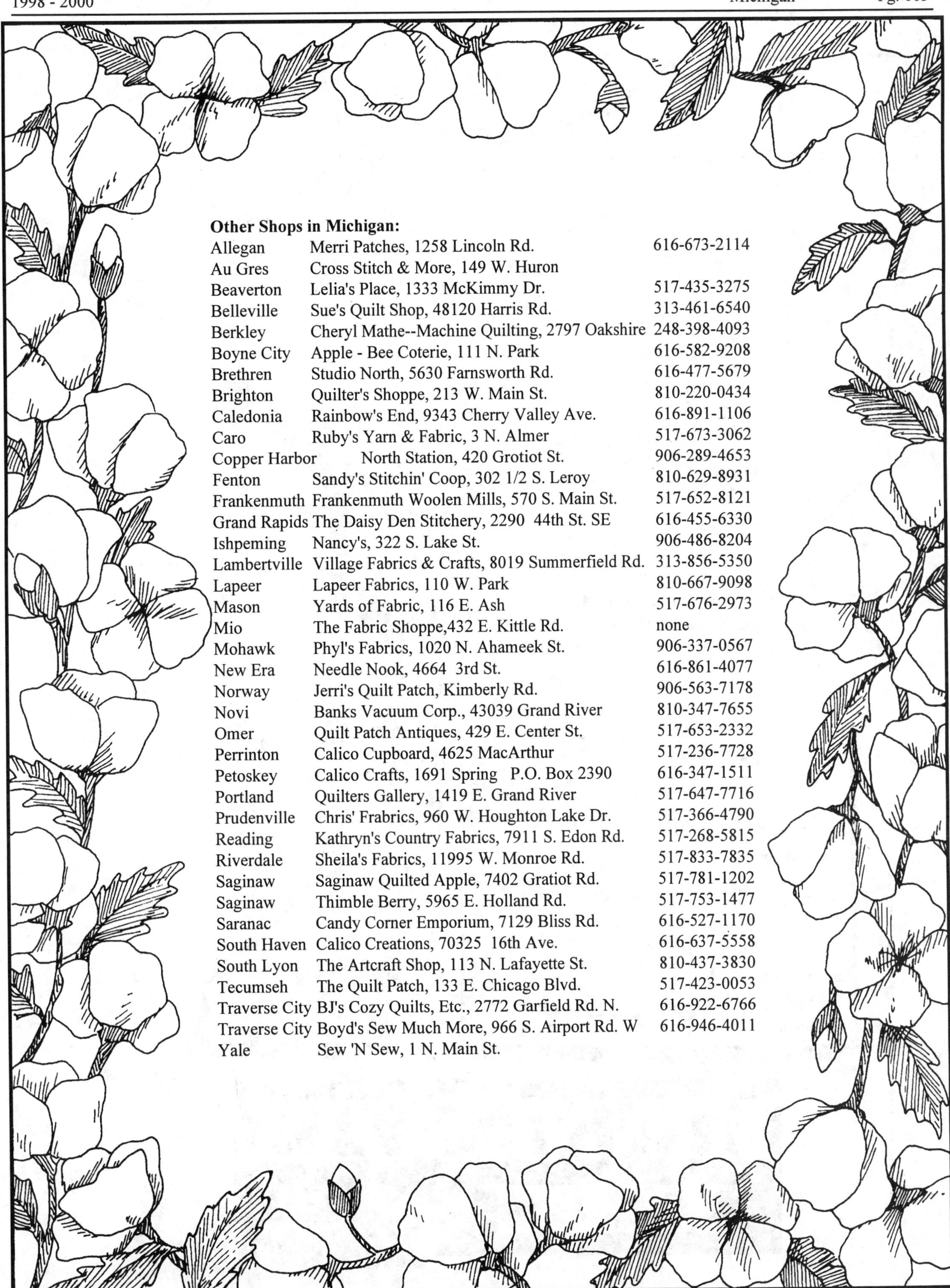

Other Shops in Michigan:

Allegan	Merri Patches, 1258 Lincoln Rd.	616-673-2114
Au Gres	Cross Stitch & More, 149 W. Huron	
Beaverton	Lelia's Place, 1333 McKimmy Dr.	517-435-3275
Belleville	Sue's Quilt Shop, 48120 Harris Rd.	313-461-6540
Berkley	Cheryl Mathe--Machine Quilting, 2797 Oakshire	248-398-4093
Boyne City	Apple - Bee Coterie, 111 N. Park	616-582-9208
Brethren	Studio North, 5630 Farnsworth Rd.	616-477-5679
Brighton	Quilter's Shoppe, 213 W. Main St.	810-220-0434
Caledonia	Rainbow's End, 9343 Cherry Valley Ave.	616-891-1106
Caro	Ruby's Yarn & Fabric, 3 N. Almer	517-673-3062
Copper Harbor	North Station, 420 Grotiot St.	906-289-4653
Fenton	Sandy's Stitchin' Coop, 302 1/2 S. Leroy	810-629-8931
Frankenmuth	Frankenmuth Woolen Mills, 570 S. Main St.	517-652-8121
Grand Rapids	The Daisy Den Stitchery, 2290 44th St. SE	616-455-6330
Ishpeming	Nancy's, 322 S. Lake St.	906-486-8204
Lambertville	Village Fabrics & Crafts, 8019 Summerfield Rd.	313-856-5350
Lapeer	Lapeer Fabrics, 110 W. Park	810-667-9098
Mason	Yards of Fabric, 116 E. Ash	517-676-2973
Mio	The Fabric Shoppe,432 E. Kittle Rd.	none
Mohawk	Phyl's Fabrics, 1020 N. Ahameek St.	906-337-0567
New Era	Needle Nook, 4664 3rd St.	616-861-4077
Norway	Jerri's Quilt Patch, Kimberly Rd.	906-563-7178
Novi	Banks Vacuum Corp., 43039 Grand River	810-347-7655
Omer	Quilt Patch Antiques, 429 E. Center St.	517-653-2332
Perrinton	Calico Cupboard, 4625 MacArthur	517-236-7728
Petoskey	Calico Crafts, 1691 Spring P.O. Box 2390	616-347-1511
Portland	Quilters Gallery, 1419 E. Grand River	517-647-7716
Prudenville	Chris' Frabrics, 960 W. Houghton Lake Dr.	517-366-4790
Reading	Kathryn's Country Fabrics, 7911 S. Edon Rd.	517-268-5815
Riverdale	Sheila's Fabrics, 11995 W. Monroe Rd.	517-833-7835
Saginaw	Saginaw Quilted Apple, 7402 Gratiot Rd.	517-781-1202
Saginaw	Thimble Berry, 5965 E. Holland Rd.	517-753-1477
Saranac	Candy Corner Emporium, 7129 Bliss Rd.	616-527-1170
South Haven	Calico Creations, 70325 16th Ave.	616-637-5558
South Lyon	The Artcraft Shop, 113 N. Lafayette St.	810-437-3830
Tecumseh	The Quilt Patch, 133 E. Chicago Blvd.	517-423-0053
Traverse City	BJ's Cozy Quilts, Etc., 2772 Garfield Rd. N.	616-922-6766
Traverse City	Boyd's Sew Much More, 966 S. Airport Rd. W	616-946-4011
Yale	Sew 'N Sew, 1 N. Main St.	

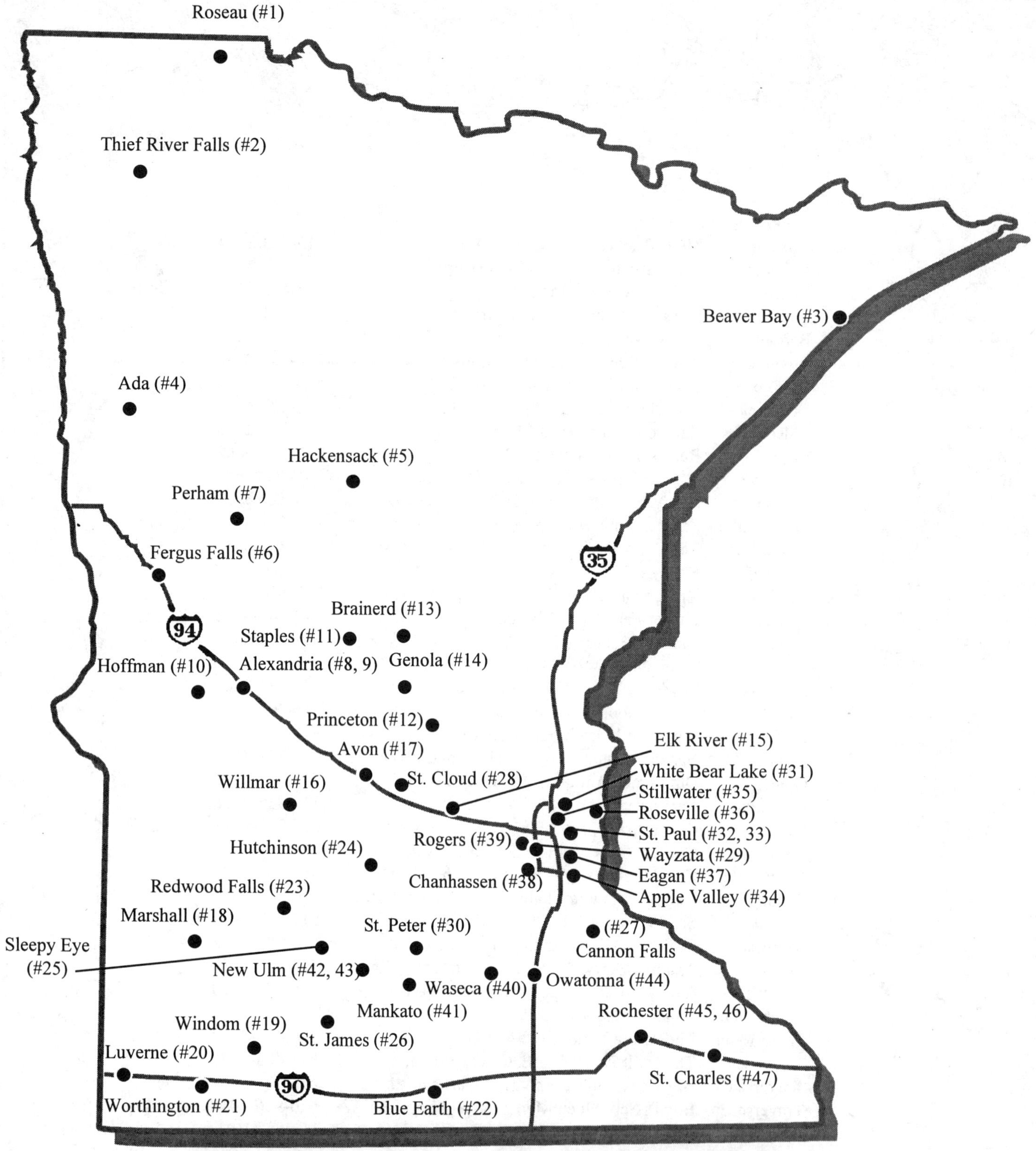

Roseau (#1)

Thief River Falls (#2)

Beaver Bay (#3)

Ada (#4)

Hackensack (#5)

Perham (#7)

Fergus Falls (#6)

35

94

Brainerd (#13)

Staples (#11)

Hoffman (#10)

Alexandria (#8, 9)

Genola (#14)

Princeton (#12)

Elk River (#15)

Avon (#17)

White Bear Lake (#31)

St. Cloud (#28)

Willmar (#16)

Stillwater (#35)

Roseville (#36)

St. Paul (#32, 33)

Rogers (#39)

Hutchinson (#24)

Wayzata (#29)

Chanhassen (#38)

Eagan (#37)

Redwood Falls (#23)

Apple Valley (#34)

Marshall (#18)

St. Peter (#30)

(#27) Cannon Falls

Sleepy Eye (#25)

New Ulm (#42, 43)

Owatonna (#44)

Waseca (#40)

Mankato (#41)

Rochester (#45, 46)

Windom (#19)

St. James (#26)

Luverne (#20)

St. Charles (#47)

90

Worthington (#21)

Blue Earth (#22)

Roseau, MN #1

The Quilt Hus

Mon - Fri 10 - 5
Thur til 7
Sat 10 - 3

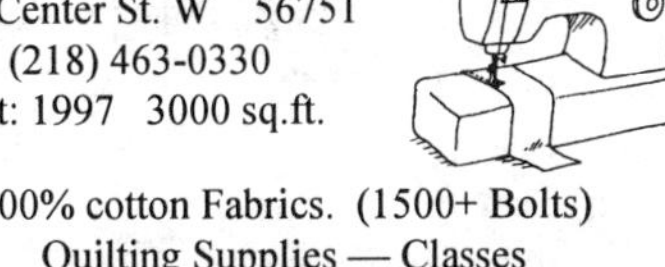

Bernina Sales & Service
216 Center St. W 56751
(218) 463-0330
Est: 1997 3000 sq.ft.

100% cotton Fabrics. (1500+ Bolts)
Quilting Supplies — Classes
Velkommen Room (Gift Shop)

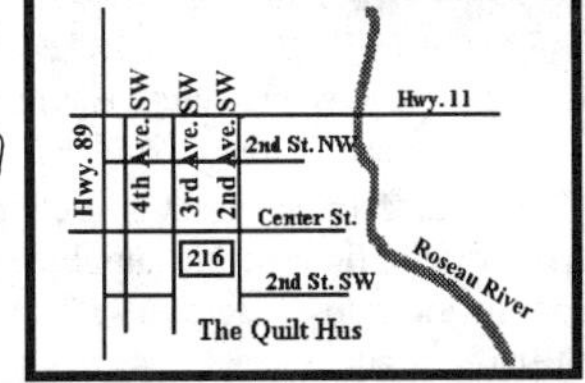

Thief River Falls, MN #2

212 E. 3rd St. 56701
(218) 681-3501 Fax: (218) 681-7466
E-Mail: slois@trf.means.net

Annette's Fabrics

Est: 1971
3000 sq.ft.

4th largest independently owned fabric store in the state of Minnesota. Our "Calico Wall" is over 35 feet long and 4 rows high. Also carry bridal and special occasion fabrics.

Mon - Fri 9 - 6
Thur til 8 Sat 9 - 5:30
Sundays 12 - 4 (School Year)

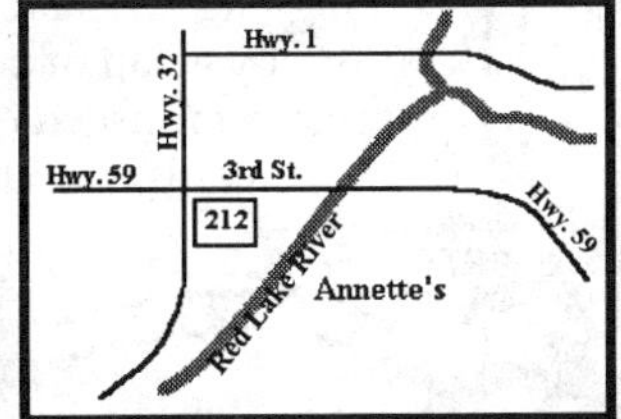

Beaver Bay, MN #3

Quilt Corner

Mon - Sat 10 - 4
Sun 12 - 4

Beaver Bay Mini Mall, P.O. Box 304
(218) 226-3517
Owner: Roxanne Johnson
Est: 1990 800 sq.ft.

Over 500 Bolts of Cotton Fabric. Books, Notions, Patterns, & Stencils. Many Quilts for sale. Gifts too.

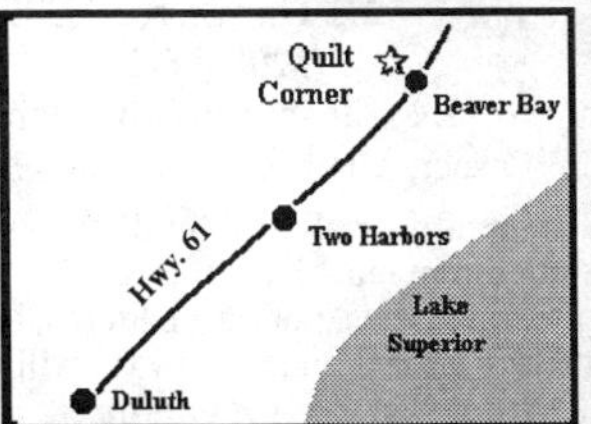

Ada, MN #4

"Just For Fun"

Mon - Fri 9 - 5:30
Sat 9 - 3

Hwy. 200 E,
P.O. Box 221 56510
(218) 784-3568

Fax: (218) 784-2123
Owner: Patricia A. Olson Est: 1997
Unique small town shop. Quilting Supplies, Books, Patterns, Fine 100% Cotton Fabric (1000 Bolts). Gifts & Home Furnishings. Warm & Personal assistance.

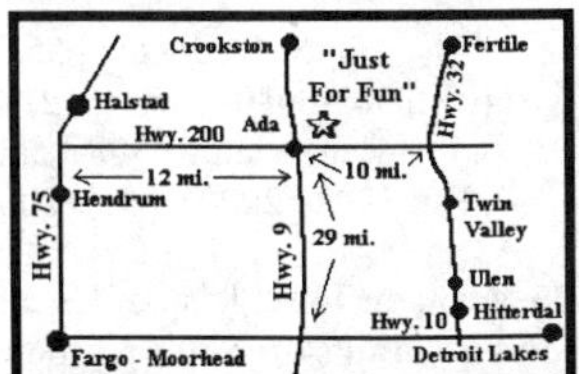

Piecemakers Quilt Shop

Hwy. 371 North
P.O. Box 129 56452
(218) 675-6271
Est: 1984

Hackensack, MN #5

Owners: Mary and Pam Curo

Nestled in the land of lakes and majestic pines this shop features over 2,000 bolts of fine 100% cottons, plus a large selection of quilting books, patterns and notions for all your quilting needs.

Over 200 dolls, santas, bears and angels on display.

New!
Gifts and Collectibles

Home of Cotton Tales Pattern Company.

Custom Machine Quilting Services now available in the store!

Quarterly newsletter featuring Mystery Quilts, Quilt Classes, Retreats, Block of the Month and mail order available at the store or by subscription.

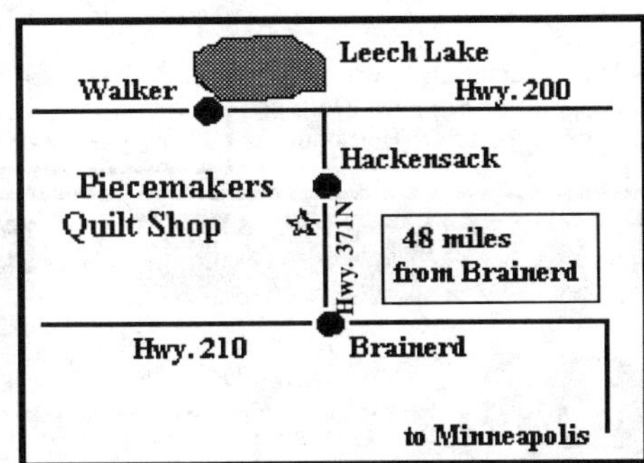

Open Monday through Saturday
10:00-5:00
Sundays 12:00-5:00

Quilters Cottage

316 N. Tower Rd. 56537
(218) 739-9652
Fax: (218) 739-0722
E-Mail: quilters@prtel.com
Owner: Jolene Miller
Est: 1988 1500 Bolts

Authorized Dealer Pfaff Sewing Machines Sales and Service.

PFAFF

Mon, Tues, Wed & Fri 10 - 5
Thur 10 - 6:30
Sat 10 - 3

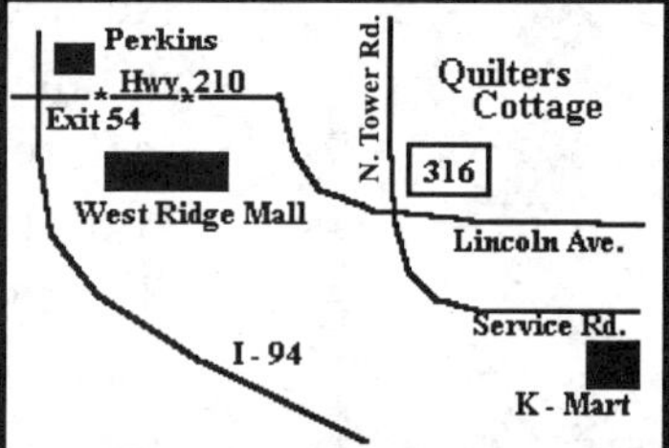

Your one stop quilt shop. We supply everything but the time.

Fergus Falls, MN #6

Perham, MN #7

Mon - Fri 9 - 5:30
Sat 9 - 4

Bay Window Crafts & Quilt Shop

116 2nd Ave. SW 56573
(218) 346-7272
Owner: Sarah Hayden
Est: 1989 2000+ Bolts

Beautiful fabrics, great selection of books, patterns, notions, craft supplies, pottery and quilts for sale. Classes. Custom Quilting. Terrific service!

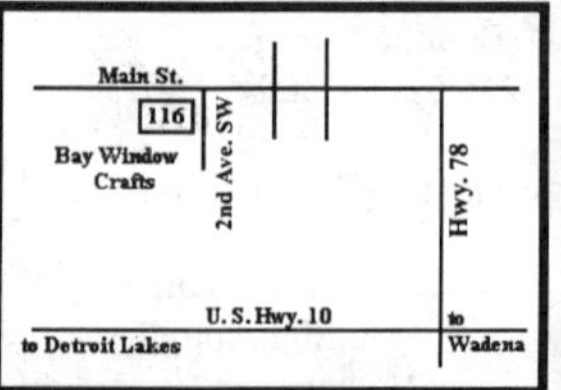

Alexandria, MN #8

109 15th Ave. E
56308
(320) 763-6771

The Common Threads Quilt Shop

Mon - Fri 10 - 5
Thur til 6
Sat 10 - 3

Your center for all your quilting needs - 100% cotton fabrics, books, patterns, and specialty quilting notions. Ongoing "Block of the Month" kits and patterns. Enjoy a cup of coffee while browsing through samples, finished quilts for sale, unique gift items, cards and ideas for home decorating.

Alexandria, MN #9

Tues - Fri 9:30 - 5
Sum Sat 10-3
Win Sat 10-1

Alexandria Stitchin' Post

110 5th Ave W 56308
(320) 763-3400 Fax: Same
E-Mail: jkennedy@gctel.com
Owners: Terilyn Kennedy & Jane McCrery
Est: 1996 1100 sq.ft.

A "Must See" Shop Featuring New Home Sewing Machines, Quilting Supplies, Dolls & Accessories. Contemporary & Heirloom Fabrics & Laces.

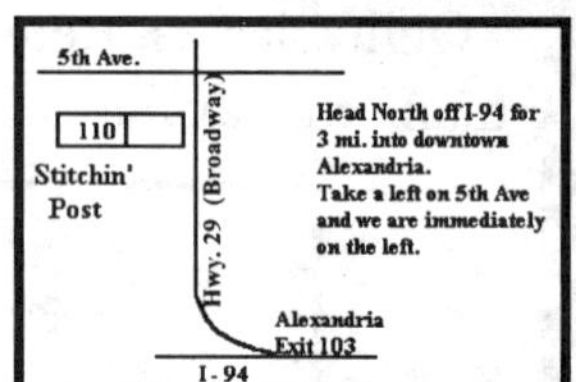

Hoffman, MN #10

Mon - Fri 9 - 5:30
(May - Dec)
Sats 9 - 12

Nuts & Bolts Quilt Shop

213 First St. N 56339
(320) 986-2447
E-Mail: jccbsjg@runestone.net
Owner: Cindy Gulbrandson Est: 1996

A friendly small town quilt shop specializing in custom machine quilting. We carry 100% cotton fabrics, notions, patterns, books, gifts, offer classes and are always willing to help with your project.

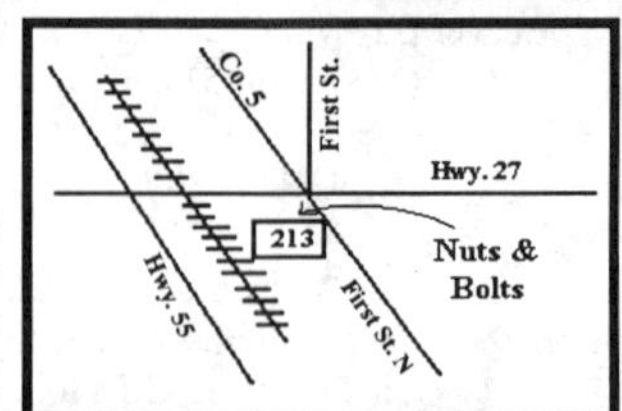

Staples, MN #11

Tues - Fri 10 - 5:30
Sat 10 - 3

216 2nd. Ave. 56479
(218) 894-1776

Owner: Linda Melby

Pfaff Sewing Machines. Custom Machine Quilting, Fabric, Quilting Supplies, Patterns, Classes.

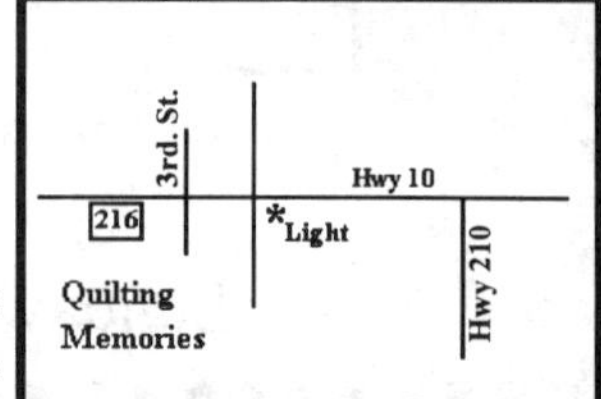

Princeton, MN #12

Mon - Fri 10 - 7
Sat 10 - 4

Country Treasures Quilt Shop

105 N. LaGrande 55371
(612) 389-0680 Fax: (612) 444-9530
E-Mail: d.lerew4308@aol.com
Est: 1992 2000 sq.ft. 2000 Bolts

We are in the lower level of Ossell's. We have over 200 Bolts of 1930's reproduction prints.

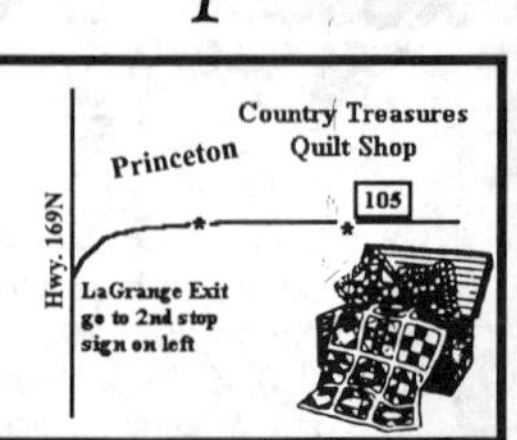

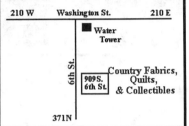

Brainerd, MN #13

909 S. 6th St. 56401 (218) 829-7273
Owner: Lou Rademacher Est: 1971

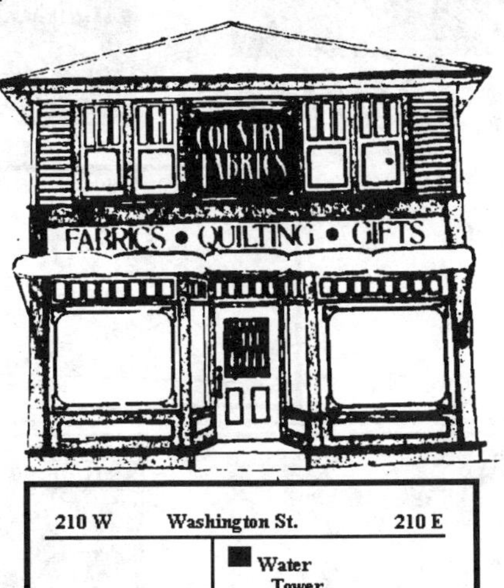

Country Fabrics, Quilts, & Collectibles

Show us this coupon and receive
10% off your purchase.
1 time only.

Mon - Fri
9:30 - 5:30
Sat 9:30 - 5

Our 1800 Mercantile is filled with over 2000 calicoes by the leading designers: Thimbleberries, Brannock & Patek, Hoffman, Horton, P & B and Marcus. We have a large selection of craft and wearable art patterns. We carry many colors of Polarfleece too. We are your authorized Viking, Elna & Brother dealer. If you are not into quilting, visit our 'quaint' 2nd floor gifts/antique shop.

P.S. Watch for our expansion—we will be doubling our space and everything else too.

Genola, MN #14

#1 Main Street 56364
(320) 468-6435
Est: 1934 8000 sq.ft.
Free Catalog
Owners: Sue Poser & Paul Gruber

Daily 7 am - 10 pm
7 Days a Week

The most unique Quilt Shop you'll ever enter.
8000 Bolts of Cotton. Home of the "Lap Hoop"
All the latest patterns & books—100's of Titles
A true General Store with German sausages, meats and more!

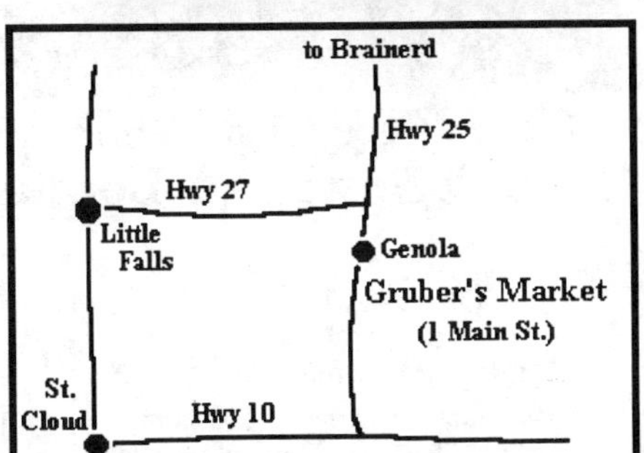

Elk River, MN #15

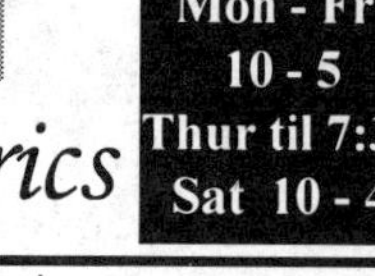

Mon - Fri 10 - 5
Thur til 7:30
Sat 10 - 4

Cottage Quilts & Fabrics

823 Main St. 55330
(612) 241-1490
Owner: Lorraine Thompson
Est: 1994 1000 Bolts

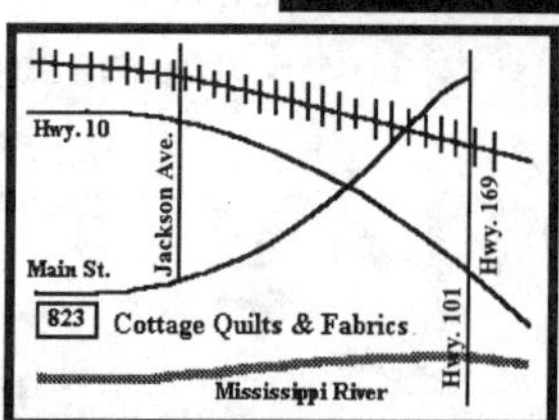

Large selection of 100% cottons, quilting supplies, notions, patterns, books and classes.
"Come Quilt With Us!"

Willmar, MN #16

Mon - Fri 9:30 - 5
Sat 10 - 2

Darlin Quilts

6691 Hwy. 71 NE 56201
(320) 235-7576
Owner: Lin Grinde

Machine Quilting, Fabrics, Patterns & Classes.
5 miles North of Willmar on Hwy. 71

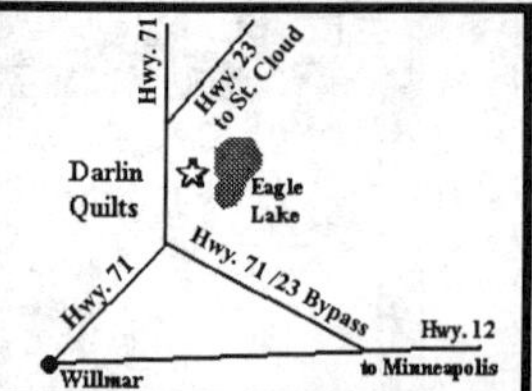

Avon, MN #17

Aunt Annie's Quilts & Silks

Visit our newly expanded shop.
Over 2400 sq.ft. of well lit shopping & classroom area.
2500+ bolts of fabrics including Liberty of London, Bali, Japanese, Australian, Hoffman, Kaufman, RJR, Moda, Kona Bay, Momen House, Monarch, Alexander Henry, Nancy Crow, hand-dyed & painted and many others.
Fine woolens, silks, rayons & flannels.
Inspiring samples & displays.
Local & international books and magazines.

Known for color assistance, enticing & unique fabrics, knowledgeable & helpful staff.
Fabrics chosen by working artists for creative quilters and sewers.

Tour groups welcome.

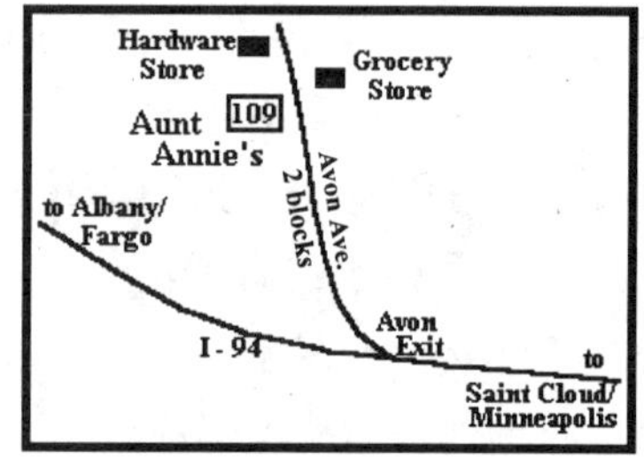

109 Avon Ave. S, P.O. Box 359 56310
(320) 356-1061
Owners: Lucy Senstad & Helen Frie

Marshall, MN #18

Mon - Fri 9:30 - 6
Thur til 9
Sat 9:30 - 5

Fabrics Plus

237 W. Main 56258
(507) 537-0835 Fax: (507) 537-1320
Owner: M. Elaine Nyquist
Est: 1985 2500 sq.ft.

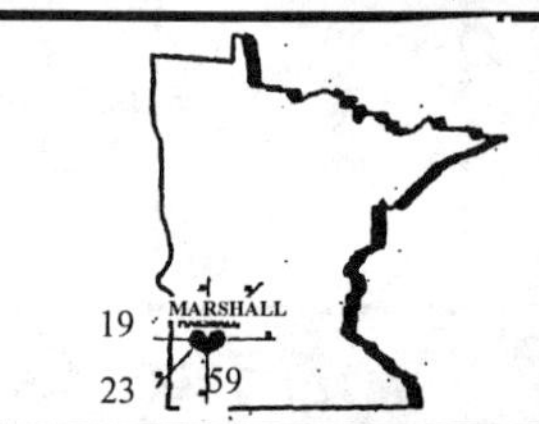

Southwest Minnesota's finest fabric selection. Over 3500 bolts of cottons for quilting plus fashion, home decor. Sewing Machines Also.

Windom, MN #19

Mon 9 - 6:30
Tues - Fri 9 - 5
Sat 9 - 3

Prairie Quilting

1293 Hale Place 56101
(507) 831-2740
Owner: Kay Peterson

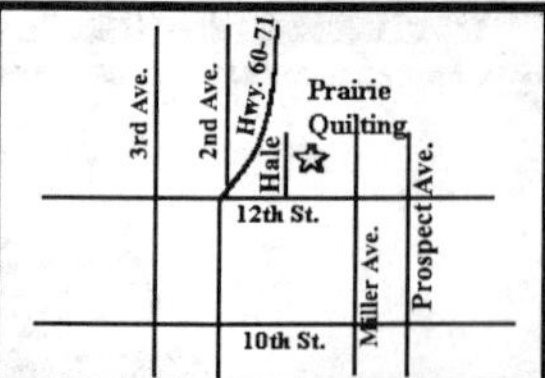

Unique Quilt Shop location next to feed store. Great selection of 100% cotton fabrics, books, patterns, and notions. Quilts for sale.

Luverne, MN #20

Mon - Sat 9 - 5
Thur til 9

The Sewing Basket

204 E. Main 56156
(507) 283-9769
Est: 1979 1200 sq.ft.

Main Street Luverne, Minnesota just north off Interstate 90

A nice selection of better quilting fabrics. Also books, patterns & supplies. Lots of samples on display.

Worthington, MN #21

Mon - Thur 9 - 5:30
Fri 9 - 9
Sat 9 - 4

CRAFTY CORNER Quilt & Sewing Shoppe

1820 Oxford St. 56187
(507) 372-2707
Owner: Zuby Jansen
Est. 1982 2600 sq.ft.

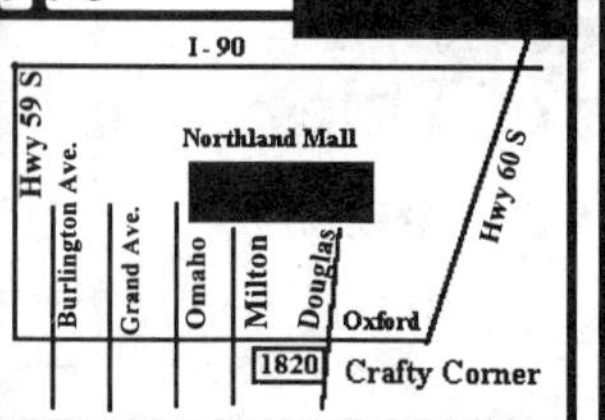

We sell 100% cotton fabrics. 1500 bolts in stock. Many Patterns Bernina Sewing Machine sales & Service. Quilting Supplies!

Blue Earth, MN #22

Mon - Sat 9 - 5
Thur til 8

Quilt Company

120 S. Main 56013
(507) 526-2647
Est: 1988 1300 sq.ft.
Owners: Lola Hendrickson, Jolyn Olson, & Tracy Peterson

Complete line of Quilting Needs.
Fabric, Patterns, Notions, Classes, Service.
Also Custom Quilting.

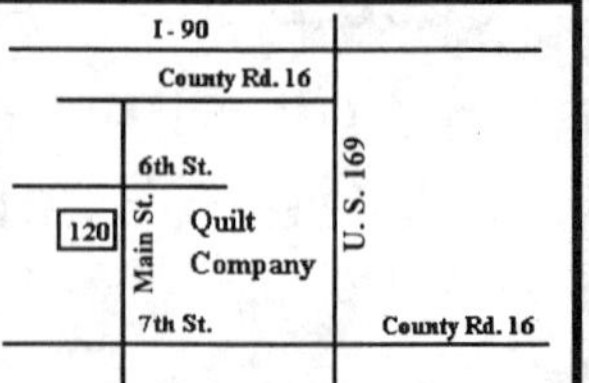

MAIN STREET COTTON SHOP

141 E. 2nd Street ~ Redwood Falls, MN 56283 #23

and

7 North Main ~ Hutchinson, MN 55350 #24

FREE FULL COLOR CATALOG • MAIL ORDER AVAILABLE 24 HRS. A DAY

1-800-624-4001 *or* 507-637-5221

Selected by...
American Patchwork and Quilting Sampler Magazine 1995
as one of the 10 top shops in North America!

Visit both stores on your next trip to Minnesota. The Redwood Falls store is a charming quilt shop located in the heart of the Minnesota River Valley, two hours west of Minneapolis. Our Hutchinson store is located one hour west of Minneapolis in a wonderful old building with tin ceilings and hardwood floors. The building is shared with Thimbleberries™, Inc. and offers an ever changing quilt display of Thimbleberries™ quilts. In addition, both shops have a large selection of unique gifts with a primitive, antique and folk art flavor that add to the charm of the Main Street Cotton Shop.

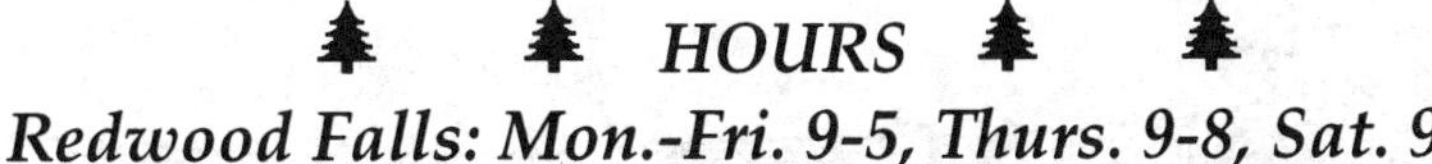

HOURS

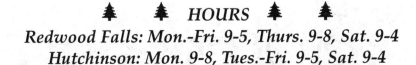

Redwood Falls: Mon.-Fri. 9-5, Thurs. 9-8, Sat. 9-4
Hutchinson: Mon. 9-8, Tues.-Fri. 9-5, Sat. 9-4

504 1st. Ave. S 56081

St. James, MN #26

(507) 375-7501
Fax: (507) 375-5522
Est: 1996 4800 sq.ft.
1600 Bolts 1500 Patterns

Grandma's Quilt Emporium

Quilting Fabrics, notions, patterns, books and many samples.
Frequent Buyers Club, Bernina Dealer, Kits and mail order available.
Large Gift Shop with Tea Room— wonderful for lunch.

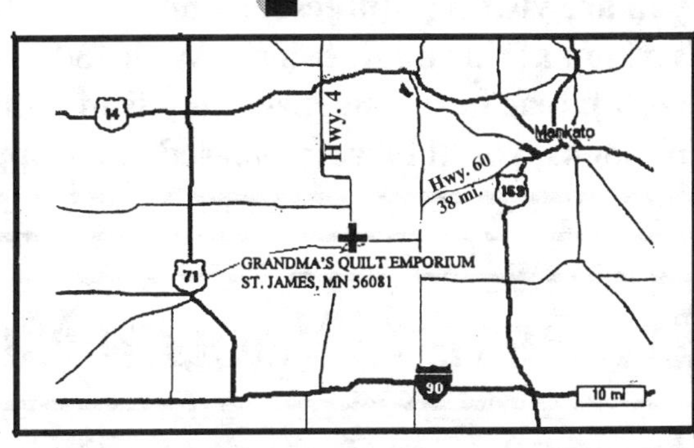

Mon - Sat 9 - 5:30 Thur til 7 Sat 9 - 5

Create a treasured heirloom for someone you love or for your own home.

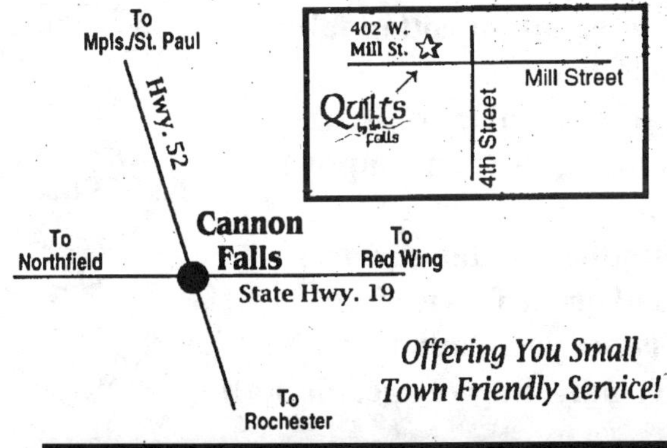

Cannon Falls, MN #27

402 W. Mill St. 55009
(507) 263-2528 or (888) 899-2528
Owners:
Marilou & Larry Welt
3000 sq.ft.

Offering You Small Town Friendly Service!

Mon - Sat 9 - 5 Thur 9 - 8

We have everything you need to create a Beautiful Handmade Quilt. 100% quality Cotton Quilting Fabrics & Homespuns.
Finished Quilts & Wall Hangings
Beautiful Gifts, Needlework Supplies
Unique Gift Bags & Cards, Classes
Quilting Samples on Display, Stencils
Free Inspiration & Advice Always Available.

St. Cloud, MN #28

Gruber's Quilt Shop

708 St. Germain
(320) 259-4360
Owner: Sue Poser

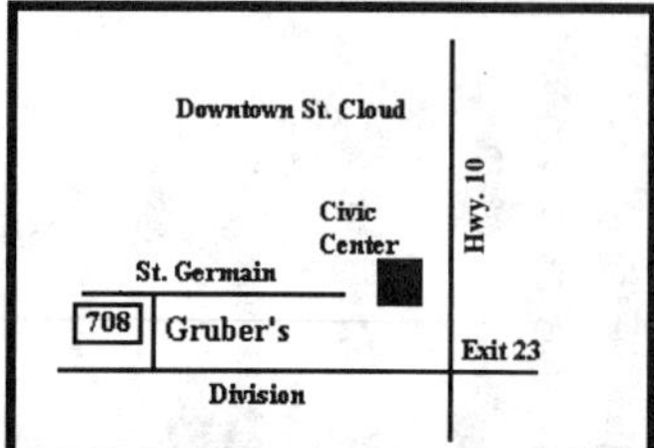

Mon, Wed, Fri 9 - 7
Tues & Thur 9 - 5:30
Sun 12 - 4

If you are visiting Minnesota's heartland, don't miss a stop at this quaint shop. With 1500+ of the newest fabric in the market and lots of patterns and books, you'll be very pleased you stopped.

St. Peter Woolen Mill

Mary Lue's Knitting World

101 W. Broadway 56082
(507) 931-3734
Fax: (507) 931-9040
E-Mail: spwoolen@prairie.lakes.com
Web Site: www.woolenmill.com
Est: 1867 6400 sq.ft.
1000 Bolts Free Catalog

Mon - Fri 9 - 5:30
Thur til 8 Sat 9 - 5 Sun 12 - 4

Large selection of fabrics, yarns, gifts, knitting & sewing machines, and quilting supplies.

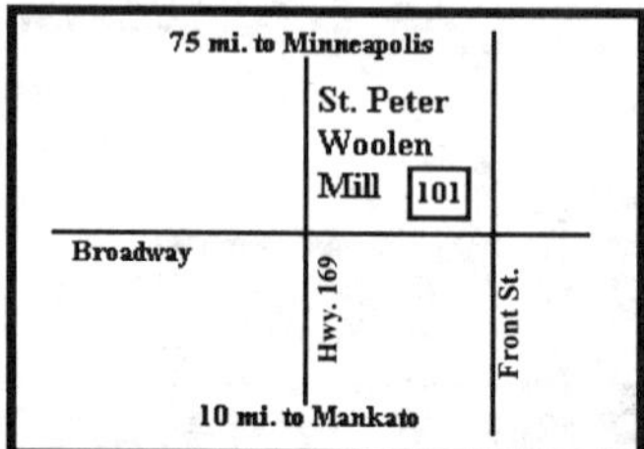

Located 1 block east of hwy. 169 at the corner of W. Broadway and Front St. in downtown St. Peter, MN

Custom wool carding since 1867. Manufacturers of NATURE'S COMFORT wool batting.

"LIKE QUILTING THROUGH AIR"

St. Peter, MN #30

WAYZATA Quilting Emporium

BF Incorporated

Wayzata, MN #29

Mon - Sat 9 - 5
Thurs til 8:30
(Sept thru April
Mon til 8:30 and
Sun 1 - 4 also)

927 East Lake Street
55391
(612) 475-2138
Owners: Deb Buchholz & Wendy Fedie
Est: 1980 1650 sq.ft.

... Eclectic Collection of fabrics — from traditional to contemporary, homespun to hand-dyed
... 2000+ bolts of cotton fabric
... 300+ book titles
... Large selection of patterns
... Quilting tools and supplies
... Kits
... Bundles and fat quarters
... Mail order fabric club
... Classes year round
... Friendly, knowledgeable staff

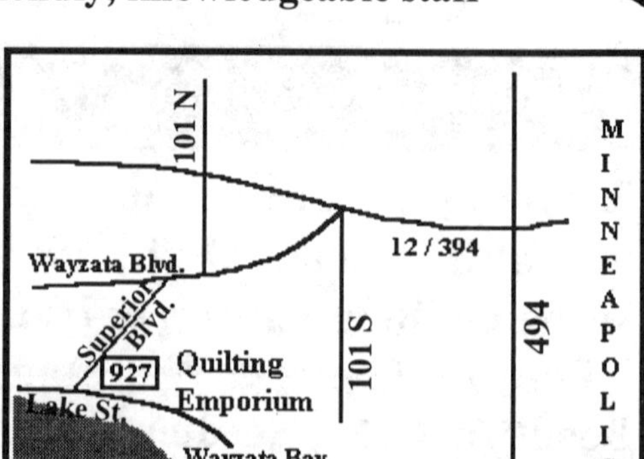

Twenty minutes west of Minneapolis — over 2000 bolts of cotton —

A complete quilt shop !

Bear Patch Quilting Co.

A Quilter's Heaven filled with 100% cotton fabrics, patterns, books, notions, and samples to inspire your creativity. Bear Patch also offers a large selection of wool and rug hooking supplies. Year round classes. Machine quilting services available. Lots of samples and great ideas!

Featuring:
Kris Lange Designs paper foundation pieced patterns
Hand dyed wools by Faye Schilling
Hand dyed cottons by Primrose Gradations.

Join us for:
Block of the Month,
Patchwork Thursdays,
and Bear Rug
Hooking Club

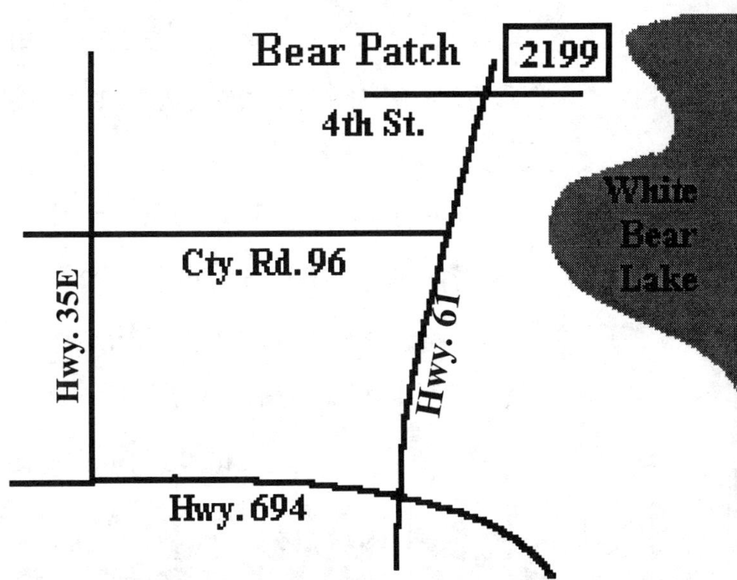

612-429-1039
2199 Fourth St. 55110
Est: May 1997
4600 sq.ft. 1500+ Bolts

Mon - Fri
9 - 9
Sat 9 - 5
Sun 12 - 4

White Bear Lake, MN #31

St. Paul, MN #32

THE COUNTRY PEDDLER QUILT SHOP

2230 CARTER AVENUE 55108
(612) 646-1756 Fax: (612) 645-6899
E-Mail: quilts@countrypeddler.com
Web Site: www.countrypeddler.com
Est: 1973 Owner: Jean Humenansky

Mon & Thur 9:30 - 9
Tues, Wed, Fri, & Sat 9:30 - 5:00
Sun 12 - 5:00

Located in historic St. Anthony Park of the Twin Cities, the shop is two stories of the latest in quilting notions, fabrics, books, classes and patterns.
With inspiration everywhere, you can choose from 5000 bolts of 100% cotton fabrics, quarterly newsletter, Peddler's Pieces monthly fabric club, 250 Club for frequent buyers, Mystery in the Mail Kits, Birthday Club, Machine Quilting Service and large selection of Block of the Month projects.
We will gladly mail order any of your quilting needs directly to your door.

Selected by American Patchwork & Quilting Magazine as one of North America's 10 Top Quilt Shops in the July 1997 issue of Quilt Sampler.

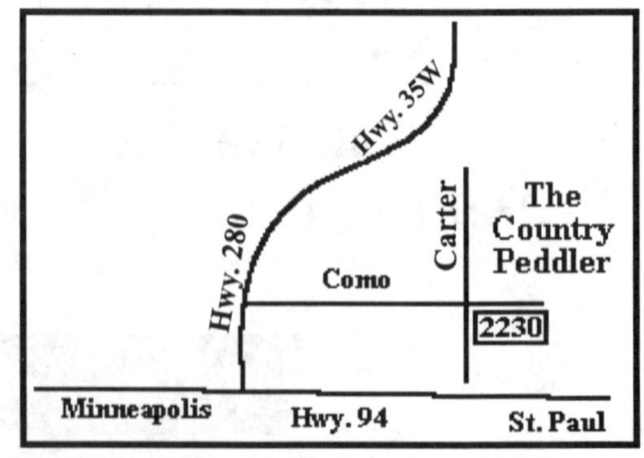

1692 Grand Ave. 55105 (612) 698-3233
E-Mail: dsloom@aol.com
Owner: Sue Loomer

St. Paul, MN #33

Quilts, Tops, Blocks

Authentic Vintage Fabric, 1930's cottons, Barkcloth, Rayon, Upholstery, Chenille. Huge selection of buttons, lace, trims. Vintage clothes & accessories, tablecloths, Fancy Linens, Antiques & more.

Mon, Tues, Wed 10 - 6
Thur 11 - 8
Fri & Sat 11 - 6
Sun 12 - 5

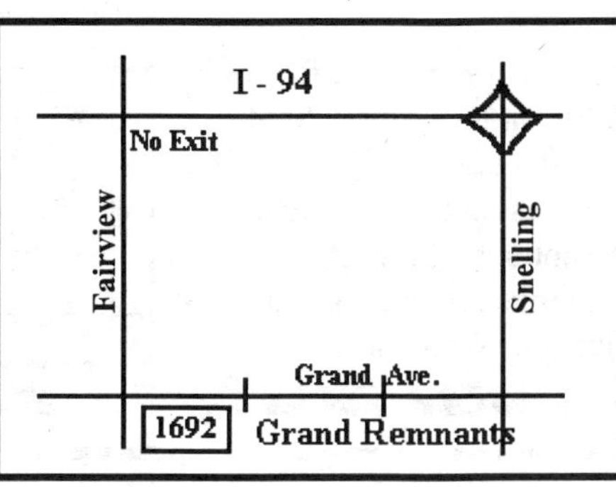

exit I - 94 at Snelling
South on Snelling to Grand Ave.
West on Grand 2 1/2 blocks

Apple Valley, MN #34

Mon. - Fri. 10 - 8:30
Sat. 10 - 5 Sun. 12 - 5

7655 W. 148th St., Apple Valley, MN 55124
Phone: 612 / 432-1827 • 1-800-475-2137
E-Mail: fabrictown@aol.com
Web Site: www.fabrictown.com
Owner: Barbara Sherman — Est. 1981

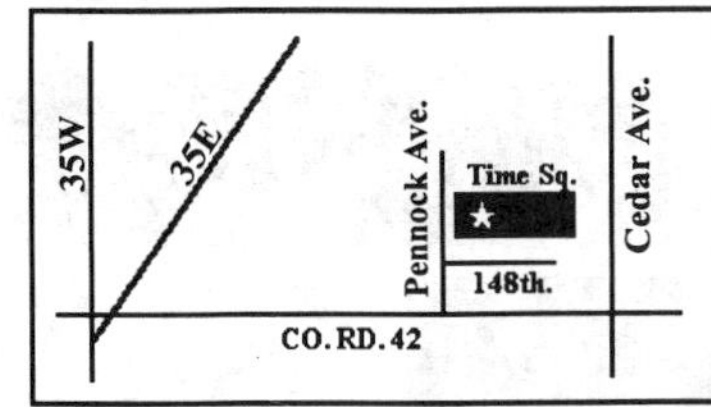

• Our 3,000 sq.ft. store features: 3,000 BOLTS OF 100% COTTON, BOOKS, PATTERNS, KITS, HUNDREDS OF SAMPLES

LOOKING FOR SOMETHING? WE SHIP!

Our friendly, knowledgeable staff is looking forward to meeting you!

Stillwater, MN #35

AND SEW ON

1672 S. Greeley St. 55082
(612) 430-9441 or (888) 641-5408
Established 1990 2000 sq.ft.
Owners: Deborah Gangnon
www.husqvarnaviking.com/and-sew-on
aso@woldnet.att.net

Mon & Wed 9:30 - 6:00
Tue & Thur 9:30 - 8:00
Fri 9:30 - 5:00
Sat 9:30 - 4:00

Located in historic Stillwater

100% cotton quilting fabrics by Hoffman, RJR, R&B, South Seas and more...
The latest in books, patterns and notions. Classes.
Authorized premier Husqvarna Viking & White dealer.

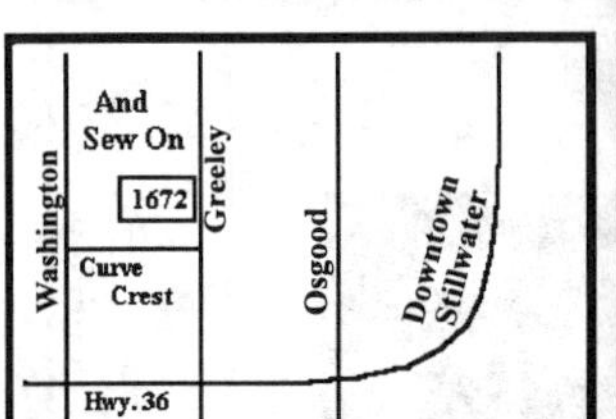

Roseville, MN #36

Mon, Fri & Sat 10 - 5:30
Tues, Wed & Thur 12 - 9

Colorful Quilts & Textiles

"Located in the Hamline Shopping Center"
2817 N. Hamline Ave. 55113
(612) 628-9664

Unique quilts & wearables our speciality! Innovative fabrics, books, classes, dyes & fabric paints. City's largest selection of hand-dyed Fabrics. Personalized service & inspiration.

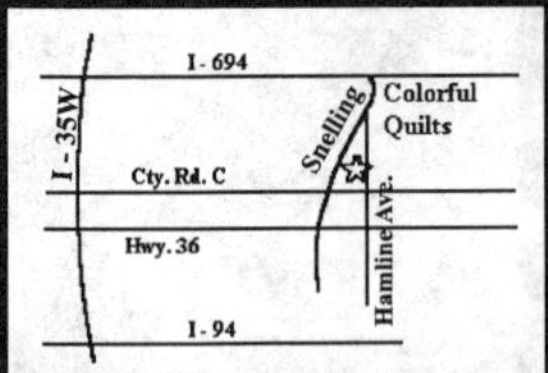

Eagan, MN #37

Mon - Thur 9:30 - 8
Fri & Sat 9:30 - 5

Country Needleworks

3924 Cedarvale Blvd. 55122
(612) 452-8891
Owner: Susan Herzberg
Est: 1989 1600 sq.ft. 1400 Bolts

A Country Shop offering the finest in cotton fabrics, books, patterns and quilting supplies. Classes & Gift Certificates Available.

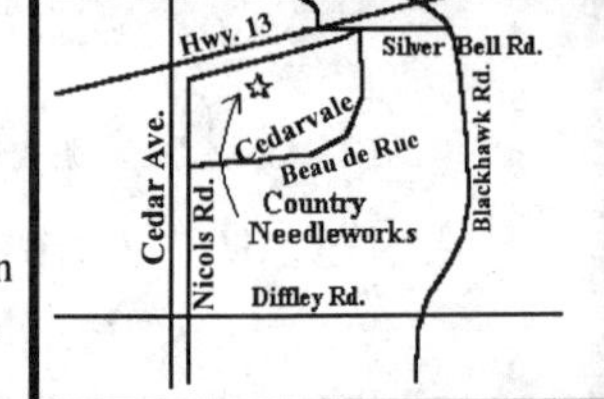

535 W. 78th St. 55317
(612) 934-5307
E-Mail: The Sampler@ pressenter.com
Owner: Karol Plocher
Est: 1977 2650 Sq.ft.

Warm, Inviting Quilt Shop. 2000 Bolts Cotton Fabrics Quilting & Wall Stencils, Rug Hooking. Lots of Patterns & Gifts. Mail Order Fabric Club, Classes

Chanhassen, MN #38

Mon, Wed, Fri 9:30 - 6:30
Tues & Thur 9:30 - 8:30
Sat 9:30 - 5:30
Sun 12 - 4:30

Directions:

Take Highway 494 to Highway 5 West - go to Great Plains Blvd (Chanhassen exit) — turn Rt. — Follow street around Chanhassen Dinner Theater to first left.

Rogers, MN #39

Mon - Thur 10 - 5
Fri 10 - 9
Sat 10 - 4

Quilted Treasures OF ROGERS

Rogers Plaza - 21317 John Milless Dr. 55374
Intersection of Cty 81 & Hwy. 101
(612) 428-1952 Owner: Rita Kroening
100% Cotton Quilting Fabrics, Notions, Books, Patterns & Kits. We offer an assortment of Quilting & Applique classes & seasonal retreats.

Waseca, MN #40

M, Th 10 - 6
T, W, F 10 - 5
Sat 10 - 4

The Happy Hands Shoppe

107 2nd St. NW
56093
(507) 835-5081
Est: 1983
Owners: Darcy Barnes & Martha Waddell

Supplies for:
Quilting, Hardanger, Stenciling, Counted Cross-stitch, Painting, Crafts. Lots of Patterns, Books, Classes.
Consignment Gifts.

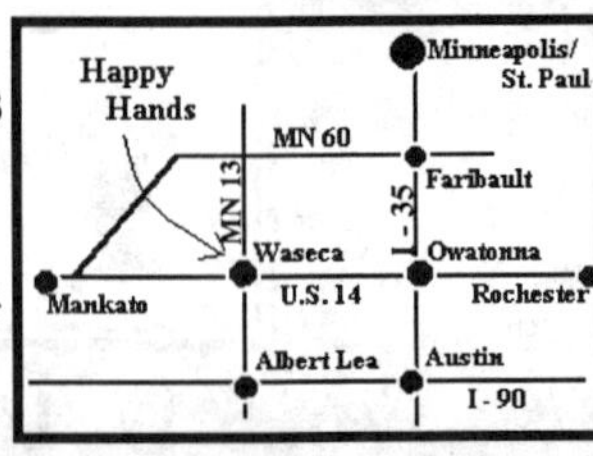

Mankato, MN #41

Mon - Sat 10 - 5
Sun 12 - 3
Winter:
Mon - Fri 10 - 6
Sat 10-5 Sun 12-4

Harts of Country

110 E. Elm 56001
(507) 345-7242
E-Mail: harts110@ic.mankato.mn.us
Owner: Jan Johnson

Mankato's only Quilt Shop. All fabrics are top quality 100% cotton. Notions, books, patterns, classes and so much more. Wire, tappers, quilt magazines and many quilted pieces on display.

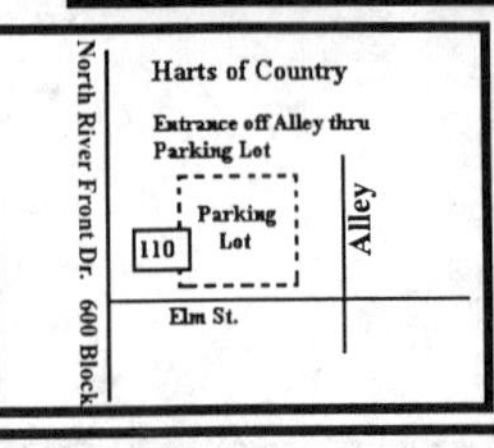

New Ulm, MN #42

Mon - Fri 9:30 - 9
Sat 9:30 - 5:30
Sun 12 - 5

Muggs Fabric & Bridal

101 N. German Marktplatz Mall
(507) 359-1515 56073
Owner: Margaret Meyer
3000 sq.ft.

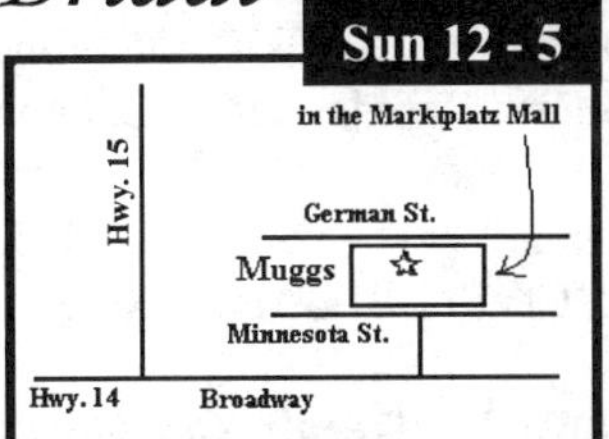

Friendly quilt shop with over 2000 bolts of quality 100% cottons including Hoffman, RJR, Debbie Mumm.

New Ulm, MN #43

Mon 10 - 8
Tues - Fri 10 - 5
Sat 10 - 4

The Thimble Box

526 S. Minnesota 56073
(507) 354-6721
E-Mail:
Thmbx@newulmtel.net

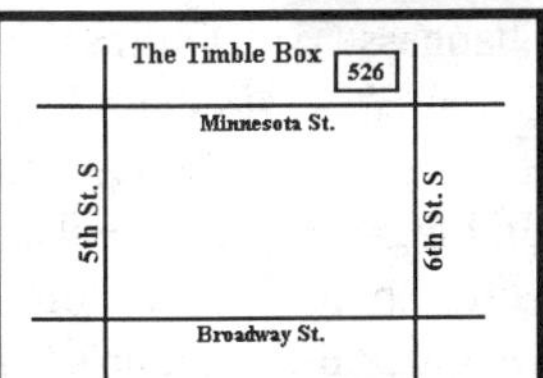

Enter the nostalgic atmosphere of a turn-of-the-century grocery store. An inviting, warm shop that combines the joy of quilting and an intriguing array of time-gone-by gifts.

Owatonna, MN #44

Mon - Fri 9 - 6
Sat 9 - 4:30

The Cotton Patch

110 W. Broadway 55060
(507) 451-5979
Est: 1993 1800 sq.ft. 1000+ Bolts
Owners: Cathy Torrey,
Jeralene Staska & Laura Wertwijn

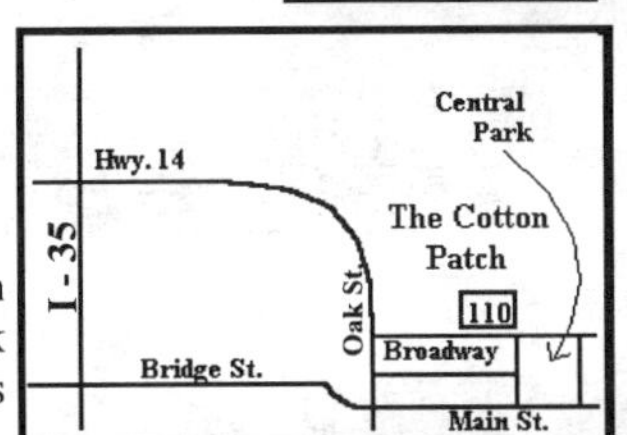

Quality 100% cotton fabrics; large selection of homespuns; patterns; books; notions; silk ribbon embroidery. Located on downtown's charming Central Park.

Rochester, MN #45

Mon - Fri 10 - 6
Sat 10 - 5

Just A Little Something

304 6th St. SW 55902
(507) 288-7172
E-Mail: jalsi@juno.com
Owner: Crystal D. Monson Est: 1996

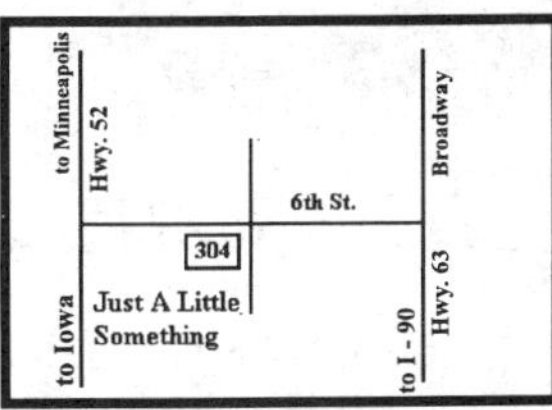

Great Selection of Quality Fabrics. Books, Patterns, Notions. Old Fashioned, Friendly Service. We will help you with your projects. Quilting Classes.

Rochester, MN #46

Mon - Thur 9 - 8
Fri 9 - 6
Sat 9 - 5

All in Stitches

1426 5th Place NW 55901
(507) 281-9872
Owner: Sandy Evans
Est: 1995 2500 sq.ft. 2000 Bolts

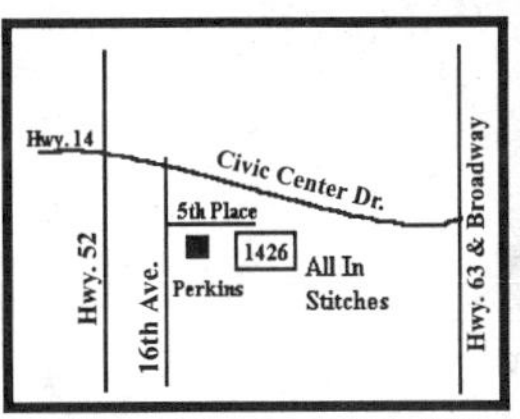

Wonderful selection of 100% cottons, books, patterns and classes. Warm, friendly service. Located next to Perkins No.

St. Charles, MN #47

Mon - Sat 8 - 6

Yoder's Quilts & Crafts

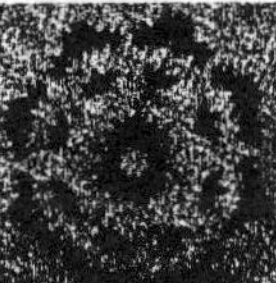

Rt. 1, Box 75 55972
Owners:
Amos & Lydia Yoder

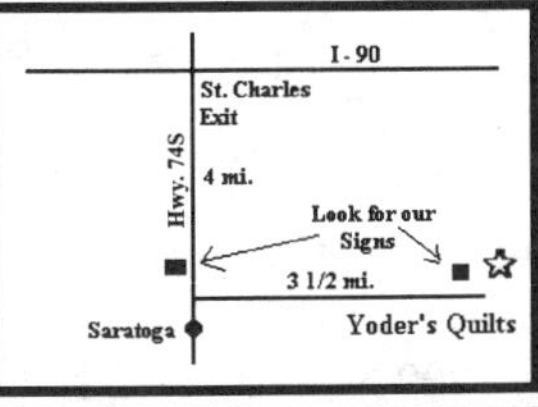

Large selection of Quilts. Hand quilted by Amish. Wallhangings, Centerpiece Runners, Placemats, Some Crafts Etc.

Minnesota Guilds:

Lakes Area Quilting Guild, 1219 S. Nokomis, Alexandria, 56308
Meets: 3rd Monday (Sept - Nov & Jan - May) 7:30 p.m. at County Historical Society

Hands all around Quilters, P.O. Box 329, Braham, 55006

Pine Tree Patchworkers, P.O. Box 935, Brainerd, 56401

Quilters along the Yellowstone, P.O. Box 261, Buffalo Lake, 55314

Piece Makers Quilting Group, Cannon Falls
Meets: 2nd Tuesday and Thursday 9:30, also 2nd Thursday 1:30 and 7 p.m. at Quilts by the Falls

Common Threads, 500 E. Minnesota St., Cannon Falls, 55009

Chaska Area Quilt Guild, P.O. Box 44, Chaska, 55318

Minnesota Quilter Inc., 8616 Darnel Rd., Eden Prairie, 55344

Country Quilters, Fergus Falls
Meets: 3rd Tuesday 9 a.m. at First Baptist Church, 629 Channing Ave. E

Evening Guild, Fergus Falls
Meets: 1st Monday 7 p.m. at Pioneer Nursing Home Comm. Room, 1006 Sheridan Ave.

Piecemakers Quilt Guild, R.R. #1, Box 150, Gibbon

Loon Country Quilters, 4646 Hwy. 2 E., Grand Rapids, 55744

Blue Mound Quilters, Luverne, MN 56156
Meets: 1st Monday 7:30 p.m. in the Library basement

Heartland Quilters, Hackensack

Threadbenders, Marshall
Meets: 1st Monday

Prairie Piecemakers, 101 N. German, New Ulm, 56073

Thimbleberries Quilt Club, Perham
Meets: 3rd Wednesday 9:30 a.m., 1 p.m., and 6 p.m. at Bay Window Crafts

Rochester Quilters' Sew-Ciety, P.O. Box 6245, Rochester, 55903
Meets: 1st Monday 7 p.m. at Christ United Methodist Church, 400 5th Ave. SW

Piecemaker's Quilt Club, P.O. Box 26, Staples, 56479
Meets: 3rd Thursday at Quilting Memories, Holds a quilt show every other year (99 next)

Thief River Falls Q. G., P.O. Box 121, Thief River Falls, 56701
Meets: 4th Tuesday at Northland Community College

Stitchers In Time Quilt Club, 107 2nd St. NW, Waseca, 56093
Meets: 2nd Tuesday 10 a.m. at Happy Hands Shoppe

Country Quilters, Willmar, 56201
Meets: 2nd Tuesday at 7 p.m.

Other Shops in Minnesota:

Alexandria Mary Ellen Larson, 1903 Cty. Rd. 22 W 320-763-7177
Austin Creations From the Heart, 400 N. Main St. 507-433-5551
Chanhassen QuiltSMART, West 96th St. 612-445-5737
Felton Lori's Quilt Factory, R.R. #1 218-494-3911
Hayward Calico Hutch, P. O. Box 51 507-377-1163
Hibbing Pins N Needles, 314 E. Howard St. 218-262-5531
Minneapolis The Quilt Works, 1055 E. 79th 312-588-5345
Minneapolis Eydie's Country Quilting, 2822 W. 43rd St. 612-929-0645
Minneapolis Glad Creations Inc., 3400 Bloomington Ave. S. 612-724-1079
Mountain Lake Quilts, 1104 6th Ave. 507-427-2728
Northfield Jacobsen's, 419 Division St. 507-645-4672
Oklee Country Stitch 'N, 204 Main St. 218-796-5744
Oklee The Oklee Quilt Shop, 128 S. Main 218-796-5151
Pelican Rapids Calico Cupboard, 25 1st Ave. NW PO Box 336 218-863-4681
Randall Sew Casual, 525 Pacific Ave. 320-749-2326
St. Charles Amish Market Sq., I - 90 & Hwy 74 507-932-5907
St. Paul Treadle Yard Goods, 1338 Grand 612-698-9690
Walnut Grove Plum Creek Patchwork, Rt. 2, Box 95
Wells The Creative Needle, 135 S. Broadway 507-553-3195
White Bear Lake Reed's Fabrics, 4425 S. Lake Ave. 612-429-5347

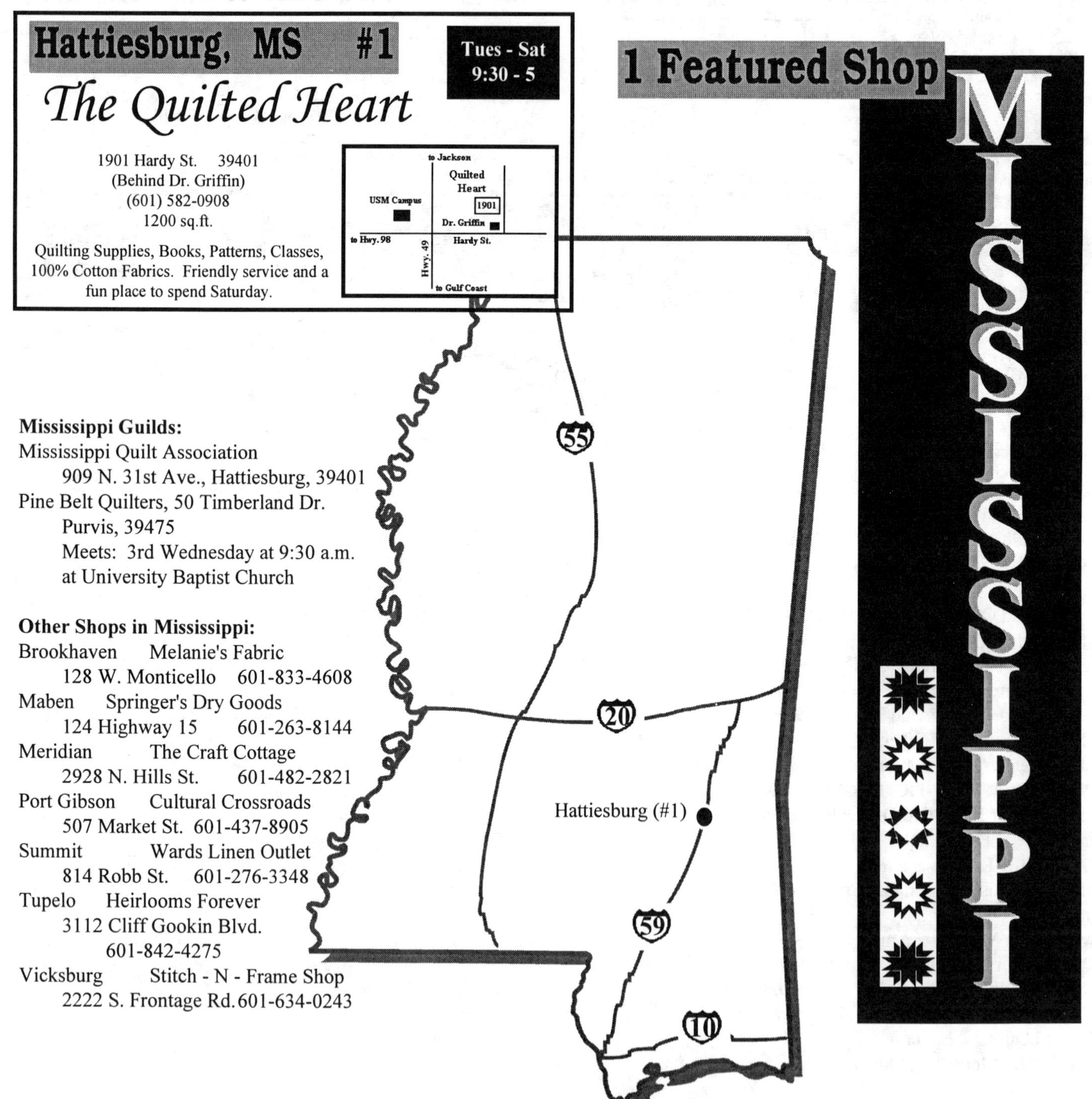

Hattiesburg, MS #1

Tues - Sat 9:30 - 5

The Quilted Heart

1901 Hardy St. 39401
(Behind Dr. Griffin)
(601) 582-0908
1200 sq.ft.

Quilting Supplies, Books, Patterns, Classes, 100% Cotton Fabrics. Friendly service and a fun place to spend Saturday.

Mississippi Guilds:

Mississippi Quilt Association
909 N. 31st Ave., Hattiesburg, 39401
Pine Belt Quilters, 50 Timberland Dr.
Purvis, 39475
Meets: 3rd Wednesday at 9:30 a.m.
at University Baptist Church

Other Shops in Mississippi:

Brookhaven Melanie's Fabric
128 W. Monticello 601-833-4608
Maben Springer's Dry Goods
124 Highway 15 601-263-8144
Meridian The Craft Cottage
2928 N. Hills St. 601-482-2821
Port Gibson Cultural Crossroads
507 Market St. 601-437-8905
Summit Wards Linen Outlet
814 Robb St. 601-276-3348
Tupelo Heirlooms Forever
3112 Cliff Gookin Blvd.
601-842-4275
Vicksburg Stitch - N - Frame Shop
2222 S. Frontage Rd. 601-634-0243

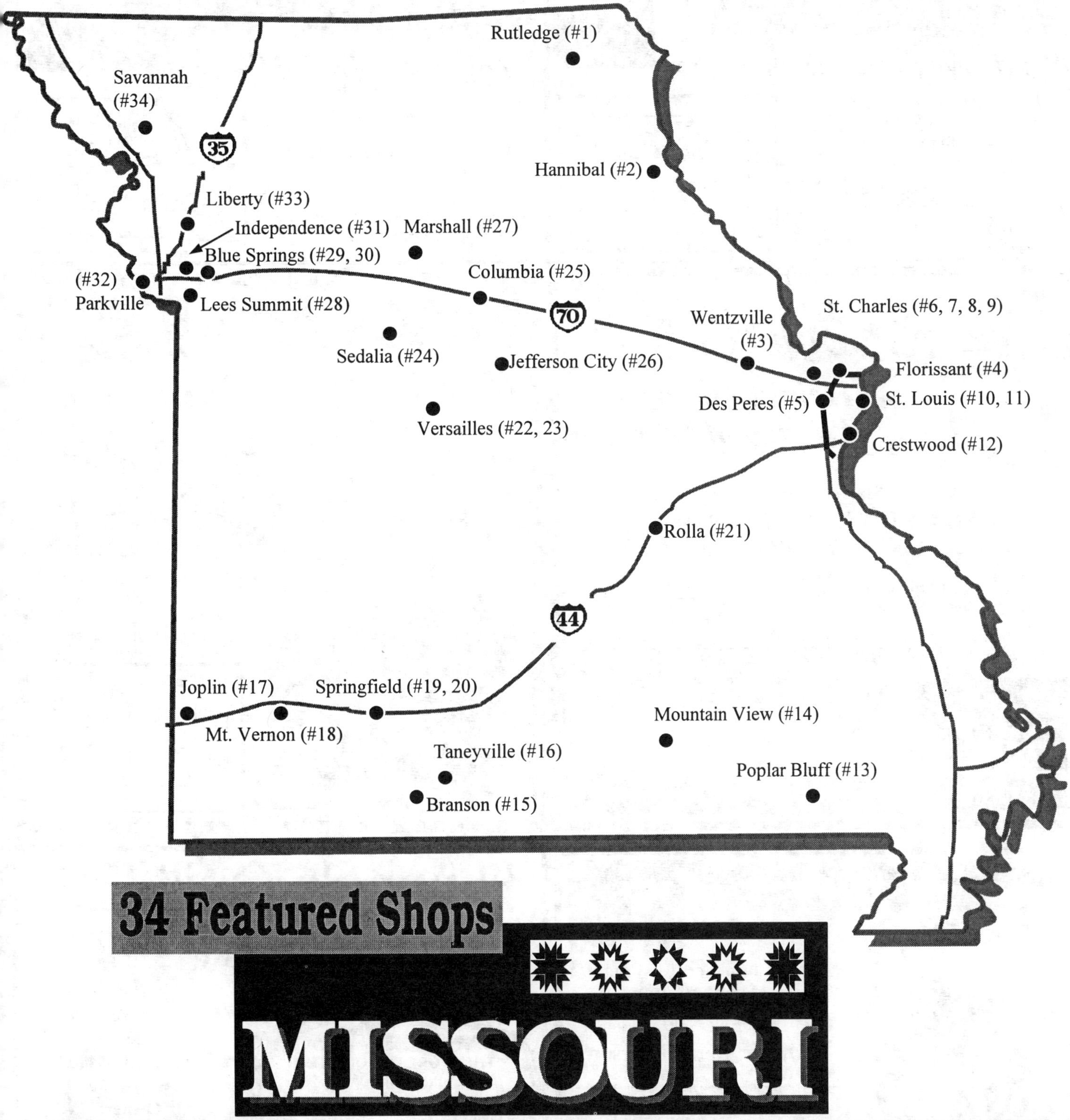

Rutledge (#1)
Savannah (#34)
35
Hannibal (#2)
Liberty (#33)
Independence (#31)
Marshall (#27)
Blue Springs (#29, 30)
(#32) Parkville
Lees Summit (#28)
Columbia (#25)
70
Wentzville (#3)
St. Charles (#6, 7, 8, 9)
Sedalia (#24)
Jefferson City (#26)
Florissant (#4)
Des Peres (#5)
St. Louis (#10, 11)
Versailles (#22, 23)
Crestwood (#12)
Rolla (#21)
44
Joplin (#17)
Springfield (#19, 20)
Mountain View (#14)
Mt. Vernon (#18)
Taneyville (#16)
Poplar Bluff (#13)
Branson (#15)

34 Featured Shops

MISSOURI

Rutledge, MO #1

Mon - Sat 8 - 5

Zimmerman's Store

Main St., Box 1 63563
(660) 883-5766 Est: 1974
Owners: Paul & Lydia Zimmerman
Mgr: Ellanor Zimmerman

1400 bolts of 100% cotton fabrics at reasonable prices. Batting, quilt patterns & books, sewing notions, hand quilted quilts, pillows, aprons etc.

136
15
Arbola
136
A
Memphis
M
M
Gorin
15
W
Rutledge
M
K
K
to Kirksville
Rt. 11
EE
15
to Edina

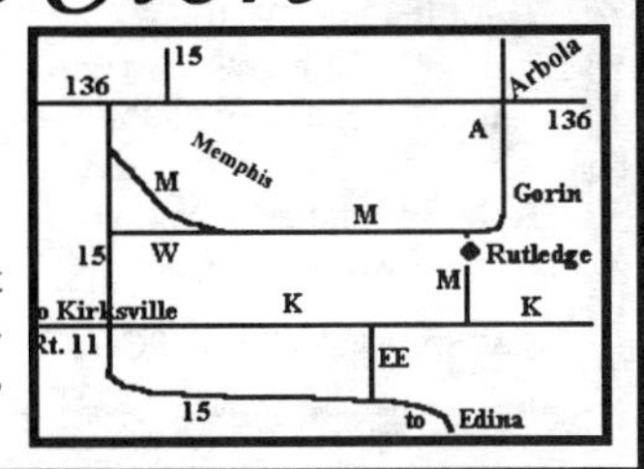

Hannibal, MO #2

Mon - Sat 9 - 5 Sun 12 - 5

Hickory Stick

326 N. Main 63401
(573) 221-4538
Owner: Patricia Waelder
Est: 1977 3000 sq.ft.
Across from Mark Twain's Home.
2000 Bolts- Calicos & Homespun. Fabrics, Cross- Stitch, Craft Patterns, Gifts.
Christmas. Open all year.

Hwy. 36 E
Bridge Over Mississippi
N. 3rd.
Hwy. 61
Hickory Stick
Located at the corner of Hill & N. Main
Mark Twain's Home
Hill St.
326
N. Main

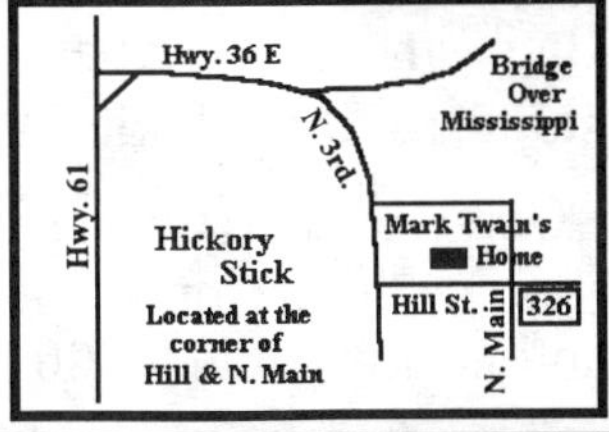

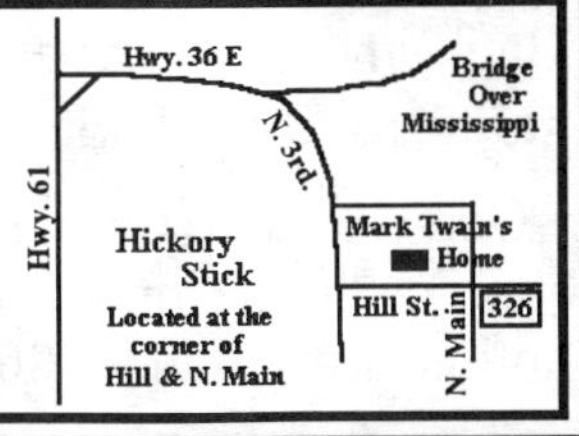

Wentzville, MO #3

Sun - Fri 9 - 3

Prairie Way Antique/Quilt Shop

110-B E. Pearce 63385
(314) 327-5609
Owners: Tom & Judy Love
Est: 1984 4000 sq.ft.

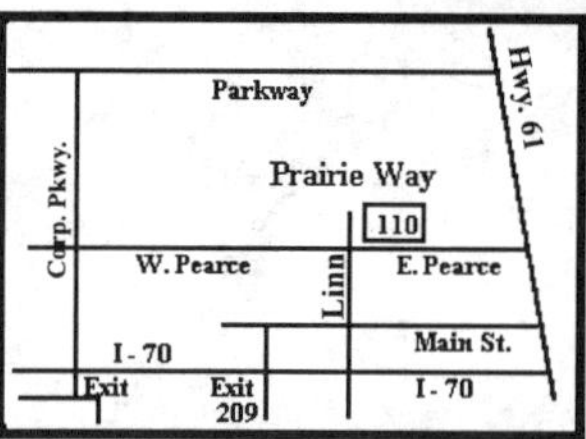

Large Selection of Antique Quilts & Tops, Quilting Templates, Cotton Feed Sacks, Kansas City Star Quilt Patterns, Hand Quilting Done.

Florissant, MO #4

Mon - Sat 10 - 4 Tues & Wed til 8

Helen's Hen House

180 Dunn Rd. 63031
(314) 837-7661
Owners: Helen Argent & Joan Nicolay
Est: 1978 1350 sq.ft.

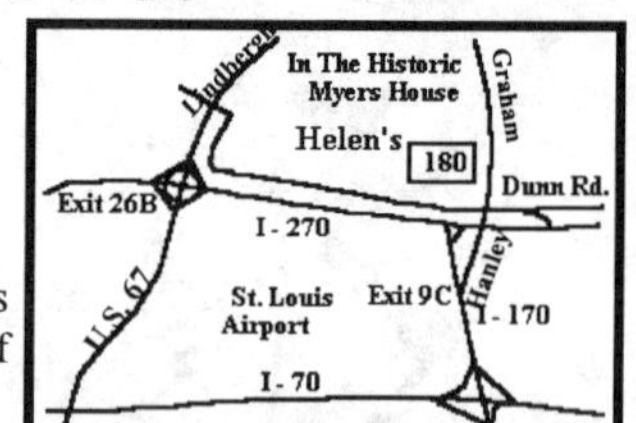

Over 2000 Bolts. Specializing in homespuns & reproduction fabrics. Complete line of quilting supplies, patterns & Books.

The Kotton Patch

Helping to create a Legacy of Warmth.

12772 Manchester 63131
(314) 965-KOTN (5686) 1800 sq.ft.
Owner: Marylu Amantea 3000 Bolts

100% Cotton Fabrics,
Quilt Books
Notions
Patterns

Complete Quilt Shop

Mon - Fri 9:30 - 5
Mon & Wed til 8
Sat 10 - 4:30
Sun 1 - 4

Des Peres, MO #5

St. Charles, MO #6

Mon - Sat 9:30 - 5 Sun 11 - 5

Patches Etc. Quilt Shop

337 South Main 63301
(314) 946-6004
Owner: Ann Watkins
Est: 1979 850 Sq.ft.
1000 Bolts Catalog $1
E-Mail:
3Patches@prodigy.net

Historic Saint Charles

Quilts, Fabric and Patterns - - Certified appraisals by Ann Watkins. Also visit our Craft Center and Button Shoppe

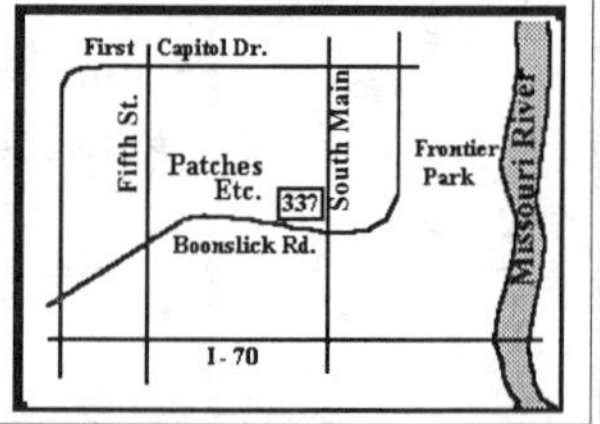

St. Charles, MO #7

Mon - Fri 10 - 7 Sat 10 - 2

1522 Caulks Hill Rd. 63303
(314) 939-0000
Est: 1995
Owner: Doris Jinkerson

I - 70
Mercantile Bank
Harvester Rd.
1522
I - 270
Hwy. 94
Caulks Hill
Quilt 'n Craft Corner
I - 40

4 ½ miles from I - 70
6½ miles from I - 40
turn on Harvester Rd. (look for the Mercantile Bank) then turn left at first stop light into parking lot.

Come browse through my 'garden' of 100% cotton fabrics, homespuns, and flannels. Books, patterns & notions available. 4000 Bolts & growing. Smiles Free!

Huning's Quilt Fair

St. Charles, MO #8

huning's quilt fair

"THE STORE FOR QUILTERS"
Hand Quilted Quilts
Stamped Embroidery Goods
Pillow Cases
Pillow Case Doll Kits
Quilt Tops (Bucilla & Tobin)
Quilt Blocks
Flosses (DMC & J & P Coats)
Quilting Stencils & Frames
Quilt Backing, Batting, Books & Patterns
Calicos & Solids of 100% Cotton & blends.
Rotary Supplies & Notions
Nursing Home Gowns

VISA MASTER DISCOVER

334 North Main Street
63301
(314) 946-5480
Est: 1860
Owner:
Monica Vandeven
2700 sq.ft.

Mon - Sat 9 - 5

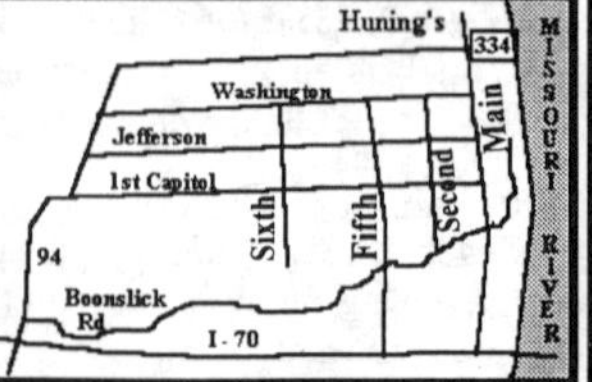

St. Charles, MO #9

"Out of the scraps of my life God has made a beautiful quilt."

330 S. Main St. 63301
(314) 946-9520
Web Site: Coming Soon
Owner: Karel Owens
Est: 1976 1000 sq.ft.

Fabric — 3000 bolts and more arriving weekly. Classes, Bears and Quilt Racks. Custom orders welcomed. Machine Quilting Available.

Karel Owens in our Aunt Gracies Corner. The Largest Selection in the Midwest. Also Moda, Homespun, VIP, Plantation, Hoffman and Cheater Cloth.

Kalico Patch

Kali, our mascot, sharing a quilt with one of our handmade bears.

We are a convenient stop for traveling quilters. Our shop is just off I - 70. To accommodate our travelers we offer half day quilting classes. If you would like a schedule of our classes, please send a SASE. If you are planning a bus tour to the St. Charles area we will schedule special classes for your quilt group. On your first visit to our store, bring this ad and you will receive a 15% discount on fabric and books. If it happens to be your birthday you will receive a 20% discount. To receive the discount bring this ad and proof of birthday (month and day only).

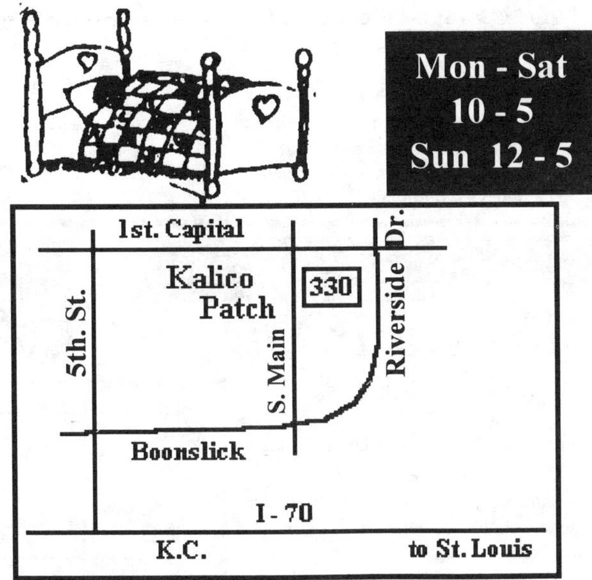

Mon - Sat
10 - 5
Sun 12 - 5

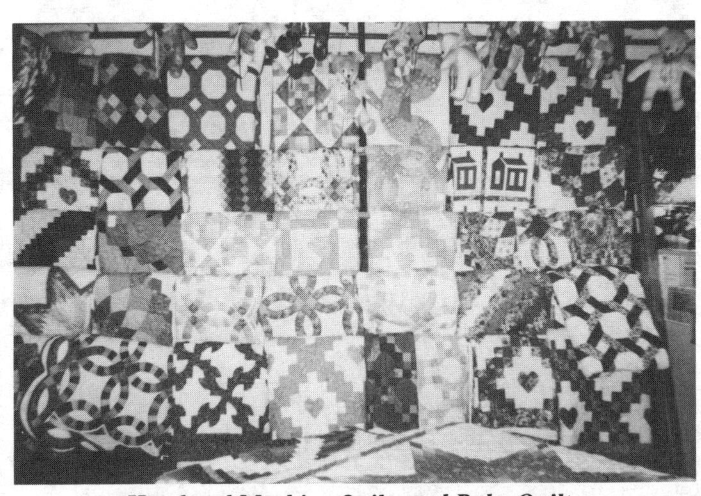

Hand and Machine Quilts and Baby Quilts. Over 200 in stock - Custom Work Available.

St. Louis, MO #10

Mon - Thur 10 - 9
Fri & Sat 10 - 5
Sun: By Appt

The Sign of the Turtle

5223 Gravois 63116
(314) 351-5550 Est: 1975
Owners: Ann & Bill Hofmann
1600 sq.ft. 300 Bolts 50 Solids

St. Louis Area's Quilting Headquarters!
By the Bevo

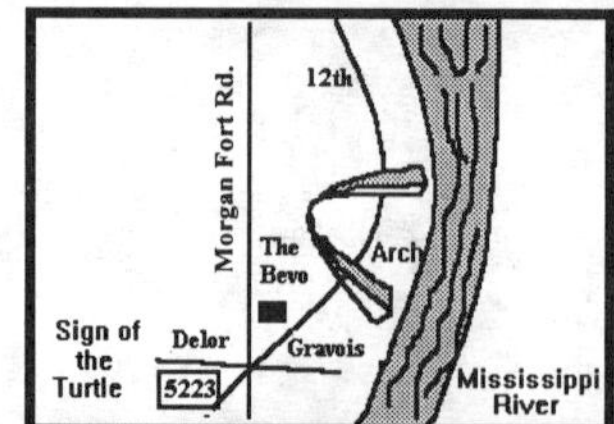

St. Louis, MO #11

M, W 9:30 - 5
T, Th 9:30 - 8
Fri & Sat
9:30 - 4:30

THE QUILTED FOX

10403 Clayton Rd. 63131
(314) 993-1181
Owner: Louise L. Georgia
Est: 1994 2500 sq.ft. 4000 Bolts

Unique Cotton fabrics found around the world for the quilter. Helpful staff, Fox Fabric Club for the out-of-town.

Crestwood, MO #12

Mon - Fri
9:30 - 5:30
Sat 9:30 - 4:30
Class Eves.

Quilt 'N' Stitch

9109 Watson Rd. 63126
(314) 961-0909 Owner: Connie Ewbank
Est: 1992 2400 sq.ft. 1500 Bolts
e-mail: STLCONSTHR@AOL.COM

Large selection of fabrics - Christmas, homespuns, contemporary. Books, patterns, notions, classes. Also counted cross stitch and silk ribbon embroidery.

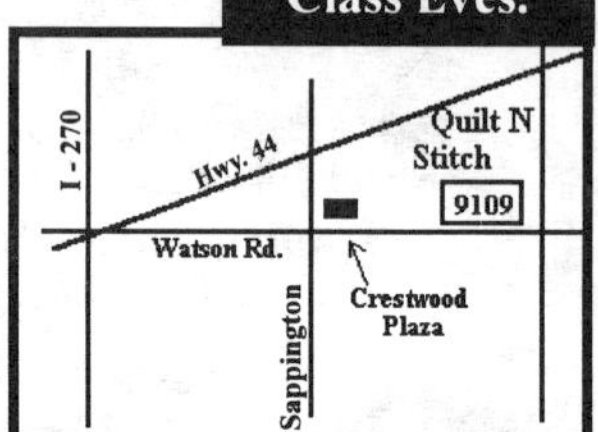

Poplar Bluff, MO #13

8:30 - 5:30
Except Fri.
close @ 5

Quilters Craft Shop

1302 South 11th 63901
(573) 785-6514
Owner: Mary L. Hoeinghaus
Est: 1984 800 sq.ft. 500 Bolts

100% cottons, books & Patterns specialize in Quilts, quilt racks and many other crafts. Machine Quilting.

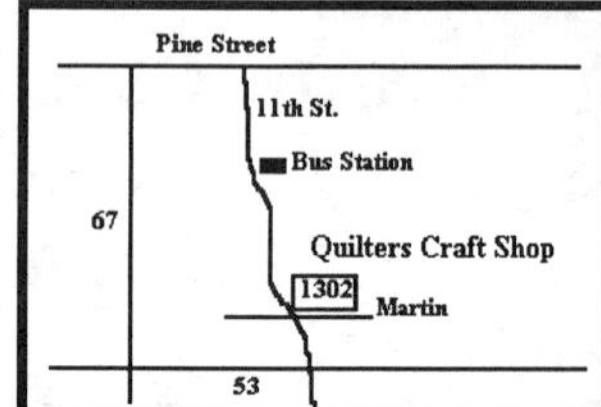

Mountain View, MO #14

Mon - Fri
10 - 5
Sat 10 - 3

Calico Cupboard

110 Oak St. 65548
(417) 934-6330
Owner: Darlene Godsy
Est: 1981 1500 sq.ft. Catalog $2.00

600 bolts of cotton fabrics, lots of patterns, books, notions, counted cross stitch books and supplies plus friendly Ozarks service.

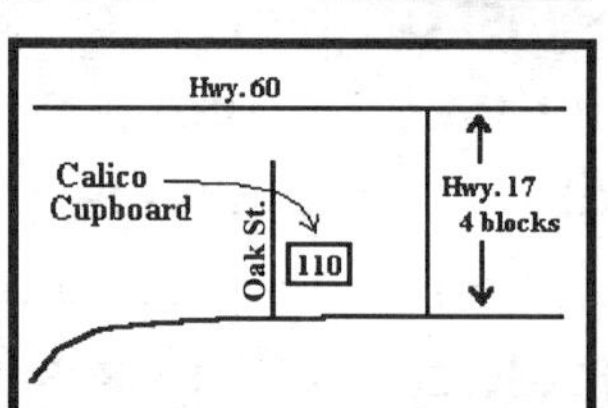

Branson, MO #15

Summer
8 - 8 Daily
Winter
9 - 6 Daily

Quilts & Quilts

1137 West Hwy. 76 65616
in Branson Heights Shopping Ctr.
(417) 334-3243
Owner: Marlys Michaelson Est: 1981

Largest and most complete quilting shop in the 4 state area. Handmade Quilts. Over 4000 bolts of Calico and Gifts !

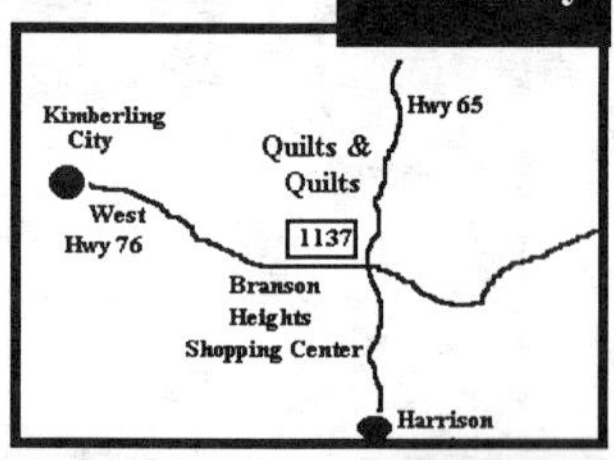

Taneyville, MO #16

Mon - Fri
9 - 5
Sat 9 - 1

Quilts 'N' More

419 Grand Ave. (Hwy. 76)
Mail: 824 St. Hwy. FF 65759
(417) 546-6330
Owners:
Evelyn Clark & Mary Sims

Quilts, Fabrics, Counted Cross Stitch, Gifts, Lace, Ribbon, Notions, Books, Patterns, Repair & Finish Quilts, Clothing, Day-Evening Classes

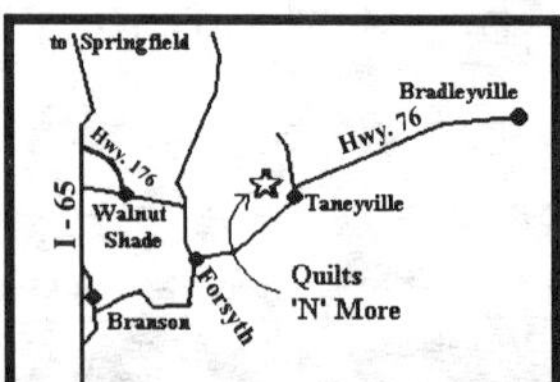

Joplin, MO #17

Mon - Fri
9 - 6
Sat 9 - 4

Sew Neat

1710 E. 32nd St. #L, Fountain Plaza
(417) 782-4242
Owner: Brenda Orban
Quilt fabric—Specialty fabric & supplies, sewing supplies. Quilt Classes, beginner & advanced. Heirloom & craft classes.
Many items not available anywhere else.
Come visit our qualified staff.

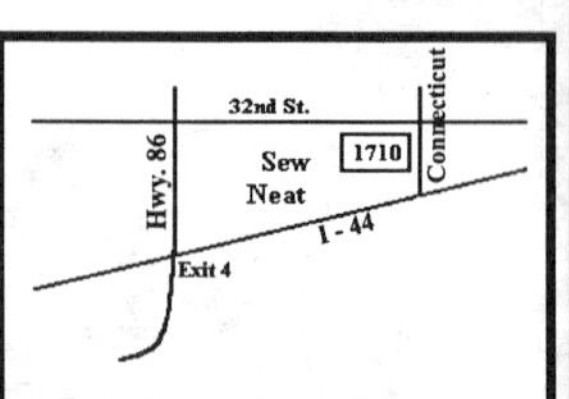

Mt. Vernon, MO #18

Mon - Sat
8:30 - 5:30
Sun 1 - 5

Turner's Calico Country
& Ben Franklin

207 E. Dallas 65712
(417) 466-3401

Quilt Show Everyday, 1000's of Calicos, Quilting Supplies, 100's of Sewing & Craft Patterns, Old Time Candy Case, Fresh Homemade Fudge, Ozark-Made Oak Baskets, Fenton and Collectibles.

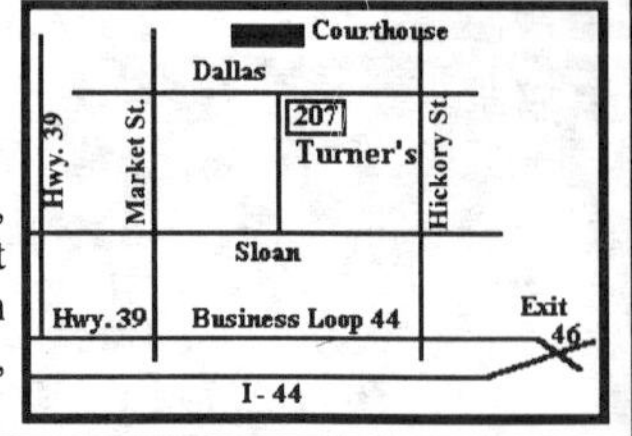

Springfield, MO #19

Tues - Fri
9:30 - 5:30
Sat 10 - 4

The Quilt Shoppe

2762 South Campbell 65807
(417) 883-1355
Owners: Rosalie Carey & Gilda Young
Est: 1978 2100 sq.ft.

100% cotton fabrics(1500 prints, 300 solids), 200 stencils, books, patterns, notions, Q-Snap frames, Hinterberg frames.
"Down the street from Bass Pro"

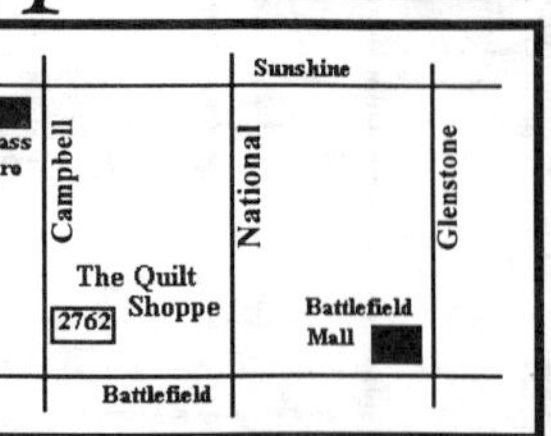

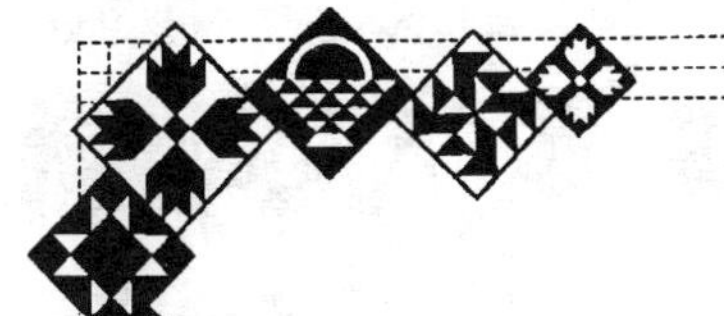

SPRINGFIELD, MO #20

The Quilt Sampler

1936B South Glenstone "On The Plaza" 65804

(417) 886-5750

e-mail: qltsampler@aol.com

web site: http://www.pcis.net/quiltsampler

Cristen Powell, owner

Est. 1994 3800 sq. ft.

3000 + bolts
of fine quality cotton fabrics
including plaids, balis, batiks
and we have a flannel room!
Block of the Month Clubs
Kits
Sewing Antiques including
Featherweight sewing
machines

Mon. - Fri.
10 - 5
Thurs. til 8
Sat. 10 - 4
1st Sunday each month
12 - 4

Books
Patterns
Notions
Buttons
Classes

Close to Bass Pro -- drop off your husband and come stay with us as long as you like!

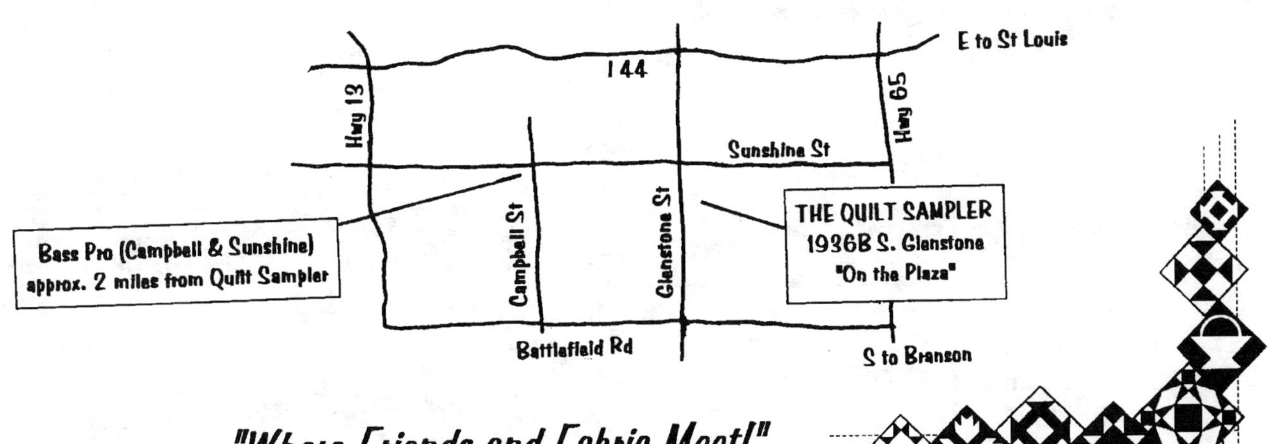

"Where Friends and Fabric Meet!"

Rolla, MO #21

Mon - Fri 9 - 6
Sat 9 - 5

Fabrics Unlimited

13795 U.S. 63 S 65401
(573) 364-5245
Owner: Betty I. Lewis 1600 sq.ft.
2500 total bolts, 1100+ quilt fabric

Quilting Fabrics, Notions, Batting, Quilt Books. Machine Quilting. Machine Binding. Our main business is quilt supplies.

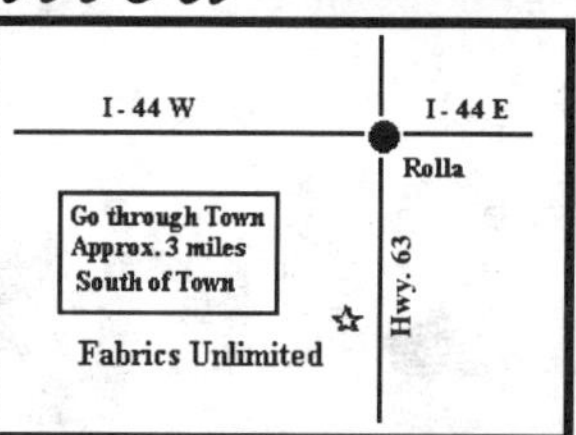

Versailles, MO #23

Mon - Sat 9 - 5

Clark's Fabrics

West Vue Shopping Center 65084
Hwy 5 & 52 W. Est: 1964
(573) 378-5696 1800 sq.ft. 1700 Bolts
Owner: Kirk Chapman

Great selection of all types of fabric, including quilting, clothing and home decorating. Buttons, Buttons, Buttons !

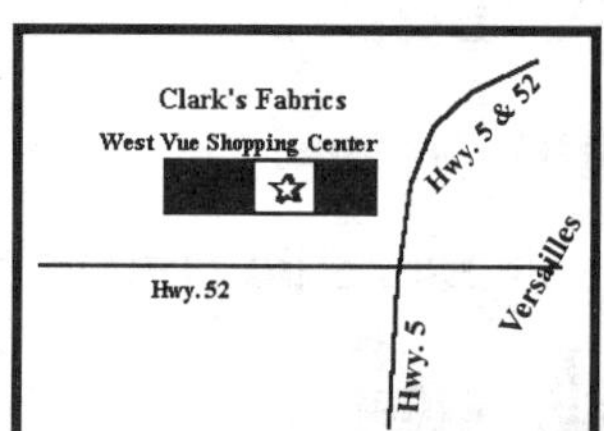

Linda's Cottonpatch

Owner: Linda Petty

Mon - Sat 9 - 5

502 W. Newton 65084 (573) 378-6191
Fax: (573) 378-5289 Est: 1993 2400 sq.ft.
E-Mail: lspetty@laurie.net

Quilt fabrics, notions, books & patterns. Fashion fabrics too. Authorized dealer.

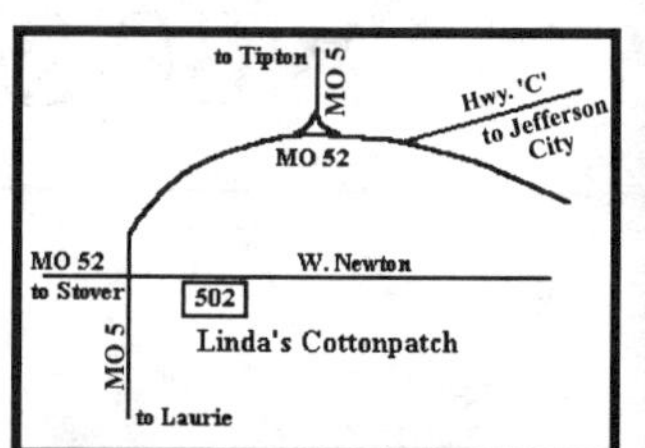

Versailles, MO #22

Sedalia, MO #24

Mon - Fri 9 - 5
Sat 9 - 4

D & T Quilt Shop

3620 S. Marshall 65301
(660) 826-4788
Owner: Theresa Gerber
Est: 1991 1200 sq.ft.

Fabrics, Notions, Embroidery Blocks, Classes. 3000+ Bolts. Buttons by the Lb. $4.99. Friendly Country Atmosphere

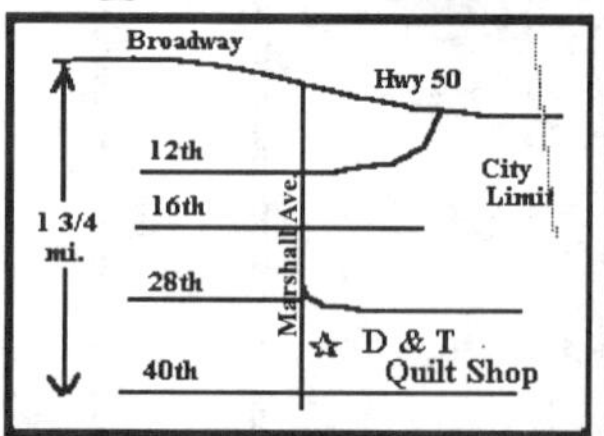

Columbia, MO #25

Mon - Thur 10 - 7
Fri & Sat 10 - 5

Silks & More Fine Fabrics

2541 Bernadette Dr. 65203-4674
(573) 446-2655
Owner: Millie Kaiser
Est: 1985 5200 sq.ft.

Large selection of beautiful 100% cotton prints and solids, designer fabrics, books, patterns, and notions. Come see us!

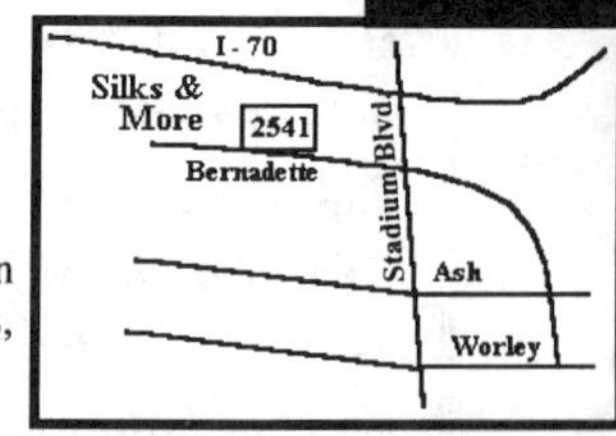

Linda's Cottonpatch

Owner: Linda Petty

Mon - Fri 9 - 6
Sat 9 - 5

3720 W. Truman Blvd. 65109
(573) 634-2371 Owner: Linda Petty
Est: 1997 1400 sq.ft.

Jefferson City, MO #26

Quilt fabrics, notions, books & patterns. Authorized Husqvarna Viking dealer.

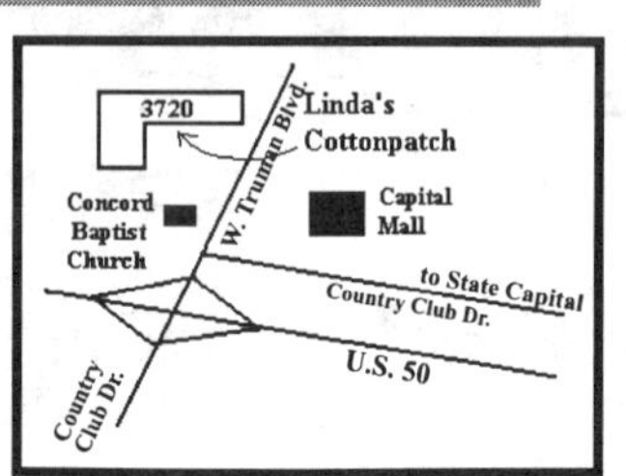

Marshall, MO #27

Mon - Fri 9:30 - 5:30
Sat 9:30 - 5

Quilt Shoppe

1322 W. Vest 65340
(816) 886-4646
Owner: Janis Eddy

Fabric, Books, Notions, & Antiques.

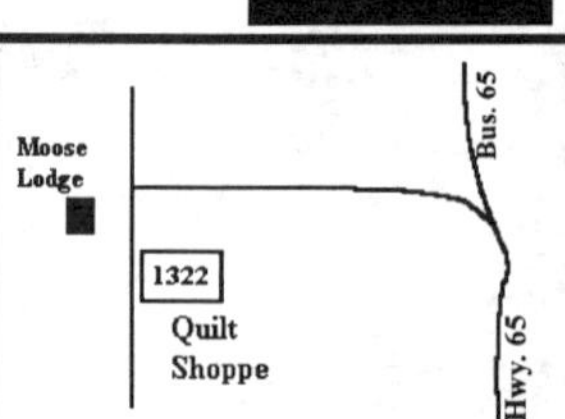

Lees Summit, MO #28

Mon - Thur 9:30 - 5:30
Fri 9:30 - 5
Sat 9:30 - 3

QUILTER'S STATION

(816) 525-8955

824 SW Blue Pkwy. 64063
Owner: Rita Briner
Large selection of 100% Cotton Fabrics.
Quilting Supplies, Books & Patterns.
Machine Quilting & Classes.

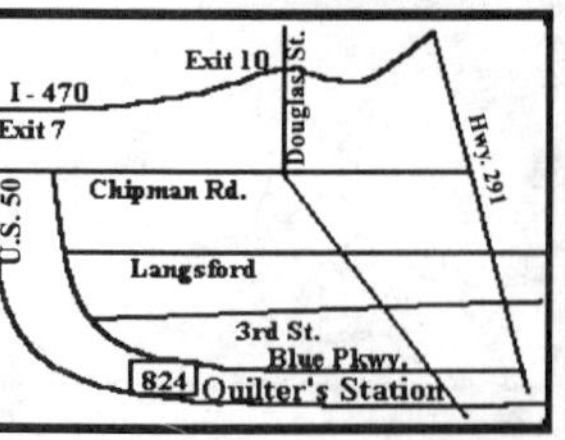

Blue Springs, MO #29

Mon - Thurs 10 - 8
Fri & Sat 10 - 4:30

ZOELEE'S FABRICS

1300 West 40 Hwy. 64015
(816) 228-5746
Owner: Zoelee Donnell
E-Mail: zoelees@discoverynet.com
Web Site: www.discoverynet.com/~zoelees
Est: 1982 3800 sq.ft. 1000 Bolts

Quilting Fabrics & Supplies. Lingerie fabrics & Accessories. Large selection of Knits, Swim Wear, Designer Fabrics, Stretch & Sew, Patterns & Notions. Juki Sales & Service

I-70
291 Hwy.
I-470
40 Hwy.
Zoelee's
14th St.
1300
Hwy. 7

Blue Springs, MO #30

Mon - Fri 10 - 5
Tues & Thur til 7
Sat 10 - 4

Cottonbelle Quilt Shoppe

805 B Main St. 64015
(816) 220-3500
Owners: Dianna Holden & Linda Kriesel
Est: 1996

Large selection of 100% cotton name brand fabrics, sewing and quilting notions, books, patterns, supplies and classes.

Independence, MO #31

RUSTIC YEARNINGS

17601 A East 40 Hwy. Colonnade Shopping Center 64055
(816) 373-2423 E-Mail: rusticy@aol.com
Est: 1993 8500 sq.ft. 5000+ Bolts

Large Selection of Books, Notions, Patterns & Fabrics for Quilting and Crafting. Also unique Home Accessories & Gifts plus P. Buckley Moss Gallery.

Mon - Sat 10 - 8
Sun 10 - 5

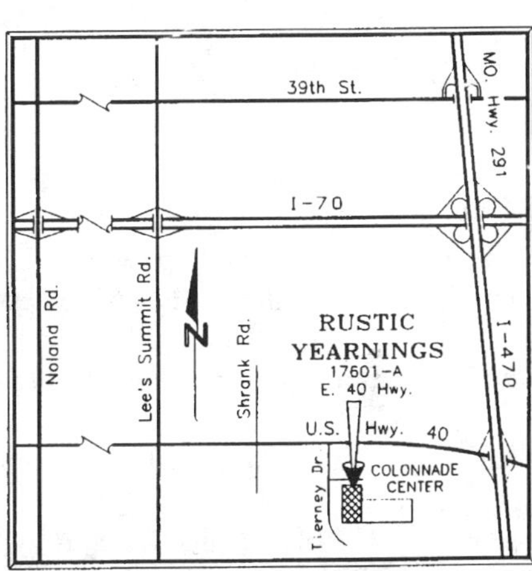

Missouri Guilds:

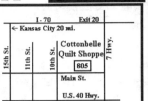

Booneslick Trail Quilters' Guild, P.O. Box 542, Columbia, 65205
Flower Valley Quilting Guild, P.O. Box 9002, Florissant, 63032
Calico Cutups, Forsyth, c/o Ioma Potter, 3549 St. Hwy. F, Rockaway Beach, MO 65740
Hannibal Piecemakers Quilt Guild, 2335 Palmyra Rd., Hannibal, 63401
Meets: 1st Tuesday 6 p.m.
Town & Country Quilters, 1710 E. 32nd, Joplin, 64804
Meets: 3rd Tuesday 12p.m.
at First Methodist Church, 4th & Byers
Quilters Guild of Greater Kansas City, P.O. Box 22561, K. C., 64113
Northland Quilters' Guild, P.O. Box 46654, Kansas City, 64118
Meets: 2nd Thursday 10 a.m. at Gashland United Methodist Church, 7715 N. Oak Trafficway
Nitetime Needlers, P.O. Box 28731, Kansas City, 64118
Meets: 2nd Thursday 7 p.m. at Gashland United Methodist Church, 7115 N. Oak, Gladstone
Stitch By Stitch, Marshall, 65340
Meets: 3rd Tuesday 6:30 p.m. at RLDS Church
Country Patchworkers, P.O. Box 365, Marshall, 65340
Missouri State Quilters Guild, 37 Johnson St., Rolla, 65401
Ozark Piecemakers Q. G., P.O. Box 4931, Springfield, 65808
The Piece Corps Quilt Guild, St. Joseph
Meets: 1st Monday 6:30 p.m. and 1st Thursday 9:30 a.m.
at Ashland Methodist Church, Ashland Ave. and Genefield Rd.
Inspired Quilters Guild, Warrensburg

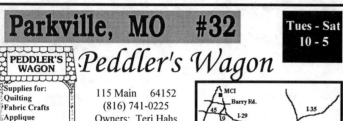

Parkville, MO #32

Tues - Sat
10 - 5

PEDDLER'S WAGON
Supplies for:
Quilting
Fabric Crafts
Applique
Silk Ribbon Emb.
Free Demos

Peddler's Wagon

115 Main 64152
(816) 741-0225
Owners: Teri Hahs
Est: 1982 3400 sq.ft.

Quilts, Fabric, Country Gifts, Ladie and Friends Dolls.

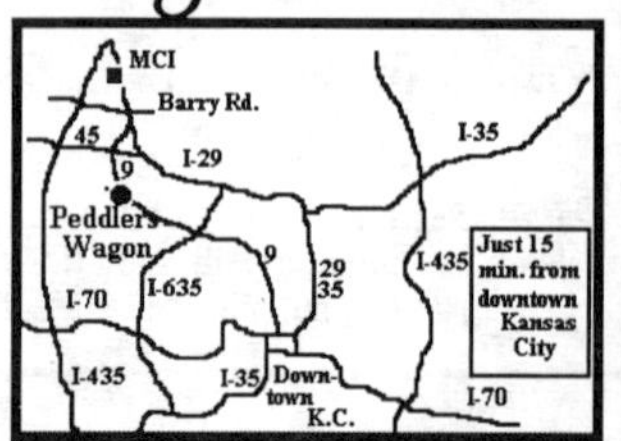

Liberty, MO #33

Mon - Sat
10 - 5
Thur til 8
Sun 1 - 5

Liberty Quilt Shop

131 South Water 64068
(816) 781-7966
Owner: Julie Kiffin
Est: 1988 3000 sq.ft.

Over 3000 bolts of 100% cotton. Books, patterns, and friendly, helpful staff !

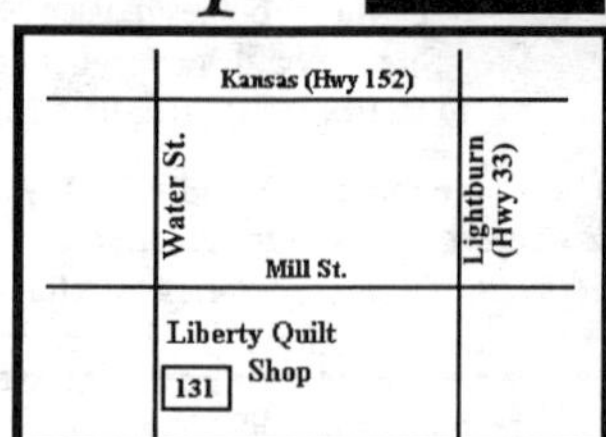

Savannah, MO #34

Mon - Fri
9 - 5
Tues til 9
Sat 9 - 4

Top Stitch Country

420 Court St. 64485
(816) 324-4053
Est: 1985 2500+ sq.ft.

Brand Name Fabrics, Books, Patterns, Notions, Sewing Machines, Classes, Quilts and Quilted Items for Sale.

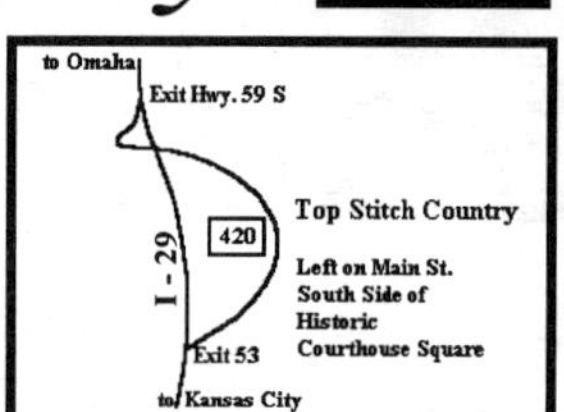

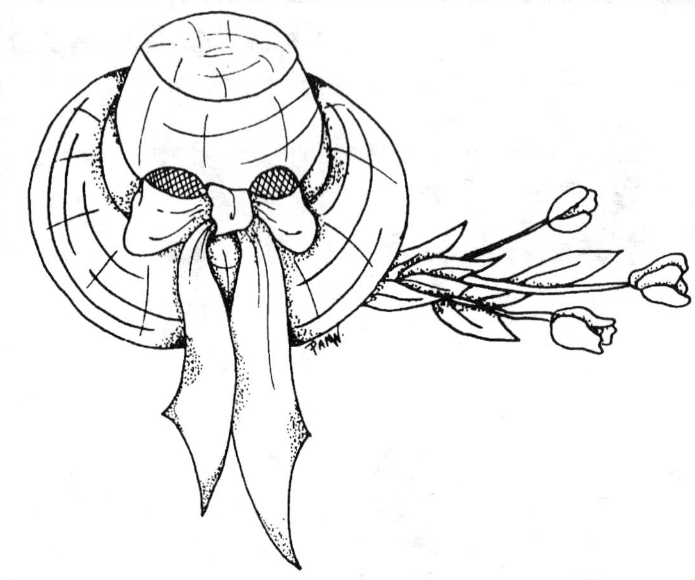

Other Shops in Missouri:

Appleton City	AC Sewing Supply, 116 E. 4th St.	
Ballwin	In Stitches, 14664 Manchester Rd.	314-394-4471
Beaufort	Quilt N Time Quilt Station, R.R. #1	573-484-3120
Boonville	Fashion Shack Fabrics, 11571 Dogwood	816-882-7001
Branson	The Cotton Patch Quilt Shop, 2420 W. Hwy. 76	417-334-2040
Branson	Carolina Mills Outlet, Hwy. 76	417-334-2291
Branson	Rosebrier Quilts, 117 E. Main St.	417-336-3436
Branson	Quilt Cottage, 122 Skyview Dr.	417-339-3445
Branson	Quilt Connection, 673 St. Hwy. 165	417-334-6523
Cape Girardeau	The Sewing Basket, 2504 William	573-339-7667
Carrollton	Quilted Thimble, 14 N. Main St.	816-542-1133
Clinton	Mary Jane's Fabrics, 109 W. Franklin St.	816-885-5651
Craig	Fabrics Unique, Rt. 1	816-683-5757
Crystal City	Quilting Bee, 520C Bailey Rd.	314-931-0307
Farmington	Old Village Quilt Shop, 113 S. Jackson St.	573-756-3353
Fredericktown	Carolina Fabric Center, 107 N. Mine La Motte St.	573-783-2222
Hannibal	Yore Quilts, 403 Broadway	573-221-2480
Jamesport	Leona's Quilts and Quaints, Rt. 2	816-684-6628
Kansas City	The Fabric Stash, 643 E. 59th	816-523-7882
Kirksville	Kaye's Fabrics, 300 N. Franklin	816-665-0123
Laquey	Country Bumpkin Enterprises Hwy. AA	314-765-4479
Lebanon	H & H Fabric and Quilt Center, 326 W. Commercial St.	417-532-2378
Marshall	Betty Sue O'Dell, 466 S. Odell	816-886-3663
Mt. Vernon	Grannie's Patchworks, 105 E. Dallas St.	417-466-7080
Oak Grove	Phanora's Variety, 1560 S. Broadway St.	816-625-8531
Osage Beach	Quilts & Things, R.R. #2 P.O. Box 2535	573-348-4146
Osceola	Quilts and Crafts, 312 Second	417-646-7746
Palmyra	Rosebrook Creations 116 W. Jefferson St.	573-769-3504
Potosi	Busy Bee Quilt Shop & Florist, 103 Fissell St.	573-438-8660
Springfield	Crafters Delight, 2709 W. Kearney St.	417-866-4184
Springfield	Patchwork Corner, 702 E. Commercial St.	417-866-6160
St. Louis	Thimble & Thread, 2629 Yeager Rd.	
St. Louis	Eunice Farmer Fabrics, 9814 Clayton Rd.	314-997-1531
Ste. Genevieve	Monia's Unlimited, 316 Market	314-883-7874
Vienna	GS Fabric and Gifts, Hwy. 42 W.	314-422-3500
Warrensburg	Traci's Crafts & Gifts, 319 N. Holden St.	816-429-6844

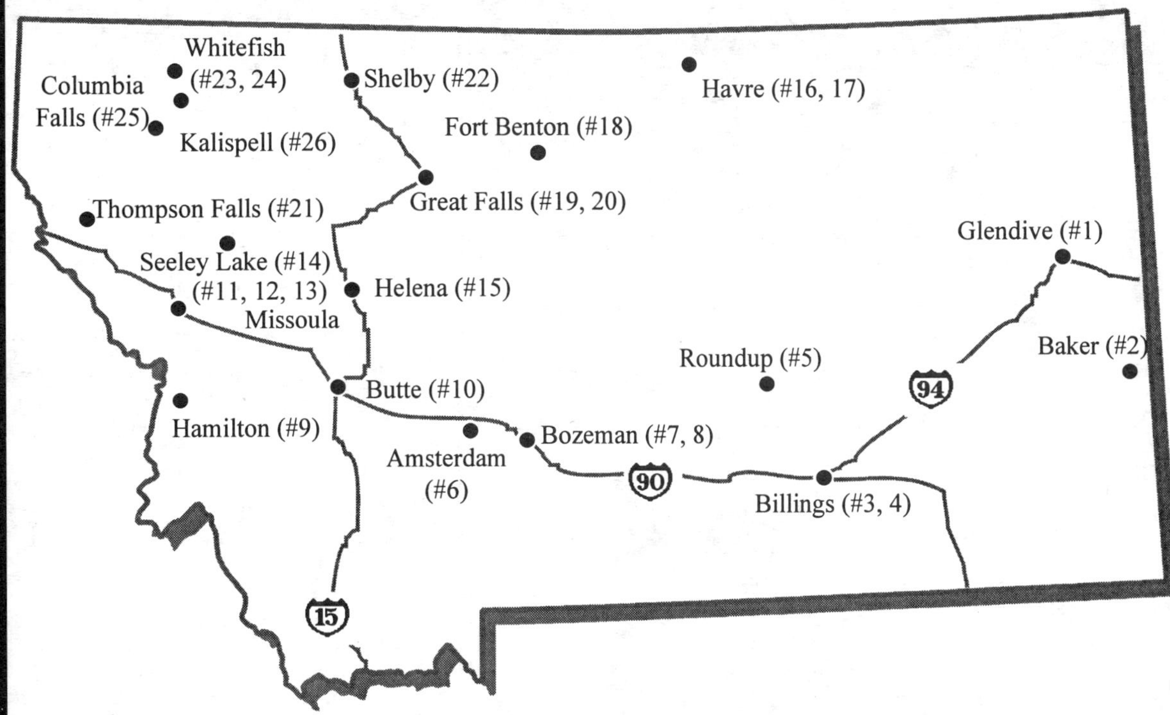

26 Featured Shops

Glendive, MT #1

Mon - Sat 10 - 5

The Enchanted Room

222 W. Towne St. 59330
(406) 365-4745
Owners: Myrna Quale & Laura Gluecker

Quilt Shop located in Restored Historic Home. Excellent Selection of Quilting Fabric, books, & notions. Unique gifts, Custom Floral, Home Decorating accessories.

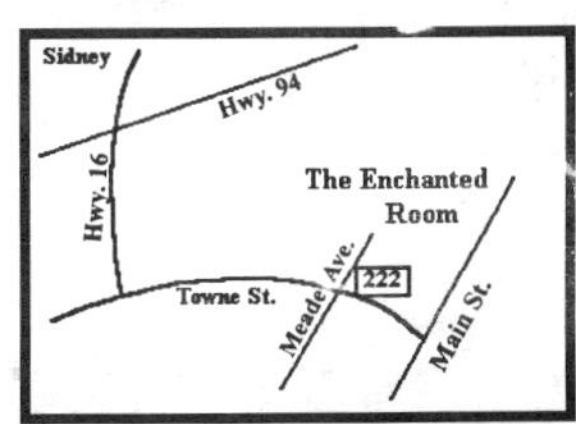

Baker, MT #2

Mon - Sat 9:30 - 5

Creative Stitches

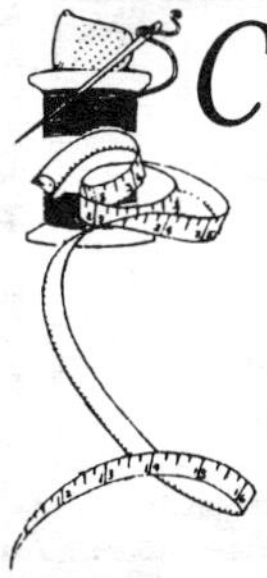

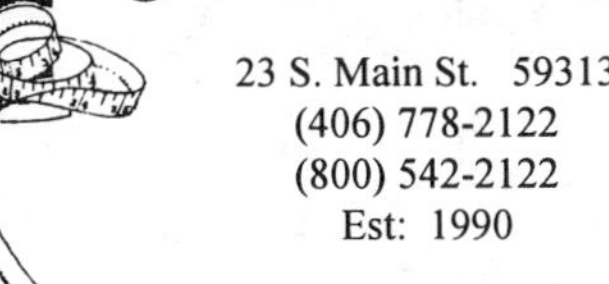

23 S. Main St. 59313
(406) 778-2122
(800) 542-2122
Est: 1990

Large selection of 100% cotton fabrics, quilt books & notions.

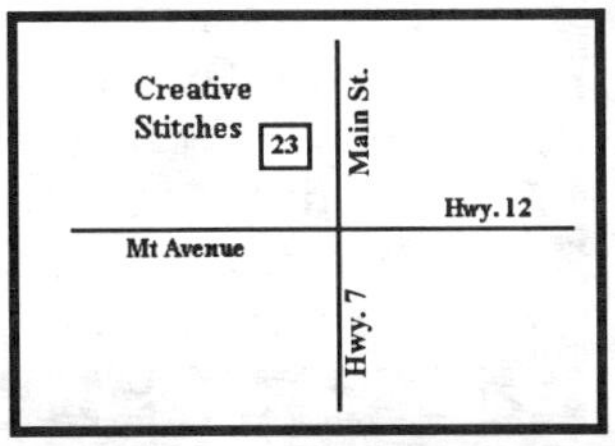

Creative Stitches
23
Main St.
Hwy. 12
Mt Avenue
Hwy. 7

Billings, MT #3

**Mon & Tues 10 - 6
Wed 10 - 8
Thur, Fri, Sat 10 - 5
Sun 12 - 5**

Fiberworks

1310 24th St. W 59102
(406) 656-6663 Fax: (406) 656-3363
Owner: Laura Heine
Est: 1994 3000 sq.ft.

Fantastic Fabrics for Flash Funk & Fashion

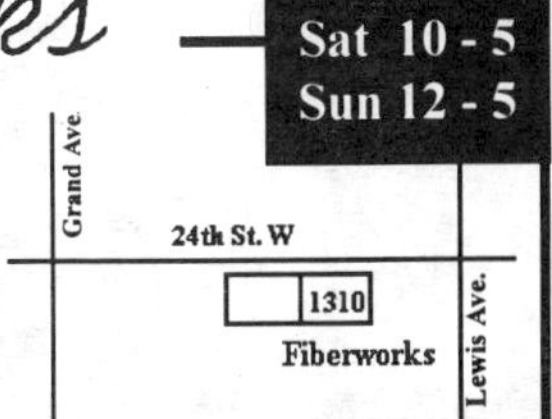

Billings, MT #4

Mon - Sat 9:30 - 5:30

Bernina Sewing Center

1505 Rehberg Ln. 59102
(406) 656-4999
Owners: Frank & Doris Holzer
900 Bolts

Authorized Bernina Dealer.
Quilting books, patterns, supplies.
100% cotton calicos & solids.
Classes. Friendly & helpful

Roundup, MT #5

9 a.m. to 9:30 or 10 p.m.

Scrap Happy Quiltworks

137 Main St. 59072
(406) 323-1616
Owner: Florence Scott

Large selection of 100% cotton fabrics, thread, books, patterns, notions, Elna & Bernina sewing machines & classes.

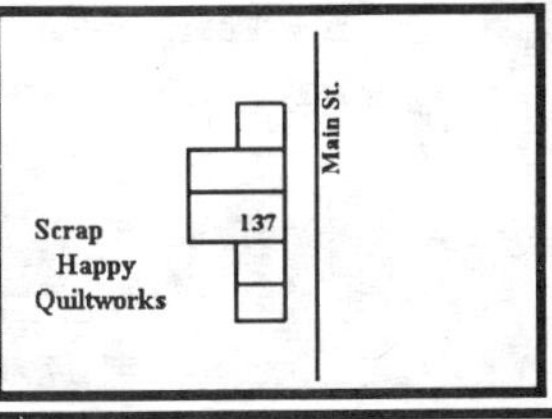

Reproduction Fabrics

Patchworks

PATCHWORKS is renowned for its large inventory of reproduction cotton fabrics and expertise in selecting authentic-looking fabrics representative of bygone eras from:

~ 1775 to 1950 ~

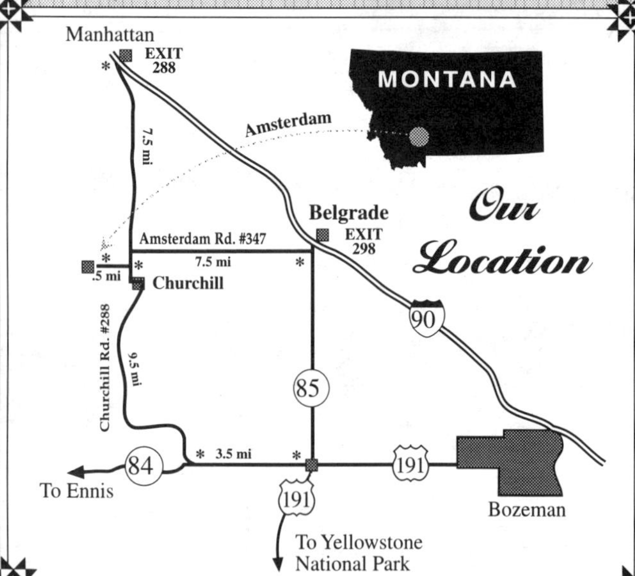

Our Location

Miles

TO PATCHWORKS FROM:

Bozeman, Montana	18 miles
Livingston	43 miles
Big Sky Ski Resort	50 miles
Yellowstone Nat'l Park	87 miles
Helena	88 miles
Billings	160 miles
Missoula	190 miles

Send $5.00 for brochure and samples to:

Hours (MST)

STORE HOURS:
9:00 a.m. - noon M-F (always)
Afternoons & Sat By appointment

PHONE HOURS:
9:00 a.m. - noon M-F (always)
Noon - 7:00 p.m. M-F (usually)

PATCHWORKS, Dept. O
6676 Amsterdam Road
Amsterdam, Montana
59741-8315 USA

PHONE: 406-282-7218
FAX: 406-282-7322

E-mail: fabric@patchworks-usa.com
Internet: www.patchworks-usa.com

Toll-free Order Line: 1-888-PATCHWK

Bozeman, MT #7

Mon - Sat 9:30 - 5:30

Bear Comforts

126 E. Main St. 59715
(406) 586-6097 Fax: (406) 586-5239
(800) 757-6097
Owner: Sandy Taylor
Est: 1977 2500 sq.ft. 2000 Bolts

Bozeman's only complete quilting store offering hundreds of bolts of 100% cotton, the latest notions, patterns & books for your selection.

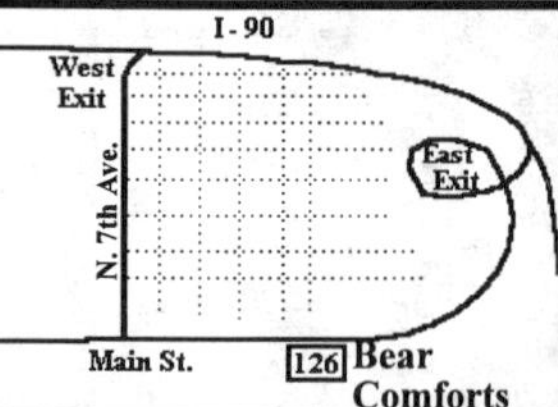

Bozeman, MT #8

Tues - Sat 11 - 4 Thurs til 6

Quilting In The Country

5100 S. 19th Rd. 59718
(406) 587-8216
Owner: Jane Quinn

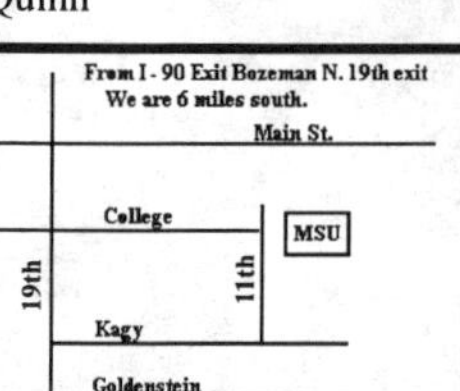

Charming shop in bunkhouse on 120 year old homestead. 3 miles south of Bozeman. Classes. Free end of summer outdoor quilt show.

Hamilton, MT #9

201 S. Second
59840
(406) 363-3471
Owner: Rosalie Reinbold
Est: 1972
3500 sq.ft.

Mon - Sat 9:30 - 5:30

Featuring over 2000 bolts of prints & Solids—Hoffman, Alexander Henry, Concord, Marcus, Peter Pan, Wamsutta & More. Quilting Supplies & large selection of books. Newsletter/Class Schedule Available.

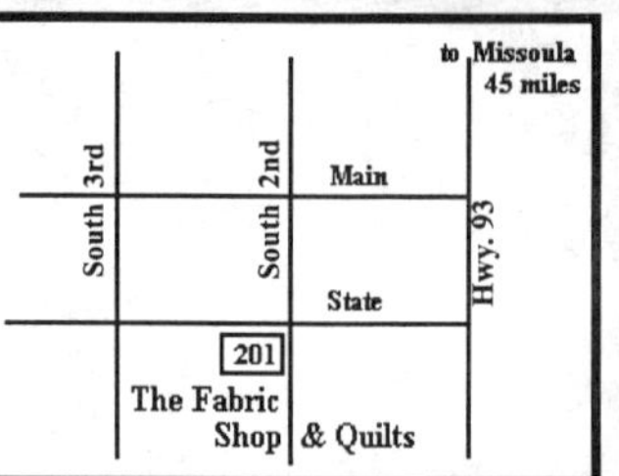

Butte, MT #10

Mon - Sat 10 - 5:30

QUILT - ESSENTIALS

3104 Busch St. 69701
(406) 494-1633 E-Mail: stilwell@in-tch.com
Owners: Carol Kirkpatrick, Robin Stilwell, & Julie Flammang

Appointments & After Hours call 494-1009 or 494-3832

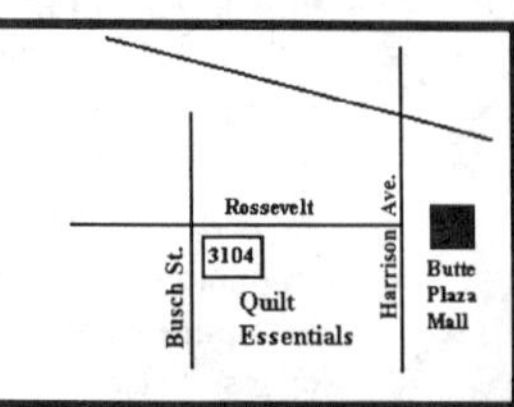

Fabrics & Supplies, Classes, Custom-Made Quilts & Gifts.

Missoula, MT #11

Mon - Fri 10 - 8
Sat 10 - 5
Sun 12 - 5

Latitudes Fabrics

Corner of 3rd & Higgins 59801
(406) 728-9171
Owner: Annette Palmgren

Quality 100% cottons including Batiks, Ethnics & Traditionals for quilting. Wearables, Dollmaking, Textile Art & Home Decor. Related Books, Patterns, Classes.

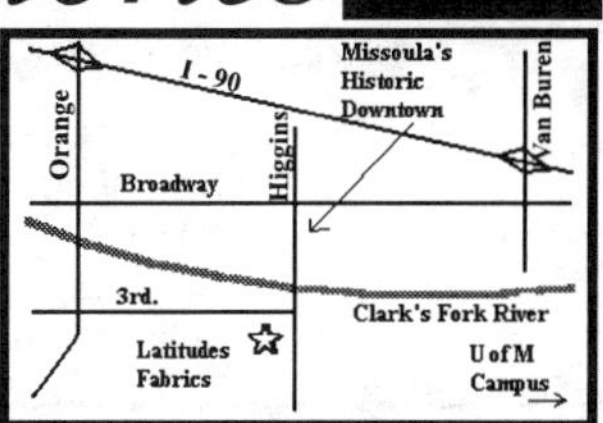

Missoula, MT #12

Mon - Sat 10 - 5

Country Friends Quilt Shop

1900 W. Broadway 59802
(406) 728-7816 Fax: (406) 327-9667
Est: 1988 4,200 sq.ft.
Owners: Cherie Jacobsen & Anna Mae Cheff

Books, Patterns, 100% Cotton Fabric, Quilts, Quilting Classes, Wonderful Country Handcrafted Gifts

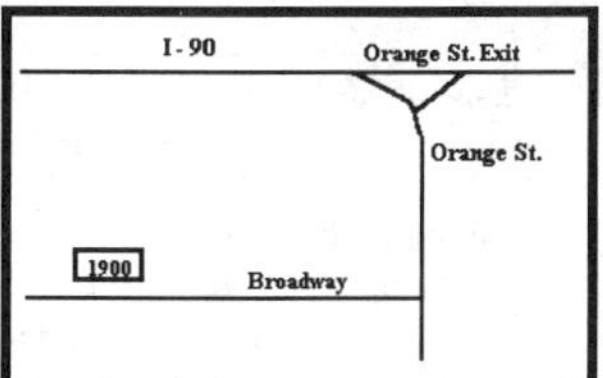

Missoula, MT #13

Timeless Treasures Quilt Shop

1519 Cooper St. 59802 (406) 542-6566
Fax: (406) 327-0742 E-Mail: quilts@montana.com

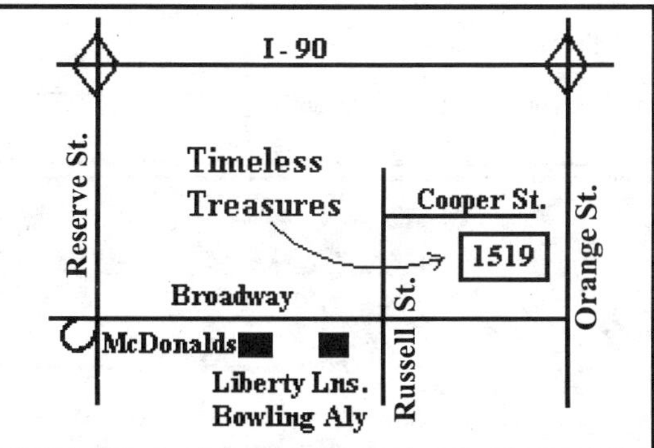

Mon - Sat 10 - 6

* Featuring Fine Cotton Fabrics *
* Books, Patterns & Notions *
* Custom Hand-Guided Machine Quilting *
* Quilts for Sale *
* Call ahead for our class schedule *

Seeley Lake, MT #14

Mon - Sat 10 - 5:30
Sun 12 - 4

Deer Country Quilts

Lazy Pine Mall, Hwy. 83 (P.O. Box 808)
(406) 677-2730 Fax: (406) 677-2885
Owner: Penny Copps
Est: 1996 1500 sq.ft. 1000+ Bolts

Stitch a memory in the beautiful Seeley-Swan Valley. Fabric, Classes, Notions—Everything you need including inspiration.

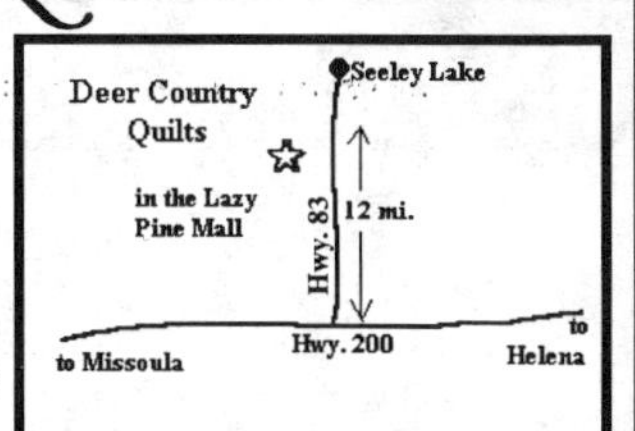

Helena, MT #15

Mon - Sat 10 - 5

Calico Cupboard

601 Euclid Ave. # C 59601
(406) 449-8440
Owners: Dianne Ducello
Est: 1989 2000 sq.ft.

Specialize in fine 100% cotton Fabric, unique patterns, quilting books, notions, classes and gifts.

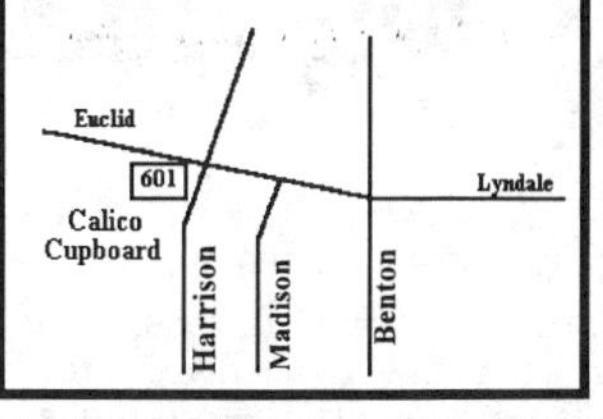

Havre, MT #16

Mon - Sat 9 - 5:30 Eves During Classes

The Silver Thimble

104 3rd Ave. 59501
(406) 265-4531 Est: 1981
E-Mail: Edna.gregory@hi-line.net
Owner: Edna Gregory 3500 sq.ft.

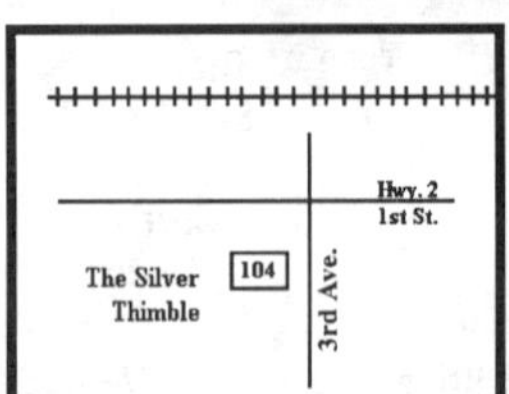

Full line of fabrics for quilting & wearables, Bernina machines, latest books & patterns, unique notions. Classes available.

Havre, MT #17

By Appt. Only

Quilters' Edge

220 3rd. Ave. 59501 (406) 265-1191
Owner: Patricia Haas Est: 1993 1500 sq.ft.

Tell me what you are looking for. I do mostly mail order. I carry top quality fabrics: Japanese, Hand-dyed, Hoffman, RJR, Kaufman, Nancy Crow, Moda, Benartex, Bali Fabrications & Island Textiles just to name a few. Also Books, Patterns, Notions, Stencils, & Batting.

"Bless My Buttons" Quilting and More...

Step into our 'little piece of heaven' and discover the endless possibilities with fabrics, threads, patterns, classes, gifts and more.

Wed, Thur, Fri 12 - 7
Sat 10 - 5 Sun 11 - 4

1514 Front St.
Box 1420 59442
(406) 622-5150

Owners: Paulette Albers, Maggie Onstad & Gini Onstad

Fort Benton, MT #18

Great Falls, MT #19

Mon - Fri 10 - 6
Sat 10 - 5

Wild Hare Quilt Shoppe

900 Second St. South, Suite 1 59405
(406) 727-1757
Owner: Bev Jonasen Est: 1996

100% Cotton Top quality Fabrics.
Books-Patterns-Notions-Classes.
Award Winning Machine Quilting.
Mail Order (visa-mastercard-discover)
Gift Shop.

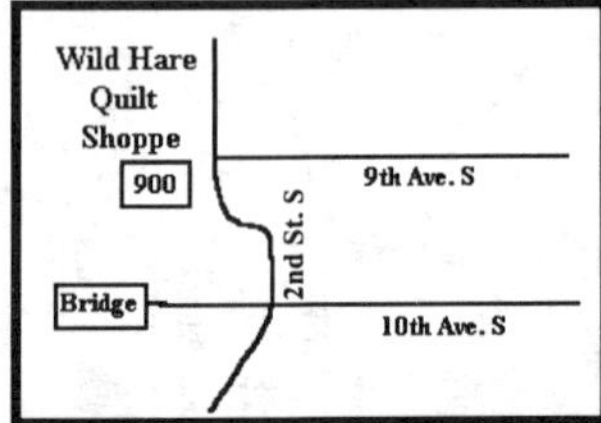

Great Falls, MT #20

Mon - Sat 10 - 6

Bernina - Silver Thimble

1323 9th Ave. S 59405
in the Montana International Ins. Bldg.
(406) 452-7222
E-Mail: Edna.gregory@hi-line.net
Owner: Edna Gregory Est: 1998

Bernina sewing machines, accessories. Many patterns & books, decorative threads and unique notions.

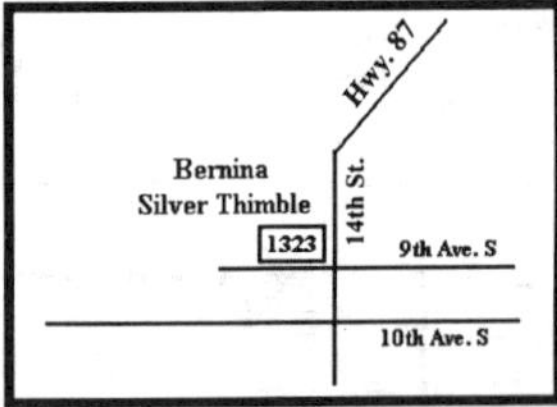

Thompson Falls, MT #21

Mon - Fri 9 - 5

Quilts "R" Us

214 Greenwood
59873
(406) 827-3450
Owner: Doris Besaw

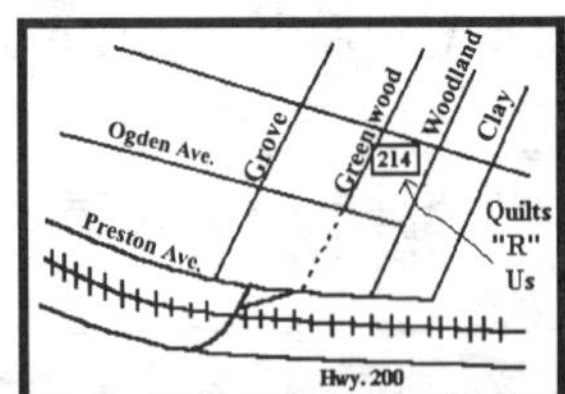

Cotton Prints and over one hundred solid colors. Hand-dyed and Marbleized fabrics. Thread, Notions and tools.

Shelby, MT #22

Mon - Sat 9 - 5:30

225 Main St. 59474
(406) 434-7106
Owner: Shelby Creative Investment

Complete Quilt Shop.
Fabric, Notions, Pfaff Sewing Machines. Plus we do commercial quilting and ship anywhere.

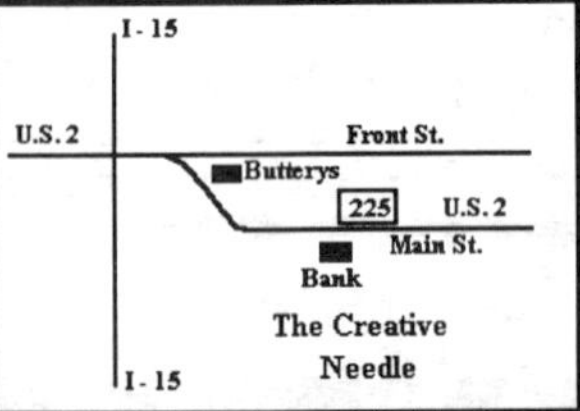

Whitefish, MT #23

Mon - Fri 9 - 6
Sat 10 - 3

Sew Excited Fabrics

550 E. 1st St. #102 59937
(406) 862-7218
Owner: Cheryl Schankin
Est: 1994 1200 sq.ft. 700+ Bolts

Lots of colors! 100% Cottons, Flannel, Linen, Books & Patterns, Quilting & Sewing Classes We also repair quilts by hand. Outerware Fabrics & patterns too!
Service with A Smile!

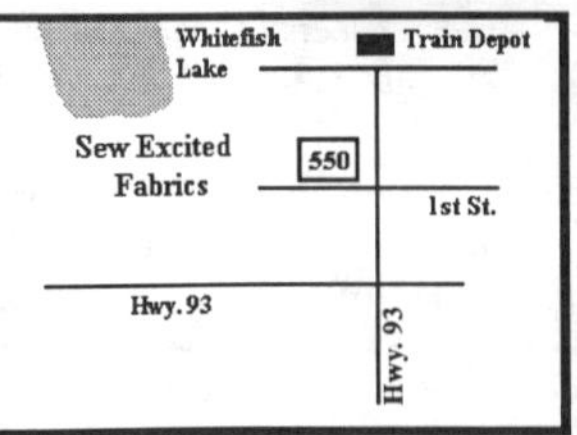

Whitefish, MT #24

Mon - Sat 9:30 - 5:30

General Store

dba QUILTS FOREVER

121 Central Ave. 59937
(406) 862-5986 Fax: (406) 862-9187
E-Mail: goldie@digisys.net
Owner: Melissa Gold

Yard Goods, Yarn, Notions, Books & Antiques. Quilt, sewing & craft classes, custom machine quilting also alterations & repairs.

Columbia Falls, MT #25

4775 Hwy. 2 W 59912
(406) 257-6966
E-Mail:
marting@cyberport.net
Owner: Susan Gilman

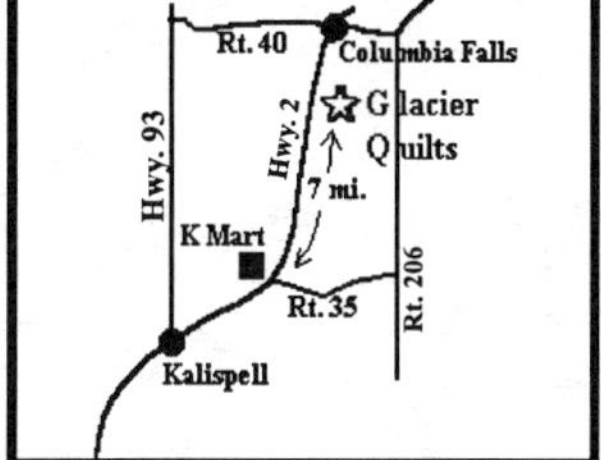

Mon - Fri 10 - 6
Sat 10 - 4

Quality 100% Cotton Fabrics and Flannels, Books, Patterns, Classes. Quilting Tools & Toys, Gifts and Quilts. Mail orders welcome. Newsletter/class schedule available.

Kalispell, MT #26

Quilts • Fabrics • Supplies
Unique Patterns • Gifts •
Lessons

Large selection of antique, handquilted, novelty and machine Quilts.
Mail Orders Welcome
Owner: Joan P. Hodgeboom
Est: 1983 4700 sq.ft.

1710 Hwy. 93 S. 59901
(406) 257-5799
Next to Diamond Lil Inn

Mon - Fri 9:30 - 5:30
Sat 9:30 - 5

Selected by American Patchwork & Quilting magazine readers as one of the Top 10 quilt shops in the nation.

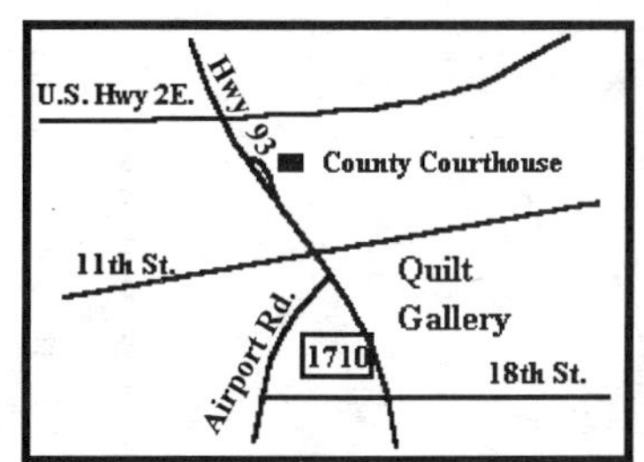

Montana Guilds:

Life's Patchwork Quilting Guild, Baker
  Meets: 4th Wednesday 1 p.m.
  at Fallon Co. Library Basement Meeting Room
Piecemakers Quilt Guild, P.O. Box 176, Big Fork, 59911
Bigfork Piecemakers Guild, Bigfork
  Meets: 3rd Thursday 7 p.m. at Senior Citizen Center
Nimble Thimble Quilters, 1917 Ave. C, Billings, 59101
Quilt by Association, P.O. Box 22233, Billings, 59104
Yellowstone Valley Q. G., 3114 Country Club Circle, Billings, 59102
Quilter's Art Guild of N. Rockies, P.O. Box 4117, Bozeman, 59772
Stitch & Chatter Quilt Club, Box 318, Broadus, 59317
  Meets: 2nd & 4th Tuesday at County Courthouse Election Room
Art Chateau Quilters, 2915 Nettie, Butte, 59701
Chateau Quilters, 3405 Eastlake, Butte, 59701
West Shore Quilters Guild, Dayton
  Meets: 1st Monday 1 p.m. at Dayton Presbyterian Church
Piecemakers, Box 212, Dillon, 59725
Scrap & Threads Quilt Guild, Eureka
  Meets: 2nd Thursday 9 a.m. at Eureka Baptist Church
Quilters Art Guild of the N. Rockies, P.O. Box 242, Great Falls, 59403
Falls Quilt Guild, P.O. Box 6592, Great Falls, 59406
  Meets: 2nd Tuesday 7 p.m.
  at Great Falls Senior Citizens Center, 1004 Central Ave.
Bitter Root Quilters Guild, P.O. Box 943, Hamilton, 59840
  Meets: 4th Wednesday 7 p.m. at Daly Elem. School
Big Horn Quilters, Rt. #1, Box 1238, Hardin, 59034
  Meets: 2nd Tuesday 7 p.m. at E&R Church, 703 N. Cheyenne
Undercover Gals Quilt Guild P.O. Box 508, Hardin, 59034
  Meets: 4th Thursday 7 p.m. at Hotel Becker
Hi-Line Quilt Guild, 67 Saddle Butte Dr., Havre, 59501
  Meets: 1st Wednesday 7 p.m. at Hill County Electric Coop
Helena Quilter's Guild, P.O. Box 429, Helena, 59624
  Meets: 2nd Tuesday 7:15 p.m.
  at Evangelical Covenant Church on Hoback
Flathead Quilters Guild, P.O. Box 9845, Kalispell, 59903
  Meets: 1st Thursday 7:30 p.m. at the Quilt Gallery
Central Montana Fiber Art Guild, Lewiston
Kootenai Valley Quilters, P.O. Box 490, Libby, 59923
  Meets: 2nd Monday 7:30 p.m. at Methodist Church
Hands All Around Quilters, P.O. Box 697, Malta, 59538
  Meets: 2nd Tuesday except Aug.
Peace Quilt Guild, 2136 Collins Ln., Missoula, 59802
Missoula Quilt Guild, P.O. Box 325, Missoula, 59802
  Meets: 2nd Wednesday 7 p.m. at Country Friends Quilt Shop
Plains Piecers, 1010 River Rd., Plains, 59859
Mission Mountain Quilters, 4185 Cheff Ln., Ronan, 59864
  Meets: 1st Tuesday 7 p.m. at Ronan High School, Home Ec Room
Cross Country Piecemakers, 137 Main St. Roundup, 59072
  Meets: 2nd Saturday at Scrap Happy
Seeley Lake Quilt Guild, P.O. Box 205, Seeley Lake, 59868
  Meets: 4th Thursday 7:30 p.m. at Deer Country Quilts
Triangle Squares Quild Guild, 124 6th Ave. S, Shelby, 59474
Sapphire Quilters, 317 Main St., Stevensville, 59870
Flat Iron Quilting Guild, P.O. Box 925, Thompson Falls, 59873
  Meets: 1st Monday 7 p.m. alternating between
  Thompson Falls & Trout Creek
Quack-N-Quilters, 63 Manor Dr., Townsend, 59644
  Meets: 2nd Thursday 7 p.m. at Elementary School
Tender Loving Quilters, 205 S. 6th, Troy, 59935
Stumptown Quilter's Society, P.O. Box 186, Whitefish, 59937
  Meets: 2nd Sat 11 a.m. at Community room North Valley Hospital

Other Shops in Montana:

Anaconda	Quilter's Rose, 401 E. Commercial	406-563-6997
Billings	Pin Cushion, 2646 Grand Ave. #9	406-652-6328
Bozeman	Silver Thimble, 11 E. Main St.	406-587-0531
Broadus	Fabric to Fashion, 106 Crane Ave.	406-436-2963
Circle	Circle of Threads, 117 W. Main St.	406-485-3332
Deer Lodge	Quilts & Stuff, 507 Main St.	406-846-3637
Dillon	Crafty Quilter, 104 N. Montana St.	406-683-5884
Helena	Fabric Garden, 101 Reeder's Alley	
Helena	Country Loft, 2893 Flamingo Rd.	
Laurel	Ben Franklin Store, 13 Colorado Ave.	406-628-7124
Lewistown	Megahertz, 223 W. Main St.	406-538-8531
Lewistown	Fabric Connections, 321 W. Main St.	406-538-2847
Libby	Quilters' Cottage, 910 Main St.	406-293-6306
Miles City	Copper Thimble, R.R. #1, Box 2216	406-232-7226
Polson	Two Bobbins Full, 323 Main St.	406-883-3643
Rexford	Ruby's Quilt & Gift Shop, 5050 W. Kootenai	None
Ronan	Ribbons, Star & Wing, 1319 U.S. Hwy 93 S	406-676-8265
Scobey	Bev's Sewing Center, 123 Main St.	406-487-2841
Seeley Lake	Quilts & Cloth, Tall Timber Mall	406-677-2730
Shelby	Quilt With Class, 860 Oilfield Ave.	406-434-5801
Stevensville	Seams Beautiful, 317 Main St.	406-777-0016
Twin Bridges	Mary R. Originals, 204 South Main	406-684-5878

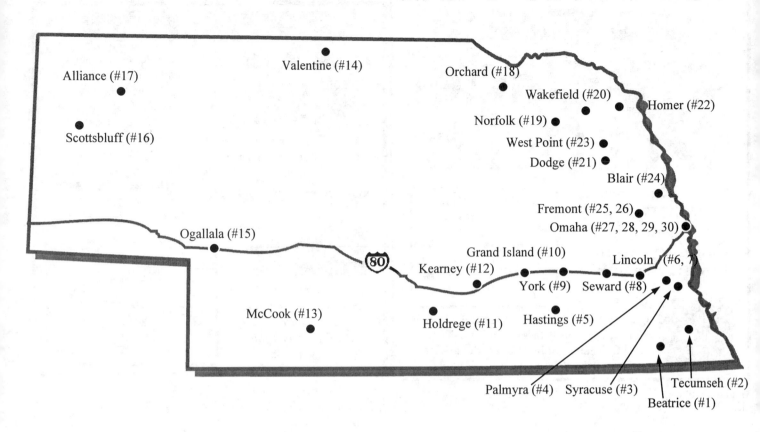

Valentine (#14)
Alliance (#17)
Orchard (#18)
Wakefield (#20)
Homer (#22)
Norfolk (#19)
Scottsbluff (#16)
West Point (#23)
Dodge (#21)
Blair (#24)
Fremont (#25, 26)
Omaha (#27, 28, 29, 30)
Ogallala (#15)
Grand Island (#10)
Lincoln (#6, 7)
80
Kearney (#12)
York (#9)
Seward (#8)
McCook (#13)
Holdrege (#11)
Hastings (#5)
Palmyra (#4)
Syracuse (#3)
Tecumseh (#2)
Beatrice (#1)

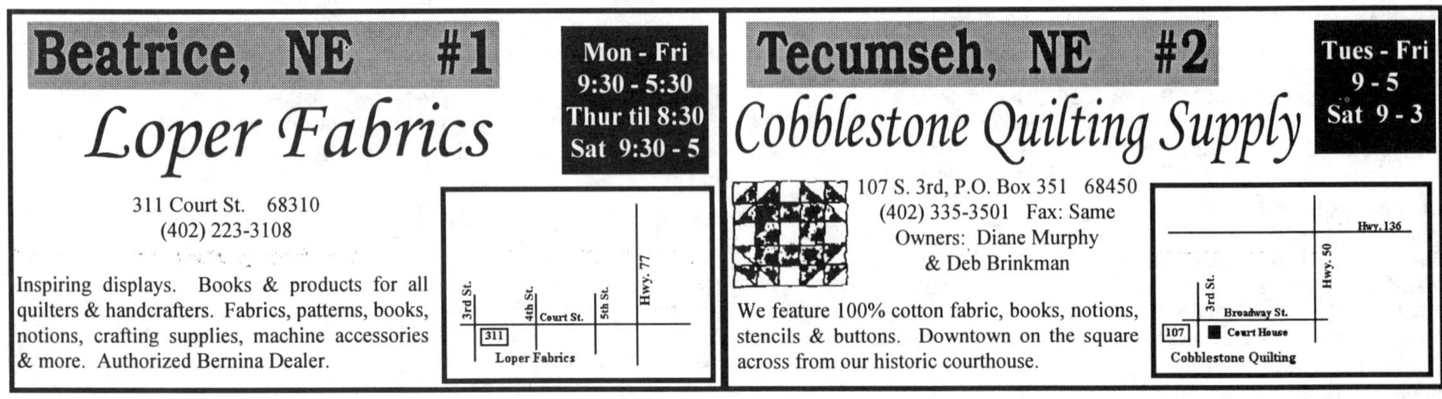

Syracuse, NE #3

COMMON THREADS

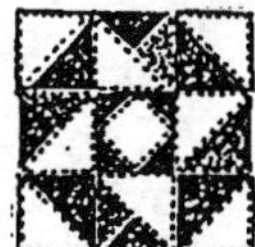

325 5th St. 68446
(402) 269-2235
Owners: Julie & David Zahn
Est: 1997 1800 sq.ft.
800 Bolts

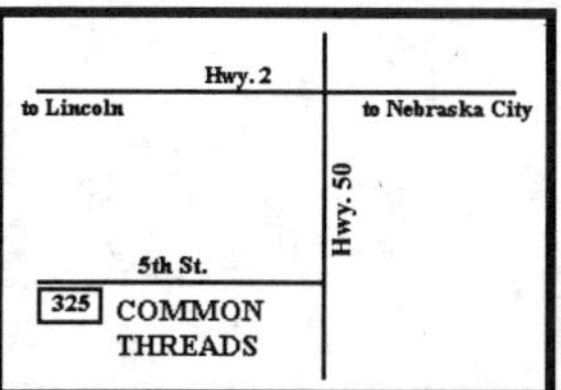

Nice selection of 100% Cotton fabrics, books, patterns & gifts.
Located in a restored 1890's Bank Building!

Palmyra, NE #4

Owner:
Gloria Hall
Est: 1989
600 sq.ft.
Price List Avail.
(800) 284-8574

By Appt.

R. R. #1 Box 255B 68418
(402) 780-5773

We have over 100 quilts dating from 1870's to 1960's Vintage Fabric, Tops, Blocks, Feed Sacks & Old Linens.

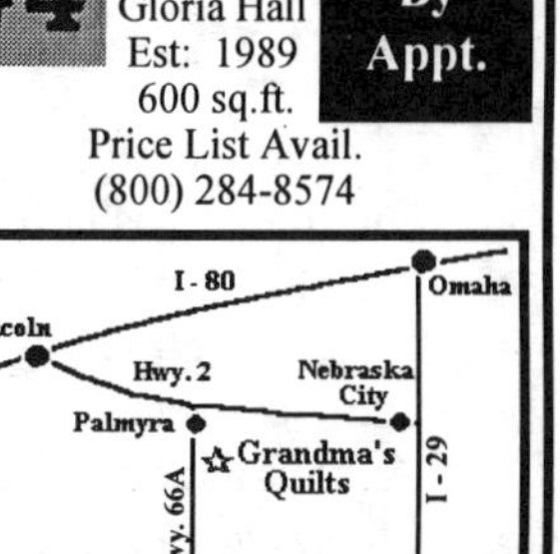

E-Mail: grandma@grandma'squilts.com
Web Site: www.grandmasquilts.com

Hastings, NE #5

**Mon - Fri 10 - 5:30
Sat 10 - 3**

Calico Cottage

306 N. Lincoln 68901
(402) 463-6767
Everything for the Quilter ! !

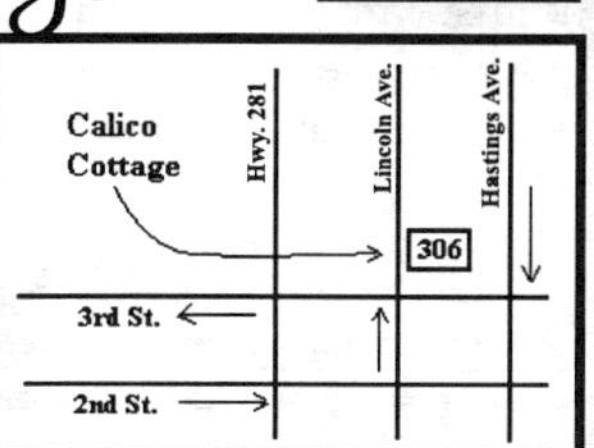

Over 1000 bolts Cotton Fabric. Quilting Notions, Books, Patterns, Classes. Authorized Bernina Dealer.

Lincoln, NE #6

**Mon - Sat 10 - 5
Sun 10 - 4**

The Calico House

5221 S. 48th 68516
In Sutter Place Mall
(402) 489-1067
Est: 1974 2300 sq. ft. 1500 Bolts

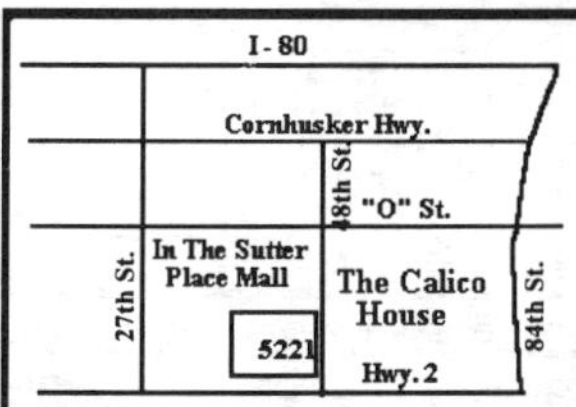

Friendly, Experienced Staff. We love plaids & flannels. Always the Latest Fabrics and the Greatest Patterns.

The Front Parlor

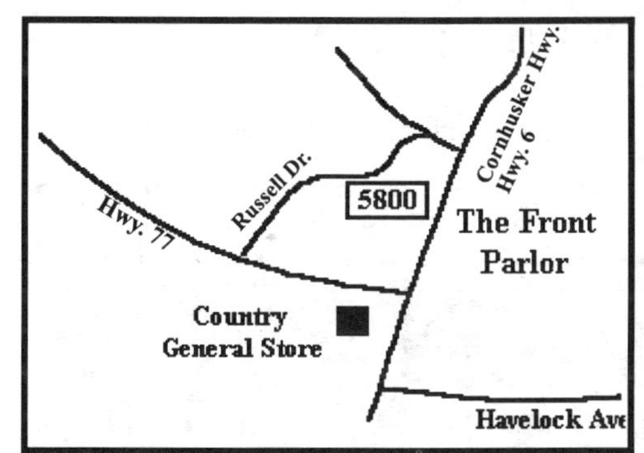

Lincoln's Newest Quilting Source

**at The Mercantile Shopping Center
5800 Cornhuster Hwy. #4
68507
(402) 466-7744
Fax: (402) 466-1513**

Unique 100% cotton fabric selection, Quilting Frames, Classes, Books, Patterns, & Notions. People Oriented

**Mon - Fri 12: 30 - 5
Wed til 7
Sat 10 - 5 Sun 1 - 4**

Lincoln, NE #7

One of Nebraska's most Complete Sewing Centers!

- Full line of Fashion & Quilt Patterns
- Pfaff Sewing Machines & Sergers
- Large Selection of Quilt Fabrics & Books
- Supplies: Templates, Frames, Needles, Etc.
- Fashion Fabric & Bridal Specialties
- Classes in Clothing Construction & Quilt Making

636 Seward St. 68434 Owner: Marian Fosler Est: 1970
Hrs: Mon -Sat 9 - 5:30 Thurs til 9 Sun 1 - 4

Seward, NE #8

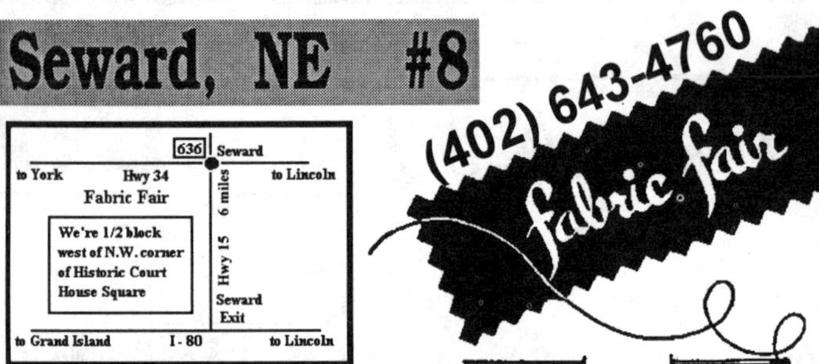

York, NE #9

BERNINA Sewing Center

Countryside Fabrics

718 Lincoln Ave. 68467
(402) 362-5737
e-mail: cf10637@navix.net
Owners: Ed & Lola Schall
Est: 1970 4000 sq.ft.

- Over 2000 Bolts of Quilting Fabric
- Quilters Supplies & Notions
- Fashion Fabrics
- Bridal & Special Occasion Fabrics
- Books & Patterns
- Bernina Sewing Machines, Sergers & Deco Embroidery Machines
- Special Interest Programs
- Free Newsletter Upon Request
- Mail Order Service
- Visa/Master & Bernina Cards Accpt.

Countryside Fabrics 718 — 8th St. — 7th St. — 3rd St. — Lincoln — Grant — Hwy. 81 — Beaver Creek — to I - 80

Mon - Fri 9:30 - 5:30
Thur til 9 Sat 9:30 - 5

York's One-Stop Fabric Center

Grand Island, NE #10

205 N. Locust St.
68801

Mon - Fri 10 - 5:30
Sat 10 - 4

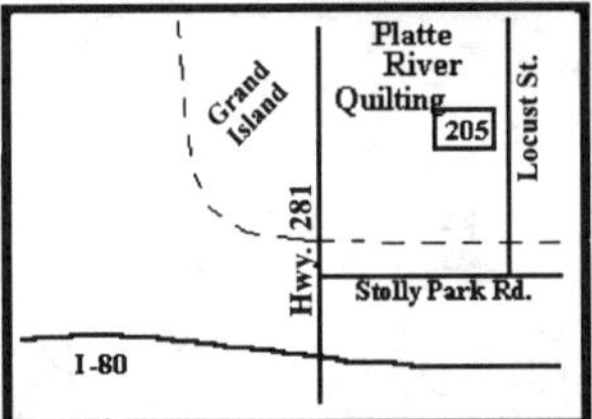

(308) 382-5535 Est: 1978
Machine Quilting Over 1000 Bolts

Quilting Supplies Bear Making Supplies
Primitive Rug Hooking Supplies.

Holdrege, NE #11

323 West Ave. 68949
(308) 995-2728
Owner: Janet Kugler
Est: 1991 1400 sq.ft.

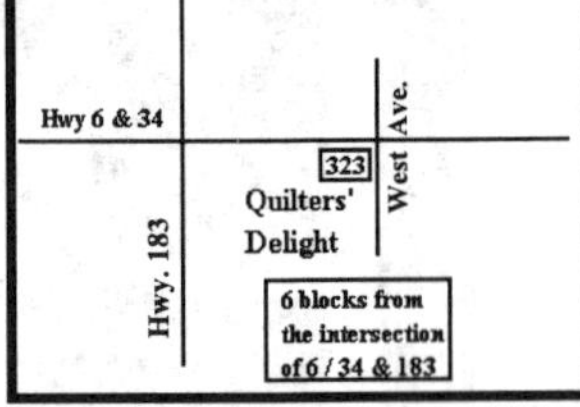

Over 2500 bolts of 100% Cotton fabric. Plus everything you need to finish your project: Books, Patterns, Notions. Also some novelty items.

Mon - Fri 9:30 - 5:30
Thurs til 8 Sat 9:30 - 5

Kearney, NE #12

Quilter's Trunk

Mon - Fri 9:30 - 5:30
Thur til 7
Sat 10 - 4

2114 Central Ave. 68847
(308) 236-6286
Fax: (308) 236-6156

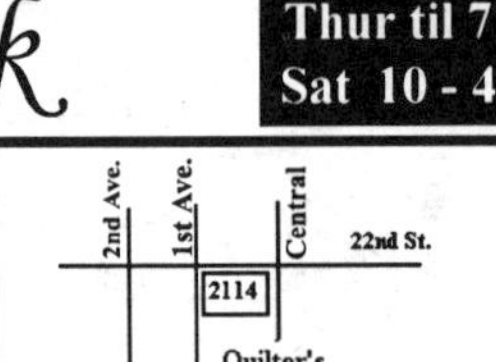

100% Cotton Fabrics — Quilting Supplies
Bernina Sewing Machines and Service.

McCook, NE #13

McCook's Fabrics and Crafts

Mon - Sat 9 - 5:30
Thur til 8
Sun 1 - 5

206 Norris Ave. 69001
(308) 345-1132 Fax: (308) 345-1434
Est: 1981 5500 sq.ft. 1750 Bolts

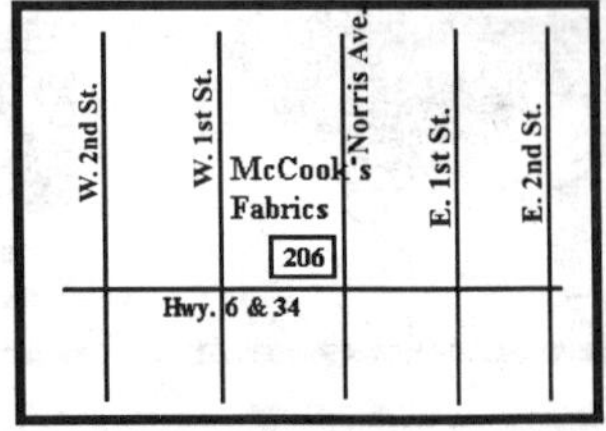

Quilting books, notions, patterns, leading brands of 100% cotton quilt fabrics, holiday fabrics year round and large selection of craft supplies.

Valentine, NE #14

Mon - Sat 9 - 6

The Gallery

226 N. Main St. 69201
(402) 376-3834
Owner: Mary Mulligan
Est: 1988 2600 sq.ft. 1500+ Bolts

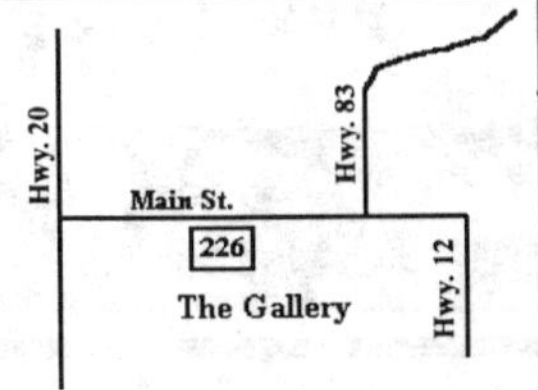

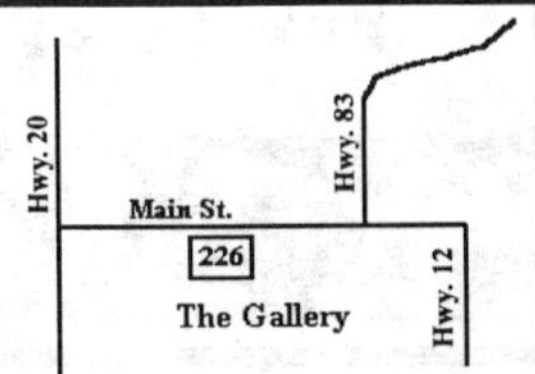

A Little Quilt Shop with Much More!
Two Floors of Gifts, Fabrics, and Quilt Supplies. Free Newsletter

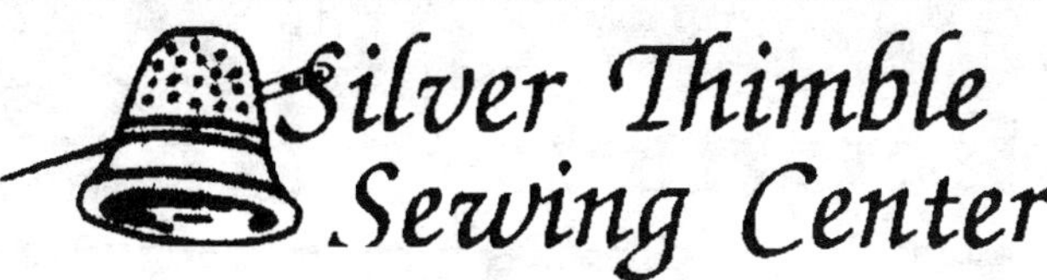

108 N. Spruce 69153
(308) 284-6838 Fax: Same
Owner: Julie Peterson
Est: 1988 2500 sq.ft.

Show us this ad and Receive a Free Gift.

Mon - Sat
9 - 5:30
Thur til 8

Ogallala, NE #15

2300+ Bolts of Cottons, Quilt Fabrics and Supplies. Books, Notions, Batting, Classes.
Elna & Pfaff Machine Sales and Service.
Full line fabric store.

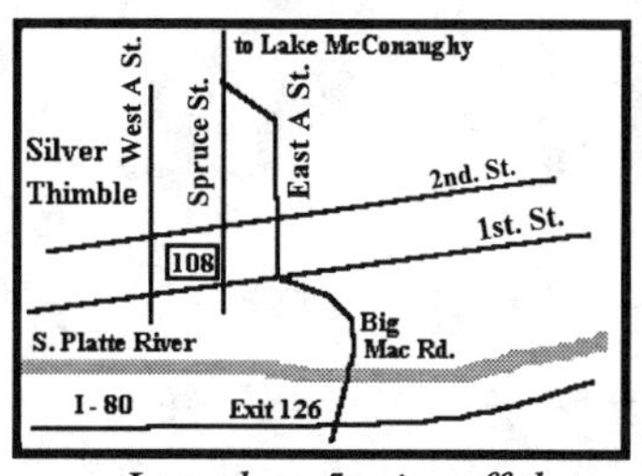

Less than 5 min. off the Interstate.

Scottsbluff, NE #16

Prairie Pines Quilt Shop

Mon 10 - 8
Tues - Sat
10 - 5

70756 County Rd. 20 69361
(308) 632-8668

Supplies and classes for Quilting and Cross-Stitch.
Including1500 bolts of 100% cotton fabrics.
Locally made gift items.

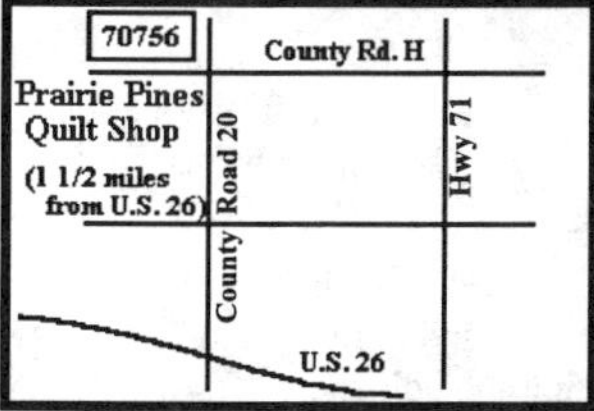

Alliance, NE #17

Mon - Sat
9 - 5:30

Special Stitches

402 Box Butte Ave. 69301
(308) 762-3784
Owner: Deb Thiems
Est: 1987

Quilting Supplies, Counted Cross Stitch, Machine Quilting, Viking Sewing Machines & Sergers.

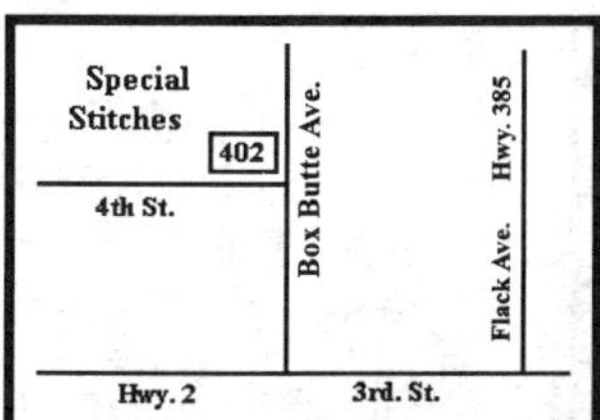

Orchard, NE #18

Mon - Sat
10 - 5

Cornerstone Quilts

410 N. Harrison St. 68764
(402) 893-2022
Owners: Jennifer Trease & Flicsha Allen

Fabric, quilting supplies, machine quilting, custom made quilts and classes.

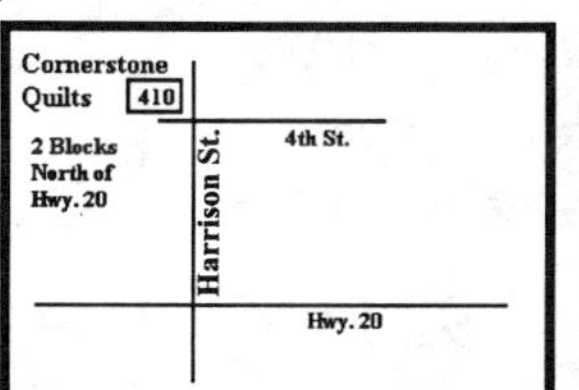

Norfolk, NE #19

Mon - Sat
9:30 - 5:30
Thur til 8

Golden Needle

509 Norfolk Ave. 68701
(402) 371-9641
Owner: Bev Dederman

Over 1500 bolts of quality 100% cotton quilt fabrics, books, patterns. Authorized Pfaff dealer. Soft sculpture, cross-stitch & custom framing.

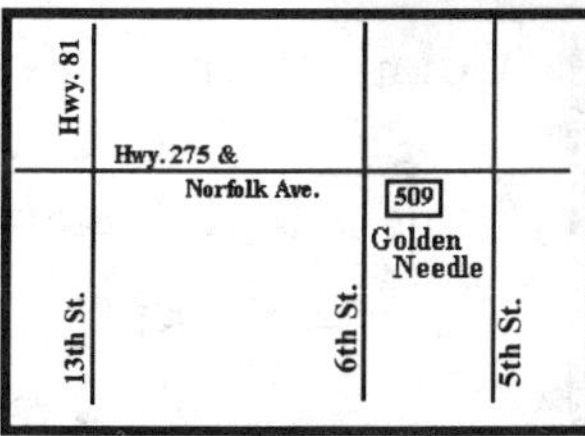

Wakefield, NE #20

Mon - Sat
9 - 5

The Quilt Shop

301 Main St., P.O. Box 88 68787
(402) 287-2325 Fax: (402) 287-2045
E-Mail: quiltshop@thenetpages.com
Web Site: www.thenetpages.com/quiltshop/

Custom & Ready made quilts - Block of the Month - Lessons - Fabric - Books - Notions. Machine & hand Quilting - machine embroidery

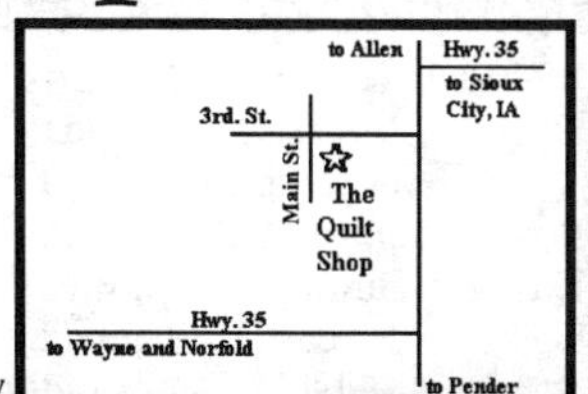

Homer, NE #22

Wed - Sat
10 - 5

A Wish & A Prayer

102 S. First St., P.O. Box 453 68030
(402) 698-2221 Fax: (402) 698-2337
E-Mail: brblia@pionet.net Est: 1994
Owners: Barb Lauritsen & Jody Rohde

"By the hand & from the heart"
Quality 100% cotton fabrics, kits, B.O.M.'s
Personal, knowledgeable, friendly service our specialty.

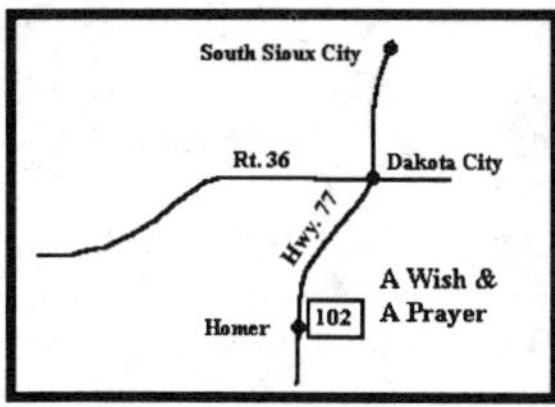

Selected by Better Homes & Gardens American Patchwork & Quilting as one of the Top Ten Quilt Shops in North America for 1997.

Dodge, NE #21

VOGIES Quilts & Treasures

Mon - Sat
9 - 5:30

Over 2500 bolts of quilting fabrics. Hundreds of Books, Patterns, and samples on display.
Also—Unique Giftware & Jewelry.
Mail Orders Welcome. Now accepting Visa & Mastercard.

153 Oak St., P.O. Box 367
Dodge, NE 68633
(402) 693-2230
Owner: Dave & June Vogltance

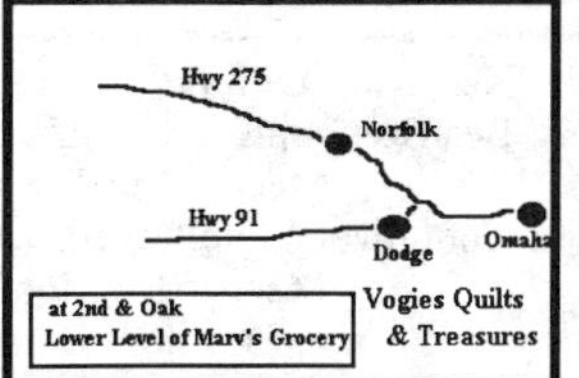

West Point, NE #23

Mon - Fri 9 - 12 & 1:30 - 5
Sat 9 - 12
or by Appt.

Creative Notions

107 N. Main St. 68788
(402) 372-2004
Owner: Deb Busch Est: 1996

Nice selection of quality 100% cotton fabrics, sewing and quilting notions, books and patterns. (quilting, doll and craft)

Blair, NE #24

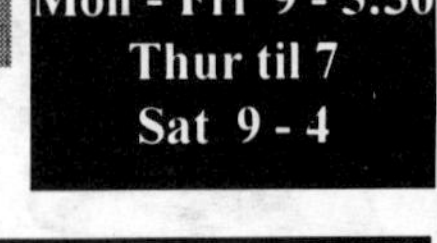

Topstitch

1646 Washington St.
68008
(402) 426-4650
Owner: Carleen Andersen

elna

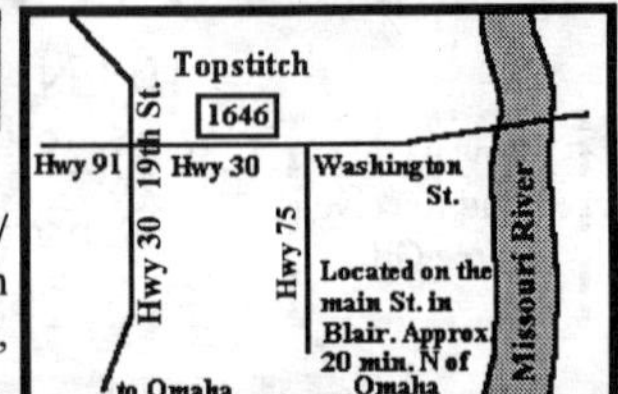

Over 1500 bolts of quality cottons including RJR / Jinny Beyer, P&B, Hoffman, Red Wagon & South Seas. Excellent selection of books, notions, patterns, & gifts. Authorized Elna Sales & Service.

Suz's Fabric Art

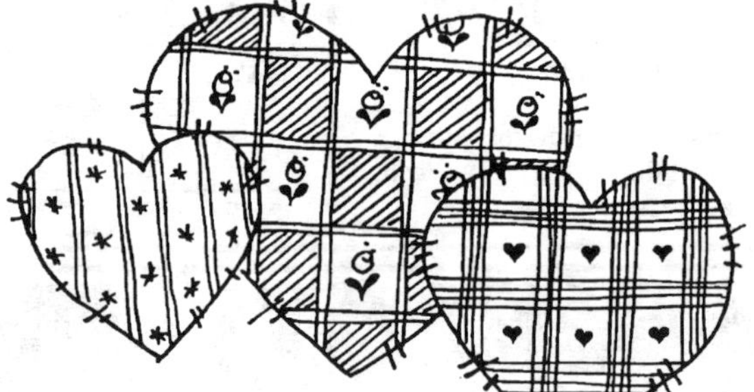

QUILTING FABRICS

Your one stop shop for all your quilting fabrics, quality quilting & sewing notions.

Professional Custom Machine Quilting

Specializing in quilting to the design of your quilt. (handguided quilting machine)

AUTHORIZED BERNINA DEALER

Complete line of Fons & Porter, Hoffmans, Marcus Bros. Civil War Prints, Aunt Gracie and over 65 Moda Marble Colors. Great Flannels, Red Wagon Mission Valley Plaids & Indigo, Debbie Mumm.

2625 N. Broad St. 68025 (402) 727-9233
Owner: Suzanne Caruso

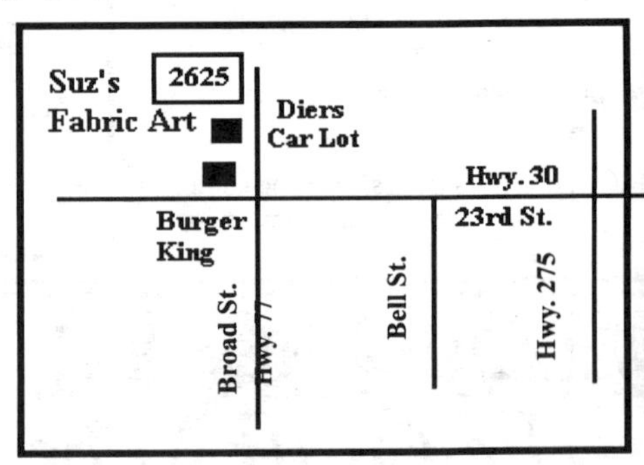

Fremont, NE #25

Monday - Friday 10 - 6, Saturday 10 - 5

Fremont, NE #26

Tues - Sat 10 - 5:30

Country Traditions

413 N. Main 68025 (402) 721-7752

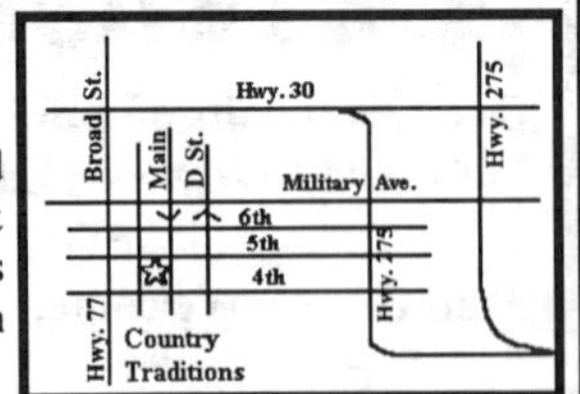

Come Visit Our Wide Selection of: Country and Reproduction Fabrics, Quilting Supplies & Classes. Folk Art Craft Patterns and Books Consignment Crafts, Gifts & Collectibles. All in a setting of a wonderful Historic Brick Bldg.

Nebraska Guilds:

Beatrice Quilters' Guild, Beatrice
Meets: 2nd Tuesday 10:30 a.m.
Cottonwood Quilters, P.O. Box 27, Elkhorn, 68022
Meets: 3rd Monday
at St. John's Lutheran Church, Bennington
Prairie Piecemakers, P.O. Box 1202, Fremont, 68025
Meets: last Monday 7:30 pm
at Good Shepherd Church, 1544 E. Military
Prairie Pioneer Quilters, P.O. Box 675, Grand Island, 68802
Hastings Quilters Guild, P.O. Box 442, Hastings, 68901
Meets: 1st Thursday 7 p.m.
at 1st St. Paul's Lutheran Church Basement
Lincoln Quilters Guild, P.O. Box 6861, Lincoln, 68506
Meets: 2nd Monday 7 p.m. at 7th Day Adventist Church
Nebraska State Quilt Guild, 6325 Tanglewood Ln., Lincoln, 68516
Heritage Quilt & Needlework Guild, 315 S. 16th, Nebraska City, 68410
Meets: 4th Tuesday at 7 p.m.
Country Piecemakers Quilt Guild, 509 Norfolk Ave., Norfolk
Meets 3rd Monday (except Dec.) 7:30 p.m.
at Norfolk Senior Center, 307 Prospect St.
Quilt Heritage Foundation--Quilt Rescue Squad & Crazy Quilt Society & Conference & Quilt Restoration Society & Conference,
P.O. Box 19452, Omaha, 68119 Fax: 800-811-1610
Omaha Quilters Guild, 108th and Grover, Omaha
Meets: 2nd Tuesday (Sept - May) at Westside Comm. Center
Blue Valley Quilters, 636 Seward St., Seward, 68434

Omaha, NE #27

Tues - Sat 10 - 5 or by Appt.

The Kirk Collection & 1860 Dry Goods

1513 Military Ave. 68111
(800) 398-2542 (402) 551-0386
E-Mail: Kirkcoll@aol.com
Web Site: www.kirkcollection.com
Owners: Nancy & Bill Kirk
Est: 1986 3000 sq.ft. Free Catalog

Antique fabric & Antique quilts, the real thing and reproductions. Quilting cottons, crazy quilt fabrics, antique lace, trim & buttons

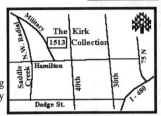

Military
N.W. Radial
The Kirk Collection
1513
75 N
Hamilton
Saddle Creek
40th
30th
I - 480
Dodge St.

Omaha, NE #28

David M. **Mangelsen's**®

3457 S. 84th St. 68124
Westgate Plaza
(402) 391-6225
Fax: (402) 391-4659
Est: 1961 33,000 sq.ft.

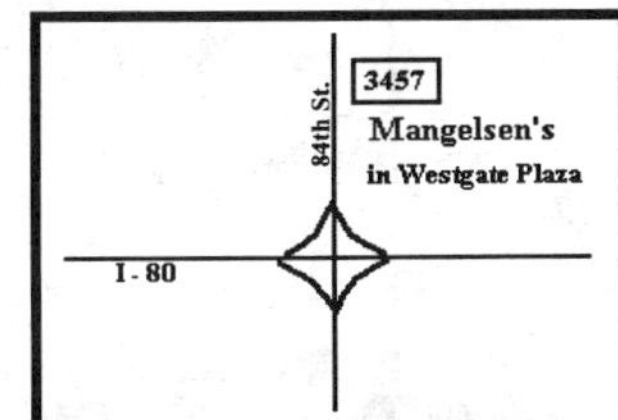

Mon - Sat 9 - 9 Sun 12 - 5

The store where you shop for FUN !

A Quilter's dream.

Fabric, Patterns, Books, Notions, Crafts, Floral, Party Goods and More !

Omaha, NE #29

Mon - Sat 9:30 - 5:30 Thur til 8

Log Cabin Quilt Shop

2809 South 125 Avenue #283 68144
In Westwood Plaza
(402) 333-5212
Est: 1980 1700 sq.ft.

Complete line of books, patterns, fabrics, and notions for quilters.
Service with a smile !

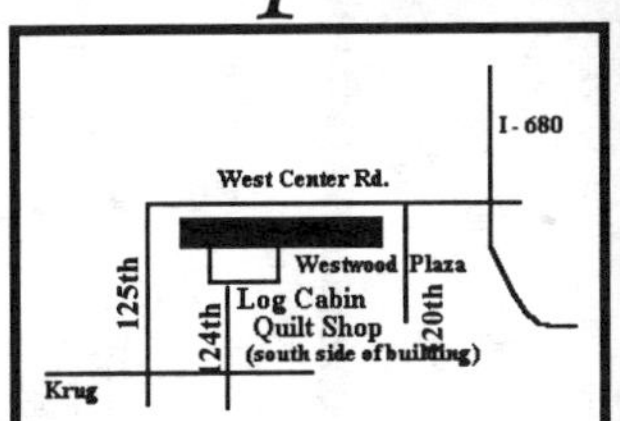

Omaha, NE #30

Open 7 days a Week Call for Hours.

Country Sampler

2516 S. 132nd Ct. 68144
(402) 333-6131
Owner: Deb Cizek
Est: 1990 3400 sq.ft. 1000+ Bolts

NE's largest selection of patterns. We specialize in homespuns & that "country look". A quilt and country store in one!

2516
Country Sampler
132nd. Ct.
Tony Roma's
132nd. St.
Center

Other Shops in Nebraska:

Heming Ford	Pat's Creative Stitchery, RR #1 Box 47	308-487-3999
Kearney	Craft-o-Rama, P.O. Box 63	308-236-8973
Lexington	Creative Fabrics, 512 N. Washington	308-324-3197
Lincoln	Creative Hands, 5220 S. 48th St. Bldg. 4	402-483-1538
Omaha	Bernina Sewing Centers, 3407 S. 84th St.	402-392-0430
Omaha	Mayfair Textiles, Inc, 1123 Howard St.	402-346-5388
Omaha	Patty Kennedy 5807 Poppleton	402-553-6954
Omaha	Country Corner 6621 Railroad Ave.	402-731-8707
Omaha	Quilting B's, 8323 Chicago St.	402-392-1084
Omaha	Quilting B's, 6342 Lafayette	402-551-9181
Papillion	Quilt Boutique, 546 N. Washington St.	402-339-6984
Red Cloud	Sewing Box, 422 N. Webster St.	402-746-3592

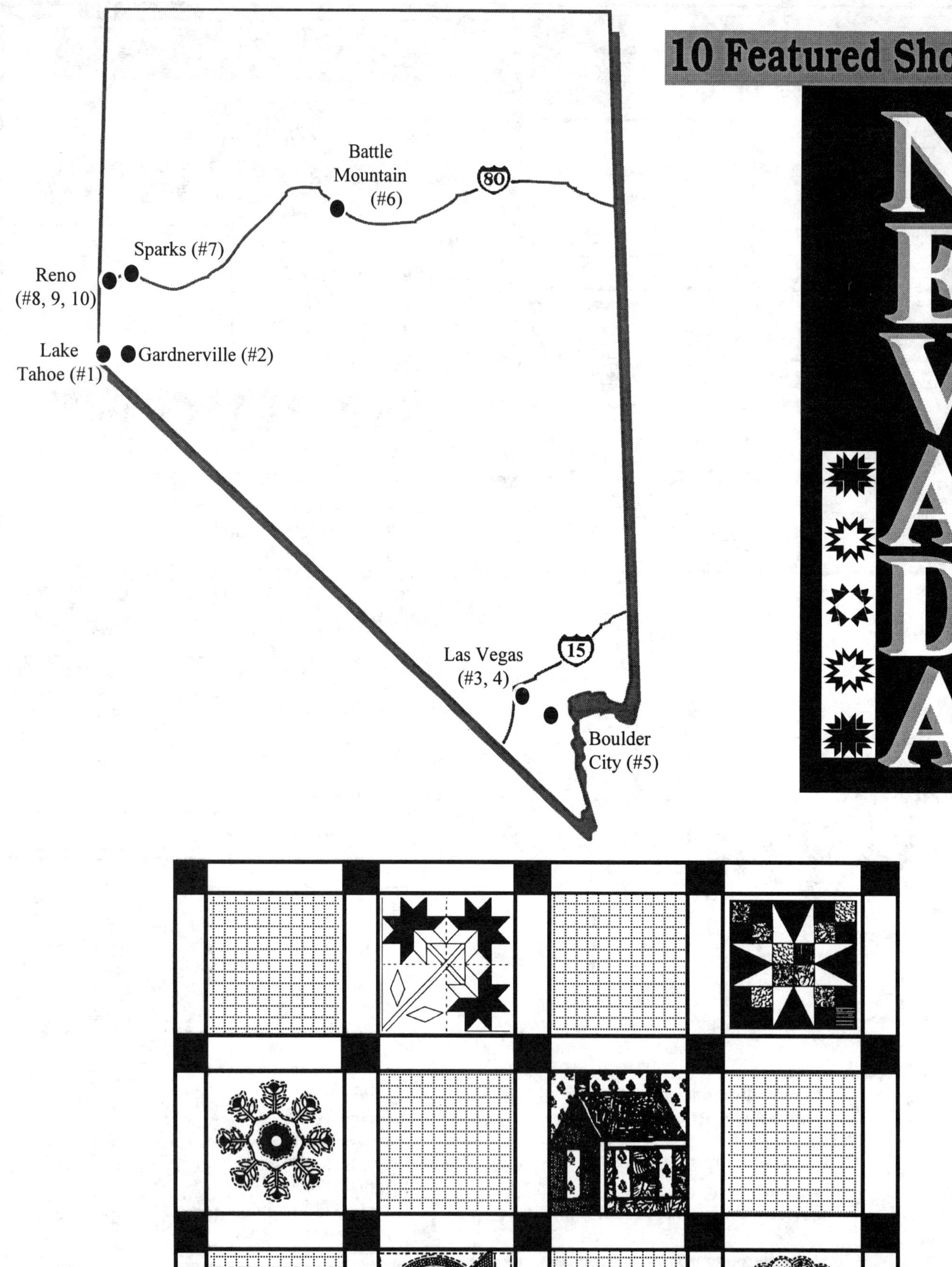
10 Featured Shops
NEVADA
Battle
Mountain
(#6)
80
Sparks (#7)
Reno
(#8, 9, 10)
Lake
Tahoe (#1)
Gardnerville (#2)
Las Vegas
(#3, 4)
15
Boulder
City (#5)

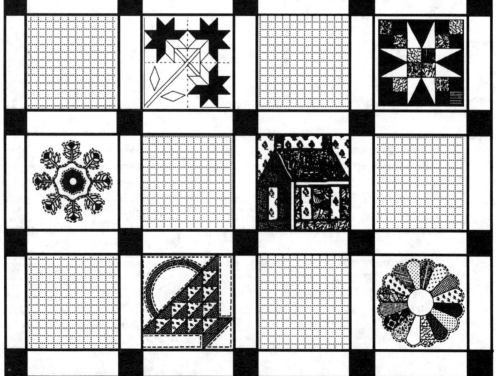

Lake Tahoe, NV #1

Near "Zephyr Cove"

ANTIQUE JUNCTION

EVERYTHING BUT ANTIQUES

1000+ Bolts — 100% Cotton Quilting Fabrics,
Books, Accessories, Notions, Patterns,
Knitting Yarns, Needlework Books and Supplies.

Animal Feed, Pet Supplies
A Dog & Cat Boarding Kennel

We are located in a resort area 2 miles from gaming casinos. Very friendly family operated store. Very knowledgeable.

Mon - Sat 9 - 5:30
Sun 10 - 4

396 Dorla Ct.,
P.O. Box 10548 89448
Web Site: www.tohoemall.com/aj/
(702) 588-3907 Fax: Same
Est: 1978 4000 sq.ft.

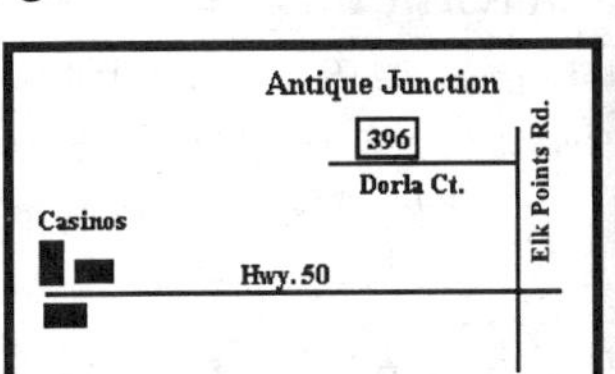

Gardnerville, NV #2

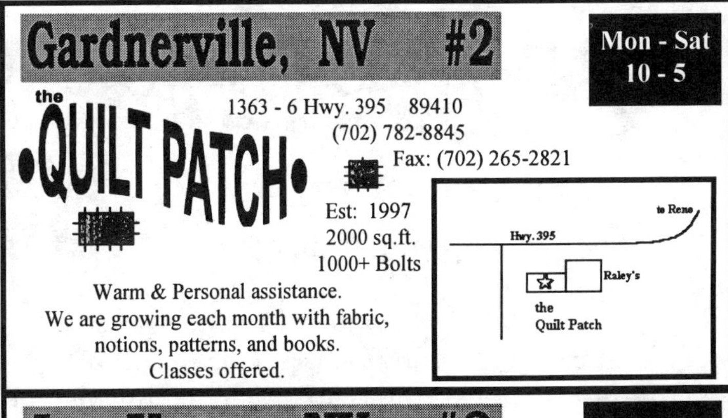

Mon - Sat 10 - 5

1363 - 6 Hwy. 395 89410
(702) 782-8845
Fax: (702) 265-2821

Est: 1997
2000 sq.ft.
1000+ Bolts

Warm & Personal assistance.
We are growing each month with fabric, notions, patterns, and books.
Classes offered.

Las Vegas, NV #3

Mon - Thur 10 - 7:30
Fri & Sat 10 - 5:30
Sun 12 - 5

4700 S. Maryland
Pkwy. #6 89119
(702) 471-7133

Close to the Strip and Quilter Friendly.
Patterns, Fabric, Books and Notions.
Drop in Quilters Welcome.
Come Sew!

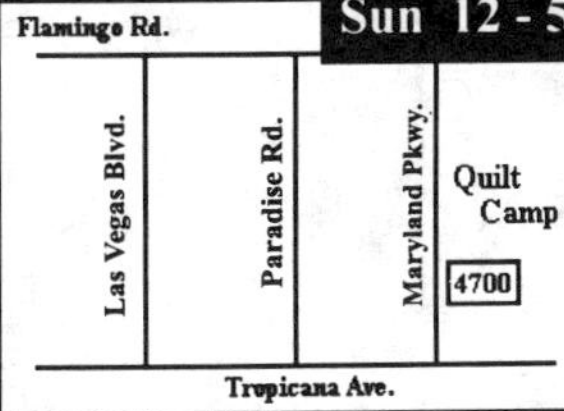

FABRIC BOUTIQUE QUILT SHOP

4465 W. Charleston, Las Vegas, NV. 89102

"One of the largest quilt shops in the country"

In Las Vegas we like to do things in a big way. So we have one of the largest quilt shops in the country. Visit us and see. You won't be disappointed. You'll find:

- 7000 BOLTS OF QUILTING COTTONS
- OVER 1200 BOOK TITLES
- HUGE SELECTION OF CRAFT PATTERNS
- CLASSES
- BLOCK OF THE MONTH PROGRAM
- PFAFF SEWING MACHINES

Owner: Darleen Ros
Est: 1982 - 11,000 sq.ft.

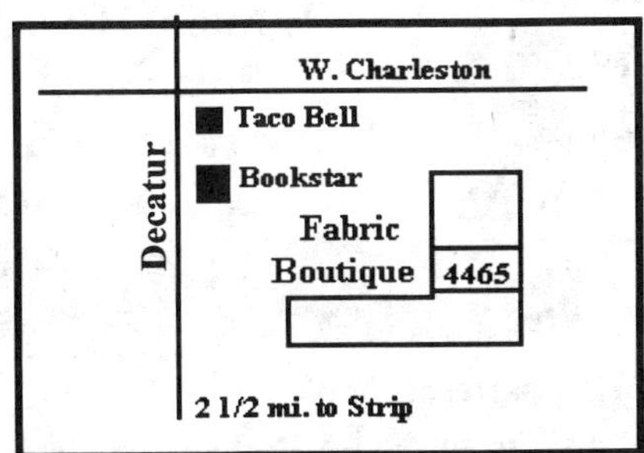

Phone: (702) 878-0068
Fax: (702)878-9004

#4

Hours: Mon to Fri 9:30-5:30, Sat 10-5, Sun 12-5

(702) 293-2979
Owner: Nanci Bowen

Tues - Sat
10 - 5:30

Periwinkle Cottage
Treasures for the Heart & Home

Owner: Jodi Kincaid
(702) 293-5767

Located in Historic Old Town... come visit a gentler time and treat your senses to beautiful music, the aromas of grandma's house and creativity to delight the eye. The shoppe is bursting with treasures new and old. We have a unique selection of quilt fabrics, books and notions. All are carefully chosen with our customers in mind... reminiscent of an old-fashioned mercantile.

You'll find romantic gifts, candles, birdhouses, body products, gourmet goodies and one of a kind treasures made by local craftspeople.

More than just a fabric store, we specialize in new ideas and personal customer service. Come pay us a visit... the tea kettle is always on.

to Las Vegas
Hwy. 95
to Lake Mead
Buchanan
1229
fiddlesticks
Arizona St.

1229 Arizona St. 89005

Boulder City, NV #5

2 Great Shops in One!!

Nevada Guilds:

Carson Valley Quilt Guild, 1417 Bumble Bee Dr.
Gardnerville, 89410

Desert Quilters of Nevada, P.O. Box 28586
Las Vegas, 89126

Truckee Meadows Quilters, P.O. Box 5502, Reno, 89513
Meets: 1st & 3rd Friday 7 p.m.
and 2nd & 4th Friday 10 a.m.
at Silver Connection, 601 W. 1st St.

Other Shops in Nevada:

Carson City	Quilts Country Charm, 3659 Green Acres Dr.	702-882-2745
Fallon	Workman's Farms Crafts & Nursery 4990 Reno Hwy.	702-867-3716

QUILTERS DON'T DO BUTTONS!

Sparks, NV #7

Mon - Sat
10 - 5

Quilt Stop

101 15th St. 89431
(702) 355-3233
Owner: Joan Carroll 1300+ Bolts

100% Cotton Fabric, Classes, Books, Patterns, Notions, Quilts on Display. Also mail order. Call for info.

Reno, NV #8

Mon - Fri 10 - 5:30
Sat 10 - 5
Sun Oct - Dec
11 - 4

Needle In A Haystack

970 W. 7th St. 89503
(702) 323-8587 Fax: (702) 323-8562
E-Mail: Mitzi@the-needle.com
Web Site: www.the-needle.com
Est: 1993 2200 sq.ft. 3000+ Bolts

Nestled in this old Victorian Home are bolts & bolts of fabric, surrounded by patterns and handcrafted gifts.

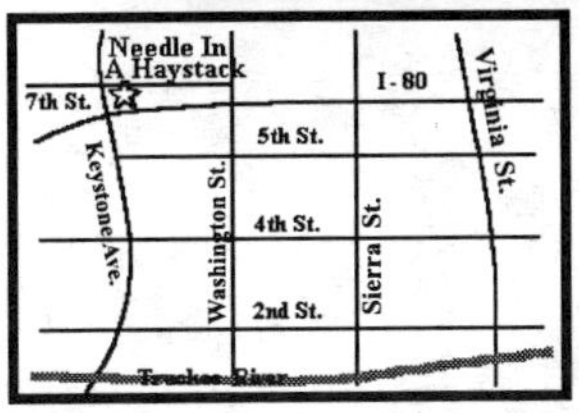

Reno, NV #9

Mon - Sat
9:30 - 5:30

Sierra Sewing

351 E. Plumb Ln. 89502
(702) 323-8555
Owners: Lae & Linda Levin

Great Quilt Fabrics and all the latest notions and Viking & Pfaff machines.

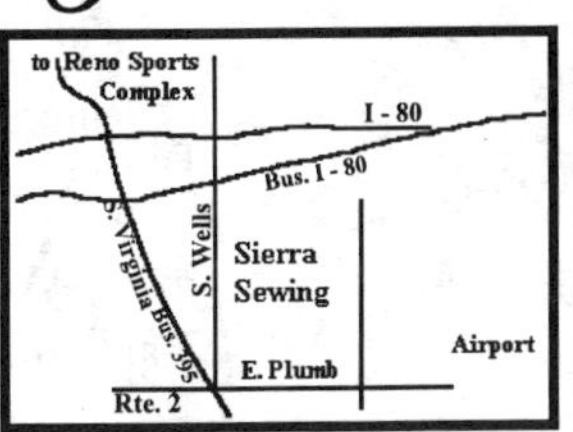

Reno, NV #10

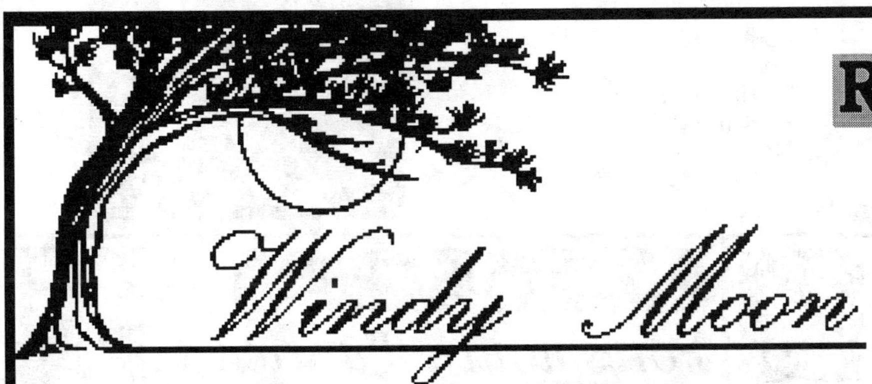

Windy Moon

- Fabrics
- Traditional
- Quilts
- Notions
- Classes
- Gifts

Biggest Little Quilt Shop in the West
Visit, Call, Fax or reach us on the web soon.
(702) 323-4777 or (800) 622-8082
Fax #: (702) 323-4790 or
Web Site: Coming Soon

Mon - Sat 10 - 6 Sun 11 - 5

The Corner of Wells Ave. & Kuenzli St. in the Historic Creamery Bldg. 4300 sq.ft. of fabric, notions, books, & patterns. All the Quilter Needs

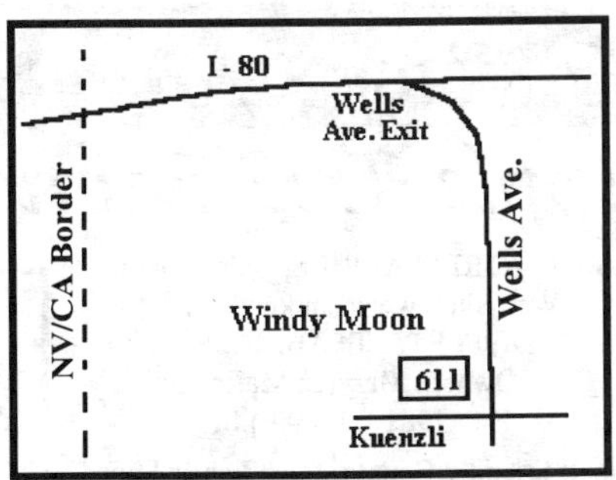

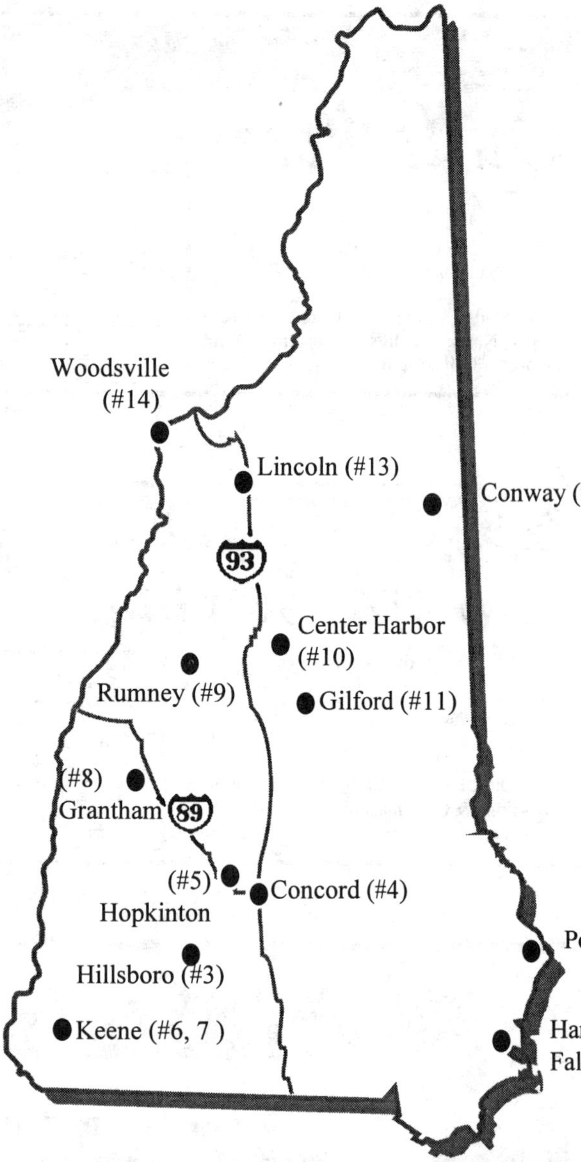

Woodsville (#14)
Lincoln (#13)
Conway (#12)
93
Center Harbor (#10)
Rumney (#9)
Gilford (#11)
(#8) Grantham
89
(#5) Hopkinton
Concord (#4)
Portsmouth (#2)
Hillsboro (#3)
Keene (#6, 7)
Hampton Falls (#1)

14 Featured Shops

Hampton Falls, NH #1

Mon - Sat 9:30 - 5
Thur til 8
Sun 1 - 5

The Silver Thimble Quilt Shop

Route 1 Shoppers Village 03844
(603) 926-3378
Owner: Patti Sanborn
Est: 1970 3000 sq.ft.

Oldest Quilt shop in New England! Over 1,500 bolts of 100% cotton Featuring Hoffman, Jinny Beyer, P&B, and more. Complete Quilt Shop!

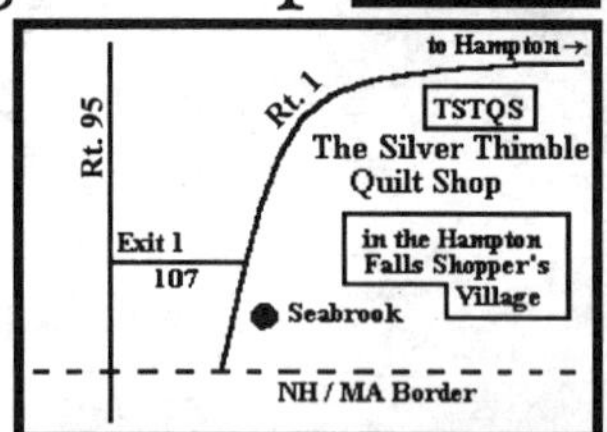

Portsmouth, NH #2

Mon - Sat 9:30 - 5:30
Summer
Sun 12 - 5

Portsmouth Fabric Co.

112 Penhallow St. 03801
(603) 436-6343 Fax: (603) 430-2943
E-Mail: berninabin@aol.com
Owner: Gretchen Rath
Est: 1979 1000 sq.ft.

We invite you to browse through our expanded collection of contemporary quilting cottons, fiber art and how-to books. Swiss Bernina Machines.

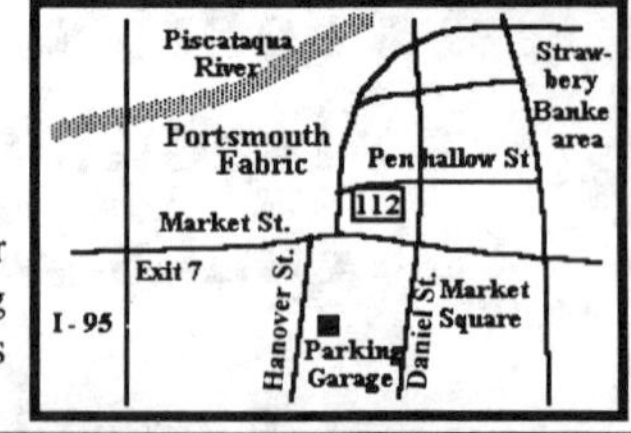

Hillsboro, NH #3

Mon - Sat 10 - 5

Apple Tree Fabrics

7 Old Drift Way 03244
(603) 478-5552

E-Mail: ATREEFABRICS@conknet.com
Web Site: www.conknet.com/APPLETREEFABRICS/
Owner: Marylyn Marin
Est: 1981 1000 sq.ft.

"Small Friendly Country town Fabric Shop" Quilting supplies, notions, fabrics, polartec, Woolfelts™, Books, Classes, Crafts, New Home

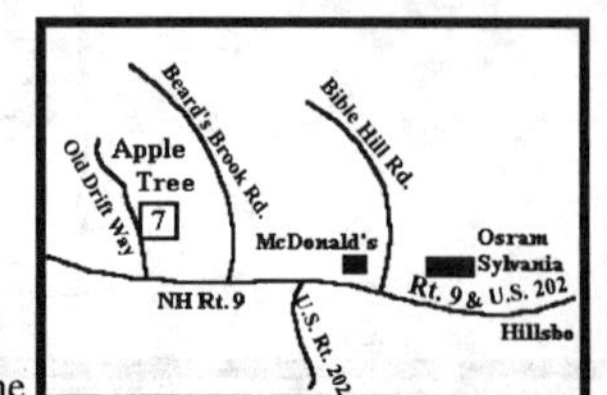

Concord, NH #4

Mon - Sat 10 - 5
June, July, Aug
Mon-Fri 10 - 5
Sat 10 - 1

Golden Gese Quilt Shop

28 South Main 03301
(603) 228-5540
Owner: Nancy Gesen
Est: 1987 1200 sq.ft. 2000 Bolts

100% Cotton Fabric, Books, Patterns, Notions & Classes. Helpful Assistance.

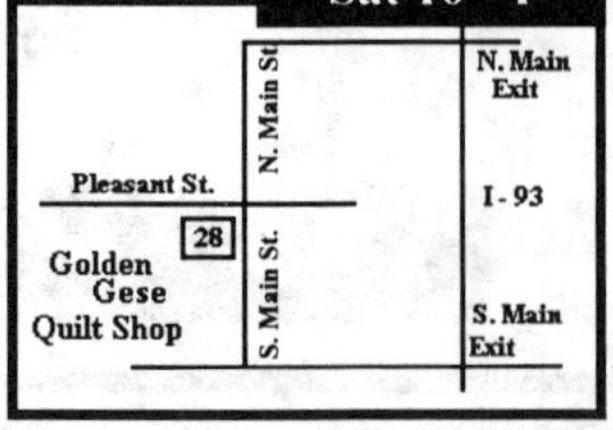

N. Main St
N. Main Exit
Pleasant St.
I - 93
28
Golden Gese Quilt Shop
S. Main St.
S. Main Exit

Hopkinton, NH #5

COUNTRY QUILTER

A Working Quilt & Gift Shop With A Homespun New England Charm

Tucked away on a scenic road in a 200-year old barn is the Country Quilter, considered by many to be one of the most unique country quilt and gift shops in New England. We offer a beautiful selection of quilts and quilt supplies, as well as hand quilted wall hangings, pillows, crib quilts, lap quilts and other carefully selected handcrafted gifts.

You will enjoy selecting fabrics from over **2,500** bolts of 100% cotton fabric (the largest inventory in the area) including Hoffman, R.J.R.,Thimbleberries, Cozy Cotton Flannels, Jinny Beyer, Marcus Brothers, a variety of Homespuns, Nancy Crow, Moda, Timeless Treasure, Northcott Silk and P & B Fabrics just to name a few.

We also carry notions, batting, stencils, and a wide assortment of the latest release books and patterns.

We welcome all visitors to our colorful shop. We enjoy taking the time to make you feel at home and unhurried. Our staff is comprised of expert quilters who welcome questions and tips from our customers and enjoy sharing what we have learned from our visitors.

369 College Hill Road, Hopkinton, NH 03229 - Phone - (603) 746 - 5521

Hours: Open all year 'round - Monday through Saturday 10:00-5:30 - Sunday Noon 'Til 5:30

Guild Members receive ***20%*** off all fabric cut from the bolt with $20.00 Minimum Purchase!

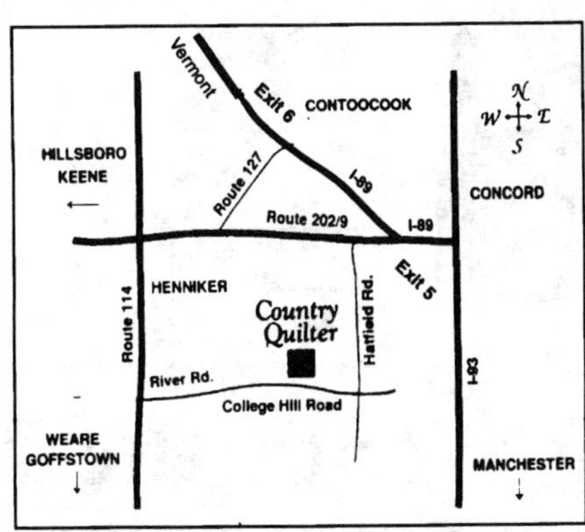

D I R E C T I O N S

__From North/Vermont__

Take Route I-89 South to NH **Exit 6**. Turn Right & follow Route 127 to Route 202/9. Turn Left to next exit at Hatfield Road and follow the well marked signs.

__From I-93 North or South__

Take I89 North to **Exit 5**, Route 202/9. Take it 3 Mi. to the Hatfield Road exit. Follow the well marked signs.

We have Air Conditioning for your summer comfort

❖

VISA/ MC/ Discover & personal checks accepted

❖

Visit us on the Web at **www.countryquilter.net**

Keene, NH #6

Mon - Sat
9:30 - 5:30
Fri til 8

NEW ENGLAND FABRICS

— & Decorating Center —

Tremendous Selection of Beautiful Fabrics for:

- Quilting • Apparel • Bridal
- Draperies • Slipcovers
- Upholstery & More!

Plus Yarn & Sewing Machines

Central New England's Largest Fabric & Home Decorating Center!

55 Ralston St., Keene, NH 03431
(603) 352-8683
www.nefabrics.com

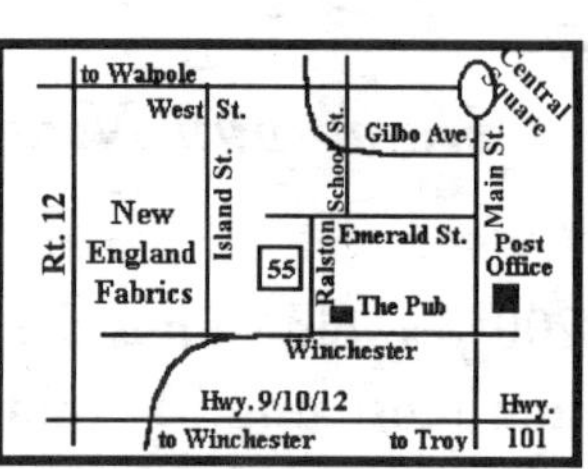

Keene, NH #7

Mon - Fri
10 - 5:30
Sat 10 - 4

The Moses House

149 Emerald St. 03431
(603) 352-2312
Owners: Fran & Russ Moline
Est: 1987 1800 sq.ft.

The best Quilting Fabrics, Books, Patterns, Supplies and Classes. Cross Stitch & Rubber Stamps. PFAFF Dealer. Featherweights, (etc.) Bought, Sold & Repaired.

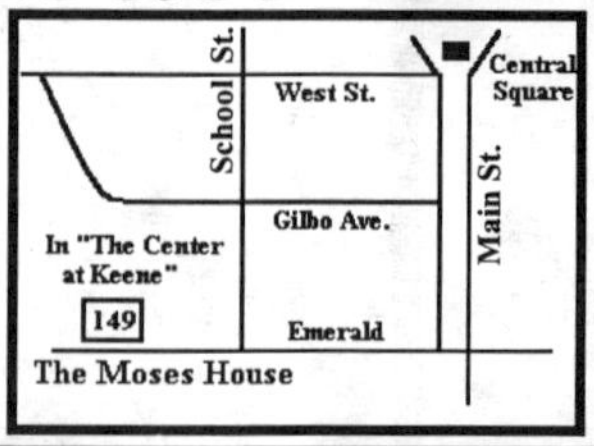

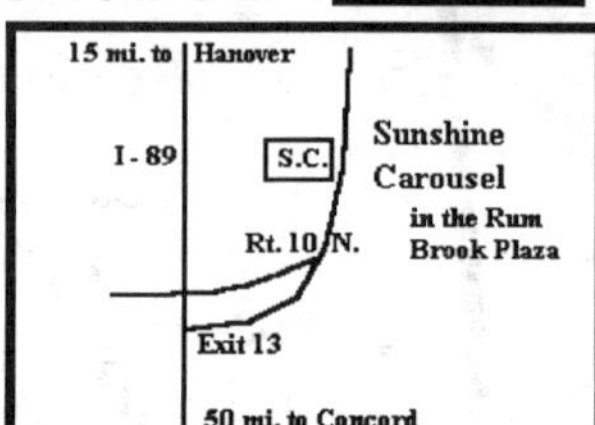

Grantham, NH #8

Tues - Sat
9:30 - 5
Thur til 7

Sunshine Carousel

95 Shaw Brook Rd. 03753
(603) 863-5754
Owner: Elaine Pillsbury
Est: 1990 1200 sq.ft.

Quilting Supplies and classes. Large assortment of cotton fabrics, books, patterns, and notions. Also handmade gifts and crafts.

15 mi. to Hanover
I - 89
S.C.
Sunshine Carousel in the Rum Brook Plaza
Rt. 10 N.
Exit 13
50 mi. to Concord

Rumney, NH #9

CALICO CUPBOARD

Quilting & Knitting Headquarters

Main Street 03266
(800) 348-9567
(603) 786-9567
Est: 1978 2000 sq.ft.
Owners: Joe & Nancy Kolb

A Delightful Experience

In A Quaint New England Village

- **Over 1500 bolts of top of the line quilting fabrics**
- **Terrific selection of homespuns and flannels**
- **Outstanding variety of quilting books**
- **Warm atmosphere and friendly service.**

Mon - Sat
9:30 - 5:30
Sun 9:30 - 5
Closed April

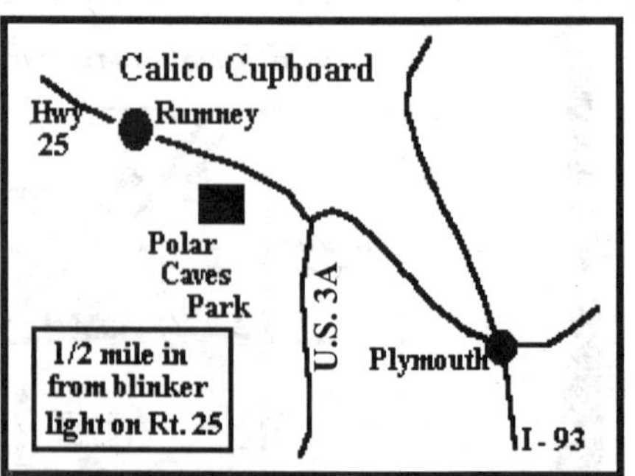

We're Worth the Trip!

Centre Harbor, NH #10

7 Days a Week 9 - 6 Extended Summer hrs.

Keepsake Quilting

In Senters Marketplace
Route 25 P.O. Box 1618
(603) 253-4026 03226
Est: 1988 Free 128 pg. Catalog

America's largest quilt shop with over 6,000 bolts of cotton! Hundreds of finished Quilts.
Don't miss it. It's a Quilter's Paradise!

Conway, NH #12

Mon-Sat 9-5:00 Sun 10-4

Rt 16 • PO Box 2322
Conway, NH 03818
Toll Free 1-888-447-3470
email wizard@ncia.net
Web Site:http://www.ncia.net/quiltshop
Owners: Judy & Neal McIlvaine

Quilter's Dream.
Over 2000 Bolts of Cottons
All at Discounted Prices.
Very Large Selection of
Books, Patterns, Notions.
Very Helpful Staff

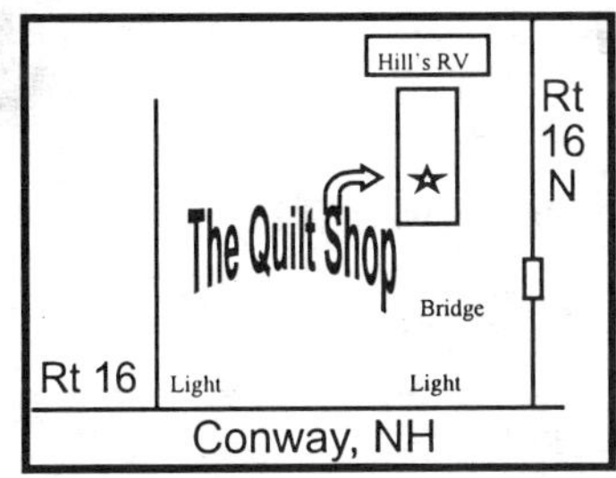

Gilford, NH #11

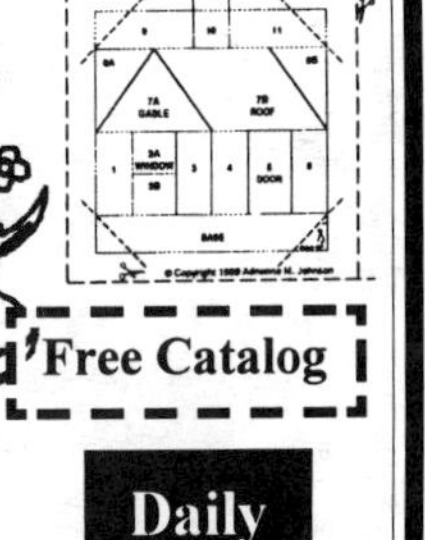

Free Catalog

36 Country Club Rd.
Village West II 03246

Daily 9-5

At Quilting Techniques we specialize in Flip & Sew® tear-away foundation sheets for precision machine piecing. Quilters' Step Saver Appliqué®Pat. Show us this ad and receive a 20% discount

(603) 524-7511
Owner: Adrienne Johnson
Est: 1988 1150 sq.ft.
E-Mail:
quiltpen@cyberportal.net

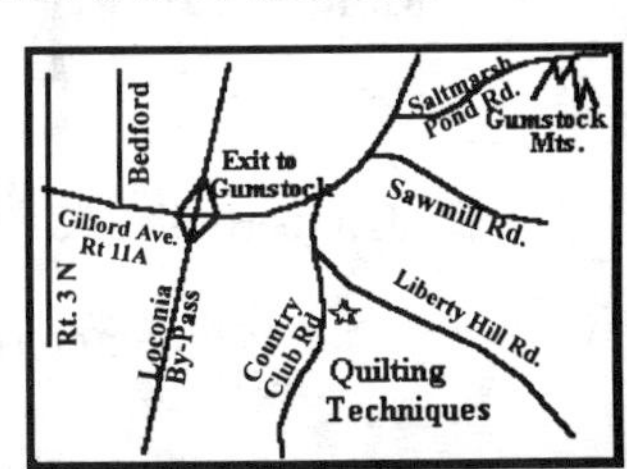

Lincoln, NH #13

10 - 5 Daily Extended Hrs July - Oct

Pinestead Quilts

Main St. 03251
(603) 745-8640
Owner: Kathleen Achorn Sherburn
Est: 1980

A personal quilt shop where your projects interest us. Quilting, knitting, cross-stitch & craft supplies. Fabric. Ready-made quilts & crafts.

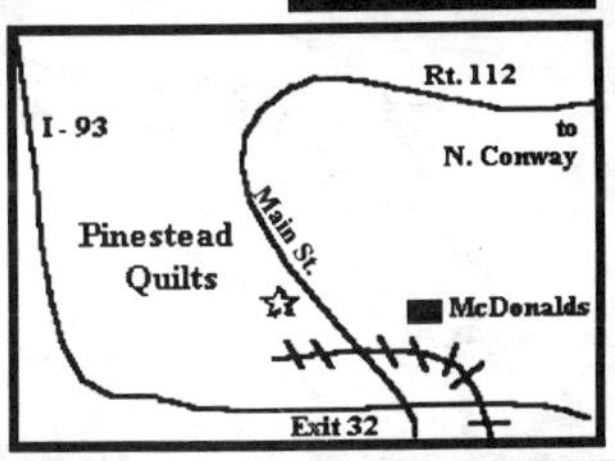

Woodsville, NH #14

Tues - Sat 9:30 - 5 Fri til 6

Seams Sew Easy Fabric Shoppe

65 Central St. 03785
(603) 747-3054
Owners: Chris & Lloyd Steeves

A complete fabric store featuring a large selection of quilting fabrics and supplies. Quality Paton's yarns.

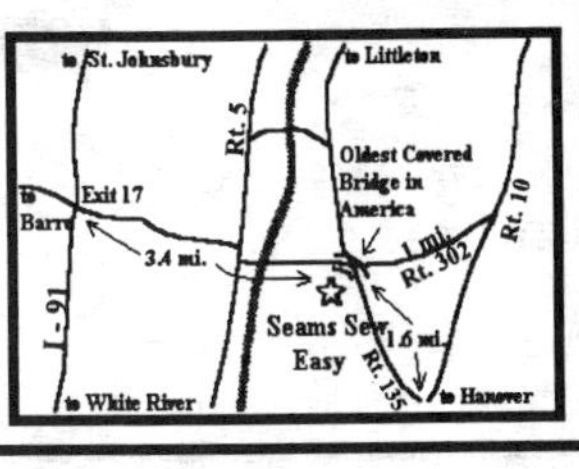

New Hampshire Guilds:

Capital Quilter's Guild, 28 S. Main St. c/o Golden Gese
Concord, 03301
Meets: Havenwood Nursing Home
Cocheco Quilt Guild, P.O. Box 1153, Dover, 03821
Meets: 3rd Tuesday at First Parish Church
Hannah Dustin Quilters Guild, P.O. Box 121, Hudson, 03051
Cheshire Quilters Guild, P.O. Box 1481, Keene, 03431
Sunshine Quilters Guild, P.O. Box 713, New London, 03257
Meets: 3rd Tuesday 7 p.m. at Grantham Town Hall
Monadnock Quilters Guild, P.O. Box 140, W. Peterboro, 03468
Meets: 3rd Friday 7 p.m.
Quilt Festival: Oct. 10-11, 1998, Middle School
Ladies of the Lakes Guild, P.O. Box 552, Wolfeboro, 03894

Other Shops in New Hampshire:

Andover	Wilcox Farm Quilts, Rt. 11, 322 Main St.	603-735-5891
Bedford	The Patchworks, 133 Bedford Center Rd.	603-472-3002
Concord	Bittersweet Fabric Shop, 8 Cottage St.	603-753-4920
Derry	Ben Franklin, 121 W. Broadway	603-432-2650
Guild	The Dorr Mill Store, P.O. Box 88	800-846-3677
Lancaster	Needleworks, 81 Main St.	603-788-2965
West Lebanon	The Quilters Nest, 94 Main St.	603-298-7232

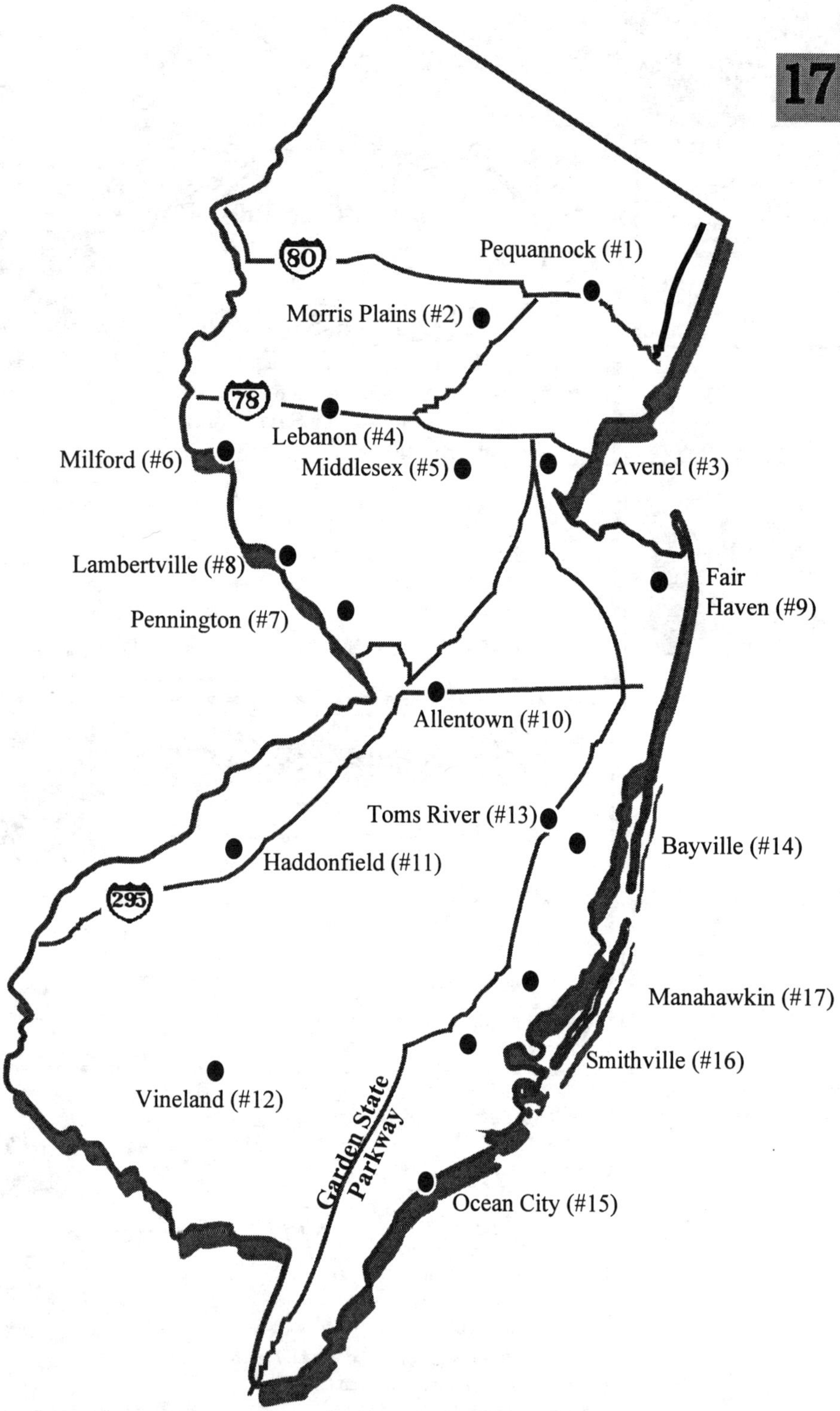

17 Featured Shops

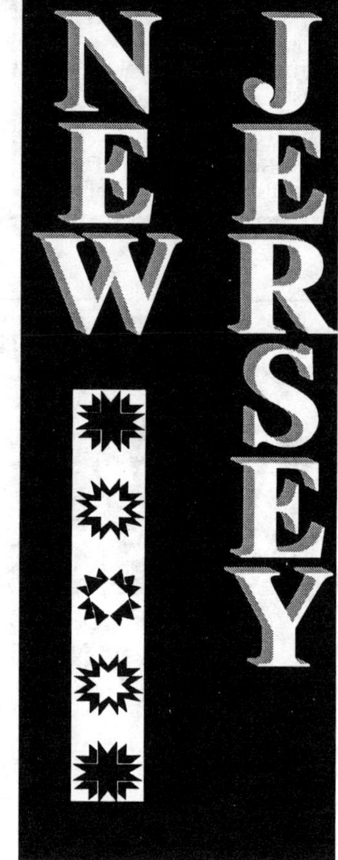

80
Pequannock (#1)
Morris Plains (#2)
78
Lebanon (#4)
Milford (#6)
Middlesex (#5)
Avenel (#3)
Lambertville (#8)
Pennington (#7)
Fair Haven (#9)
Allentown (#10)
Toms River (#13)
Bayville (#14)
Haddonfield (#11)
295
Manahawkin (#17)
Smithville (#16)
Vineland (#12)
Garden State Parkway
Ocean City (#15)

Pequannock, NJ #1

Mon - Sat 10 - 5
Tue & Wed eves 7 - 8:30
Check for summer eves

Acme Country Fabrics

24 Newark Pompton Tpk.
(201) 696-1784 07440
Owners: Alyce Vander Stad & Janet Grimal
Est: 1945

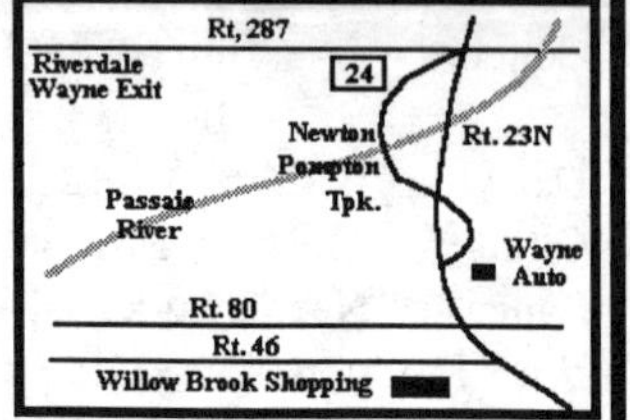

North Jersey's largest fabric selection. Over 4000 bolts of quilting fabrics. Full service sewing store. Bernina sewing machines.

Morris Plains, NJ #2

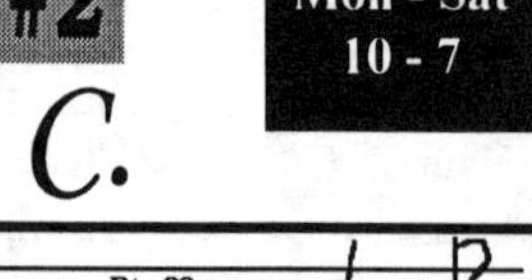

Aardvark & C.

748 Speedwell Ave. 07950
(201) 539-9033
Owner: Sally Alworth
Est: 1987 3400 sq.ft. 2500 Bolts

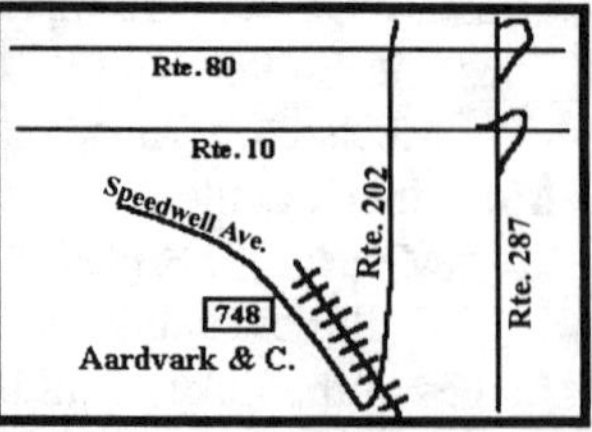

Great selection of fabrics, books, notions and classes. Also cross stitch, lace and ribbons. 30 minutes from NYC.

Mon - Fri
10 - 5
Thur til 8
Sat 10 - 4:30

Quilter's Corner

Avenel, NJ #3

511 Avenel St. 07001
(732) 602-1413
E-Mail: pbqc@earthlink.net
Web Site:
www.vikinghusqvarna.com/quilters-corner
Owner: Pat Brown
Est: 1987
2000 sq.ft.

Complete line of Fabrics, Books, Frames, Etc. for the Quilter. Husqvarna Viking Dealer.

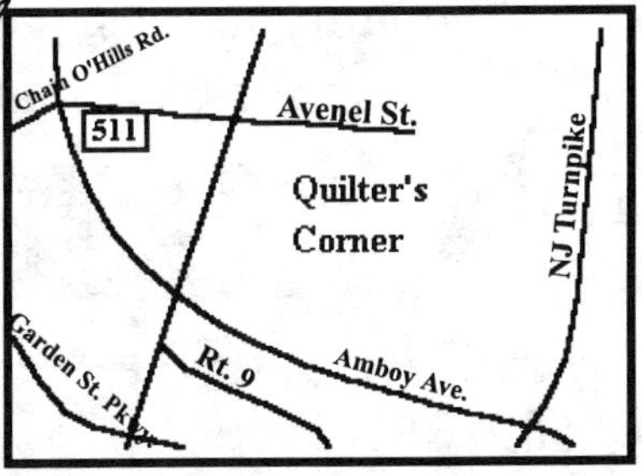

Chain O'Hills Rd.
511
Avenel St.
Quilter's Corner
NJ Turnpike
Garden St. Pkwy.
Rt. 9
Amboy Ave.

One Stop Quilt Shop!

Lebanon, NJ #4

Budding Star Quilts

Mon - Sat
10 - 5:30
Thur til 8
Sun 1 - 4

Rt. 22 E, Lebanon Plaza 08833
(908) 236-7676
Owner: Kathy Verser Est: 1987 1800 Bolts

We Specialize in Kits for all Levels!

Over 1500 Bolts 100% Cotton Fabric.
Large selection of flannels. Classes.
Bernina Sewing Machine Dealer and Service.

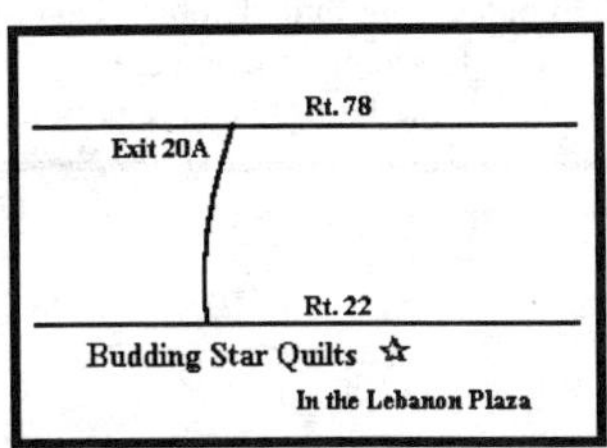

Middlesex, NJ #5

Prints Charming

109 Harris Ave. 08846
Barbieri Plaza
(732) 469-4700
E-Mail: prints@blast.net
Web Site: www.westfifth.com/quilting
Owner: Claudia Menendez
Est: 1981 1800 sq.ft.

Mon - Fri 10 - 5
Thur til 7
Sat 10-4:30
Sun 11 - 4

A complete quilt shop with 2000 bolts, books on quilting & sewing, notions, a great thread department and unique gifts — Boyd's bears, doll & bear furniture and much more.
Authorized Elna dealer.
Mail Order Available.

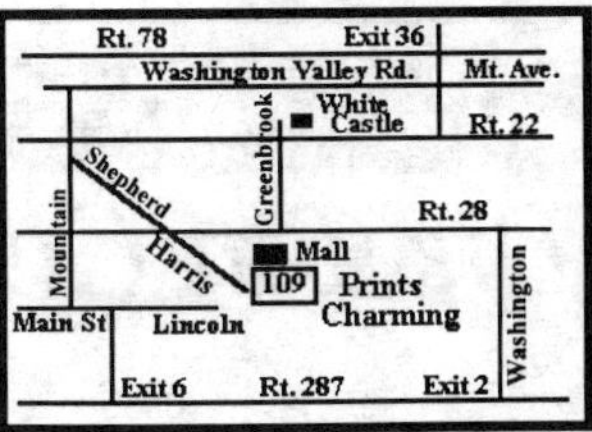

It's Worth the Trip

Milford, NJ #6

By Appt. Only

Grandmother's Flower Garden

2 Walden Rd. 08848
(908) 995-7899 Est: 1989
Owners: Sibby & George Hillman

Singer 221 Featherweights and tables, antique quilts and tops. Quilt restoration and laundering. Shipping available. Call for directions.

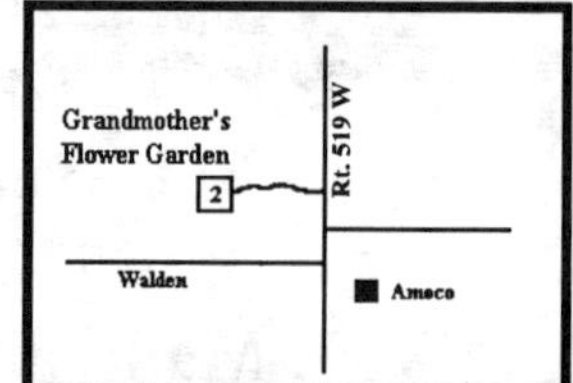

Pennington, NJ #7

Tues, Wed, Thur 10 - 5
Fri 10 - 7
Sat 10 - 4
Sun 12 - 4

Pennington Quilt Works

Pennytown Shopping Village
Route 31 North
(609) 466-5722
Owner: Jan Crane Est: 1996

Wonderful selection of fabrics, books and supplies. All the basics, but always something new. Fun Classes. Warm expert service.

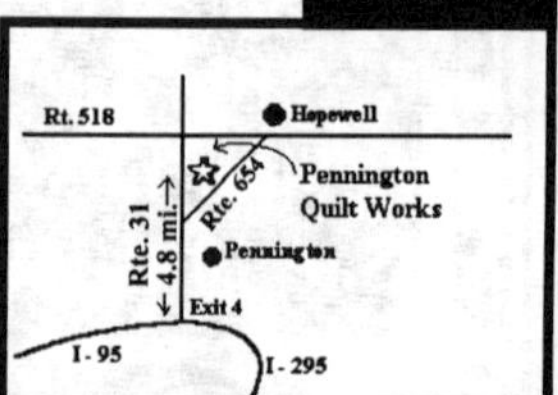

Lambertville, NJ #8

"One Stitch at a Time"

A nostalgic quilt shop featuring old quilts, quality fabrics, patterns, books, supplies, gifts and antiques.

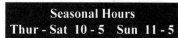

Seasonal Hours
Thur - Sat 10 - 5 Sun 11 - 5

17 Church St. 08530
(609) 397-4545
E-Mail:
Quilter111@aol.com
Owner:
Catherine Giambalvo
Est: 1996

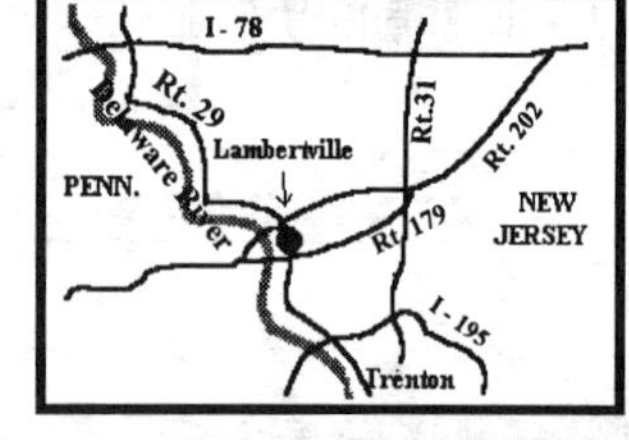

Fair Haven, NJ #9

West End Fabrics

588 River Road 07704
(732) 747-4838 Est: 1989
Owner: Joy Bohanan 2200 sq.ft.

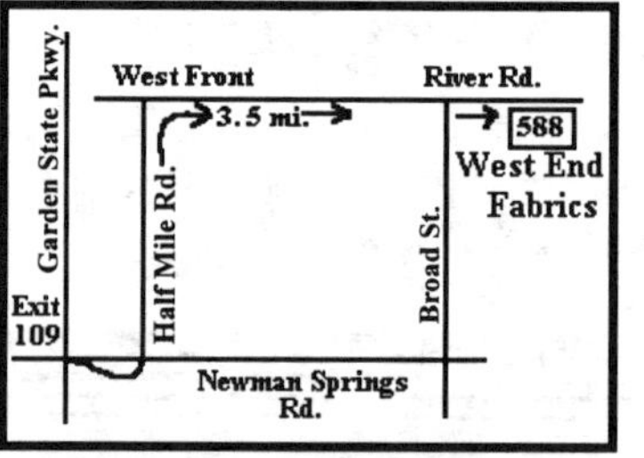

Mon - Fri 9 - 5:30
Wed til 7 Sat 9 - 5

Known for beautiful fabrics, innovative classes, friendly, knowledgeable help, and creative machine quilting. **Every Day is "show and tell" at West End.**

Allentown, NJ #10

Tues - Sat 9:30 - 4
Thur til 7:30
Sun 12 - 5

Quilter's Barn

34 South Main St. P.O. Box 295
(609) 259-2504 08501
Est: 1975

... all 100% cotton fabrics
... Books ... Patterns ... Notions,
... Batting ... classes ... personal service

I - 95E
Exit 8 (Allentown-Hightstown)
NJ Turnpike N.
Rt. 539 S. (Main St.)
Quilter's Barn 34

Haddonfield, NJ #11

Mon - Sat 10 - 5
Sun 12:30 - 4
Class Nights 7 - 9

The Little Shop

143 Kings Hwy. East 08033
(609) 429-7573
Owner: Deborah Hagy Moore
Est: 1960 1700 sq.ft.

10 minutes from Philadelphia. Quality cotton fabric. Instruction & Gifts. All the latest books & notions.

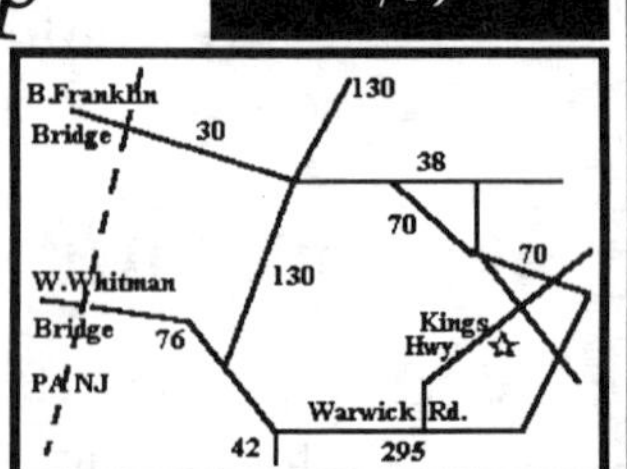

Vineland, NJ #12

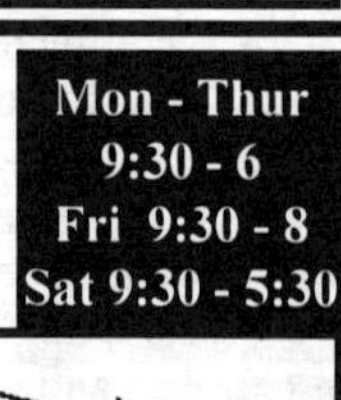

The Pin Cushion

36 Landis Ave. 08360
(609) 692-5460
Est: 1972 4000 sq.ft.
2000 Bolts (Quilt Prints)

Dress, Bridal, Quilt Fabrics.
Notions, Patterns & Accessories.

Toms River, NJ #13

CRAFTY Fabrics

2479 Church Rd. 08753
(732) 255-8342
Owner: Diane McColley
Est: 1983 1400 sq.ft.

Quilting Supplies and Classes. 100% Cotton Fabrics, Books, Patterns, Batting & Notions. Also Handmade Pillows and Crafts

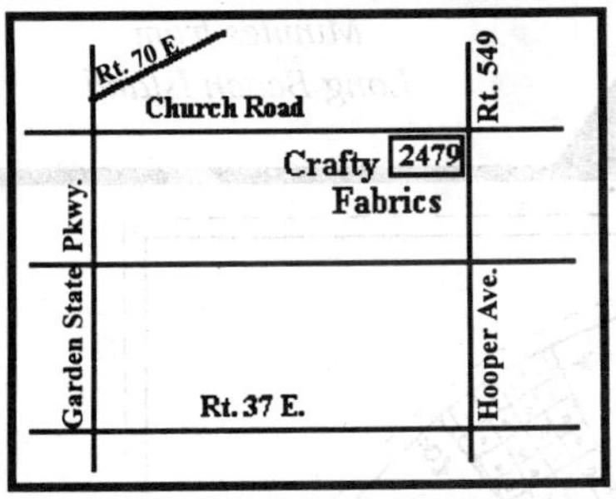

Rt. 70 E.
Church Road
Crafty Fabrics 2479
Rt. 549
Garden State Pkwy.
Hooper Ave.
Rt. 37 E.

Tues - Sat
10 - 5
Class Nights
7 - 9

Bayville, NJ #14

Est: 1994
3300 sq.ft.

Quilting Possibilities

500 Rt. 9 08721 08721
(732) 269-8383
Owners:
Debbie & Jim Welch
E-Mail: qps@quiltingposs.com
Web Site: www.quiltingposs.com

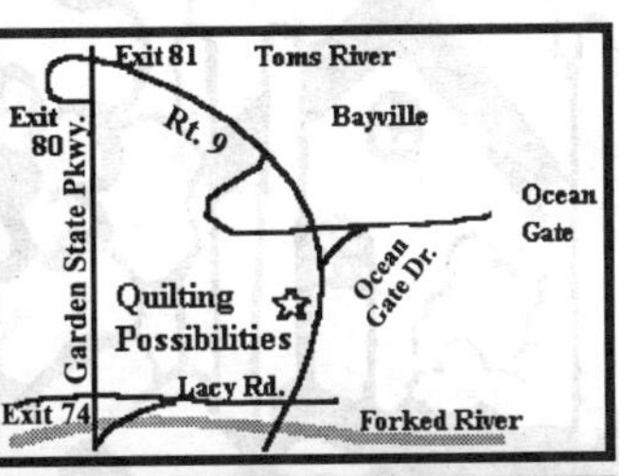

We are an authorized Bernina and Elna dealer, and carry a full line of sewing machines, sergers, and supplies. We repair and service all brands of sewing machines. Name Brand 100% cotton fabric (2000+ bolts), books, notions, patterns. Horn of American dealer plus custom built sewing centers.

Tues - Sat 10 - 5 Sun 12 - 4

Nothing Sews Like A Bernina. Nothing.
BERNINA elna

Ocean City, NJ #15

715 Asbury Ave. 08226
(609) 399-7166
Owner: Bea Minor
Est: 1990 1900 sq.ft.

Summer
Mon - Fri
10 - 7:30
Sat 10 - 5
Sun 12 - 4
Winter
Mon - Sat
10 - 5
Sun 12 - 4

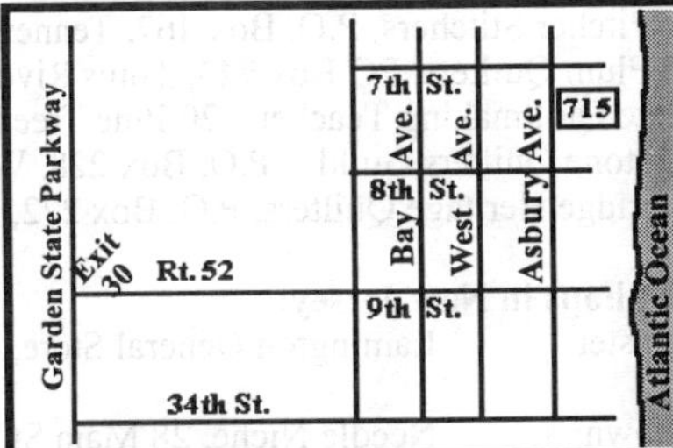

1500 Bolts of 100% Cotton
Classes ◆ Books ◆ Notions
Craft Patterns ◆ Gifts

Smithville, NJ #16

Sew Distinctive

Open 7 Days
Winter
10 - 6
Summer
10 - 8

At the Village Greene in Historic Smithville
615 E. Moss Mill Rd. 08201
(609) 652-2260
Owner: Mona Bawgus
Emphasizing Quilting and Sewing instruction. Broad selection of fabrics, unusual buttons, unique threads, patterns and books. Everything to create that distinctive look.

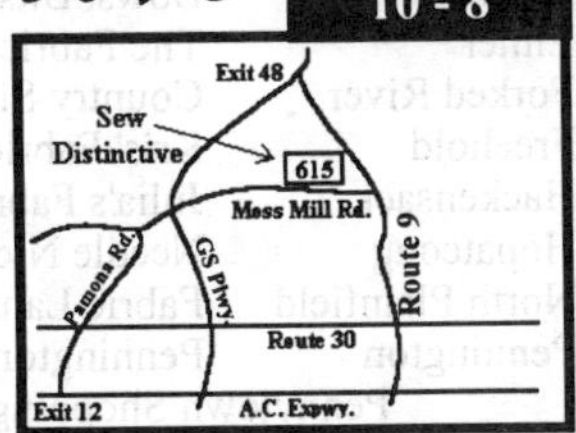

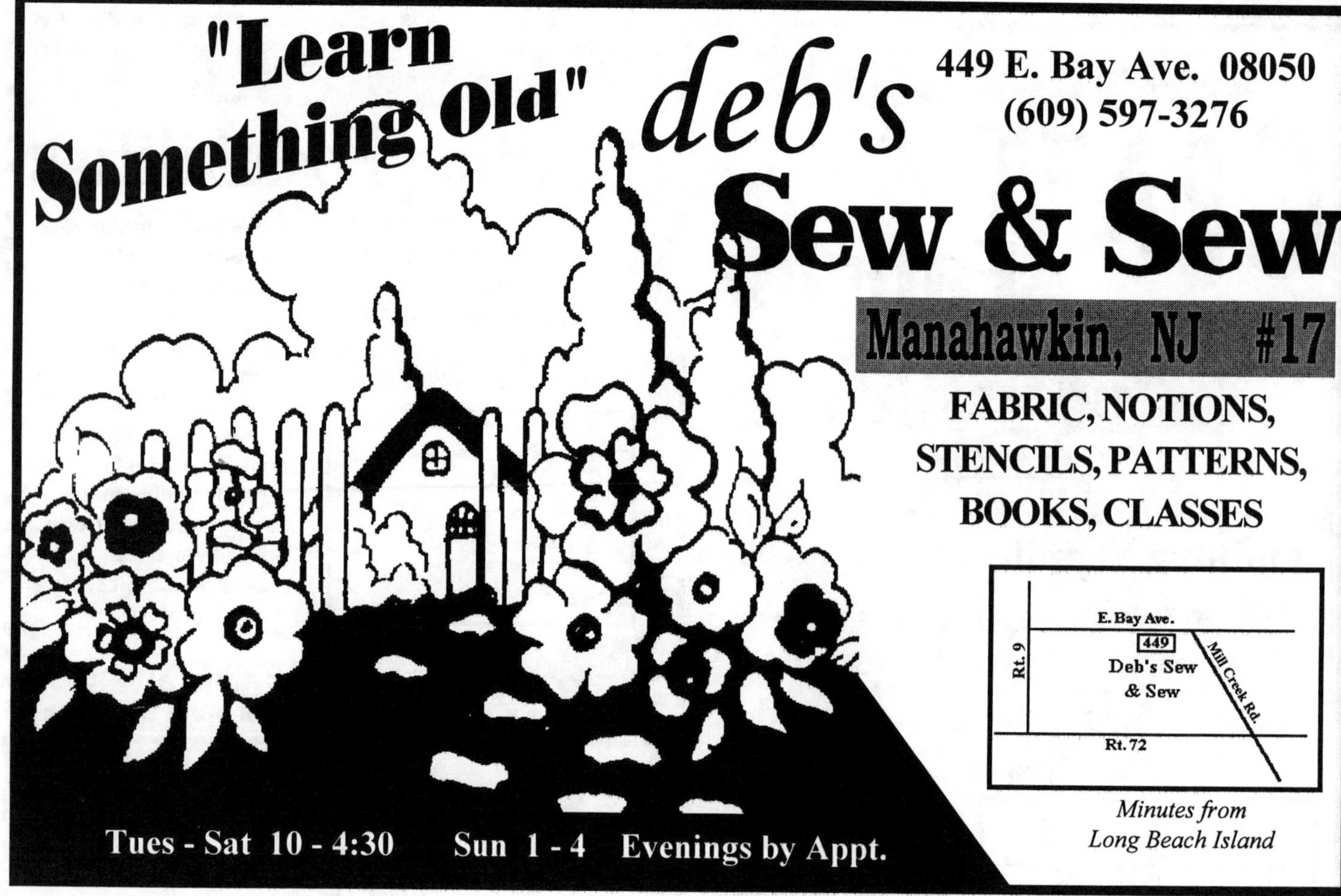

New Jersey Guilds:

Garden State Quilters, P.O. Box 424, Chatham, 07928
Meets: 2nd Monday.
Cinnaminson Quilters, Cinnaminson
Lafayette Quilters Guild, Egg Harbor City, NJ
Meets: 2nd Saturday at the Senior Nutrition Ctr., Cincinnati and Buerger Sts.
Molly Pitcher Stitchers, Freehold
Love Apples, P.O. Box 89, Glendora, 08029
Beach Plum Quilters, P.O. Box 204, Island Heights, 08732
Turtle Creek Quilters, 27 W. Church St., Jamesburg, 08831
The Jersey City Quilters, 181 Pearsall Ave., Jersey City, 07305
Pieceful Shores Quilters Guild, P.O. Box 351, Manahawkin, 08050
South Shores Stitchers, P.O. Box 1103, Marmora, 08223
Rebecca's Reel Quilters, P.O. Box 36, Middletown, 07748
Moorestown Area Quilters, Moorestown, 08057
Jersey Shore Quilters, 415 Foreman Ave., Point Pleasant, 08742
Courthouse Quilters Guild, 121 Back Brook Rd., Ringoes, 08551
Berry Basket Quilters, 509 Paige Dr., Southampton, 08088
Molly Pitcher Stitchers, P.O. Box 467, Tennent, 07763
Beach Plum Quilters, PO Box 743, Toms River, 08753
Tri-State Quiltmaking Teachers, 20 Pine Tree Rd, Toms River, 08753
Brownstone Quilters Guild P.O. Box 228, Waldwick, 07463
Woodbridge Heritage Quilters, P.O. Box 272, Woodbridge, 07095

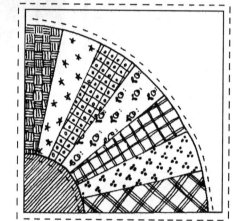

Other Shops in New Jersey:

Bedminster	Lamington General Store, 285 Lamington Rd. 523 Rt.	908-439-2034
Blairstown	Needle Niche, 28 Main St.	908-362-8773
Bridgeton	The Strawberry Patch, 73 Landis Ave.	609-451-8572
Bridgeton	Broad Meadows Country Fabrics, 100 Mary Elmer Dr.	
Cape May Courthouse	Quilted Gull, 1909 N. Rt. 9	609-624-1630
Chester	Natalie S. Hart Antique Quilts, North Rd. R. R. #1	973-584-3319
Clinton	Seams Like Home, 14 Main St.	908-730-8896
Delran	Simply Stitches, 263 Southview Dr.	
Denville	Bows, Bits & Stitches, 9 Broadway	
Elmer	The Fabric Place, 160 Dutch Row Rd.	609-358-7375
Forked River	Country Sisters, 110 N. Main St.	609-693-7224
Freehold	Kris' Fabric Corner, 3333 Hwy. 9 N	732-303-8211
Hackensack	Julia's Fabrics, 137 Main St.	201-487-4110
Hopatcong	Needle Niche, P.O. Box 592	973-398-8412
North Plainfield	Fabric Land, 855 Rte. 22	908-755-4700
Pennington	Pennington Quilt Works, Pennytown Shopping Center, 145 Rt. 31 N	609-466-5722
Perrineville	Golden Sunshine Inc., P.O. Box 293	908-446-0240
Rio Grande	Olsen Sew & Vac Center, 1121 Rt. 47 S. Robbins Nest Plaza	609-886-5510
Scotch Plains	Cozy Corner Creations Quilt Shop, Front & Park Sts.	908-322-8480
Somerville	Millstone Workshop, 1393 Main St.	908-874-3649
Somerville	Somerville Sewing, 45 West Main St.	908-725-0044
Trenton	Raymond's, 528 Route No. 33	609-586-1440
Westfield	Village Curtains, 169 E. Broad St.	908-789-2555

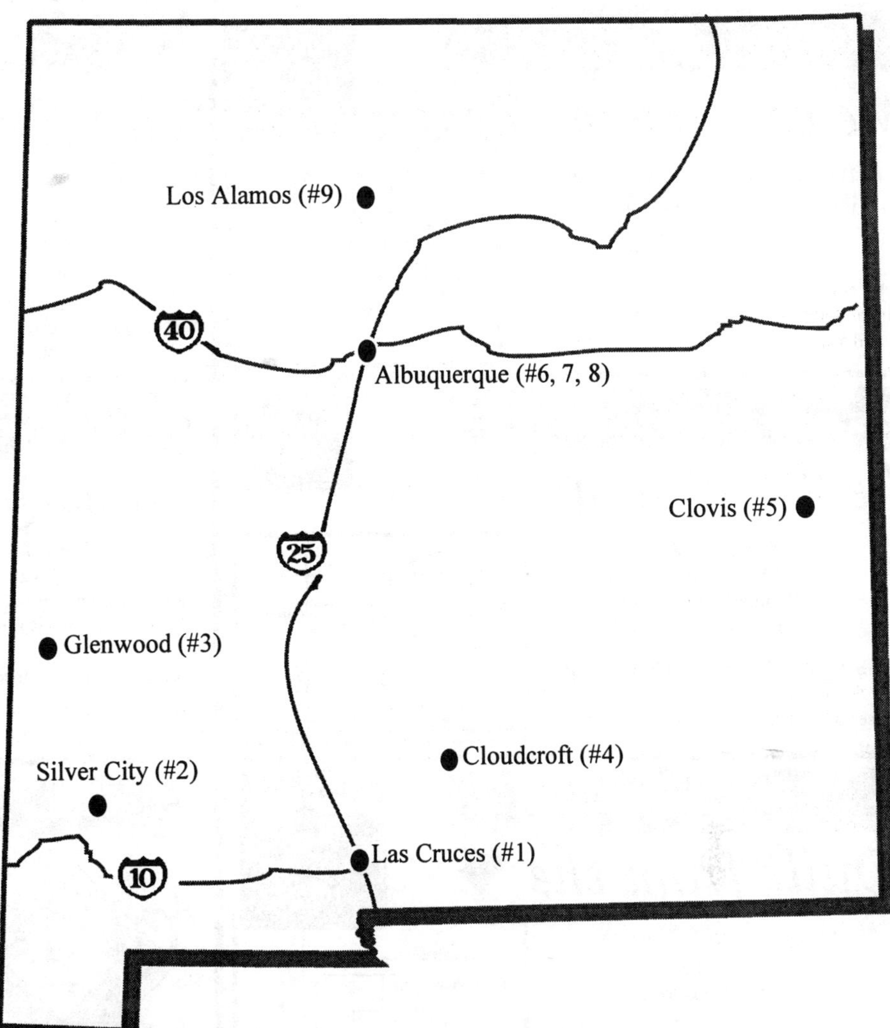

NEW MEXICO

9 Featured Shops

Las Cruces, NM #1

Mon - Thur 9:30 - 5:30
Fri 9:30 - 7
Sat 9:30 - 4

Soft Creations

203 Avenida de Mesilla 88005
(505) 525-8155 Fax: Same
E-Mail: tinadal@zia.net
Owner: Tina Dalcour
Est: 1996 2000+ sq.ft.

Come for inspiration, ideas and the greatest place to buy supplies and fabric!

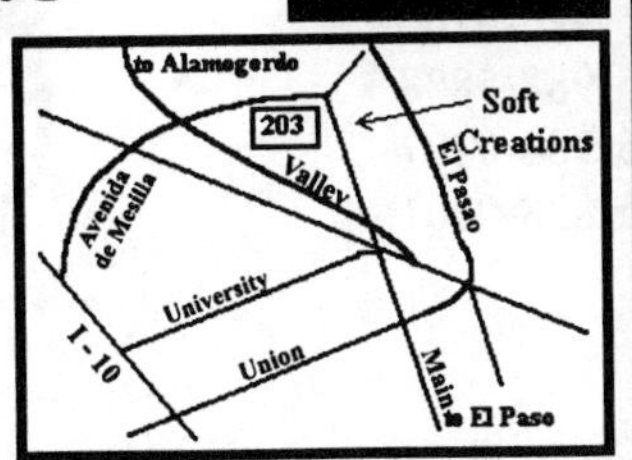

Silver City, NM #2

Mon - Sat 9 - 5

Thunder Creek Quilt Company

1330 N. Hudson St. 88061
(505) 538-2284 or (800) 376-4201
Owners: Cindy Ugarte & Nancy Coryell
Est: 1995 700+ Bolts

Cotton Fabric. Notions, Sulky & Gutermann Threads. Gingher Scissors. Classes. Gifts.

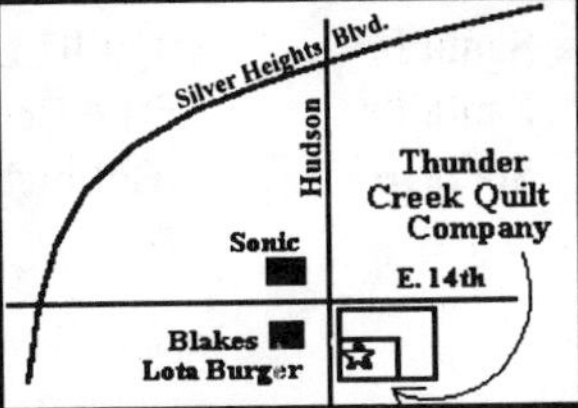

Glenwood, NM #3

Mon - Sat 10 - 5
Sun 12 - 4

Melba's Sewing Basket

Hwy. 180 West Main St. 88039
(888) 411-0545 or (505) 539-2463
Owner: Melba Johnston
Est: 1993 600 Bolts

This "country in the city" shop boasts 1000+ bolts of cotton fabric, books, patterns, notions and a friendly, helpful staff of quilters.

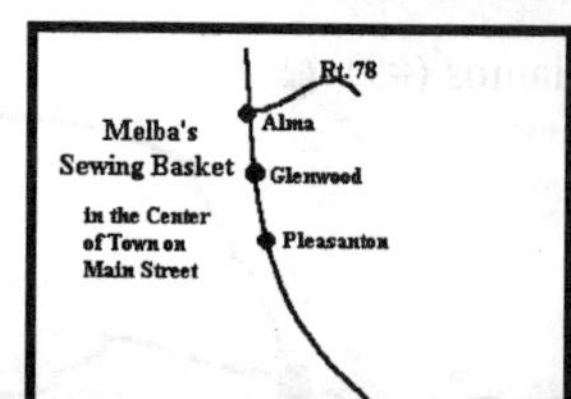

Cloudcroft, NM #4

Daily 10 - 5

The Scrap Basket

Located in Artisan Alley
206 Burro Ave. 88317
(505) 682-1468
Owner: Patricia Drake

Small shop in a mountain village.
Retail Quilts, Fabric, Supplies, Related Gifts, Books & Patterns.

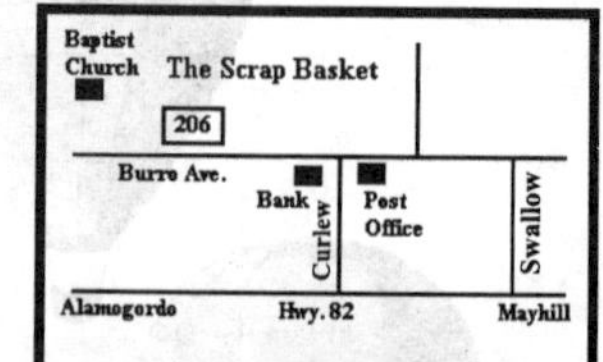

Clovis, NM #5

Mon - Sat 10 -5

the Patchwork House

519 Main St. 88101
(505) 769-8072
E-Mail: judy@pdrpip.com
Owner: Judy Matthews

Best Selection of Quality Quilting Fabrics, Books, Patterns, Notions for 100 miles.
Classes and custom Quilting Service Avail.

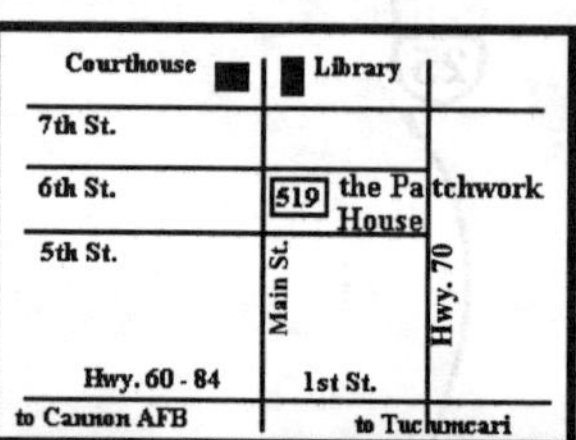

Albuquerque, NM #6

Mon - Fri 9 - 6
Sat 9 - 5
Sun 2 - 5

The Quilt Works

11117 Menaul N.E. 87112
(505) 298-8210
E-Mail: quilt@thuntek.net
Web Site: www.quiltworksabq.com
Est: 1985 1750 sq.ft.
Owners: Shirley Brabson & Margaret Prina

We have over 2700 bolts of cotton fabric.
We're Friendly and Helpful !

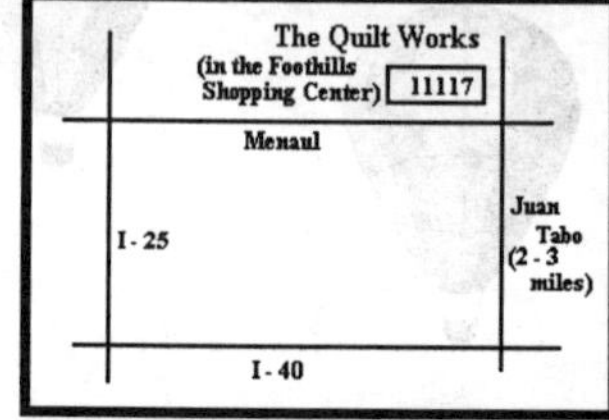

Albuquerque, NM #7

Mon - Thur 10 - 6
Fri & Sat 10 - 5

Quilt from the ♥

417 Tramway NE #1 87123
(505) 292-8560
Owner: Leta Brazell

A Full Service Quilt Shop !
Quilts for Sale, Custom Quilts, Finishing, Classes, Fabric, Books, Notions & More.

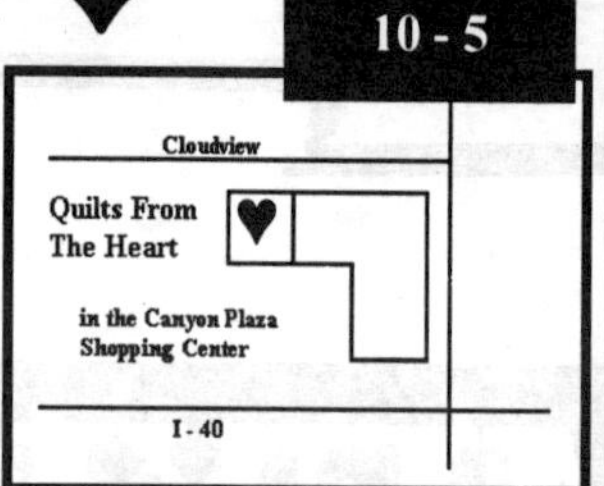

Albuquerque, NM #8

Mon - Fri 10 - 6
Thur 10 - 8
Sat 10 - 5
Sun 12 - 5

A Quilter's Affaire Inc.

12500 Montgomery 87111
(505) 292-8925
Owner: Kathy Heger
Est: 1994
2500 sq.ft.

Featuring over 1500 bolts of fabric, notions, books, & patterns for quilting and crafting. Classes Too!

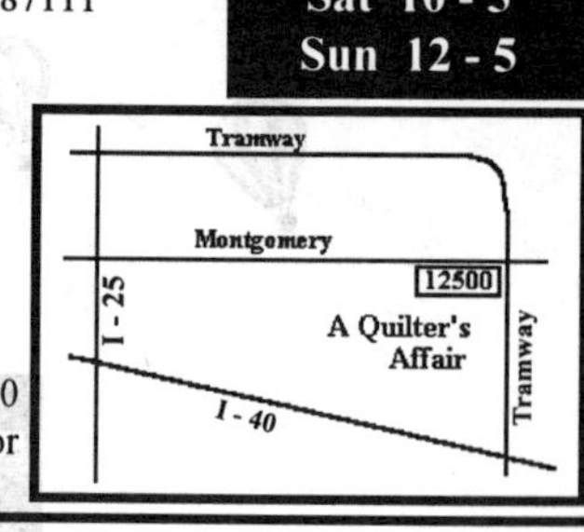

New Mexico Guilds:

Enchanted Quilter's Guild, 900 Catalina, Alamogordo, 88301
New Mexico Quilters' Association, P.O. Box 20562, Albuquerque, 87154
Los Alamos Piecemakers Quilters, P.O. Box 261, Los Alamos, 87544
Pecos Valley Quilters, 807 N. Missouri, Roswell, 88201
Northern New Mexico Quilters, P.O. Box 8350, Santa Fe, 87504

Other Shops in New Mexico:

Albuquerque	Ann Silva's, 3300 San Mateo E.	505-881-5253
Carlsbad	Chrisden Craft,1316 W. Mermod St.	505-885-0789
Farmington	Apple Barn, 5991 Hwy. 64	505-632-9631
Farmington	Quilt Garden, 2501 E. 20th St.	505-325-2116
Farmington	Knit One Quilt Two, 3024 E. Main St. #Y4	505-326-7324
Lincoln	Lincolnworks, P.O. Box 32	505-653-4693
Santa Fe	Moxie, 205 W. San Francisco St.	505-986-9265
Santa Fe	Quilts Ltd., 652 Canyon Rd.	505-988-5888
Santa Fe	The Bedroom, 304 Catron St.	505-984-0207
Socorro	Bobbie's Bobbin, P.O. Box 1125	505-838-0001

Hogansburg (#36)
Marcellus (#20)
Skaneateles (#21)
Savannah (#15)
Fairport (#16)
Tonawanda (#4)
East Rochester (#17)
Medina (#5)
Niagara Falls (#2)
Holley (#6)
Lockport (#1)
Williamsville (#3)
Alexander (#7)
Clarence (#12)
East Aurora (#11, 13)
Hamburg (#8)
Boston (#10)
Dansville (#24)
Canandaigua (#22)
Rushville (#23)
Aurora (#26)
Penn Yan (#25)
Brewerton (#14)
Liverpool (#18)
(#34) Manlius
Oneida (#35)
Utica (#40)
McLean (#19)
(#29) Ithaca
Big Flats (#30)
Olean (#9)
Andover (#28)
Hammondsport (#27)
Endwell (#31)
Binghamton (#32)
Queensbury (#37)
Gloversville (#39)
Fultonville (#41)
Schenectady (#38)
Fly Creek (#33)
Cobleskill (#42)
(#43) Ravena
Sidney Center (#44)
Hillsdale (#47)
Pine Bush (#45)
Wappingers Falls (#48)
Somers (#46)
Cold Spring Harbor (#55)
New York (#52, 53)
Brooklyn (#49, 50)
Southampton (#54)
Sayville (#51)
87
81
90
88
390
NEW YORK
55 Featured Shops

Lockport, NY #1

5410 Stone Rd. 14094
(716) 433-5377
Owner: Judith Farnham
Est: 1982

Pine Grove Workshop

Mon - Sat 10 - 4:30

2000 Bolts 100% Cotton
Old and New Quilts
Hundreds of Books, Patterns, & Notions
Classes—Spring Seminar

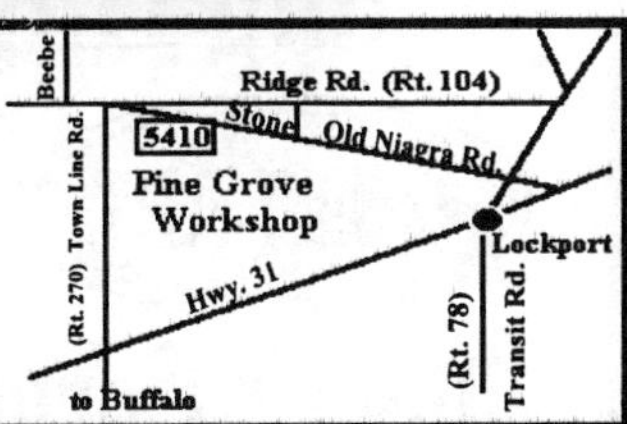

Niagara Falls, NY #2

Tues 10 - 2:30
Wed & Fri 10 - 8:30
Thur 10 - 4:30
Sat 10 - 3

Quiltmakers & Friends

4716 Military Rd. 14304
(716) 297-4069
Owner: Florence M. Rhodes

Hundreds of bolts — 100% cotton fabrics. Large selection of quilt books, notions, patterns & gifts. Classes offered.

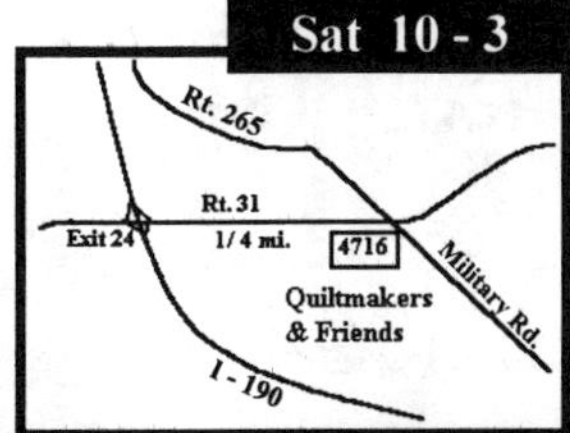

Williamsville, NY #3

Mon & Wed 10 - 9
Thur - Sat 10 - 5

Sew What

8226 Main Street 14221
(716) 632-8801
Owner: Ann Shaw
Est: 1990 600 Bolts 1100 sq.ft.

Specializing in Quilting & Cross Stitch, we offer a large selection of unique and unusual fabrics, 100's of patterns & notions.
Come Browse!

Sew What
8226
Rt. 5 Main St.
to I - 290
I - 90 Exit 49
Rt. 78
Rt. 33

Tonawanda, NY #4

Flash your Quilt Guild Card for a discount on your purchases.

Threads of Time

Mon - Fri 10 - 5
Mon & Thur til 9
Sat 10 - 4

347 Somerville Ave. 14150
(716) 837-1372
Owners: Mari Wojcik & Jeanette Rogers

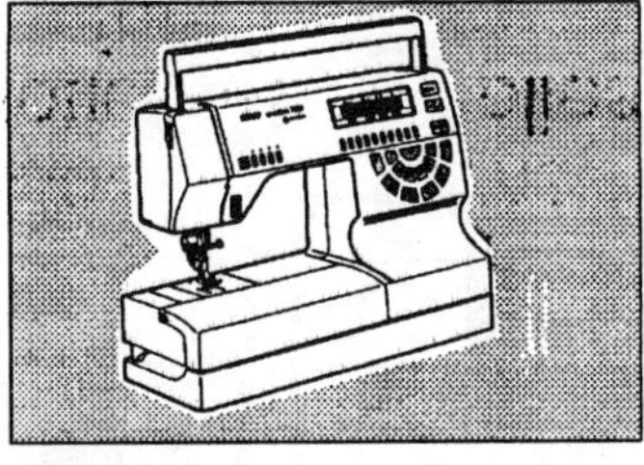

We carry hundreds of bolts of fine cotton fabrics for all your quilt dreams.
Also classes, books, patterns, a great variety of threads, notions & . . . lots of ideas.
PFAFF Authorized Sales & Service

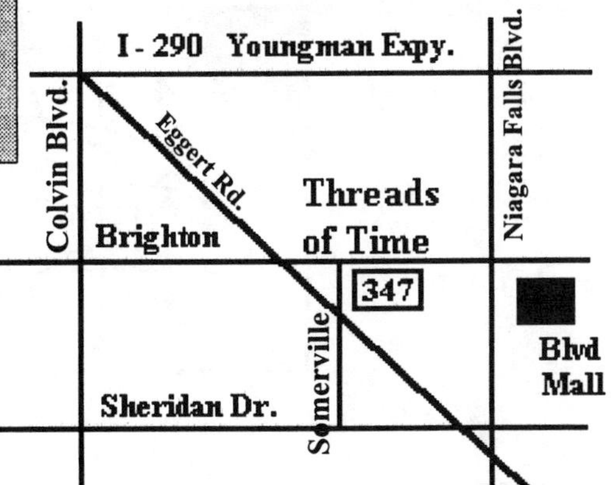

"If You're a Quilter -- Then You're a Friend"

Medina, NY #5

The Personal Touch

Complete Quilt Shop
Specializing in Traditional & Homespun

Mon - Sat 9:30 - 5 Fri til 6

435 Main St. 14103
(716) 798-4760
Owner: Nancy Berger
Est: 1981 2000 sq.ft.

Come in and Browse
Half Quilt Shop and Half Gift Shop.
Books, patterns, notions & supplies for Quilters.
Lace & Ribbon also.
Juried gifts by local artisans Co-op.
Large 'garden' and flower shop with a large selection of Bears and their "makings".

Lake Ontario
The Personal Touch
Medina
Hwy 31A
Hwy 31
I - 90
to Buffalo
Hwy. 63
on Main St. in Medina

On the Banks of the Erie Canal

"We're not Just a Quilt Shop"

Holley, NY #6

Tues - Sat 10 - 4

Apple Country Quilt Shop

4701 Bennetts Corners Rd. 14470
(716) 638-5262
Owner: Linda Glantz Est: 1994

Large variety of 100% cottons, quilting supplies, classes and gifts. Friendly & helpful staff.
Home of 2 Quilt Guilds

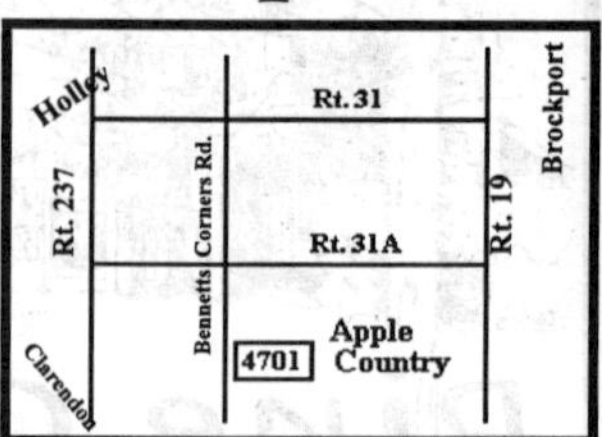

Hamburg, NY #8

18 Buffalo St. 14075
(716) 646-0090

THE SEWIN' STORE

Mon - Fri 10 - 6 Thur 10 - 8 Sat 10 - 5

Fabric, books, classes in quilting, applique, wearable arts, machine embroidery and heirloom techniques.

Machine Quilting Services.
Machine Repairs on all Makes/Models

Owner:
Wilhelmina Fiedler
Est: 1994
3000 sq.ft.
E-Mail:
sewin@buffnet.net

20% Discount for Guild Members with cards

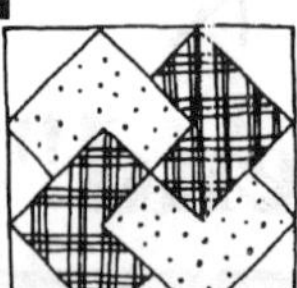

Rolling Hills

Mon - Fri 10 - 4
Tues til 9
Sat 12 - 4

Quilter's Corner

(716) 591-3606
3274 Broadway 14005
1200 sq.ft. Est: 1988

Exit 48
Thruway
Batavia
Hwy. 5
Hwy 33
Corfu
Buffalo
Hwy 77
Hwy 98
Hwy 63
Rochester
Alexander
Route 20
Pavilion
3274
Rolling Hills Quilters Corner

E-Mail: superquilt@usa.net
Owners: Jennie Peck & Ann Kroll

Alexander, NY #7

Your Complete Quilt Shop.
Quilts, Fabric, Notions, Classes, 100% Cottons, Books.
We specialize in unique & unusual fabrics from different parts of the globe.

Olean, NY #9

Mon - Sat 10 - 5 Fri til 8

Calico Country

803 W. State St. 14760
(716) 372-5446
Owner: Betsy Leute
Est: 1983 1600 sq.ft.

Nine rooms full of 1700 bolts of 100% cotton fabric, books, patterns, quilts, gift items and much more.

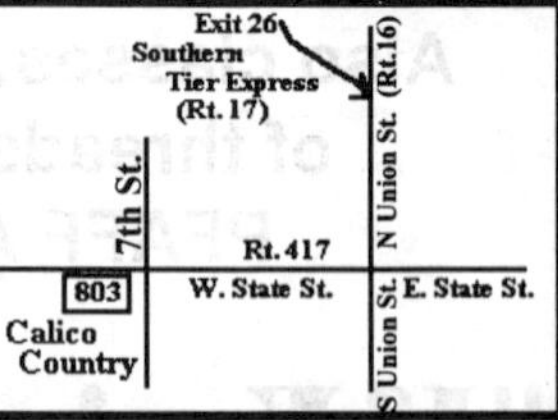

Boston, NY #10

Tues - Sat
10 - 5
Tues & Thurs
evenings til 9
Sunday 12 - 5
Closed Sun July & Aug.

The Quilt FARM

est. 1989

3600 sq. ft.

5623 South Feddick Road 14025
(716) 941-3140 Owners: Chris North & Isabell Schmit
Staffed by Family and Friends

DIRECTIONS: (a scenic country drive 30 minutes South of Buffalo)
I - 90 to Route 219 South, Exit at Rice Road
Off exit ramp turn right & go (up hill) to first intersection,
left on Zimmerman, then right on South Feddick Road
Call for specifics . . . It's a challenge.

"WORTH THE DRIVE"

The Answer to a Quilter's Prayers in God's Country

"ANNIVERSARY EVENT"
June 20th 1998 and
June 19th 1999
Starting @ 6 a.m.
40% off all fabrics
35% after 7 a.m. and so on

A barnful of quilters supplies:

- ... 3,000+ bolts of 100% cotton
- ... large selection of notions
- ... elna sewing machines
- ... 450+ books & patterns plus kits
- ... Gammil Quilting machine
- ... Finished and Custom order Quilts
- ... Origin of "Quilt Farm" Patterns
- ... Classes

"Shop 'til the Cows come home."

East Aurora, NY #11

659 Main St. 14052
(716) 652-2811
Fax: (716) 652-2863
Est: 1978
3500 sq.ft.

Clarence, NY #12

10750 Main St. 14031
(716) 759-8081
Fax: (716) 759-1715
Est: 1996
3000 sq.ft.

Aurora Sewing Center

Mon 10 - 8
Thur 10 - 9
Tues, Wed, Fri
10 - 5:30

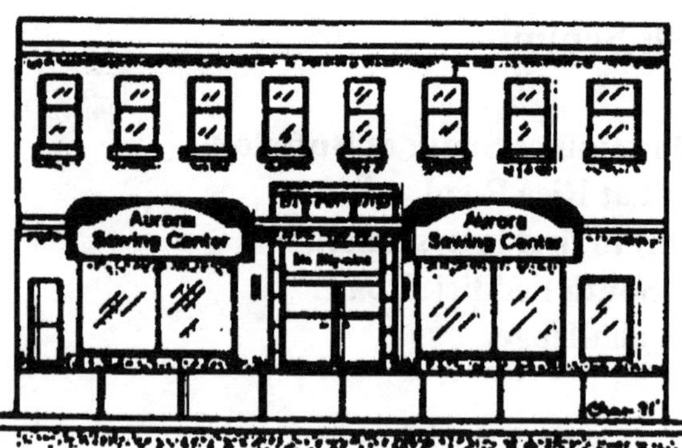

Stop in and visit our shops — You'll be pleasantly surprised!

- *We have over a 1000 Bolts of fabric to choose from.*
- *Thousands of book titles, quilting, sewing, applique and more.*
- *The latest in craft, quilting, teddy bear & applique patterns — with lots of displayed samples!*
- *Look-in on our classroom activities — we have over 90 different classes offered each semester.*
- *Bernina sewing machines, sales and service.*
- *Service of all makes and models*
- *Large display of Horn cabinets.*

BERNINA®

Owners: Regis Boire & Barb Perry
Web Site Coming Soon . . .
E-Mail Questions ASCBARB@aol.com

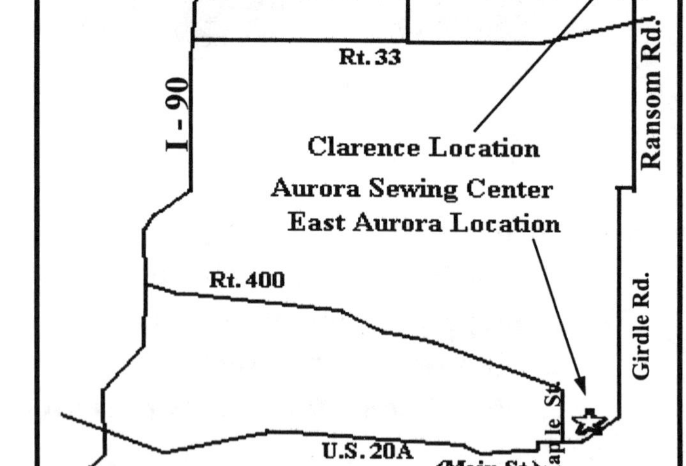

2 Great Locations ! !

East Aurora, NY #13

Vidler's 5 & 10

Mon - Sat 9 - 5:30
Fri til 9
Sun 12 - 4

680 - 694 Main Street 14052
(716) 652-0481
Owners: Bob & Ed Vidler
Est: 1930 13,000 sq. ft. 1000+ Bolts

10,000 yards of calicos. Hundreds of Instruction books on quilting, sewing, crafts, knitting & needle crafts.

"It's a Fun Place to Shop"

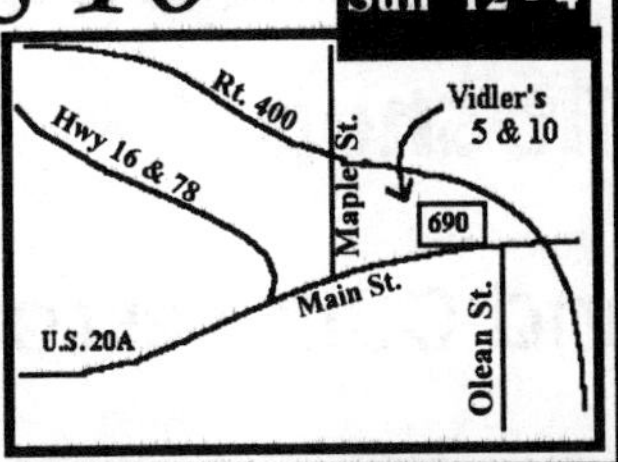

Brewerton, NY #14

Tues & Thur 10 - 1
Wed & Fri 10 - 3
Sat 1 - 5
or by Appt.
Extended Summer Hrs.

Simpkin's Quilt Shoppe

9687 Rt. 11, P.O. Box 936 13029
(315) 668-6423 Est: 1998
Owner: Marlene N. Verity

Fabrics, classes and gifts.
"We're small with a BIG love for Quilters."

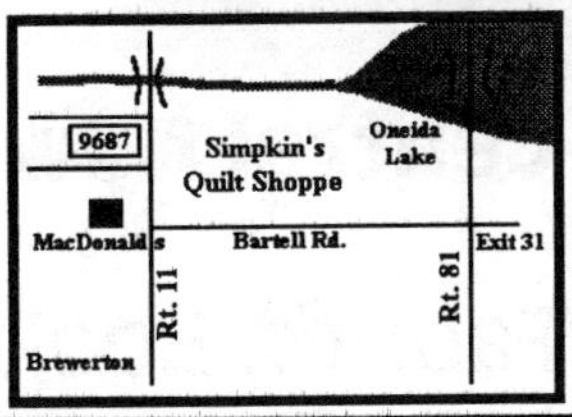

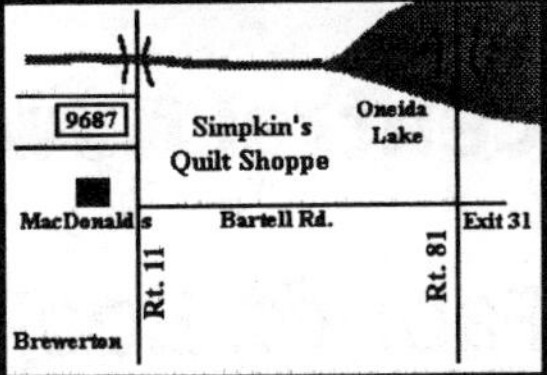

Savannah, NY #15

Mon - Sat 9 - 5
Thur & Fri til 8

4219 Yates Rd. 13146
(315) 594-8485
Owner: Arlene Zimmerman

One of a Kind Store!

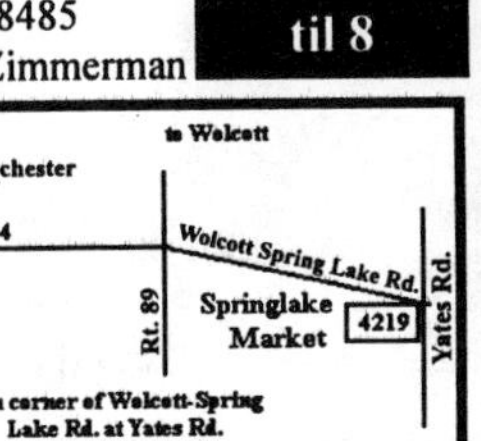

Great selection ... name brand fabrics unbeatable prices ... with a dutch country flair ... notions ... books ... crafts.

Fairport, NY #16

Tues - Fri 10 - 5
Sat 10 - 4

150 N. Main St. 14450
(716) 377-3650
Owner: Marion Skrynski

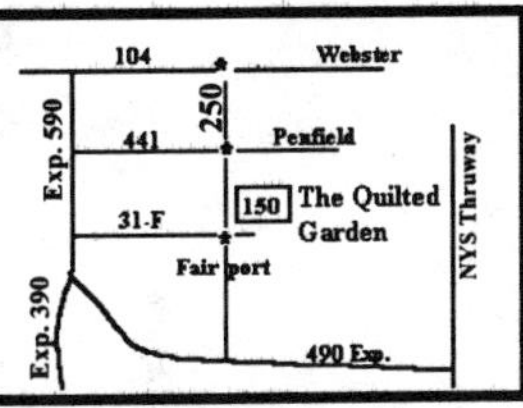

Hand guided machine quilting. Special fabrics.
Full Service Quilt Shop.

East Rochester, NY #17

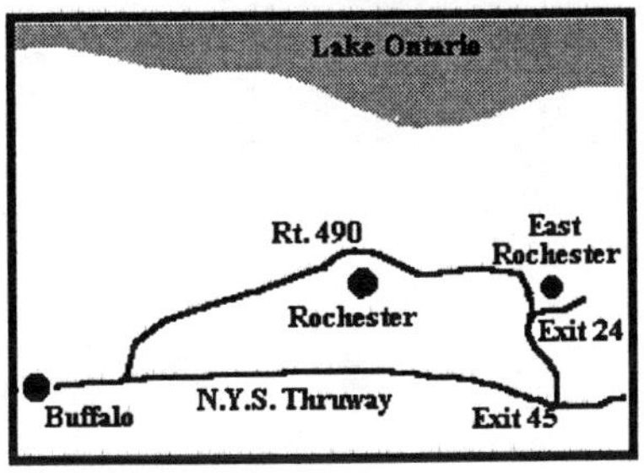

Lake Ontario
Rt. 490
East Rochester
Rochester
Exit 24
Buffalo
N.Y.S. Thruway
Exit 45

333 W. Commercial St. 14445
(716) 248-2362
Owner: Kitty Keller
4400 sq.ft. 3500+ Bolts

patricias'
Fabric House

VAST Collection of Fine Quilting Cottons.
Including Rose & Hubble, Alexander Henry, Kona Bay, Moda, Hoffman and many others.
Stencils, Books, Patterns, Notions, Classes.

ONE STOP SHOPPING FOR ALL YOUR QUILTING NEEDS

Mon - Thur 10 - 9
Fri & Sat 10 - 5

Chickadee Fabrics
526 Old Liverpool Road • Liverpool, New York 13088 • 315/453-4059

Central New York's Premier Quilt Shop

Fabrics, Books, Notions, Classes, and Quilt restoration. Staffed by knowledgeable quilters

1865 square feet with over 1800 bolts of fabric and 2 dedicated classrooms

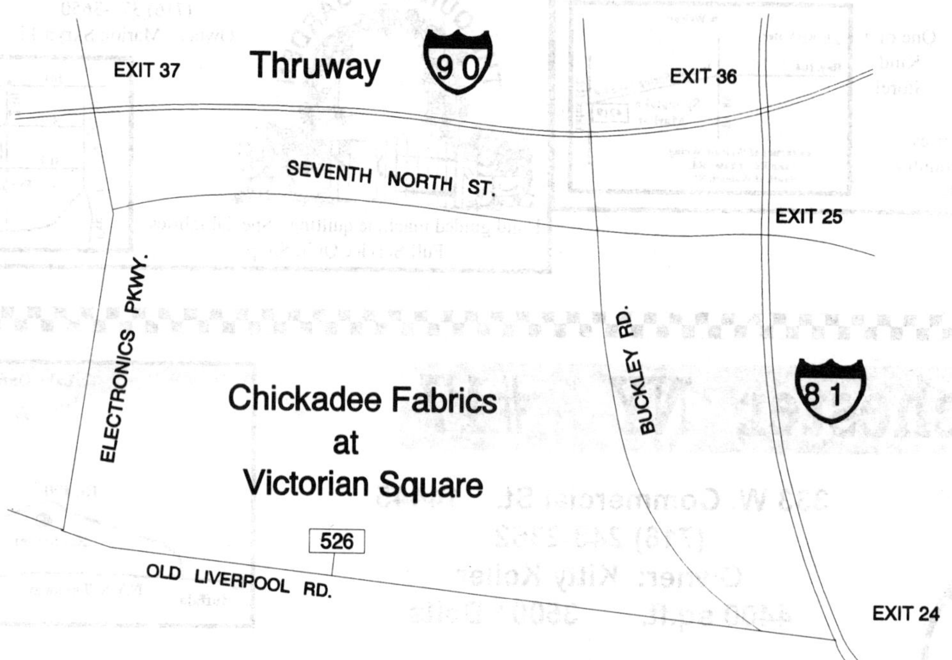

Featuring fabrics by Hoffman, P&B Textiles, Kona Bay, RJR, and many others.

Books by That Patchwork Place, C&T Publishing, and Quilt Digest Press.

Over 160 classes offered per year with day, night, Saturday, custom, and private classes

Easily accessible from both interstate highways
Store Hours: Mon - Sat 10:00 - 5:00

Liverpool, NY #18

McLean, NY #19

THE SQUARE, 3 Stevens Rd.
McLean, New York 13102
Phone: (607) 838 - 3095
Owner: Clara Travis

Featured in Patchwork and Quilting Ideas Magazine, Winter '97 Issue

Quilting Gadgets, Gismos and Gottahaves
Bus Tours and Quilt Guilds welcome but do call ahead
*100% cotton fabrics *Notions * Books * Patterns * Gifts

We are located in an old country store at the five crossroads in the historic village of McLean, NY. Come and browse through one of New York State's most unique quilt stores and enjoy home made pie, sweet rolls and coffee before returning to the lovely scenery of the beautiful Finger Lakes. Ten minutes from Interstate 81 and Route 13.

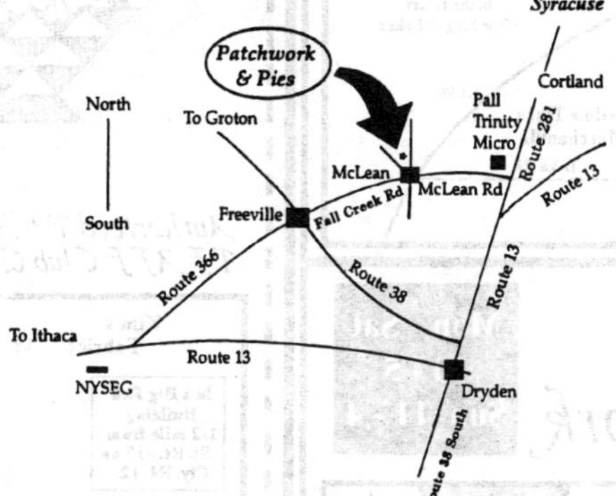

Tuesday - Friday 10 - 5:00 & Saturday 10 - 4:00

Closed between Christmas and New Years. Please call for other special holiday hours.

Fax: (607) 838-0108 E-Mail 75021.1111@compuserve.com

www.patchworkandpies.com

Marcellus, NY #20

Mon - Sat 9 - 5 Or by Appt.

The Quilting Shoppe

2162 Lawrence Rd. 13108
(315) 673-1126
Owner: Elaine Lyon
Est: 1983 1800 sq.ft. 1800+ Bolts

100% Cotton Fabrics, Notions, Batting, Books, Hoops, Frames, Lessons.
Quilted Jackets, Quilt Repairs & Washing.
Quilts for Sale.

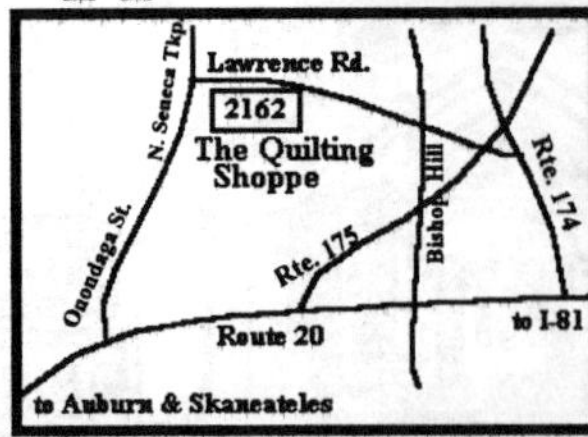

Skaneateles, NY #21

Mon - Sat 10 - 4

Patchwork Plus

36 Jordan Street 13152
(315) 685-6979
Owners: Judi West
Est: 1987

2500 bolts of 100% cottons, books, notions, patterns; Plus friendly service in Skaneateles; Gateway to the Finger Lakes

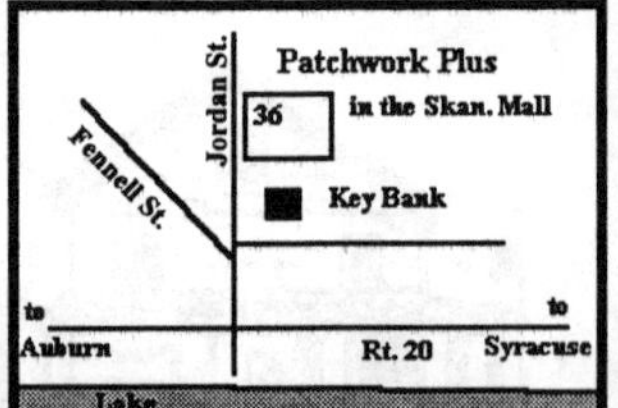

Canandaigua, NY #22

Mon - Wed 10 - 6 Thur 10 - 8 Fri & Sat 10 - 5

FABRICS, etc.

71 S. Main St. 14424
(716) 394-6350 Fax: (716) 394-6533
E-Mail: fabric@frontiernet.net
Owner: Mary Hoffman
Est: 1993 1500 sq.ft.

In the heart of the beautiful Finger Lakes. Quilt supplies, Fashion fabrics, patterns, books, classes & much more. Pfaff & Babylock.

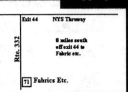

Exit 44 NYS Thruway
Rte. 332
8 miles south off exit 44 to Fabric etc.
71 Fabrics Etc.

Rushville, NY #23

Mon - Sat 9 - 5

Quilting on a Country Lane

4594 Harvey Lane 14544
(716) 554-6507
Owner: Arlene Lee
Est: 1980

Quilt making supplies. Notions, Books, Fabric, Patterns, and Machine Quilting.

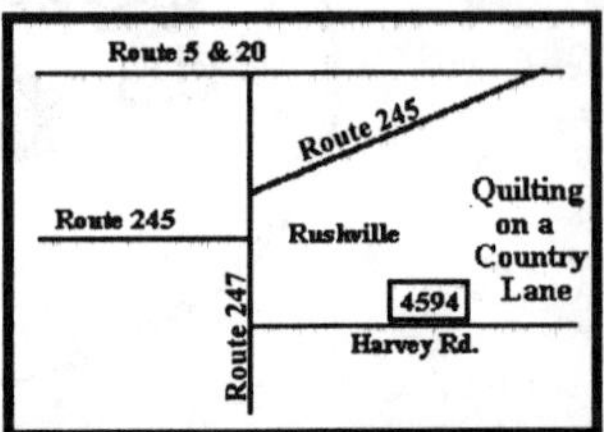

Dansville, NY #24

Mon - Fri 9:30 - 5:30 Sat 9:30 - 5

MATERIAL REWARDS

10348 Sandy Hill Rd. 14437
(716) 335-2050 Est: 1986
Owners: Teri & Marty Wilson
2500 sq.ft. 1500 Bolts

Hundreds of bolts of 100% cottons, books, notions and patterns. Gifts for Quilters and Machine quilting available.
Quilt Show Sept. 4, 5, 6 1998

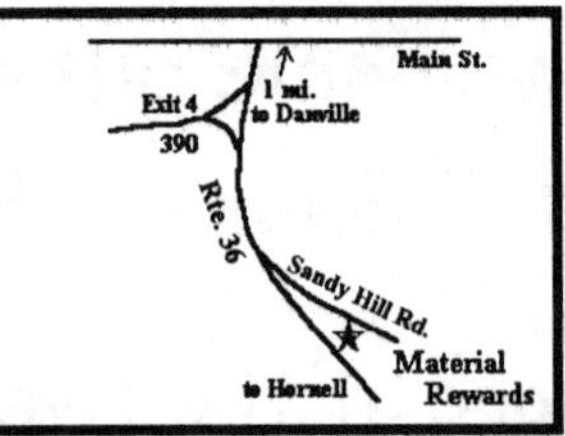

Penn Yan, NY #25

Mon - Sat 10 - 4:30

The Quilt Room

1870 Hoyt Rd. 14527
(315) 536-5964 E-Mail: quilt@eznet.net
Web Site: www.quiltroom.com
Owners: Glenn & Naomi Lapp
Est: 1981 1000 sq.ft.
Our specialty is Hand-Made Quilts.
Made Locally by the Amish & Mennonites with 80-100 in stock.
We Repair and make custom Quilts also.

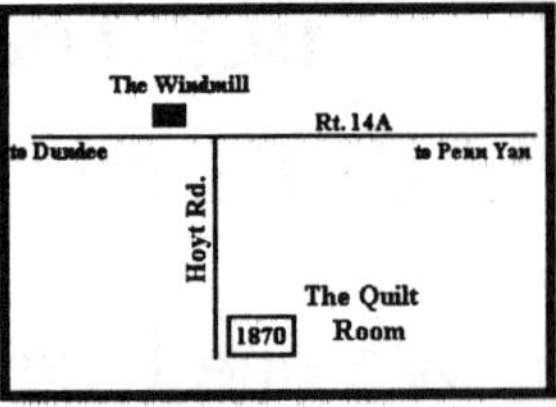

Aurora, NY #26

Thur - Sat 10 - 5 And By Chance or Appt.

Gosline Place Merchantile

2306 Lake Rd. 13026
(315) 364-8169
Owner: Yvonne Jordan
Est: 1995

A Quilt Shop overlooking the East Shore Cayuga Lake. Features premium 100% cottons, books, patterns, notions.

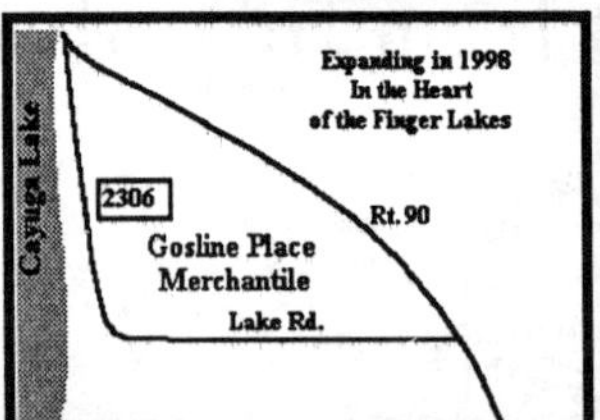

Hammondsport, NY #27

Mon - Sat 10 - 5 Sun 11 - 4

Lake Country Patchwork

67 Shether St. P.O. Box 332 14840
(607) 569-3530 Est: 1996
Owner: Candace Hosier

Let the natural beauty of the Finger Lakes inspire your next quilt. We have 100% cotton fabrics, quilting supplies and books. Quilts & gift items.

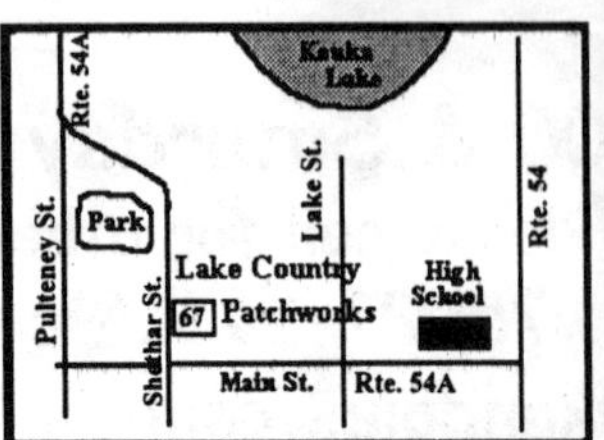

Kim's Fabrics

Authorized PFAFF Dealer
PFAFF Club Quilt Classes

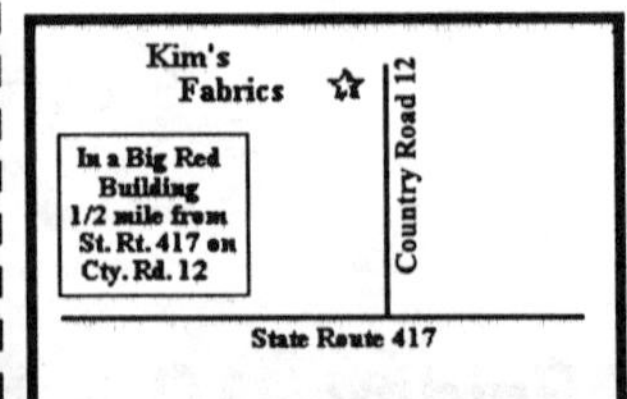

3591 County Rd. 12
14806-9709
(607) 478-5284

A Fun and Friendly Shop

Mon 9:30 - 8
Tues - Fri 9:30 - 5
Sat 9 - 3

Hundreds of bolts of 100% Cotton fabric. Books. Notions, and Patterns. Gifts for Quilters.

Andover, NY #28

Owner: Kim Waters Est: 1993

Ithaca, NY #29

Mon - Fri 10 - 6
Sat 10 - 5
Sun 1 - 4

Quilters Corner

200 Pleasant Grove Rd. 14850
(607) 266-0850 Est: 1995
Owners: Katie Barnaby, Sherry Haefele, Cyndi Slothower, Linda Van Nederynen
1400 sq.ft. 2000 Bolts & Merrie Wilent

A diverse collection of exciting fabric selected by five wild women. Huge book selection, patterns, notions, and gifts. Authorized Pfaff dealer.

Big Flats, NY #30

Mon - Sat 10 - 5
Thur 10 - 8:00

The Village Sampler

18 Canal St. 14814
(607) 562-7596
Owner: Carol A. Blakeslee
Est: 1986 4500 sq.ft.

Extraordinary Fabrics, Ideas, & Notions for the Quilter & Cross Stitcher. A Doll Crafter's Paradise. Gifts Too!

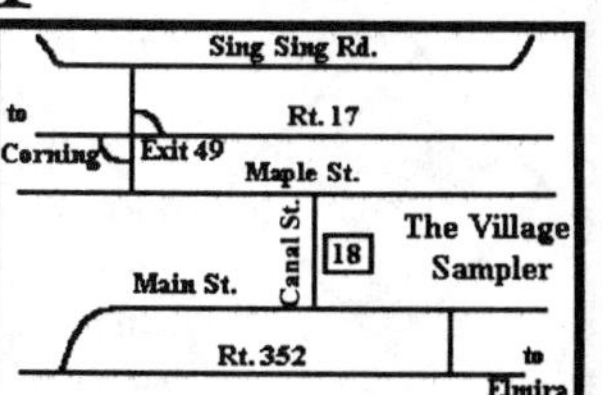

Endwell, NY #31

Mon - Fri
9 - 5:30
Sat 9 - 1

Sew Much More

2723 East Main St. 13760
(607) 748-8340
Owner: Nancy Valenta
Est: 1990 1750 sq.ft.

Over 2000 bolts of 100% cottons. Heirloom sewing, specialty threads, books and patterns galore. A delightful experience for your palette. HUSQVARNA VIKING Authorized Dealer.

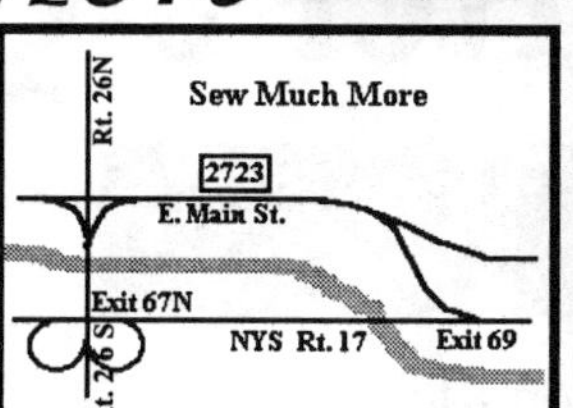

Binghamton, NY #32

Mon - Fri 10 - 5
Thurs til 6:30
Sat 10 - 4

Grandmother's Thimble

29 Kattelville Rd. 13901
(607) 648-9009 (800) 646-9009
Owner: Carol Darrow Est: 1988
e-mail: XQHD79A@Prodigy.com
www.thecomputerpros.com/thimble

Totally devoted to Quilters!
Over 1300 bolts of 100% cotton fabric.
Bernina Sewing Machines, Sergers,
Embroidery Systems, Classes.

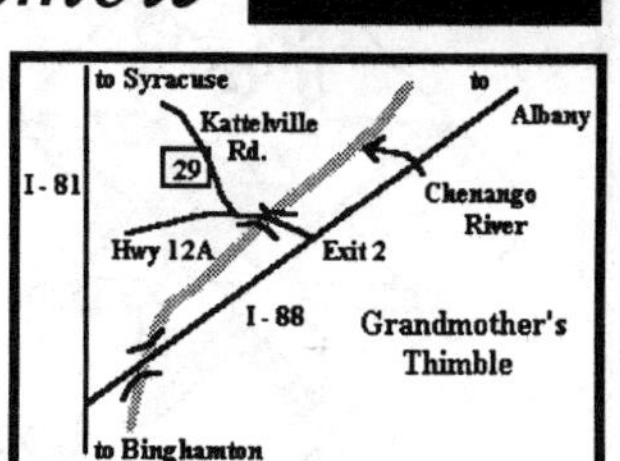

Est: 1989

Fly Creek, NY #33

3 miles North of Cooperstown, NY

Heartworks

Quilts  Fabrics

A real country quilt shop with over 2,000 bolts of Fine Cotton Fabrics and Cotton Flannel Fabrics, Batting, Books, Stencils and a full line of notions. One-of-a-kind full size quilts (made here in NY,USA), quilt repair, custom design of quilts for interior decorators, and hand quilting of your quilt tops. Authorized dealer for Bernina and Elna Sewing Machines.

Rte. 28 P.O. Box 148 13337
Owners:
Margaret & Jim Wolff

(607) 547-2501
E-Mail:
hrtworks@telenet.net

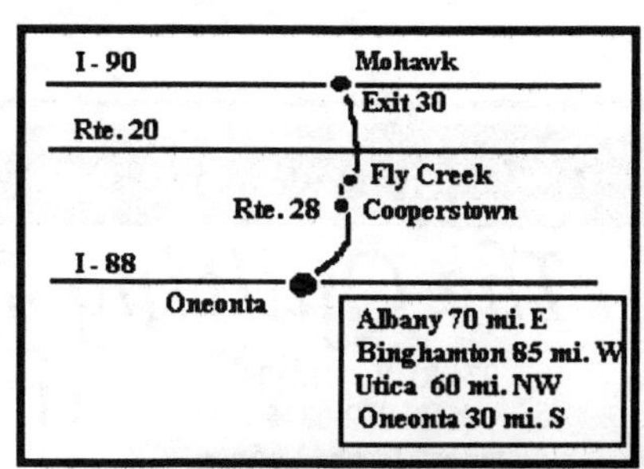

Between visits to our shop, please visit us on the world wide web at: www.heartworksquilts.com featuring our applique kits & is updated monthly

Open Year Round
Mon - Sat 10 - 5

Manlius, NY #34

Mon - Sat
9:30 - 5
Wed til 7

Cazenovia Quilt Shop

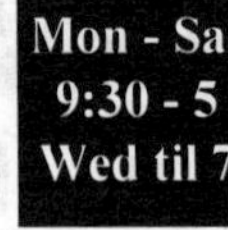

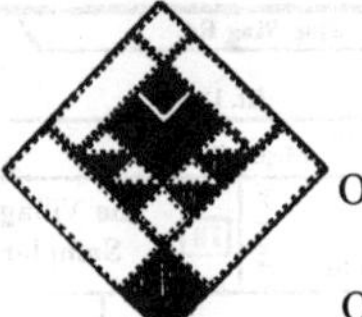

125 E. Seneca St.
13104
(315) 682-6777
Owner: Ruth A. Roickle

Books, Patterns, Quilting Supplies 100% cotton fabric, gifts, classes, warm & friendly assistance.

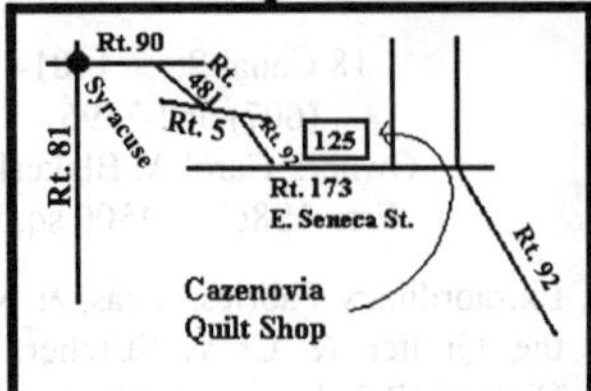

Oneida, NY #35

Mon - Sat
10 - 5
Thur til 8

Cottons Etc.

228 Genesee Street 13421
(315) 363-6834 Est: 1980
Owner: Paula Schultz 1700 sq.ft.
Swatch Set $2 and LSASE.
e-mail: cottons@ny.tds.net

Our motto is "You Can Never Have Too Much Fabric!" A Pot-pourri of Quilting & Fashion Fabrics, Notions, Books & Patterns. Ask for free gift!

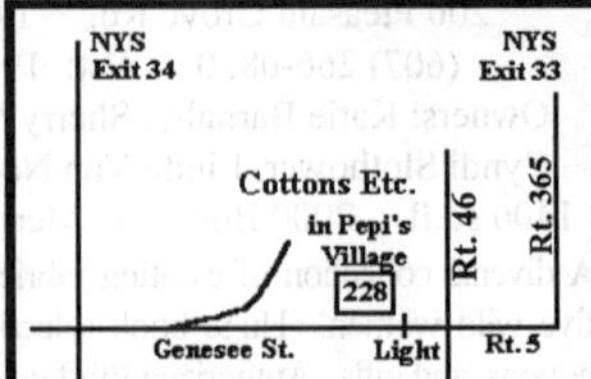

Dreamcrafter's Quilt Shop

Hogansburg, NY #36

Located at the Wolf Pack Gift Shop on Rte. 37
Rte. 37, Box 121 - B, Bombay, NY 12914
(518) 358-4285
E-Mail: Dreamcrftr@aol.com
Owner: Dyan Swamp Est: 1997 2000 Bolts
We welcome all visitors to our colorful shop.
We enjoy taking the time to help you.
All purchases are tax-free.

Mon - Sat
9 - 9
Sun 10 - 9

Just 6 miles from the Canadian border on the Akwesasne Mohawk Indian Reservation.

SUPPLIES FOR ALL YOUR "DREAM" CREATIONS

* 2000+ Bolts of 100% Cottons, Hoffman, Nancy Crow, P&B, Maywood
* Notions: Quilters' Tools, Batting, Thread.
* Huge Selection of Books, Patterns & Stencils
* Amish Patterns & Books
* Fat Quarters Galore!!!
* Hand-Dyed and Marbled Fabrics
* New Classes every month
* Great assortment of Quilter's Gifts
* Quilts for Sale

Queensbury, NY #37

Mon - Sat
10 - 5
Sun 12 - 5

The Quilting Bee

974 Rt. 9 12804
(518) 792-0845
Owner: Joanne Loftus
Est: 1987 1500 sq.ft.

Cotton fabrics include designer's calicos & solids, books, patterns & notions. Banner flag supplies, Antiques. Gifts and Quilts. Bernina Dealer.

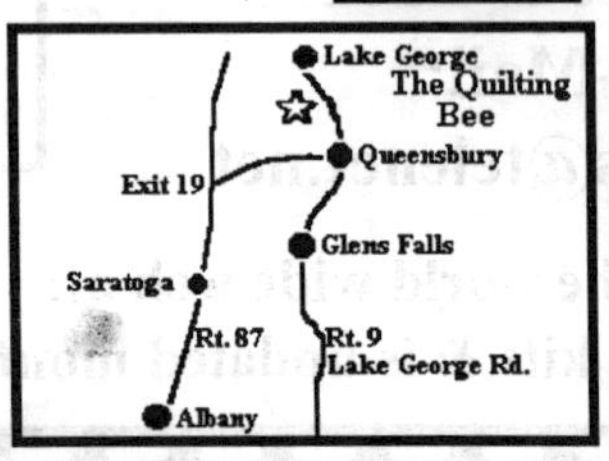

Schenectady, NY #38

Mon - Fri
10 - 5
Sat 10 - 4

Flying Geese Fabrics

Shaker Pine Mall 145 Vly Road 12309
(518) 456-8885 Est: 1985 1700 Bolts
Owners: Donnie Brownsey,
Tara Conlon & Joanne Skudder.

The latest in 100% Cotton Fabrics & Quilting supplies, Classes, Books, Patterns all designed for the enthusiastic Quilter!

Gloversville, NY #39

385 S. Main St. 12078
(518) 725-4919 Fax: (518) 773-4166
(800) 336-9998
Owners: Diana & John Marshall
Est: 1981 4600 sq.ft. 2000+ Bolts

Specializing in Sales & Service of
Bernina • Brother
Including Brother Personal Embroidery Machine

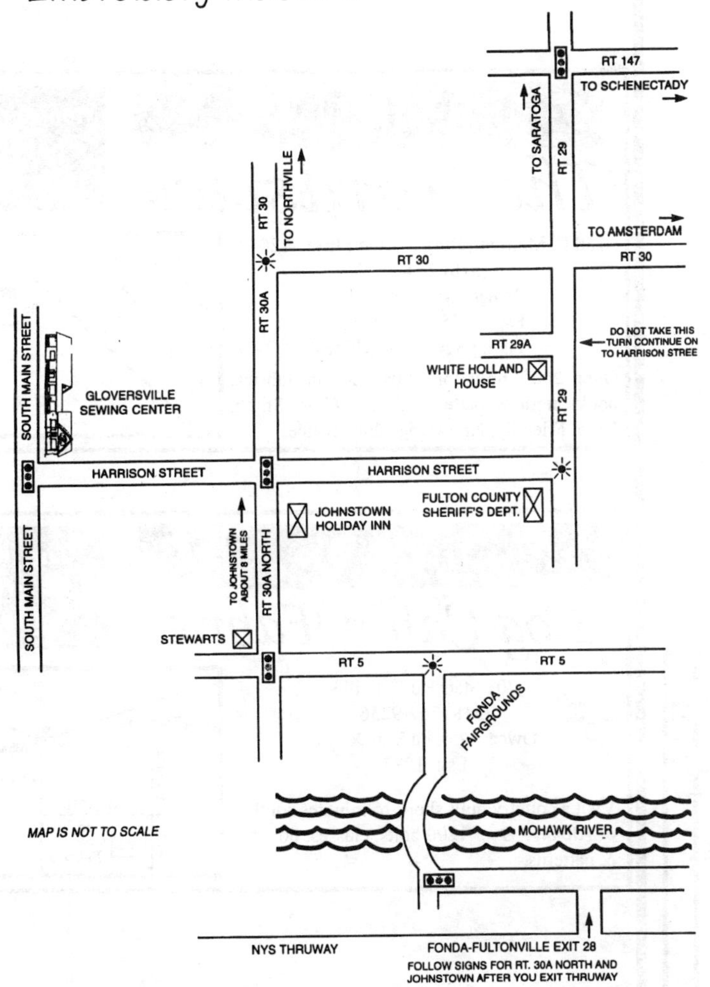

Area's Largest Selection of
Quilting Books & Patterns

Over 2000 Broadcloths in Stock
Including Hoffman
Alexander Henry
P & B • RJR • Moda

Large Assortment of
Decorative Threads
Silk Ribbons
Specialty Needles
Sewing Machine Attachments

Classes in Everything
8 Instructors to Assist You

From A to Z — It's all here!

Mon - Fri 9 - 5:30
Thur til 8:30 Sat 9 - 5

Utica, NY #40

2336 West Whitesboro St. 13502
(315) 735-5328 Owners:
Susan Kowalczyk & Sandra Jones
Est: 1991 2000 sq.ft.

Mon - Fri 9:30 - 5:30
Sat 10 - 5

A shop with unusual fabrics for quilting & sewing.
Books, notions, patterns, gifts, classes and newsletter.
Bernina Affiliate.
Services Offered:
Private Lessons, Quilt Basting,
Specific classes for 4 or more.
Fabric always discounted 10%
(no s&h added.)

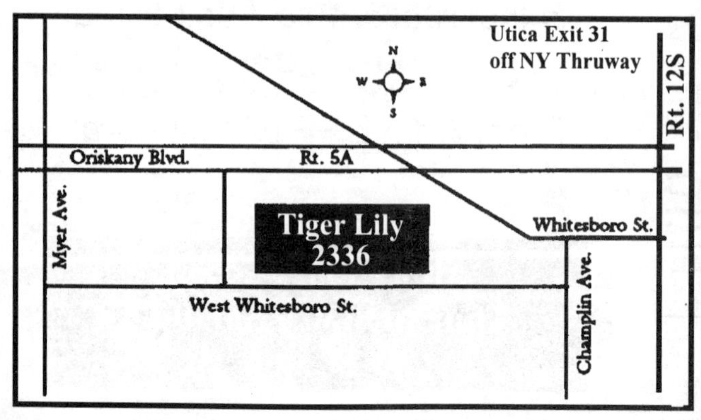

Fultonville, NY #41

Morning Glory Fabrics

Tues - Sat
10 - 5

1555 State Hwy. 161 12072
(518) 922-8720
Owners: Linda & John Anderson
Est: 1993 1200 sq.ft. 700 Bolts

A full service quilting and sewing shop with 100's of bolts of quilt fabric. Large selection of Polartec® & other clothing fabrics. Pfaff Dealer.

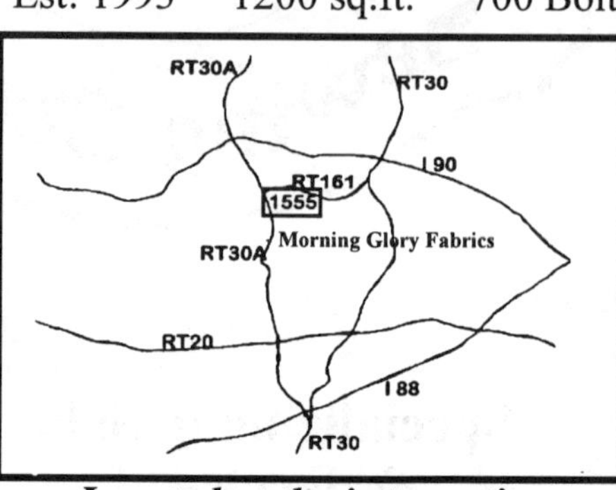

Located at the intersection of St. Hwys. 161 & 30A

Cobleskill, NY #42

The Yardstick

Mon - Fri 9 - 9
Sat 9 - 6
Sun 11 - 5

150 E. Main St., Burger King Plaza 12043
(518) 234-2179
Owner: Merilyn Ludwig
Est: 1975 2500 sq.ft.
Viking Sewing Machines

Over 2000 bolts of 100% cotton fabrics, books, notions, patterns, classes, Cross-Stitch, Yarn. Friendly, Knowledgeable service.

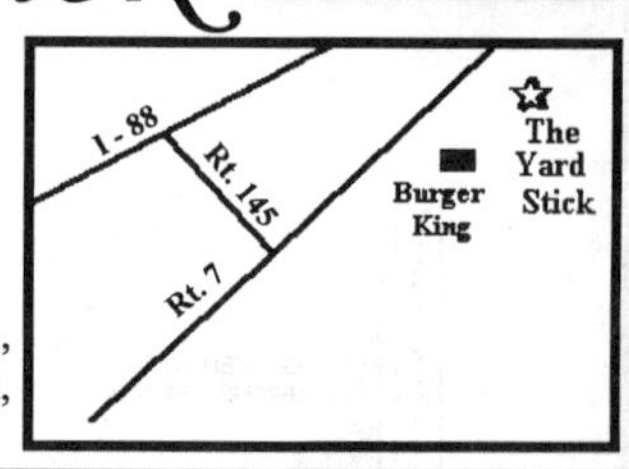

Ravena, NY #43

Log Cabin Fabrics

Tue 10 - 9
Wed - Fri 10 - 5
Sat 10 - 4

702 Starr Rd. 12143
(518) 767-9236
Owner: Londa VanDerzee
Est: 1987

Visit a country quilt shop, 15 minutes south of Albany. Over 1200 bolts, classes, books & patterns.

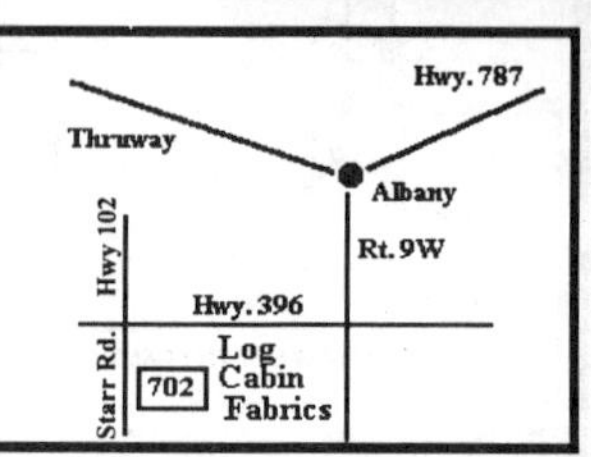

The Fieldstone House

to Oneonta
to Unadilla
Exit 11
I - 88
NY 357
to Binghamton
The Fieldstone House
East Sidney Dam
Wheat Hill Rd. to Sidney Center
to Franklin

RD 2, Box 307A 13839
(607) 369-9177
Proprietors: Jane & Allan Kirby

Sidney Center, NY #44

featuring: **Fabric Shop**
Gift Collection
Country Tea Room
Bed & Breakfast

The Fabric Shop

Three rooms are filled to capacity with more than 8000 bolts

This outstanding selection includes all of your favorite designs from . . .

Alexander Henry • Benartex • Concord • Cute as a Button
Debbie Mumm • Gutcheon • Hoffman • Kaufman • Libas • Marcus Brothers
Mary Ellen Hopkins • Northcott/Monarch • P&B • Peter Pan • Red Wagon
RJR • Roberta Horton • Spiegel • Timeless Treasures ... and more.

Books, Threads, Needles, Muslin, Battings, Templates
Buttons, Cutting Tools, Flannels
Cross-Stitch Patterns/Fabric, Clothing Patterns

"A quilter's dream come true"

The Gift Collection

Baskets ❖ Candles ❖ Pottery ❖ Stuffed Animals
Wrought Iron ❖ Tinware

"Come Browse for that Special Gift"

Hours: 7 day a week 11 - 5
Closed Occasionally for Quilt Shows and Family Events
Other Times by Appointment

The Country Tea Room

A delightful lunch is served daily; reservations recommended. Breakfast & dinner are also available by reservation only. Small group gatherings such as quilt guilds, showers, birthday parties are a specialty.

"Relax & Enjoy with Friends & Family"

The Bed and Breakfast

The Kirby Homestead, a fieldstone house on a quiet country hill side, is located on the same property approximately one-half mile from the shop. Four comfortable rooms are available, each with a double bed. A full breakfast is served to guests at the Country Tea Room. This is the perfect location for a quilting retreat!

"Enjoy the Peace & Quiet of this Country Home"

Pine Bush, NY #45

QUILTER'S ATTIC

- 1500 bolts of fabrics, including Hoffman, RJR, P&B, Benartex, Mission Valley, Rose & Hubble, South Seas, Timeless Treasures, Northcott, Kaufmann, Clothworks & more.
- Nice selection of wovens, flannels, wools, and synthetic furs.
- Complete supply of books, patterns, notions & batting.
- Silk Ribbon & Rug Hooking supplies.
- Supplies for dolls, bears & Santas.
- Gift Items.
- Large Classroom with a continuous schedule of classes year round taught by an extremely talented staff of teachers.
- Thimbleberries & Piecemakers club.
- Lots of samples on display at all times.
- Numerous Block of the month programs including Applique, Pieced, Paper Pieced & embroidery. Featuring traditional as well as contemporary designs. Pick up monthly or have them mailed.
- Our friendly & knowledgeable shop owners invite you to visit soon!

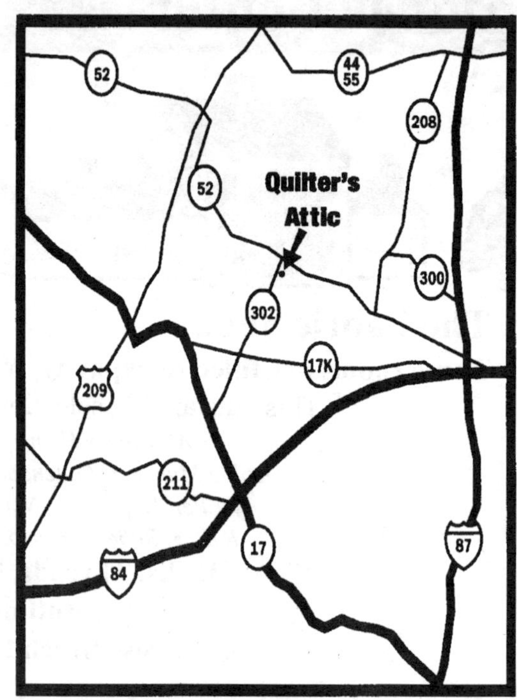

JUST MINUTES FROM MAJOR HIGHWAYS:

***From Route 17**: Take exit 119 (Route 302 N) to Pine Bush. Less than 10 miles from exit on right.*
***From Route 84**: Take exit 8 (Route 52 W) to Pine Bush. Left on Route 302 - 1/10th mile on left.*

Tues - Sat
10 - 4
Evenings during classes

Route 302, P.O. Box 656 12566
(914) 744-5888
Owners: Wayne & Kathy Joray
Est: 1994 1800 sq.ft. 1500 Bolts

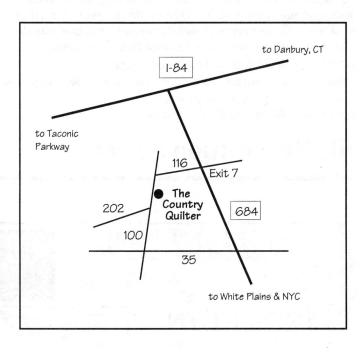

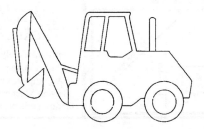

K & K Quilteds

Rt. 23, P.O. Box 23 12529
(518) 325-4502
Director: Camille Cognac

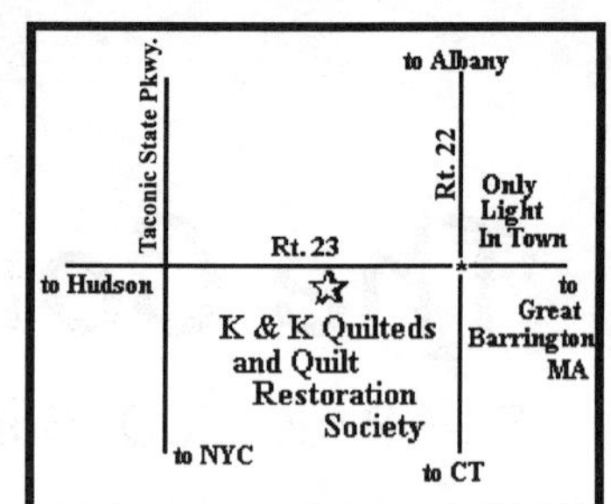

Hillsdale, NY #47

When quilters come into our shop with color swatches clutched in their hands, they stop at the door, remain silent and quizzically ask, "Where's the fabric?" The sign suggests fabric, hoops, walls of batting and size #12 quilting needles. We sell none of these. *K & K Quilteds is not a traditional quilt shop.*

Although not a traditional quilt shop, K & K Quilteds does fill a need in the quilt world. Those old quilts, treasures from the past, can gain a new life. Our deepest satisfaction comes from transforming a severely damaged quilt into a usable quilt that can be enjoyed into the 21st century. K & K Quilteds has evolved into a textile and sewing studio which specializes in quilt restoration and the sale of custom wall-hangings and antique quilts. Often called a "quilt hospital', we jokingly refer to ourselves as "quilt doctors" who specialize in plastic surgery with cotton, tweezers, stilettos, fine tip scissors and #12 sharps. We know we've done our job well when the quilt owner cannot find the repairs.

If you have a quilt in need of restoration, please follow this procedure:

Call or write (include photo), Arrange time & method of shipment, when quilt has been examined, we will discuss options
Shipping Guidelines: Notify K & K, Ship in secured plastic bag
Include address and phone, Insure quilt fully, Allow 2 weeks for estimate

Also the Home of the: **Quilt Restoration Society**

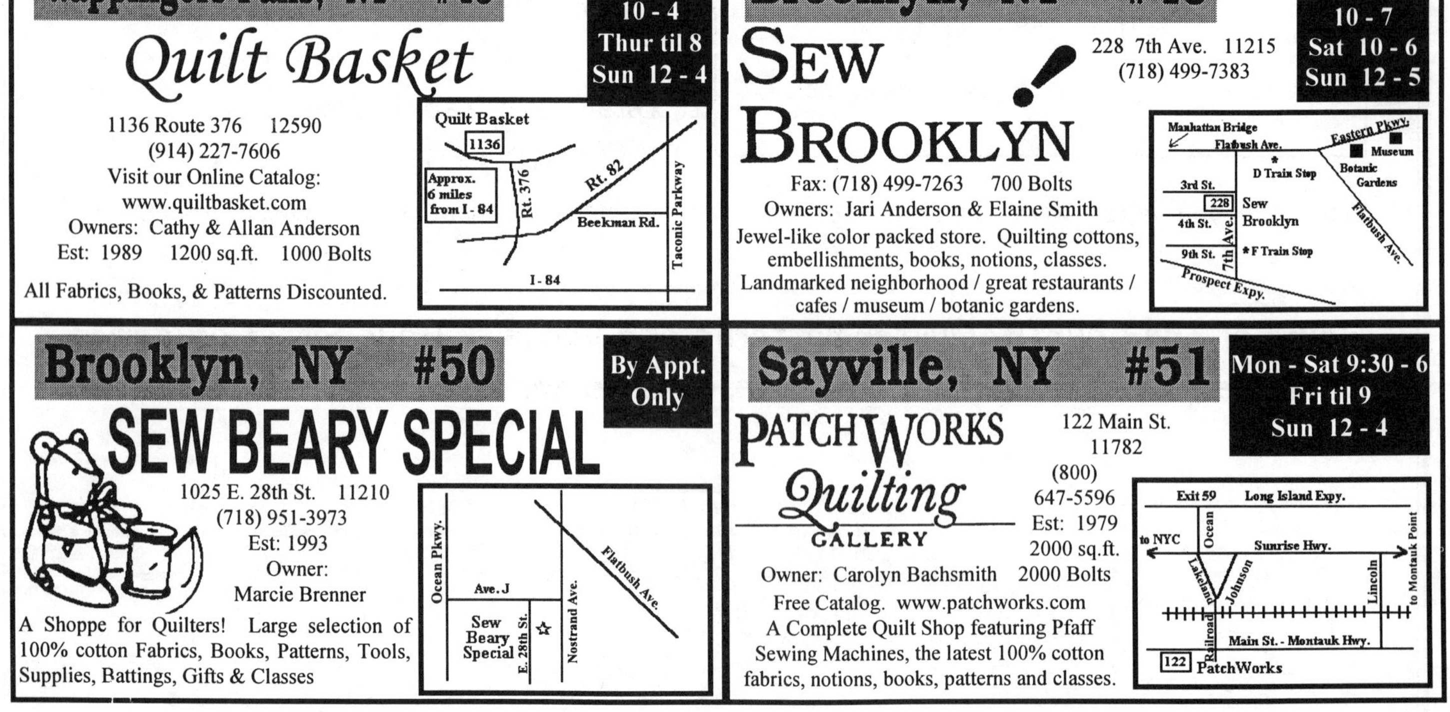

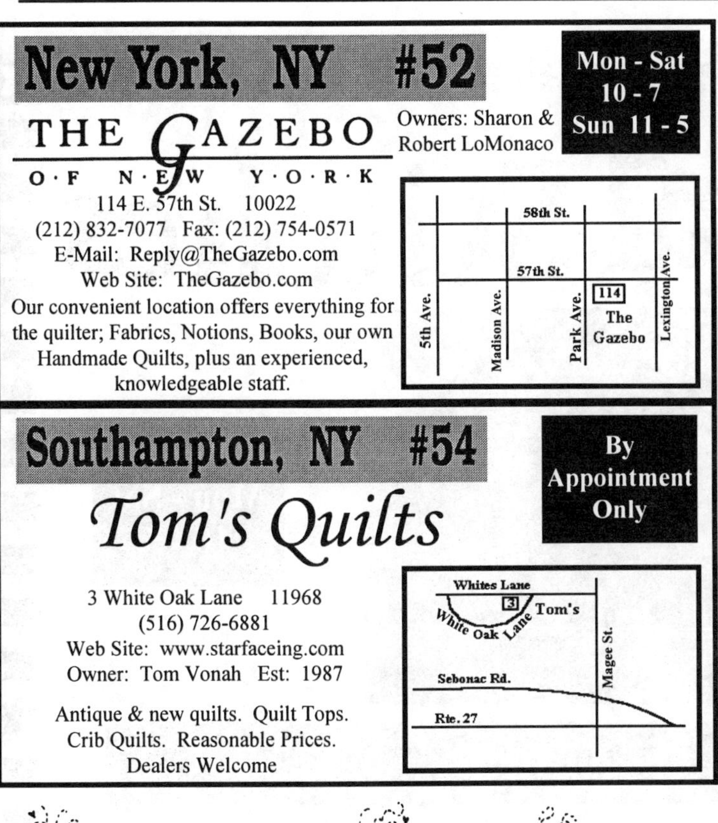

New York, NY #52
Mon - Sat 10 - 7
Sun 11 - 5
THE GAZEBO
OF NEW YORK
Owners: Sharon & Robert LoMonaco
114 E. 57th St. 10022
(212) 832-7077 Fax: (212) 754-0571
E-Mail: Reply@TheGazebo.com
Web Site: TheGazebo.com
Our convenient location offers everything for the quilter; Fabrics, Notions, Books, our own Handmade Quilts, plus an experienced, knowledgeable staff.
58th St.
57th St.
5th Ave.
Madison Ave.
Park Ave.
Lexington Ave.
114
The Gazebo
Southampton, NY #54
By Appointment Only
Tom's Quilts
3 White Oak Lane 11968
(516) 726-6881
Web Site: www.starfaceing.com
Owner: Tom Vonah Est: 1987
Antique & new quilts. Quilt Tops.
Crib Quilts. Reasonable Prices.
Dealers Welcome
Whites Lane
3
Tom's
White Oak Lane
Magee St.
Sebonac Rd.
Rte. 27

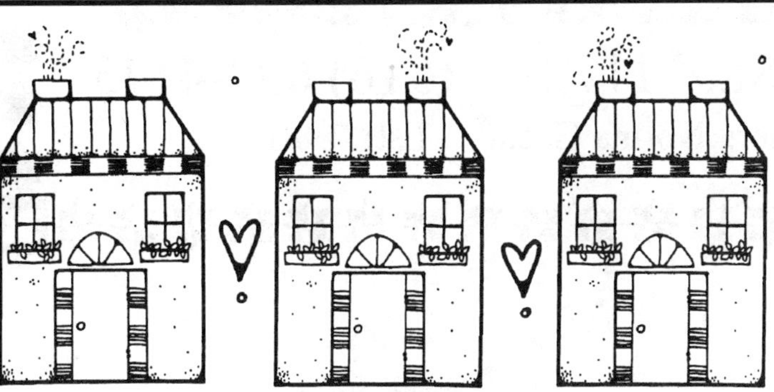

New York, NY #53

Tues - Fri 11 - 7
Sat 10 - 6
Sun 11 - 5

157 West 24th St. 10011
(212) 807-0390
Fax: (212) 807-9451
E-Mail:
71611.3030@compuserve.com

THE CITY QUILTER

Outstanding selection of 100% Cotton Fabrics.
Gifts, books, patterns, notions and classes.
Bernina machines and accessories.

7th Ave.
parking garage
THE CITY QUILTER
6th Ave.
157 West 24 St.
Subway/ bus stop
23rd St.
Subway/ bus stop

Owner:
Cathy Izzo

New York Guilds:

Q.U.I.L.T., 79 Edgecomb St., Albany, 12209
Athens Schoolhouse Quilters, Athens
Candlelight Quilter's, Baldwinsville
Tea Time Quilters, Brewerton
The Quilter's Guild of Brooklyn, 239 E 5th St., Brooklyn, 11218
  Meets: 3rd Saturday (sometimes Sunday)
Quilting By the Lake, Cazenovia
Huntington Quilters, Little Neck Rd., Centerport
  Meets: 2nd Tuesday at Centerport Methodist Church
Champlain Valley Quilter's Guild, Chazy
Clarence Log Cabin Quilters, 4895 Kraus Rd., Clarence, 14031
Creative Sewing Club, Clarence, 14031
Plankroad Quilt Guild, Clay
Twilight Stitchers, Clay
Q.U.I.L.T., Kenwood Ave., Delmar, 12054
  Meets: 2nd Friday 9:45 a.m. at United Methodist Church
Lake to Lake Quilt Guild, Dresden
Southtown Piecemakers Quilting, Box 340, East Aurora, 14052
Eden Quilt Guild, Church St., Eden, 14057
  Meets: 3rd Monday (alternate months) 7 p.m.
  at United Methodist Church of Eden
Perinton Quilt Guild, Fairport
Towpath Quilt Guild, P.O. Box 188, Fayetteville, 13066
Lake Country Quilt Guild, Fulton
Wings Falls Quilter's Guild, Bay & Washington Sts., Glens Falls
Sew Busy Quilt Guild, 385 S. Main St., Gloversville, 12078
  Meets: 3rd Monday 7 p.m.
  at Gloversville Sewing Center Working guild with
  demos, classes, instruction given every month.
Lake to Lake Quilt Guild, Box 67, Gorham, 14461
  Meets: 1st Wednesday (Sept - June) 10:30 a.m.
  at Gorham Methodist Church
Empire Quilters, P.O. Box 6175, Grand Central Station, 10163
River Lea Quilters Guild, Grand Island
Americana Village Quilters, P.O. Box 292, Hamilton, 13346
Mohawk Valley Quilt Guild, Holland Patent
Country Neighbors Q.G., 4719 Bennetts Corners Rd., Holley, 14470
Tompkins County Quilters, Women's Community Bldg.,
  Senecca St., Ithaca, 14850
Wiltwyck Quilter's Guild, P.O. Box 3731, Kingston, 12401
Borderline Quilters c/o Rena Patty, 525 Murphy Rd., Lisbon, 13658
  Meets: 1st Wednesday 12 noon & 7 p.m. at Canton Library
Plank Road Quilters Guild, Liverpool, 13090
Kenan Quilters Guild, 433 Locust Street, Lockport, 14094

Towpath Quilt Guild, Manlius
Tumbstall Quilt Guild, Marcellus
Long Island Quilters' Society, P.O. Box 1660, Mineola, 11501
The Scriba Quilter's, Oswega
Country Quilters Guild, Pine Bush, 12566
Meets: 2nd Wednesday 7 p.m. at Pine Bush Schools
Hudson River Piecemakers, Porter Corners
First Dutchess Quilters' Guild, P.O. Box 3182, Poughkeepsie, 12603
Meets: 3rd Wednesday 7:30 p.m. at Arlington High School South Campus, Stringham Rd, LaGrangeville
Genesee Valley Quilt Club, P.O. Box 18321, Rochester, 14618
Lake to Lake Quilt Guild, 4594 Harvey Rd., Rushville, 14544
Cabin Fever Quilters, Saranac Lake
Q.U.I.L.T.S., 1068 Maryland Avenue, Schenectady, 12308
Thumbstall Quilt Guild, Skaneateles
Smithtown Stitchers, P.O. Box 311, Smithtown, 11787
Northern Star Quilters Guild, P.O. Box 232, Somers, 10589
East Long Island Q. G., P.O. Box 1514, Southampton, 11968
Cayuga Lake Quilt Guild, 5 Park St., Union Springs, 13021
Meets: 2nd Wednesday 7 p.m. at A. J. Smith Elementary School
Quilter's Consortium of NY, P.O. Box 769, Waverly, 14892
Endless Mountain Quilt Guild, Waverly
Westfield Quilt Guild, S. Portage St., Westfield, 14787
Meets: 4th Monday 7 p.m. at Westfield YMCA, biannual Quilt Show, Sept. 18-19th 1998
Mohawk Valley Quilt Club, 31 Capardo Dr., Whitesboro, 13492

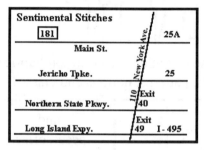

Other Shops in New York:

Albany	The Sewing Store, 265 Osborne Rd.	518-482-9088
Auburn	Finger Lakes Quilting, 65 Washington St.	
Averill Park	Quilt Lady, Rt. 43	518-674-0913
Boheima	Boheima Sewing and Knitting Center, 4109 Sunrise Hwy.	
Brockport	Country Treasures, 27 Market St.	716-637-5148
Brooklyn	Sew Materialistic, 1310 Coney Island Ave.	718-338-6104
Brooklyn	Park Slope Sewing Center, 297 7th Ave.	718-832-2556
Chatham	Sarris Quilts, 46 Main St.	518-392-6323
Croton-on-Hudson	Pinwheels, 5 Old Post Rd. S	914-271-1045
Depauville	Patchwork North, NY 12, P.O. Box 223	315-686-1714
Dundee	The Fabric Shop, 8 Main St.	607-243-7052
Farmingdale	Phillips-Boyne, 1646 New Hwy.	516-755-1230
Fayetteville	Bear's Paw, 7070 Cedar Bay Rd.	315-445-2055
Floral Park	Patchwork Patch, 32 Hemlock St.	516-326-0774
Fulton	Herron's Fabric Center, 121 Cayuga St.	315-592-4031
Greenwood Lake	It's About Time, 274 Pine Hill Rd.	914-477-0066
Hamilton	The Pin Cushion, 37 Milford	315-824-5410
Hartsdale	Hartsdale Fabrics, 275 S. Central Ave.	914-428-7780
Hudson	Fabrications Quilt Shop, 558 Warren St.	
Hurleyville	Chris-Sans Nubian Quilt House, Meyerhoff Rd.	914-434-6667
Ithaca	Homespun Boutique, 101 The Commons	607-277-0954
Lockport	Martha's Cupboard, 3362 Hess Rd.	716-434-4535
Mahopac	Sue's Fabric, R.R. #6	914-628-8338
Malden Bridge	Claudia Kingsley Quilts & Antiques, Box 118	518-766-4759
Manhasset	The Watermelon Patch, 500 Plandome Rd.	516-365-6166
Mastic	Addie's Corner Shoppe, 1484 Montuk Hwy.	516-281-3966
Monsey	Patchwork Sampler, 7 Fieldcrest St.	914-357-1011
Mt. Kisco	Pins and Needles, 161 Main St.	914-666-0824
New York	B&J Fabrics, 263 W. 40th St.	212-354-8150
New York	Laura Fisher Antique Quilts, 1050 2nd. Ave. #57	212-838-2596
New York	Paron Fabrics, 56 W. 57th	212-247-6451
New York	Quilts Plus, 86 Forsyth	212-334-0123
Norwich	Kinsley Creations, 8 Pleasant St.	607-334-9989
Norwood	Martha Drologio, 1140 River Rd.	
Oneonta	Stitching Post, 363 Chestnut,	607-432-7500
Plainview	Melanis Moods Ltd. 14 Manetto Hill Mall	516-935-4644
Port Chester	Nimble Thimble 509 N. Main St.	914-934-2934
Port Jefferson	Stitchin Time, Inc., 326 Main St.	516-928-4544
Rockville Center	Bramson House, 5 Nassau	516-764-5006
Roslyn	Arbor House, 22 Arbor Lane	516-538-0009
Saugerties	A Stitch in Tyme Quilt Shop, 27 Scotti Ln. #R32	914-336-7306
Sea Cliff	Calico Square, 347 Glen Cove Ave.	516-676-5577
Seneca Falls	Country Quilting Shoppe, 3600 Rt. 89	
South Dayton	Block in the Square Quilt Shop, 30 Maple St.	716-988-3013
St. James	Corner Cupboard, 367 Lake Ave.	516-584-7288
Summit	Haybarn Gift & Quilting Shop, Hwy. 10	518-287-1368
Warrensburg	I Love Fabric & Co., 30 Main St.	518-623-9814
West Oneonta	Country Fabrics HCR Box 620	607-432-9726

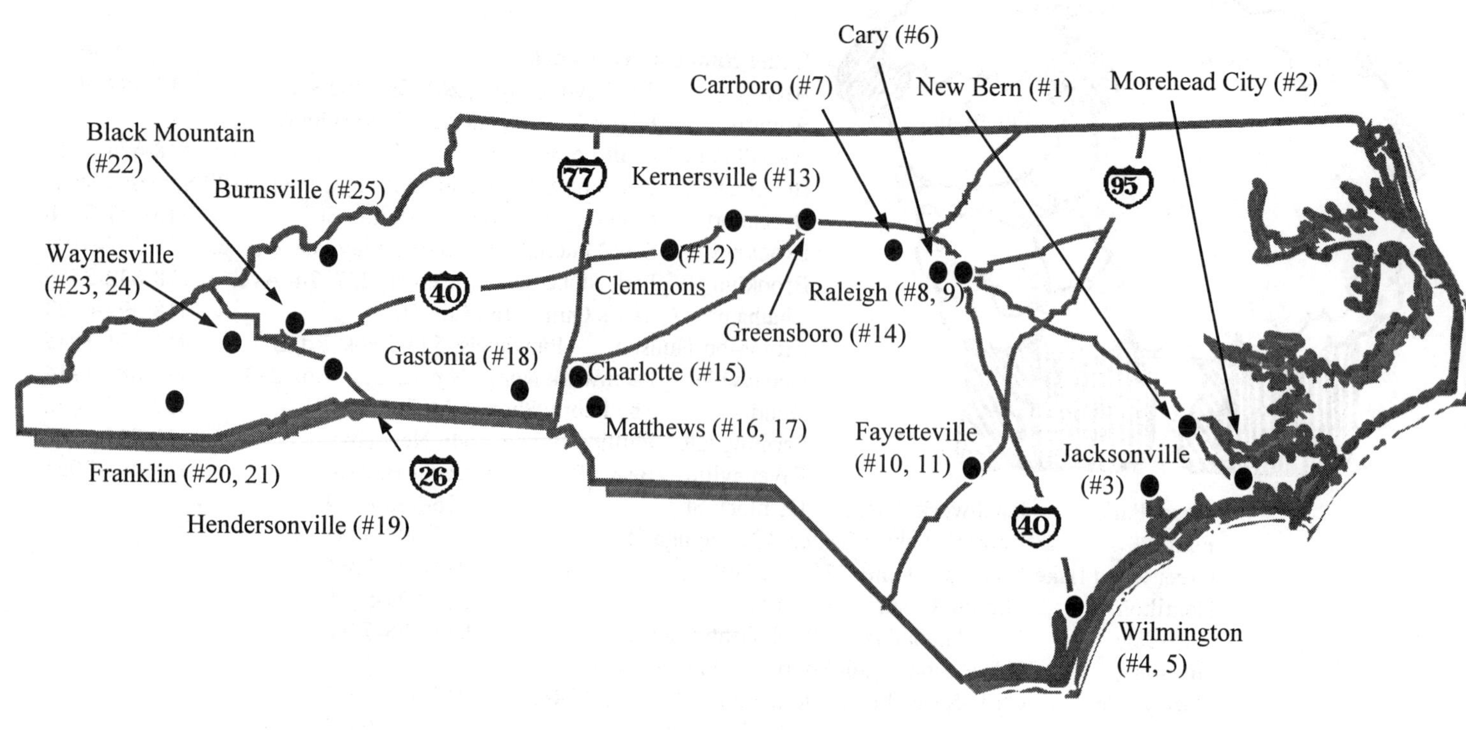
Cary (#6)
Carrboro (#7)
New Bern (#1)
Morehead City (#2)
Black Mountain (#22)
Burnsville (#25)
77
Kernersville (#13)
95
Waynesville (#23, 24)
(#12)
Clemmons
40
Raleigh (#8, 9)
Greensboro (#14)
Gastonia (#18)
Charlotte (#15)
Matthews (#16, 17)
Fayetteville (#10, 11)
Jacksonville (#3)
Franklin (#20, 21)
26
Hendersonville (#19)
40
Wilmington (#4, 5)

NORTH CAROLINA
25 Featured Shops

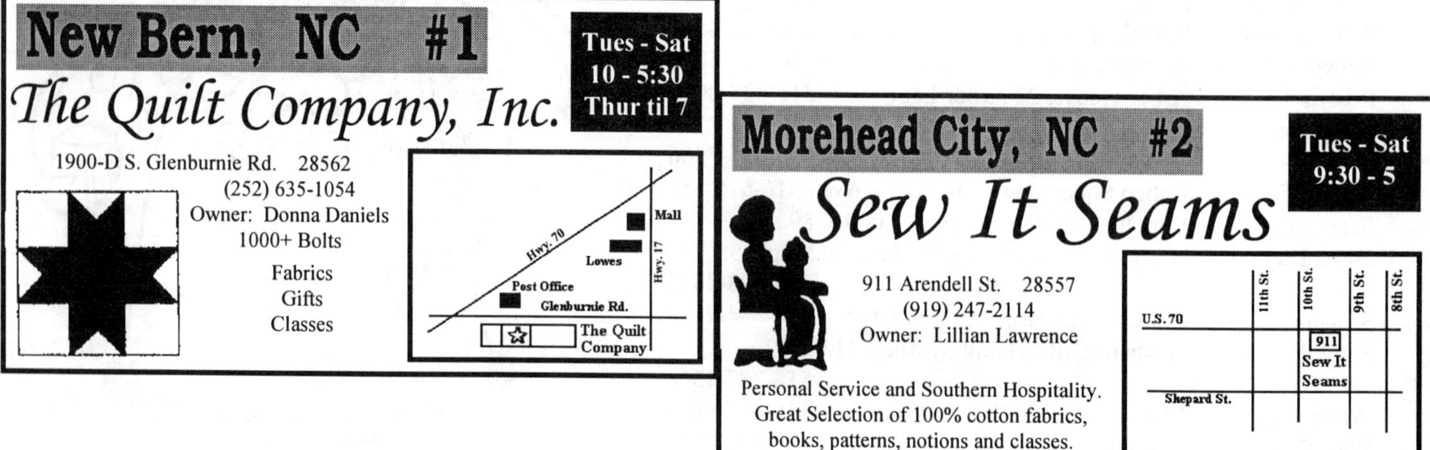
New Bern, NC #1
Tues - Sat
10 - 5:30
Thur til 7
The Quilt Company, Inc.
1900-D S. Glenburnie Rd. 28562
(252) 635-1054
Owner: Donna Daniels
1000+ Bolts
Fabrics
Gifts
Classes
Hwy. 70
Mall
Lowes
Hwy. 17
Post Office
Glenburnie Rd.
The Quilt Company
Morehead City, NC #2
Tues - Sat
9:30 - 5
Sew It Seams
911 Arendell St. 28557
(919) 247-2114
Owner: Lillian Lawrence
Personal Service and Southern Hospitality.
Great Selection of 100% cotton fabrics,
books, patterns, notions and classes.
11th St.
10th St.
9th St.
8th St.
U.S. 70
911
Sew It Seams
Shepard St.

Jacksonville, NC #3

Mon - Sat
10 - 5

The Cotton Patch Quilt Shoppe

1122 Gum Branch Rd. 28540
(910) 938-1395 Fax: Same
Owner: Sharon C. Turner
Est: 1993 1600 sq.ft. 4200 Bolts

Large selection Fabrics, Books & Patterns, Notions, Ceramic Buttons, Classes.
"A Really Great Quilt Store."

Wilmington, NC #4

Mon - Sat
10 - 5

The Quilting Bee

4545 Fountain Dr. 28403
(910) 395-0223
Owner: Heather G. Tighe
Est: 1996
1200 sq.ft.

Large selection of fabrics, patterns, notions, books and gifts. Day and evening classes for all levels. Friendly and knowledgeable staff. Authorized Bernina sales & service.

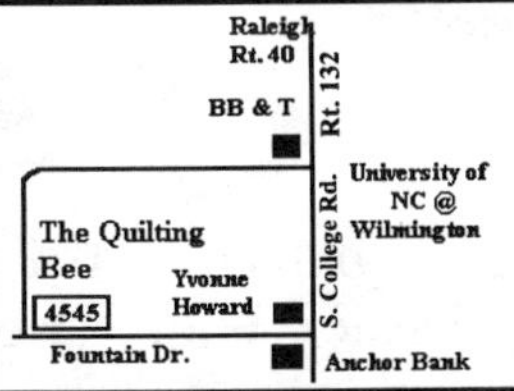

Fabrics, Supplies, and Classes. PFAFF Sewing Center

Mon - Sat 10 - 5

Fabric—Over 1500 Bolts
Hoffman, Alexander Henry, Jinny Beyer, Robert Kaufman and P&B
Books —100 Titles and More
Notions—Great Variety of Threads
Mettler, Cotty, Luny, Mez Alcezar, Sulky, Finishing Touch, Madera
Classes—All Skill Levels

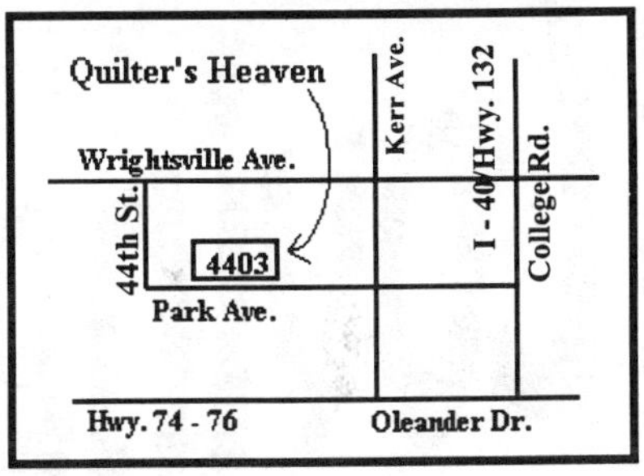

Quilter's Heaven
Wrightsville Ave.
Kerr Ave.
I - 40/Hwy. 132
College Rd.
44th St.
4403
Park Ave.
Hwy. 74 - 76
Oleander Dr.

Wilmington, NC #5

4403 Park Ave 28403 (910) 395-0200
Owners: Mary Sneeden Est: 1991 2200 sq.ft.

Cary, NC #6

Mon - Fri
10 - 6
Sat 10 - 5

Etc. Crafts

226 E. Chatham St. 27511
(919) 467-7636
Owner: Jean Petersen

Large selection of 100% Cotton Quilting Fabrics. Books and Notions.

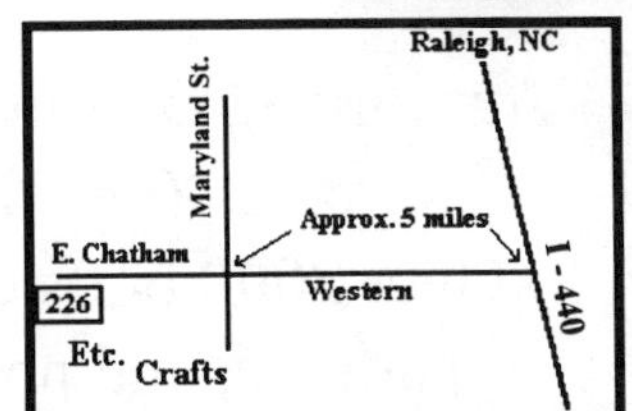

Carrboro, NC #7

Mon - Sat
10 - 6
Sun 1 - 4

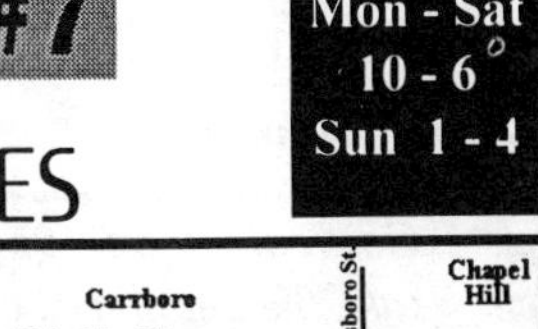

THIMBLE PLEASURES

205 W. Main St. 27510
(919) 968-6050
Owner: Julie Holbrook
Est: 1993 1400 sq.ft.

Over 2,500 Bolts of 100% Cotton Designer Fabrics. Books, Patterns, Notions. Wide variety of classes. Quarterly Newsletter.

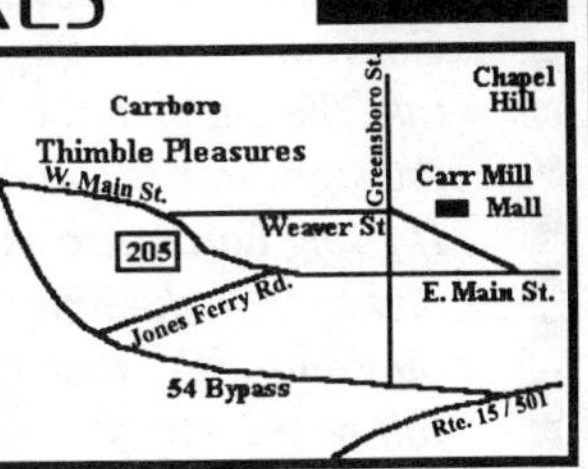

Raleigh, NC #8

Bernina World of Sewing

3000 bolts of 100% cotton fabric. Authorized Bernina Dealer. Wide variety of specialty patterns, threads, notions and sewing accessories. Large selection of sewing cabinets and work tables.

"Come Visit Us and be a part of the excitement"

Mon - Sat 10 - 5
Thur til 8

6017 Glenwood Ave. 27612
(919) 782-2945
Visit Us on the internet:
www.citysearch.com/rdu/berninaworld

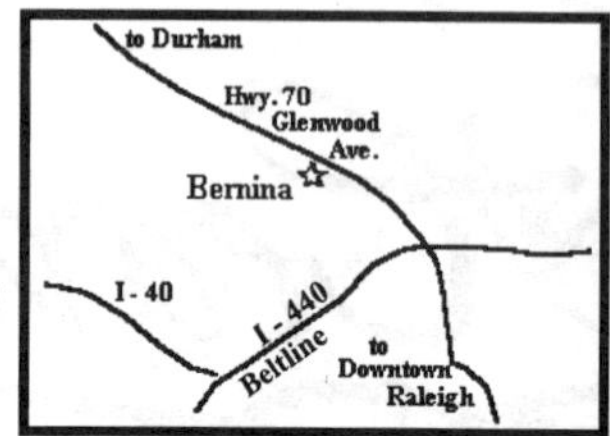

Located 1- 1/4 miles West of Crabtree Valley Mall on Hwy. 70 in Oak Park Shopping Center.

Raleigh, NC #9

Mon - Thur 10 - 6
Fri & Sat 10 - 5
Sun 1 - 5

1612 N. Market Dr. 27609
(919) 790-7792
Fax: (919) 790-1834
E-Mail: archangelfabrics@mindspring.com
Web Site: www.citysearch.com/rdu/archangel
Owner: Sandy McKenzie Est: 1995 2250 sq.ft.

Over 3000 bolts 100% designer cottons, classes, supplies, gifts, notions, books & patterns. Machine quilting service available.

Fayetteville, NC #10

Magnolia Station

Mon - Sat 10 - 4
Closed Tues & Sun.

623 Wakefield Dr. 28303
(910) 867-2170
Owners: Dee Dalton

Full service Quilt Shop.
Quilting supplies.
"Sharing Things We Love"

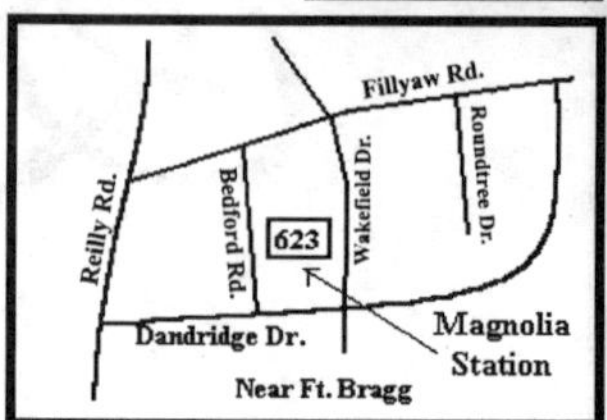

Fayetteville, NC #11

Loving Stitches

Est: 1996
2400 sq.ft.

150 Andrews Rd. 28311
Northeast of Fayetteville
Andrews Commons
Shopping Center
(910) 630-3912

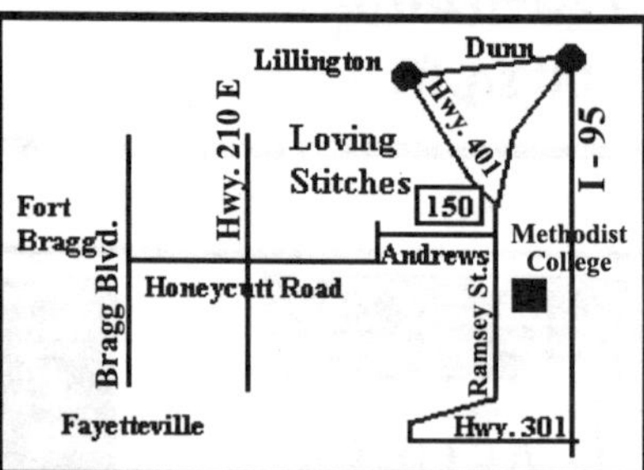

Convenient to I - 95. If going south take the Dunn, NC exit and follow the signs to Hwy. 401 / Fayetteville. If going north take exit for Hwy. 87 and stay on the Frwy. until it ends on Ramsey St., then turn left and follow the map.

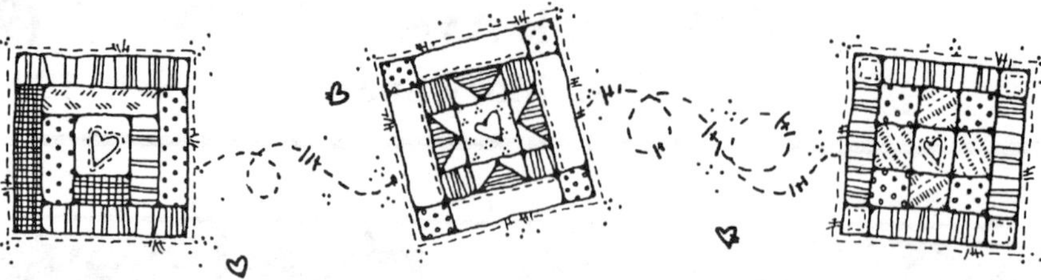

Fax: (910) 630-0916 E-Mail: jrw28311@msn.com
Web Site: www.Fayettevillenc.com/lovingstitches

Mon - Fri 10 - 6
Thur til 9
Sat 10 - 4

Authorized Bernina Dealer. Repairs for all brands. (On-site repair technician)
Over 2000 bolts of cotton fabric, books, patterns, and notions. Great Classes!

We're Brimming with new Fabrics, Classes, and Quilting Goodies! & Lots of Samples!

Fabric Village

2668 Lewisville-Clemmons RD.
P.O. Box 1605 27012
(336) 766-5273
Owner: Ann Roth Est: 1992

Mon - Fri 10 - 5:30
Sat 10 - 3

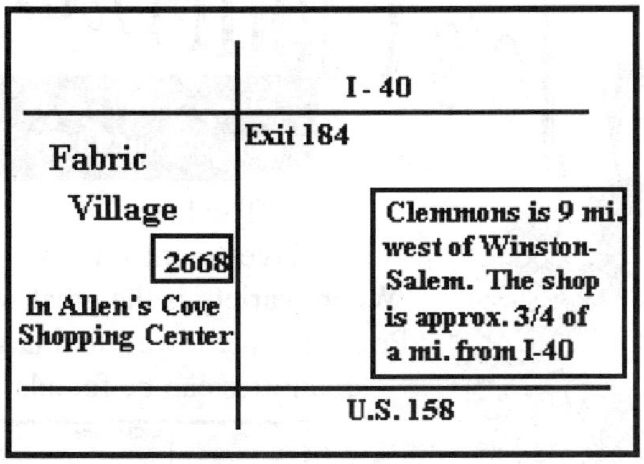

I - 40
Exit 184
Fabric Village
2668
In Allen's Cove Shopping Center
Clemmons is 9 mi. west of Winston-Salem. The shop is approx. 3/4 of a mi. from I-40
U.S. 158

Clemmons, NC #12

Fabrics include:
RJR, Thimbleberries, RJR, Hoffman, Benartex, Alexander Henry, Red Wagon, R. Kaufman, Northcott, Bali, Mumm's the Word, Timeless Treasures and many others.

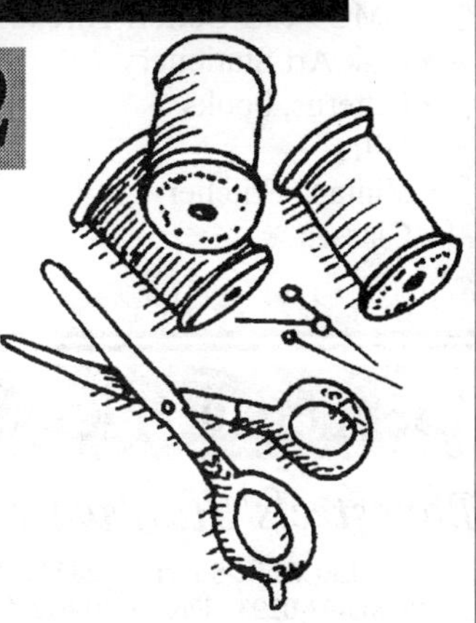

509 N. Main St. 27284
(336) 993-7770

Quilting Peace by Piece

Visit a charming 1922 restored home filled with rooms of fabric, notions, books, patterns, and plenty of class samples. Friendship extraordinaire!!

Mon - Fri 10 - 5 Thur til 8
Sat 10 - 5 Sun 1 - 5

Owner: Terri LaRue
Est: 1994 2000 sq.ft. 1000 Bolts
Free Newsletter

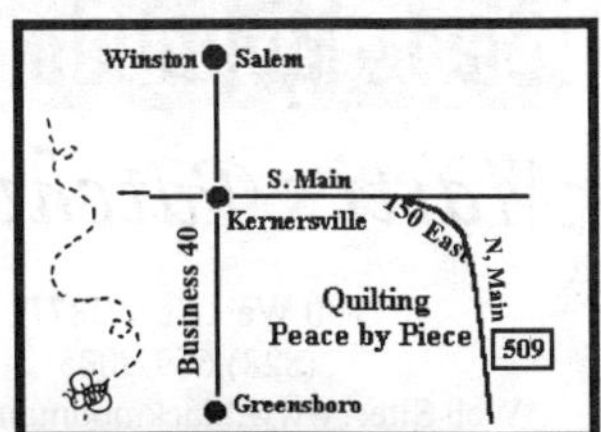

Kernersville, NC #13

Greensboro, NC #14

Mon - Fri 10 - 5:30
Sat 10 - 5

Fran's Quilt Shop

519 State St. 27405
(336) 274-9805
Fax: (336) 275-7227

Area's Largest Selection of Quilting Fabric, Books, Notions, and gadgets. Classes for beginning, intermediate & advanced students. Authorized Bernina Dealer.

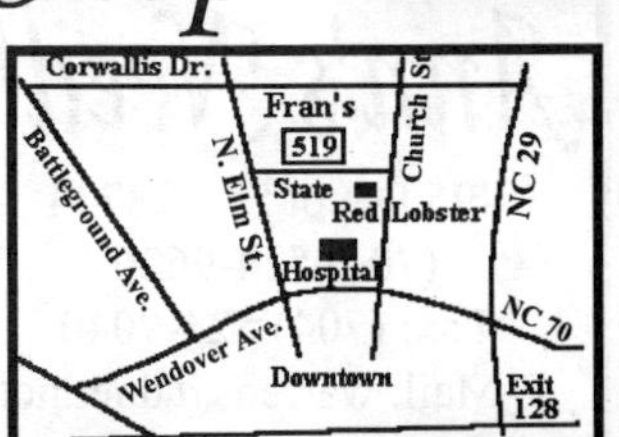

Charlotte, NC #15

Mon - Sat
10 - 4:30

Quilter's Gallery

901 South Kings Dr. Suite # 135
(704) 376-2531 28204
Owner: Patti Cline & Cindy Page
Est: 1981 2000 sq.ft. 2000+ Bolts

Cotton Fabrics--Traditional and unusual prints, Batiks, and Homespuns. Wide range of books and patterns. German Mohair & Teddy Bear Supplies. French Heirloom Sewing Supplies. Buttons and trims.

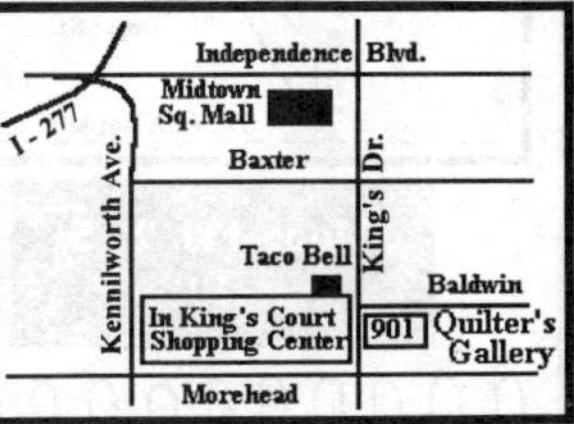

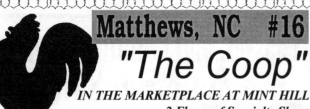

Matthews, NC #16

"The Coop"

IN THE MARKETPLACE AT MINT HILL
2 Floors of Specialty Shops

11237 Lawyers Rd. Hwy 51 28227
(704) 545-3117

Owner: Teri Coop Green
Hm: (704) 882-9342
E-Mail: THECOOP104@aol.com

Mon - Sat 10 - 6

Specializing in:

- Brushed Cotton
- Homespuns by (Moda) Red Wagon
- Rug Hooking kits
- Supplies
- Wool
- DMC Pearl Cotton Threads
- Folk Art Stationery
- Patterns, books
- Gifts
- Vintage Stitchery
- Classes

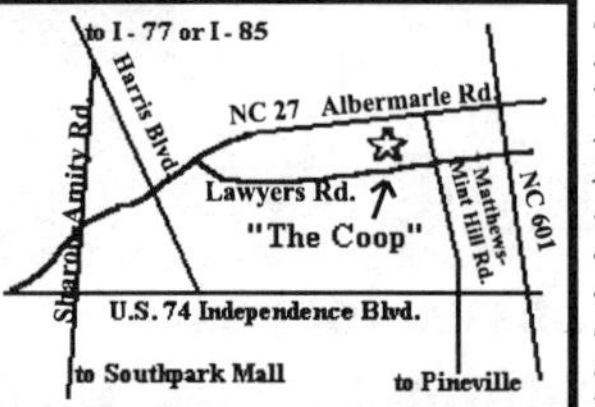

Matthews, NC #17

Mon - Wed 10 - 5
Thur til 7
Fri & Sat 10 - 4

Quilt Patch Fabrics

3555 - 3 Matthews - Mint Hill Rd.
(704) 844-8577 28105
E-Mail: troublemaker@tarheel.net
Web Site: www.angelfire.com/ne/quiltpatch/index.html
Owners: Charlotte Harkey, Bryan Gregory, Janice Cooper Est: 1996 2500 sq.ft.
Full color range of 100% cotton fabrics (1000+ bolts), books & patterns, notions, hand & machine technique classes, machine quilting

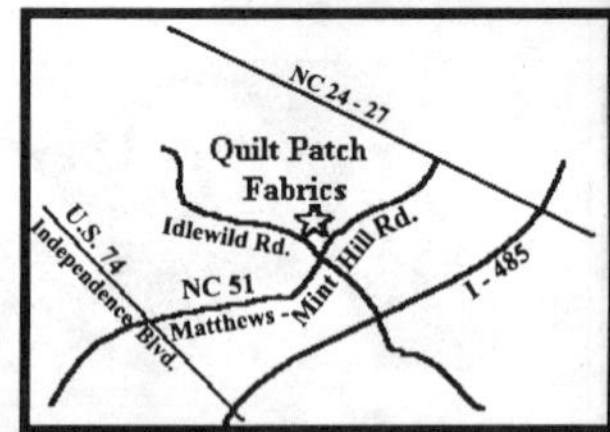

Gastonia, NC #18

Est: 1951
32,000 sq.ft.

(800) 627-9567

Mary Jo's Cloth Store

Mon - Sat 9 - 5:45
Mon & Thur til 8:45

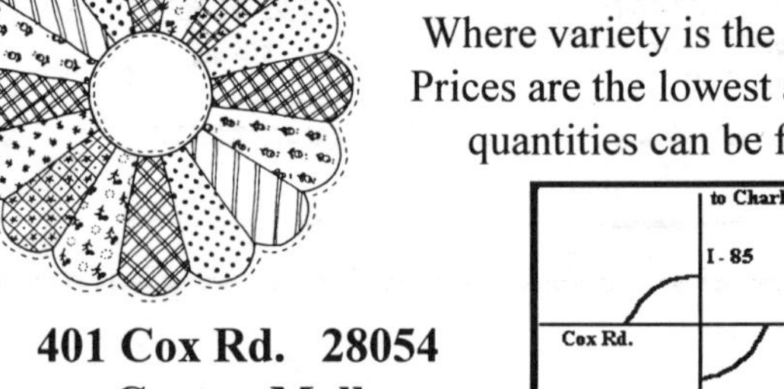

"The Place"
for investment sewers.
Where variety is the greatest.
Prices are the lowest and large quantities can be found.

401 Cox Rd. 28054
Gaston Mall
Owner: Mary Jo Cloninger

to Charlotte
I-85
Cox Rd.
Gaston Mall
401
Mary Jo's Cloth Store
to Spartanburg

Hendersonville, NC #19

Mon - Fri
9 - 5:30
Sat 9 - 4

Bonesteels' Hardware & Quilt Corner

150 White Street 28739
(828) 692-0293 Fax: (828) 692-6053
Owners: Pete & Georgia Bonesteel
Web Site: www.lapquilter.com

BERNINA
The Art and Science of Sewing

Home of Georgia Bonesteel, Hostess of the PBS series "Lap Quilting". Quilt Fabrics, Notions, Books and Patterns Available.

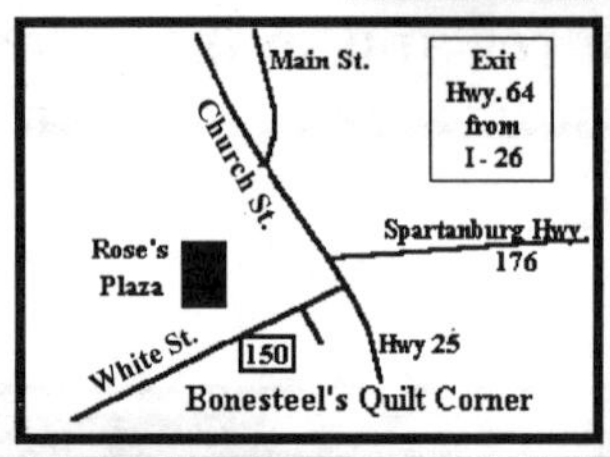

Franklin, NC #20

Ann's Needle & Hook Depot

495 Depot St. 28734
(704) 524-9626
Fax: (704) 524-9040
E-Mail: warrens@dnet.net
Owner: Ann Warren

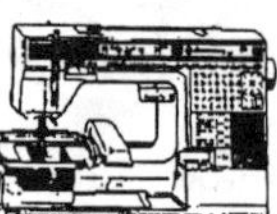

Husqvarna VIKING

- Competitive Prices
- Ask For A Demo

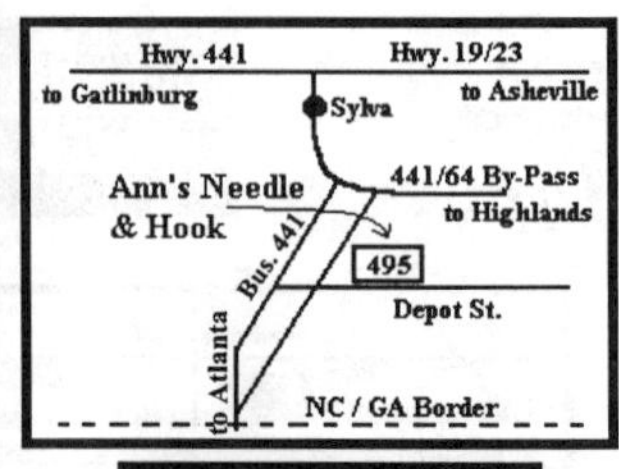

Mon - Fri 9 - 5
Sat 10 - 4

- ✣ Quilting Fabrics— Homespuns, Wool, Cottons, Batiks, Bear Fur
- ✣ Rug Hooking & Braiding
- ✣ Patterns & Books
- ✣ Wearable Arts / Classes
- ✣ Lots of Gifts
- ✣ Jewelry-Snowmen, Cats, Bears, etc.

"The Fun Place To Be"

Franklin, NC #21

Nov - May
Mon - Sat 10 - 5
June - Oct
Mon - Sat 9 - 5:30
Sun 1 - 5:30

Maco Crafts Cooperative

2846 Georgia Rd. 28734
(704) 524-7878
Mgr: Shelia Moffitt 200 members
Est: 1969 3000+ sq.ft.

FABRIC & QUILT SHOP:1000+ Bolts
Latest cotton fabrics, quilting & sewing notions, PATTERNS, BOOKS, supplies; classes, demos, also quality juried local crafts.

Black Mountain, NC #22

Mon - Fri
10 - 5
Sat 11 - 4

Marti's Patchwork Cottage

100 West St. 28711
(828) 669-9005
Web Site: www.blackmountain-nc.com
Owner: Marti Cummins
Est: 1996 800 sq.ft.

We're small but we're growing. The best of Hoffman, South Sea Imports and other brands plus our own line of hand-dyed fabrics.

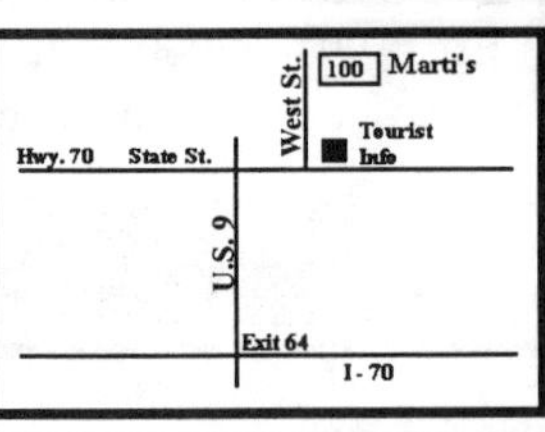

Waynesville, NC #23

Mon - Sat 9:30 - 5:30 Sun 12:30 - 5

W. K. Fabrics

2348 Russ Ave. 28786
(828) 456-3250

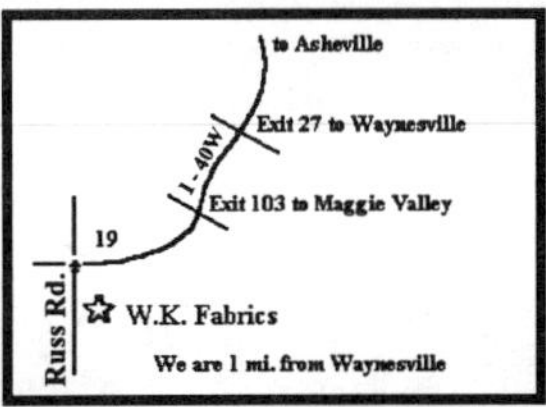

Husqvarna Viking Dealer.
Large selection of quilting fabrics.
Upholstery. Complete Sewing Center.

Burnsville, NC #25

Mon - Fri 9 - 5 Sat 9 - 4

The Country Peddler

3 Town Square 28714
(704) 682-7810
Owners: Barbara & Tommy Pittman
Est: 1980

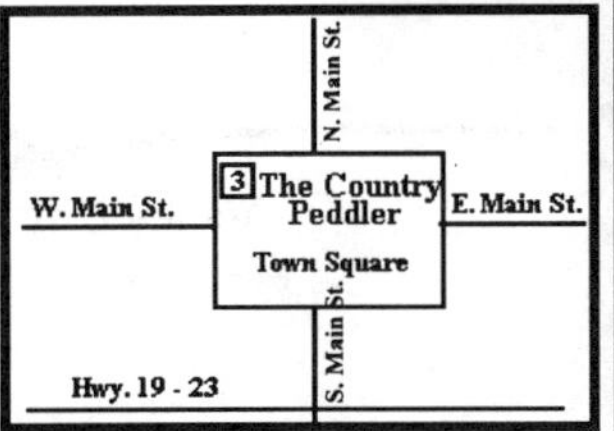

Great selection of quilts, fabrics, & notions. Custom quilts made to order. Quilted and fabric gifts.

#24

Western North Carolina's best source for quality fabrics, supplies & books suitable for Quilting, Heirloom Sewing, Fine Handsewing, Needlearts & Doll Clothes!

Beautiful French & English Laces,
Silk Ribbon Embroidery Materials
Australian Periodicals including
Australian Patchwork & Quilting Magazine
Dolls Bears & Collectibles
Australian Smocking & Embroidery
Australian Inspirations
Australian Cross Stitch & Embroidery

. . . .

Mimi's Fabrications
77 Howell St., Waynesville, NC 28786
(828) 452-3455 Fax (828) 456-7011

DIRECTIONS

(Located approximately 25 miles west of Asheville, NC)

From Main Street Waynesville (downtown) go North on Main (US Business 23) to Howell which runs between **Haywood Savings Bank and Garrett Funeral Home.** Turn East on Howell and go one and a half blocks. Mimi's is behind the photography studio at the intersection of Howell and Wall Street — across from the driveway of Angelo's Family Pizza.

Hours: April through October
Monday - Fri 10AM - 5 PM Saturday 10 AM - 2 PM
November through March
Monday & Tuesday by appointment — Wednesday thru Saturday as above.
Call before coming in inclement weather.

North Carolina Guilds:

Three Rivers Q. G. c/o HPC,245 E. Main St., Albemarle, 28001
Asheville Quilt Guild, P.O. Box 412, Asheville, 28793
    Meets: 3rd Tuesday, alternates day and night,
    at Trinity United Methodist Church
Charlotte Quilter's Guild, P.O. Box 221035, Charlotte, 28222
Durham-Orange Quilters' Guild, P.O. Box 51492, Durham, 27717
    Meets: 3rd Monday 7:30 p.m. at Church of Reconciliation,
    110 N. Elliott Rd., Chapel Hill
Tarheel Quilters Guild, P.O. Box 36253, Fayetteville, 28303
    Meets: 3rd Sunday 2 p.m.
    at Westminister Presbyterian Church
Cape Fear Quilters Guild, 500 Southland Dr., Fayetteville, 28311
    Meets: 3rd Sunday 1:30 p.m. at Loving Stitches
Smoky Mtn. Quilt Guild, P.O. Box 1381, Franklin, 28734
    Meets: 2nd Monday 9 a.m. and 7 p.m.
    at Jaycee Bldg., West Main
    Quilt Show Oct. 1998, and every other year.
Piedmont Quilters Guild, P.O. Box 10673, Greensboro, 27404
Misty Mountain Quilter's Guild, P.O. Box 913, Hayesville, 28904
    Meets: 4th Monday 1 p.m.
    at Sharp Memorial Church, Young Harris, GA
Vance Quilts R Us, Henderson, 27536
Western North Carolina Quilters Guild, 1735 5th Ave. W
    Hendersonville, 28793
    Meets: 3rd Thursday, alternates day & night,
    at First Congregational Church
Heart of the Triad Quilt Guild, P.O. Box 874, Kernersville, 27284
    Meets: 1st Monday 6:30 p.m.
    at Good Shepherd Moravian Church
Crystal Coast Quilter's Guild, P.O. Box 1819, Morehead City, 28557
    Meets: 3rd Thursday 7 p.m.
    at St. Paul's Episcopal Church, Beaufort
Twin Rivers Quilters Guild, P.O. Box 151, New Bern, 28563
    Meets: Every Thursday 10 a.m.
    at the Tabernacle Baptist Church, 616 Broad St.
North Carolina Quilt Symposium, 200 Transylvania Ave., Raleigh
Sandhills Smocking Guild, 2816 Stonecliff Ln., Sanford, 27330
    Meets: Last Thursday 7 p.m. at Loving Stitches
Sandhill Quilter's Guild, PO Box 1444, Southern Pines
    Meets: 3rd Tuesday 9:30 a.m.
    at Brownson Memorial Presbyterian Church
Quilters by the Sea, P.O. Box , Wilmington, 28401
Forsyth Piecers & Quilters, P.O. Box 10666, Winston-Salem, 27108

Other Shops in North Carolina

Asheville	Street Fair, 42 Battery Park Ave.	704-253-0836
Burnsville	Young's Fabrics, Crafts & Antiques, 724 S. Main St.	704-682-6633
Burnsville	Needle Me This, 112 W. Main St.	704-682-9462
Chapel Hill	Cotton Boll Creative Sewing Center, 91 S. Elliott Rd.	919-942-9661
Cherokee	Quilt and Comfort Gallery, Acquoni Rd.	704-497-4103
Fletcher	Carolina Fabric Outlet, 6024 Hendersonville Rd.	704-684-0801
Franklin	Carolina Sew & Vac, 214 A Palmer St. Shopping Ctr.	704-524-3046
Franklin	La Poma & La Poma, P.O. Box 777	704-524-5114
Franklin	Sew Creative, 91 Highlands Rd.	
Goldston	Calico Quilt Antiques, Belview Ave.	919-898-4998
Greensboro	Log Cabin Craftshop, 5435 N. Church	910-282-7331
Hendersonville	Cloth of Gold, 1220 Spartanburg Hwy.	704-697-2100
Newland	Brenda Kay Crafts, Library St.	

Williston (#1)
29
Mayville (#7)
Dickinson (#2)
Bismarck (#3)
94
Valley City (#4)
Fargo (#6)
Lisbon (#5)

NORTH DAKOTA

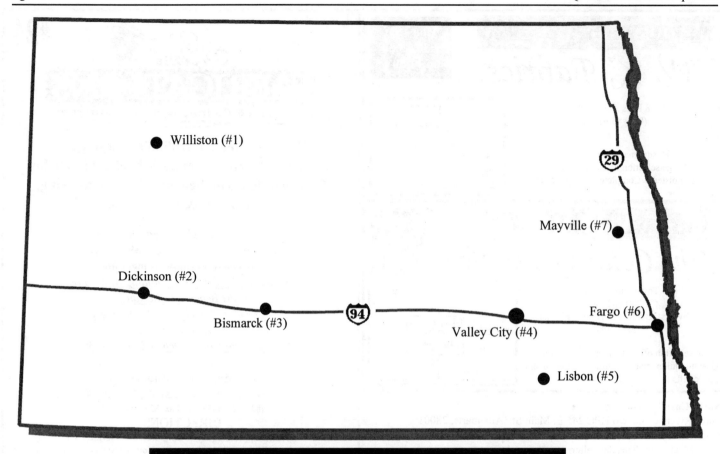

7 Featured Shops

Williston, ND #1

Mon - Sat
10 - 5:30

QuiltMakins

16 East Broadway 58801
(701) 774-3315
Owners: Dory Harstad
Est: 1988 2200 sq. ft.

100% Cottons, Notions, Large Selection of books, classes, and Friendly Folk !

4th.
Main
1st. Ave.
W. Broadway
E. Broadway
16
QuiltMakins
2nd.

Dickinson, ND #2

Mon - Sat
9:30 - 5:30

Bernina Sew and So

38 1st St. W 58601
(701) 225-1408 7200 sq.ft.
Owners: Bev Haas & Betty Volesky

Dakota's Largest Fabric Store.
Mail order and newsletter available upon request. Quilt, Bridal, Fashion Fabrics. Bernina and New Home Dealer.

Bismarck, ND #3

Mon 10 - 8
Tues - Fri
10 - 5:30
Sat 9:30 - 5:30

Inside J & R Vacuum & Sewing
223 E. Main 58501
(701) 258-5619
(800) 371-5515
Owners: Jim & Rene Barnhardt

Quilt Supplies, classes, name brand 100% cotton quilting fabrics, books, patterns, notions, cabinets & PFAFF sewing machines.

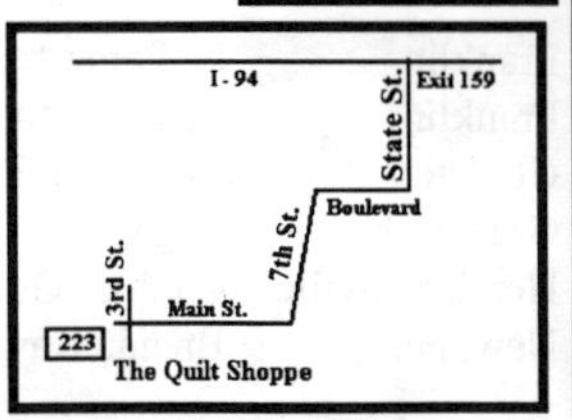

Valley City, ND #4

Mon - Sat
9:30 - 5:30

Cotton Patch Treasures

330 Central Ave. N 58072
(701) 845-4926
Owner: Georgia Manstrom
Est: 1993 2100 sq.ft.

Distinctive gifts such as Boyds Bears. Fabrics, classes, Books, Patterns, Quilting Supplies. Pfaff Sewing Machine Dealer.

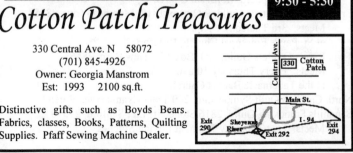

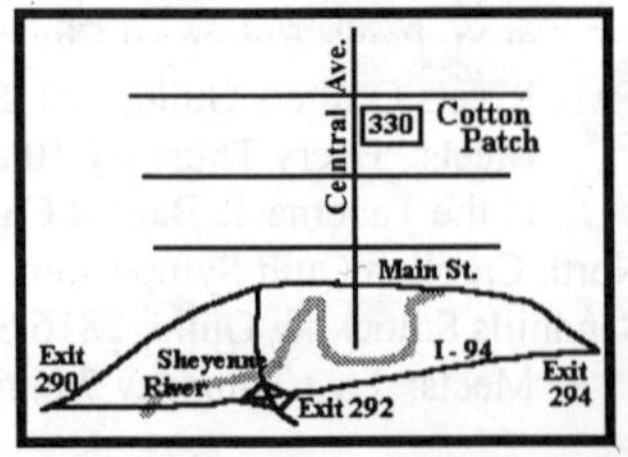

Lisbon, ND #5

Mon - Fri 9 - 5:30
Sat 9 - 5
Sun 12 - 4

Ingeborg & Frannies

416 Main St., P.O. Box 189 58054
(701) 683-4193
Owner: Bonnie Bauman
Est: 1996 1900 sq.ft.

Large selection of brand name 100% cottons. Patterns, Notions, Coffee Shop, Gifts and Antiques under one roof. Classes & Displays.

Mayville, ND #7

Mon - Sat 9 - 5:30

Homespun Treasures

28 Main St. W 58257
(701) 786-3790
Owner: Faye Grandalen
Est: 1996 1600 sq.ft. 800+ Bolts

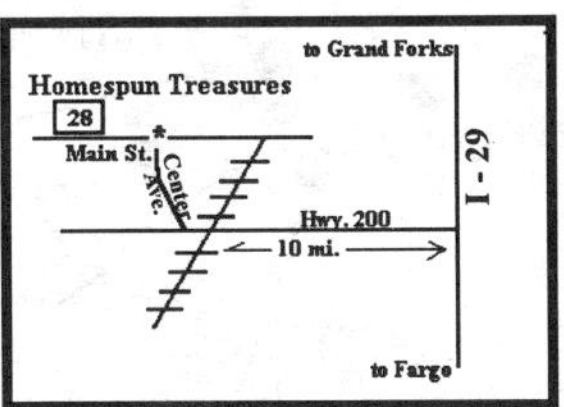

Fine cotton fabrics, quilting supplies, books, patterns, notions, custom machine quilting, classes, consignment/crafts and gift items, quilt racks.

Fargo, ND #6

QUILTER'S QUARTERS

604 Main Ave. 58103
(701) 235-6525
Owner: Barbara Bunnell
Fax: (701) 293-3145
E-Mail: QQinFargo@aol.com
Est: 1979
2500 sq.ft. 2000 Bolts

Mon 10 - 9
Tues - Sat 10 - 5:30

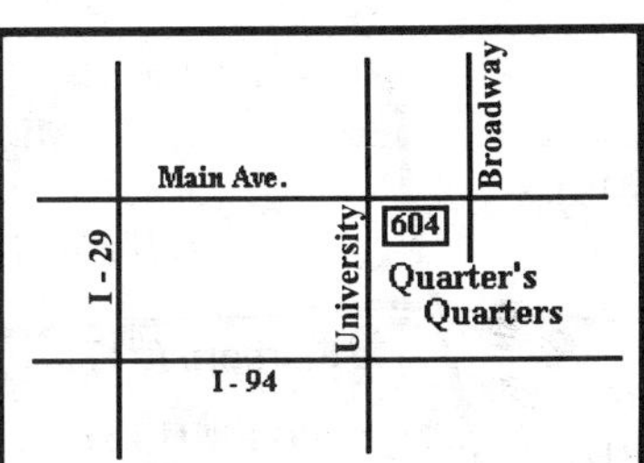

Nothing Sews Like A Bernina. Nothing.
BERNINA®

Authorized Bernina dealer. 100% cotton fabrics, books, patterns, notions, classes, supplies, friendly staff!

North Dakota Guilds:

Quilters' Guild of North Dakota, P.O. Box 2662, Fargo, 58107
Meets: 3rd Saturday

In Stitches Quilt Club, Lisbon
Meets: 2nd Thursday 7 p.m.
at Ingeborg & Frannie's Quilt Shop

Other Shops in North Dakota:

Carrington	Designer Fabrics, 929 Main St.	701-652-3527
Devils Lake	The Garden Gate, 410 4th St.	701-662-6388
Grand Forks	Quilted Rabbit, 1826 S. Washington St.	701-772-7173
Minot	Carol's Etc., 112 S. Main St.	701-839-6183

Painesville (#54)
South Amherst (#52)
Port Clinton (#33)
80
90
Archbold (#30)
Maumee (#31)
Willoughby (#53)
Chesterland (#55)
Cortland (#56)
Bettsville (#32)
Findlay (#34)
Medina (#35)
Wadsworth (#36)
Rootstown (#58)
Akron (#50)
(#57)
Youngstown
Wooster (#51)
Ashland (#48)
Mansfield (#49)
Kenton (#29)
Kidron (#38)
Canton (#59)
Mt. Hope (#42)
Loudonville (#44)
Shreve (#37)
75
(#45, 46) Sugarcreek
Uhrichville (#47)
Middleburg (#20)
Mt. Vernon (#28)
Palestine (#19)
Charm (#43)
Berlin (#39, 40, 41)
Hilliard (#21)
Westerville (#22)
Hebron (#26)
Fairborn (#17)
70
Brookville (#18)
(#27) Millersport
Centerville (#16)
71
Columbus (#23, 24, 25)
Cumberland (#3)
Caldwell (#2)
Kettering (#15)
Camden (#14)
McConnelsville (#4)
77
Waynesville (#13)
Wilmington (#12)
Chillicothe (#1)
Fairfield (#11)
Pomeroy (#5)
Cincinnati (#8, 9, 10)
Portsmouth (#7)
Galliopolis (#6)

OHIO

59 Featured Shops

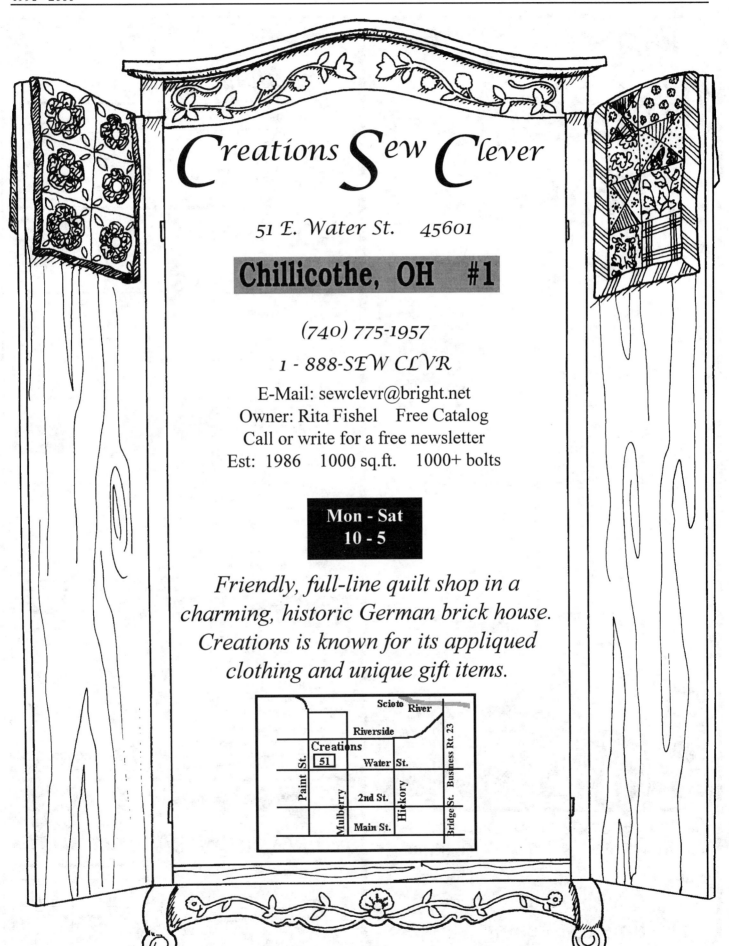

Creations Sew Clever

51 E. Water St. 45601

Chillicothe, OH #1

(740) 775-1957

1 - 888-SEW CLVR

E-Mail: sewclevr@bright.net

Owner: Rita Fishel Free Catalog

Call or write for a free newsletter

Est: 1986 1000 sq.ft. 1000+ bolts

Mon - Sat
10 - 5

Friendly, full-line quilt shop in a charming, historic German brick house. Creations is known for its appliqued clothing and unique gift items.

Scioto River
Riverside
Creations
51
Water St.
Paint St.
Mulberry
2nd St.
Hickory
Main St.
Bridge St.
Business Rt. 23

Caldwell, OH #2

Townsquare Fabrics
& Quilt Shop

507 Main Street 43724
(614) 732-5351
www.twinbridges.com/townsquare
Owner: Effie Townsend
Est: 1985
Over 1000 Bolts of Fabric

Mon - Fri 10 - 4
Tues til 6
Sat 10 - 2

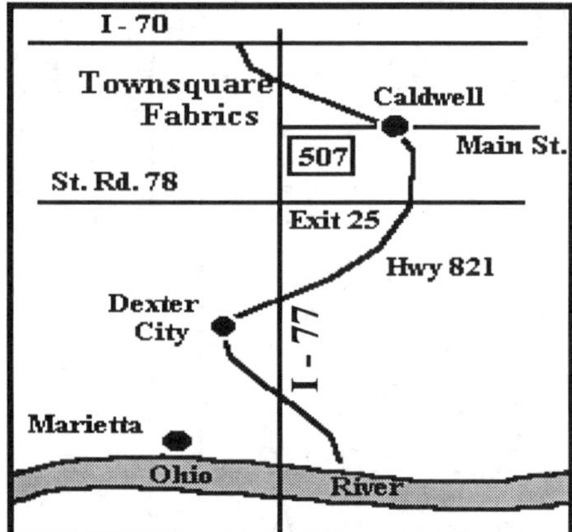

Cotton Fabric
Quilting Supplies
Patterns
Stencils
Batting
Books
Q-Snap Quilting Frames
Daytime & Evening Classes

Cumberland, OH #3

Tues - Sat 11 - 5

Cumberland Quilt Shop

424 Main St., P.O. Box 73 43732
(740) 638-2626 Fax: (740) 962-4276
Owners: Rita & Phil Lawrence
Est: 1996
Top quality 100% cotton quilt Fabric, Books, Patterns, Notions & Classes. Custom Machine Quilting. Handcrafted Gifts. Located in the historic Cumberland Bank Building.

McConnelsville, OH #4

Mon - Sat 9 - 5

32 E. Main St. 43756
(740) 962-6206
Est: 1988
Authorized Pfaff Dealer,
Quilt Fabrics, Supplies,
Decorative Threads, Classes, Books.

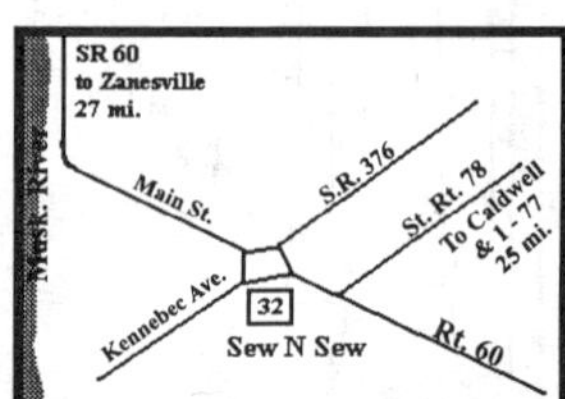

Pomeroy, OH #5

Mon - Sat 9 - 5

The Fabric Shop

110 W. Main St. 45769
(740) 992-2284 Fax: (740) 992-4189
E-Mail: fabricshop@eurekanet.com
Web Site: www.eurekanet.com/~fabricshop
Owner: Becky Anderson Est: 1959
We specialize in Quilting fabric and supplies. Singer Sewing Machine Dealer. Located on the beautiful Ohio River in historic Pomeroy, OH.

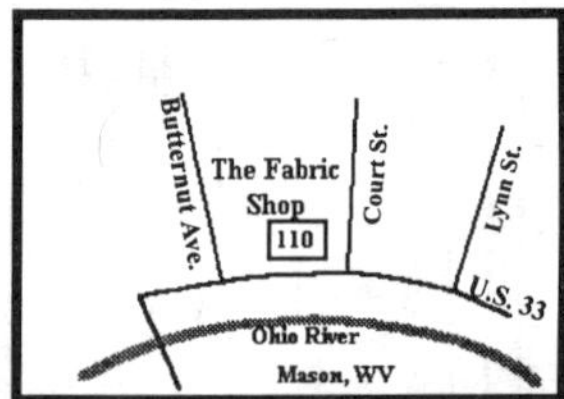

Gallipolis, OH #6

Mon - Sat 10 - 5

Mary Lee's "The Quilt Shop"

322 2nd Ave. 45631
(740) 446-2202 1000 Bolts
E-Mail: mlmquilt@zoomnet.net
Owner: Mary Lee Marchi
We Cater to Quilters.
Complete line of notions & fabric. Hoffman, Jinny Beyer and many others. Machine Quilting. We have quilted over 2300 quilts.

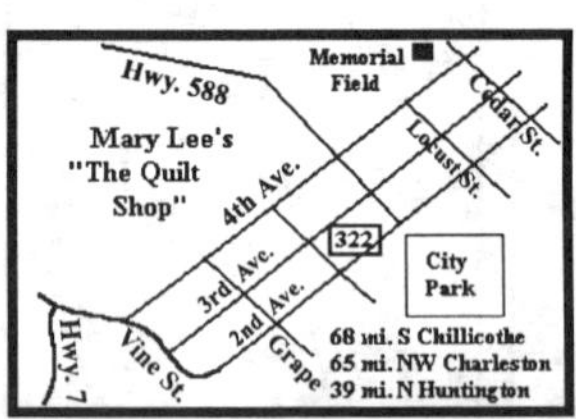

Portsmouth, OH #7

Mon - Fri 10 - 5
Sat 9 - 4

Homespun Treasures

319 Chillicothe St. 45662
(740) 353-8426
Owner: Robin Berry Est: 1998
Right in the Heart of Downtown Southern Ohio. Moda, Mumm, RJR, Indo & More. Quilting Supplies, Books, Patterns, Classes, Country Gifts & More.

Cincinnati, OH #8

6934 Miami Ave. 45243 in "Madeira"
(513) 271-2028

Owner:
Marie Tsacalis
Est: 1988 3300 sq.ft.
15 min. from downtown Cincinnati

Creative Cottage

Quilting & Cross Stitch

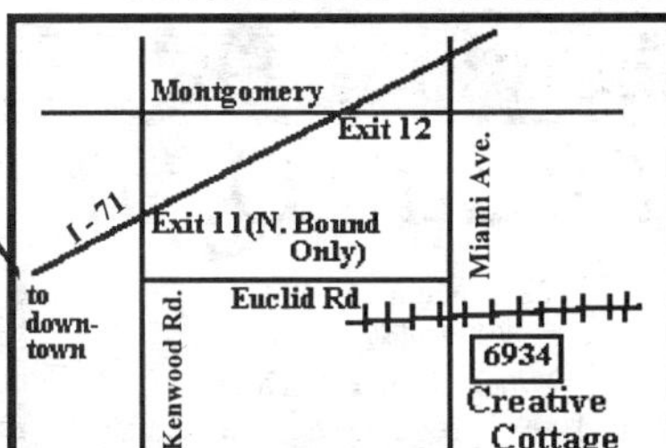

Mon - Sat 9:30 - 5:30
Wed & Thurs til 8:30
Sun 1 - 4

__QUILTING__ - Large selection of books, patterns, stencils & tools.
__FABRIC__ - 1200+ bolts of exciting cotton plus large selection of homespun and flannels.
__CRAZY QUILTING & SILK RIBBON EMB. SUPPLIES__
__CROSS STITCH__ - Huge selection of cross stitch books, fabrics, exciting fibers and notions.
__CLASSES AND WORKSHOPS__
__SPONSOR OF "GOLDEN NEEDLES"__ - Annual Show at Cincinnati Convention Center (August/September) featuring National teachers, Vendor Mall & Exhibits
AND LOTS OF FUN, FUN, FUN...

Cincinnati, OH #9

Mon - Fri 10 - 5
Call for Saturday Hours

Creations by Country Love

9384 Loveland-Madeira Rd.
(513) 984-1484 Est: 1986
Owner: Beverly Dickerson

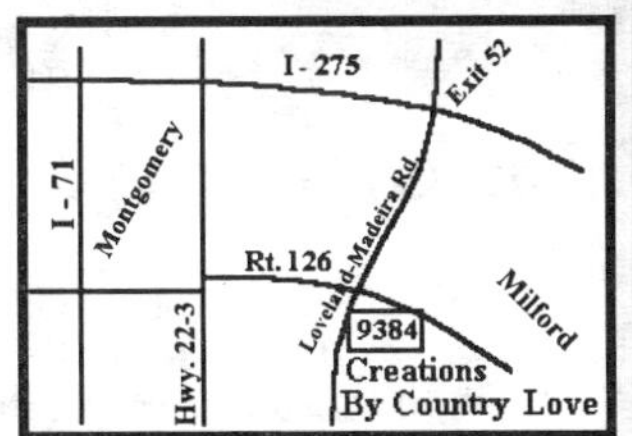

Quilting Fabric, Books, & Supplies. Classes. Custom Machine Quilting & Binding Service. Quilt Racks & Hangers. Baskets of all kinds.

Cincinnati, OH #10

Ohio Star Quilt Shop

Mon - Fri 10 - 8
Sat 10 - 5
Sun 12 - 5

8556 Beechmont Ave. #450 45255
(513) 474-9355
Owners: Marianne & Mark Schmitt
Est: 1993 3800 sq.ft.

Huge Selection of Quilting Supplies, Books, Classes and Notions. 1000 Bolts of Designer Fabric including RJR, Hoffman, Jinny Beyer, P&B.

Five Mile Rd. Eight Mile Rd. I - 275 Ohio Star Quilt Shop Beechmont Mall 8556 Ohio Pike Rt. 125 Beechmont Ave.

Also Yarn, Knitting & Crocheting Supplies

Fairfield, OH #11

Mon - Thur 10 - 8
Fri & Sat 10 - 4

Stitches 'n Such

702 Nilles Road 45014
(513) 829-2999
Web Site: www.stitchesnsuch.com
located 5 miles north of Cincinnati

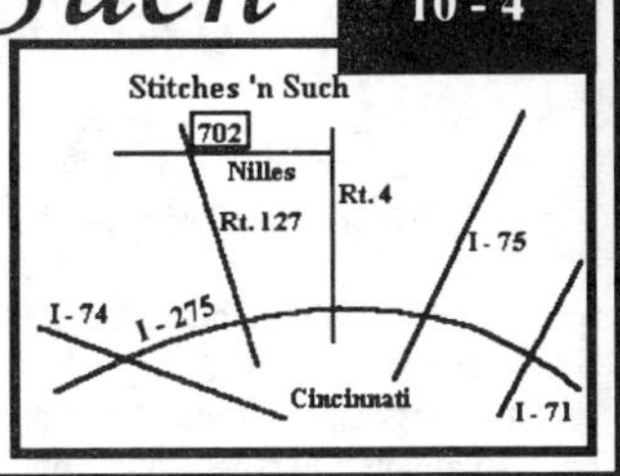

Fabric, fabric, fabric - over 2,000 bolts including homespuns, flannels, fleece, wool. Patterns, books, notions. We also carry rug hooking supplies.

Wilmington, OH #12

Mon - Sat 10 - 5

In Stitches

100 1/2 W. Main St. 45177
(937) 382-5559 Fax: (937) 382-2554
Web Site: www.institchesinc.com
Est: 1993

100% Cottons, Patterns, Books, Notions, Classes. Viking & White Sewing Machines & Sergers. Unique Country Gifts.

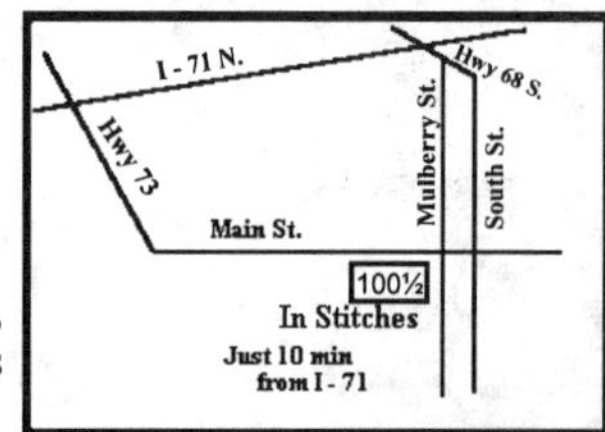

Waynesville, OH #13

**Mon - Sat 10 - 5
Thur til 8
Sun 12 - 5**

Fabric Shack

99 S. Marvin Ln. & Miami St. 45068
(513) 897-0092 Fax: (513) 897-7176
E-Mail: info@fabricshack.com
Web Site: www.fabricshack.com
Owner: Maxine Young
Est: 1986 3000 sq.ft. 7000+ Bolts
The ultimate quilt shop . . .
All the fabrics, colors, designers, the biggest in the midwest . . .
Notions, patterns, and books too!

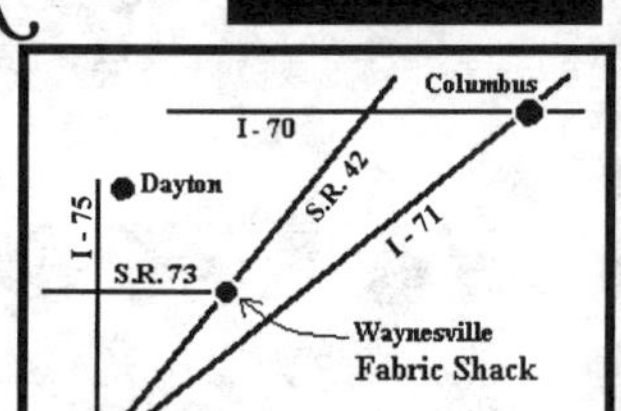

Camden, OH #14

**Wed - Fri 10 - 4:30
Sat 10 - 2**

Linda's Quilt Shop

22 S. Main St. 45311
(937) 452-0600
Owner: Linda M. Knott
Est: 1990 1000 sq.ft. 800 Bolts

Quilting Fabrics for traditional Quilters. Classes, Supplies, Books, Patterns, Notions, & Quilting Frames (custom made).
Instructional Videos.

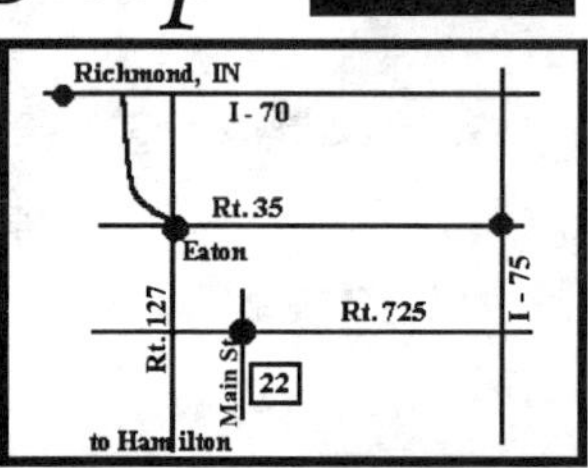

Kettering, OH #15

**Mon - Fri 10 - 6
Sat 10 - 4**

Sew Biz

3098 Woodman Dr. 45420
(937) 299-3391
Owners: Linda Adams, Jacie Rinne & Susan Oppenheim
Est: 1959 3000 sq.ft.

Books, Patterns. Quilting, Heirloom and Silk Ribbon Supplies. Classes — Hand and Machine. Bernina, Babylock and Service.

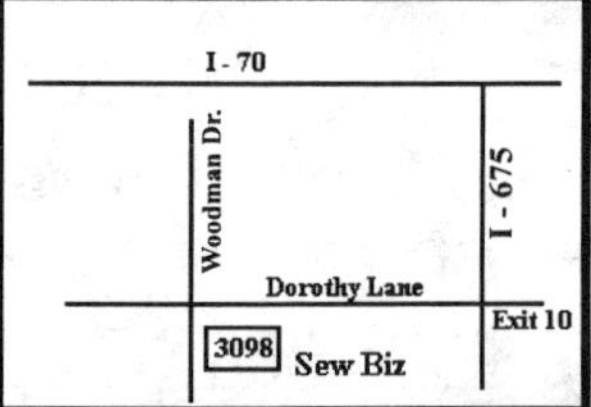

Centerville, OH #16

**Mon - Thur 10 - 8
Fri & Sat 10 - 5**

Sew-A-Lot

232 N. Main St. 45459
(937) 433-7474 Fax: (937) 433-0757
E-Mail: sew-a-lot@juno.com
Owner: Debbie Bernhard
Est: 1982 3500 sq.ft. 2500 Bolts

Sales & Service of Pfaff & Elna machines.
Great selection of 100% cotton fabrics, patterns, books & machine threads. Classes.
Historic building built in 1874.

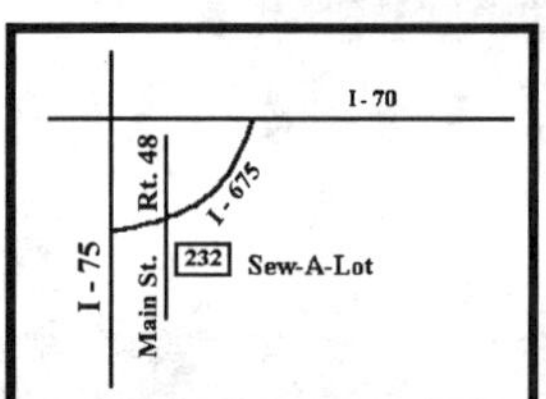

Fairborn, OH #17

**Tues, Wed, Fri, & Sat 10 - 4
Mon & Thur 10 - 8**

Daisy Barrel, Inc.

19 West Main Street 45324
(937) 879-0111
Owners: Marjorie, Sandy, Judy, Phyllis, & Gretchen
Est: 1972 5000 sq.ft. 2000+ Bolts

We specialize in best quality materials for the quilter, cross-stitcher, teddy bear maker, (including mohair) and stenciler. Our experienced staff will be glad to help.

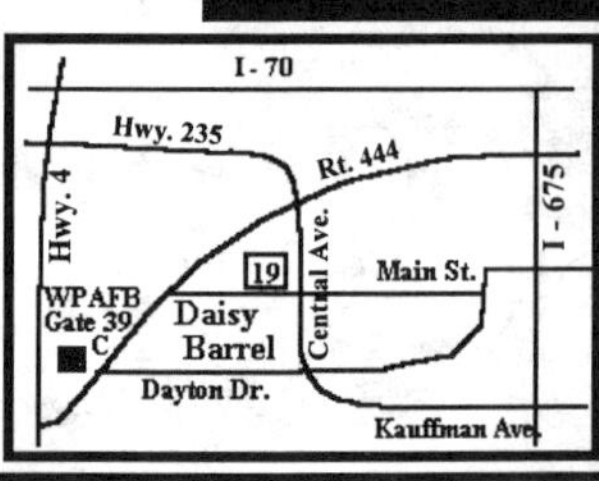

Brookville, OH #18

**Brookside Plaza
428 N. Wolf Creek
45309
(937) 833-5188
Owner:
Joanne Zirkle
Est: 1984 5200 sq.ft.**

Quilts N' Things

2500 Bolts Finest Cottons, Oriental Prints, Notions, Books, Stencils, Finished Quilts, Wallhangings, Gifts, Classes. Machine Quilting

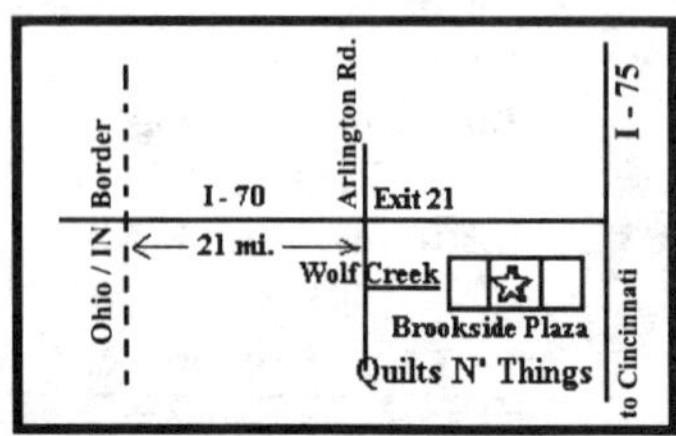

Mon - Fri 10 - 5
Thur til 8:30 Sat 9:30 - 1:30

Palestine, OH #19

**Tues - Fri 1 - 6
Sat 1 - 5**

Pap & Granny's Quilt & Antiques

211 W. Cross St. 45352
(937) 548-8508
Owners: Don & Maryalice Brewer
Est: 1993

Fabrics - Hoffman, RJR, South Seas & many others. Books, Notions, Classes, Gifts. Quilts & Wall Hangings for Sale.

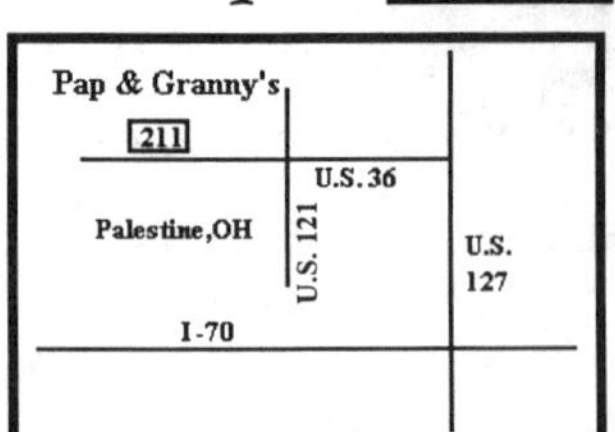

Middleburg, OH #20

Tues - Sat 10 - 6

Sweet Mountain Quiltery

6079 C. R. 158, P.O. Box 31 43336
(937) 666-2085
Owner: Jill Hardman Est: 1997

100% cotton Fabrics, Books, Patterns, Accessories, Quilts, Singer Featherweights, Classes. Custom piecing & hand quilting available. Personal Assistance — Free!

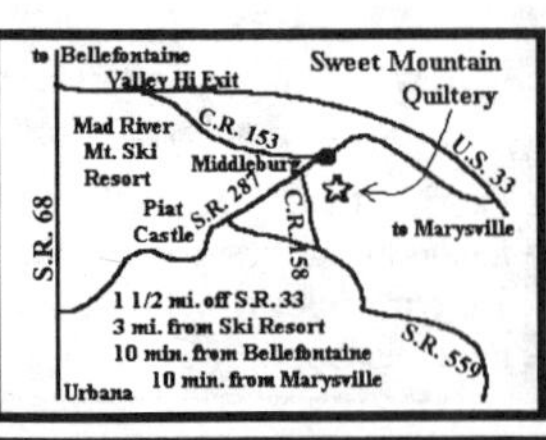

Quilt Pox Shoppe & More

Owner: Karen Sue Weiler

We carry over 300 Hand-dyed, Bali & Batik Fabrics alone. Custom Machine Quilting. Classes. Notions.

Bus tours: By appt. only please. Plus: We have a childs play area for your little ones and two reclining easy chairs and color T.V. for those who are with you that have not been infected with "***Quilt Pox***" yet.

3840 Lattimer St.
43026
(614) 771-0657
2400 sq.ft.
1500+ Bolts

Mon - Sat 10 - 5
Thur & Fri til 8

Hilliard, OH #21

Westerville, OH #22

Mon - Fri 10 - 8;30
Sat 10 - 5
Sun 12 - 5

Calico Cupboard

24 N. State St. 43081
(614) 891-0938
Owner: Marcie Collucia
Est: 1971 5000 sq.ft.

3000+ bolts of cotton fabrics, plus hundreds of patterns, books, notions and much more. Craft supplies & Gifts too! We're worth the trip.

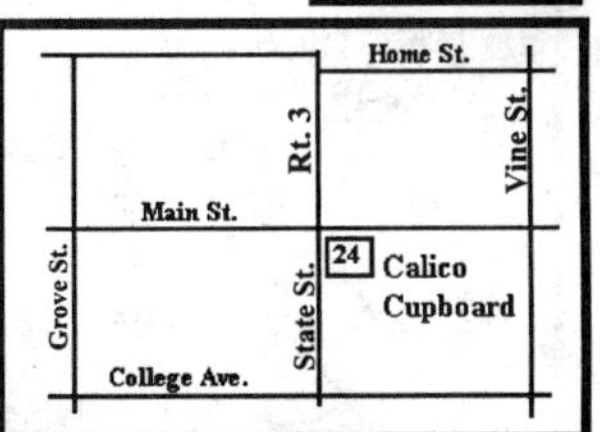

Columbus, OH #23

Picking Up The Pieces/Helyn's Hoops

We share one shop in German Village near Downtown
911 City Park Avenue 43206
(614) 443-9988
E-mail: QLTPATI97@aol.com

Original products invented by Gay Dell, owner of ***Helyn's Hoops***, include:

"Emma Sings"

Picking Up The Pieces is the retail Quilt Shop owned by Pati Shambaugh. Pati carries fabrics, books, patterns, notions & supplies. Pati also designs original patterns, techniques & tools; lectures & teaches quilting at the shop, guilds & quilt shows wherever they may be. Wholesale inquiries are invited on all original items listed here.

The ORIGINAL as developed by Pati Shambaugh
Quilt Patis
Picking Up The Pieces
911 City Park Ave.
Columbus, OH 43206
(614) 443-9988

Open
Mon. - Sat.
9 - 6
Other times by appointment.

Columbus, OH #24

Mon & Wed 10 - 6
Tues & Thur 10 - 8
Fri & Sat 10 - 5

The Glass Thimble

3434 N. High St. 43214
(614) 267-9566
Web Site: www.glassthimble.com
Owners: Bev & Gary Young
Est: 1979 5800 sq.ft.

Over 3500 bolts of cotton Fabrics, lots of books & patterns plus stained glass supplies. We love quilting and it shows

Columbus, OH #25

By Appt. Only

QUILTS

128 W. 2nd Ave. 43201
(614) 299-9099
Owner: Michael Council
E-Mail:
havana1@webtv.net

Buying and selling antique Quilts before 1950. Send Photo or call.

Hebron, OH #26

Tues, Wed, Thur 10 - 8
Fri & Sat 10 - 5
Sun 1 - 5

Patchwork Cottage Quilt Shop & Heavy Metal Quilting

224 National Rd. (corner St. Rts. 37 & 40)
(740) 929-3940 43025
Owners: Judi Kirby (PCQS) & Barb Whyte (HMQ)

Shop in Victorian Elegance. Unusual Cotton Fabrics, notions, books, patterns, classes, & encouragement! Machine Quilting Available. The coffee's always on!

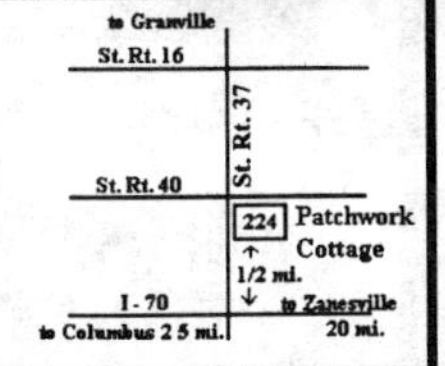

Millersport, OH #27

Thurs, Fri Sat 10 - 5 or by Appt.

The Quilters' Retreat

2595 Canal Dr., Box 667 43046
(740) 467-2366 or (800) 895-2366
E-Mail: quilt@ascenture.net
Web Site: www.ascenture.net/quilt
Owner: Nita Cook Est: 1994 1000 Bolts

We have something for everyone, a great variety of designer fabrics (100% cottons), books, patterns, notions and gifts.

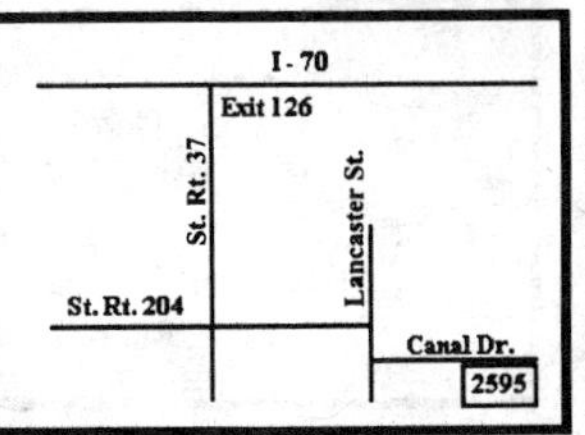

Mount Vernon, OH #28

Mon - Sat 10 - 5

Jordan's Quilt Shop

16 S. Main St. 43050
(740) 393-7463
Fax: Same
E-Mail: djord@ecr.com
Est: 1987 2000 sq.ft.

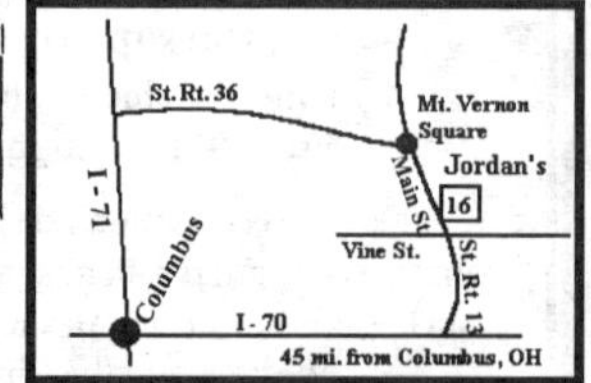

Over 1500 bolts of 100% cotton fabric, books, patterns, classes, quilts.
Bernina and Viking Sewing Machines.

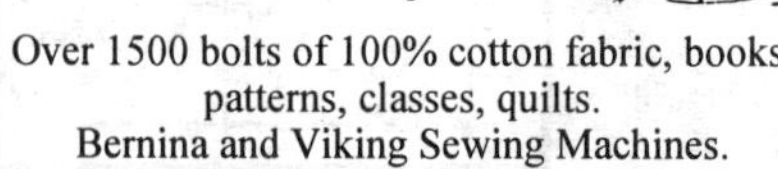

Kenton, OH #29

First Sun of Month 1 - 5 Tues, Wed, Thur, Sat 12 - 5

Ye Olde Schoolhouse

10389 C.R. 190 43326
(419) 675-1652
Owner: Dolores D. Phillips-Layman
Est: 1978

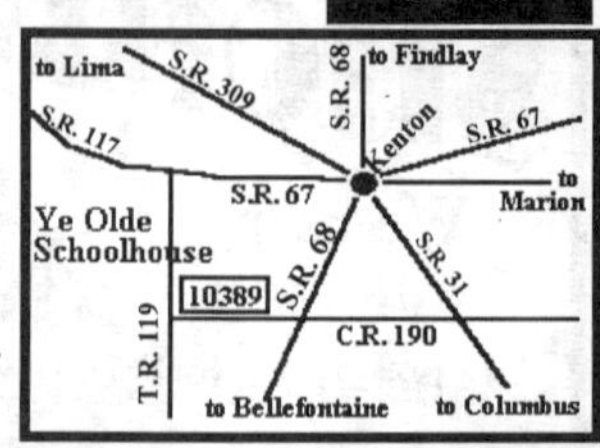

Full Line Quilt Shop Notions & Novelties Books & Patterns Featuring Hoffman, RJR, Benartex, Kona Bay, Kauffman, Alexander Henry and more.

Archbold, OH #30

Sauder Village Quilt Shop

- Over 1,000 bolts of 100% cotton fabrics including RJR, Hoffman, Moda, P & B and homespuns.
- Large selection of books, patterns and notions.
- Open year 'round - Monday-Saturday 10:00-5:00 (Mid-April thru October - also open on Sunday from 1:00-5:00)
- Classes for all skill levels
- Custom-ordered quilts
- Six-day Quilt Fair every spring
- Located inside Historic Sauder Village
- Never an entrance fee to shop!

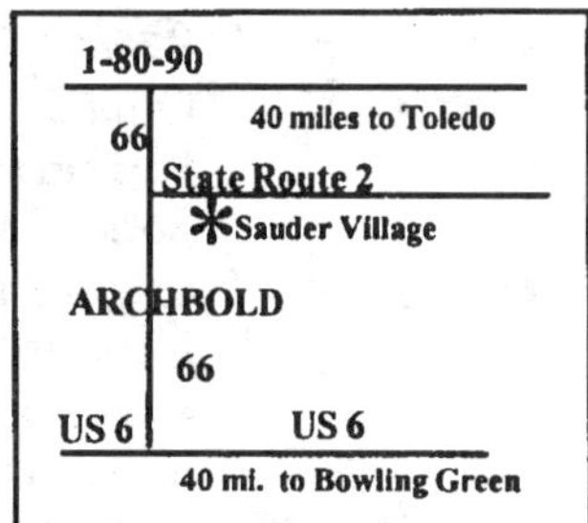

St. Rt. 2, P.O. Box 235, Archbold, OH 43502
1-800-590-9755 village@bright.net

Maumee, OH #31

Mon - Sat 10 - 4 Tues eve 7 - 9

The Quilt Foundry

234 W. Wayne 43537
(419) 893-5703
Owners: Mary Beham, Margaret Okuley, Peg Sawyer, Gretchen Schultz
Est: 1981 1000 sq.ft.

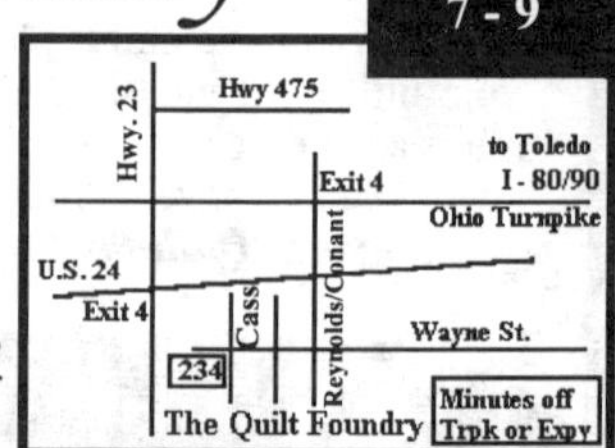

The Quilt Foundry offers friendly, personalized service in your search for wonderful fabric, supplies, books and classes.

THE DOOR MOUSE

Over 7000 bolts of cotton, patterns, and quilting supplies in a barn setting. Featuring quilts and many handcrafted memories, legends and heirlooms which capture the beauty and simplicity of rural life. Join our friendly staff for classes in the corn crib.

Mail Orders Welcome. We accept Visa/MC & Discover

5047 W. SR 12
P.O. Box 455 44815
(419) 986-5667
E-Mail:
doormouse@nwohio.com
Web Site:
www.thedoormouse.com
Owner: Mary Ann Sorg

Mon - Thur 10 - 8
Fri & Sat 10 - 5
Last Sunday of Month 12 - 5

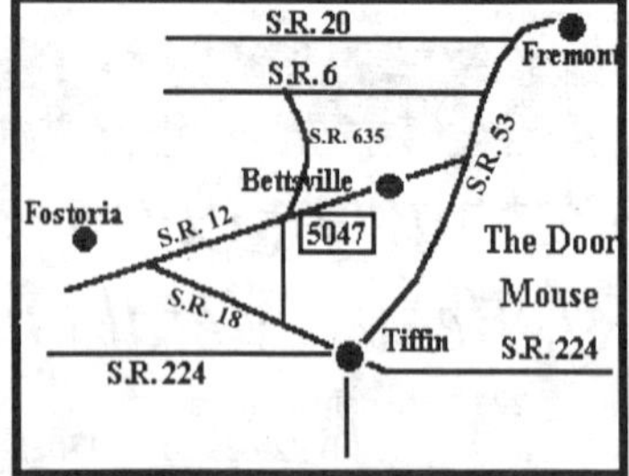

Est: 1979 3600 sq.ft.

Bettsville, OH #32

Port Clinton, OH #33

Tues - Sat 10 - 5 Tue & Thur eve 6:30 - 9 Closed Wed.

Carol's Fabric Art

312 W. Third St. 43452
(419) 734-3650
Owner: Carol Swope
Est: 1984

Fabrics, Books, Patterns, Notions, Cross - Stitch Stencils.

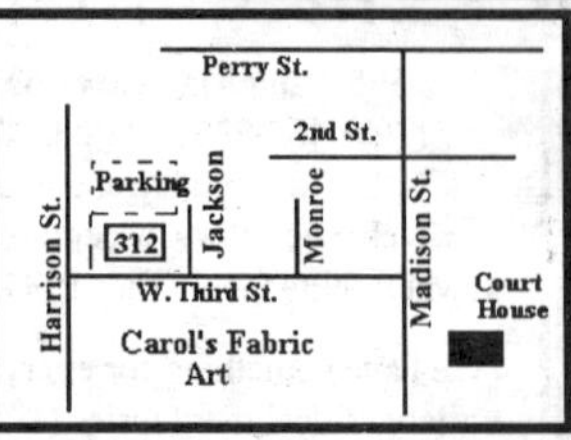

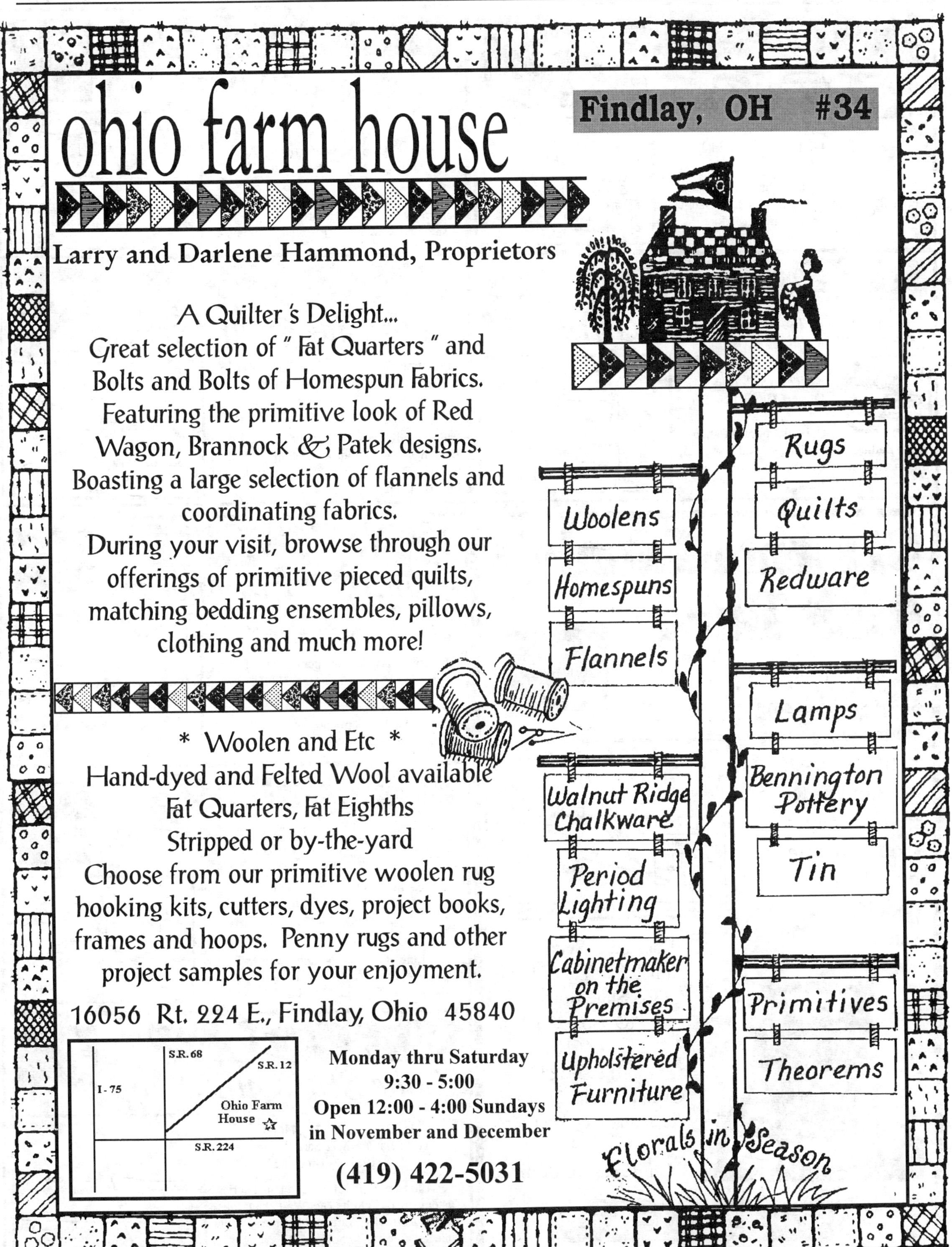
ohio farm house
Findlay, OH #34
Larry and Darlene Hammond, Proprietors
A Quilter's Delight...
Great selection of " Fat Quarters " and
Bolts and Bolts of Homespun Fabrics.
Featuring the primitive look of Red
Wagon, Brannock & Patek designs.
Boasting a large selection of flannels and
coordinating fabrics.
During your visit, browse through our
offerings of primitive pieced quilts,
matching bedding ensembles, pillows,
clothing and much more!
* Woolen and Etc *
Hand-dyed and Felted Wool available
Fat Quarters, Fat Eighths
Stripped or by-the-yard
Choose from our primitive woolen rug
hooking kits, cutters, dyes, project books,
frames and hoops. Penny rugs and other
project samples for your enjoyment.
16056 Rt. 224 E., Findlay, Ohio 45840
S.R. 68
S.R. 12
I-75
Ohio Farm House
S.R. 224
Monday thru Saturday
9:30 - 5:00
Open 12:00 - 4:00 Sundays
in November and December
(419) 422-5031
Rugs
Quilts
Redware
Woolens
Homespuns
Flannels
Lamps
Bennington Pottery
Tin
Walnut Ridge Chalkware
Period Lighting
Cabinetmaker on the Premises
Upholstered Furniture
Primitives
Theorems
Florals in Season

Medina, OH #35

Mon - Sat 10 - 5 Tues & Thur til 7

Medina's Quilting Bee

228 S. Court St.
44256
(330) 764-3333

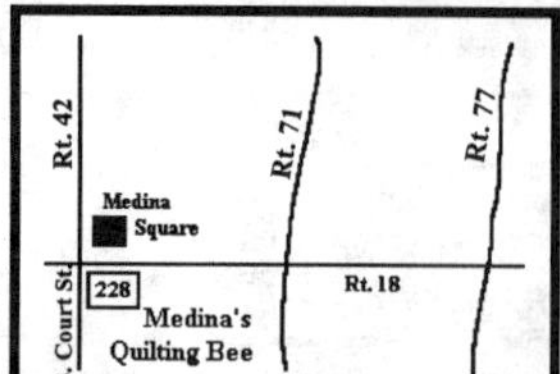

Owners: Linda & Jim McCauley
Est: 1997

Located in Historic downtown Medina. Friendly service. Cotton, wool & felt fabrics. Books, Patterns, Notions & More. Classes always forming.

Wadsworth, OH #36

Mon - Fri 10 - 5:30 Sat 10 - 3

Sally's Shop

139 College Street 44281
(330) 334-1996
Owner: Sally Morrison
Est: 1975 2400 sq.ft.

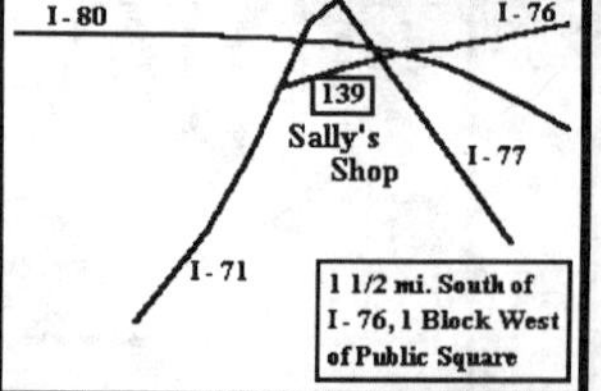

Over 500 bolts of calicos + other fabrics -- patterns & books -- Also needlework -- yarns -- spinning & weaving fibers and equipment.

Shreve, OH #37

Mon - Sat 10 - 5

Gloria's Fabrics & Gifts

202 S. Market St. 44676
(330) 567-9146
Owner: Gloria Landfair

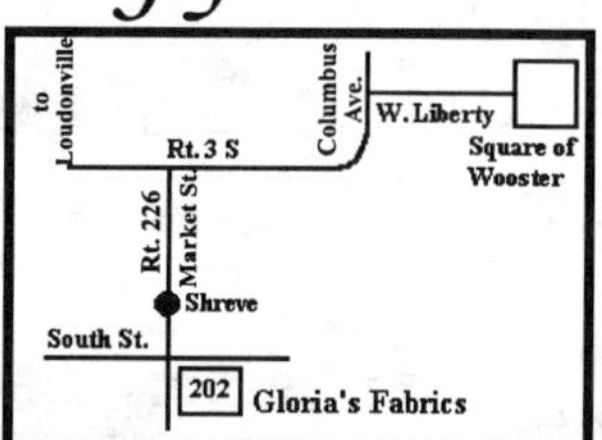

Quilters Cottons, Calico Prints, Batting, Pillow Panels, Wall Hangings, Muslin, Juvenile Prints, craft patterns, country crafts, quilts and notions.

Kidron, OH #38

Mon - Sat 9:30 - 5 closed major holidays

Hearthside Quilt Shoppe

13110 Emerson Rd. Box 222 44636
(216) 857-4004 Est: 1990
Owners: Clifford & Lena Lehman
2400 sq.ft. Mgr. Cheryl Gerber

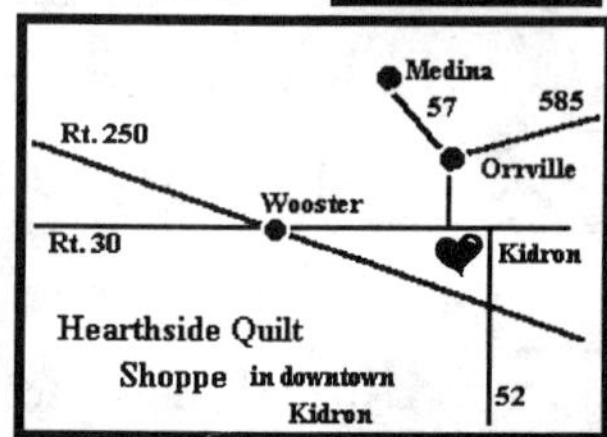

Amish and Swiss Mennonite Quilts, Wall Hangings made in our area. Large selection to choose from. Custom orders welcome! Free Brochure.

Gramma Fannie's Quilt Barn

Mon - Fri 10 - 5 Sat 10 - 6

Visit our unique shop specializing in:

- our own line of patterns & kits
- custom order quilts
- top of the line quilt fabrics
- books
- stencils.

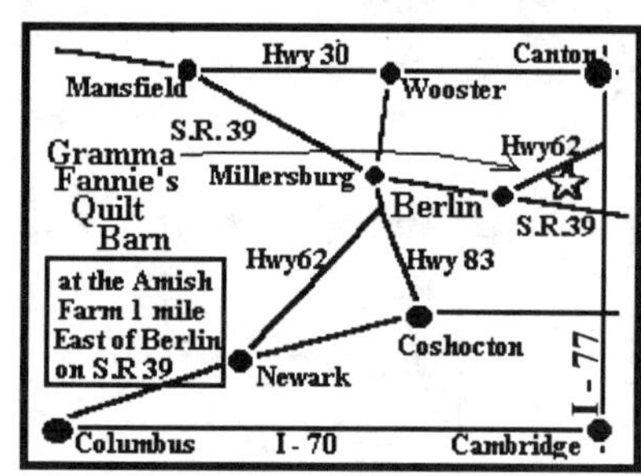

Located at Schrock's Amish Farm and Home
4363 State Route 39
P.O. Box 270
44610
(330) 893-3232
Owners: John Schrock & Joann Hershberger
Est: 1991
1 mile east of Berlin

Berlin, OH #39

Berlin, OH #40

Mon - Sat 10 - 6

Country Craft Cupboard

P.O. Box 419, 4813 E. Main St.
(330) 893-3163 44610
Owners: Mary Sundheimer & Karen Lamp
Est: 1984 3500 sq.ft. 1000 Bolts

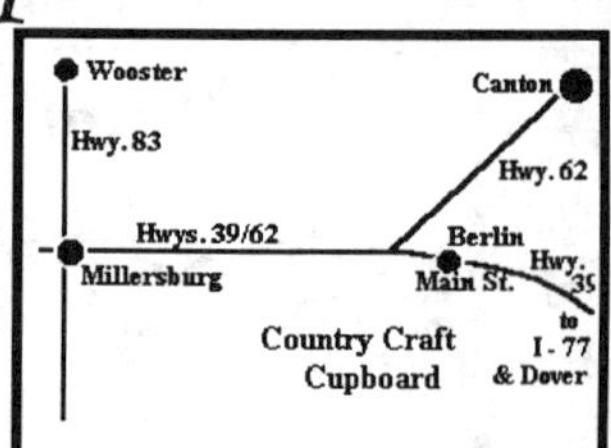

1000 bolts of specialty fabrics, plus craft supplies. Hundreds of books & patterns! Models galore! In an old country store!

Berlin, OH #41

Mon - Fri 8 - 8 Sat 8 - 6

Spector's Plain & Fancy

German Village Shopping Center
Oak St. 44610
(330) 893-3935

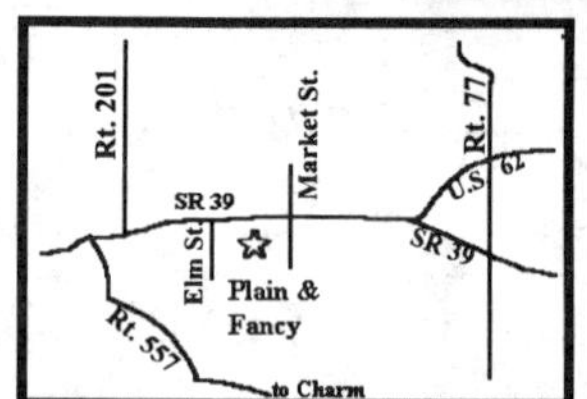

Full Line of Fabrics, Notion, Quilt & Craft Supplies & Patterns. Excellent Values on solid & Printed Fabrics.

Mt. Hope, OH #42

Mon - Sat 8 - 5

Lone Star Quilt Shop

Box 32 C. R. 77 44660
Owners: Ervin & Sara Yoder
Est: 1981 Brochure $1

Over 1000 bolts of Print and Plain Fabrics. Custom made Quilts & Wall hangings. Notions & Books Crafts— Placemats, Table Runners, Pillows, Potholders, etc.

Charm, OH #43

Mon - Sat
8 - 5

Miller's Dry Goods

4500 S.R. 557 Est: 1965
Mail—Millersburg, OH 44654
Owners: The Miller Family
Also—a whole barn full of quilts.

Beautiful selection of ready-made Quilts. Custom Quilting. Over 5000 bolts of fabric. Wall hangings, pillows, quillows, etc. Nice selection of quilt and pattern books.

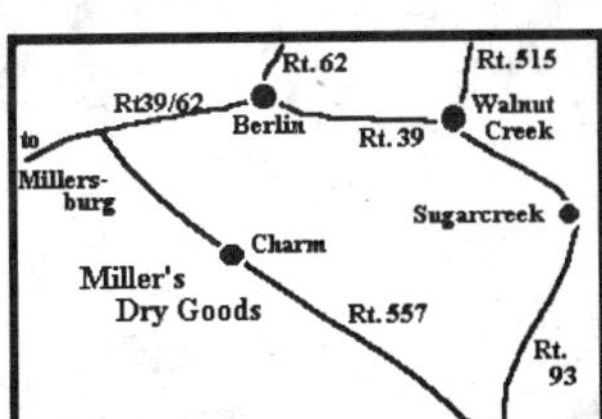

Loudonville, OH #44

Mon - Sat
10 - 5:30
Wed 12 - 5

Piecemaker Fabric Shop

141 W. Main St. 44842
(419) 994-5179 or
(800) 871-3492 (Ohio Only)
Owner: Becki Smith Est: 1993

The shop for crafters in the heart of Mohican Country. Cotton Fabrics (Over 600 Bolts), Books, Patterns, Notions, Craft and Cross Stitch Supplies.

Sugarcreek, OH #45

Mon - Sat
8:30 - 5
Fri til 8

Spector's Store

122 E. Main 44681
(330) 852-2113
Mgr: Mary Mullet

Full Line of Fabric and notions. Quilt and Craft supplies. Excellent Values on Solid & Printed fabrics.

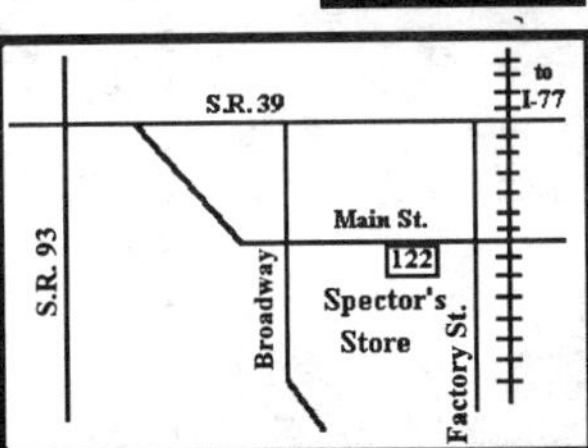

Sugarcreek, OH #46

Mon - Sat
9 - 5

Swiss Village Quilts and Crafts

113 S. Broadway P.O. Box 514 44681
(330) 852-4855
Owners: Aden & Anna Hochstetler
Est: 1982 1250 sq.ft. Free Brochure

Quality, local-made Quilts, Wallhangings and related items. Wooden toys Etc. Most items made locally by Amish
Special orders gladly Accepted.

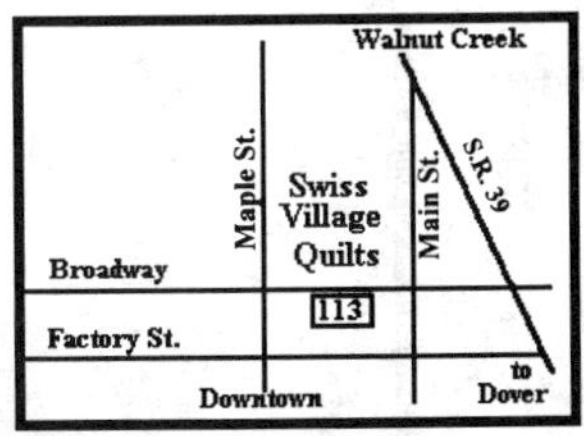

Uhrichsville, OH #47

Mon by Chance
Tues, Thur, Fri
9 - 5
Wed & Sat 9 - 12

Material Things

109 N. Water St. 44683
(740) 922-2310

Quaint family atmosphere provides patterns, lace, notions, buttons, quilt supplies... many charming gift items by owner/artist Karla Armstrong... Christmas Room... Classes. 10 min. SE on Rte 250 from New Philadelphia's New Town Mall.

Mansfield, OH #49

Mon - Thur
10 - 5:30
Fri & Sat
10 - 4

Quilt Connection

415 Park Ave. W 44906
(419) 522-2330
Owner: Janet Williams
Est: 1980 1200 sq.ft.

Visit us for quality products & personal, friendly service!
Fabrics, Quilt & Sewing Supplies, Bernina & New Home Sewing Machines. Classes.

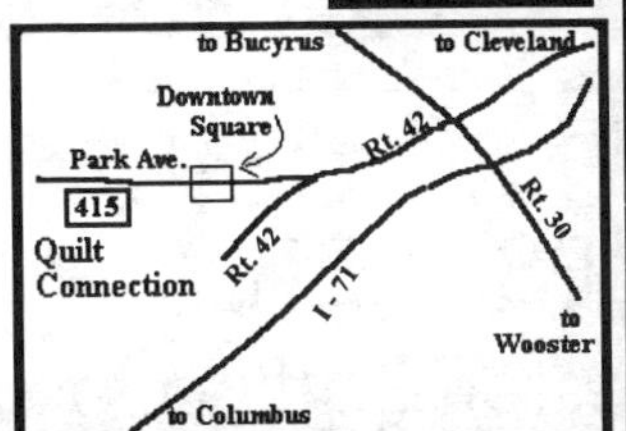

Akron, OH #50

Mon-Thur 10 - 8
Fri & Sat 10 - 5
Sun 12 - 4

A Piece In Time

5485 Manchester Rd. 44319
(330) 882-9626 (800) SANDY98
Owner: Sandy Heminger
6000 sq.ft. Catalog LSASE

Truly Wonderful Fabrics, Elna Sewing Machines, Incredible Selection of Books & Notions & (Nation wide) Exquisite Custom Machine Quilting.

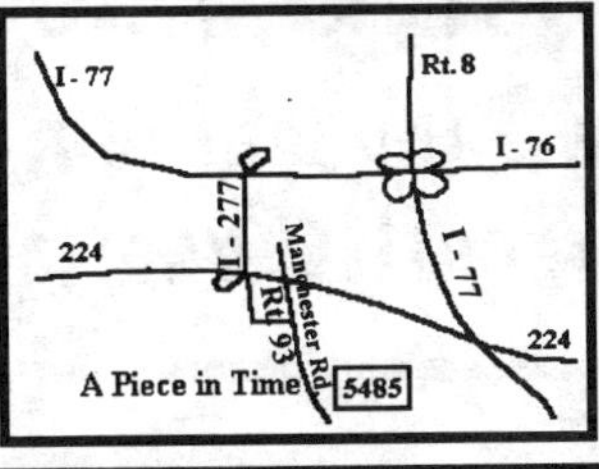

Ashland, OH #48

Country Charm Fabrics and Sew Crazy

Est: 1975

1422 Township Road 593 44805
Country Charm—(419) 281-2341
Sew Crazy—(419) 281-9422
Owners: Cindy Doggett & George Finley

Mon, Tues,
Thur, Fri
10 - 5
Sat 10 - 4

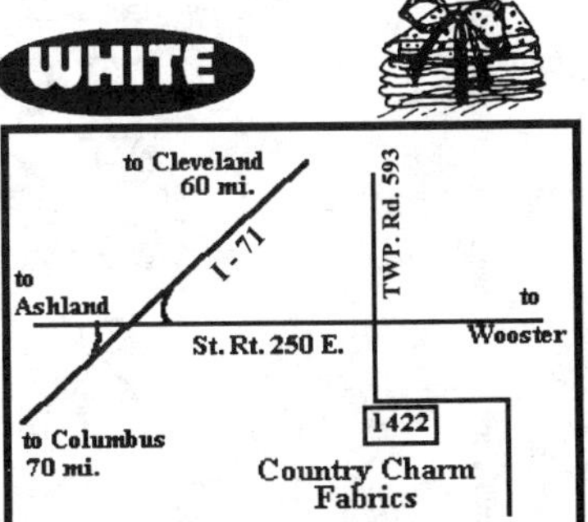

A Complete array of Quilting fabrics from the best mills in America. Notions, Quilt Frames, Classes, and all of the essentials for the Quilting Enthusiast. Viking & White Dealer Sewing Machines & Serger Repair

LOG CABIN QUILTS

#51

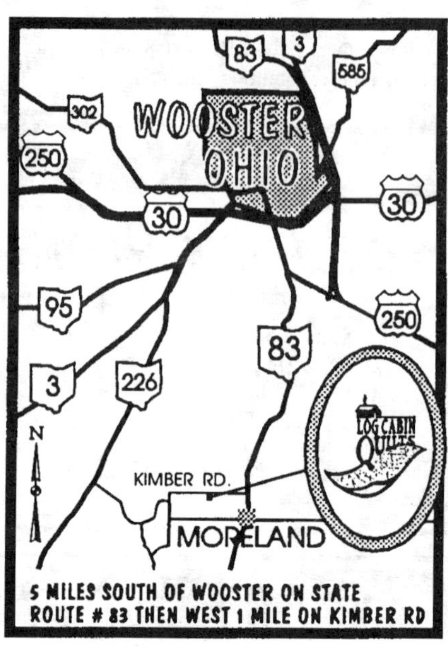

CLOSED JANUARY & FEBRUARY

* We Do Machine Quilting
* Machine Basting
* Hand & Machine Binding

We have the Largest Selection
in Northeast Ohio of
90" wide 100% Cotton Fabrics

We Also Stock 108" & 120" Linings

40,000 Yards of 100% Cotton Fabric
AT or near WHOLESALE Prices

We Also Stock 90" Polyester Batting on the Roll

CALL PHYLLIS AT (330) 264-6690

910 KIMBER RD., WOOSTER, OHIO 44691

Visit us at our website: www.logcabinquilts.com
Email: mrsquilts@aol.com

QUILTS & KREATIONS

South Amherst, OH #52

101 E. Main St. 44001
Phone / Fax (440) 986-4132
Owner: Sandra Whitaker

QUILTS & KREATIONS was established in 1980 and we have grown in size throughout the years. We offer you over 3600 sq.ft. of shopping area in our 100+ year old building. There are over 3500 bolts of designer fabric to choose from. We stock the area's largest selection of 100% cotton fabrics, patterns, books, and unique craft patterns.

We are Lorain County's only authorized Bernina Dealer and Lorain County's most complete quilt shop.

BERNINA®

Mon - Sat 10 - 5 Thur til 7

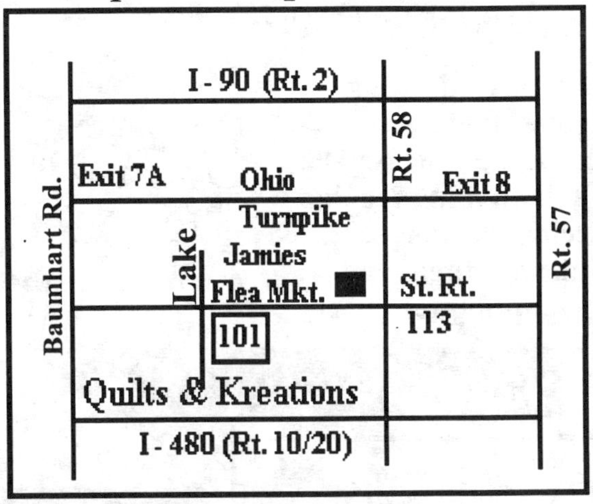

I - 90 (Rt. 2)
Rt. 58
Exit 7A
Ohio Turnpike
Exit 8
Baumhart Rd.
Lake
James Flea Mkt.
St. Rt. 113
Rt. 57
101
Quilts & Kreations
I - 480 (Rt. 10/20)

Easily accessible from either the Ohio Turnpike or Interstate Route 90.
We are 1.6 miles west of State Route 58 on State Route 113 in South Amherst, Ohio.
We are on the southeast corner of the street at the light.

Willoughby, OH #53

Mon & Thur 10 - 8
Tues & Wed 10 -6
Fri & Sat 10 - 5

Erie Street Fabrics

4134 Erie Street (Rt. 20) 44094
(440) 953-1340
Owner: Mary Huey
Est: 1979 3000 sq.ft.

Stocked with a unique assortment of cotton fabrics. Offering year-round classes in Quiltmaking, Smocking & Clothing. Authorized Bernina Dealer.

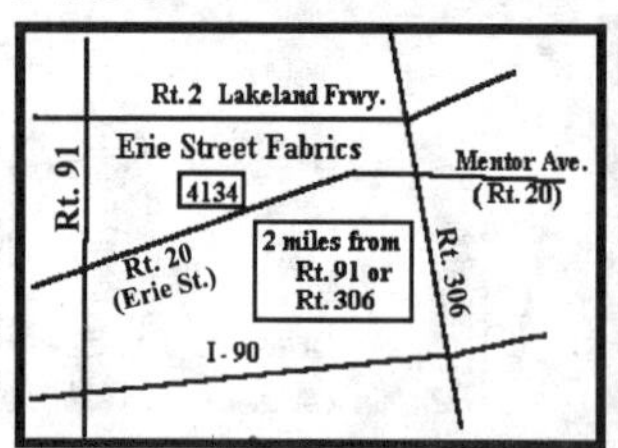

Painesville, OH #54

Tues - Sat
10 - 5

Parlour Quilts, Inc.

216 E. Main St. 44077
(440) 357-0055
Owners: Nancy Gelsinger & Sue Kane
1400 sq.ft. 1000 Bolts

Top Quality 100% Cotton Fabrics, Classes, Books, Patterns, Notions, Batting, Quilts, Readymades. Special Orders. Classes by Request.

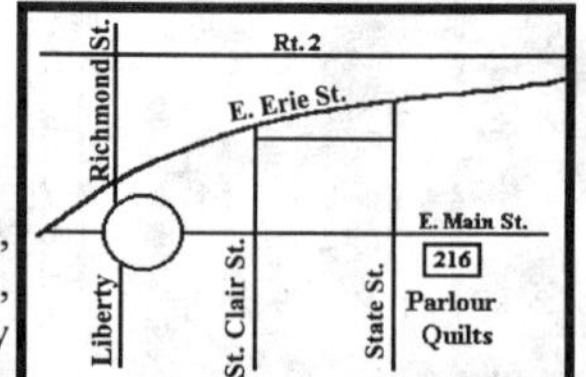

Chesterland, OH #55

Mon - Sat
10 - 5

Remembrances

12570 Chillicothe Rd. 44026
(440) 729-1650
Owner: Cheryl Pedersen
Est: 1984 1200 sq.ft.

Cotton Fabrics, Notions, Books.
Classes: quilting & dollmaking.
Finished crafts also available.

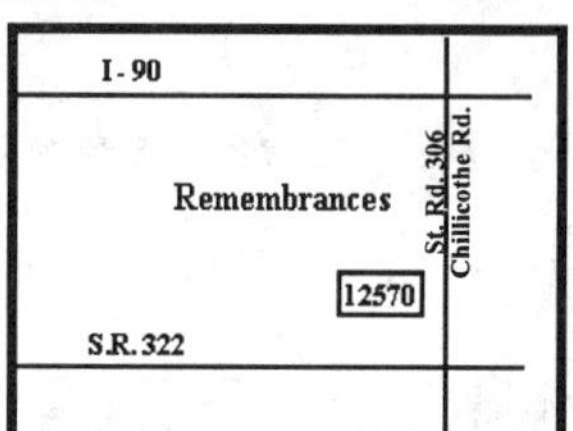

Cortland, OH #56

Tues - Fri 10 - 5
Sat 10 - 4
Summer
Tues - Sat
10 - 4

Simple Pleasures Quilt Shop

112 Park Ave. 44410
(330) 638-1733
Owners: June Karovic & Betty Kerner
Est: 1986 700 Bolts

Complete quilt shop 100% cotton fabrics. Latest in flannels and homespuns. Books & craft-sewing patterns.

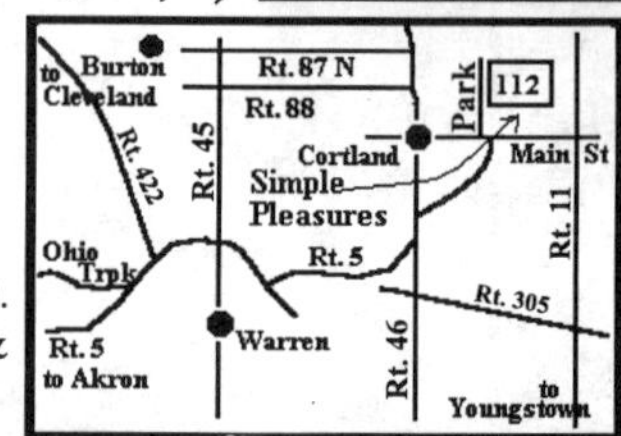

Quilter's Quarters

8458 Market Street 44512
(330) 758-7072
Owner: Julie Maruskin
Est: 1989 900 sq.ft. 900+ Bolts

We carry quilting supplies, fabrics, tools, books and patterns. We teach hand and machine piecing, masterpiece quilting stitch, and applique.

Youngstown, OH #57

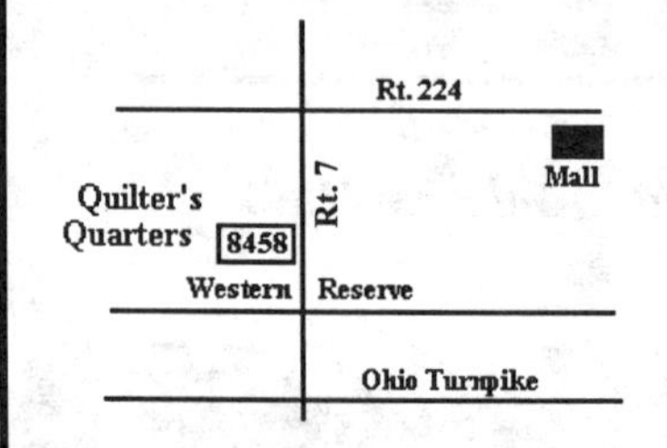

Mon - Fri
9 - 5
Sat 9 - 4

Rootstown, OH #58

Tues - Fri
10 - 6
Thur til 8
Sat 10 - 4

A Quilter's Corner

4169 Tallmadge Rd. 44272
(330) 325-1880
Owner: Bernadette Sanders
Est: 1998 1400 sq.ft.

Large selection of 100% cotton quilting fabrics, books, notions, quilts & soft patterns. Quality custom quilting services.

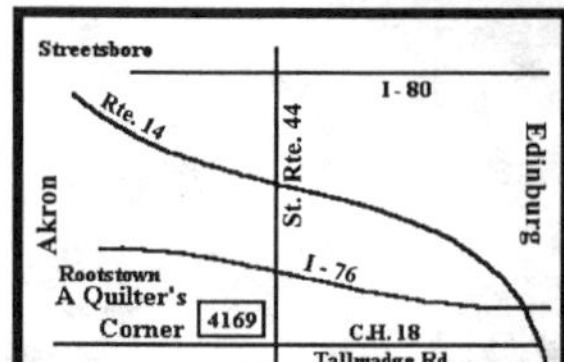

Canton, OH #59

Schoolhouse Quilt Shoppe

Mon - Sat 9:30 - 5

2872 Whipple Ave. 44708
(330) 477-4767
Est: 1976
Owners: Judie & Bob Rolhernal

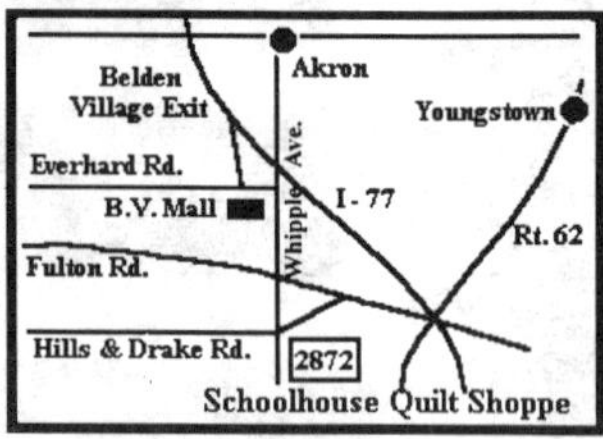

4000 Bolts of Fabric, Quilts, & Supplies.
Over 350 swatches.
We have a catalog of fabrics and original quilt kits available. Send $7.00
Come Visit Us.

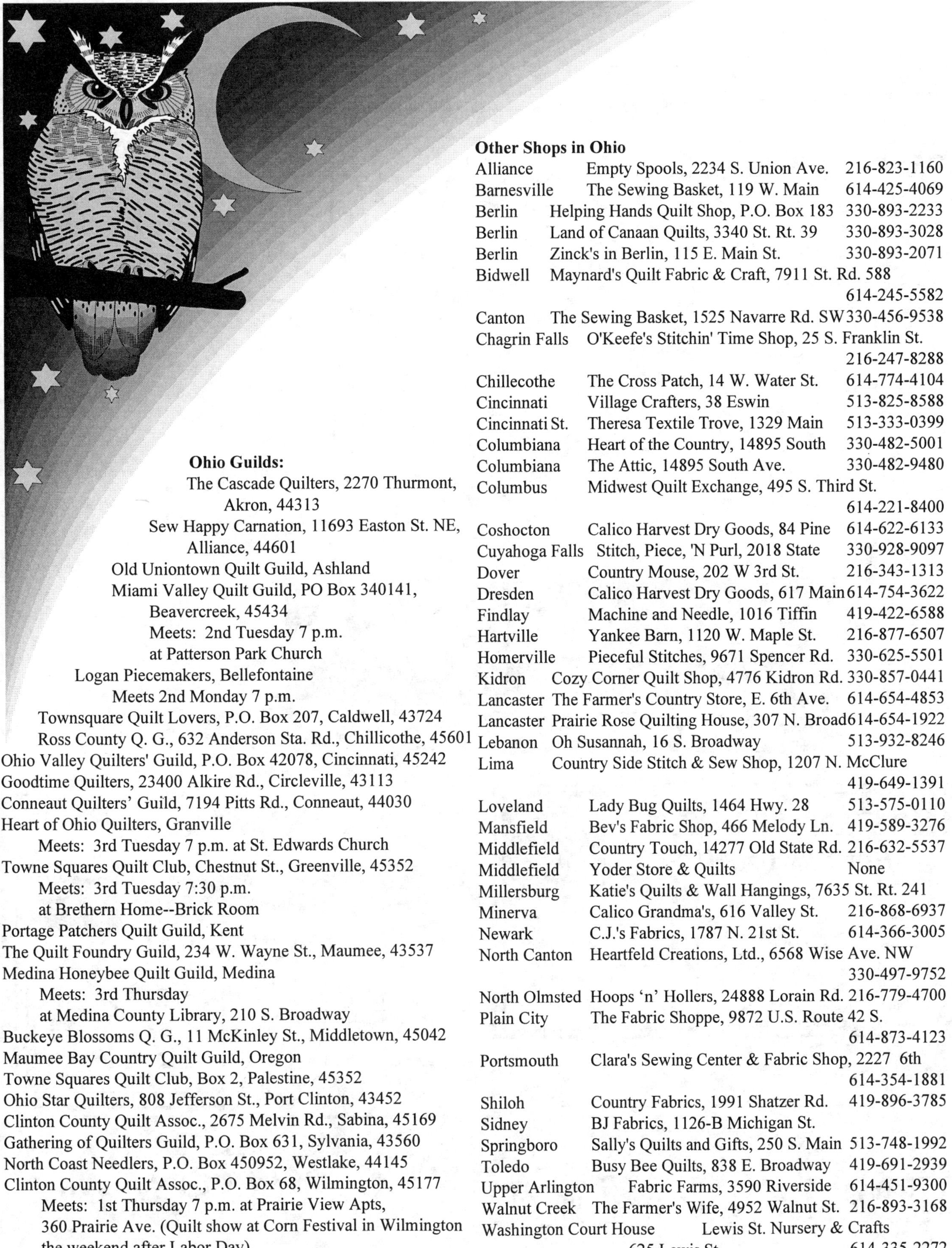

Other Shops in Ohio

Alliance	Empty Spools, 2234 S. Union Ave.	216-823-1160
Barnesville	The Sewing Basket, 119 W. Main	614-425-4069
Berlin	Helping Hands Quilt Shop, P.O. Box 183	330-893-2233
Berlin	Land of Canaan Quilts, 3340 St. Rt. 39	330-893-3028
Berlin	Zinck's in Berlin, 115 E. Main St.	330-893-2071
Bidwell	Maynard's Quilt Fabric & Craft, 7911 St. Rd. 588	614-245-5582
Canton	The Sewing Basket, 1525 Navarre Rd. SW	330-456-9538
Chagrin Falls	O'Keefe's Stitchin' Time Shop, 25 S. Franklin St.	216-247-8288
Chillecothe	The Cross Patch, 14 W. Water St.	614-774-4104
Cincinnati	Village Crafters, 38 Eswin	513-825-8588
Cincinnati St.	Theresa Textile Trove, 1329 Main	513-333-0399
Columbiana	Heart of the Country, 14895 South	330-482-5001
Columbiana	The Attic, 14895 South Ave.	330-482-9480
Columbus	Midwest Quilt Exchange, 495 S. Third St.	614-221-8400
Coshocton	Calico Harvest Dry Goods, 84 Pine	614-622-6133
Cuyahoga Falls	Stitch, Piece, 'N Purl, 2018 State	330-928-9097
Dover	Country Mouse, 202 W 3rd St.	216-343-1313
Dresden	Calico Harvest Dry Goods, 617 Main	614-754-3622
Findlay	Machine and Needle, 1016 Tiffin	419-422-6588
Hartville	Yankee Barn, 1120 W. Maple St.	216-877-6507
Homerville	Pieceful Stitches, 9671 Spencer Rd.	330-625-5501
Kidron	Cozy Corner Quilt Shop, 4776 Kidron Rd.	330-857-0441
Lancaster	The Farmer's Country Store, E. 6th Ave.	614-654-4853
Lancaster	Prairie Rose Quilting House, 307 N. Broad	614-654-1922
Lebanon	Oh Susannah, 16 S. Broadway	513-932-8246
Lima	Country Side Stitch & Sew Shop, 1207 N. McClure	419-649-1391
Loveland	Lady Bug Quilts, 1464 Hwy. 28	513-575-0110
Mansfield	Bev's Fabric Shop, 466 Melody Ln.	419-589-3276
Middlefield	Country Touch, 14277 Old State Rd.	216-632-5537
Middlefield	Yoder Store & Quilts	None
Millersburg	Katie's Quilts & Wall Hangings, 7635 St. Rt. 241	
Minerva	Calico Grandma's, 616 Valley St.	216-868-6937
Newark	C.J.'s Fabrics, 1787 N. 21st St.	614-366-3005
North Canton	Heartfeld Creations, Ltd., 6568 Wise Ave. NW	330-497-9752
North Olmsted	Hoops 'n' Hollers, 24888 Lorain Rd.	216-779-4700
Plain City	The Fabric Shoppe, 9872 U.S. Route 42 S.	614-873-4123
Portsmouth	Clara's Sewing Center & Fabric Shop, 2227 6th	614-354-1881
Shiloh	Country Fabrics, 1991 Shatzer Rd.	419-896-3785
Sidney	BJ Fabrics, 1126-B Michigan St.	
Springboro	Sally's Quilts and Gifts, 250 S. Main	513-748-1992
Toledo	Busy Bee Quilts, 838 E. Broadway	419-691-2939
Upper Arlington	Fabric Farms, 3590 Riverside	614-451-9300
Walnut Creek	The Farmer's Wife, 4952 Walnut St.	216-893-3168
Washington Court House	Lewis St. Nursery & Crafts, 625 Lewis St.	614-335-2272

Ohio Guilds:

The Cascade Quilters, 2270 Thurmont, Akron, 44313

Sew Happy Carnation, 11693 Easton St. NE, Alliance, 44601

Old Uniontown Quilt Guild, Ashland

Miami Valley Quilt Guild, PO Box 340141, Beavercreek, 45434
Meets: 2nd Tuesday 7 p.m.
at Patterson Park Church

Logan Piecemakers, Bellefontaine
Meets 2nd Monday 7 p.m.

Townsquare Quilt Lovers, P.O. Box 207, Caldwell, 43724

Ross County Q. G., 632 Anderson Sta. Rd., Chillicothe, 45601

Ohio Valley Quilters' Guild, P.O. Box 42078, Cincinnati, 45242

Goodtime Quilters, 23400 Alkire Rd., Circleville, 43113

Conneaut Quilters' Guild, 7194 Pitts Rd., Conneaut, 44030

Heart of Ohio Quilters, Granville
Meets: 3rd Tuesday 7 p.m. at St. Edwards Church

Towne Squares Quilt Club, Chestnut St., Greenville, 45352
Meets: 3rd Tuesday 7:30 p.m.
at Brethern Home--Brick Room

Portage Patchers Quilt Guild, Kent

The Quilt Foundry Guild, 234 W. Wayne St., Maumee, 43537

Medina Honeybee Quilt Guild, Medina
Meets: 3rd Thursday
at Medina County Library, 210 S. Broadway

Buckeye Blossoms Q. G., 11 McKinley St., Middletown, 45042

Maumee Bay Country Quilt Guild, Oregon

Towne Squares Quilt Club, Box 2, Palestine, 45352

Ohio Star Quilters, 808 Jefferson St., Port Clinton, 43452

Clinton County Quilt Assoc., 2675 Melvin Rd., Sabina, 45169

Gathering of Quilters Guild, P.O. Box 631, Sylvania, 43560

North Coast Needlers, P.O. Box 450952, Westlake, 44145

Clinton County Quilt Assoc., P.O. Box 68, Wilmington, 45177
Meets: 1st Thursday 7 p.m. at Prairie View Apts,
360 Prairie Ave. (Quilt show at Corn Festival in Wilmington the weekend after Labor Day)

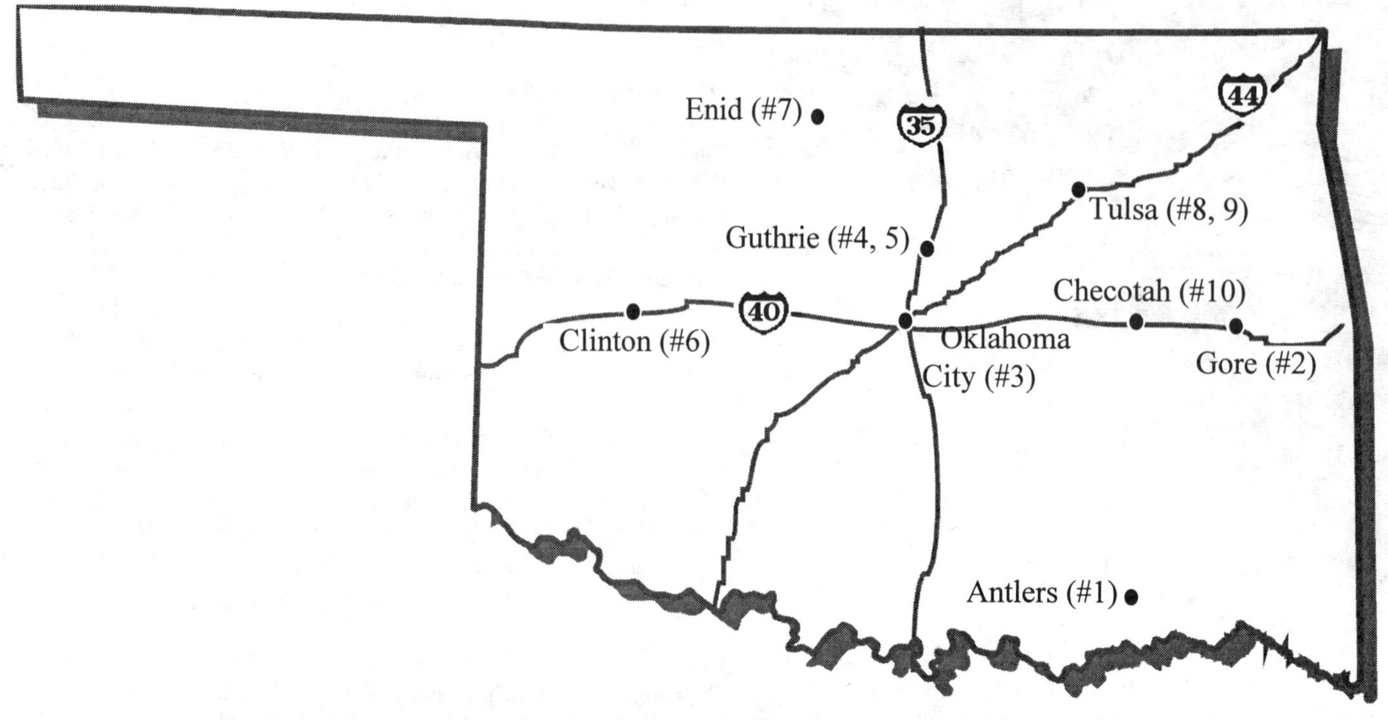

10 Featured Shops

Antlers, OK #1

Mon - Fri 9 - 5 Evenings & weekends by Chance or Appt.

Betsy's Quilts

HC 70, Box 870, P.O. Box 947 74523
(580) 298-5821 Est: 1994
(888) 817-5821 (OK only)
Owner: Betty Hairfield 2000 sq.ft.

Over 1000 Bolts of Name Brand Fabrics.
Books, Patterns, Notions.
Quilts & Quillows for Sale.
Machine Quilting Pattern or Outlined.

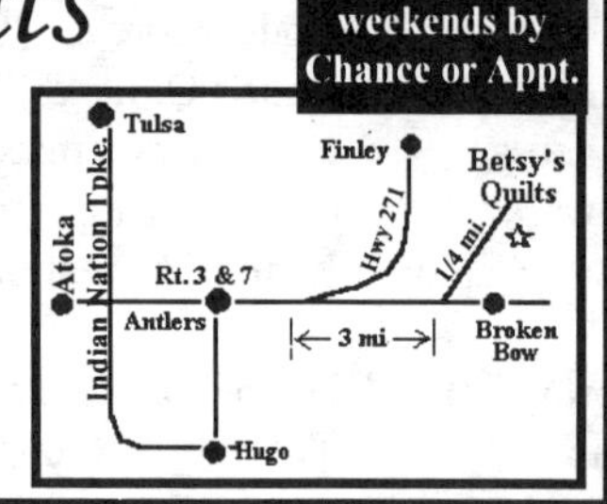

Gore, OK #2

Thur - Sat 10 - 5

Round Top Quilt Shop

Box 217 Ray Fine Dr. 74435
(918) 489-5652
Owner: Mardena Matthews
Est: 1985

Quilting Supplies, Fabric, Patterns, Books
Notions, Classes
Plus Finished Quilts & Wallhangings.

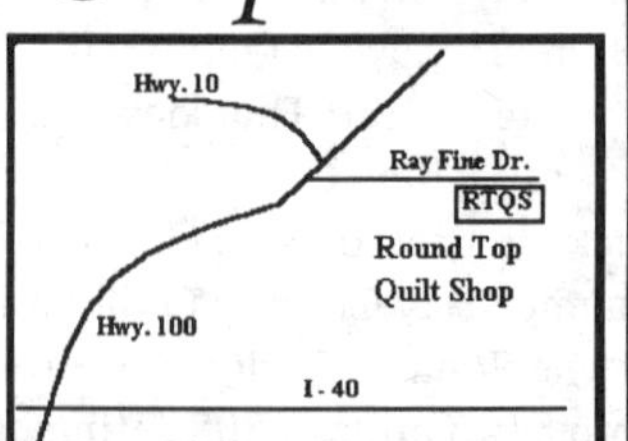

Have you hugged your sewing machine today?

Oklahoma City, OK #3

Oklahoma QUILTWORKS

9323 N. Pennsylvania 73120 (405) 842-4778
Barbara Stanfield & Carole Jo Evans Est: 1988 2400 sq.ft.

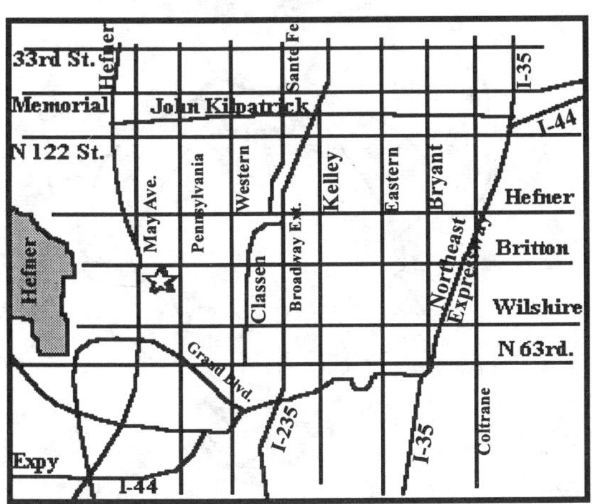

3500+ bolts of Cotton Fabric
500+ Quilting Book Titles
Notions, Patterns, Classes & Gifts

Mon - Fri 10 - 5
Thur til 8 Sat 10 - 3

Come Visit us in August of Odd Numbered years for the "Celebration of Quilts" Quilt Show

Guthrie, OK #4

Mon - Thur 10 - 6
Fri & Sat 10 - 8
Sun 12 - 5
Shorter Hrs. Jan - March

Quilted Classics

206 S. Second 73044
(405) 282-5439 Fax: (405) 282-6834
E-Mail: clair@quiltedclassics.com
Web Site: www.quiltedclassics.com
Catalog $3

We sell quality Hand-Quilted Quilts at affordable prices. We also have table linens and gifts.

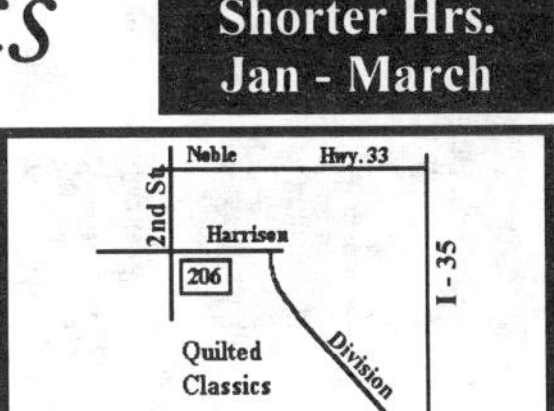

Guthrie, OK #5

Mon - Sat 9 - 5
Sun 1 - 4

Pincushion, Inc.

124 W. Oklahoma 73044
(405) 282-2666
Owner: Cynthia Baker
Est: 1974 2400 sq.ft.

Cottons and fashion fabric. Stocking the unique and distinctive in fabric. We carry the Vintage Western Pattern line—"Buckaroo Bobbins". Located in historic Guthrie.

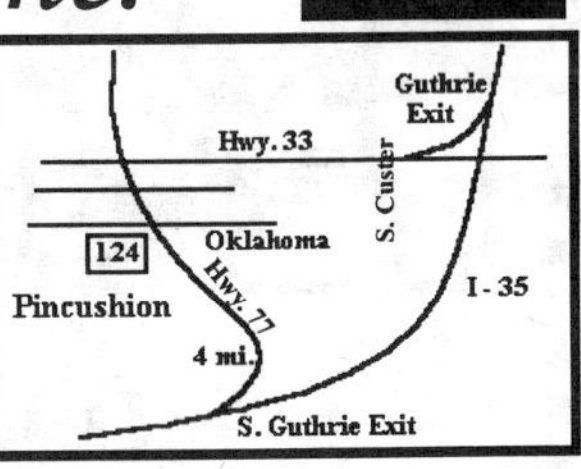

Clinton, OK #6

Mon - Fri 10 - 5
Sat 10 - 3

AL-Bar Fabric

711 Frisco St. 73601
(580) 323-4230
Owners: Rex & Terri Finnell
Est: 1972 5000 sq.ft. 2000 Bolts

Authorized Pfaff Dealer. Quilting Books and all Quilting Supplies. Classes Fashion Fabrics and a lot more. Machine Quilting. Look for new web site.

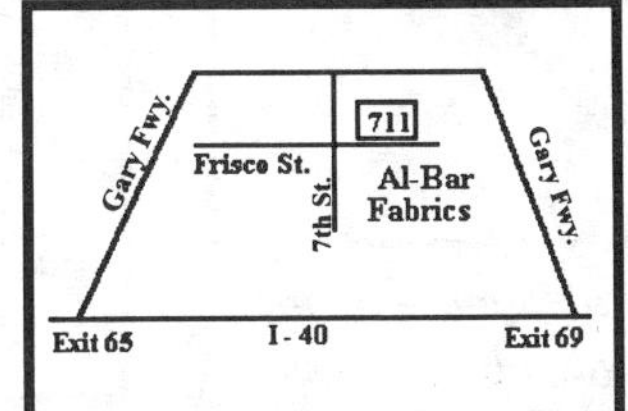

Enid, OK #7

Mon - Sat 10 - 5

The Quilting Parlor

118 North Independence 73701
(405) 234-3087
Owner: Patricia M. Russell
Est: 1981 3000 sq.ft.

2000 Bolts 100% Cotton Fabrics, Notions, Books, Classes. Quilt Camp - A weekend retreat of classes for the quilter.

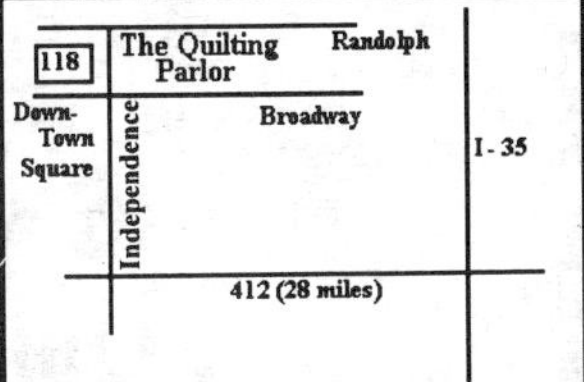

Tulsa, OK #8

The Quilters' Nook

1740 S. Harvard 74112
(918) 747-NOOK
(6665)
Owners: Glen Jones
& Anne Seereiter
Est: 1987 6000 sq.ft.

Mon 9:30 - 7
Tues - Fri
9:30 - 5:30
Sat 9:30 - 4:30

Fabric - Always 100% Cottons (2500+ bolts).
Notions - To ease tasks.
Patterns & Books - For inspiration & instruction (400+ titles).
FRIENDLY SERVICE !

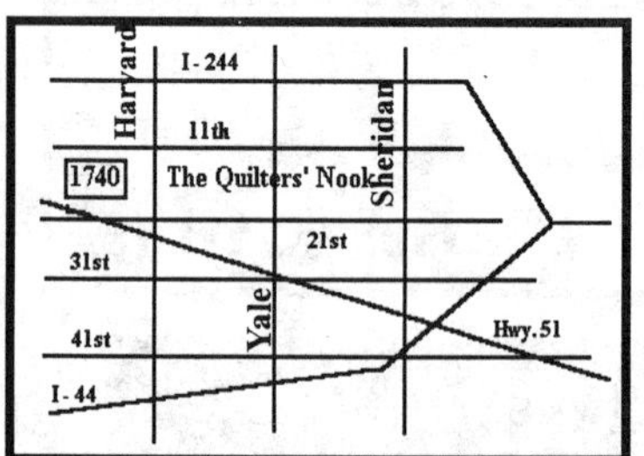

Tulsa, OK #9

Cotton Patch

Mon - Fri
10 - 5:30
Tues til 7
Sat 10 - 5

8250 East 71st St. 74133
(918) 252-1995
Owner: Nancy & Mike Mullman
Est: 1977 1200 sq.ft.

Large quilt fabric selection, books, notions, and patterns.

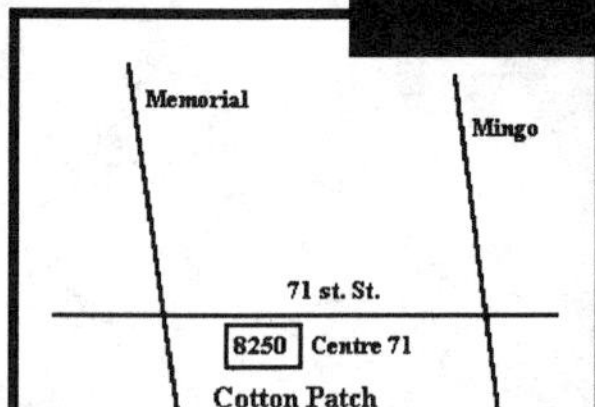

Checotah, OK #10

Mon - Sat
9 - 5

Davis' Log Store

H.C. 60, Box 1315 74426
(918) 473-7020

Quilters Fabrics and "Necessarys" nestled among Antiques & Collectibles on Lake Eufaula
State Highway # 150.

New & Antique Quilts

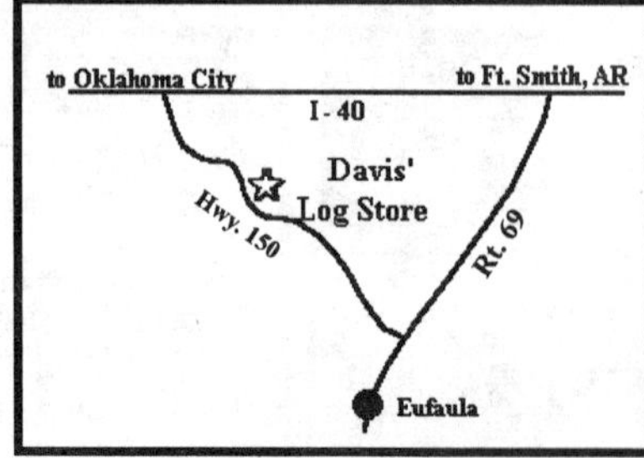

Exit #259 on I - 40 3 miles S. or 4 miles N. of Fountainhead Resort

QUILTERS CABIN RETREAT

FOR QUILTERS & TRAVELERS
AN EXTENSION OF DAVIS' LOG STORE
SLEEPS 2 TO 12
CALL FOR MORE INFO.

Oklahoma Guilds:

Southwest Oklahoma Quilters, 1021 S. Fowler, Altus, 73521
Oklahoma Prairie Quilters Guild, 312 W. Colorado, Anadarko, 73005
Pushmataha County Quilt Guild, P.O. Box 910, Antlers, 74523
Meets: Last Tuesday 10 a.m. & 6 p.m. at Church of Christ Annex Bldg.
Southern Oklahoma Quilters, 4244 S. Plainview Rd., Ardmore, 73401
Jubilee Quilters Guild, P.O. Box 3113, Bartlesville, 74006
Oklahoma Quilters State Org., P.O. Box 5015, Bartlesville, 74005
Northside Quilters of OKC, 7500 NW 25th Terr., Bethany, 73008
Country Fare Quilters Guild, 2614 SE Crestview, Claremore, 74017
Western Oklahoma Quilters Guild, 323 S. 8th, Clinton
Meets: 4th Monday (except Dec.) 7:30 p.m. at Senior Citizen Center
Patchwork Quilters Guild, 1528 W. Oak, El Reno, 73036
Grand Lake O'Cherokees, 60451 E. 317th Ct., Grove, 74344
First Capital Quilters, 1206 Magnolia Ct., Guthrie, 73044
Timeless Treasures Quilt Guild, Rt. 3, Box 32K, Guymon, 73942
Panhandle Piecers Quilt Guild, 721 NW 5th, Guymon, 73942
Wichita Mountains Quilt Guild, 816 NW Ferris Ave., Lawton, 73507
Kiamichi Quilt Guild, 200 E. Adams, McAlester, 74501
Meets: at McAlester Bldg. Room 311
Muskogee Area Quilters Guild, 2175 S. 72nd St. E, Muskogee, 74403
Washita Valley Churndashers, 914 W. Main, Norman, 73069
Town & Country Quilters, Rt. 1, Box 186, Okemah, 74859
Central Oklahoma Quilters Guild, P.O. Box 23916, Oklahoma City, 73123
Cherokee Strip Quilters Guild, 1914 Lakeview Dr., Perry, 73077
P.M. Patches & Pieces, 2700 Mockingbird Dr., Ponca City, 74604
Pioneer Area Quilters' Guild, P.O. Box 2726, Ponca City, 74604
Spinning Spools Quilt Guild, 46506 Westech Rd., Shawnee, 74801
Cimarron Valley Quilters Guild, P.O. Box 1113, Stillwater, 74076
Green Country Quilter's Guild, P.O. Box 35021, Tulsa, 74153
Western Oklahoma Quilter Guild, 122 Grandview, Weatherford, 73096

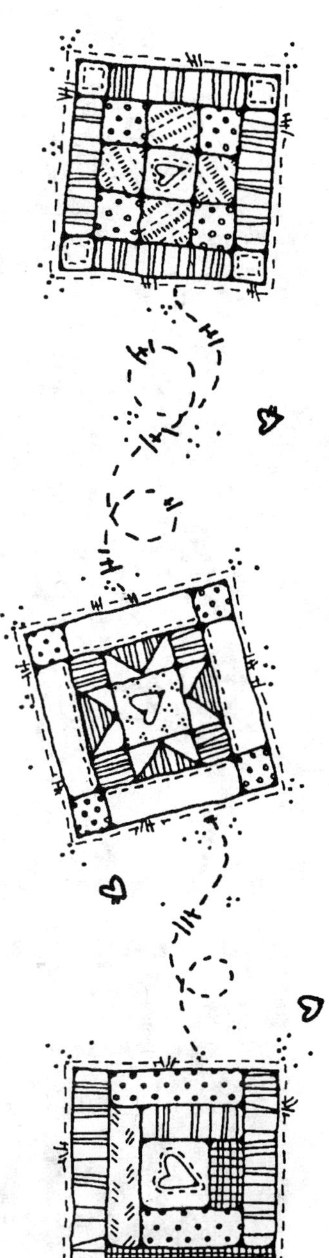

Other Shops in Oklahoma

Anadarko	Calico Patch Sewing Center, 105 W. Broadway St.	405-247-3251
Atoka	Sewing Basket, 210 E. Court St.	405-889-3470
Boise	City Stitches, Hwy. 287 S	405-544-2226
Chickasha	Off the Bolt, 407 W. Chickasha Ave.	405-224-2280
Chickasha	Becky's, 2227 Carolina	405-224-0332
Clinton	Cindy's Quilts, P.O. Box 1212	580-323-1174
Duncan	Cook's Sew Biz, 427 S. Hwy. 81	405-255-2843
Fargo	Calico Gal Quilt Shop, 121 1st St.	405-698-2440
Grove	Linda's Thread Basket, 2112 U.S. Hwy. 59 N	918-786-2046
Guymon	Heritage Quilts, 1907 Blue Sage Dr.	405-338-1402
Harrah	Martin Fabric Shop, 1960 N. Church Ave.	405-454-2960
Henryetta	Tiger Mountain Quilt Barn, Box 296A Route 2	918-466-3244
Jenks	Victorian Charm Quilt Shoppe, 225 E. Main St.	918-298-9090
Lawton	Hilltop Fabrics, P.O. Box 169 8202 W. Lee RR #4	405-536-5776
Mooreland	Heartland Quilt Works, 110 N. Elm St.	405-994-6090
Muskogee	Chief's Classics & Collectables, 429 Eastside Blvd.	918-683-7825
Norman	Patchwork Place, 104 E. Gray St.	405-321-4569
Nowata	Shrum's Country Quilters, 520 E. Cherokee Ave.	918-273-3393
Oakwood	J & J's Quilting Place, R.R. #2, Box 28	405-891-3575
Oklahoma City	Buckboard Antiques & Quilts, 1411 N. May Ave.	405-943-7020
Ponca City	Linda's Creative Sewing, 405 E. Grand Ave.	405-762-6694
Shawnee	Sue's Sewing Shoppe, 2301 North Kickapoo	405-273-4600
Tulsa	The Quilting B, 9433 E. 51st St.	918-622-4787
Tulsa	Quilts & Handcrafts, 908 W. 24th St.	918-584-8617
Valliant	Quilts Unlimited, 48 E. Wilson	405-933-4641

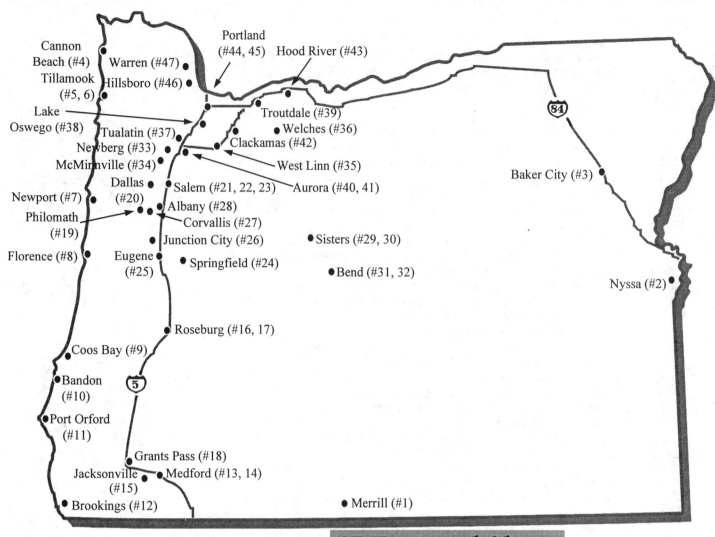

Cannon Beach (#4)
Warren (#47)
Tillamook (#5, 6)
Hillsboro (#46)
Portland (#44, 45)
Hood River (#43)
Lake Oswego (#38)
Troutdale (#39)
Tualatin (#37)
Welches (#36)
Newberg (#33)
Clackamas (#42)
McMinnville (#34)
West Linn (#35)
Dallas (#20)
Salem (#21, 22, 23)
Aurora (#40, 41)
Baker City (#3)
Newport (#7)
Albany (#28)
Philomath (#19)
Corvallis (#27)
Junction City (#26)
Sisters (#29, 30)
Florence (#8)
Eugene (#25)
Springfield (#24)
Bend (#31, 32)
Nyssa (#2)
Roseburg (#16, 17)
Coos Bay (#9)
Bandon (#10)
Port Orford (#11)
Grants Pass (#18)
Jacksonville (#15)
Medford (#13, 14)
Brookings (#12)
Merrill (#1)
84
5

47 Featured Shops

Merrill, OR #1

Tues - Fri 10 - 5
Sat 10 - 2

132 E. Front St.
97633
(541) 798-5955
Est: 1996
2100 sq.ft.

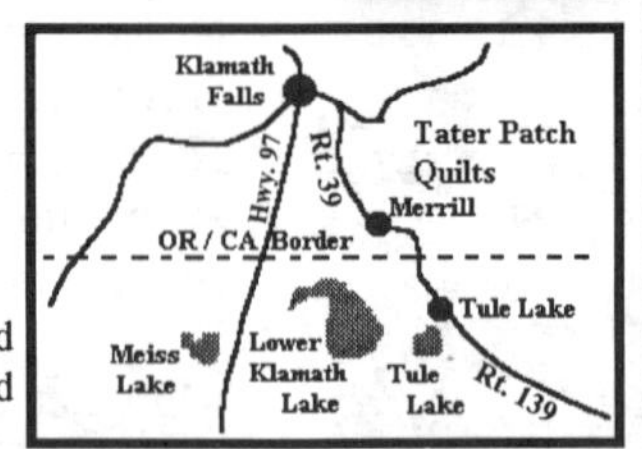

Large Selection of 100% Cotton Fabrics and Flannels. Books, Patterns, Notions and Classes. "On the Road to Reno"

Nyssa, OR #2

Mon - Sat 10 - 6

Marilynn's Pickets & Patchwork

124 Main St. 97913
(541) 372-5336

1500 Bolts
Books, Patterns, Classes, Gifts.
Best Selection of flannels in Eastern OR & Western ID.
Friendly, helpful "down home" atmosphere!

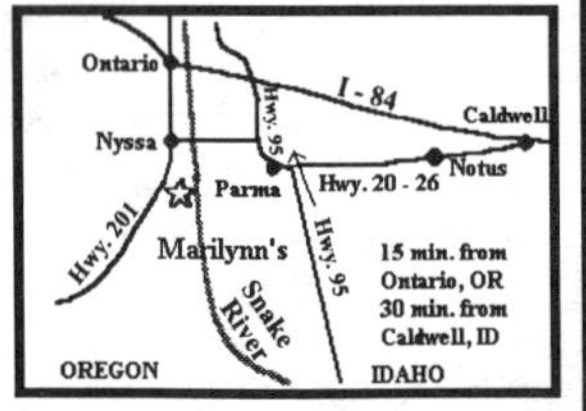

Baker City, OR #3

Mon - Fri 9:30 - 5:30
Sat 9:30 - 5

Jan's Pastimes

2101 Main St. 97814
(541) 523-6919
Owner: Jan Mahugh
Est: 1993 1400 sq.ft. 900 Bolts

Fabrics. Books. Decorative Painting.
Quilting Supplies. Notions.
Classes and More.
Authorized Elna Dealer.

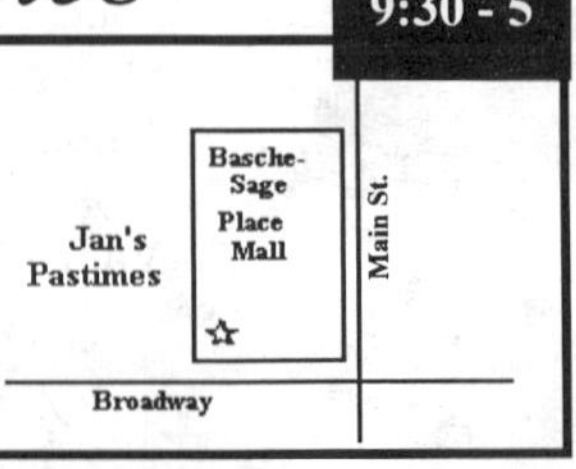

Cannon Beach, OR #4

7 Days a Week 10 - 5

Center Diamond

1065 S. Hemlock 97110
(503) 436-0833 Fax: (503) 436-2540
E-Mail: Bonniewa@aol.com
Web-Site: www.centerdiamond.com
Owners: Julie & Bonnie Walker
Est: 1994 1500 sq.ft. 2000+ Bolts
Over 2000 bolts of the most gorgeous 100% cotton fabrics. Books, patterns, notions & gifts. Located 1 block from the beach.

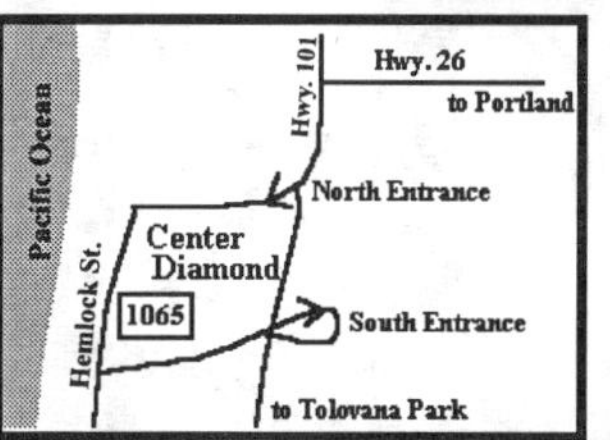

Jane's Fabric Patch

Tillamook, OR #5

1110 Main St. 97141
(503) 842-9392
Owner: Jane Wise
Est: 1981 2500+ Bolts

Mon - Fri 1 - 5:30
Sat 10 - 4
Summer - Sundays & Holidays 11 - 3

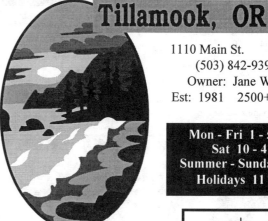

Coastal Retreat.
Multi-facetted Quilt shop.
Large fabric selection, creative, knowledgeable and friendly ideas and assistance.

9th St. / Main St. / 10th St. / Pacific / 11th St. / Jane's Fabric Patch 1110

Tillamook, OR #6

Tues - Sat 10 - 4
Sun 12 - 4

Latimer Quilt & Textile Center

2105 Wilson River Loop 97141
(503) 842-8622

A museum dedicated to the textile arts. We have classes for quilting, spinners, & weavers.
Shows change every 2 months.

We are located north of Tillamook one block off 101 N by the Coronet Store and the Shilo Inn.

Newport, OR #7

Mon - Sat 10 - 5

The Newport Quilt & Gift Co.

644 S.W. Coast Hwy. 97365
(541) 265-3492
E-Mail: newportquilt@newportnet.com
Web Site: www.newportnet.com/newportquilt
Owner: Julie Golimowski
Est: 1989 2400 sq.ft. Free Catalog
"The Most Complete Quilt shop on the Oregon Coast" Fabric, books & notions.
Home of Block Party by Mail 2000 Bolts

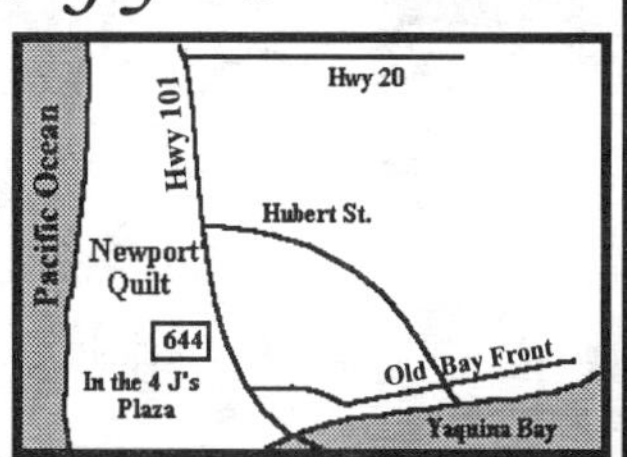

Florence, OR #8

Mon - Sat 9 - 5:30

2876 Hwy. 101 97439
(541) 997-3313 Est: 1969
Owner: Frieda Doyle 2000 sq.ft.
We carry 100% cottons & fashion fabrics. Quilting Supplies. We sell quilt books & patterns and we offer friendly service.

BERNINA

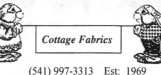

Pacific Ocean / 29th St. / 2876 Cottage Fabrics / Hwy. 101 / Hwy. 126

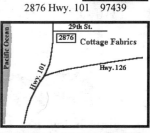

Coos Bay, OR #9

Mon - Fri 10 - 6
Sat 10 - 5

Threads That Bind

169 N. 2nd 97420
(541) 267-0749 Est: 1996
E-Mail: Threads@harborside.com
1300 sq.ft. 500+ Bolts & growing

100% Cottons; Large Book Selection; Notions; Classes—day/evening; Machine Quilting; Revolving Mini Quilt Show; Newsletter.

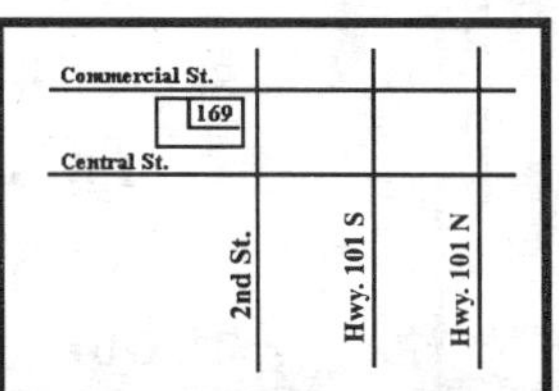

Bandon, OR #10

Mon - Sat 10 -5
Sun 11 - 4

Forget-Me-Knots

230 2nd St. 97411
(541) 347-9021
Owners: Janice Mottau & Melody Johnson
Est: 1988 1000 sq.ft. 1000 Bolts
A unique & charming shop specializing in quilting, dollmaking, silk ribbon embroidery. Supplies, patterns, books, classes & a large selection of 100% cottons

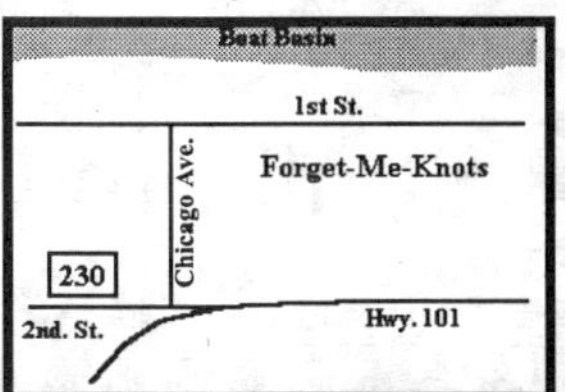

Port Orford, OR #11

Mon - Sat 10 - 5
Summer Sundays

Quilter's Corner

335 W. 7th, P.O. Box 69
(541) 332-0502 97465
Owners: Dottie Barnes, Dolores Purdy & Debbie Dorman
Est: 1994 1800 sq.ft. 2500 Bolts
Fabric, Notions, Patterns and Books. Machine Quilting, Classes and Quilts. Friendly, Spacious and Wonderful Lighting.

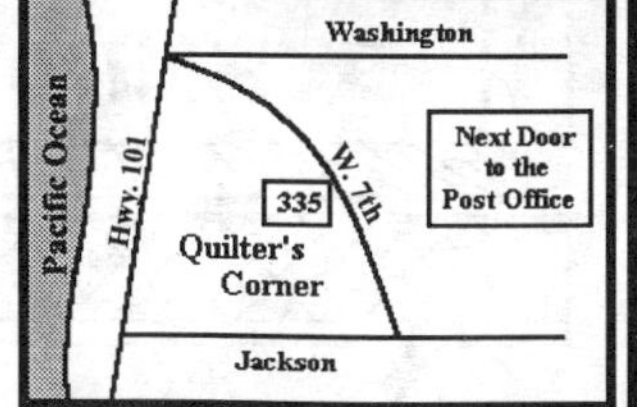

Brookings, OR #12

Mon - Sat 10 - 5

Country Keepsakes

802 Chetco Ave., P.O. Box 4012 97415
(541) 469-6117 (800) 469-6117
Owners: Michelle Fallert & Laurie Mitts
Est: 1988 2000 Bolts

We have a great variety of classes. Choose from over 2000 bolts of cotton fabric. Quilting supplies and books.

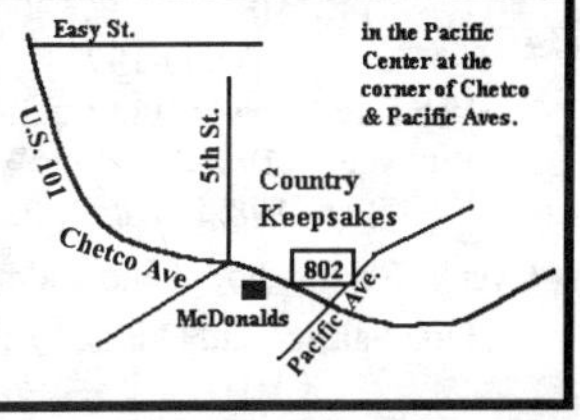

Medford, OR #13

Mon - Sat 10 - 5

Rosebud Quilts & Cottons

35 S. Bartlett 97501
(541) 779-2410
Owner: Beth Allison
Est: 1993 2000 sq.ft. 2000 Bolts

A Charming Shop with a beautiful selection of 100% cotton fabrics. Large selection of quilt books & patterns. Sewing notions & classes.

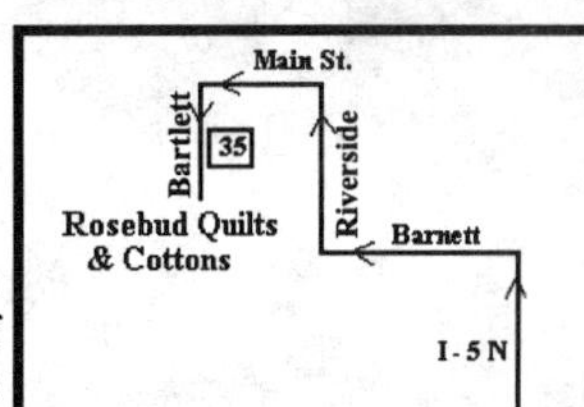

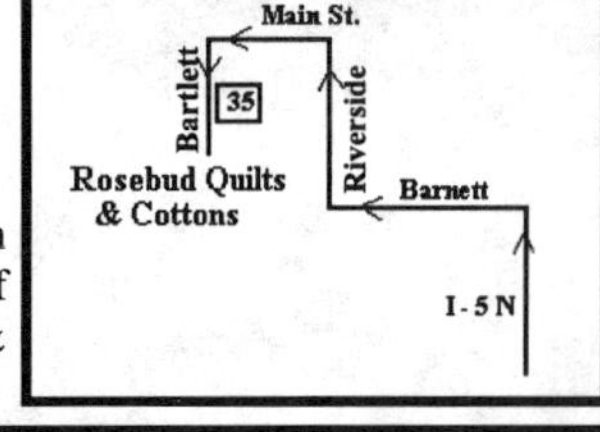

Medford, OR #14

Calico Junction

1310 - C Center Dr. 97501 (541) 770-8001
Owner: Vickie Kiser
Est: 1977 1500 sq.ft. 500 Bolts

Mon - Sat 10 - 6 Sun 12 - 5

500+ bolts of Hoffman, Kona Bay, South Seas, Maywood and Moda.

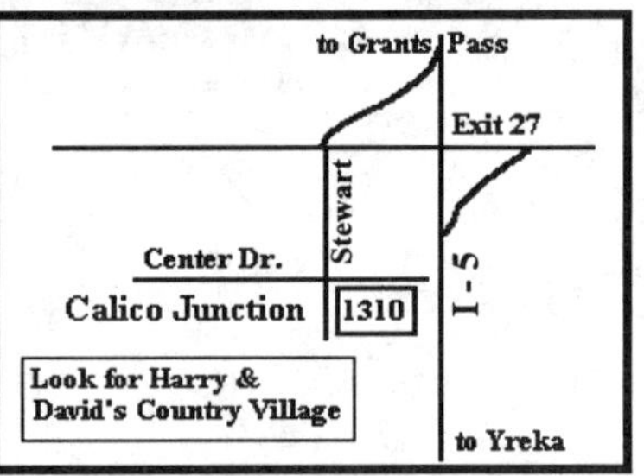

Southern Oregon's Largest Pattern Selection

Jacksonville, OR #15

Mon - Sat 10 - 5 Sun 11 - 4

Country Quilts & Crafts

110 5th St. 97530
(541) 899-1972
Web Site: www.countryquilts.com
Owners: Bob & Marge Wall
Est: 1988 650 Sq.ft.
Over 100 quilts both hand and machine.
Fine Fabrics and Quilts, Quilts, Quilts ! !

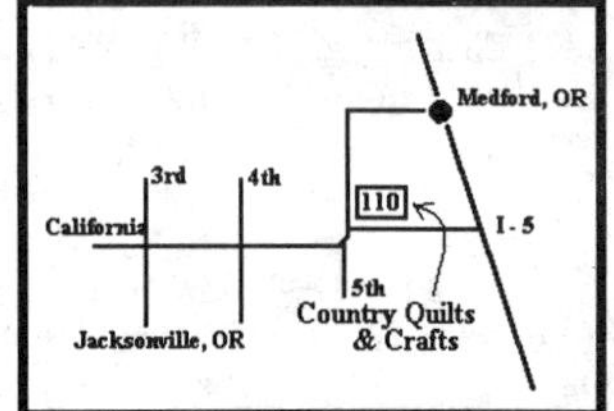

Roseburg, OR #16

Seams Like Old Times Quilt Studio

(541) 672-5396

780 NW Garden Valley Blvd. #154 Garden Valley Shopping Center

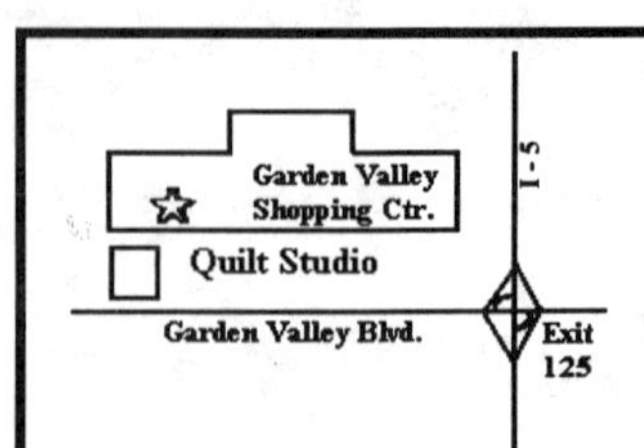

Mon - Fri 10 - 6 Sat 10 - 4

Owner: Sandra Thomas

10% Discount w/ Ad

Your Full Service Quilt Studio offering the finest in:

Classes, 100% Cotton Fabric
Tools & Notions
Books & Patterns
Silk Ribbon & Heirloom Supplies
Friendly and Supportive Staff
On Site Quilting Machine

Sales & Service **Est: 1994**

Nothing sews like a Bernina. Nothing.
BERNINA®

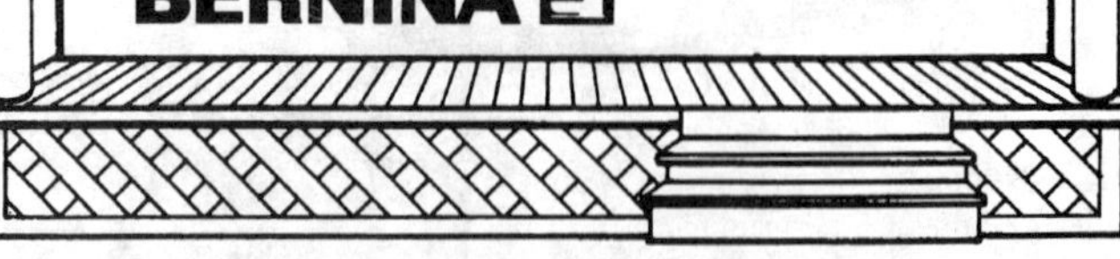

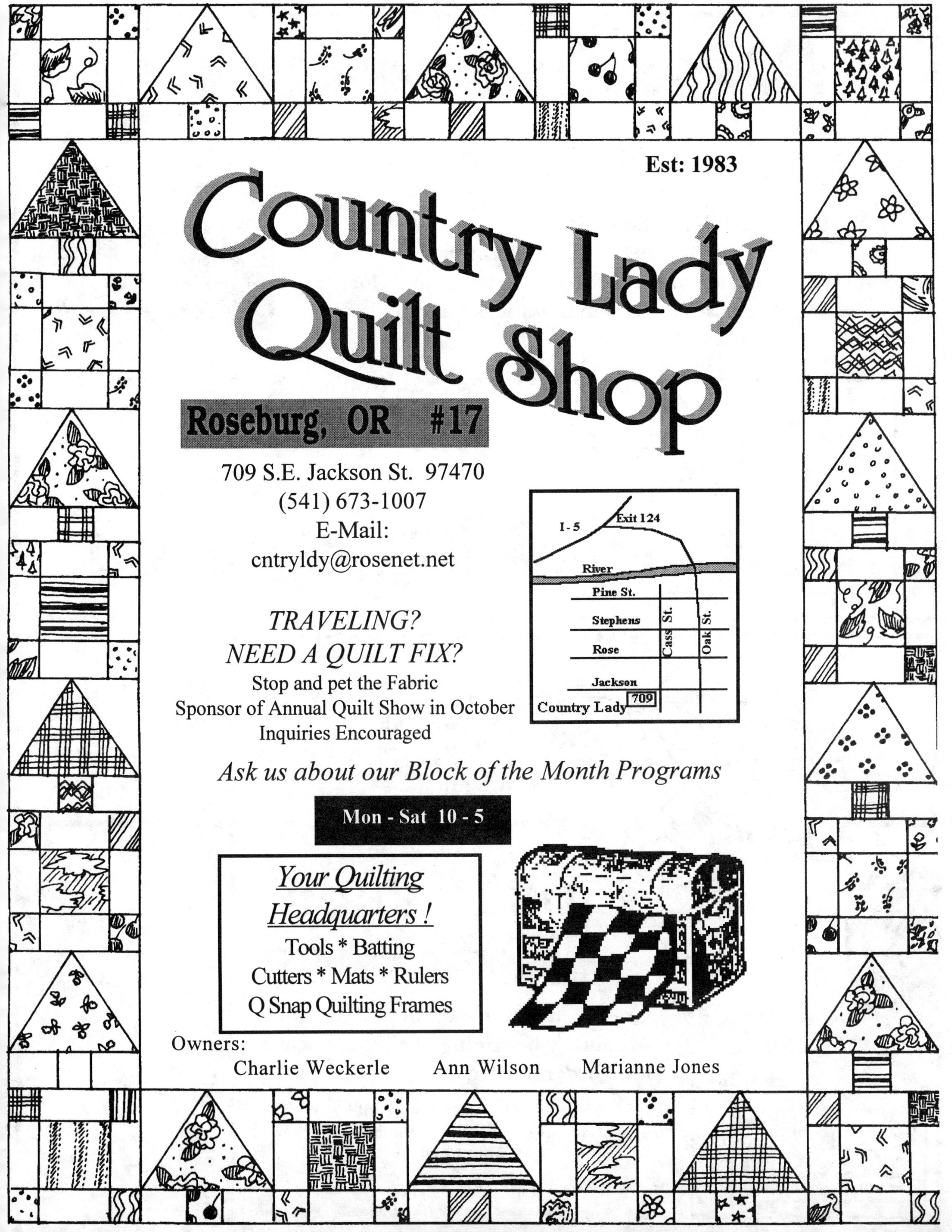
Est: 1983
Country Lady Quilt Shop
Roseburg, OR #17
709 S.E. Jackson St. 97470
(541) 673-1007
E-Mail:
cntryldy@rosenet.net
I-5
Exit 124
River
Pine St.
Stephens
Rose
Jackson
Cass St.
Oak St.
Country Lady
709
TRAVELING?
NEED A QUILT FIX?
Stop and pet the Fabric
Sponsor of Annual Quilt Show in October
Inquiries Encouraged
Ask us about our Block of the Month Programs
Mon - Sat 10 - 5
Your Quilting Headquarters !
Tools * Batting
Cutters * Mats * Rulers
Q Snap Quilting Frames
Owners:
Charlie Weckerle
Ann Wilson
Marianne Jones

Plaza Sewing Center

We have a full line of fabrics for the Quilter. Over 200 Solids & over 1800 printed cottons.
A Great Selection of Quilt & Craft Patterns and Books.
Also a Great Selection of aids, notions and threads.

Mon - Fri 9:30 - 6
Sat 9:30 - 5:30
Sun 11 - 5

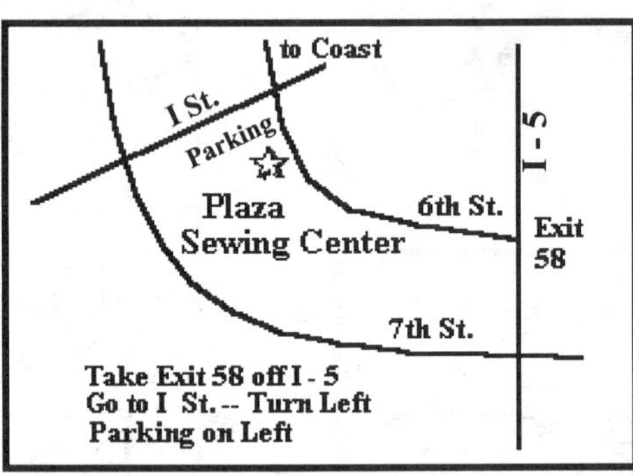

311 SE 6th St. Golden Rule Plaza 97526
(541) 479-5757
Owners: Rick & Mary Chapman
Est: 1967 5000 sq.ft.

Grants Pass, OR #18

1243 Main - P.O. Box 333 97370
(541) 929-3795 Fax: (541) 929-3597
E-Mail: jannilou@proaxis.com
Est: 1985 3700 sq.ft. 800+ Bolts
Owners: Jan Bressler & Lou Shafer

QUILT SHOP

Philomath, OR #19

- Great Patterns, books, notions & more.
- Absolutely beginning to advanced classes
- Mail order catalog $1

Next time you're in Philomath, drop by to see us "on location" at the old Waucomah movie theater building.

Mon, Wed, Fri and Sat, 9:30a-5:30p
Tues & Thurs 9:30a-9:00p

Admit One ... or many!
Your ticket to successful Quiltmaking

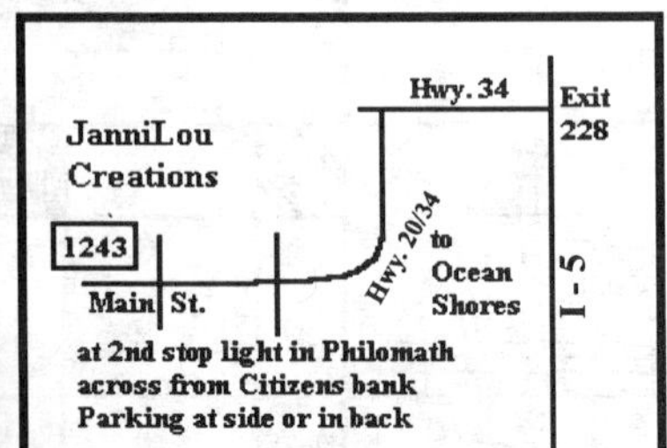

Rachel Greco, Owner

Grandma's Attic Sewing Emporium, Inc.

- 100% cotton fabrics for Quilting/Sewing
- Patterns, Books, Notions and More!
- Block of the Month/Fabric Clubs by Mail
- Send for FREE catalog!

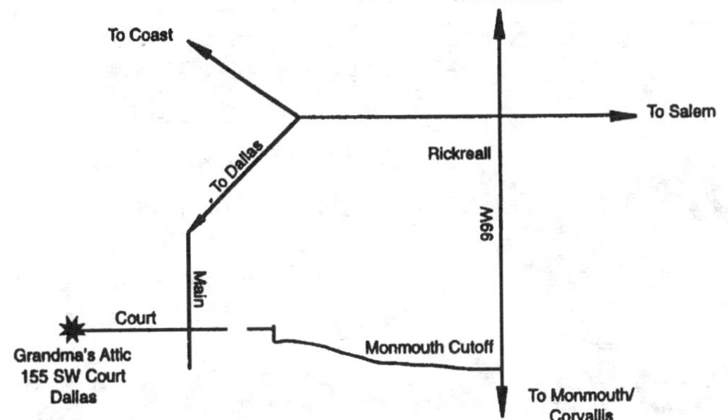

Dallas, OR #20

155 SW Court St. 97338
Est: 1995 2000 sq.ft.
1500+ Bolts

Mon - Fri
9:30 - 5:30
Sat 10 - 5
Sun 12 - 4

(503) 623-0451 Fax: (503) 623-6523
E-Mail: GrandmasAttic@compuserve.com
Web: www.GrandmasAtticQuilting.com

GREENBAUM'S Quilted Forest

240 Commercial St. N.E. 97301

Salem, OR #21

We carry the largest selection of books, quilting supplies and shop samples in the area, displayed in a historic building with high ceilings to give you a quilt show every time you walk in.

(503) 363-7973

3000 square feet with a large selection of Hoffman, Batiks, and Thimbleberries fabrics.

greenqf@cyberis.net

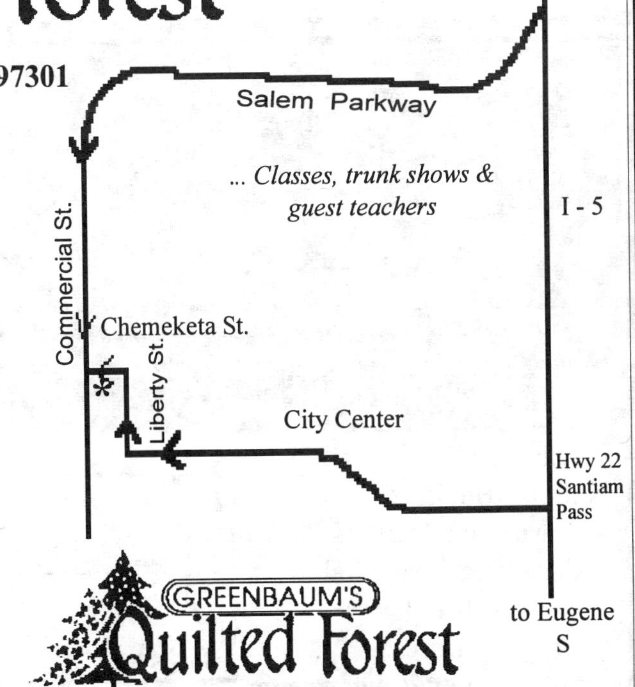

Hours: Mon - Sat 9:30 - 5:30 & Sun 12 - 5

Established 1900 as a General Store

Salem, OR #22

Tues - Sat 10 - 4:30

Simply Friends

1313 Mill St. SE 97301
(In the Mission Mill Village)
(503) 363-9230
Owner: Bonnie McNeely

Located in the Historic Woolen Mill. A charming shop with 100% cottons, books, notions and over 200 doll and quilt patterns.

Salem, OR #23

Mon - Sat 9 - 5:30

Salem Bernina

910 Commercial St. SE 97302
(503) 362-8523
Owner: Gloria & Roland Gille
Est: 1990 2000 sq.ft.

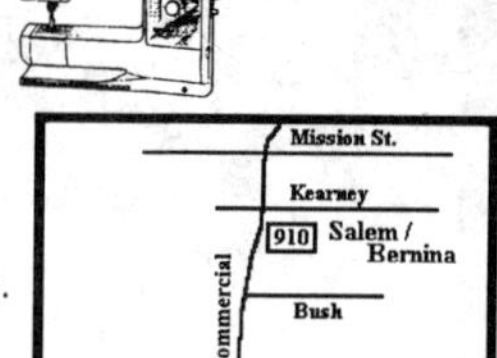

Authorized Bernina Dealer for all your sewing needs. Quilt Books & Supplies. 100% cotton fabrics by Hoffman, P&B, RJR, & more. Call about our quilting classes.

Springfield, OR #24

4227-C Main St. 97478
(541) 746-3256
Est: 1993 1400 sq.ft.
Owners: Joan Karagavoorian & Teri Harter

Something to Crow About

Mon - Sat 10 - 5:30 Sun 12:30 - 5

Over 1,500 Bolts of Cottons, Flannels & Homespun Fabrics. Patterns, Craft Supplies & Gifts. Home of "Something to Crow About" & "Sweet Gatherings" Patterns.

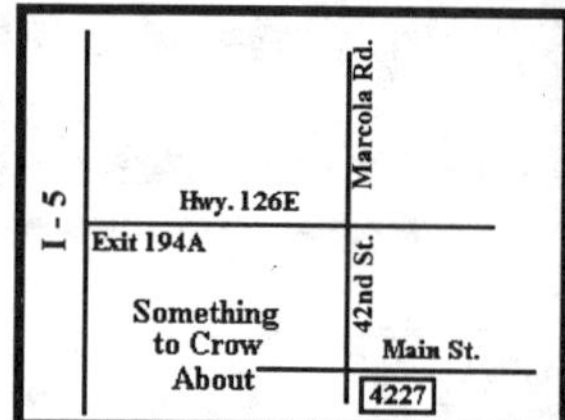

Classes: Quilting, Doll making & Tole

Eugene, OR #25

Mon - Sat 10 - 5 Sun 12 - 4

The Quilt Patch

23 E. 28th Ave. 97405
(541) 484-1925
Owner: Kathy Myrick
Est: 1974 2400 sq.ft.

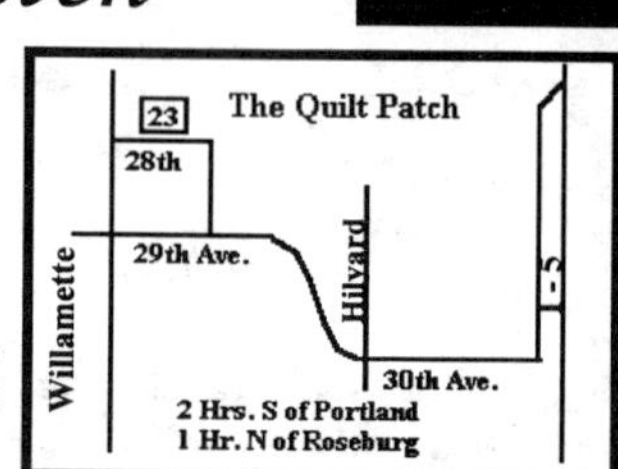

Over 2000 bolts 100% cotton fabric, notions, patterns, books, classes, charm and watercolor packets. Block-of-the-Month.

Mon - Fri 10 - 5 Thur til 8 Sun 1 - 5

Complete line of Fabric, Notions, Books, & Patterns. Machine Quilting, Custom & Ready to buy Quilts & Gifts. Classes.
e-mail: junction@eugene.com

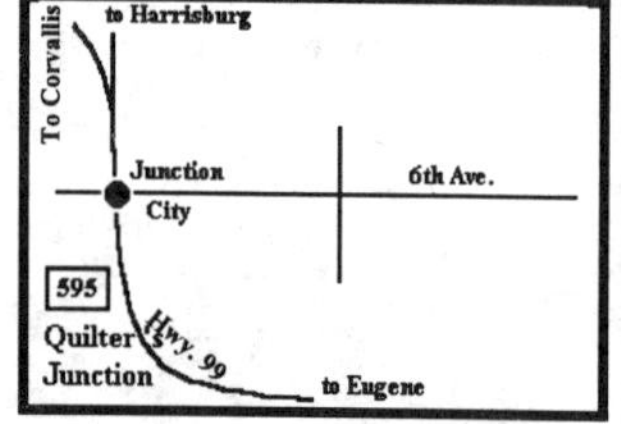

Junction City, OR #26

Corvallis, OR #27

Mon - Sat 9:30 - 5:30

Quiltwork Patches

209 S.W. 2nd St. 97333
(541) 752-4820
Owners: Brian & Jessy Yorgey
Est: 1979 650 sq.ft. 1800 Bolts

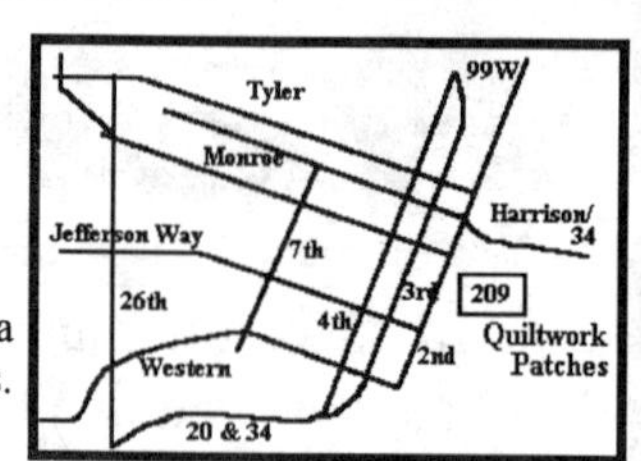

Over 1800 bolts of fine quality fabrics, plus a large selection of Quilter's tools and books. Free Brochure

Albany, OR #28

Mon - Sat 10 - 5

The Quilt Loft

126 Ferry SW 97321
(541) 928-7242
Fax: (541) 917-0058
E-Mail: robertsd@peak.org
Owner: Karen Roberts Est: 1996

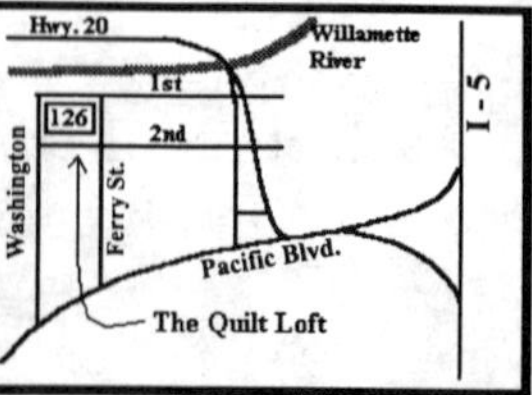

Quilts, Classes, Supplies and Gifts in historic downtown Albany.

Sisters, OR #29

Pieceful Expressions & Hucklebeary's

391 W. Cascade 97759
(541) 549-0955
Owners: Bev Gunson & Leslie Ellis
Est: 1996 1400 sq.ft.

7 Days a Week 10 - 5

2 Shops in 1 !
Quilted wearable art, hand-crafted gifts, antiques & collectibles. Just down the block from the Stitchin' Post

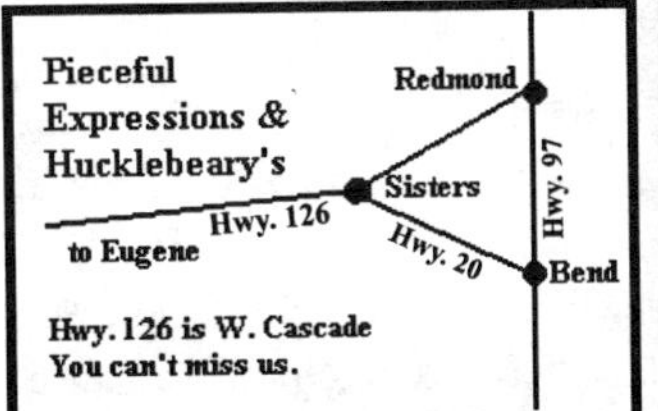

Sisters, OR #30

Sisters Outdoor Quilt Show, 2nd Sat. in July

Mon - Sat 9 - 5
Sun 10 - 5

311 W. Cascade St., P.O. Box 280 97759
(541) 549-6061 Fax: (541) 549-1922
Fabric Finders Fabric Club $20 a year.
E-Mail: stitchin@empnet.com
Owner: Jean Wells
Est: 1975 5000 Bolts Catalog $2

A fantasy of cotton fabrics for quilting. Stitchin' Post Patterns. Books and ideas galore. Gifts for Quilters & Gardeners.

The Stitchin' Post
311 W. Cascade
Hwy 97
Hwy 126 Sisters Redmond
Hwy. 20 Bend

Inquire about our "To Be Continued" quilt clubs.
*Gardening with Angels block of the month
*Northwest Look Sampler club

Bend, OR #31

Mon - Sat 9:30 - 5:30
Sun 12 - 4

Scandia Square 1155 SW Division
(541) 383-4310 97702
Owner:
Barbara Schreiner
Est: 1992
1400 sq.ft. 2500 Bolts
E-Mail: bjqltbsk@transport.com
Web Site: www.transport.com/~bjqltbsk
Top Quality fabrics, 600 book titles, silk ribbon, wearables, dolls, classes, fat quarters, fabric packets, mail order.

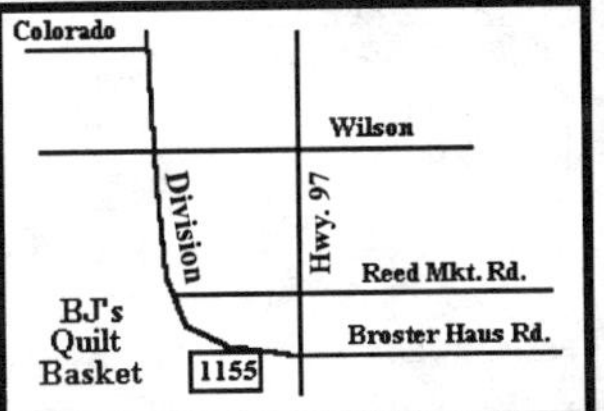

Bend, OR #32

Mon - Sat 10 - 5:30

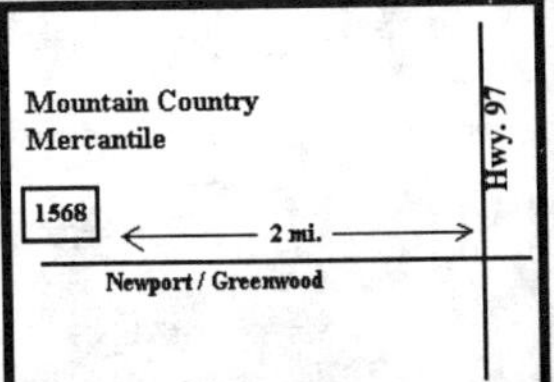

1568 NW Newport Ave. 97701
(541) 382-5984
6500 square feet of fabric, mostly calico - flannel - wool. 6000-7000 bolts of fabric.

Newberg, OR #33

Mon & Thur 10 - 9
Tues, Wed Sat 10 - 5:30
Fri 10 - 6

Hands to Heart Quilt Shoppe

315 E. First St. 97132
(503) 537-0424 Fax: (503) 537-0243
E-Mail: handstoheart@juno.com
Owners: Gordon & Jane Weir
Est: 1995 2000 sq.ft. 1500 Bolts

Fine cottons, notions, books, patterns. We offer classes for different levels of quilters & crafters. Antiques, Bears & Gift Items.

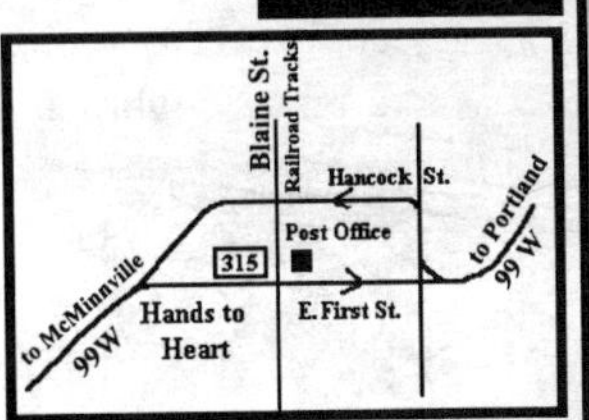

BOERSMA'S

It's SEW Much Better!

McMinnville, OR #34

203 E. 3rd St. 97128
(503) 472-4611 (800) VAC-SEWS
Owners: Jack & Michelle Boersma
Est: 1976
20,000 sq.ft. 5000 Bolts

Fine 100% Cottons, Quilt Books, Supplies, Notions, Classes.
Also Antiques, Collectibles, and Gift Items.
Sewing machine sales and service.
Experienced Staff

Mon - Thur 8:30 - 6
Fri 8:30 - 7
Sat 9 - 5

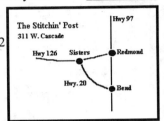

West Linn, OR #35

Country Dry Goods

Mon - Fri 10 - 5
Sat 10 - 4:30

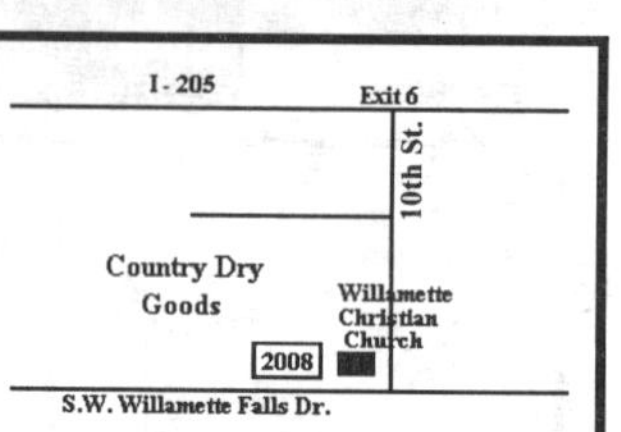

2008 S.W. Willamette Falls Dr. 97068
(503) 655-4046
Est: 1987 1600 sq.ft.
Owner: Linda Peck

DEDICATED TO THE QUILTER AND WOULD BE QUILTER.
We carry the latest books, patterns and 100% cotton fabrics.

Welches, OR #36

Tues - Sat
10 - 7
Sun 10 - 4

E. Hwy. 26, P.O. Box 97067
(503) 622-5792
E-Mail: RUT-ROW@worldnet.att.net

For The Love of Quilts

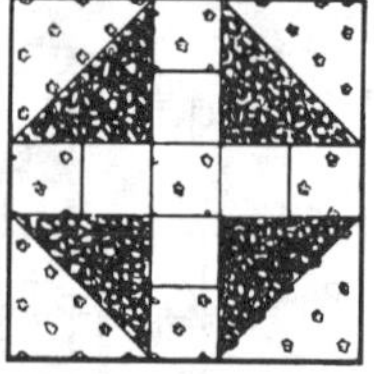

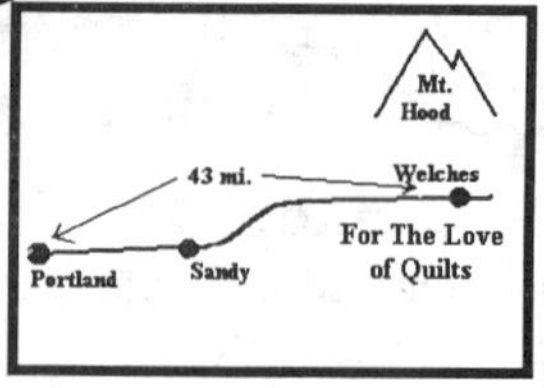

Mt. Hood
43 mi.
Welches
Portland
Sandy
For The Love of Quilts

"For The Love of Quilts" is located on Hwy. 26 in the shadow of beautiful Mt. Hood, in the Mt. Hood recreational area. We feature over 2000 bolts of fabric, 300 book titles, patterns, swatch club & classes. Machine quilting.
ANNUAL QUILT SHOW—Last weekend of July

Tualatin, OR #37

Mon - Fri
9:30 - 5:30
Sat 10 - 5
Sun 11 - 5

The Quilt Shoppe

19285 SW Martinazzi 97062
(503) 691-7933 Fax: (503) 650-5165
Owner: Valerie Lynn Johnston

- Over 1500 bolts of 100% Cotton Fabrics.
- Quilting/Bear Supplies, Classes.
- 100's of patterns, books, etc.

"We pride ourselves in friendly customer service"

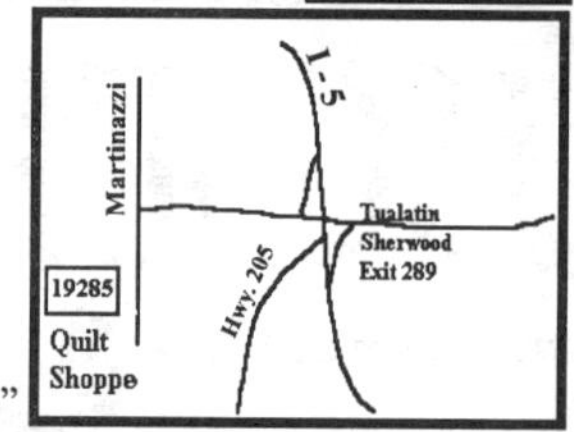

Lake Oswego, OR #38

Mon - Sat
10 - 5:30
Sun 12 - 5

The Pine Needle

429 First St. 97034
(503) 635-1353
Owner: Geri Grasvik
Est: 1992 6000 sq.ft. 1500 Bolts

Discover the most unique quilt - gift shop in Oregon.
Fabric, gifts, patterns, classes & crafts.

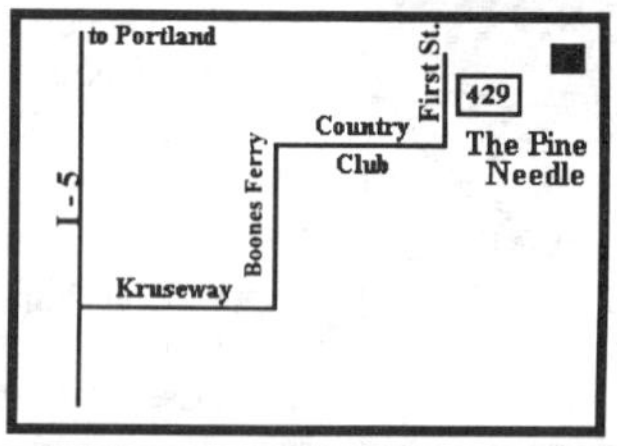

to Portland
First St.
429
The Pine Needle
Country Club
Boones Ferry
I - 5
Kruseway

Troutdale, OR #39

Oregon Country Quilts & Fabrics

Tues - Sat
9:30 - 5
Tues & Wed til 9

236 E. Historic Columbia River Hwy. 97060
(503) 669-9739
Est: 1991 2000 sq.ft.
Owners: Vickie Peterson & Susan Miller

Troutdale's only Quilting Store.
EASY ACCESS From I - 84 at exit 17.
Hoffman, Jinny Beyer, P&B, plus many books, patterns & notions.

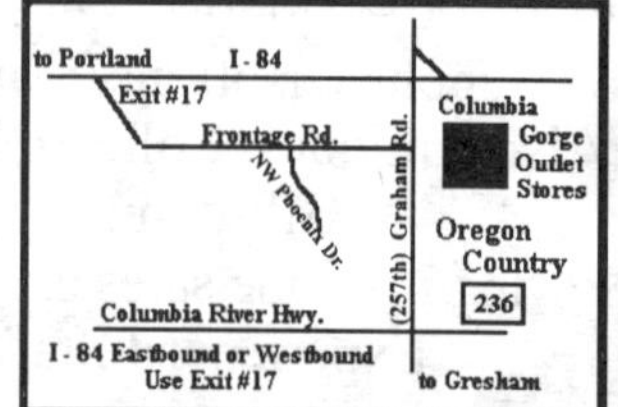

Aurora, OR #40

JACOB'S HOUSE

21641 Main St. NE
Aurora, OR 97002
(503) 678-3078
Owner: Karen Stephens

Quilt Supplies, Antiques and Collectibles.

Jacob's House is a wonderful collection of antiques, primitives, kitchen, sewing & country collectibles, homespun and vintage fabrics

Tues - Sat
11 - 5
Sun 12 - 5

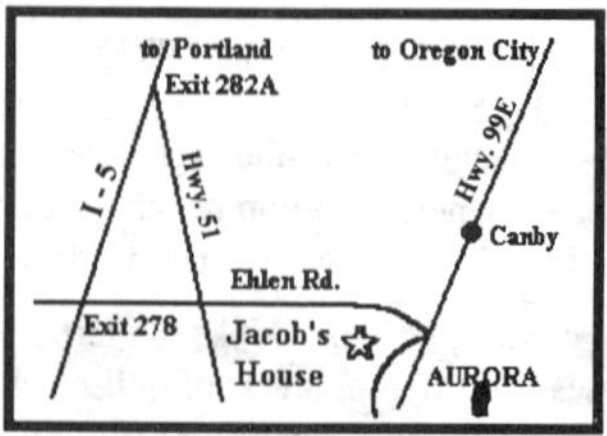

Est: 1993

Aurora - Butteville, OR #41

Mon - Sat 10 - 5
Sun 12 - 5

Linden House Quilt Shop

Free Fat Quarter with this ad!

Specializing in reproduction fabrics—all era's Patterns, & kits. Over 2500 bolts. Machine quilting, repair & restoration.

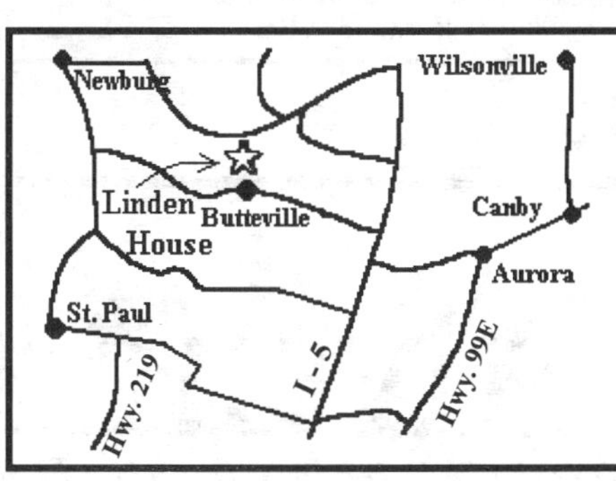

10791 Arndt Rd. NE 97002
(503) 678-1236 Fax: (503) 678-1238
e-mail: pckosta@aol.com
Owner: Pearl Kosta

I - 5 northbound take exit 278
I - 5 southbound take exit 282A

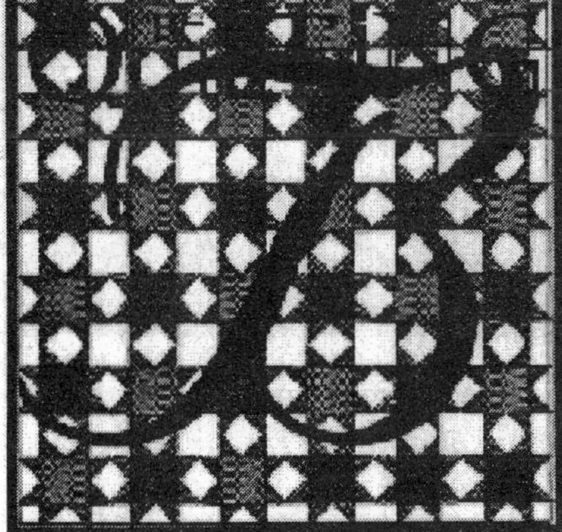

15410 SE 94th St. 97015
(503) 656-2999
Owner: Betty Anderson
Est: 1995 2000 sq.ft.
1500+ Bolts

Mon - Sat 10 - 5

Clackamas, OR #42

Cozy shop located in 100 year old Grange Building.
We feature flannels, homespuns & warm country colors.
Classes. Patterns. Tea anytime.

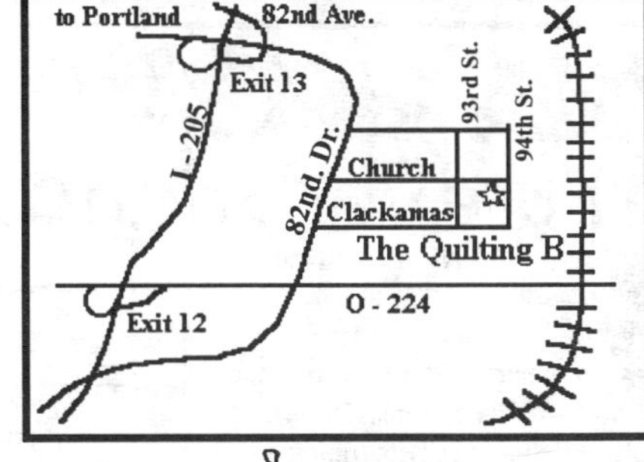
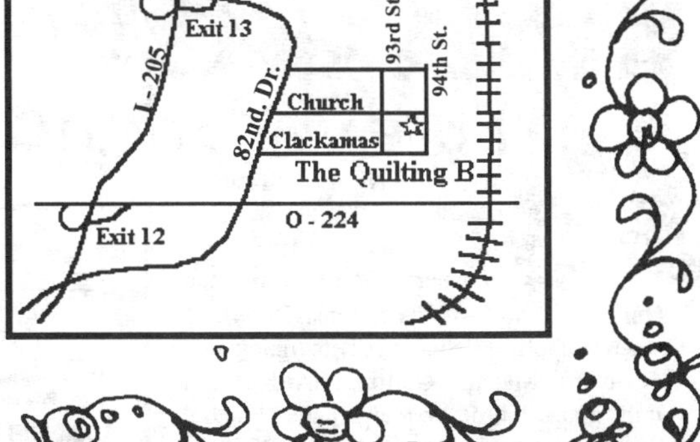

Hood River, OR #43

Mon - Sat
10 - 6

E.T.C.

1215 "C" Street 97031
(541) 386-5044
Est: 1987
Owner: Ann Zuehlke

Fabric, Books, Quilting Supplies, Patterns, Threads, Notions. Hand-Crafted Gifts, Classes for "kids" of all ages.
900+ Bolts and 150+ Books

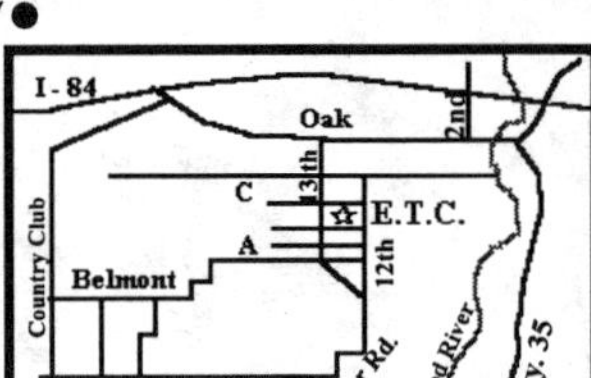

Portland, OR #44

Tues-Sat
10 - 4
Wed til 6

Patchwork Peddlers

4107 NE Tillamook
(503) 287-5987 97212
Owner: Gail Pope
Est: 1977 1200 sq.ft.

Largest selection of quilt books in the Northwest; 1200 bolts of 100% cotton fabric.

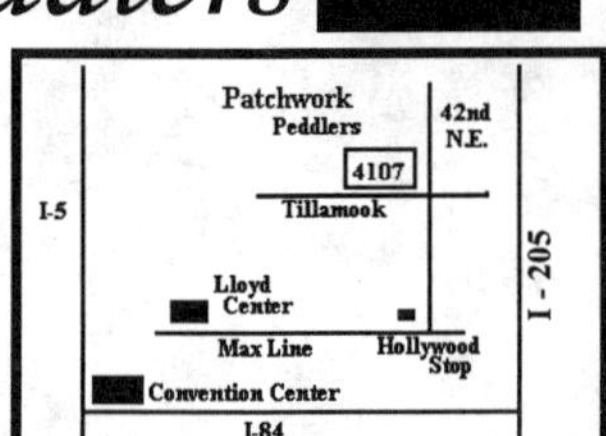

Portland, OR #45

Alyen* Creations

Exotic Materials for the Daring Fiber Artist

- Vintage Japanese Kimonos
  (Dozens to choose from)
- Kimono Fabrics (sold by the foot)
- Hand-Dyed and
  Hand-Painted Fabrics (Hundreds of yards)

***Alyen is pronounced "Alien," like a Martian.**
Your source for inspiration since 1992.

Call Alycia Allen Tolmach, Fiber Artist and Surface Designer, at (503) 236-2968, for an appointment and directions.

E-Mail: alyen@teleport.com
Web Site: www.teleport.com/~alyen

Visa / Mastercard Accepted

Phone for an appointment and directions. Give me a call; I am very flexible.

Hillsboro, OR #46

Mon 2 - 6
Tues - Fri 12 - 6
Sat 12 - 4

Furever Friends

2209 NE Cornell Rd.
97124
(503) 640-1907
Owners: Don & Nola Aman

Quilting fabrics—100% cottons. Books, Classes, Supplies, Patterns & Kits (many our own). Machine Quilting: SASE
Quilts made to order & ready made. Photo Quilts & Shirts our speciality since 1988.

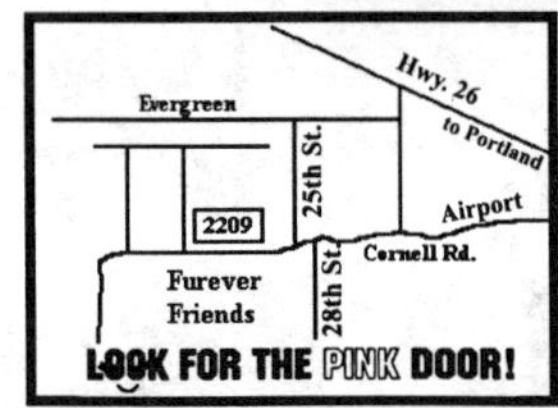

Warren, OR #47

Tues - Fri
9:30 - 6
Sat 9:30 - 5

Fibers & Stitches

58093 Columbia Hwy. 97053
(503) 397-5536 Fax: Same
Owner: Sue Widmer

Large selection of Cotton Fabrics, Books, Patterns & Quilting Notions. X-stitch patterns, fabric, notions also available.

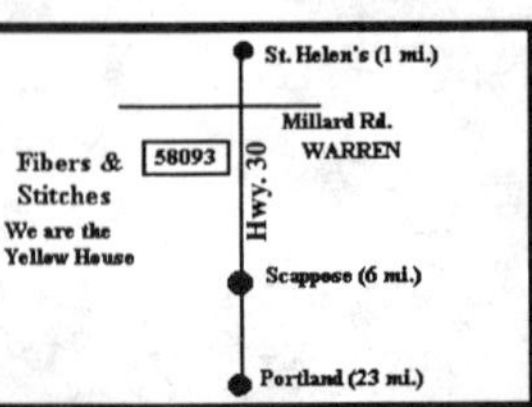

Oregon Guilds:

Albany Sew & Chat Quilt Club, 1215 W. 37th, Albany, 97321
Meets: Thursday 9 a.m. at United Methodist Church
Beulah Rebkah Lodge #35 Quilters, 540 SE 2nd, Albany, 97321
Meets: Weekly at Hill St. Church of Christ
Tualatin Hills Quilters, 8005 SW Grabhorn Rd., Aloha, 97007
PHD, 18490 SW La Paz Court, Aloha, 97007
Meets: Weekly in member's home
School House Quilters, Box 640, Astoria, 97103
Meets: 2nd & 4th Monday 7 p.m. at Astoria Middle School
Baker City Quilters R.R. 1, Box 27, Baker City, 97814
Meets: Wednesday 8 a.m. at County Extension Office
Tillamook County Quilters, 6735 Tillamook Ave., Bay City, 97107
Beaverton Comm, Center Quilters, 14185 SW Alibhai, Beaverton, 97005
Meets: Thursday 9 a.m.
Mt. Bachelor Quilt Guild, 1972 NE 3rd St. #127, Bend, 97701
Bend Quilters, 1665 SE Ramsey, Bend 97702
Meets: Weekly during the day
Summit Quilters, 20445 Marval Pl., Blodgett, 97326
Azalea Quilt Guild, P.O. Box 994, Brookings, 97415
Brookings Quilt Guild, P.O. Box 994, Brookings, 97415
Gladstone Chautauqua Quilters, 190 W. Gloucester, Clackamas, 97027
Meets: Weekly 6:30 p.m. at Senior Center
Castle Quilters Guild, P.O. Box 992, Clatskanie, 97016
Coos Sand N' Sea Quilters, P.O. Box 1234, Coos Bay, 97420
Meets: 1st Thursday 7 p.m. (Sept. - June) at Gloria Dei Lutheran Church, 1290 Thompson or 3rd Wednesday 10 a.m. at First Christian Church, 2420 Sherman, North Bend
Coquille Valley Art Center, Coquille Meets: 2nd & 4th Tuesday
Quilts from Caring Hands, 889 NW Grant Ave., Corvallis, 97330
Meets: Weekly afternoons, at Briar Rose Quilt Shop
Garfield Skip-a-Week Quilters, P.O. Box 234, Estacada, 97023
Meets: Wednesday at Garfield Grange Hall
Pioneer Quilters, 2130 Bedford Way, Eugene, 97401
Emerald Valley Quilters, P.O. Box 70755, Eugene, 97401
Meets: 3rd Wednesday 6:30 p.m.
at Trinity United Methodist Church, 440 Maxwell Rd.
Rhododendron Quilt Guild, 160 Florentine Ave., Florence, 97439
Meets: 2nd & 4th Wednesday 10 a.m.
at Church of the Nazarene
Satellite Meets: 1st & 3rd Tuesday 7 p.m. at Cottage Fabrics
Sweet Home Quilters, P.O. Box 175, Foster, 97345
North Santiam Quilters, 824 W. Central St., Gates, 97346
Meets: Thursday at Gates Church of Christ
Gold Beach Quilters Guild, P.O. Box 138, Gold Beach, 97444
Meets: 3rd Thursday 7 p.m. at Curry County Fairgrounds
Pine Tree Quilters, 128 Covey Ln., Grants Pass, 97527
Meets: 2nd Tuesday in member's home
Hugo Ladies Club Quilters, 201 Hitching Post Rd., Grants Pass, 97526
Mountain Stars, 404 Pavillian, Grants Pass, 97526
Meets: 2nd Saturday 1 p.m. or March, June & Sept
Furever Friends, 2209 NE Cornell Rd., Hillsboro, 97124
Meets: 1st & 3rd Tuesday 6 p.m. "Quilts for Warmth" project
Dog River Quilters 1215 C St., Hood River, 97031
Meets 1st Monday 6:30 p.m. at E.T.C. shop
Jacksonville Museum Quilters, P.O. Box 284, Jacksonville, 97527
Meets: 9 a.m. Wednesdays & Thursdays at US Bank Bldg.
Junction City Quilt Guild, 1225 W. 10th St., Junction City, 97448
Pelican Piecemakers, 1915 Carlson, Klamath Falls, 97603
Quilt Questers, 2006 Washington Ave., La Grande, 97850
Jefferson County Country Quilters, 3576 W. Franklin Ln., Madras, 97741
McMinnville Piecemakers, 106 Kingwood St., McMinnville, 97128
Meets; 2nd Monday 7 p.m. at McMinnville Residential Estates
Mountain Stars Quilters, 80 High Oak Dr., Medford, 97504
The Tater Patchers, 132 E. Front, Merrill, 97633
Meets: 2nd Thursday 7 p.m. at Tater Patch Quilts
Quaint Quilters, 130 Cottonwood Ct., Monmouth, 97361
Meets: Weekly (except summer) in member's home
Tillamook County Quilters, 41325 N. Fork Rd., Nehalem, 97131
Meets: 3rd Thursday at Latimer Quilt & Textile Center
Chehalem Park & Recreation Quilters, 3300 Victoria Way, Newberg, 97132 Meets: Tuesday 1 p.m. at Senior Community Center, 2nd & Howard and Thursday 7 p.m. at Vittoria Square Rec Hall, Springbrook & Vittoria Way
Chehalem Valley Quilt Guild, Newberg, OR
Meets: Thursday 7 p.m. at Hands to Heart Shop, 315 E. 1st
Coast Quilters, P.O. Box 436, North Bend, 97459
Baker City Quilt Club, P.O. Box 89, North Powder, 97867
Uper Willamette Piecemakers, P.O. Box 1101, Oakridge, 97463
Meets: 1st Tuesday at the Museum
Treasure Valley Quiltmakers, P.O. Box 1198, Ontario, 97914
Meets: 3rd Thursday 1 p.m. at Pilgrim Lutheran, 208 SW 1st
Blue Mtn. Piecemakers Q. G., 3307 NE Riverside Ave., Pendleton, 97801
Meets: Monthly at First Christian Church
Mary's River Quilt Guild, P.O. Box 1317, Philomath, 97370
Meets: Last Thursday (except Nov. & Dec) 7:30 p.m.
at Benton County History Museum, 1101 Main St.
Northwest Quilters, P.O. Box 3405, Portland, 97208
Meets: 2nd Monday alternates morning and evening
at Emmanuel Lutheran Church, 7810 SE 15th,
annual quilt show early Oct. at Aurora Colony Museum
High Fiber Diet, 6920 SW 3rd Ave., Portland, 97219
Heirloom Quilters, 8805 SW Woodside Dr., Portland, 97225
Meets: Thursday 9:30 a.m. at Beaverton Mill End Store
Columbia Stitchery Guild, P.O. Box 19645, Portland, 97280
Meets: Quarterly (Sept, Dec, March, June)
at Lakewood Center, 368 S. State St., Lake Oswego
Fabric Depot Quilters, 3651 SE Washington St., Portland, 97214
Meets: Wednesdays 1 p.m. at 122nd & SE Washington
Coast Quilters, Reedsport, 97467
Meets: 1st Wednesday 10 a.m. (Sept. - May)
at United Presbyterian, 2360 Longwood Dr.
Piecemakers, P.O. Box 550, Rogue River, 97537
Meets: 1st & 3rd Monday 9 a.m. at Civic Club, 1st & Pine
Umpqua Valley Quilt Guild, P.O. Box 1105, Roseburg, 97470
Capitol Quilters, 4211 Gardner SE, Salem, 97302
Meets: Every Other Week, day time at Mission Mill Museum
Mid Valley Quilt Guild, P.O. Box 621, Salem, 97308
Summerplace Quilters, 31942 Raymond Creek Rd., Scappoose, 97056
East of the Cascade Quilters, P.O. Box 280, Sisters, 97759
Meets: 4th Wednesday 7 p.m. at Stitchin Post Classroom
Sublimity Quilters, P.O. Box 36, Sublimity, 97385
Meets: Thursday 9 a.m. at St. Boniface Rectory Basement
Sun River Quilters, P.O. Box 3219, Sunriver, 97707

Other Shops in Oregon:

Astoria	Custom Threads, 1370 Commercial St.	503-325-7780
Baker City	High Mountain Fabrics, 3210 H St.	503-523-5722
Beaverton	Mill End, 12155 SW Broadway	503-646-3000
Canyonville	J & J Fabric and Crafts, 413 SE Main	541-839-4319
Corvallis	Country Calico, 6120 S.W. Country Club Dr.	541-758-3323
Cottage Grove	Pandora's Box, 517 Main	
Eugene	Factory Fabrics, 2165 W. 7th	503-687-1732
Florence	Laurel Street Fabrics, 208 Laurel St.	541-997-7038
Forest Grove	Main Street Mercantile, 2001 Main	503-359-4616
Grants Pass	Cotton Shop, 125 Dorry Ln.	541-476-0214
Grants Pass	Quilt Country, 2175 NW Vine St.	541-479-2700
Hermiston	Craft Corner, 395 NE 1st	541-567-8824
King City	Itchin' to Stitch, 15715 SW 116th Ave.	503-620-8167
Lake Oswego	Bernina Sew n' Vac, 16925 SW 65th	503-624-7440
Lincoln City	Oceanlake Sewing Ctr., 1337 NW 12th	541-996-9696
McMinnville	Sew Much More!, 416 NE 3rd St.	503-435-1701
Milton Freewater	Quilt Garden, 1310 Main	
Milwaukee	Mill End Store, 9701 S.E. McLoughlin	503-786-1234
Newberg	Threads and More, 602 B E. 1st	503-538-3577
Portland	Scarborough Flair, 4442 N. E. 131 Pl.	503-254-3882
Portland	Mona's Ethnic Fabric, 4831 NE Fremont	503-284-6043
Portland	Daisy Kingdom, 134 NW 8th Ave.	503-222-9033
Portland	Fabric Depot, 700 SE 122nd Ave.	503-252-9530
Reedsport	Quilt Connections, 850 Broadway Ave.	541-271-3179
Salem	... And Old Lace, 320 Court St.	503-585-6010
Salem	Heartland Quilts, 4939 Countryside NE	541-962-5374
Silverton	Quilt and Fabric, 103 S. Water St.	503-873-7042
Springfield	Jean Marie's Fabrics, 637 Main St.	541-746-0433
Tigard	Calico Corners, 9120 SW Hall Blvd.	503-624-7218
Wheeler	Creative Fabrics, 475 Nehalem Blvd.	503-368-5900
Winchester Bay	Quilt Connections, 850 Broadway	541-271-3179

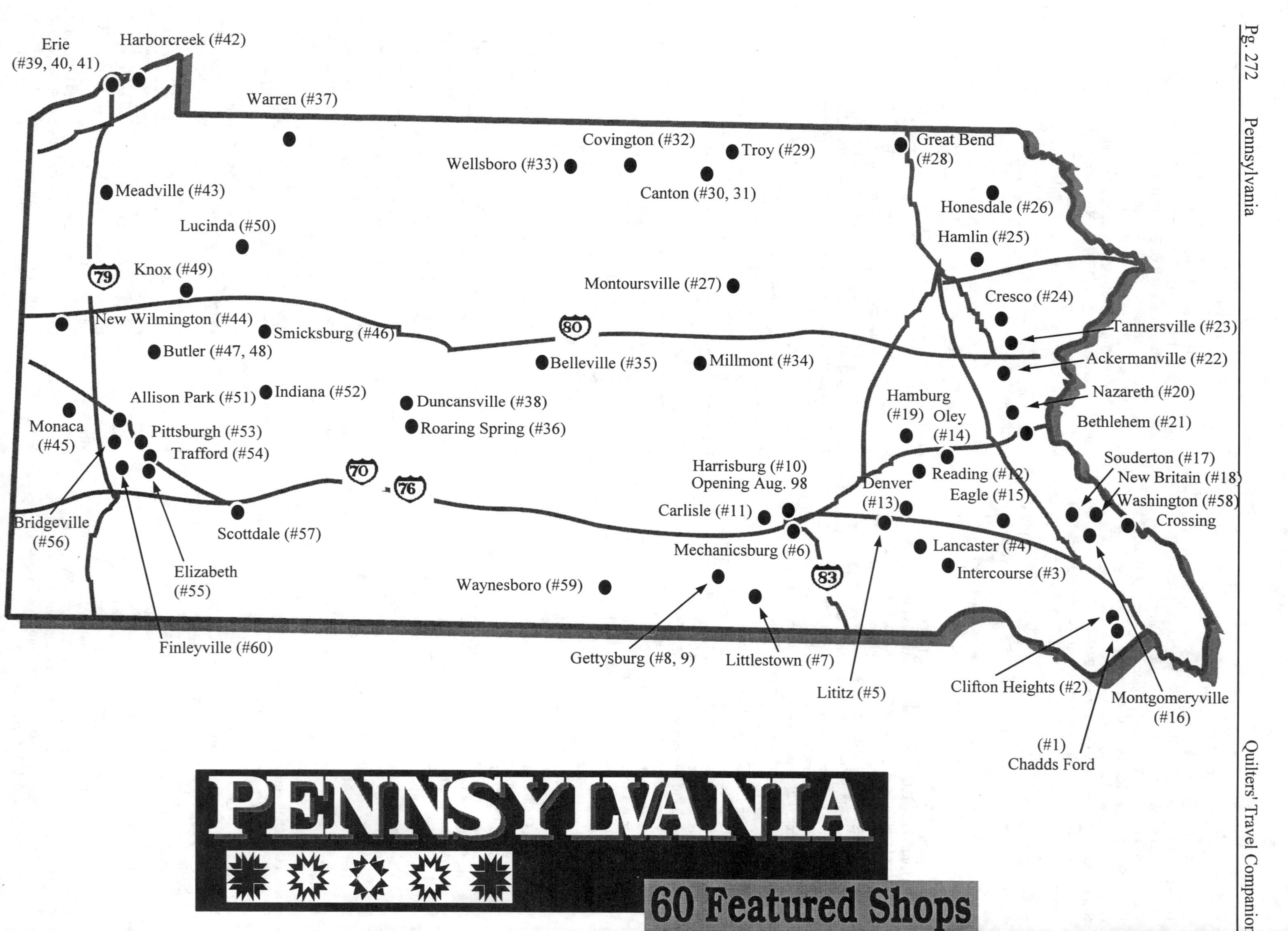
Erie (#39, 40, 41)
Harborcreek (#42)
Warren (#37)
Covington (#32)
Troy (#29)
Wellsboro (#33)
Canton (#30, 31)
Great Bend (#28)
Honesdale (#26)
Hamlin (#25)
Meadville (#43)
Lucinda (#50)
Knox (#49)
Montoursville (#27)
Cresco (#24)
New Wilmington (#44)
Smicksburg (#46)
Butler (#47, 48)
Belleville (#35)
Millmont (#34)
Tannersville (#23)
Ackermanville (#22)
Allison Park (#51)
Indiana (#52)
Duncansville (#38)
Roaring Spring (#36)
Hamburg (#19)
Oley (#14)
Nazareth (#20)
Bethlehem (#21)
Monaca (#45)
Pittsburgh (#53)
Trafford (#54)
Harrisburg (#10) Opening Aug. 98
Reading (#12)
Denver (#13)
Eagle (#15)
Souderton (#17)
New Britain (#18)
Washington (#58) Crossing
Bridgeville (#56)
Scottdale (#57)
Carlisle (#11)
Mechanicsburg (#6)
Lancaster (#4)
Intercourse (#3)
Elizabeth (#55)
Waynesboro (#59)
Finleyville (#60)
Gettysburg (#8, 9)
Littlestown (#7)
Lititz (#5)
Clifton Heights (#2)
Montgomeryville (#16)
(#1) Chadds Ford
79
80
70
76
83
PENNSYLVANIA
60 Featured Shops

Celebrating Our 15th Anniversary

A Patch of Country

Owner: Karen Reed
Est: 1983 2200 sq.ft.

Chadds Ford, PA #1

22 Olde Ridge Village 19317 (610) 459-8993

Mon - Sat
10 - 5
Thurs til 8
Sun 12 - 5

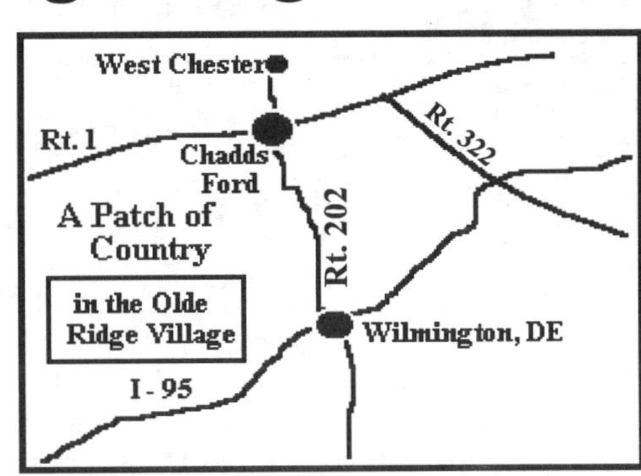

Located 1 mile south of Route 1 on Route 202. Within half an hour of the New Jersey & Maryland state lines. 1 mile north of the Delaware state line. Minutes from Brandywine River Museum, Winterthur Museum, Longwood Gardens, Brandywine Battlefield State Park and Valley Forge.

- Block of the Month Programs for hand, machine or applique techniques
- Highest Quality Cottons & Quilter's Tools
- 250+ Book Titles, Patterns
- Staffed exclusively by Quilters
- Bear Making Supplies
- Special Order & Mail Order Services Available
- Year-round classes for all skill levels with full student support.

Announcing New, Exclusive Block Of The Month Kits
GINGER BABIES™
Designed just for
A Patch of Country
Join any time!
Available year 'round
Distinctive Pieces
© 1997 Susan R.DuLaney
Distinctive Pieces

Clifton Heights, PA #2

Mon & Fri 10 - 9
Tues, Wed, Thur 10 - 6
Sat 10 - 5

Hayes Sewing Machine Co.

9 E. Baltimore Pike 19018
(610) 259-5959 Fax: (610) 259-6915
E-Mail: trevhayes@aol.com
Web Site: www.trevhayes.com
Est: 1969 1500+ Bolts

Large selection of Quilting Cottons, Books, and Sewing Notions. Award Winning Bernina and Elna Dealer. Come see us!

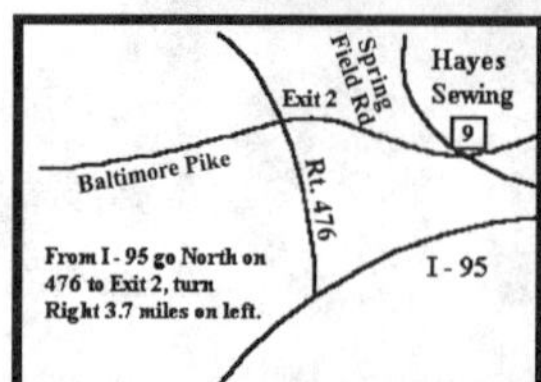

Intercourse, PA #3

Mon - Sat 8 - 5

Zook's Fabrics

3535 Old Philadelphia Rd. 17534
(717) 768-8153 Fax: Same
Est: 1966 5000 sq.ft.

Large Selection of quilting fabric, books, patterns, quilting notions & hand made gifts. Also a large selection of sale fabric.

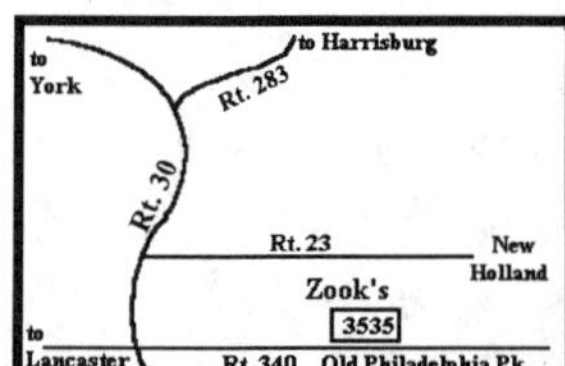

Lancaster, PA #4

Mon, Tues, Thur, Sat 10 - 4
Wed 10 - 6
Fri 10 - 8

Patchwork Dollhouse

8 Meadow Lane 17601
(717) 569-4447
Owner: Brenda Watson
Est: 1980 1500 sq.ft. 1500 Bolts

Classes, Fabric for Quilting and Smocking, Books, Patterns, Notions. Bernina machines and accessories.

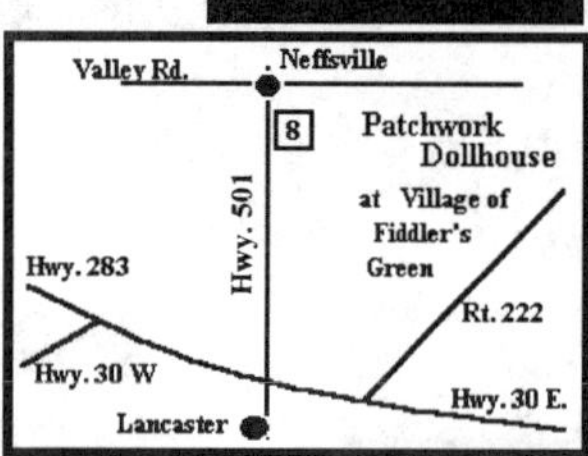

Lititz, PA #5

Mon, Thur, Fri 8 - 9
Tue, Wed, Sat 8 - 5

Weaver's Dry Goods

108 W. Brubaker Valley Rd.
(717) 627-1724 17543
Owners: Ivan & Lena Weaver
Est: 1978 2000 sq.ft.
Visa, MC, & Discover Welcome

One of Lancaster County's Largest Fabric Shops

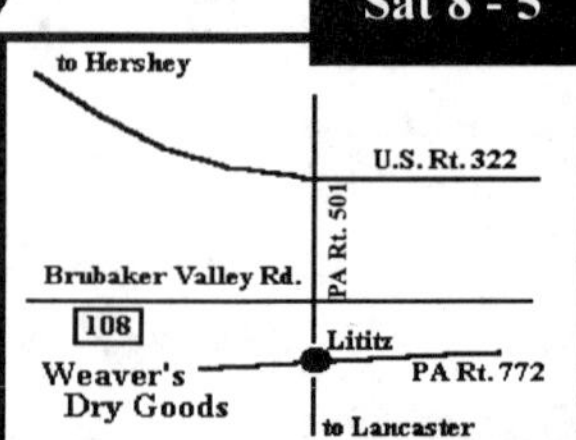

Mechanicsburg, PA #6

Mon - Sat 9:30 - 9
Sun 11 - 6

Ben Franklin Crafts

4880 Carlisle Pike 17055
(717) 975-0490
Est: 1989 2000+ Bolts

100% Cotton Fabric. Patterns, Books, Notions, Battings, Classes, Stitchery and basic craft supplies.

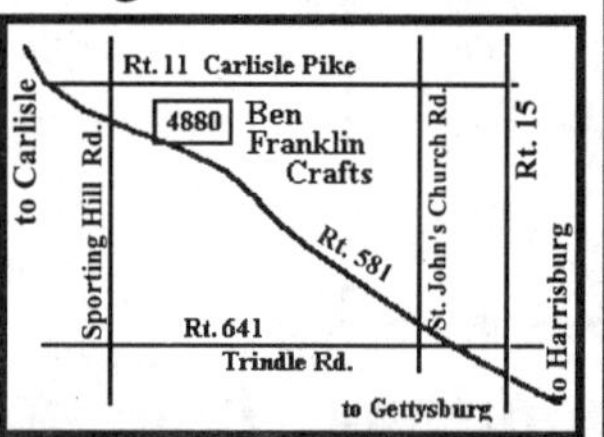

Littlestown, PA #7

Mon - Sat 9:30 - 5
Sun 1 - 5

The Quilt Patch

1897 Hanover Pike 17340
(717) 359-4121 Fax: (717) 359-8124
Owners: Scott & Debra Cromer
Est: 1979 12,000 sq.ft.

1500 Calicoes, D. Mumm, Hoffman, Homespuns, Waverlys, Quilts & Supplies. Art Gallery. Gifts, Collectibles (Dept. 56, Hummel, Swarovski, Etc.), Curtains, Heritage Lace.

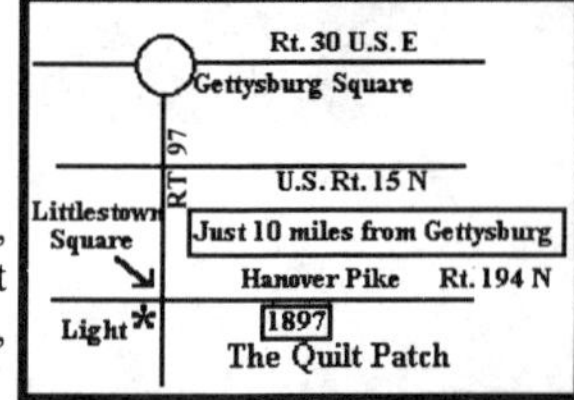

Gettysburg, PA #8

Mon- Sat 9 - 6
Sun 12 - 5

Gettysburg Quilting Center

523 Baltimore St. 17325
(800) 676-2658
(717) 338-0665 Fax: (717) 338-0846
E-Mail: holted@cvn.net
Owners: Ann & Dale Holte

"Everything a Quilter Needs." Designer fabrics, books, notions & tools, patterns, and classes. Near the historic battlefield.

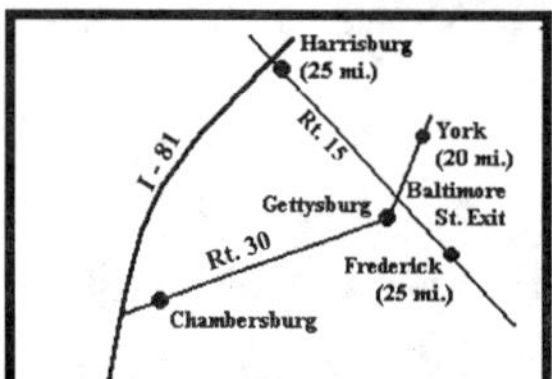

Gettysburg, PA #9

Mon - Thur 9:30 - 6
Fri 9:30 - 8
Sat 9:30 - 5

Needle & Thread

2215 Fairfield Rd. 17325
(717) 334-4011
Owner: Darlene Grube
Est: 1985 7000 sq.ft.

FULL LINE FABRIC STORE
10,000 bolts to Choose from—Pendleton, wools, silks, cottons. Books & Patterns

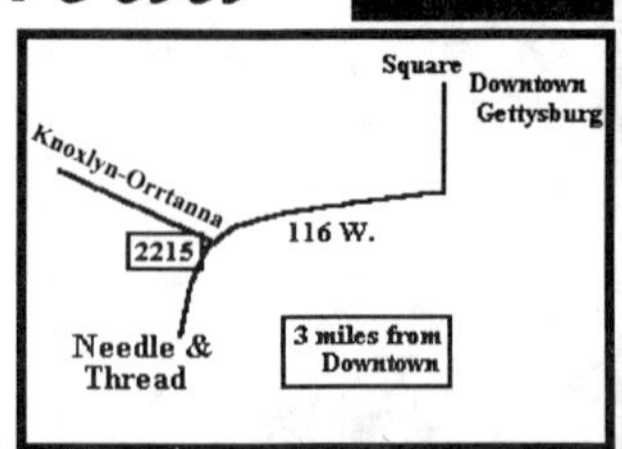

Harrisburg, PA #10

Mon - Fri 10 - 6
Wed til 8
Sat 10 - 4

Quilters Gathering

OPENING IN AUGUST 1998

5490 Derry St. 17111
Owner: Stephanie DeMuro

Quilters Gathering offers a complete line of quilting fabrics, notions, books, and patterns, plus an extensive schedule of quilting classes.

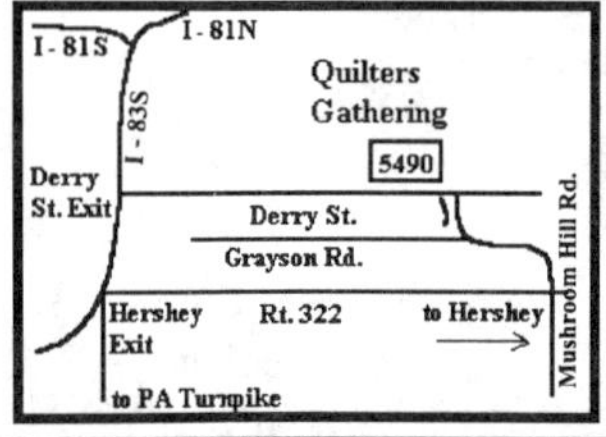

Carlisle, PA #11

Tues- Fri 9 - 4
Or By Appt.
July Hrs. Vary
Please Call

Calico Corner

341 Barnstable Road 17013
(717) 249-8644
Owner: Janet Shultzabarger
Est: 1984 400+ Bolts

Personal attention to quilters needs. 100% cottons, notions, books, classes. Very reasonable prices and service with a smile.

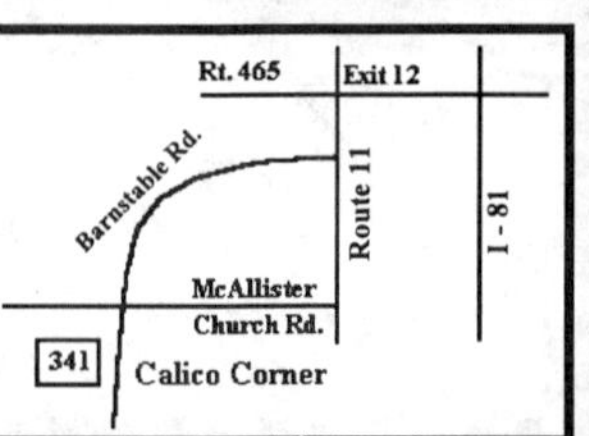

Reading, PA #12

By Appt. Only

Julie Wegelin's Sewing Cellar

945 N. 4th St. 19601
(610) 376-3490 Catalog $1
E-Mail: jwsewingcellar@juno.com
Web Site: www.sewnet.com/SewingCellar

Original Patchwork clothing patterns. Classes, workshops, sewing camps for children, sewing vacations and trips for adults.
-Sewing-Quilting-Bearmaking-

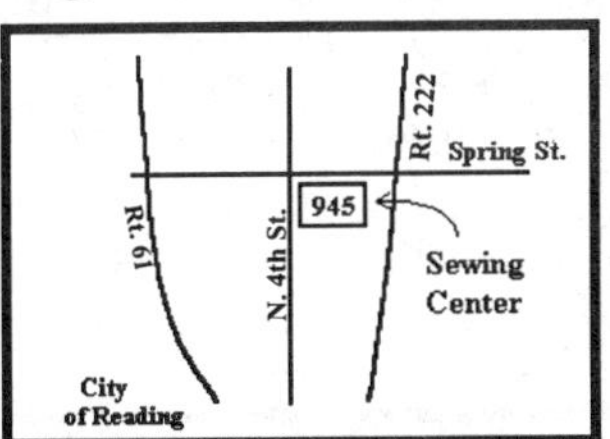

Denver, PA #13

**Mon, Tues & Fri 8:30 - 8:30
Wed, Thur & Sat 8:30 - 5**

Burkholder's Fabrics

2155 W. Rt. 897 17517
(717) 336-6692
Owners: Jacob & Martha Burkholder
Est: 1972 3000 sq.ft.

Sewing notions, quilt supplies, lace, fabrics, including VIP, Debbie Mumm, Springmaid, Concord, Hoffman, Peter Pan, knits & more.

Oley, PA #14

**Mon - Sat 10 - 4
Thur til 6**

The Summer House Needleworks

6375 Oley Turnpike Rd. 19547
(610) 689-9090 Fax: (610) 689-4713
Owner: Gail Kessler Free Catalog
Est: 1975 3500 sq.ft. 4500 Bolts

Vast collection of the most beautiful, unusual fabrics in cotton, flannel, silk & wool. Needle-point, Quilting & Rug Hooking Supplies. Mail order service with 30 Block-of-the Month Programs.

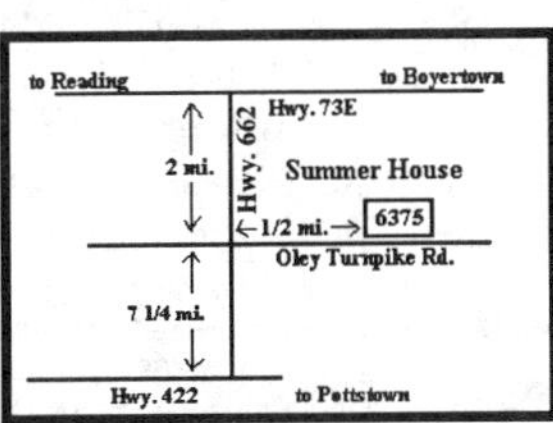

Eagle, PA #15

**Mon - Sat 10 - 5
Wed til 8
Sun 12 - 4**

Tudor Rose Quilt Shop

Route 100 at Byers Rd. (P.O. Box 21)
(610) 458-5255 19480
Web Site: www.tudorrose.com
Owner: Jane Russell
Est: 1990 1200 sq.ft. 2000+ Bolts

100% cotton fabrics. Plus silks & wools. Everything a quilter needs plus friendly smiles, expert help.

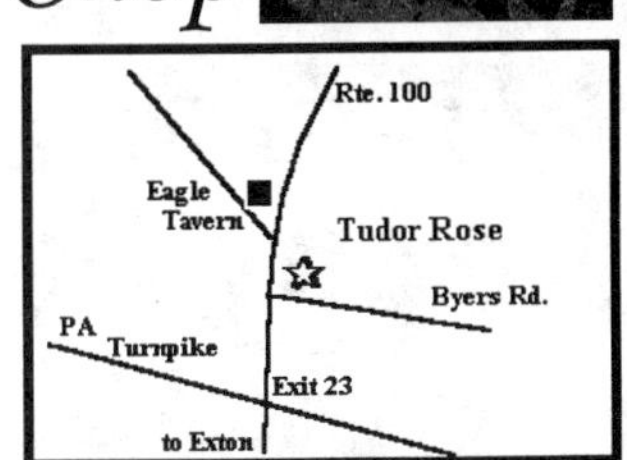

Montgomeryville, PA #16

THE COUNTRY QUILT SHOP

**515 Stump Rd.
P.O. Box 828 18936-0828
(215) 855-5554
E-Mail: cqs515@aol.com**

**Mon, Fri, & Sat 10 - 5
Tue, Wed, & Thur 10 - 9
Sun 1 - 5**

**An assortment of over 4500 bolts of the finest 100% cotton fabrics--Hoffman, RJR, P&B, Timeless Treasures & more! One of the largest selections of homespun in the area. A large & complete display of books, patterns, tools & notions. Classes for all levels with a courteous & professional staff of quilters that are happy to help with any project.
Stop in and experience the excitement!**

**Owner: Cyndi Hershey
Est: 1987 3600 sq.ft.
CHECK OUT OUR WEB SITE
http://members.aol.com/cqs515**

Souderton, PA #17

Mon- Fri 9 - 9
Sat 9 - 5

The Souder Store

357 Main St. 18964
(215) 723-2017
Est: 1922

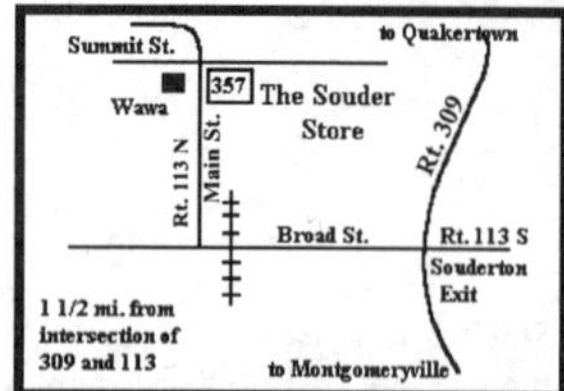

Extensive collection of 100% cotton quilting fabrics and supplies. Large selection of bridal fabrics, silks, wools and dress goods.

New Britian, PA #18

Tues - Sat 10 - 5
Sun 12 - 4:30

Hentown Country Store

326 W. Butler Ave. 18901
(215) 345-8286 Est: 1962
Owner: Midge Smith 2500 sq.ft.
Newsletter Avail. 500+ Bolts

100% Cotton Fabric, Homespun. Very Large (7000+) selection of Craft & Quilt Patterns. Teddy Bear Making Supplies. Handmade Folkart.

Rt. 202
Clemens Shp. Ctr.
to Quakertown
County Lane Rd.
Bristol Rd.
326 Hentown Country Store
Almshouse Rd.
Doylestown
Rt. 313
Rt. 413
Rt. 202
Rt. 611
Rt. 263
to Newtown VA

Hamburg, PA #19

260 N. 4th St. 19526
(610) 562-7173
Owner: Jean Boyd
Est: 1990 1000 sq.ft.

Happy Sewing Room

We offer beautiful cotton fabrics, quilting supplies, patterns, books, sewing machines, classes & most important the personal service every quilter deserves.

Mon, Tues, Thur, & Fri 9:30 - 6
Wed & Sat 9:30 - 12

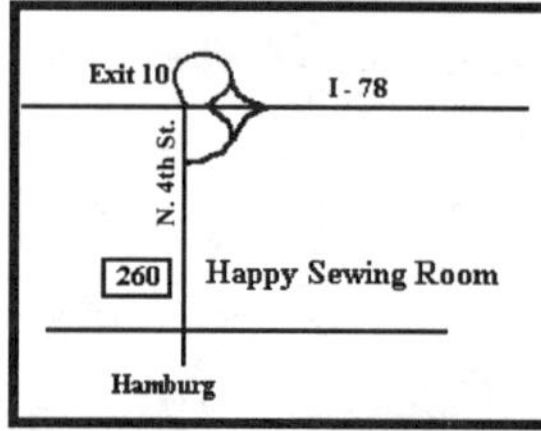

Nazareth, PA #20

Tues, Wed, Fri 10 - 5
Thur 12 - 7
Sat 10 - 4

The Quiltery

140 W. Center St. 18064
(610) 759-9699
Owner: Diane Noraas
Est: 1982

A Complete Quilt Shop.

100% Cotton Fabric -- books, notions, patterns, and classes. Special quilt orders made. And always friendly service.

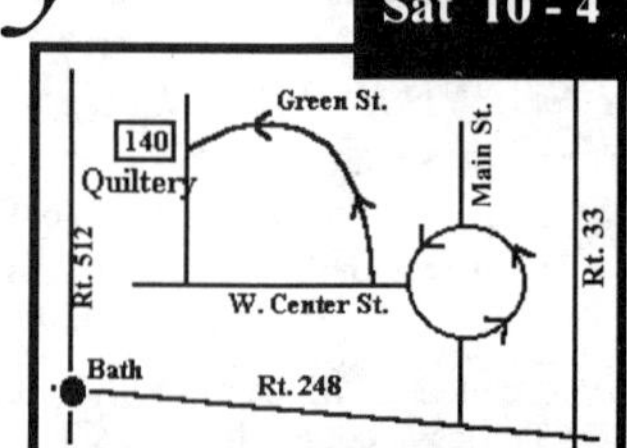

Bethlehem, PA #21

Mon - Fri 10 - 5
Thur til 8
Sat 10 - 4

Schlosser Quality Quilt Frames

25 Club Avenue 18018
(610) 758-8488 Est: 1989
Owner: Wilma Schlosser

Fabric--Notions- -Books--Patterns
Frames for both quilter and needleworkers.
Antique Quilts. Singer Featherweights.
Notions for Cross Stitchers.

Ackermanville, PA #22

Mon - Thur 9:30 - 5:30
Sat 9:30-4

The Village Barn

1547 Mill Road 18013
(610) 588-3127 Est: 1975
Owners: Ditta Van Gemen & Marijke Philipsen
1000 sq.ft.

Complete Quilt Shop. 1000 Bolts 100% Cotton Fabrics, Books, Notions, Classes. Machine Quilting Service. Helpful Staff. Large selection of Country Gifts.

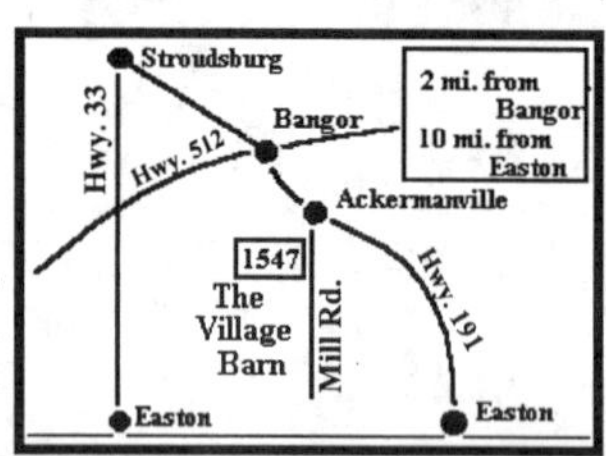

Tannersville, PA #23

Tue - Sat 10 - 4

Stencil 'N Stitch

Pocono Peddlers Village
P.O. Box 291 18372
(717) 629-3533
Located in the Pocono Mountains.

Quilting fabric, notions, lap hoops, frames, books, patterns, warm & natural cotton batting, stencils.

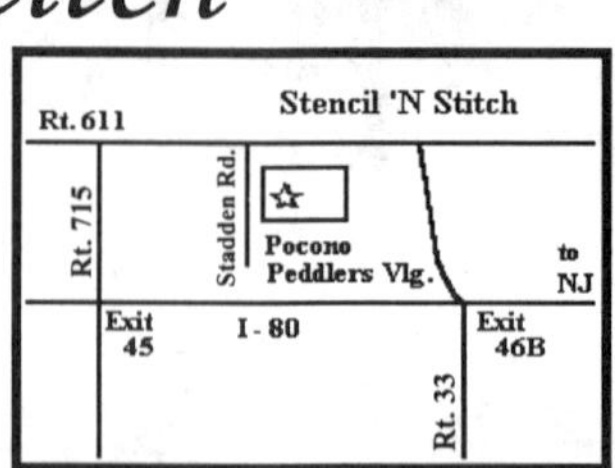

Cresco, PA #24

Mon - Sat 9 - 5
Fri til 8
extended hours in summer/fall

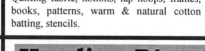

Paradise Inn Quilting

RD #1, Box 489B 18326
(717) 595-2611
E-Mail: chessy@ptd.net
Owners: Sandy Singer-Dietz & Family
Est: 1995 900+ Bolts

A unique shop in Historic Paradise Inn in the Pocono Mountains. Featuring 100% cottons, books, classes, Fabric Dyeing supplies.

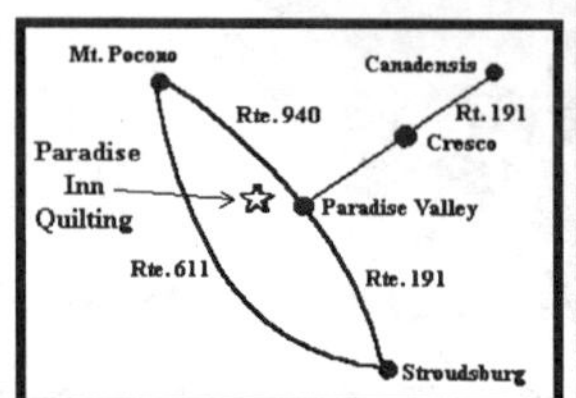

Hamlin, PA #25

Thurs, Fri Sat 10 - 5
Summer May Vary

Ye Olde Sewing Emporium

Rt. 191, St. John's Centre Box 190
(717) 689-3480 18427
Owner: Sandra Cinfo Est: 1991

A Unique Shop Specializing in Fabrics, Notions, Books, Classes, Ribbons, and Gifts for Quilters, Sewers and Needlecrafters.

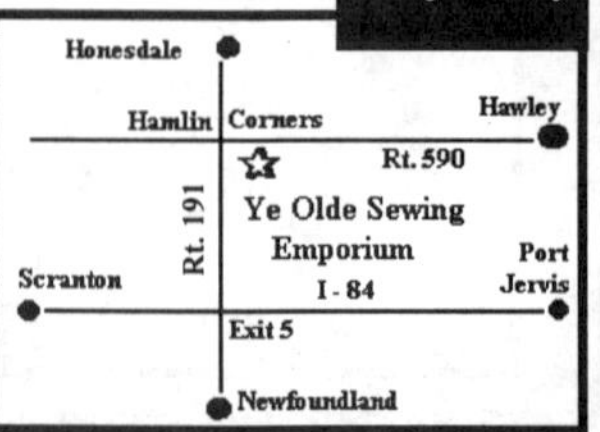

Honesdale, PA #26

Tues - Sat 10 - 5

The Mountain Quiltworks

R.R. #4, Box 395 18431
(717) 253-9510
Owner: Amy R. Dunn
325+ Bolts 1100 sq.ft

Find everything you need to create tomorrow's heirlooms. From various source books, stencils & patterns too of course, top quality cotton fabrics.

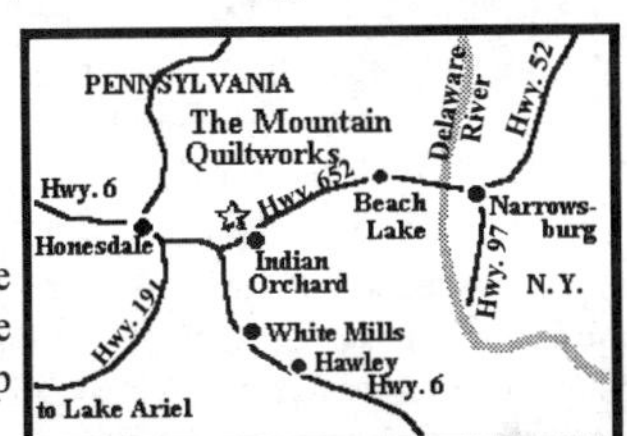

Montoursville, PA #27

Thur 10 - 5
Fri 10 - 7
Sat 10 - 3

Our Gathering Place

233 Broad St. 17754
(717) 368-1130
Owner: Chris Kroboth 1000 Bolts

Fine cotton fabrics and quilting supplies.
Many books and patterns plus classes.
Come Gather, share & enjoy!

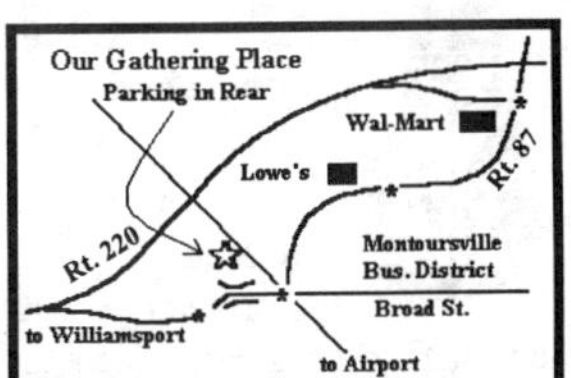

Great Bend, PA #28

Mon - Sat 10 - 4
Tues til 8

Sister's Choice Quilt Studio

P.O. Box 772, Randolph Rd. 18821
(717) 879-4196
Est: 1991
Owners: Bettie Armondi & Marjorie Cook

100% Cotton Fabric, Books, Patterns, Quilting Supplies, Classes Handmade Gifts & Quilted Items. Buses Welcome

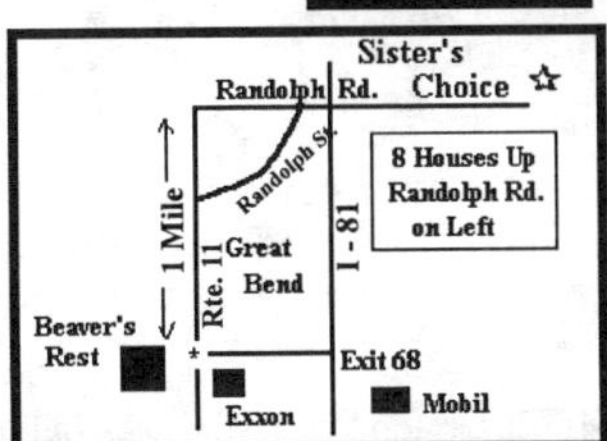

Troy, PA #29

Cotton Fields

R.R. #3, Box 496 16947
(717) 297-3776
Fax: (717) 297-4446
E-Mail: tandm@epix.net

Wed - Sat 10 - 5

Est: 1996
1100 sq.ft.
700 Bolts

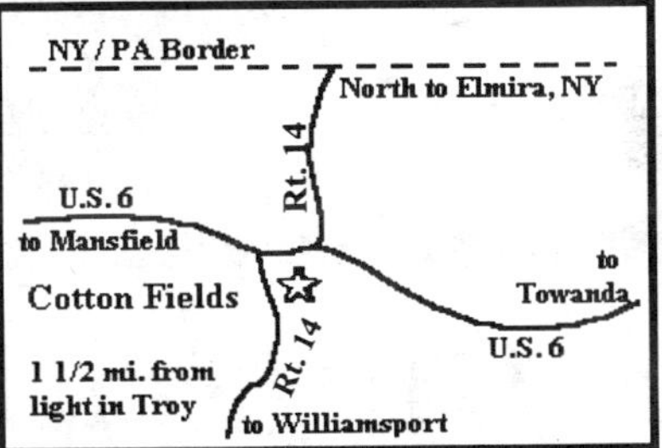

Owner: Mitzie H. Christine

Fine 100% cotton fabrics in a shop just like home (gifts downstairs). RJR-Thimbleberries, Moda, Homespuns. Books, patterns and classes.

Canton, PA #30

M, W, Th, F 9 - 5
Sat 9 - 12

The Four Hands Fabric Shop

158 N. Center St. 17724
(717) 673-5280
Owners: Barbara & David
Est: 1995 Groover

Growing inventory of 100% cotton fabrics & homespuns, quilting notions, stencils, books and patterns. Class schedule and newsletter upon request.

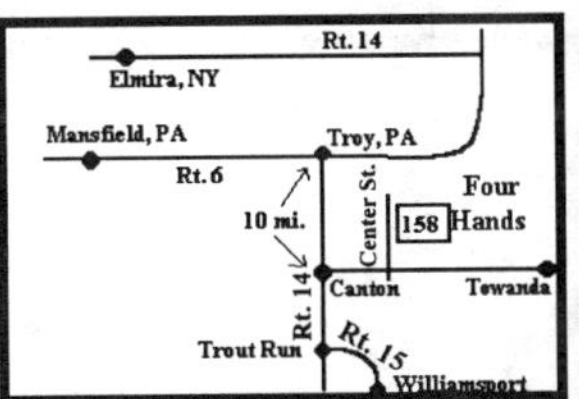

Canton, PA #31

Tues - Sat 10 - 5

The Weathervane Quilt Shop

R.R. #2, Box 26, Rt. 14 17724
(717) 673-4944 Fax: 297-3074
E-Mail: nortsned@epix.net
Owner: Nancy Swatsworth
Est: 1996 3000 sq.ft.

1000+ Bolts of 100% fine cotton fabrics, books, patterns, notions. Lovely handmade gifts. Featherweight Singer Sewing machines.

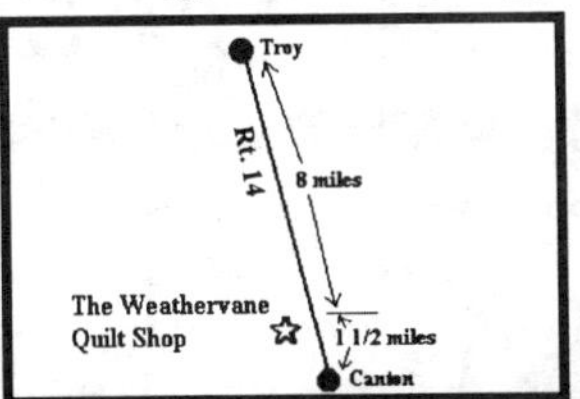

Covington, PA #32

Tues - Fri 10 - 5
Sat 10 - 3

Williams General Craft Supplies

1 Main St. 16917
(717) 659-5079
Owner: Joyce Williams

100% name brand cotton fabrics, craft and quilting supplies, books, patterns. Classes. Quilted items and crafts for sale.

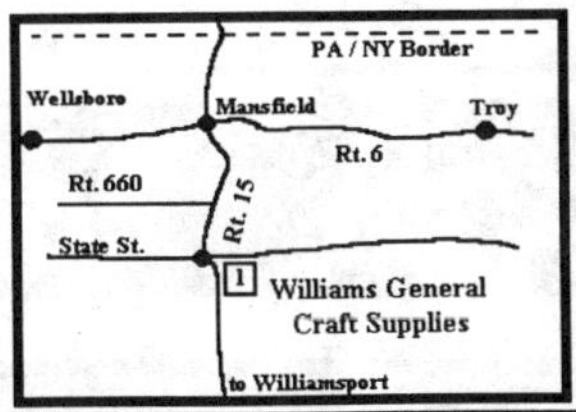

Wellsboro, PA #33

Tues - Sat 10 - 5

Gammie's Attic

RD #6, Box 128 16901
(717) 724-6151 Est: 1997
E-Mail: Eagle40@ptd.net
Owner: June Cooper 1800 Bolts

My Customers Call Gammies the gathering place of all kinds of sewing information and fabric. Also enjoy our old fashioned soda fountain. Craft Fair & Auction Oct. 10, '98.

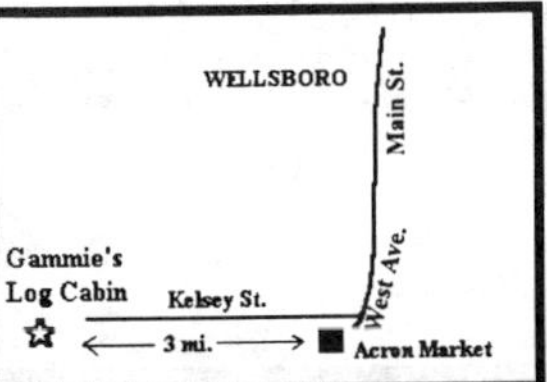

Millmont, PA #34

M. T. Th, & F 9 - 9 Sat 9 - 5

Nora's Quilts & Crafts

R.D. #2, Box 111 17845
(717) 922-1849
Owners: Eli & Nora Martin
Est: 1972

Complete line of quilts, tablerunners, wall hangings, placemats, pillows, potholders, dolls, wooden crafts, shelves & all kinds of quilted items.

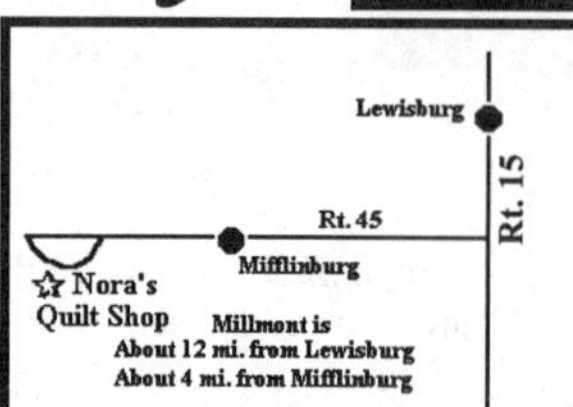

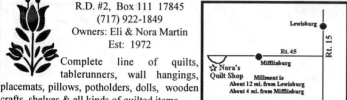

Belleville, PA #35

Mon - Sat 9 - 5

A.M. Buchanan Dry Goods

2459 S.R. 655 17004
(717) 483-6428
Owner: Anna M. Buchanan
Est: 1983 1700 sq.ft. 2000 sq.ft.

Largest selection of fabrics, patterns, books & quilting supplies in the area. Hand made Quilts, hangings, Pillows & more. Great Gifts in stock. Located 2 mi. south of Belleville on Rt. 655

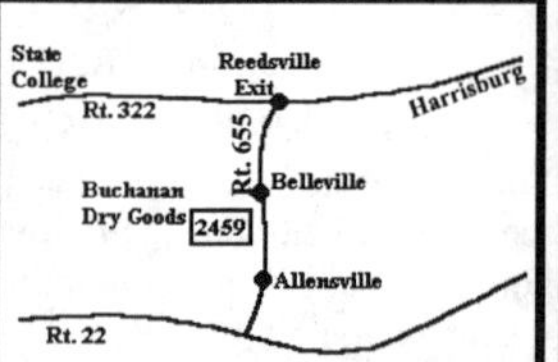

Roaring Spring, PA #36

Mon - Fri 9:30 - 4:30 Saturdays May - Sept 10 - 2 Oct - Apr 10 - 4

Country Beefers

RD #1, Box 495 16673
(814) 224-4818 Est: 1981
Owners: Louann Ferraro & Betty Beegle

Cotton fabrics, homespuns, books, craft patterns, notions, stencils. Also locally made gift items, appliqued clothing and Yankee Candles.

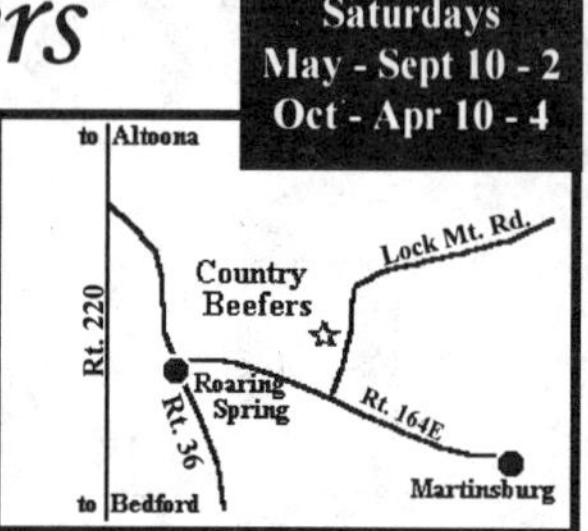

Warren, PA #37

Mon - Fri 10 - 5:30 Sat 10 - 4

Sew Necessary

209 Liberty St. 16365
(814) 723-3188 Fax: (814) 723-3192
Owner: Karen Eggleston
Est: 1995

100% Cotton Fabrics! Check out our classes. Books, patterns, notions, quilting supplies, yarns and cross-stitch supplies.

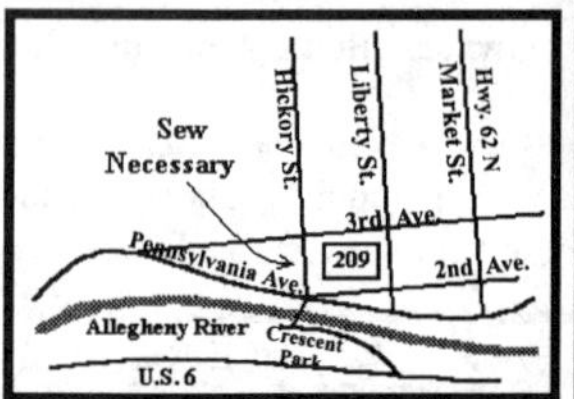

Est: 1995

Spring Meadow
(Municipal Dr.)
(814) 695-8098
Fax: (814) 695-8234

The Rainbow's End Quilt Shop

Owners:
Ruth and Arthur Briggs

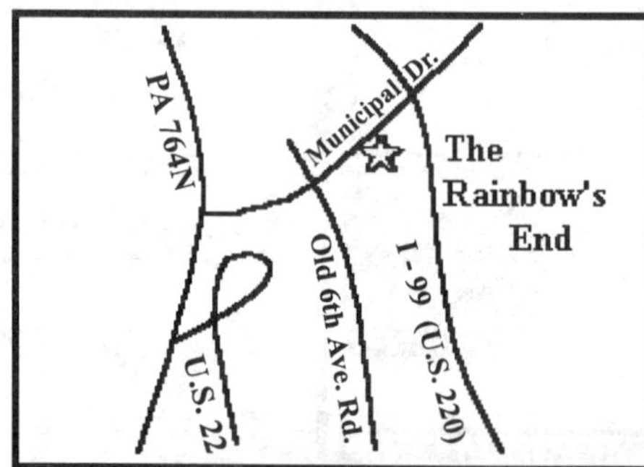

Duncansville, PA #38

The Rainbow's End caters to the needs of contemporary Quilters and carries

* Hoffman
* P&B
* Kauffman
* Kona Bay . . .
* and more!

900 Bolts & growing

BUY THE YARD QUILT SHOP BUY THE YARD QUILT SHOP

BUY THE YARD QUILT SHOP

BUY THE YARD QUILT SHOP

Erie, PA #39

Buy The Yard QUILT SHOP

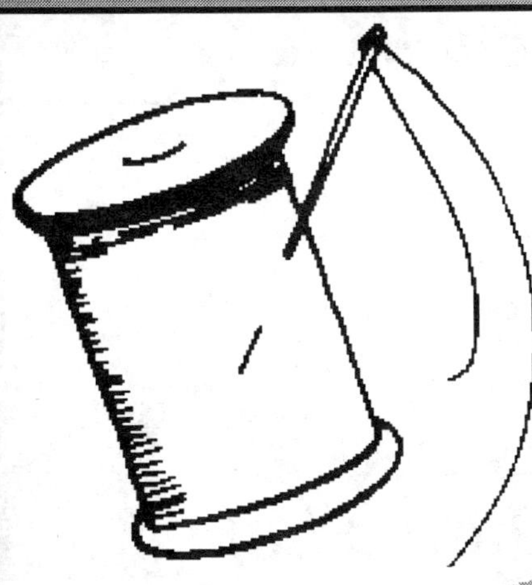

Largest fabric selection in the area. Complete line of quilting supplies, books, patterns & classes. Bus tours welcome - please call ahead.

Corner 10th & Holland
202 E. 10th St. 16503
(814) 454-4000

Tues - Sat 10 - 5
Fri til 6

Est: 1997
2500 sq.ft.
1200+ Bolts
Owners:
Geraldine J. Bork
Tracey M. Peterson
Michelle D. Samson

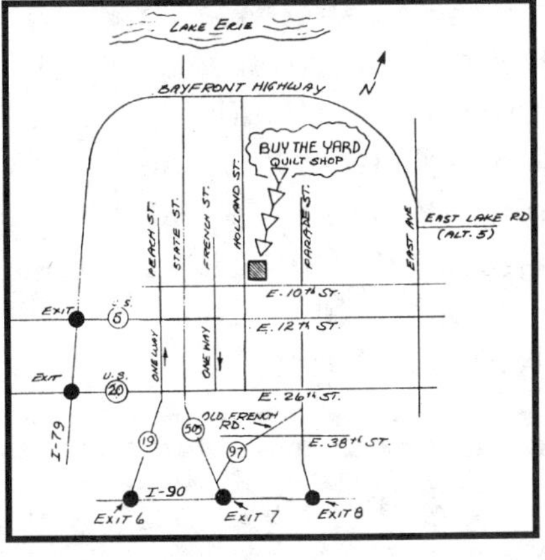

Free Parking in Rear & On-Street Parking

BUY THE YARD QUILT SHOP BUY THE YARD QUILT SHOP

Erie, PA #40

Threads & Treasures

Mon 10 - 7
Tues, Thur, Fri 10 - 5
Sat 10 - 4

2010 Interchange Rd. 16509
(814) 868-2226
Owner: Judy Dykins

Quilts, Wallhangings, Antiques, Gifts. We also carry a wide variety of Hoffman, RJR, Roberta Horton Plaids, Books, Patterns, Quilt Supplies & Classes.

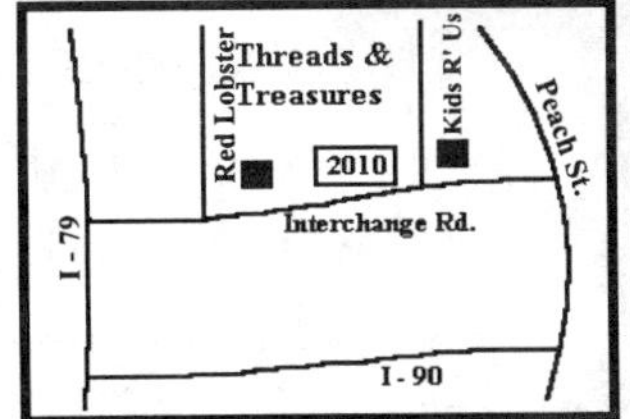

Erie, PA #41

International Fabric Collection

Thursday 10 - 3 and by Appt. or chance.

3445 West Lake Rd. 16505
(814) 838-0740 Est: 1987
E-Mail: info@intfab.com 1500 sq.ft.
Web Site: www.intfab.com
Owner: Dorothy Brown Catalog $3

Cottons from Japan, Italy, Holland, Africa. Yukata, mud cloth, Kente cloth, Liberty of London. Unusual Books & Patterns. Sashiko Supplies.

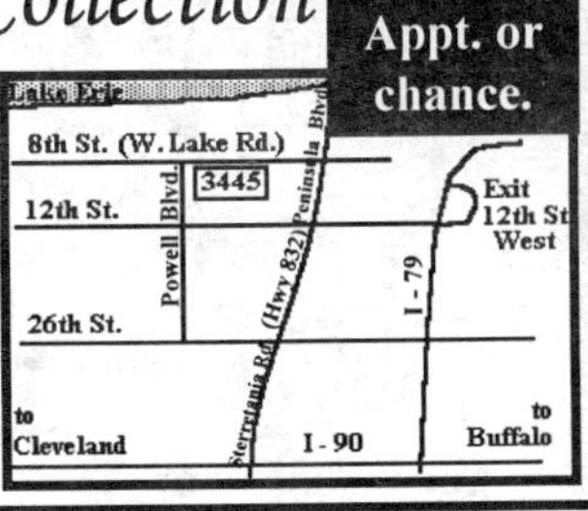

Harborcreek, PA #42

Calico Patch Quilt Shoppe

Mon - Fri 10 - 5
Thur til 6:30
Sat 10 - 4

3229 Davison Road 16421
(814) 898-2978
Owners: Jim & Millie Ward
Est: 1984 1400 sq.ft. 2500 Bolts

Largest Quilt Shop in tri-state area with country prices; home of original **"Puncture Proof" & "Magic Tip" Leather Thimble.**

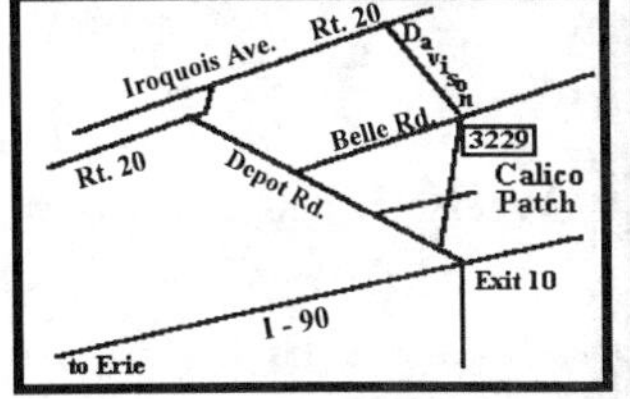

Meadville, PA #43

The Quilt Square

Mon - Fri 10 - 5
Tues til 8
Sat 10 - 3

560 Washington St. 16335
(814) 333-4383
Owner: Gail McClure
Est: 1981 3200 sq.ft. 2000 Bolts

RJR, Hoffman, South Seas and many more designer fabrics. Latest books and patterns. A staff who loves to see what you've done, so bring it in.

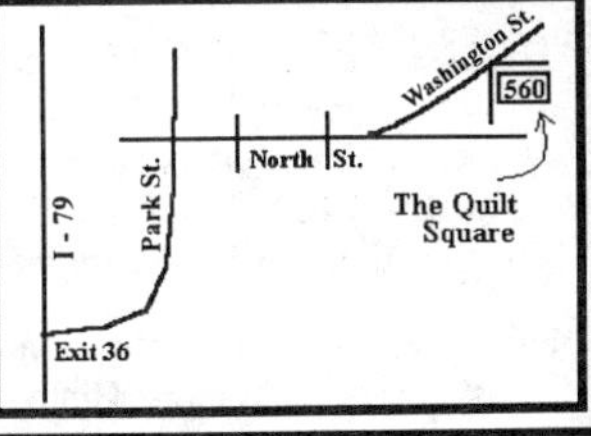

New Wilmington, PA #44

The Quilting Bee

126 South Market St. 16142
(724) 946-8566

1000+ Bolts Cotton/ Designer fabrics. Complete line of books, patterns. In the heart of W. Pennsylvania Amish farmlands, Just South of I - 80 and Sharon, PA. and minutes West of I - 79 and the Grove City Outlet Mall on Rt. 208. Come Visit!

Tues - Sat 10 - 4:30

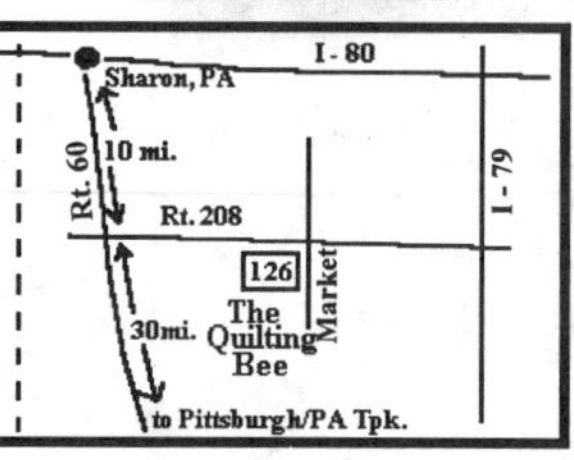

Owner: Linda Miller
Est: 1981
1200 sq.ft.

Monaca, PA #45

Mon - Sat 10 - 4

The Quilt Basket

1116 Pennsylvania 15061
(724) 775-7774
Owner: M. Maxine Holmes
Est: 1984

The Quilt Basket is a complete quilt shop offering lots of classes & all the supplies: i.e. fabrics, patterns, books, and notions.

Smicksburg, PA #46

Sept - May
Mon - Sat 9 - 5
June - Aug
Mon - Sat 9 - 7

Yoder's Quilt Shop

RD #1 Box 267 Hwy 954 N
(412) 397-9645 16256
Owners: Sue & Jay Hurtt
Est: 1988

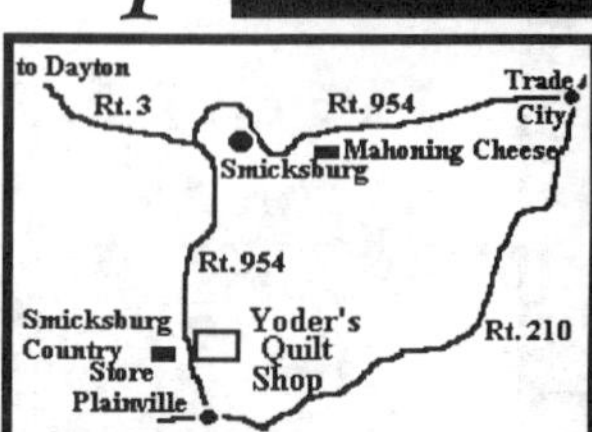

A large assortment of Amish-made quilts, wallhangings, fabric, notions, patterns, and quilting supplies. Over 1000 bolts of fabric at an everyday discount.

Butler, PA #47

QUILTING at "HOME"

225 Morton Ave.
16001
Home: (724) 284-1382
Studio: (724) 353-2891
Owner: Paulette Cole
Est: 1995

By Appointment Only

Machine Quilting

Ask about our 3 day, 2 night Quilting Weekends. Would you like to be on our mailing list?

Butler, PA #48

Mon - Fri 10 - 5
Thur til 8
Sat 10 - 3
1st Sun 12 - 4

Patches, Pretties N Lace

317 W. Jefferson 16001
(724) 287-2901 Est: 1989
New Location: 3 Story Victorian Quilt Shop

Red Wagon's Homespuns, Flannels, Kona Solids, Books & Patterns, Hinterburg Frames & Hoop on Display. Exclusive Amish Stencils. Brother & Elna Sewing Systems.

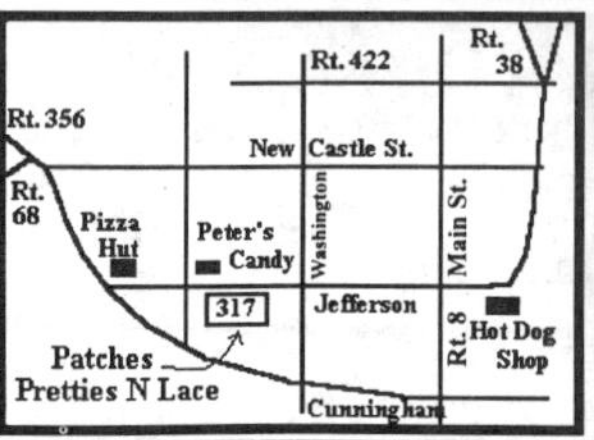

Knox, PA #49

Est: 1987

Countryside Crafts & Countryside Quilts

Owners:
Jolinda Tharan (Crafts)
& Sally Byers (Quilts)
P.O. Box 255 RD # 2 16232
Exit 7 from I - 80
(814) 797-2434

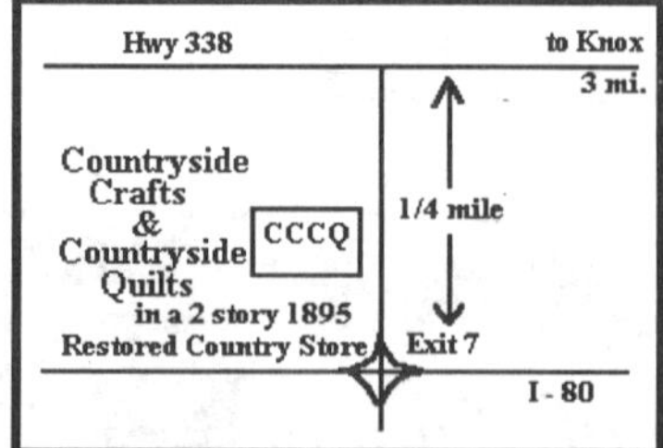

Mon - Sat 10 - 4:30
Sun 1 - 4:30

In the heart of Clarion County. We are the area's Largest and Most Unique Country gift, craft and Quilting supply shop. With 100% Cottons, Books, Quilting Patterns and the area's largest supply of craft patterns. Homespuns and flannels. Handmade Country Clothing. Free Newsletter.

Country Bear Creations

Lucinda, PA #50

Mon - Sat
9:30 - 5:30

34 Maple Drive 16235
(814) 226-8893
Owners: Keith & Sharon Kennedy
Mail Orders Welcome
MC Visa Discover
E-Mail: ear@csonline.net

Custom Made Shelves, Quilting Frames, & Quilt Racks

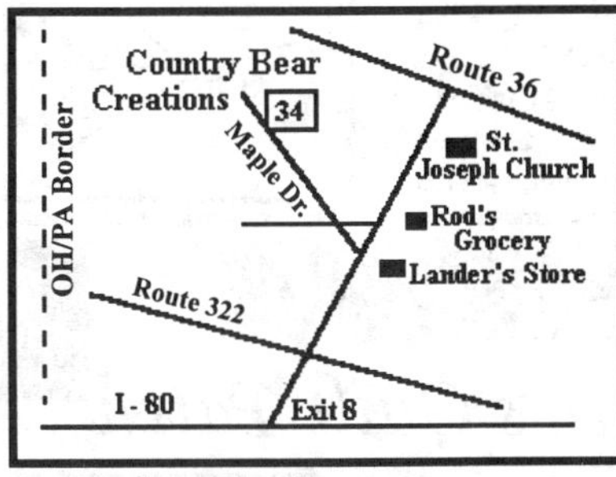

Over 500 bolts of 100% cotton fabric 90", 108" & 120" quilt backing. Large selection of Stencils, Books, Patterns, Tools and Quilt Kits.
Wide variety of classes.
We are the home of applique quilt designers Mary Alice Schmader and Sharon Kennedy.

Allison Park, PA #51

3940 Middle Rd. 15101
(412) 487-9532
Fax: (412) 487-9581
Owner: Karen Montgomery
Est: 1994 3500 sq.ft.

Mon - Sat
9:30 - 5
Mon & Thur
til 9

THE QUILT COMPANY

Pittsburgh's Largest Quilt Shop!

Featuring 100% cottons, books, and original patterns.
Quilting Supplies & Notions.
Featured by American Patchwork & Quilting as one of the top 10 shops in the Country for 1997.

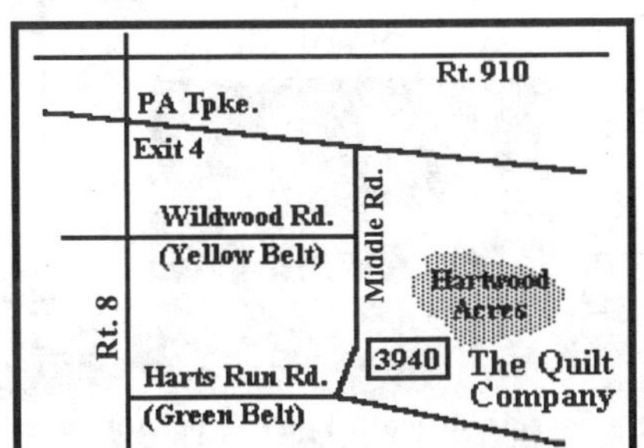

Indiana, PA #52

Mon - Fri 10 - 5
Sat 10 - 3

Harriet's Quilt Shop

271 Philadelphia St. 15701
(724) 465-4990
Owner: Harriet Yatsko
Est: 1980 3000 sq.ft.

A nice selection of cotton fabrics, stencils, books, patterns, thimbles and notions. Classes: Basic hand sewn sampler to quick machine piecing

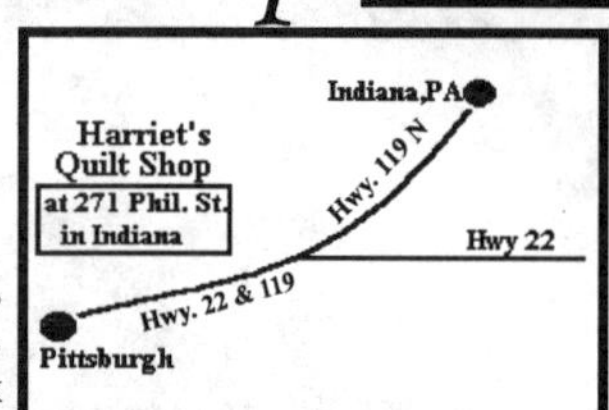

Pittsburgh, PA #53

Mon - Sat 10 - 5
Thur til 8

Piecing It Together

3458 Babcock Blvd. 15237
(412) 364-2440
Owners: Johanna Blanavik
Est: 1986 1200 sq.ft.

Complete line of quilting supplies, 100% cotton fabrics, books, notions, patterns, and classes. Lots of samples. Personal, friendly.

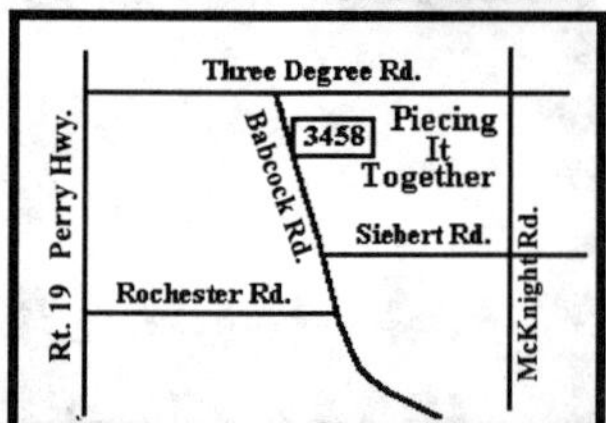

Trafford, PA #54

Mon - Fri 10 - 5
Thur til 8
Sat 10 - 4

The Quilter's Shop

329 Cavitt Ave. 15085
(412) 856-6088

100% Cotton Fabrics, Quilting Supplies, Books, Classes and great Service.
Exit 6 off PA Turnpike.

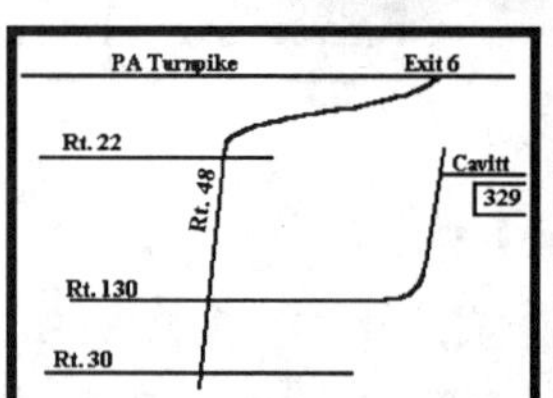

Elizabeth, PA #55

Tues - Sat 9 - 4
Tues til 8

Banners & Blankets

1125 Swiss Alpine Village 15037
South of Pittsburgh on Route 48
(412) 751-3707
Owners: Michele Shepler Est: 1995
Top Quality 100% Cotton Quilt Fabrics
Notions - Books - Patterns - Classes
New Home Sewing Machines & Sergers
Banner Making Supplies, Catalog - $1.00

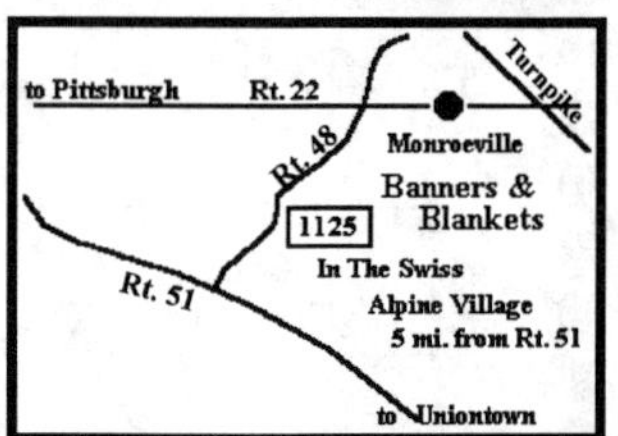

Bridgeville, PA #56

Mon - Sat 10 - 5
Wed til 9
Sun 12 - 4

Sister's Choice

533 Washington Ave. #104
15017
(412) 220-9596
E-Mail: sisters@nb.net
Owners: Karen Grabowski & Kathi Parli
Est: 1995 1200 sq.ft.

Large selection of 100% cotton fabrics, books and patterns. Bear making supplies.
BERNINA sewing machines.

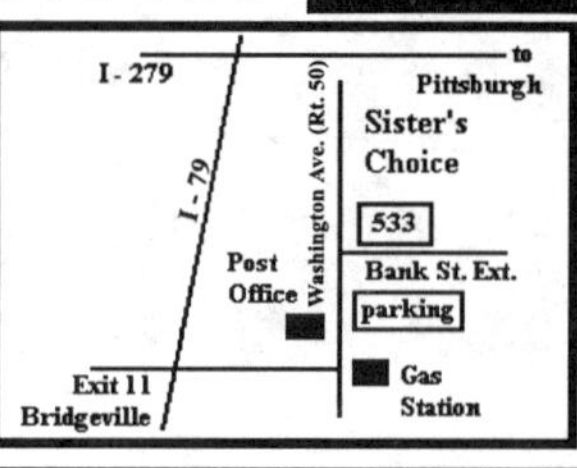

Scottdale, PA #57

Mon - Sat 10:30 - 5

Kate & Becca's Quilt Patch

103 Pittsburgh St. 15683
(724) 887-4160
Owners: Kate Hepler & Becca Flack

Calico Prints, Stencils, Quilt Books, Templates, Quilt Kits. Selection of Handmade Quilts—Contemporary and Traditional. Done by craftspeople who do only the finest work. Gifts for all occasions.

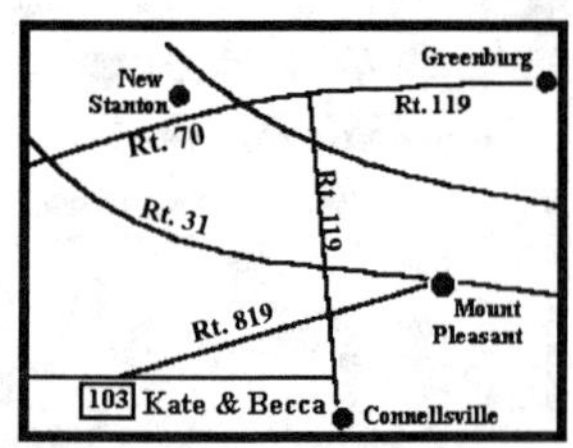

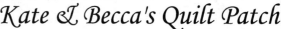

Bittersweet Designs

Bittersweet is a unique quilters' resource center featuring a special collection of quality fabrics, a large selection of stencils, museum grade quilt hangers and lots of ideas.

1116 Taylorsville Rd.
18977
(215) 493-2752

NJ Rt. 29
Delaware River
National Park
Rt. 532
I - 95
Bitter sweet
1116
Taylorsville Rd.
Exit 31

Tues - Fri 10 - 5
Thur til 8
Sat 10 - 4 Sun 12 - 4

Washington Crossing, PA #58

Conveniently located just 3½ miles from the New Hope exit (#31) of I - 95. Follow the historic Delaware Canal to our shop which is near Washington Crossing National Park in the heart of scenic Bucks County.

Waynesboro, PA #59

Mon & Fri 8 - 8
Tues - Thur 8 - 5
Sat 8 - 4

Benedict's Country Store

6205 Marsh Rd. 17268
(717) 762-6788
Est: 1980 2200 sq.ft. 3000 Bolts

Over 3000 Bolts Fabric in stock.
Large selection Quilt Books, Patterns and Quilting Supplies.

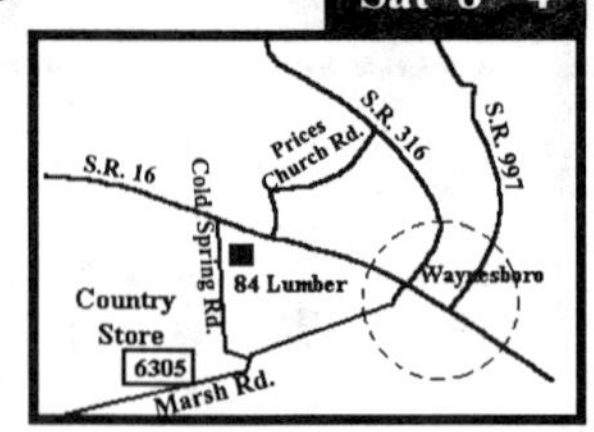

Happiness is finishing a quilt!

Pennsylvania Guilds:

Keystone Quilters, 806 Mill Grove Dr., Audubon, 19403
Beaver Valley Piecemakers, P.O. Box 1725, Beaver
Meets: 1st Wednesday 7 p.m. at Mt. Olive Lutheran Church
Colonial Quilters' Guild, P.O. Box 4033, Bethlehem, 18018
Centre Pieces, P.O. Box 657, Boalsburg, 16827
LeTort Quilters, P.O. Box 260, Carlisle, 17013
Meets: 1st Sunday 2 p.m. and 3rd Monday 7 p.m. at First United Methodist Church
Three Rivers Quilters, Castle Shannon, 15234
Mon Valley Quilters, Charleroi, 15120
Quilt Company East, Churchill
Brandywine Valley Quilters, P.O. Box 953, Concordville, 19331
Mid-Appalachian Quilters, Dover
Pocono Mountain Q. G., P.O. Box 1465, East Stroudsburg, 18301
Meets: 2nd Wednesday (Sept-June) 7 p.m. at Stroudsburg High School Cafeteria
Hands All Around Erie Quilt Guild, 1420 Lord Rd., Fairview, 16415
Stitch-in-Peace Quilt Guild, Gettysburg
Meets: 4th Monday 1 & 7 p.m. at Gettysburg Quilting Ctr
Sisters Choice Quilt Guild Randolph Rd., Great Bend, 18821
Hands all Around Erie Quilt Guild, Harborcreek
North East Crazy Quilters Guild, Harborcreek
Pieceful Patchers, Hollidaysburg
Meets: 2nd & 4th Tuesday 7 p.m. at Hillcrest Apts.
Calico Quilters, Hollidaysburg
Meets: 1st Tuesday 7 p.m. at Hillcrest Apts.
Pine Tree Quilters, 271 Phila St., Indiana, 15701
Meets: 1st Monday at Harriets Quilt Shop
Log House Quilt Guild, P.O. Box 5351, Johnstown, 15904
Heart and Home Quilters Guild, Kutztown
Meets: 3rd Wednesday 7 p.m. at St. Pauls United Church of Christ, 47 S. Whiteoak St.
Lebanon Quilt Guild, Lebanon
Meets: 1st Monday 7:30 p.m. at Cornwall Manor, Contact: Claudia Lawrence (717) 274-3169
Heart & Home Q. G., 24 Schock Rd., Lenhartsville, 19534
Laurel Mountain Quilters, Ligonier Town Hall, Ligonier, 15658
Ligonier Quilters, Ligonier Town Hall, Ligonier, 15658
Keystone Quilters, 5540 Beverly Pl., Pittsburgh, 15206
Tri-County Quilters Guild, P.O. Box 318, Portersville, 16051
Loyal Hannahs Quilt Guild, 512 Chestnut St., Saltsburg, 15681
Schuylkill County Q. G., P.O. Box 85, Schuylkill Haven, 17972
Meets: 3rd Monday 6:30 p.m. at First United Methodist Church, 420 Saylor St.
PA Quilters Assoc., 825 N. Webster Ave., Scranton, 18510
Tradaghton Quilt Guild, Williamsport
Meets: 2nd and 4th Wednesday 7 p.m. at New Covenant United Church
Berks Quilters Guild, P.O. Box 6942, Wyomissing, 19610
Meets: 3rd Tuesday 6:30 p.m. at GPU, Rt. 183, just north of the Reading Airport

Other Shops in Pennsylvania

Allentown Tucker Yarn Co., 950 Hamilton Mall 610-434-1846
Altoona R Quilt Shop, 2700 Windwood Rd. 814-942-2606
Altoona Moore Stitches, 1635 E. Pleasant Valley 814-943-2977
Altoona Ben Franklin Crafts, 120 Park Hills Plaza 814-944-7788
Bellevue The Quilted Cottage, 690 Lincoln Ave. 412-734-5141
Bethlehem Creative Quilting Workshop, 415 High St. 610-868-0376
Bethlehem Fabric Mart of Bethlehem, 2485 Willow Park Rd. 610-866-3400
Biglerville Craft Cupboard, 13 S. Main St. 717-677-9588
Bird in Hand Fisher's Hand Made Quilts, P.O. Box 286 2713-A Old Philadelphia Pike 717-392-5440
Bird in Hand Quilt Barn, 207 N. Harvest Rd. 717-656-9495
Bird-in-Hand Lapp's Dry Goods, 3137 Old Philadelphia Pike No Phone
Camp Hill Country Patchwork, 1603 Carlisle Rd. 717-761-2586
Clarks-Summit Carriage Barn Antiques, 1550 Fairview Rd. 717-587-5405
Columbia Sew Nice Too, 515 Chestnut St. 717-684-0896
Connoquenessing Added Touch, 1366 Evans City Rd., P.O. Box 137 412-789-7019
Corry Pansy's Fabrics, 109 N. Center St. 814-664-9424
Dallas Back Mountain Quiltworks, 52 Mill St. 717-675-4018
Doylestown Sew Smart Fabrics, 53 W. State St. 215-345-7990
Eagle Little Bit Country, Rt. 100 610-458-0363
Easton Tucker Yarn Co., 414 N. Hampton St.
Effort Country Quilterie, R. R. #3, Box 2482 717-620-9707
Elkland Golden Thimble, 114 W. Main St. 814-258-5677
Equinunk Janos Quilt Shop, P.O. Box 246 717-224-6008
Gap M & N Hand Made Quilts, 270 Octorara 717-768-8673
Gipsy Village Variety Store, 33 Main St. 814-845-7503
Glenside Granny's Sewing Den, 243 Keswick Ave. 215-885-4959
Goodville Obie's Country Store, 1585 Main St. 717-445-4616
Intercourse The Old Country Store, 3510 Old Philadelphia Pike 717-768-7101
Intercourse Dutchland Quilt Patch, 3461 Old Philadelphia Pike 717-768-3981
Intercourse Nancy's Corner, 3503 Old Philadelphia Pike 717-768-8790
Intercourse The Country Market at Intercourse, P.O. Box 555 3504 Old Philadelphia Pike 717-768-8058
Jeannette Chris' Country Closet, 616 Clay Ave. 412-523-0607
King of Prussia King of Prussia Sewing Center Route 202, 156 W. Dekalb Pike 610-768-9453
Kinzers Countryside Crafts, 326 Springville Rd. 717-354-8699
Lahaska The Fabric Cottage, 5788 York Rd. 215-794-2440
Lahaska Quilts Incredible, P.O. Box 492 215-794-3107
Lancaster Sawtooth, 11 W. King St. 717-295-3961
Lancaster Strawberry Patch, 112 Willow Valley Sq. 717-464-2224
Landenburg Gail Bush, 8 Springer Way 610-255-0548
Lansdale Lansdale Discount Linens, 816 W. Second 215-855-7162
Lewisburg Keister Antiques, 209 Market 717-523-3945
Mahanoy City Chesko Fabrics, 301 E. Centre 717-773-0140
Mansfield Lucia's Fabric Shop, Rte. 15 S 717-662-7024
Media Hen House, 100 W. Baltimore Pike 610-565-5152
Mifflinburg Mary Koons Quilts, 408 Chestnut St. 717-966-0341
Montoursville Stere Sewing Machine Center, 1116 S. Broad St. 717-368-8819
New Brighton Boyde's Country Stitch, 81 E. Inman Dr. 412-846-4175
New Holland Cedar Lane Dry Goods, 204 Orlan Rd. 717-354-0030
Northampton Dave Iron's Antiques , 223 Covered Bridge Rd. 610-262-9335
Pebersburg Brush Valley Dry Goods, Star Route Box 33
Philadelphia Byrne Fabrics, 8434 Germantown Ave. 215-247-3485
Philadelphia A&J Fabrics, 752 S. 4th St. 215-592-7011
Pittston Edelstein's Fabrics, R.R. 141 S. Main 717-655-1930
Punxsutawney Lydia's Quilt Shop, R.D.7 814-938-5533
Ronks Dutchland Quilt Patch, 2851A Lincoln Hwy. E 717-687-0534
Ronks Family Farm Quilt, 3511 W. Newport 717-768-8375
Saltsburg Patchwork at Heart, 219 Point St. 412-639-8441
Sayre General Store, 927 W. Lockhart 717-888-2320
Scranton Scranton Fabric Center, 1779 N. Keyser Ave. 717-346-0721
Sewickley Tapas, 441-1/2 Walnut St. 412-741-9575
Toughkenamon Antiques at New Garden, Box 212 215-265-3603
Volant Quilted Collectibles, Main St. 412-533-3863
West Chester Gone to Pieces, 325 E. Gay St. 610-918-9101
Wilkes Barre Touch of Eyelet, 1006 Wyoming Ave. 717-283-3048
Willow Grove Yours, Mine & Ours Sewing, 219 Easton Rd. 215-659-3347

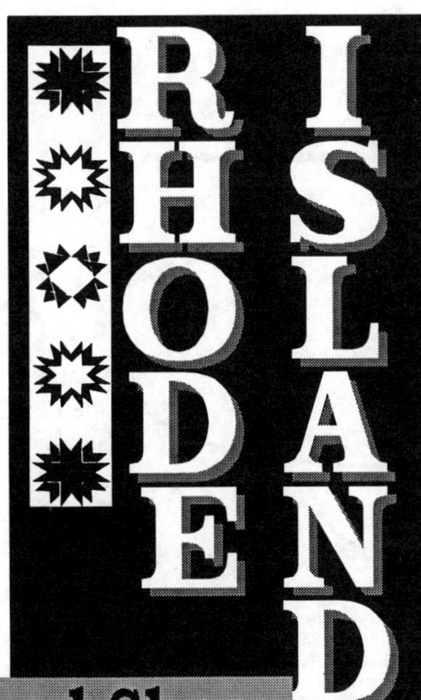

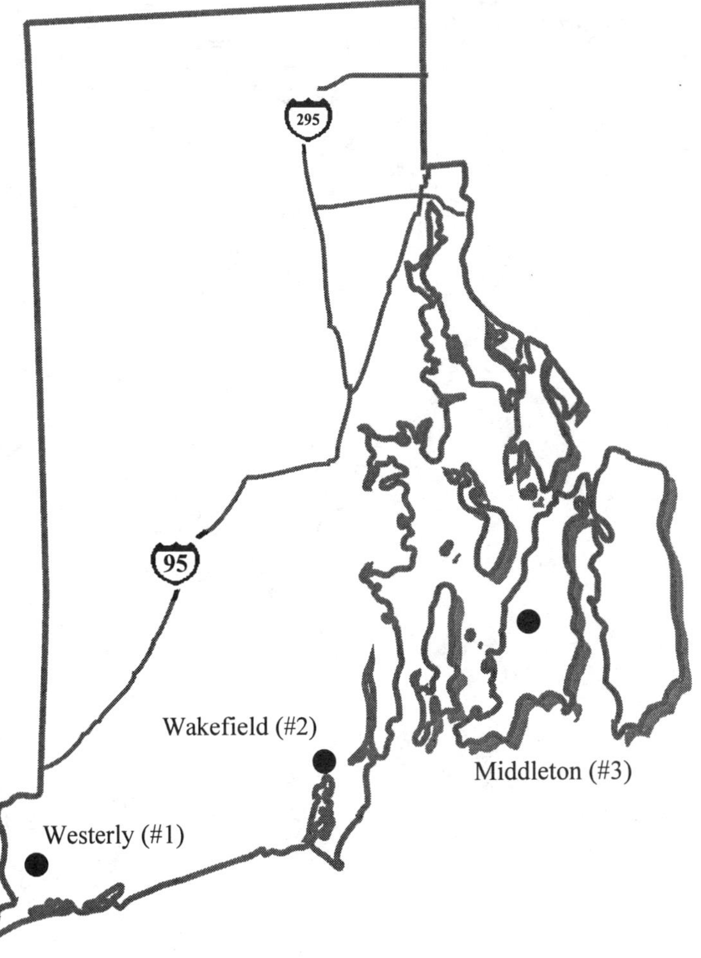

3 Featured Shops

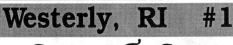

Westerly, RI #1

Mon - Thur 9:30 - 7
Fri & Sat 9:30 - 5:30

Sew & Sew

271 Post Rd. 02891
(401) 322-9194 Fax: (401) 322-7030
E-Mail: sewetsew@aol.com
Owner: Yvette G. Drurey Est: 1990

Fashion Fabrics, Quilting Cottons, Supplies and Books, Classes, Bernina Sewing Machines and Accessories.

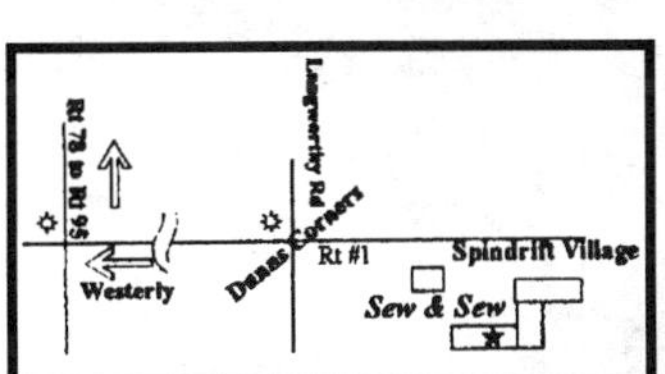

Wakefield, RI #2

Tues - Sat 10 - 5

Folk Art Quilts

269 Main St. 02879
(401) 789-5985
Owners: Evie Cherms & Mary Loftes

100% Cottons—Moda, Hoffman, P&B, Benartex and More. Quilting supplies, notions & patterns.

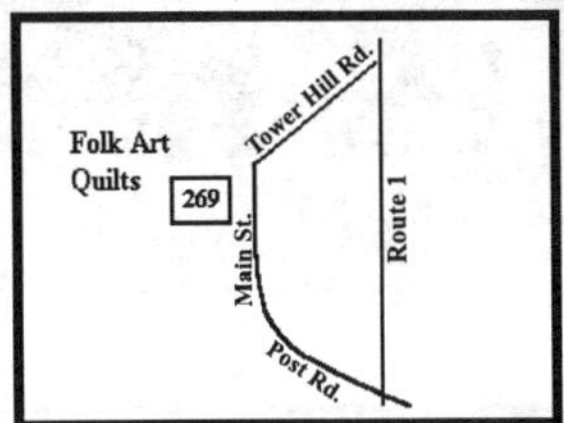

Rhode Island's largest selection of Quilting Fabrics.
Hoffman, Henry's etc.
Books, Sterling Thimbles, Classes & Workshops, Quilts & Gifts

Mon - Wed 12 - 7
Thur - Sat 10 -4

Middletown, RI #3

747 Aquidneck Avenue
02842
(401) 846-2127 or
(800) 736-4364
Owners: Linda Hilliard & Irene King
Est: 1984 2500 sq.ft.

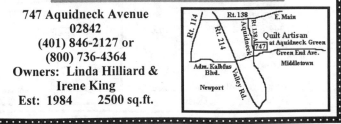

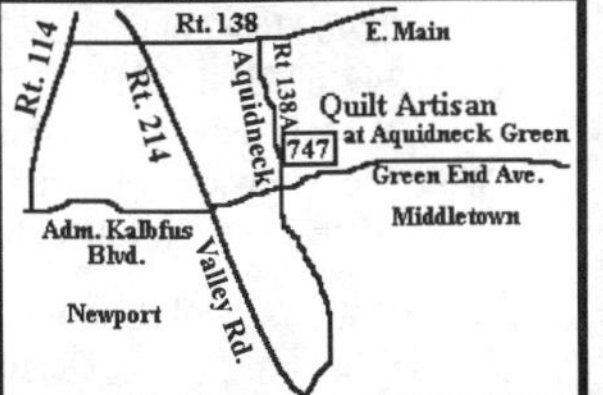

Rhode Island Guilds:
Narragansett Bay Quilters, Box 614, East Greenville, 02818
Blackstone Piecemakers, 15 Harkness Rd. W, N. Smithfield, 02896
Quilters by the Sea, P.O. Box 708, Portsmouth, 02871

Other Shops in Rhode Island:

Harmony	Country Hang-Up, Inc., Box 228	401-949-0049
Pawtucket	Lorraine Fabrics, 593 Mineral Spg.	401-722-9500
West Greenwich	The Quilt Shoppe, 74 Gooseneck Hill Rd.	401-397-4040
West Warwick	Fabric Place, 300 Quaker Lane	401-823-5400

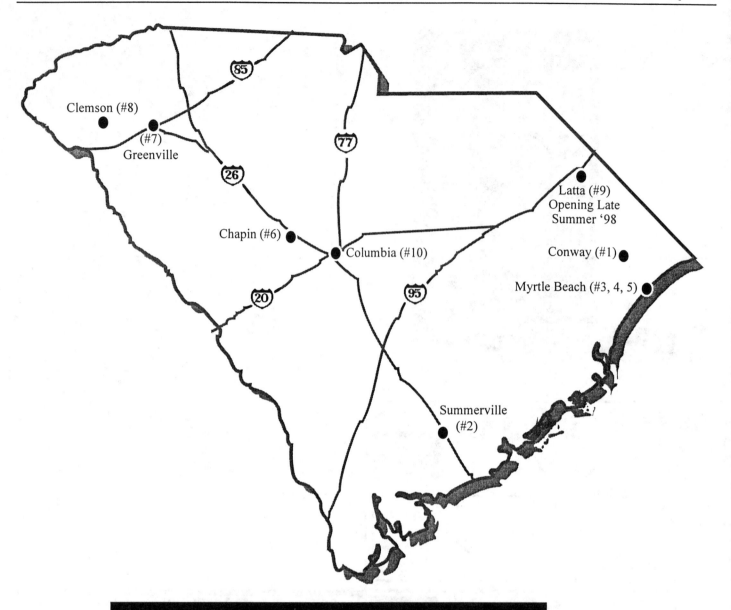

Clemson (#8)
(#7) Greenville
Chapin (#6)
Columbia (#10)
Latta (#9) Opening Late Summer '98
Conway (#1)
Myrtle Beach (#3, 4, 5)
Summerville (#2)
85
77
26
20
95

SOUTH CAROLINA

10 Featured Shops

Conway, SC #1

Mon - Fri 10 - 6
Sat 10 - 3

Sew Many Common Threads

2290 Hwy. 544 29526
(843) 347-6263 Fax: (843) 397-1056
E-Mail: sew@sccoast.net
Web Site: www.commonthreads.com
Est: 1996 1500 sq.ft.

fabrics, patterns, books, notions, classes
Husqvarna Viking Dealer.

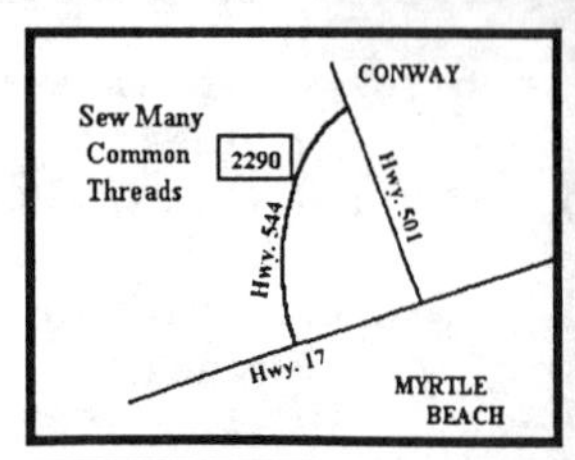

Summerville, SC #2

Mon - Sat 10 - 5:30
Sun by Appt. Call
871-4000

People, Places, & Quilts

Est: 1990

129 West Richardson Ave.
In Cauthen's old Hardware Store
(803) 871-8872 29483

Fabric & Quilting Supplies. Antiques, Folk Art, and Quilts. OF COURSE ! Everything one of a kind and hand made in the U.S.A.
Free Newsletter

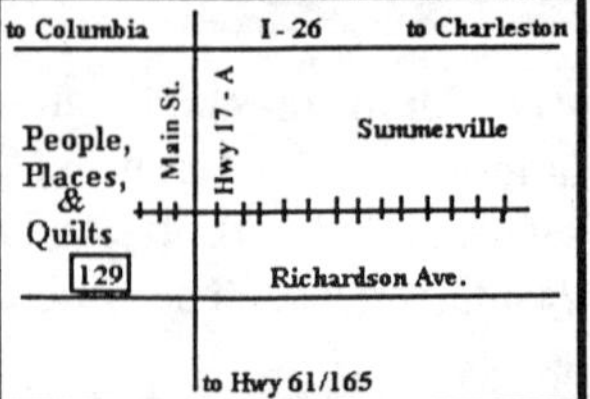

Fabrics, Supplies, and Classes. PFAFF Sewing Center

Fabric—Over 1500 Bolts
Hoffman, Alexander Henry, Jinny Beyer, Robert Kaufman and P&B
Books —100 Titles and More
Notions—Great Variety of Threads
Mettler, Cotty, Luny, Mez Alcezar, Sulky, Finishing Touch, Madera
Classes—All Skill Levels

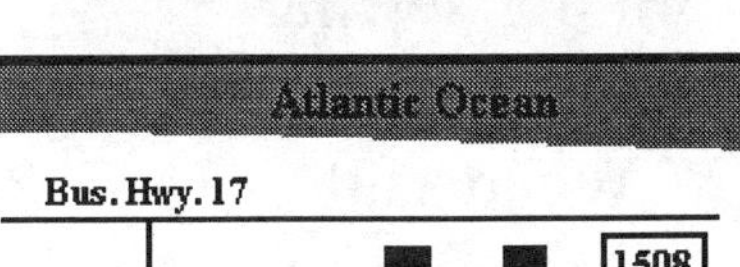

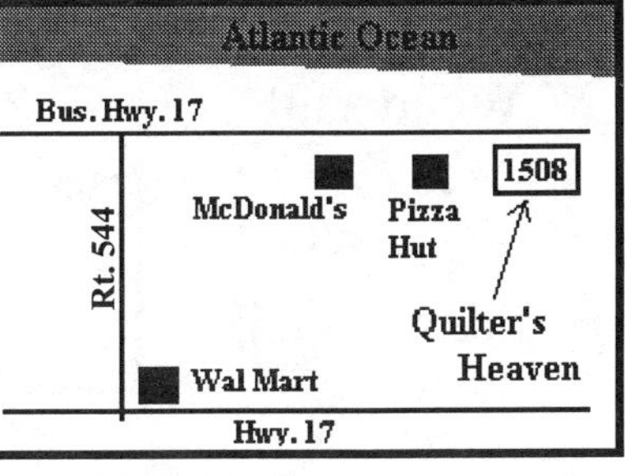

Myrtle Beach, SC #3

1508 Hwy. 17 N 29575 (843) 477-1611
Owners: Mary Sneeden Est: 1994 2000 sq.ft.

Myrtle Beach, SC #4

Mon - Fri 9 - 5
Sat 9 - 3

Oak Street Fabrics

504-C 27th Ave. N 29577
(843) 448-8021
E-Mail: Oakstfab@aol.com
Owners: James Thomas Jr. & Dorothy Tyson
Est: 1971
Specializing in quilt fabrics. Quilting service available. Also children's fabric and smocking supplies.

Oak Street Fabrics 504
27th Ave.
Oak St.
Myrtle Square Mall
Bus. 17
21st Ave.

Myrtle Beach, SC #5

Mon - Fri 9:30 - 5
Sat 9:30 - 4

Quilting By the Sea

5706 S. Kings Hwy. 29575
(843) 828-4443
Est: 1997 3000 sq.ft. 2000 Bolts

Large selection of 100% cotton fabrics along with flannels and wools.
Quilting books and notions.
Wonderful gift items and nautical treasures.

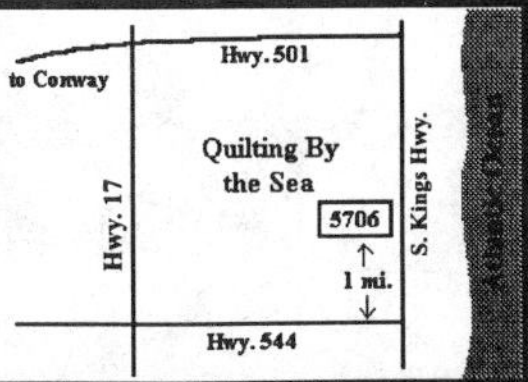

Pieces From The Heart
Quilt & Gift Shop

103 Clark St. 29036
(803) 345-8722
Fax: (803) 345-8726
Owner: Rose M. Azarigian
Est: 1997 1400 sq.ft.

Viking Sewing Machine Dealer. Wonderful selection of Fabrics, Notions, Patterns & Books.

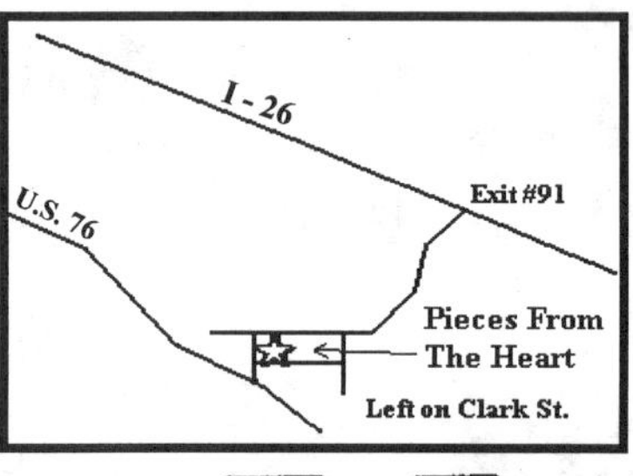

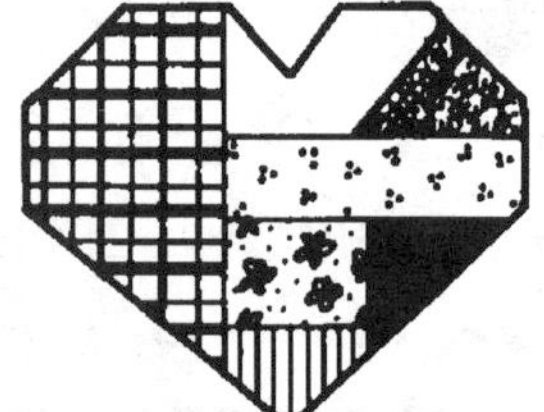

Mon - Fri 10 - 6
Thur til 7
Sat 10 - 5

Chapin, SC #6

Greenville, SC #7

Mon - Fri
9:30 - 5:30
Sat 10 - 4

Classic Keepsakes

626 Congaree Rd. 29607
(864) 288-0273
Owner: Elizabeth Be Den
website: www.classickeepsake.com

Quality Fabrics & Notions for all your sewing needs. Large selection of buttons, Creative Classes, Viking sewing machine dealer.

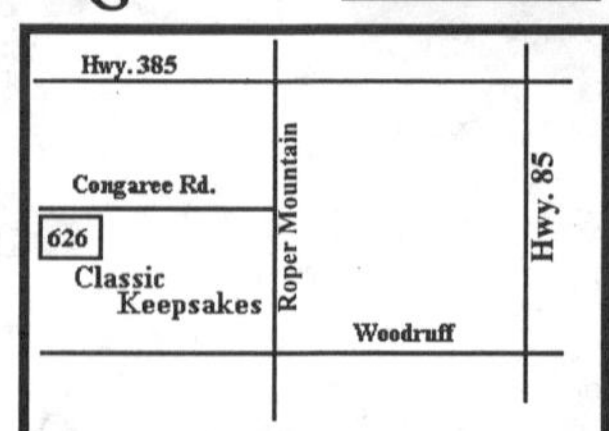

Clemson, SC #8

Mon - Fri
9:30 - 5:30
Sat 9:30 - 4

Heirlooms & Comforts

405 - 160 College Ave.
(864) 654-9507 29631
Owner: Sara Ballentine
Est: 1984 1300 sq.ft. 1700 Bolts

Upstate's most complete quilt shop--fabrics, tools, books, patterns, notions, classes--in a friendly atmosphere.

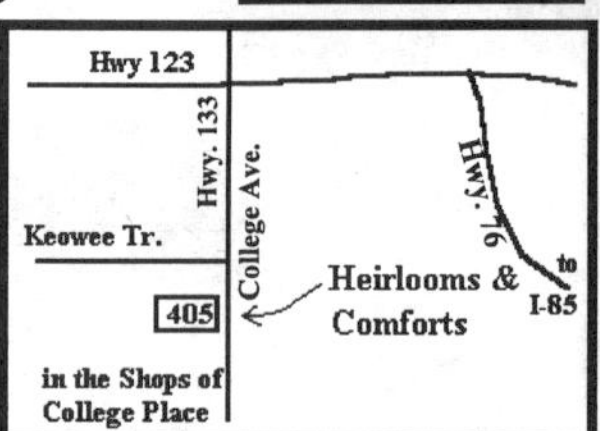

Latta, SC #9

Tues - Fri
10 - 5
Sat 10 - 3

Pieces from the Attic

Opening Late Summer 1998
Located in RJK Frames and Things
112 E. Main St. 29565
(843) 752-9319
Owner: Rebecca Grant

Fabric, Supplies and Patterns related to Quilting.

Exit 181 from I - 95 follow 917E to Latta, Cross RR, Building is on left before red light.

South Carolina Guilds:

Palmetto Crafty Quilters Meets: At Grand Strand Senior Center
Foothills Piecemakers Quilting Guild
Cobblestone Quilters Guild, P.O. Box 39114, Northbridge Station, Charleston, 29407
Meets: 2nd Thursday at Lutheran Church of the Redeemer
Greater Columbia Quilters, Columbia
Meets: 3rd Tuesday 10 a.m., 2nd Tuesday 9:30 a.m. and last Thursday 7 p.m. at McGregor Prebyterian Church, 6505 St. Andrews Rd.
Logan Lap Quilters, P.O. Box 7034, Columbia, 29201
Meets: 3rd Tuesday 9:30 a.m. at St. Andrews Recreation Center, 920 Beatty Rd.
For Bees: 1st Tuesday 6:30 p.m. and 3rd Thursday 6 p.m. in members homes
Mauldin Quilt Guild, Fountain Inn, 29644
Foothills Piecemakers, P.O. Box 26482, Greenville, 29616
Meets: 1st Thursday at Greenville Technical College
PD Patchwork Quilters, 112 E. Main St., Latta, 29565 Meets: last Thursday 7 p.m. at RJK Frames & Things
Grand Strand Quilters, Oak Street, Myrtle Beach
Piedmont Piecers, 1484 E. Main St., Spartanburg, 29307
Coastal Carolina, Surfside Beach

Other Shops in South Carolina:

Beaufort	Patches of the Heart, 3016 Ashwood Cir.	803-522-3303
Beaufort	Mother Hubbards Cupboard, 412 Charles St.	803-524-1892
Charleston	Margiotta's Sewing Machine Co., 874 Orleans Rd.	803-766-3621
Johns Island	Veronica's Boutique & Fabrics, 3375 Maybank Hwy.	864-559-2530
Reevesville	Quilt House, 6841 Johnston Ave.	803-563-3890
Salem	Calico House, 22 Cardinal Point	

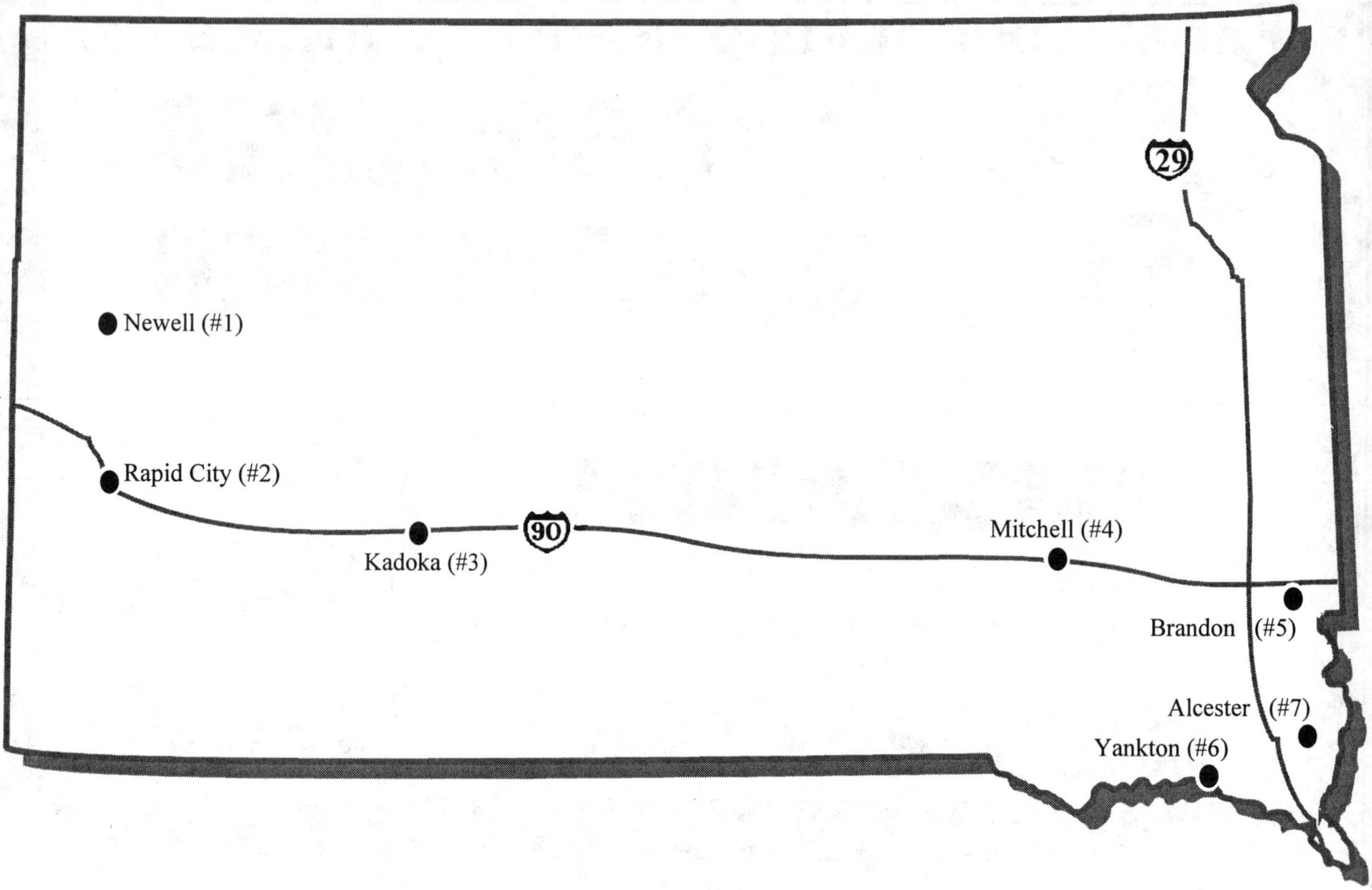

Newell (#1)
Rapid City (#2)
Kadoka (#3)
90
Mitchell (#4)
29
Brandon (#5)
Alcester (#7)
Yankton (#6)

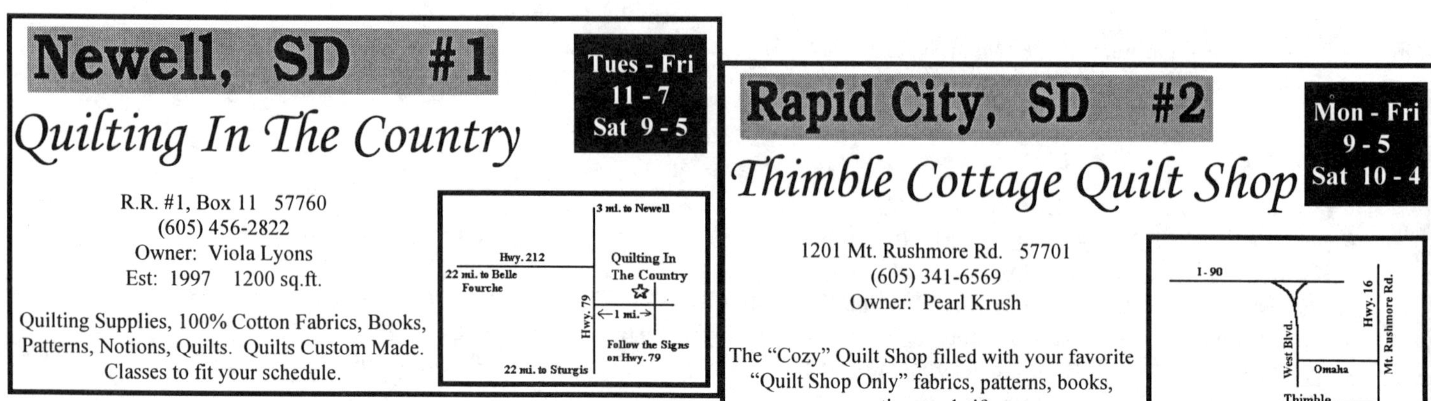

Newell, SD #1
Tues - Fri
11 - 7
Sat 9 - 5
Quilting In The Country
R.R. #1, Box 11 57760
(605) 456-2822
Owner: Viola Lyons
Est: 1997 1200 sq.ft.
Quilting Supplies, 100% Cotton Fabrics, Books, Patterns, Notions, Quilts. Quilts Custom Made. Classes to fit your schedule.
3 mi. to Newell
Hwy. 212
22 mi. to Belle Fourche
Quilting In The Country
Hwy. 79
1 mi.
Follow the Signs on Hwy. 79
22 mi. to Sturgis
Rapid City, SD #2
Mon - Fri
9 - 5
Sat 10 - 4
Thimble Cottage Quilt Shop
1201 Mt. Rushmore Rd. 57701
(605) 341-6569
Owner: Pearl Krush
The "Cozy" Quilt Shop filled with your favorite "Quilt Shop Only" fabrics, patterns, books, notions and gifts.
I-90
Hwy. 16
Mt. Rushmore Rd.
West Blvd.
Omaha
Thimble Cottage
1201

Kadoka, SD #3

Mon -Sat 9 - 6

Dakota Winds Fabric & Crafts

306 Main St., P.O. Box 45 57543
(605) 837-2145 or (888) 849-2199
E-Mail: kathy@dakotawinds.com
Web Site: www.dakotawinds.com
Owner: Kathy Jobgen
Est: 1991 1200 sq.ft. 300 Bolts
We carry a mix of fabrics including:
Hoffman, Debbie Mumm, Concord & VIP
plus much more.

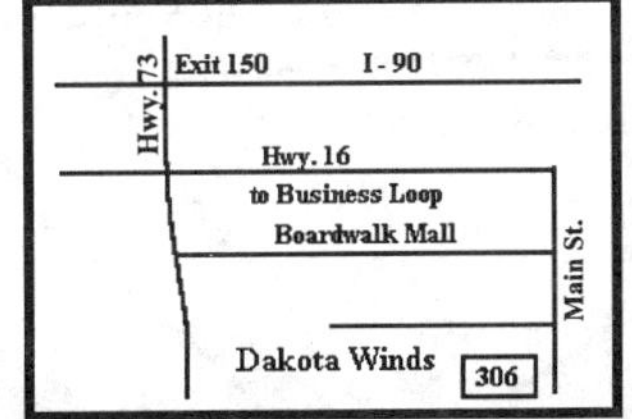

Mitchell, SD #4

Mon - Sat 9 - 5:30

314 North Main Street
(605) 996-0947
Owners:
Carma Popp
Est: 1987
1200 sq.ft.

100% cottons, Books, and Patterns. Classes. Friendly, helpful staff.
Authorized Pfaff Dealer

PFAFF

Brandon, SD #5

Mon - Fri 9 - 5:30
Sat Summer 9 - 3
Sat Winter 9 - 5

Quilted Memories

600 N. Splitrock Blvd. 57005
(605) 582-7411 Fax: (605) 757-6520
Owner: Twyla Lacey
Est: 1997 600 Bolts

Great 100% cotton fabrics, patterns & books, lot of classes to choose from, quality notions, gifts. Right off I - 90 Interstate.

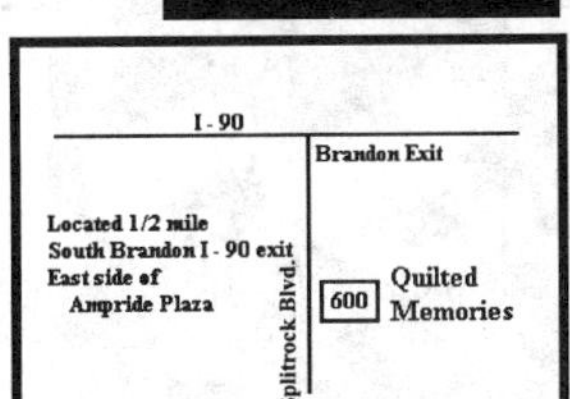

Yankton, SD #6

Mon - Fri 10 - 5:30
Thur til 8
Sat 10 - 5

Riverrun Fabrics

909 Broadway #4 57078
(605) 665-3406
Owners: Misty Winter-Nockels
& Jon Nockels

A great array of cottons, books, patterns, notions and other quilting goodies plus apparel fabrics and super classes!

Alcester, SD #7

Mon - Sat 9 - 5:30

Lacy Lovelies

Second St., P.O. Box 317 57001
(605) 934-1994
Owner: Millie Gubbrud
Est: 1968 5000 sq.ft.

The ultimate in privately owned fabric shops. Huge selection of Cottons, Silk, Wool, Ultra Suede, Fashion, Bridal and Decorator.

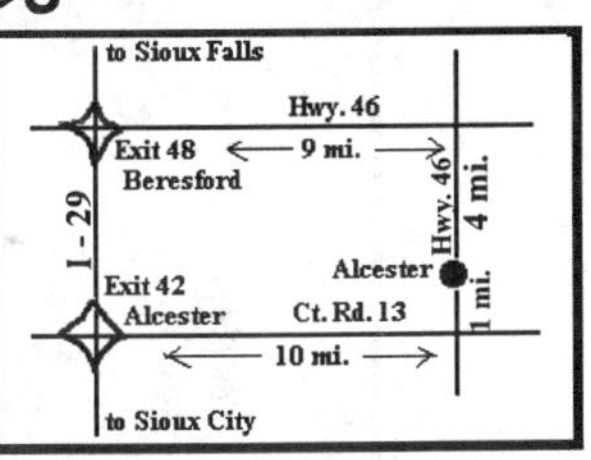

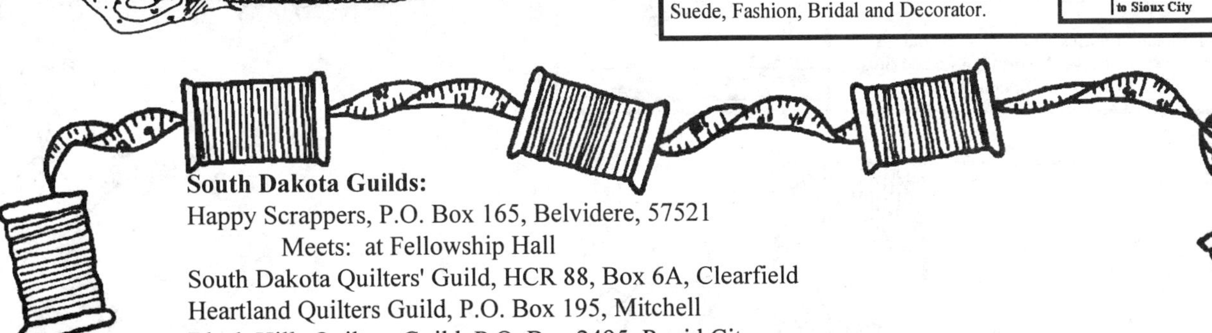

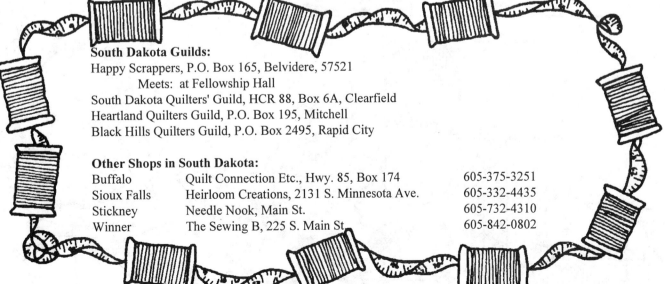

South Dakota Guilds:

Happy Scrappers, P.O. Box 165, Belvidere, 57521
Meets: at Fellowship Hall
South Dakota Quilters' Guild, HCR 88, Box 6A, Clearfield
Heartland Quilters Guild, P.O. Box 195, Mitchell
Black Hills Quilters Guild, P.O. Box 2495, Rapid City

Other Shops in South Dakota:

Buffalo	Quilt Connection Etc., Hwy. 85, Box 174	605-375-3251
Sioux Falls	Heirloom Creations, 2131 S. Minnesota Ave.	605-332-4435
Stickney	Needle Nook, Main St.	605-732-4310
Winner	The Sewing B, 225 S. Main St.	605-842-0802

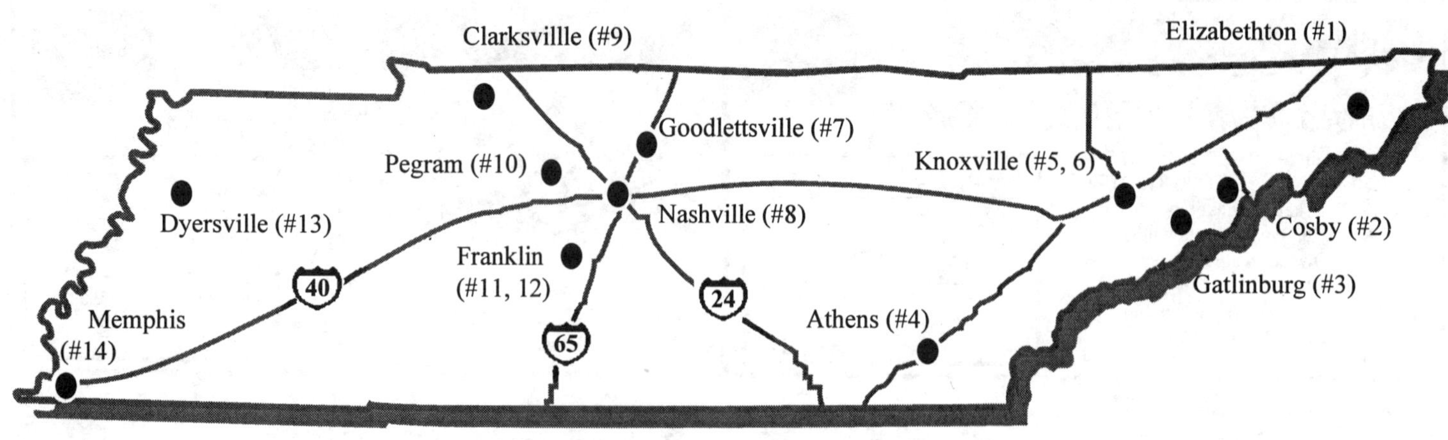

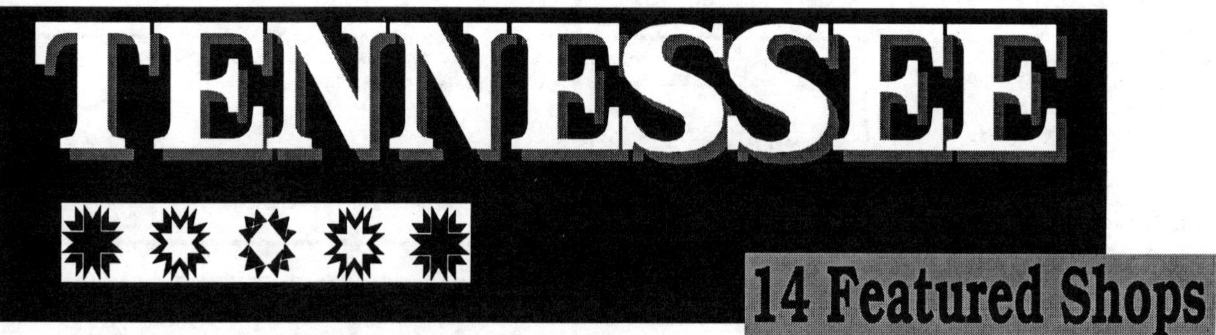

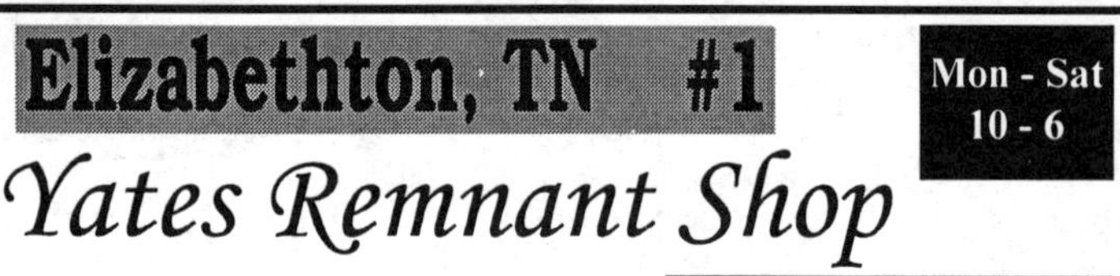

1008 Bristol Hwy. 37643
(423) 542-9251
Owner: Pauline Shell
Est: 1962

Full Line Fabrics — Quilt — Bridal —
Upholstry — Large Assortment Lace Trims.
User Friendly — Special Orders.

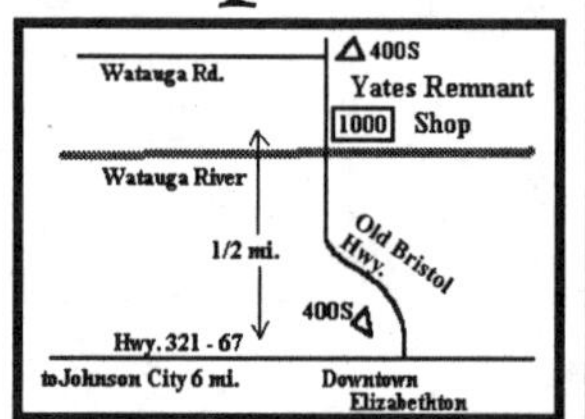

Holloway's Country Home Quilts

Daily 9:00 - 5:00

Our Main Shop

Holloway's Country Home welcomes a host of well known artists and craftspeople to:

Our House Next Door

For a unique shopping experience we now have five buildings for you to browse through.

- **Wood Workers**
- **Doll Artist**
- **Wood Carvers**

A husbands room, where the coffee pot is always on and the T.V. too!!

Our House Next Door

HAND QUILTED WITH AMERICAN PRIDE

Uniquely designed quilts, wall hangings. Fabrics, quilt kits, supplies and much more.

THE LARGEST SELECTION OF FINE VINTAGE QUILTS IN THE AREA!

Be sure to visit Maria's Country Closet and Sewing Room where you will find ...

- **Fashions by Maria**
- **Quilted Vests and Jackets**
- **Ponchos**
- **Afghans, locally woven and embroidered at great prices**

If you are a collector of American Quilts or other American hand crafts, visit us in our historical log building in the quiet country atmosphere of the small Tennessee community of Cosby.

For a walking tour through our shops please send for a video catalog. $5.00 charge refundable with $25.00 or more purchase.

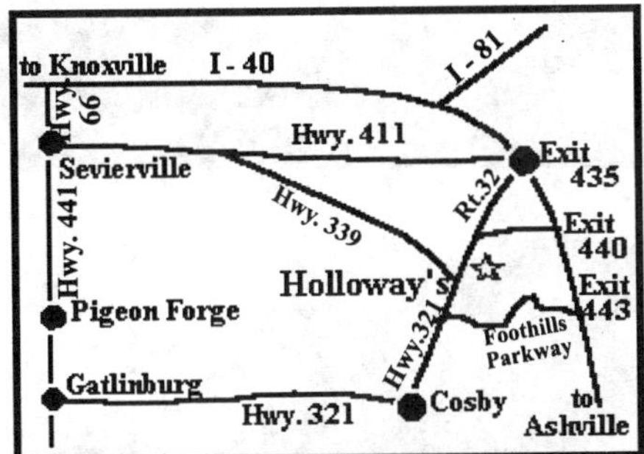

3892 Cosby Highway (Scenic Hwy. 321)
(just 19 miles from Gatlinburg)
(423) 487-3866
Owners: Maria & John Holloway

Cosby, TN #2

Gatlinburg, TN #3

Quilts By Wilma

1662 E. Parkway 37738
(423) 436-5664
Owner: Wilma Prebor

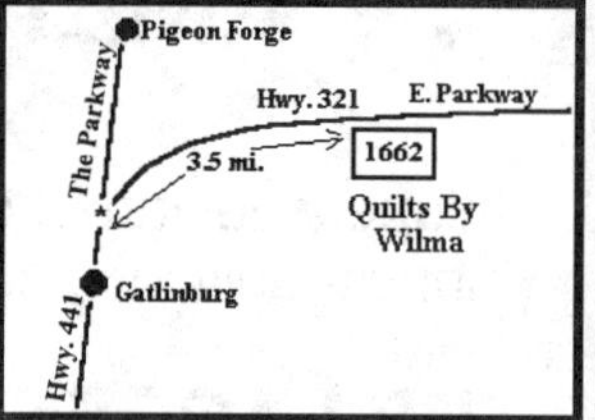

"Home of Regina's Quilt Kits.

Daily 9 - 6
Call for Winter Hours

Hundreds of quilting tools, books, stencils, patterns and designer fabric. Plus the largest selection in the U.S.A. of Regina's Pre-Cut Quilt Kits. Over 300 locally made Quilts.

If You Need It, We've Got It

Athens, TN #4

Tues - Fri 10 - 4:30
Sat 10 - 1
or by Appt.

Cotton Patch

154 County Rd. 653
(423) 745-1914
Owner: Mary Ann Sheffey
Est: 1996 1000+ Bolts

100% Cotton Fabrics including Hoffman, Bali, RJR, Benartex, 30's reprints. Quilting Supplies, Notions, Books and Patterns.

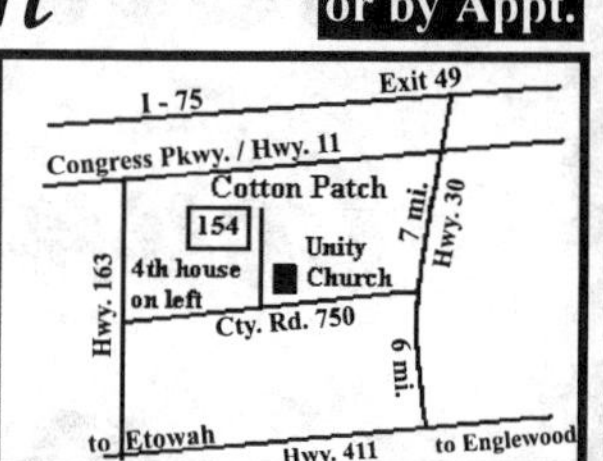

Knoxville, TN #5

Tues - Fri 9 - 5
Sat 9 - 6

Quilt Craft

"The Quilters Service Center"
4630 Mill Branch Ln. 37938
(423) 922-0769 Est: 1985
Mgr. Renna Kent

100% Cotton fabrics including homespun & reproduction fabrics. Also Quilting Books, Supplies & gifts. Q-Snap & Norwood frame dealer.

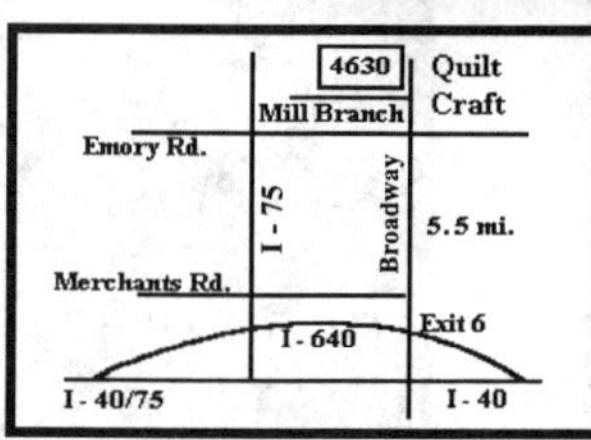

Knoxville, TN #6

Gina's

Bernina Sewing Center

30 minutes from the Great Smoky Mountains including Dollywood and Gatlinburg!!

Mon - Thur 9:30 - 6
Fri 9:30 - 5
Sat 9:30 - 4

120 Farlow Dr. Knoxville, TN 37922
(423) 966-5941 fax: (423) 966-6924
Owner: Regina Owen Est: 1980 5000 sq.ft.

Gina's is also the place for all your BERNINA needs.

Gina's has over 3000 bolts of quality cotton fabric, quilting books, notions, bridal fabrics, silks and woolens.
We specialize in heirloom sewing, smocking, machine work and a <u>lot</u> more.
Call for our extensive class schedule.

Gina's

... in the BIG RED BARN!

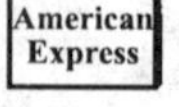

BERNINA®

Goodlettsville, TN #7

126 N. Main St. 37072
(14 Miles North of
Downtown Nashville)

(615) 859-5603

Established 1987

Mon - Fri 9 - 4
Thurs til 8 Sat 10 - 4

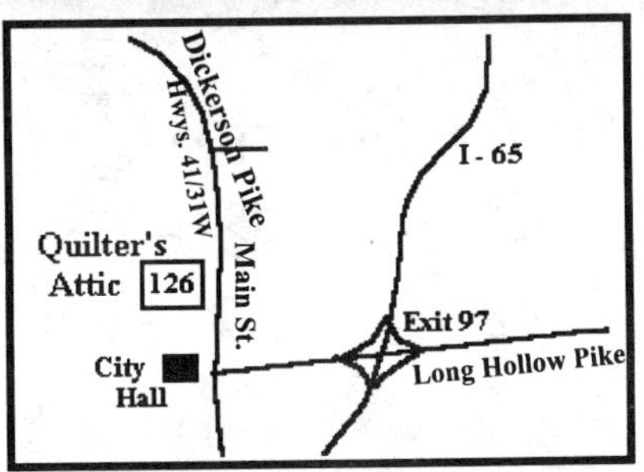

One stop shopping for quilters and bear makers...

Classes, fabric, books, patterns and notions...

Set in the midst of an antique mall...

4500 sq.ft. Over 2000 Bolts

Owners: Karen Gibson & Jean Shaw

Easy Access From I - 65

Southeastern Quilting Co., Inc.

Nashville, TN #8

748 Douglas Ave. 37207
(615) 262-4765
Fax: (615) 262-7653
Family owned and operated
since 1984

Mon - Fri 8 - 4:30

LOVE TO PIECE TOPS? CAN'T FIND TIME TO QUILT THEM?
We multi-needle machine quilt pieced tops or fabrics with quality backing, filler & thread. Fast, economical service.
Average cost: $29.25. Binding: Add $10.00. Outlining & pantographing also available for comforters, bedspreads & quilts.

Call or write for our free flyer.

Web Site: www.citysearch.com/nas/sequilting

Clarksville, TN #9

Country Quilting

1953 Madison St.
37043
(In the Tradewinds
South Shopping Center)
(615) 551-3650
E-Mail: CQuiltn@aol
2 Web Sites: www.Clarksville.com
or www.CountryQuilting.com

Mon - Fri
10 - 5
Sat 10 - 4

Smocking & Heirloom
Sewing Fabrics, Notions,
Gifts, Books, Patterns,
Classes, Workshops,
Seminars.
Authorized Bernina Dealer

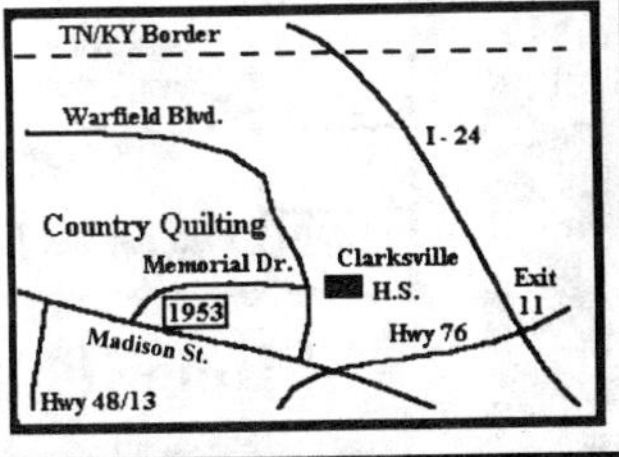

Pegram, TN #10

Mon - Sat 9 - 5

Harpeth Clock & Quilt Company

462 Hwy 70 P.O. Box 40
(615) 646-0938 or (800) 238-4284
Owners: Richard & Margaret Murray
Est: 1978 4500 sq.ft.

Quilting supplies & Instructions. Large assortment of cotton fabrics, books, patterns, notions and Handmade Quilts. Plus Clocks.

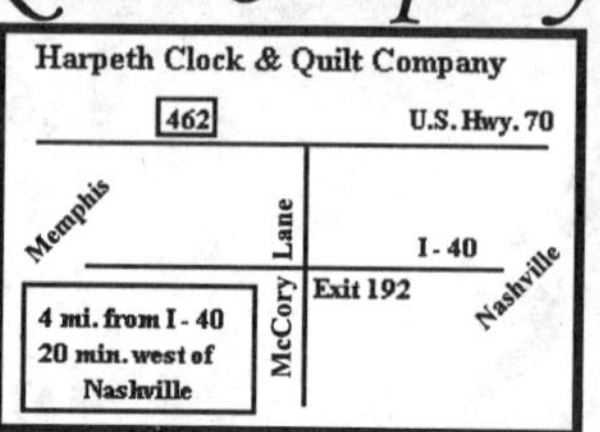

Franklin, TN #11

Mon - Sat 9:30 - 6

Stitchers Garden

413 Main St. 37064
(615) 790-0603
Owner: Myra Nickolaus
Est: 1988 3000 sq.ft.

Middle Tennessee's Most Complete Quilting Shop! Over 8000 bolts of all cotton fabrics, complete Jinny Beyer palette, Q-Snap frames, stencils, books, templates, patterns, and classes.

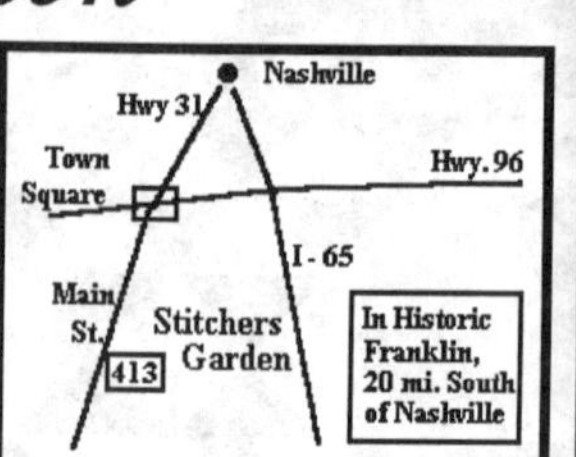

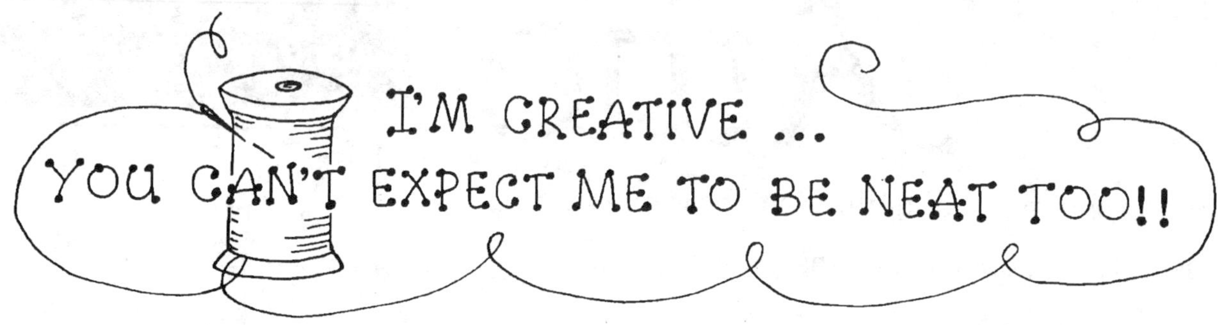

I'M CREATIVE ...
YOU CAN'T EXPECT ME TO BE NEAT TOO!!

Patchwork Palace

"Antique Salvations"

Largest Selection of Vintage Quilts in the Southern States — 400 to 500 in stock.
Fine Handmade Tennessee Quilts — All Sizes
We carry a full line of Handcrafts made from Antique Linens & Quilts.
Antiques — Bears — Angels — Pillows — Dolls
Most are one-of-a-kind designed & made by local Artisans

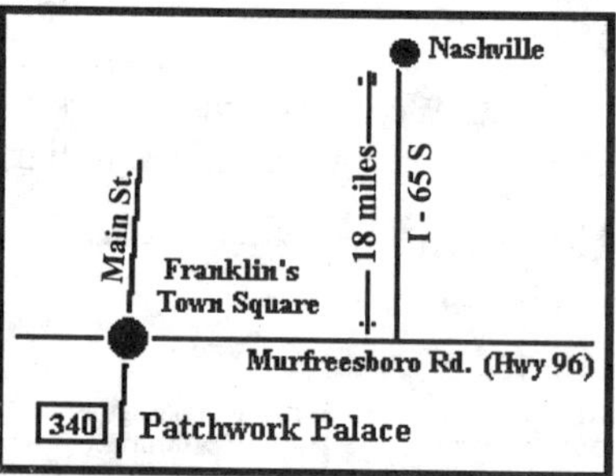

340 Main St. 37064

Franklin, TN #12

(615) 790-1382
After Hrs.
(615) 790-8301

Collectibles
Ty Beanie Babies
"Little Souls": Dolls
The Boyd's Collection
Debbee Thibault Folkart

Mon - Thur 9:30 - 5 Fri & Sat 9:30 - 5:30

Dyersburg, TN #13

Mon - Fri 10 - 5
Sat 10 - 3

Sew Many Ideas

219 S. Mill Avenue 38024
(901) 286-4721
Owners: Jeanne Bird McClain & Betty Bird
Est: 1988 4000 sq.ft.

Authorized Bernina Dealer. 100% cotton fabric by Hoffman, Jinny Beyer, M.E. Hopkins, P&B + many more. Notions, Books, Q-snap frames, craft patterns.

Memphis, TN #14

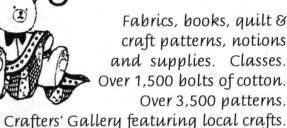

Quilts & Crafts

Fabrics, books, quilt & craft patterns, notions and supplies. Classes. Over 1,500 bolts of cotton. Over 3,500 patterns. Crafters' Gallery featuring local crafts.

Mon - Sat 9:30 - 4:30

2830 Austin Peay #9
38128
(901) 373-4004
Owner: Marie May
Est: 1991 2,000 sq.ft.

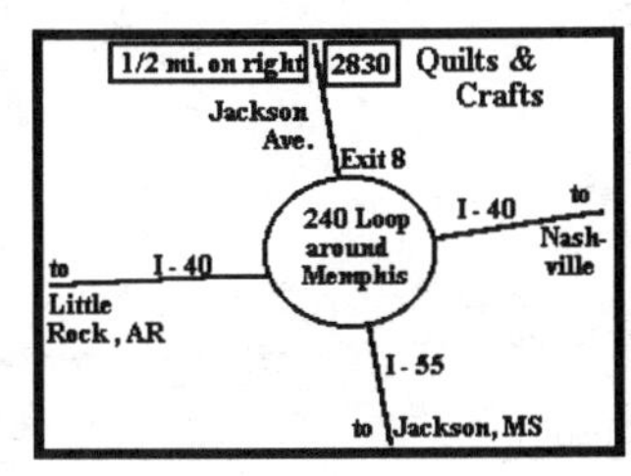

Tenessee Guilds:

Sycamore Stitchers
Meets: 2nd Thursday 9:15 a.m.
at Sycamore Shoals State Park
Heritage Quilt Guild, Athens
Meets: 1st Tuesday 7 p.m. at Heritage Museum
Chattanooga Quilters, 808 Windy Hill Dr., Chattanooga, 37421
Country Quilters, 1953 Madison St., Clarksville, 37043
Tennessee Valley Quilters, P.O. Box 92, Crab Orchard, 37723
Heritage Quilters, 121 Valley Lane, Englewood, 37329
Blue Ridge Quilters Guild, 5 White Oak St., Johnson City, 37604
Smoky Mountain Quilters of Tennessee, Knoxville
Meets: 2nd Monday 7 p.m.
Cherokee Blossom, 1430 Brymer Ck. Rd. SW, McDonald, 37353
Millington Quilt Guild, 9130 Ellen Davies Rd., Memphis, 38133
Boll Weevil Quilt Guild, 253 Brierview, Memphis, 38120
Cotton Patchers Q. G., 494 St. Nick Dr., Memphis, 38117
Uncommon Threads, 2582 Van Eaton Lane, Memphis, 38133
Heirloom Quilters, 1918 Battleground Dr., Murfreesboro, 37129
Music City Quilters Guild, P.O. Box 140876, Nashville, 37214

Other Shops in Tennessee:

Bell Buckle	Bingham's, 3 Webb Rd. E	615-389-6908
Brentwood	Sew Much More, 6939 Nolensville Rd.	615-776-3424
Chattanooga	Ann's Quilt Shop, 3609 Ringgold Rd.	423-698-8000
Cleveland	The Sewing Connection, 3354 Keith St.	423-479-8468
Cleveland	Lofty Creative Fabrics, 54 Mouse Creek Rd.	423-478-5815
Cookeville	The Quilt Shop #2, 210 W. Spring St.	931-528-1213
Cookeville	Country Patchworks, 134 S. Willow Ave.	931-526-7276
Cookeville	Glenda's Fabric, 739 S. Jefferson Ave.	931-528-2734
Cookeville	Parrott's Fabric House, 396 Short St.	931-526-1788
Fayetteville	The Flower House Needle Shop, 401 S. Main	931-433-7132
Jackson	The Fabric Source, 1090 U.S. Highway 45 Bypass	901-668-1877
Johnson City	CMQ Outlet and Sewing Center, 1600 E. Jackson	423-753-9220
Johnson City	Nimble Thimble, 2230 N. Roan St.	423-282-1075
Jonesborough	Sewing Bee, 104 E. Jackson Blvd.	423-753-7399
Jonesborough	Tennessee Quilts 123 E. Main St.	423-753-6644
Kingsport	Ramblin Rose, 216 Colonial Hghts	423-239-7408
Knoxville	Edith's Cloth, 2828 Broadway	423-687-5272
Lawrenceburg	Discount Fabric Store, 110 N. Military Ave.	931-762-4147
Maryville	Dorothy's, 2510 E. Lamar Alexander Pkwy.	423-983-4969
McMinnville	B & J Quilt Shop, 1202 Sparta St.	931-473-8141
Memphis	Cloth Connections - Quilt Shop, 3724 Summer	901-458-7129
Nashville	Quilt Patch Co., 2416 Music Valley	615-883-7404
Oak Ridge	The Quilting Corner, 37 E. Tennessee Ave.	423-483-7778
Paris	Thimble Fabric, 11 Henderson Dr.	901-642-5733
Pegram	Stitchin Station, 4515 Hwy. 70 E	615-797-9477
Pigeon Forge	Quilts International, 2662 Teaster	423-429-2772
Pikeville	Fabric House, Main St.	423-447-6195
Red Boiling Springs	Quilts & More, 3606 Carthage	615-699-3776
Signal Mountain	Toll House Fabrics & Quilts, 1404 James Blvd.	423-886-5977
Sparta	Peggy's Sew-Shop, 16 E. Bockman	931-836-2888
Union City	Stitchin Post, 611 S. 1st St.	901-885-1800
Woodbury	Cloth Shop, 227 W. Main St.	615-563-5201

TEXAS

67 Featured Shops

Spearman, TX #1

Mon - Fri 9:30 - 5:30 Sat 9:30 - 5

Jo's This N' That

214 Main 79081
(806) 659-3999
Owner: Joan Farr

We are a Traditional Quilt Shop.

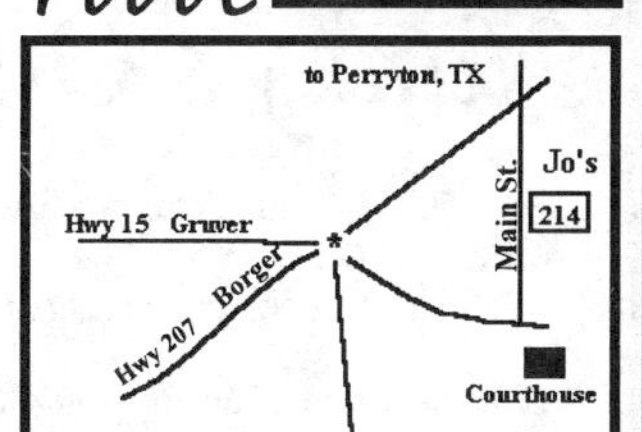

Amarillo, TX #2

Mon - Sat 9:30 - 5:30

R & R Quilts and More

2821 Civic Circle 79109
(806) 359-6235
Millie Riggs

Friendliest Little Shop in Texas. Over 2000 Bolts of 100% Cotton Fabrics. Classes, Supplies, books, and Patterns.

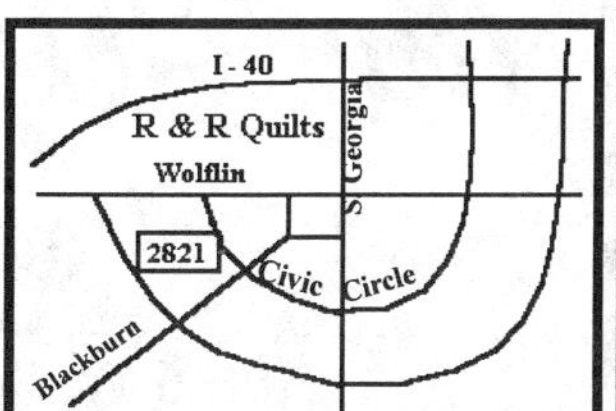

Amarillo, TX #3

Mon - Sat 10 - 5

Old 66 Quilts & More

3614 W. 6th Ave. 79106
(806) 373-7777
E-Mail: aliceama@arn.net
Owner: Alice Grant
Est: 1996 7500 sq.ft. 650 Bolts

Located on Historic Route 66. Classes, Custom Quilts, Old & New Quilts, Fabrics & Notions. Quilt Machine (do your own quilt).

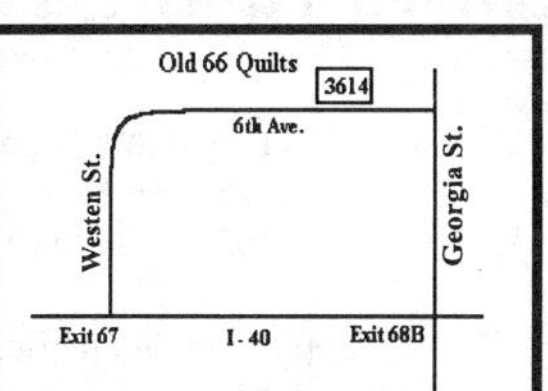

Lubbock, TX #4

Mon - Sat 10 - 5

The Quilt Shop

4525 50th St. 79414
(In the Sunshine Sq. Shopping Center)
(806) 793-2485
Owner: Sharon Newman
Certified Appraiser Est 1979

We have 1500 bolts of cotton, books, supplies & classes. Appraisals by appointment.

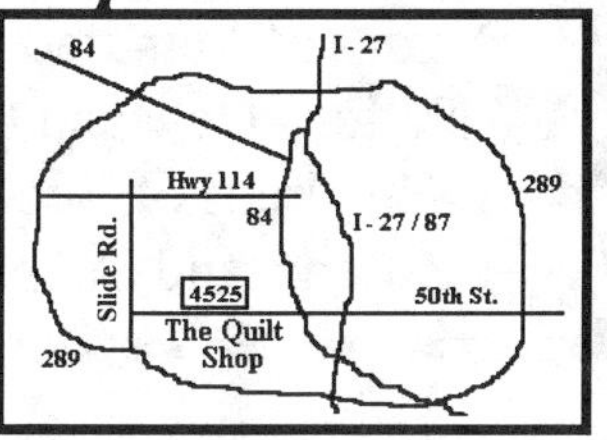

Needle Nook

Midland, TX #5

3211 W. Wadley 79705
#12 Imperial Shopping Ctr.
(915) 694-9331
In Texas & New Mexico
(800) 843-6962
Fax: (915) 520-0111
Owner: Joyce Sledge
Est: 1975 2100 sq.ft. 1200 Bolts

Mon - Fri 10 - 5:30 Sat 10 - 4

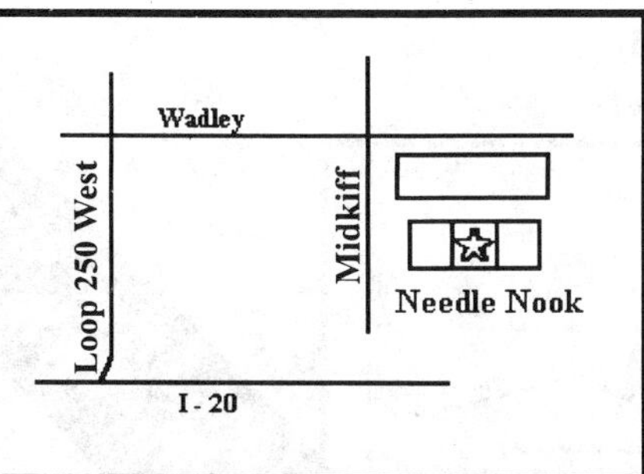

Everything a Quilter Needs

Wonderful fabric selection, Quilting Books & Patterns,
Wearable Art, Full line of Sulky & Mettler Threads,
Machine & Hand Quilting, Classes, Stencils,
Silk Ribbon, Horn Sewing Cabinets,
Bernina Machines

BERNINA®

Stephenville, TX #6

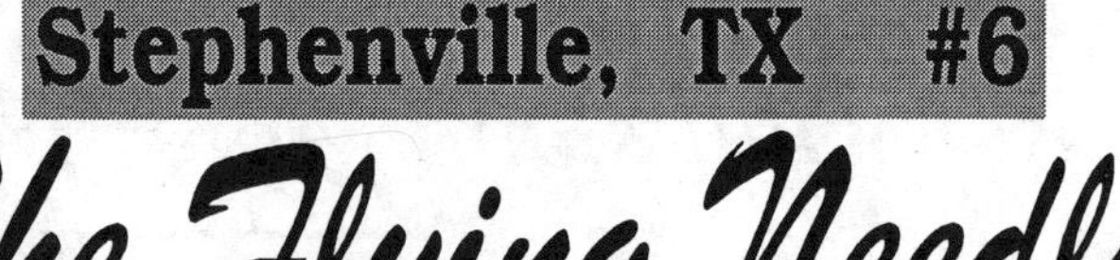

Mon - Sat 9 - 6

1495 W. South Loop 76401
(254) 965-7577 Est: 1971

1400+ Bolts of Cotton from Dozens of Manufacturers, Notions New and Old, Hundreds of Books, Patterns and Supplies.

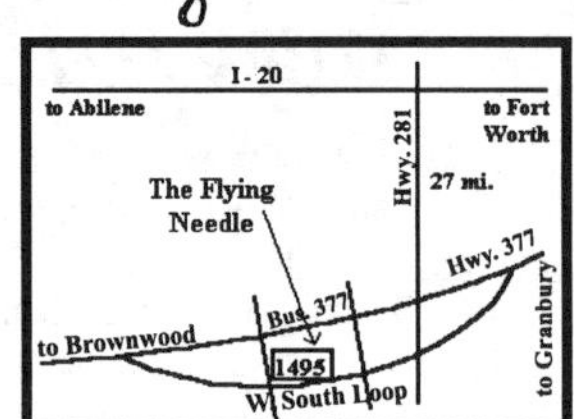

Waco, TX #7

Nancy's Quilt Block

Tues - Fri 10 - 5:30
Sat 10 - 4

502 B Austin Ave. 76701
(254) 757-2843
E-Mail: NPughl@compuserv.com

Good selection of quality 100% cotton fabrics, books, patterns & notions. Classes available. Friendly Service.
"To God be the Glory."

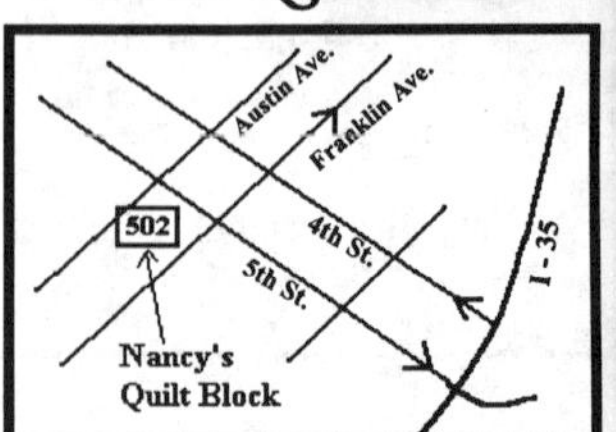

Lampasas, TX #8

M.J.'s Fabrics, Fashions, and Quilts

Mon - Sat 9 - 5

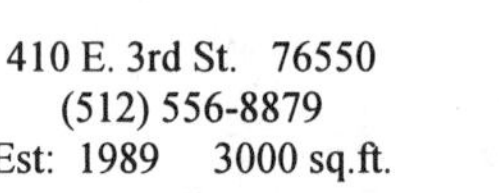

410 E. 3rd St. 76550
(512) 556-8879
Est: 1989 3000 sq.ft.

Top of the line fabrics.
Unique Patterns. Friendly Clerks.
Info on places of interest in the area.

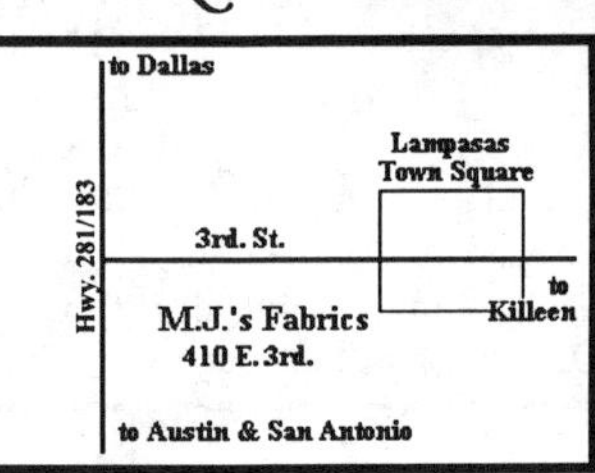

Temple & Killeen Sewing Machine & Quilt Stores

Temple, TX #9

1709 W. Ave "M"
76504
(254) 774-9797 or
(800) 506-9797
1000+ Bolts

Mon - Fri 10 - 6
Sat 10 - 5
Or Call, We'll be happy to stay late.

Killeen, TX #10

1002 E. Elms #113
76542
(254) 616-2200
650 Bolts

Quilting & Sewing Machine Classes
Notions & Books & Patterns
Authorized Dealer for Bernina,
New Home & Brother Machines
20 years experience in repairing all brands.
Help in choosing a commercial quilting machine.
Kid's Camp: Kids come and learn to sew!

Owners:
It's a Family Affair!
Sue & John Weathers
Pat & Stephen Weathers

2 Shops!

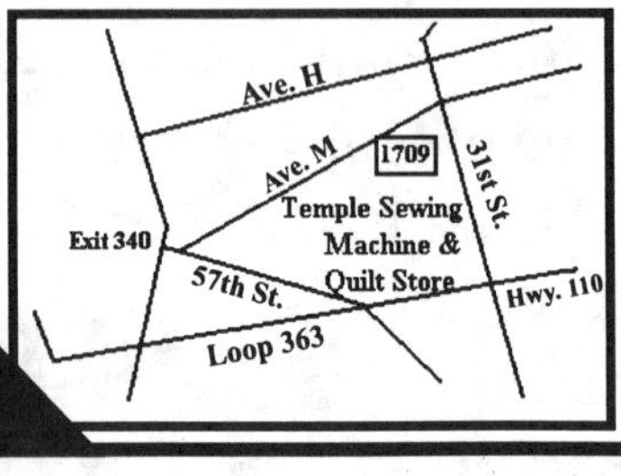

Ave. H
Ave. M
1709
31st St.
Temple Sewing Machine & Quilt Store
Exit 340
57th St.
Hwy. 110
Loop 363

Web Site:
www.ufindm
.com/quilt

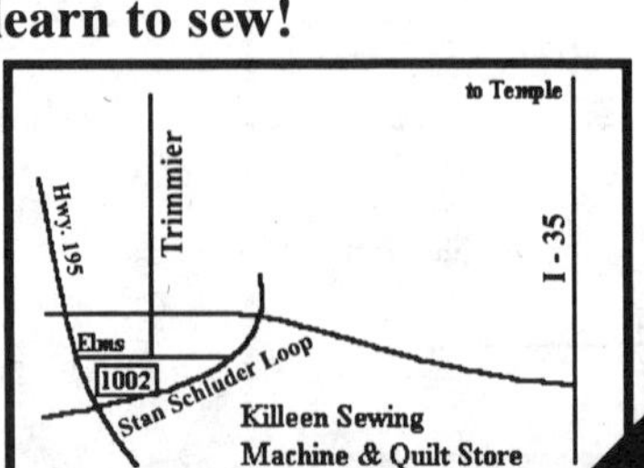

10% off to Quilt Guild Members

Pruitt's Fabric and Quilt Shop

318 George Bush Dr. 77840
(409) 693-9357 Fax: (409) 696-6264
E-Mail: pruitt@cy-net.net
Est: 1946

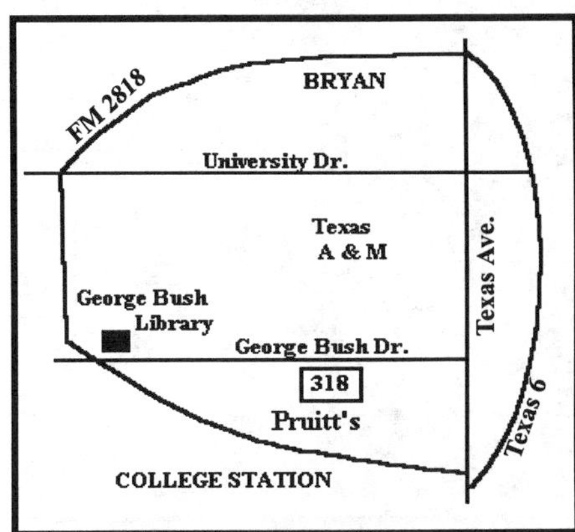

College Station, TX #11

Everything A Quilter Needs.

Large selection of vibrant colored cottons (5000+ Bolts), quilting books, patterns, & supplies, plus Silk, Wool, Linen, Velvet, Ultra Suede, Bridal Laces and Trims. Special orders Welcome

OPEN:
Mon - Sat 10 - 6

Bryan, TX #12

Tue - Fri 10 - 6
Sat 10 - 4

Polly's Quilt Cottage

3705 E. 29th St. 77802
(409) 846-7735 Fax: (409) 822-0769
Owner: Polly Trant

Largest in the Brazos Valley.
Only Aggie Quilt Dealer.
Top quality fabrics & notions.
Hand-made gifts. Super Sunday Sales!

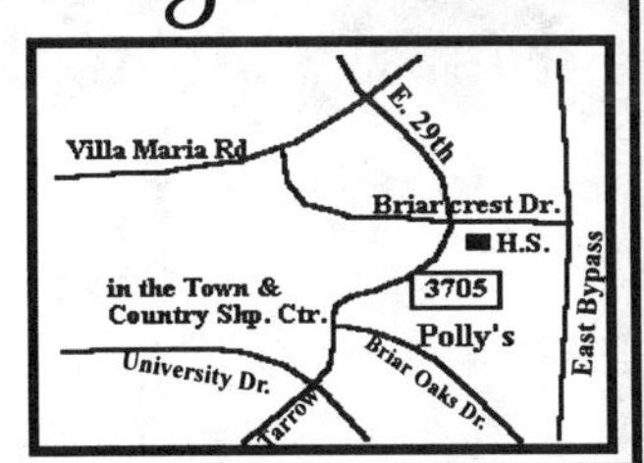

Brenham, TX #13

Stitch Haven

For Those Who Love Quilting Needlework and Fine Fabrics

Tues - Fri 10 - 5:30
Sat 10 - 3

Featuring Cotton Fabrics and Supplies for Quilting, Wearable Art, Smocking, and Silk Ribbon Embroidery

1600 S. Day St. 77833
(409) 836-3200

Round Rock, TX #14

Tues - Sat
10 - 5

Mini Stitches

208 W. Bagdad Ave. #7 78664
Corner of Brown & Bagdad
(512) 255-8545
Owner: Carol Kussmaul Est: 1994

Fulfill your creative destiny with our select fabrics, patterns, classes, and personalized assistance. Silk Ribbon also available.

Austin, TX #15

The Quilt Store, Inc.

2700 W. Anderson Lane #301 78757
(512) 453-1145

We have a fantastic selection of 5,000 bolts of 100% cotton fabrics, books, patterns and other supplies for quiltmakers.

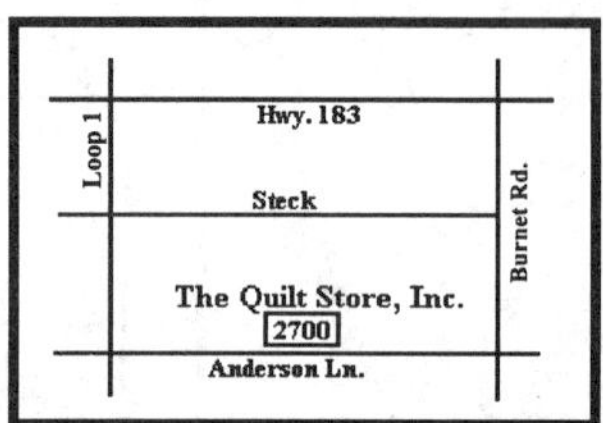

Mon - Sat 10 - 5
Thurs til 8

Austin, TX #16

Gem Fabrics

Mon, Tues, Thur 10 - 8
Wed, Fri, Sat 10 - 6
Sun 12 - 5

13776 Hwy. 183 N. #142 78750
(512) 258-8061
E-Mail: GemBixler@aol.com
Web Site: www.gemfabric.com
Owners: Dorothy & Reynolds Bixler
Est: 1968 2400 sq.ft. 2000 Bolts

Beautiful Fabrics, Books, Patterns, Helpful Tools, Lots of Classes, Authorized Dealer: New Home & Viking

Austin, TX #17

Homestead Sewing & Quilting

Mon - Fri 9 - 5:30
Sat by Appt.

10209A FM 812 78719
(512) 243-2772

We make custom handmade quilts & comforters, quilt your quilt tops, custom mongram quilt signatures & do repairing & rebinding.

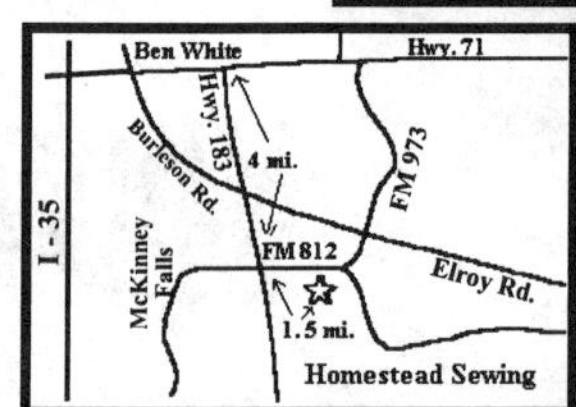

New Braunfels, TX #18

Millstream Cottons

Mon - Fri 9:30 - 5
Sat 10 - 4

125 N. Castell 78130
(830) 620-1382 Fax: (830) 620-1387
E-Mail: millstream@compuvision.net
Owner: Sally Shimek
Est: 1997 2000 sq.ft.

Large selection of top name 100% cotton fabrics. Quilting supplies, books, patterns, notions, kits & classes.

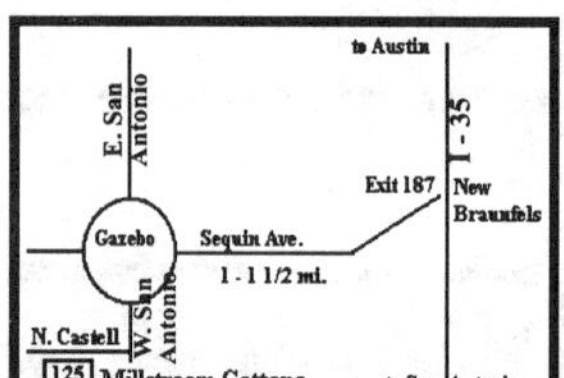

Boerne, TX #19

Sew Special

Mon - Sat 9 - 5
Sun 12 - 5

1014 N. Main Street 78006
(210) 249-8038
Owners: Four Quilting Nuts !
Est: 1987 1800 sq.ft. 1200 Bolts

"The Best Little Quilt Shop by a Country Smile" Cottons, books, patterns, notions, classes, & Help ! Ask about our Fabric Club.

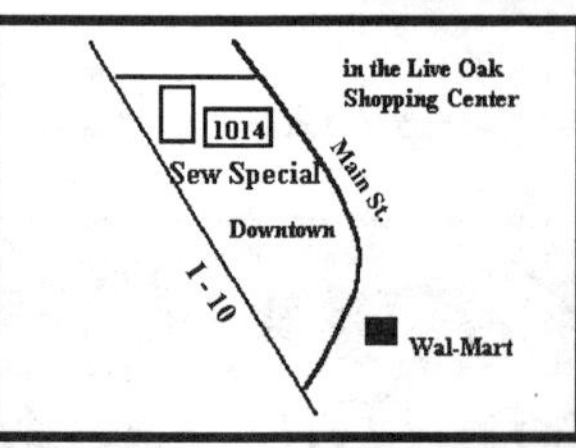

San Antonio, TX #20

Bernina - New Home Sewing Center

Mon - Sat 9:30 - 6

11777 West Ave. 78216
(210) 344-0791
Owners: Terry & Vince Soll

Beautiful fabric. Books & patterns. Quilt & Sewing Machine Acc. Threads. Sewing & Embroidery, Machines. Sergers. Heirloom Lace & Cabinets.

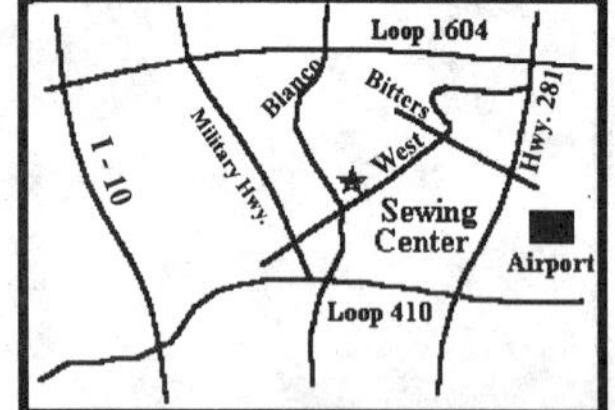

San Antonio, TX #21

Seventh Heaven

Mon - Fri 9 - 5:30
Sat 9 - 3

5860 Hwy 87 E. 78222
(210) 648-1381
Owner: Dixie Bradbury
Est: 1990 3600 sq.ft. 1000 Bolts

Heavenly delight 100% Cotton Fabrics, Supplies. Hoffman, RJR, P&B, and Moda. Patterns, Books and more. Singer Sewing Machines.

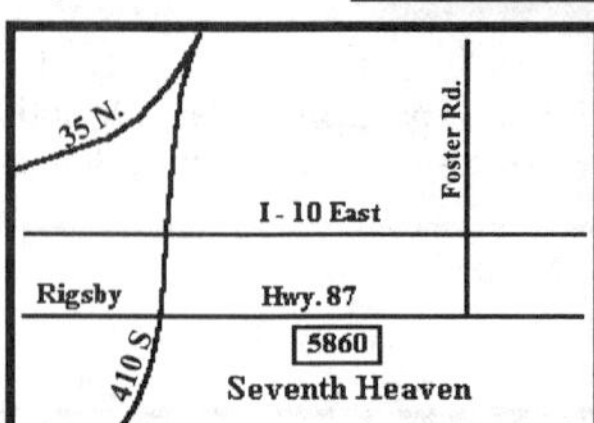

San Antonio, TX #22

Las Colchas

Tue - Sat 10 - 5
Tue & Thur til 7

110 Ogden St. 78212
(210) 223-2405

100% Cotton Fabrics - checks, plaids, Homespuns. Supplies & Classes Patterns, Books, Kits. Year Round Christmas Room all in a cozy Victorian House.

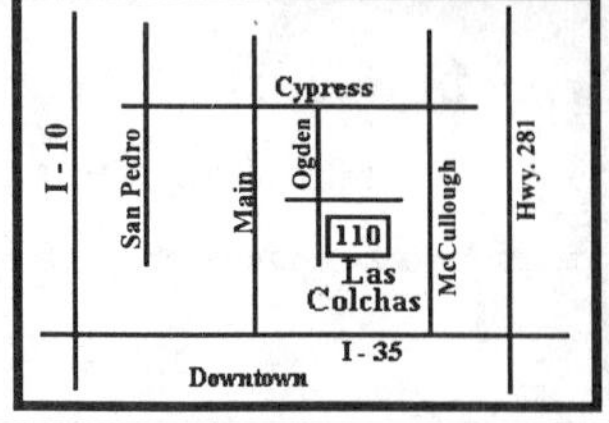

Lytle, TX #23

Kalico & Keepsakes

Mon - Sat 9 - 6

14945 Main St., P.O. Box 329 78052
(830) 772-4721
Owner: Dee Cromer
Est: 1997 2300 sq.ft.

Full line quality Fabric and Notions. Classes — day, night and Saturdays. Professional finishing on Gammill Machine. Our Customers are soon Friends.

Good Fabrics and lots of neat stuff that quilters and sewers love!!

Rug Hooking
Silk Ribbon
Burda Patterns
Brother Embroidery Machines
Elna Sewing Machines
Featured in the Summer '96 edition of *American Patchwork and Quilting.*

Kerrville, TX #24

832 Water St. 78028
(830) 896-8088
or (800) 853-1108
Owner:
Kathy Thompson
Est: 1978

A UNIQUE FABRIC BOUTIQUE

Sponsoring Electric Quilt 3 Retreats. Call for Scheduling Information.

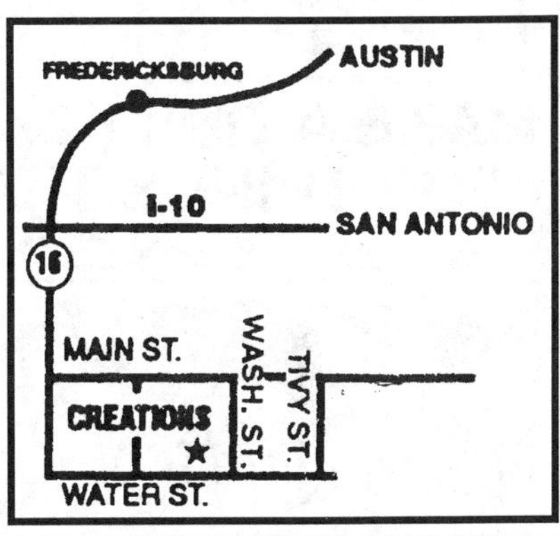

E-Mail: creation@hilconet.com
Web Site: www.creations-online.com

Mon - Sat
9:30 - 5:30

Converse, TX #25

Tues - Fri 1 - 5
Sat 10 - 3

General Store/Quilt Studio

305 S. Seguin 78109
(210) 659-7278
Owners: Rosalie & Les Bourland
Est: 1985 2094 sq.ft.

400 Bolts 100% Cotton Fabric, Books, Patterns, Quilt Frames, Batting and other supplies. Quilt Classes.

Victoria, TX #26

Mon - Fri 10 - 5:30
Sat 10 - 2

Quilters Patch

205 N. Star, Suite Q 77904
(512) 578-0380
E-Mail: qpatch@ibm.net
Owners: Karen Leach & Sherry Ware
Est: 1996 2000 sq.ft. 2000 Bolts

2000 Bolts of Cotton Fabric, Hoffman, Moda, RJR, Aunt Graces, Kaufman, Hi-Fashion, Batiks, P&B, & Kona Bay. Located off Hwy. 77

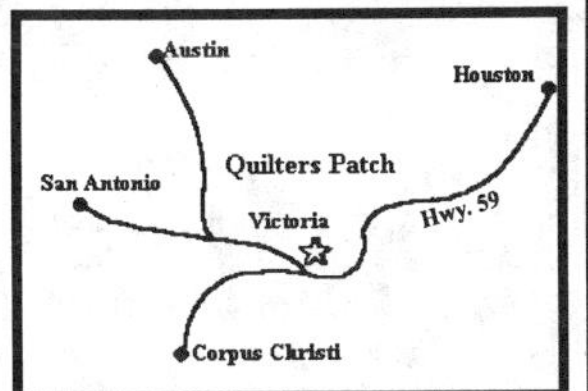

Harlingen, TX #27

Mon - Sat 9:30 - 6

SCAIEFS FABRICS

805 S. Dixieland Rd. 78552
(956) 425-4082 or (800) 221-1-SEW
Est: 1978

Home of Bernina, New Home, Pacesetter by Brother. A fabulous assortment of good quilting cottons - color sorted. Plus threads, cutters, mats, templates, patterns, books, and sewing machine accessories.

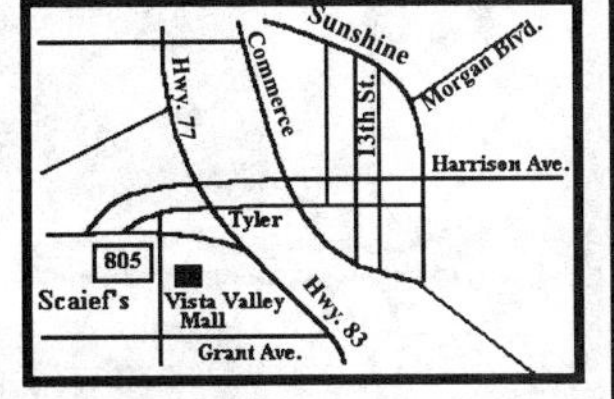

Rockport, TX #28

Mon - Fri 10 - 5
Sat 10 - 4

Golden Needles & Quilts

701 N. Allen 78382
(512) 729-7873 Fax: Same
E-Mail: KTSTAN@aol.com
Owner: Kay Stanley
Est: 1989 2800 sq.ft. 1000+ Bolts

Original Blocks of the Month & Patterns. 100% cotton fabrics, books, notions. Custom Machine Quilting. Silk ribbon, cross stitch, yarns needlework supplies.

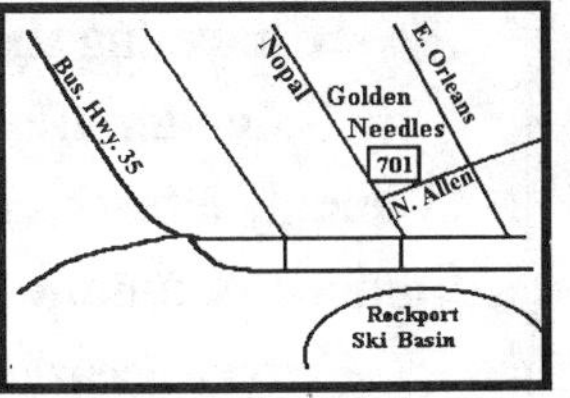

Your Complete Quilting Shop

Corpus Christi, TX #29

The Quilt Bee

Mon - Fri 9 - 5
Sat 9 - 3

(512) 225-4493 or
(800) 527-4515
Mail Orders Welcome
Est: 1990

6410 Weber #13

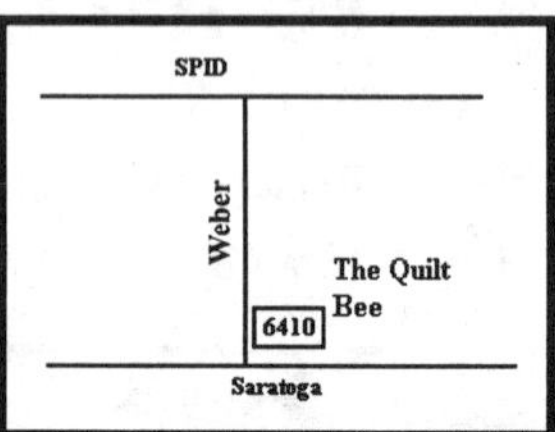

Patterns, Notions, Books, Fabric & Classes

Janome-New Home Sewing Machines

MAKE A QUILT . . .TAKE TIME FOR THINGS THAT MATTER

Corpus Christi, TX #30

Mon - Fri 10 - 6
Sat 10 - 5

The Quilt Cottage

5433 S. Staples 78411
(512) 985-0908
Owner: Lynda Butler
Est: 1994 1600 sq.ft.

A very warm & friendly shop. We have over 1500 bolts all cotton fabric. Loads of Books, Patterns, Notions, Classes, etc. Professional Machine Quilting

Staples
The Quilt Cottage
5433
S.P.I.D.
Everhart
Bonner
Holly

Bay City, TX #31

Mon - Sat 9 - 4
Thurs til 7

Bailey Mercantile

1732 6th St. 77414
(409) 244-8420 Fax: (409) 244-8479
E-Mail: rgbailey@compuserve.com
Web Site: www.baileyhouse.com Est: 1996
Owner: Sue Bailey 3000 sq.ft. 1500 Bolts

Great selection of 100% cotton fabrics. Quilting supplies, books, notions, classes. New Home Machines. Call or write for newsletter.

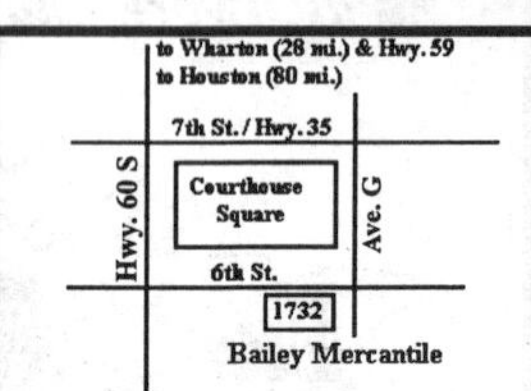

Bay City, TX #32

Mon - Sat 9:30 - 7:30
Most Sun 1 - 5:30

Threads, Quilts, & Creations

1728 6th St. 77414
(409) 245-5347 Fax: (409) 244-5886
Owner: Beverly Runyan
Est: 1995 3200 sq.ft. 1500 Bolts

Wonderful gifts. Dolls, bears, candles, etc. Over 1500 bolts of 100% Cotton Fabric. Books, patterns, notions, classes. Christmas Room. Antiques.

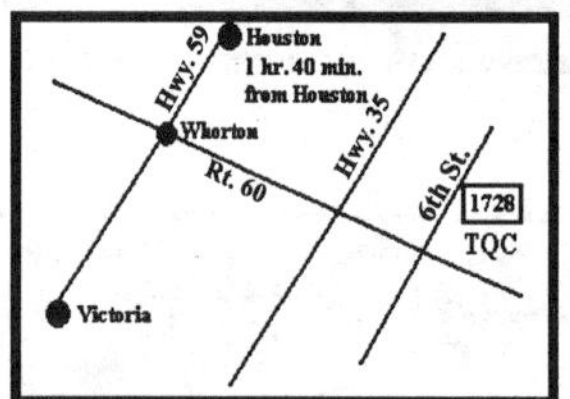

Galveston, TX #33

Quilts by the Bay

5923 Stewart Rd. 77551
(409) 740-9296 Est: 1991
Owner: Patricia Stephenson
2500 sq.ft. 1500 Bolts

Mon - Sat 10 - 5:30 Sun 12:30 - 5

Charming shop by Galveston Bay with top quality fabrics, classes, notions, & unique gifts for every occasion.

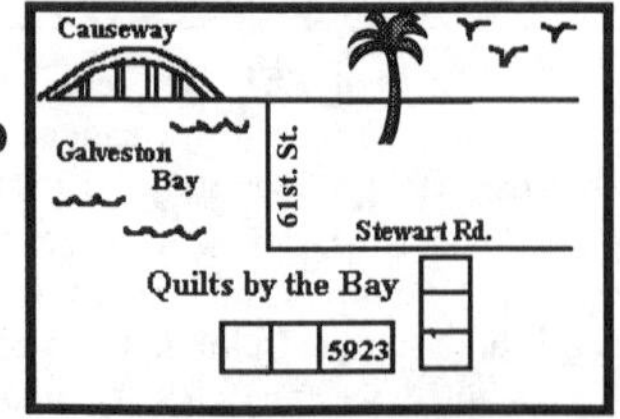

Front Porch Quilts

5050 FM 1960 W, #127 77069
(281) 444-2882 Fax: Same
Owners: Misty Odenweller & Amy Cranford
Est: 1996 3250 sq.ft. 1200+ Bolts

We are a full service quilt store with classes, fabric, notions, patterns, books, commercial quilting machine, living room & children's corner. Newsletter with Mail Order Available.

Mon - Fri 9:30 - 5
Thur til 8
Sat 10 - 5

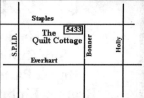

Houston, TX #34

Quilts Fabrics Gifts Classes

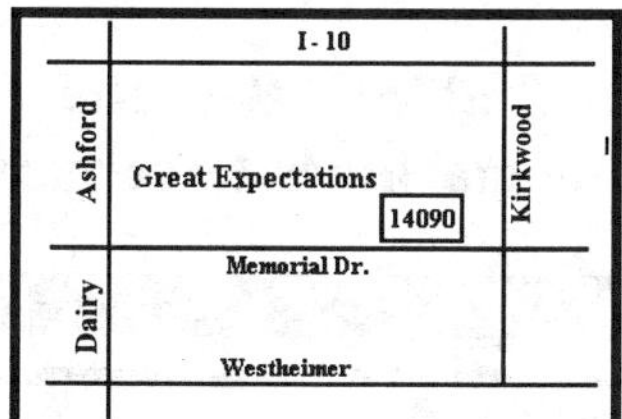

Houston, TX #35

Visit Our New Location

14090 Memorial Drive 77079
(713) 496-1366
Owner: Karey Bresenhan Est: 1974

Featured in Quilt Sampler Magazine Summer 1996

Mon - Fri 10 - 6
Wed 10 - 8 Sat 10 - 5

Houston, TX #36

Mon 10 - 9
Tues - Sat
10 - 4

Quilt Quarters

1410 B Blalock 77055
Off I - 10
(713) 468-5886
Owner: Kay Tanner
Est: 1986 2400 sq.ft.

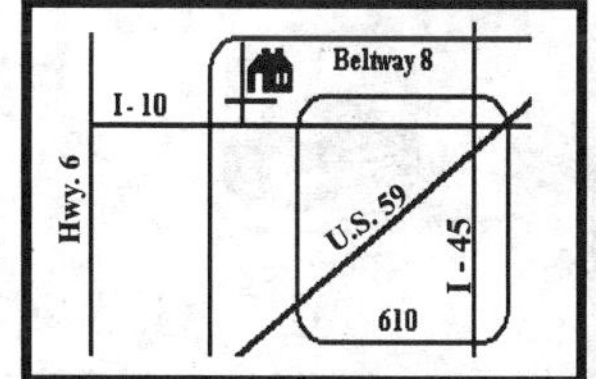

Friendly, helpful, All cotton fabrics, large book & stencil selection, silk ribbon supplies.
Services: Restoration & Repair, Appraisals, Basting. Let us quilt your top.

Katy, TX #37

Mon 10 - 7
Tues - Fri
10 - 4:30
Sat 10 - 3

Quilt 'n Sew Studio

1841 N. Mason Rd. 77449
(281) 347-0470 Fax: (281) 347-0474
Owners: Terri Burton
Est: 1993 1895 sq.ft.

100% cotton Fabrics, Quilting supplies, books, patterns, kits, classes (kids too!).
We Quilt - Quilt Tops in the Shop!
Custom Quilting

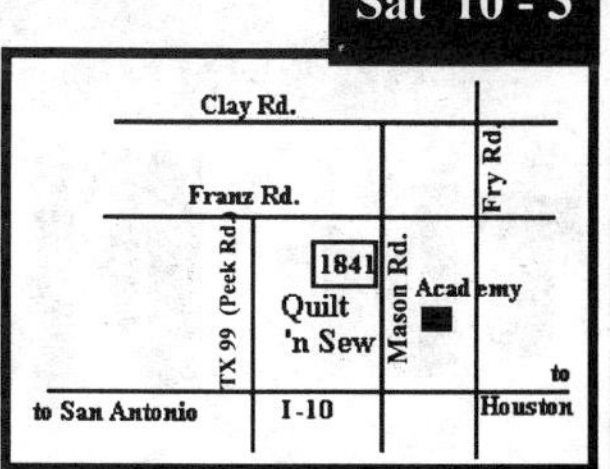

Friendswood, TX #38

Mon - Fri
10 - 5:30
Tues til 7
Sat 10 - 4

Quakertown Quilts

607 S. Friendswood Dr. 77546
(281) 996-1756 Fax: (281) 648-9090
Owner: Pat Forke Est: 1988 3000 sq.ft.

Complete Quilt Shop.
1400+ bolts of cotton fabric.
Books, Patterns, Notions & Gift Items
Blocks of the Month
Wholesale inquiries welcome.

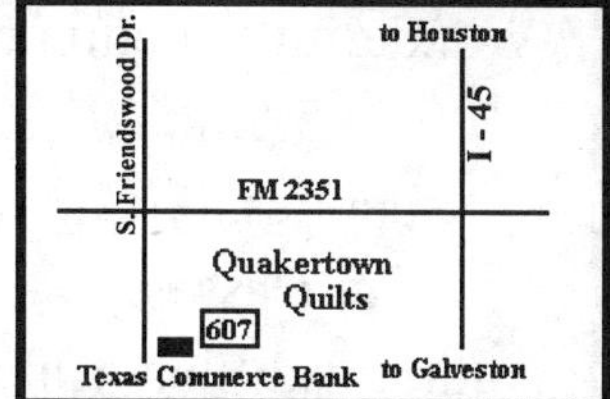

La Porte, TX #39

Mon - Sat
10 - 5

The Painted Pony 'N Quilts

1015 S. Broadway 77571
(281) 471-5735 Fax: (281) 471-1713
E-Mail: ppnq@aol.com
Owner: Sherrie S. Thomas Est: 1986

5000+ top name quilting fabrics. Extensive selection Reproductions, Plaids, Notions, Gifts. Janome New Home Dealer. Friendly, Knowledgeable staff to assist in all areas.

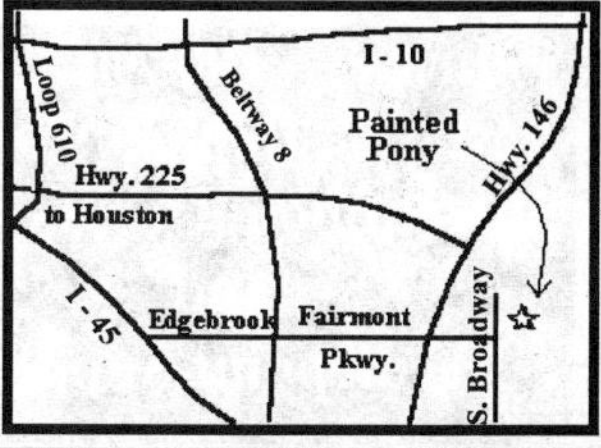

Spring, TX #40

Juliene's Quilts

26303 Preston #B & C 77373
(281) 355-9820
or (800) 976-0633
Owners: Juliene & John Pickens
Est: 1993 2400 sq.ft.

Tues - Sat
10 - 5
Sun 12 - 5

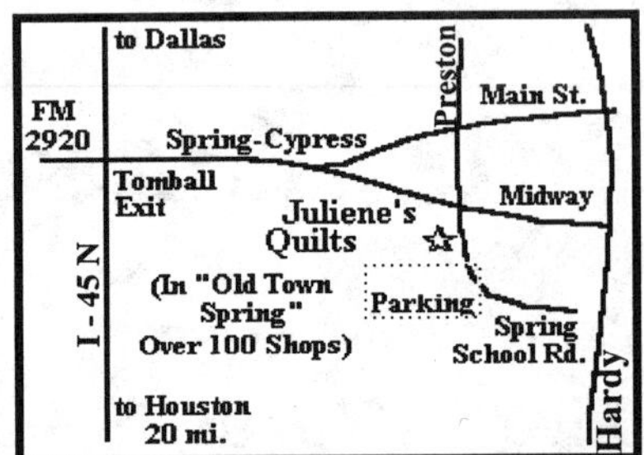

- Fabrics (2500 Bolts)
- Patterns & Notions
- Great Selection of Buttons
- Quilt Frames, Racks, Hoops & Hangers
- Classes or Individual Instruction
- Authorized Viking Dealer
- Hand Guided Machine Quilting (Pantograph, Outlining or Freehand) Send Us Your Tops
- Quilted Gifts, Collectibles
- Collector Thimbles
- Located in Historic Old Town Spring amongst 150 other great shops.

Humble, TX #41

It's A Stitch

(281) 446-4999
9759 FM 1960 Bypass
77338
Owners: Judy
& John Curtis
Est: 1992 3000 sq.ft.

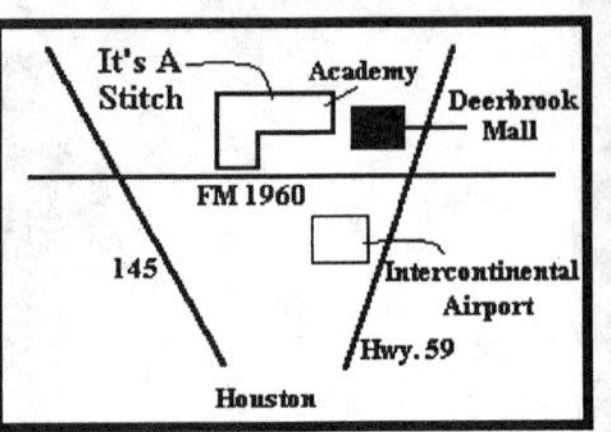

Mon - Fri
10 - 5:30
Sat 10 - 5
Sun 12 - 5

- Large selection of quilting fabrics
- Patterns, books, notions
- Classes
- Bernina, Pfaff and Bernette sewing machines & sergers

Beaumont, TX #42

The Piecemaker

Mon - Fri 10 - 5 Sat 10 - 3

3677 Calder Ave. 77706
(409) 835-4736
Owner: Noel Ann McCord

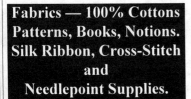

Fabrics — 100% Cottons
Patterns, Books, Notions.
Silk Ribbon, Cross-Stitch
and
Needlepoint Supplies.

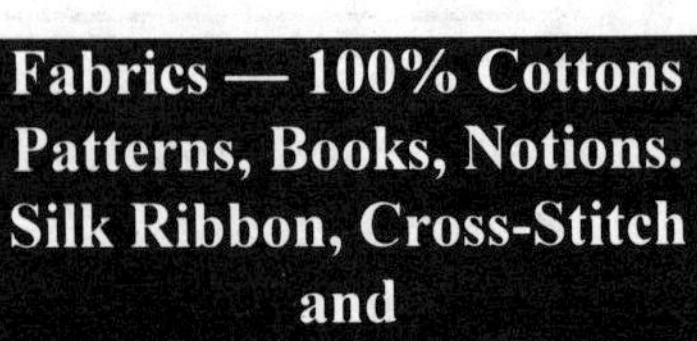

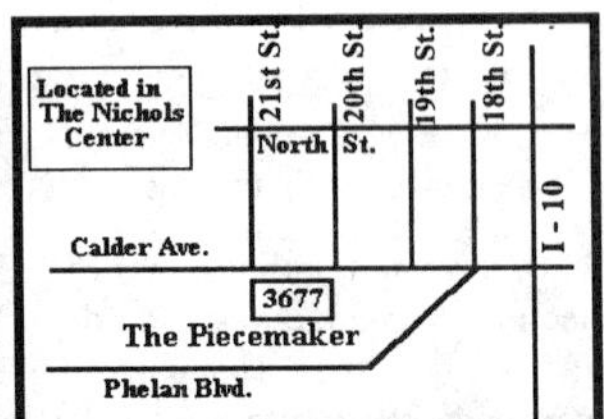

Mon - Sat 10 - 5

502 E. Goode, P.O. Box 1190 75783
(903) 763-5048 Fax: (903) 763-4683
E-Mail: stitchin@stitchinheaven.com
Owner: Debby Luttrell Est: 1996 2500 sq.ft.
Visit our Web-Site at: www.stitchinheaven.com

Quitman, TX #43

Wonderful selection of 100% cotton fabrics, supplies, books & classes.
Authorized Elna dealer.
Newsletter Available.

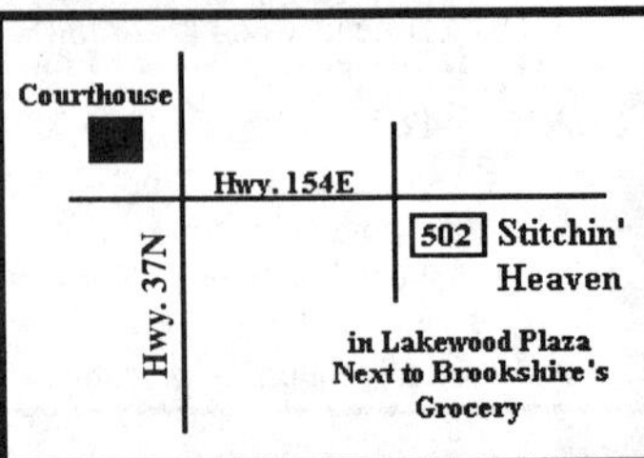

The Woodlands, TX #44

Mon - Sat 9 - 5

Plain & Fancy

418 Sawdust Rd.
77380
(281) 367-1021
Owner: Sandra Contestabile

Largest Selection of Fabric in Houston

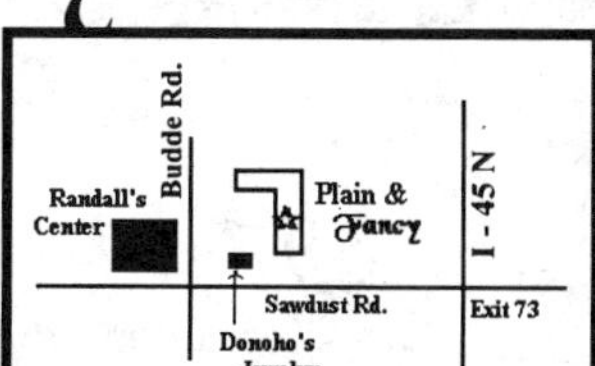

Livingston, TX #45

Mon - Fri 8 - 5:30 Sat 8 - 1

Jean's Corner of Feeder's Supply

712 N. Jackson 77351
(409) 327-8817 Fax: (409) 327-6411
E-Mail: sew712@livingston.net
Owner: Jean Yarbrough

Brand name 100% cotton Fabrics
Books - Notions
New Home Sewing Machines

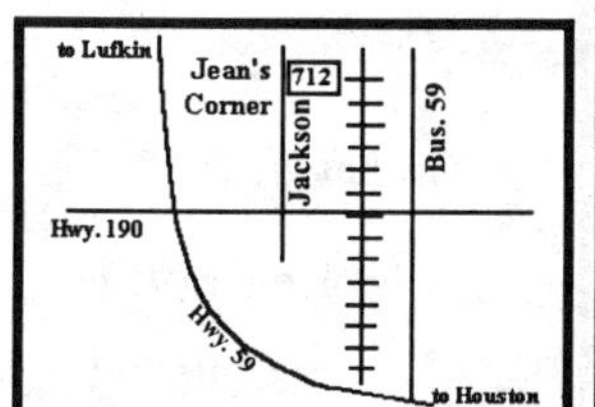

Jefferson, TX #46

Mon - Fri 10 - 5

Quilters Corner

Rt. 4, Box 1354 A 75657
(903) 665-3385
Owners: Janis Mayfield, Gail Thomas & Dorothy Thompson Est: 1990

Specializing in machine quilting. Quilting Supplies, books and fabric. Quilts of all sizes. Crafts and antiques for sale.

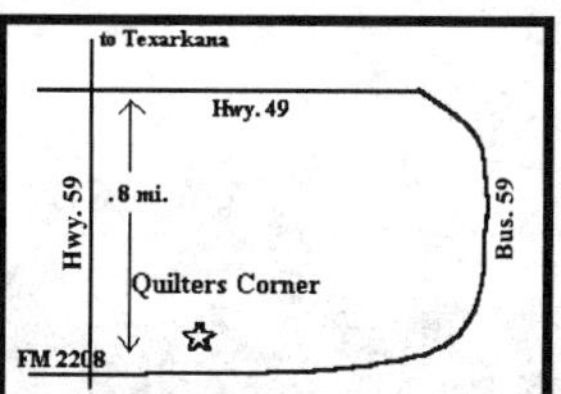

Canton, TX #47

Tues - Sat 10 - 5 Wed 10 - 4

Sew Wright Designs & Gifts

100 W. Dallas 75103
(903) 567-1062 or (800) 480-2739
Fax: (903) 887-6644
E-Mail: swfabrics@aol.com
Owner: Greg & Kim Wright

Quilting, Crafts, Wearables. Needlearts—Cross Stitch, Needlepoint, Hardanger. Fabrics, Notions, Patterns & Classes.

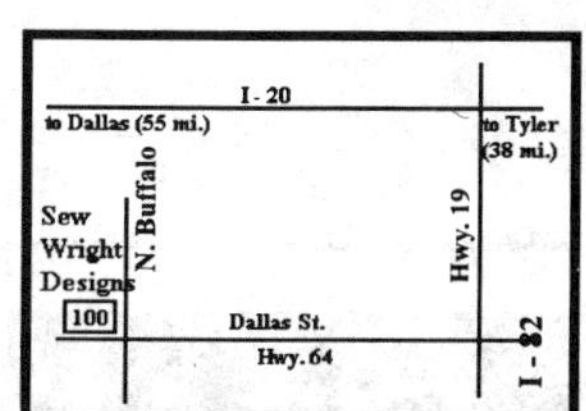

Calico Junction

Mon - Fri 10 - 5:30 Sat 10 - 5

(903) 342-3399

107 E. Elm St. 75494

5000 sq.ft. 1000 Bolts

Fax: (903) 342-3399 E-Mail: ksmisek@bluebonnet.net

Winnsboro, TX #48

Sewing Notions * Patterns * Classes * Gifts * Antiques * Cappucino & Pie * Quilts * Antique Sewing Machines * Custom Machine Quilting

Calico Junction offers excellent Custom Monogramming by Marilyn
(903) 342-3477 or (800) 957-7607

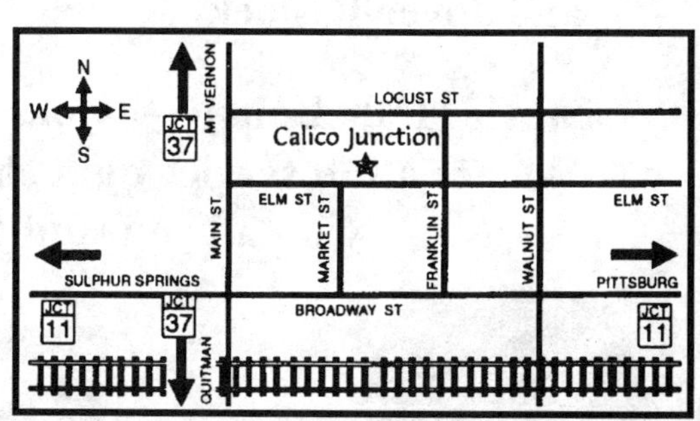

When you're planning a trip to pass thru East Texas, call and we'll send you our newsletter...

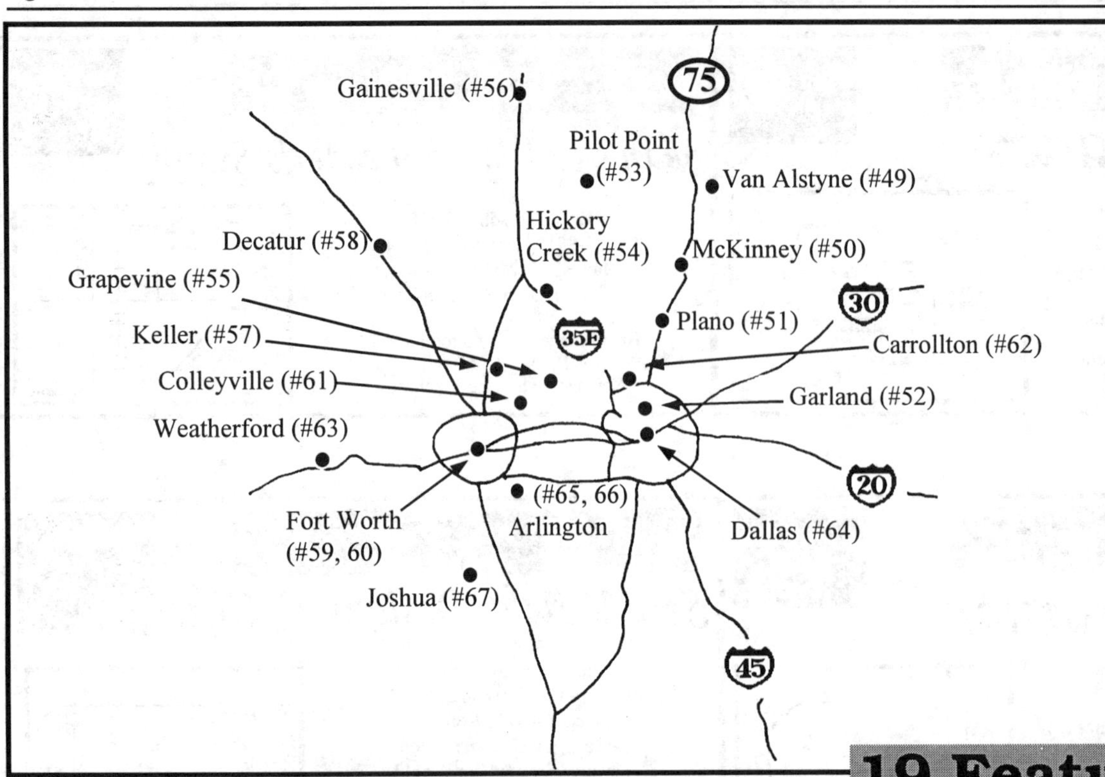

19 Featured Shops

Dallas / Fort Worth Area

Van Alstyne, TX #49

204 E. Jefferson
P.O. Box 1236
75495
(800) 482-5023
E-Mail: chqs@airmail.net
Owners: Roxanne Rentzel and Joyce Kislack

Carriage House Quilt Shoppe

Fabric (1500 Bolts) — Books — Classes — Notions
We are a full service quilt shop that can help you with all your quilting needs.

Mon - Sat 10 - 5

12 Miles North of McKinney on The Square Downtown

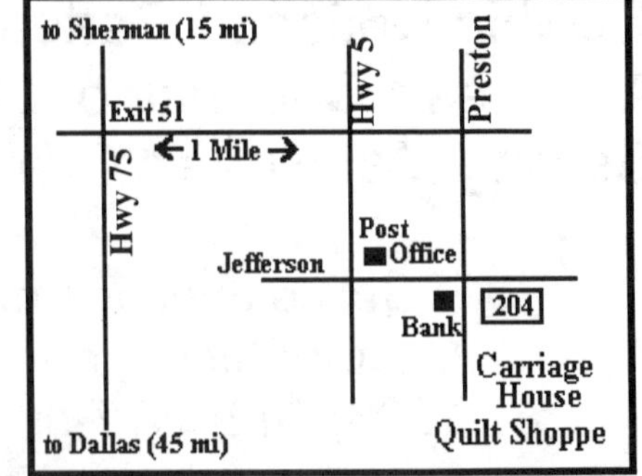

- 100% Cotton Fabric - Classes - Notions -

- 100% Cotton Fabric - Patterns - Classes - Notions - Embroidery - Gifts -

McKinney, TX #50

Open Late Mondays
9:30AM-9:00PM
Tuesday-Saturday
9:30AM-5:00PM

215 E. Louisiana St. McKinney, Texas 75069
Metro 972-562-7700 Fax 972-548-8008

EST: 1989 **6850 SQ.FT.**

Owners: Sharon Blevins, Dan & Jane Mitchell

30 Minutes North of Dallas on Hwy 75

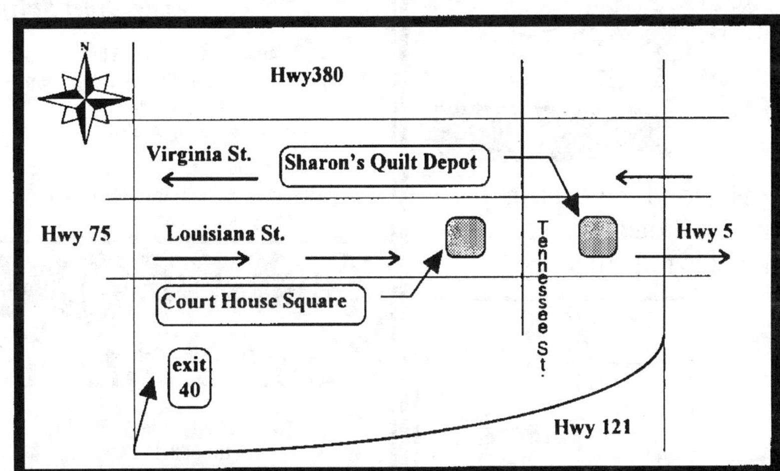

Great friendly knowledgable employees...willing to help you or just ooh & aah. Located in Historic downtown McKinney among many antique and specialty stores.

Visa, Mastercard, Discover Accepted

- 100% Cotton Fabric - Patterns - Classes - Notions - Embroidery - Gifts -

- 100% Cotton Fabric - Classes - Notions -

Country Calico's Quilt Shop

701 E. Plano Pkwy. #110
Plano, Texas 75074
(972) 423-2499
(972) 509-2721(fax)

A LARGE, BRIGHT, AIRY SHOP LOADED WITH ALL THE NEWEST QUILTING BOOKS AND NOTIONS

THE LATEST FABRIC LINES, INCLUDING AUNT GRACE'S, THIMBLEBERRIES, MODA, BENARTEX

- *over 2500 bolts*
- *knowledgeable, friendly staff*
- *open Sundays*
- *open Monday evenings*
- *lots of flannels*
- *free pattern of the month*
- *numerous classes ranging from beginner to advanced*
- *Frequent Shopper Card*

#51

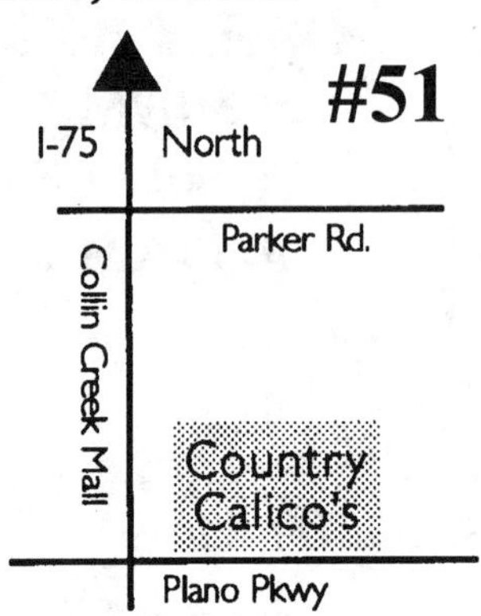

EASY ACCESS TO I-75

Garland, TX #52

Mon - Fri 10 - 5
Sat 10 - 3

Suzy's

111 North 6th 75040
(972) 272-8180
Owner: Suzanne Cook
Est: 1989 4200 sq.ft.

A Complete Quilt Shop
Gifts & Accessories, Candles, Classes

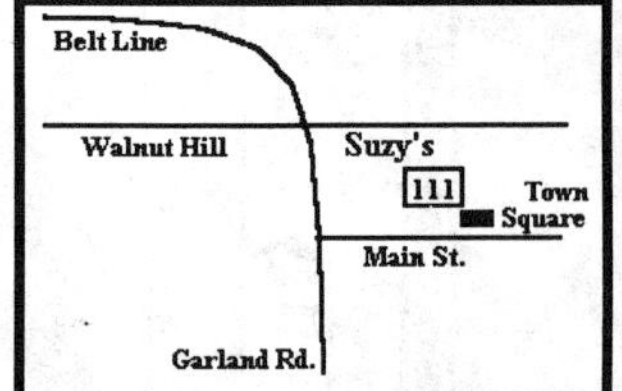

Pilot Point, TX #53

Mon - Fri 9:30 - 5
Sat 9:30 - 3

Stitching Post

1045 S. Hwy. 377, P.O. Box 678 76258
(940) 686-5847 Fax: (940) 686-2783
E-Mail: spgraves@gte.net
Owner: Donna Graves 3000+ Bolts

Large selection of fabric, books and quilting supplies. Mail order available.

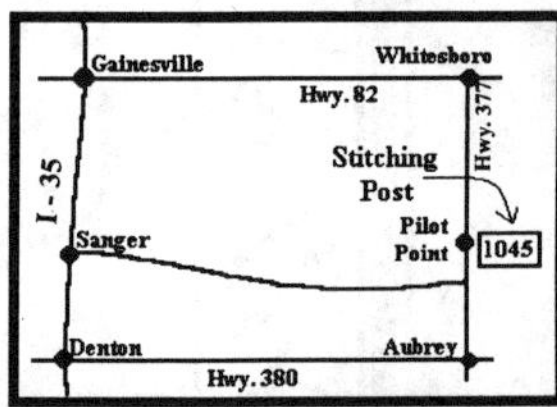

Quilt Country

6060-B S. Stemmons 75065
(940) 321-9216

Mon - Sat 10 - 5

Lots of original patterns, kitted projects, and beautiful models compliment a broad range of fabric inventory from plaids to batiks.

Owner: Sandy Brawner

Fax: (940) 497-2486
E-Mail:
quiltcountry@centuryinter.net
Est: 1995 3000 sq.ft. 1700+ Bolts

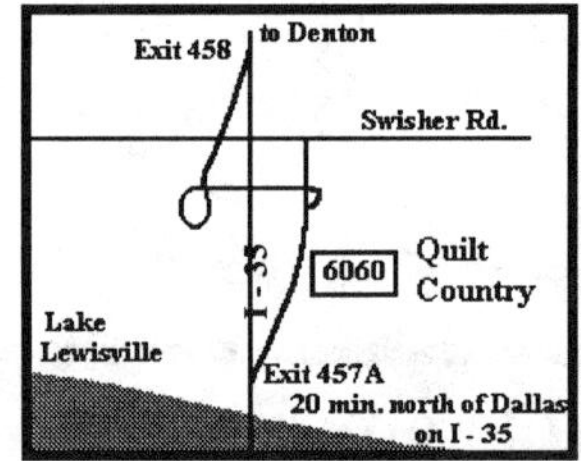

Hickory Creek, TX #54

Grapevine, TX #55

Mon - Fri 10 - 5
Sat 10 - 4

2-Sisters' Quilts
and Other Stuff

408 S. Main 76051
(817) 488-0144 E-Mail: 2sisters@gte.net
Owner: Linda Morrell
1 exit from DFW airport

2 minutes from airport.
Fabrics, classes, notions, gifts & quilts.
Friendly, knowledgeable staff.

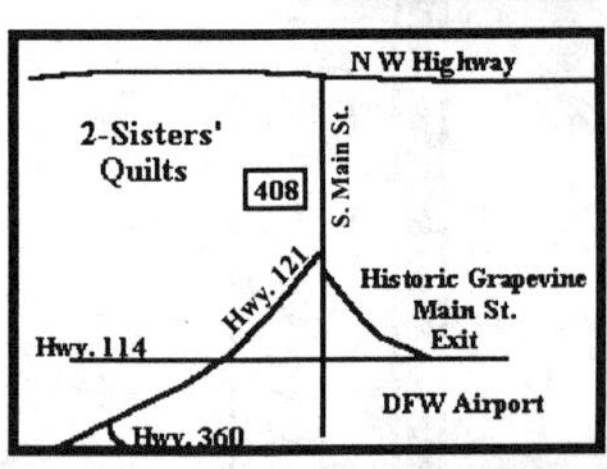

Gainesville, TX #56

Tues - Sat 10 - 5

Pass Time Fabrics

1218 East California 76240
(940) 668-1747
Owner: Fran Scott
Est: 1986

Full line of 100% cotton calicos and solids. Books, notions, patterns, classes - everything for quilters!

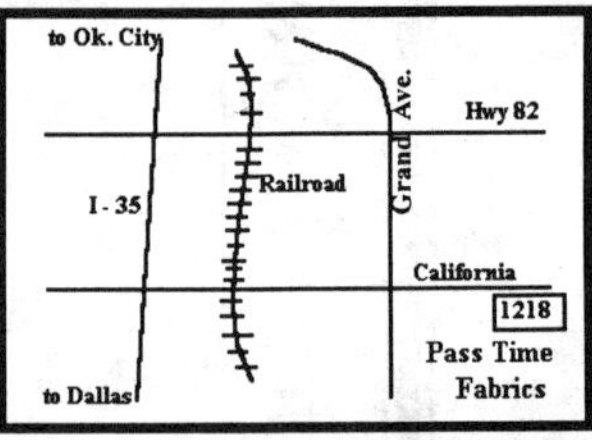

Keller, TX #57

Mon - Fri 10 - 6
Sat 10 - 3

Grandma's Quilts

111 W. Vine St 76248
(817) 431-1348
(800) 305-5547
Owner: Helen L. Madden
Est: 1991

100% Cotton Fabrics for Quilters. Notions, Patterns, Books, Etc. Etc. **Machine Quilting.**

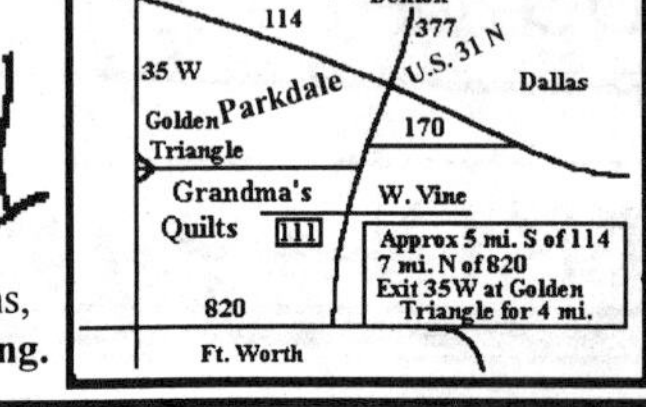

Decatur, TX #58

Mon - Sat 10 - 5:30
Thur til 7

The Nine Patch Quilt Shop

208 W. Main
(940) 627-4220 or (888) 736-5765
Fax: (940) 627-4222
Owner: Sandy Smith
Est: 1997 1800 sq.ft. 1000 Bolts

Full Service Quilt Shop

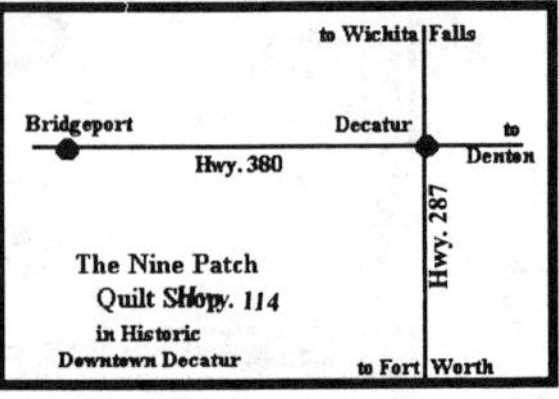

Ft. Worth, TX #59

Tues - Sat
10 - 4
Thur til 7

Cabbage Rose

Quilts & Gifts

3526 W. Vickery Blvd. 76107
(817) 377-3993
Est: 1998 5000 sq.ft.

Complete line of quilting supplies & fabric; Antique furniture; Clothing; Gifts

Exit 11
Montgomery
Downtown Ft. Worth
I - 30
Cabbage Rows
3526
Vickery Blvd.
I - 35W

Fort Worth, TX #60

Tues - Fri
10 - 5:30
Sat 10 - 3
or by Appt.

Quilting by Design

5628-B Camp Bowie Blvd. 76107
(817) 735-8686
E-Mail: mitzib@hawkpci.net
Owner: Mitzi Boyd

Complete Custom Hand-Guided Machine Quilting Service. Stand-Up (commercial) machine classes & time rental. We finish and repair Antique Quilts.

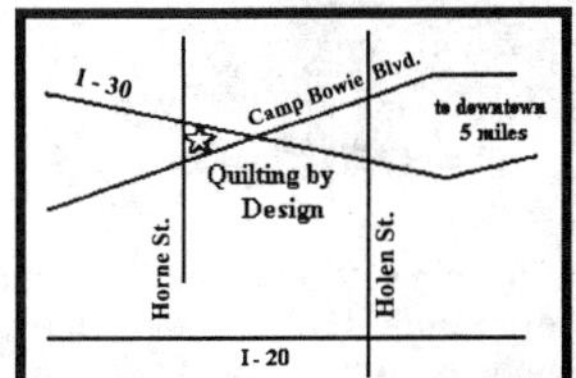

Colleyville, TX #61

Mon & Thur
9 - 6
Tues, Wed,
& Fri 9 - 5
Sat 10 - 4

Quilter's Dream

6409 Colleyville Blvd. 76054
(817) 481-7105
Owner: Beverly Ingram

We are known for our knowledgeable, friendly staff and large selection of beautiful 100% cotton fabrics, books & notions.

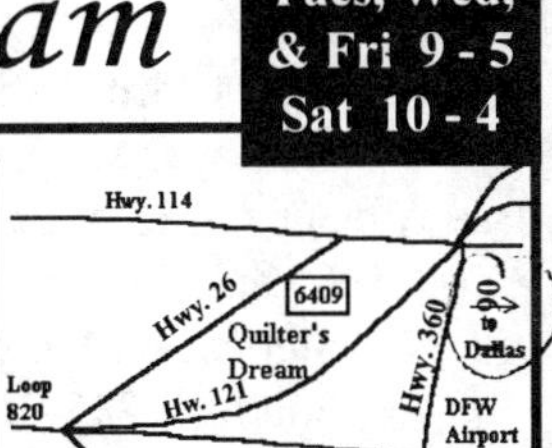

Carrollton, TX #62

Mon - Sat
10 - 5
Thurs til 7

The Old Craft Store

1110 W. Main Street 75006
(972) 242-9111 Fax: (972) 245-0407
Owner: Melba Hamrick
Est: 1971 3000 sq.ft. 2500 Bolts

100% Cottons, full-service quilt shop. Patterns, notions - nestled among antiques & old-fashioned U.S. Post Office.

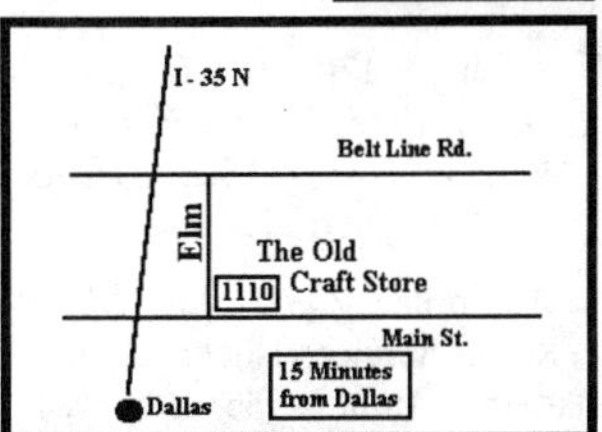

Weatherford, TX #63

Grandma Lynn's Quilts

133 N. Waco St. 76086
(817) 599-4114
Owner: Lynn Harris
Est: 1994 1200+ Bolts

- Exclusive Pre-cut Quilt Kits - Free Brochure
- Over 1200 bolts 100% Cotton Quilt Fabrics including Batiks & Designer Fabrics
- Hundreds of Books & Patterns
- Stencils & Batting
- Quilting Supplies
- Photo Transfer Service
- Mail Order Available

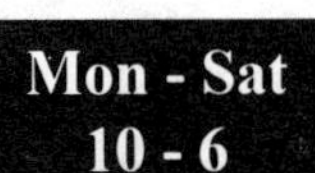

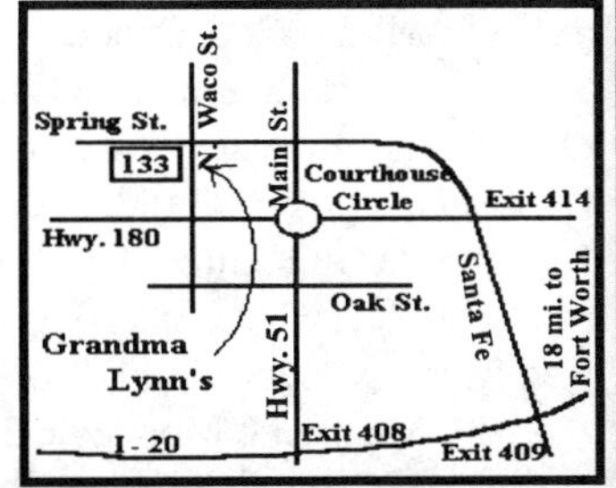

Dallas, TX #64

9658 Plano Rd. 75238
(214) 343-1440
or (888) 494-0291
Fax: (214) 343-2223
E-Mail:
KBaird4939@aol.com
Owner: Kelly J. Baird
Est: 1994 3000 sq.ft.

If you love color, this is the place to find it! 3000 bolts of bright, fun, unusual quilting fabrics. 150+ bolts of balis and batiks. Extensive notions, books and patterns. Home of Creative Copy™ Textile Transfer Papers, making transferring photos to fabric fun and easy.

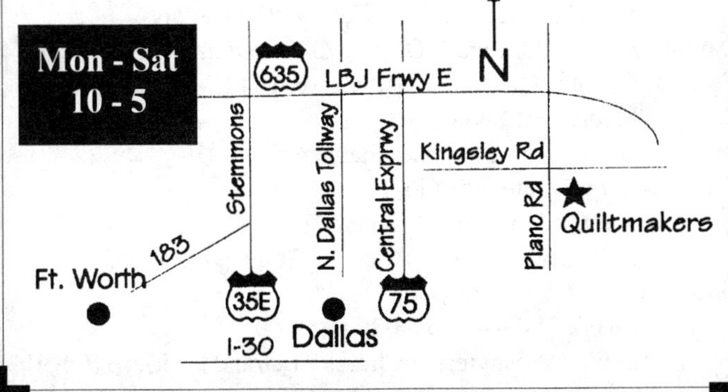

Arlington, TX #65

Abram House Quilt Shop

1210 W. Abram
76013
(817) 277-4749
2100+ sq.ft.

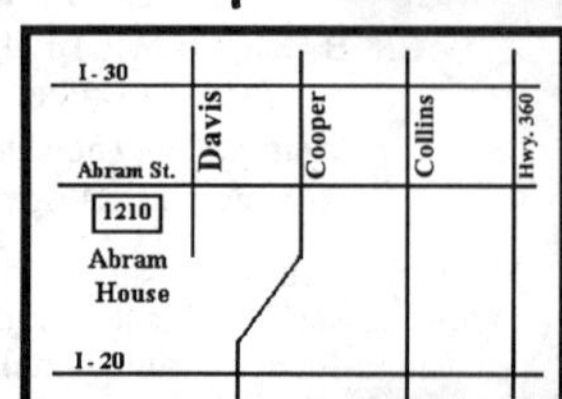

Charming 1903 house filled with large selection of quality 100% cotton fabrics. Books and notions. Antiques and gifts.

Arlington, TX #66

Mon - Sat
10 - 5

Sewing Machine Museum

804 W. Abram St. 76013
(817) 275-0971
Owners: Frank & Halaina Smith

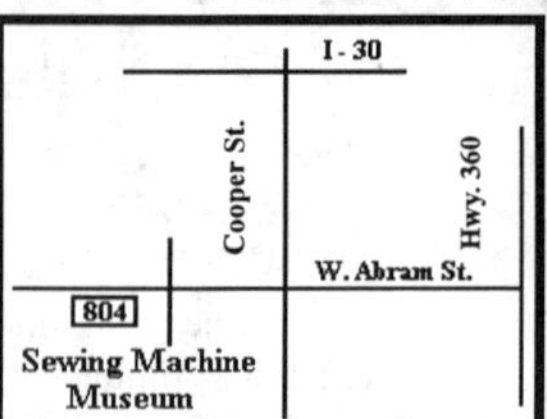

America's First Sewing Machine Museum. We sell "Feather Weights" and the new replica "Little John". 30 Years in the Making. 8 Years at present location. 156 machines displayed from 1853

Joshua, TX #67

Mon - Fri
10 - 5:30
Thur til 9
Sat 9 - 5

Sandy's Quilt Shop

301 B 12th St., P.O. Box 448 76058
(817) 558-2882 or (800) 775-7034
Owner: Sandy Hammons
Est: 1996 1200 sq.ft. 2500 Bolts

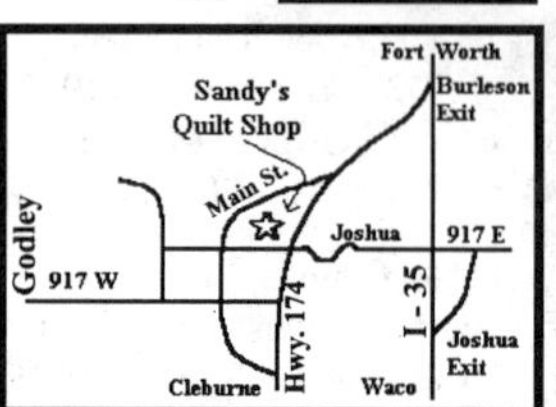

Authorized Pfaff Sewing Machine Sales and Repair Service. Books, Quilting Notions and Patterns. At the corner of Hwy. 174 & Hwy. 917

Texas Guilds:

Denton Quilt Guild, Denton
McKinney Quilter's Guild, McKinney
Quilter's Guild of Arlington, Arlington
Allen Quilt Guild, Allen
  Meets: 3rd Thurs. at First Utd. Methodist Churc, Hwy. 5
High Plains Quilters Guild, 2433 I-40 West, Amarillo, 79109
New Horizons Quilt Guild, 4224 S. Van Buren, Amarillo, 79110
  Meets: 1st Thursday 7 p.m.
  at Amarillo Federated Women's Bldg., East Room
Arlington Guild, Arlington
  Meets: 2nd Tuesday 7 p.m.
  at Vandergriff Convention Center, 2800 S. Center St.
Austin Area Quilt Guild, P.O. Box 5757, Austin, 78763
  Meets: 1st Monday 7 p.m.
  at Faith Lutheran Church, 6600 Woodrow
Memory Makers Quilt Guild, 1732 6th St., Bay City, 77414
  Meets: Last Wednesday
Golden Triangle Quilt Guild, Beaumont
Coastal Beand Quilt Guild, Box 181074, Corpus Christi, 78480
  Meets: 2nd Thursday at Ethel Eyerly Community Center
Quilters Guild of Dallas, 15775 N. Hillcrest, Dallas, 75248
  Meets: 1st Thursday 7 p.m. at Congressional Shearith Isreal, Kaplan Hall, 9401 Douglas
Dayton Quilt Guild, Inc., P.O. Box 231, Dayton, 77535
Town & Country Quilt Club, Rt. 4, Box 104 HV, Dublin, 76446
  Meets: 1st Saturday 1 p.m.
  at The Flying Needle, Stephenville
Trinity Valley Quilters' Guild, Fort Worth
  Meets: 3rd Friday 9:30 am
  at Central Christian Church, 3205 Hamilton St.
Grand Prairie, Grand Prairie
  Meets: 1st Monday 7:30 p.m.
  at First Presbyterian Church of Grand Prairie, 310 SW 3rd
Homespun Quilter's Guild, P.O. Box 2228, Hewitt, 76643
  Meets: 4th Monday 7 p.m. at Harrison Senior Citizen's Center, 1716 N. 42nd St., Waco
The West Houston Q. G., 17731 Mossy Ridge Ln., Houston, 77095
  Meets: 3rd Wednesday 7 p.m.
  at Bear Creek Ext. Center, 2 Abercrombie
Bay Area Q. G., 1094 Scarsdale, P.O. Box M237, Houston, 77089
  Meets: Evening--3rd Wednesday 7 p.m. at J D Bruce Student Building (Second Floor), San Jacinto College South, 13735 Beamer Rd. Daytime-- 3rd Thursday 10 a.m. at M.U.D. Building, 11610 Sageyork
Jefferson Quilt Guild, Jefferson
  Meets: 3rd Tuesday 10 a.m. at Quilters Corner
Crossroads to Texas, Killeen
  Meets: 2nd and 4th Monday
  at 7 p.m. at 1st United Methodist Church
Plantation Quilt Guild, Lake Jackson Meets: 2nd Tuesday
Keystone Square Quilters, 410 E. 3rd St., Lampasas, 76550
  Meets: Every Wednesday 10 a.m. at M.J.'s Fabrics
Lampasas Quilt Guild, 303 South Western, Lampasas, 76550
Land O' Lakes Quilt Guild, Lewisville
  Meets: 1st Monday 7 p.m.
  at Garden Ridge Church of Christ, Main & Garden Ridge
Lakeview Quilters Guild, P.O. Box 580365, Nassau Bay, 77258
  Meets: 3rd Monday 7 p.m.
  at St. Paul's Catholic Church, 18223 Point Lookout
Medina County Quilters Guild, Natalia
Quilters Guild of Plano, P.O. Box 260216, Plano, 75026
  Meets: 2nd Thursday 7:30 p.m.
  at Pitman Church of Christ, 1815 W. 15th St.
Alamo Heritage Quilter's Guild, P.O. Box 781134, San Antonio
Greater San Antonio QG, P.O. Box 65124, San Antonio, 78265
Wildflower Quilt Guild, 3011 N. 3rd., Temple
  Meets: 3rd Tuesday 6:30 p.m.
  at Cultural Activity Center
Woodlands Area Quilt Guild, Box 8494, The Woodlands, 77381
  Meets: 1st Wednesday at South Montgomery County Community Center, Lake Robbins & Grogan's Mill Rds.
East Texas Quilt Guild, P.O. Box 130773, Tyler, 75713-1773
  Meets: 2nd Thursday 9:30 a.m.
  at Trinity Lutheran Church, 2001 Hunter St.
Quilt Guild of Greater Victoria, Victoria
Homespun Quilters Guild, 5009 Lake Highlands Dr., Waco, 76710
Rio Grande Quilt Guild, P.O. Box 32, Wesbaco, 78599
  Meets: 2nd Saturday 10 a.m. at First Christian Church
Red River Quilters' Guild, P.O. Box 8372, Wichita Falls, 76307
  Meets: 1st Monday 6:30 p.m.
  at Central Christian Church, 3122 Grant St, Wichita Falls.

Other Shops in Texas:

Abilene	Country Pleasures, 2508 S. 7th St.	915-676-8691
Austin	Gingers Needlearts, 5322 Cameron Rd.	512-454-5344
Austin	Quilts 'N Things, 4406 Burnet Rd.	512-451-7073
Bonham	The Quilt Cottage, 202 E. Sam Rayburn Dr.	903-583-5201
Brashear	Quilts Galore & More, 1 Main St.	903-582-2609
Burleson	Little By Little, 206 Hoover Rd., P. O. Box 2017	817-295-4416
Caldwell	My Spare Time, Rt. 3 Box 264	
Comanche	Quilts & Tops, 605 E. Central Ave.	915-356-2047
Conroe	Quilt 'N Time Sisters, 17641 Linda Ln.	409-231-3322
Dallas	The Copper Lamp, 5500 Greenville Ave. #402	214-521-3711
Fort Worth	Cherrie's Quilt Shop, 4320 Wichita St.	817-531-0074
Fort Worth	Cotton Works, 8507 Hwy. 377 S.	817-249-0424
Fredericksburg	Tea Rose Quilts & Gifts, 809 W. Main St.	830-997-9948
Killeen	Skyline Gallery & Framing, 425 N. Gray St.	817-634-6062
League City	The Fabric Hut, 2214 Fair Pointe Dr.	713-477-7531
Lewisville	The Pepper Tree, 112 W. Main St.	972-221-6345
Lockney	The Old Blue Quilt Box, 200 S. Main St.	806-652-2183
Longview	Sharman's Sewing Center, 1017 McCann Rd.	903-753-8014
Lufkin	Country Quilting & More, 1200 S. 1st. St.	409-639-1503
Memphis	Greene Dry Goods Company, 109 S. Sixth St.	806-259-2912
Monahans	Ye Olde Quilt Shoppe, 104 W. 2nd St.	915-943-5855
New Braunfels	The Quilt Barn, 186 E. Garden St. PO Box 312554	830-620-5810
Pittsburg	Quilts & More, R.R. #4, P.O. Box 264	903-856-2870
Plano	Singer & New Home Center, 2129 B W. Parker	972-596-0660
Richardson	The Fabric Affair, 339 Dal-Rich Village	972-234-1937
Richardson	MJ Designs, 970 N. Coit Rd.	214-437-2744
Richardson	Kay Fabrics, 518 W. Arapaho Rd.	972-234-5111
San Antonio	Plain Jane's Folk Art, 555 Bitters Rd.	210-496-5436
Spearman	Country Stitches, 512 S. Townsend St.	806-659-2080
Sulphur Springs	Sew Many Quilts, 101 Radio Rd. #3	903-885-8916
Sunrise Beach	Patches, 103 Sunrise Dr.	
Tyler	Granny's Needle Haus, 6004 S. Broadway Ave.	903-561-4637
Webster	Fabrics Etcetera, 571 W. Bay Area Blvd.	281-338-1904
Wichita Falls	Sewin' In Style, 4708 K-Mart Dr. #G	940-691-5575
Wimberly	The Peacemakers, R.R. # 12	

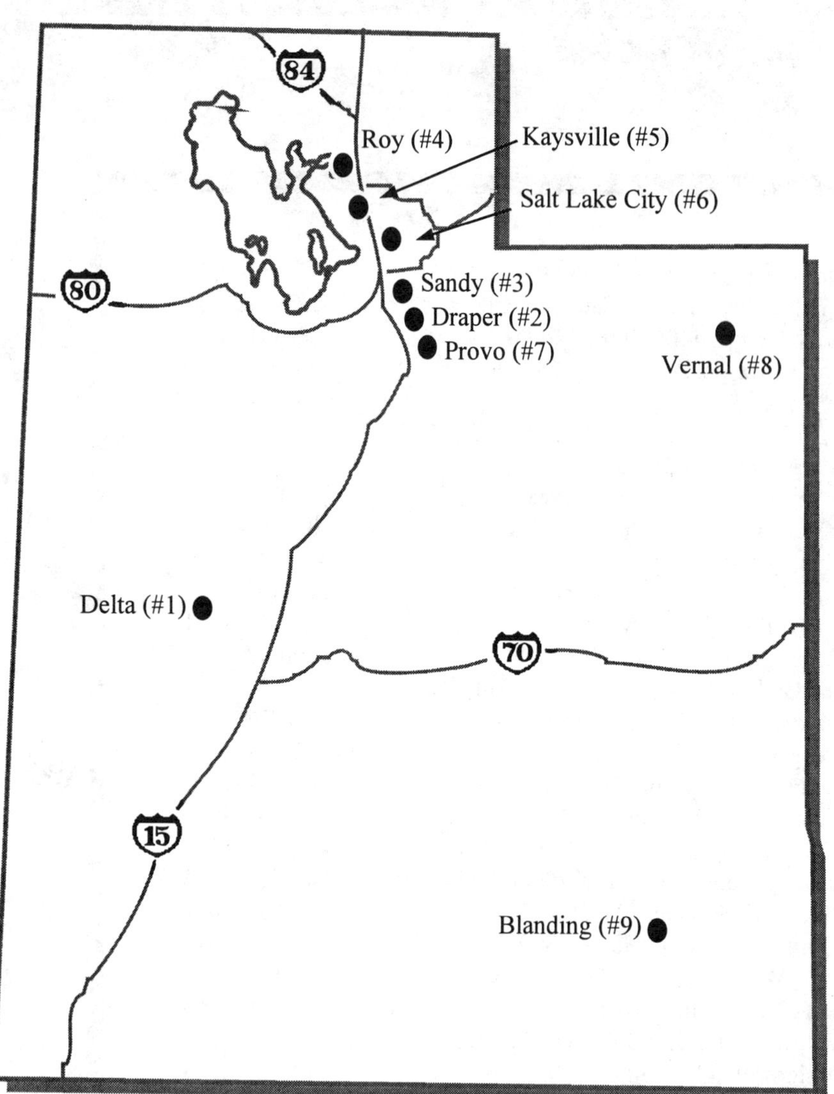

9 Featured Shops

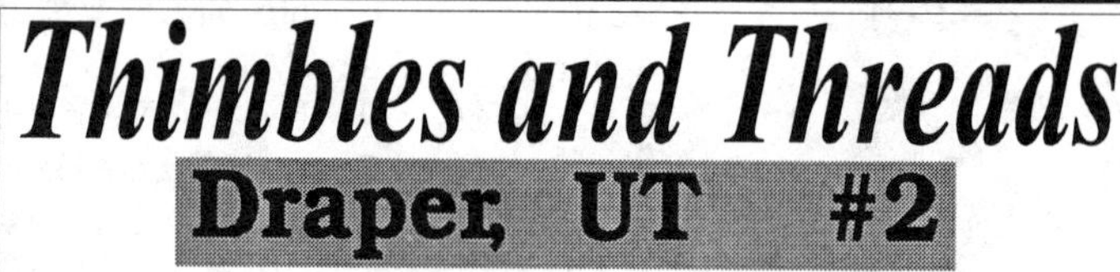

#1 in Knowledgeable, Friendly Service

12215 South 900 East 84020
115 Draper exit #294
(801) 576-0390
Est: 1994 2000 bolts

Cotton Fabrics
Wonderful Quilt Samples
Books * Kits
Classes * Supplies

Mon - Sat 10 - 5

Delightful country setting 25 min. South of S.L.C. Located in the Historical Draper Poultry Feed & Egg Warehouse built in 1910

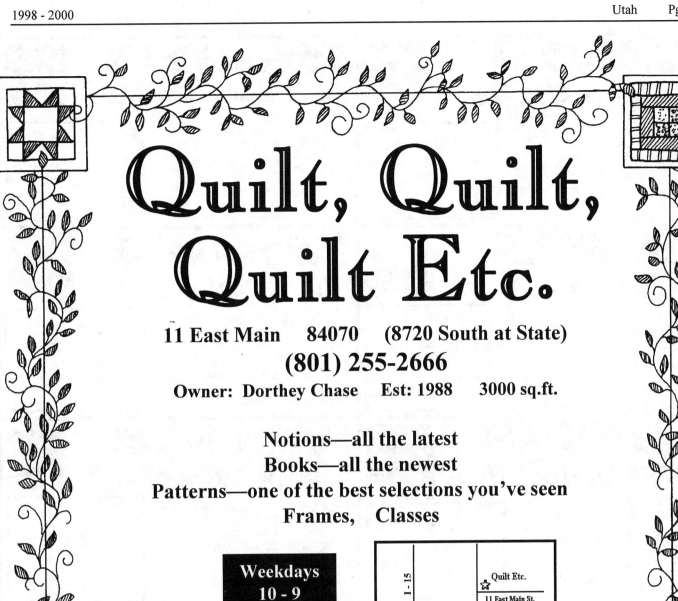

Quilt, Quilt, Quilt Etc.

11 East Main 84070 (8720 South at State)

(801) 255-2666

Owner: Dorthey Chase Est: 1988 3000 sq.ft.

Notions—all the latest
Books—all the newest
Patterns—one of the best selections you've seen
Frames, Classes

Weekdays
10 - 9
Saturdays
10 - 5

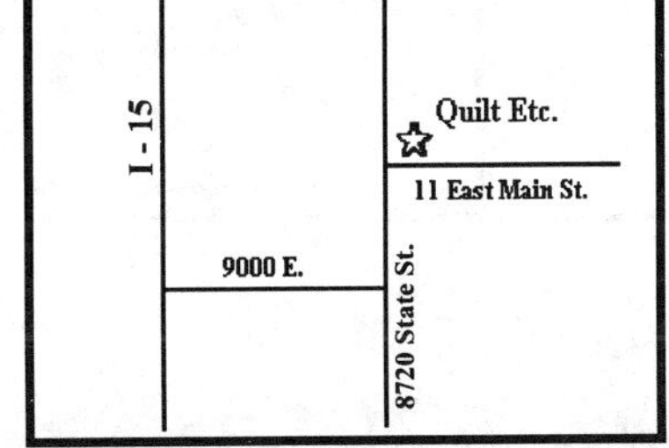

Quilt
Etc.

Sandy, UT #3

15 Minutes South of Salt Lake City

Over 9000 Bolts of Fabric

Roy, UT #4

Mon - Fri 9 - 9
Sat 9 - 7

Ben Franklin Crafts®

1946 W 5600 S 84067
(801) 825-7037 Fax: (801) 773-1666
E-Mail: mbennion@ix.netcom.com
Owners: David, Sharon, & Michael Bennion
Est: 1957 21,000 sq.ft. 2000+ Bolts

Over 2000 bolts of hand picked fabric. Great selection of sewing & quilt supplies. Quilt books and patterns, yarn. Plus much more!

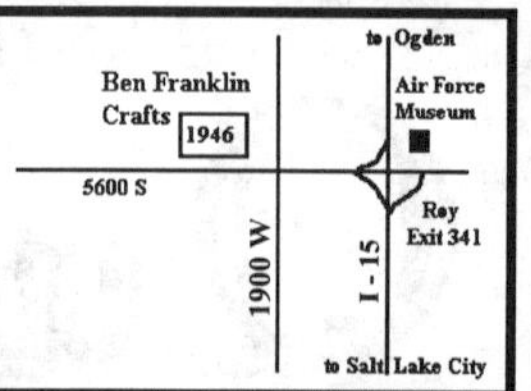

Kaysville, UT #5

Mon - Fri 9 - 9
Sat 9 - 7

Ben Franklin Crafts®

354 N. Main (801) 444-1177
Fax: (801) 444-0429
E-Mail: sbennion@ix.netcom.com
Owners: Steven & Scott Bennion
Est: 1997 20,000 sq.ft. 1500+ Bolts

Over 1500 Bolts of hand picked fabric. Great selection of sewing & quilt items. We also have floral & frame supplies.

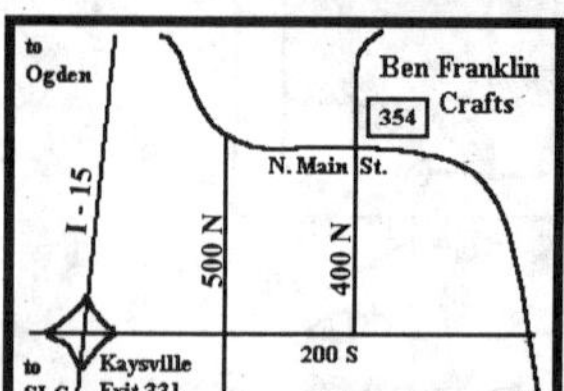

Salt Lake City, UT #6

Mon - Fri 10 - 9
Sat 10 - 7

Mormon Handicraft

36 S. State St. #220 84111
(801) 355-2141 or (800) 843-1480
Fax: (801) 531-9337 Est: 1937
E-Mail: edanzig@deseretbook.com
Web Site: www.mormonhandicraft.com

Quality handmade gifts and a wonderful selection of fabrics, patterns, books and notions for beginning to advanced quilters.

N. Temple St.
Temple Square
Church Office Bldg.
S. Temple St.
Main St.
ZCMI Mall
Mormon Handicraft
Level 2
State St.

Provo, UT #7

Mon - Sat 10 - 6

The Stitching Corner

480 N Freedom Blvd. 84601
(801) 374-1200
Owner: Scott Blackham
Est: 1990 3500 sq.ft.

Pfaff authorized dealer; 3000+ bolts of cotton; classes daily; quilting notions, patterns, threads. Knowledgeable Quilters.

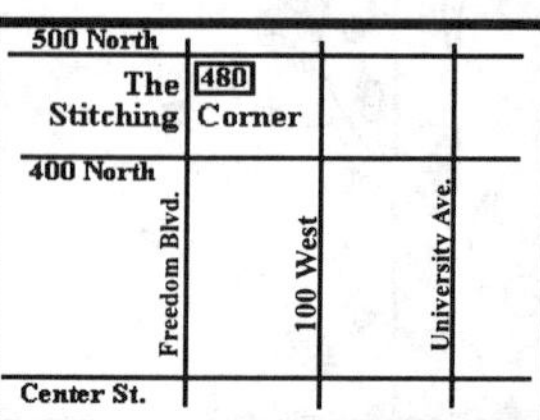

Vernal, UT #8

Mon - Fri 10 - 6
Sat 11 - 4:30

Quilted Hens

38 South 600 West
84078
(435) 789-2411

We have a simple abundance of Flannels and Quilting Cottons. Bernina Sales and Service.

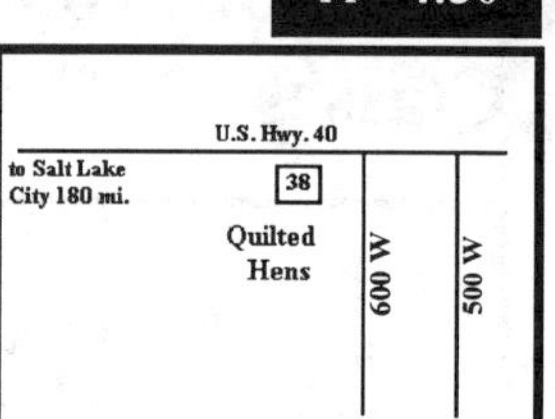

Blanding, UT #9

Mon - Sat 8 - 6

"A Stitch in Time"

82 S. Main 84511
(801) 678-2228 Fax: (801) 678-2856
Owners: Bryce & Cathy Redd
Est: 1911 2000 sq.ft.
Large selection of 100% cotton fabrics.
Quilt Books—Quilt supplies—Notions—Classes

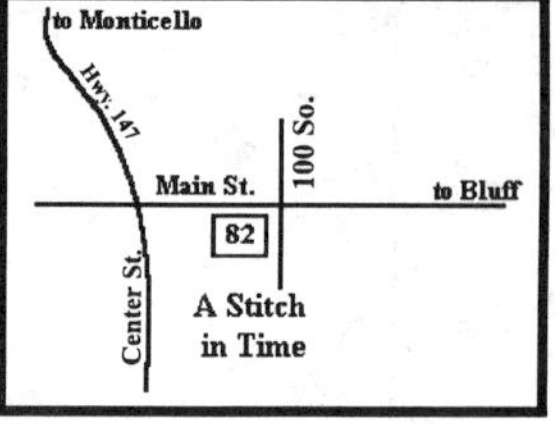

Utah Guilds:

Piece in the Valley c/o Ann Morgan, 647 E. Bristlecone, Delta, 84624
Meets: 2nd Thursday 7 p.m. at Losee Variety--Upstairs
Ogden Quilt Guild, 340 N. Washington Blvd., Ogden, 84404
Roy Pioneer Quilters, 4232 S. 2275 West, Roy, 84067
Utah Quilt Guild, P.O. Box 17032, Salt Lake City, 84117
Dixie Quilt Guild, P.O. Box 507, St. George, 84771

Other Shops in Utah:

Bountiful	Quilter's Haven, 5 Points Mall, 1642 S. Main	801-292-1846
Cedar City	Color Country Crafts, 622 S. Main	801-865-7060
Cedar City	Country Fabrics, 169 N 100 W	801-586-4544
Centerville	A Quilter's Retreat, 158 W. Parish	801-294-0640
Layton	Nuttalls' Crazy Quilt Shop, 21 E. Gentile St.	801-544-5911
Logan	Grandma's Quilts, 93 E. 100 S.	435-753-5670
Logan	Thistlehill Quilts, 7 N. Main	435-752-3225
Logan	Needles N Neighbors, 128 S. 1170 E	801-753-6589
Ogden	Bernina Sewing Center, 2318 Washington Blvd.	801-392-5081
Ogden	Gardiner's Sewing, 2233 Grant	801-394-4466
Ogden	Fibers & Twigs, 159 23rd St.	801-627-5005
Orem	Fabric Mill, 390 E 1300 S	801-225-3123
Pleasant Grove	Piece Goods Craft & Fabric, 460 W. State Rd.	801-785-0437
Providence	The Quilt House, 135 S. 100 E	801-752-5429
Provo	Fabric Mill, 90 W. Center St.	801-375-4818
Richfield	Marcia's, 44 W 100 N	801-896-8354
Roy	Marlene's Quilts, 3118 W 5200 S	801-825-0547
Salt Lake City	Quilter's Patch, 2370 S. 3600 W.	801-973-6117
Salt Lake City	Nuttall Bernina, ZCMI Mall, 36 S. State St	
Salt Lake City	Gentler Times Quilt Shop, 4880 S. Highland Circle	801-277-9233
Salt Lake City	The Grace Co.-Quilting Frames, 801 W 1850 S	801-972-5801
Sandy	Fabric Warehouse, 9251 S 700 E	801-565-8465
Sandy	The Cotton Shop, 9441 S 700 E	801-572-1412
St. George	Sew Suite, 34 W. Tabernacle #E	435-673-9117
Tremonton	Miller's Buttons & Bolts, 25 W. Main St.	435-257-5604
West Jordan	Stitching Corner, 1550 W. 7800 S.	801-566-1400
West Jordan	Village Quilt Shop, 1095 W 7800 S	801-566-1846
West Valley City	Quilt Shop, 3601 S 2700 W	801-966-7915

10 Featured Shops

Winooski (#1)
Shelburne (#2)
Stowe (#3)
Waitsfield (#4)
89
91
Rutland (#5)
Plymouth (#6)
Weston (#7)
Chester (#8)
Westminster (#10)
Wilmington (#9)

Vermont Guilds:

Champlain Valley Quilt Guild, 05482
Meets: 1st Tuesday 7 p.m.
at Essex Alliance Church,
Essex Junction

Oxbee Quilter's Guild, P.O. Box 148
Bradford, 05033

Green Mt. Quilters State Guild
P.O. Box 56, Fairfax, 05454

Heart of the Land Quilter's Guild
R.R. #1, Box 263,
Hartland, 05048

Maple Leaf Quilter's Guild, Box 7400
Mendon, 05701

Winooski, VT #1

Mon - Sat 10 - 9
Sun 12 - 5

Yankee Pride

Champlain Mill 05404
(802) 655-0500
Est: 1981 2500 Bolts

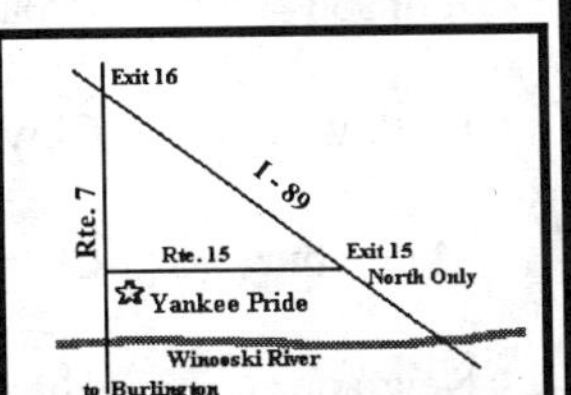

All the top brands of fabrics, the newest books and notions, classes. Friendly, knowledgeable service.

Shelburne, VT #2

Mon - Sat 10 - 5
Sunday
Call First

Quiltsmith Fabrics

65 Falls Rd. 05482
(802) 985-3688
Owner: Julie Sopher
Est: 1981 2400 sq.ft.

Everything for the Quilter: Fabric, Books & Notions. Also ribbon embroidery, crewel & needlepoint supplies. Plus Heirloom Sewing & Smocking.

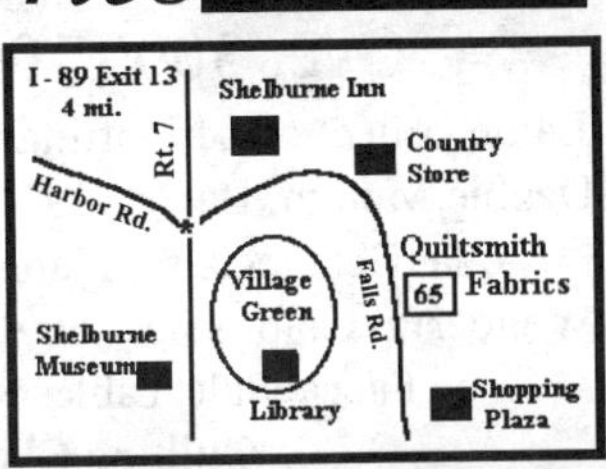

Stowe, VT #3

Mon - Sat
10 - 5

Prints & Patches

Main St., P.O. Box 1205 05672
(802) 253-8643
Owner: Mary Johnson
Est: 1979 800 sq.ft.

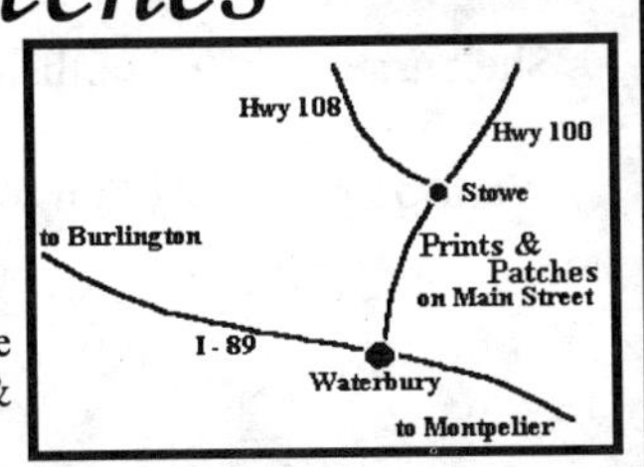

Come on into our Retail shop in Stowe, where we create our own Vermont quilts. Antique & Hand quilted quilts also.

Waitsfield, VT #4

Mon &
Wed - Sat
10 - 5

Cabin Fever Quilts

The Old Church Route 100
P.O. Box 443 05673
(802) 496-2287 Owner: Vee Lowell
Est: 1976 1200 Sq.ft.

Cabin Fever Quilts offers Amish/ Mennonite hand quilted quilts plus custom made tied comforters. Fabric, Quilting Supplies, Quilt Kits & much more!

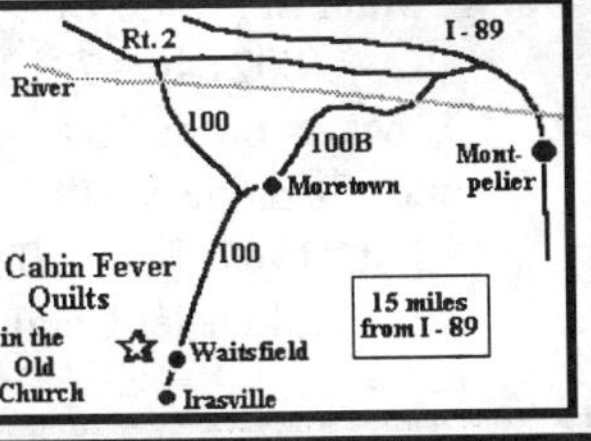

Rutland, VT #5

Mon - Sat 9:30 - 5
Sun 12 - 5

Country Quilt & Fabric

4 U.S. Rt. 4 (Rt. 4E) Mendon, VT 05701
(802) 773-3470
Owners: Pat & Lynne Benard
Est: 1982 1400 sq.ft.
3000+ bolts of 100% cotton fabrics -- Hoffman, South Seas, P&B, RJR, plus notions, Books & Patterns
Custom Orders too

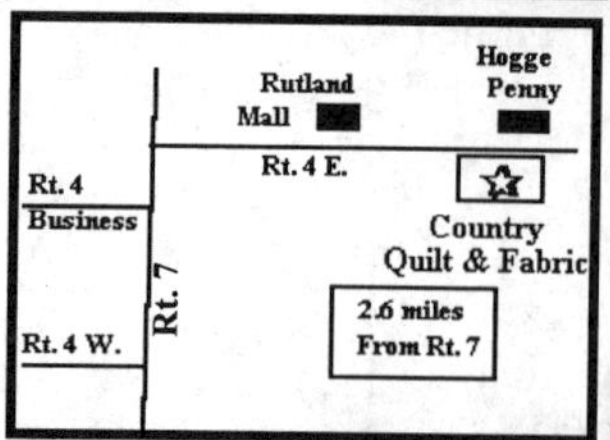

Plymouth, VT #6

Daily Late May - mid Oct 9:30 - 5

President Calvin Coolidge State Historic Site

Plymouth Notch Historic District
(802) 672-3773 Est: 1956
P.O. Box 247 05056
10 Museums Buildings

Several late 19th Century Quilts on Permanent exhibition. Including one pieced by Calvin Coolidge when he was 10 years old. (Tumbling Blocks)

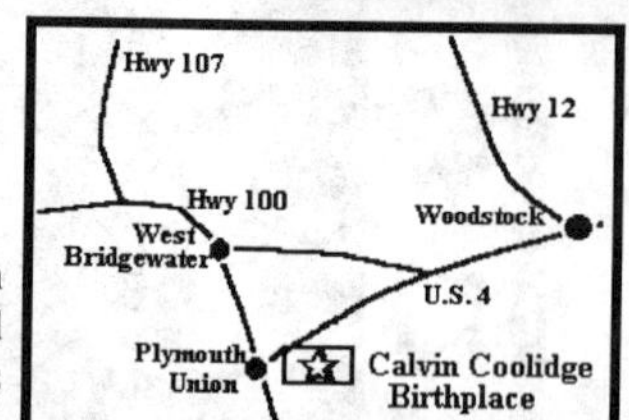

Weston, VT #7

June - Oct 7 days 10-5
Nov - May Fri - Mon 10 - 5

Weston House

Route 100, P.O. Box 82 05161
(802) 824-3636
Owners: Joanne & Richard Eggert
Est: 1978 1500 sq.ft. 650+ Bolts
Quilting Supplies, books and patterns. Huge selection of yard goods--including Roberta Horton's "LINES" fabrics.
Finished Quilts, wallhangings, pillows too!

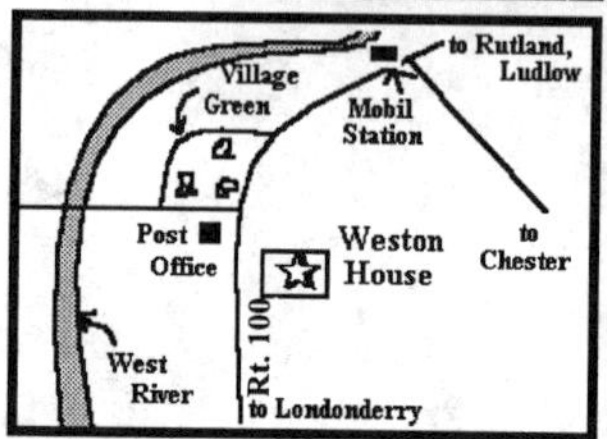

Chester, VT #8

Wed - Sat 10 - 5
Sun 12 - 4
Extended Hours During Foliage Season

Country Treasures

"On the Green" P.O. Box 994
(802) 875-4377 05143
E mail: countrytreasures@nelta.com
www.nelta.com/country/treasures
Est: 1990 1700 sq.ft. 900 Bolts
Quilters will discover a fine selection of patterns, books, fabric, flannels and homespun. Our gift line includes folk art, wall hangings, dried flowers and VT Maple Syrup.

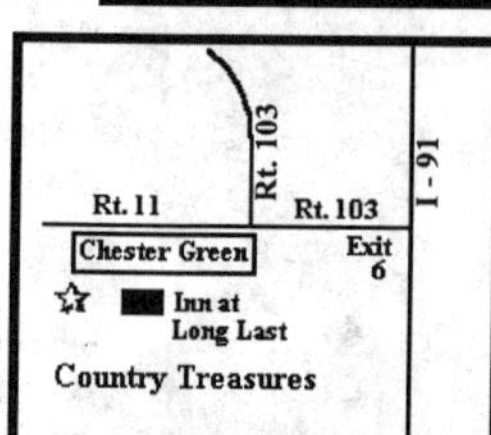

Wilmington, VT #9

Norton House

A Quilter's Paradise !

Over 3000 100% Cotton Fabrics.
Large collection of Hoffman, Jinny Beyer, Reproduction Prints, Debbie Mumm, Batiks, 1920's & 1930's prints, Mission Valley, Moda, Chanteclaire, Flannel Florals & Prints, Solid Fabrics.
Wonderful Color selection • Expert Help in Fabric Coordination
Fabric Sale Tables • Books • Patterns • Notions
Quilting Classes • Quilt Gallery
Needlework Kits • Candles • Country Gifts

Open 7 Days a Week 9 - 5

30 W. Main St., P.O. Box 579 05363
(802) 464-7213
E-Mail: norquilt@sover.net
Owner: Suzanne Wells Wurzberger
Est: 1967 2000 sq.ft.
Mail Order Catalog

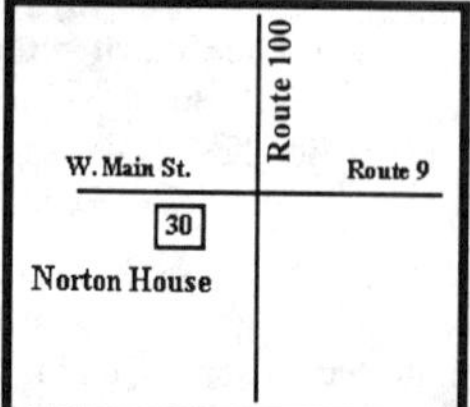

Westminster, VT #10

M, T, Th, F 12 - 4
Sat 10 - 4
Other Times by Chance or Appt.

Quilt-a-way

540 Back Westminster Rd.
(802) 722-4743 05159
Owner: Carol Coski
2000 sq.ft. 600+ Bolts

"She who dies with the most fabric wins!"
Every day is a sale day & we discount everything we sell.

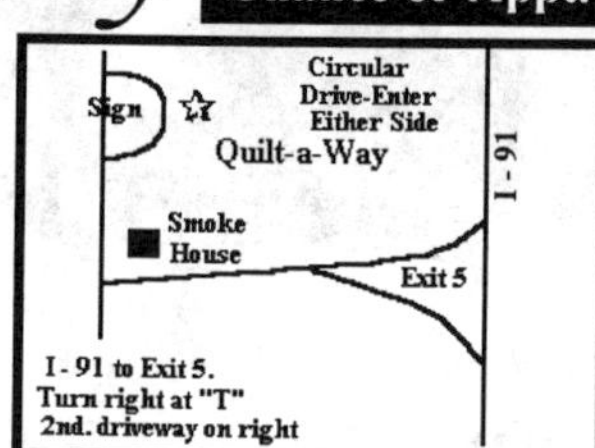

Other Shops in Vermont:

Johnson	Broadwoven Fabric Mill, R.R. # 2 #1035 802-635-7880
Ludlow	Clover Knoll Crafter, 140 Main St. 802-228-4830
Middlebury	Charlotte's Collections, 3 Merchant's Row 802-388-3895
Newfane	The Log Cabin Quilting Shop, R.R. #1, 802-365-7974
Newfane	Newfane Country Store, Route 30 802-365-7916
North Clarendon	Quilt Barn of Vermont, 286 East St. 802-775-0988
Shelburne	Hearthside Quilts, 2048 Shelburne Rd. 802-985-8077
Wardsboro	Anton of Vermont, Rt. 100 802-896-6007

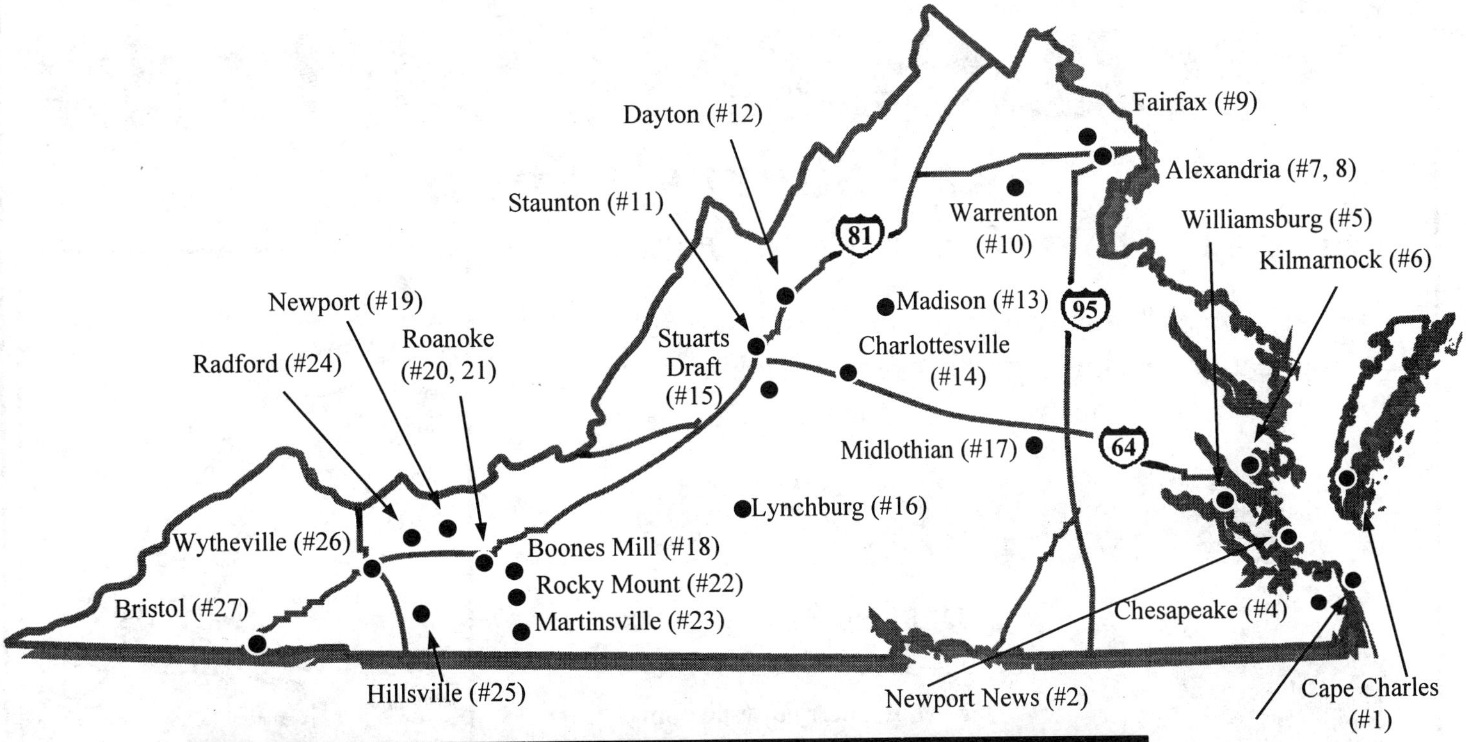

Dayton (#12)
Fairfax (#9)
Alexandria (#7, 8)
Staunton (#11)
Warrenton (#10)
Williamsburg (#5)
Kilmarnock (#6)
Newport (#19)
Madison (#13)
Roanoke (#20, 21)
Stuarts Draft (#15)
Charlottesville (#14)
Radford (#24)
Midlothian (#17)
Lynchburg (#16)
Wytheville (#26)
Boones Mill (#18)
Rocky Mount (#22)
Bristol (#27)
Martinsville (#23)
Chesapeake (#4)
Hillsville (#25)
Newport News (#2)
Cape Charles (#1)
Virginia Beach (#3)
81
95
64

VIRGINIA

27 Featured Shops

Cape Charles, VA #1

Mon - Sat 10 - 5

315 Mason Avenue 23310
(757) 331- 3642
Owner: Henrietta Morris
Est: 1990 600 sq.ft.

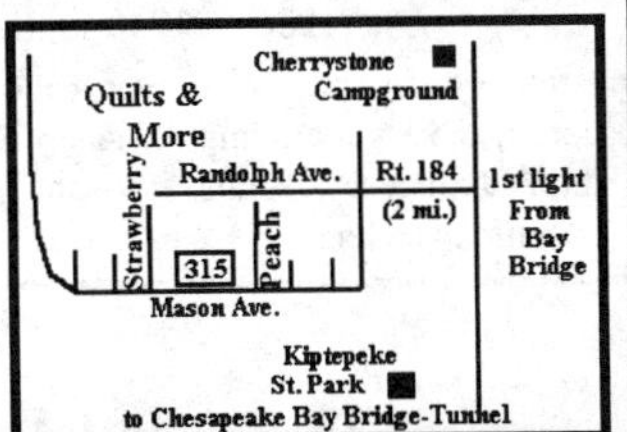

Quilts, other handmade items by owner. Quilting, X-stitch craft supplies. Fabrics of all kinds, patterns, notions and more.

Newport News, VA #2

Mon - Sat 10 - 5 Sun 1- 4

Nancy's Calico Patch

21 Hiddenwood Shopping Center 23606
(757) 596-SEWS (7397)
Owner: Nancy Gloss Est: 1987

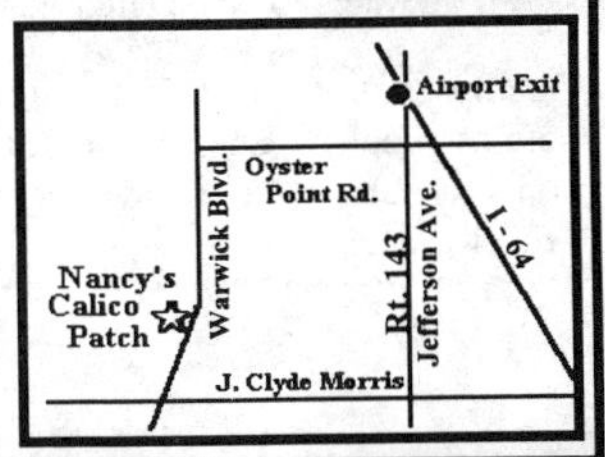

We have fabrics, books, patterns, supplies, & classes for Quilting, Smocking, & Heirloom sewing plus Elna & Pfaff sewing machine sales & service.

Virginia Beach, VA #3

Mon - Sat 10 - 5:30 Thur til 8 Sun 12 - 4

What's Your Stitch 'N Stuff, Inc.

5350 Kempsriver Dr. #104 23464
(757) 523-2711
Owners: Holly Erdei-Zuber & Irene Erdei

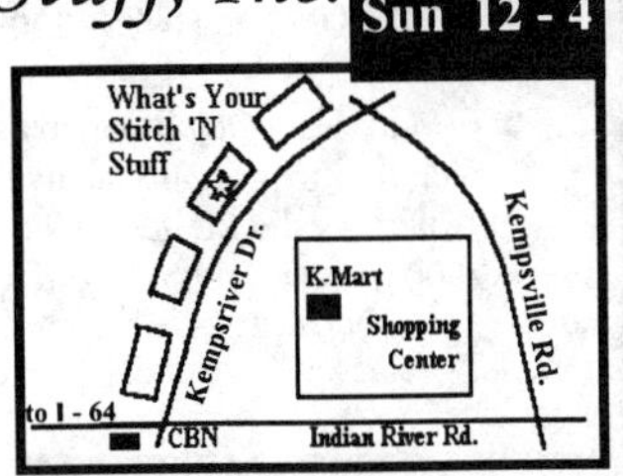

100% Cotton Fabrics and Thread, Books, Patterns, Notions, Dolls, Primitive Rug Hooking. PLUS ALWAYS FRIENDLY SERVICE!

Chesapeake, VA #4

Mon - Fri 10 - 6 Thur til 8 Sat 10 - 5 Sun 12 - 4

Sis 'N Me Quilt Shoppe

3361 Western Branch Blvd. (Hwy 17)
(757) 686-2050 23321
www.sis-n-me.com
Owner: Carole King
Est: 1987 2000 sq.ft. 1500 Bolts

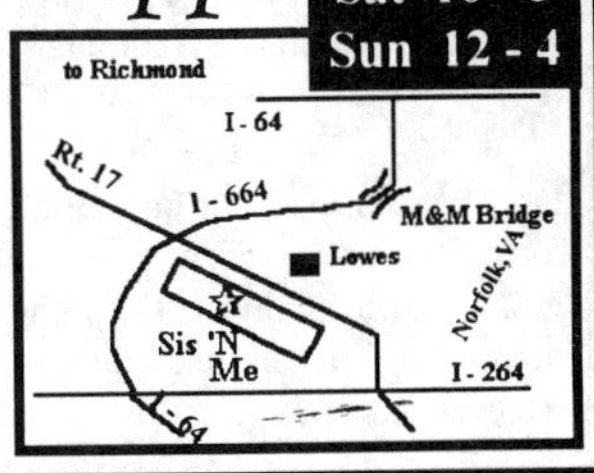

Large selection of 100% cotton Fabrics, Books, Notions, Patterns, Stencils, "Quilter's Cotton" Batting, Prismatic Foil (Glitz Magic) Classes. Mail Order. "Block-a-Month"

Needlecraft Corner

aka "Sherry's Shop"

Over 4,000 bolts of 100% Cotton Fabrics.

Home of "Granny Nanny's Quilting Gadgets" foundation piecing patterns, needlework kits, fibers, books and accessories.

Williamsburg, VA #5

Mon - Sat 9 - 7
Sun 10 - 6

7521 Richmond Rd. 23188
(757) 564-3354 Fax: (757) 564-8453
E-Mail: sherry@wsac.com
Est: 1977
Owner: Jack Barnett

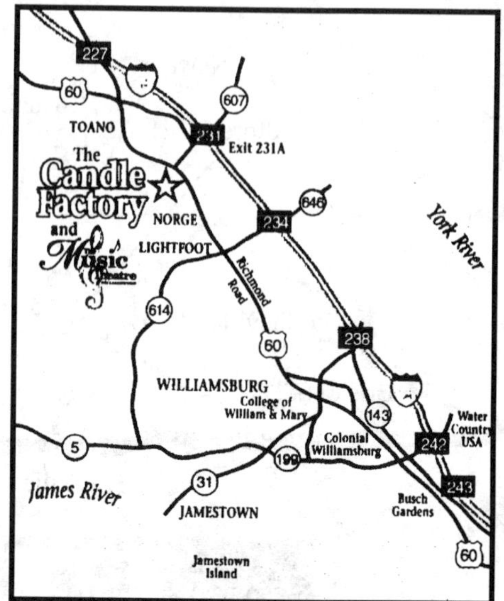

One mile from I - 64 at exit 231A

Kilmarnock, VA #6

The Briar Patch, Inc.

Mon - Fri 10 - 5
Sat 10 - 4

81 N. Main St. 22482
(804) 435-9065
Owners: Jeanne and Lacy Rose

Quality cotton fabrics, quilting supplies, notions, books, patterns, classes. Quilts and crafts for sale. Custom ordered quilts available. Friendly service.

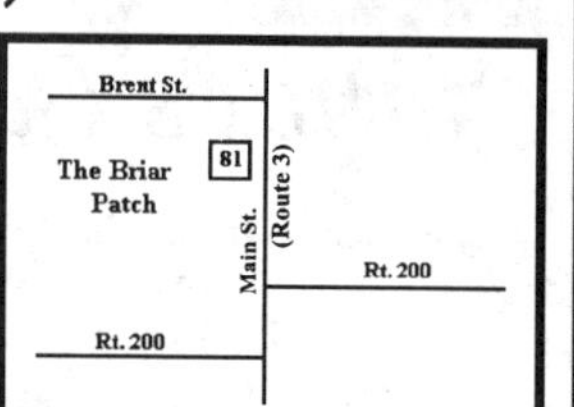

Alexandria, VA #7

Quilt N Stuff

Mon - Sat 10 - 5
Wed til 8

1630 King Street 22314
(703) 836-0070
Owner: Madeline Shepperson
Est: 1986 1740 sq.ft.

Bright, open shop with over 1500 bolts of cotton fabrics including African, Indonesian and Japanese Prints. Viking Sewing Machine Dealer.

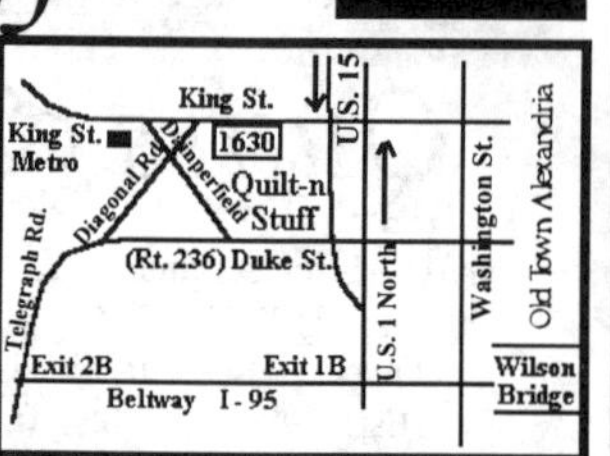

Alexandria, VA #8

Rocky Road to Kansas

Mon - Sat 11 - 5
Sun 1 - 5

215 South Union Street 22314
(703) 683-0116 Est: 1980
Owner: Dixie Kaufman 986 sq.ft.

Large selection antique/vintage Quilts. Tops, Patches, Feedsacks. Quilt Related Items. An assortment of the Old and Interesting: Lighting, Linens, Decorative Pieces, Rugs . . . .

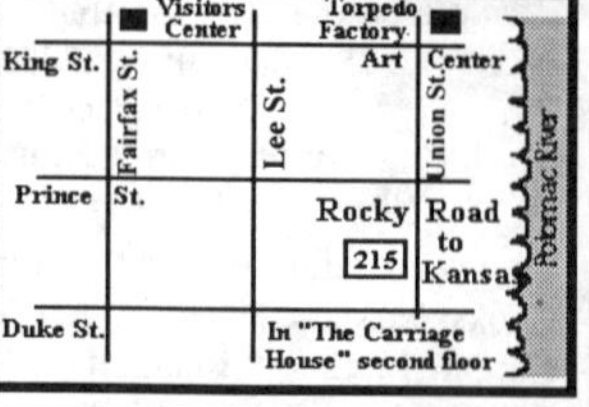

Fairfax, VA #9

The Quilt Patch

Mon - Sat 10 - 5
Thur til 8

3932 Old Lee Hwy. 22030
(703) 273-6937
E-Mail: leslie@quiltpatchva.com
Web Site: www.quiltpatchva.com
Owner: Leslie Pfeifer Est: 1974

Over 2000 bolts 100% cotton fabrics. Hundreds of book titles. Notions, patterns, stencils, classes, friendly professional assistance.

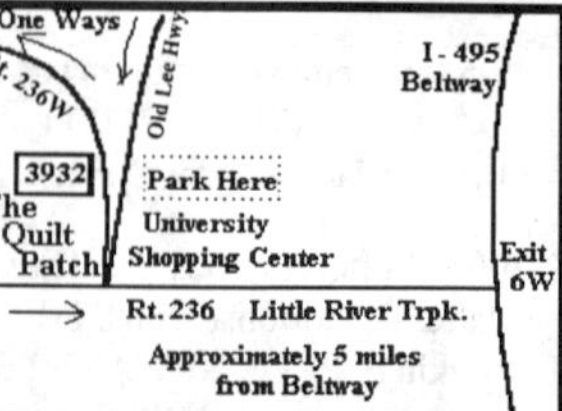

Warrenton, VA #10

Mon - Sat 9:30 - 5

Quilter's Confectionery

79 W. Lee Hwy. 20186
(540) 347-3631
E-Mail: qltconf@mnsinc.com
Owner: Karen S. Walker
Est: 1993 2700 sq.ft. 3000+ Bolts

"Candy" Shop for Quilters. No Fat
No Cholesterol! No Calories!
Cross Stitch, Too!
Very High in Fiber.

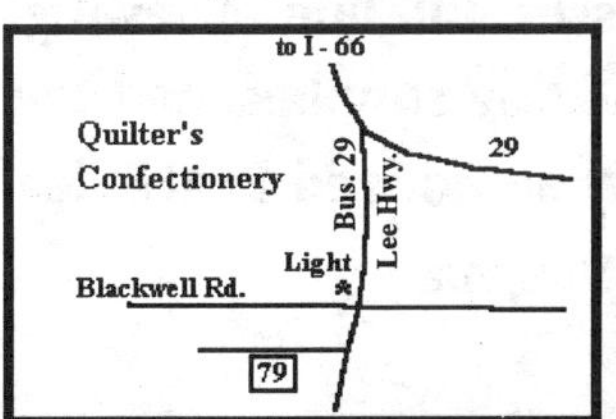

Dayton, VA #12

Mon, Wed, Sat 9 - 5 Tues, Thur, Fri 9 - 9

Clothes Line

Hwy. 42 S, P.O. Box 70 22821
(540) 879-2505
Owners: Oren & Margaret Heatwole
Est: 1972 7000 sq.ft.

Quality selection of 100% Cotton Fabrics, Fashion Fabrics, Quilting Supplies, Books, Patterns, Notions, Classes
Bernina authorized sales and service.

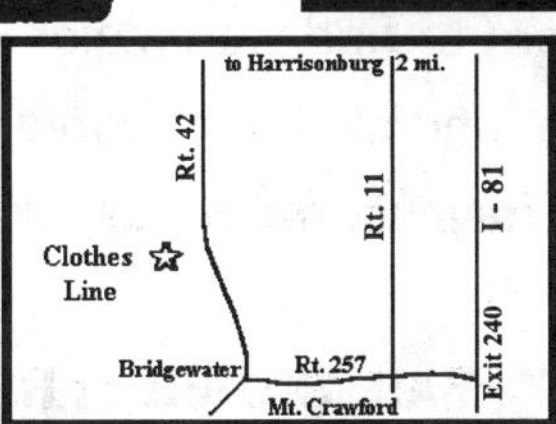

Madison, VA #13

Tues - Sat 10 - 4

Little Shop of Madison

320 S. Main St. P.O. Box 452 22727
(540) 948-4147
Owner: Thelma Shirley
Est: 1978

Hundreds of Fabrics and
All other Quilters' Indulgences.

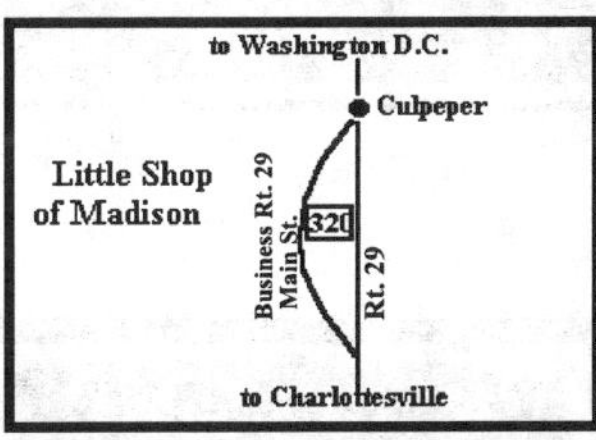

Charlottesville, VA #14

Tues - Fri 10 - 5 Sat 10 - 4

Quilter's Fare

182 Zan Rd. Seminole Sq. Shp. Ctr.
(804) 973-4422 22901
Owner: Sandy Hopkinson
Est: 1995

Specializing in the finest cottons and quilting supplies on the market today. Teaching quilting classes in the newest techniques.

Express Car Wash
Zan Rd.
Rt. 29
Chili's
182
Quilter's Fare
Holiday Inn
Rt. 250 By-Pass
I - 64

Stuarts Draft, VA #15

Mon - Sat 9:30 - 5

The Candy Shop & Fern's Fabrics

10 Highland Drive 24477
(540) 337-0297
Owners: Tom & Connie Almarode
Est: 1983 1000 sq.ft.

Unique country store, owned & operated by Mennonite family. Beautiful quilts, fabrics, patterns, books & more.

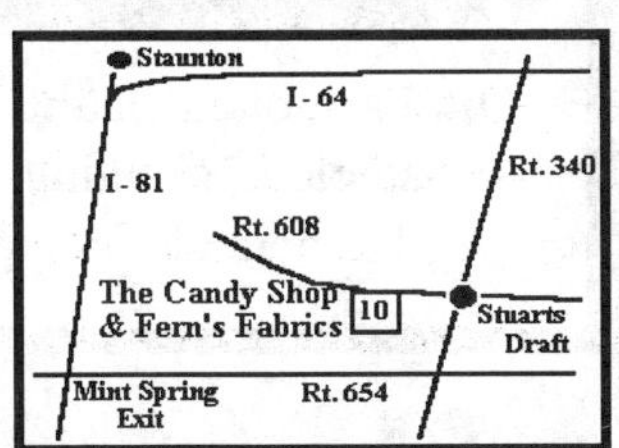

Enjoy a unique shop
in Historic Downtown Staunton
at the Train Station

Our shop features
100% cotton fabric collections
from top of the line
designers and manufacturers,
as well as
Patterns, Books, & Notions
selected for today's
Quilter and Fabric Crafter.

*Ask us about
ongoing classes for
quilters and crafters.
Custom made dinner napkins
and ties are available.*

40 Middlebrook Ave. 24401
(540) 886-7728
Owner: Rachel W. N. Brown

Hours
Mon. Wed. Fri. & Sat.
10:00 a.m.- 5:00 p.m.
Tues. & Thurs.
10:00 a.m.- 8:00 p.m.

We are experienced quilters dedicated to offering personal service.

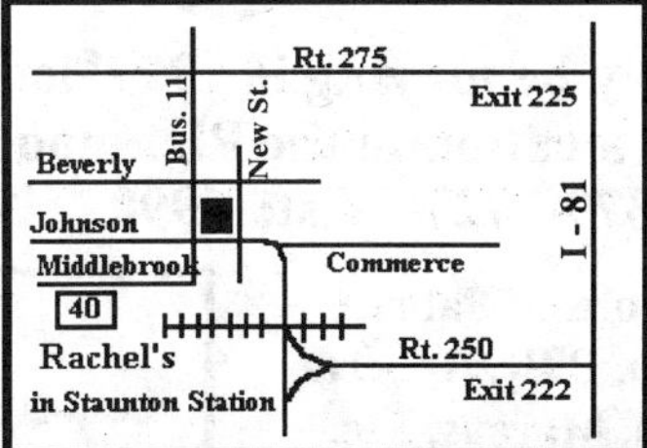

Staunton, VA #11

Quilted Expressions

3226 Old Forest Road Lynchburg VA 24501

(804) 385-6765

Hours: Mon.-Sat. 10-5 Open till 8 on Thursdays

OWNER: ROBERTA WHITT OPENED:1992

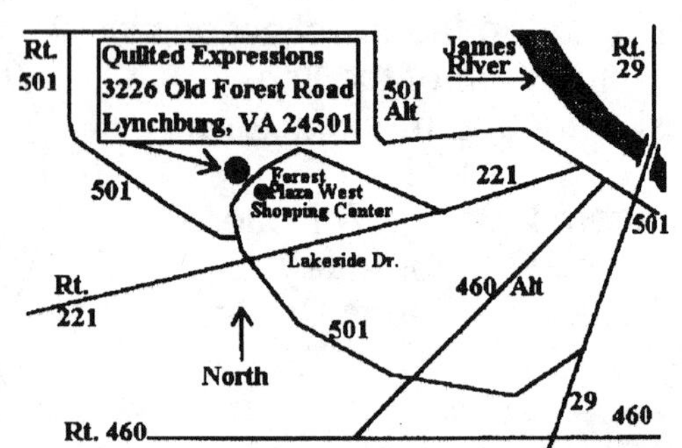

Quilted Expressions **is your source for top-quality 100% cotton fabrics, unique classes, full line of sewing notions, quilting supplies, and the only factory authorized PFAFF dealer in Central Virginia.**

SALES AND SERVICE OF PFAFF PRODUCTS.
Active PFAFF Club and the full line of sergers/sewing machines, featuring the PFAFF 7570 with Creative Fantasy Embroidery Unit. Machine instruction classes. **Over 3,000 bolts in-stock,** including hard-to-find watercolor batiks, Dutch wax prints, imported linen, and all your favorite name brands. **PLUS the latest in gadgets, instruction books, and patterns.**

MAIL ORDER SERVICE AVAILABLE
TRAVEL GROUP INQUIRIES ARE WELCOME!
Call ahead and let us prepare a special event for your group!!

IF THE FLAG IS FLYING, COME ON IN!

Lynchburg, VA #16

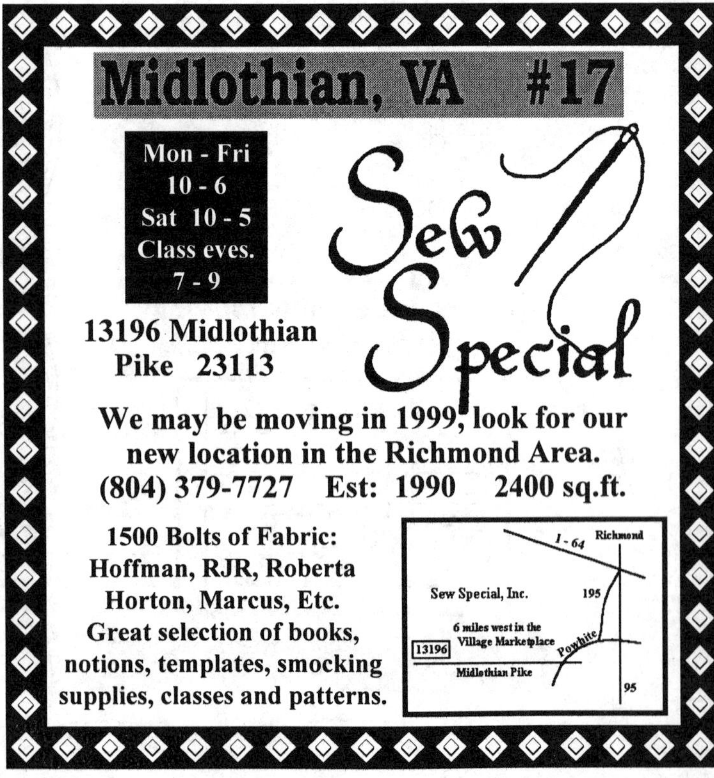

Boones Mill, VA #18

Boone's Country Store

2699 Jubal Early Hwy. 24065
(540) 721-2478
Owners:
Randy & Elva Boone
Est: 1975 3588 sq.ft

I - 81
ROANOKE
Hwy 581
Elm Ave.
24 East
Roanoke River
Windy Gap Mt.
Jubal Early Hwy.
116 S
Blue Ridge Pkwy.
to Bedford and Smith Mt. Lake
220 S
Rt. 684
Boones Mill Rd.
Boone's Country Store
122
Boones Mill
Rocky Mount
Hwy. 40 E

9 miles from Boones Mill

Tues - Sat 9:30 - 5:30

Old Fashioned Quality -- Up to date Values. Calicoes, broad cloth, sheetings, quilting supplies, books, gifts. Homemade breads, pies, cakes & sweet rolls.

Newport, VA #19

The Quilted Garden

Home of The Foundation Piecer

The Pattern Journal for Quilters who Love Foundation Piecing

High quality designer fabrics at a reasonable price

Featuring quilting cottons from : Benartex, Hoffman, RJR, P&B, Kaufman, Kona Bay, Northcott, Bali Fabrications

"Dedicated to the Advancement of Foundation Piecing"

- Books
- Patterns
- Quilting Notions
- Classes
- Japanese Seed Beads
- Beading Supplies
- Gifts
- Friendly Service

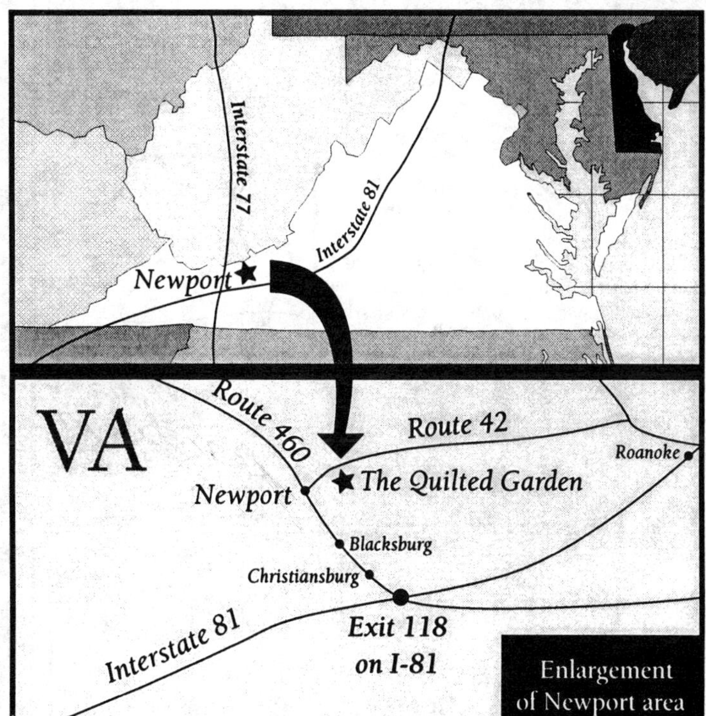

How to Find us

Rt 42 Box 187M
Newport, VA 24128
(540) 544-7143
Owners: Liz Schwartz & Stephen Seifert
Mon-Fri 10-5; Sat 12-5

Visit us on-line! www.quiltersweb.com

Roanoke, VA #20

Mon - Fri 9:30 - 4
Tues til 6
Sat 10 - 2

The Quilting Connection

2825 Brambleton Ave. 24015
(540) 776-0794
Owner: Jill Setchel
Est: 1994 1200 sq.ft.

Large selection of 100% Designer Cottons, Quilting Supplies, Wearable Art, patterns, books, notions and gifts. Personal Service. Classes Available.

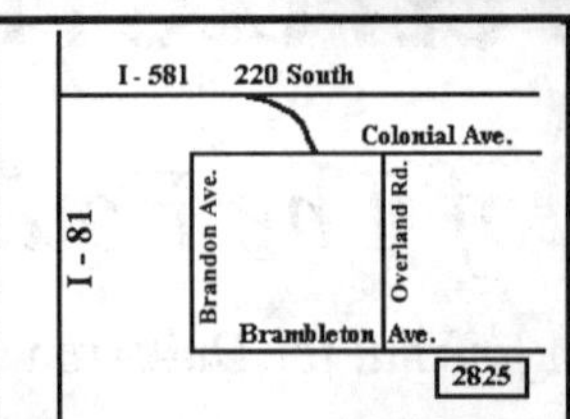

Roanoke, VA #21

By Appt. Only

Touch of Country

611 Greenwich Dr. 24019
(540) 362-5558
Owner: Lula Parker

Machine Quilting Service.

Rocky Mount, VA #22

Mon 9 - 6
Tues - Fri 9 - 5
Sat 9 - 3

Fabric Mill Outlet

453 S. Main St. 24151
(540) 483-2822
Owner: Linda Brown
Est: 1993 3000 sq.ft. 1000+ Bolts

Over 1000 bolts of fabric for your sewing needs. Flat Folds and Designer Fabrics. Complete line of Sewing and Quilting Supplies.

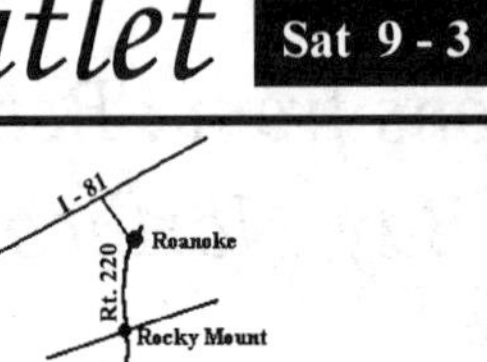

Martinsville, VA #23

Mon - Fri 8:30 - 5
Sat 10 - 2

The Sewing Studio, Inc.

1310 S. Memorial Blvd. 24112
(540) 632-5700 Fax: Same
E-Mail: jfeeny@neocomm.net
Owner: Brenda S. Feeny
Est: 1992 5000 sq.ft. 1100+ Bolts

Large selection of fabric, books & notions. BabyLock dealer. Sales - Service. Classes.

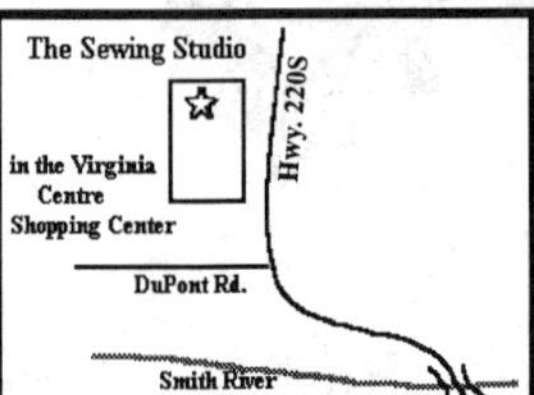

Radford, VA #24

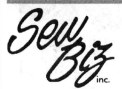

Mon - Sat 9 - 5:30
Thur til 8

Sew Biz inc.

92 & 94 Harvey St. 24141
(540) 639-1138
E-Mail: sewoften@aol.com
Est: 1981
3600 sq.ft.
2000+ Bolts

Two floors of beautiful fabrics for quilting and apparel. Historic building (1889). Extensive selection books, patterns, tools, accessories for Bernina & Elna.

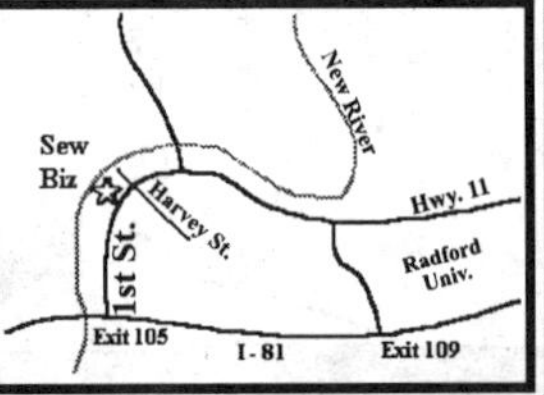

Wytheville, VA #26

Mon - Sat 10 - 5:30

Sew What Fabrics

200 B W. Main St. 24382
(540) 228-6400
Owner: Carol C. Britt
Est: 1982 2100 sq.ft. 1600 Bolts

Wonderful cottons, books, notions, & art to wear supplies. Friendly assistance! Ask about our auto-ship programs. Pfaff Dealer.

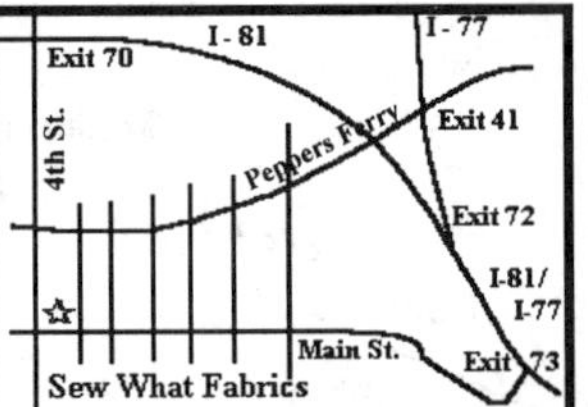

Bristol, VA #27

By Appt. Only

Handcrafted Quilts

1113 Prospect Ave. 24201
(540) 466-5186
Owner: Iva N. Gross

Finished hand quilted quilts, all size, many patterns. Will hand quilt your tops. I don't have any supplies. Custom hand quilting.

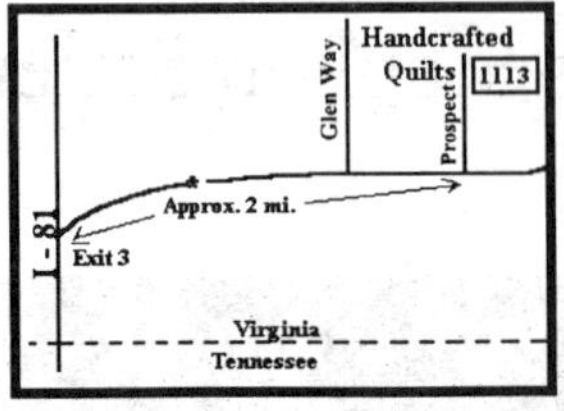

Hillsville, VA #25

Mountain Plains Fabrics

Rt. 1, Box 175A 24343
Located on highway 52, 4505 Fancy Gap Hwy.
5 miles S. of Hillsville, VA
(540) 728-7517
E-Mail: mtnplnfab@pixelmaster.com
Web Site: www.pixelmaster.com/mtnpln/
Owners: Freddie & Hallie Currin

Quilting Fabric & Supplies * Quilt Batting
Buttons * Polyfoan * Lace * Drapery
Upholstery Material * Vinyl * Pillow Tops
Pound Goods such as:
sheeting, lace, fake fur, comforters.

Mon - Sat 9 - 5

Est: 1960
8000 sq.ft.
2500 Bolts

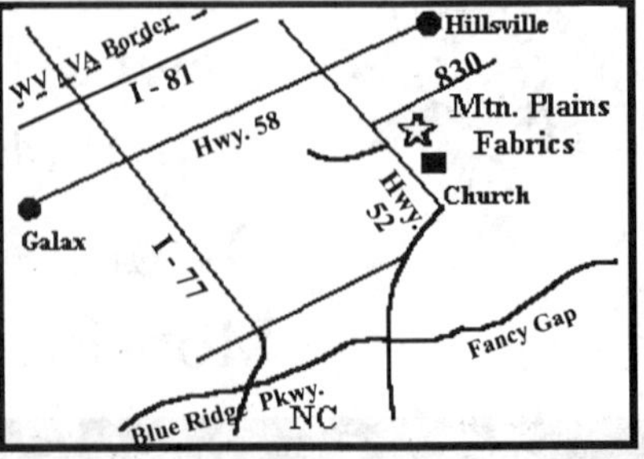

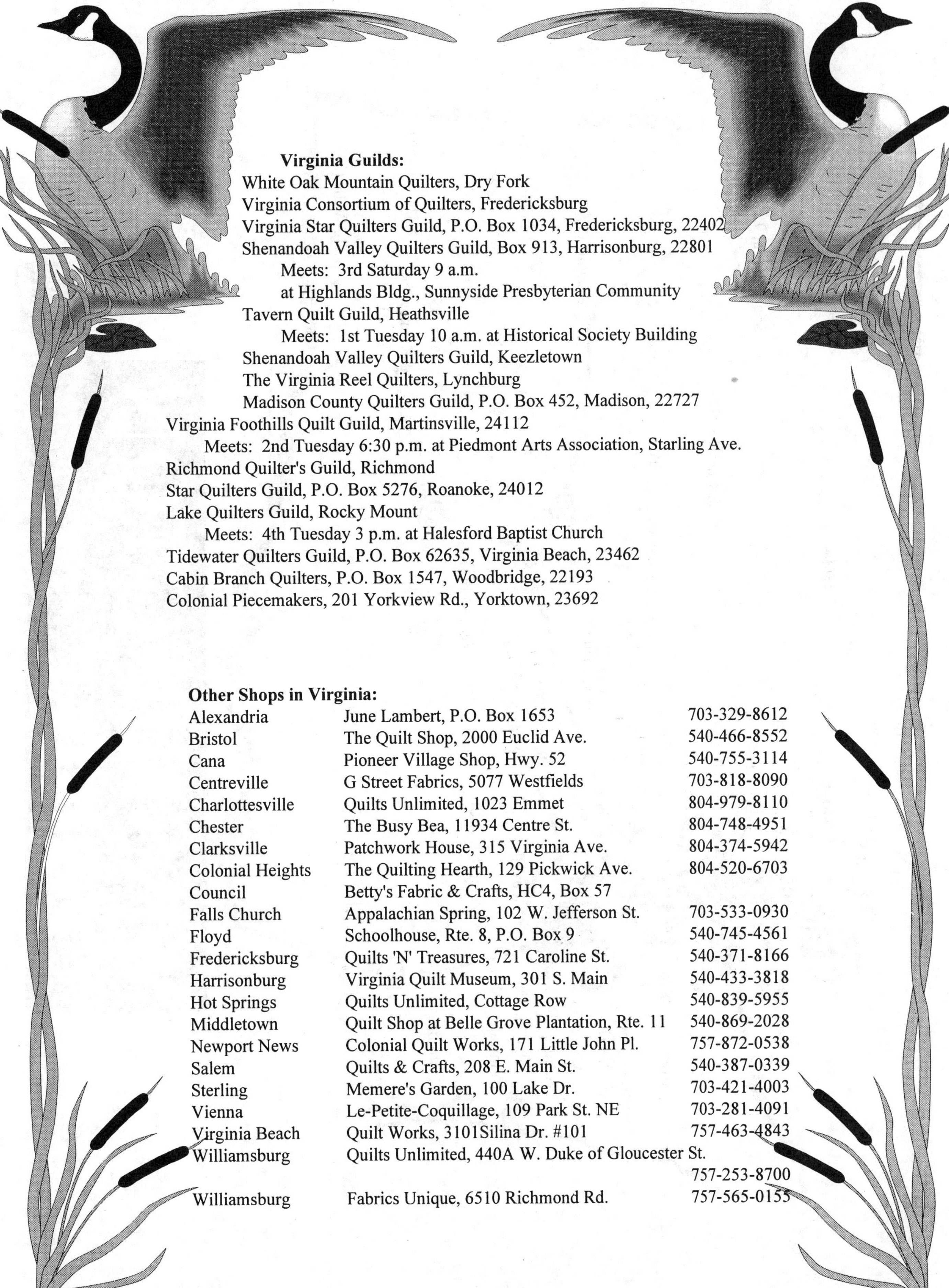

Virginia Guilds:

White Oak Mountain Quilters, Dry Fork
Virginia Consortium of Quilters, Fredericksburg
Virginia Star Quilters Guild, P.O. Box 1034, Fredericksburg, 22402
Shenandoah Valley Quilters Guild, Box 913, Harrisonburg, 22801
Meets: 3rd Saturday 9 a.m.
at Highlands Bldg., Sunnyside Presbyterian Community
Tavern Quilt Guild, Heathsville
Meets: 1st Tuesday 10 a.m. at Historical Society Building
Shenandoah Valley Quilters Guild, Keezletown
The Virginia Reel Quilters, Lynchburg
Madison County Quilters Guild, P.O. Box 452, Madison, 22727
Virginia Foothills Quilt Guild, Martinsville, 24112
Meets: 2nd Tuesday 6:30 p.m. at Piedmont Arts Association, Starling Ave.
Richmond Quilter's Guild, Richmond
Star Quilters Guild, P.O. Box 5276, Roanoke, 24012
Lake Quilters Guild, Rocky Mount
Meets: 4th Tuesday 3 p.m. at Halesford Baptist Church
Tidewater Quilters Guild, P.O. Box 62635, Virginia Beach, 23462
Cabin Branch Quilters, P.O. Box 1547, Woodbridge, 22193
Colonial Piecemakers, 201 Yorkview Rd., Yorktown, 23692

Other Shops in Virginia:

Alexandria	June Lambert, P.O. Box 1653	703-329-8612
Bristol	The Quilt Shop, 2000 Euclid Ave.	540-466-8552
Cana	Pioneer Village Shop, Hwy. 52	540-755-3114
Centreville	G Street Fabrics, 5077 Westfields	703-818-8090
Charlottesville	Quilts Unlimited, 1023 Emmet	804-979-8110
Chester	The Busy Bea, 11934 Centre St.	804-748-4951
Clarksville	Patchwork House, 315 Virginia Ave.	804-374-5942
Colonial Heights	The Quilting Hearth, 129 Pickwick Ave.	804-520-6703
Council	Betty's Fabric & Crafts, HC4, Box 57	
Falls Church	Appalachian Spring, 102 W. Jefferson St.	703-533-0930
Floyd	Schoolhouse, Rte. 8, P.O. Box 9	540-745-4561
Fredericksburg	Quilts 'N' Treasures, 721 Caroline St.	540-371-8166
Harrisonburg	Virginia Quilt Museum, 301 S. Main	540-433-3818
Hot Springs	Quilts Unlimited, Cottage Row	540-839-5955
Middletown	Quilt Shop at Belle Grove Plantation, Rte. 11	540-869-2028
Newport News	Colonial Quilt Works, 171 Little John Pl.	757-872-0538
Salem	Quilts & Crafts, 208 E. Main St.	540-387-0339
Sterling	Memere's Garden, 100 Lake Dr.	703-421-4003
Vienna	Le-Petite-Coquillage, 109 Park St. NE	703-281-4091
Virginia Beach	Quilt Works, 3101Silina Dr. #101	757-463-4843
Williamsburg	Quilts Unlimited, 440A W. Duke of Gloucester St.	757-253-8700
Williamsburg	Fabrics Unique, 6510 Richmond Rd.	757-565-0155

Lynden (#16, 17)
Eastsound (#18)
Bellingham (#19)
Colville (#11)
Sedro Woolley (#20)
Omak (#12)
Port Townsend
(#47, 48)
LaConner (#21, 22)
Langley (#24)
Spokane (#8, 9, 10)
Everett (#23)
Chelan (#13)
Poulsbo (#46)
Bothell (#26)
Bremerton (#45)
Woodinville (#25)
Leavenworth (#14)
Seattle (#28, 29)
Port Orchard
(#43, 44)
Bellevue (#30)
Issaquah (#27)
Ritzville (#7)
Federal Way (#33)
90
Tacoma (#34)
Renton (#31)
Olympia (#41)
Puyallup (#37)
Auburn (#32)
Colfax (#15)
Tumwater (#42)
Yelm (#35, 36)
Yakima (#5)
Centralia (#40)
82
Richland (#4)
Kennewick
(#1, 2)
Dayton (#6)
5
Longview (#38, 39)
Walla Walla (#3)
WASHINGTON
48 Featured Shops

Est: 1991

Kennewick, WA #1

Pieceable Dry Goods

"A Country Quilt Store"

Selected by American Patchwork & Quilting magazine as one of the Top 10 Quilt Shops for 1998.

Featuring great service, merchandise displays and samples, every quilter needs to visit Pieceable Dry Goods. Customers come from miles around to shop. You will always enjoy popping into the shop to savor the warm, cozy feeling that has been created. We specialize in reproductions of prints from the 1820's to 1930's. You'll also be pleased at the array of gifts, patterns, fabric, rug hooking, silk ribbon, paper piecing and supplies in addition to extensive and creative classes.

Professional quilting machine service offered to help you get those projects done.

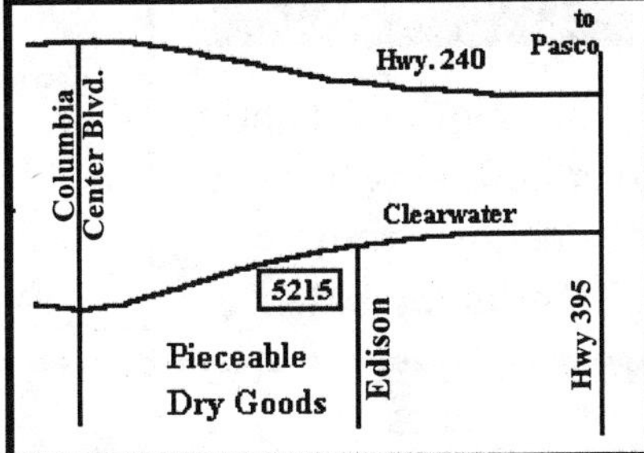

We have wonderful neighbors including: Countryside Cottage (a wonderful gift shop), Sweet Cravings (homemade candies) & Fun 2 Learn (educational toys).

No matter what your age...It's time to start quilting!

Join our 1998 Block of the Month Clubs!

Flowers of the month by Linda Brannock $7.49 per month
"American from Sea to Shining Sea" $6.50 per month
Charming Raggedy Kids $6.50 per month
Calendar Quilt of the Month from Picket Fence $13.99 per month
"Stitchin' Up The Year '98" $6.50 per month
CALL FOR MORE DETAILS

Treasures from the Past Fabric Club

Let us become your source of yesterday's prints in today's quality fabric! These reproduction fabrics will add an authentic touch to your new quilts—perfect for that traditional block, a little quilt, or a charming doll quilt. When this pack arrives each month it will warm your heart and make you smile! Contains 3/8 yd. border fabric and 13 fat eights that coordinate for $19.99 per month.

5215 W. Clearwater #106 Marineland Village 99336

(509) 735-6080

Owners: Terry Guizzo & Barbara Ward

Mon - Fri 10 - 5:30 Sat 10 - 5

Kennewick, WA #2

Mon - Sat 10 - 6

Fantasticks

135 Vista Way 99336
(509) 735-3844 Fax: (509) 735-1592
Est: 1983 1000 sq.ft.

Friendly shop with quality fabric, notions, quilt books and classes. Also home decor, gifts, collectables, Dept. 56, Williraye & Model Trains.

Walla Walla, WA #3

Tues - Sat 10 - 6 Winter 10 - 5

Suzanne's Quilt Shop

413 "B" St. at the Walla Walla Airport
(509) 526-9398 99362

Quilter's Fabric, Notions, Books, Patterns. Machine quilting Service. Day and Evening Classes.

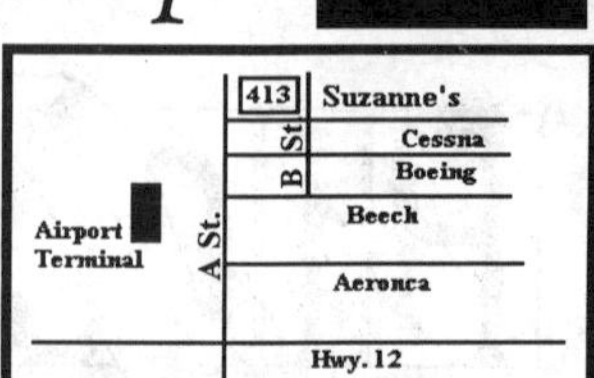

Richland, WA #4

Quiltmania!!

248 Williams 99352
(509) 946-PINS (7467)
Owner: Debi Merhar
Est: 1991 1000 Bolts

Mon - Thur 10 - 9
Fri & Sat 10 - 5

Classes, Notions, Fabric. Over 400 book titles to choose from.
Quilts for Sale.

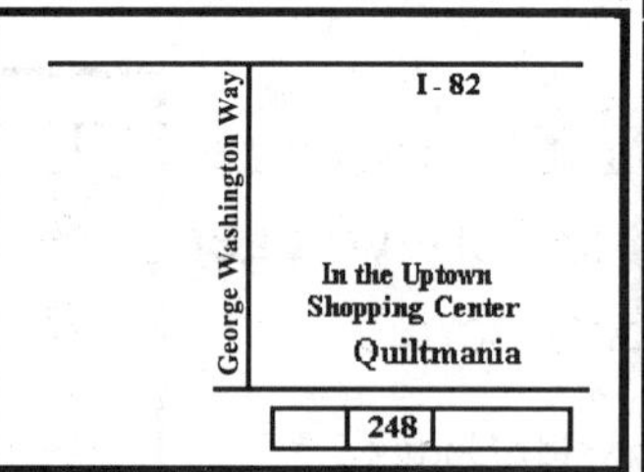

Yakima, WA #5

BERNINA® Sewing Center & Quilt Shop

521 W. Yakima Ave. 98902
(509) 248-0078 Fax: (509) 248-0348
E-Mail: bernina@wolfenet.com
Owners: Brad & Sue McMillan
Est: 1968 3500 sq.ft.

Moon - Fri 9 - 5:30 Sat 9 - 5

Over 2500 Bolts of Quilt Fabric. Large Selection of Books, Patterns, Notions, Classes. Brennan & New Home Sales & Service.

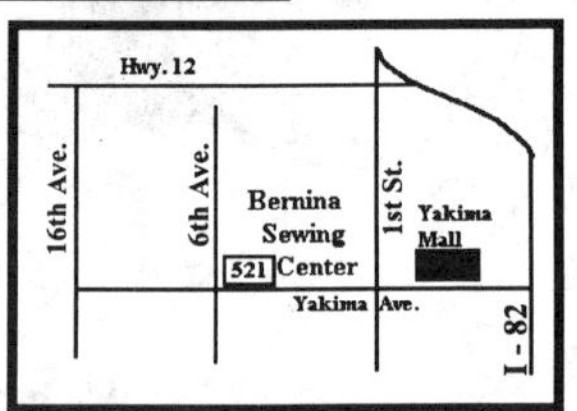

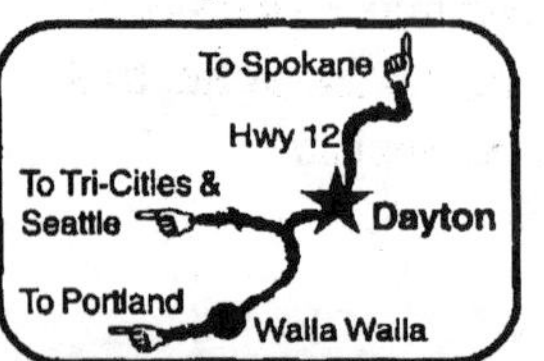

Hawthorne Gallery

• Gifts • Antiques • Treasures •

Located on Dayton's Main Street in the middle of the block—Hwy 12

Specializing in flannels and vintage reproduction cotton fabrics. Also, rug hooking supplier; wool, tools, books and classes.
• 7,500 sq. ft. old time country store •

• M-F 10-5 • Sat 10-3 •
• 245 E. Main • Dayton, WA 99328 •
• (509) 382-3137 •

Dayton, WA #6

Ritzville, WA #7

Garden Gate Quilt Shop

107 W. Main 99169
(509) 659-1370
Owner: Celia Benzel 1500 Bolts

A fun and friendly quilt shop located in historical downtown Ritzville. Lots of great ideas displayed in our shop with fabrics, notions, books & patterns. You won't be disappointed.

Mon - Sat 10 - 5

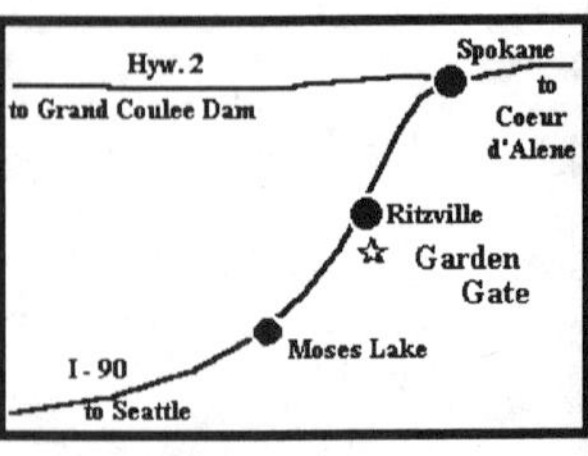

Spokane, WA #8

Selected by American Patchwork & Quilting magazine readers as one of the Top 10 quilt shops in the nation for 1998.

Mon - Fri
9:30 - 9
Sat 9:30 - 5:30
Sun 12 - 5

12117 E. Mission 99206
(509) 928-6037 Fax: 928-6903
Owner: Jackie Wolff Est: 1984 5000 sq.ft.

Spokane's finest Quilting Store!

Filled with quilting books, notions, tools, & 3000 bolts of fabric. Friendly staff and Spokane's only Bernina Dealer.

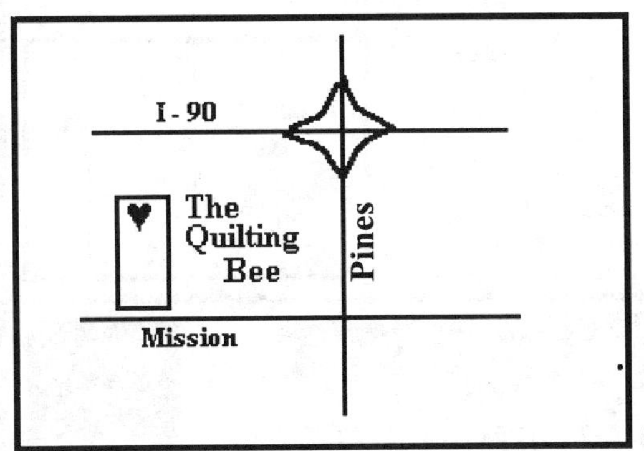

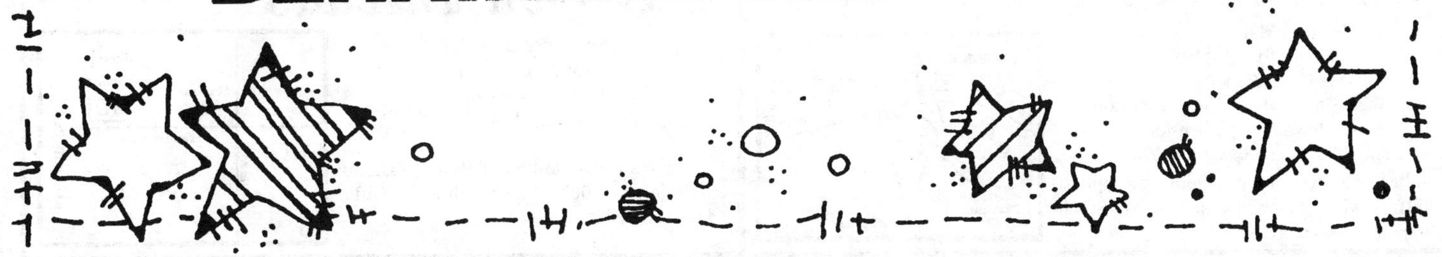

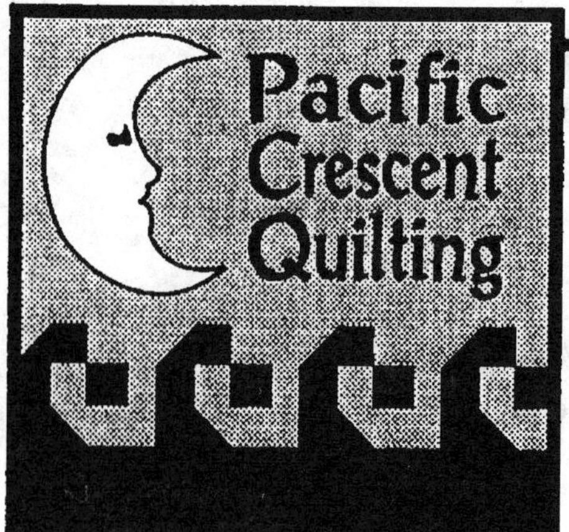

Spokane's
QUALITY SHOP FOR QUILTERS

**Great fabric, Books, patterns and notions.
We provide mail order service anywhere.
Warm, friendly service in a bright & sunny shop.**

(509) 484-4808

7454 N. Division 99208
Fax #: (509) 484-4918
E-Mail: pcq@pcqspokane.com

Division
The Onion
PCQ

**Mon - Fri 10 - 8
Sat 10 - 6
Sun 11 - 5**

Spokane, WA #9

Owners: Sandy & Larry McCauley Est: 1995 3200 sq.ft. 4000 Bolts

Quality Fabric & Notions for Quilting & Fabric Crafts

Spokane, WA #10

**Mon - Sat
9 - 6**

Sew E-Z, Too

2901 W. Northwest Blvd. 99205
(509) 325-6644
Owner: Vickie Black
Est: 1997

Designer Fabrics and More.
Large selection quality cottons, books, patterns.

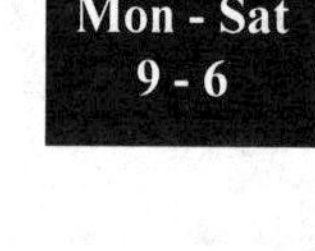

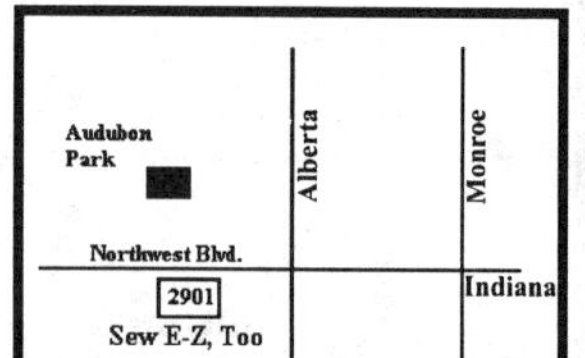

Colville, WA #11

**Mon - Thur
10 - 6
Fri 10 - 8
Sat 10 - 5
Sun 12 - 4**

E - Z Knit Fabrics

165 N. Main 99114
(509) 684-2644 Fax: (509) 684-6659
E-Mail: vlb1311@plix.com
Owners: Vickie Black & Helen West
Est: 1969 3000 sq.ft.

3 stores in one — Beads — Fabrics — Yarn
One of the largest selections of fabric in Washington.

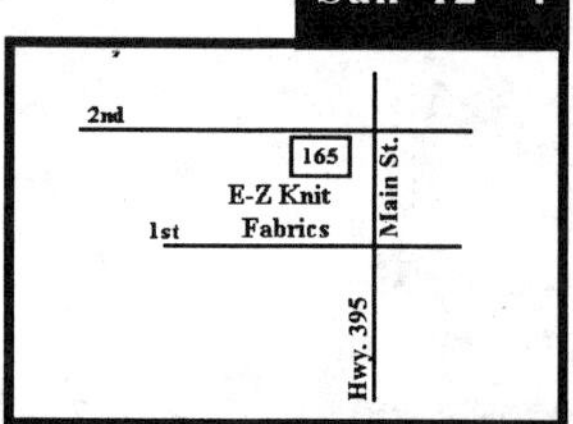

Omak, WA #12

**Mon - Sat
9 - 6**

Needlelyn Time

9 North Main 98841
(509) 826-1198
E-Mail: needlyn@televar.com
Web Site: www.needlelyntime.com
Owner: Lyn Hruska
Est: 1986 3000 sq.ft. 1900 Bolts

Quilter's Fabrics, Notions, Quilting Supplies. Pfaff Sewing Machines and Cross-Stitch Supplies. Also Classes.

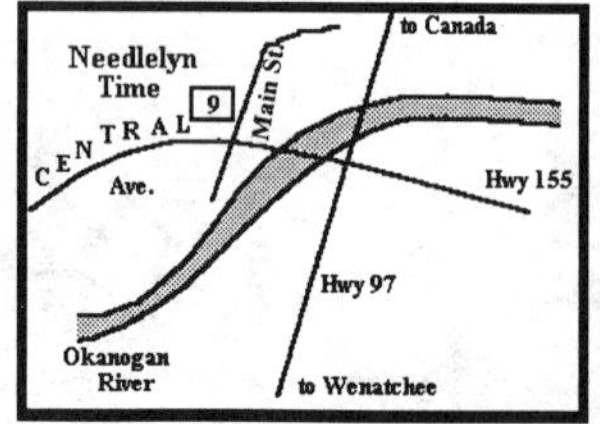

Chelan, WA #13

**Mon - Sat
9:30 - 5:30**

Woven Threads

115 S. Emerson 98816
(509) 682-7714
Owner: Rose Buhl
Est: 1995

We carry a complete line of Books, Patterns & Notions. 100% cotton fabrics. Gifts. Classes. Free Newsletter

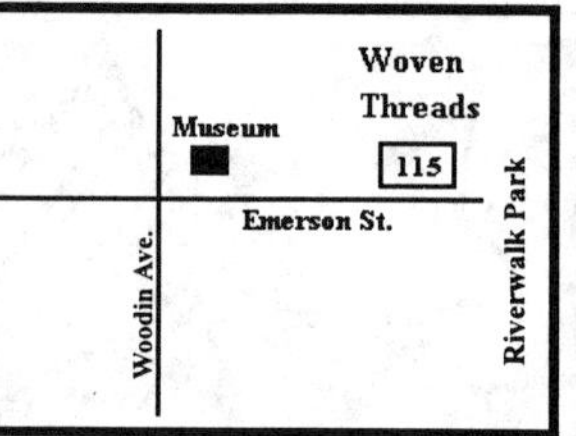

Leavenworth, WA #14

All Year 9 a.m. to 8 p.m.

Dee's Country Accents

917 Commercial St. 98826
(800) 829-5311
Owners: Dee & Al Howie
Est: 1987 1500 Bolts

Incredible Fabrics, Largest selection in the Pacific Northwest of Quilt Books and Patterns. PLUS a Bed & Breakfast decorated with quilts and antiques.

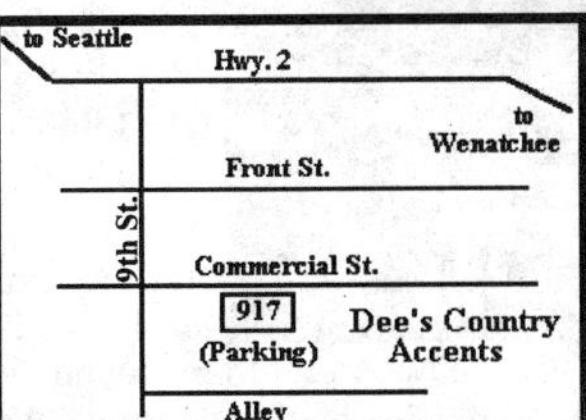

Lynden, WA #16

Mon - Sat 9 - 5:30

Fabric Cottage

510 Front St. 98264
(360) 354-5566
Owner: Grace Mulder
Est: 1979 2500 sq.ft.

Lynden's greatest selection for the enthusiastic quilter and crafter. Wonderful samples to inspire you. A friendly staff to help you.

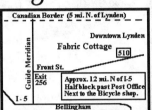

Canadian Border (5 mi. N. of Lynden)
Downtown Lynden
Fabric Cottage
510
Guide Meridian
Front St.
Exit 256
Approx. 12 mi. N of I-5
Half block past Post Office
Next to the Bicycle shop.
I-5
Bellingham

Lynden, WA #17

Mon - Sat 9:30 - 5:30

Boomers

1722 Front St. 98264
(360) 354-1533 Fax: (360) 354-4789
E-Mail: boomers@sos.net
Est: 1989 2000 sq.ft. 1200 Bolts

Pfaff Sewing Machines, over 1000 bolts 100% Cottons, Quilt Books, Craft Patterns, Notions, Friendly, Knowledgeable Staff.

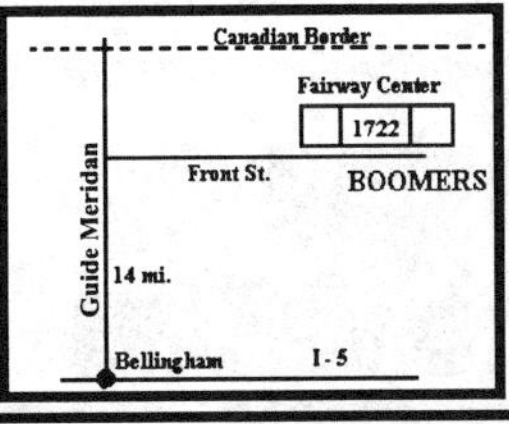

Becky's Fabrics and Bernina

114 N. Main 99111
(509) 397-6171

Colfax, WA #15

Owner: Rebecca Keck
Est: 1992
1200 sq.ft. 1800+ Bolts
Fabric Club and
Mail Order Available.

Nothing Sews Like A Bernina. Nothing.
BERNINA®

Mon - Sat 10 - 5
Thur til 6

to Spokane
Becky's Fabrics N. 114 Main
Hwy. 195
Colfax
Hwy. 26
to Moscow ID
Pullman
to Lewiston, ID

Becky's Fabrics is an authorized Bernina Dealership. We stock a complete line of Bernina sewing machines, sergers and accessories and have our own in-store technician available for service and repair on any machine. We also stock an assortment of the finest 100% cotton quilting fabrics available and a complete selection of books, patterns and a very friendly and knowledgeable staff to assist you. As you are meandering through the rolling hills of the Palouse, stop by and say hello.

Eastsound, WA #18

Mon - Sat 10 - 5

The Cotton Club

11 "A" St. 98245
P.O. Box 1075

(360) 376-2686
Est: 1993
Owner: Ruth Vandestraat
1000 sq.ft. 1000 Bolts

On Lovely Orcas Island — A Complete Quilting Shop plus Yarn, Stitchery, Kits, Notions. Across from the Post Office.

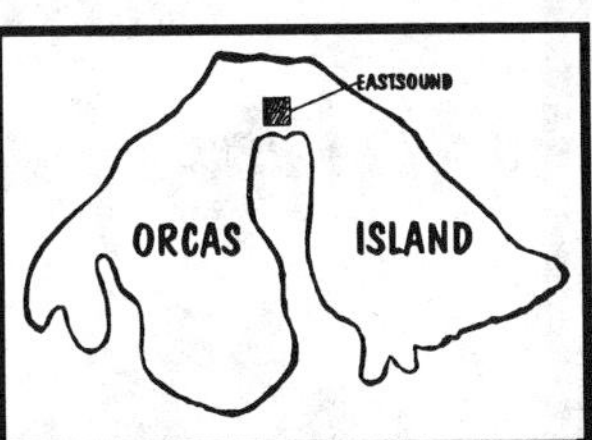

Bellingham, WA #19

Mon - Sat 10 - 5 Sun 12 - 4

Quilt Basket

A Quilter's Haven

2108 13th St. 98225
(360) 734-7080 Est: 1977
Owner: Jyl Peterson 2300 sq.ft.

Over 650 bolts of 100% cottons.
Books, patterns, notions,
gift items, Classes. Kids Play Area.

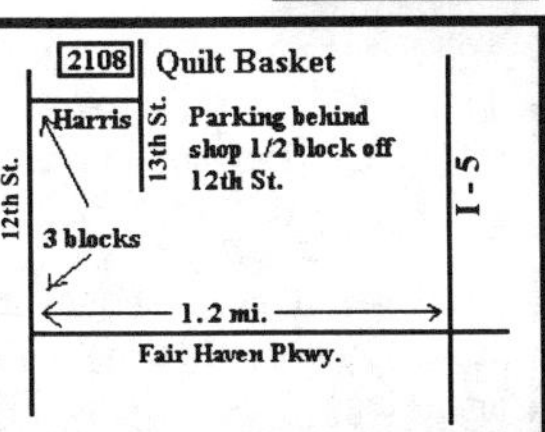

Sedro Woolley, WA #20

Mon - Fri 9:30 - 5:30 Sat 9:30 - 5

Cascade Fabrics

824 Metcalf 98284
(360) 855-0323
Owner: Paul Kelley
Est: 1978 3000 sq.ft.

Quilting Supplies and Books, Classes. Experienced Staff. 20% off all quilting cotton always. Additional non-quilting fabrics also.

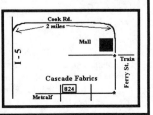

Cook Rd.
2 miles
Mall
I-5
Train
Ferry St.
Cascade Fabrics
824
Metcalf

LaConner, WA #21

Open Daily 10 - 5

Creighton's Quilts

503 E. Morris St. Est: 1988
(in the Morris St. Antique Mall)
(360) 766-5010 E-Mail: annbow@cio.net
Owner: Ann Bodle-Nash
AQS Certified Quilt Appraiser since 1994.
Appraisals by Appointment.
Antique & New Amish quilts for sale. Books, notions, countrywares, folk art, & rugs.

LaConner, WA #22

Wed - Sun 11 - 5

La Conner Quilt Museum

703 S. 2nd St.,
P.O. Box 1270 98257
(360) 466-4288
Director: Rita Hupy

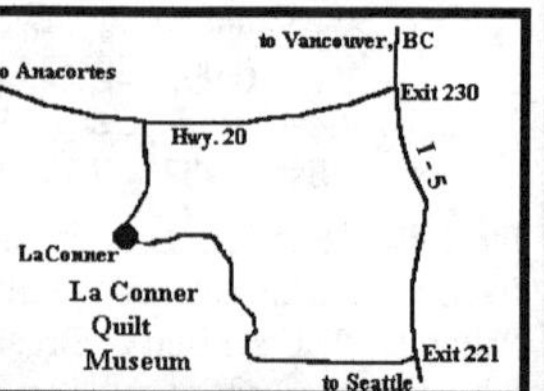

The only Quilt Museum in the State of Washington. Five shows a year from around the country and the world. Memberships Available.

Everett, WA #23

Mon - Sat 9 - 7

3122 Broadway
98201
(425) 259-6579

Fax: (425) 743-3344
Owner: Diane Coombs Est: 1982

Over 2500 Bolts of 100% Cotton, Books, Notions, Classes & Quilts!
Plus Quilt Related Tours to National Shows

Woodinville, WA #25

Office Tours Mon & Wed at 1 p.m.

That Patchwork Place

20205 144th Ave. NE 98072
(800) 426-3126
Web Site: www.patchwork.com
Free Catalog

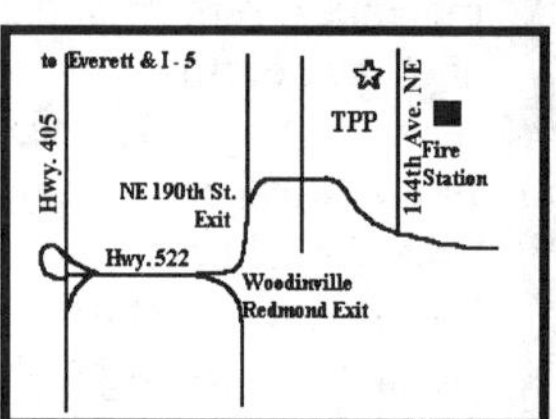

Visit the Publisher of America's Best-Loved Quilt Books™. Call to reserve a spot on our tour (and buy "hurt" books) !

Quilting by the Sea

221 Second St. #6, (Langley Village)
P.O. Box 844 98260 (360) 221-8171
Owner: Mary Darby Est: 1995
1800 sq.ft. 1,100+ Bolts 450+ Quilt Titles
Classroom & Retreat Space with view of Puget Sound.

Fabrics, books, patterns, supplies, gifts, & quilts. The friendliest quilt shop for service, inspiration & sharing of ideas.

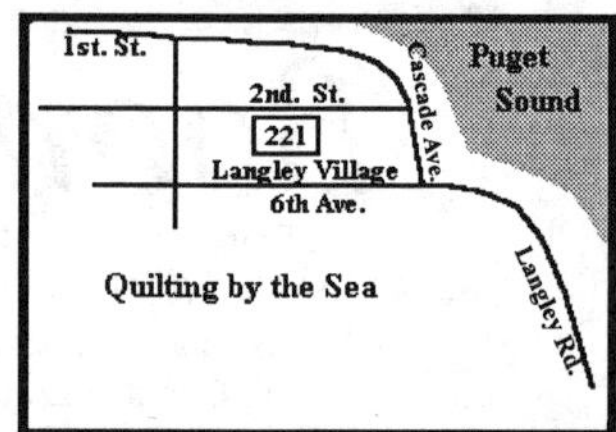

Open Daily 10 - 5
Sun 12 - 5
Closed Tues

Langley, WA #24

Bothell, WA #26

Mon - Sat 10 - 6
Thurs til 8
Sun 11 - 5

Keepsake Cottage Fabrics

23732 Bothell-Everett Hwy. 98021
(425) 486-3483
Owners: Delberta Murray & Julie Stewart
Est: 1985 1000 sq.ft.

Quilting Fabrics, patterns and notions. In the heart of Bothell's Country Village. Also English Smocking.

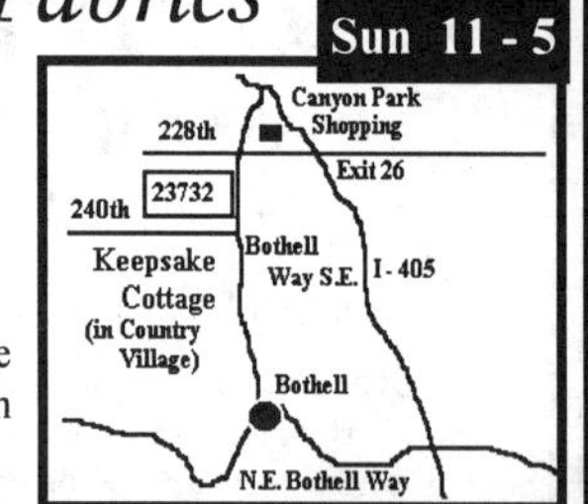

Issaquah, WA #27

Mon - Sat 10 - 6
Wed til 7
Sun 12 - 5

The Loft

1480 N.W. Gilman Blvd. #2 98027
(425) 392-5877 Est: 1972
Owners: Deborah Doty
& Jacquie Vaughn

Complete Quilt Shop. Experienced and personable help. Great selection of samples for inspiration. Fabric, Books, Patterns, Classes galore !!

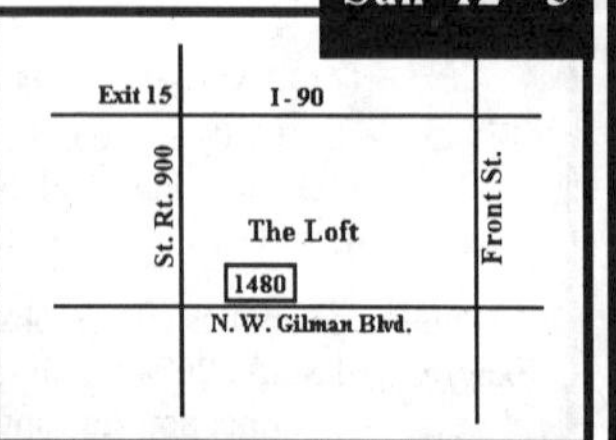

Seattle, WA #28

Mon - Sat 10 - 6

Undercover Quilts from the U.S.A.

1411 1st Ave. #106 98101
(800) 469-6511 or (206) 622-6382
Fax: (206) 622-7704
E-Mail: quilts@serv.net
Owner: Linda Hitchcock
Web Site: www.undercoverquilts.com
Est: 1990 1000 sq.ft. 1000 Bolts

Largest Selection of American Made New and Antique Quilts in the Pacific Northwest!
Fabrics, Books, Supplies, gifts, antique tops, and blocks.

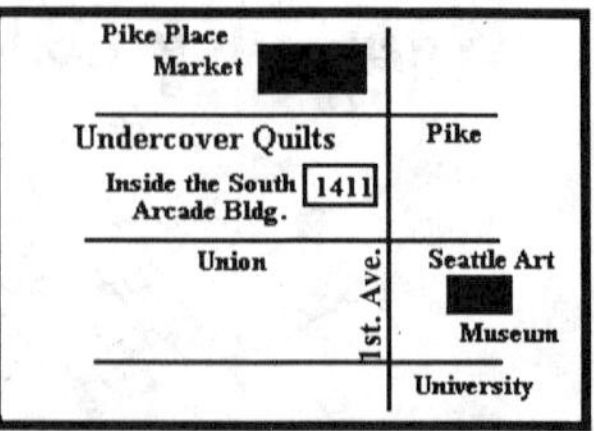

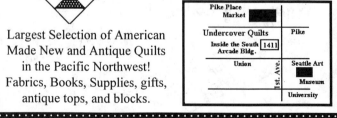

"The N.W.'s Largest Quilting Resource!"

Seattle, WA #29

In The Beginning *fabrics*

1000's of Fabrics!
100's of Books!
Patterns, Notions, and More!
A new quilt show each month!

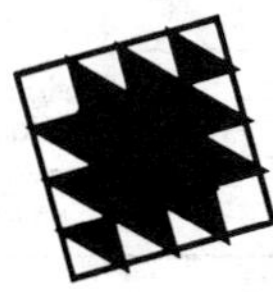

Mail Order

(206) 523-1121

Catalog Available

See our internet catalog at:

http://www.inthebeginningfabrics.com

Collector's Society

How would you like to receive four wonderful fabrics each month? They might be a beautiful collection of florals, a group of fun novelties, a coordinated group from the likes of Hoffman, Nancy Crow, or ITB. Whatever the monthly selections might include they will all have something in common. These groups will be high quality fabrics that we feel all serious fabric enthusiasts should have in their collections. You might use them in a project or you might just admire them, take them off the shelf and "pet" them once in awhile. You may also order extra yardage once you receive your selections.

We will send you 4 fat 1/4 yd. pieces (18" x 22") each month. Your credit card number will be kept on file and your account will be charged monthly. You continue as long as you want and may choose to discontinue your membership at any time. **The charge is $11.50 per month for residents of the U.S. and Canada and $14.00 per month for all others. If you prefer not to be charged monthly you may prepay for 6 months at a time, $69.00 for residents of U.S. and Canada and $84.00 for all others. (All prices subject to change) As an added bonus, each mailing will include Marsha McCloskey's Pattern of the Month.**

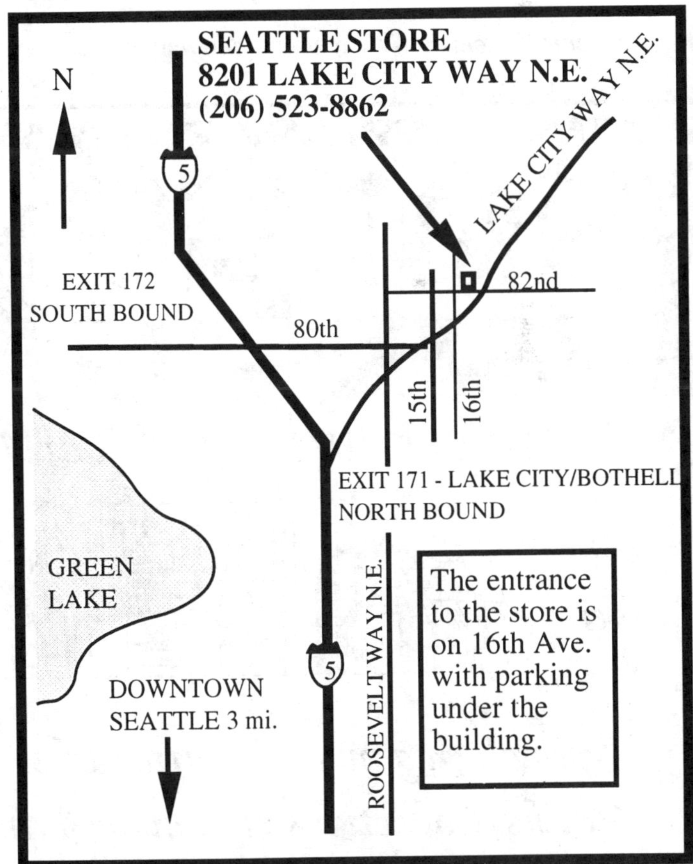

Hours: Mon., Tues., Fri. & Sat. 10 - 5:30, Wed. & Thur. 10 - 9, Sun. 12 - 5

Bellevue, WA #30

Conveniently located east of Seattle
just off of I-405 in the Design Market of Bellevue

- We carry the complete line of Electric Quilt products, plus Quilt Pro (Mac & PC versions) and the Quilt Pro foundation piecing CD.
- Our class schedule is packed with dynamic, "hands-on" classes in EQ3, photo transfer, fabric painting & dyeing, all types of quilting, clothing, and more!
- Browse through our large selection of books, patterns, and notions. (Have you tried silk thread for appliqué yet?)
- And with mountains of wonderful cotton, ikat, batik and imported fabrics you are certain to find something perfect for your next project.
- For the first-time quilter to the expert; from traditional favorites to art quilts, we strive to meet all your quilting needs.
- Can't come in person? Visit us on our website at www.quiltworksnw.com

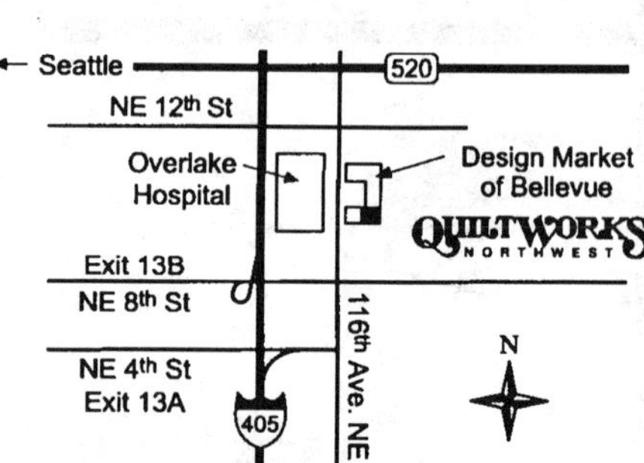

1014 116th Ave NE
Bellevue, WA 98004-4610
(425) 453-6005

Monday, Wednesday, Friday & Saturday
10:00 am–6:00 pm.
Tuesday & Thursday 10:00 am–9:00 pm.
Sunday 12:00 noon–5:00 pm.

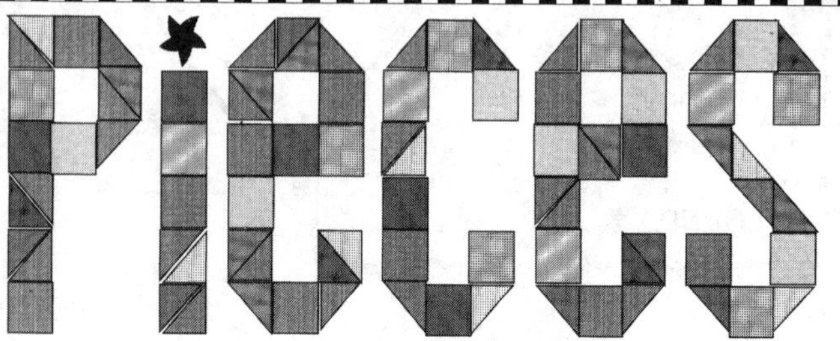

Mon - Sat
10 - 7
Sun 12 - 5

332 Burnett Ave. S 98055
(425) 271-7160
E-Mail: pieces@gte.net
Web Site: Coming Soon
Est: 1996
1900 sq.ft. 2600 Bolts

Quality Fabrics & Quilting

Mail Orders.

Quarterly Newsletter.

Specializing in a wide array of color!
Batiks, Collections & Unique Prints !
Classes & Kits year round !

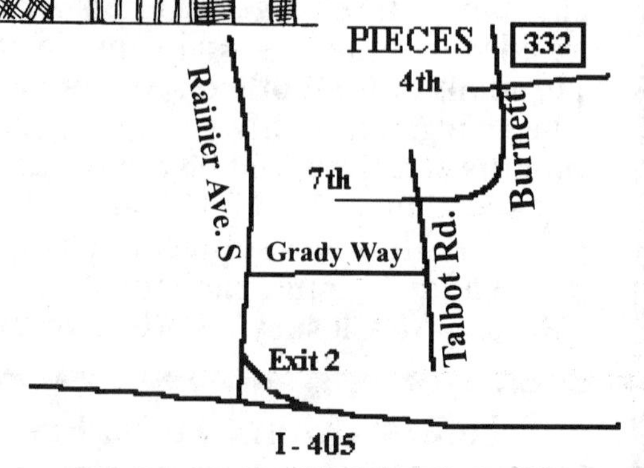

Renton, WA #31

CALICO CAT and

other Fine Fabrics

204 E. Main 98002
(800) 908-0885 or (253) 939-0885

Mon - Fri 10 - 8
Sat 10 - 5
Sun 12- 5

Wheel-Chair Accessible

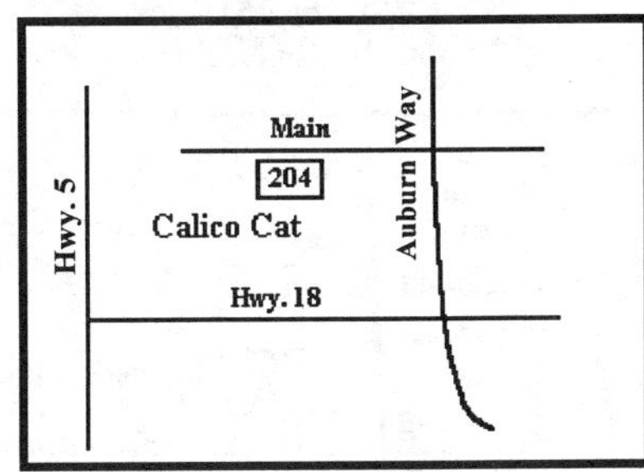

Over 2800 fine cotton fabrics.
Extensive book collection.
Notions, Patterns, Classes.
We Accept Visa, MC, Discover
Mail Order Available
Free Newsletter/Catalog
Block of the Month - By Mail - $6 per month
Customer receives a fabric kit and pattern each month and creates a sampler quilt.
Owner: Mary Stanton Est: 1992 2500 sq.ft. E-Mail: calicocat@mci2000.com

Federal Way, WA #33

Mon - Fri 10 - 6
Sat 10 - 5

Rags To Britches

1612 SW Dash Point Rd. 98023
(253) 661-5976
E-Mail: suesrags@aol.com
Web Site: www.suesrags.com/suesrags
Est: 1994 1500 Bolts

Quilting Fabrics, Books, Notions, Smocking and Heirloom Sewing Supplies, Patterns. Classes and Friendly Staff.

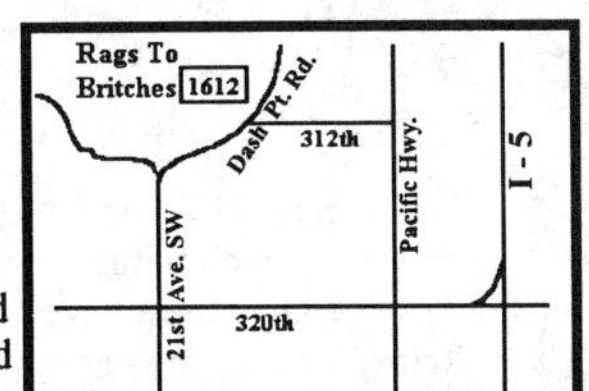

Tacoma, WA #34

Mon - Fri 10 - 7
Sat 10 - 6

Comfy Quilt Shop

3617 Bridgeport Way W 98466
(253) 565-5745 or (800) 889-0371
Owners: JoAnn Wick & Valerie Brown
Est: 1995

Large selection of Books, Patterns, etc.
Lots of Ethnic Fabric.
Classes available year around.

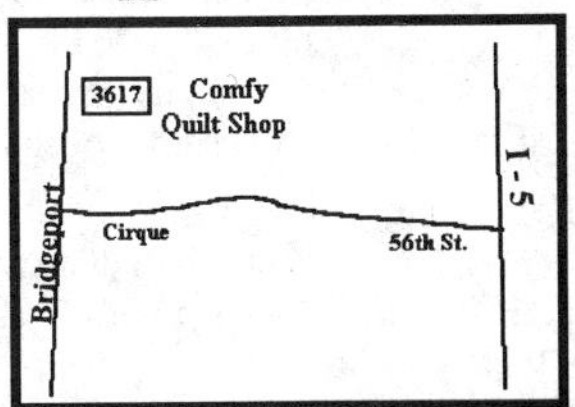

Yelm, WA #35

Mon - Fri 9 - 6
Sat 9 - 5
Sun 10 - 4

GEE-GEE'S Crafts & Fabrics

601 Yelm Ave. W, P.O. Box 926 98597
(360) 458-5616
Est: 1978 6000 sq.ft. 3500+ Bolts

100% Cotton Fabrics, over 200 Quilting Books, Quilting frames, stencils, notions, craft supplies,and yarns.
Plus Collectible Gifts & Finished Quilts.

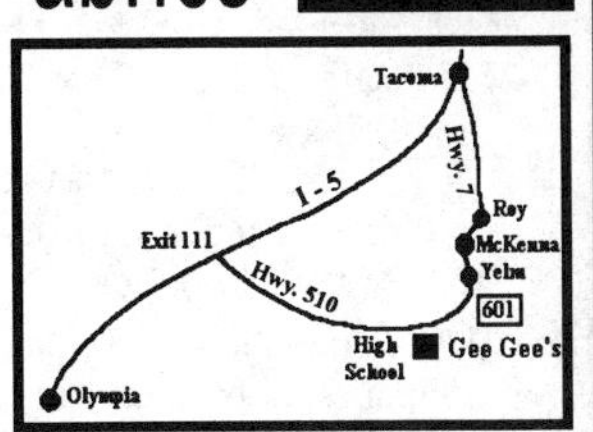

Yelm, WA #36

By Appt. Only

Quilts by Flo

13242 Rocking "S" Lane SE 98597
(360) 458-6667
Owner: Florence M. Schirman
Est: 1979 784 sq.ft. 380 Bolts
RV Turnaround

Classes, Notions, Fabric, Supplies, Quilts, Quilted Gifts. Relaxed Atmosphere in the Country.

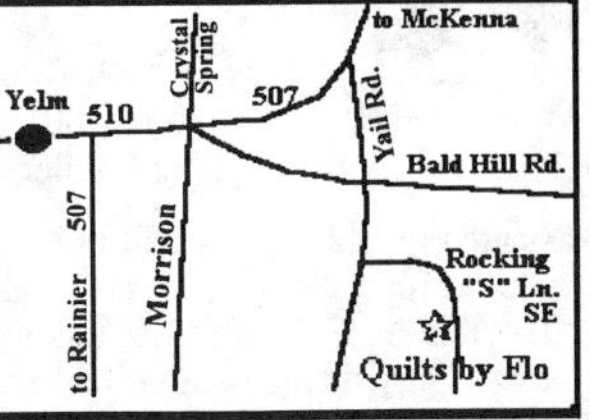

Serving Quilters for over 16 years!

The Quilt Barn

1206 E. Main 98372
1-(800) 988-BARN or (253) 845-1532
Owner: Evie Griffin 2000 sq.ft.

Puyallup, WA #37

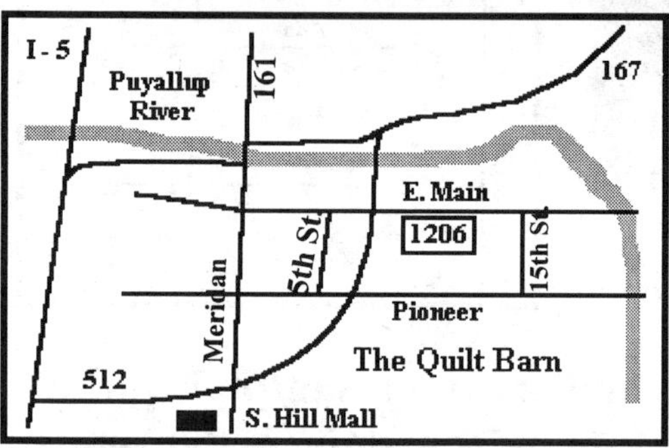

Mon - Sat 10 - 6
Thur til 9
Sun 12 - 5

- Fine 100% Cotton Quilting Fabrics
- Complete Quilting Supplies & Notions
- Lots of Patterns & Books
- Knowledgeable Staff
- Day & Evening Classes
- Open 7 days a week
- Fabric Ensemble Fabric Club
- Personalized Fabric Partner Club
- Mail Order

Call for our catalog or details on our Fabric Clubs.

Longview, WA #38

Mon - Thur 10 - 6
Fri 10 - 4
Sat 10 - 5

Heirloom Stitches

1414 Commerce Ave. 98632
(360) 425-7038
Owners:Ron & Vivian Spreadborough
Est: 1991 2500 sq.ft. over 4000 Bolts

Everything for quilting. 100% cottons, books, patterns, charts, notions. Hoffman, P&B Textiles, Moda, South Seas and more. Classes Available.

Maple
Broadway
1414
Heirloom Stitches
Commerce
12th
I-5
Hwy. 432
Exit 36

Longview, WA #39

Mon - Thur 10 - 6
Fri 10 - 5
Sat 10 - 4

Momma Made It

2035 9th Ave. 98632
(360) 636-5631
Est: 1996 1200+ Bolts

Located in a 1930's era cottage and specializing in reproduction fabrics. Staffed by friendly, knowledgeable quilters. Relax, browse, and get inspired!

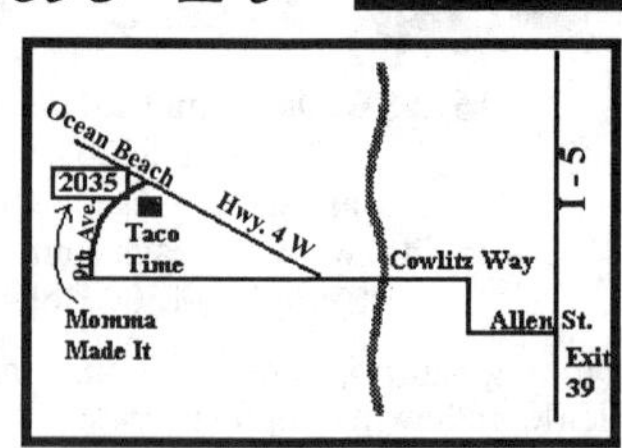

Centralia, WA #40

Mon - Sat 10 - 6
Thur til 9

Quilters Junction

1131 Mellen St. 98531
(360) 807-1255
Owner: Evelyna Liotta Manier Est: 1997

Located in a large house built in 1916. Owner loves reproduction fabrics. Take Exit 81 (Mellen St. Exit) off I - 5, and go one block east. Only house with quilts hanging on the porch. Fabrics, Patterns, Books & Notions.

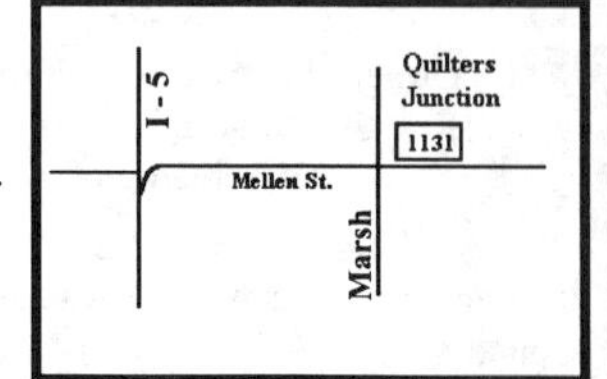

Olympia, WA #41

Mon - Fri 10 - 6
Sat 9 - 5

The Quilt Patch

2747 Pacific Ave. SE, Suite C-1 98506
(360) 754-6732 or (888) 737-2724
Fax: (360) 754-8182
Owner: Pat Seely Est: 1995
1600 sq.ft. 2500+ Bolts Newsletter

100% Cotton Fabric, Quilting & Sewing Supplies, Books, Patterns, Classes. Industrial Quilting Machine.

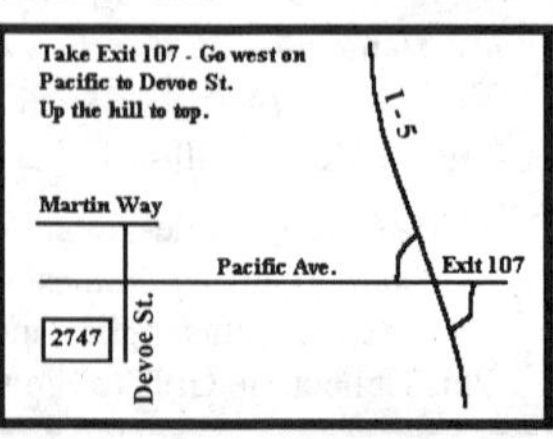

Quilter's Quarters

100 Ruby Street S.E Tumwater, WA 98501-4546 360-236-0596
Owners: Julie and Joan Bonin
Established: 1998 2700 Square Feet

"Your Full Service Quilting Headquarters"

Offering the finest and latest in quality

- 100% Cotton Fabric
- Books and Patterns
- Quilting Supplies and Notions
- Classes at all levels
- Authorized Bernina Dealership

Store Hours: Monday - Saturday 10-6
Tuesday 10-8 Sunday 12-4

From I-5 North: Take exit 102 Trosper Road. Turn right onto Trosper, right on Capital Blvd, and then left on Ruby. (Corner of Citgo and Seven-Eleven) We are located behind Pizza Hut.

From I-5 South: Take exit 102 Trosper Road. Turn left onto Trosper, right on Capital Blvd, and then left on Ruby. (Corner of Citgo and Seven-Eleven) We are located behind Pizza Hut.

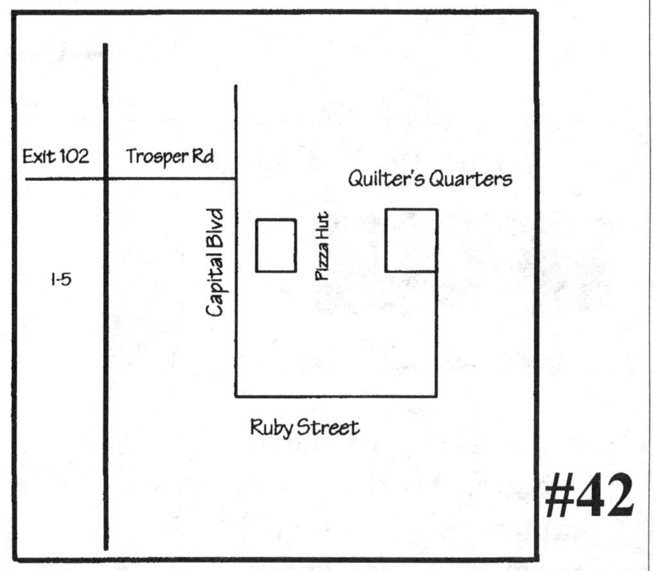

#42

Port Orchard, WA #43

Mon - Sat 10 - 6

Christina's Heritage

2516 Bethel Rd. SE 98366
(360) 895-1034

We specialize in reproduction fabrics 1820's - 1930's, Aunt Grace's also Hoffman, RJR, P&B, quilt supplies, books, classes. We also are trained in dating, appraising and restoring quilts.

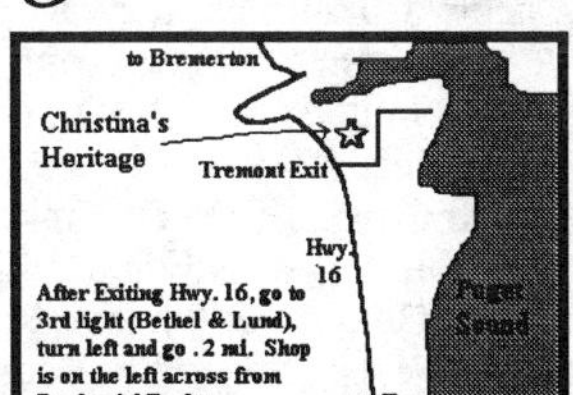

Port Orchard, WA #44

Mon - Fri 10 - 8
Sat 10 - 6
Sun 12 - 5

Rochelle's Fine Fabric & Quilting

1700 Mile Hill Drive #200C
South Kitsap Mall: Upper Level
(360) 895-1515 98366
E-Mail: rochelle@oz.net
Owner: Rochelle Savage
Est: 1981 5500 sq.ft.

A complete collection of cotton solids & prints from all the best manufacturers. A large selection of books & notions. Classes too!

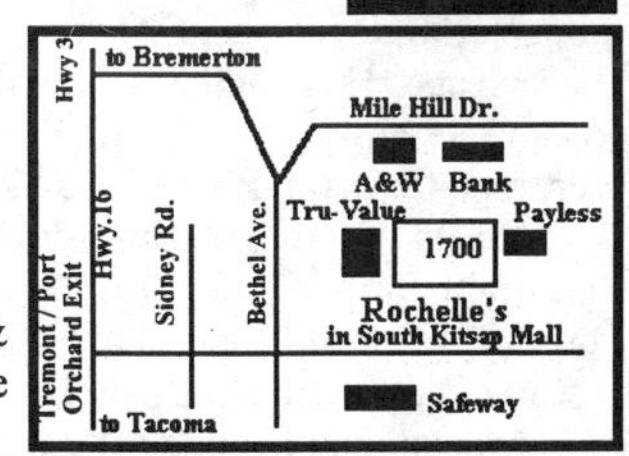

Bremerton, WA #45

7 Days a Week 10 - 6

The QUILT SHOP

6710-A Kitsap Way 98312
Off Hwy. 3 at Kitsap Lake
(360) 479-5970
Owner: Tish Smith Est: 1994
Aunt Grace's Headquarters

Bright Fabrics.
Books, Notions, Stencils, Classes.

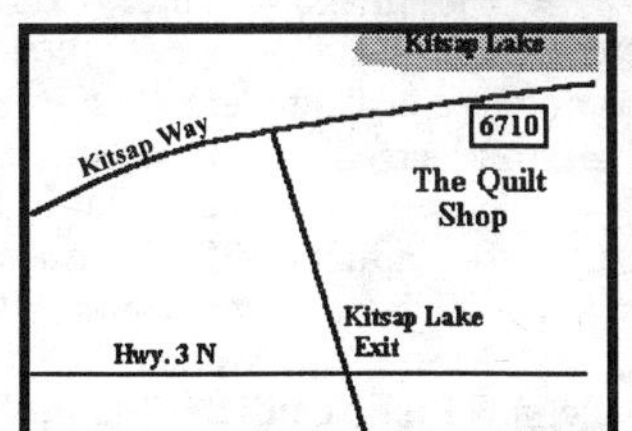

Poulsbo, WA #46

Mon - Sat 10 - 5:30
Sun 11 - 4

Heirloom Quilts & Fabrics

18833B Front St., P.O. Box 1957 98370
(360) 697-2222 Fax: (360) 697-4495
Est: 1986 3000 sq.ft. 2500 Bolts

Fabrics, Books, Notions, Cross-Stitch, Smocking Supplies, Classes.

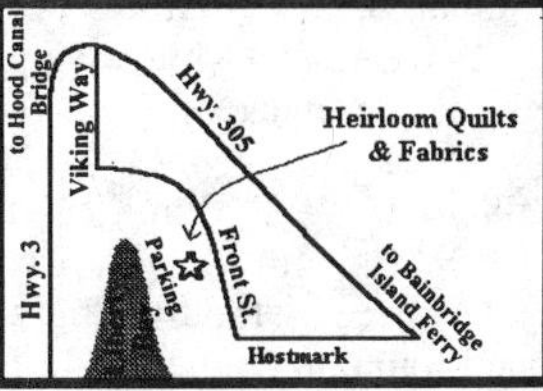

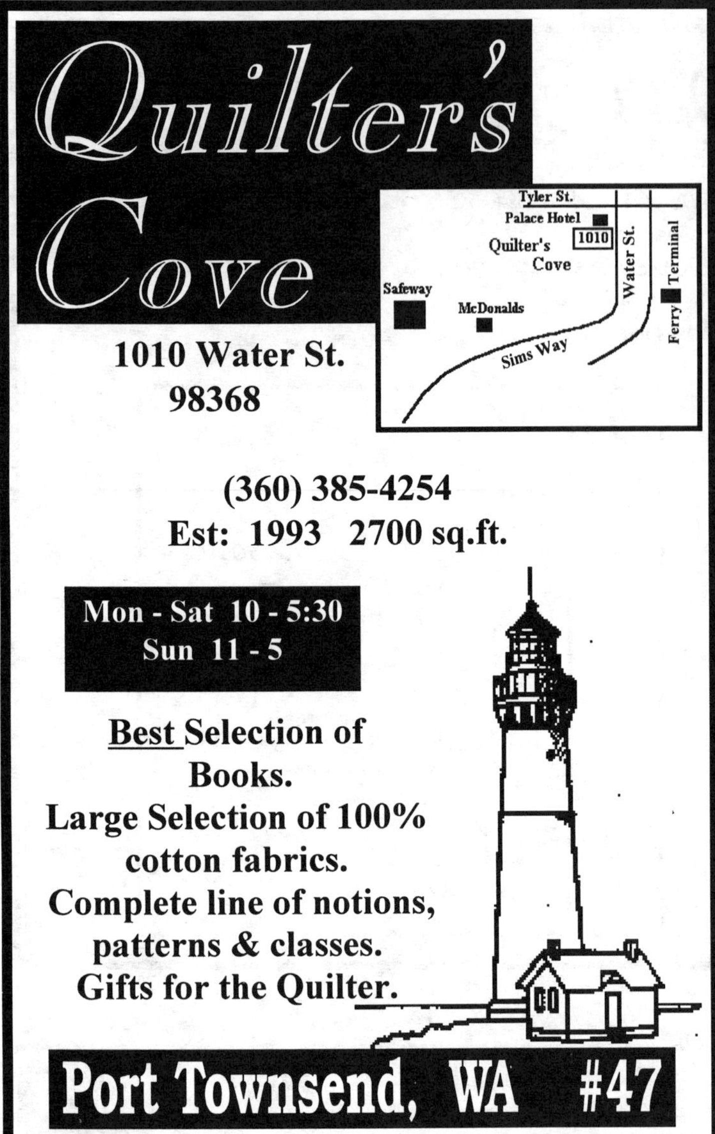

Port Townsend, WA #48

Mon - Sat 9:30 - 5:30

Seaport Fabrics, Inc.

2427 Sims Way 98368
(360) 385-3992 Fax: (360) 379-3961
Owners: Jim & Linda Dornan
3800 sq.ft.

Quilting, Clothing, Curtain and Upholstery Fabrics Available. A full service fabric store plus custom machine quilting. Advice is always free!

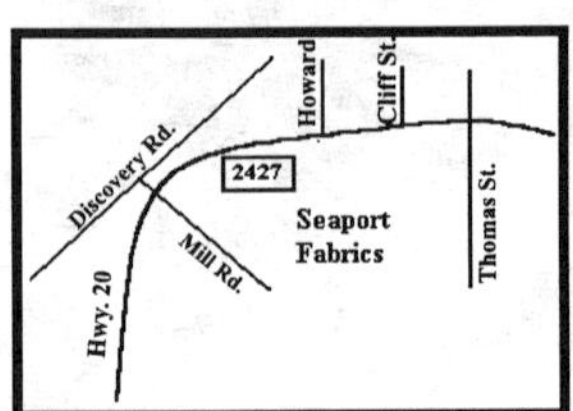

Washington Guilds:

Fidalgo Island Quilters, P.O. Box 1302, Anacortes, 98221
Meets: 1st Monday 1 p.m. at OACW Union Hall, 902 5th St
Northwest Quilting Connection, 906 35th St., Anacortes, 98221
Evergreen Quilters, P.O. Box 5344, Bellingham, 98227
Meets: 1st & 3rd Thuesday 10 a.m. at Garden St. Methodist Church
Moonlight Quilters, 336 36th St., Bellingham, 98226
Meets: 2nd Monday 6:30 p.m.
Cascade Quilters, 1273 Eagle Dr., Burlington, 98233
Meets: 2nd Monday (Sept - June) 2 p.m. at Conway Fire Hall
Camano Island Quilters, Camano Island
Meets: 1st Wednesday 10 a.m. (Sept. - June) at Country Club Fire Station, 1326 S. Elger Bay Rd. or 1st Thursday 6:30 p.m. at Stanwood Library
Country Quilters, 975 NW Pennsylvania Ave., Chehalis, 98532
Meets: Weekly in member's home
Cabin Fever Quilt Club, P.O. Box 207, Chimicum, 98325
Meets: Mondays at Tri-Area Community Center
Whitman Samplers Guild, 114 N. Main, Colfax, 99111
Meets: 2nd Monday 7 p.m. at Becky's Fabrics
Colville Piecemakers, 1496 Q Hwy. 20 E, Colville, 99114
Meets: 3rd Tuesday 6:30 p.m. at Lutheran Church, 295 E. Dominion
Quilters II, 129 E. Elm, Colville, 99114
Meets: 4th Monday 1 p.m. at Free Methodist Church, E. 1st & S. Elm
Blue Mountain Quilters, 245 E. Main, Dayton, 99328
Meets: 4th Monday 7:30 p.m. at Methodist Church
Fat Quarter Quilters, W 2024 Antler Rd., Deer Park, 99006
IRBQ Quilters, P.O. Box 1547, Eatonville, 98328
Mountain Quilters, 39615 Meridan E., Eatonville, 98328
Fairfield Quilt Guild, Rt. #1, Box 134A, Fairfield, 99205
Rock Creek Quilters, Fairfield
Crazy Quilters, 615 SW 346th St., Federal Way, 98023
Meets: 2nd & 4th Thursday 6 p.m. at Light of Christ Lutheran Church, 2400 SW 344th
Peninsula Lutheran Church Women Quilters, 6509 38th Ave. NW Gig Harbor, 98335
One Block Short, 8711 92nd St. NW, Gig Harbor, 98332
Mountain Valley Guild, 24809 50th Ave. E, Graham, 98338
Horizon Quilters Ultd., P.O. Box 202, Grandview, 98930
Meets: 2nd Tuesday 9:30 a.m. at Immanuel Lutheran Church, 300 S. Euclid
Pieceful Discovers Q. C., 42 Panhandle Rd., Grays Harbor, 98550
Meets: Twice a month Tuesdays 6:30 p.m. (Except Nov. & Dec) at Cosmopolis School
Quilters on the Rock, 1188 E. Sherwood Ln., Greenbank, 98253
Ladies of the Lake, P.O. Box 363, Hoodsport, 98548
Pieceful Discovers Quilt Guild, Hoquaim
Issaquah Quilters Guild, P.O. Box 337, Issaquah, 98029
Meets: 2nd Friday 10 a.m. at Our Savior Lutheran Church
Quacky Quilters, 417 Modrow Rd., Kalama, 98625
Quilts From the Heart, P.O. Box 82133, Kenmore, 98028
Service organization making quilts for "at risk" children.
Senior Center Quilters, 500 S. Auburn, Kennewick, 99336
Covington Quilters, 26503 168th Pl. SE, Kent, 98042
Evergreen Piecemakers, P.O. Box 5817, Kent, 98064
Meets: 2nd & 4th Monday at First Christian Church
Narrows Conn. Quiltmakers, 1604 A St. KPN, Lake Bay, 98349
Cheney Country Quilters, Rt. #2, Box 70, Lamont, 99017
Meets: Mondays 1 p.m. at Ben Franklin store, Cheney
Crazy Quilters, 2845 E. St., Hwy. 525, Langley, 98260
Meets: Weekly 10 a.m. at Bayview Senior Services
Calico Quilter, 4723 Olympia Way, Longview, 98632
Meets: Weekly in member's home
Chatty Quilters, 250 Niemi Rd., Longview, 98632
Meets: 2nd & 4th Wednesday 10 a.m. (except Dec)
Enchanted Quilters, Rt. #2, Box 3030, Lopez Island, 98261
Meets: 2nd Tuesday, Lopez Senior Center
Pieceable Quilters, 830 E. Wiser Lake Rd., Lynden, 98264
Meets: 1st Tuesday 7 p.m. at the Fabric Cottage
Sew and Sews, 825 Fern Dr., Lynden, 98264
Meets: 3rd Friday at 825 Fern Dr.
Quilters Anonymous, P.O. Box 322, Lynnwood, 98046
Meets: 2nd Wednesday 10 a.m. and the Tuesday night before 7 p.m. at Church of Christ, 21507 52nd Ave. W, Mountlake Terrance. Largest guild in Washington.
Chelan Vly. Undercover Quilters, 1385 Totem Pole, Manson
Quilters Les Complete, P.O. Box 594, Milton, 98354
Basin Piecemakers, 8504 Hillcrest Dr., Moses Lake, 98837
Meets: 4th Tuesday at Frontier Fabrics
Cascade Quilters, 1302 E. Kincaid St., Mt. Vernon, 98273
Apple Valley Piecemakers, P.O. Box 819, Naches, 98937
Meets: 3rd Monday 7 p.m. at Naches Fire Hall
Pend O'Reille Quilters, 306 S. Washington, Newport, 99156
Sea Gal Quilters, P.O. Box 1022, Ocean Shores, 98569

Fronen Stepdecker Odessa Q. C., P.O. Box 151, Odessa, 99159
Meets: Mondays 1 p.m. & 7 p.m.
Quiltmakers of Olympia, P.O. Box 7751, Olympia, 98507
Creative Quilters, P.O. Box 264, Orcas Island, 98245
Night Court Quilters, 1114 E. 3rd., Port Angeles, 98362
Crazy Quilters, 727 S. Alder St., Port Angeles, 98362
Meets: 2nd & 4th Tuesday 1 p.m. at member's home
Court House Quilters, 305 W. 3rd, Port Angeles, 98362
West Sound Quilt Guild, c/o Teri Emmons, 1860 SE Van Skiver Rd. Port Orchard, 98367
Meets: 1st Wednesday 7 p.m. at Givens Community Center, e-mail address: gemmons@ix.netcom.com
Port Orchard Quilters Guild, P.O. Box 842, Port Orchard, 98366
West Sound Quilters, Port Orchard
Cabin Fever Quilters, 581 Pinecrest Dr., Port Townsend, 98368
Kitsap Quilters, P.O. Box 2787, Poulsbo, 98370
Meets: 4th Tuesday at St. Charles Episcopal Hall
Patchin People, 405 SE Grant, Pullman, 99163
Meets: Monthly 1:30 p.m. at Rec Hall Statesman Condo
Puyallup Valley Quilters, P.O. Box 1421, Puyallup, 98371
Tacoma Quilters, 2028 Historic Way, Puyallup, 98371
Chapel Women's Quilters, 13902 Finian Rd. SE, Rainier, 98576
Willapa Harbor Quilters, Rt. #3, Box 39A, Raymond, 98577
Meets: Tuesdays 11 a.m. & Thursdays 7 p.m. at First Baptist Church, 9th & Duryea
The Country Samples Quilts Club, Rt. #1, Box 15E, Reardan, 99029
Block Party Quilters, P.O. Box 932, Redmond, 98073
Meets: 1st Thursday 7 p.m. at Eastside Catholic High School, 11650 SE 60th, Bellevue
Cedar River Quilters, Renton
Meets: 3rd Wednesday 6:30 p.m. at Lutheran Church, South 2nd & Whitworth
South Eastern Washington Quilters P.O. Box 1201, Richland, 99352
Meets: 1st Tuesday 6:30 p.m. at Benton Co. PUD, Kennewick
Tri City Quilters, P.O. Box 215, Richland, 99352
Meets: 2nd Monday 7 p.m. at PUD & 3rd. Monday 10 a.m. at Central United Protestant Church
Peaceby Piece Ritzville Quilter Guild, 107 W. Main, Ritzville, 99169
Meets: 2nd Monday night at Zion Congregational Church
Eatonville Quilt Club, 32425 S.R. 507, Roy, 98580
Contemporary Quilt Assoc., P.O. Box 95685, Seattle, 98145
Meets: 2nd Saturday 10:30 a.m. at University Unitarian Church, 6556 35th Ave. NE
Big Pretty Girls, Seattle
Seattle Quilt Troupe, 6203 Vassar Ave. NE, Seattle, 98115
Pacific Northwest Quilters, P.O. Box 22073, Seattle, 98122
Pacific NW Needle Arts Guild, 4649 Sunnyside Ave. N, Seattle, 98103
Three general meetings each year and approx. nine workshops
The Y's Piecemakers, 7740 17th Ave. SW, Seattle, 98106
Riverton Pk United Meth. Women, 13508 34th Ave. S, Seattle, 98168
Northwest Assoc. of Quilt Artists, 8361 30th Ave. NW, Seattle 98117
Around the Sound Q. G., 350 N. 190th St. #418-C, Seattle, 98133
Sunbonnet Sue Quilt Club, P.O. Box 211, Sequim, 98382
Meets: Wednesdays at Masonic Hall
Christmastown Quilters, E. 200 Tramac Pl., Shelton, 98584
Meets: 2nd Thursday 7 p.m. at Mason General Hospital
Wednesday Friendship Quilters, 19342 1st NW, Shoreline, 98177
Busy Bee Quilters, P.O. Box 26, Snohomish, 98291
Meets: 3rd Thursday 6:30 p.m. at St. Michaels Catholic Church, 1512 Pine Ave.
Q.U.I.L.T. Connection, P.O. Box 61, Snohomish, 98291
Meets: 2nd Thursday in member's home
West Sound Quilt Guild, P.O. Box 4306, South Colby, 98384
Rock Creek Quilters, Rt. #1, Box 158, Spokane, 99012
Spokane Valley Quilters Guild, P.O. Box 13516, Spokane, 99213
Meets: 1st Tuesday evenings (Feb, March, June, Sept, Oct, Dec) at Valley Senior Center
Washington State Quilters, Spokane Chapter, Box 7117, Spokane, 99207
Meets: Jan, April, July & Oct at Mukigawa Ft. Wright Institute
Northwest Quilting Connection, 1641 County Line Rd., Stanwood, 98292
Meets: 1st or 2nd Sat (Jan, March, May, Sept, Nov) in various locations
Piecemakers, 405 Isaac Pincus St., Steilacoom, 98388
Steady Stitchers, 83 Chapman Loom, Steilacoom, 98388
Meets: Tuesdays 9 a.m. in member's home
Fat Quarters, 821 4th St., Sultan, 98294
Meets: 1st Wednesday in member's home
Lower Valley Quilters of Sunnyside, 5881 Hwy. 241, Sunnyside, 98944
Meets: Monthly in member's home
Around the Sound Quilters Guild, Tacoma
Comforters, 4639 S. Thompson, Tacoma, 98408
Meets: 4th Thursday at South End Community Center
Narrows Connection Quiltmakers, Tacoma
Needle Arts Guild of Puget Sound, P.O. Box 99093, Tacoma
Titlow Lodge Quilters, 8425 6th Ave., Tacoma, 98465
Mt. Tahoma Quilt Guild, 871 S. 142nd St., Tacoma, 98444
PM Patchers, 1239 E. 54th St., Tacoma, 98404
Cowlitz Prairie Crazy Quilters, P.O. Box 56, Toledo, 98591
Clark County Quilters, P.O. Box 5857, Vancouver, 98668
Meets: 2nd Thursday (Sept - June) 6:30 p.m. at Church of Christ, 800 NE Andresen Rd.
Ongoing Quilters of Marshall Ctr, 13316 SE McGillivray, Vancouver, 98684
Vashon Island Quilters, P.O. Box 1132, Vashon, 98070
Needle & I Night 13714 SW 240th St., Vashon Island, 98070
Meets: 2nd Monday 7 p.m. at Shoreline Center, 18560 1st Ave. NE, Seattle
North Central Washington Quilters, P.O. Box 2715, Wenatchee, 98807
Meets: last Wednesday 7 p.m. at Wenatchee Museum
New Kids on the Block Quilters, 407 N. Western Ave., Wenatchee, 98801
South Beach Quilter's Guild, P.O. Box 1315, Westport, 98595
White Salmon Quilters, 161 Tunnel Rd., White Salmon, 98672
Yakima Quilt Guild, Yakima
Meets: 1st and 3rd Wednesdays at Franklin School
Yakima Valley Quilter's Guild, P.O. Box 10771, Yakima, 98909
Meets: Every other month 1st & 3rd Wednesday evenings at Camlu Retirement Home Rec room
Yakima Valley Museum Quilters, 2105 Tieton Ave., Yakima, 98902
Meets: Thursdays 9 a.m. at the museum

Other Shops in Washington:

Anacortes	Fabrics Plus, 608 Commercial Ave	360-293-7641
Arlington	Bunny Patch, 24613 27th Ave. NE	360-435-8414
Battle Ground	Country Manor Fabric & Crafts, 7702 NE 179th	360-573-6084
Burlington	Stitch and Quilt, 415 Pease Rd.	360-757-1889
Chehalis	Sisters, 476 N. Market Blvd.	360-748-9747
Edmonds	The Calico Basket, 550 A Main St.	425-774-6446
Ellensburg	Moser's Clothing Store, 118 E. 4th	509-925-1272
Long Beach	Jean's Fabrics, 811 Pacific S	
Lopez	Enchanted Needle, P.O. Box 178	360-468-2777
Lynden	Calico Country, 527 Front St.	360-354-4832
Marysville	Fudge & Funnies, 1515 3rd St.	360-659-8455
Metaline Falls	Sweet Creek Creations, E 219 5th	509-446-2429
Mt. Vernon	Calico Creations, 400 S. 1st. St.	360-336-3241
Newport	The Pin Cushion, 306 S. Washington	509-447-5913
Prosser	Sew Delightful, 1119 Meade Ave	509-786-4441
Pullman	Quilted Heart, 1709 NW Lamont St.	509-332-1905
Puyallup	Puyallup Sewing & Vacuum, 111 N. Meridian	253-841-4288
Richland	Perks Sewing, 621 The Parkway	509-943-1149
Seattle	Nancy's Sewing Basket, 2221 Queen Anne N.	206-282-9112
Sequim	The Pine Cupboard, 127 W. Washington	360-683-7026
Snohomish	Clearview Triangle, 8311 180th SE	360-668-4151
Stevenson	Rock Creek Fabrics, 390 SW 2nd	509-427-8662
Union Gap	The Quilter, 2640 Main St.	509-575-7569
Yakima	Fiddlesticks, 1601 Summitview	509-452-7718
Yakima	Ann's Quilts and Things, 3504 Ahtanum	509-965-2313

7 Featured Shops

WEST VIRGINIA

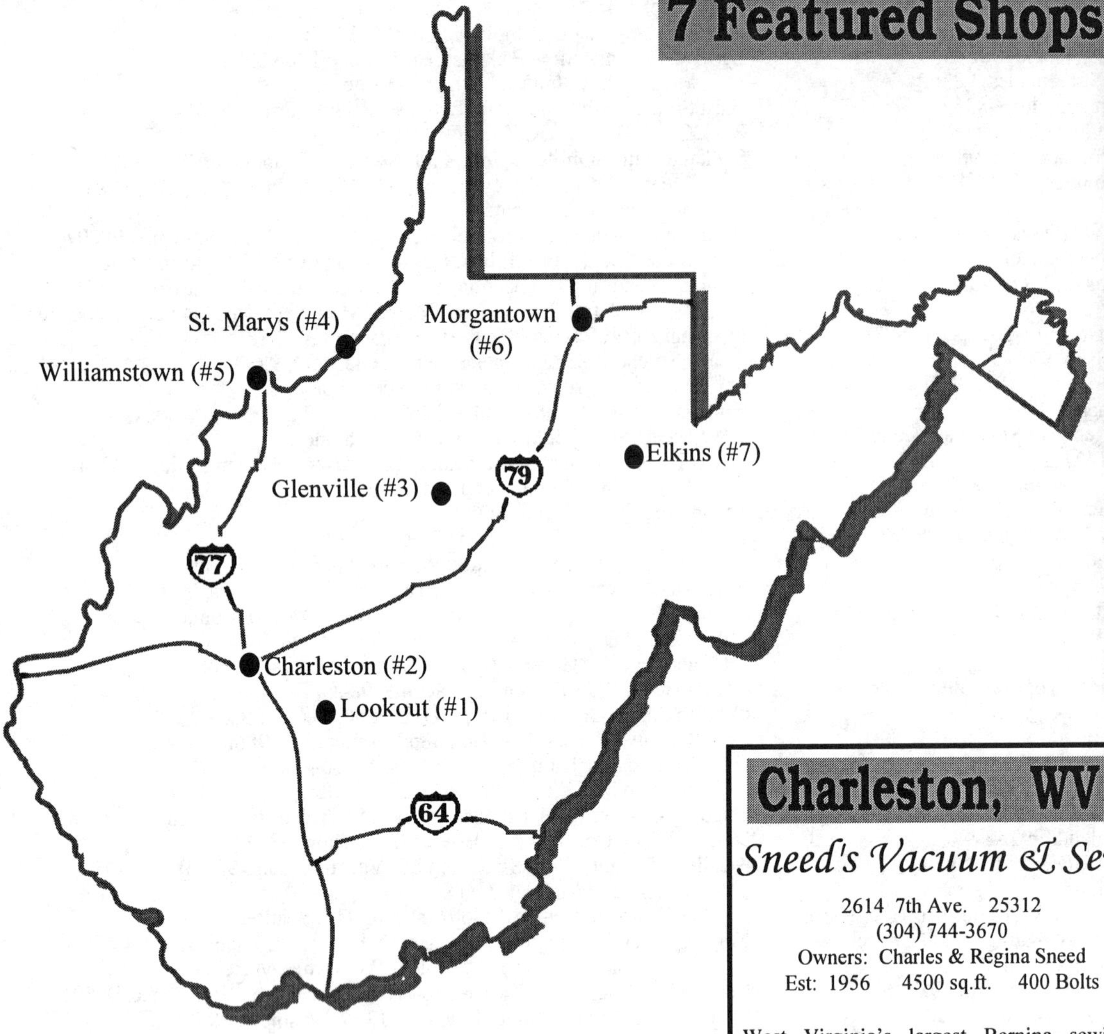

St. Marys (#4)
Morgantown (#6)
Williamstown (#5)
Elkins (#7)
79
Glenville (#3)
77
Charleston (#2)
Lookout (#1)
64

Charleston, WV #2

Mon - Fri 8 - 5:30
Sat 9 - 1

Sneed's Vacuum & Sewing Center

2614 7th Ave. 25312
(304) 744-3670
Owners: Charles & Regina Sneed
Est: 1956 4500 sq.ft. 400 Bolts

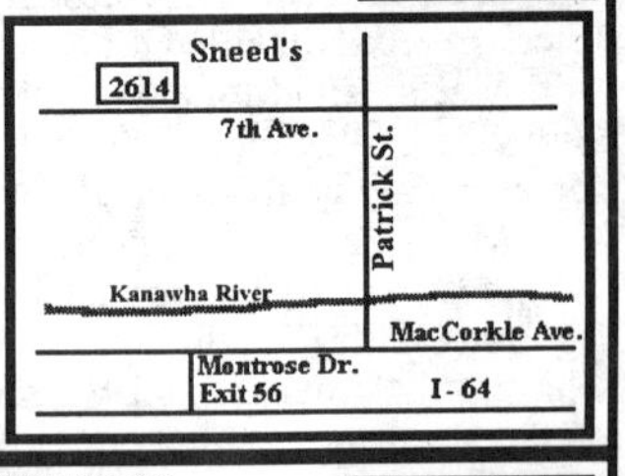

West Virginia's largest Bernina sewing machine dealer. Quilting Supplies, Fabrics, and lots of classes.

Sneed's
2614
7th Ave.
Patrick St.
Kanawha River
MacCorkle Ave.
Montrose Dr. Exit 56
I - 64

Glenville, WV #3

Tues - Sat 9 - 5

The Crafter's Patch

Main and Morris Sts. 26351
(304) 462-4010
Owner: Sadie Kelble
Est: 1994 1500 sq.ft. 500 Bolts

The Best 100% Cotton Quilt Fabrics. P&B, Benartex, RJR, South Seas. Quilting and Sewing Notions. Year round classes. Helpful information when needed.

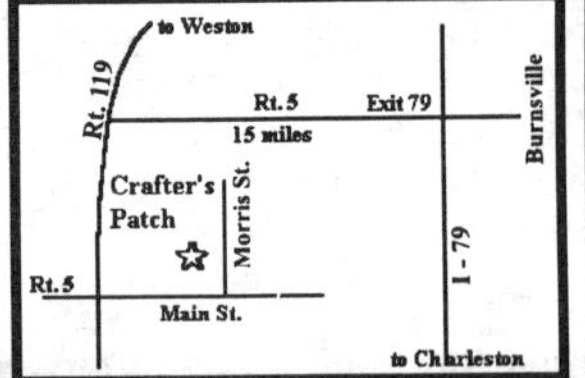

St. Marys, WV #4

Tues - Sat 9 - 4

Zepora's Quilt Shop

116 Lafayette St. 26170
(304) 684-7113
Owner: Zepora Morgan Hughes
Est: 1977 1600 sq.ft. 1500 Bolts

Everything to make a quilt under one roof. Educational department. Custom Made Quilts.

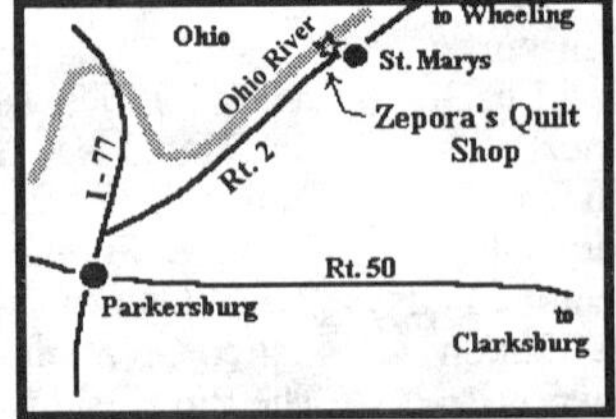

West Virginia Guilds:

Hands All Around, Beckley
  Meets: 1st Monday at United Methodist Temple
Penthouse Quilters, Beckley
  Meets: Every Monday & Thursday
  at Earhart Dodge Bldg.
Log Cabin Quilters, Elkins
  Meets: 1st Thursday at Elkins Manor
Mountain Quilters c/o Mary Burdette, 104 Greenberry Dr., Elkview, 25071
Nimble Thimbles, Fayetteville
  Meets: 3rd Tuesday at American Legion Bldg.
Thimbles & Thread Quilt Guild, Main & Morris St., Glenville, 26351
Quilt Lovers Guild c/o Edna Ross, Rt. 4, Box 386, Hurricane, 25526
Country Roads Quilt Guild, 120 High St., Morgantown, 26505
  Meets: 2nd Thursday 7 p.m. at South Middle School
Mercer Co. Quilting Bee c/o Margaret Meador, Box 109, Princeton, 24740
West Virginia Quilters Inc., P.O. Box 18016, South Charleston, 25302
Kanawha Valley Quilters, P.O. Box 8252, South Charleston, 25303
Moon & Stars Quilt Guild, P.O. Box 18040, South Charleston, 25303
Mountain Heritage Quilters Guild, Union

Other Shops in West Virginia:

Buckhannon	Marlene's, 7 W. Main St.	304-472-7269
Clarksburg	Clarksburg Sewing Center, Route 2	304-622-8112
Cross Lanes	Ben Franklin, 5512 Big Tyler Rd.	304-776-3434
Farmington	Cotton Patch, Route 250 N.	304-825-6225
Huntington	The Cherry Tree Quilt Shop, 6306 E. Pea Ridge	304-736-8086
Jane Lew	Homestead Fabric Shoppe, Main	304-884-7666
Lewisburg	Threads, 157 Seneca Trail	304-645-3956
Lewisburg	Quilts Unlimited, 203 E. Washington St.	304-647-4208
Malden	Cabin Creek Quilts, 4208 Malden	304-925-9499
Point Pleasant	Ruth's Fabric Shop, 705 22nd St.	304-675-6454
Reedsville	Eleanor's Quilts, Rt. 7 E.	304-864-5762
Sophia	Quilt Fabrics, Main St.	304-683-9429
Winfield	Fern's Fabric and Quilt Shoppe, 6130 St. Rt. 34	304-757-3047

Superior (#58, 59)
Hayward (#57)
Park Falls (#49)
Minocqua (#48)
Eagle River (#47)
Frederic (#56)
Rhinelander (#50)
Rice Lake (#55)
Tomahawk (#46)
Turtle Lake (#53)
53
New Richmond (#54)
Chippewa Falls (#42)
Antigo (#52)
Wausau (#45)
Eau Claire (#40)
Withee (#41)
Menomonie (#39)
Osseo (#51)
Waupaca (#16)
Stevens Point (#44)
94
Wisconsin Rapids (#43)
Green Bay (#12, 13)
Appleton (#14, 15)
Denmark (#11)
Berlin (#17)
Oshkosh (#18)
Manitowoc (#8)
La Crosse (#38)
Fond du Lac (#20, 21)
Sheboygan (#10)
Princeton (#19)
Reedsburg (#37)
(#5, 6)
West Bend
Beaver Dam (#22, 23)
Prairie du Sac (#36)
Slinger (#9)
Cedarburg (#7)
Waunakee (#26)
Sun Prairie (#24, 25)
Ferryville (#35)
Madison (#27, 28)
Elm Grove (#1)
Cambridge (#29)
Genesee Depot (#2)
90
Fennimore (#34)
Hales Corners (#4)
Montfort (#33)
Janesville(#30)
Racine (#3)
Platteville (#32)
Monroe (#31)

WISCONSIN

59 Featured Shops

Elm Grove, WI #1

Patched Works, Inc.

In a Western Suburb of Milwaukee
13330 Watertown Plank Rd.
Elm Grove, WI 53122
(414) 786-1523
Owner: Trudie Hughes
Est: 1978 6000 sq.ft.

Books
Patterns

"Home of Trudie Hughes' Summer Camps"

Mon - Fri 9 - 5 Wed til 8
Sat 9 - 4 Sun 12 - 4

5000 bolts of Cotton Fabric
Hundreds of Books &
Patterns for the Quiltmaker

Owned by a Master Fabricaholic

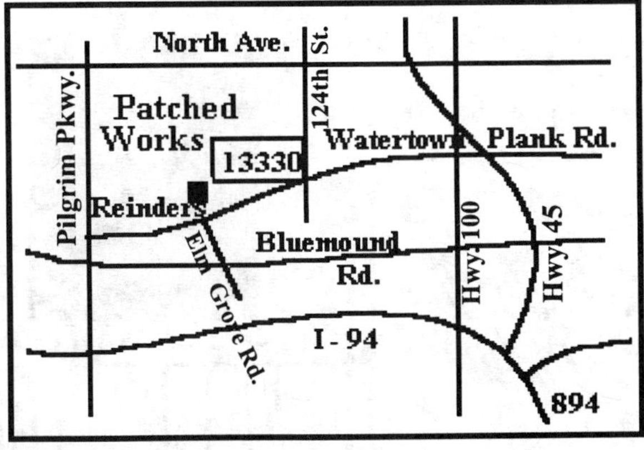

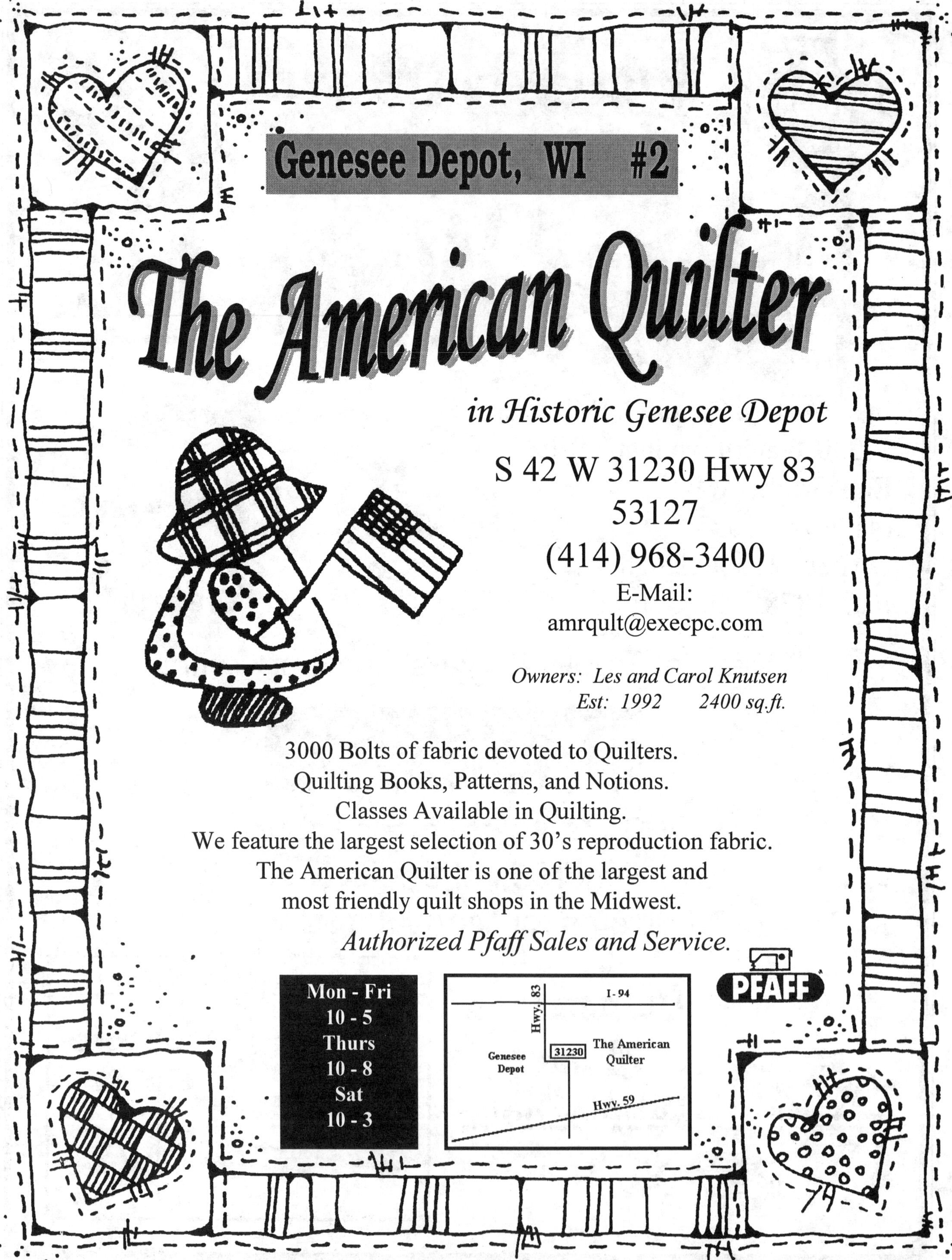

Genesee Depot, WI #2
The American Quilter
in Historic Genesee Depot
S 42 W 31230 Hwy 83
53127
(414) 968-3400
E-Mail:
amrqult@execpc.com
Owners: Les and Carol Knutsen
Est: 1992 2400 sq.ft.
3000 Bolts of fabric devoted to Quilters.
Quilting Books, Patterns, and Notions.
Classes Available in Quilting.
We feature the largest selection of 30's reproduction fabric.
The American Quilter is one of the largest and
most friendly quilt shops in the Midwest.
Authorized Pfaff Sales and Service.
PFAFF
Mon - Fri
10 - 5
Thurs
10 - 8
Sat
10 - 3
I-94
Hwy. 83
31230
The American Quilter
Genesee Depot
Hwy. 59

Complete Quilt & Cross-Stitch Shop

Racine, WI #3

Mon, Wed, Fri	10:00 a.m. - 5:00 p.m.
Tues, Thurs	10:00 a.m. - 8:00 p.m.
Saturday	10:00 a.m. - 4:00 p.m.
Sunday	11:00 a.m. - 4:00 p.m.

We'd love to have you visit us - in person or on our new web site! We also have a new toll-free telephone number to make ordering easier.

(888) 3CALICO
(888) 322-5426
Fax: (414) 632-2457
E-Mail: calicocc@execpc.com
Web Site: www.execpc.com/~calicocc
Est: 1979 3000 sq.ft.

3305 Washington Ave. 53405 (414) 632-4224

Calico, Canvas & Colors

Two stories of Wonderful Fabrics, Graphs, Patterns and Gifts with a friendly, knowledgeable staff to help.

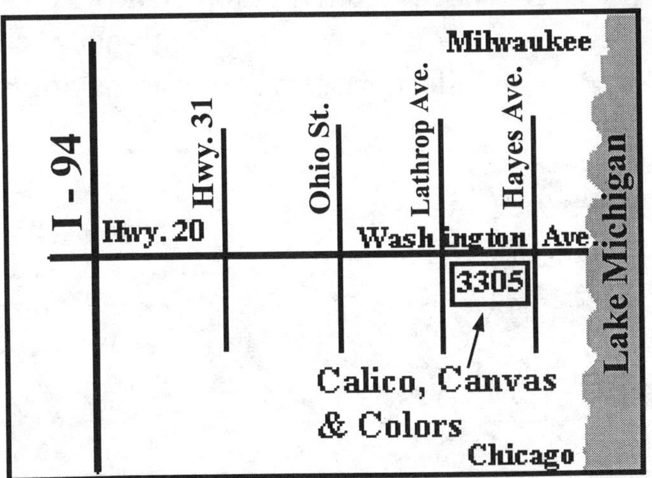

Hales Corners, WI #4

Mon - Fri 9 - 9
Sat 9 - 5
Sun 12 - 4

Hearthside Quilters Nook

10731 W. Forest Home Ave. 53130
(414) 425-2474
Owners: Carol Baker & Jan Krueger
Est: 1979 2800 sq.ft. 2000 Bolts

Beautiful Fabric, Great Selection, Books, Patterns, Notions, Heirloom & Silk Ribbon Sewing Supplies. Christmas year Round. "Where Friendly service is a Tradition!"

West Bend, WI #6

Mon - Fri 8:30 - 4

Hinterberg Design, Inc.

2805 E. Progress 53095
(800) 443-5800
Owner: Kris Hinterberg
Est: 1981 Free Catalog

Factory Store
Quilting Frames and Hoops

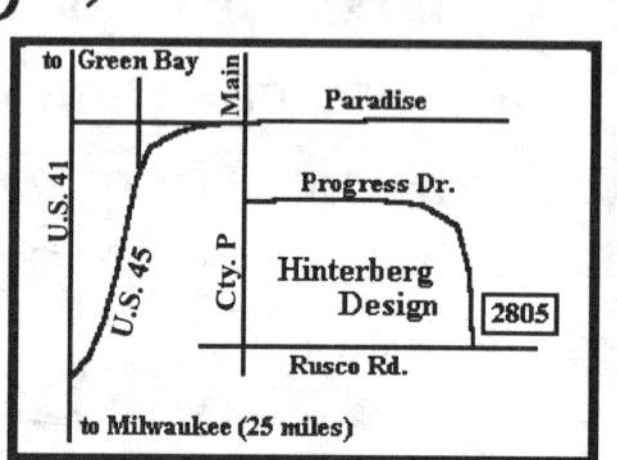

Royce Fabrics

Est: 1971

Mon - Fri 9:30 - 8
Sat 9:30 - 5
Sun 11 - 4

West Bend, WI #5

846 S. Main 53095
(414) 338-0597
Fax: (414) 338-1492
E-Mail:
roycefabrics @hnet.net
Owner: Jerry Quasius
3200 sq.ft.

2000 Quilting Fabrics.
Books, Soft Patterns,
Quilting Classes.

BERNINA

Authorized Sales & Service Dealer for 25 Years.

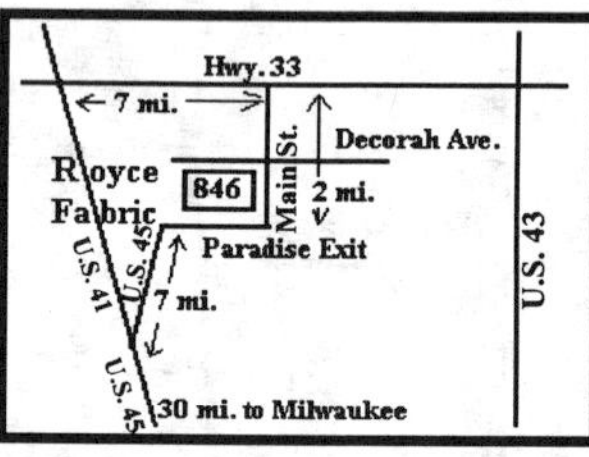

Cedarburg, WI #7

W62 N228 Washington Ave. 53012
(414) 377-8400
Fax: (414) 375-8958
Owner: Vikki Hahn

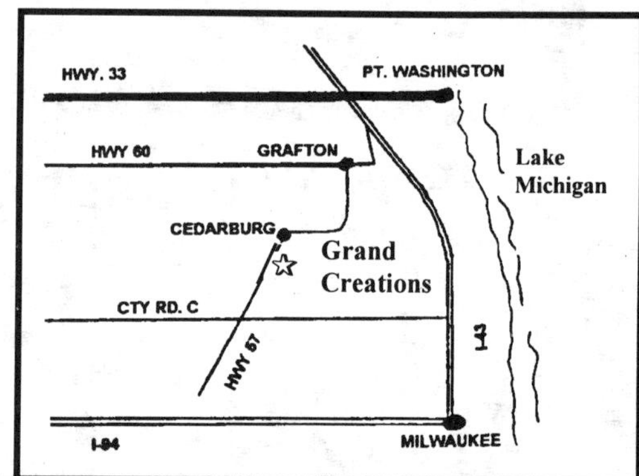

Growing selection of top quality 100% cottons for quilting, Patterns & Books.
Continuous schedule of classes.
Collector Bears and bear making supplies including Imported Mohair.

Mon - Thur 10 - 9
Fri 10 - 6 Sat 10 - 3

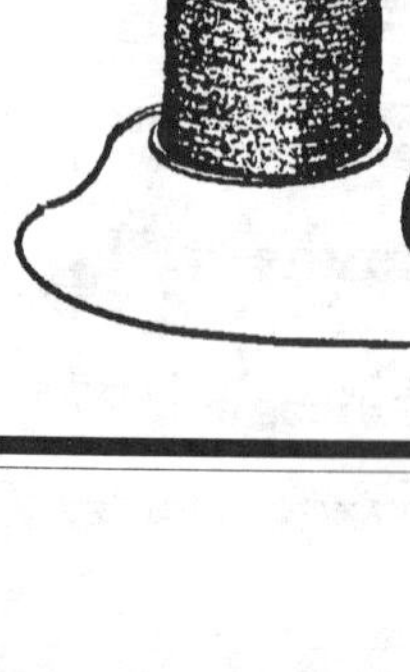

Grand Creations by Vikki

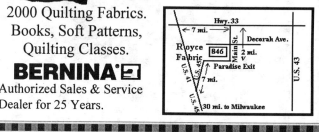

Quilts n' Silks

Fabrics and Supplies

Manitowoc, WI #8

Mon - Fri
9 - 6
Sat 9 - 3

711 York St. 54221-2232
(800) 933-1161
(920) 686-0839 Fax: (920) 686-0876
Owner: Elaine A. Springer
Est: 1995 2400 sq.ft. 2500 Bolts

Authorized
PFAFF
Dealer

For all of your quilting fabrics, books, patterns, notions and quilting classes visit Quilts n' Silks!

Spiegel ❖ Kona ❖ South Seas ❖ Debbie Mumm Collections
Thimbleberries ❖ Benartex ❖ P&B ❖ Hoffman
RJR Jinny Beyer ❖ Moda ❖ Bali ❖ Robert Kaufman

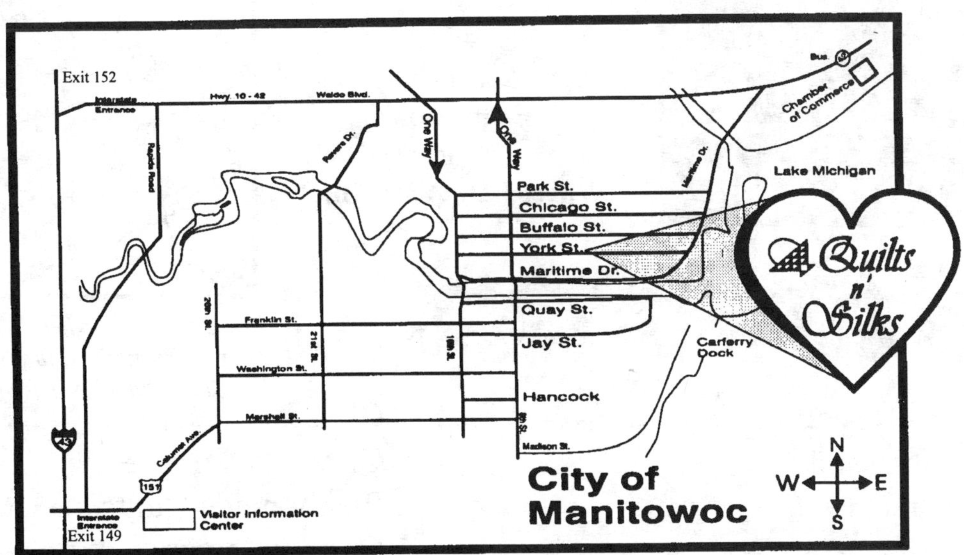

Overlooking the Wisconsin Maritime Museum in historic downtown Manitowoc. Near the Car Ferry dock.

Slinger, WI #9

Mon, Wed, Fri 9 - 5
Tues & Thur 9 - 7
Sat 10 - 4

Common Threads

425 C East Washington St. 53086
(414) 644-0613
E-Mail: common@nconnect.net
Louanne & Bill Spenner
Est: 1995 1500 sq.ft. 1000 Bolts

For women who take pride in their quilting & sewing. Friendly, Expert Service by Knowledgeable Staff. Husqvarna Viking Authorized Dealer.

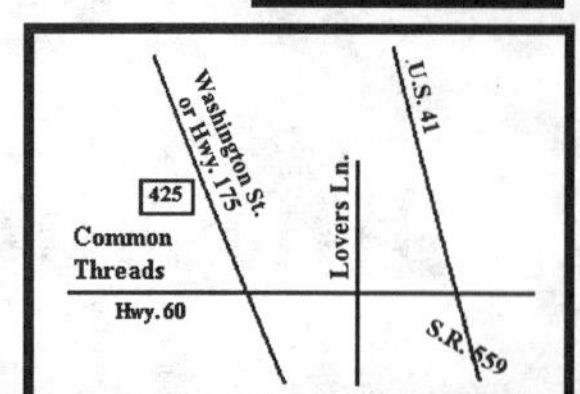

Sheboygan, WI #10

Tues, Thur, Fri 10 - 5
Wed 12 - 7
Sat 10 - 4

Piece By Piece Quilt Shop

1947A N. 8th St. 53081
(920) 458-1251
Owner: Mary Kaufman
Est: 1994 700 Bolts

Quilting Supplies, Books, Patterns, Great Line of 100% Cotton Fabrics. Classes for all levels.

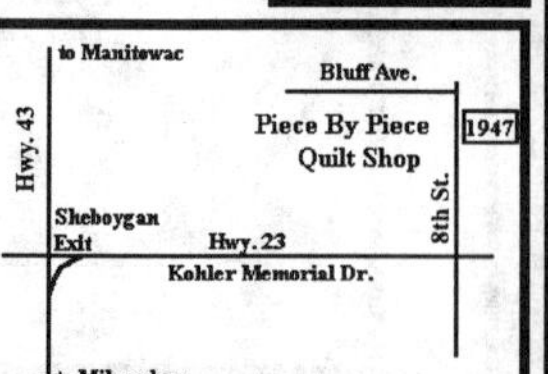

Denmark, WI #11

Mon - Fri 9 - 5
Sat 9 - 3
Or By Appt.

Handworks

116 W. Main St., P.O. Box 636
(920) 863-8843 54208
Owner: Ramona Gillaume
Est: 1994

Quilting Supplies, Crafts, Books, Patterns, Fine 100% Cotton Fabrics, Notions, Classes. Quilts and Crafts for sale.
Knowledgeable Staff

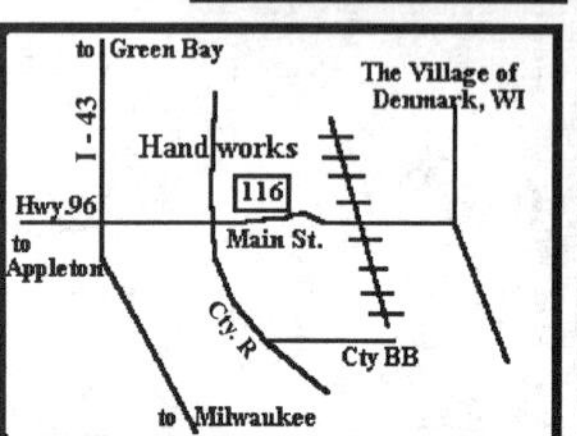

Green Bay, WI #12

Mon - Fri 10 - 6
Tues & Thur til 8
Sat 10 - 4
Sun 12 - 4

Main Street Cotton Works

1812 Main St. 54302
(920) 469-5694
Owners: Patt and Gil Nowak
Est: 1995 1000 Bolts

Located in a 50 yr. old home featuring 100% cotton fabrics, books, patterns & quilting supplies, classes and Friendly, Knowledgeable Staff

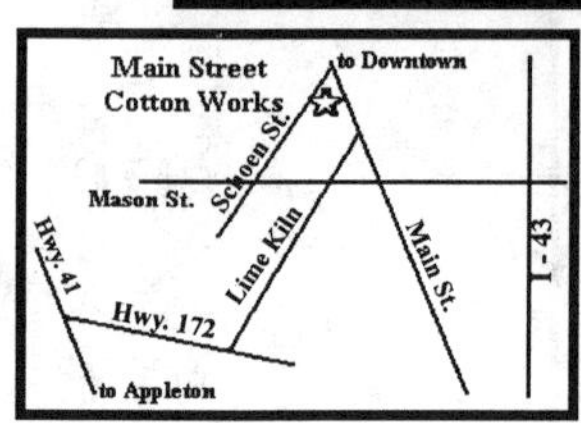

2475 University Ave.
University Courtyard
54302
(800) 469-1495
(414) 468-1495
Owners: Nanette Guzzonato & Elaine Corson
Est: 1990
Wheelchair Accessible

Mon & Thur 9:30 - 8
Tues & Wed 9:30 - 5
Fri 9:30 - 4 Sun 11 - 4

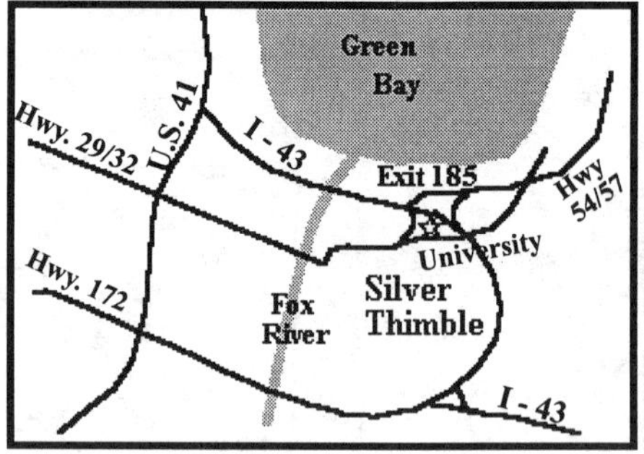

Take I - 43, exit 185, to Green Bay
Turn left at first stoplight.
Go one block & left into parking lot

Green Bay, WI #13

- ★ 1800 bolts 100% cotton fabric
- ★ Over 200 bolts solids
- ★ Books & Patterns
- ★ Notions
- ★ Help selection colors/fabrics
- ★ Pfaff Sewing Machine Sales
- ★ Classes
- ★ Gifts
- ★ Ready-made Quilts
- ★ Custom Sewing
- ★ Graph patterns
- ★ Help to increase/decrease patterns
- ★ Complete line Thimbleberries fabric, books & patterns at reduced prices

Appleton, WI #14

Mon - Fri 9:30 - 5
Thur til 8
Sat 9:30 - 4

Quilters' Corner

2009A N. Richmond St. 54911
(414) 749-1957

Great selection of quality 100% cotton fabrics. Books, patterns, notions & classes.

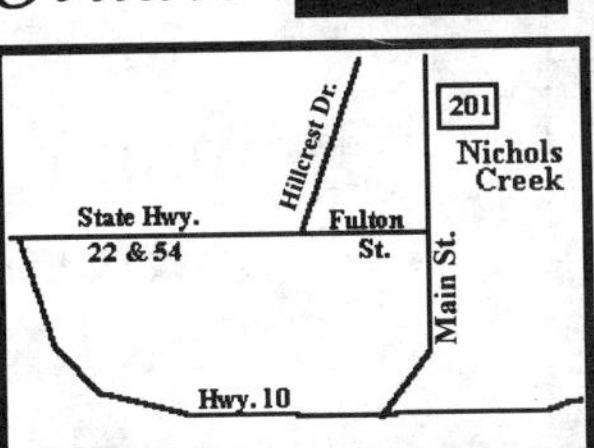

Waupaca, WI #16

Mon - Fri 10 - 5
Sat 10 - 4

Nichols Creek Quilt Studio

201 N. Main 54981
(715) 256-1024 or (888) 256-1024
Owners: Nancy M. Oftedahl & Janice Keil Robbins
Est: 1994 1200 sq.ft. 1500 Bolts

Finished Quilts, Cotton Fabric, Large selection of Patterns, Books. Quilting Supplies and Notions. Classes Offered.

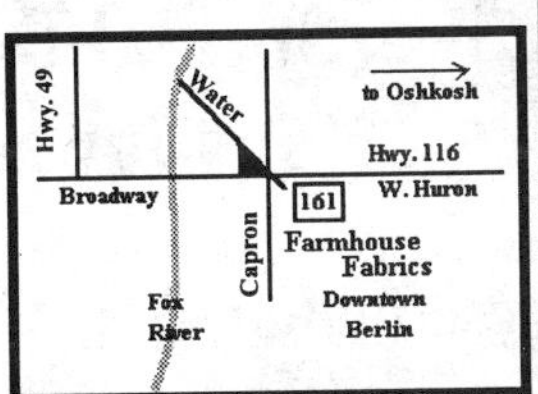

Berlin, WI #17

Seasonal
Please Call First

FARMHOUSE FABRICS

161 W. Huron St. 54923
(920) 361-1324
E-Mail: farmfab@vbe.com
Owner: Jean Teal Est: 1980
1000 bolts of 100% Cotton fabrics, specializing in Antique Reproductions. Please visit our website featuring online catalog at: www.farmfab.com

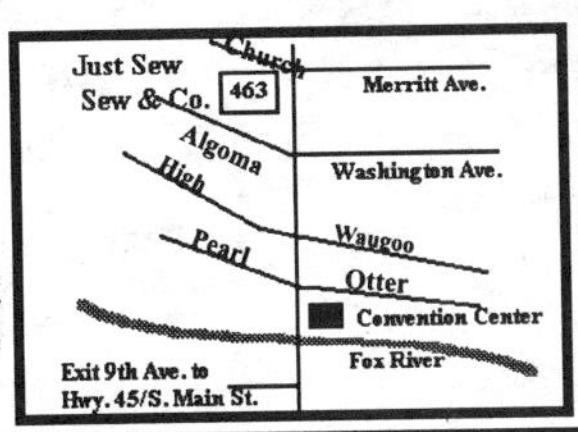

(920) 991-9021
201 N. Richmond St. 54911.

Patchwork Sampler

Quality fabrics including homespuns, Florals, flannels, wools, batiks, neutrals
— Books & Patterns — Classes —
— Bernina Sewing Machines —
— Friendly, Knowledgeable Staff —

Appleton, WI #15

Mon - Fri 9:30 - 5
Thur til 8 Sat 9:30 - 4

Owners: Kim Teigen & Rhonda Roberts
Est: 1997 1300 sq.ft. 1500+ Bolts

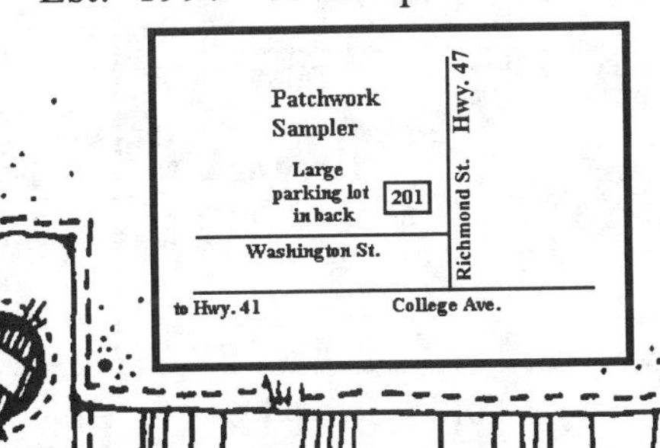

Oshkosh, WI #18

Mon - Fri 10 - 6
Sat 10 - 4:30

JUST SEW SEW & CO.

463 N. Main St. 54901
(920) 303-1166
Owner: Pat Schneider

Large selection of cotton Fabric, Books, Craft Patterns, Quilting & Sewing needs. A Welcome for everyone coming in. I enjoy meeting all.

Just Sew Sew & Co. | 463 | Church | Merritt Ave. | Algoma | Washington Ave. | High | Waugoo | Pearl | Otter | Convention Center | Fox River | Exit 9th Ave. to Hwy. 45/S. Main St.

Princeton, WI #19

Mon -Fri 8:30 - 5
Sat 9 - 3

Quilts & Quilting

607 W. Main St. (414) 295-6506
P.O. Box 362 54968 Est: 1971
Owners: Sandy & Ron Mason
Machine Quilting & Kit Brochure SASE

Custom Machine Quilting Since 1971
Fabric, Notions, Books, Classes.
Die-Cut Quilt Top Kits—pillows to king size.

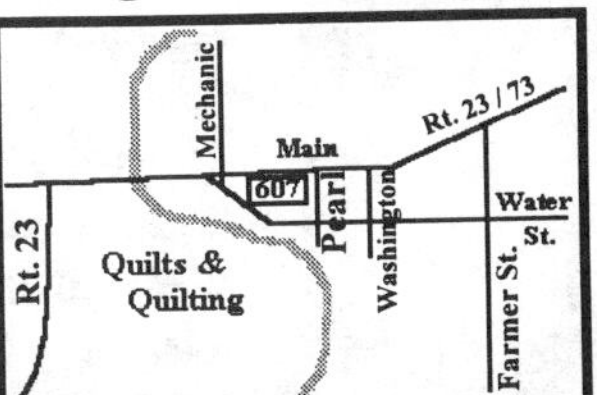

Fond du Lac, WI #20

Mon - Fri 10 - 5:30
Sat 10 - 4:30

Gingerbread Junction

46 N. Main St. 54935
(920) 924-6050
Owners: Kathy Decker & Sharon Rasmussen
Est: 1995

Quilting and craft supplies, kits, rug hooking, country gifts and home decor. Friendly, helpful service in a cozy, nostalgic atmosphere.

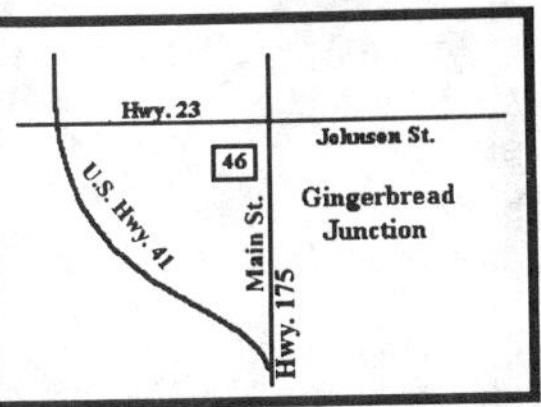

Fond du Lac, WI #21

Fond du Lac Quilting

15 North Main Street 54935
(920) 921-3816 or (800) 594-9064
Owner: Peggy Eckerstorfer

Monday thru Thursday 9:30 to 5:00
Friday - 9:30 to 7:00
Saturday - 9:30 to 4:00

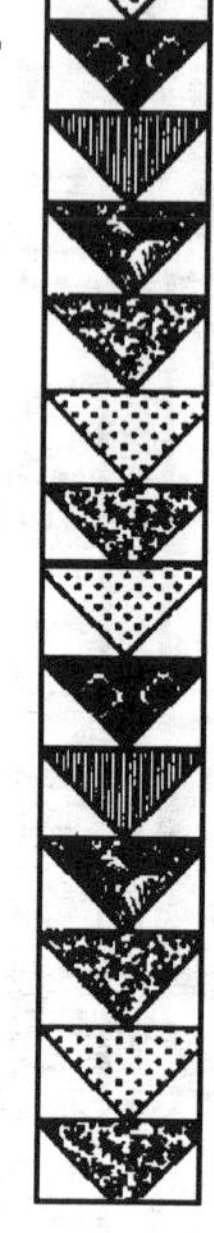

Fond du Lac Quilting is one of Wisconsin's Largest Quilt Shops ! !
The best selection of Quilting Fabrics, Books, and Patterns in the state !
FREE CATALOG
Bernina Dealer for over Twenty Years !

Bus Tours Welcome
Special Demo's for tour groups

We are the Host of two of the largest quilting events in the mid-west:
Quilter's Escape & Summer School for Quilters

Summer School for Quilters
July 17, 18 & 19, 1998
Featuring National Instructors:

- ♥ Eleanor Burns — Quilt in a Day: 3 days of hands on classes.
- ♥ Darlene Zimmerman — Granny's Apron Prints & Tri-Recs tool
- ♥ Barbara Vlack — Applique-Electric Quilt 3.0 Hands-on Workshops
- ♥ Helen Hopka — 23rd Psalm Liturgical Quilt
- ♥ Wendy Gilbert — Machine Quilting: Snail Trail Mystery Quilt
- ♥ Rosemany Kurtz — Celtic Quilting (Learn from the best)
- ♥ Sue Kruger — A new twist to Applique
- ♥ Bill Eckerstorfer — Amish Quilt Basket
- ♥ Jean Edkins — Wonderful Woodsmen
- ♥ Chantelle Beal — Beautiful Bindings & Exquisite Edgings
- ♥ Karls Spinks — Wearable Art

Quilter's Escape XI
February 5, 6 & 7, 1999
elinor peace bailey — her wonderful dolls
Bonnie Kaster — Sweet Memories Applique
and 6 other national teachers to be announced.
Our Quilting Events consist of Seminars, Quilt Show, Workshops and Merchants Mall

Embroidery Retreat November 6, 7 & 8th, 1998
Attn: Artista, Midwest BBD Friends and all Embroidery Machine Owners.
Special 3 day retreat in Fond du Lac.
For information call our 800 No. or E-mail amyrob@centuryinter.net

For More Information send a 52 cent stamp.

Beaver Dam, WI #22

Mon.–Fri. 9–5
Wed. 'til 8
Sat. 9–4

Nancy's Notions

333 Beichl Ave. 53916
(920) 887-7321
Owners: Nancy & Richard Zieman
Est: 1985 • 3000 sq. ft. • Free Catalog

Large selection of brand name 100% cottons, sewing and quilting notions, patterns, and supplies.

Home of *"Sewing With Nancy"*

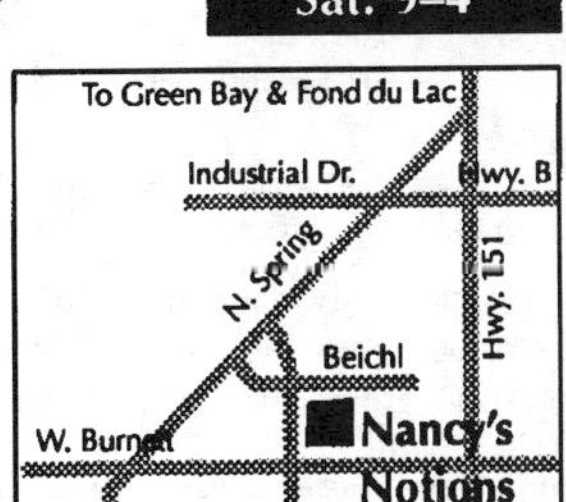

Beaver Dam, WI #23

Mon - Sat
10 - 5
Thur til 8

The Peddler's Etc.

152 Front St. 53916
(920) 887-3060
Owner: Marilyn Cooper
Est: 1995 2400 sq.ft. 800+ Bolts

Large selection of fabric, books, patterns & quilting supplies. Classes offered. Friendly atmosphere—personal service.

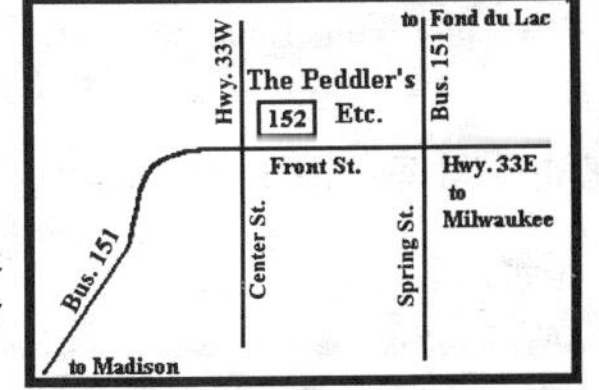

Sun Prairie, WI #24

Mon - Fri
9:30 - 5:30
Sat 10 - 5

J.J. Stitches & Co.

221 E. Main St. 53590
(608) 837-2266
Est: 1975 5000 Bolts

Located in a Turn-of-the-Century downtown shop. Combines designer fabric lines with homespuns, tickings & vintage replica fabrics.

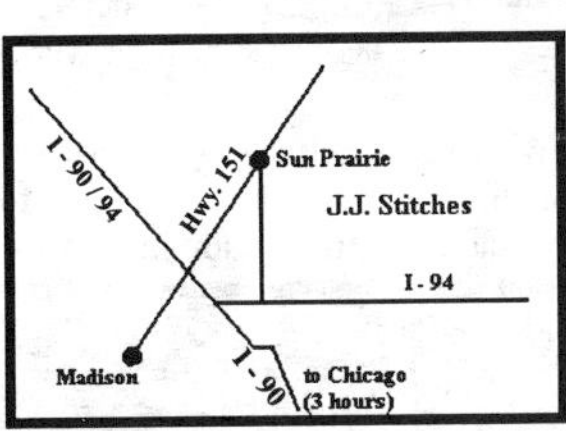

Sun Prairie, WI #25

Mon - Fri
10 - 5
Thur 12 - 5
Sat 10 - 4

Prairie Quiltworks, LLC

229 E. Main St. 53590
(608) 837-9201
Owner: Sue Alstad

Quilting fabrics and supplies. Classes.
Hand guided machine quilting.
Warm and friendly atmosphere.

Waunakee, WI #26

100 Baker St. 53597 (608) 849-6473
Owners: Mike & Debbie Kuehn
Est: 1995 8000 sq.ft. 4800 Bolts

Mill House Quilts

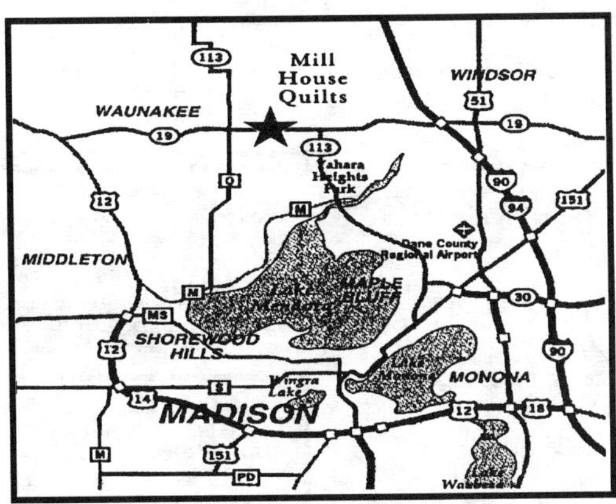

Off 90 - 94 exit Hwy. 19 West to Waunakee

A Refurbished 1875 Feed Mill featuring over 4800 bolts of fine quilting fabrics, quilting supplies, books, patterns & classes.
Newsletter and mail orders available upon Request.

Mon - Sat
9 - 5
Thurs til 8

Madison, WI #27

Mon - Fri 9:30 - 6
Thur til 8:30
Sat 9:30 -5

The Stitcher's Crossing

6108 Mineral Point Rd. 53705
(608) 232-1500 Fax: (608) 232-1750
Owners: Elaine Boehlke & Kit Thomsen
Est: 1980 2400 sq.ft.

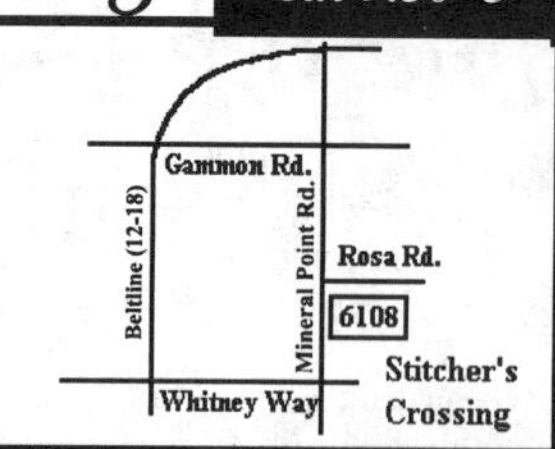

Unique shop for all your quilting and cross stitch needs. All of our wonderful models and displays will inspire you.

Madison, WI #28

Mon - Fri 9:30 - 5:30
Thur til 8:30
Sat 9:30 - 5

Quilter's Workshop

6101 Odana Road 53719
(608) 271-4693
Owner: Joan Pariza
Est: 1990 2400 sq.ft.

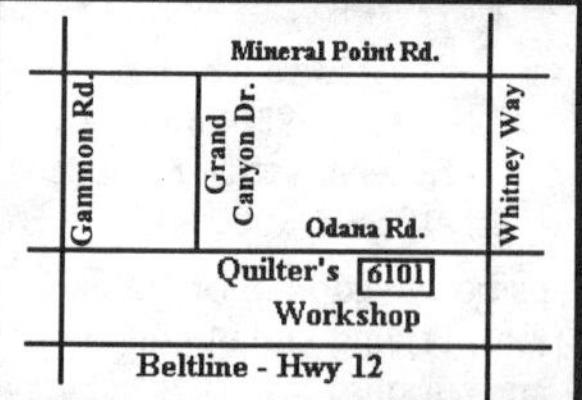

Madison's only shop devoted to Quilters -- over 2000 bolts -- all 100% cotton -- includes latest in Hoffman, Jinny Beyer -- Patterns, Books, Notions ...

Cambridge, WI #29

Mon - Sat 9:30 - 5
Sun 12 - 5

The Quilt Shop

236 W. Main St., P.O. Box 280 53523
(608) 423-3185
E-Mail: TheQuiltSh@aol.com
Owner: Cindy Imhoff
Est: 1996 1000 sq.ft. 1000 Bolts

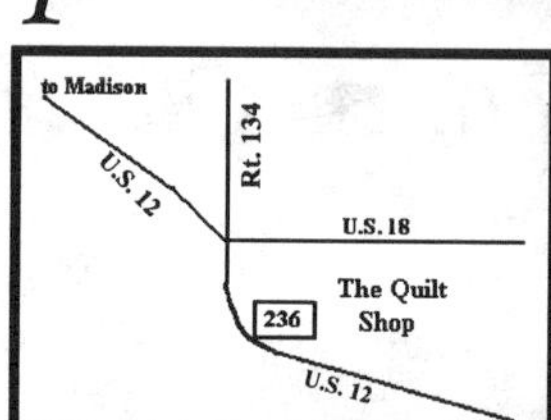

100% cotton fabrics, books, patterns, notions & gift items. Newsletter avail. with class schedule. Project & fabric selection assistance avail.

Janesville, WI #30

Fri 10 - 5
or By Appt.

Sew Bee Quilting

343 S. Lexington Dr.
53545
(608) 754-2488
Owner: Lynda Short
E-Mail: sbqltr@inware.com
Est: 1990 500 sq.ft. Catalog LSASE

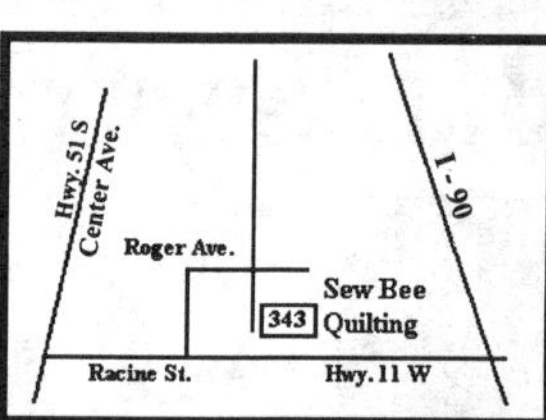

Sew Bee Quilting specializes in custom machine quilting as well as hand-dyed fabrics and features quilts made in Wisconsin.

Monroe, WI #31

Mon - Fri 10 - 6
Sat 9- 5
Sun 12 - 4

Uniquely Yours

128 W. 8th St. West Court 53566
(608) 325-1433
Owner: Sandy Haffele
Est: 1990 2600 sq.ft. 3000 Bolts

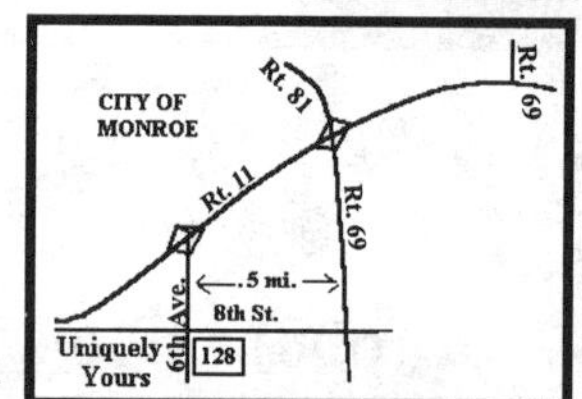

High quality 100% cotton fabric. Large selection of books, patterns & quilt supplies. Wide variety of gift items. Warm, friendly staff.

Platteville, WI #32

Mon - Fri 9 - 5:30
Sat 9 - 5

Creative STITCHES

125 East Main 53818
(608) 348-9276 Fax: (608) 348-9214
E-Mail: creative@pcii.net
Owner: Rhonda Simmons
2100 sq.ft. of quilting, cross-stitch & yarn supplies, books & patterns; classes.
elna™ sewing machines, sergers & presses
Yarn Club.

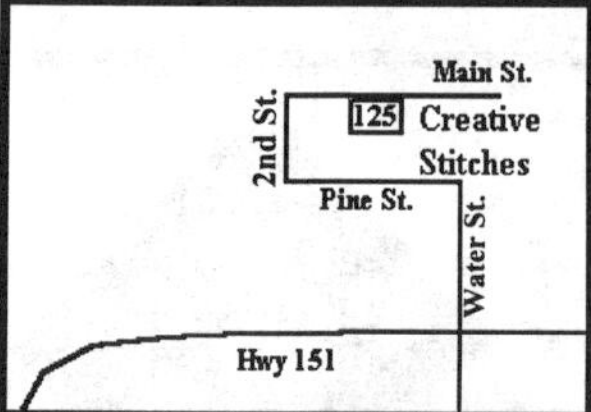

Montfort, WI #33

Mon - Fri 10 - 6
Sat 10 - 4
Shortened hrs. Jan - April

Moments in Time

200 E. Hwy. 18 53569
(608) 943-6632

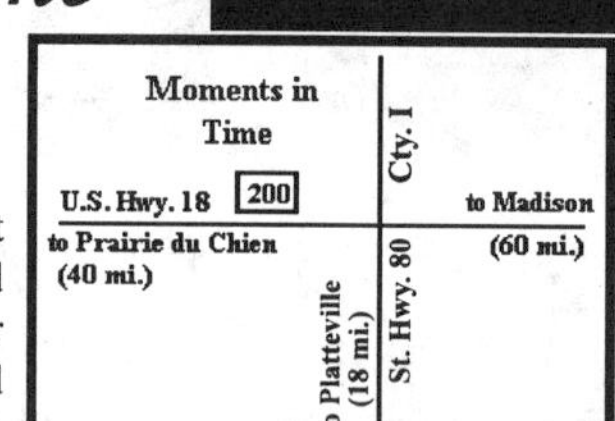

We feature ready made quilts and wood quilt display items. Nice selection of wood accessories, floral arrangements. Collector dolls, clocks. Christmas items displayed and for sale all year.

Fennimore, WI #34

Mon - Fri 9 - 5
Sat 9 - 3

Yard & Yard Shop

960 Lincoln Ave. 53809
(608) 822-6014
Owner: Doris Monroe
Est: 1974

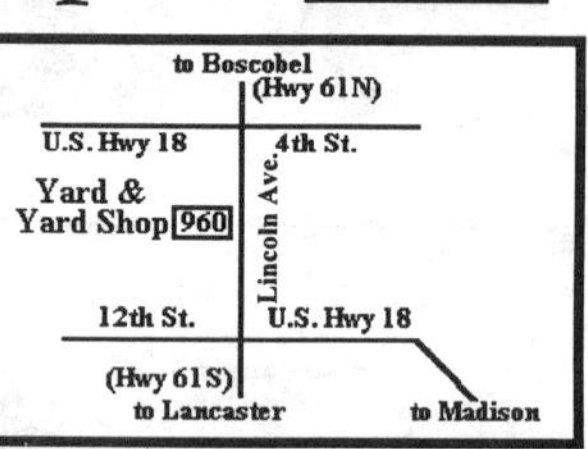

Quilt Supplies, Classes, Fashion Fabric Patterns. New Home Sewing Machines — Sales and Service.

Ferryville, WI #35

Mon - Fri 9 - 5
Weekends by chance or appt.

Olde Tyme Quilt Shoppe

R.R. #2 Rush Creek Rd. Box 215
(608) 648-2081 54628
Owner: Virginia Johnson
Est: 1986 900 sq.ft.

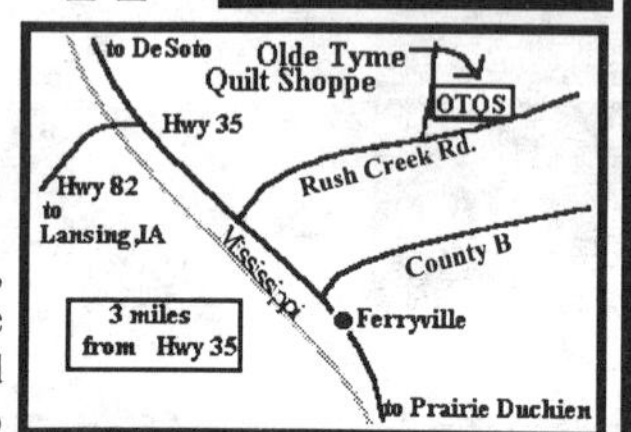

Custom made Quilts--Hand dyed fabric, notions. Hand or machine quilting, outline quilting. 100% cotton threads, 1200 yard spools. Virginia's original quilts. Classes also

Prairie du Sac, WI #36

Mon - Fri 9 - 6
Sat 9 - 5
(3rd Sun Nov-March 1)
Sun 12 - 4

Homespun Fabrics

585 Water St. 53555
(608) 643-5083
Owner: Louise Back
Est: 1995 1000 Bolts

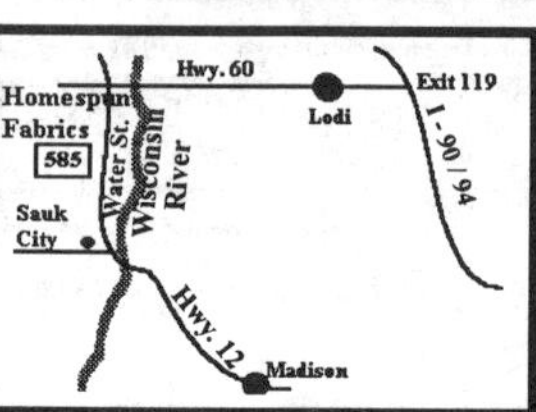

Great Selection of 100% Cotton Fabrics, Books, Notions & Patterns. 100% Wools for Hooking. Quarterly Newsletter.

Reedsburg, WI #37

Quintessential Quilts

940 East Main 53959 (608) 524-8435
Owner: Terry Antholz Est: 1989 4800 sq.ft. 9 - 10,000 Bolts

Large selection of fabric, books, patterns, & quilting supplies.

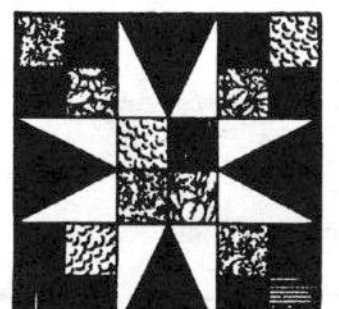

All your quilting needs located under one roof!
Continuous schedule of classes.
Mail orders and newsletter available upon request.
WISCONSIN'S BEST KEPT QUILTING SECRET!

Mon - Sat 9 - 5
Sun 12 - 4.

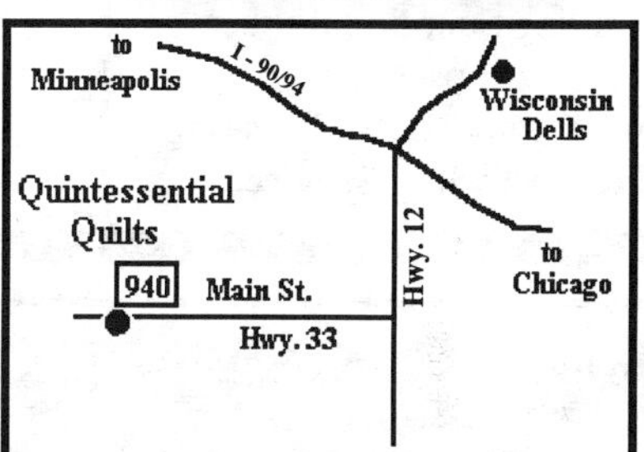

LaCrosse, WI #38

A Stitch In Time

Mon - Sat 10 - 5 Thur til 8

BERNINA

225 N. 3rd St. 54601
(608) 782-3257 Est: 1992
Owner: Monica Campbell
2400 sq.ft. 1800 Bolts

Large selection of fabric, books, patterns, & quilting supplies. The friendliest quilt shop for service, inspiration and sharing of ideas.

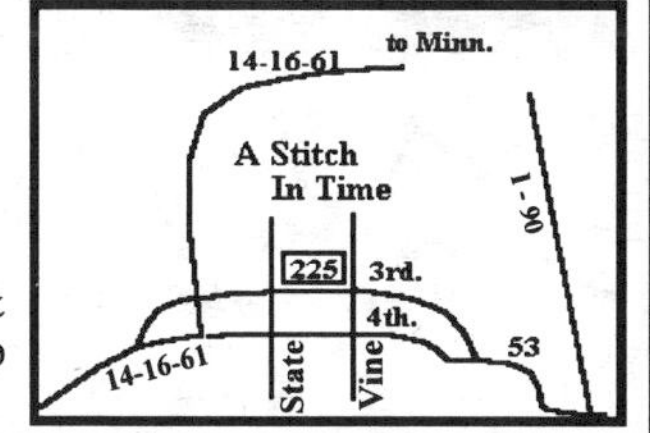

Menomonie, WI #39

Carol's Golden Needle

Tues - Sat 10 - 5

620 Wilson Ave. 54751
(715) 235-8828
Owner: Carol Thompson

Enjoy the atmosphere of our 1910 Victorian House while browsing through our high quality quilting fabrics, notions, books and patterns.

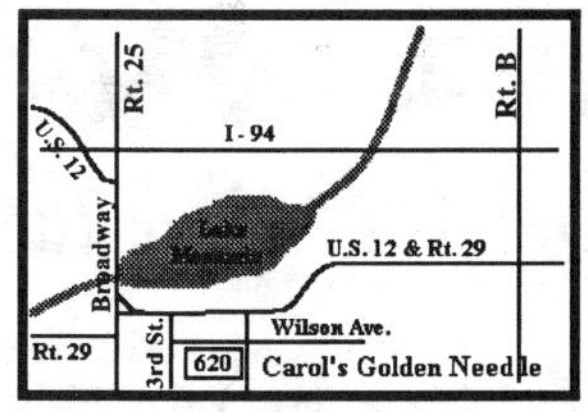

Eau Claire, WI #40

The Calico Shoppe

Mon - Fri 10 - 5 Sat 10 - 4

214 S. Barstow St. 54701
(715) 834-9990
Owner: Lynn Goelzer
Est: 1993 1000+ Bolts

Great selection of fabrics, patterns, books & quilting supplies. A charming shop specializing in friendly service and abundant ideas!

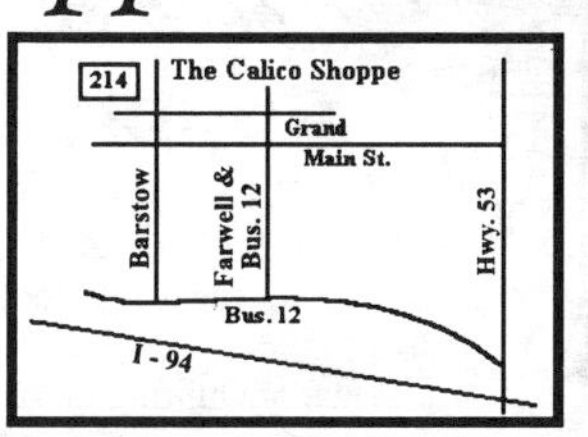

Withee, WI #41

Dutch Country Fabrics

Mon - Fri 9 - 5 Sat 9 - 4

W 6463 Cty. Rd. X 54498
Owners: Louis & Verna Martin
Home Phone: (715) 229-4796

Fabric, Quilts & Batting, Baby Supplies, Hosiery, Underwear, Childrens Shoes, Boxed Greeting Cards, Sweaters, Sewing Notions, Disposable Diapers, Stationery & Hair Accessories.

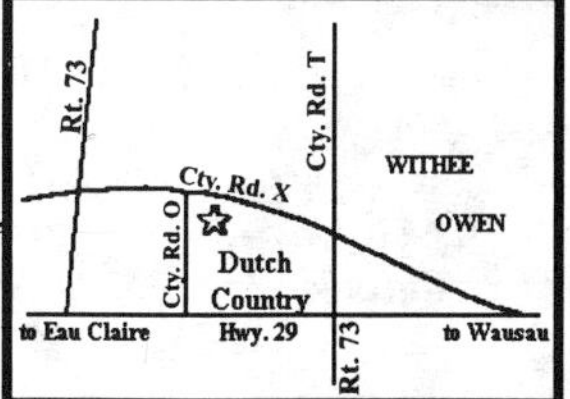

Chippewa Falls, WI #42

Kay's NINE PATCH & CHIPPEWA CARDING

17 W. Central Street 54729
(715) 723-5931
Owner: Kay Hanson
Est: 1993 1500 sq.ft. 750 Bolts

Mon - Fri 9 - 5
Sat 9 - 3

Pieced Quilts & Comforters, Fine Quality Yarns, Quilting & Knitting Supplies, Rubber Stamps, Gifts.
Wool & Poly Batts. Washing & Recarding Service.

Wisconsin Rapids, WI #43

240 W. Grand Ave.
(715) 424-1122 54495
Owner: Carol Prahl
Est: 1993

Tues - Fri 10 - 5
Sat 10 - 4

Over 2500 Bolts of 100% Cottons Books, Patterns, Stencils, & Quilting Notions.

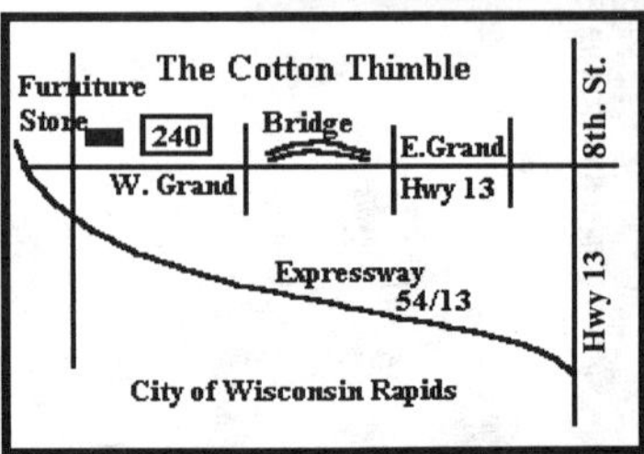

Stevens Point, WI #44

Mon - Thur 10 - 5
Fri 10 - 7
Sat 10 - 4
Changes in Summer

1125 Main St. 54481
(715) 341-5540
Owner: Nina McVeigh

Quaint Shop with quilting, silk ribbon, English smocking & Heirloom Sewing. Dealer of Bernina Sewing Machines. Classes & Workshops

Centerpoint on Main
Main St.
1125
The Sampler House
Church St.
Bus. 51
Hwy.10
Hwy. 51/39
Clark St.

Wausau, WI #45

Mon - Thur 10 - 5
Fri 10 - 7
Sat 10 - 4

Owner: Nina McVeigh

304 S. 1st Ave. 54401
(715) 848-1199

Small shop with loads of Books, Patterns and Fabric. Features patterns by local designers. Dealer of Bernina Sewing Machines. Workshops & Classes.

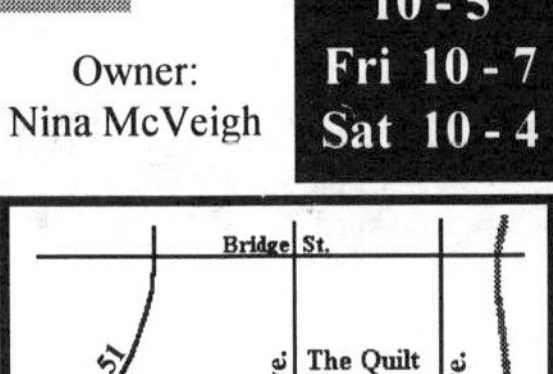

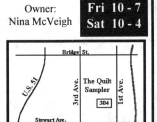

Tomahawk, WI #46

Between Friends Quilting & Supplies

14 W. Wisconsin Ave. 54487
(715) 453-8884 Fax: (715) 453-9026
Est: 1997

Quilting Books, Fabrics, Quilting Supplies, Thread, Floss, Ribbon Embroidery, Classes. Free Newsletter, friendly Service, Inspiration & sharing of ideas.

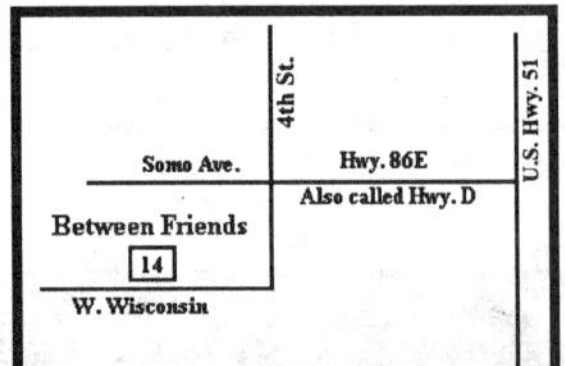

Eagle River, WI #47

Mon - Fri 10 - 5
Thur til 9
Sat 10 - 3

220 S. Main St.,
P.O. Box 194 54521
(715) 479-2313
Owner: Lisa Wood

Est: 1995 1000 sq.ft. 800+ Bolts

North Woods Quilting at its Best! Fabrics, Patterns, Books, Wool Rug Hooking Supplies, Viking Sewing Machines and Classes.

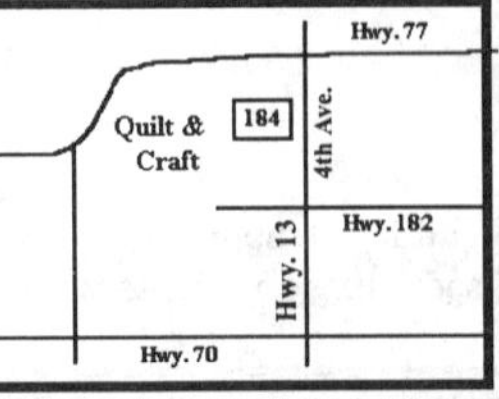

Minocqua, WI #48

Labor Day - Mem.
Mon - Fri 10 - 4
Sat 10 - 3
Memorial - Labor
Mon - Fri 10 - 5
Sat 10 - 3

510 Chicago Ave.
P.O. Box 910 54548
(715) 358-7074
Fax: (715) 479-3849
Est: 1995 2000+ Bolts
Owners: Barb Zawistowski & Pam Micheau

Friendly cottage on the lake carrying fabrics, notions, books, and patterns for your quilting, crafting and silk ribbon embroidery.

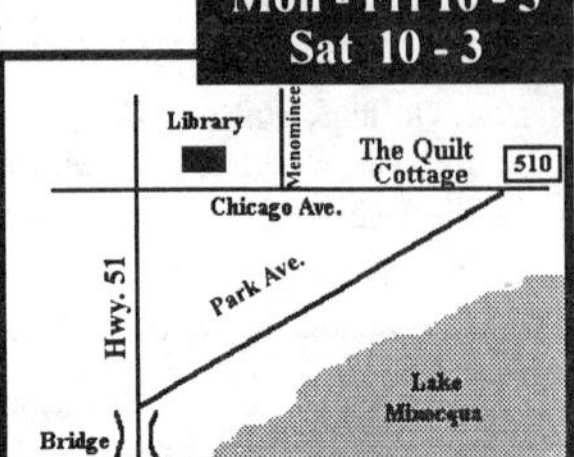

Park Falls, WI #49

Mon - Fri 9 - 6
Sat 10 - 4
Sun 10 - 2

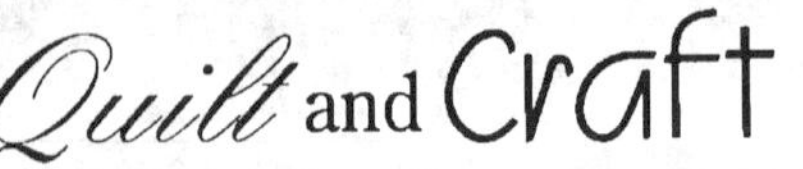

Supply Center

184 S. 4th Ave. 54552
(715) 762-4353
Owner: Pat Radlinger

Quality Quilting fabrics—
Books & Crafting Supplies.

Wall St.
Railroad St.
Heartstrings Quilts 220
Main St.
Pine St.

Rhinelander, WI #50

Mon - Fri 9 - 5
Sat 9 - 3

Geri's Fabric Patch

Largest & Newest supply of Books, Patterns, and Tools.

Collector of Antique Reds, Greens and Crazy Quilts.

Happy to fill telephone requests.

Newsletter and Classes

Also X-Stitch—fabrics, floss & patterns

Continuous Quilt Show

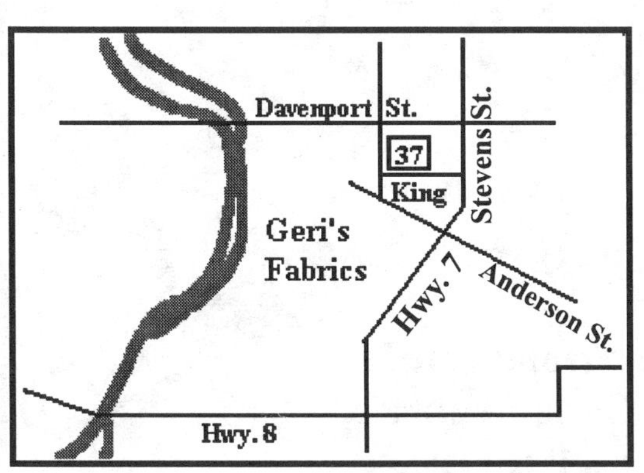

37 S. Brown St. 54501
(715) 362-6294
E-Mail:
ragview@newnorth.net
Owners: Geri and Dick Vieaux
Est: 1979
5000 sq.ft. 4000 Bolts

Osseo, WI #51

Mon - Sat
9:30 - 5

E 10725 Country Rd. HH 54758 (715) 597-2452

Owner: Betty Wolff Est: 1996 2000 sq.ft. 3000 bolts

The Quilt Yard

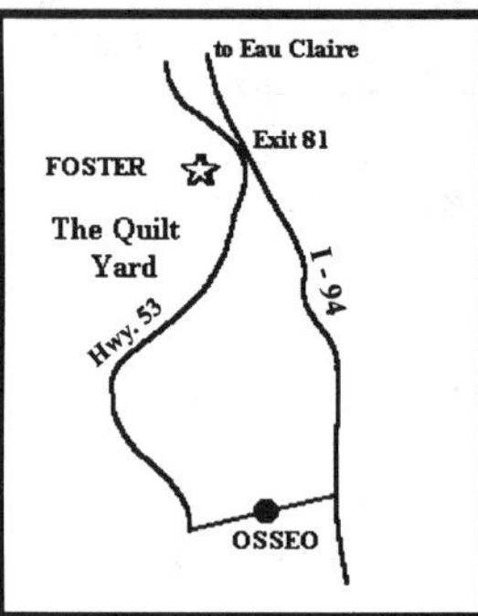

Located just off I - 94, Exit 81 — 2 blocks West in the Unincorporated town of Foster.

Books, Patterns, Notions and Namebrand 100% cotton Fabrics. Featuring Vintage Dry goods and Giftware.

Betty, Jane, Norma, and Val invite you to stop by and visit.

Antigo, WI #52

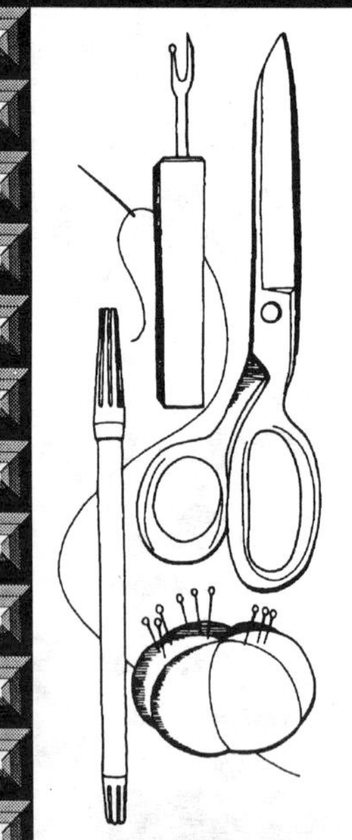

The Cutting Edge

816 5th Ave. 54409
(715) 623-3590

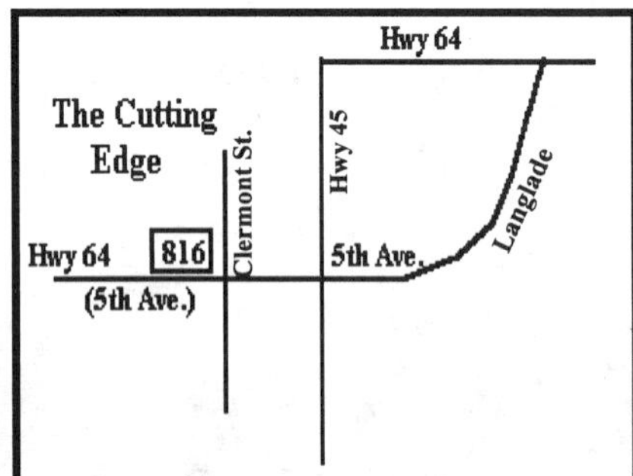

Wide Assortment of 100% Cotton Fabrics, Notions, Patterns & Books
Day & Evening Classes.

Mon - Thur 9 - 6
Fri 9 - 7
Sat 9 - 4

Owner:
Marla Arndt
Est: 1990
6000 sq.ft.

We do Custom work and Machine Quilting

Tues - Sat
9:30 - 5
April 1 - Dec 31
Mondays
also 9:30 - 5

Turtle Lake, WI #53

Quilting, Cross Stitch & Yarn. Wool—rug hooking supplies. Books, patterns, buttons & notions. Fabrics include: cottons, flannels, polar fleece and hand-dyed wool.

P.O. Box 200 54889
612 U.S. Hwy. 8 & 63 W
(715) 986-2983

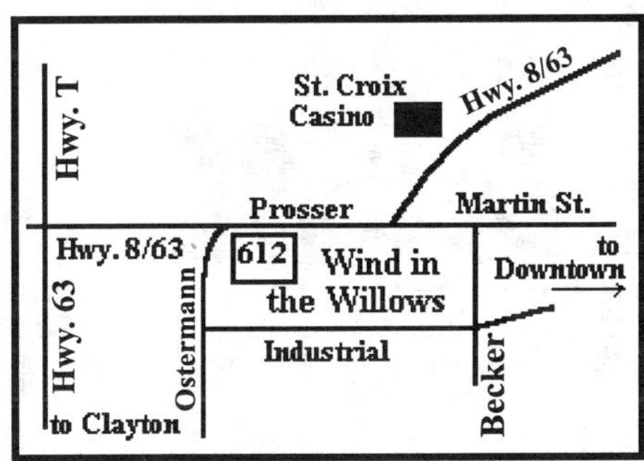

Also Visit The Gallery Barn.

We carry Lexington Furniture, home accessories, gifts & collectables including: Sedgefield lamps, reproductions, The Boyd's Bear Collection, Candles & much more.

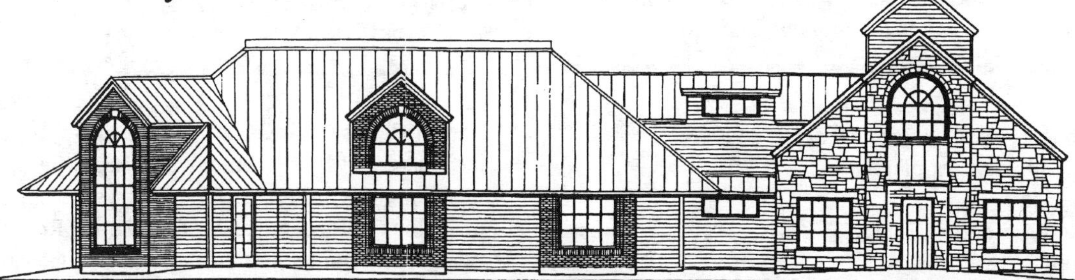

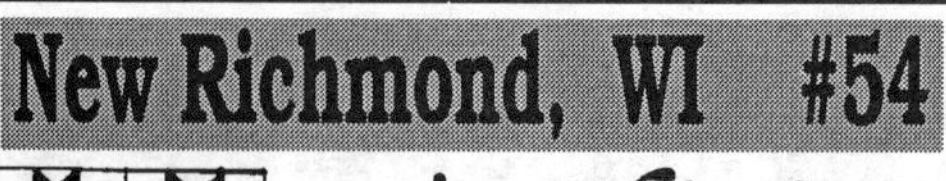

Mon - Fri 10 - 6
Wed til 9
Sat 10 - 3

228 Paperjack Plaza #9
(715) 246-9910
Fax: (715) 246-9912
E-Mail: traditio@frontiernet.net
Owners: Anna Dzik & Mary Jensen
Annual Sale August 1st & 2nd. 600+ Bolts fabric, patterns, books, notions, stencils, cross stitch, yarn, classes, newsletter.

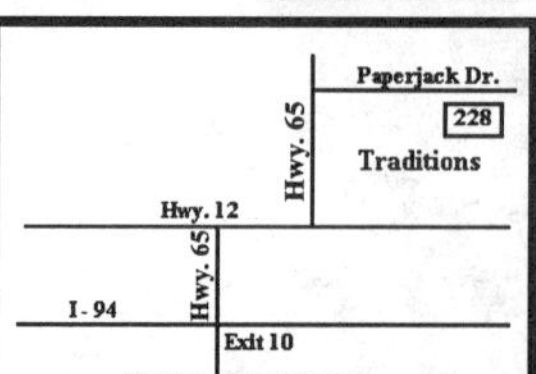

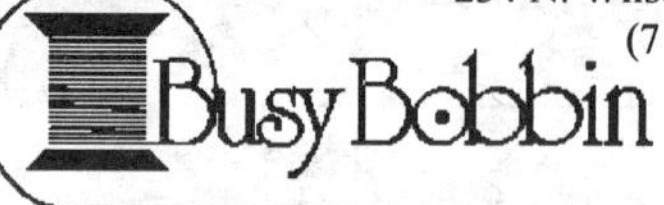

Mon - Fri 9:30 - 5
Sat 9:30 - 3

234 N. Wilson Ave. 54868
(715) 234-1217

Busy Bobbin

Owner: Diann Raymond
Est: 1981 1000 sq.ft. 2000 Bolts
Large selection 100% Cotton fabrics, patterns, books, and quilting notions.
Classes offered.

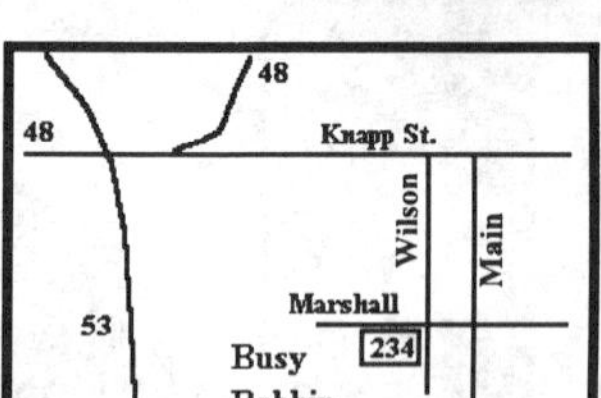

Frederic, WI #56

Cheri's Country Quilting

1425 - 305th Ave. 54837
(715) 327-4519
Owner: Cheri Moats

100% Cotton Fabrics (Over 1000 Bolts), Books, Patterns, Notions, Stencils, Classes. Custom Machine Quilting.

Wed - Sat 9:30 - 5:30
Or By Appointment

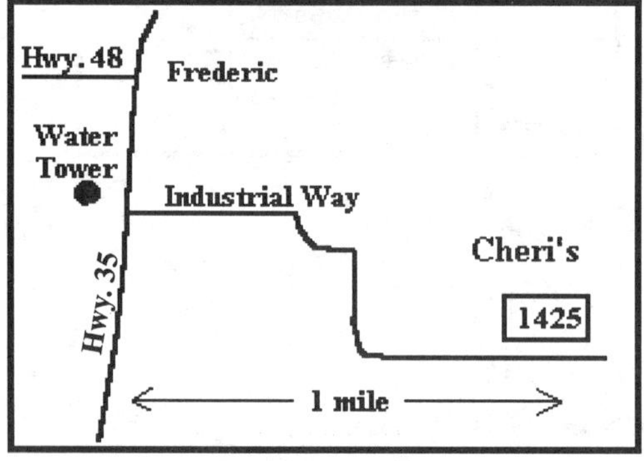

1 1/2 miles east of Downtown Frederic

Hayward, WI #57

Mon - Fri 10 - 5
Sat 10 - 3

Windmill Square, 15776 N. State Rd. 27
(715) 634-3260 54843

Hayward QuiltersQuarters

Owner: Diann Raymond
Est: 1995 1500 sq.ft. 1600 Bolts

Large selection 100% Cotton fabrics, patterns, books, and quilting notions.
Classes offered.

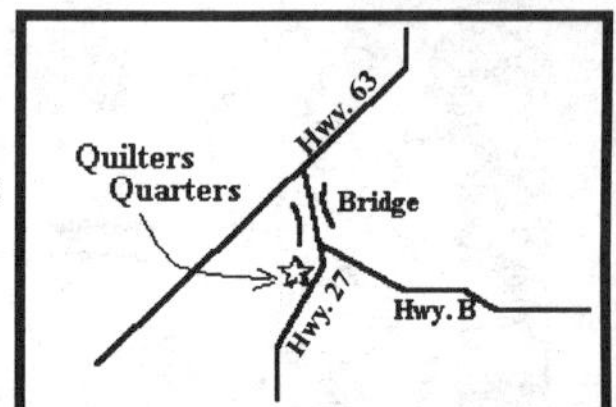

Superior, WI #58

Mon, Wed, Thur, Fri 9:30 - 5
Sat 10 - 5

Pine Haven Quilts & Furnishings

5535 E. County Rd. B 54874
(715) 399-2223 Est: 1997
Owner: Andrea Lien 600+ Bolts

Friendly Country Quilt Shop with fine 100% Cotton Fabrics, Books, Patterns, Gifts, Classes. We also carry hardwood Quilt Racks, Cedar Chests and Quilt Frames. Custom Orders Avail.
10% off on your first visit!

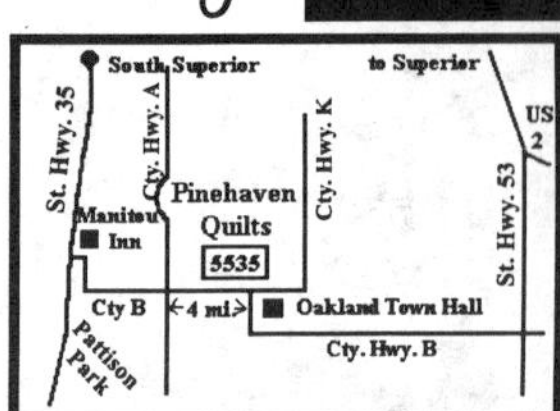

Superior, WI #59

Mon - Fri 9:30 - 5
Thur til 8
Sat 10 - 4

Fabric Works

1320 Tower Ave. 54880
(715) 392-7060
Owner: Barb Engelking
Est: 1991

Over 2000 Bolts of 100% Cotton Fabric. Quilting Books, Patterns and Supplies.

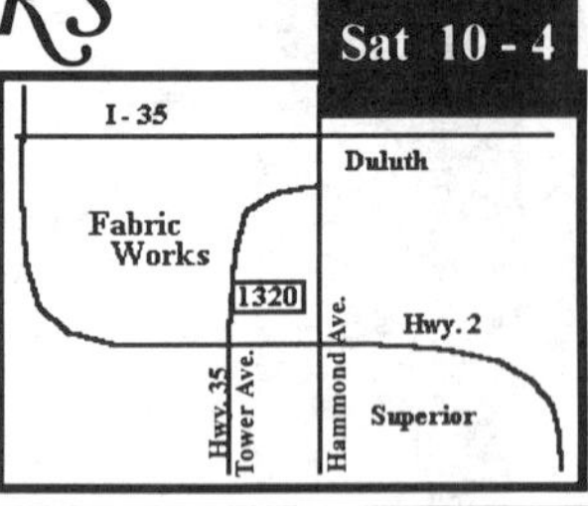

Wisconsin Guilds:

Tomorrow's Quilters, P.O. Box 248, Amherst, 54406
Darting Needles, P.O. Box, Appleton
Meets: 3rd Monday 7 p.m.
at First United Methodist Church
Augusta Quilt Addicts, Augusta, 54722
Meets: Mondays 1 p.m. at Augusta Senior Center
Baraboo Quilters, 901 Moore Street #15, Baraboo, 53913
Phi Beta Cabin Quilter's Sorority, W 8834 Niblick, Beaver Dam, 53916
Meets: 2nd Wednesday 6:30 p.m.
at Trinity Methodist Church, 308 Oneida St.
Heart in Hands Quilt Guild, Box 12A, Boyceville, 54725
Piecemaker's, 1165 Parkmoor Dr., Brookfield, 53005
Lake Country Quilters, 1385 Countryside Ln., Brookfield, 53045
Fort Atkinson Piecemakers, 163 Hoopen Rd., Cambridge, 53523
Cedar Creek Quilters, 1654 Summit Dr., Cedarsburg, 53012
Old World Quilters, 304 Larkin St., Eagle, 53119
Cranberry Country Q. G., c/o P.O. Box 194, Eagle River, 54521
Meets: 3rd Monday 10 a.m.
at Prince of Peace Church
Clear Water Quilters, 2112 Rudolph Rd., Eau Claire

A Piece at a Time, 440 W. Washington, Fall Creek, 54742
Meets: 4th Monday 7 p.m. at Faith Evangelical Church
Village Quilters of Harvard, 212 Abbey Springs, Fontana, 53125
Piecemakers Quilt Guild, 510 Grove St., Fort Atkinson, 53538
Mixed Sampler Quilt Club, Box 133, Frederic, 54837
Menomonee Falls Quilters, W. 154 N. 11666 Daniels, Germantown, 53022
Heritage Quilters, 203 Beech, Grafton, 53024
Evergreen Quilters, P.O. Box 783, Green Bay, 54305
LaCrosse Area Quilters, W. 8154 Holland Dr., Holmen, 54636
Hudson Heritage Quilters, 874 Willow Ridge, Hudson, 54016
It's a Stitch Quilt Club, 3280 Highway P, Jackson, 53037
Rock Valley Quilters Guild, P.O. Box 904, Janesville, 53547
Southport Quilter's Guild, P.O. Box 1523, Kenosha, 53141
Prairie Sampler Quilt Club, N2173 Smith Park Rd., Lodi, 53555
Meets: 3rd Tuesday at Sauk City Library
Mad City Quilters, 157 Nautilus Dr., Madison, 53705
Twilight Quilters Guild, 9 Leyton Circle, Madison, 53713
A Patch of Lakeshore, 1696 Skyline Dr., Manitowoc, 54220
Meets: 2nd Thursday 6:45 p.m. at St. Mary's Home
Northwoods Quilters, P.O. Box 595, Marinette, 54143
Darting Needles Quilt Guild, P.O. Box 603, Menasha, 54952
Covered Bridge Quilters, 13907 N. Port Washington Rd. Mequon, 53092
North Shore Quilters Guild, Box 17263, Milwaukee, 53217
Orchard Inn Quilters, 5510 W. Calumet Rd., Milwaukee, 53223
Wisconsin's Quilter's Inc., P.O. Box 83144, Milwaukee, 53223
West Suburban Quilters Guild, 2621 N. 65th St., Milwaukee, 53213
Stitch it or Stuff it Quilters, 6551 N. 66th St., Milwaukee, 53223
Ladies of the Lake, P.O. Box 481, Minocqua, 54548
Evergreen Quilters, Box 426, Montello, 53949
Calico Capers Quilt Guild, RR 1 Gem Ave., Montello, 53949
Crazy Quilters, S 70 W 32864 Oak Pl., Mukwonago, 53149
Patched Lives Q. G., N. 53 W. 33511 Cumberland Dr., Nashotah, 53058
Pine Tree Needlers, 1177 Dakota Lane, Neshkoro, 54960
Willow River Piecemakers, New Richmond, 54017
Meets: 2nd Thursday at St. Lukes
Wandering Foot Quilters, 8620 S. Howell Ave., Oak Creek, 53154
Lake Side Quilters, 1350 Menominee Dr., Oshkosh, 54901
Meets: 3rd Wednesday 6:30 p.m. at Marion Manor
Plum Creek Quilters, W 601 210th Ave., Plum City, 54761
Lighthouse Quilters, P.O. Box 124, Racine, 53403
Around the Block Quilters, 940 E. Main, Reedsburg, 53959
Cornerstone Quilt Guild, 337 K St., Reedsburg, 53959
Rhinelander Northwoods Quilters, 49 Lake Creek Rd., Rhinelander 54501 Meets: 1st Tuesday 7 p.m. at Senior Center
Friendship Quilter's Guild, 587 N. Park St., Richland Center, 53581
Ladies of the Lake Quilters, 9200 Longs Rd., Sayner, 54560
Shawano Area Quilters, 225 S. Main, Shawano, 54166
Sheboygan County Q. G., 2426 N. 25th St., Sheboygan, 53083
Ties That Bind Quilt Guild, Slinger
Meets: 3rd Wednesday 7 p.m. at Common Threads Quilt Shop
Scrap Happy Quilters c/o Patti Johnson, 5595 E. Neuman Rd. South Range, 54874
Meets: 2nd Thursday 6:30 at Darrow Rd. Church
Wild Rivers Quilting Guild, Box 1065, Spooner, 54801
Star Point Quilters Guild, P.O. Box 607, Stevens Point, 54481
The Stoughton Quilters, 404 W. Wilson, Stoughton, 53589
Prairie Heritage Quilters, P.O. Box 253, Sun Prairie, 53590
Casda Quilts, 2231 Catlin Ave., Superior, 54880
North Woods Quilters, 709 W. Third Street, Washburn, 54891
Pine Tree Quilters Guild, P.O. Box 692, Wausau, 54402
Meets: 2nd Tuesday 7 p.m. at Wausau Mall meeting room
Pine Tree Needlers, P.O. Box 431-2, Wautoma, 54982
Kettle Moraine Quilt Club, 4991 Hillside Dr., West Bend, 53095
Dells Country Quilters, #530 Hwy. 23 E., Wisconsin Dells, 53965

Other Shops in Wisconsin:

Algoma	Ben Franklin Store, 513 4th St.	414-487-3101
Cashton	Borntreger Furniture, Box 1978	
Cedarburg	Woolen Mill, W. 62 N. 580 Washington Ave.	414-377-0345
Delavan	The Stitchery, R. R. # 4, Box 232	414-728-6318
Delevan	3rd. St. Cotton Shop 117 S. 3rd St.	414-728-7868
Elmwood	Simple Pleasures, 125 E. Race Ave.	715-639-6201
Fish Creek	Door County Quiltworks, 3903 St. Hwy.42,	920-868-3660
Herbster	Cabin Fever Quilt Co., P.O. Box 6	715-774-3309
Hudson	St. Croix Country Dry Goods, 220 Locust St.	715-386-7405
Janesville	Prairie Point Quilt Shoppe, 2525 Woodlane Dr.	608-756-4228
Luck	Quilt Country, 129 S. Main St.	715-472-8088
Menomonee Falls	Fall's Sewing Center, W 155 N 8833 Main	414-253-3600
Mukwonago	NinePatch Quilters' Hutch, 955 Main St.	414-363-9566
Neenah	Holz's Pfaff Sewing Center, 132 W. Wisconsin Ave.	920-722-8262
North Prairie	Pamella's Place 129 N. Harrison St.	414-392-3855
Omro	YDS, 5530 St. Hwy. 116	414-582-7196
Oshkosh	J-K Fabric & Crafts, 362 S. Koeller	920-231-7430
Spring Green	Country Sampler, 133 E. Jefferson St.	608-588-2510
Spring Green	Sew 'N Sew, 122 N. Lexington	608-588-2273
Stetsonville	Betty White's Fabrics, 109 Mink Ave.	715-678-2294
Stockholm	Amish Country, 119 Spring St.	715-442-2015
Sun Prairie	Itchin' to Stitch, 509 W. Main	608-837-4131
Superior	Best Friends, 6006 Tower Ave.	715-392-1991
Tomah	Threads Through Time, 408 Superior Ave.	608-372-4000
Verona	Maple Springs Farm, 1828 Hwy. PB	608-845-9482
Waukesha	Genesee Woolen Mill, S 40 W 28178 Hwy. 59	414-521-2121

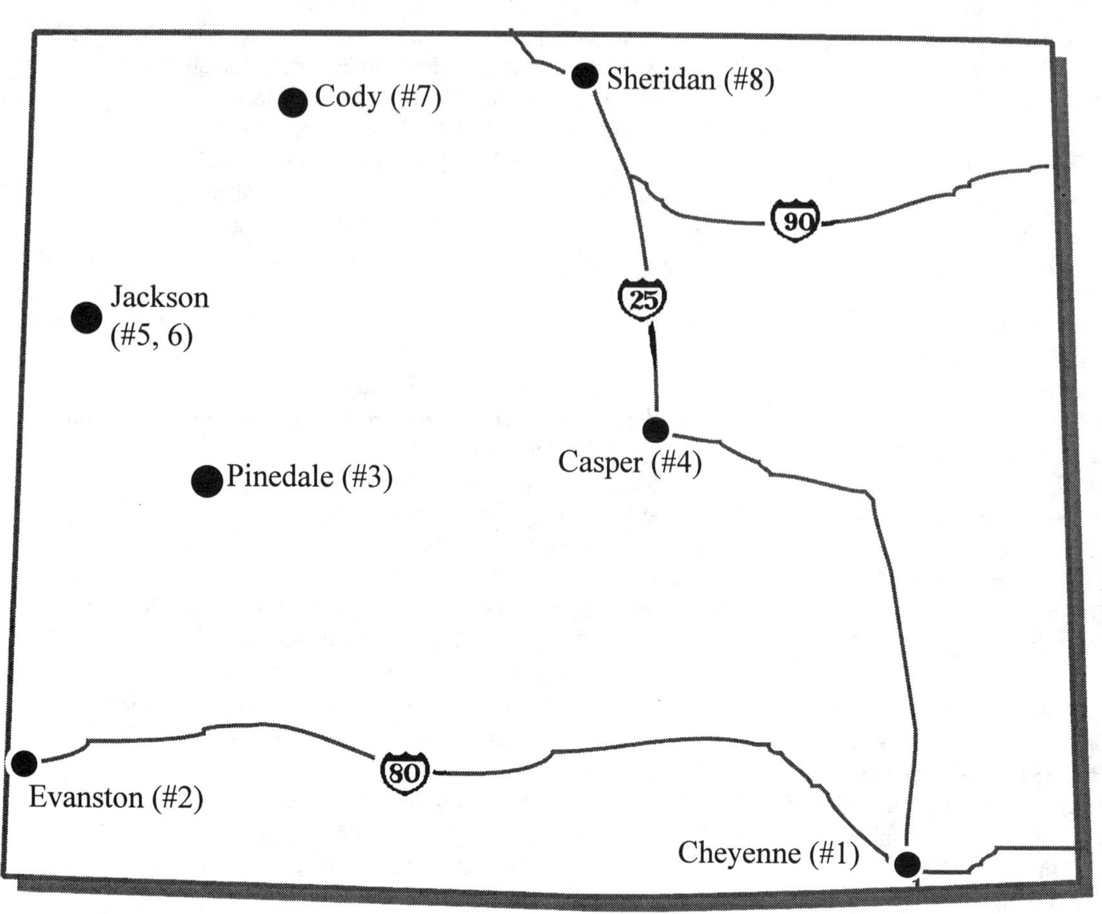

8 Featured Shops

Cheyenne, WY #1

Mon - Fri 10 - 4
Sat 10 - 3

The Quilted Corner

2015 Warren Ave. 82001
(307) 638-2002

Cheyenne's only shop devoted to Quilters. Located in historic Home. Large selection of 100% cotton Fabric, Books, Notions & Patterns.

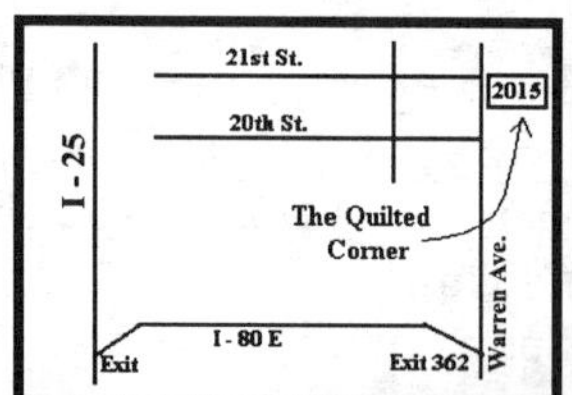

Evanston, WY #2

Mon - Sat 10 - 6

Quilt Trappings

927 Main St. 82930
(307) 789-1675
E-Mail: sleroy@tcd.net
Est: 1995 2000 sq.ft.

Located in the historic Blythe & Fargo Building. Large selection of fabrics, notions, patterns and books. Pfaff sewing machines.

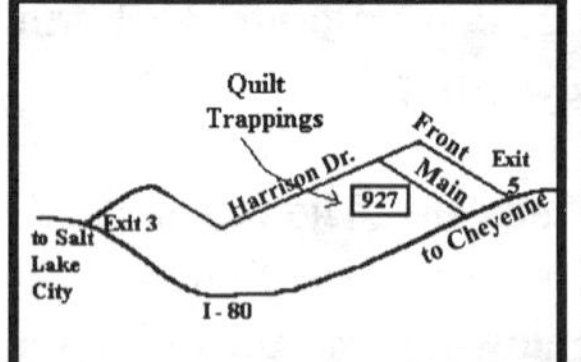

Pinedale, WY #3

Winter Tues - Sat 10:30 - 5:30
Summer Mon - Sat 9:30 - 5:30

Joan's Country

215 W. Pine, P.O. Box 1916 82941
(307) 367-4341
Owner: Joan Dobbs
Est: 1992 1200 sq.ft. 800+ Bolts

100% Cotton Quilt Fabrics, Kits, Books, Patterns & Gifts. Catalog, Swatches, Classes and more. All Major Credit Cards Accepted. Come in and Say Hi!

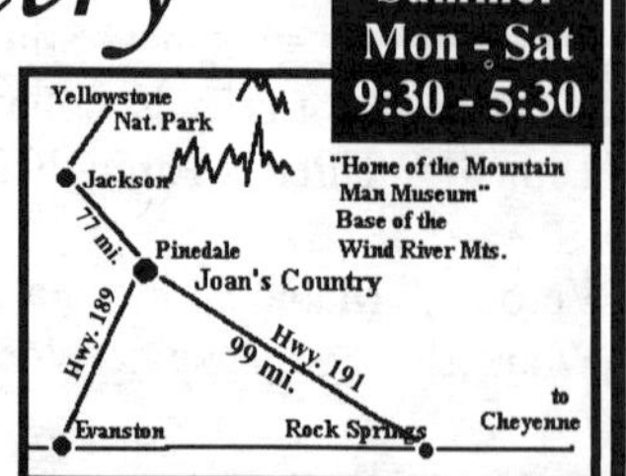

Casper, WY #4

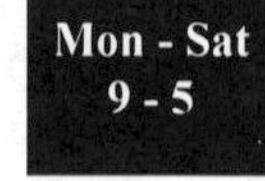

Prism Quilt

114 E. 2nd St. 82601
(307) 234-4841
Owners: Becki & Bill Marsh
Est: 1987 4800 sq.ft. 3000+ Bolts

3000+ cotton fabrics, Pfaff, Sewing Machines, Quilts, Books, Patterns, Notions, Classes, Quilting Supplies and Service.

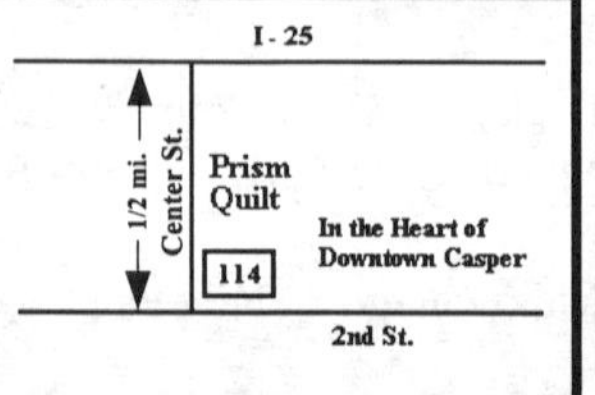

Jackson, WY #5

545 N. Cache 83001
(307) 734-7919 Fax: (307) 734-2772
E-Mail: QUILTSOUTH@aol.com
Owner: Susan Southworth
Freelance Writer for Quilt Magazine

Summer Hours:
Mon - Fri
10 - 6
Winter Hours
depend on Snow

Jackson Hole Quilt Connection

We're not just quilts! Stop in and check out the large selection of wildlife buttons; those 'hard to find' elk, buffalo, bear claws, cat paws, and many more. Browse around the shop and see our nice gifts, hemp, hemp kits and books that will help you make the latest in hemp jewelry. We stock beads, embellishments, quilting and sewing supplies, quilting books, patterns and kits. 100% cotton fabrics and 'fancy' fabrics for that special Victorian project or crazy quilt. We specialize in wildlife fabrics and also carry Jinny Beyer and Hoffman.

Looking for something different or out of the ordinary? You'll find patterns here that you won't find elsewhere, patterns that will make you chuckle. Designers Nancy Ahern and Julie Russell keep this shop stocked with their unique patterns and kits. You'll see Nancy's take on the Rockefellers of Jackson Hole...4 big boys from the parks hanging around a big rock under the Wyoming sky. In addition to the Wildside patterns, there are eight patterns in the "Grace the Cat" series, featuring a gray cat who gets into all sorts of trouble. You can make 'your' cat by simply changing it using fabric colors that match such as calico or black and white etc. Julie's Mortimer the Moose has become very popular because of its 'One of a Kind' quality. Her 'Moose Angels' simply fly out the door because they are so adorable and you just want to take one home with you!

Don't get 'top heavy'; bring in your quilt tops for me to quilt at reasonable prices and I'll mail them back to you so they will be waiting on your return from your vacation.

A little bit of everything for everyone. Unique, special and distinct. Unlike any shop you've visited. Just like the saying about Wyoming... "Unlike any other place on earth..." So is the Jackson Hole Quilt Connection!

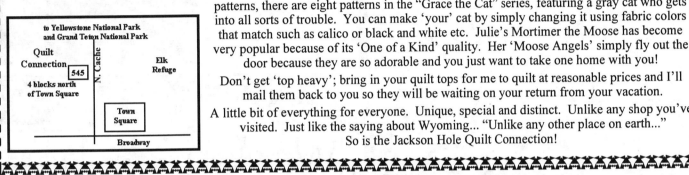

to Yellowstone National Park and Grand Teton National Park
Quilt Connection
545
4 blocks north of Town Square
N. Cache
Elk Refuge
Town Square
Broadway

Jackson, WY #6

Stitch 'n Time

Mon - Fri
9 - 6
Sat 9 - 5

185 S. Scott Ln. P.O. Box 8819
(307) 733-6800 83002
Owners: Edward & Shirley Christian
Est: 1971 4500 sq.ft. 4000 Bolts

A unique array of fabrics and notions that expand the imagination to creative expression.

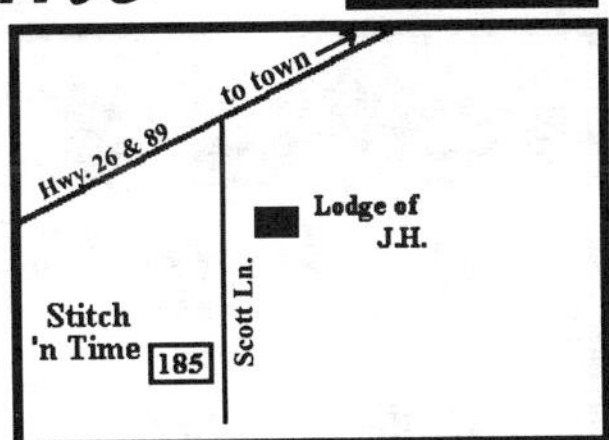

Cody, WY #7

Crafty Quilter

Mon - Fri
10 - 5:30
Sat 10 - 4

1262 Sheridan Ave. 82414
(307) 527-6305 Est: 1981
Owner: Susy McCall
Mgr: Terri Lightman

2000+ bolts quality cotton fabrics.
Many Hoffmans
Books, Patterns, Notions.
Close to Buffalo Bill Historical Center.

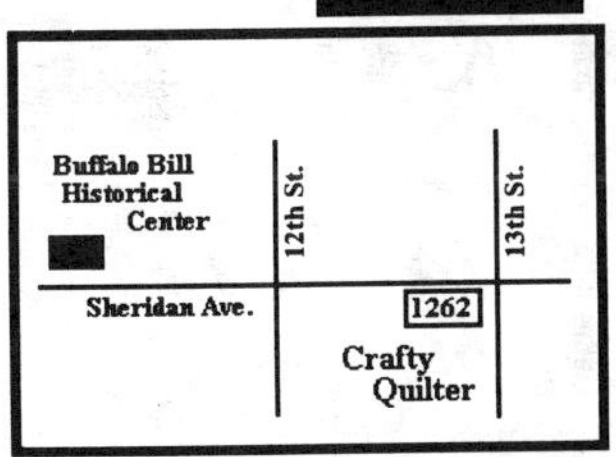

Wyoming Guilds:
Wyoming Heritage Quilters, P.O. Box 19081, Cheyenne, 82003
NE Wyoming Quilt Guild, 3508 S. Douglas Hwy., Gillette, 82718
Jackson Hole Guild, P.O. Box 8819, Jackson, 83001
Paintbrush Piecers Quilt Guild, P.O. Box 258, Powell, 82435

Sheridan, WY #8

Treasured Stitches

Mon - Fri
10 - 5
Tues til 9
Sat 10 - 4

155 W. Loucks St. 82801
(307) 674-0558
Owners: Josephine Schreibeis & Rita Barker
Est: 1996

Top quality Fabrics, Patterns, Books, Quilter's Notions, and Supplies. Classes. Silk Flowers & some Finished Crafts.

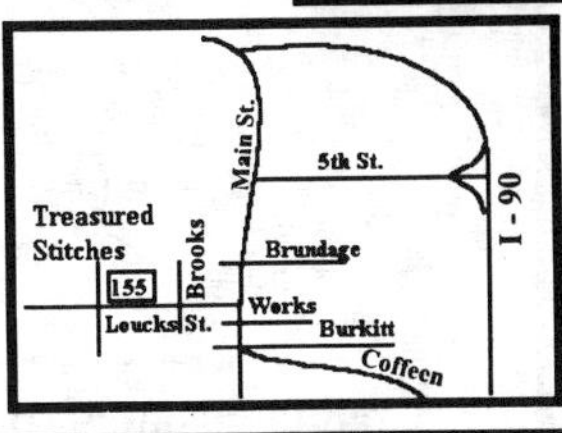

Other Shops in Wyoming:

Douglas	Sheila's Fabrics, 515 S. 4th St.	307-358-5333
Dubois	Sew What?, 132 E. Ramshorn	307-455-3373
Evanston	Quilted Quacker, 112 Yellow Creek Rd.	307-789-9050
Lander	Quilting Bee, 637 W. Main St.	307-332-4123
Lyman	Valley Fabric Shop, 102 Meadow	307-786-2653
Rock Springs	Threads 'n Things, 2646 Commercial Way	307-382-2897
Torrington	Homesteaders Quilting Shop, 2140 Main St.	307-532-8989
Worland	Hansen's Fabric, 734 Big Horn Ave.	307-347-4895

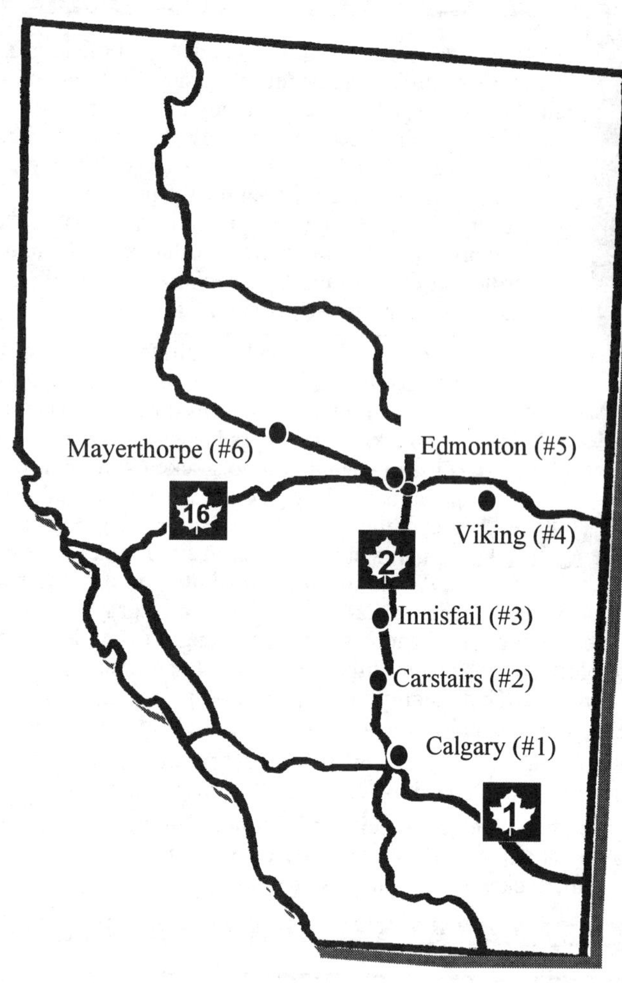

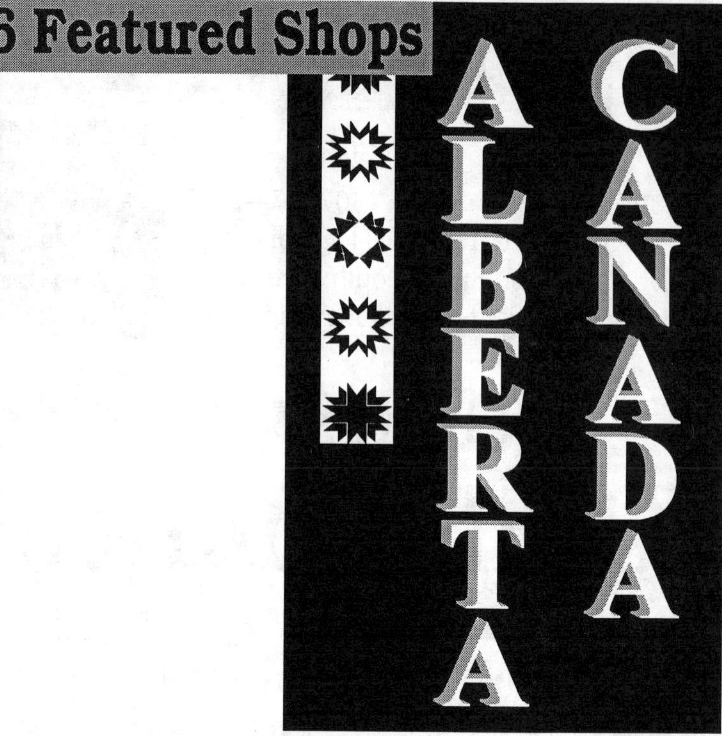

Carstairs, AB #2

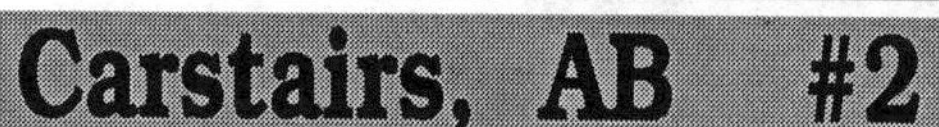

Custom Woolen Mills ltd.

Mon - Fri
8 - 5

R.R. # 1 T0M 0N0
(403) 337-2221
Fax: Same
E-Mail: smithwr@cadvision.com

Est: 1975
Free Catalog

Owners: Fen & Bill Purves - Smith

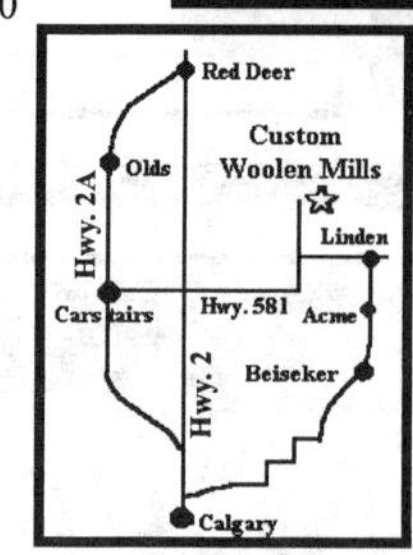

Small woolen mill, machinery dating 1860 to 1910, gift shop, quilting batts, comforter sewing.

Calgary, AB #1

The Fabric Cottage

16 Crowfoot Terrace NW
T3G 4JB 3700 sq.ft.
(403) 241-3070
Fax: (403) 547-8743
Owners:
Doreen Folk & Joan Vogel

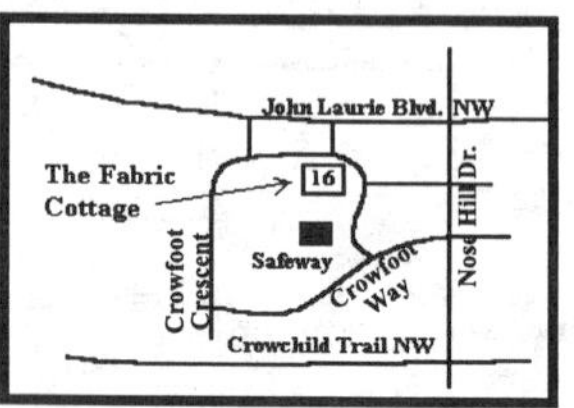

Mon - Sat 10 - 5:30
Thur til 8:30

100% quilting cottons, books, patterns, notions & classes. Fully authorized Bernina dealership in sales & service.

"From traditional to contemporary"

Innisfail, AB #3

Fabric Fantasy

Mon - Fri
9:30 - 5:30
Sat 10 - 5

5028 - 49th St. T4G 1M1
(403) 227-4618

Large selection of top quality 100% cotton Fabrics, polar Fleece, patterns and specialty cross stitch supplies.

to Edmonton
Hwy. 2
50th Ave.
Red Deer
50th St.
Fabric Fantasy
Innisfail
49th St.
5028
to Calgary

Viking, AB #4

Viking Fabric & Gifts

Mon - Sat
9 - 5:30
Summer
9:30 - 4:30

5116 - 50 St. T0B 4N0
(403) 336-3000
Owner: Patricia Winter

Great selection of fabrics for quilting & fashion sewing, notions, books, patterns and Husqvarna/White Sewing Machines.

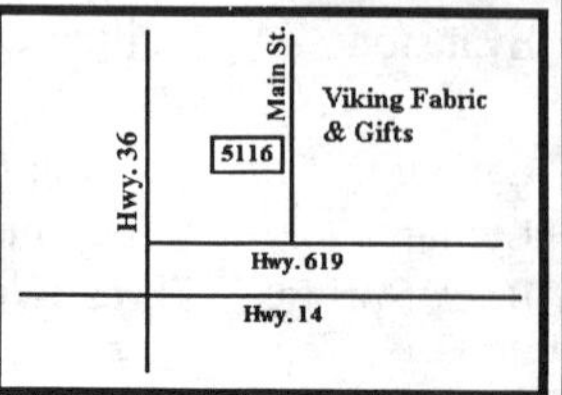

Alberta Guilds:

Alberta Handicrafts Guild, Beisiker Branch, Box 59, Beisiker, T0M 0G0
Country Quilters, Box 37, Blue Ridge, T0E 0B0
  Meets: 2nd Monday 7 p.m. at Anselmo Hall
Heartland Quilters' Guild, Box 218, Botha, T0C 0N0
Piecemakers Guild, 42 Hampstead Circle NW, Calgary, T3A 5P1
  Meets: 3rd Monday (Sept - June) at St. Peters Anglican Church
Stitch-In Witches, 5003 Balhart Rd. NW, Calgary, T3A 1C1
  Meets: 2nd Tuesday 7 p.m. in member's home
Stitch-In time, 89 Flavelle Rd. SE, Calgary, T2H 1E8
St. Stephens Quilt Group, 1312 - 106th Ave. SW, Calgary, T2W 0B7
  Meets: Wednesdays 9:30 a.m. at St. Stephen's Church
St. Cyprian Quilters, 927 Ranch Estates Pl. NW, Calgary, T3G 1M5
  Meets: Mondays 9:30 a.m. in member's home
Springbank Quilters, Box 18, Site 18, RR #12, Calgary, T3E 6W3
  Meets: Every other Thursday 1 p.m. in member's home
Prairie Wind Quilters, 856 Lake Twintree SE, Calgary, T2J 2W3
  Meets: 2nd Wednesday 11:30 a.m. in a members home
Newcomers Club, 171 Woodsman Lane SW, Calgary, T2W 4Z5
Calgary Silver Thimble Q. G., #1 - 8203 Silver Springs Rd. NW, Calgary
  Meets: 1st & 3rd Wednesdays 7:30 p.m. at Silver Springs Community Centre, 5720 Silver Ridge Dr. NW, Calgary
Calgary Guild of Needle & Fibre Arts, Box 52146, Edmonton Tr RPO Calgary, T2E 8K9 Meets: 2nd Wednesday (Sept - June) 7 p.m. at the Scandinavian Centre, 738 - 20th Ave. NW, Calgary
Bow River Quilters, 2188 Brownsea Dr. NW, Calgary, T2N 3G9
  Meets: 1st Friday (except July & Aug) 9:30 a.m. at 2188 Brownsea Dr. NW, Calgary
Alberta Handicrafts Guild, P.O. Box 34085, Calgary, T3C 2W0
  Meets: Mon. 9 a.m. at Rossacarrock Comm., 1406 - 40th St. SW
Sew & Sew Quilters, 4623 - 26th Ave NE, Calgary, T1Y 2R9
  Meets: Tuesdays 7 p.m. in member's home
Mountain Cabin Quilters, Box 2868, Canmore, T0L 0M0
Big Hill Quilters, 50 Glenwood Pl, Cochrane, T0L 0W3
Alberta Handicrafts Guild, Dalmead Branch, Box 312, Dalmead, T0J 0V0
Hearts & Hands Quilters Guild, Box 6321, Drayton Valley, T0E 0M0
Edmonton District Quilt Guild, Box 68004, 70 Bonnie Doon Mall P.O. Edmonton, T6E 4N6 Meets: at the Provincial Museum
Quilt Guild, 9104 - 116th St., Edmonton, T6G 1P9
Quilter's Co-op, 1016 - 46th St., Edmonton, T6L 5V8
Southeast Quilters Guild, 10519 - 52nd St., Edmonton, T6A 2G7
Alberta Handicrafts Guild, 75 Sunset Blvd., Edmonton, T8N 0P2
Alberta Handicraft Guild, Box 5733, High River, T1V 1T3
  Meets: Fridays 9 a.m. at the Cultural Centre, 251 9th Ave.
Western Rocky Mountain Quilters Guild, 111 Tamarack Ave., Hinton, T7V 1C6
Central Alberta Quilters Guild, Box 5462, Lacombe, T4L 1X2
  Meets: 1st Monday at Lacombe Jr. High Home Ec Room
Lacombe Quilters, Box 2577, Lacombe, T0C 1S0
Lethbridge Centennial Q. G., 811 - 5th Ave. S, Lethbridge, T1J 0V2
  Meets: 4th Tuesday (except Dec, July & Aug), at the Bowman Arts Center, 811 0 5th Ave. S
Log Cabin Quilters Guild, 5301 - 23rd St., Lloydminster, T9V 2P9
Medicine Hat Quilters, 45 - 1st St., Medicine Hat, T1A 6G9
Country Lane Quilters, Box 89, Millarville, T0L 1K0
  Meets: 1st Tuesday (Sept - June) at Millarville Church House
Chinook Country Quilters, 32 Downey Rd., Okotoks, T0L 1T2
Lebel House Quilters Guild, Box 2434, Pincher Creek, T0K 1W0
  Meets: 3rd Thursday at Lebel House
High Country Quilters, 6 Wolf Court, Redwood Meadows, T3Z 1A3
  Meets: 2nd Wednesday 7:30 p.m. at Redwood House
Rimbey & District Quilters, P.O. Box 1131, Rimbey, T0C 2J0
St. Albert Quilters Guild, 94 Finch Crescent, St. Albert, T8N 1Y6
Stony Plain Quilters, Box 866, Stony Plain, T0E 2G0

Other Shops in Alberta:

Boyle	Crystal's Crafts, 5021 - 3rd St.	
Brooks	Family Fabrics, Box 862	
Calgary	Country Quilts, 816A 16th Ave. SW	403-228-2217
Calgary	Quilter's Cabin, 118 - 10816 Macleod	403-278-4433
Calgary	Rocky Mountain Quilt Co., Box 2, Site 11, R.R. 5	
Calgary	Freckles, 126 10th St. NW	403-270-2104
Calgary	D & D Fabric Place, 6020 1Ast. SW	403-259-8442
Calgary	Traditional Pastimes, Box 57, Site 19, R. R. 2	
Calgary	Ant Hill, 148 10th St. NW	403-283-8989
Camrose	Cotton Berry Fabrics, 5028 50th St.	403-679-0636
Canmore	The Sugar Pine Co., 801 Main St. #8	403-678-9603
Cardston	Imagination Unlimited, 257 Main St.	403-653-2633
Claresholm	Fabric Boutique, Box 1418	
Cochrane	Fab-Bric House, 2056 3 Ave	403-932-3944
Drayton Valley	Material Matters, 5119 51st St.	403-542-3233
Edmonton	The Quilter's Palette, 522 Carse Ln.	
Edmonton	Quilter's Dream, 10732 - 124 St.	403-452-1133
Edmonton	The Notion Place, 4748 - 99th St.	
Edmonton	MacPhee Whorkshop, 13704 - 113A St.	
Grand Centre	Material World, 5408 - 55A St.	
Grande Prairie	Patchwork Cottage, 10209 - 102nd St.	
Hanna	Yesterday's Dreams, Box 34	403-854-2622
High River	Chinook Fabrics, Box 5482	
Hinton	Sew with Sue, Hills Shopping Center, 201 Penbina Ave.	
Killam	Tatters, 5007 - 50th St.	
Lacombe	Wildflower Creations, 5025 50 Ave	403-782-4141
Leduc	Seams to Be, 5212 - 50th St.	
Lethbridge	Fanny's Fabrics, 1245 2nd Ave. S	403-329-3355
Lethbridge	Thistle Down Quilts, #3 - 1021 2 Ave.	403-329-1551
Lethbridge	Village Crafts, #3, 1240 - 2nd Ave. N	
Linden	Jo-Al Styles & Fabrics, 113 Central Ave.	403-546-3882
Lloydminster	Patchwork Junction, 5732 44th St.	403-875-5935
Mayerthrope	Kountry Krafts, PO Box 1109	403-786-2821
Milk River	Stitch in Time, 207 Main St. NW	
Nanton	Fabrique Boutique, 2119 20 St	403-646-2106
Okotoks	Rainbow End, 2 Elma St. W	
Okotoks	Old Country Store, 64 N. Railway St.	
Okotoks	Patchwork Plus, 1100 Village Ln. Bay 6	403-938-6107
Olos	D Mentions, 14 Balsam Crescent	
Oyen	The Country Fabric Shop, Box 442	
Red Deer	Cotton Threads Quilt Co., 5020 Gaetz	403-346-4005
Sherwood Park	Lori's Fabric, 20-975 Broadmoor	403-464-9697
Spruce Grove	Materiai Women, 206 B McLeod Ave.	
St. Albert	Sherry's Calico Cupboard, 31A Perron St.	
Stettler	Stettler Fabric Place, 4909 B 50 St.	403-742-6145
Stony Plain	Patt's Niche, 109 - 50th St.	
Strathmore	Country Creations, P.O. Box 2142	403-934-4054
Taber	Lacey's Fabrics, 5328 - 48th Ave.	
Three Hills	Three Hills Sewing Center, 411 Main St.	
Vegreville	McFabrics & More, Box 668	
Wainwright	Sewing Basket, 213 - 10th St.	
White Court	Sew Right, 5106 50th St.	403-778-5717

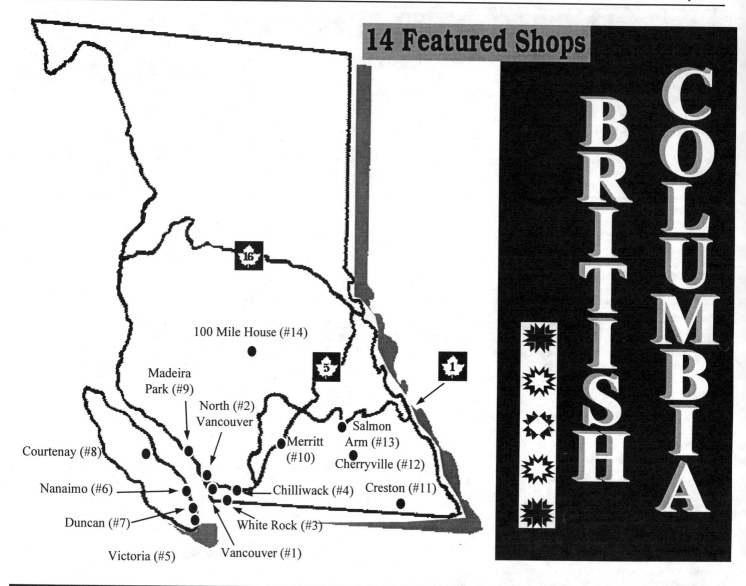

14 Featured Shops

BRITISH COLUMBIA

100 Mile House (#14)
Madeira Park (#9)
North (#2) Vancouver
Courtenay (#8)
Merritt (#10)
Salmon Arm (#13)
Cherryville (#12)
Nanaimo (#6)
Chilliwack (#4)
Creston (#11)
Duncan (#7)
White Rock (#3)
Victoria (#5)
Vancouver (#1)
16
5
1

The Cloth Shop

2 Great Shops!

Vancouver, BC #1

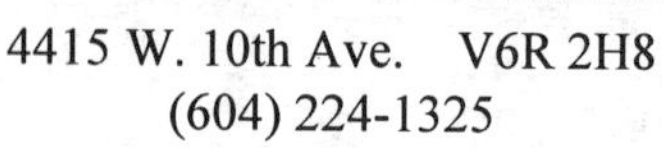

4415 W. 10th Ave. V6R 2H8
(604) 224-1325

Mon - Sat 10 - 5:30
Thur til 9 Sun 12 - 5

Beautiful selection of pure cotton fabrics. Books, patterns and quilting notions. Mohair and bear making supplies. Year round classes, excellent friendly service.

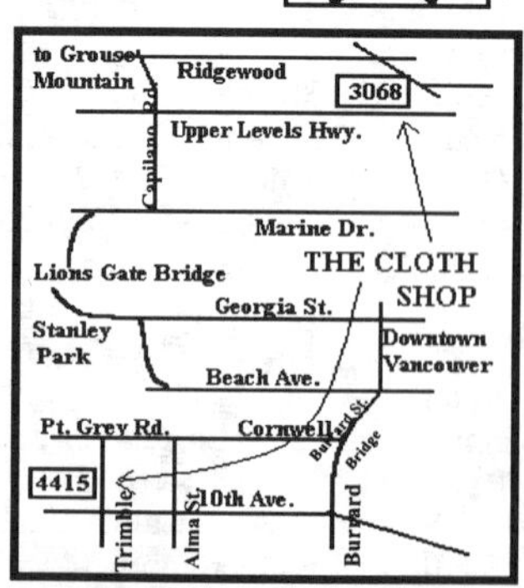

North Vancouver, BC #2

3068 Highland Blvd. V7R 2X4
(604) 990-1325

Mon - Sat 9:30 - 5:30
Sun 12 - 5

White Rock, BC #3

Mon - Sat
10 - 5:30
Sun 12 - 4

Creations III Fabrics

13979 - 16th Ave. V4A 1P8
(604) 531-9311
Owners: Beverly, Bonnie & Jacqueline Alp

Great selection of cottons, patterns & books.
Country craft kits our specialty.
Lots of novel ideas!

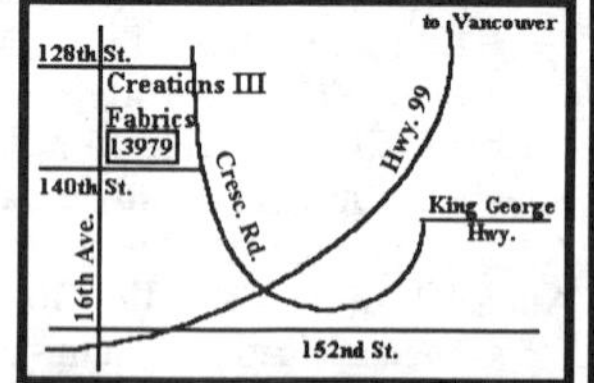

Chilliwack, BC #4

Mon - Sat
9 - 5:30

Hamels Fabrics

9339 Mary St. V2P 4G9
(604) 792-4506 Fax: (604) 792-9633
Owner: Pauline Southgate
Est: 1958 2300 sq.ft.

Specialize in Quality Quilting and Fashion Fabrics. Large selection of Notions and Books. Janome & Bernina Dealer.

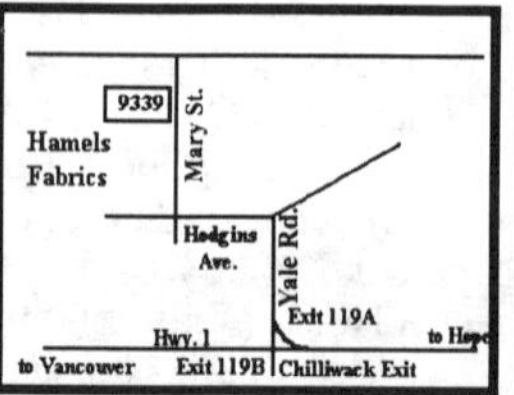

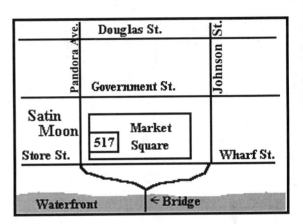

Snip & Stitch
SEWING CENTRE
NANAIMO

Wander through our store for a refreshing experience. You will find a relaxing atmosphere, warm and friendly staff, and that "something special" you've been looking for!

Conveniently situated, one block off the Island Highway in North Nanaimo, Snip & Stitch offers a wide selection of classes, books and notions as well as the "BEST" selection of quilting cottons on Vancouver Island.

We look forward to meeting you.

Betty MacLean & Staff

Your "One-Stop Quilting & Sewing Machine Store" on Vancouver Island!

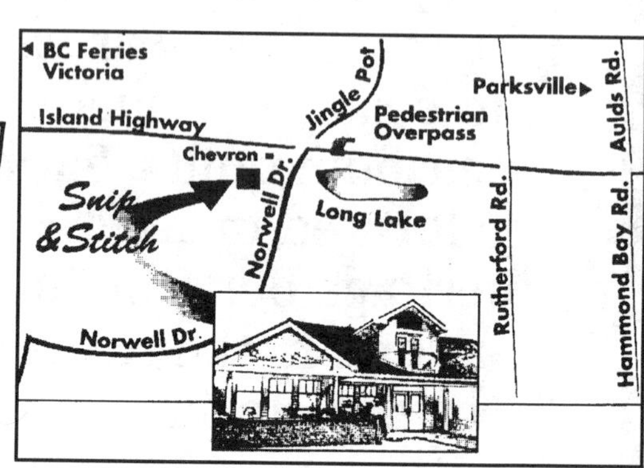

I - 4047 Norwell Dr. V9T 1Y6
(250) 756-2176

Fax: (250) 756-2178
E-Mail: snip@nanaimo.ark.com
Web-Site: nanaimo.ark.com/~snip

Nanaimo, BC #6

9:30 - 5:30 Six days a week
12:00 - 4:00 Sundays

Duncan, BC #7

Mon - Sat 9:30 - 5

Robin's Fabric Garden

40 Ingram St. V9L 1N7
(250) 748-3441 Fax: (250) 748-4195
Owner: Robin Duke

Quilt Country!
Beautiful Cottons. Great Classes. Patterns. Notions. Quilt Gallery

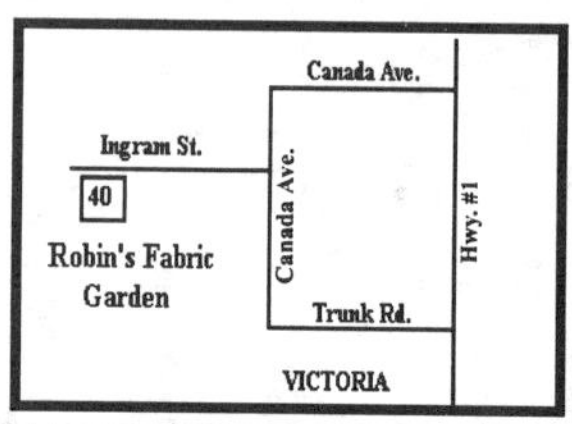

Courtenay, BC #8

Mon - Sat 10 - 5

Huckleberry's Fabrics, Inc.

779 Rye Rd. V9N 3R7
(250) 338-4054
Fax: (250) 338-4025
Owners: Cecil & Ann Marie Potter

Our 100% cotton fabrics are hand picked. We carry a full line of the latest books and patterns.

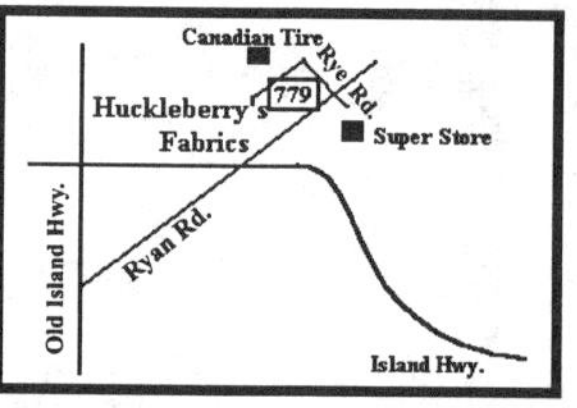

Madeira Park, BC #9

**Mon - Fri 9:30 - 5
Sat 10 - 4:30**

The Quilted Path and Country Pleasures

4982 Gonzales Rd., Box 181 V0N 2H0
(604) 883-2274 (Fax Same) Est: 1995

Langdale ferry from Horseshoe Bay. One hour north on Hwy. 101 to Madeira Park. Quilting fabrics, supplies, books, crafts, yarns & Gifts.

Merritt, BC #10

Mon - Sat 9 - 5

Pablo's Decorating Centre

2074 Quilchena Ave., Box 2819
(250) 378-9733 V1K 1B8
Fax: (250) 378-9736
Ray & Brenda Thompson

Pablo's has a great selection of quality name brand quilting cottons, patterns, and notions. Have fun at Pablo's

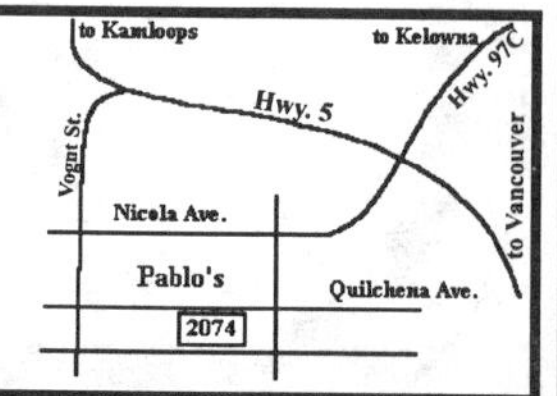

Creston, BC #11

Mon - Sat 10 - 5:30

Quiltview Corner

115 - 20th Ave. S V0B 1G5
(250) 428-4891
E-Mail: quilt@cancom.net
Owners: Terri Morris & Jean Swalwell

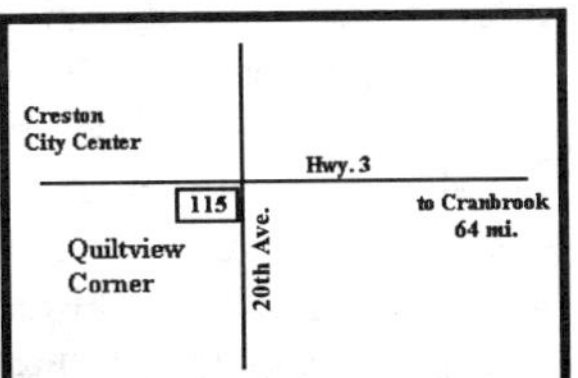

Inspiration comes in fabric, classes, notions, books, patterns, gizmos, & gotta haves!

Cherryville, BC #12

Daily 9 - 5

Cherry Ridge Crafts and Bed & Breakfast

648 N. Fork Rd., R.R. #1 V0E 2G0
(250) 547-2257 or 547-8919
Owners: Dave & Jill De Vries
Est: 1992 700 Bolts

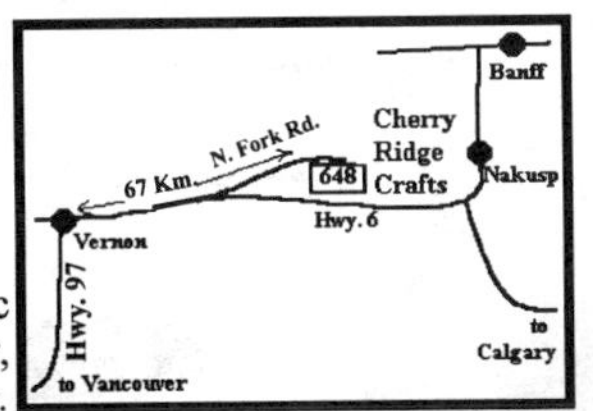

Quilt Shop and Bed & Breakfast. Fabricaholic Owner. Willow Chair & Quilting Classes. Deer, Birdwatching. Near Monashee Wilderness Park.

100 Mile House, BC #14

Mon - Sat 9 - 5:30 Fri til 9

Country Fabrics & Things

P.O. Box 13 (Cariboo Mall)
(250) 395-3377 Fax: Same
Est: 1986 1200 sq.ft.

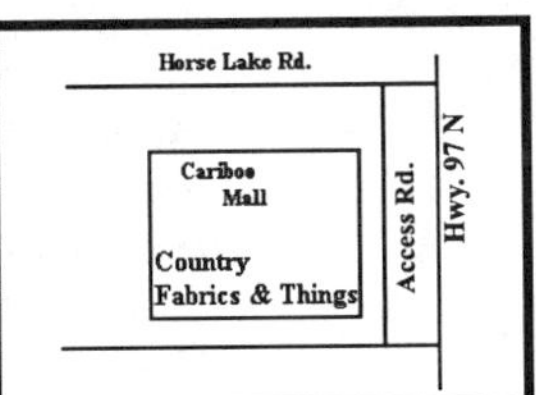

Very large selection of pillow and crib panels; Quilting fabrics & supplies, lace & trims, denims & Navaho fabrics.

The Sewing Basket

Mon - Sat 9:00 - 5:30

168 MacLeod
P.O. 327
V1E 4N2
(250) 832-3937
Fax: Same
Est: 1983
2500 sq.ft.

Stop by for your free Angel Pattern!

Salmon Arm, BC #13

We carry thousands of bolts of unique fabrics... all for the seamstress at home, or the most selective quilter! We're also a "MacPhee Workshop Dealer" with a great selection of MacPhee Fabrics and Patterns.

~ Craft Supplies ~ Craft Kits ~
~ Needlework ~ Quilting Supplies ~
Plus Many Hard to Find Notions and Accessories...

We offer over 50 'Year Round' Classes
Keeping you Up-to-Date with the latest Techniques.

British Columbia Guilds:

Timberline Quilters Guild, Box 194, Blubber Bay, V8A 1S9
Meets: Thursday eve at Villa Soccer Center, Timberlane Park
Piecemakers, 1019 Marchant Rd., Brentwood, V5O 1A0
North Star Quilter's Guild, Box 476, Burns Lake, V0J 1E0
Campbell River Friendship Quilter's Guild, Campbell River
Nell Hamilton Quilters, 1854 South Isd Hwy., Campbell River, V9N 1B8
Cherryville Quilting Guild, 648 N. Fork Rd., Cherryville, V0E 2G0
Meets: 1st & 3rd Wednesday 9 a.m. at 648 N. Fork Rd.
Quintessential Quilters, P.O. Box 1454, Chetwynd, V0C 1J0
Chilliwack Quilters Guild, 45899 Henderson Ave., Chilliwack
Meets: 3rd Tuesday 9:30 a.m.
The Schoolhouse Quilter's Guild, P.O. Box 1507, Comox, V9N 8A2
Como Lake Quilters Guild, 2345 Huron Dr., Coquitlam, V3J 1A6
Pacific Spirit Quilter's Guild, #53 2905 Norman, Coquitlam, Z3C 4H9
Meets: 3rd Friday 7 p.m.
at New Vista Care Home, 7550 Rosewood, Burnaby
Schoolhouse Quilter's Guild, Courtenay
Creston Valley Quilters Guild, P.O. Box 2178, Creston, V0B 1G0
Heritage Quilters, 355 Dogwood Pl, Duncan, V9I 1M3
Meets: Mondays 10 a.m. and Thursdays 8 p.m.
at Girl Guide Hall, 321 Cairnsmore
Fernie Quilter's Guild, Box 2577, Fernie, V0B 1M0
Meets: 2nd & 4th Tuesday at Fernie Arts Station
Fort St. John Country Quilters, P.O. Box 6474, Fort St. John, V1J 4H9
Meets: 2nd & 4th Monday (except July, Aug & Dec.)
at North Peace Cultural Centre
Beaver Valley Quilters, Box 1079, Fruitvale, V0G 1L0
Sunshine Coast Quilters G., R.R. #4, S-18A C27, Gibsons, V0N 1V0
Meets: Saturday every other month from Sept.
at Davis Bay School, Sechelt
Mountain Magic Quilters, Box 2414, Golden, V0H 1Z0
Grand Forks Quilt Connection, Box 1708, Grand Forks, V0H 1H0
Meets: 2nd Thursday 7 p.m. at Grand Forks Art Gallery
Calico Quilters, 253 Beach Ave., Kamloops, V2B 1C4
Sagebrush Quilters Guild, 1717 N. River Dr., Kamloops, V2B 7N4
Orchard Valley Q. G., P.O. Box 585 Stn A, Kelowna, V1Y 7P2
Meets: Tuesday 9 a.m. (Sept to mid-Dec & Jan to mid-May)
at Kelowna Curling Club
St. Pius X Quilters, 679 Clifton Rd., Kelowna, V1V 1A7
Kitimat Quilters' Guild, 35 Dease St., Kitimat, V8C 2M2
Kitwanga Patchwork Partners, Box 147, Kitwanga, V0J 2A0
Meets: 7 p.m. Monday (Sept - June)
at K.E.S. School Home Ec Room
Pender Harbour Piecemakers, Site 2 Camp 28 R.R. #1, Madeira Park V0N 2H0
Ridge Meadows Quilters, 12073 Rothsay St., Maple Ridge, V2X 8X8

Marysville Quilters, 612 - 305th St., Marysville, V0B 1Z0
Quilters Guild, 397 Neil Rd., R.R. #1, Mayne Island, V0N 2J0
Nicola Valley Quilter's Guild, Box 938, Merritt, V0K 2B0
Highland United Church Quilters, 3255 Edgemont Blvd., N. Vancouver V5K 4H8
Lion's Gate Q. G., Box 54194, Lonsdale W, N. Vancouver, V7M 3K5
Meets: 4th Thursday 7 p.m.
at Community Services Bldg, 285 Prideaux St.
Nanaimo Quilter's Guild, Nanaimo
Oona River Sewing Circle, Box 1132, Oona River, V0V 1E0
Osoyoos Quilters, P.O. Box 958, Osoyoos, V0H 1V0
Meets: 1st & 3rd Tuesday 9 a.m.
at St. Christophers Anglican Church
Quilt House Quilters Guild, P.O. Box 1177, Parksville, V9P 2H2
Meets: 2nd Monday (Sept - June) at Parksville Legion Hall
Pentiction Quilters' Guild, P.O. Box 20165, Penticton, V2A 8K3
Meets: 2nd & 4th Wednesday (Sept - May)
at the Library Museum building, 785 Main St.
Bitts & Batts, Log Cabin Quilters, 2616 - 9th, Port Alberni, V9Y 2M7
Timberlane Quilters' Guild, 7296 Field St., Powell River, V8A 1S9
Meets: Thursday eve. at Villa Soccer Center, Timberlane Park
Prince George Q. G., 2880 - 15th Ave., Prince George, V2M 1T1
Meets: Last Wednesday at Studio 2880
Salmo Quilters Guild, Box 83, Salmo, V0G 1Z0
Meets: 2nd Thursday (except July & Aug)
in member's home
Chilliwack Quilter's Guild, P.O. Box 455, Sardis, V2R 1A8
Meets: 4th Wednesday 7 p.m.
at Mt. Slesse Middle School, 5871 Tyson
Calico Cats, #4 - 10110 St., Sidney, V8L 3B3
Fraser Valley Quilters Guild, 18971 - 59th Ave., Surrey, V3F 7R8
Meets: 2nd Monday 11:30 p.m. at Chamber of Commerce,
Guildford Centennial Library, Guildford
Windy Willow Quilt Guild, P.O. Box 501, Taylor, V0C 2K0
Vancouver Guild of Fabric Arts, 4397 West 2, Vancouver, V6R 1K4
Vancouver Quilters Guild, 4085 W. 35th Ave., Vancouver, V6N 2P4
Meets: 1st Wednesday 7:30 p.m. (Sept - June)
at St. Marys Anglican Church, 2490 W 37th Ave. (Larch)
Silver Star Quilting Squares, Box 1853, Vernon, V1T 8C3
Meets: 1st & 3rd Thurs 9 a.m. at St. Johns Lutheran Church
Ceilidh Quilters, 3205 Kenya Pl, Victoria, V8P 3T9
Victoria Quilters' Guild, P.O. Box 6453, Stn C, Victoria, V8P 5M4
Cariboo Piecemakers, Box 6065, Williams Lake, V2G 3W2

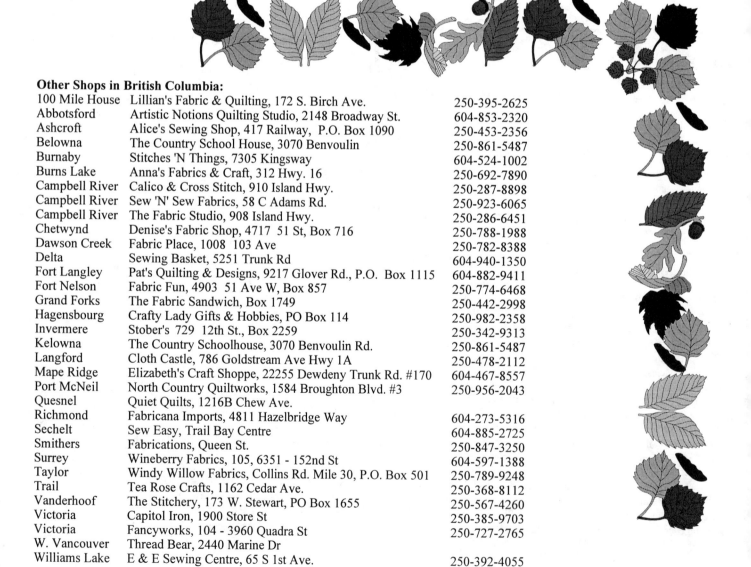

Other Shops in British Columbia:

100 Mile House	Lillian's Fabric & Quilting, 172 S. Birch Ave.	250-395-2625
Abbotsford	Artistic Notions Quilting Studio, 2148 Broadway St.	604-853-2320
Ashcroft	Alice's Sewing Shop, 417 Railway, P.O. Box 1090	250-453-2356
Belowna	The Country School House, 3070 Benvoulin	250-861-5487
Burnaby	Stitches 'N Things, 7305 Kingsway	604-524-1002
Burns Lake	Anna's Fabrics & Craft, 312 Hwy. 16	250-692-7890
Campbell River	Calico & Cross Stitch, 910 Island Hwy.	250-287-8898
Campbell River	Sew 'N' Sew Fabrics, 58 C Adams Rd.	250-923-6065
Campbell River	The Fabric Studio, 908 Island Hwy.	250-286-6451
Chetwynd	Denise's Fabric Shop, 4717 51 St, Box 716	250-788-1988
Dawson Creek	Fabric Place, 1008 103 Ave	250-782-8388
Delta	Sewing Basket, 5251 Trunk Rd	604-940-1350
Fort Langley	Pat's Quilting & Designs, 9217 Glover Rd., P.O. Box 1115	604-882-9411
Fort Nelson	Fabric Fun, 4903 51 Ave W, Box 857	250-774-6468
Grand Forks	The Fabric Sandwich, Box 1749	250-442-2998
Hagensbourg	Crafty Lady Gifts & Hobbies, PO Box 114	250-982-2358
Invermere	Stober's 729 12th St., Box 2259	250-342-9313
Kelowna	The Country Schoolhouse, 3070 Benvoulin Rd.	250-861-5487
Langford	Cloth Castle, 786 Goldstream Ave Hwy 1A	250-478-2112
Mape Ridge	Elizabeth's Craft Shoppe, 22255 Dewdeny Trunk Rd. #170	604-467-8557
Port McNeil	North Country Quiltworks, 1584 Broughton Blvd. #3	250-956-2043
Quesnel	Quiet Quilts, 1216B Chew Ave.	
Richmond	Fabricana Imports, 4811 Hazelbridge Way	604-273-5316
Sechelt	Sew Easy, Trail Bay Centre	604-885-2725
Smithers	Fabrications, Queen St.	250-847-3250
Surrey	Wineberry Fabrics, 105, 6351 - 152nd St	604-597-1388
Taylor	Windy Willow Fabrics, Collins Rd. Mile 30, P.O. Box 501	250-789-9248
Trail	Tea Rose Crafts, 1162 Cedar Ave.	250-368-8112
Vanderhoof	The Stitchery, 173 W. Stewart, PO Box 1655	250-567-4260
Victoria	Capitol Iron, 1900 Store St	250-385-9703
Victoria	Fancyworks, 104 - 3960 Quadra St	250-727-2765
W. Vancouver	Thread Bear, 2440 Marine Dr	
Williams Lake	E & E Sewing Centre, 65 S 1st Ave.	250-392-4055

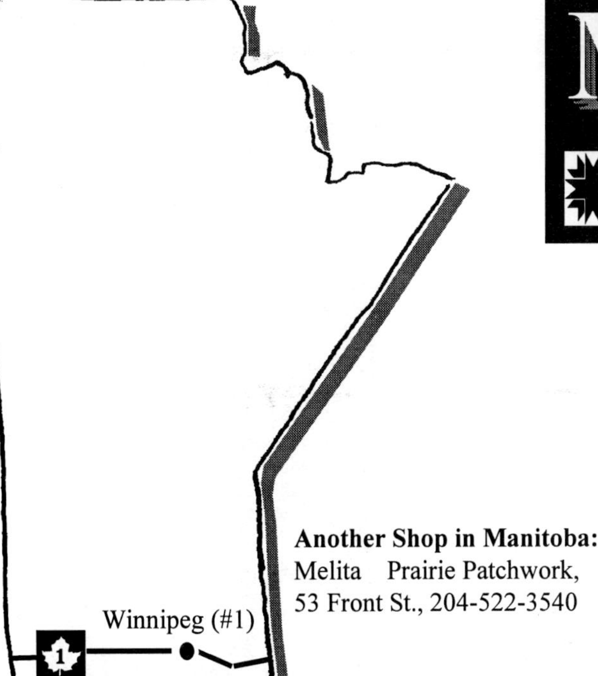

MANITOBA

1 Featured Shop

Winnipeg, MB #1

Mon - Sat 10 - 5 Thur til 7

The Quilting Bee

1026 St. Mary's Rd. R2M 3S6
(204) 254-7870 or (888) 518-3300
Fax: (204) 254-7895
Owners: Maria & Gwyneth Ball
1400 Bolts Free Newsletter

Biggest and friendliest shop in Manitoba. Wonderful selection of fabrics, notions, books, patterns and classes. Authorized PFAFF Dealer.

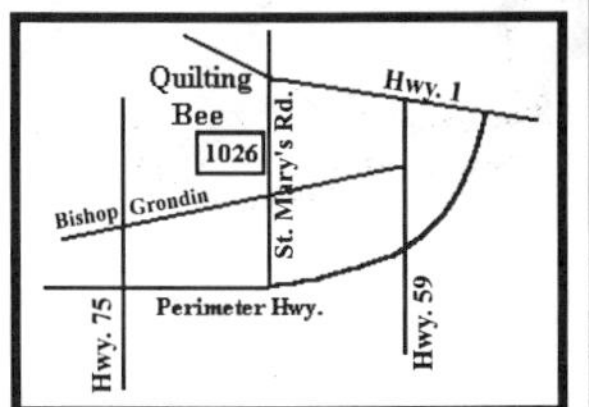

Another Shop in Manitoba:
Melita Prairie Patchwork,
53 Front St., 204-522-3540

Bedford, NS #1

Mon - Sat 10 - 5 Thurs & Fri til 9

The Cotton Patch

1717 Bedford Hwy. B4A 3X1
(902) 832-0155
Owner: Jackie Harris
Est: 1981 1600 sq.ft. 2000 Bolts

Quilting supplies including 2000 bolts of 100% cotton fabrics. Hundreds of books & patterns. A full line of notions. Knowledgeable staff.

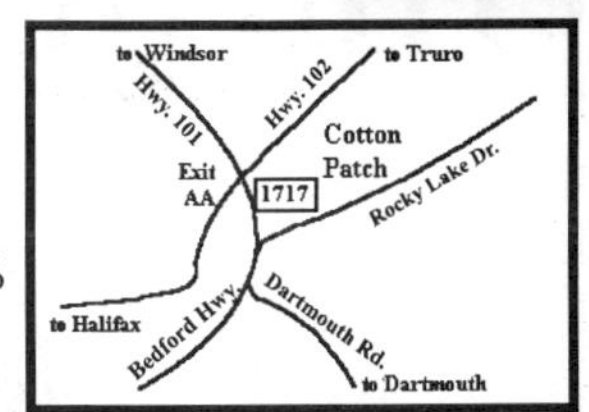

1 Featured Shop

NOVA SCOTIA

Other Shops in Nova Scotia:
Halifax Quilter's Hope Chest, 2483 Agricola St. 902-425-5002
Head of St. Margarets River B Quilts, 5001 St. Margaret's Bay Rd. 902-826-1991
Margaret's Bay River 'B' Quilts, 6001 St. 902-826-1991
Victoria County Lorraines Yarns & Crafts P.O. Box 49 902-336-2605

A Shop in Newfoundland:
St. John's Fabric Expressions, Inc., 17 Elizabeth Ave. 709-722-5000

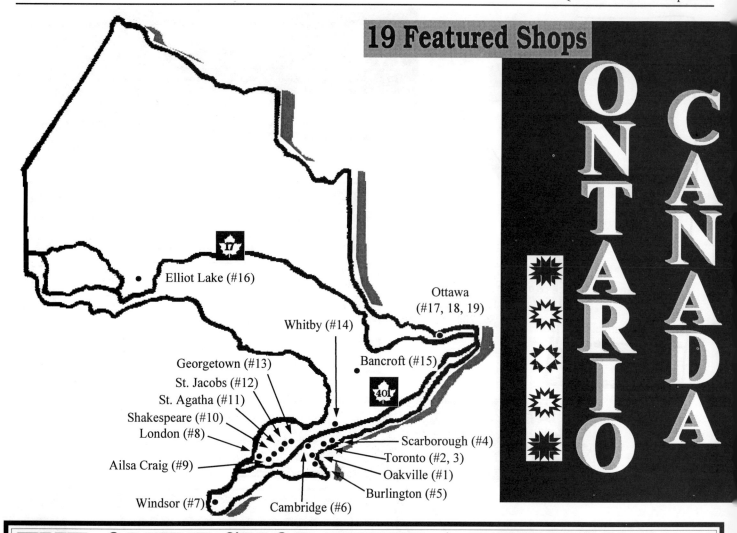

19 Featured Shops

ONTARIO CANADA

Elliot Lake (#16)
Ottawa (#17, 18, 19)
Whitby (#14)
Georgetown (#13)
Bancroft (#15)
St. Jacobs (#12)
St. Agatha (#11)
Shakespeare (#10)
London (#8)
Scarborough (#4)
Ailsa Craig (#9)
Toronto (#2, 3)
Oakville (#1)
Burlington (#5)
Windsor (#7)
Cambridge (#6)
17
401

THE QUILT SHOP WITH A DIFFERENCE!

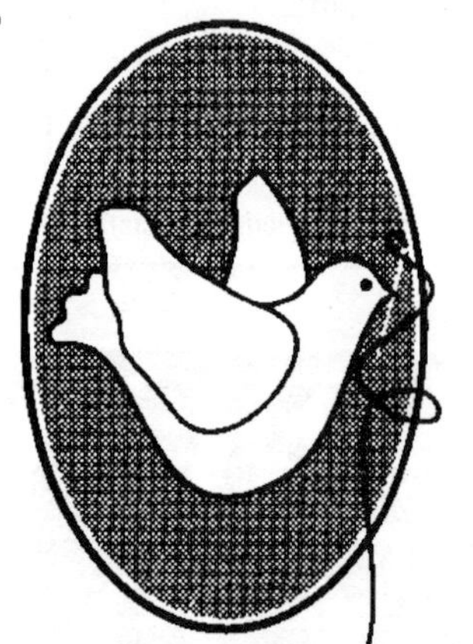

VISIT US AT
222 Lakeshore Rd. E L6J 1H6
(905) 844-1793
Owner: Jill Pettit

Mon - Sat
10 - 5:30
Fri til 9

Oakville, ON #1

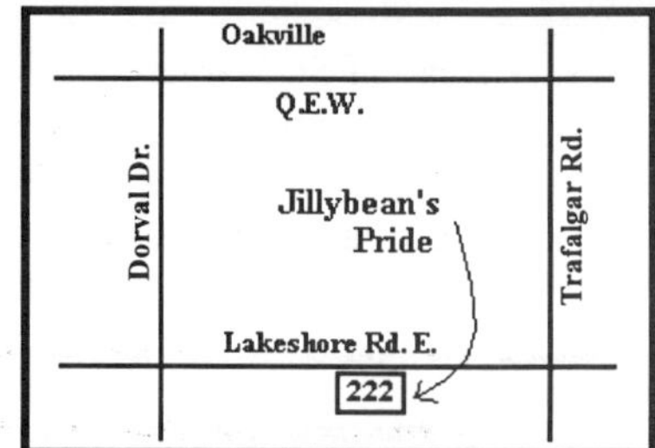

JILLYBEAN'S PRIDE

E-Mail: info@jillybeans.com
Web Site: www.jillybeans.com

Quilting Supplies, Needlework, and Unique Gifts

Toronto, ON #2

Quilters' Quarters

Close to downtown hotels, easy to get to by public transit or car.
Antique shops, restaurants, specialty shops and gift shops very nearby.

Mon - Fri 10 - 6
Sat 10 - 5:30

595 Mt. Pleasant Rd. M4S 2M5
(416) 487-1047 Est: 1990
(800) 561-5132 (Canada & U.S.)
Owner: Connie Archambault
900 sq.ft. 1500+ Bolts
Free newsletter & class schedule

Lots of 100% cotton fabrics from traditional to dramatic. Plus books, patterns, classes, & notions. Teddybear making supplies, mohair, glass eyes, joints and patterns. Mail order fabric club and **free Smiles !**

Toronto, ON #3

Quilters' Fancy Ltd.

Tues - Sat 10 - 6
Thur til 8

Free Catalogue

2877 Bloor St. West M8X 1B3
(416) 232-1199 in Canada (800) 363-3948
E-Mail: qfancy@idirect.com
Web Site: web.onramp.ca/quiltersfancy
Est: 1979 900 sq.ft. 2500+ Bolts

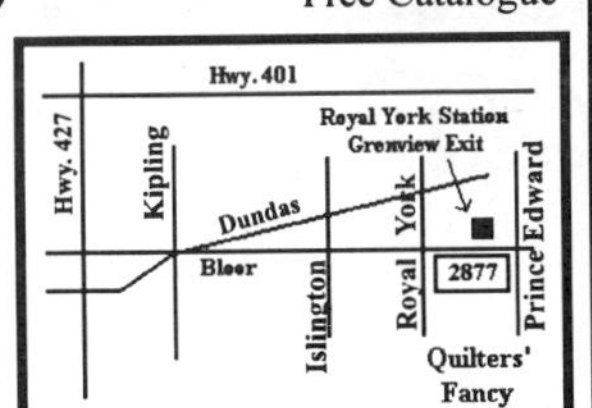

Teaching store. Great Fabric collection. Over 100 batiks. Wide selection of books. Low prices. Quilt Software. Specialty threads.

Scarborough, ON #4

The Quilting Patch

Tues - Sat 10 - 5
Thur til 9
July & Aug
Wed - Sat 10 - 4

88 Dearham Wood M1E 1S4
(416) 281-5561
Owner: Donna Edwards
Est: 1984 800 sq.ft. 1400 Bolts

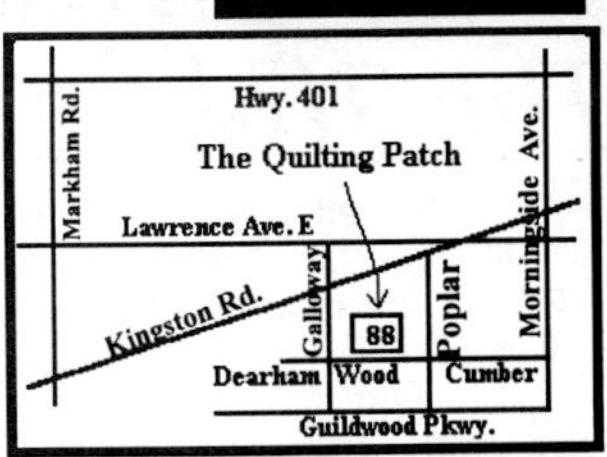

Large Selection of Quality Cotton Fabrics, Books, Patterns, & Supplies. Classes and made to Order Quilts Available.

Burlington, ON #5

The Quilter's Cupboard, Inc.

Mon - Sat 9:30 - 5
Wed & Thur til 9

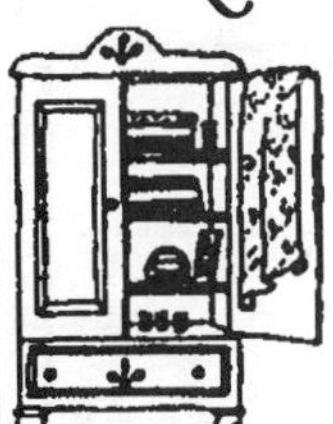

2501 Guelph Line #11
L7M 2A3
(905) 332-6640
1000+ Bolts of 100% cotton. Books, Notions, Patterns, Classes. All your quilting needs in one friendly shop.

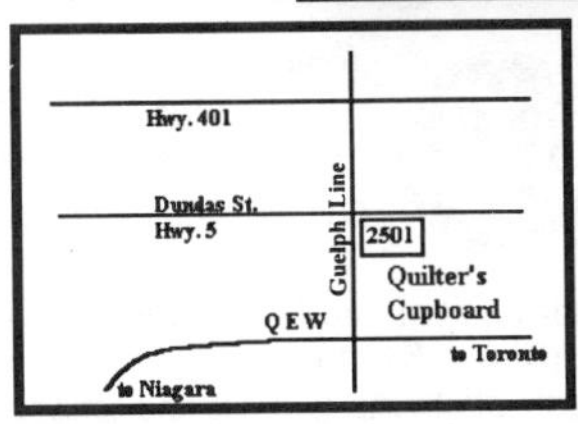

Cambridge, ON #6

Fibre Feats

Mon - Sat 9:30 - 4:30

1660 Blair Rd. N3H 4R8
(519) 653-4489
Owner: Phyllis Brown
Est: 1985 2000 Bolts

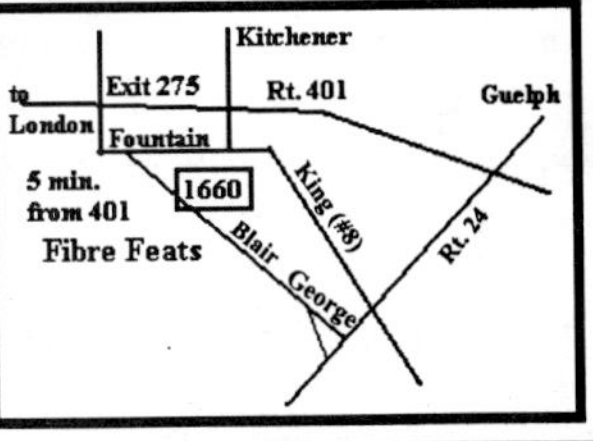

This old barn is overflowing with an unusual selection of inspiring cottons. Great books, classes. Waterloo County Quilt Festival Participant.

Windsor, ON #7

Mon - Thur 9 - 5:30
Fri 9 - 9
Sat 9 - 5:30

The Dresden Rose Sewing Centre

3850 Dougall (at Cabana) N9G 1X2
(519) 966-3355 Fax: (519) 966-9066
E-Mail: dresden.rose@sympatico.ca
Owner: Gail Millson Est: 1988 2000 sq.ft.

Husqvarna Viking dealer of distinction; classes, 100% cotton fabrics. Free Lessons with machine purchase. Service to all brand machines.

London, ON #8

Tues - Sat 10 - 5
Thur til 8

Quilters' Supply

1634 Hyde Park Rd. N6H 5L7
(519) 472-3907
Owner: Sharon Whatford
Est: 1978 2600 sq.ft. 2000 Bolts

Quilts, fabrics and over 200 books for the Quilter and fabric artist. Phone, write or visit for ongoing workshop schedules.

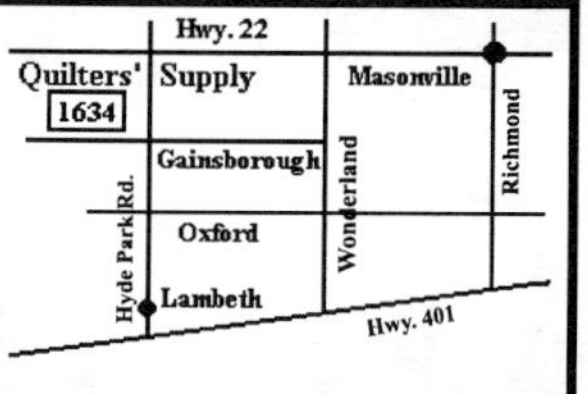

Ailsa Craig, ON #9

Mon - Sat 10 - 5
Fri til 8

Cotton-By-Post Quilt Shoppe

153 Main St. N0M 1A0
(519) 293-3499 Fax: (519) 232-9199
E-Mail: seagnew@wwdc.com
Web Site: www.cotton-by-post.com
Owners: Suzanne Agnew & Heather Stewart
Est: 1995 On-line Catalogue

Quality cotton fabrics, cotton batting, books, patterns and all the latest quilting notions. Classes available for all skill levels.

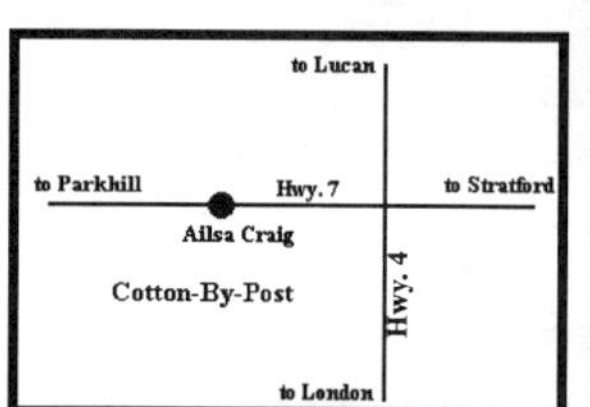

Shakespeare, ON #10

Open Daily

27 Shakespeare St. N0B 2P0
(519) 625-8435 Est: 1986
Owner: Heather Stock
1200 sq.ft.
1500 Bolts

Your place to find a timeless and elegant quilt for your home or choose the supplies to make a family heirloom. Lots of Shops for Everyone To Enjoy in Canada's Antique Capital

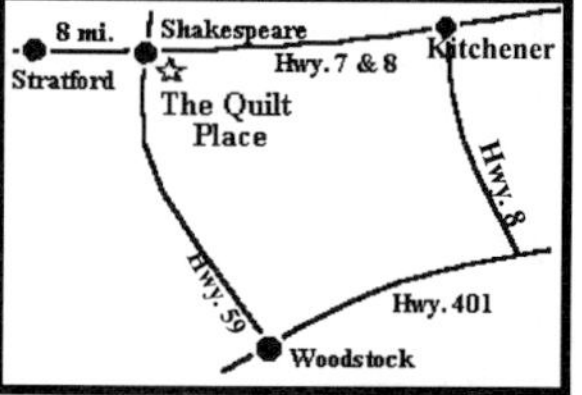

St. Agatha, ON #11

Tues - Sat 10 - 5:30
Sun 12:30 - 5:30

Miller's Country Store

221 Erb St. E. N0B 2L0
(519) 747-1575
Owner: Barb Elliott
Est: 1986 2000 sq.ft. 900 Bolts

Mennonite Quilts. Area's largest selection of plaids for quilts, curtains & upholstery. Country gifts and custom crafted furniture.

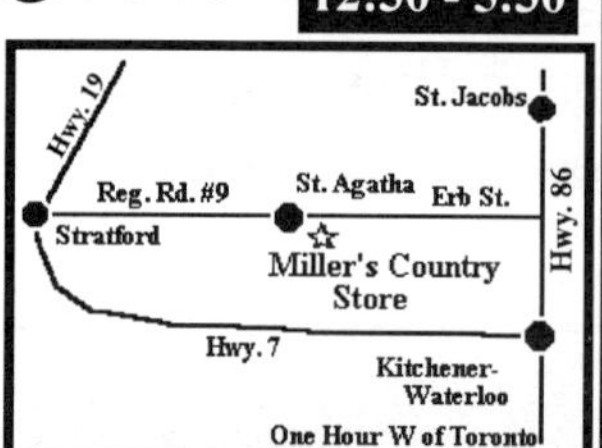

St. Jacobs, ON #12

Mon - Sat 9:30 - 5:30
Sun 1 - 5

Ruffled Elegance & Calico

38 King St. N0B 2N0
(519) 664-2665 Est: 1984
E-Mail: ruffled@ionline.net
Web Site: www.stjacobs.com/ruffledelegance
Owner: Marion Martin 1800 sq.ft.

"A Quilter's Delight — A Decorators Dream" Name brand fabrics, patterns, notions. Classes Curtains & Pillows. Handmade quilts by local Mennonite quiltmakers.

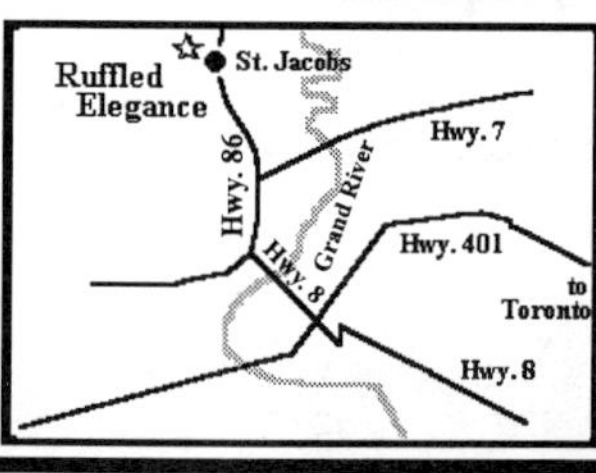

Georgetown, ON #13

Mon - Sat 9:30 - 5:30
Sundays & Holiday Mon 12 - 5

The Hobby Horse

12707 9th Line L7G 4S8
(905) 877-9292 or (800) 565-5366
E-Mail: orders@thehobbyhorse.on.ca
Web Site: www.thehobbyhorse.on.ca
Owner: Gail Spence
Est: 1982 Free Catalog

We're filled to the brim with bolts of cotton fabrics, quilting supplies, patterns, books, kits and much more. Come Visit Our Store.

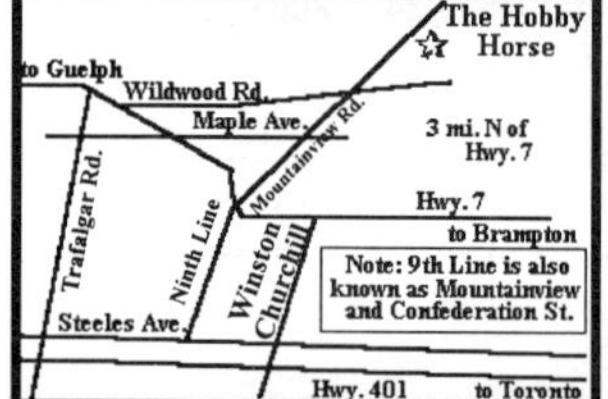

Whitby, ON #14

Mon - Fri 10 - 8
Sat 9:30 - 5
Summer 11 - 7

Olde Silver Thimble

1380 Hopkins St. #1 L1N 2C3
(905) 436-0297
Owner: Barbara Day
Est: 1987 2000 sq.ft. 1500 Bolts

Quilting, Jacket and Bear classes all year. Batiks, Jinny Beyer, Concord, Flannels, Hoffman, Kauffman, Mumms the Word, Northcott & South Seas

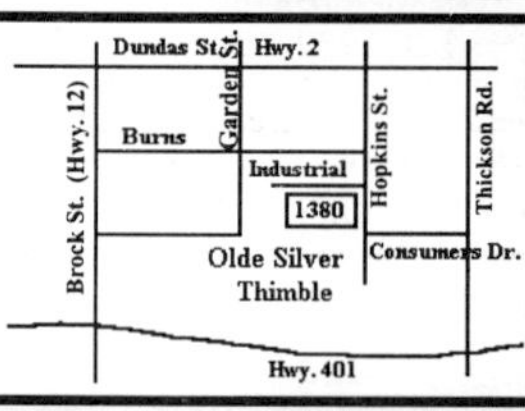

Bancroft, ON #15

Mon - Sat 9 - 5:30

Country Quilts & Fabrics

10 Hastings St., Box 398
K0L 1C0
(613) 332-2540
Owner: Gwen Schock
Est: 1991 900 sq.ft. 3000+ Bolts

Quilts, Fabrics, Quilting Supplies, Books, Laces, Ribbons, DMC Floss, Stencils, Beads, Patterns, Trims.

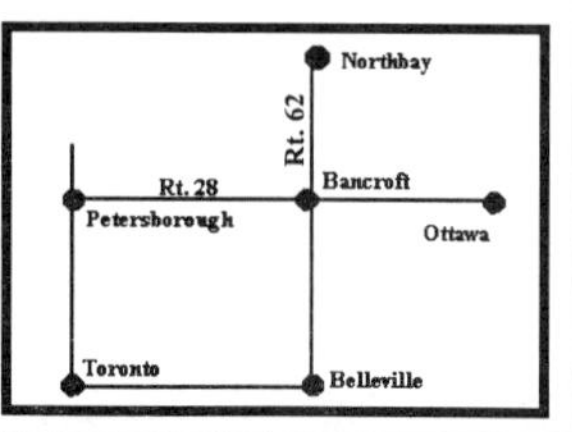

Elliot Lake, ON #16

Mon - Fri 9:30 - 5:30
Sat 9:30 - 5

A Stitch in Time

6 Saskatchewan Rd. P5A 1Z1
(705) 848-8277
E-Mail: wills@onlink.net
Owner: Nancy Wills Est: 1997

Fabric, Yarn and Notions for all your Sewing, Quilting, Knitting and Cross-stitch needs. Books, Patterns, Classes and scissor sharpening.

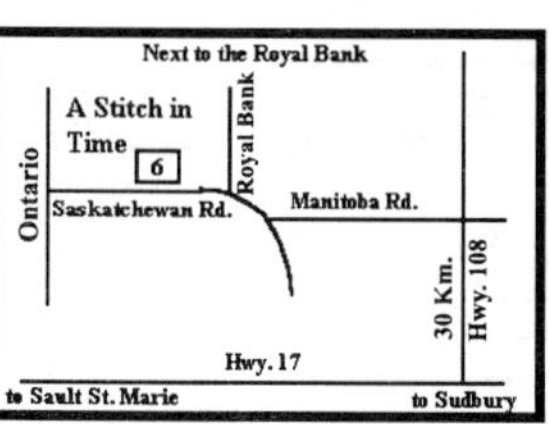

Ottawa, ON #17

Mon - Sat 10 - 5:30 Fri til 7

Quilts & Seams

313 Richmond Rd. K1Z 6X3
(613) 725-5113 Fax: (613) 798-1952
E-Mail: qwpope@msn.com
Owner: Sandi Pope Est: 1982 2000 sq.ft.

A shop for the discerning quiltmaker featuring quality fabrics, notions, books, patterns & classes. Authorized babylock, Bernina & Elna dealer.

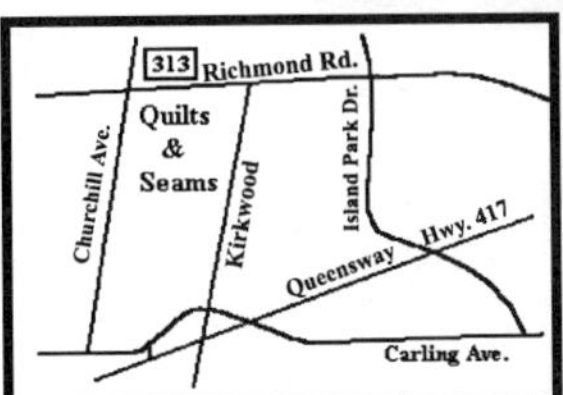

Ottawa, ON #18

Mon - Thur 10 - 6 Fri 10 - 8 Sat 10 - 5 Sun 12 - 4

Maple Tree Quilts

846 Bank St. K1S 3W1
(613) 234-2337
Fax: (613) 234-1403
Owner: Mary Pal 1100 sq.ft.

Exquisite quilting supplies, classes & gifts. Name-brand 100% cotton fabrics. Canadian quilters and artists proudly featured. Warm, personal assistance.

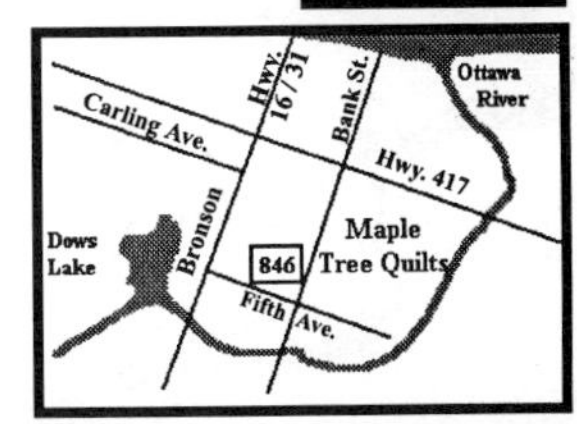

Ottawa, ON #19

Tues - Sat 10 - 5

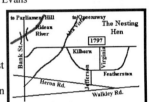

THE NESTING HEN

1797 Kilborn Ave. at Virginia Dr.
K1H 6N1
Owner: Sandra Evans
(613) 521-9839
Est: 1987

All inclusive Quilt Shop. Ottawa's loveliest Fabrics. Best Books and Supplies. Fine Needlearts and Gifts. Located in Pretty Residential Area.

Ontario Guilds:

Elliot Lake Quilt Guild, P.O. Box 411, Elliot Lake, P5A 2J8
Meets: Every Tuesday 7 p.m. at Moose Lodge, 25 Oakland Blvd.
Brant Heritage Quilters Guild, Box 23047, Brantford, N3T 6K4
Hamilton Quilt Guild, c/o 8259 - 20 Rd., Hamilton, L9B 1P9
Halton Quilters Guild, Box 171, Oakville, L6J 4Z5
Stoney Creek Q. G., c/o 22 Pembroke St., Stoney Creek, L8J 1N8

Other Shops in Ontario:

Aylmer	Quality Handmade Quilts, R.R. #1	None
Barrie	The Quilters Shop, Horseshoe Valley Rd.	705-739-6875
Callander	Country Quilting & Fabrics, 80 Lansdowne E	705-752-4813
Cookstown	Quilt & Wool Shoppe, 25 Queen St.	705-458-9233
Elmira	Reichard's Dry Goods, 3 Arthur St. S	519-669-3307
Elmira	Busy Bee Quilts, 48 Arthur St. S	519-669-3441
Kingston	Abbey Dawn Quilts & Antiques, 1519 Abbey Dawn	613-542-6247
Kingston	The Quilter's Choice, 646 Progress Ave.	613-384-8932
Kirkland	Applique & Patchwork, 3646 St. Charles Blvd.	519-426-8289
Leamington	A Stitch in Time, 260 Oak St. E	519-322-4690
Minesing	Quilters Shop, R.R. #1, Box 77	705-739-6875
Navuan	Aunt Beth's Quilt World, 3217 Navan Rd., R.R. #2	613-837-6222
Nepean	Sew for It!, 418 Moodie Dr.	613-820-2201
North Bay	Quilts & Other Comforts, 151 Main St. W	705-476-7811
Oakville	Quilt Patch, 101A Bronte Rd.	905-847-5105
Red Lake	The Yarn Shop, 150 Harvey St.	807-727-2564
Richmond	Country Quilter, 3444 McBean, P.O. Box 968	613-838-5541
Streetsville	Quiltessential, 228 Quilt St. S	905-542-9194
Stroud	Marge's Fabric & Fancys, 205 Yonge St. N	705-431-3698
Thunder Bay	Patchworks, 221 Algona St. S	807-345-6111
Toronto	Quilter's Garden, 931 Kingston Rd.	416-693-1616
Toronto	Sawtooth Borders Quilt Gallery, 110 Park Rd.	416-961-8187
Uxbridge	Quilter's Cupboard, 4 Sandy Hook Rd.	905-852-3617

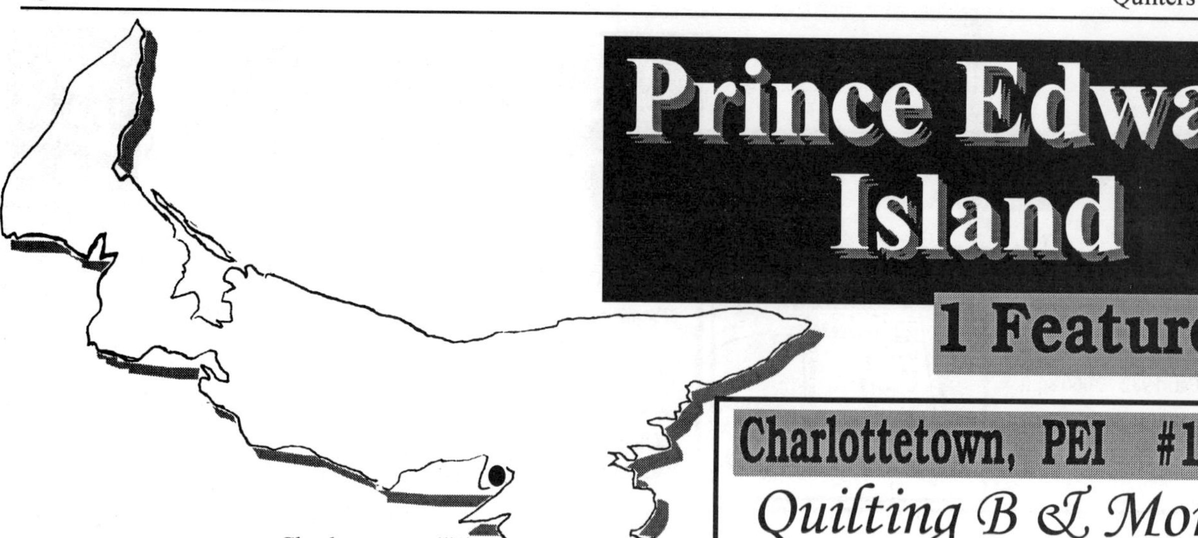

Prince Edward Island

1 Featured Shop

Charlottetown (#1)

Charlottetown, PEI #1

Summer
Mon - Fri
8:30 - 8

Quilting B & More

155 Queen St. C1A 4B1
(902) 628-1998
900 sq.ft. 1000+ Bolts

Come visit us in our new location.
Charlottetown offers lots to see and do.

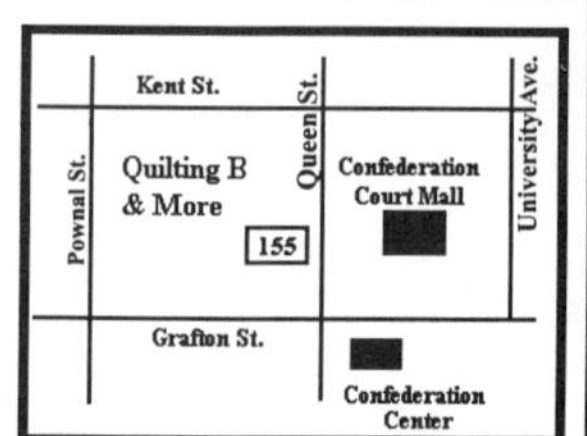

Another Shop on Prince Edward Island:
Souris Jean's Quilting Crafts & Things, Main St., McPhee Mall 902-687-1367

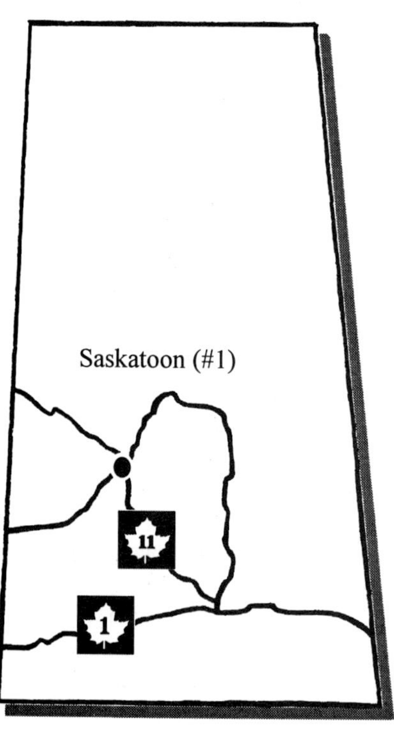

Saskatoon, SK #1

Mon - Sat
9 - 5:30
Thur til 9

Homespun Craft Emporium, Inc.

250-A Second Ave. S S7K 1K9
(306) 652-3585
Owners: Isabelle McDonald
& Peggy Grandberg
Est: 1986 1200 Bolts

Your one stop quilting shop. 100% cotton fabric. Wide selection of books and tools. Quality Saskatchewan made crafts.

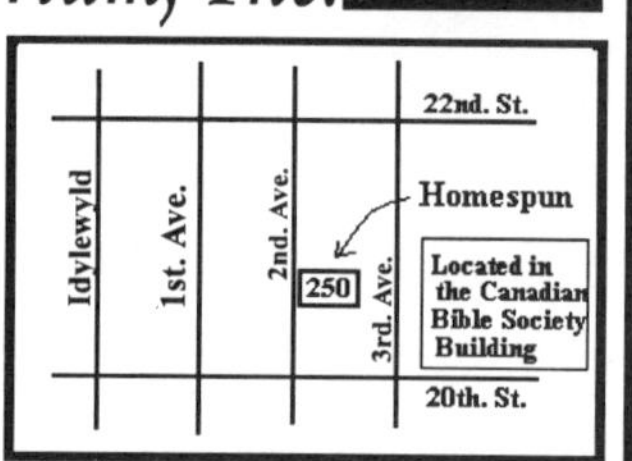

Another Shop in Saskatchewan:
Spirit Wood Thoughts & Things, 332 First St. E., Box 97 306-883-3800

SASKATCHEWAN CANADA

1 Featured Shop

A Shop in Quebec:
Pointe-Claire La Maison de Calico, 324 Bord du Lac 514-695-0728

A Shop in the Yukon Territory:
White Horse A Stitch in Time, 3121 Third Ave. 403-667-6133

INDEX
An Alphabetical listing of featured shops by name

Order Form for "*Quilters' Travel Companion*"
1998 - 2000 Edition

Name ____________________ $13.00 each copy

(Plus $2.50 shipping)

Address ______________________________________

____

Phone ______________

Copy this form or Detach and send to:

We will continue to update our guide on a regular basis. If you own a shop or know of one we should be sure to include in future editions of this guide, please drop us a note or call (719) 685-5041. Also if you have any suggestions for other information we could include that would be helpful when you're traveling, we'd appreciate hearing them.

We welcome wholesale inquiries.

We also publish another travel guide much like this one for cross-stitchers, needlepointers, and knitters (1 book), namely the Needlecrafters' Travel Companion (1997 - 1999 edition). It is 208 pages and features over 400 shops. The cost is $9.00 plus $2.00 shipping.

Index of Web Sites

A listing of shops who have a Web Site (in order by page) for you to visit when you can't be there in person.
Shop in your bathrobe!
(Please refer to the shop's ad for the address, most need the prefix http:// added)

Index of Shop Offers

A listing of shops who offer Catalogs, Newsletters, Fabric Clubs, Block of the Months, etc.
In order by page number.
(If there is no cost indicated in their ad, please call first.)

Index of Shop Offers Continued:

3 Featured "On-Line" Shops

P.O. Box 490
Pine Grove, CA
95665
(888) 878-5803

Owner:
Margie Andermatt

Web Site: www.foothill-fabric.com
E-Mail: sewwhat@cdepot.net

We have a wide variety of foundation paper piecing patterns and books and a large selection of fabric on the web page.
We accept Master Card, Visa, American Express and Discover.

We also have a Packet of the Month Club. Each month we send out either 5 fat quarters or 5 - ½ yard pieces of bright and unusual fabric. The cost to join the club is $13.50 for the fat quarter packet and $23.50 for the ½ yard packet, including shipping. There is also sales tax in California and international shipping is a little more. The last six months' packets can be seen on our web page.

"On-Line" Fabric Shop

A Must For Any Quilter Who Travels

With this edition of the Quilters' Travel Companion we now have over 1350 Featured Shops across the United States and Canada.

(Over 500 shops not in previous editions)

Each shop's listing includes address, telephone, shop hours, directions and a description of merchandise.

Plus state-by-state guild information and over 1000 more store addresses.

ISBN 0-9635290-7-2